WORLD CITY GUIDE

30 TOP CITIES WORLDWIDE

HIGHBURY
Columbus Travel Publishing
A DIVISION OF HIGHBURY HOUSE COMMUNICATIONS PLC

ISBN: 1-902221-81-8

Booksales
Tel: +44 (0)1322 660070.
E-mail: booksales@columbus-group.co.uk
Website: www.columbustravelguides.com

Design, layout and production by Space DPS Ltd, London
Printed by Wyndeham Grange

Publisher	Peter Korniczky
UK Sales and Marketing Manager	Helen Argent
Head of Editorial	Gary Bowerman
Editor	Sarah Chatwin
Assistant Editor	Beth Notten
Sub-editors	Karen Henderson, Kate Roberts
Cartographer	David Burles
Picture Researcher	Sarada de Villeneuve
Front cover design	Space DPS

Thanks to...
The Publishers would like to thank all the tourist offices, chambers of commerce, airlines and other organisations and individuals who assisted in the preparation of this edition. Most of the photographs used in this publication were supplied by the respective tourist office. The Publishers would also like to thank other organisations and individuals whose photographs appear. Special thanks to Corel, Hong Kong Tourism Board, Los Angeles Convention and Visitors Bureau (Michele and Tom Grimm) for their contribution to the front cover design.

Important Notice
The information in this book is compiled from many sources, including tour operators, airlines, national and city tourist offices and governmental bodies. While every effort has been made to ensure the accuracy of the information, the Publishers accept no responsibility for any loss occasioned to any person acting or refraining from acting as a result of the material contained in this publication or liability for any financial or other agreements that may be entered into with any organisations or individuals listed in the text.

By its very nature much of the information contained in the publication is susceptible to change or alteration, for instance in response to changing political, health and environmental situations. These changes or alterations are beyond the control of the Publishers. To assist users in obtaining up-to-date information, the Publishers have provided as many contact telephone numbers and website addresses as possible. In any case of doubt, or in response to any change in a domestic or international situation, users are urged to verify information upon which they are relying with the relevant authority.

CONTENTS

World map	iv
Credits	vi
Introduction	vii
Amsterdam	1
Athens	15
Auckland	29
Bangkok	43
Barcelona	55
Berlin	69
Brussels	83
Cape Town	97
Copenhagen	117
Delhi	131
Dubai	145
Dublin	157
Hong Kong	169
London	185
Los Angeles	205
Madrid	221
Mexico City	233
Miami	247
Moscow	263
New York City	279
Paris	295
Prague	311
Rio de Janeiro	325
Rome	339
Singapore	353
Stockholm	369
Sydney	383
Tokyo	397
Toronto	411
Vienna	427

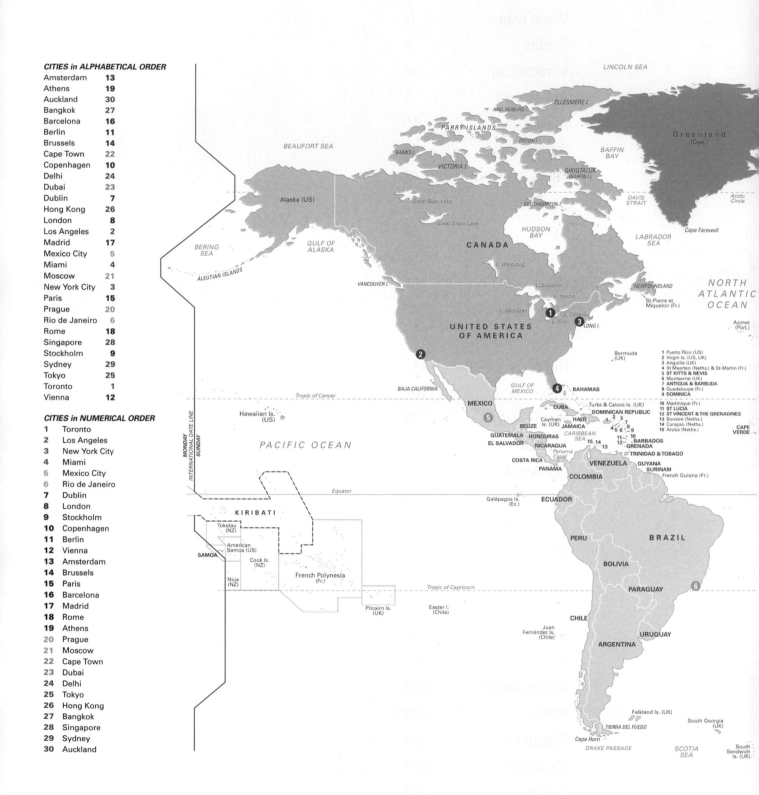

CITIES in ALPHABETICAL ORDER

Amsterdam	**13**
Athens	**19**
Auckland	**30**
Bangkok	**27**
Barcelona	**16**
Berlin	**11**
Brussels	**14**
Cape Town	**22**
Copenhagen	**10**
Delhi	**24**
Dubai	**23**
Dublin	**7**
Hong Kong	**26**
London	**8**
Los Angeles	**2**
Madrid	**17**
Mexico City	**5**
Miami	**4**
Moscow	**21**
New York City	**3**
Paris	**15**
Prague	**20**
Rio de Janeiro	6
Rome	**18**
Singapore	**28**
Stockholm	**9**
Sydney	**29**
Tokyo	**25**
Toronto	**1**
Vienna	**12**

CITIES in NUMERICAL ORDER

1	Toronto
2	Los Angeles
3	New York City
4	Miami
5	Mexico City
6	Rio de Janeiro
7	Dublin
8	London
9	Stockholm
10	Copenhagen
11	Berlin
12	Vienna
13	Amsterdam
14	Brussels
15	Paris
16	Barcelona
17	Madrid
18	Rome
19	Athens
20	Prague
21	Moscow
22	Cape Town
23	Dubai
24	Delhi
25	Tokyo
26	Hong Kong
27	Bangkok
28	Singapore
29	Sydney
30	Auckland

1 Puerto Rico (US)
2 Virgin Is. (US, UK)
3 Anguilla (UK)
4 St Maarten (Neths.) & St-Martin (Fr.)
5 ST KITTS & NEVIS
6 Montserrat (UK)
7 ANTIGUA & BARBUDA
8 Guadeloupe (Fr.)
9 DOMINICA
10 Martinique (Fr.)
11 ST LUCIA
12 ST VINCENT & THE GRENADINES
13 Bonaire (Neths.)
14 Curaçao (Neths.)
15 Aruba (Neths.)

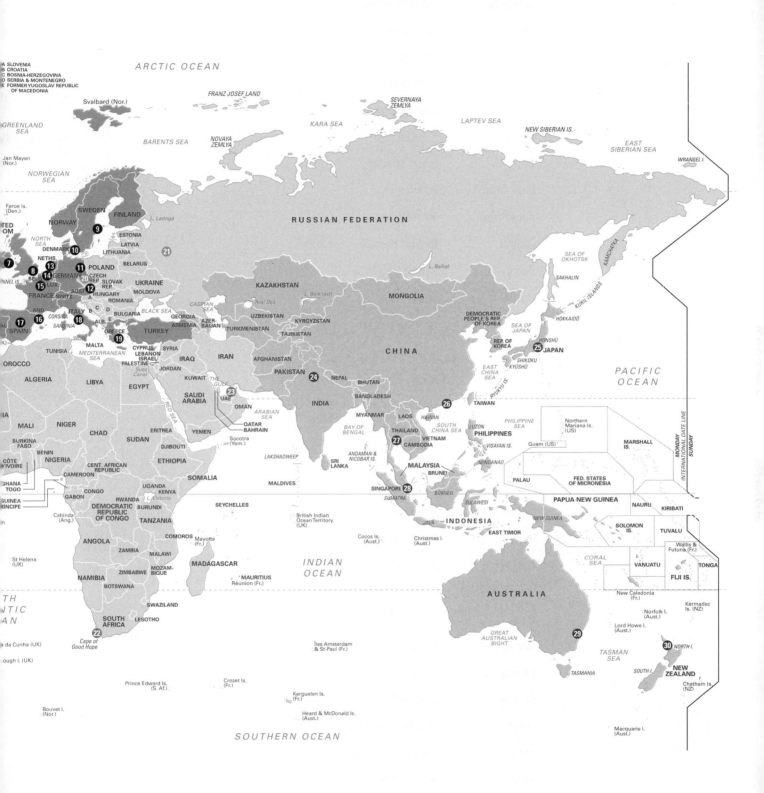

A SLOVENIA
B CROATIA
C BOSNIA-HERZEGOVINA
D SERBIA & MONTENEGRO
E FORMER YUGOSLAV REPUBLIC
  OF MACEDONIA

ARCTIC OCEAN

FRANZ JOSEF LAND

SEVERNAYA
ZEMLYA

Svalbard (Nor.)

KARA SEA

LAPTEV SEA

NEW SIBERIAN IS.

GREENLAND
SEA

BARENTS SEA

NOVAYA
ZEMLYA

EAST
SIBERIAN SEA

WRANGEL I.

Jan Mayen
(Nor.)

NORWEGIAN
SEA

RUSSIAN FEDERATION

SEA OF
OKHOTSK

KAMCHATKA

Faroe Is.
(Den.)

SWEDEN

FINLAND

L. Ladoga

SAKHALIN

KURIL ISLANDS

TED
OM

NORWAY

9

ESTONIA

NORTH
SEA

DENMARK

10

LATVIA

LITHUANIA

L. Baikal

HOKKAIDŌ

7

NETHS.

13

POLAND

BELARUS

SEA OF
JAPAN

HONSHŪ

8

11

KAZAKHSTAN

BEL.

14

GERMANY

CZECH
REP.

SLOVAK
REP.

NNEL IS.

15

LUX.

AUST.

HUNGARY

UKRAINE

MOLDOVA

L. Balkhash

MONGOLIA

SHIKOKU

KYŪSHŪ

25

JAPAN

FRANCE

SWITZ.

12

A

ROMANIA

CASPIAN
SEA

Aral Sea

REP. OF
KOREA

DEMOCRATIC
PEOPLE'S REP.
OF KOREA

AND

ITALY

B

C

D

BULGARIA

BLACK SEA

GEORGIA

UZBEKISTAN

KYRGYZSTAN

EAST
CHINA
SEA

PACIFIC
OCEAN

16

CORSICA

SARDINIA

18

E

ALB.

ARMENIA

AZER-
BAIJAN

TURKMENISTAN

TAJIKISTAN

CHINA

17

SPAIN

SICILY

GREECE

19

TURKEY

MALTA

MEDITERRANEAN
SEA

CYPRUS

LEBANON

ISRAEL

PALESTINE

SYRIA

IRAQ

IRAN

AFGHANISTAN

PAKISTAN

24

NEPAL

BHUTAN

TAIWAN

26

RYUKYU IS.

MONDAY   SUNDAY
INTERNATIONAL DATE LINE

TUNISIA

JORDAN

Suez
Canal

KUWAIT

THE
GULF

23

UAE

SAUDI
ARABIA

INDIA

BANGLADESH

PHILIPPINE
SEA

Northern
Mariana Is.
(US)

MARSHALL
IS.

OROCCO

ALGERIA

LIBYA

EGYPT

RED
SEA

OMAN

QATAR
BAHRAIN

ARABIAN
SEA

MYANMAR

LAOS

HAINAN

SOUTH
CHINA SEA

PHILIPPINES

LUZON

Guam (US)

A

MALI

NIGER

CHAD

SUDAN

ERITREA

YEMEN

Socotra
(Yem.)

BAY OF
BENGAL

THAILAND

27

CAMBODIA

VIETNAM

VISAYAN IS.

PALAU

FED. STATES
OF MICRONESIA

BURKINA
FASO

BENIN

NIGERIA

CENT. AFRICAN
REPUBLIC

DJIBOUTI

ETHIOPIA

LAKSHADWEEP

SRI
LANKA

ANDAMAN &
NICOBAR IS.

MINDANAO

'IVOIRE

CAMEROON

MALDIVES

MALAYSIA

BRUNEI

PAPUA NEW GUINEA

NAURU

KIRIBATI

HANA
TOGO

GUINEA
RINCIPE

GABON

CONGO

DEMOCRATIC
REPUBLIC
OF CONGO

UGANDA

RWANDA

BURUNDI

KENYA

L. Victoria

SEYCHELLES

British Indian
Ocean Territory
(UK)

SINGAPORE

28

SUMATRA

BORNEO

SULAWESI

INDONESIA

NEW GUINEA

SOLOMON
IS.

TUVALU

n

Cabinda
(Ang.)

TANZANIA

COMOROS

Mayotte
(Fr.)

Cocos Is.
(Aust.)

Christmas I.
(Aust.)

JAVA

EAST TIMOR

CORAL
SEA

VANUATU

Wallis &
Futuna (Fr.)

TONGA

St Helena
(UK)

ANGOLA

ZAMBIA

MALAWI

MOZAM-
BIQUE

MADAGASCAR

INDIAN
OCEAN

New Caledonia
(Fr.)

FIJI IS.

NAMIBIA

ZIMBABWE

MAURITIUS

Réunion (Fr.)

AUSTRALIA

Kermadec
Is. (NZ)

TH
NTIC
AN

BOTSWANA

SWAZILAND

Norfolk I.
(Aust.)

da Cunha (UK)

SOUTH
AFRICA

LESOTHO

22

Cape of
Good Hope

Lord Howe I.
(Aust.)

GREAT
AUSTRALIAN
BIGHT

29

TASMAN
SEA

NORTH I.

30

ough I. (UK)

Îles Amsterdam
& St-Paul (Fr.)

SOUTH I.

NEW
ZEALAND

Chatham Is.
(NZ)

Prince Edward Is.
(S. Af.)

Crozet Is.
(Fr.)

TASMANIA

Bouvet I.
(Nor.)

Kerguelen Is.
(Fr.)

Heard & McDonald Is.
(Aust.)

Macquarie I.
(Aust.)

SOUTHERN OCEAN

CREDITS

Amsterdam	Robin McKelvie
Athens	Jane Foster
Auckland	Tony Mudd
Bangkok	Anita Sach
Barcelona	Teresa Fisher
Berlin	Rebecca Ford
Brussels	Stuart Bowden
Cape Town	Beth Notten
Copenhagen	Terry Marsh
Delhi	Richard Hopton
Dubai	Robin McKelvie
Dublin	Teresa Fisher
Hong Kong	Paul Mackintosh
London	Sarah Chatwin
Los Angeles	Angela Songui
Madrid	Chris and Melanie Rice
Mexico City	Lizzie Fullerton
Miami	Melisse Gelula
Moscow	Rachel Atkinson
New York City	Melisse Gelula
Paris	Teresa Fisher
Prague	Jon Gillaspie
Rio de Janeiro	Elliot Walker
Rome	Jane Foster
Singapore	Emma Levine
Stockholm	Rebecca Ford
Sydney	Nick Dent
Tokyo	Lucy Hornberger
Toronto	John Watson
Vienna	Jon Gillaspie

INTRODUCTION

Welcome to the *World City Guide* – the most comprehensive guide to the top 30 cities around the world.

The *World City Guide* is published by Highbury Columbus Travel Publishing, the travel publishing division of Highbury House Communications Plc. Over the last 20 years, Highbury Columbus Travel Publishing has become established as the leading provider of destination information to the global travel industry and, in that time, our flagship title, the *World Travel Guide*, has sold close to 500,000 copies worldwide. Our new publication, the *World City Guide* builds on this reputation and follows in the footsteps of *The Columbus City Guide – Europe*, which was published in 1999 and featured 35 European cities.

The *World City Guide* is designed to give travellers everything they need when visiting a city – whether for business or leisure. Each city combines practical information with local insight and includes a detailed street map. The cities are divided into Travel, Sightseeing, Accommodation, Restaurants and Entertainment, covering sections from Getting There By Air to Bicycle Hire, Key Attractions to Excursions, Luxury Hotels to Budget Restaurants, Nightlife to Literary Notes. There are also extra factual boxes – Business Profile, Business Etiquette, City Statistics, Cost of Living, Tourist Information and Special Events.

All 30 cities in the *World City Guide* have been written by expert travel writers on the scene and updated in 2003 – making this publication the most up-to-date, comprehensive source of worldwide city information available.

AMSTERDAM

Amsterdam is a city that everyone thinks they know. Images of scantily clad women turning on those red lights and wafts of cannabis smoke are as much ingrained on the consciousness as the myriad canals and the tragic story of Anne Frank. While popular preconceptions about the Dutch capital ring true for many arriving visitors, they really only tell half the story.

Amsterdam is a real, living and breathing city, not just an oasis for tourists, those who like 'a smoke' and men in search of extra-marital sex. In the canals beneath the stag parties and working girls, young Internet entrepreneurs strike deals across Europe from their houseboats and just outside the old core is the RAI, one of the continent's key conference and business hubs. As well as the chugging canal boats, the city's waterways also increasingly play home to massive cruise ships and cargo vessels from all over the world. Today, Amsterdam peddles tourists almost as slickly as it has peddled goods and services over the centuries.

Located at the southern end of the Markermeer, in Noord Holland, the city has clearly come a long way since it was founded, as legend has it, by two fishermen and a seasick dog. The story goes that the dog jumped ship to deposit the contents of his stomach and the two fishermen became the founders of Amsterdam. The reality might have been slightly more prosaic, with the River Amstel being dammed in the 13th century and spawning a settlement, which took the name of *Aemstelledamme*.

The lifeblood of Amsterdam has long been its aquatic locale, close as it is to the North Sea and built on myriad canals, which neatly divide the city into easily navigable districts and imbue it with a small town ambience. There seems to be a canal around every corner in Amsterdam – not too surprising, considering that the city is home to a staggering 165 of them. It is also a busy museum city, as well as a buzzing cultural centre, particularly after dark. Here, beside the tourists and visiting businesspeople, the tolerant locals get on with their lives. Despite the bad publicity surrounding the rise and murder of far right politician Pim Fortuyn, in 2002, Amsterdam's tolerance is still famed. But it does not only extend to practical solutions on how to deal with one of the world's oldest industries and the controlled use of soft drugs. The city is also a haven for many nationalities, various sexualities and people of radically different political and religious persuasions. Whatever visitors make of the sex and drugs, it is difficult not to be impressed by this live-and-let-live mentality.

As well as being a nefarious oasis, the local tourist board is keen to stress that Amsterdam boasts more museums per square inch than anywhere else on the planet. And, in a sense, the whole city is a living museum – a crucial part of Amsterdam's charm.

During the summer, all of the city's eclectic groups come together in Vondelpark, to relax in the balmy weather. Amsterdam statistically might be one of Europe's wettest capitals but as soon as the clouds clear and the sun is allowed to shine, its inhabitants spill out onto the streets, to sit in the numerous pavement cafés, take a cruise on a canal or even partake in that most ubiquitous of Amsterdam pastimes – ride their bicycles. Amsterdam's winters tend to be cold with plenty of rain but this seldom seems to deter the tourists, who flock to the city all year round. Particularly cold winters also offer the unique chance for visitors to witness Amsterdamers uniting in skating across the picturesquely frozen canals.

Photo: Netherlands Board of Tourism

A typical street scene

TRAVEL

Getting There By Air

Amsterdam Airport Schiphol (AMS)

Tel: (0900) 7244 7465. Fax: (020) 604 1475.
Website: www.schiphol.nl
Schiphol, located 15km (nine miles) southwest of Amsterdam, is the fourth largest airport in Europe, with over 90 airlines flying to over 220 destinations. Schiphol ranks fourth behind London Heathrow, Frankfurt and Paris Charles de Gaulle, and has repeatedly been voted 'Best Airport in Europe' by readers of *Business Traveller Magazine*.

Major airlines: The national airline, *KLM – Royal Dutch Airlines* (tel: (020) 474 7747; website: www.klm.nl), flies direct to all major European, North American and Asia-Pacific cities. *KLM UK* (tel: (020) 474 7747; website: www.klmuk.com) flies to London Stansted and several regional airports throughout the UK. *Transavia* (tel: (020) 406 0406; website: www.transavia.nl), 80% of which is owned by KLM, operates scheduled flights to London Gatwick and Barcelona. Transavia has also recently launched a budget offshoot, using Schiphol as its hub, called *Basiq Air* (tel: (0900) 0737; website: www.basiqair.com). On the domestic front, *KLM Cityhopper* (tel: (020) 648 3456; website: www.klmcityhopper.nl) operates services between Amsterdam and Eindhoven. Other major airlines serving the airport include *Air France, British Airways, Cathay Pacific, China Airlines, Easyjet, Egypt Air, Northwest Airlines* and *Virgin Express*.

Approximate flight times to Amsterdam: From London is 50 minutes; from New York is 7 hours; from Los Angeles is 10 hours 25 minutes; from Toronto is 7 hours and from Sydney is 21 hours 20 minutes.

Airport facilities: Facilities at Schiphol are first rate, with bureaux de change, currency exchange machines, restaurants, duty-free shops, left-luggage, tour operators, a hotel reservation service and prayer rooms. Departure lounges also have funky chairs and plenty of space in which to relax before flying.

Shower facilities and day rooms are available at the airport hotels. Car hire companies include *Avis, Budget, Europcar* and *Hertz*.

Business facilities: The *Schiphol Business Centre* (tel: (020) 653 2480; fax: (020) 653 2566) is open to all passengers. Facilities include fax, personal computer, telephone and secretarial services. The centre is open Monday to Friday 0830–1900. There is one conference room in the terminal, which can cater for groups of up to 55 delegates and must be booked in advance through the business centre. Coin operated fax machines are located throughout the airport terminal. Computers, printers and mobile telephones – for making and receiving both local and international calls – can be hired from *KPN Telecom Rentcentre* (tel: (020) 653 0999; fax: (020) 653 0998), which is open 0700–2200. There is also a press centre. Some major airlines provide executive lounges, which offer some business facilities.

Arrival/departure tax: None.

Transport to the city: *Connexxtions* (tel: (020) 653 4975) operates a shuttle bus service to the city centre, every 20 minutes daily between 0600–2100 (journey time – approximately 20–30 minutes, although due to numerous stops, journeys can sometimes take up to an hour). Hotels serviced include the Carlton, Crowne Plaza, Golden Tulip Barbizon, Holiday Inn, Krasnapolsky, Novotel, Okura, Park, Pulitzer, Renaissance, Sofitel and Tulip Inn. The cost is €10.50 for a single ticket and €19 for a return, although there is an extra charge for non-contracted hotels.
NS (tel: (0900) 9292/6; website: www.ns.nl) trains run between the airport and Amsterdam's Centraal Station, daily every 15 minutes 0600–2400 (journey time – 20 minutes) and every hour throughout the night. A second-class ticket costs €3.10 one way or €5.50 return. There is also a direct link between Schiphol and Amsterdam's RAI Congress Centre, with trains running every 15 minutes 0525–2410. Schiphol also has direct links to The Hague, Rotterdam and Vlissingen.
Official airport taxis pick up passengers from outside the arrivals hall. The journey to the city costs from €30 and takes approximately 15–25 minutes, depending on which part of the city is required.

Getting There By Water

Amsterdam is a busy port city and one of the top ten most important cruise ship harbours in Europe, although less than 100 cruise ships visited the city in 2002 and cruise passenger levels dropped to below 100,000 over the same period. Amsterdam's business ports are run by *Ports of Amsterdam* (tel: (020) 523 4500; website: www.amsterdamports.nl), while information on cruise ship services is available from *Amsterdamcruise* (tel: (020) 551 2557; fax: (020) 625 2869; website: www.amsterdamcruise.com). The main cruise hub, which can handle two cruise ships at one time, is based at the funky new passenger terminal at *Oostelijke Handelskade*, located on the edge of the city centre (tel: (020) 5091 000; website: www.ptamsterdam.com), which is equipped with restaurants, bars and ATMs. The new *Felison Terminal*, on the IJ meer (tel: (0255) 545 420; website: www.felisonterminal.nl), was opened by the same operator in time for the summer 2003 season. The main ferry terminal for services around Europe is situated further south, at *Hook of Holland* (tel: (017) 438 9333), where the terminal has a restaurant but no banking or exchange facilities.

Ferry services: Cross-channel ferries are run by *Stena Line* (tel: (08705) 455 455; website: www. stenaline.co.uk), which operates a rail/fast-ferry service from London (Liverpool Street) to Amsterdam (Centraal Station), via Harwich and the Hook of Holland. There are two services daily, one in the morning and one in the evening (journey time – 8 hour 40 minutes).

Transport to the city: Although within walking distance, trains and buses connect the new cruise terminals with Amsterdam city centre. The Hook of Holland is connected by an express rail link with Centraal Station.

Getting There By Rail

Centraal Station, Stationsplein, is one of the largest railway terminals in Europe. The station has an impressive array of facilities, from showers and restaurants to hotel and travel booking services. Over the last few years, the station has become increasingly seedy and insalubrious; many locals avoid it after dark. The national rail provider is *Nederlandse Spoorwegen – NS* (tel: (0900) 9292/6; website: www.ns.nl), which runs an increasingly creaking network covering destinations all over Holland and further afield into the rest of Europe. International tickets should be reserved at least a week in advance.

Rail services: There are regular *Eurostar* trains (tel: (0990) 186 186, in the UK; website: www.eurostar. com) from London to Brussels (journey time – 3 hours 40 minutes), where a direct connection to Amsterdam can be caught after a short wait (journey time – 3 hours). *THALYS* (tel: (0900) 9228; website: www.thalys.com) high-speed services also connect Amsterdam with Brussels (journey time – approximately 2 hours 30 minutes). There are frequent daytime services from most large Western European cities and night services from all over the continent.
Over the last few years, the reputation of The Netherlands' railway network has suffered, after part-privatisation led to maintenance problems, cancelled services and a public perception that the railways are in a dire state. There might be some light at the end of the train tunnel, with recent talk of new high-speed connections to France and Germany and an extension of the Eurostar service to Amsterdam.

Transport to the city: Centraal Station is located in the city centre. A number of trams and buses, as well as taxis, are available in the area immediately outside the main building.

Getting There By Road

The Netherlands is connected to the rest of Europe by a superb network of motorways. Green 'E's indicate international highways, red 'A's indicate national highways and yellow 'N's indicate smaller routes. Although frontier formalities between The Netherlands, Germany and Belgium have now all but vanished, motorists – particularly on smaller roads – should be prepared to stop when asked to do so by a customs official.

Driving is on the right. Speed limits are 120kph (75mph) on motorways, 80kph (50mph) on major roads and 50kph (30mph) in towns. Children under 12 years should not travel in the front seat. Seatbelts are compulsory. The maximum legal alcohol to blood ratio for driving is 0.05%. The minimum driving age in The Netherlands is 18 years. An International Driving Permit is not required, as long as a national driving licence from the country of origin is held. EU pink format licences are accepted. Trailers and caravans are allowed in without documentation. A Green Card is advisable but not compulsory. Without it, drivers with motor insurance policies in their home country are granted only the minimum legal cover in The Netherlands –

CITY STATISTICS

Location: Noord-Holland, The Netherlands.
Country dialling code: 31.
Population: 735,328 (city); 1,268,908 (metropolitan area).
Ethnic mix: 145 nationalities in The Netherlands, 96% Dutch, 4% other nationalities.
Religion: 38% Roman Catholic, 30% Protestant, 32% do not profess any religion.
Time zone: GMT + 1 (GMT +2 from last Sunday in March to Saturday before last Sunday in October).
Electricity: 220 volts AC (moving at the rate of one volt per year towards the European standard of 230 volts), 50Hz; round two-pin plugs are standard.
Average January temp: 3°C (36°F).
Average July temp: 17°C (61°F).
Annual rainfall: 804mm (31.5 inches).

the Green Card tops this up to the level of cover provided by the driver's own policy.

The yellow cars of the *Royal Dutch Touring Club, ANWB/Wegenwacht* (tel: (070) 314 1420) patrol major roads 24 hours a day, with qualified mechanics equipped to handle routine repairs.

Emergency breakdown service: *ANWB* (0800) 0888.

Routes to the city: Schiphol lies on the E19, from where it is an easy 18km (11 miles) drive into Amsterdam. The A10 is the Amsterdam ring road. The main route out of Amsterdam, toward Brussels, is the

A2, heading south to join the A27 and finally the A16/E19 at Breda, which continues across the border to Antwerp. The A2 also connects with Utrecht, from where the A12/E35 travels directly through the Duisburg-Essen conurbation, passing Düsseldorf, Cologne and continuing southeast until Frankfurt. Hanover is best reached by taking the E231 out of the city to connect with the A1/E30, becoming the A30/E30, which continues east to Hanover.

Approximate driving times to Amsterdam: From Brussels – 2 hours 30 minutes; Hanover – 4 hours; Frankfurt – 6 hours 30 minutes.

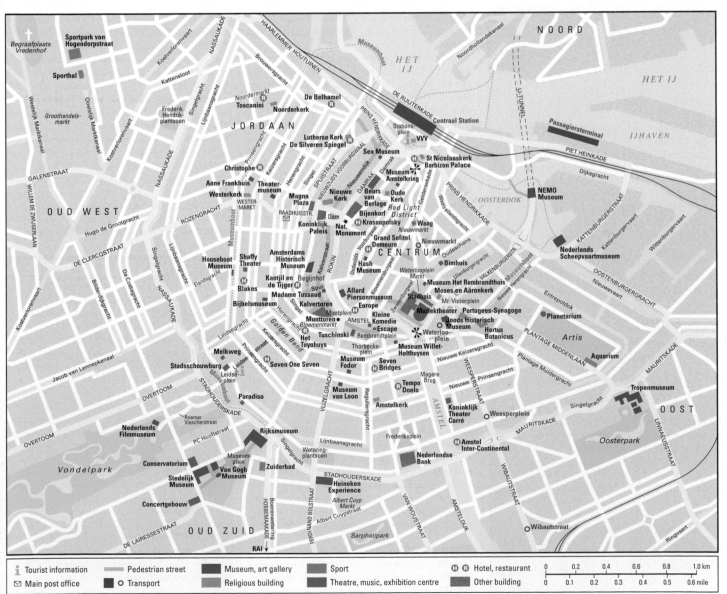

ℹ Tourist information	▬ Pedestrian street	▮ Museum, art gallery	▮ Sport	ⒽⓇ Hotel, restaurant	
✉ Main post office	○ Transport	▮ Religious building	▮ Theatre, music, exhibition centre	▮ Other building	

Scale: 0 – 1.0 km / 0 – 0.6 mile

Amsterdam likes to see itself as being at the heart of Europe and its location does give it easy access to a number of major European markets. *European Cities Monitor* recognised the Dutch capital as one of the top five business locations in Europe in 2002.

The country has suffered as a whole during the global downturn but has not yet endured problems on anything approaching the scale of Germany's predicament, despite its close economic ties with this neighbour. In fact, Germany is The Netherlands' biggest trading partner, with 25% of import and export trade, while other major players include Belgium, Luxembourg, France and the UK. On average, approximately 70–100 foreign companies set up in The Netherlands every year. They are attracted by Amsterdam's prime position within Europe, with excellent international connections from the ever-expanding Schiphol airport and Amsterdam port, a strong infrastructure, a multi-lingual workforce, a stable political and economic climate and business-friendly policies.

Major companies with a presence in Amsterdam include *ABM Amro Bank, Phillips* and *Shell*, with *Canon, IBM* and *Sony* all having their European headquarters in the city. It is fitting in a city that was home to the world's first ever public stock exchange that finance is a major part of the business world, with the financial sector employing approximately 8% of Amsterdam's workforce and some 70 banks having a presence in the city. After finance, fashion and flowers are key sectors. Of all Amsterdam's exports, tulips are probably the most famous. In terms of exports, fresh flowers are a large market and Heineken is the largest export brewery in the world, with sales to 150 countries. Heineken was one of the few major European breweries to offer positive results for 2002. Over the last 20 years, Amsterdam has also emerged as a strong base in advanced technological industries, computing, telecommunications and biotechnology.

One key industry currently facing difficulties is tourism, with both the lucrative North American and Japanese markets suffering due to the instability in the Middle East. Unemployment levels have risen slightly in Amsterdam recently, with city-wide unemployment running at a rate of 5.7% by the end of 2002, still lower than the national average of 6.9%.

The facilities provided for businesses in Amsterdam are extensive. The Amsterdam *RAI International Exhibition & Congress Center,* Europaplein 8 (tel: (020) 549 1212; fax: (020) 646 4469; e-mail: mail@rai.nl; website: www.rai.nl), is one of the country's largest and one of the world's leading convention centres. Business activity in Amsterdam is largely focused around the city centre, although also important are the port area and the new business parks on the city fringes. Commercial information is available from the *Amsterdam Chamber of Commerce and Industry* (tel: (020) 531 4000; fax: (020) 531 4699; e-mail: post@amsterdam.kvk.nl; website: www.kvk.nl) and from *Amsterdam Promotion Foundation* (website: www.amsterdampromotion.nl).

Coach services: *Eurolines* (tel: (020) 560 8788; e-mail: info@eurolines.nl; website: www.eurolines.nl) operates coach services, sometimes in conjunction with other national companies, to major cities throughout Europe, including London, Paris, Brussels and Frankfurt. Offices are located at Rokin 10 and the coach station, *Amstelstation*, Julianaplein 5 (tel: (020) 560 8787).

Getting Around

Public Transport

Amsterdam's integrated public transport system is run by the municipal transport company, *GVB* (tel: (020) 460 6060; website: www.gvb.nl), which has an information office at Centraal Station. The best way to get around the city is either on foot or by using the extensive tram, metro, bus and ferry networks. A map of all tram and bus routes in Amsterdam is available from tourist offices or the *GVB* office by Centraal Station, costing €0.80.

The Circle Tram 20 that used to ferry tourists around a city loop is no more but **trams** are still a great way of getting around. Trams operate Monday to Friday 0600–2400 (Saturday from 0630 and Sunday from 0730). All trams leave from Centraal Station – trams 1 and 2 traverse the main canals, tram 17 provides a frequent, fast and dependable service, tram 16 takes a route to Museumplein and Concertgebouw, while trams 9 and 14 go to the Muziektheater and Waterlooplein market.

Amsterdam's four **metro** lines all start at Centraal Station and serve the southeastern business district and the suburbs. The trains run Monday to Friday 0600–2415 (Saturday from 0630 and Sunday from 0730).

The outlying areas of the city – mostly the suburbs that the trams do not reach – are served by 30 **bus** lines, which run until midnight. Night buses run nightly from 0030–0730, after the other services have stopped (numbered from 71 to 79).

A free **ferry** service provides cyclists and pedestrians with connections to Amsterdam Noord, the area across the IJ. The main ferry landing is on De Ruijterkade (behind the Centraal Station). Ferries are frequent and operate between 0615–2057, with a limited service at the weekend (most ferries do not operate on Sunday). When taking a bicycle aboard, passengers should make sure to not break local etiquette and always go through the cyclist channel rather than the pedestrian one. The Noord Canal across the IJ is a quiet and less taxing cycle route for visitors who find navigating the busy city too traumatic. For single rides, a *strippenkaart* can be used. This needs to be stamped every time a tram, bus or metro is boarded – each journey uses one strip, plus a strip for every zone travelled. Once stamped, a ticket is valid for an hour, regardless of how often a change of tram or bus is made. It is cheaper to buy a strippenkaart before boarding the public transport system than it is to pay a cash fare. Strippenkaarten are available from tourist offices, tobacconists and large hotels for €1.60 for two units (the minimum required for travel in one zone), €6.20 for 15 units or €18.30 for 45 units. Not having a valid ticket incurs a spot fine of €29.10, plus the cost of the ticket; ticket inspections are common. Visitors spending plenty of time travelling around the city are advised to buy a *dagkaarten* day **pass**, for €5.60.

Water Travel

Not surprisingly, there are several modes of water travel in Amsterdam. In addition to public ferries, canal buses travel between Centraal Station and the Rijksmuseum,

Tram

every 25–45 minutes – fares vary between the different service providers. The special Museum Boat departs from Prins Hendrikkade, every 30 minutes in summer and every 45 minutes in winter, stopping off at the city's main museums. This costs €13.50.

Canal taxis, which can carry up to 40 passengers, are also available. They can either be hailed from the canal-side or ordered in advance daily 0800–0100, from *WaterTaxis* (tel: (020) 535 6363; website: www.water-taxi.nl). The smallest taxi costs €75 for the first 30 minutes and €60 for each subsequent 30 minutes within the city limits. Alternatively, visitors can hire pedalos (also known as canal bikes) and boats to explore the canals. These are available from *Canal Bike*, Weteringschans 24 (tel: (020) 626 5574; fax: (020) 624 1033; website: www.canal.nl), who have 100 canal bikes and are open daily 0900–1800. A four-person canal bike costs €8 per person per hour, if there is only one or two passengers, and €7 per person per hour, if there are three or four passengers. A deposit of €50 per canal bike is required. Canal Bike also organises group tours of Amsterdam and Utrecht.

Taxis

Rather than hailing a taxi in the street, it is more usual in Amsterdam either to order one by phoning the *Central Taxi Office* (tel: (020) 677 7777) or to pick one up at one of the taxi ranks, which are located at Centraal Station, Rembrandtplein and Leidseplein. Taxis, which have an illuminated 'taxi' sign on the roof, usually come quickly – unless it is raining or a Friday or Saturday night. Although they provide a good service, taxis are relatively expensive. The starting fare is €2.90, with every kilometre costing €1.80 – regardless of the time of day or night – for the first 25km (16 miles) and then €1.30 thereafter. A meter indicates the fare, on top of which a small tip will be appreciated.

Limousines

There are a number of limousine companies in Amsterdam, offering airport transfers and hourly or daily hire. Two possibilities are *CS Limousine Service* (tel: (020) 673 7888; fax: (020) 673 9045; website: www.limousineamsterdam.com) and *Delden Limousine Service* (tel: (020) 684 8408; fax: (020) 686 3638). Prices start at €110 for an airport transfer or €75 per hour, plus an extra €1.40 per kilometre travelled over 15km (nine miles). Many of the drivers provide an informal guide service.

Driving in the City

Driving in Amsterdam is not recommended. Even for excursions outside the city, it is preferable to take the train. The city's streets are not big enough to accommodate the tens of thousands of cars owned by the city's residents, let alone the 500,000 tourists who annually arrive in their cars. As a result, parking spots are limited and expensive. Visitors are advised to park their car at a P+R (park and ride) lot, from where there are bus, tram and subway lines into the city centre. Motorists also need to watch out for cyclists and the special cycle lanes. Rush hours (0700–0900 and 1700–1900) are best avoided. Car headlights should be dimmed in built-up areas and it is illegal to use sidelights only.
Parking at the massive ArenA P+R, reached by the A1, A2 and A9 into the city, or the Stadionplein P+R, situated next to the Olympisch Stadion, costs €5.70 per day, which includes two free public transport tickets. In the city centre, cars must be parked in a designated parking space or in a car park. Parking meters can be recognised by a yellow sign with the letter 'P' and charges are split into three zones. Parking tickets for the most central zone A and zone B cost €2.80 per hour, while parking in zone C costs €1.70 per hour. City centre parking spaces can be reserved in advance, by going online (website: www.parkeerlijn.nl). Parking regulations are quite strict and there are tough measures for violating the city's car parking laws, with wheel clamping common. The car pound (tel: (020) 555 9833) is located at Cruquiuskade 25 in Havens Oost, the Eastern Harbour district.

Car Hire

Conditions of hire vary, although, in most cases, the driver will have to be 25 years old and have held a valid national licence for one year. An International Driving Permit (IDP) is not needed, as long as a valid national licence is produced. Payment is usually made with a credit card bearing the name of the driver. The major European firms are represented in Amsterdam. Cars are also available for hire through the airport and most hotels. The companies that have branches in the city centre include *Avis*, Polderweg 98–100 (tel: (020) 465 1115; fax: (020) 665 9038; website: www.avis.com), *Budget*, Overtoom 121 (tel: (020) 612 6066; fax: (020) 689 0694; website: www.budget.com), and *Hertz*, Engelsegade 4 (tel: (020) 612 2441; fax: (020) 626 2395; website: www.hertz.com).

Rates start at approximately €50 per day and €220 a week. Fare conditions vary and some companies have an additional mileage charge. Those hiring a car should always check that the rates include the minimum insurance cover required in Amsterdam.

Bicycle Hire

There are bicycle lanes that are marked out by white lines but cyclists will still need to watch out for cars, trams and pedestrians. Bicycles can be hired from *Bike City*, Bloemgracht 68–70 in Westerkerk (tel: (020) 626 3721; website: www.bikecity.nl), *Damstraat Rent-A-Bike*, Damstraat 20–22 (tel: (020) 625 5029; website: www.bikes.nl) and *Macbike Too*, Marnixstraat 220 (tel: (020) 626 6964; website: www.macbike.nl). Bike hire (for a one-speed bicycle) costs approximately €7 for the first day and €5 for subsequent days. A deposit of €30–100 or a credit card imprint is usually required, along with an additional form of identification. Optional insurance, at around 50% of the hire charge, can also be taken. When cycling around Amsterdam, cycling two abreast is illegal, as is a bicycle without reflector bands on both front and back wheels. Bikes should always be securely locked with two locks – one connecting the front wheel to a lamppost or railing and one securing the frame to something similarly as solid – there is a thriving stolen bike market in the city.

SIGHTSEEING

Sightseeing Overview

With its flat and compact city centre, Amsterdam is an easy city to get around on foot. But perhaps the best way for visitors to get a real feel for the place is to head straight out on a canal tour, something that many locals have never done. Most of the main attractions are located within the historical core, usually within walking distance of each other, although the efficient tram and bus networks are close at hand for attractions further afield.
The most visited sites in the city are the many excellent museums, such as the *Rijksmuseum*, *Anne Frank Museum*, *Amsterdams Historisch Museum*, *Stedelijk Museum*, *Van Gogh Museum* and the new *NEMO Museum*. Less cerebral pursuits are on offer among the grand façades and elegant museums, with brown bars and prostitutes adorning windows all day and night in the *red light districts*. Away from these busy places, the city is also blessed with quiet canals and leafy parks, which provide an escape all year round, especially *Vondelpark*, with its open-air, free concerts during summer. Breaking away from the main tourist throng is the best way for one to discover the 'real' Amsterdam of grand old canal-side merchants' houses where modern Amsterdamers still live, in an almost bucolic setting. As well as being the transport hub for the city, Amsterdam's grand Centraal Station is also the gateway to a myriad half- and full-day trips, with regular and inexpensive train services all over The Netherlands.

Key Attractions

Rijksmuseum (State Museum)

The largest and most popular museum in The Netherlands was opened in 1885 and has grown

steadily ever since. Today, it includes paintings dating from the 15th century up until 1850, as well as some quite stunning pieces of furniture. Visitors with a limited amount of time should head straight for the Dutch Masters on the first floor, where the star painting, Rembrandt's *Nightwatch*, hangs alongside several Vermeers and Van Hals. A pamphlet describes all of the museum's highlights and there are audio tours available. Although part of the Rijksmuseum and included in the price of the museum ticket, the *South Wing* has its own entrance, at Hobbemastraat 19. Exhibits include 18th- and 19th-century paintings, Oriental objets d'art and a textile and costume section. Stadhouderskade 42
Tel: (020) 674 7047. Fax: (020) 674 7001.
E-mail: info@rijksmuseum.nl
Website: www.rijksmuseum.nl
Transport: Trams 2, 5, 6, 7 or 10.
Opening hours: Daily 1000–1700.
Admission: €9 (concessions available).

Anne Frankhuis (Anne Frank House)

The queues can be horrendous at the small but very popular *Anne Frank House*, which annually attracts roughly half a million people. It is the historic home where Anne Frank, her family and four other Jewish people hid from the occupying Germans during World War II, after fleeing their native Germany. Finally

Photo: Netherlands Board of Tourism

Rijksmuseum

caught by the Nazis, after two years in hiding, they were taken off to concentration camps, where Anne died. However, her father survived and published her diary, which has been translated into 50 languages.
Prinsengracht 263, Westerkerk
Tel: (020) 556 7100. Fax: (020) 620 7999.
E-mail: museumsecretariaat@annefrank.nl
Website: www.annefrank.nl
Transport: Trams 13, 14 or 17.
Opening hours: Daily 0900–1900 (Sep–Mar); daily 0900–2100 (Apr–Aug).
Admission: €6.50 (concessions available).

Van Gogh Museum

This spacious museum houses a permanent display of 200 paintings and 500 drawings by Van Gogh, as well as works by Toulouse-Lautrec and Gauguin. A new wing is being used to display temporary exhibitions.
Paulus Potterstraat 7
Tel: (020) 570 5200. Fax: (020) 673 5053.
E-mail: info@vangogh.nl
Website: www.vangoghmuseum.nl
Transport: Trams 2, 3, 5, 12 or 16.
Opening hours: Daily 1000–1800.
Admission: €9 (concessions available).

Museum Het Rembrandthuis (Rembrandt House Museum)

This museum, a charming three-storey house, built in the early 17th century, is where Rembrandt lived for nearly 20 years. Recently, a museum wing has been added, with more space for a permanent collection of his work. It is home to a comprehensive collection of 250 of the artist's etchings and self-portraits. The work of Rembrandt's teachers and students are also on display, which adds depth and dialogue to Rembrandt's own work.
Jodenbreestraat 4–6
Tel: (020) 520 0400. Fax: (020) 520 0401.
E-mail: museum@rembrandthuis.nl
Website: www.rembrandthuis.nl
Transport: Trams 4, 9 or 14; metro Nieuwmarkt; boat to Waterlooplein or Zwanenburgerwal.
Opening hours: Mon–Sat 1000–1700, Sun 1300–1700.
Admission: €7 (concessions available).

Stedelijk Museum

The best collection of modern art in Amsterdam is housed in a neo-Renaissance building, designed by A W Weissmann in 1895 – another wing was added in the 1950s. The permanent collection includes Dutch and international art from the second half of the 19th century onwards, with works by Picasso, Cézanne, Chagall and Monet, as well as photography,

video, film and industrial design. Recent Dutch artists on display include Mondrian, De Kooning and Lichtenstein. Frequently changing temporary exhibitions are displayed in the New Wing. The museum has a restaurant with a terrace overlooking the sculpture garden – a lovely place in which to sit, on a sunny day. The Stedelijk Museum will be closed for alterations from 1 January 2004 until 2006.
Paulus Potterstraat 13
Tel: (020) 573 2737. Fax: (020) 573 2789.
E-mail: dir@stedelijk.nl
Website: www.stedelijk.nl
Transport: Trams 2, 3, 5, 12 or 16; bus 63.
Opening hours: Daily 1000–1800 (Apr–Oct); daily 1100–1700 (Nov–Mar).
Admission: €5.

Amsterdams Historisch Museum (Amsterdam Historical Museum)

The Amsterdam Historical Museum shows how this city grew from a small medieval town into a modern city. Housed in a former orphanage that dates back to 1524, the museum is filled with paintings, prints and archaeological finds. One of the most interesting exhibits is an 18th-century coach without wheels. According to council regulations – and to reduce the noise of wheels on the cobbled streets – wealthy Amsterdammers had to travel by sleigh, even in summer. The entrance fee to the museum includes free entry to the Civic Guards Gallery, a glass-roofed 'street' between Kalverstraat and the Begijnhof, which is lined with 15 massive portraits of the Amsterdam Civic Guards, dating from the 17th century. However, the Rijksmuseum (see above) has the most famous painting of the Civic Guard – Rembrandt's Nightwatch.
Kalverstraat 92 or Nieuwezijds Voorburgwal 359
Tel: (020) 523 1822. Fax: (020) 620 7789.
E-mail: info@ahm.nl
Website: www.ahm.nl
Transport: Trams 1, 2, 4, 5, 9, 14, 16, 24 or 25.
Opening hours: Mon–Fri 1000–1700, Sat and Sun 1100–1700.
Admission: €6 (concessions available).

Heineken Experience

Voted 'Best Amsterdam Visitor Attraction' in 2001, the Heineken Experience is a self-guided, multimedia exploration of the workings of the world's largest beer exporter. There is plenty of information on the company's rich history and also the 'Bottle Ride', where visitors get to feel what it is like to be a beer bottle during the production process. At the end of the tour, there is, of course, the chance to sample the hallowed brew.

Stadhouderskade 78
Tel: (020) 523 9666.
E-mail: info@heinekenexperience.nl
Website: www.heinekenexperience.nl
Transport: Trams 16, 24 or 25.
Opening hours: Tues–Sun 1000–1800.
Admission: €7.50 (concessions available).

Sub-Culture Museums

Amsterdam is infamous for its Sexmuseum but it also boasts the dubious charms of the Hash Museum and the Torture Museum. The extremely tacky Sexmuseum Amsterdam, the only one in Europe, is full of erotica – objets d'art, photos, prints, paintings and videos – dating from the Roman era to about 1960, although it somehow manages to be totally devoid of eroticism. The Hash Museum is of interest to those visitors who come to Amsterdam in search of coffee shops and would like to learn a little more about the hallowed weed, while the Torture Museum caters for another sub-group of society altogether. Nevertheless, it is tongue-in-cheek enough to be of interest to all. The three museums are all within walking distance in the city centre.
Hash Museum
Oudezijds Achterburgwal 130
Tel: (020) 623 5961.
Transport: Trams 4, 9, 14, 16, 24 or 25.
Opening hours: Daily 1100–2200.
Admission: €5.70.
Sexmuseum Amsterdam
Damrak 18
Tel: (020) 622 8376.
Website: www.sexmuseumamsterdam.com
Transport: A short walk from Centraal Station.
Opening hours: Daily 1000–2300.
Admission: €2.60.
Torture Museum
Singel 449
Tel: (020) 639 2027.
Transport: A short walk from Centraal Station.
Opening hours: Daily 1100–2200.
Admission: €5.70.

Koninklijk Paleis (Royal Palace)

The Royal Palace, designed by Jacob van Campen, was built in 1648, as Amsterdam's city hall. When King Louis Napoleon arrived in Amsterdam, in 1808, he had the city hall turned into a palace. The large collection of Empire-style furniture, chandeliers and clocks date from this period. Although the palace is still the official royal residence, the royal family lives in The Hague. However, Queen Beatrix does host official functions here.
Nieuwezijds Voorburgwal 147
Tel: (020) 620 4060.
E-mail: info@koninklijkhuis.nl
Website: www.koninklijkhuis.nl
Transport: Trams 1, 2, 4, 5, 9, 13, 14, 16, 17, 24 or 25.
Opening hours: Tues, Wed, Thurs, Sat and Sun 1230–1700; guided tours need to be booked two weeks in advance.
Admission: €4.50 (concessions available).

NEMO Museum

The funky new NEMO Museum is an unmistakable sight on the banks of the IJ. Just a short stroll away from Centraal Station is this museum, which attempts to defy the crusty image of some traditional museums by offering plenty of hands-on exhibits to stimulate young minds and keep them occupied, as well as provide more information on science and technology for older visitors. This bright, relaxed venue is a good antidote to Amsterdam's other, perhaps more stuffy, museums, especially for younger visitors.

Oosterdok 2
Tel: (0900) 919 1100. Fax: (020) 531 3535.
Website: www.e-nemo.nl
Transport: Bus 22.
Opening hours: Tues–Sun 1000–1700.
Admission: €10 (concessions available).

Further Distractions

Vondelpark

Named after a famous Dutch poet, the *Vondelpark* is known as the 'green lung' of Amsterdam. It contains 49 hectares (120 acres) of ponds, gardens, lakes, playgrounds, cafés and a bandstand. During summer, there are regular free concerts. At times, palm readers and buskers – African drummers, classical quartets and jazz singers – provide entertainment. Just a short walk from the Leidseplein, the Vondelpark is an ideal place for visitors to get away from it all.
Vondelpark, Roemer Visscherstraat
Tel: (020) 676 5860.
E-mail: info@vondelpark.tv
Website: www.vondelpark.tv
Transport: Tram 1, 2, 3, 5, 6, 7, 10 or 12.
Opening hours: Daily dawn until dusk.
Admission: Free.

Nieuwe Kerk (New Church)

Despite its name, the building of the original church that stood on this site was started in 1408, as the congregation had outgrown the Oude Kerk (Old Church). The present structure dates from the 17th century, the previous wooden church having been badly damaged by fire. One of the most interesting pieces inside the church is the pulpit. Rising to a height of more than 10m (33ft), it took sculptor Albert Jansz Vinckenbrinck almost 20 years (1645–1664) to create. A close look at the carved 'rope' of the handrail will reveal mischievous angels sliding down it. Located next door to the Royal Palace, on the Dam, the *Nieuwe Kerk* has been used for the inauguration of Dutch monarchs since 1815 – Queen Beatrix was crowned here in 1980. The church is also renowned for excellent exhibitions and it is rated as one of the top three exhibition locations in The Netherlands.
Nieuwezijds Voorburgwal
Tel: (020) 638 6909 (recorded information).
E-mail: mail@nieuwekerk.nl
Website: www.nieuwekerk.nl
Transport: Tram 1, 2, 4, 5, 9, 13, 14, 16, 17, 24 or 25.
Opening hours: Mon–Fri 1000–1600, Sat and Sun 1100–1700 (can vary).
Admission: Varies according to exhibition; often free.

Hortus Botanicus

The very pretty *Hortus Botanicus* is home to more than 800 plants from all over the world. It is also one of the oldest botanical gardens in the world, established as a 'Hortus Medicus' herb garden in 1638. The garden became an ornamental garden, displaying foreign plants brought back by the East India Company, from as far afield as South Africa, India, Indonesia, Australia and Japan. Conducted tours take place on Sunday at 1300 and last for 60–90 minutes.
Plantage Middenlaan 2A
Tel: (020) 625 9021. Fax: (020) 625 7006.
E-mail: hortus.amsterdam@wxs.nl
Website: www.hortus-botanicus.nl
Transport: Metro Waterlooplein; tram 7 or 9.
Opening hours: Mon–Fri 0900–1700, Sat and Sun

1100–1700 (Apr–Oct); Mon–Fri 0900–1600, Sat and Sun 1100–1600 (Nov–Mar).
Admission: €3.40 (Nov–Mar); €6 (Apr–Oct); concessions available.

Roemer Visscherstraat

Also known as United Europe, or Seven Countries Houses, the extraordinary street, *Roemer Visscherstraat*, was built in 1894, by architect Tjeerd Kuipers, with the intention of focusing on the history of European architecture. Lying between the Vondelpark and Leidseplein, numbers 20 to 30A of this street provide a one-minute excursion through seven European cities. Number 20, with its Gothic windows, is based on romantic German architecture. Number 22 is a miniature French Loire château, while 24 is a Moorish masterpiece reminiscent of Granada's Alhambra. There is an Italian palazzo at number 26, next door to which, with its onion-shaped dome, is a house reminiscent of a Russian cathedral. Number 30 is a Renaissance-style Dutch house, while 30A is an English cottage.
Roemer Visscherstraat 20–30A
Transport: Tram 1, 2, 3, 5, 6, 7, 10 or 12.

Houseboat Museum

Living on a houseboat sounds like an alluring way of life and it is increasingly popular in the Amsterdam area. This modest museum, reputed to be the only one of its kind in the world, delves into this unique way of life, answering questions about what it is like to live on a boat in this historic city. The boat is quite like a house – with a living room, shower, toilet and bedroom – and is a far better way of seeing into a houseboat than poking through the windows of a real one, as many curious tourists cannot help themselves doing.
Opposite Prinsengracht 296
Tel: (020) 427 0750.
E-mail: info@houseboatmuseum.nl
Website: www.houseboatmuseum.nl
Transport: Trams 13, 14 or 17.
Opening hours: Wed–Sun 1100–1700 (Mar–Oct); Fri–Sun 1100–1700 (Nov–Feb).
Admission: €2.50.

Tours of the City

Walking Tours

The VVV *Amsterdam Tourist Office* – (tel: (020) 551 2525 *or* 201 880 *or* (0900) 400 4040; fax: (020) 201 8850; e-mail: info@amsterdamtourist.nl; website: www. visitamsterdam.nl) publishes a number of brochures detailing informative and interesting walking tours of the city. The series 'A Walk Through…' includes 'Maritime Amsterdam', 'Jewish Amsterdam' and 'The Jordaan'. Another, 'Amsterdam in the Footsteps of Vincent Van Gogh', covers places associated with the artist.
Mee in Mokum, Hartenstraat 18 (tel: (020) 625 1390), offers guided tours around the Old Town and Jordaan. All tour guides are long-term residents over the age of 50. The content of the tours varies between guides, as each has their own very personal and individual perspective on the city. The three-hour tours, which run from Tuesday to Sunday, set off from the Historisch Museum and cost €3.50 – advanced booking is essential.

Bus Tours

The new *De Opstapper* minibus is run by GVB (tel: (0900) 9292; website: www.gvb.nl). The hop-on hop-off bus circles away from the Centraal Station and curves around Prinsengracht towards Waterlooplein and then back. It leaves every ten minutes and, as there are no

dedicated stops, passengers just tell the driver where they want to get off. Standard public transport *strippenkaarten* for one zone, at €1.60, are valid, as are *dagkaarten* passes (see *Public Transport* in *Getting Around*), otherwise tickets are available for purchase from the driver, also at €1.60.

Bicycle Tours

Yellow Bike, Nieuwezijds Kolk 29 (tel: (020) 620 6940; fax: (020) 620 7140; website: www.yellowbike.nl), operates tours between April and November, with prices starting at €17 for a two-hour tour of the city, including the Vondelpark and the Jordaan. Tours are conducted in English but German, French, Spanish or Italian tours can also be arranged on request. All tours depart from Nieuwezijds Kolk 29, which is a five-minute walk from the Centraal Station.

Boat Tours

Probably the best way to see Amsterdam is from one of the many canal tour boats available. There are a number of companies operating these tours. The hour-long itinerary varies little but the price and delivery of information does. Visitors should choose from *The Best of Holland*, Damrak 34 (tel: (020) 624 6340; website: www.asiacompass.nl), *Lindbergh*, Damrak 26 (tel: (020) 622 2766), *Lovers*, opposite Prins Hendrikkade 25–27 (tel: (020) 622 2181; website: www.lovers.nl), and *Rondvaarten*, opposite Kooy BV Rokin 125 (tel: (020) 623 3810). The tours run throughout the year, at regular intervals during the day. Passengers can choose either to go once in a loop or use the boats as a hop-on hop-off way of getting around the main attractions. The price per adult starts at €8, for the basic once-round loop. Other boat tours that combine the cruises with visits to various museums or take in the canals by night are also available.

Excursions

The national tourist office (website: www. visitholland.com) can provide information on travelling outside Amsterdam.

For a Half Day

Castricum: A 25-minute train journey from Centraal Station, approximately 40km (25 miles) north of Amsterdam, this coastal town is wonderful for getting away from it all. Bicycles are available for hire, costing €6 per day, at the train station (tel: (0251) 654 035 (reservations). Maps can be obtained from the station restaurant, before cycling through

Self portrait by Vincent Van Gogh

Photo: Netherlands Board of Tourism

Photo: Netherlands Board of Tourism

Keukenhof Gardens

beautiful woodlands and meadows to reach the dunes. *VVV Castricum*, Dorpsstraat 62 (tel: (0251) 652 009; fax: (0251) 672 363; e-mail: info@ vvvcastricum.nl) can provide further information.

Marken and Volendam: Two of the region's prime tourist attractions, these pretty fishing villages are easily accessible from Amsterdam. *Marken* is situated on an island, joined to the mainland by a bridge, while *Volendam* is situated on the banks of the IJsselmeer, both approximately 15km (nine miles) north of the city. The locations both have plenty of atmosphere – there are lots of wooden houses and many of the locals still wear traditional dress. Visitors can wander through streets of quaint old houses, dress up in traditional costume and learn how to buy and sell fish at the Volendam fish auction. The outing can be extended into a full-day tour, by stopping off for a fresh fish lunch and visiting the *Volendams Museum*, where an old sailor's collection of over one million cigar bands is on display. Volendam offers a variety of watersports, including excellent windsurfing. Transport is through an organised coach tour or the excellent bus service from Centraal Station. Departure times are available from the public transport information line (tel: (0900) 9292). *VVV Marken*, De Zarken 2, Monnickendam (tel: (0299) 651 998) and *VVV Volendam*, Zeestraat 37, Volendam (tel: (0299) 363 747; fax (0299) 363 484) can provide further information.

For a Whole Day

Tulips: Between the last week in March and the last week in May is the best time to head for the 28 hectares (69 acres) of the *Keukenhof Gardens*, Stationsweg 166A (tel: (0252) 465 555; fax: (0252) 465 565; e-mail: info@keukenhof.nl; website: www.keukenhof.nl). Open daily 0900–1800, the themed gardens are filled with tulips, narcissi and hyacinths; entrance costs €11.50. Trains run from Amsterdam's Centraal Station to Leiden, from where a shuttle bus connects to Keukenhof. Eight kilometres (five miles) north of *Keukenhof* is *Haarlem*, where the *Frans Roozen Nurseries and Tulip Show*, Vogelenzangweg 49 (tel: (023) 584 7245), can be visited from late March to late May, daily 0800–1930; entrance is free. Haarlem town centre is a beautiful mixture of 16th- and 17th-century buildings, with two fine museums. The *Frans Hals Museum*,

Heiligland 62, is home to paintings by the artist of the same name, while *St Bavokerk Cathedral*, contains a 5000-pipe organ, which Mozart is reputed to have played. Regular trains from Amsterdam's Centraal Station run to Haarlem. *VVV Haarlem*, Stationsplein 1, Haarlem (tel: (0900) 616 1600, at 100c per minute; fax: (023) 534 0537; e-mail: info@wvzk.nl) can provide further information.

Rotterdam: Holland's second largest city is often neglected by tourists but has a lot to offer. It might be most renowned as the home to Europe's largest port and it is, to some extent, blighted by the mass of industrial infrastructure that goes with this. Nevertheless, *Europoort* is an attraction in itself, with daily boat tours of the massive port. *Rotterdam* has a buzz and character, which was further enhanced by its recent stint as European City of Culture. Situated 45km (28 miles) south of Amsterdam and neighbouring The Hague, this city boasts a number of first-rate museums, an impressively modern city centre and plenty of shopping opportunities. The city's nightlife is also legendary, with a more cutting edge and raffish feel than touristy Amsterdam. In addition to this, the red light districts of Rotterdam have a harder edge that is a million miles away from the much tamer tourist venues in Amsterdam. Over the last few decades, the city has boldly let itself become a testing ground for the avant-garde ideas of some of the world's more esoteric architects, with a variety of stunning and challenging buildings dotted around the city. Regular trains run to Rotterdam from Amsterdam's Centraal Station. *ANWB/VVV Rotterdam*, Coolsingel 67, Rotterdam (tel: (0900) 403 4065; fax: (010) 413 3124; e-mail: info@vvv. rotterdam.nl; website: www.vvv.rotterdam.nl) can provide further information.

ACCOMMODATION

Hotel prices generally include VAT, which currently stands at 6%, although do not include visitors' tax, which currently stands at 5%. The visitors' tax is usually added to the bill at the end, although it is a good idea for one to check whether it is included when making a reservation.

The prices quoted below are the lowest standard rates for a double room, including VAT but excluding visitors' tax and breakfast, unless otherwise specified.

Business

Golden Tulip Barbizon Palace

Situated in the city centre, opposite Centraal Station, and providing easy access to Schiphol airport via frequent train connections or shuttle buses, this grand five-star hotel provides modern luxury within a chain of 19 splendid 17th-century townhouses. Many of the guest rooms feature ancient oak beams and split-level designs and all are fitted with full mod cons. Business facilities include a variety of meeting rooms and a magnificent congress centre, housed in a restored 15th-century chapel and connected to the hotel by an underground passage. Other amenities include a health and fitness club, a private mooring, a gourmet restaurant and classy cocktail lounge.
Prins Hendrikkade 59–72
Tel: (020) 556 4564. Fax: (020) 624 3353.
E-mail: info@gtbpalace.goldentulip.nl
Website: www.goldentuliphotels.nl/gtbpalace
Price: From €160.

Golden Tulip Grand Hotel Krasnapolsky

The dazzling list of former guests at this well-respected city centre hotel includes William III, Brahms, Mahler, Verlaine, Conrad, Joyce and President Mitterand. And it was here that Omar Shariff worked for a short spell as a porter, having lost at the poker table. Located on Amsterdam's Dam Square, opposite the Royal Palace, this 468-room hotel is vast and unprepossessing from the outside, however, once inside, there is a great atmosphere of calm, efficiency and comfort. A popular business choice, it is one of the largest congress hotels in Benelux, with 22 modern conference rooms able to accommodate up to 2000 people. It also offers excellent dining options, including the celebrated Art Deco *Winter Garden*, which is among the most popular breakfast-meeting venues in Amsterdam.
Dam 9
Tel: (020) 554 9111. Fax: (020) 622 8607.
E-mail: info@krasnapolsky.nl
Website: www.krasnapolsky.nl
Price: From €175.

The Grand Sofitel Demeure Amsterdam

Originally a 16th-century royal inn, then the Admiralty, and later the City Hall, this splendidly restored historic building is now a world-class hotel, located near Dam Square. The 182 deluxe bedrooms are individually designed to suit both business and leisure guests and they all offer views of the surrounding canals, private gardens and courtyards. There is a dedicated business centre and 19 conference rooms of varying sizes. Other facilities include an indoor heated swimming pool, sauna and massage facilities, and the smart but informal canalside *Café Roux*, set up by world-renowned chef Albert Roux.
Oudezijds Voorburgwal 197
Tel: (020) 555 3111. Fax: (020) 555 3222.
E-mail: hotel@thegrand.nl
Website: www.thegrand.nl
Price: From €380.

Hotel Okura

The *Hotel Okura* is a top-notch Japanese-owned tower hotel in a great location between the airport and the city centre and only a short distance from the

RAI. Guestrooms have all mod cons with Internet connection through TVs and large, well-lit desks. The Executive Lounge is useful for those looking for a more exclusive place to take breakfast, entertain guests or hold small meetings; it also allows for guests in a hurry to check out without the hassle of going to the main reception. For long-haul travellers, the spa is a must, with a full jet lag recovery package including a special work out programme, massage and meals. The hi-tech gym has a good selection of exercise equipment, as well as a pool and sauna. There are myriad dining outlets at this 370-bed hotel – one with a Michelin star and another with a view of the city – as well as a sprinkling of bars. The hotel has everything busy executives need during their stay. The Okura's Grand Ballroom is the largest dining location and can seat 1050 (or 1200 standing). There are also 18 other meeting places and a dedicated flexible conference team to tailor them to individual requirements.
Ferdinand Bolstraat 333
Tel: (020) 678 7111. Fax: (020) 671 2344.
E-mail: sales@okura.nl
Website: www.okura.nl
Price: From €205.

Luxury

Amstel InterContinental Amsterdam
One of Holland's most luxurious and prestigious hotels occupies a tranquil, scenic location on the banks of the Amstel River. Since its opening in 1867, it has played host to countless kings, queens and celebrities, such as Princess Diana, Audrey Hepburn, Madonna and members of The Rolling Stones. With opulent, traditional-style rooms of stately grandeur containing Delft porcelain, spacious conference facilities, an impressive health club and swimming pool, magnificent riverside terraces, limousine service and private motor launches, the hotel fully lives up to its motto 'Tradition meets excellence'. Even the restaurant, *La Rive* (see *Restaurants*), headed by chef Edwin Katz, boasts two Michelin stars.
Professor Tulpplein 1
Tel: (020) 622 6060. Fax: (020) 622 5808.
E-mail: amstel@interconti.com
Website: www.amsterdam.interconti.com
Price: From €450.

Hotel de l'Europe
Although its legendary owner, Freddy Heineken, passed away in 2002, the *Hotel de l'Europe* is still among Amsterdam's most prestigious five-star hotels – a grand, Victorian, redbrick hotel, combining Old World style and elegance with modern comfort and a warm, relaxed atmosphere. Attention to detail and real class are hallmarks of the hotel, with the 19th-century paintings, which adorn the public areas, no mere copies. Each bedroom is equipped with full mod cons to suit the most discerning professional or leisure traveller and many afford magnificent views over the Amstel River and the Munt Tower. The hotel offers top-notch business facilities, including six elegant function rooms with built-in mod cons that are perfect for meetings, cocktails, luncheons and dinners. There is also an indoor heated swimming pool and a fitness centre. Complimentary boxes of sweets, fresh fruit and snazzy soapboxes are a nice touch in all rooms. The superior suites are opulent and have balconies overlooking the canals, with suite 102 a stand-out with its large dreamy dark-blue bed, hot tub and twin balconies. The Penthouse Suite is a palatial home from home, with

two levels connected by a spiral staircase, a choice of balconies and a kitchenette. A rolling renovation throughout 2003 ensures Hotel de l'Europe stays among the cream of the Amsterdam crop.
Nieuwe Doelenstraat 2–8
Tel: (020) 531 1777. Fax: (020) 531 1778.
E-mail: hotel@leurope.nl
Website: www.leurope.nl
Price: From €335.

Moderate

Seven Bridges
This delightful, quiet guesthouse counts among the city's best budget options. It is ideally located on one of the loveliest canals with a view of seven bridges, just a stone's throw from lively Rembrandtplein. Each room is a comfortable, stylish double, individually furnished and filled with antiques and there are hand-painted tiles in the en-suite bathrooms. Some have TVs but none have telephones. Guests are assured a warm welcome and, with no dining room at the 300-year-old building, breakfasts are served on fine china in the guestrooms. As there are only 11 bedrooms, it is vital to book in advance.
Reguliersgracht 31
Tel: (020) 623 1329.
Price: From €110.

Van Ostade
It would be difficult to miss this hotel, because the outside walls are decorated with bicycles. The best way for one to see Amsterdam is, without doubt, by bicycle and so where better to stay in town than the two-wheel-friendly *Van Ostade* hotel? Situated in the lively De Pijp district, yet only ten minutes by tram from the city centre, this clean, basic bed and breakfast hires out bicycles for just €5 a day. On arrival, guests receive maps showing the city's main cycle routes and the young, friendly staff can also provide advice on how to discover hidden Amsterdam. Rooms are light, airy and simple, although not all are en suite. There is a relaxing communal area and Internet access is available in the breakfast room. Children are also welcome. No credit cards.
Van Ostadestraat 123
Tel: (020) 679 3452. Fax: (020) 671 5213.
E-mail: info@bicyclehotel.com
Website: www.bicyclehotel.com
Price: From €65 (including breakfast).

Other Recommendations

Blakes Hotel
Blakes is the Amsterdam branch of the Anouska Hempel-designed *Blakes of London*. Located in the trendy Jordaan district, this small boutique hotel is one of the Small Luxury Hotels of the World and is the epitome of style and sophistication. It is housed in a former 17th-century theatre, which, in its heyday, premiered plays by Holland's 'Shakespeare', Joost van den Vondel, and staged concerts conducted by the great Italian composer, Antonio Vivaldi. Today, the minimalist East-meets-West designer decor of the 26 guest rooms – including every imaginable mod con from modem points and voice-mail to CD players and fax machines – combined with an intimate courtyard garden, spectacular canal views, young, efficient staff and a top-notch French-meets-Asian restaurant, ensures an exclusive and luxurious stay. Business services are available upon request and there are conference facilities for up to 30 people.
Keizersgracht 384
Tel: (020) 530 2010. Fax: (020) 530 2030.
E-mail: blakes@slh.com
Website: www.slh.com/blakes
Price: From €370.

Hotel Seven One Seven
This ultra-stylish boutique hotel is situated in an excellent location, right on the edge of the Prinsengracht canal. *Hotel Seven One Seven* only has eight units (rooms and suites), with all of them boasting large beds, Bang & Olusen DVDs, as well as CD players, modem connections and fresh Dutch flowers. There are two patios where guests can take breakfast during the summer months. 'The Library' is a small and cosy conference venue that can house up to half a dozen delegates. On entering the hotel, it is soon apparent that it is owned by a designer – in this case Dutchman Kees can der Valk – with lush fabrics and ornate touches all part of a decor scheme that oozes class and understated sophistication.
Prinsengracht 717
Tel: (020) 427 0717. Fax: (020) 423 0717.
E-mail: info@717hotel.nl
Website: www.717hotel.nl
Price: From €375 (including breakfast).

Hotel de l'Europe

Photo: Leonardo

RESTAURANTS

The selected restaurants have been divided into five categories: Gastronomic, Business, Trendy, Budget and Personal Recommendations. The restaurants are listed alphabetically within these different categories, which serve as guidelines rather than absolute definitions of the establishments.

Most restaurants in Amsterdam include the BTW tax, which currently stands at 17%, and a service charge of 10–15%, within their prices. Nevertheless, Amsterdammers generally round up small bills to the nearest € and leave tips as change rather than include them on credit card payments.

The prices quoted below are for an average three-course meal for one person and for a bottle of house wine or cheapest equivalent; they include BTW tax and service charge but not tip.

Gastronomic

Christophe

Chef Jean-Christophe Royer is fully deserving of his Michelin star for his clever blending of French style with US experience and East Asian influences to great effect. The result is exotic flavour combinations, such as cod with chorizo, pimentos and fennel or deep-fried sea scallops with coconut, avocado mousse, celery, curry and lime sauce. His culinary creations are served with flair in a chic, ultra-modern, canalside restaurant. Reservations essential. No lunch.
Leliegracht 46
Tel: (020) 625 0807. Fax: (020) 638 9132.
E-mail: info@christophe.nl
Website: www.christophe.nl
Price: €65. Wine: €30.

De Silveren Spiegel

Fish is a speciality on the haute cuisine menu of this intimate, candlelit restaurant, housed in two beautifully restored 17th-century townhouses near the Centraal Station. Menu highlights include Zaandam mustard soup with bacon crackling, lukewarm smoked eel from Volendam with cucumber salad and white wine and horseradish sauce, a sensational calf's liver terrine with bacon and apple sauce or grilled filet of brill with seasonal

Beer garden by one of the many canals

vinaigrettes. The wine list is first class, with a rare selection of Dutch wines on offer. No lunch.
Kattengatt 4–6
Tel: (020) 624 6589. Fax: (020) 620 3867.
E-mail: restaurant@desilverenspiegel.com
Website: www.desilverenspiegel.com
Price: €45. Wine: €25.

Excelsior

The *Excelsior* is the signature restaurant of the Hotel de l'Europe (see *Hotels*) and as grand as the famous hotel that houses it. Located on the ground floor, the elegant dining room hovers just above canal level, so diners should be sure to reserve a window table. Award-winning head chef Jean Jacques Menanteau has been at the helm since 1994. He has perfected a decadent menu that includes starters such as jelly of oysters with Basque pepper or brochette of scallops with bourbon vanilla marrow. The mains are equally impressive, with beef tournedos and foie gras, truffle and Madeira sauce, or turbot panfried with Parma ham. Indulgent desserts include soufflé with Grand Marnier and orange salad or mango cannelloni with champagne sorbet. The six-course gastronomic menu at €90 is excellent value for food of this quality and is a real treat.
Nieuwe Doelenstraat 2–8
Tel: (020) 531 1777. Fax: (020) 531 1778.
E-mail: hotel@leurope.nl
Website: www.leurope.nl
Price: €70. Wine: €30.

La Rive

Everything about *La Rive* is superlative, thanks to Edwin Katz, one of The Netherlands' most acclaimed chefs. It is one of the country's finest restaurants, located in the city's most expensive hotel, Amstel InterContinental Hotel, and boasting two Michelin stars. The decor is intimate yet sumptuous with warm tones, soft lighting and silver service. North Sea crab salad with green herbs or lemon biscuits and spicy gazpacho, followed by poached rabbit with gratinated leeks, onion and truffle ravioli and creamy rosemary sauce, with marinated pineapple souflée, honey ice cream and nougat for dessert count among Katz's signature dishes. The formal dining room affords spectacular views over the Amstel River. Reservations essential.
Amstel InterContinental Hotel, Professor Tulpplein 1
Tel: (020) 622 6060. Fax: (020) 622 5808.
E-mail: amstel@interconti.com
Website: www.amsterdam.interconti.com
Price: €80. Wine: €35.

Le Ciel Bleu

The celebrated modern restaurant, located on the 23rd floor of the deluxe Okura Hotel in the De Pijp district (see *Hotels*), offers diners the ultimate in French cuisine. Set in stylish surroundings, with blue skies portrayed on the ceiling and the night sky reflected on a carpet of stars, *Le Ciel Bleu*'s menu boasts many delights, such as lobster soufflé and sautéed scampi topped with melted goat's cheese. The spectacular bird's-eye view of the city skyline helps to make the meal an especially memorable one. There is also a small bar, where guests can take an aperitif or enjoy a glass of fine Scottish single malt whisky after the meal. For special occasions or for special clients, there are also two elegant private dining rooms.
Ferdinand Bolstraat 333
Tel: (020) 678 7111. Fax: (020) 671 2344.
E-mail: sales@okura.nl
Website: www.okura.nl
Price: €60. Wine: €25.

Business

De Belhamel

Stylish continental cuisine at affordable prices is the speciality of chef Victor Kerbosch at this sumptuous Art Nouveau-style restaurant, overlooking a picturesque, leafy canal in the bohemian Jordaan district. The signature dish – beef with poached shallots and armagnac and chanterelle mushroom sauce – is an absolute must, followed by crème brûlée with vanilla ice cream and a cinnamon galette or Dutch cookies served with vanilla mascarpone and red fruits. Reservations advisable, especially for the sought-after tables on the terrace. No lunch.
Brouwersgracht 60
Tel: (020) 622 1095. Fax: (020) 623 8840.
E-mail: stein.vd.linden@belhamel.nl
Website: www.diningcity.nl/debelhamel
Price: €45. Wine: €15.

Dorrius

Established in 1890, *Dorrius* is a popular, central restaurant located in the Crowne Plaza hotel, close to Dam Square. The traditional menu in this long-established, old-style restaurant offers a sophisticated take on hearty, rustic Dutch specialities, such as thick split-pea soup, herring dishes or chicory casserole with meatballs, as well as quality oysters from Zeeland. Reservations recommended; the restaurant is especially popular for business lunches.
Crowne Plaza Amsterdam City Centre, Nieuwezijds Voorburgwal 5
Tel: (020) 420 2224. Fax: (020) 521 1794.
E-mail: roomeyer.jaap@crowneplaza.nl
Website: www.dorrius.nl
Price: €40. Wine: €20.

Het Tuynhuys

Het Tuynhuys (The Garden House) offers discreet service, an eclectic menu of gourmet European cuisine and an exemplary wine list. Typical dishes include exotic salads combinations, such as sweetbreads, prawns, duck liver and smoked salmon, followed by roasted duck filet with Moroccan seasoning and a warm lentil and raisin salad. Guests can either dine in the formal restaurant, located in a converted coach house, or outside in the elegant garden during fine weather. The restaurant is located a short walk from the city's famous floating flower market.
Reguliersdwarsstraat 28
Tel: (020) 627 6603. Fax: (020) 423 5999.
Price: €41. Wine: €17.

Kantjil en de Tijger

A successful combination of modern decor, relaxed but efficient service and spicy, imaginative cuisine makes *Kantjil en de Tijger* (The Deer and the Tiger) one of the capital's most popular Indonesian restaurants. The sensational *rijsttafel* is a favoured speciality (literally meaning 'rice table', this is a traditional Indonesian feast of up to 20 rice, vegetable, meat and fish dishes), although only for those with big appetites. The sharing dishes can be a helpful tool in breaking the ice during that all important business lunch.
Spuistraat 291–3
Tel: (020) 620 0994. Fax: (020) 623 2166.
Website: www.kantjil.nl
Price: €20. Wine: €15.

Vis aan de Schelde

This popular restaurant, conveniently located near the RAI International Exhibition & Congress Center in the De Pijp district, is arguably the best fish restaurant in Amsterdam, with chef Michiel Deenik at the helm. Its classy, modern black-and-white interior with shiny floor tiles and crisp white linens, is artfully counterbalanced by an impressive menu of dishes from around the world, ranging from sushi to bouillabaisse. Diners can expect superb seafood creations such as sautéed pike-perch filet on creamed cauliflower with truffle-polenta biscuit and Sauternes wine essence or ray wing with zucchini flower filled with scallop mousse.
Scheldeplein 4
Tel: (020) 675 1583. Fax: (020) 670 4617.
Website: www.visaandeschelde.nl
Price: €50. Wine: €20.

Trendy

Inez IPSC

Inez IPSC (International Private Society Club) is one of the hottest restaurants in Amsterdam, drawing a hip crowd to its spartan, modern dining room, for inventive dishes, such as lobster ravioli with caviar sauce or cauliflower pannacotta. Inez is so trendy that even the word 'fusion' food is considered *passé* here. Instead, the menu is described as 'IMF' (International Modern Freestyle). Diners can enjoy as many courses as they like (three starters then a dessert for example) while admiring one of the best urban vistas in town.
Amstel 2
Tel: (020) 639 2899.
Website: www.inezipsc.com
Price: €42.50 (fixed price). Wine: €20.

Le Garage

This trendy brasserie, located in a converted garage near Vondelpark and headed by celebrity chef Joop Braakhekke, is currently one of the places to see and be seen. The flamboyant decor of plush red banquettes and mirrored walls is reflected in the ambitious menu, which mixes regional French cuisine with strong Eastern influences, also including all-time favourites such as prawn cocktail, ribeye steak or duck in orange sauce.
Ruysdaelstraat 54–56
Tel: (020) 679 7176. Fax: (020) 662 2249.
Price: €40. Wine: €18.

L'Indochine

This new Vietnamese restaurant manages both style and serenity with a slightly colonial decor; it is a firm favourite with those who have their finger on the fashion pulse. The Thai- and Cantonese-influenced Vietnamese menu at *L'Indochine* focuses on seafood with excellent dishes like squid stuffed with shrimp, red onions and shitake mushrooms, or spicy sea bass in sweet and sour sauce. Carnivores also are catered for with the unusual *filet mignon* in satay spice and basil with snow peas. The set menus are very good value and allow for sharing and sampling of a number of dishes.
Beulingstraat 9
Tel: (020) 627 5755.
Website: www.indochine.nl
Price: €45. Wine: €19.50.

Supper Club

It might not be as painfully hip as it once was – largely thanks to the savvy tourists who have discovered it – but a meal at *Supper Club* is always unforgettable and not just for the food. In this innovative restaurant, the predominantly white interior is transformed into various theatrical backdrops that change weekly, according to the cuisine – one night it is a beach, the next a Greek temple, with a sophisticated, five-course gastronomic menu to match the decor. Underneath the restaurant is the *Supper Club Lounge*, a small and ultra-cool bar. Diners might enjoy dishes such as Portuguese oysters, grilled spiced chicken or seared tuna.
Jonge Roelensteeg 21
Tel: (020) 344 6400. Fax: (020) 344 6405.
E-mail: info@supperclub.nl
Website: www.supperclub.nl
Price: €60 (five-course meal). Wine: €22.

Zushi

Zushi, a futuristically decorated restaurant of predominantly wood, glass and stainless steel, serves one of Amsterdam's latest food trends – conveyor-belt-style Japanese fast food. Here, guests select sushi from different coloured plates, then pay at the end of the meal, according to the number and colour of the empty plates – definitely a fun place, with dishes ranging from €2.20 to €8. Options include a range of sushi favourites, including California Maki (king crab, avocado and mayonnaise), *maguro* (tuna), *sake* (salmon) and *gyunik* (beef) sashimi, as well as hot dishes such as *gyoza* (pork and garlic dumplings) and shrimp net roll (prawn wrapped in rice paper). For dessert, diners can try the *tempura mochi* (ice cream tempura).
Amstel 20
Tel: (020) 330 6882. Fax: (020) 330 6883.
Website: www.zushi.nl
Price: €20 (average amount spent). Wine: €13.

Budget

Café de Jaren

Café de Jaren has been named 'Best Grand Café in Holland' with good reason. This smart, spacious and modern Grand Café, situated nearby the Hotel de l'Europe, is best known for its trendy clientele and sunny waterfront terraces overlooking the Amstel River. Even during winter, the huge glass windows offer sweeping views of the waterway, although diners should not expect to get a seat outside anywhere around lunchtime or at all during the height of the summer season (reservations are not accepted). Food ranges from simple soups, snacks and sandwiches – including no less than three smoked salmon options – to well priced, full menus on the first floor, including a selection of vegetarian dishes and Dutch staples, such as *hutspot* (meat stew) or *haring* (herring). For dessert, the chocolate pear mousse is difficult to resist. Not quite as hip as it used to be, Café de Jaren is still a good place to fill up in comfortable, central surrounds. The salad bar is good value for those on a budget.
Nieuwe Doelenstraat 20–22
Tel: (020) 625 5771. Fax: (020) 624 0801.
Website: www.café-de-jaren.nl
Price: €25. Wine: €15.

Café Van Puffelen

At the back of this intimate, sawdust-strewn brown bar, there is a cosy restaurant that serves generous portions of tasty, modern Dutch food to a young and lively crowd. The mustard soup with mussels, followed by salmon marinated in beetroot with a saffron dressing, with delicious cherry *clafoutis* for dessert, is highly recommended. The handmade

Frozen canal

chocolates served with coffee should not be overlooked. During the summer, a barge moored outside doubles up as a terrace venue.
Prinsengracht 375–7
Tel: (020) 624 6270. Fax: (020) 627 6900.
E-mail: vanpuffelen@diningcity.nl
Website: www.diningcity.nl/vanpuffelen
Price: €30. Wine: €15.

De Keuken van 1870

Once a soup kitchen, this basic, old-fashioned establishment now serves huge platefuls of cheap, no-frills Dutch fare to workers and tourists alike, all seated at communal tables. Visitors should expect traditional staples, such as *stamppot* (a meaty stew) and *paling* (smoked eel).
Spuistraat 4
Tel: (020) 624 8965. Fax: (020) 624 8965.
Price: €15. Wine: €10.

Pancake Bakery

Situated in a lovely, old, gabled canal house, the *Pancake Bakery* is a friendly restaurant that claims to produce 'the best pancakes in town', cooked on an old Dutch griddle. With over 70 different sweet and savoury toppings, the choice can be bewildering. Choices range from the simple syrup or sugar pancake variety to gourmet creations such as the pancake with cheese, sunflower seeds, onions and mushrooms. Dessert is just as adventurous, including the Dutch favourite of a hot cherry, vanilla ice cream, cherry liqueur and whipped cream pancake. The restaurant is cheery and inviting, with tasselled lights and large paintings decorating the walls.
Prinsengracht 191
Tel: (020) 625 1333. Fax: (020) 330 4442.
Website: www.pancake.nl
Price: €15. Wine: €12.

Wagamama

The ridiculously successful *Wagamama* formula has arrived in Amsterdam. Those in the know will be pleased to hear that all of the Wagamama staples are here – the communal seating, the rushed off their feet staff, the chopsticks and, of course, the great big bowls of noodles. Prices are reasonable for large and healthy portions of ramen noodle dishes and spicy curries. A major downside is that communal seating is not to everyone's liking and, in particular, not popular with

Photo: Netherlands Board of Tourism

couples or small groups looking to have a cosy chat or intimate meal. Lone diners could also find themselves engulfed in a rowdy group.

Max Eeuweplein 10
Tel: (020) 528 7778. Fax: (020) 330 4422.
Website: www.wagamama.com
Price: €25. Wine: €12.

Personal Recommendations

D'Vijff Vlieghen

This cosy, candlelit restaurant, meaning 'The Five Flies' in English, is popular with both tourists and locals. Set in a series of period rooms and spread over five ancient, rambling, 17th-century canal houses, the dark wooden panelling, crisp white linens and antique furnishings of the interiors – including four original Rembrandt etchings – create a formal yet intimate setting for the impressive and fanatically organic 'new Dutch cuisine' menu. Typical dishes include spring onion soup laced with berry-flavoured Dutch gin or red perch with sauerkraut, with tangy plum compote for dessert. The main course of wild sea bass with *rilettes* of smoked trout on a coulis of fresh vine tomatoes and basil is excellent. No lunch.

294–302 Spuistraat
Tel: (020) 624 8369. Fax: (020) 638 8171.
Website: www.d-vijffvlieghen.com
Price: €40. Wine: €20.

Krua Thai Classic

Arguably the city's finest Thai restaurant and definitely the most stylish, with subdued lighting, sleek chairs and candles on the tables. Diners are ushered into *Krua Thai Classic* by smooth Thai staff in suave rather than overblown traditional dress. The upper level is the place to be to survey the action below. It is advisable to decide what to order before the appetiser arrives, as the delicate prawn toast can lead to diners ordering too much food. Highlights include juicy chicken satay with a rich peanut sauce to start and mains such as Penang Beef (thin strips of succulent beef in a perfectly spiced sauce). Sticky rice with coconut milk and mango is a good way for diners to cool down after some of the more authentically hot dishes, as is the Thai Singha beer. The theatre menu, available 1700–1900, offers especially good value, as does the expansive banquet for two.

Staalstraat 22
Tel: (020) 622 9533. Fax: (020) 624 9062.
E-mail: p.s.kruathai@zonnet.nl *or* info@kruathai.nl
Website: www.kruathai.nl
Price: €45. Wine: €20.

Tempo Doelo

Tempo Doelo is arguably Amsterdam's best Indonesian restaurant, famous for its western-style interior, exotic flower arrangements, impressive wine list and some of the spiciest dishes in town. The satays and *gado-gado* (vegetables in peanut sauce) are particularly tasty, while the mango dessert is a deliciously tangy and refreshing way to round off a meal. No lunch.

Utrechtsestraat 75
Tel: (020) 625 6718. Fax: (020) 639 2342.
Price: €30. Wine: €15.

Toscanini

Toscanini, situated in the Jordaan, offers authentic Italian cuisine prepared in an open-plan kitchen, a bustling yet relaxed atmosphere, first-class service and excellent value for money. The menu includes sensational handmade pasta and risotto, as well as simple meat and fish dishes. The standard Italian staples such as melon and proscuitto to start, followed by lasagne, are to be found here. It really is little wonder that this is one of Amsterdam's most popular Italian restaurants. Reservations essential. No lunch.

Lindengracht 75
Tel: (020) 623 2813. Fax: (020) 638 8949.
Website: www.toscanini.nl
Price: €35. Wine: €15.

Yamazato

The Hotel Okura's signature restaurant has recently been awarded the Michelin star it so richly deserves. Under the expert guidance of Executive Chef Akira Oshima – a congenial and knowledgeable host – *Yamazato* brings the best of Japan to Amsterdam, both on the plate and with the ambience and seamless service provided by kimono-clad staff. The decor is traditional Japanese, with low tables and stylish, lightweight furnishings. Only the freshest of ingredients are used in Yamazato's menu items and this is reflected in the mouth-watering sushi and sashimi on offer. As much of the seafood as possible is locally sourced, while specialities, such as scallops, are flown in from France and Ireland. Mains include lobster tempura, eel steak with *kabayaki* (broiled fish) sauce and salt grilled sea bass, or for meat lovers, excellent beef fillets that are placed on charcoal stoves on the table and left to cook to the diner's preference. The 'Sou-Syun Menu' at €90 (minimum two people) is excellent value and perfect for those who want to taste a range of dishes but are unsure of what to order.

Ferdinand Bolstraat 333
Tel: (020) 678 7111. Fax: (020) 671 2344.
E-mail: sales@okura.nl
Website: www.okura.nl
Price: €70. Wine: €30.

ENTERTAINMENT

Nightlife

Amsterdam is one of Europe's top party cities. At night, it is like a human zoo, with all sorts of weird and wonderful activities on offer. The city can be the venue for a romantic stroll, with the lights of the bridges and old houses reflected in the canals, or a night spent bar hopping from buzzing bar to buzzing bar, before partying until dawn in one of Europe's top clubs. It could even be a nefarious evening, dipping into the dirty underbelly of a city with few inhibitions. There are hundreds, if not thousands, of bars dotted around Amsterdam and it can be just as pleasant to idle away a few hours in a neighbourhood bar as it is to spend the night in one of the trendier venues in the centre of the city. If, however, you are interested in listening to live bands and dancing the night away, then you should head for the Rembrantsplein-Leidseplein area. If you want seedy, then head for Walletjes and indulge. Over the last few years, the trend in Amsterdam has been away from smoky pubs towards 'grand cafés', a mixture of bar and café, where it is equally as acceptable to explore the excellent range of Dutch beers as it is to flick through a newspaper over a latte.

Amsterdam's clubs usually open at 1000 and, by law, must close promptly at 0400 during the week and 0500 at the weekend. The best nights to go out tend to be Thursday and Saturday. The mainstream clubs prefer a smart-casual dress, with no trainers or jeans. Anything goes at the funkier, more cutting-edge venues. Only those over 18 years are allowed to purchase alcohol in bars and clubs and drinks cost in the region of €5. Amsterdam tolerates the sale and use of soft drugs, which centres around smoking cafés or coffee shops. These are easy to recognise, as their names normally include words like 'free', 'high', 'happy' and 'space', and, of course, you can smell them too. These places usually have a drugs 'menu', with all sorts of nefarious offerings available. However, Amsterdam's coffee houses will be affected by new legislation banning smoking in public places. Bars, restaurants and cafés will be smoke-free from January 2004 but the coffee houses have been given until January 2005 to get used to the idea. Legally, this will mean that punters can buy marijuana in a coffee house but will have to go outside to smoke it.

The best listing for Amsterdam's nightlife is *Time Out*, also updated online (website: www.timeout.com).

Bars

De Waag, Nieuwmarkt, is a trendy bar in the red light district, which also stages cultural performances and exhibitions. Whisky lovers should head for *De Stil*, Spuistraat 326, which boasts over 150 single malt whiskies. The owners are friendly and will coach whisky virgins through the first stages of discovering whisky unaided by cola or water as a mixer. Meanwhile, beer aficionados should make a beeline for *De Wildman*, Nieuwezijds Kolk 3, which has an array of over 200 bottled beers from all over Europe. *Satellite Sports Café*, Leidseplein 11, is tacky and touristy but a great venue for those missing their football and rugby.

Nieuwezijds Voorburgwal is currently the most hip area in the city for bars/clubs. *Seymour Lounge*, Nieuwezijds Voorburgwal 200, is a funky place with a bizarre fish tank full of bricks behind the bar, where live DJs entertain Amsterdam's party set before they move on to the clubs. Just across the road, at Nieuwezijds Voorburgwal 169, is the ultra trendy *NL Lounge*, with its cutting-edge sounds, discerning crowd and nightmare bouncers – dress to impress. The gay and lesbian scene thrives in Amsterdam, with Reguliersdwarsstraat one of the more cutting edge nightlife areas, with *April*, at Reguliersdwarsstraat 37, and *Soho*, Reguliersdwarsstraat 36, two of the most popular venues.

Casinos

Two places in which to win or lose money are *Holland Casino Amsterdam*, Max Euweplein 62, open daily 1330–0300 (last entry at 0200), and *Holland Casino Schiphol Airport*, in Terminal West at Amsterdam Airport Schiphol, open daily 0600–1930. Smart attire is requisite and only those over 18 years are admitted – passports are required.

Clubs

Old dames *Paradiso*, Weteringschans 6–8, and *Melkweg*, Lijnbaansgracht 234, seem like they have been around forever and can look a little tired. They might not always get the big contemporary names anymore – you are more likely to see the Stereo MCs than Sasha – but they are both good bets at the weekend for an unpretentious and fun night out. *Escape*, Rembrandtplein 11, is a massive venue that can hold up to 2000 revellers. Its Saturday 'Chemistry' night is a Dutch institution, attracting some big name international DJs, although the queues to get in can be a nightmare. A more intimate club venue is *Sinners in Heaven*, Wagenstraat 3–7, with a trendier and older crowd than many of the city's larger, more mainstream clubs. Newcomer *Panama*, Oostelijke Handelskade 4, also caters for an older crowd in the up-and-coming Zeeburg warehouse district. *More*, Rozengracht 133, is an exclusive club by the people behind the Supper Club restaurant, with the same chic feel and smattering of beautiful people.

Live Music

Jazz has always been popular in Amsterdam. Many of the jazz greats have lived in the city, including Chet Baker, who died here. Head for *Bourbon Street Jazz and Blues Club*, Leidsekruisstraat 6–8, or the main jazz venue, *Bimhuis*, Oude Schans 73–77, in the historic centre, where the *Dutch Jazz Orchestra* (website: www.dutchjazz.nl) plays on Wednesday and musicians from all over Europe perform on other days of the week. *Paradiso*, Weteringschans 6–8, and *Melkweg*, Lijnbaansgracht 234, both often have rock gigs and sets by alternative acts.

Sport

Football is the favourite sport in Amsterdam and the city is home to *Ajax* (website: www.ajax.nl), one of the top Dutch football teams, along with *PSV Eindhoven* and *Feyenoord Rotterdam*. Ajax is ranked among the top European clubs, thanks to their success in the 2002/2003 UEFA Champions League. The team plays at the spectacularly high-tech *Amsterdam Arena*, Arena Boulevard 29 (tel: (020) 311 1444; fax: (020) 311 1480). If there are no matches being played, visitors can still look around the Arena's *World of Ajax* museum (tel: (020) 311 1333), which charts the history of the club, as well as take a tour of the stadium. Admission to the museum is €3.50. A valid passport is required to buy match tickets. The *Royal Dutch Football Association (KNVB)* organises the Dutch Football League, which is divided into the Eredivisie (major league) and Eerste Divisie (premier league).

A truly spectacular sight in Amsterdam in winter is a frozen canal – all the more so when the local people don their skates and claim the smart Keizergracht as their own ice rink.

Formula One racing fans might want to visit *Zandvoort*, five kilometres (three miles) west of Haarlem, where the Dutch Grand Prix used to be held, before it was cancelled due to safety reasons.

Tickets to sporting events are available for purchase direct from the football clubs and individual venues.

Fitness Centres

Club Sportif, Valkenburgerstraat 28 (tel: (020) 620 6631; fax: (020) 638 3531), offers aerobics, tennis and fitness facilities. It is open Monday to Friday 1000–2400 and Saturday to Sunday 1000–1800. A day pass costs €15. *Fitness Aerobic Centre Jansen*, Rokin 109–111 (tel: (020) 626 9366), is open Monday to Friday 1000–2230 and Saturday to Sunday 1200–2000. A day pass costs €12.

Golf

Amstelborgh, Borchlandweg 6–12 (tel: (020) 563 3333; fax: (020) 697 1306), is a nine-hole public course, where the green fees are €15. It is located a ten-minute walk from Duivendrecht metro station. *Amsterdamse Golfclub*, Bauduinlaan 35 (tel: (020) 497 7866), is an 18-hole course built in a reclaimed polder. Green fees are between €30 and €35 and membership is not required.

Tennis

Frans Otten Stadium, Stadionstraat 10 (tel: (020) 662 8767; fax: (020) 679 0138; website: www.

Canal at night

fransottenstadion.nl), has tennis courts. It is open Monday to Friday 0700–0100 and Saturday and Sunday 1000–1800. Hire of a court costs from €16.35.

Shopping

Amsterdam has much to offer the avid shopper. On the one hand, there are international fashion labels, books, arts and antiques, while on the other, there are local specialities to buy, such as tulip bulbs, chocolates, cumin cheese, stoneware bottles of *jenever* (Dutch gin), blue Delft china and diamonds.

The main shopping areas are Leidsestraat, between the Leidseplein and Spui, Kalverstraat and Nieuwendijk, leading from the Munt Tower via the Dam to near Centraal Station. Pedestrianised Leidsestraat, which – with its fashion boutiques, large fashion store (*Metz & Co*), souvenir shops and newsagents – is Amsterdam's answer to Oxford Street and the perfect place for tourists to combine a spot of shopping with canal views and café stops. At the northern end of Leidsestraat is Singel, the floating flower market. Kalverstraat offers a combination of classy department stores, fashion boutiques and the luxurious shopping centre, Kalvertoren, while Nieuwendijk, one of Amsterdam's oldest shopping streets, is home to moderately priced fashion, shoe and CD stores.

Amsterdam has recently gained a reputation for cool clubbing clobber, with *Clubwear House*, Spuistraat 242, and *ZX Fashion*, Kerkstraat 113, two of the funkiest outlets, with the latter also boasting a hair salon that specialises in outlandish styles. Both shops also provide insider information on the city's coolest parties, which few tourists ever get to hear about. *DKNY* is located on PC Hooftstraat 60, while *Armani* is at number 39–41, in the same upmarket shopping street. *Maison de Bonneterie*, Rokin 140–2, is the Harrods of Amsterdam – here one can find top quality men's and women's clothing and fine household goods. The Dam offers a couple of options, including *Bijenkorf*, Dam 1, the premier department store in Amsterdam, which sells a good range of clothing, accessories, cosmetics and household items. *Magna Plaza*, Nieuwezijds Voorburgwal 182, is located in a fairy-tale, neo-Gothic pile that was once the General Post Office. Inside are 40 shops ranging from *Virgin Megastore* to *Shu Uemura Cosmetics*. Emerging shopping areas include KNSM island, with its designer outlets, and Haarlemmerdijk and Tussen de Bogen, with their speciality and niche shops. *Wini*, Haarlemstraat 29, is a favourite of the local clubbing set with hip clothes and retro fashion.

Amsterdam has 25 markets for those seeking a bargain; they are open during normal shopping hours

(see below), weather permitting. There is an interesting flea market around the City Hall and Opera. The busy, cosmopolitan, food and clothes market is in Albert Cuypstraat. The colourful *Bloemenmarkt* (flower market) on the Singel is not to be missed, while the organic food *Boerenmarkt* (farmers' market) is in *Noordermarkt*, which is open Saturday 0900–1600 (in winter until 1500). The *Vogelmarkt* (bird market), also at Noordermarkt, is open Saturday 0800–1300.

Traditional shopping hours are Tuesday to Friday 0900/1000–1800 and Saturday 0900–1700. However, some shops now stay open later, particularly on Thursday. Generally, shops are closed all day on Sunday and on Monday morning. There is a 20% sales tax on luxury goods and 5% on other items. Visitors from outside the EU can obtain a tax refund at shops displaying the tax-free shopping sign. Shoppers must fill in the appropriate forms and present this to customs at the airport, before check-in. The signed form is then handed to *ABN AMRO* banks in the departure terminals. *Global Refund* (tel: (023) 524 1909; fax: (023) 524 6164; e-mail: taxfree@ nl.globalrefund.com; website: www.globalrefund.com) can provide further information.

Culture

Amsterdam has always had a vibrant and varied cultural scene but over the past few decades it has blossomed, thanks to a renewed interest in Dutch culture. First and foremost, Amsterdam is a musical city, offering a range of musical styles from street performers and carillons to the more highbrow midday and evening performances in the *Concertgebouw* (Concert Hall), Concertgebouwplein 2–6 (tel: (020) 671 8345 (reservations) *or* 675 4411 (information); website: www.concertgebouw.nl), which is noted for its superb acoustics. On most summer evenings, it is possible for punters to attend an organ concert or a recital of Baroque chamber music in one of Amsterdam's magnificent old churches, such as *Oude Kerk* and *Nieuwe Kerk*.

Amsterdam stages around 15,000 performances every year (roughly 40 a day), although there is a more concentrated cultural season lasting from September to the end of June. Shows do not cost a fortune and a relaxed dress code means that even the opera can be attended in fairly casual clothes.

Tickets to cultural events can be booked through *AUB*, Leidseplein 26, open 0900–2100 (tel: (0900) 0191 (€0.40 per minute); website: www.aub.nl). AUB only accepts payment by credit card. Online listings for cultural events (website: www. whatsonwhen.com *or* www.timeout.com) are updated regularly.

Photo: Leonardo

Canal bridge at Brouwersgracht and Prinsengracht

Music

The *Concertgebouw*, Concertgebouwplein 2–6 (tel: (020) 671 8345 (reservations) *or* 675 4411 (information); website: www.concertgebouw.nl), is not only home to the world-famous *Royal Concertgebouw Orchestra* (website: www. concertgebouworkest.nl) conducted by Riccardo Chailly but also plays host to visiting companies and international soloists. Free concerts take place in either the *Grote Zaal* (Great Hall) or *Kleine Zaal* (Recital Hall) of the Concertgebouw, on Wednesday 1230–1300.

The *Beurs de Berlage*, Damrak 62A (tel: (020) 530 4141; fax: (020) 620 4701; website: www.beursvanberlage.net), is an architecturally fascinating building, where the 140-member *Netherlands Philharmonic Orchestra* (website: www.orkest.nl) is based. The *Netherlands Chamber Orchestra* (website: www.orkest.nl) and guest artists tend to perform in the building's 'glass box', the *Aga Zaal*. The *Boekmanzaal* is part of the *Muziektheater* (Opera House), Amstel 3 (tel: (020) 551 8911; fax: (020) 551 8025), home of *Netherlands Opera* (website: www.dno.nl). It holds a free lunchtime concert at 1230–1300 on Tuesday (October to June), often performed by members of the *Netherlands Philharmonic Orchestra*, the *Choir of the Netherlands Opera* (website: www.dno.nl) and the *Netherlands Ballet Orchestra* (website: www. balletorkest.nl/paginaas/engels/textENG1.html).

Less formal concerts are performed by four of the city's 17th-century carillons, on a weekly basis. Bell ringing takes place on Tuesday 1200–1300 at *Westertoren* (Western Tower), Thursday at *Zuidertoren* (Southern Tower) and Friday at *Munttoren*. The bell ringer at *Oude Kerkstoren* (Old Church Tower) gets to sleep in – concerts are Saturday 1600–1700.

Theatre

Some international fringe theatre companies perform in English and the *Stadsschouwburg* (Municipal Theatre), Leidseplein 26 (tel: (020) 624 2311; fax: (020) 623 8685; website: www. stadsschouwburgamsterdam.nl), often stages English-language theatre productions, as well as dance performances. Musicals and cabaret find a home in the *Koninklijk Theater Carré* (Royal Carré Theatre), Amstel 115–125 (tel: (020) 353 5355; fax: (020) 624 8499; website: www.theatercarre.nl), situated on the River Amstel, and in the nearby *Kleine Komedie*, Amstel 56–58 (tel: (020) 624 0534 (tickets) *or* 626 5917 (information); e-mail: algemeen@dekleinekomedie.nl; website: www. dekleinekomedie.nl), a charming little theatre dating back to 1788.

Dance

The *Dutch National Ballet* (website: www. het-nationale-ballet.nl) is considered one of the best and most versatile companies in Western Europe. Its many devotees flock to the *Muziektheater* (Opera House), Amstel 3 (tel: (020) 551 8911; fax: (020) 551 8025), a 1600-seat coliseum overlooking the Amstel River, to see the great classical ballets as well as works by 20th-century dance innovators. The Muziektheater also plays host to the *Netherlands Dance Theatre* (website: www.ndt.nl), Holland's other world-class ballet company, as well as foreign companies. Situated on a curve of the Amstel, in the heart of the city, this latest cultural landmark is, despite its size, amazingly intimate. The venue is closed in July.

Film

The multi-screen *City*, Kleine Gartmanplantsoen 13–25 (tel: (0900) 1458), on the Leidseplein, shows Hollywood blockbusters. But Amsterdam is also known for its arty cinemas, such as the newly renovated *Tuschinski*, Reguliersbreestraat 26–28 (tel: (0900) 1458), which shows films from all over the world. Films are rarely dubbed into Dutch but are shown in the original language with subtitles.

Films shot in Amsterdam include Mike van Diem's *Karakter* (1997), Dick Maas's *Amsterdamned* (1987) and the Bond film, *Diamonds are Forever* (1971).

Cultural Events

Every 30 April, a huge street party and carnival marks *Queen's Day* and the city is awash with orange. *Floating Amsterdam* occupies the last two weeks of May, when outdoor productions are staged on the River Amstel. Every June, the month-long *Holland Festival*, featuring music, dance and drama, takes place. Tickets can be booked in advance through tourist offices but some same-day sale tickets are always held at the Musiektheater box office. In August, concerts are performed on boats ringing the Prinsengracht canal. All summer long there are regular cultural events in Vondelpark.

Literary Notes

Ian McEwan won the 1998 Booker Prize for his *Amsterdam* (1998), which is partly set in the city. Amsterdam also provided the inspiration for part of John Irving's novel, *A Widow for One Year* (1999), and Sidney Sheldon's *If Tomorrow Comes* (1986). Albert Camus wrote *La Chute* (1970) while based here. More recently, Deborah Moggach's *Tulip Fever* (1998) depicted life in 16th-century Amsterdam. The city has played a prominent role in the works of Dutch authors – two well-known books that have been translated into English include *Blue Mondays* (1994) by Arnon Grunberg and *Bitter Herbs* (1957) by Marga Minco. The unique ambience of Amsterdam permeates the work of Nicolas Freeling, in his detective novel, *A Long Silence* (1972). Perhaps the most famous work to come out of Amsterdam, however, is *The Diary of Anne Frank* (1947). Marga Minco's *Empty House* (1986) might be less famous but it explores some of the same issues. A lighter work is Janwillem van de Wetering's *Amsterdam Cops* (2001), a collection of cop stories that are mainly set in the capital's underworld. Geert Mak's *Amsterdam: A Brief Life* (2001) is ostensibly a guide to the city but its historical depth and highly personalised detail make it an interesting read for repeat visitors wanting to delve further under Amsterdam's skin.

SPECIAL EVENTS

Remembrance Day, some 20,000 locals remember the war dead with the Dutch Royal Family, 4 Mar, Dam Square
National Museum Weekend, free entry to many of Amsterdam's museums, Apr, throughout the city
Queen's Day, parades, fireworks and celebrations, 30 Apr, throughout the city
Liberation Day, celebrations to mark the end of German occupation in 1945, 5 May, throughout the city
National Biking Day, locals take to the streets on their bikes, 11 May, throughout the city
National Windmill Day, Amsterdam's six working windmills open to the public, 11 May, various windmills
Floating Amsterdam, outdoor productions, last two weeks May, River Amstel
Holland Festival, music, dance and drama, Jun, various venues
Canal Run, race around the canals, Jun, Prinsengracht and Vijzelgracht canals
Over Het IJ, festival of experimental theatre, Jul, NDSM Shipyard, Neveritaweg
Parade, circus and fair, first two weeks Aug, Martin Luther Kingpark
Grachtenfestival, over 70 classical concerts, Aug, various venues
Amsterdam Pride, gay festival with a canalside parade, Aug, various venues
Amsterdam Marathon, Oct, around the city
Christmas Day, 25 Dec, throughout the city
New Year's Eve, street party, 31 Dec, Dam Square

Athens (*Athina*) is named after Athena – the goddess of wisdom – who, according to legend, won the city after defeating Poseidon in a duel. The goddess' victory was celebrated by the construction of a temple on the Acropolis, the site of the city's earliest settlement in Attica.

As a city state, the coastal capital of Athens reached its heyday in the fifth century BC. The office of the statesman, Pericles, between 461BC and his death in 429BC, saw an unprecedented spate of construction, resulting in many of the great classical buildings – the Parthenon, Erechtheion, Hephaisteion and the temple at Sounion – now regarded as icons of ancient Greece. Physical evidence of the city's success was matched by achievements in the intellectual arts. Democracy was born, drama flourished and Socrates conceived the foundations of Western philosophy. Remarkably, although the cultural legacy of this period has influenced Western civilisation ever since, the classical age in Athens only lasted for five decades. Under the Macedonians and Romans, the city retained a privileged cultural and political position but became a prestigious backwater of the Empire rather than a major player. The birth of Christianity heralded a long period of occupation and decline, culminating in 1456

and four centuries of Turkish domination, which has left an indelible cultural mark on the city. By the end of the 18th century, Athens was also suffering the indignity of having the artistic achievements of its classical past removed by looting collectors.

Modern Athens was born in 1834, when the city was restored as the capital of a newly independent Greece. Greek refugees flooded the city at the end of the Greek–Turkish war, swelling the population. After World War II, American money funded a massive expansion and industrialisation programme. The rapid growth of the post-war years and the high temperatures of its Mediterranean climate have created a city that can often be polluted and could be described as an urban sprawl. Excessive traffic creates a gridlock on the streets and noxious fumes (*néfos*) in the air, although great efforts are being made to reduce this. Visitors with visions of gleaming marble and philosophers in white robes are understandably perturbed that the architectural achievements of Athens' classical past are surrounded by the unforgiving concrete of indiscriminate 20th-century urbanisation. Over three million visitors come to the city each year, but the majority see the sights as quickly as possible – as if fulfilling some cultural duty – before heading off for the easy hedonism of the Greek islands.

However, Athens repays a closer acquaintance. In addition to the celebrated classical sites, the city boasts Byzantine, medieval and 19th-century monuments, as well as one of the best museums in the world and areas of surprising natural beauty. Despite the traffic, an appealing village-like quality becomes evident in the cafés, tavernas, markets and the maze of streets around the Pláka. Moreover, Athens has the finest restaurants and the most varied nightlife in the country and remains a major European centre of culture, celebrated each year at the Athens Festival. The metropolitan area, including the port at Piraeus, is the indisputable industrial and economic powerhouse of the country, while the return of the Olympic Games in 2004 is prompting a flurry of new development. Major projects include the extension of the Athens metro system, the building of new sports venues, the upgrading of hotel accommodation and the revitalisation of the Piraeus port area. The world-renowned National Archaeological Museum, which was closed for renovation through 2003, is due to reopen for the Olympics, although the long-awaited New Acropolis Museum has fallen way behind schedule. In addition, ancient sites within the city centre are being linked by a traffic-free 'archaeological promenade' intended to enhance the urban environment for locals and visitors alike.

Parthenon

Photo: Corel

TRAVEL

Getting There By Air

Athens International Airport S.A. Eleftherios Venizelos (ATH)

Tel: 21035 30000. Fax: 21035 32284.
E-mail: info@aia.gr
Website: www.aia.gr *or* www.athensairport-2001.gr
Opened in 2001, Athens International Airport (Eleftherios Venizelos), located 27km (17 miles) northeast of the city, can now serve up to 16 million passengers annually – a capacity that should rise to 50 million annually by 2004.

Major airlines: Greece's national airline, *Olympic Airways*, Syngrou 96–100 (tel: 21092 69111 *or* 21093 63363 (flight information) *or* 21096 66666 (reservations); fax: 21092 67154; website: www. olympic-airways.gr), operates flights to major cities in Europe and the Middle East, as well as to New York, Montreal, Toronto and Johannesburg. Its domestic flights cover destinations throughout mainland Greece and the islands. Other international airlines serving Athens include *Air Canada, Air France, Alitalia, Austrian Airlines, British Airways, Delta Airlines, Iberia Airlines, KLM, LOT Polish Airlines, Lufthansa, Singapore Airlines, TAP Air Portugal* and *Virgin Atlantic.*

Approximate flight times to Athens: From London is 3 hours 15 minutes; from New York is 10 hours 10 minutes; from Los Angeles is 18 hours 35 minutes; from Toronto is 12 hours and from Sydney is 22 hours 5 minutes.

Airport facilities: These include banks, bureaux de change, duty-free shops, bars, restaurants, a post office, a GNTO tourist information office (tel: 21035 30448; open daily 0800–2200) and car hire companies *Alamo/National, Avis, Budget, Europcar, Hertz* and *Sixt.*

Business facilities: In addition to the business lounge, there is the *Athens International Airport Business Centre* (tel: 21035 30000), which is equipped with booths furnished with PCs, Internet access, telephones, printers, photocopy machines, faxes, and offering secretarial services. A meeting room is also available.

Arrival/departure tax: None.

Transport to the city: The *Athens Urban Transport Organisation* (tel: 185) runs 24-hour express bus services linking the airport to the city (journey time – approximately 40 minutes, depending on traffic). Bus Line E94 runs to Ethniki Amyna metro station, Line E95 runs to Syntagma Square, in the city centre, and Line E96 runs to Piraeus Port. Tickets, which must be validated in the orange machines on the buses, cost €2.90 and allow for 24 hours of unlimited travel on all forms of public transport (bus, tram and metro). These are available for purchase from the bus driver. Taxi services are also available – the cost is approximately €25 to the city centre or €30 to Piraeus Port.

Getting There By Water

Athens is served by the major port at *Pireás* (Piraeus), run by the *Piraeus Port Organisation – OLP* (tel: 21042 26000). Facilities at the port include left-luggage, ATMs, banks, bureaux de change, bars, restaurants, taxis, car hire and numerous travel agencies selling ferry tickets – agencies can also arrange accommodation on the islands.

Ferry services: Many visitors to Greece head straight from Athens International Airport to Piraeus, for a ferry to the Greek islands (website: www. greekislands.gr). From Piraeus, there are regular crossings to ports in the following areas of Greece: *Dodecanese, Cyclades, Peloponnese, Saronic Gulf Islands, Crete, Samos,* northeastern *Aegean Islands* and northern Greece.

Schedules change frequently and services are reduced out of season. Travellers can obtain up-to-date information from the service provider or from the *Athens News,* which lists daily departure times. The local port police, *limenarhío* (tel: 108), are also a good source of information, although their English is limited. Tickets can be bought from the shipping lines' offices located around the quaysides – the larger lines also have offices in the city centre. Three classes of ticket offer varying degrees of comfort and cabin bunks can also be booked. Most ships have limited restaurant facilities. During high season (March/April and August), it is wise for visitors to buy tickets in advance, as inter-island travel is very popular.

Hydrofoils are a fast alternative to the ferries, although services are more expensive and drastically reduced in adverse weather conditions. The majority of hydrofoils from Piraeus are operated by *Hellas Flying Dolphins* (website: www.dolphins.gr). Reservations and tickets can be purchased at the main booking office at Akti Kondili (tel: 21041 99100), in Piraeus, or from authorised agents in the city centre.

There are also international services between Piraeus and Limassol (Cyprus), Port Said (Egypt), and Haifa (Israel), although services to Israel are currently suspended due to the situation there.

Transport to the city: A metro line runs between the centre of Athens and the Piraeus Port terminus (journey time – approximately 25 minutes). There is also an express bus, Line E96, every 30 minutes from the airport to Piraeus Port. A taxi between the port and the centre of Athens will cost approximately €9.

Getting There By Rail

The Greek railway service is run by *Hellenic Railways Organisation (OSE)*, Karolou 1 (tel: 21052 97777 (international services); website: www.osenet.gr).

Greek trains have first- and second-class accommodation and there are luxury sleeper trains on selected routes. However, the rail service is limited to the northern and eastern mainland and parts of the Peloponnese. Trains are cheaper than buses but generally much slower. Reservations are available for no extra charge and there is a 20% rebate on return fares. Touring cards, issued by OSE, entitle the holder to unlimited second-class travel at a reduced cost for ten, 20 or 30 days – there are further discounts for groups. The main railway stations in Athens are *Larissis* (tel: 21052 98837) and *Pelopónnisos* (tel: 21051 31601), both situated off Dheliyáni. Facilities at these stations are minimal, basically left-luggage and a couple of bars.

Rail services: The domestic railway network is limited to the mainland and is generally slower than travel by road. Destinations include Patra (journey time – 4 hours), Kalamata (journey time – 7 hours) and Argos (journey time – 3 hours). Trains to the Peloponnese depart from Pelopónnisos station. Trains for destinations in northern Greece, Evia and the rest of Europe depart from Larissis station. International train services require changing at Thessaloníki (journey time – 6 hours), from where the only direct services are to Bulgaria, FYROM (the Former Yugoslav Republic of Macedonia) and Turkey. A train to London, for example, requires a complicated series of changes and takes three and a half days.

Transport to the city: Buses and taxis are readily available at both stations, while Larissis station is connected directly to the city centre (Syntagma) by metro (Line 2).

Getting There By Road

Main roads are designated by blue signs. Traffic drives on the right. The maximum speed limit for cars is 120kph (70mph) on motorways, 110kph (60mph) outside built-up areas and 50kph (31mph) in built-up areas. It is illegal to carry spare petrol (*venzeni*) in the vehicle. The minimum age for driving is 18 years. Seatbelts must be worn and children under ten must sit in the back seat. Penalties for drinking and driving over the limit are severe – the maximum legal alcohol to blood ratio for driving is 0.05%, above 0.08% is considered a criminal offence.

A national driving licence is acceptable for EU nationals but nationals of other countries may need an International Driving Permit. EU nationals in possession of a Green Card, which provides international third-party insurance, are permitted to import a foreign-registered car, caravan, motorcycle, boat or trailer, for a maximum of six months (or up to 15 months for a fee). A Green Card is no longer a legal requirement in Greece for visits of less than three months, however, without it, insurance is limited to the minimum legal cover. Car registration documents must be carried at all times.

The *Greek Automobile and Touring Club (ELPA)*, Messogion 2–4 (tel: 21077 91615; fax: 21077 86642; website: www.elpa.gr), provides members of associated national automobile clubs with 24-hour assistance on main roads.

Emergency breakdown service: *ELPA* 104.

Routes to the city: The *PATHE* (Patra, Athens and Thessaloníki) motorway runs from Patra in the west via Athens to Thessaloníki and Tsoliades on the FYROM (Former Yugoslav Republic of Macedonia) border. To reach both Istanbul and Sofia, drivers must head north on the E75 to Thessaloníki. From there, Istanbul is east on the E90, crossing the border at Kipi, while Sofia lies northeast on the E79, crossing the border at Promahonas.

Approximate driving times to Athens: From Thessaloníki – 6 hours 45 minutes; Sofia – 11 hours 30 minutes; Istanbul – 16 hours 45 minutes.

Coach services: There are two domestic long-distance bus terminals in Athens – terminal A, Kifissou 100, and terminal B, Liossion 260. Buses

link Athens and all the main towns in Attica, northern Greece and the Peloponnese. Bus schedule information is available from the bus operator, *KTEL* (tel: 21051 24910; website: www.ktel.org).

Hellenic Railways Organisation (OSE), Karolou 1 (tel: 21052 97777 (international services); website: www.osenet.gr), runs regular international bus services to Albania, Turkey and Bulgaria, departing from Pelopónnisos train station, Dheliyáni (tel: 21052 98739).

CITY STATISTICS

Location: Attica, Greece.

Country dialling code: 30. The old Athens code of '010' has been replaced with '210', however, '210' must be dialled even within Athens. All numbers throughout the country now have ten digits, which must all be dialled.

Population: 3,196,000 (metropolitan area).

Ethnic mix: Vast majority Greek, with small minority of other nationalities.

Religion: 98% Greek Orthodox majority, with Muslim, Roman Catholic and Jewish minorities.

Time zone: GMT + 2 (GMT + 3 from last Sunday in March to Saturday before last Sunday in October).

Electricity: 220 volts AC, 50Hz; round two- or three-pin plugs are standard.

Average January temp: 9.5°C (49°F).

Average July temp: 27.5°C (81.5°F).

Annual rainfall: 376mm (14.5 inches).

Getting Around

Public Transport

Public transport in the city is run by the *Athens Urban Transport Organisation* (tel: 185; website: www.oasa.gr). The extensive transport system consists of **buses**, **trolley buses**, **city-centre minibuses** and a **metro/electric train** service, which is being rapidly expanded, due to the Olympic Games.

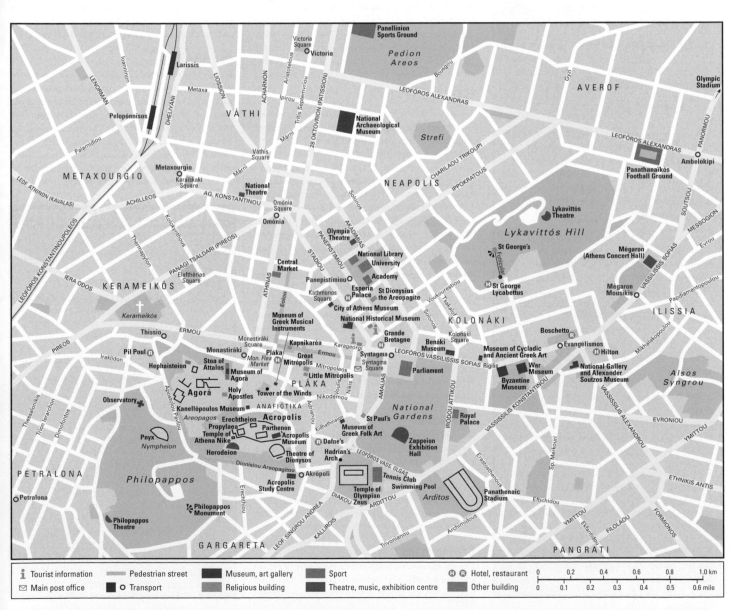

ℹ Tourist information	Pedestrian street	Museum, art gallery	Sport	ℋ ℛ Hotel, restaurant		
✉ Main post office	○ Transport	Religious building	Theatre, music, exhibition centre	Other building		

BUSINESS PROFILE

The public sector is still a dominant force in the Greek economy, accounting for about half the GDP, despite increasing deregulation and privatisation. GDP increased by 3.8% in 2002, compared to a 4.0% increase in 2001. Unemployment in Greece stood at 9.7% (fourth quarter of 2002), showing a notable decrease on the 2000 figure of 11.1%, while unemployment in Athens remained the same at around 10%.

The country receives substantial funding from the European Union (equivalent to about 3.3% GDP per annum). Greece is a key link to the emerging markets in the Balkans and the eastern Mediterranean. As the only EU state in this part of Europe, the country is regarded as a zone of relative economic and political stability within a particularly volatile region. Greece has the largest merchant marine fleet in the world, with an 18% share of international commercial tonnage. Greater Athens, including the port of Piraeus, is a major hub for international transport and trade – a role that has been enhanced by the opening of Eleftherios Venizelo, the new international airport. The metropolitan area also accounts for most of the country's industry — tourism, textiles, machine tools and shipping are among the key sectors.

Outside Athens, the agricultural sector continues to be a major employer (16% in 2001), although its contribution to national GDP is declining. Tourism is the country's largest industry, with a turnover of €10.248 million in 2001, accounting for about 8.5% of GDP.

The top three Greek companies on the Athens Stock Exchange (website: www.ase.gr) in 2002 were *Hellenic Telecommunications Organisation* (OTE), the *National Bank of Greece* and *EFG Eurobank Ergasias*. Most big business is centred around Syntagma Square and the neighbouring area of Kolonáki.

The award of the 2004 Olympic Games has prompted a surge of investment. Athens is experiencing a building boom and the construction industry is projected to be producing annual revenues of nine billion Euros (or 20% of GDP) by 2004. Major projects include the Athens metro extension, the building of new sports venues around town and the creation of a further 4000 hotel rooms to accommodate the influx of visitors. Greece's admission to the single European currency in January 2002 was another boost to the country's economy. Austerity measures introduced to meet the EMU's (European Monetary Union) requirements have resulted in a downward rate of inflation - 3.4% in 2001, compared to an average of 3.9% between 1997 and 2000.

The *Athens Chamber of Commerce and Industry*, Akademias 7, just off Syntagma Square (tel: 21036 04815; website: www.acci.gr), gives information about business opportunities in the city, while the *British-Hellenic Chamber of Commerce*, 25 Vassilissis Sofias (tel: 21072 10361; website: www.bhcc.gr), can provide British people with information about doing business in Greece.

Public transport is cheap and extensive but often overcrowded, particularly during the siesta rush hour (1300–1500). Fares are low – a bus ticket within the city centre costs €0.45 and a metro ticket €0.70. Tickets are sold at bus terminals and some street kiosks (*periptera*) and must be validated in orange machines located on-board the buses or in the metro station. Failure to produce a validated ticket on request results in a heavy fine. Monthly **passes** for the entire urban network are available for €35.

Blue **buses** run daily 0500–2430; there is also a limited night service on the major routes. Services are often disrupted by traffic jams and strikes. The most visited parts of the city, including the major attractions, are served by several yellow **trolley bus** routes. In most cases, however, it is preferable to walk. **Minibuses** 100, 150 and 200, in the historic triangle and commercial centre, operate Monday to Friday 0630–1700 (Tuesday until 2100) stopping regularly at red signs. Minibus 150, which runs along the street Stadiou, connecting Omonia Square and Syntagma Square, is free. The other routes charge €0.45 like normal buses.

The original **electric train/metro** line (Line 1) runs north–south between the suburb of Kifissia and Piraeus Port daily 0500–2415. The metro (website: www.ametro.gr) is undergoing an expansion. Line 2, with its new Acropolis station, now brings sightseers within a ten-minute walk of the upper city, and should be extended south to the coastal resort of Glyfada for 2004. The new east–west line (Line 3) runs from Syntagma to Ethniki Amyna and should be extended to Stavros by 2004, from where a new suburban railway line will run to Eleftherios Venizelos airport.

Taxis

A number of companies operate radio taxis in Athens, which can be reserved over the phone for a €2 charge. Reputable companies include *Athina 1* (tel: 21092 17942), *Ermis* (tel: 21041 15200), *Hellas* (tel: 21064 57000) and *Ikaros* (tel: 21051 52800). Official yellow taxis with red-on-white number plates can also be hailed on the street. During the siesta rush hour of 1300–1500, taxis are in demand and it is not unusual to share the ride (but not the fare) with other passengers. This practice is safe, if not entirely legal. Tipping is not customary, although taxi drivers may expect to 'keep the change' when handed a note. Taxis in Athens are probably cheaper than in any other European capital but unscrupulous drivers may occasionally try to overcharge naïve tourists, so it is wise for travellers to ensure that the meter is switched on and functioning before departure. The meter starts at €1.17 and is non-negotiable. Within the city, the rate is €0.24 per kilometre; outside the city, the rate is €0.40 and there is a minimum charge of €1.50. Extra charges for baggage, trips to the airport and late-night journeys are explained in English on charts inside the taxis.

Limousines

The *Greek Limousine Drivers' Union* (tel: 21032 33957) provides information on limousine services in Athens. Providers include *Astra Limousine Service* (tel: 21092 36755), *Limousine Service* (tel: 21032 34120) and *Convecta Travel Agency and Limousine Services*, Amalias 46 (tel: 21032 25090; website:www.travelling.gr/convecta). Rates start at around €270 for an eight-hour hire period.

Driving in the City

Despite the government's efforts, the centre of Athens still has a traffic and pollution problem. There are times when the streets become completely clogged with traffic and pollution levels are high. The tradition of the afternoon siesta means that, in summer, there are four daily rush hours. The busiest is 1300–1500, when people are going to and from their homes, offices, shops and schools during the siesta. The other busy periods are 0800–0900, 1700–1800 and 2000–2100. The latest traffic-reduction scheme bans all motor vehicles from the commercial centre of Athens – defined as the area around Stadiou, Mitropoleos, Athinas, Omonia Square, Syntagma Square and Monastiráki Square. There is, however, limited access for cars to and from hotels and car parks along the streets Nikis–Karageorgi Servias–Voulis and N. Nikodemou. The scheme is slowly being extended to create a traffic-free zone in the whole central area. Parking is extremely difficult in central Athens, as it is restricted in many streets. Vehicles contravening these regulations may be towed away. Pavements are often blocked by desperate drivers who have been unable to find a parking place. Luxury hotels have their own garages, otherwise drivers can try the central but very crowded car park at Kathmonos Square (a ten-minute walk from Syntagma Square). The main parking lot on the outskirts of the city centre is at the new Olympic Stadium, at Irini. From here it is a 25-minute metro ride into the centre.

For all these reasons, driving in Athens cannot really be recommended to visitors. A car is more of a problem than an asset in Athens, although visitors may wish to hire a car for a trip out of the city.

Car Hire

Regulations vary from company to company, however, in all cases, drivers require a valid driving licence. A national driving licence is sufficient for nationals of EU states. Other nationalities should obtain an International Driving Permit. The minimum age for hiring a car ranges from 21 to 25 years.

Most car hire companies have offices in Athens and at the airport. Major providers include *Avis* (tel: 21032 24951; website: www.avis.gr), *Budget* (tel: 21034

BUSINESS ETIQUETTE

The working day in Athens is fairly flexible. In general, offices are open 0830–1630, although shops and banks may have different hours – smaller organisations still close for a siesta in the afternoon during summer. Punctuality is expected for meetings, although a Greek host may keep a business visitor waiting for a short time. It is usual to shake hands to greet a business contact but embracing and kissing colleagues is not uncommon, although not upon first acquaintance. Business cards are exchanged after introductions have been made. Business attire is relatively formal – men are expected to wear suits and ties and women should wear suits. More casual wear is sometimes acceptable during the summer but local businesspeople tend to dress conservatively.

Hospitality is an important part of Greek culture and visiting businesspeople may well be taken to lunch. Greeks do not drink excessively but they will appreciate it if foreigners show enthusiasm to sample Greek wines and spirits. Almost everyone smokes, so visitors should not be surprised by endless offers of cigarettes. Gifts from abroad are well received but not expected, unless a visitor is invited to a colleague's home, in which case a gift of wine, sweets or flowers is usual.

98800; website: www.budget.gr), *Europcar* (tel: 21092 48810; website: www.europcar.com) and *Hertz* (tel: 21099 82902; website: www.hertz.gr). Hire rates for a small car start at around €50 per day (with a surcharge if the vehicle is picked up at the airport).

Bicycle & Scooter Hire

Scooters are a popular means of transport in Athens, although riding a bicycle cannot be advised. *Rent Moto*, Robertou Gali 1, Makrigiani (tel: 21092 34939; website: www.motorent.gr), hires out scooters and bicycles. Rent Moto has a second office in Piraeus. Rates for scooter hire start at €20 for 24 hours (plus a credit card deposit).

SIGHTSEEING

Sightseeing Overview

Modern Athens is divided into districts but *Plateía Síndagmatos* (Syntagma or Constitution Square) is the epicentre of the city – almost everything worth seeing in Athens is within a half an hour's walk of here. Other useful landmarks are the unavoidable *Akrópoli* (Acropolis) and *Lykavittós Hill*. The *Pláka* covers the area below the Acropolis, to the east of the *Agorá*. Despite being heavily commercialised, this is the most pleasant part of the city to explore on foot. Narrow winding streets are lined with 19th-century buildings, souvenir shops and bustling tavernas. In particular, *Anafiótika* – at the base of the Acropolis – is a delightful area that recreates the style and atmosphere of a Greek village. The area was settled by workers from the island of Anafi, who came to Athens to build a palace for King Otto. In addition to simply wandering the streets or watching the world go by over a lengthy coffee, the highlights of the Pláka include several specialist museums. On the edge of this district, the Monastiráki bazaar is a grimy bustling slice of authentic Athenian life, with neighbouring Psirri the currently fashionable area for bars, restaurants and nightlife. At the other end of the scale, the Kolonáki district, on the edge of Lykavittós, is wealthy and fashionable, providing a welcome retreat from the harder edges of the city.

The tourist season lasts from April to October and is at its peak in August, when the city is crowded and often horribly hot. The Ministry of Culture's website provides information on the main monuments in Athens (website: www.culture.gr).

Key Attractions

Akrópoli (Acropolis)

The *Acropolis* (upper city) dominates both the city's skyline and any tourist's itinerary. The name refers to the rocky outcrop that formed the site of the original settlement in Athens. Foundations for a temple dedicated to Athena were laid in 490BC, however, work did not begin in earnest until the Golden Age of Pericles (461–429BC). The Acropolis site includes the *Acropolis Museum* and four sacred buildings, all from the fifth century BC. The steep ascent to the summit leads to the *Propylaea*, a monumental gateway in the Ionic and Doric styles, which serves as the entrance to the site. The *Temple of Athena Nike* is to the left of the Propylaea – the original was destroyed by Turkish forces in the 17th century but has been beautifully restored. The *Parthenon* is the largest

Porch of the Caryatids, Acropolis

building on the Acropolis and an icon of Western civilisation. Built entirely from marble that glows gold at sunset, the Parthenon was intended as a sanctuary for Athena and housed a statue (no longer in existence) of the goddess. Despite the tourists, the perfect harmony of the structure is still awe-inspiring. On the southern slopes, the *Théatro Dionysou* (Theatre of Dionysus) was home to the original performances of the tragedies of Aeschylus, Sophocles and Euripedes and the comedies of Aristophanes. This stone auditorium, from the fourth century BC, held 17,000 spectators and the ruins remain one of the most atmospheric of Athens' ancient sites.

The *Erechtheion* temple is a dual shrine to Athena and Poseidon-Erechtheus and was built on the site of the mythical battle between the two deities. The south side features a series of six support columns designed as maidens or *caryatids*. Due to severe environmental damage, the *caryatids* have been replaced by models. Many of the treasures from the Acropolis can be found in the *Acropolis Museum*, in the southeast corner of the complex. Nine rooms house objects from the four buildings, including five original *caryatids*. Building work is underway on the *New Acropolis Museum*, which will be located at the foot of the Acropolis Hill. An all-glass structure designed by Swiss architect Bernard Tschumi, the museum will be a new home for statues and artefacts from the Acropolis and will hopefully persuade the British Museum in London to return the controversial Parthenon Marbles, seized by Lord Elgin in 1799. However, although originally scheduled for 2004, the museum looks unlikely to be completed until 2007.

Acropolis Hill, centre of Athens
Tel: 21032 10219 (Acropolis) *or* 36665 (museum).
Fax: 21032 14172 (Acropolis and museum).
Transport: Acropolis or Monastiráki metro.
Opening hours: Daily 0800–1900 (summer); daily 0830–1500 (winter).
Admission: €12 (all-inclusive).

Agorá (Market)

Although the site is now a jumble of monuments and ruins from different periods, in Athens' heyday, the *Agorá* was the focus of city life, serving not only as a place of trade but also as the city's political, administrative and cultural heart. Law courts, temples

and public offices were all based in this area, where ordinary Athenians, stall holders and merchants mingled with officials, politicians and philosophers. The site is dominated by the *Hephaisteion* (Temple of Haephaistos), from the fifth century BC, one of the best-preserved ancient temples in Greece. Its name comes from the god of fire and metalwork – this area of the city was originally the blacksmiths quarter – but it is also known as the *Thiseío* (Theseion), because its friezes depict images of Theseus from Greek mythology. The *Ágioi Apóstoloi* (Church of the Holy Apostles) dates from the second century AD and was restored in the 1950s. Interior features include post-Byzantine frescoes and early wall paintings.

Other attractions around the *Agorá* include the statues of the ten eponymous heroes, *Poikile Stoa* and the *Basileios Stoa*. The fascinating *Museo tis Agoras* (Museum of Agorá) contains an eccentric array of everyday artefacts found in the area. It is housed in the *Stoa Attalou* (Stoa of Attalos). This two-storey structure from the second century BC was restored

TOURIST INFORMATION

The *Greek National Tourism Organisation* (GNTO) did have an Infodesk at Amerikis 2. This has now closed, however, at the time of going to press, there was no information available on the replacement locations, although central tourist information centres are planned.

Head Office
Tsocha 2, Ampelokipoi
Tel: 21087 07141.
E-mail: info@gnto.gr
Website: www.gnto.gr

Passes
It is possible to buy a block ticket for the 'Archaeological Sites of Athens'. The ticket is valid for three days, costs €12 and can be bought at any of the participating sites. These include the Acropolis, the Theatre of Dionysus, the Agorá, Kerameikós and the Temple of Olympian Zeus.

Photo: Corel

Jockey of Artemision, National Archaeological Museum

by the American School of Archaeology and is thought to have been an early shopping arcade containing 42 separate shops.
Adrianou 24, Monastiráki
Tel/fax: 21032 10185.
Transport: Thissio or Monastiráki metro.
Opening hours: Daily 0800–1900 (summer); daily 0800–1500 (winter).
Admission: €4 (all-inclusive).

Ethnikó Archaiologikó Mouseio (National Archaeological Museum)

Following extensive renovation, this world-famous museum is scheduled to reopen in April 2004. Housed in a late 19th-century building, it is undoubtedly the best museum in Greece, with one of the finest collections of ancient and classical Greek artefacts. Fascinating pieces include: the 17th-century BC *Thira Frescoes* from Akrotiri, on the island of Santorini; the *Mycenaen Collection*, featuring hordes of finely crafted gold work dating from between the 16th and 11th centuries BC; and the *Bronze Collection*, including an imposing larger-than-life bronze statue of Poseidon from 460BC. Also worth checking out is the recently added *Egyptian Wing*.
Patission 44, Omonia
Tel: 21082 17717.
Opening hours: Mon 1230–1900, Tues–Fri 0800–1900, Sat and Sun 0830–1500 (summer); Mon 1100–1700, Tues–Fri 0800–1700, Sat and Sun 0830–1500 (winter).
Admission: Not yet available.

Vizantino Mouseio (Byzantine Museum)

Housed in a delightful neo-classical building, this museum traces the course of Byzantine art through the centuries. Besides boasting one of the richest collections of icons in the world, the museum exhibits mosaics, sculptural works and jewellery from the area that is now Greece, as well as from other regions of the former Byzantine Empire. Also of interest are three reconstructions of period churches – early Christian, Byzantine and post-Byzantine.
Vassilissis Sofias 22, Kolonáki
Tel: 21072 31570.
Transport: Evangelismos metro.
Opening hours: Tues–Sun 0830–1500.
Admission: €4.

Mouseío Ellinikis Laikis Technis (Museum of Greek Folk Art)

Lying on the edge of Pláka, this museum displays a vast and colourful collection of folk art that dates from 1650 onwards. Works are divided into specific sections devoted to costumes, embroidery, weaving, gold and silver jewellery, woodwork, weaponry, Greek shadow theatre and hand-painted ceramics. The highlights are the traditional costumes, set off against suggestive reconstructions of houses relating to their specific regions. Another highlight is the *Theofilis Room*, the reconstruction of a house on the island of Lesvos, which was frescoed by Theofilis Hadjimichael (1868–1934), a self-taught artist who took his inspiration from both Greek mythology and the socio-political situation of his country at that time.
Kidathineon 17, Pláka
Tel: 21032 13018.
Transport: Monastiráki metro.
Opening hours: Tues–Sun 1000–1400.
Admission: €2.

Mouseío Ellinikón Mousikon Orgánon (Museum of Greek Musical Instruments)

Housed in a renovated 19th-century mansion in the heart of Pláka, the *Mouseío Ellinikón Mousikon Orgánon* displays a collection accumulated by the musicologist, Fivos Anoyanakis. This museum is great fun – each display case is accompanied by a headset, so that visitors can listen to the sound of the instruments. Films in the entrance feature their construction and performance. Information is provided in English.
Diogenous 1–3, Pláka
Tel: 21032 50198.
Transport: Monastiráki metro.
Opening hours: Tues and Thurs–Sun 1000–1400, Wed 1200–1800.
Admission: Free.

Mouseío Kykladikís kai Archaías Ellinikís Téchnis (Museum of Cycladic and Ancient Greek Art)

The museum houses the private collection of Nikolas P Goulandris. Beautiful exhibits from the Cycladic civilisation (3000–2000BC) form the focus of the collection but other artefacts cover the pre-Minoan Bronze Age and the post-Mycenaen age up to 700BC. The museum makes good use of multimedia information and is less daunting than the National Archaeological Museum. The museum shop offers an excellent selection of quality reproduction pieces.
Neofitou Dhouká 4, Kolonáki
Tel: 21072 28321 *or* 49706 (museum shop).
Website: www.cycladic.gr
Transport: Bus 234.
Opening hours: Mon and Wed–Fri 1000–1600, Sat 1000–1500.
Admission: €3.50 (concessions available).

Panathinaiko Stádios (Panathenaic Stadium)

The elegant three-sided stone stadium was built in 1896, for the first of the modern-day Olympic Games. The design by Ernst Ziller was based on the plan of a fourth-century-BC stadium that originally stood on the site. During the 2004 Olympic Games, this stadium will host the fencing contests and the marathon will end here. It should not be confused with the modern Olympic Stadium that was built in the north of the city in 1982.
Leoforos Ardhittou
Transport: Bus 2, 4, 11 or 12.
Opening hours: Daily dawn–dusk.
Admission: Free.

Olympieion (Temple of Olympian Zeus)

Lying close to the National Gardens and Pláka, this was one of largest temples in the ancient world, being dedicated to the god of all gods, Zeus. Building work began in 515BC, but was only completed some 700 years later in AD131, under the Roman Emperor Hadrian. Today, 16 of the original 104 marble columns, which are 17m (56ft) high, survive. On the edge of the site stands the triumphal arch named Hadrian's Arch.
Leoforos Vas. Olgas and Amalias
Tel: 21092 26330.
Transport: Syntagma metro.
Opening hours: Daily 0800–1900 (summer); daily 0800–1500 (winter).
Admission: €2.

Further Distractions

Green Spaces

The *Ethnikós Kipos* (National Gardens) are a welcome green haven in the centre of the city. The gardens have peacocks and a small botanical museum. Another calm spot is the *Kerameikós Cemetery* (currently closed for refurbishment, although due to reopen in April 2004), named after the patron saint of potters and ceramics and dating from the 12th century BC. Tombstones range from the grand to the poignantly simple. There is also a small museum on site, which houses the originals of some of the more valuable tombstones that have been replaced with replicas in the actual cemetery.
Ethnikós Kipos
Amalias, Syntagma
Tel: 21072 11178.
Transport: Syntagma metro.
Opening hours: Daily dawn–dusk.
Admission: Free.
Kerameikós Cemetery and Museum
Ermou 148, Kerameikós
Tel: 21034 63552.
Transport: Thissio metro.
Opening hours: Daily 0800–1900 (summer); Tues–Sun 0830–1500 (winter).
Admission: €2.

Mikrí Mitrópoli (Little Mitrópolis)

Although *Megáli Mitrópoli* (Great Mitrópolis), which serves as Athens' cathedral, dominates the square of the same name, visitors may well prefer *Mikrí Mitrópoli* (Little Mitrópolis), an exquisite 12th-century church with a mystical atmosphere and charming name – *Panaghía Gorgoepiíkoös* (the Madonna who swiftly hears).
Mitropoleos Square, Pláka
Tel: 21032 21308.
Transport: Monastiráki metro.
Opening hours: Daily 0700–1300.
Admission: Free.

Tours of the City

Walking Tours

Athens is well suited to walking, as most of the sights are centrally located. The 'Unification of Archaeological Sites' is a project currently underway to link the city's ancient sites by a four-kilometre (2.5-mile) traffic-free promenade. The first phase of the route, leading from the Acropolis metro station along Dionissiou Areopagitou on the south side of the Acropolis, has already been inaugurated. The entire project should be completed for 2004.

For private guided tours, visitors are advised to contact the *Association of Tourist Guides of Athens*, Apollonas 9A (tel: 21032 20090), which provides guides for individual and group tours and supplies licensed guides to the travel agencies.

It is often more satisfactory to go it alone, armed with a map and a guidebook. Syntagma Square makes a logical starting point. From here, walkers can either advance up Vassilissis Sofias and then left through the well-to-do district around Kolonáki Square and on to Lykavittós Hill, or go south along Amalias past the National Gardens, turning right towards the Pláka and the Acropolis. Another route to the Acropolis might start at the bazaar on Monastiráki Square, leading uphill past the Agorá. A wander around the Pláka, using the main thoroughfares of Adrianou and Kidhathinaion for orientation, is equally rewarding.

Bus Tours

Numerous companies and travel agencies offer tailor-made tours for groups, whether walking or bus or a combination of both. For example, *Fantasy Travel* (tel: 21033 10530; website: www.fantasy.gr) offers a condensed half-day 'Athens Sightseeing Tour', which is a bus tour with various stops for walking about, including the Parliament building on Syntagma Square, Hadrian's Arch, the Temple of Olympian Zeus, the Acropolis and the Acropolis Museum. Fantasy Travel offers this for groups of up to 50, at a cost of €44.50 per person.

Excursions

For a Half Day

Temple of Poseidon: Built in 444BC, the *Temple of Poseidon* stands on the tip of Cape Sounion, overlooking the Aegean Sea, and is a spectacular sight, particularly when there is a good sunset. The site (tel: 22920 39363) is open daily from 1000 until sunset and admission is €4. The coastal road from Athens offers a dramatic route to the ruins – by car or bus. From the city centre, the regular local bus departs from Mavromateon, a side street next to the National Archaeological Museum.

For a Whole Day

Delphi: Pilgrims visited *Delphi* until the fourth century AD, to seek advice from its famous oracles. Situated on dramatic cliffs to the west of Athens, the site includes the *Temple of Apollo*, the *Sacred Way*, a vast amphitheatre (offering the best view of the site), a stadium and an excellent museum (currently closed but due to reopen in spring 2004). The site is open daily 0730–1900 in summer and 0800–1700 in winter. The museum (tel: 22650 82312) is usually open Monday 1200–1830 and Tuesday to Sunday 0730–1900 in summer, with reduced hours in winter. Admission costs €9 (site and museum) or €6 (site only). Regular buses make the three-hour journey from terminal B, at Liossion 260, in Athens.

Argo-Saronic Islands: *Aígina* (Aegina) is the closest island to the city and therefore gets very crowded on summer weekends. However, for visitors based in Athens, Aegina can make a pleasant and accessible day trip. The island boasts good beaches, the pleasant town of Aegina and a beautifully preserved Doric temple – *the Temple of Aphaia* (490BC). There are frequent ferries to Aegina from Piraeus Port and the journey by hydrofoil (see *Getting There By Water*) takes just 40 minutes. The tourist office in Aegina (tel: 22970 25690 *or* 23613) can provide further information. Alternatives to Aegina include *Ýdra* (Hydra), which is 90 minutes by hydrofoil, *Póros*, one hour, and *Spetsai*, just over two hours. Each has its own appeal. Hydra has a beautiful harbour and several delightful fishing villages, the capital of Póros is a pleasant harbour-side town with an archaeological museum, while Spetsai benefits from a partial ban on cars, a covering of pine trees and good beaches. For those short of time, an organised tour group is a good idea. *Epirotiki Tours* (tel: 21042 91501; website: www.epirotiki.gr) runs a one-day cruise around the islands of Aegina, Poros and Hydra, with a short stop at each. Cruises cost about €80 per person, including lunch on-board.

Peloponnese: It is possible to take trips from Athens to the major classical sites in the *Peloponnese*, including *Corinth*, *Epidaurus* and *Mycenae*. Although the modern town of *Kórinthos* (Corinth) is fairly unpleasant, the surrounding attractions include *Ancient Corinth* (the Roman capital of Greece), the acropolis of *Acrocorinth* and the *Corinth Canal*.

The vast ancient theatre at *Epidaurus* enjoys a spectacular setting, pin-drop acoustics and is remarkably well preserved. It was built in the fourth century BC, rediscovered in the 19th century and is currently used for the Epidaurus Festival in July and August (website: www.greekfestival.gr). The site (tel: 27530 22009), which is open daily 0800–1900 in summer and 0800–1700 in winter, includes the ruins of an extensive spa and sanctuary, as well as a museum. Admission costs €6 and regular buses make the journey from terminal A, Kifissou 100, in Athens.

Although research suggests *Mykínes* (Mycenae) was probably not the home of Agamemnon, as archaeologist Heinrich Schliemann famously claimed, the site (tel: 27510 76585) is undeniably impressive and remains one of the most popular in Greece. Highlights include the *Lion Gate*, the *Royal Cemetery* and the *Treasury of Atreus*. Mycenae can be reached on the Náfplio bus from terminal A, Kifissou 100, in Athens, and is open daily 0800–1900 in summer (closes at 2100 during August but at 1500 in winter). Admission costs €6.

Outdoors: For visitors who need a break from so much culture, there are reasonable beaches south of Athens at *Glyfada*, *Vouliagméni* and *Varkiza*. Bus A3 from Syntagma Square goes to all three places.

Temple of Aphaia, Aegina

Photo: Corel

Alternatively, the mountains that surround the city offer excellent opportunities for walking and hiking and are delightful in spring, when the slopes are covered with flowers and wildlife. Mount Párnitha, a one-hour drive north of the city, is easily accessible and has well-marked paths.

ACCOMMODATION

A service charge of 12% and a local tax of 10% is usually included in hotel prices, rather than added to the bill at the end, but visitors should check.

The prices quoted below are the lowest standard rates for a double room, including service charge and tax, but excluding breakfast, unless otherwise specified.

Business

Andromeda Athens

This exclusive boutique-style hotel lies east of Kolonáki, close to the US Embassy and the Athens Concert Hall and away from the bustle of the city centre. Secluded and private, the interior is adorned with Persian carpets, Italian pastels and modern, designer furniture. The 30 spacious guest rooms are elegantly decorated and offer full modern comforts. Across the road lie 12 suites with kitchenettes, which are perfect for longer stays. Executive services include a business centre and a conference room with seating for up to 100 delegates. It is located seconds from the Megaro Mousikis metro station and ten minutes by taxi from Syntagma Square.
Timoleontos Vassou 22
Tel: 21064 15000. Fax: 21064 66361.
E-mail: andromeda@slh.com
Website: www.slh.com/andromeda
Price: From €450.

Athenaeum InterContinental

Purpose built for business travellers and tourists, the *Athenaeum InterContinental* is situated on a busy thoroughfare south of the Acropolis. Its 489 rooms

and 54 suites are well equipped, modern and stylish. Conference facilities include the *Athenaeum Ballroom*, one of the largest function rooms in Greece (seating 2200), and the *Athenaeum Conference Centre*, designed to accommodate up to 150 delegates. There is an excellent business centre and two floors are devoted to the *Executive Club*. The rooftop restaurant offers splendid views over the capital, while leisure facilities include a gym, sauna, solarium and open-air swimming pool. A hotel shuttle bus makes regular ten-minute departures to the city centre.
Syngrou 89–93
Tel: 21092 06000. Fax: 21092 06500.
E-mail: athens@interconti.com
Website: www.athens.intercontinental.com
Price: From €352 (including breakfast).

Hilton Hotel

Situated opposite the National Art Gallery, within walking distance of the British and American Embassies and close to the Evangelismos metro station, on the edge of Kolonáki, the *Hilton Hotel* reopened in February 2003, following a total make-over. This chic, modern hotel is popular with business travellers and has 527 rooms (including 119 executive rooms and 19 suites). All guest rooms have balconies, as well as telephone, satellite TV, air conditioning and mini-bar. Executive rooms have a few extra perks, such as bathrobe, iron and ironing board, two telephones, modem point and a complimentary *Wall Street Journal*. Of the guest rooms, 220 have views of the Acropolis, for which a small supplement is payable. The 14 meeting rooms, business centre and vast exhibition space also make this hotel an ideal conference venue. There are six restaurants and bars (one on the rooftop), a swimming pool and a health centre.
Vassilissis Sofias 46
Tel: 21072 81000. Fax: 21072 81111.
E-mail: gm_athens@hilton.com
Website: www.athens.hilton.com
Price: From €375.

Plaka Hotel

Fully refurbished in 2001, the 67 rooms of the *Plaka Hotel* have pine floors, minimalist Italian-style furniture and cheerful, primary-coloured fabrics. Each has an en-suite bathroom and is equipped with telephone, air conditioning, TV, safe and mini-fridge. The modern comforts and central location – it is close to the Monastiráki metro station and a five-minute walk from Syntagma Square – make this hotel popular with Greek business travellers and tourists. There is a roof garden overlooking the jumbled rooftops of Pláka, with a summer snack bar. The nearby *Hotel Achilleas*, just off Syntagma Square, at Lekka 21, is under the same management.
Kapnikareas 7
Tel: 21032 22096. Fax: 21032 22412.
E-mail: plaka@tourhotel.gr
Website: www.plakahotel.gr
Price: From €125 (including breakfast).

Luxury

Astir Palace Resort

Lying 25km (15.6 miles) south of the city centre, this exclusive seaside resort is Athens' top retreat for the rich and famous. The complex occupies an entire peninsular, totally 30 hectares (75 acres) of landscaped parkland, with an indented coastline, several beaches and three hotels totalling 476 rooms, 72 suites and 73 bungalows. The hotels are modernist white structures with ample glazing offering views over the sea and grounds. The rooms and their facilities vary within each of the three hotels but all are fresh, modern and very comfortable. As well as the private beaches, the complex offers an indoor pool, three outdoor seawater pools, a fitness club with sauna and massage and four tennis courts. For transport to the city centre, there is a hotel shuttle bus, a limousine service and even a heliport.
Apollonos 40, Vouliagmeni
Tel: 21089 02000. Fax: 21089 62582.
E-mail: aspa-res@astir.gr
Website: www.astir.gr
Price: From €440 (including breakfast).

Hotel Grande Bretagne

Reopened in March 2003, this exclusive hotel has finally been restored to its former opulence and is now part of *Starwood Hotels*' 'Luxury Collection'. The city's oldest and most prestigious hotel was originally built in 1842, as a private mansion, located opposite the former Royal Palace (now the Parliament), but it was converted into a hotel in 1872, since then royalty, heads of state, film and rock stars have all stayed here. The elegant marble lobby is tastefully arranged with Oriental rugs and chandeliers, while the newly refurbished 290 guest rooms and 37 suites are equally refined. All rooms have air conditioning, 24-hour room service, laundry and dry cleaning, a mini-bar and a safe, while suites have extra facilities, such as Internet access, DVD and hi-fi system. There is a rooftop restaurant offering stunning views over the Acropolis, a health club and spa, an indoor pool, as well as an outdoor rooftop pool and bar.
Vassilissis Georgiou 1, Syntagma Square
Tel: 21033 30000. Fax: 21032 28034.
E-mail: info@grandebretagne.gr
Website: www.grandebretagne.gr
Price: From €285.

Moderate

Art Gallery Hotel

Housed in the former studio and gallery of Greek artist Dora Bouki, this hotel lies in a quiet residential street in Koukaki, a ten-minute walk from Pláka, south of the Acropolis. Bouki's niece now runs the establishment and offers friendly and endlessly patient advice at the reception. There are 20 rooms, all with wooden floors, ceiling fans and bathrooms; many also have balconies affording views of the Acropolis. Long-distance travellers will appreciate the hotel laundry service. Colourful oil paintings by Bouki are on display throughout the building and the resident cat adds to the homely atmosphere. Through the winter (November to March), rooms are hired out at reduced rates on a monthly basis.
Erecthiou 5
Tel: 21092 38376. Fax: 21092 33025.
E-mail: ecotec@otenet.gr
Price: From €90.

Marble House Pension

Hidden away in a cul-de-sac off An Zinni, this reasonably priced pension lies in the peaceful residential area of Koukaki, south of the Acropolis. There is a good public bus service to the city centre and Pláka is just a ten-minute walk away. Fully refurbished in 2000, the 16 rooms are still looking good – most have private bathrooms and balconies and all have mini-fridges. Air conditioning is available at a small surcharge. There is a homely, family atmosphere, with a small bougainvillea-covered

Acropolis at night

Photo: Corel

terrace out front, where guests can have breakfast, plus a communal lounge with satellite TV. Through the winter (November to March), rooms are hired out on a monthly basis at bargain rates.
An Zinni 35
Tel: 21092 34058 *or* 28294. Fax: 21092 26461.
E-mail: info@marblehouse.gr
Website: www.marblehouse.gr
Price: From €32 (without bathroom), €36 (with bathroom).

Other Recommendations

Hotel Pentelikon
This impressive 1920s building is set in its own grounds in the exclusive northern suburb of Kifissia. It is a 30-minute ride by car or metro from the city centre but the area's tree-lined boulevards and fresh air (4°C cooler than in town) make it a welcome retreat. Each of the 44 rooms (including 14 suites) is uniquely decorated in Belle Epoque style, with floral wallpaper and fabrics and select antiques. All rooms have plush bathrooms, air conditioning, mini-bar and safe. The hotel's peaceful garden is enhanced by a swimming pool and its five conference and banqueting halls make it a classy venue for business meetings and celebrations. Gourmets come here specifically to dine at *Vardis* (see *Restaurants*).
Diligianni 66, Kifissia
Tel: 21062 30650. Fax: 21080 19223.
E-mail: reservations@hotelpentelikon.gr
Website: www.hotelpentelikon.gr
Price: From €320.

St George Lycabettus
This luxury hotel, located in Kolonáki, on the way up Lykavittós Hill and close to the funicular for St George's Church, affords fantastic views over Athens. Its 158 rooms are individually furnished in modern style with a classical touch, while each floor follows a theme, with the corridors exhibiting paintings and objects related to various aspects of Greek culture, such as shipping or Byzantine icons. Room facilities include satellite TV, direct-dial telephone, voice-mail, radio and CD player, mini-bar, complimentary shoeshine, hairdryer and safe. The *Grand Balcon* restaurant is set in a lovely roof garden and there is a rooftop swimming pool and bar, as well as a gym and sauna. Additional facilities include four conference rooms, a business room and a minibus shuttle service to Syntagma Square.
Kleomenous 2
Tel: 21072 90711. Fax: 21072 90439.
E-mail: info@sglycabettus.gr
Website: www.sglycabettus.gr
Price: From €342 (including breakfast).

RESTAURANTS

The selected restaurants have been divided into five categories: Gastronomic, Business, Trendy, Budget and Personal Recommendations. The restaurants are listed alphabetically within these different categories, which serve as guidelines rather than absolute definitions of the establishments.
Some Athens restaurants are closed for the summer break, between mid-July and mid-September. Prices in Greek restaurants will usually already include the 10% sales tax. However, all Greek restaurants are

Temple of Olympian Zeus

required by law to add a 13% service charge to the bill and it is still customary to leave the waiter an additional 10% tip on top of this.
The prices quoted below are for an average three-course meal for one person and for a bottle of house wine or cheapest equivalent; they include sales tax but do not include service charge or tip.

Gastronomic

Beau Brummel
Once Athens' most expensive restaurant, prices at *Beau Brummel*, in the smart suburb of Kifissia, have eased up of late. The chef, Jean de Grylleau, has moved away from the former butter-heavy French style of cooking and introduced a lighter and healthier Mediterranean slant, with an emphasis on fresh local garden produce and seafood, such as the sea bass marinated in Noilly Prat and served with fennel sauce. The first-floor dining room exudes quiet charm and elegance – parquet flooring, exposed stonework, silver cutlery and crystal glass – while the recently opened ground-floor *Brasserie* now offers a cheerful €30 set menu for Sunday lunch.
Ag Dimitriou 9, Kifissia
Tel: 21062 36780. Fax: 21062 36981.
Website: www.beaubrummel.gr
Price: €70. Wine: €30.

Pil Poul
Housed in a neo-classical building in Thissio, *Pil Poul* specialises in creative Mediterranean cuisine. One might begin with warm foie gras with chicory and caramelised port sauce, followed by stuffed lamb fillet with white Greek cheese, tomato and olives, rounded off by pineapple cream with almonds. The dining rooms are adorned with floor-to-ceiling sweeping curtains and glass chandeliers and, in summer, there is a roof terrace with views of the Acropolis. Aficionados include French fashion designer Jean-Paul Gaultier.
Apostolou Pavlou 5, Thissio
Tel: 21034 23665. Fax: 21034 13046.
Price: €60. Wine: €30.

Spondi
Frequently cited as the Athens' top restaurant, the Michelin-starred *Spondi* is situated in the Pangrati district and occupies a vaulted stone cellar, with tasteful minimalist furnishing and subtle lighting. In summer, there are tables outside in a pretty courtyard. The menu features fusion cuisine, with an abundant use of aromatic herbs and spices. Diners can choose from main dishes like pigeon breast with artichoke sauce or sea bass with rose petal and vanilla sauce. The desserts are equally tempting and extravagant. Reservations recommended. No lunch.
Pirronos 5, Pangrati
Tel: 21075 64021 *or* 20658.
E-mail: info@spondi.gr
Website: www.spondi.gr
Price: €60. Wine: €20.

To Varoulko
Awarded one Michelin star in 2002, this excellent fish restaurant is based in Piraeus most of the year but transfers to the nearby *Yacht Club*, at Mikrolimano, in summer. It is best known for excellent monkfish and creative presentation. The menu varies daily, according to what is available in the fish market, but tempting starters might include courgettes stuffed with crab, shrimp and rice, followed by monkfish cooked in wild celery and topped with sautéed hot pepper, or swordfish with porcini mushrooms.
Deligeorgi 14, Piraeus
Tel: 21041 12043.
Price: €60. Wine: €17.

Vardis
This Michelin-starred restaurant lies within the Pentelikon Hotel, in the northern suburb of Kifissia. The menu features creative Mediterranean cuisine, with an emphasis on seafood and game. Diners could begin with perch and crayfish cream soup with basil, followed by guinea fowl breast and potato purée with marjoram. The dining room is striking – black leather chairs and sofas, parquet flooring, lemon-coloured table linens and candles. In summer, there are tables in the garden by the pool. Reservations essential. No lunch.
Pentelikon Hotel, Diligianni 66, Kifissia
Tel: 21062 30650. Fax: 21080 10314.
E-mail: pentelik@otenet.gr
Website: www.hotelpentelikon.gr
Price: €80. Wine: €25.

Poseidon, National Archaeological Museum

Business

Azul

Kolonáki may be the centre of commerce by day but by night it is also a glamorous quarter for wining and dining. Azul has earned itself a reputation for innovative Greek-Mediterranean cuisine, with exquisite meat and fish dishes complemented by light sauces and aromatic herbs, such as sole in caper and lemon sauce. The interior dining room is small, with just a dozen or so tables, but, during summer, tables spill out onto the pedestrian walkway. Reservations recommended.
Haritos 43, Kolonáki
Tel: 21072 53817.
Price: €30. Wine: €18.

Boschetto

Set in a small park, close to the Evangelismos metro station, *Boschetto* specialises in Italian nouvelle cuisine. Tables are arranged in a glass conservatory, as well as outside beneath the trees. Fresh pasta dishes – such as penne with prosciutto, asparagus and pecorino – are a favourite. Also of note are the chilled smoked tomato soup with crabmeat, and the sautéed turbot with wild mushrooms and fresh thyme. The service is efficient and professional and the espresso coffee reputedly the best in town.
Alsos Evangelismos
Tel: 21072 10893. Fax: 21072 23598.
Price: €60. Wine: €30.

Deals

Located in Neo Psihiko, *Deals* is frequented by smart young professionals. The interior comprises an airy, wood-beamed, split-level space, while outside there is an ample, leafy patio, sheltered by canvas awnings. For a light lunch, diners can order a colourful salad of mixed lettuce, avocado and salmon. For something more robust, seafood croquettes (shrimp and crab with herb mayonnaise) could be followed by duck fillets with orange, honey, thyme and red pepper. Select cigars are available at the bar.
Vasiliou Dimitriou 10, Neo Psihiko
Tel: 21067 73183.

E-mail: iceman@otenet.gr
Website: www.cafedeals.com
Price: €30. Wine: €20.

Jimmy and the Fish

Overlooking the delightful harbour of Mikrolimano, in Piraeus, this excellent fish restaurant offers a refined ambience indoors and a rather more informal and breezy atmosphere at the waterside tables outside. Discreet waiters, clad in hallmark blue and white aprons, deliver vast pans of sizzling spaghetti with lobster, or simply grilled fresh fish with lemon and parsley, or colourful seasonal salads to discerning diners ranging from shipping magnates to Orthodox priests. Reservations recommended.
Akti Koumoundrou 46, Piraeus
Tel: 21041 24417.
Price: €80. Wine: €18.

To Kafeneio

A popular spot for lunch among embassy staff, *To Kafeneio* is located in the fashionable Kolonáki business district. The air-conditioned dining room is refined but relaxed, with wood-panelled walls and pink tablecloths. One might begin with *melitzanes imam baildi* (aubergine in garlic and tomato), followed by *hirino me selino* (pork casserole with wild celery) served with a creamy lemon *avgolemono* sauce.
Loukianou 26, Kolonáki
Tel: 21072 29056 *or* 37277.
Price: €24. Wine: €14.

Trendy

Aristera-Dexia

Gazi means 'gas' and the district of Athens where *Aristera-Dexia* is located, once down-at-heel but now rather trendy, takes its name from the city gasworks. Young, sophisticated Athenians come here to eat fusion cuisine, with main dishes including pheasant sausage with parsnips in Madeira sauce. Diners should save room for a dessert – the chocolate mousse with passion fruit purée is exquisite. The interior is quite impressive, with a glass catwalk leading over an underground wine cellar. On warm evenings, there are tables outside in the courtyard.
Andronikou 3, Gazi
Tel: 21034 22380.
Price: €50. Wine: €20.

Balthazar

Possibly Athens' most fashionable summer venue, *Balthazar* is only open between early May and late October, as it transfers to the *Rock'n'Roll Café* during the winter (see *Bars* in *Nightlife*). It is a chic bar-restaurant, contained within a subtly lit, walled garden planted with trees and shrubs. Some people come here just to drink (and be seen) but there is also a tempting choice of dishes, such as goat's cheese wrapped in grilled vegetables, octopus and beans scented with truffle oil and caramelised onions, or grilled swordfish with green beans and mussel sauce. Reservations recommended.
Tsoha 27, Kolonáki
Tel: 21064 12300. Fax: 21064 12310.
Price: €50. Wine: €25.

Cosmos

Taking up the ground floor of the Deste Foundation Centre for Contemporary Art, in Neo Psihiko, the interior of this chic bar-restaurant comprises

minimalist furniture, modern paintings and industrial-style lighting. The menu includes an inspiring range of appetisers, pasta, meat, fish and cheese dishes, as well as sandwiches at lunchtime. The second-floor gallery hosts contemporary art exhibitions and remains open until 2400.
Omirou 8, Neo Psihiko
Tel: 21067 29150.
Price: €35. Wine: €20.

De Luxe

Located in the Makrigiani district, this open-plan, split-level bar-restaurant is popular with the hip media crowd. The entrance opens onto the lively bar area with funky music, while the more sedate dining space is located on an upper level. Beautifully presented dishes include grilled goat's cheese salad, fish in lemon *avgolemono* sauce with capers, or octopus with black-eyed peas.
Falirou 15, Makrigiani
Tel: 21092 43184.
Price: €30. Wine: €20.

Mamacas

Another fine restaurant in Gazi, *Mamacas* is situated at a crossroads and, in summer, this location is quite surreal, with candlelit, whitewashed wooden tables on four street corners and the towering gasworks in the background. The colour is supplied by the people and the food, which includes starters such as *spetzofai* (spicy sausage) or *revithia* (chickpea soup), and main courses such as fillet steak with grilled tomato, parsley and onion. There is a wine bar annex across the street.
Persefonis 14, Gazi
Tel: 21034 64984.
Website: www.mamacas.gr
Price: €28. Wine: €16.

Budget

Damigos (Bakalarakia)

Situated in a basement in Pláka, *Damigos* first opened in 1865, making it possibly the oldest taverna in Athens. One of the two rooms in which it is housed has several enormous wine barrels on display. The menu features hearty local dishes, notably *bakaliaros tiganitos* (deep-fried cod) and *melitzanes tiganites* (fried aubergine), both of which are served with delicious *skorthalia* (potato,

Kouros, National Archaeological Museum

garlic and olive oil sauce). The house white wine, a pine-scented retsina, comes from the family vineyard.
Kidathineon 41, Pláka
Tel: 21032 25084.
Price: €10. Wine: €4 (one-litre carafe).

O Platanos

One of Pláka's oldest tavernas, located near the Tower of the Winds, *O Platanos* has served up home cooking since 1932. There is a good choice of stews, predominantly lamb or veal cooked with either okra, potatoes, spinach or aubergines, while the only dessert on offer is syrup-drenched *baklava*. The house wine, a barrel retsina, is excellent. The interior is simple – green and white tablecloths and wooden chairs – while tables outside are arranged on a pretty bougainvillea-covered terrace.
Diogenous 4, Pláka
Tel: 21032 20666.
Price: €16. Wine: €4.80 (one-litre carafe).

Scholiarhio

Located in the heart of Pláka, close to small Byzantine church of Ag Nikolaos, this charming *ouzerí* occupies two floors, linked by a head-spinning spiral staircase. The menu is in Greek only but waiters bring a selection of dishes on trays, so diners can chose what they like the look of. Highly recommended are the *bakaliaros tiganitos* (deep-fried cod) served with garlicky *skorthalia* (potato, garlic and olive oil sauce) and the homemade *taramasalata*. The restaurant stays open until 0200 and diners get a complimentary sticky, syrupy sweet at the end of their meal.
Tripidon 14, Pláka
Tel: 21032 47605.
Price: €12. Wine: €6 (one-litre carafe).

Taverna Efimero

Up a steep flight of steps, just off Exarhia Square, this friendly taverna offers a relaxed, romantic atmosphere amid rustic bohemian decor. There is no menu – waiters bring a selection of dishes on large trays to the tables, Thessaloníki style. Customers can choose from a colourful array of *mezethes*, such as *saganaki* (fried cheese), *dolmathes* (stuffed vine leaves), *htapothi krasato* (octopus in wine), *papoutsakia* (stuffed aubergines) and *horiatiki salata* (Greek salad). There is live music some evenings.
Corner of Methonis and Themistokleous, Exarhia
Tel: 21038 41848.
Price: €12. Wine: €5 (one-litre carafe).

Thanasis

A classic place to stop for *souvlaki kalamaki* (shish kebab) served with pita bread and chips, *Thanasis* is popular with locals and gets unbelievably busy, especially at weekends. The atmosphere is fast and chaotic but traditional and fun. Tables are set in a lofty space above the open-plan kitchen area, as well as outside on the street, just around the corner from the Monastiráki metro station.
Mitropoleos 69, Monastiráki
Tel: 21032 44705.
Price: €7. Wine: €3 (half-litre bottle).

Personal Recommendations

Abyssinia Café

This small bistro, close to the Monastiráki metro station, overlooks the furniture restorers' workshops of the antique market. The marble-top tables, polished

Temple of Athena Nike

dark-wood furniture and large mirrors create a pleasant atmosphere for morning coffee, lunch or dinner. Everything is made on the premises – favourites include *gavros* (marinated anchovies), *keftedes* (meatballs in tomato sauce) and stuffed prunes with nuts, syrup and whipped cream. Those who come here in the evening can enjoy *mezethes*, ouzo and occasional live accordion music.
Kinetou 7, Avisinia Square, Monastiráki
Tel: 21032 17047.
Price: €16. Wine: €12.

Achinos

This beautifully designed split-level restaurant is built into a cliffside on the coast, offering fantastic views over the sea. The atmosphere is romantic but relaxed, and the waiters professional but friendly. The kitchen employs authentic regional ingredients to turn out carefully presented dishes, such as grilled *manouri* cheese from the island of Crete, as well as creative salads and delicious stewed meats. The wine goes down well too.
Akti Themistokleous 51, Freatida, Piraeus
Tel: 21045 26944.
Price: €22. Wine: €18.

Archeon Gefsis

Archeon Gefsis means 'ancient flavours' and the menu here features the long-forgotten cuisine of Epicouros. Main dishes include suckling pig stuffed with liver, apple, chestnuts and raisins, while the desserts – such as apple, pomegranate and yoghurt with honey – are heavenly. Food is served in ancient style, with a spoon and knife but no fork. There is also a central branch, however, the Piraeus establishment lies in a beautiful neo-classical building close to Mikrolimano marina.
Epidaurou 10, Kastella, Piraeus
Tel: 21041 38617. Fax: 21041 38618.
E-mail: info@arxaion.gr
Website: www.arxaion.gr
Price: €30. Wine: €10.
Branch:
22 Kodratou, Omonio
Tel: 21052 39661. Fax: 21052 00372.

Photo: Corel

Market stalls

Dafne's

Situated on the edge of Pláka, opposite Hadrian's Arch, the interior of this romantic restaurant is frescoed in warm ochre, rusty red and muted green hues. The sheltered courtyard is heated in winter, making open-air dining possible throughout the year. Sophisticated Athenians and foreigners alike come here to savour traditional Greek dishes, such as lamb *souvlaki* with yoghurt and mint, *stifado* (stew) of rabbit in Mavrodaphne sweet wine sauce, and delicious homemade *kaimaki* (ice cream).
Lyssikratous 4, Pláka
Tel/fax: 21032 27971.
Price: €45. Wine: €18.

Eden

Located in the heart of Pláka, just below the Acropolis, *Eden* struck instant success when it opened in 1982, as the country's first vegetarian restaurant. Everything on the menu is organic, from the soya *souvlaki* served with brown rice and *tzatziki*, to the aubergines stuffed with nuts and cheese. Drinks include organic wines, freshly squeezed juices and a choice of herbal teas. It is a relaxed and cheerful place, with salmon-pink walls hung with framed art posters.
Lissiou 12, Pláka
Tel: 21032 48858.
Price: €13. Wine: €10.

ENTERTAINMENT

Nightlife

Athens has a lively nightlife scene that takes place in the streets as well as in the hundreds of bars, tavernas and clubs throughout the city. Bars open until around 0400 and nightclubs until 0400 or 0600. The legal drinking age in bars and clubs is 18 years. Prices vary, although punters can expect to pay around €5 for a beer or €7 for a whisky. It is not usual to drink wine by the glass in bars in Greece, although wine is always served in restaurants, usually by the half-litre. Admission prices vary dramatically from place to place, often increasing at the weekend. Greeks tend to dress informally for a night out.

Winter is the best time to enjoy the full range of after-dark entertainment, as many establishments follow the tourists out to the islands during the summer. For an authentic Athenian evening, find a bar or club offering *bouzouki* or *rembétika* music. Alternatively, numerous nightclubs and bars cater for European and international tastes. These are to be found mainly in the Syntagma, Thissio, Psirri and Kolonáki areas of central Athens, as well as in the suburbs, such as Kifissia, Faliro, Glyfada, Vouliagméni, Voula and Varkiza. *Kathimerini*, an English-language insert available with the *Herald Tribune*, provides information on 'what's on' in Athens.

Bars

The most 'happening' bar in town has to be *Rock'n'Roll*, Loukianou 6, Kolonáki. The rich and beautiful of all ages flock here to enjoy late-night drinking and good music. The central dancefloor dominates the place, so it is noisy and crowded, but there are a few tables where it is possible to sit and drink and even eat as well. Rock'n'Roll has a selective admission policy and, at weekends, it's almost impossible to get in if you don't know the right people. Close by, *Mommy*, Delphon 4, Pefkakia, is a glamorous bar-restaurant with a rather more sedate atmosphere. *Guru*, Plateía Theatrou 10, Psirri, behind the central vegetable market, is another extremely popular bar-restaurant. Thai food is served in the eastern-style lounge on the first floor, while the ground floor is given over to house and disco music. A ten-minute walk away, *Bee*, on the corner of Miaouli and Themidos, Psirri, also combines drinking, dining and music, pulling in a mixed gay crowd. For a taste of traditional Greece, visit an *ouzerí* (also known as *ouzédhika* and *mezedhopolía*). These are bars selling ouzo (usually beer and wine as well) accompanied by *mezédhes* (Greek hors d'oeuvres). A good place to try is *Scholiarhio*, Tripódon 14, Pláka (see *Restaurants*). For an early evening aperitif or an after-dinner nightcap, stop off at *Filomousou*, Plateía Filomousou 1, a charming old-fashioned café, also in the heart of Pláka, with tables outside on Plateía Filomousou.

Casinos

An hour's drive to the north of Athens, in Loutraki, a spa and resort town at the gateway to the Peloponnese, lies *Loutraki Casino*, Posseido 48, Loutraki (website: www.club-hotel-loutraki.gr), a glittering modern establishment that claims to be one of the largest casinos in Europe. It is open 24 hours daily except Wednesday. The minimum age is 23 years. In contrast, on Mount Párnitha, the *Parnes Casino* operates in old-fashioned style from the Mont Parnes Hotel, 2 Karageorgi Servias (website: www.mont-parnes.gr). A mountain cable car carries visitors up to the hotel, day and night. The casino is open daily 1930–0145 (until 0245 on Saturday) except for Wednesday. Evening dress and a valid passport are required for both establishments.

Clubs

The city's most exclusive nightclub, frequented by rich and glamorous under-40s, is *Privilege*, which recently relocated to Ag Eleoussis and Kakourgodikiou, just a five-minute walk from Monastiráki metro station. During summer, the club moves out to the beach. Some of Europe's top DJs come to play at the renowned *Plus Soda*, Ermou 161, Thissio. In summer, Plus Soda also transfers to the seaside. Another chic and trendy club is *Venue*, L Kifoias 101, Marousi, where house and techno rule the dancefloor. For a more informal but very colourful night out, try *Folie*, Eslin 4, Ambelokipi, where guests of all ages let their hair down to reggae, funk, Latin and ethnic music.

Live Music

For the best jazz in town, visit *Halfnote Jazz Club*, Trivonianou 17, Mets. This sophisticated venue stages contemporary and classic jazz, jazz funk and blues concerts, featuring international musicians. Alternatively, try *Blues Hall*, Ardittou 44 (close to the Panathenaic Stadium), to hear both Greek and foreign blues artists perform. Rock music enthusiasts might prefer *Rodhon*, Marni 24, Omonia. The mood here is informal and fun and the club stages some excellent rock and pop concerts. Many of Greece's top bouzouki stars play at the highly popular music hall *Apollon Palace*, Singrou 259, Nea Smirni. To hear authentic rembétika (blues sung by immigrants from Asia Minor who came to Greece in 1920s), try either the notorious *Stoa Athanaton*, in the arcade inside the Central Market (reservations necessary on Friday and Saturday nights), or *Boemissa*, Solomou 19, Exarhia.

Sport

As if Athens' cultural and architectural achievements are not enough, the city can also boast the modern *Olympic Games* and the marathon among its lasting legacies. Panhellenic athletic contests were held in Athens from the fourth century BC and reinstated as the modern Olympic Games in 1896. After the initial disappointment of seeing the millennium Olympic Games go to Sydney, Athens is ready to welcome the Games home again in 2004. The marathon commemorates the Greek soldier, Phidippides, who ran 42km (26 miles) from the battlefield at Marathon to Athens, to announce Greek victory over the Persians (490BC). He delivered his one word message – 'Nenikamen' (we have won) – and then collapsed and died. The annual *Athens Marathon* retraces his footsteps from the battleground to the 1896 Olympic Stadium. Although the Greek national team has not seen much success in recent years, football is by far the nation's favourite sport. In the domestic league, the local giants are *Panathanaïkós* (website: www.pao.gr) and *AEK* (website: www.aek.com) in Athens and *Olympiakós* (website: www.olympiakos.gr) in Piraeus. The season runs from September to June and most major football matches are played at the *Athens Olympic*

Stadium, Athens Olympic Sports Complex, Maroussi. Basketball and volleyball are also hugely popular. Individual venue ticket offices sell tickets for national sporting events, while *SEGAS*, Syngrou 137 (tel: 21093 59346; website: www.segas.gr), sells tickets to international events. The *Olympic Committee* (tel: 21020 04000; website: www.athens.olympic.org) can provide information on the forthcoming 2004 Olympic Games. The *General Secretariat of Sports*, Panepistimiou 25 (tel: 21032 94227; website: www.sport.gov.gr), provides information on sport in Athens.

Golf

There is a professional (18-hole, 72-par) golf course at Glyfada. The *Glyfada Golf Course*, Kypros/Panopis 15, Glyfada (tel: 21089 46820; website: www. glyfadagolf.gr), is open Tuesday to Sunday from 0730 until sunset and Monday from 1300 to sunset. Membership is not required and admission costs €70 on weekdays and €82 on weekends. A handicap card is requested.

Horseracing

The *Faliro Ippodromo* racetrack is located at the end of Syngrou (tel: 21094 26331). There is racing on Monday, Wednesday and Friday from 1700 in summer and from 1500 in winter.

Riding

The *Attikos Riding Club* (tel: 21066 26429) is based at Alopekis 5A, Kolonáki.

Running

The *Athens Marathon* (website: www.athens marathon.com) provides the opportunity to run along the original marathon route. It takes place each year in November and details can be obtained from *SEGAS*, Syngrou 137 (tel: 21093 59346; website: www.segas.gr).

Sailing

The *Greek National Tourist Organisation* website (www.gnto.gr – click on 'Marine Tourism') has a list of over 50 charter companies offering yachts for hire. Information on races and clubs is available from *Hellenic Sailing Federation* (tel: 21032 35560).

Scuba Diving

The *Aegean Dive Center*, in Glyfada (tel: 21089 45409; website: www.adc.gr), organises scuba diving tuition (with English-speaking instructors) and one-day diving trips along the coast between Glyfada and Cape Sounion.

Swimming

The best beaches are located at Glyfada, Vouliagméni and Varkiza (see *Excursions*).

Tennis

Tennis courts are open to visitors at the *Glyfada Golf Course*, Kypros/Panopis 15, Glyfada (tel: 21089 46820). The *Athens Tennis Club* (tel: 21092 32872) also welcomes non-members on weekdays 0800–1400.

Windsurfing

All *GNTO*-run beaches have windsurfing equipment for hire. The *Hellenic Windsurfing Association* (tel: 21032 30068) can provide more information.

Shopping

Athens' busiest shopping street is the pedestrian-only Ermou, off Syntagma Square, where shoppers can pick up the season's latest clothing and accessories. The most upmarket shopping district in Athens is nearby Kolonáki, where designer boutiques (such as the Italian classic *Versace* and the newest Greek talent, *Eleftheriades*) rub shoulders with coffee shops and chic restaurants. This area includes Tsakalof, one of the most expensive streets in the world. Thankfully, Athens has not adopted mall culture and no massive retail emporiums taint the city's shopping scene. The city's best bookshop is the vast seven-storey *Eleftheroudakis*, on Panepistimiou, which stocks an excellent selection of English-language fiction, non-fiction and travel guides.

There is a long tradition of silver and gold craftsmanship in Athens and jewellery made here can be of a particularly high quality. Jewellers are concentrated in chic Kolonáki, with the expensive international outlets, such as *Bulgari*, lining Voukourestiou, while up-and-coming Greek designers, such as *Elean Votsi*, have shops in the surrounding side streets.

Other good-value items include spirits, ceramics and leather goods. Typical Greek gifts include hand-woven rugs, known as *flokati*, copper coffee pots, virgin olive oil and honey, all of which can be found in the souvenir shops in Pláka. In Athens, there is a big market in reproductions of museum pieces and religious icons – the best places for visitors to buy these are at the shops in the museums themselves.

In the *Monastiráki* area, on the edge of Pláka, shops sell everything from combat army boots and second-hand books to fake designer sunglasses and ancient coins. Shops open out directly onto the street, bazaar style, while Sundays bring the *Monastiráki Flea Market*, 0800–1400, where goods range from carefully restored antique furniture to rather dubious bric-a-brac. *Kentrikí Agorá* (Central Market) is housed in a huge 19th-century metal structure near Omonia Square and is open early morning to early evening, often taking a break for siesta during summer, selling fresh fish, meat and fresh produce. Smaller markets radiate out from the central building. Household items, fresh fruit and vegetables are sold weekly in *Laiki* (People's Markets) all over Athens.

Shops generally open Monday and Wednesday 0900–1430, Tuesday, Thursday and Friday 0900–1330 and 1730–2030 and Saturday 0900–1500. Small, family-run shops may stay open as late as 2200, for the sale of food, drinks and newspapers. Bargains can be snapped up at the sales in August and February. Haggling is standard practice in the tourist areas of Athens and is essential in order to avoid paying extortionate prices.

Visitors from outside the European Union who have been in Greece for less than three months can claim back VAT of up to 18% on purchases over €120. A 'tax-free cheque' will be issued in the shop, to be presented along with the receipt to customs when leaving the county. *Global Refund* (website: www. globalrefund.com) can provide more information.

Culture

Athens probably has the most long-standing and impressive cultural heritage of any city in Europe. However, this pedigree is not confined to past greatness – the city has a number of international performance groups and a continued enthusiasm for the arts is expressed annually at the *Athens Festival*. In 1985, Athens became the first European City of Culture. The idea to showcase the cultural achievements of cities around the continent was conceived by Melina Mercouri, a Greek actress turned politician.

In addition to the venues detailed below, a variety of English-language cultural events are also on offer at the *British Council*, Kolonáki Square 17 (tel: 21036 92333; fax: 21036 34769; website: www. britishcoucil.gr), or at the *Hellenic American Union*, Massalías 22 (tel: 21036 80000; website: www.hau.gr). The Ministry of Culture's website (www. cultureguide.gr) has full listings for forthcoming cultural events throughout Greece (predominantly in Athens).

During the summer, tickets for all performances included within the Athens Festival and the Athens International Jazz and Blues Festival are sold at the *Hellenic Festival Box Office*, Panepistimiou 39 (tel: 21032 21459; website: www.greekfestival.gr), which is open Monday to Friday 0900–1600 and Saturday 0900–1430. Tickets to other cultural events are available for purchase direct from the venue box offices.

Metropolitan Radio Athens (98.4FM) broadcasts a listing of cultural events in English at 0730 and 2030 daily.

Music

Many tavernas, particularly in the Pláka, put on music and dance shows at night. Most shows are designed for tourists but are nonetheless lively and entertaining. The more authentic Greek music in Athens consists of *dhimotiká* (folk songs accompanied by guitar, clarinet and violin) and *rembétika* (a kind of Greek blues, developed by refugees from Asia Minor in the 1920s; see *Live Music* in *Nightlife*). The music combines

Odeon of Herod Atticus

Photo: Corel

Middle Eastern and Greek influences and the lyrics deal with the lives of the city's poor and outcast.

The city's major orchestra is *Athens State Orchestra*, who hold many of their performances at the *Mégaron Mousikis Athenon* (Athens Concert Hall), Leofóros Vassilissis Sofias (tel: 21072 82333; website: www.megaron.gr). This modern venue hosts ballet, opera and classical music events, as well as conferences and exhibitions. The main auditorium seats 2000 and there is also a 500-seat recital hall named after the Greek conductor and composer Dimitri Mitropoulos. The *Greek National Opera* (website: www.nationalopera.gr) is based at the *Olympia Theatre*, Akadimias 59–61 (tel: 21036 12461), which also hosts operas and musical events performed by touring companies and musicians.

Theatre

The tragedies of Aeschylus, Sophocles and Euripedes and the comedies of Aristophanes represent the highpoints of ancient Greek theatre and heralded the birth of Western drama. The original performances were held in the *Théatro Dionysou* (Theatre of Dionysus), on the southern slopes of the Acropolis (see *Key Attractions*). Nearby, the *Odion Iródou Attikou* (Odeon of Herod Atticus) is a Roman theatre from the second century AD, also known as the *Herodeion* (tel: 21072 27209). The auditorium is usually only open on summer evenings, for the *Athens Festival*, when it provides an impressive setting for performances of music and classical drama. The outdoor *Lykavittós* theatre, on Lykavittós Hill (tel: 21072 27209), hosts a range of plays and concerts throughout the summer.

The *National Theatre of Greece* (tel: 21052 88100; website: www.national-theater.gr) encompasses five theatre groups – the *Central Theatre* (*Kentriki Skini*), the *New Theatre* (*Nea Skini*) and the *Experimental Theatre* – all of which are based at Agiou Konstantinou 24–26, as well as the *Kotopouli-Rex Theatre* and the *Katina Paxinou Children's Theatre*, both of which are based at Panepistimiou 48.

Altogether, there are around 50 theatres in Athens performing between October and May. However, visitors without fluent Greek may be restricted to the English-language performances of touring companies.

Dance

The *Dora Stratou Dance Theatre* (tel: 21032 44395) was founded 35 years ago, by a dancer and devotee of Greek folk culture. Each evening from May to September, the troupe – dressed in traditional costume – puts on a show of exuberant Greek song and dance at an open-air theatre on *Filopáppou* (Philopapps Hill), opposite the Acropolis. The *National Ballet Company* (website: www.nationalopera.gr) also perform in the *Olympia Theatre* (see *Music* above).

Film

Athens may not be Hollywood but, with hundreds of traditional and modern cinemas throughout the city, the Greek capital is an excellent place to see a film. Many are closed in summer, when dozens of open-air screens take over to create impromptu cinemas, such as *Cine Pallini,* Venizelou 3 and Marathonos Aveneu, Pallini (tel: 21066 66815 *or* 66284), which provides chairs and tables in a garden setting, and *Thission*, Paylou 7, Thissio (tel: 21034 70980 *or* 20864), with a view of the Acropolis. *Asty*, Korai 4 (tel: 21032 21925), off Panepistimou, shows arthouse movies. About 90% of films are shown in the original language. The local press provides listings of English-language films.

One of the most respected Greek film directors is Theo Angelopoulos, whose credits include the 1995 film *To*

Vlemma tou Odyssea (Ulysses' Gaze), starring Harvey Keitel. His 1998 film, *Mia Aioniotita ke Mia Mera* (Eternity and a Day), won the Palme D'Or at the 51st Cannes Film Festival. Other directors to watch out for are Michael Cacoyannis – director of *Zorba the Greek* (1962) – Alexis Damianos, Kostas Ferris, Pandelis Voulgaris, Tonia Marketaki and Nikos Panayotopoulos. However, for many people, the all-time classic remains *Never on Sunday* (1960), filmed in the Piraeus port area, directed by Jules Dassin and starring Melina Mercouri as a prostitute with a heart of gold.

Cultural Events

The *Athens Festival* (website: www.greekfestival.gr) takes place every summer (June to September). This major international festival was inaugurated in 1955 and combines music, modern and classical theatre, and contemporary and traditional dance. Venues for the festival are the Roman Odeon of Herod Atticus, the open-air theatre on Lykavittós Hill, the Veákio amphitheatre in Piraeus, and the amphitheatre at Epidaurus. Tickets are available from the *Hellenic Festival Box Office* (see above). Unsold tickets are available from 1800 at the Odeon of Herod Atticus box office on the evening of the performance. The *Athens International Jazz and Blues Festival* takes place in June – tickets are also available from the Hellenic Festival Box Office.

Literary Notes

This classical city is most closely revisited through the classical authors. Of particular interest are *The Histories* (fifth century BC) by Herodotus, *The Rise and Fall of Athens* (first century) by Plutarch, and *History of the Peloponnesian War* (fifth century BC) by Thucydides.

The Greek myths provide an essential background to the achievements of classical Athens – the most celebrated sources being the *Iliad* and the *Odyssey* (ninth century BC) by Homer, as well as works by Hesiod. Classical drama is at its best on stage but is also available to read in translation. Some of the most important works include the tragedies, *Prometheus Bound* and the *Oresteia* (fifth century BC) trilogy by Aeschylus, *Antigone*, *Oedipus Rex* and *Electra* (fifth century BC) by Sophocles, *Trojan Women* and *Iphigeneia in Taurus* (fifth century BC) by Euripedes; and the comedies, *The Frogs* and *The Birds* (fifth century BC) by Aristophanes.

More recent accounts of the city include *The Longest Night – Chronicles of a Dead City* (1985), a collection of stories by Petros Haris, evoking the atmosphere in Athens during World War II. The Noble Prize winner, Odysseus Elytis, died in Athens in 1996. His poems can be read in English in *The Collected Poems of Odysseus Elytis. Dinner with Persephone* (1997) by the American poet, Patricia Storace, is an amusing glimpse of life in modern-day Athens.

Temple of Haephaistos

It used to be joked that visitors arriving in New Zealand should turn their watches back 30 years. However, one look at Auckland, with its vibrant waterfront life – not for nothing is it called the 'City of Sails' – and its busy Downtown district, and it soon becomes clear that this joke is well past its sell-by date. Auckland may not be New Zealand's capital – that distinction belongs to Wellington – but it is the country's largest city and, along with Christchurch on the South Island, the major gateway for most travellers.

Just over 300km (190 miles) from the northern tip of the North Island, Auckland bestrides a narrow isthmus, the city's districts weaving their way around bays and harbours, large and small. Around the city sit numerous rugged hills, reminders of the eruptions of the 48 volcanoes that created the isthmus some 50,000 years ago. The earth's crust is very thin between Waitemata and Manukau harbours and fissures in the surface burst forth with magma every few thousand years, to create more volcanoes – the last some six hundred years ago, which formed Rangitoto Island, much to the consternation of the Maori settled on neighbouring Motutapu Island.

Current thinking has it that over 1000 years ago, the first of many waves of Polynesian migrants arrived in New Zealand in double-hulled canoes, to begin hunting and limited cultivation on the fertile volcanic land. Highly defensible and numerous, the sites on volcano tops covered by rich soil made wonderful settlements, which consequently flourished. However, after the arrival of Europeans in the 1820s, the introduction of the gun – which led to a massive increase in inter-tribal warfare – and European-carried diseases, the Maori population was decimated. In 1840, the British bought land in the area from the local Maori tribe, for £55 and some blankets. Auckland was made the capital city of New Zealand, which it remained until 1865, when Wellington took over.

As well as the harbours and fertile land, the city's maritime climate is appealing. Its situation by the sea means that it never gets too hot in summer or too cold in winter. There may be occasional frosts during wintertime (June to August) but seldom anything too severe, while summer temperatures usually stay in the mid-20s Celsius (upper-70s Fahrenheit), although it can become quite humid. Such a climate naturally leads to a healthy – and hedonistic – outdoor lifestyle. Although exact figures vary, it is said that there are more boats per capita here than in any other city in the world. There are over 500km (310 miles) of walking trails within Greater Auckland, as well as 22 leafy parks. But when the city palls, its inhabitants escape to the offshore Hauraki Gulf Islands, the Coromandel Peninsula or up the coast to another of the country's seaside beauty spots, the Bay of Islands.

Boats to the islands leave from the ferry terminal on Auckland's waterfront, regenerated for the 2000 America's Cup, the subsequent 2002 challenge and the 2003 competition. Slightly east of here is Queen Elizabeth II Square and running south from the Square is Queen Street. This is the city's main thoroughfare, upon which stands the impressive Auckland Town Hall. Queen Street eventually reaches Karangahape Road, which everyone calls K Road. Between K Road and the waterfront, is the heart of Auckland City. To the southeast is the sophisticated Parnell district, with the Auckland Museum and Auckland Domain Park, while to the northwest of the centre is Herne Bay and Ponsonby. These are the hip and happening areas, with bohemian bars and cafés.

To support the aforementioned hedonistic outdoor lifestyle requires a prosperous economy and that is what Auckland is re-experiencing, after a few years in the doldrums. Tourism, the country's biggest earner, is on the up, especially since the film release of parts one and two of the *Lord of the Rings* trilogy, filmed in New Zealand – with a knock-on effect for the city's other sectors, such as business and finance. It may not be 'boom city' but Auckland is certainly blossoming.

Photo: Tourism New Zealand

The QE2 joins other cruise ships at Auckland Harbour

TRAVEL

Getting There By Air

Auckland International Airport (AKL)

Tel: (09) 276 0789.

E-mail: admin@akl-airport.co.nz

Website: www.auckland-airport.co.nz

Auckland International Airport is located 21km (14 miles) south of central Auckland, in the suburb of Mangere. It is one of the two main international gateways to New Zealand – the other being Christchurch, on the South Island. The airport handles, on average, more than 23,000 passengers per day, travelling on 81 international and 324 domestic flights. There are direct flights to several countries including Australia, Canada, Europe, Great Britain, Japan, Singapore, Thailand and the USA. There is one international terminal and are two domestic terminals. The terminals are linked by a free shuttle bus service. There is also a marked footpath between the terminals.

Major airlines: *Air New Zealand* (tel: (0800) 737 767; website: www.airnz.com) is the national airline. Other major carriers include *Aerolíneas Argentinas, Air Canada, British Airways, Canadian Airlines, Cathay Pacific, Garuda, Japan Airlines, Korean Air, Lufthansa, Malaysia Airlines, Qantas, Singapore Airlines, Thai Airways* and *United Airlines.*

Approximate flight times to Auckland: From London is 24 hours; from New York is 21 hours; from Los Angeles is 15 hours; from Toronto is 21 hours and from Sydney is 3 hours.

Airport facilities: Facilities include a bank, tourist information centre, Bureau de Change, snack bars, newsagent, duty-free shops, restaurant, courtesy telephones, left-luggage and car hire from *Avis, Budget* and *Hertz,* as well as a variety of domestic operators.

Business facilities: There is no business centre as such, although the *Airport Camera Centre* (tel: (09) 256 8660; fax: (09) 256 8664; website: www.airport-camera.com), located on the first floor of the International Terminal and open daily 0700–1900, has photocopying, courier and faxing services as well as a post shop. Within the airport, there are also

Internet kiosks that cost NZ$2 for ten minutes. Two conference rooms, the *Marlborough and Blenheim Conference Rooms* (tel: (09) 256 8782), situated on the top floor, are available to hire, with full catering facilities available. Space for private meetings can be booked in one of three areas in the Air New Zealand Domestic Terminal – *The Club House, The Cabin* or *The Coachroom* (tel: (09) 256 8851). All international airlines provide VIP lounges.

Arrival/departure tax: A departure tax of NZ$25 on all international flights is payable at the airport, although it is often included in the ticket price.

Transport to the city: There is an *Airbus* service (tel: (09) 275 9396; website: www.airbus.co.nz) that connects all three terminals with the Downtown Airline Terminal, every 20–30 minutes, daily 0620–2200 (journey time – approximately 40 minutes). Tickets cost NZ$14 one way and are available from the driver. Private shuttle services into the city are also available at the airport, meeting all flights and costing NZ$14–22, with a possible reduction for travellers in possession of a YHA or VIP card. A taxi to the city centre will cost approximately NZ$40.

Getting There By Water

Only two ways exist for getting to New Zealand by water – as part of a round-the-world cruise or by crewing on somebody's yacht, picking up a berth in South America or Australia. Most cruise ships call at Auckland Harbour in February, stopping for a couple of days before continuing on their way. The Tasman Sea, between Australia and New Zealand, is some 3200km (2000 miles) of lumpy water that can cut up rough at the drop of a hat. The Pacific Ocean between South America and New Zealand is also renowned for being mischievous. This probably explains why the majority of visitors prefer to fly. However, Auckland's popularity as a cruise stop is growing and the 2002–03 season will see no less than 21 cruise ships docking here, bringing some 53,000 visitors to the city.

Auckland is the 'City of Sails' and the harbour is extremely important to the city's economic and cultural life, which is primarily one of outdoor hedonism. The titular sails are those of an enormous number of private yachts, which compete for space with privately owned pleasure boats ranging from small single-engine crafts to luxury cruises, upon which people sip cocktails while watching the back wash and listening to the bumble bee-like drone of jet-skis hooning around.

Auckland Harbour, located in central Auckland, on the Waitemata Harbour (opposite Queen Elizabeth II Square), is New Zealand's maritime hub, providing shipping links to 160 ports in 73 countries. *Ports of Auckland* (tel: (09) 366 0055; website: www.poal.co.nz) owns and operates ports in the east and west coast of North Island, including Auckland Harbour. The main passenger sectors are the *Overseas Passenger Terminal, Queens Wharf* and *Princes Wharf,* which stand alongside each other, off Quay Street, right at the heart of Auckland Harbour. Cruise liners call at the Overseas Passenger Terminal and Queens Wharf, where facilities are numerous. Since this was also the focus of the America's Cup, the whole area is awash with smart restaurants, trendy pubs and other entertainment options.

Ferry services: Ferry services operated by *Fullers* (tel: (09) 367 9111; website: www.fullers.co.nz) depart from the ferry terminal on Quay Street. Destinations are largely limited to local routes, such as Devonport, Bayswater, Birkenhead and Stanley Bay

COST OF LIVING

One-litre bottle of mineral water: NZ$1.80

33cl bottle of beer: NZ$2–4

***Financial Times* newspaper:** NZ$5

36-exposure colour film: NZ$12

City-centre bus ticket: NZ$1.20

Adult rugby or cricket ticket: From NZ$20

Three-course meal with wine/beer: From NZ$50

1 New Zealand Dollar (NZ$1) = £0.36; US$0.59; C$0.82; A$0.90; €0.53

Currency conversion rates as of July 2003

(see *Public Transport* in *Getting Around*). However, there are also regular services to the Hauraki Gulf Islands.

Transport to the city: The waterfront area is located at the heart of the city. The public bus service (see *Getting Around*) stops at the nearby Queen Elizabeth II Square, where taxis are also readily available. The harbour is only a two-minute walk from the Britomart Centre, a 15–20-minute walk from the train station and approximately ten minutes from almost anywhere in downtown Auckland. The Explorer Bus service runs from the ferry terminal on Quay Street every half hour from 0900–1600 (October to April), hourly for the rest of the year (see *Tours of the City*). Tickets are available from the driver, for NZ$25 (one-day unlimited use of the Explorer Bus) or NZ$40 (two days). A museum bus also operates from the National Maritime Museum, corner of Quay Street and Hobson Street, to the Auckland Museum, in the Auckland Domain.

Getting There By Rail

New Zealand's rail services are operated by *Tranz Scenic* (tel: (0800) 802 802; website: www.tranzrailtravel.co.nz/ tranzscenic/default.asp). Trains are efficient, reasonably priced but rare, operating more as a tourist service than a business or commuter network. *Auckland Station* is currently located on Beach Road. However, by the end of 2003, the station will be in the Britomart, a purpose-designed combined train and local bus station, incorporating the old post office building on Queen Elizabeth II Square, at the harbour end of Queen Street. As far as facilities go, the train station has a ticket office, which is rarely used, and very little else, seeing as it is being decommissioned at the end of this year.

Rail services: The only service, apart from infrequent local suburban commuter trains, is the daily early morning service to New Zealand's capital, Wellington, on the southern tip of North Island, as well as an overnight service from Sunday to Friday (journey time – approximately 11 hours).

Transport to the city: Auckland Station is located approximately one kilometre (0.6 miles) east of the city centre. The station is located on public bus routes and taxis are also available, although at the end of 2003, it will be relocated to the more centrally located Britomart, with a bus interchange and an underground walkway connecting the station to Queen Elizabeth II Square.

Getting There By Road

Driving in New Zealand is easy, inexpensive and, although Auckland is one of the busiest areas, in terms of traffic, it is still relatively quiet by European standards. Nearly all roads are State Highways, designated by 'SH' and a number. Small numbers refer to the major routes between destinations – such as SH1 from Auckland to Wellington – while larger numbers indicate smaller roads linking smaller destinations – such as SH94 from Te Anau to Milford Sound. All other roads, of which there are a few, are known, although not officially, as 'B' roads. These are often little more than ribbons of tarmac or, on some occasions, 'metalled' roads, where the surface is made of loose chippings.

A valid national driving licence is required for driving in New Zealand, for up to 12 months. The legal driving age is 18 years. Insurance is not mandatory but is recommended. Traffic drives on the left and most roads are quiet. The maximum legal alcohol to blood ratio for driving is 0.08% (0.03% for drivers under 20 years). Speed limits are 100kph (62mph) on open roads, 50kph (31mph) in urban areas and 20kph (12mph) in the vicinity of schools and stopped school buses. There are 'Limited Speed Zones' where the speed limit is often reduced from 100kph (62mph) to 50kph (31mph) in adverse conditions.

The *New Zealand Automobile Association* (website: www.nzaa.co.nz) provides information on road conditions (tel: (0900) 33222) and general information (tel: (0800) 500 222) and has a reciprocal

CITY STATISTICS

Location: Auckland Region, North Island, New Zealand.
Country dialling code: 64.
Population: 1.25 million (greater Auckland region).
Ethnic mix: 73% European descent, 12% Maori descent, 6% other Pacific Islanders (including Tonga, Samoa and Cook Islands), 5% Asian, 4% other.
Religion: Christian majority; minorities include Muslim, Buddhist, Hindu, Jewish and other religious communities, including traditional Maori religion.
Time zone: GMT + 12.
Electricity: 240–250 volts AC, 50Hz; flat three-pin plugs are used. Converters are available for standard UK, European and American plugs in New Zealand and all major airports and it is a good idea for visitors to take a voltage surge protector for sensitive equipment, such as computers.
Average January temp: 24°C (75°F).
Average July temp: 14°C (57°F).
Annual rainfall: 1185mm (46.2 inches).

agreement with the British AA, whereby visiting drivers can get maps for free.

Emergency breakdown service: *NZ AA* (0800) 500 222.

Routes to the city: SH1 north runs parallel to the east coast of North Island to Warkworth and then on to the Bay of Islands, Northland Forest Park and Cape Reinga. SH1 south heads toward Hamilton and Wellington, which links with SH5 to Rotorua, SH29 to Taurangia, SH2 to Gisborne,

SH3 to New Plymouth (via the west coast and linking with Raglan or Waitomo), SH5 to Napier and SH4 to Wanganui.

Approximate driving times to Auckland: From Rotorua – 2 hours 30 minutes; Bay of Islands – 3 hours; Wellington – 8–9 hours.

Coach services: Auckland has good coach links with other major New Zealand towns and cities, as well as the more popular tourist areas. Coaches operate from the *InterCity Coach Terminal*, at the Sky

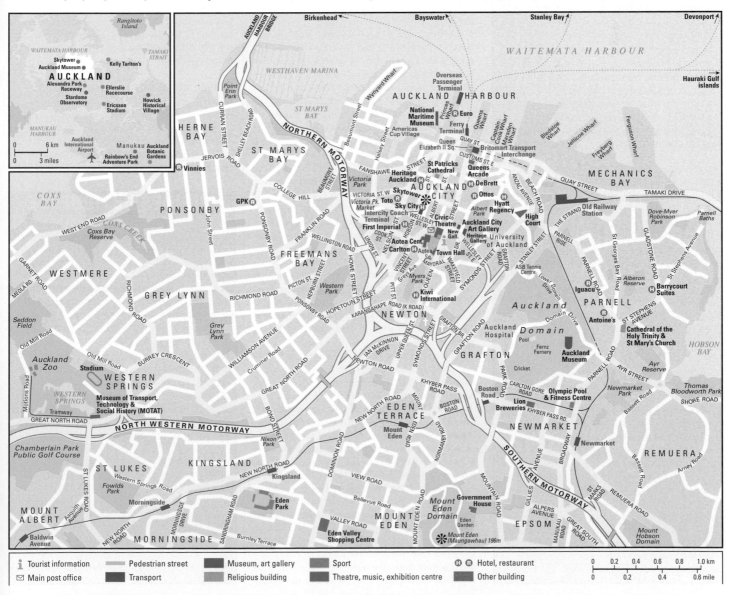

i Tourist information	Pedestrian street	Museum, art gallery	Sport	H R Hotel, restaurant	0 0.2 0.4 0.6 0.8 1.0 km
✉ Main post office	Transport	Religious building	Theatre, music, exhibition centre	Other building	0 0.2 0.4 0.6 mile

BUSINESS PROFILE

The New Zealand economy is predominantly based on exporting wool, dairy products, wood, minerals, seafood and meat. It is also largely dependent on tourism. However, there is a growing reliance on high-tech industries and expertise, fashion, TV and film production and special effects. Auckland has a mostly business and services-oriented economy. The majority city-dwellers work in the service industries, while a lesser number are employed in import and export. The business directory shows familiar corporate names, such as IBM, 3M, Microsoft, Cisco, Merrill Lynch, KPMG, Citibank and Price Waterhouse. The city's mainstays are business and financial services, manufacturing, transport, communications and the trade and hospitality industries. These last two reflect the importance of tourism to New Zealand, and to its biggest city. Auckland also contains the country's biggest port, handling 50% of container traffic. Although there is no specific Central Business District, most of Auckland's businesses are located around Queen Street, from Cook Street down to the waterfront.

The city's GDP is over NZ$20 million per annum and, thanks to current low interest and exchange rates, this is estimated to increase at a steady rate of about 4% per annum for the next three years. This is 1% higher than the growth anticipated for the whole country, which reflects the constant population drift towards Auckland. This drift does, however, contribute to the city's unemployment rate of 6.9%, which is relatively high when compared to the national rate of 6.1%. The Auckland region contains roughly 30% of New Zealand's population, which is, on average, younger, more highly paid and better educated than the general population – although this is due in part to the number of people who move to Auckland after they have finished tertiary education.

Tourism is New Zealand's single biggest revenue earner, currently estimated to be worth well in excess NZ$4.5 billion. This figure constantly increases, because of the country's high profile as the world's safest tourist destination and the location for the filming of the Lord of the Rings trilogy. This greatly benefits Auckland, as has hosting the America's Cup for 2003.

Asian visitors traditionally have accounted for almost one fifth of New Zealand's tourists, so the 30% drop in visitor numbers at the start of 1999 was attributed to the Asian financial crisis, although Asian visitors are once again on the increase. Economic recovery, following the impact of this crisis, has naturally been welcomed – tourism arrivals at Auckland International Airport rose by 8.7% during 1999 and retail spending rose by 4.2% for the year ending 30 September 1999. However, this is fairly small in comparison with the projections for spending increases as a result of a massive rise in visitor numbers. Despite fears that the 11 September 2001 terrorist attacks and voluntary administration of Ansett Australia, by Air New Zealand, would lead to a drop in tourist numbers – which have increased every year since 1999 – the weekly entry figures, compiled by the government's statistics department, indicate a continued healthy rise in tourists hungry for that unique kiwi experience.

City Casino, 102 Hobson Street (tel: (09) 913 6100), where there are basic facilities, such as left-luggage, a café and toilets. Coaches also operate from the *Northliner Travel Centre*, 172 Quay Street, opposite the ferry terminal.

The biggest coach service provider throughout New Zealand is *InterCity* (tel: (09) 913 6100; website: www.intercitycoach.co.nz), in conjunction with its partner, *Newmans* (tel: (09) 913 6200; website: www.newmanscoach.co.nz). Apart from these two, there are other smaller operators and shuttle bus companies, all of which provide an alternative way of getting beyond the city limits. *Go Kiwi Shuttles* (tel: (0800) 446 549) runs to the Coromandel Peninsula and Rotorua, while *Gutherys* (tel: (0800) 759 999) travels to Hamilton and *Northliner Express* (tel: (09) 307 5873) to the Bay of Islands.

Getting Around

Public Transport

Stagecoach Auckland (tel: (0800) 103 080; website: www.rideline.co.nz) operates a reasonable **bus** network around Auckland, most of which leave from the *Downtown Bus Centre*, Commerce Street, although this will be changing by the end of 2003 (see *Getting There By Rail*). Buses operate Monday to Thursday 0600–2200, Friday 6000–2330, Saturday and Sunday 0700–2300.

A flat fare in the city centre costs NZ$1.20, and NZ$1.20 thereafter for each zone travelled through. A ticket for 'The Link', a city centre loop-route bus, costs just NZ$1.20. The *Auckland Pass* is available for NZ$8 and provides unlimited travel on all buses and all ferries (see below) to the North Shore (including Devonport) for the day of purchase. Tickets are available for purchase upon boarding, at stations and at visitor centres. There is a free *Auckland Busabout Guide* available from newsagents and visitor centres, which lists routes and fares.

Auckland also has a small, unloved **metro** service, called the *Tranz Metro* (tel: (0800) 103 080; website: www.tranzmetro.co.nz), with two main lines. One divides into two – from Central Auckland via Glen Innes to Papakura (Eastern Line) or Central Auckland via Ellerslie to Papakura (Southern line). The other heads west from Central Auckland via Newmarket to Waitahere. The Eastern line operates Monday to Friday 0540–1939, with no weekend service, while the Southern line operates Monday to Friday 0550–2000 and Saturday 0630–1930 and the Western Line Monday to Friday 0605–2000 and Saturday 0705–2000.

The metro fare from the city centre to the end of each line is approximately NZ$8. For a single in stage one, the fare is NZ$1.10; there are six stages in total. A *Day Rover* **pass** costs NZ$10 and is valid from 0900 Monday to Saturday. A ten-trip carnet and a monthly pass are also available for NZ$10–64 and NZ$96–199 respectively. All tickets and passes are available for purchase on the train (exact change is recommended) or more cheaply at Central Auckland.

Ferries, operated by *Fullers* (tel: (09) 367 9111; website: www.fullers.co.nz), link the ferry terminal on Quay Street with some of the further suburbs, such as Devonport, Bayswater, Birkenhead and Stanley Bay. Ferries operate Monday to Thursday approximately 0615–2300, Friday and Saturday 0630–0130 and Sunday 0700–2200. Ferry fares vary and fluctuate with the price of oil – the main Auckland Devonport Ferry currently costs NZ$8.

Tickets are available for purchase on board, at the terminals and in visitor centres.

Auckland's *Rideline* (tel: (09) 366 6400; website: www.rideline.co.nz) provides further information on all public transport services.

The main service that visitors will find useful is the Explorer Bus, with one bus running every half hour from 0900–1600 (October to April), hourly for the rest of the year (see *Tours of the City*), linking up all the major tourist attractions. The hop-on hop-off bus starts and terminates at the ferry terminal on Quay Street. Tickets are available from the driver, for NZ$25 (one day) and NZ$40 (two days).

Taxis

There are several private taxi companies in Auckland, with ranks situated around the city. Taxis can also be hailed in the street, although booking by telephone is the usual option. One of the biggest companies is the *Auckland Co-operative Taxi Society* (tel: (09) 300 3000). Alternatively, visitors could try *Alert* (tel: (09) 309 2000) or *Corporate* (tel (09) 631 1111). Taxis are metered, with a minimum charge of NZ$3. Tipping is not expected.

Limousines

Limousines are not common in laid-back Auckland. *Prestige Limousines* (tel: (0800) 765 577) and *Corporate Cars* (tel: (0800) 733 833) both provide a variety of limousines with chauffeurs. Rates start from NZ$200 per hour. The *Auckland Co-operative Taxi Society* (tel: (09) 300 3000) offers business-class cars for hire from NZ$65 per hour.

Driving in the City

Auckland is as big and busy as any other major city but driving is not the stressful experience it can be elsewhere. Drivers in New Zealand are much more courteous out in the country but are still fairly tolerant in the city. A car is useful, because of the sprawling nature of Auckland and roads are in good

BUSINESS ETIQUETTE

Conducting business in Auckland is no different from any other major Western city. There are no cultural pitfalls to watch out for, unless dealing directly with Maori (who will outline relevant protocols before any meetings), and the only noticeable difference lies with the nature of the country's people. They are notably friendlier, more informal and more relaxed. Although ties and jackets are worn, jackets may soon be discarded and shirtsleeves rolled up. A more informal dress code also exists in restaurants and bars, although the smartest restaurants may still expect a jacket and tie to be worn. Business hours are generally Monday to Friday 0900–1700 and punctuality is appreciated, although no one will be offended if the visitor is a little late, especially at times when the traffic is busy.

As dinner is seen as a time for socialising and not business, meetings mainly take place over lunch. Invitations to dine out or to visit someone's home are far more readily issued than in many other countries and are genuine, not merely as a gesture. The native host will expect to pay for a meal or a round of drinks but guests can step in and pay their turn without creating arguments or offence. Friendliness not formality is the Auckland watchword.

condition and mostly well signposted. However, the Downtown area gets very congested, especially in the morning and evening rush hours and, in particular, on a Friday afternoon. Parking Downtown can also be a problem. Central 24-hour car parks include Albert Street (to the west of Queen Street and close to the waterfront), Customs Street West and Beresford Street, near Karangahape (K) Road. Metered parking is generally NZ$1–3 per hour and approximately NZ$1–5 per hour in a secure car park.

Car Hire

All the major international car hire companies have offices in Auckland, as well as several domestic companies. Drivers must be over 21 years of age – some companies add on a hefty surcharge if the driver is less than 25 years. A valid national or international driving licence is required – in some cases, if the licence has been held for less than three–five years, an extra insurance excess may apply. Fully comprehensive insurance is not compulsory but is advisable and often included as part of the car hire deal, as many local drivers in rural areas take a very relaxed attitude to driving regulations and may not be insured themselves. However, extra insurance is not really necessary, as with each hire, there is a refundable accident bond – a credit card slip for anything from NZ$500 to NZ$1000 – which goes toward the cost of repairs (either part of it or in its entirety), should the driver have a prang. Drivers will probably find, when hunting around, that the best deals are available from mid-range domestic firms and that money can be saved by booking a car upon arrival in New Zealand, rather than beforehand. The main car hire companies include *Ace Tourist Rentals* (tel: (09) 303 3112; website: www.acerentalcars.co.nz), *A2B* (tel: (0800) 616 333; website: www.a2brentals.co.nz), *Avis* (tel: (09) 526 2800; website: www.avis.com), *Budget* (tel: (0800) 652 227; website: www.budget.co.nz), *Hertz* (tel: (0800) 654 321; website: www.hertz.com) and *Maui* (tel: (0800) 737 070; website: www.maui-rentals.com), which only hires out campervans. In the high season, rates start at approximately NZ$60 per day, for the short-term hire of a small car.

Bicycle & Scooter Hire

Cycling is popular in New Zealand and Auckland is a pleasant city in which to practise this pastime – away from the centre and the rush-hour traffic. A signposted cycle route runs for 50km (31 miles) along the waterfront and around the city. There are several bicycle hire companies, including *Adventure Cycles*, 36 Customs Street East (tel: (09) 309 5566; website: www.adventure-auckland.co.nz), which hires out a sit-up-and-beg bike for NZ$18, or a mountain bike from NZ$25. The company also hires out bikes for a month-long period, for those who fancy a quick pedal around the North Island, costing around NZ$180. *Penny Farthing*, corner of Khyber Pass Road and Symonds Street (tel: (09) 379 2524), hires out entry level mountain bikes for NZ$30 a day. Most companies offer similar hire rates. Auckland has many motorcycle hire companies, with the minimum size of bike usually being 250cc, which requires a full motorcycle licence. Smaller scooters and mopeds, where an ordinary car driving licence is all that is required, can be hired for short trips but are of limited value when touring the city and no value at all on longer trips. Motorbikes cost NZ$115 per day for a minimum of seven days and NZ$140 a day for a minimum of three days; scooter hire starts at approximately NZ$40 for two hours or NZ$70 for a day. Providers include *Bike Adventure New Zealand*, Drury, Pukekohe (tel: (0800) 498 600), *New Zealand*

Youth culture

Motorcycle Rentals, 31 Beach Road (tel: (09) 377 2005), and *Te Waipounamu Motorcycle Tours*, 54 Barry Point Road, Takapuna (tel: (09) 489 9242), although, of these, only New Zealand Motorcycle Rentals hires out scooters (at NZ$75 per day). *Waiheke Island Rental Cars*, Waiheke Island (tel: (09) 372 8635), the only place a scooter comes into its own, offers a similar deal as those available on the mainland.

SIGHTSEEING

Sightseeing Overview

Despite Auckland's urban sprawl, the major tourist sites are situated around the city centre, while those that are further afield can be reached by public transport, the Explorer Bus, which links many of the attractions, public transport or a hire car. The city centre is easily explored on foot, starting with the waterfront, which epitomises the lively feel of the 'City of Sails'. Here too can be found the Downtown Tourist Centre, some useful transport stops, such as the Stagecoach Bus Terminal (soon to be relocated to Queen Elizabeth II Square) and the Ferry Terminal, Department of Conservation Office, the National Maritime Museum and the America's Cup Village.

The city's main street, Queen Street, and the roads and malls that flank it, give a sense of the shopping options, including the two-storey Queens Arcade. Queen Street continues past the Town Hall and close by Albert Park, although it is worth remembering that there are many specialised shopping options in the various suburbs that surround the centre, which form self-contained village-like satellites.

Albert Park is one of 22 parks in the city and is home to the more ornate half of the Auckland City Art Gallery, the Heritage Gallery – the other half, the New Gallery, is located on the other side of Wellesley Street – and the Bruce Wilkinson Collection, a charming small display of ornate clocks and figures. Southeast of the centre is the huge 81-hectare (202-acre) Auckland Domain, crowned by the city's main 'must-see' site, the Auckland Museum – packed with Maori and Pacific Island artefacts. From the museum, an extra loop on the Explorer Bus circuit takes visitors further out to Mount Eden, Auckland Zoo and the Museum of Transport, Technology and Social History (MOTAT).

Venturing further afield requires a car, taxis or more public transport. East of the city are golf courses, the Ellerslie Racecourse, attractions like Howick Historical Village, the Botanic Gardens and the Rainbow's End adventure theme park. Heading west brings more golf courses, orchards, vineyards and a sense of why Aucklanders love their city so much – inside it is lively and outside simply lovely.

Key Attractions

Auckland Domain and Auckland Museum

Created in 1845, *Auckland Domain* is the city's oldest, largest and most attractive park, with gardens and statues, pathways and ponds, a winter garden with cool and tropical houses, and the *Fernz Fernery*, with over 100 types of fern. The 81-hectare (202-acre) domain is situated on an extinct volcano, known as *pukekawa* or 'hill of bitter memories'. Within the domain is the *Auckland Museum*, the city's most visited attraction, combining its Greco-Roman style architecture with a contemporary take on the displays. The ground floor is devoted to 'The People', the middle to 'The Place' and the top to 'New Zealand at War', while a small area on the middle floor is given over to the Children's Discovery Centre. The displays tend not to be confined to Victorian-style glass cases but include various interactive and audiovisual components. The museum also houses one of New Zealand's most important collection of Maori and South Pacific artefacts and the Manaia cultural performances of song,

heralded by a conch blast that reverberates through the museum at 1100, 1200 and 1330.
Auckland Domain
Tel: (09) 303 1530 (domain) *or* 306 7067 (museum).
Fax: (09) 379 9956 (museum).
Website: www.akmuseum.co.nz
Transport: Public, Link or Explorer buses.
Opening hours: Daily dawn–dusk (domain); daily 1000–1700 (museum).
Admission: Free (domain); NZ$5 suggested donation, valid for repeated entry (museum); NZ$15 (cultural performance).

Auckland City Art Gallery

The city's main art gallery has the country's largest collections of both native and international art. The *Heritage Gallery*, which was opened in 1888, contains the bulk of the collection, with the *New Gallery* – opened across the street in 1995 – concentrating on contemporary art, with revolving exhibitions. In the Heritage Gallery, international artists include Breughel and Millais, with Reynolds and Gainsborough providing a link back to colonial days. Some of the most memorable images are those by Gottfried Lindauer and Charles F Goldie, which depict passive portraits of Maori with *moko* (facial tattoos). A free guided tour is available daily at 1400 and there is a regular programme of talks.
Heritage Gallery
Corner of Wellesley Street and Kitchener Street
Tel: (09) 379 1349.
E-mail: gallery@akcity.govt.nz
Website: www.akcity.govt.nz/attractions/artgallery
Transport: Public, Link and Explorer buses.
Opening hours: Daily 1000–1700.
Admission: NZ$4; NZ5–15 (special exhibitions).
New Gallery
Corner of Wellesley Street and Lorne Street
Tel: (09) 307 4540 *or* 309 0831.
E-mail: gallery@akcity.govt.nz
Website: www.akcity.govt.nz/attractions/artgallery
Transport: Public, Link and Explorer buses.
Opening hours: Daily 1000–1700.
Admission: NZ$4 (each section).

New Zealand National Maritime Museum

In the heart of the Downtown waterfront, this museum pays homage to the debt an island nation owes to its maritime history. It covers almost a millennium of history – from the arrival of Maori and then European settlers, to the 2000 America's Cup. Displays also deal with navigation skills, whaling, sealing and other fishing activities, the first freezer ships to export farm produce (sheep and dairy products) to Europe, and the invention of the jet boat. Visitors can see historical boats, make their own model boats and take a trip out into Auckland Harbour. The one-hour guided cruises on the *Ted Ashby*, a replica of one of the traditional, flat-bottomed, ketch-rigged scows that once worked the North Island waterways, sail Monday to Friday 1100 and Saturday, either 1100 or 1400, costing NZ$15.
Eastern Viaduct, corner of Quay Street and Hobson Street
Tel: (09) 373 0800. Fax: (09) 377 6000.
E-mail: mmuseum@wave.co.nz
Website: www.nzmaritime.org
Transport: Satellite Bus from Auckland Museum.
Opening hours: Daily 0900–1800 (Nov–Easter); daily 0900–1700 (Easter–Oct).
Admission: NZ$12.

Museum of Transport, Technology and Social History (MOTAT)

Commonly known as MOTAT – from the days before 'and Social History' was added to the name – this is the country's largest transport collection. It has a working tramway that links its two sections, the main museum and the *Sir Keith Park Memorial Site* (NZ$2 return). The latter is the collection of aircraft, including vintage aircraft from the two World Wars and a replica of the Richard Pearse plane – the first successful powered aircraft, long before the Wright brothers. The main museum has displays on all other modes of transport, a reproduction Victorian village and the Science Centre, with interactive exhibits on technology and communications.
Great North Road, Western Springs
Tel: (09) 846 7020.
Website: www.akcity.govt.nz/motat
Transport: Public bus 45 or the Link.
Opening hours: Daily 1000–1700.
Admission: NZ$10.

Howick Historical Village

In 1840, Auckland only had 1500 inhabitants. This living museum deals with the dramatic and turbulent events of the next 50 years, when the bulk of the settlers arrived from Britain, Ireland and Australia and Maori were forcibly removed from their land. The 33 period buildings have been set in a landscape of reproduction gardens, streets and even a village pond. Staff dress in period costume and, on the third Sunday of each month, there are special displays relating to different aspects of this period in the city's past.
Bells Road, Lloyd Elsmore Park, Pakuranga
Tel: (09) 576 9506. Fax: (09) 576 9708.
E-mail: fencible@ihug.co.nz
Website: www.fencible.org.nz
Transport: Public buses to Howick or Eastern (alight opposite Lloyd Elsmore Park).
Opening hours: Daily 1000–1700 (last admission 1600).
Admission: NZ$9.

Kelly Tarlton's Antarctic Encounter and Underwater World

Kelly Tarlton was a local diver who designed this centre, which opened in 1985, so non-divers could experience the underwater world that he found so fascinating. The perspex walk-through tunnels of *Underwater World* were the first to give visitors the illusion of walking underwater, for close encounters with sharks, rays and other creatures of the deep. The additional *Antarctic Encounter* includes a reconstruction of the hut in which Captain Scott and his expedition perished, modern-day studies of life on Earth's frozen continent and a Disney-like ride on the Snow Cat through artificial icebergs and snow drifts.
23 Tamaki Drive, Orakei
Tel: (09) 528 0603. Fax: (09) 375 4732.
E-mail: ktinfo@kellytarltons.co.nz
Website: www.kellytarltons.co.nz
Transport: Explorer Bus and public buses.
Opening hours: Daily 0900–2100 (Nov–Mar); daily 0900–1800 (Apr–Oct).
Admission: NZ$25.

Auckland Zoo

Almost 1000 creatures from around the world are housed at this forward-looking zoo, which tries to place the animals in surroundings that closely recreate their natural environment. New Zealand's native species are well represented, in particular the hard-to-see national bird, the kiwi, in a nocturnal enclosure, as well as the Tuatara – the most famous national

Sky Tower

lizard-cum-dinosaur. There is also a large walk-through aviary. The rainforest is such a popular feature that it even has its own website. Here monkeys and apes, parrots, spiders and other rainforest creatures can be seen in their natural habitat. *Pridelands* is an area that is home to the animals of Africa, including lions, rhinos and giraffes, while *Hippo River* allows very close-up views of hippopotami. Guided tours are available and there is an informative Visitor Centre.
Motions Road, Western Springs
Tel: (09) 360 3800 *or* 3819.
Website: www.zoorainforest.co.nz
Transport: Satellite Bus from Auckland Museum; public buses and tram from MOTAT.
Opening hours: Daily 0930–1730.
Admission: NZ$13.

Sky Tower

New Zealand's tallest building stands 328m (1076ft) high in the centre of Auckland, dominating the skyline in the same way as Seattle's Space Needle. A lift service takes 40 seconds to whizz visitors to the first observation platforms. From here, the views are breathtaking enough but even more so from the very top level, where visitors can look out over the harbour as well as the city. The tower is part of the *Sky City* complex – a casino with cafés, bars and a restaurant. Visitors should note that anyone spending a minimum amount dining here (currently NZ$25.50) receives a free pass to the very top of the tower. It is possible for visitors to climb even higher, to the *Sky Deck*, a further 50m (164ft) up, as part of the *Vertigo* experience (costing NZ$95), which involves wannabe climbers being put through a simulator to make sure they are up for it. Alternatively, for NZ$195, there is the world's longest tower-based jump, where a harness and attached wire allow for a 25-second, arrested free-fall, eye-popping descent. Adrenaline junkies can keep their suits on and repeat the experience for NZ$75.

Sky City, corner of Federal and Victoria Streets
Tel: (09) 912 6400 *or* (09) 363 6422 *or* (0800) 483 784 (Vertigo) *or* (0800) 759 586 (Skyjump). Fax: (09) 363 6374.
E-mail: skytower@skycity.co.nz
Website: www.skycity.co.nz
Transport: Explorer, public and link buses.
Opening hours: Sun–Thurs 0830–2300, Fri and Sat 0830–2400.
Admission: NZ$15 to observation platforms, plus NZ$3 to the top; concessions available.

Further Distractions

Stardome Observatory

This large site is operated by the Auckland Observatory and Planetarium Trust, to give the public an insight into what the heavens are all about. The planetarium and extensions were built in 1996, at a cost NZ$3 million, making for a high-tech modern attraction. Displays include New Zealand's first known meteorite, a piece of a meteorite that struck Arizona and model rockets. The planetarium shows 45-minute multimedia features, including what it is like to be an astronaut and the story of a young Polynesian learning the art of navigating by the stars to steer his canoe to New Zealand. Night sky and weather permitting, there is also 30-minutes of telescope gazing, during which visitors might catch a glimpse of Jupiter or Saturn's rings.
One Tree Hill Domain, off Manukau Road, Royal Oak
Tel: (09) 624 1246 or 625 6945. Fax: (09) 625 2394.
E-mail: info@stardome.org.nz
Website: www.stardome.org.nz
Transport: Buses 302, 305 or 312.
Opening hours: Shows at Tues–Sat 1900 and 2000.
Admission: NZ$10, plus NZ$5 for a guided telescope tour of the sky.

Rainbow's End

New Zealand's largest theme park has over 20 major rides and attractions, including the country's only double-corkscrew rollercoaster, dodgems, bumper boats, a pirate ship, an interactive games arcade and rides for small children.
Corner of Great South Road and Wiri Station Road
Tel: (09) 262 2030. Fax: (09) 262 1958.
E-mail: info@rainbowsend.co.nz
Website: www.rainbowsend.co.nz
Transport: Bus 47 to Westfield Shopping Town.
Opening hours: Daily 1000–1700.
Admission: NZ$35; NZ$25 (children).

Auckland Botanic Gardens

These beautiful gardens were eight years in the making before opening to the public in 1982. They cover 64 hectares (160 acres) and contain more than 10,000 individual plants, along with a lake, a nature trail, a library and an attractive outdoor café. Plants are well labelled for the enthusiast and pathways clearly signposted for visitors who only wish to walk in pleasant surroundings. The *Auckland Botanic Gardens* are now also home to the Ellerslie Flower Show.
102 Hill Road, Manurewa
Tel: (09) 303 1530 (Parks line) *or* 267 1457 (Visitor Centre). Fax: (09) 266 3698.
Website: www.arc.govt.nz/arc/parks/botanic-gardens
Transport: Buses to Drury, Papakura or Pukehohe.
Opening hours: Daily 0800–dusk (gardens); Mon–Fri

0900–1600, Sat and Sun 1000–1600 (Visitor Centre).
Admission: Free.

Eden Garden

A few minutes from Downtown Auckland lies the green oasis of *Eden Garden*. The 2.25-hectare (5.5-acre) garden on the volcanic slopes of Mount Eden – the highest point in the area and extremely popular with tour buses – was once a quarry. This was until 1965, when a group of dedicated volunteers began to transform it into what is now a national showcase garden of international status, which has won many awards. It has the largest collection of camellias in the Southern Hemisphere, as well as large numbers of rhododendrons and azaleas. Plants from around the world give year-round colour but it is also a good place for visitors to see a large number of native plants too. The landscaped gardens have some statues and a 13.5m (45ft) waterfall.
24 Omana Avenue, Epsom
Tel: (09) 638 8395. Fax: (09) 638 7685.
E-mail: eden@edengarden.co.nz
Website: www.edengarden.co.nz
Transport: Bus 274 or 275.
Opening hours: Daily 0900–1630.
Admission: NZ$5.

Auckland Bridge Climb

The most recent adventure activity in the city involves getting kitted out in overalls and a harness and then walking across the upper girders of the *Auckland Harbour Bridge*, some 65m (213ft) above the harbour, with the traffic rushing along on the road below. The views are spectacular, even at night, although this is not for the faint-hearted.
70 Nelson Street
Tel: (0800) 000 808. Fax: (09) 625 0445.
Website: www.aucklandbridgeclimb.co.nz
Transport: Public, Link and Explorer buses.
Opening hours: Day climbs Mon–Thurs 1000–1500, Fri–Sun 1000–1800; Night climbs Sat 1800 (Apr–Sep), Sat 1940 (Oct–Mar).
Admission: NZ$125 (Mon–Fri), NZ$135 (Sat and Sun).

Tours of the City

Walking Tours

The *Auckland Visitor Centre* (tel: (09) 979 2333) provides leaflets giving details of the many marked trails around the city. These include heritage walks that visit historic buildings in the city's various suburbs, as well as nature walks near the city and way out in the 'back-blocks' (more remote areas). However, as Auckland is a sprawling city and most tourists prefer walking in the natural terrain (see *Excursions*), there are no dedicated walking tours of the city.

Bus Tours

The *United Airlines Explorer Bus* (tel: (0800) 439 756; website: www.explorerbus.co.nz) links many of the visitor attractions in central Auckland. A day pass costs NZ$25, while a two-day pass is NZ$40. The bus leaves from the ferry terminal, hourly 1000–1600 and as this is a hop-on hop-off experience, the tour can take as long as it takes. At the Auckland Museum, there is an additional summer satellite link that takes passengers on to more outlying attractions, including the Auckland Zoo and the Auckland Art Gallery.
Several companies offer city tours, which last half a day and cost around NZ$50, including hotel pick-up and drop-off. Companies include *Claud 9 Tours* (tel: (09) 818 2562) and *Great Sights* (tel: (0800) 744 487; website: www.greatsights.co.nz).
Auckland Adventures (tel: (09) 379 4545; website: www.aucklandadventures.co.nz), offers half-day tours that include sights, wineries and wildlife, for NZ$60, as well as an all-day Wilderness Adventure, costing NZ$89, which includes more of the same.

Boat Tours

Tours of Auckland harbour are available through *Fullers* (tel: (09) 367 9111). The most popular tours are the 90-minute to two-hour 'Harbour Cruises', costing NZ$30 and departing 1030 and 1330. Most call in at Devonport and sail across to Rangitoto Island in the Hauraki Gulf, while some also visit Kelly Tarlton's. For the more romantic tourist, there are *NZL 40* (tel:

Waterfront

(0800) 724 569) sailing cruises on a racing yacht, costing NZ$75, and a 45-minute *Pride of Auckland* (tel: (09) 373 4557) cruise, costing NZ$45. A coffee cruise costing NZ$55, a luncheon cruise for NZ$65 and a dinner cruise at NZ$90 are other options. Alternatively, visitors could try a cruise on the *Soren Larson* (tel: (0800) 707265; website: www.sorenlarson.co.nz), a Danish Baltic trader made of oak and built in 1949. Tours take three to four hours and cost NZ$89, including lunch. Departures are from opposite the Ferry Building and Dock office, on the weekend (mid-November to mid-February).

Other Tours

An *Auckland Adventures* (tel: (09) 379 4545; website: www.aucklandadventures.co.nz) mountain bike half-day tour costs NZ$89 and include sights, wineries and wildlife. Hotel pick-up can be arranged.

Excursions

For a Half Day

Hauraki Gulf Islands: The *Hauraki Gulf Maritime Park* (tel: (09) 379 6476; fax: (09) 379 3609; e-mail: aucklandvc@doc.govt.nz; website: www.doc.govt.nz) contains 47 islands, some just a few minutes' sail away from Auckland. Not all can be visited, as some are nature reserves with no access to the general public, although others are devoted to human pleasures, with all the usual holiday facilities.

The volcanic island of *Rangitoto* is one of the most popular islands and is the largest volcanic cone in Auckland. There are several ferries per day from Auckland's ferry building and the trip takes 30 minutes. Details are available from *Fullers Cruise Centre* (tel: (09) 367 9111). Guided walking tours of Rangitoto Island in the Hauraki Gulf are available from *The New Zealand Walking Company* (tel: (09) 590 0087; website: www.nzwalkingcompany.com/itinnz.htm). Tours cost NZ$385 and NZ$698 for a two-day (three-night) taster and a four-day (six-night) explorer tour (including accommodation, lunch, guide and transfers). Walkers with a nose for New Zealand wildlife in the raw will enjoy *Tiritiri Matangi Island*, some 30km (19 miles) north, a re-stocked and re-forested sanctuary for many rare species of native bird. A *Fullers Ferry* (see above) to the island from the ferry terminal costs NZ$45 (day return). Visitors should not forget to take lunch, because there is nowhere to buy any. Once there, the *Department of Conservation* (or DOC) (tel: (09) 379 6476; fax: (09) 379 3609; e-mail: aucklandvc@doc.govt.nz; website: www.doc.govt.nz), has tour guides on the beach, imparting bush and bird lore for NZ$5 per hour.

For a Whole Day

Auckland vineyards: New Zealand makes some of the best wines in the world, especially sauvignon blanc, chardonnay and pinot noir. The best-known vineyards are situated further south, such as in Hawke's Bay and Marlborough, although Auckland has several good vineyards to the west of the city, notably in the Henderson and Kumeu areas. Several tour companies organise day trips, which normally include visits to at least four vineyards and lunch at one of them. Cost is in the region of NZ$50–110 per half day, depending on the number of people – some tours require a minimum number of passengers. Companies include *Auckland Adventures* (tel: (09) 379 4545; website: www.aucklandadventures.co.nz), *Bush and Beach* (tel: (09) 575 1458), *Waitakere Scenic Tours*

(tel: (09) 817 4547) and, best of all, *Fine Wine Tours* (tel: (09)849 4519).

ACCOMMODATION

The most important thing for visitors to remember about hotels in New Zealand is that, being in the Southern Hemisphere, the seasons are reversed. It is therefore advisable to book ahead during the Christmas period, as this is the main summer and school holiday season. Cheaper room rates might be available on the day, although some hotels are likely to be full.

The prices quoted below are the lowest standard rates for a double room, excluding Goods and Services Tax (GST), currently standing at 12.5%, and excluding breakfast, unless otherwise specified.

Business

Barrycourt Suites, Hotel and Conference Centre

This Best Western Hotel is a large white block house of a building with bright blue balconies and is situated in 1.2 hectares (three acres) of glorious greenery and trees, providing the ideal setting in which to work and play. Located in Parnell, the hotel is within walking distance of downtown Auckland and the domain. There are 67 suites with a sunny aspect, 40 well-equipped rooms and seven function rooms at guests' disposal, as well as free parking and splendid views of the Waitemata Harbour and the city. Within the conference rooms is a 440cm (170-inch) screen for video and other visual presentations, conference telephones, most forms of presentation technology, power points for computers, function bars and catering staff to deal with any requests.

10–20 Gladstone Road, Parnell
Tel: (09) 303 3789. Fax: (09) 377 3309.
E-mail: barrycourt@xtra.co.nz
Website: www.barrycourt.co.nz
Price: From NZ$99.

Carlton Hotel

This centrally located, architecturally spectacular 12-storey hotel has a glass-walled atrium that extends to its full height and 455 rooms ranging from royal through executive to studio suites, as well as large well-appointed, air-conditioned standard rooms with floor-to-ceiling windows and great views. Along with a dedicated business centre, complete with secretarial support, the hotel also contains five meeting rooms and one of the largest capacity ballrooms in the city, all just 25km (16 miles) from the airport. Other valuable facilities are safe deposit boxes, faxes in all rooms, excellent security, catering facilities, a choice of two excellent restaurants – one fusion and one Japanese – and two comfortable and relaxing bars.

Corner of Mayoral Drive and Vincent Street
Tel: (09) 366 3000. Fax: (09) 366 0121.
E-mail: res@carlton-auckland.co.nz
Website: www.carlton-auckland.co.nz
Price: From NZ$340.

First Imperial Auckland

This high-class hotel of 60 rooms – including three that are specifically designed for disabled guests – is situated in the centre of Auckland and just a five-minute walk from the main shopping streets and

waterfront. The tall redbrick, apartment-house-style block has balconies and contains an excellent variety of modern, air-conditioned rooms, executive studios and executive two-bedroom apartments. Each room has IDD telephones, PC connectors and modem points. The hotel also contains one large and one smaller conference facility with video and presentation equipment hire and secretarial support.

131–139 Hobson Street
Tel: (09) 357 6770. Fax: (09) 357 6793.
E-mail: res@firstimperial.co.nz
Website: www.firstimperial.co.nz
Price: From NZ$145.

Hyatt Regency Auckland

This unmistakable, tall, broad and handsome building in central Auckland is just a five-minute walk from the Central Business District and 25km (16 miles) from the airport. The 274 rooms on offer in this modern hotel may not match the presidential suite but all are air-conditioned and have IDD telephones, Internet access via infrared keyboards, voice-mail and in-room safes. There is also a business centre with equipment hire, secretarial services, courier delivery, translators, an airport limousine and a ballroom, as well as eight additional conference rooms with full staff back-up. In addition, the hotel boasts two restaurants, a fitness centre and jogging track, with panoramic views of the harbour and outlying city.

Corner of Princess Street and Waterloo Quadrant
Tel: (09) 355 1234. Fax: (09) 302 3269.
E-mail: auckland@hyatt.co.nz
Website: www.hyatt.co.nz
Price: From NZ$170.

Luxury

The Heritage Auckland

Auckland's most interesting international-class luxury hotel was originally the city's most historic and spectacular department store, Farmers. The landmark building has an iconic reputation and is a wonderful example of Southern Hemisphere Art Deco styling. *The Heritage* has two separate accommodation wings, made up of 467 rooms and suites, a tennis court, two swimming pools (one roof-top), a health club, a business centre, spa pools, saunas, gyms, restaurants, café bars, lobby bars, a glass atrium and, best of all, a grand tea room with fantastic views of the harbour and the America's Cup Village. Quite simply, this hotel is style and luxury personified.

35 Hobson Street
Tel: (09) 379 8553. Fax: (09) 379 8554.
E-mail: res.heritageakl@dynasty.co.nz
Website: www.dynasty.co.nz
Price: From NZ$350.

Sky City Hotel

Part of Auckland's most famous and most recent landmark, the Sky Tower, this massive and lavish hotel in the centre of the city has 344 rooms, various restaurants and bars, conference and business facilities, a roof-top pool, gym, saunas and casino, as well as stunning harbour and city views. The best of the vistas are seen from the circular viewing gallery at the top of the space-needle-like tower. All the rooms, from premier suites to standard luxury, are tastefully decorated in the style, and to the standard,

of world-class luxury hotels across the globe, while the service is efficient, friendly and respectful.
Corner of Victoria Street and Hobson Street
Tel: (09) 363 6000. Fax: (09) 363 6032.
E-mail: reservations@skycity.co.nz
Website: www.skycity.co.nz
Price: From NZ$340.

Moderate

Hotel DeBrett
Only minutes from the city centre, *DeBrett* is the place to sample the joys of an Art Deco hotel, at a fraction of the price of The Heritage (see *Luxury*). The corner-block building leans out over the pavement, to provide covered sidewalks and shows its history in the decorations on the façade. This interesting building, which crouches in the middle of the fashion and café districts, was constructed on the site of one of Auckland's first hotels and, despite showing its age a little at the edges, contains some comfortable and airy double rooms that offer good value for the tourist.
2 High Street
Tel: (09) 377 2389. Fax: (09) 377 2391.
E-mail: debrett@acb.co.nz
Website: www.acb.co.nz/debrett
Price: NZ$60 (shared bathroom), NZ$82 (en suite), including breakfast.

Kiwi International Hotel
This modest albeit perfectly adequate hotel is located in the middle of the city, only a 25-minute drive from the airport. The *Kiwi International Hotel* contains a bar and restaurant, laundry, 24-hour reception, off-street parking, conference facilities and 120 comfortable and functional rooms with their own en-suite facilities. Although the decor is rather lacking in character and the interior gives the impression of an ageing warren, there is sufficient compensation in the number and quality of the facilities on offer, the eagerness of the staff, the variety of accommodation available and the surprisingly low daily or long-term rates.
411 Queen Street
Tel: (09) 379 6487. Fax: (09) 379 6496.
E-mail: kiwihotel@xtra.co.nz
Website: www.kiwihotel.co.nz
Price: From NZ$79 (including GST and breakfast).

Other Recommendations

Peace & Plenty Inn
Without exaggeration, this is one of the finest bed and breakfasts in the entire country, with sumptuous, restored kauri-timber floors that feel like silk beneath bare feet, leading to exquisite en-suite rooms filled with fresh flowers, antique furniture and sherry or port decanters. There is a delightful verandah for breakfast – weather permitting – and the meal itself is an event of major proportions and large, healthy and hearty portions. It is served by an ultra-friendly couple, who offer sailing trips around the bay on their boat.
6 Flagstaff Terrace
Tel: (09) 445 2925. Fax: (09) 445 2901.
E-mail: peaceandplenty@xtra.com
Website: www.peaceandplenty.co.nz
Price: From NZ$220 (including GST and breakfast).

St Georges Bay Lodge
Undoubtedly one of the best types of accommodation in all of New Zealand is the bed and breakfast. In this case, *St Georges Bay Lodge* is situated in a beautiful Victorian villa in the airy and quiet suburb of Parnell, just a short ferry ride from the city centre. The white-board villa was built in the 1890s and boasts the original sash windows, turned verandah posts – supporting verdant green climbing plants – and a conservatory leading out onto a wooden balcony that overlooks Auckland's city centre from across the bay. The house is full of native timber furniture and original Kiwi artworks. There are three en-suite rooms of glorious comfort and elegance and the breakfasts (full English or Continental) are to die for.
43 St Georges Bay Road, Parnell
Tel: (09) 303 1050. Fax: (09) 303 0155.
E-mail: enquiry@stgeorge.co.nz
Website: www.stgeorge.co.nz
Price: From NZ$165 (including GST and breakfast).

RESTAURANTS

The selected restaurants have been divided into five categories: Gastronomic, Business, Trendy, Budget and Personal Recommendations. The restaurants are listed alphabetically within these different categories, which serve as guidelines rather than absolute definitions of the establishments.

Many of Auckland's restaurants operate as cafés, bars, music venues and nightclubs, as well as serving food. They do not generally have a pre-book service, although when they do, they rarely book far in advance and do not readily give out telephone or fax numbers, or e-mail addresses.

GST (Goods and Services Tax) will be mentioned on the menu, indicating whether it is included in the price or not. In the vast majority of cases it will be included as a percentage of the total bill, currently 12.5%. Tipping is rarely included in the bill and until recently was not expected, in fact it was even frowned upon. Globalisation has, however, led to a more 'American' attitude and it is now advisable for diners to tip 10–15% – but only if the service is good.

The prices quoted below are for an average three-course meal for one person and for a bottle of house wine or cheapest equivalent; they do not include GST or tip.

Gastronomic

Antoine's Restaurant
Despite its conservative tone and decor, this sophisticated silver service restaurant is a favourite, of some 27 years standing, among Auckland's gastronomes and widely held to be one of the best French restaurants in the country. Situated just ten minutes from the city centre, the restaurant offers some splendid dishes. Particularly high on the must-try list are the wonderful salmon dishes, tripe dishes and duckling, all from fresh New Zealand produce but with Gaelic flare. The menu changes weekly.
333 Parnell Road, Parnell
Tel: (09) 379 8756. Fax: (09) 524 0684.
E-mail: info@antoines.co.nz
Website: www.antoinesrestaurant.co.nz
Price: NZ$80. Wine: NZ$20.

Hammerheads Seafood Restaurant & Bar
This is a very popular waterfront restaurant with a balcony, where it pays to be seen. White awning and views of the Auckland skyline and harbour supplement the restaurant's effortless style. It has a reputation for slow service, although the cocktails are dynamite and the food is well worth the wait. Specialities include very fresh fish and shellfish, with some lamb, poultry and beef dishes, although diners are well advised to go with the fish.
19 Tamaki Drive, Okahu Bay
Tel: (09) 521 4400. Fax: (09) 521 4499.
E-mail: info@hammerheads.co.nz
Website: www.hammerheads.co.nz
Price: NZ$65. Wine: NZ$18.

Otto's
Once a magistrates court, this lovely building is now one of the premier restaurants in the city, with tasteful

Waterfront dining

Photo: Tourism New Zealand

Alfresco dining

decor and loads of potted plants. The food is catholic in its influences and melts on the taste buds, especially the duck confit, dressed in coconut and palm sugar, and the seared venison with onion ravioli.
40 Kitchener Street
Tel: (09) 300 9595. Fax: (09) 300 9596.
E-mail: enquiry@ottos.co.nz
Website: www.ottos.co.nz
Price: NZ$80. Wine: NZ$25.

Toto Restaurant

Possibly the city's finest Italian restaurant, this open and airy opera-filled room – with live opera on Thursday and Saturday – leads to a sunny terrace where it is good to be seen eating at the white-clad tables. The *ripieno* (stuffed breads) make mouthwatering appetisers and the roasted scallops and lobster are delicious menu options.
53 Nelson Street
Tel: (09) 302 2665. Fax: (09) 302 2047.
E-mail: toto@totorestaurant.co.nz
Website: www.totorestaurant.co.nz
Price: NZ$70. Wine: NZ$18.

Vinnie's Restaurant

Best bib and tucker is advised when visiting one of the few formal restaurants in Auckland, located just five minutes from the city centre. With immaculate white linen tablecloths and an exclusive, intimate atmosphere, the food is prepared on wood-fired ovens, so dishes like braised lamb and snapper ceviche in a raspberry citrus vinaigrette, have a delicious and highly distinctive flavour.
166 Jervois Road, Herne Bay
Tel: (09) 376 5597. Fax: (09) 376 5559.
E-mail: vinnies@xtra.co.nz
Price: NZ$80. Wine: NZ$25.

Business

Euro

Euro opened just in time for the America's Cup defence and since then has been the place to be seen in town. It has superb service, bare wood and tastefully refined decor, as well as a fantastically imaginative and varied menu, including rotisserie chicken on a bed of mashed potato and peanut slaw.
Shed 22, Princes Wharf, Quay Street
Tel: (09) 309 9866.
Price: NZ$70. Wine: NZ$18.

GPK

Another delicious fusion house combining Italian pizza bases (and sometimes toppings) with Pacific rim toppings, such as Thai green curry or octopus, which are then all finished off in large wood-fired ovens. The surroundings are a combination of smart restaurant and bare-wood bar with a relaxed atmosphere.
262 Ponsonby Road
Tel: (09) 360 1113.
Price: NZ$30 or NZ$20 for a pizza. Wine: NZ$15.

Iguacu

Often the haunt of young corporate wannabes and their hangers-on, *Iguacu* is a wood and flash brasserie. It has large glass windows through which patrons look out and passers-by look in at lucky folk indulging in good but expensive steaks, pan-fired lamb and fresh fish. There is also excellent jazz during Sunday brunchtime.
269 Parnell Road, Parnell
Tel: (09) 358 4804.
E-mail: info@iguacu.co.nz
Website: www.iguacu.co.nz
Price: NZ$50. Wine: NZ$20.

Porterhouse Blue

The decor is tasteful, the service faultless and the quality of the food on offer is top draw in Devonport's most well-thought-of restaurant. Particular favourites are lamb's brains, roasted ribeye, artichoke ravioli and a selection of tangy and creamy goat's cheeses.
58 Caliope Road, Devonport
Tel: (09) 445 0309.
Price: NZ$70. Wine: NZ$19.

Sake Bar Rikka

This is the best Japanese restaurant in town, done up with wall hangings and gleaming clean surfaces. Dishes include chicken teriyaki, a dazzling variety of sushi, miso and a never-ending tempura platter with hot sauce and pickled ginger, all washed down by authentic sake.
Victoria Park Market
Tel: (09) 377 8239.
Price: NZ$65. Wine: NZ$20.

Trendy

Ding How

This is a lively yet intimate Cantonese restaurant with some traditional East Asian decor, with a tendency to fill early and stay that way. Located on St Patrick's Square, there are the inevitable inner city business folk grabbing a snack, although they are outnumbered by the Chinese diners, who are a testament to the authenticity and quality of the food on offer. Trays of steaming dim sum are carried around the floor, while the waiters shout out the various options to guests who stop them to peek under the lids and make a difficult but delicious decision. The sticky rice is delicious, served with pork, chicken and steamed in a lotus leaf, as is the standard *sui mai* prawn or scallop dumplings.
Second Floor, 55 Albert Street, St Patrick's Square
Tel: (09) 358 4838. Fax: (09) 358 4855.
Price: NZ$60. Wine: NZ$15.

Kermadec

A large, fashionable and imaginatively decorated seafood specialist with a big bustling and music-filled brasserie, *Kermadec* serves classier versions of bistro favourites – pan-fried snapper, Cajun-spiced fish, fish curry and scallops. The adjacent Pacific Room dances to the beat of an altogether quieter, more expensive and refined drum.
First Floor Viaduct Basin, corner of Hobson Street and Quay Street
Tel: (09) 309 0413. Fax: (09) 307 0072.
E-mail: info@kermadec.co.nz
Website: www.kermadec.co.nz
Price: NZ$70. Wine: NZ$20.

Sails Restaurant

Only a five-minute walk from the city centre, overlooking the marina and the Harbour Bridge, this stylish and contemporary restaurant has recently been renovated and is, as a result, bright, spacious and airy. The food is not cheap but the seafood bisque, sashimi, rack of lamb, sautéed scallops, oven-baked salmon and Cajun-style Hapuka are all worth it. *Sails* also serves up its very own signature fish and chips with beer batter and the chocolate mocha tart is to die for.
Westhaven Marina, Westhaven Drive, Westhaven
Tel: (09) 378 9890.
Price: NZ$85. Wine: NZ$80.

Wildfire

A flashy new kid on the block, with black-topped waterside tables and massive fiery grills inside. Gourmet pizzas are produced, which, although good, are put completely in the shade by rotisserie specials of quail, duck, venison, steak and many more, marinated in herbs and spices and roasted over manuka coals.
Princes Wharf
Tel: (09) 353 7595. Fax: (09) 353 7590.
E-mail: wildfirerestaurant@xtra.co.nz
Website: www.wildfirerestaurant.co.nz
Price: NZ$40. Wine: NZ$20.

Zarbo

The finest deli café in Auckland, *Zarbo* is renowned for its fabulous range of products from all over the world, which are used to forge delicious breakfasts and lunches, either from the menu or picked from the display counter. The decor in this 120-seat deli and café is simple but stylish. The food takes pride of place in a long glass-covered deli counter, stuffed to overflowing with fresh cheeses, meats, dips, spreads and breads from which diners will be hard pushed to make a quick selection. There are salads of seasonal roasted vegetables, Asian sweet chilli kumara, and orzo pasta with pumpkin and feta, alongside filled rolls, lasagne, chicken breasts, roast beef and glazed ham. The breakfast menu is accompanied by scones, muffins and Eccles cakes. Lunch finishes at 1500 but the restaurant is open until 1700 for salads and some dreamy cakes and brilliant brownies.
24 Morrow Street, Newmarket.
Tel: (09) 520 2721. Fax: (09) 520 3665.
E-mail: zarbo@zarbo.co.nz.
Website: www.zarbo.co.nz
Price: NZ$15. Wine: From NZ$15.

Budget

Java Room

Described as Pacific Rim, the predominant influence in this intimate, light-hued and comfortable restaurant is Indonesian, although it serves up some fantastic Szechuan dishes, particularly the prawn offerings. The spicy fish cakes also take some beating, as does the whole snapper in sambal.

317 Parnell Road, Parnell
Tel: (09) 366 1606. Fax: (09) 358 1881.
E-mail: hooi@javaroom.co.nz
Website: www.javaroom.co.nz
Price: NZ$60. Wine: NZ$20.

Kamo

This stripped-down-to-keep-the-prices-down restaurant has functional furniture and a rowdy atmosphere. Pacific Rim is mixed with Mediterranean flavours, to come up with menu items such as fresh fish marinated in coconut cream and finely diced vegetables.
383 Karangahape Road
Tel: (09) 377 2313.
Price: NZ$50. Wine: NZ$18.

Merchant Mezze Bar

This buzzing, café-style restaurant has Turkish rugs thrown around and an intimate little deck area. It serves dishes from the Mediterranean, the Middle East and beyond, including Spanish tortilla, grilled mushroom on polenta, ceviche, and Thai green curries.
430 Queen Street
Tel/fax: (09) 307 0349.
E-mail: mezzebar@pl.net
Website: www.menus.co.nz/mezzebar
Price: NZ$30. Wine: NZ$18.

Monsoon

A heady mixture of Thai and Malay food makes for an exotic eating experience at a surprisingly low price. Functional decor takes second place to wonderful satay dishes with peanut and chilli sauce, and fish and tiger prawns in a vibrant red curry sauce.
71 Victoria Road, Devonport
Tel: (09) 445 4263. Fax: (09) 446 0170.
E-mail: monsoon1@xtra.co.nz
Website: www.monsoon.co.nz
Price: NZ$35. Wine: NZ$18.

Sri Penang

A very popular, although simplistic Malaysian restaurant, *Sri Penang* starts diners off with half a dozen chicken satay skewers and follows those with some gorgeous sambal okra, beef redang, grilled tamarin fish or claypot chicken and rice, all scooped into the mouth on a tasty roti. A fresh coat of paint on the walls has freshened up the interior somewhat but no money has been wasted on the décor, which explains why the food stays cheap and tastes so good.
356 Karangahape Road
Tel: (09) 358 3886.
Price: NZ$40. Wine: NZ$1 corkage.

Personal Recommendations

Bluefins

This is yet another informal, friendly, hanging-basket-strewn, wooden-floored and apparently simple seafood specialist but this time in the glorious surroundings of Okahu Bay. The fish is fresh, the seared scallops melt in the mouth, the tuna is just pink in the centre and the paua is large, golden and tastes of the sea.
Corner of Tamaki Drive and Aitkin Avenue, Okahu Bay
Tel: (09) 528 4551.
Website: www.bluefins.co.nz
Price: NZ$50. Wine: NZ$20.

Bolliwood

A vast Indian restaurant in the style of Bollywood films, *Bolliwood* has a retina-alarming, bright colour

Viaduct Basin

scheme and a company of waiters who play to the crowd so much so that it is quite obvious they are all actors waiting for the big break. The food is just as engaging – the dairy dishes are worth trying for a bit of richness or the spicier southern dishes for some real steam heat. The menu contains traditional Indian favourites and signature dishes, such as tandoori chicken, burrak kebab (marinated lamb chops), whole snapper, chicken tikka masala, lamb dosas and vegetarian kormas.
110 Ponsonby Road
Tel: (09) 376 8966.
Price: NZ$50. Wine: NZ$15.

Harbourside Seafood Bar and Grill

This is a typically informal Kiwi seafood restaurant, which is extremely classy, because of the beauty of the location and the quality of the food and wine. Located in a historical building, *Harbourside* affords magnificent views of the harbour from its balcony and terracotta-tiled terrace. Meanwhile, the contemporary interior is spacious, airy and stylish. The restaurant offers a myriad of prepared and presented fish and crustaceans – such as pan-fried John Dory with watercress, shiitake mushrooms and citrus zest risotto – with inland fare for the unenlightened.
99 Quay Street
Tel: (09) 307 0486. Fax: (09) 307 0523.
E-mail: harbourside.auck@xtra.co.nz
Website: www.harboursiderestaurant.co.nz
Price: NZ$50. Wine: NZ$20.

Simple Cottage

Bare-wood furniture, simple decor and a homey relaxed atmosphere mark out this vegetarian establishment and all-day coffee house as a good place for visitors to stop off for a caffeine buzz or herbal tea.

This should be followed by tofu burgers, salads, lasagne, falafel or moussaka. If given adequate notice, the restaurant will happily cater for people with specialist diets, such as gluten- or wheat-free dishes.
50 High Street
Tel: (09) 303 4599. Fax: (09) 634 1801.
Price: NZ$40. Wine: NZ$15.

Tony's

Tony's is a no-fuss or bother steakhouse (and that goes for the decor too), where the portions are about the size of the animals from which they were removed. The massive sides of juicy beef and lamb are cooked beautifully, while the accompaniments, which include pumpkin mash and sweet potato wedges, are wholesome and delicious in equal measure.
32 Lorne Street
Tel/fax: (09) 373 2138.
Website: www.menus.co.nz/tonys
Price: NZ$50. Wine: NZ$19.

ENTERTAINMENT

Nightlife

Auckland may not be New York or Paris but it has its share of night entertainment. The waterfront is where most of the smarter venues are, in particular around the America's Cup Village and the new Princes Wharf development. High Street, to the south of Queens Wharf, also has a number of good bars, including some with live music.
In bars and clubs the dress code tends to be casual, although some places enforce a smarter rule and are

particularly against black jeans and leathers, since these tend to be clothes favoured by gangs. Licensing laws are not strict and some bars have a 24-hour licence, while others remain open until the early hours. The age limit for drinking alcohol is 18 years. On average, a pint of beer will cost approximately NZ$3–5, while a glass of wine can be anything from NZ$4–12, depending upon where you do your drinking.

To find out what is on, read the Thursday and Saturday editions of the *New Zealand Herald*, the free monthly listings magazine, *What's Happening*, or the free newspaper, *Tourist Times*.

Bars

Lots of local favourites are situated down by the waterfront – such as the vast glass-walled bar, *The Loaded Hog*, Quay Street, in the Viaduct Basin – with newly fashionable hangouts in Princes Wharf, refurbished in time for the 2000 America's Cup. These include *Bellini*, in the Hilton Auckland, Princes Wharf, 147 Quay Street, and the decidedly un-Russian vodka bar, *Lenin Bar*, Princes Wharf, 201 Quay Street. With the city's British-influenced past, it is not surprising that there are numerous British-style bars in Auckland, the biggest being the *Civic Tavern*, 1 Wellesley Street West. This has an Irish bar, *Murphy's*, and an English bar, the *London Bar*, both situated downstairs, with live music and a bistro restaurant. *The Immigrant Irish Bar*, 104 Fanshawe Street, is an out-and-out Irish pub, with live music at the weekend. *The Rose and Crown*, 69 Customs Street, is an English bar with music, open from Wednesday to Saturday, while the *Kiwi Tavern*, 3 Britomart Place, is a pool bar with drink specials. The *Shakespeare Tavern*, 61 Albert Street, is a micro-brewery producing its own beer, while the *Tabac*, 6 Mills Lane, is renowned for its comfortable velvet room and for being part-owned by former Crowded House singer-songwriter Neil Finn.

Casinos

Sky City Casino, in the Sky Tower, on the corner of Victoria Street and Federal Street, is a gambling haven and an entertainment complex that includes a theatre, restaurant, bars and a hotel, as well as the casino itself. There is a minimum age of 20 years for entering the casino, although a passport is not required. Dress code is smart-casual and T-shirts, jeans and sandals are not permitted.

Clubs

The Club, 371 Queen Street, is a good place to start, with DJs from 2200 on Friday and Saturday. At the harbour, *The Loaded Hog*, Quay Street, in the Viaduct Basin, has long been a favoured hangout for yachties and yuppies alike. The younger and wilder crowd go to *Calibre*, St Kevin's Arcade, 179 Karangahape (K) Road, although not before 2300 (Thursday to Saturday), as it is open until 0800. Alternatives include *Galatos*, 17 Galatos Street, a mellow lounge bar with DJ-led dancing, *Java Jive*, 12 Pompallier Terrace, a basement bar full of live acoustic, jazz and blues music, *Khuja Lounge*, 536 Queen Street, a music lover's bar for the more mellow, older crowd and *The Power Station*, 33 Mount Eden Road, the most happening of the rock and rap dance venues. For a late-night club full of DJs spinning reggae, Cuban and African beats, try *Roots*, 322 Karangahape Road, or if what you want is more traditional Kiwi acoustic, go to *Temple*, 486 Queen Street.

Comedy

Classic, 31 Queen Street, is a well-known comedy venue that showcases local talent as well as up-and-coming

international acts. There is also the *Aotea Centre*, Aotea Square, Queen Street, *Silo Theatre*, Lower Grays Avenue, *Maidment Theatre*, corner of Princess Street and Alfred Street, and the *Civic Theatre*, corner of Queen Street and Wellesley Street.

Live Music

There is plenty of choice at the weekend, mostly in the Downtown area, along Karangahape (K) Road and in Ponsonby. Try *The Temple*, 486 Queen Street, which has music every night after 1700, *Java Jive*, 12 Pompallier Terrace, for live jazz, acoustic and blues sessions (Wednesday to Sunday), or *Papa Jack's Voodoo Lounge*, 9 Vulcan Street, which has live touring bands and DJs. If you are looking for some sweaty, touring, alternative rock, rap and dance acts, head for *The Power Station*, 33 Mount Eden Road, Mount Eden.

Sport

In New Zealand, it is popularly held that sport has taken the place of religion at the weekend. Frankly, Kiwi sports fans have a lot to be proud of on the fields of sporting endeavour. This small nation is very successful on an international scale – and at several sports, notably rugby, cricket and netball.

Rugby has enormous appeal in Auckland and throughout New Zealand. The Rugby League season is April to September and the local team is the *Vodafone Warriors* (website: www.warriors.co.nz), who play at the *Ericsson Stadium*, Maurice Road, Penrose

(tel: (09) 526 0888). The *New Zealand Rugby Football League* (tel: (09) 524 4013) can provide further information. The Rugby Union season is also April to September and the national team, the *All Blacks* (website: www.allblacks.com), play either at *Eden Park*, Reimers Avenue, Kingsland (tel: (09) 849 5555), or the *Ericsson Stadium*, when they are in Auckland, although they also play in Wellington, Chrsitchurch and Dunedin. The *New Zealand Rugby Football Union* (tel: (04) 499 4995; website: www.nzrugby.co.nz) can provide further information.

Six cricket grounds reflect the city's interest in this colonial game – the most famous is Eden Park, which has staged 225 first-class games since 1913.

Tickets to sporting events are available for purchase through *Ticketek* (tel: (09) 307 5000). The *Visitor Information Centre* (tel: (09) 979 2333) can provide details of all sporting events.

Equestrian Sports

There are several racecourses in Auckland, with night trotting each Friday and Saturday, at the *Alexandra Park Raceway*, in Epsom. Visitors should contact the *Recorded Racing Information Service* (tel: (09) 520 7507) for further details. Horseriding is also very popular in New Zealand and there are several stables within easy reach of the city. Most offer lessons, independent or guided rides, with horses for all levels of ability. Stables include *Horse Riding Warkworth* (tel: (09) 425 8517), *Ti Tree Hills Horse Treks* (tel: (09) 426 7003), *Pakiri Beach Horse Riding* (tel: (09) 422 6275) and *Shepherds Point Horse Riding* (tel: (09) 372 8194). Prices start at

Dining in Vulcan Lane

approximately NZ$25 per hour. Closer to the city centre is the *Muriwai Riding Centre*, Muriwai (tel: (09) 411 8480), which organises treks on the beach and in the forest, providing excellent views of the local gannet colony and costing NZ$45 for two hours.

Fitness Centres

The *Olympic Pool and Fitness Centre*, Broadway, Newmarket (tel: (09) 522 4414), is open to the public and has excellent facilities, as well as two swimming pools, a spa and sauna. Visitors planning to use the gym will need to do an induction course, for insurance purposes. Admission is around NZ$15.

Golf

There are several golf courses in and around Auckland, including the *Chamberlain Park Public Golf Course*, 46a Linwood Avenue, Western Springs (tel: (09) 815 4999), where 18 holes costs around NZ$30, and the *Gulf Harbour Country Club*, on the Hibiscus Coast (tel: (09) 424 0971), where 18 holes costs NZ$74, a set of hire clubs NZ$25 and shoes NZ$8. Visiting golfers can play guest rounds for a nominal fee at public courses and annual membership costs at other clubs are usually low by European standards.

Swimming

The best swimming is off the beaches that are easily reached from central Auckland, including several along Tamaki Drive and Cheltenham Beach in Northshore, on the east coast of the Devonport peninsula. There are also ten major swimming pools in the city, the most notable being the *Olympic Pool and Fitness Centre*, Broadway, Newmarket (tel: (09) 522 4414). This was built for the 1950 Empire Games and, in addition to the main 50m (164ft) pool, there is a smaller pool, fitness centre, sauna and spa. The *Visitor Information Centre* (tel: (09) 979 2333) provides a booklet listing the city's pools and recreation centres.

Tennis

The country's main international tennis venue is in Auckland – the *ASB Tennis Centre*, 72 Stanley Street (tel: (09) 373 3623). There are five indoor and seven floodlit outdoor courts, with equipment hire and coaching facilities available. Court hire costs from NZ$25 per hour. More courts are available at the *Vodafone Tennis Park*, 69 Merton Road, Glen Innes (tel: (09) 528 9782), with six indoor and 17 outdoor courts, equipment hire and coaching available.

Watersports

Needless to say, the city is a prime watersports destination. It is claimed that roughly one in six Aucklanders owns a boat, while one in three goes boating on a regular basis. The city's world profile was increased even further by the America's Cup – the finals were held in Auckland in February 2000, when New Zealand secured the cup – and was the venue for the battle for the 'old mug', until the summer of 2003. The chance to sail an America's Cup yacht is available from *Viking Cruises* (tel: (0800) 724 569), costing around NZ$85 for two hours.
Kayaking can be arranged through *Outdoor Recreations and Challenges*, in the Birkenhead Leisure Centre, Mahara Avenue, Birkenhead (tel: (09) 418 4109), and through *Fergs Kayaks*, 12 Tamaki Drive (tel: (09) 529 2230). Hire starts from approximately NZ$12 per hour for a plastic sea kayak, with guided tours from NZ$60 for a four-hour trip. Windsurfing can be arranged at several of the beaches along Tamaki Drive, while jet-skiing is available from *Jet Ski Tours* (tel: (09) 486 088).

Shopping

Auckland has an ever-increasing reputation for being an excellent shopping destination, with a vibrant homegrown fashion industry and retailers stocking all the latest international designer labels. The Kiwi fashion industry is at the cutting edge, taking – as the food industry once did – influences from Europe, Polynesia and the Pacific Rim and then, through the process of fusion, coming up with a unique style. This can range from the simple and sophisticated to the avant-garde, or from the downright practical to the high-art creations of the World of Wearable Arts (an internationally recognised fashion festival in Nelson). Good fashion outlets are mainly located in the city centre, notably the High Street. Local names include Karen Walker (worn by Madonna), Zambesi, Workshop and World.
New Zealand's fine foodstuffs may not make practical purchases to take home but its wine certainly does. The relative lack of fine wine merchants in the country is a positive advantage, as most people go direct to the vineyards and thus avoid paying inflated prices, because of the middleman's mark up. Visitors should watch out for names such as Coopers Creek, Kumeu River, Nobilo and Matua Valley or check out the free *Winemakers of Auckland* leaflet, available at the visitor centre. As for wineries from further afield, the best are in the Martinborough, Hawkes Bay, Marlborough and Gold Country regions.
Woollen and leather goods are also good options for souvenirs and gifts, as are Maori traditional crafts and items made from *pounamu* (greenstone). For jewellery, *Fingers*, 2 Kitchener Street (tel: (09) 373 3974), stocks creations from dozens of top native designers, while *Compendium*, 5 Lorne Street (tel: (09) 300 3212), is the best all-round store for general crafts. Some of the best designer gear for outdoors and in, made from natural fabrics, is available from *Untouched World*, 20 High Street (tel: (09) 303 1382). This is an up-and-coming label, with high quality, designer products that cross a broad range, from food to clothing, rather than just the usual range of knitwear.
Shops are usually open on weekdays from 0900–1700, with late-night shopping on Friday until 2100 in some parts of central Auckland, such as Queen Street. Areas such as this and some of the larger suburban shopping malls, also open on Saturday 0900–1700, as well as some on Sunday from about 1000 until 1600. Visitors should note that the suburbs of Auckland are also renowned for their shopping opportunities – some for fashion, others for sparklers and stinkies – so it is always worth straying off the beaten track.
Aotea Square, next to the IMAX Cinema and opposite the Town Hall, has a market on Friday and Saturday mornings, selling arts and crafts, clothes and jewellery. The Victoria Park Market is open daily from 0900–1800 and is a big flea market where shoppers can get virtually anything. The Polynesian Market is situated just south of Mount Eden and is open on Saturday morning.
Goods and Sales Tax (GST) is 12.5%. Provided receipts are kept, visitors can claim a tax refund at the airport or through their local New Zealand embassy upon return home.

Culture

The New Zealand cultural scene is vibrant and receives a lot more attention these days than it did in

Shopping in Newmarket

the past, principally because of the release of the first two films from the *Lord of the Rings* trilogy. Auckland, as a cultural melting pot, has a particularly healthy and diverse cultural scene, although not everything that the city generates gets beyond its own shores.
One of the centres of Auckland cultural life is *The Edge*, a conglomeration of buildings around the junctions of Queen Street, Wellesley Street West, Albert Street and Mayoral Drive. *Auckland Town Hall*, Queen Street (tel: (09) 309 2677) is an impressively renovated building, with its Great Hall said to have some of the finest acoustics in the world. Behind the Town Hall, the *Aotea Centre*, Queen Street (tel: (09) 307 5060), has main and small stages, for drama, music, ballet and opera.
For a taste of the alternative culture, with a bit more of a Polynesian influence, visitors should take a Saturday trip up the Karangahape (K) Road, or for that matter to any of the cultural or flea markets that spring up around the city on Saturday. K Road is awash with mainly Maori and Polynesian shops, butchers, fishmongers, grocers, craft shops, clothes shops, cafés and restaurants, all of which offer a colourful view of one side of New Zealand's bi-cultural society.
Tickets can be booked through *Ticketek*, at the *Aotea Centre*, Queen Street (tel: (09) 307 5000). The Thursday and Saturday editions of the *New Zealand Herald*, the free monthly listings magazine, *What's Happening*, and the free newspaper, *Tourist Times*, all provide listings and information on cultural

Photo: Tourism New Zealand

performance and events in Auckland. Listings are also available online (website: www.aucklandnz.com).

Music

The *Auckland Philharmonia* (tel: (09) 638 7073 *or* (0800) 744 542 for bookings; fax: (09) 630 9687; e-mail: ap@aucklandphil.co.nz; website: www.aucklandphil.co.nz) performs mainly at the *Auckland Town Hall*, Queen Street (tel: (09) 309 2677), which has classical music, opera and ballet regularly featured on the cultural menu. Although based in Wellington, the *New Zealand Symphony Orchestra* (tel: (04) 801 3890; fax: (04) 801 3851; e-mail: info@nzso.co.nz; website: www.nzso.co.nz) also frequently performs in Auckland, usually at the Town Hall or the *Aotea Centre*, Queen Street (tel: (09) 307 5060). Outdoor concerts are also held regularly in the Auckland Domain during summer.

Theatre

The main venue, with various sized auditoriums, is the *Aotea Centre*, Queen Street (tel: (09) 307 5060). The beautifully restored *Civic Theatre*, Queen Street and Wellesley Street West (tel: (09) 309 2677), north of the Town Hall, is used for plays and musicals. More modern rock, dance, drama and cabaret performances take place at the *Sky City Theatre*, corner of Federal Street and Victoria Street (tel: (09) 912 6000). Local productions can be seen at the *Dolphin Theatre*, Spring Street, Onehunga (tel: (09) 636 7322) and the *Howick Little Theatre Inc*, Lloyd Elsmore Park, Howick (tel: (09) 534 1406).

Dance

Numerous local dance groups include the *Auckland Dance Company*. There are regular visits from the *Royal New Zealand Ballet Company*, which is based in Wellington. Most performances are given at the *Aotea Centre*, Queen Street (tel: (09) 307 5060). *Black Grace* is an all-male dance troupe from the Pacific Islands, while the *Pounamu Maori Performance Group* gives regular displays of Polynesian song and dance at the *Auckland Museum*, Auckland Domain (tel: (09) 306 7067).

Film

The city has numerous cinemas, with the best listings in the daily *New Zealand Herald*. Most of the mainstream cinemas are situated along Queen Street, at the junction with Wellesley Street, including the *Mid-City Cinema Centre*, 239 Queen Street (tel: (09) 302 0277), and the *St James Theatre*, 312 Queen Street (tel: (09) 377 4241). The main arthouse cinema is the *Academy*, situated beneath the city library, 64 Lorne Street (tel: (09) 373 2761). There is also a seven-storey high IMAX screen at *Force Entertainment Centre*, next to Aotea Square, Queen Street (tel: (09) 979 2400).

The two best-known films to come out of New Zealand are undoubtedly *The Fellowship of the Ring* (2001) and *The Two Towers* (2002), parts one and two of the *Lord of the Rings* trilogy, directed by Peter Jackson. Parts of both films were filmed not far from Auckland. The city has achieved more serious celluloid acclaim for itself, with the 1994 film, *Once Were Warriors*, made from Alan Duff's harrowing novel about the struggle of a poor Maori family in south Auckland.

Cultural Events

Opera in the Park, in February, is a family-orientated concert staged at Auckland Domain. The *Pasifika Festival* celebrates Polynesian culture and takes place in Western Springs, each March. There are numerous small food, wine and music festivals throughout the

SPECIAL EVENTS

Auckland Anniversary Day Regatta (website: www.regatta.org.nz), late Jan, Waitemata Harbour
Opera in the Park, Feb, Auckland Domain
Devonport Food and Wine Festival (website: www.devonportwinefestival.co.nz) third week in Feb, Devonport
Pasifika Festival, Polynesian Festival, 1 Mar, Western Springs Reserve
Round the Bays Run (website: www.roundthebays.co.nz), 70,000-plus people jog ten kilometres (six miles), 30 Mar, Tawaki Drive
Waiheke Jazz Festival (website: www.waihekejazz.co.nz), Apr, various venues
Auckland Comedy Festival Apr–May, various venues
Royal New Zealand Easter Show, equestrian events, wine tastings and arts and crafts (website: www.royaleastershow.co.nz), Apr, Auckland Showgrounds, Greenlane
Auckland International Film Festival (website: www.nzff.co.nz), early Jul, various cinemas and Town Hall
Wine Waitakere, wine festival (website: www.waitakerenz.co.nz), Oct, Waitakere
Auckland–Russell Yacht Race, Oct, Auckland Harbour, starting at the yacht basin
Ellerslie Flower Show (website: www.ellerslieflowershow.co.nz), late Nov, Auckland Botanic Gardens, Manurewa
Auckland Cup, horseracing event, Dec, Ellerslie Racecourse
Christmas in the Park, seasonal family event, Dec, Auckland Domain

year, especially during summer. The year ends with *Christmas in the Park*, another family-orientated concert at the Auckland Domain, in December.

Literary Notes

New Zealand, rather than just Auckland, has several literary figures, many of whom are known internationally, such as Katherine Mansfield, most noted for her short stories. Janet Frame deals largely with the emotional crises that she herself experienced, while Keri Hulme, of mixed Maori, English and Orkney descent, won the Booker Prize for *The Bone People* (1983). This was an experimental work drawing on Maori culture and the best selling book ever by any living New Zealand author. Maurice Gee, who worked in Auckland as a teacher and later a librarian, sets several of his novels in the city. Alan Duff, whose kitchen-sink dramas, such as *Once Were Warriors* (1990), examine the place of Maori in modern society.

Yachting regatta

BANGKOK

Love it or hate it, buzzing, sweaty, exotic Bangkok is a city that really is larger than life. For some, the frenetic pace, heat, traffic and lack of personal space can be overpowering and are good reasons to pass through the city as quickly as possible but, for many others, the sheer dynamism is intoxicating.

A curious blend of the traditional East with the modern West, Bangkok's every street has a surprise in store for the visitor. Ramshackle buildings crouch next to exotic temples surrounded by delightful gardens, which are in turn overlooked by modern hotels and offices. Bangkok has emerged as a major world city with the traffic jams to match, as well as the all-pervasive mobile phones and designer clothes that are a prominent feature on the streets. The chaos on the roads is mirrored by the busy traffic on the Chao Phraya River, which dissects the city and is regularly crisscrossed by long-tailed boats, river taxis and small rowing boats, all miraculously missing each other.

But traditional Thai life is never very far away. Weaving among the nose-to-tail traffic in the morning rush hour, saffron-robed monks can still be seen collecting alms, while just moments from the city centre, whole communities live in stilt houses by the river, eking out a living using skills that have not changed for centuries.

In 1782, Bangkok became the capital of what was then Siam, following the destruction of the previous capital, Ayutthaya. Bangkok is not the name used by the Thais – they call it Krung Thep, which is actually a very shortened version of its extremely long full title. The absolute rule of the monarchy ended in 1932, when it was replaced by a system of constitutional monarchy. To this day, the monarchy is regarded with almost religious reverence and it is an offence, punishable by imprisonment, to insult the royal family. His Majesty King Bhumibol is the longest reigning monarch in the world, having come to power in 1946. Following the end of absolute monarchy, Thailand moved towards democracy but this has been thwarted by the military, which has often staged coups in protest of government policies. The role of the military in domestic politics has now been curtailed but the 1990s saw governments come and go, although there has been some stability since the government took on the job of tackling the economic crisis in the late 1990s.

Thailand is staunchly anti-Communist, as seen during the Vietnam War when it was a strategic ally for the USA. Latterly, it has softened its stance and relations have improved with its Communist neighbours who have now become members of the Association of South East Asian Nations (ASEAN), of which Thailand is an influential member. Thailand's main industries are tourism, textiles and electronics. Despite over half of Thai citizens working in agriculture, the industry only accounts for 15% of the GDP, although Thailand is still the world's largest exporter of rice. The difference in growth between industry and agriculture during the past few decades has resulted in enormous inequality between the city and countryside.

Thailand is a tropical country, so it is hot throughout the year. The best time to visit is between November and March, during the dry season. During the rainy season, humidity is very high and the downpours are short but violent and the streets of Bangkok often flood.

Bangkok skyline at sunset

Photo: Tourism Authority of Thailand

TRAVEL

Getting There By Air

Bangkok Don Muang International Airport (BKK)

Tel: (02) 535 1111.

Website: www.airportthai.co.th

Bangkok International Airport, located 25km (15miles) north of the city centre, is operated by the *Airports Authority of Thailand*. It is a major gateway to South-East Asia and one of the region's busiest airports, catering for 88 international carriers. Over 25 million passengers annually use the airport. The new international terminal has relieved congestion and handles passengers efficiently. A second international airport – Suvarnabhumi Airport – is currently under construction at Nong Ngu Hao, to the southeast of Bangkok, which will be in operation by 2005.

Major airlines: *Thai International* (tel: (02) 513 0121; website: www.thaiair.com) is the national airline and *Bangkok Airways* (tel: (02) 265 5555; website: www.bangkokair.com) and *Angel Airlines* (tel: (02) 937 8908; website: www.angelairlines.com) operate domestic flights and a small number of international routes in the region. Other major airlines include *Air China, Air France, British Airways, Cathay Pacific, Garuda Indonesia, Gulf Air, Japan Airlines, Lufthansa, Malaysian Airlines, Northwest, Qantas, SAS, Singapore Airlines* and *United Airlines*.

Approximate flight times to Bangkok: From London is 11 hours 35 minutes; from New York is 16 hours 55 minutes; from Los Angeles is 18 hours 50 minutes; from Toronto is 19 hours 50 minutes and from Sydney is 9 hours 25 minutes.

Airport facilities: These include 24-hour shopping, duty free, restaurants, snack bars, postal services, bureaux de change, tourist information, hotel reservations, left-luggage and a medical service. Car hire companies include *Avis* and *Budget*.

Business facilities: There is a business centre (tel: (02) 535 3711, ext 44) at the airport, as well as executive lounges and services like limousine hire and mobile phone hire.

Arrival/departure tax: There is no arrival tax but B500 (international) is payable in cash on departure. There is also a tax of B50 on domestic flights but this is included in the price of the ticket.

Transport to the city: Taxis can be pre-paid for at the Arrivals Hall in the airport; visitors should expect to pay B500–650 to the city centre (journey time – 40–90 minutes) plus road tolls of B70 at the booths. Airport buses (tel: (02) 995 1252) operate four different routes into the city every 30 minutes (0530–2430). Route A-1 goes to the Silom Road business district, A-2 goes to Sanam Luang (Royal Grand Palace), A-3 goes to Sukhumvit Road and A-4 goes to Hualampong Railway Station (approximate journey times – one hour; cost: B100). *Bangkok Airport Express* trains operate every 90 minutes (0800–1900) from the railway station adjacent to the airport (journey time – 35 minutes; fare: B100). The tourist information booth in the Arrivals Hall has the schedule.

Getting There By Rail

The *State Railways of Thailand* (tel: (02) 225 0300 *or* 222 0175; website: www.thailandrailway.com) operates four lines, all terminating in Bangkok. It runs trains with air-conditioned and non-air-conditioned carriages. The main station in Bangkok is *Hualampong*, Rama IV Road (tel: (02) 223 3762 *or* 224 7788 (advance booking)), which serves most of the long-distance routes. Facilities at the station include cafés, bureau de change, ATM, left-luggage, a post office and hotel reservation service. It is advisable to book tickets for long-distance trains in advance. *Noi* station across the river in Thonburi (tel: (02) 411 3102) serves Kanchanaburi and a few destinations to the south, so visitors should check which station to depart from.

Rail services: The four lines run from Chiang Mai in the north, Nong Khai in the northeast, Pattaya in the east and from Surat Thani and Butterworth (Malaysia) in the south. Direct trains take from 3 hours 45 minutes to Pattaya, 10 hours 40 minutes to Chiang Mai and 21 hours 10 minutes to Butterworth. A special *Thailand Rail Pass* is available for B3000, which includes unlimited travel in second or third class within Thailand and is valid for 20 days.

Transport to the city: Each station is served by numerous buses to the city. The National Stadium Skytrain station is situated relatively close by.

Getting There By Road

Thailand has a reasonable network of roads and highways throughout the country, designated by numbers. Traffic drives on the left and the wearing of seat belts is compulsory with on-the-spot fines for offenders. The speed limits are 60kph (37mph) in the city, 90kph (56mph) on main country roads and 120kph (74mph) on expressways. A national driving licence or International Driving Permit is required but long-term visitors staying over three months would need to obtain a Thai driving licence. The minimum age for driving is 21 years. It is illegal to drink and drive in Thailand.

Driving in Thailand is not for the faint hearted, as drivers tend to take risks and overtake on bends and hills, while buses and lorries drive as if they own the road. Driving at night is to be avoided, as most heavy trucks travel at this time. The incidence of traffic accidents is high and, when foreigners are involved in accidents, it is always assumed that they are the ones at

COST OF LIVING

Some prices in this guide are quoted in US Dollars. This is where a particular establishment quotes its prices in this way and it will usually mean that US Dollars are accepted as payment there.

One-litre bottle of mineral water: B20
33cl bottle of beer: B230 (local beer B45)
Financial Times newspaper: B200
36-exposure colour film: B140
City-centre bus ticket: B3.50–18
Adult football ticket: B50–100
Three-course meal with wine/beer: From B850

1 Thai Baht (B1) = £0.01; US$0.02; C$0.03; A$0.04; €0.02

Currency conversion rates as of July 2003

fault and they are expected to pay the costs. Having said all that, driving is the best way to see the country and reach out-of-the-way places.

Emergency breakdown service: There is no national breakdown service but all car hire companies will provide a telephone number to their clients for use in case of a breakdown or emergency.

Routes to the city: The national highways are all designated by numbers. National Highway 4 goes south to Hua Hin; National Highway 3 goes east to Pattaya; and National Highways 32 and 11 go to Phitsanulok.

Approximate driving times to Bangkok: From Hua Hin – 3 hours; Pattaya – 3 hours; Phitsanulok – 5 hours 30 minutes.

Coach services: Bangkok has three main bus terminals serving different areas of the country. Both air-conditioned and non-air-conditioned buses operate, although the air-conditioned ones tend to be faster and make less stops en route. Buses south to Hua Hin, Phuket and the Thai–Malaysian border operate from the *Southern Bus Terminal*, Pinklao-Nakonchaisri Road (tel: (02) 435 1200). Buses to Chiang Mai and Chiang Rai in the north and Ubon Ratchathani and Nong Khai in the northeast operate from the *North/northeastern Bus Terminal*, Kampaeng Petch 2 Road (tel: (02) 272 0296 *or* 279 4484). Buses to Pattaya and Trat in the east operate from the *Eastern Bus Terminal*, Soi 40 Sukhumvit Road (tel: (02) 391 2504).

Getting Around

Public Transport

The public transport system within Bangkok is plentiful and cheap, although most visitors use the taxis or the three-wheeled taxis called *tuk tuks* (see below). An **elevated monorail**, called the *Bangkok Transit System* (tel: (02) 617 7300; e-mail: nuduan@bts.co.th; website: www.bts.co.th) but known as *Skytrain*, operates on two lines across the city. The Sukhumvit Line runs from On Nut along Sukhumvit Road to Siam Square, Phaya Thai Road, Victory Monument and Mo Chit. The Silom Line starts at Saphan Taksin and runs through Silom's business area, Siam Square, ending at the National Stadium. Since opening around four years ago, the efficient Skytrain has vastly improved the time it takes to move around the city. The government has approved extension of the lines across the river and to the south. Trains operate 0600–2400, running every 3–4 minutes during the rush hour and every 5–6 minutes off peak. Tickets should be purchased from automatic ticket machines, with prices costing B10–40 across seven zones. **Passes** can be bought for ten, 15 and 30 journeys, costing B250, B300 and B540 respectively, to be used within 30 days. Three-day tourist passes are available for B280.

The *Bangkok Mass Transit Authority* (tel: (02) 246 0973; e-mail: 184.bmta@motc.go.th; website: www.bmta. motc.go.th) runs a comprehensive and highly complex **bus** system, which operates across the city 0500–2300. Fares on regular buses range from B3.50 (cream and red) to B5 (white and blue), while on air-conditioned buses (cream and blue) they range from B6 to B16 depending on distance travelled. The yellow and orange Euro II air-conditioned buses cost B18 and use fuel-efficient engines to belatedly attempt to reduce air pollution in the city. There is also a limited **night bus** service (cream and red) operating 2300–0500, with a fare of B5. Bus route maps are widely available in hotels and bookshops.

Work is underway on a 20km (12-mile) **subway** system, which is scheduled for completion in August 2004. The traffic jams in Bangkok are legendary and pollution extreme and this is aggravated by the roadworks preparing the tunnels and stations for the new subway.

Taxis

Taxis can be hailed on the streets. If they are metered taxis, they will have a taxi meter sign on the roof. Visitors should check that the meter is turned on. The meter rate starts at B35 for the first two

CITY STATISTICS

Location: Central Plain, Thailand.
Country dialling code: 66.
Population: 6 million (city); 10 million (metropolitan area).
Ethnic mix: 80% Thai, 10% Chinese, 4% Malaysian, with the remainder a mix of Lao, Khmer, Indian and Burmese.
Religion: 95% Buddhist, 4% Muslim, with the remainder a mix of Christians, Hindus and Sikhs.
Time zone: GMT + 7 (GMT + 6 from last Sunday in March to Saturday before last Sunday in October).
Electricity: 220 volts AC, 50Hz; two-pin plugs are standard.
Average January temp: 26˚C (79˚F).
Average July temp: 29˚C (84˚F).
Annual rainfall: 1500mm (58.5 inches).

kilometres, increasing by B2 for each subsequent kilometre. If stuck in heavy traffic, the meter will start increasing by the minute. There are also unmetered taxis where the fare must be agreed upon in advance. Passengers always have to pay for any road tolls incurred and should ensure they have plenty of small change to pay the taxi fare. Many people arrange a taxi through the concierge at their hotel, where the rate is fixed and paid to the hotel before departure. It is also possible to hire a taxi for longer trips. In these cases, a fare should always be agreed in advance, even with metered taxis. Tipping is not expected but much appreciated.

Tuk Tuks

These three-wheeled taxis ply the streets and are ideal for short journeys. Fares must be negotiated before getting in and range from B40 to B150 depending on the distance travelled. The number of tuk tuks in the

city is decreasing but they can still be found around hotels and visitor attractions.

River Taxis

Numerous river taxis, operated by *Chao Phraya Express River Taxi* (tel: (02) 222 5330), travel upstream and downstream on the Chao Phraya River, acting more like buses than taxis. Fares range between B5 and B15 and the hours of operation are daily 0600–1840. Some special express boats operate only during the morning and evening rush hours, with limited stops. The destinations/stops are indicated by different coloured flags. Other smaller boats just shuttle from one side of the river to the other. A new service from *Chao Phraya Tourist Boat* (tel: (02) 623 6001) operates from Sathorn Pier near the Saphan Taksin Skytrain station to ten piers near major attractions and ends at Bamglumpoo Pier. The service operates daily 0900–1500 and a one-day unlimited pass costs B75.

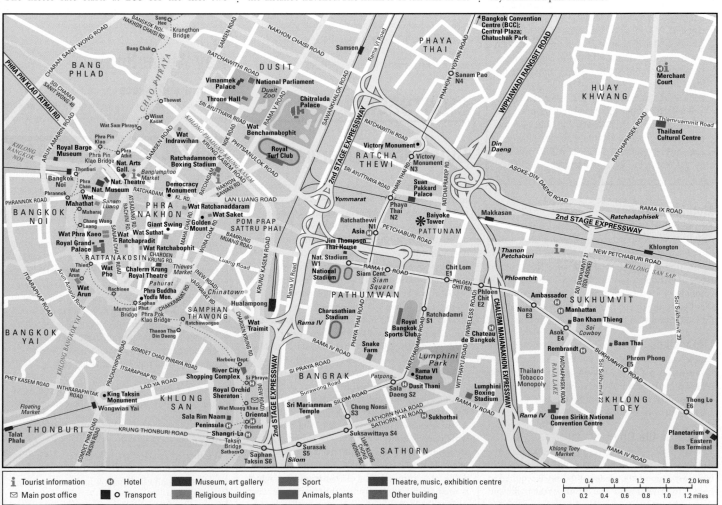

Tourist information		Hotel	Museum, art gallery	Sport	Theatre, music, exhibition centre
Main post office	Transport	Religious building	Animals, plants	Other building

0 0.4 0.8 1.2 1.6 2.0 kms
0 0.2 0.4 0.6 0.8 1.0 1.2 miles

BUSINESS PROFILE

Thailand and Bangkok were at the heart of the Asian economic collapse in 1997. The economy had been growing at a steady pace throughout the 1980s and 1990s and it was perceived to be one of the Asian Tiger economies. In 1997, the economy shrunk and unemployment increased dramatically. The government took swift action to control the economy and stabilise the currency, and there was improvement during 2000. It looked like the health of the economy would return, although this faltered in 2001, following the events of 11 September, and exports from Thailand decreased. However, the situation rapidly improved and economic growth for 2002 was 5% and this is expected to be maintained.

Tourism continues to be a particular success story for Thailand. Following the economic collapse and the flotation of the Baht in July 1997, the government launched its 'Amazing Thailand' campaign, which saw a dramatic increase in the number of visitors, many of whom were keen to take advantage of the favourable exchange rate. Tourist arrivals have continued to increase year on year and 2002 saw 10.9 million tourists – an increase of 7.31% on 2001.

As Thailand is perceived to be at the heart of South-East Asia and the gateway to other markets in the region, many multinational companies have a presence in the city. Companies from all industries have offices or manufacturing companies in Bangkok, such as *Toyota, Unilever, Proctor and Gamble, Philips, Sony, Compaq* and even *Tesco*, who bought a 75% share in a retail group with 12 stores. Despite the downturn of business and the erosion of profits for all markets, most foreign investors have stayed put and favour a long-term commitment to Bangkok and Thailand as a whole. There is still a huge difference in the standard of living between city dwellers and those in the countryside. The national rate of unemployment decreased slightly in 2002 to 3.2%, which is comparable to the figure for Bangkok.

Motorcycle Taxis

As a result of the gridlock experienced during the rush hour, motorcycle taxis are now available, as they can manoeuvre between the cars to reach their destination more quickly. Fares range from B20 to B100 depending on the distance travelled. It is compulsory for passengers to wear helmets, which are supplied by the driver. Drivers wear coloured tabards for identification and wait at road intersections.

Limousines

These can be provided by the main car hire companies (see *Car Hire* below) or at the airport (tel: (02) 535 2801), terminal one, counter 7, and terminal two, counter 5. Limousines to the city from the airport cost from B650.

Driving in the City

Driving in Bangkok requires a great deal of patience and a certain stubbornness. Few visitors attempt to hire a car, as good knowledge of the city is required to be able to drive around. The density of the traffic and the number of lanes mean that drivers always need to know which lane to be in. There are a number of expressways crossing the city, with clearly signposted exits, although traffic is often gridlocked during rush hour (0700–0900 and 1600–1800). Traffic direction and entry/exit locations change during the day without warning. Bangkok drivers – in particular taxis, buses and motorbikes – are very aggressive and unlikely to give way.

For those who do risk driving, many of the large shopping complexes and hotels have a car park attached and a convenient location is the Siam Centre on Rama I Road, which is open 24 hours. Car parks cost in the region of B20 for up to three hours and B10 for each subsequent hour.

Car Hire

Many visitors to Thailand now choose to hire a car, although few hire one within Bangkok, because of the difficulties of moving through the constantly heavy traffic. Car hire companies vary but drivers must either be at least 21 or 23 years old and have held a driving licence for one to two years. A national licence and International Driving Permit are required. It is compulsory to purchase Collision Damage Waiver and Theft Protection and these are generally included in the hire price. Payment must be made by credit card. *Avis* have an office at 2–12 Wireless Road (tel: (02) 255 5300; website: www.avisthailand.com), and *Budget* at 19/23 Building A, Royal City Avenue, New Petchburi Road (tel: (02) 203 0250; website: www.budget.co.th). Hire of a standard saloon car costs from B2000 per day or B12,000 per week.

Bicycle Hire

On Rattanakosin Island, footpaths have been converted into cycle paths, which pass places such as the Royal Grand Palace and Sanam Luang. Bicycles can be hired from the *Bangkok Tourist Bureau* (tel: (02) 225 7612) at a cost of B200 for a full day (deposit B500).

SIGHTSEEING

Sightseeing Overview

The sprawling city of Bangkok is full of interesting attractions for tourists, however, the heavily congested traffic means that it is difficult to cover a lot of ground in a single day. Sightseeing should be selective if time is short or restricted to one area per day, although the Skytrain does help visitors travel more quickly across town. An excellent way to appreciate the layout of the city is to go to the observation deck on the 77th floor of the *Baiyoke Sky Hotel*, one of the tallest hotels in the world.

Many of the main places of interest, such as the *Royal Grand Palace*, *Wat Pho* and the *National Museum*, are to the east of the Chao Phraya River (west of the north–south railway line), in an area called Rattanakosin Island, which is also home to many hotels. However, some visitors may stay to the east of the railway line in the Sukhumvit Road area, where there is excellent shopping, nightlife and tourist sights, such as *Suan Pakkard Palace Museum* and *Jim Thompson Thai House*.

Apart from the major sights (see *Key Attractions*), which are all 'must-see', there are numerous other attractions, including over 400 temples. To the north of the Royal Grand Palace is *Sanam Luang*, a huge public area surrounded by old tamarind trees, which is used for many ceremonies throughout the year, such as the Ploughing Ceremony, as well as being a popular place for kite-flying and just passing the time. The 19th-century *Wat Suthat*, on Bamrung Muang Road, is renowned for its murals depicting the lives of Buddha. In front of the temple is *Sao Ching Cha* (Giant Swing), which was the site of a Brahmin ceremony until the 1920s. Only the posts of the swing remain.

Chinatown is a lively area located between the river and Hualampong railway station. The area is fascinating for its maze of narrow lanes and open-fronted shops selling a cornucopia of items. On Yaowarat Road, *Wat Trai Mit* houses a gleaming solid gold Buddha, three metres (ten feet) high and weighing over five tons. Close to Chinatown is *Phahurat*, the main Indian area, crammed with colourful fabric shops and excellent Indian restaurants. On Si Ayutthaya Road, in an elegant area full of government buildings and the current royal residence, is *Wat Benjamabopit*, mainly built with Italian marble and a mix of European and Thai architecture. *Lumphini Park* is a haven of tranquillity in the heart of the city, dotted with pavilions and boasting two small lakes. For visitors who do not have time to travel in the rest of Thailand, the *Ancient City* is an open-air museum with full-size and scaled-down replicas of famous buildings, monuments and temples from all over the country. It covers an area of 112 hectares (280 acres) and is 33km (20 miles) southeast of the city centre.

Well worth a visit is *Bang Pa In*, 60km (37 miles) north of Bangkok, the former summer residence of the royal family in the 17th century, which is a collection of buildings reflecting Oriental and European influences. Whether visiting palaces or temples, it is important to dress respectfully. Entry can and will be refused if this rule is not followed.

Key Attractions

Royal Grand Palace

The *Royal Grand Palace* is a glittering walled complex that houses several palaces, all highly decorated with

BUSINESS ETIQUETTE

Most senior businesspeople in large or international companies will speak English but it is not common in smaller companies. It is essential to make appointments for business meetings and to exchange business cards. Punctuality is also very important (although the visitor is quite often likely to be kept waiting after arrival), so the Bangkok traffic must be taken into consideration when going to appointments. Thai hosts are quite likely to give small gifts to visitors, so it is a good idea to reciprocate with a typical national gift of one's own. Visitors should never get angry or raise their voice if things are not going according to plan, as this will mean the loss of face on both sides. Much more progress will be made by remaining calm.

Meetings often take place over lunch and these are generally held in a Thai restaurant. Thai businesspeople are quite formal in their dress but, because of the extreme heat, it is quite acceptable and practical to dispense with the wearing of a suit jacket. Office hours are usually Monday to Friday 0900–1700. There is a large ex-pat community in Bangkok and there is a big after-work drinking scene.

tiles and ceramics. Building was begun in 1782, when Bangkok was founded as the capital of Thailand. The complex houses *Wat Phra Kaeo*, the holiest of all Thai temples, where the sacred Emerald Buddha rests, not covered in emeralds but jade. There is even a scale model of Angkor Wat. There is a strict dress code and visitors wearing shorts, mini-skirts, sleeveless shirts or flip-flops will be refused entry, although it is possible to hire trousers and plastic shoes.
Na Phra Lan Road
Tel: (02) 222 6889.
Website: www.palaces.thai.net
Transport: Served by numerous buses.
Opening hours: Daily 0830–1530.
Admission: B200.

Vimanmek Palace

Vimanmek Palace is the world's largest building made entirely of golden teak. It used to be a royal summer retreat and was dismantled and rebuilt in Bangkok in 1900. The 81-room mansion stands in carefully manicured lawns, located close to the current royal residence, and contains 31 exhibition rooms. Visitors are not free to wander but must take the guided tour, which takes place every 30 minutes. Highlights include Thailand's first indoor bathroom and the oldest typewriter with Thai characters. The dress code is the same as for the Royal Grand Palace (see above).
Ratchawithi Road
Tel: (02) 228 6300.
Website: www.palaces.thai.net
Transport: Served by numerous buses.
Opening hours: Daily 0930–1600 (last tour at 1515).
Admission: B50; free once a ticket to the Royal Grand Palace has been purchased (ticket valid for 30 days).

Wat Pho (Temple of the Reclining Buddha)

Wat Pho is the oldest and largest temple in Bangkok and houses an enormous gold-plated Reclining Buddha, which is 46m (150ft) long and 15m (49ft) high. Today, it is also renowned for its teaching of herbal medicine and traditional massage.
Thai Wang Road
Tel: (02) 222 0933.
Transport: Served by numerous buses.
Opening hours: Daily 0800–1700.
Admission: B20.

National Museum

One of the largest and most comprehensive museums in the region, the *National Museum* houses a vast collection of artefacts from the Neolithic period through to more recent periods. The building, begun in 1782, is fascinating in its own right, having been built in traditional Thai style. The museum is so large that it needs more than one visit, however, if time is short, it must be spent in the lovely teak pavilion, which houses personal royal belongings. Free guided tours are given by volunteers at 0930 on Wednesdays and Thursdays and are highly recommended.
Na Phrathat Road
Tel: (02) 224 1333.
Transport: Served by numerous buses.
Opening hours: Wed–Sun 0900–1600.
Admission: B40.

Wat Arun (Temple of Dawn)

Located on the west bank of the Chao Phraya River, the 17th-century *Wat Arun* has a 79m-high (259ft) tower decorated with multicoloured ceramic tiles, which makes it a landmark along the river. The effect of the tiles is best observed at a distance. It was the first home of the Emerald Buddha, before it was transferred to Wat Phra Kaeo in 1785. There is a nightly light and sound show between October and May.
Arun Amarin Road
Tel: (02) 465 5640.
Transport: Boat from Tha Tien Pier.
Opening hours: Daily 0700–1700.
Admission: B10.

Jim Thompson Thai House

Jim Thompson was an American who came to Bangkok after World War II and the *Jim Thompson Thai House* was his home until he mysteriously disappeared in Malaysia in 1967. He completely revived the Thai silk industry and his house, traditionally Thai in style, is now a museum showing his collection of Asian artefacts. The house is a complex of six traditional Thai teak structures brought to Bangkok from various parts of Thailand and its construction was completed in 1955. The house can only be visited on a guided tour.
6 Soi Kasemsan 2 Song, Rama I Road
Tel: (02) 216 7368.
E-mail: info@jimthompsonhouse.com
Website: www.jimthompsonhouse.com
Transport: Skytrain National Stadium station.
Opening hours: Daily 0900–1700 (last tour at 1630).
Admission: B100.

Royal Barge National Museum

The royal barges are rarely used by the royal family, because of their age, and a few of them are now preserved in the *Royal Barge National Museum*, on the Thonburi side of the Chao Phraya River. The eight long, narrow boats on display are intricately gilded and each need between 50 and 60 rowers to take their oars. The figure on the bow of each boat signifies whether it carries the King and Queen or other members of the royal family. The most important barge is the Suphannahong, exclusively used by the King.
Khlong Bangkok Noi
Tel: (02) 424 0004.
Transport: River taxi.
Opening hours: Daily 0900–1700.
Admission: B30.

Further Distractions

Suan Pakkard Palace Museum

Suan Pakkard Palace used to be the residence of Princess Chumphot, one of Thailand's leading art collectors. Five traditional wooden Thai houses, brought to Bangkok from around the country, are set in one of the loveliest gardens in the city. The museum houses an important collection of antiques.
Si Ayutthaya Road
Tel: (02) 245 4934.
Transport: Skytrain Phaya Thai station.
Opening hours: Daily 0900–1600.
Admission: B100.

Ban Kham Thieng

Ban Kham Thieng is a 200-year-old classic northern-style teak house, brought from Chiang Mai and reconstructed in Bangkok. The house was owned by a worker and shows the simplicity of rural life in the north during the last century. It contains a collection of traditional implements used by farmers and ricefield fishermen.
131 Soi Asoke (Soi 21), Sukhumvit Road
Tel: (02) 661 6470.
Transport: Skytrain Asoke station.

Chianatown

Opening hours: Tues–Sat 0900–1700.
Admission: B100.

Ko Kret

Beyond the airport, 20km (12 miles) to the north of the city, *Ko Kret* is a tiny island community virtually untouched by the nearby metropolis. There are no roads on the island and many of its residents rely on its potteries for employment, as well as fruit and flowers from its many plantations. The island can be reached via Highways 31 and 35, then ferry from Pak Kret Pier.

Tours of the City

Walking Tours

Although Bangkok is not really the best city for much exploration on foot, *Diethelm Travel* (tel: (02) 255 9150; website: www.diethelm-travel.com) offers a walking tour of Chinatown, called 'Bangkok Way of Life', which lasts 3 hours 30 minutes and costs US$17.90 per person as part of a group.

TOURIST INFORMATION

Tourism Authority of Thailand (TAT)
1st Floor, 1600 New Phetburi Road, Makkasan, Rachathewi
Tel: (02) 250 5500. Fax: (02) 250 5511.
E-mail: center@tat.or.th
Website: www.tat.or.th
Opening hours: Mon–Fri 0830–1630.

There is another office at 4 Ratchadamnoen Nok Avenue, Pomprab (open daily 0830–1630). The *Tourist Service Centre* on Khao San Road (in front of Chana Songkram Police Station) is open daily 0800–2400. The tourist police provide 24-hour assistance for complaints and emergencies from their office on Ratchadamnoen Nok Avenue or through the toll-free hotline (tel: 1155).

Passes
There are no dedicated tourist passes in Bangkok.

Photo: Corel

Chao Phraya River

Bus Tours

World Travel Service (tel: (02) 233 5900; website: www.wts.co.th) runs small group tours with free pick-up from numerous hotels throughout Bangkok. Tours can be booked direct or through the tour desk in some hotels. Half-day city tours include the 'Royal Grand Palace Tour' (including Wat Phra Kaeo) and the 'Temples Tour' (covering Wat Pho, Wat Trai Mit and Wat Benjamabopit). Both last 3 hours 30 minutes; the 'Royal Grand Palace Tour' costs B850, while the 'Temples Tour' costs B750. *Diethelm Travel* (tel: (02) 255 9150; website: www.diethelm-travel.com) also offers similar tours.

The *Bangkok Tourist Bureau* (tel: (02) 225 7612) runs daily 90-minute tours past the main places of interest, on a vintage-style double-decker bus. The bus leaves the Grand Palace at 0900, 1030, 1230, 1330 and 1500 and Vimanmek Palace at 0930, 1100, 1230, 1400 and 1630. The fare is B200.

Bicycle Tours

Every Saturday at 1900 there is a two-and-a-half-hour bicycle trip around the historical heart of Bangkok, operated by the *Bangkok Tourist Bureau* (tel: (02) 225 7612; fax: (02) 225 7616). The tour departs from the offices at 17/1 Phra Arthit Road, Phra Nakhon, and passes Sanam Luang, Wat Pho, the Democracy Monument and the Khao San Road backpacker area. The charge is B290 per person, which includes the hire of a bicycle, snacks and drinks.

Boat Tours

Bangkok is laced with *khlongs* (canals) and life alongside the *khlongs* is far removed from the hustle and bustle of downtown Bangkok. An ideal way to see this side of Bangkok is a boat trip, passing tiny temples, orchards, orchid farms and typical houses on stilts. These are organised by *World Travel Service* (tel: (02) 233 5900; website: www.wts.co.th) and *Diethelm Travel* (tel: (02) 255 9150; website: www.diethelm-travel.com). Some examples of what Diethelm offers are a four-hour boat trip for US$25.10 per person or a full-day

visit to the floating market at Damnoan Saduak for US$58.90 per person (prices as part of a group).

Excursions

For a Half Day

Rose Garden: The *Rose Garden* (tel: (034) 322 588; fax: (034) 322 775; website: www.rose-garden.com) is a popular tourist attraction located 32km (20 miles) to the southwest of Bangkok. It features daily cultural shows at 1445, including dancing, Thai boxing and an elephant show. The resort is set in well-kept gardens and is open 0800–1800. Entrance to the resort costs B20, while tickets for the show are B380.

Damnoan Saduak Floating Market: Although this market is 80km (50 miles) west of Bangkok, it is far more interesting than the floating market in Bangkok, as it has not been turned into a tourist attraction. In the early morning, the narrow canals are full of small boats carrying fruit and vegetables sold by local women. The market is very colourful and atmospheric – but it is all over by 1100, which necessitates an early start from Bangkok. Although it is possible to take a bus from the Southern Bus Terminal to within a mile of the market, it is probably easier to join an organised tour from a hotel (see *Tours of the City*).

For a Whole Day

Kanchanaburi: Located 122km (76 miles) from Bangkok is the site of the infamous *Bridge over the River Kwai*. Built by Allied PoWs during World War II, this is an area of exceptional natural beauty, with forested mountains and wooded valleys. Two immaculately maintained Allied war cemeteries are located just outside of the town. Kanchanaburi can be reached by either bus or train or by tour bus from Bangkok. The local *Tourist Authority of Thailand* office (tel: (034) 511 200; website: www.tat.or.th) is open daily 0830–1630 and can provide further information.

Ayutthaya: This was the Thai capital for over 400 years until its destruction in 1767. Ruins of numerous

temples and palace buildings cover a vast area. The beauty of the place is such that it was declared a World Heritage Site by UNESCO. It is located 76km (47 miles) north of Bangkok and can be reached by bus or train or on a boat trip. The local *Tourist Authority of Thailand* office (tel: (035) 246 076/7; website: www.tat.or.th) is open daily 0830–1630 and can provide further information.

ACCOMMODATION

Many of the more upmarket hotels quote their prices in US Dollars. Prices here have been quoted in the currency that the particular establishment uses for their prices. Payment can usually be made in either Thai Baht or US Dollars.

Hotels will usually add a service charge of 10% service charge and VAT at 7% to the hotel bill at the end. This tax could change, as it is a government levy. The prices quoted below are the lowest standard rates for a double room, excluding VAT and excluding breakfast, unless otherwise specified.

Business

Chateau de Bangkok

Located close to Lumphini Park, at the heart of the business district and near to Ploenchit Skytrain station, this exclusive complex consists of one- or two-bedroom serviced apartments, which can be booked for a night or a month or longer to cater for long-term business visitors. The modern apartments are bright and fresh with light modern decor and furniture. They all have excellent facilities, including a fully equipped separate kitchen, a bathroom with Jacuzzi, voice-mail and satellite TV. In addition, there is an Italian restaurant, *Paparazzi*, a fitness centre, a Jacuzzi, sauna, rooftop pool and one meeting room that can hold up to 30 people.

29 Soi Ruamrudee, Ploenchit Road
Tel: (02) 651 4400. Fax: (02) 651 4500.
E-mail: chateau1@loxinfo.co.th
Website: www.chateaudebangkok.com
Price: From B2122.

The Dusit Thani

This opulent hotel is a Bangkok landmark conveniently located off the Silom Road in the business and entertainment district overlooking Lumphini Park. The 532 rooms are all sumptuously decorated in Thai style and all have satellite TV, VCR, mini-bar, voice-mail and direct-dial telephones with fax/modem point. Meeting facilities are excellent, offering a range of meeting and function rooms, as well as the *Napalai Ballroom*, which can comfortably seat up to 1500 people. State-of-the-art audio-visual equipment is available. Other facilities include a business centre, spa and fitness club, swimming pool, sauna, golf driving range and boutiques. Restaurants include the Thai *Benjarong*, the Japanese *Shogun* and Western food at the rooftop *Tiara*, with panoramic views of the city.
946 Rama IV Road
Tel: (02) 236 9999. Fax: (02) 236 6400.
E-mail: dusitbkk@dusit.com
Website: www.dusit.com
Price: From US$190.

Rembrandt Hotel

Located off the busy Sukhumvit Road and within easy reach of the commercial and entertainment areas, the *Rembrandt* is a popular business hotel. The 407 rooms are very tastefully furnished with cool colours and have the usual range of facilities, such as satellite TV, international direct-dial telephone and a safe. There are Executive Floors for travellers who require a little extra luxury and additional services, such as broadband Internet and express check-in. The hotel has a number of excellent dining outlets, including the highly rated *Rang Mahal* Indian restaurant and *Senor Pico* Mexican restaurant (see *Restaurants*). In addition, there is a pool, fitness room and various shops, as well as a business centre with seminar rooms accommodating up to 20 people, with audiovisual equipment available.
19 Soi 18 Sukhumvit Road
Tel: (02) 261 7100. Fax: (02) 261 7017.
E-mail: reservations@rembrandtbkk.com
Website: www.rembrandtbkk.com
Price: From US$125.

Sofitel Central Plaza

This modern hotel is ideally placed for convention delegates, being very close to the Bangkok Convention Centre and only ten minutes from the airport. There are 607 rooms and suites, including 'Dynasty Club' executive rooms for corporate travellers. Rooms feature satellite TV, air conditioning and coffee/tea making facilities. Business facilities are excellent with 25 meeting rooms, including three ballrooms, which can hold up to 600 people. Diners are also well catered for with nine restaurants offering Thai, Vietnamese, Chinese, Japanese, Italian and international food. Leisure facilities include a fitness centre, pool set in lush tropical gardens, sauna and Jacuzzi and plenty of parking.
1695 Phaholyothin Road
Tel: (02) 541 1234. Fax: (02) 541 1087.
E-mail: scp@chr.co.th
Website: www.sofitel.com
Price: From US$159.

Luxury

The Oriental

One of the most famous hotels in the world, *The Oriental* is located by the Chao Phraya River and is the hotel of choice for royalty and celebrities, past and present, such as Somerset Maugham, the Prince of Wales and Elizabeth Taylor. Although the original Author's Wing was built around 125 years ago and is very much colonial in style, two more modern wings tend to dominate the appearance of the hotel. However, the 393 rooms (including 35 suites) are all sumptuously decorated and have satellite TV, CD player, fridge, mini-bar and telephone lines with Internet access, while some have a split-level layout. The business centre has four meeting rooms and two boardrooms capable of holding up to 14 people. In addition, there are several exquisite restaurants, including *Le Normandie* (see *Restaurants*), as well as various bars, two swimming pools, a spa, a Thai cooking school, a fitness centre and a shopping arcade.
48 Oriental Avenue
Tel: (02) 659 9000. Fax: (02) 659 0000.
E-mail: bscorbkk@loxinfo.co.th
Website: www.mandarinoriental.com
Price: From US$300.

Shangri-La

The *Shangri-La* is set in tropical gardens on the banks of the river, close to the business district, and has an enviable reputation. The rooms are decorated in relaxing colours and all have a big executive desk, voice-mail and modem point. Some rooms even have broadband Internet connection. There are 23 function rooms, all equipped with the most advanced conference equipment, while the *Grand Ballroom* can accommodate up to 1000 seated guests. Additional facilities include a pool, fully equipped gym, tennis and squash courts, sauna and Jacuzzi. There is a good choice of dining outlets, including the *Maenam Terrace* for evening barbecues and Sunday brunch.
90 Soi Wat Suan Plu, New Road
Tel: (02) 236 7777. Fax: (02) 236 8579.
E-mail: slbk@shangri-la.com
Website: www.shangri-la.com
Price: From US$195 (including breakfast).

Moderate

Ambassador Hotel

The *Ambassador* is an excellent good-value choice of hotel, mainly because of its location on the Sukhumvit Road, right by the shopping and entertainment areas but within easy reach of the business district. The large, modern hotel has 755 good-sized comfortable rooms with private bathrooms and satellite TV. There are extensive business facilities, including a business centre, convention centre for up to 2000 people, three function rooms for between 50 and 500 people and several smaller meeting rooms. There are a number of restaurants and bars including the Dickens Pub, a Cantonese restaurant and a beer garden. In addition, there is a shopping arcade, health club, swimming pool, squash court and outdoor jogging track.
171 Soi 11 Sukhumvit Road
Tel: (02) 254 0444. Fax: (02) 253 4123.
E-mail: bangkok@amtel.co.th
Website: www.amtel.co.th/bangkok
Price: From US$88 (including breakfast).

Wat Phra Keo

Hotel Manhattan

Although modern and fairly uninspiring, this hotel is very friendly and, located off the Sukhumvit Road, just a few minutes from the airport expressway, also convenient for the business district. The 200 rooms are comfortable with private bathrooms, satellite TV, air conditioning, international direct-dial telephone and mini-bar. Additional facilities include a fitness room, an outdoor swimming pool and an Internet café. There is the *Broadway* coffee shop, serving Western food, and the *Miyako* Japanese restaurant and the Korean *Ara* restaurant.
13 Soi 15 Sukhumvit Road
Tel: (02) 255 0166. Fax: (02) 255 0188.
E-mail: hotelmanhattan@bigfoot.com
Website: www.hotelmanhattan.com
Price: From B1600.

Other Recommendations

Merchant Court Hotel

This hotel, conveniently located just a few minutes from the central business district and within easy reach of the airport, is managed by the prestigious Raffles International Group and lives up to the luxurious standard of the group's more famous hotels. The 407 tastefully furnished rooms have all the facilities expected of such a luxury hotel, such as a large executive table and modem point, while many of the rooms have additional facilities, as part of the Executive Club, exclusively for corporate businesspeople. The hotel also has a business centre, ballroom and eight meeting rooms. There are five restaurants, including international and Japanese cuisine, and a fitness centre and swimming pool.
202 Ratchadapisek Road, Huaykwang
Tel: (02) 694 2222. Fax: (02) 694 2223.
E-mail: info@merchantcourt.th.com
Website: www.raffles.com
Price: From B6500.

The Sukhothai

The decor of *The Sukhothai*, situated in the Silom area, is pure Thai and imparts a feeling of serenity throughout the hotel. All rooms incorporate Thai fabrics, teak and furnishings, while the public rooms are exquisitely furnished with many Thai artefacts.

Chinatown

Guest rooms all feature satellite TV, electronic safe, high-speed Internet connection and fax machine. There is a delightful cool inner courtyard with a water garden. There are several restaurants, including *The Celadon*, which serves excellent Thai food. There is a business centre, three meeting rooms and a ballroom, with timber and granite flooring, catering for up to 300 people. State-of-the-art audio-visual equipment is available for hire. The hotel facilities include a pool, health club, Jacuzzi, sauna, tennis and squash courts and a shopping arcade.
13/3 South Sathorn Road
Tel: (02) 287 0222. Fax: (02) 287 4986.
E-mail: info@sukhothai.com
Website: www.sukhothai.com
Price: From US$280.

RESTAURANTS

The selected restaurants have been divided into five categories: Gastronomic, Business, Trendy, Budget and Personal Recommendations. The restaurants are listed alphabetically within these different categories, which serve as guidelines rather than absolute definitions of the establishments.
There is VAT of 7% added to restaurant bills in Bangkok and this is usually added to the bill at the end. In addition, many restaurants also add a service charge of around 10%. Where this is not added, visitors should tip around 10%. The prices quoted below are for an average three-course meal for one person and for a bottle of house wine or cheapest equivalent; they do not include VAT or service charge, unless otherwise specified.

Gastronomic

Auberge DAB

This elegant but friendly restaurant has dark wood-panelled walls and a cool tiled floor. The sumptuous

French food is served at tables with crisp white tablecloths and elegant fine dinnerware. The excellent service and their superb speciality seafood, such as Maine lobster roasted in its shell with sautéed girolle mushrooms, make this a very special place. A good-value three-course set lunch is also available for B340. Ground Floor, Mercury Tower, 540 Ploenchit Road
Tel: (02) 658 6222/3. Fax: (02) 658 7892.
E-mail: auberge@aubergedab.com
Website: www.aubergedab.com
Price: B1400. Wine: B850.

Baan Khanitha

This restaurant, located off Sukhumvit Road, has won the *Bangkok Dining and Entertainment Award* for 'Best Thai Restaurant' for the past six years and its popularity is proof of this. The converted villa has stylish and typically Thai decor, a mainly wooden interior with antiques and works of art creating a very calm atmosphere. The exquisite presentation of the food is as stylish as the decor. A signature dish is the deep-fried, freshwater, sun-dried cotton fish served with mango sauce. Set menus are available for two people, ranging from B800 to B1000.
36/1 Soi 23 Sukhumvit Road
Tel: (02) 258 4181
Fax: (02) 260 9601
Price: B800. Wine: B750.

Le Banyan

Le Banyan is one of those restaurants where the welcome is genuine, the decor elegant and the food superb. This intimate classy restaurant, located off Sukhumvit Road, serves French haute cuisine, including the fabulous lightly roasted breast of duck served with a sauce made from the juice of the duck. No lunch.
59 Soi 8 Sukhumvit Road
Tel: (02) 253 5556. Fax: (02) 253 4560.
E-mail: lebanyan@loxinfo.co.th
Website: www.lebanyan.net
Price: B1300. Wine: B1100.

Le Normandie

This small plush restaurant with a rarefied atmosphere serves up what has to be the best French cuisine in Bangkok, if not in the region. Located in the original part of The Oriental hotel, the floor-to-ceiling windows have unrivalled views over the Chao Phraya River. The menu is extensive and an excellent choice is the truffle-coated breast of pigeon and duck liver with truffled leek. There is a three-course lunch for B1250 per person and a set dinner menu for B3800. No lunch Sunday.
The Oriental, 48 Oriental Avenue
Tel: (02) 659 9000. Fax: (02) 659 0000.
E-mail: philippe@mohg.com
Website: www.mandarinoriental.com
Price: B4500. Wine: B1200.

Rang Mahal

This restaurant, situated on the rooftop of the Rembrandt Hotel (see *Hotels*), with superb views of the city, serves gourmet Indian food at its best. The decor is sumptuous with Indian wall hangings and plush colours and the atmosphere very tranquil with Indian music playing unobtrusively in the background. The food is all excellent but a particularly fine dish is *murgh makhanwala*, succulent chicken simmered in creamy fenugreek-flavoured tomato gravy. Sunday brunch is very popular at B510 per person.

Rembrandt Hotel, 19 Soi 18 Sukhumvit Road
Tel: (02) 261 7100. Fax: (02) 261 7016.
E-mail: catering@rembrandtbkk.com
Website: www.rembrandtbkk.com
Price: B750. Wine: B1200.

Business

Admiral's Pub & Restaurant

This cool, colonial-style, wood-panelled restaurant, a converted Thai house with teak decor, is owned by a Dane, which explains the photos of Scandinavians who served in the Siam Imperial Navy. It is really a place in which to while away the hours, as it is a combination of restaurant, library, meeting room, wine cellar and terrace. The food is predominantly Scandinavian, such as meatballs with cold potato salad. The all-you-can-eat barbecue on Wednesdays and Saturdays costs B395, including the salad bar.
20 Soi 18 Sukhumvit Road
Tel: (02) 663 4396/7. Fax: (02) 262 1616.
E-mail: admirals@adisti.com
Website: www.adisti.com
Price: B500 (including VAT). Wine: B800 (including VAT).

Ban Chiang

Ban Chiang is a restored wooden house with lush garden (lit up at night), situated in the Silom area, and serving up traditional Thai food. The food is beautifully presented, with a magnificent selection including fried grouper fish with Thai peppers, pineapple and chilli sauce. Ban Chiang is popular with businesspeople at lunchtimes, but the simple classic decor make it ideal for a special evening meal.
14 Surasak Road
Tel: (02) 236 7045 *or* 266 6994.
Price: B350. Wine: B530.

Cairns Stonegrill Restaurant

Australia comes to Bangkok with a restaurant serving tempting dishes cooked on a volcanic rock at 400°C. A choice of pork, chicken, seafood, lamb, beef and venison is offered together with an unlimited salad bar. The restaurant is simple but classic, with boomerangs on the wall as a testimony to its origins. No lunch weekends.
Soi 8 Sukhumvit Road
Tel: (02) 653 1323/3. Fax: (02) 253 2758.
Price: B300 (including VAT). Wine: B550 (including VAT).

Le Dalat Indochine

Down from the busy Sukhumvit Road, the upmarket *Le Dalat Indochine* serves probably the best Vietnamese food in Bangkok. Located in a gorgeous old house in a big garden, dining here is really a delightful experience. The elegant interior has a colonial feel and photos and memorabilia covering the walls. Well known for its seafood, an excellent choice here would be the crispy fried crab served with salad. Set lunches are available from B290 per person. Its equally superb sister restaurant, *Le Dalat*, is just across the road.
14 Soi 23 Sukhumvit Road
Tel: (02) 661 7967. Fax: (02) 661 7968.
Price: B500 (including VAT). Wine: B1100 (including VAT).

Zanotti

The simple but stylish decor contributes to a relaxed ambience in this Italian restaurant off the Silom Road. The restaurant appeals more to a business clientele rather than romantic diners, as it can be quite busy in the evenings. There is an extensive menu put together by the Italian chef, with such specialities as black squid ink linguine with clams and shrimp sauce.

21/2 Saladaeng Colonnade Soi Saladaeng, Silom Road
Tel: (02) 636 0002 or 0266. Fax: (02) 636 0221.
E-mail: info@zanotti-ristorante.com
Website: www.zanotti-ristorante.com
Price: B700. Wine: B370.

Trendy

The Barbican

In a quiet soi off the Silom Road, *The Barbican* is a music café with a small contemporary area with stools and tables downstairs and a simple, teak restaurant upstairs. Tapas snacks are available, as well as Thai food, including a tasty roast chicken breast rolled with aubergine and served with saffron sauce. There is a good-value three-course set lunch for B245. No lunch weekends (restaurant).

9/4–5 Soi Thaniya, Silom Road
Tel: (02) 233 4141/2. Fax: (02) 266 7747.
E-mail: somchart@greatbritishpub.com
Website: www.greatbritishpub.com
Price: B500 (including VAT). Wine: B610 (including VAT).

Jesters

Located in the Peninsula Hotel, this restaurant, spread over two levels, is a great place to dine, with fun contemporary decor and stunning views of the Chao Phraya River. It serves an eclectic mix of Pacific Rim food, such as tikka marinated rack of lamb with madras-style potatoes and mint chutney. No children 12 years or under. No lunch.

Peninsula Hotel, 333 Charoennakorn Road
Tel: (02) 861 2888. Fax: (02) 861 1112.
E-mail: pbk@peninsula.com
Website: www.peninsula.com
Price: B850. Wine: B950.

Joke Club Restaurant & Bar

The *Joke Club* is one of the places to be seen in Bangkok, often frequented by Thai royalty, politicians and Hollywood stars. This modern, Hong Kong-style restaurant serves Chinese and Cantonese food cooked in an open kitchen. Located off busy Sukhumvit Road, the restaurant is particularly well known for its congee (white rice porridge served with various meats and vegetables) – all 46 varieties – and dried abalone, at a fraction of Hong Kong prices. Nine-course set meals are available for B350–1680 per person for groups of ten people or more.

155 Soi 11 Sukhumvit Road
Tel: (02) 651 2888/9. Fax: (02) 651 3535.
E-mail: jokeclub@samart.co.th
Price: B500. Wine: B815.

Marmalade

A new arrival on the Bangkok restaurant scene, *Marmalade* is already creating waves. The interior reflects the name of the restaurant, with a dominant funky orange complemented by black sculptures. This is a place for the young at heart, with loud music and truly excellent food, such as the fried mackerel with sweet and hot topping.

Emporium Office Tower, Lobby 2, Soi 24 Sukhumvit Road
Tel: (02) 664 9988.
Website: www.marmaladebkk.com
Price: B300 (including VAT). Wine: B450 (including VAT).

Zanzibar

This chic and contemporary restaurant in a converted Thai house is situated in the Sukhumvit area. The ground floor is loud and buzzing with live music, while upstairs is more mellow with comfy seating. Thai and Italian dishes are on offer, including excellent pizza and seared beef with parmesan and baby spinach. No lunch.

139 Soi 11 Sukhumvit Road
Tel: (02) 651 2700. Fax: (02) 651 2800.
Price: B500 (including VAT). Wine: B520 (including VAT).

Budget

Mango Tree

Tucked in a quiet soi between the busy Silom and Surawongse Roads, *Mango Tree* is made up of two old houses, with intriguing photos of a past Bangkok on the wall and a collection of old cameras. Although cheap, this restaurant is not really a budget place, as it serves fantastic fine Thai food. The dishes are influenced from all corners of Thailand and the spicy green and red curries are particularly tasty. There is also a selection of set menus ranging from B300 to B700 in price.

37 Soi Tantawan, Surawongse Road
Tel: (02) 236 1681 or 2820. Fax: (02) 238 2649.
E-mail: mangotree@coca.com
Price: B300 (including VAT). Wine: B800 (including VAT).

O'Reillys Irish Pub

This traditional Irish pub on the Silom Road has a comfortable bar with a great atmosphere. The floor is wooden and there are photographs of traditional Irish scenes adorning the walls. A good selection of Thai and European food is on offer, including a wholesome beef and Guinness pie. A popular daily set lunch for B192 is also available.

62/1–4 Silom Road
Tel: (02) 632 7515. Fax: (02) 235 1572.
E-mail: irish@loxinfo.co.th

Price: B330 (including VAT). Wine: B800 (including VAT).

Singapore Chicken Rice

At first sight, the functional white tiles, practical tables and frenetic atmosphere of this small restaurant are not particularly appealing. However, it is frequented by ex-pats, visitors and many locals, who all come for the fantastic food. Diners can watch dishes, such as the scrumptious wonton, being prepared out the front. No credit cards.

440/5 Soi 53 Suhumvit Road
Tel: (02) 392 4247.
Price: B120 (including VAT). Beer: B50 (including VAT).

The Whole Earth

The Whole Earth is set in a large candlelit garden of an old Thai house, just off a busy soi off Sukhumvit Road. There is an excellent choice of Thai and Indian food, including a large vegetarian selection. The simple calm interior with wooden floors (shoes have to be removed before entering) is a very relaxing place to enjoy an excellent choice of food. The vegetable dopiaza with nan is highly recommended.

71 Soi 26 Sukhumvit Road
Tel: (02) 258 4900.
Price: B250. Wine: B750.

Witch's Tavern

This friendly local in the Thonglor area is done up in an English pub style, with comfy leather sofas in which to relax and watch the large screen TVs or the live jazz at the weekend. The restaurant serves English and Thai food and particularly delicious is the spaghetti with hard shell clams, onions and white wine. There is a special three-course lunch available Monday to Saturday for B250 and a jazz brunch at the weekend.

306/1 Soi 55 Sukhumvit Road
Tel: (02) 391 9791. Fax: (02) 381 1924.
E-mail: witched@samart.colth
Website: www.witch-tavern.com
Price: B420. Wine: B1300.

Egg-fried rice

Photo: Tourism Authority of Thailand

Carvings in Chatuchak Market

Personal Recommendations

Cabbages & Condoms

Cabbages & Condoms is nearly as strange as its name, with displays of condoms of all shapes, sizes and colours and a tableau of vasectomy equipment in the restaurant. However, the place goes from strength to strength and combines its work to improve life for rural Thailand through contraception, hygiene programmes and AIDS education with great Thai cuisine. Located off busy Sukhumvit Road, the restaurant is surprisingly relaxing, with a lush garden and delicious food, and the addition of a deserving cause makes it well worth a visit. A particularly tasty dish is the hot and sour salad of Shanghai noodles with shrimp and chicken.
10 Soi 12 Sukhumvit Road
Tel: (02) 229 4610/11. Fax: (02) 229 4632.
Price: B600 (including VAT). Wine: B600 (including VAT).

Harmonique

Situated fairly close to the river and the famed hotel The Oriental, the family-run *Harmonique* is incredibly welcoming. The restaurant is located in an old house, dating back more than 100 years, with a lush garden, Thai antiques and fans. The fantastic appetisers, including the steamed shrimp in coconut, are particularly recommended. A selection of appetisers is available for B250 for two people. Closed Sunday.
22 Charoenkrung 34
Tel: (02) 237 8175. Fax: (02) 630 6269.
Price: B650 (including VAT). Wine: B660 (including VAT).

Ma Be Ba

Leaving the hot steamy streets of the Phloenjit area of Bangkok to enter *Ma Be Ba* feels like stepping into Italy. The smell of the bakery and the tiled mosaic floor,

warm colours, plants and open kitchen are very evocative of southern Italy. Family friendly, the place is as popular with ex-pats as it is with locals. The restaurant offers a set lunch for B329 for three courses. Seafood is a speciality, such as the pan-fried crispy sea bass fillet.
93 Lung Suan Road, Phloenjit, Lumpinee
Tel: (02) 253 9426.
Price: B1000. Wine: B1000.

Manorah Cruise

There can be no better way to experience the Chao Phraya River than on a dinner cruise on a beautifully restored rice barge. Operated by the Marriott Resort & Spa Hotel, the *Manorah Cruise* welcomes visitors for daily lunch and dinner cruises, which pass riverside temples and waterfront homes, providing the opportunity to see river life close up. There is a choice of three set menus of beautifully presented Thai food, including tasty river prawns in hot curry sauce. The cruise departs from the Marriott Hotel listed below but can be boarded from different piers: Sathorn Bridge, River City or Oriental Public. Reservations recommended.
Marriott Resort & Spa Hotel, 257 Charoennakorn Road
Tel: (02) 476 0022. Fax: (02) 476 1120.
Website: www.marriottdining.com
Price: B1200. Wine: B1750.

Senor Pico

Located in the Rembrant Hotel (see *Hotels*), this is one of the best Mexican restaurants in Bangkok. The vibrant restaurant is cantina style, with terracotta pots, Mexican bric-a-brac around the walls and low lighting. A resident band adds to the atmosphere. The subtle blend of spices is evident in the charcoal-grilled prawns marinated in lemon juice and herbs. Combination meals of chicken enchilada and beef fajitas with refried beans and rice are good value at B380. No lunch.

Rembrandt Hotel, 19 Soi 18 Sukhumvit Road
Tel: (02) 261 7100. Fax: (02) 261 7016.
E-mail: catering@rembrandtbkk.com
Website: www.rembrandtbkk.com
Price: B650. Wine: B1190.

ENTERTAINMENT

Nightlife

Much of Bangkok's nightlife is concentrated in the two red light districts of Bangkok – Patpong (between Silom and Surawong Roads) and Soi Cowboy (Sukhumvit Road), named after the first bar that opened there called the Cowboy Bar. Bangkok's sex industry is as blatant and booming as ever. However, in addition to the numerous sex clubs and massage parlours, there are many excellent cocktail bars and restaurants and, at night, the area is always thronging with people. Most venues are open all day and late into the night, although bars and clubs are supposed to close at 0200. Sometimes, there is an admission fee but this usually includes one or two drinks. The dress code is very relaxed, although a few of the nightclubs do enforce smarter dress.
As in any city, nightlife venues come and go and news of the latest hotspots can be found in the city's listings magazine, *Bangkok Metro* (website: www.bkkmetro.com).

Bars

The *Bull's Head*, 33/1 Sukhumvit Road, is popular with many ex-pat residents of Bangkok. It is a British-style pub, with regular quiz and theme nights. Irish pubs are popular in most cities in the world and the busy *Dubliner Irish Pub*, on Sukhumvit Road (Washington Square), is no exception. A stylish watering hole is *The Barbican*, Soi Thaniya, Silom Road, with a good selection of drinks and good food. The attractively named *Skunk*, Ekamai Soi 10, Soi 63 Sukhumvit Road, draws a regular crowd and has interesting decor, such as car parts on the walls.

Casinos

Gambling is illegal in Thailand.

Clubs

Concept CM2, a huge disco and bar in the basement of the Novotel Hotel on Siam Square, continues to be very popular, in particular on Thursday, its retro night. The amazing light and sound system and ostentatious Art Deco-style interior of *Narcissus*, 112 Soi 23 Sukhumvit Road, attracts the smart set keen on house, trance and techno. *Ministry of Sound*, 2 Soi 12 Sukhumvit Road, has regular guest slots with internationally known DJs. The hangout for trendy locals and ex-pats is the *Q Bar*, 34 Soi 11 Sukhumvit Road, which also imports top international DJs. Both clubs offer a range of music from house to hip hop.

Live Music

Ad-Makers, 51 Soi Lang Suan (off Ploenchit), has live bands that play folk, pop and hard rock and the crowd often sing along. *Saxophone Pub*, 3/8 Victory Monument, Phayathai Road, has great acoustics, a lively atmosphere and a variety of live music including funk, jazz, blues and ska. Top-quality live bands frequent *La Lunar*, Soi 26 Sukhumvit Road, which has a multi-screen video system and impressive lights and lasers. The *Bamboo Bar*, in the upmarket hotel, The Oriental (see *Hotels*), is an intimate and refined club with an excellent reputation for its guest jazz bands. *Radio City*, Patpong Soi 1, is a great live music venue with bands playing old rock music.

Sport

Bangkok and Thailand are synonymous with Thai Boxing *(Muay Thai)*, the traditional sport of kick-boxing, where feet, knees and elbows can be used as well as fists. Its popularity means that fights are held every night of the week around the city, particularly at *Ratchadamnoen Stadium*, Ratchadamnoen Nok Road (tel: (02) 281 4205), on Monday, Wednesday, Thursday and Sunday nights, and *Lumphini Stadium*, Rama IV Road (tel: (02) 251 4303), on Tuesday, Friday and Saturday nights.

Two other sports are also popular in Thailand. Kite fighting takes place in the hot season, where opposing teams fly male Chula and female Pakpao kites in a surrogate battle of the sexes. Visitors can witness spectacular events most weekends at Sanam Luang (see *Sightseeing Overview*). *Takraw* is played using a woven rattan ball – a circle of men use their feet, knees, thighs, chests and shoulders to acrobatically pass the ball to each other, endeavouring to keep it airborne and to kick it into a suspended basket. Tournaments are periodically held at Sanam Luang. The local press will have details.

The Thailand football league (website: www.thaifootball.com) has two divisions, the premier and the first, and the teams have names such as *Air Force*, *Bangkok Bank* and the *Navy and Telephone Organisation of Thailand*. Information on games can be obtained from the *Football Association of Thailand* (tel: (02) 216 2954). Tickets for all sporting events can be bought at the venue up to an hour before the match starts.

Fitness Centres

Many of the fitness centres throughout the city are attached to hotels and are for members only. However, daily membership is available at the *Grande Spa and Fitness Club*, in the Sheraton Grande Sukhumvit, 250 Sukhumvit Road (tel: (02) 653 0282; website: www.sheratongrandesukhumvit.com).

Golf

Thailand has many excellent golf courses and some are open to visitors. The *Royal Golf & Country Club* (tel: (02) 738 0133; website:www.thailandgolf paradise.com/royalgolf), is located within easy reach of Bangkok, southeast of the city, at 69 Moo 7, Sukhumvit 17, Bang Sao Thong, Samut Prakan – best reached by taxi. It has a beautiful 18-hole course, with green fees for visitors of B800 during the week and B1300 at the weekend. The *Rose Garden Golf Club* (tel: (034) 322 780; website: www.thailandgolf paradise.com/rosegarden) is located 32km (20 miles) southwest of the city, at Tha Talad Sub District, Sampran, Nakhon Pathom – reached along National Highway Number 4. It has an 18-hole championship golf course with green fees of B700 during the week and B1300 at weekends (closed Monday).

Swimming

Siam Water Park, to the north of the city, on Sukhaphibun 2 Road (tel: (02) 517 0075), has waterslides and artificial surf. *Nawasri Pool*, 209 Ramkhamhaeng Soi 21 (tel: (02) 318 0134), is open to non-members.

Tennis

Tennis clubs that are open to the public include *Asoke Sport Club*, 302/81 Mooban Tawaamit, Asoke-Din Daeng (tel: (02) 246 2260), *Sawadee Soi*, 35/5 Soi 31 Sukhumvit Road (tel: (02) 258 4502), and *Central Tennis Court*, 13/1 Soi Attakarn Prasit, Sathorn Tai Road (tel: (02) 213 1909).

Shopping

Bangkok is arguably the best place in Asia for shopping and visitors will be spoilt for choice with the extensive shopping malls, department stores, small shops and markets. The city is also a bargain hunter's paradise and haggling with street vendors is to be expected and all part of the fun enjoyed by both buyer and seller. The Silom Road area is one of the main shopping centres, which boasts numerous specialist shops and department stores, including *Robinsons*, several shopping plazas and a wide range of silk and antique shops, as well as many tailors. The *River City Shopping Complex*, adjacent to the Royal Orchid Sheraton Hotel, has two floors devoted to antiques. Prices are fixed in most department stores but they do frequently offer discounts to interested buyers. The ultimate shopping experience is to be had at *The Emporium*, on Sukhumvit Road, with brand-name clothing and accessories, as well as cinemas, supermarkets and restaurants.

However, most visitors will head to the many street markets for their colourful atmosphere and lower prices. The Sukhumvit Road area has a street market that runs most of the day but is busiest at night. Dozens of stalls sell clothes, bags, silk items and gifts. Apart from the colourful nightlife in Patpong, the area also has a bustling night market where clothes and souvenirs are a real bargain. The weekend market at *Chatuchak Park*, on Phaholyothin Road, sells virtually everything that Thailand makes or grows, such as furniture, carpets, ceramics, watches, clothes, food and flowers. Chinatown is full of gold shops and the nearby cloth market at Phahurat has a huge range of superb fabrics. *Woeng Nakhon Kasem*, better known as the 'Thieves' Market', located between Yaowarat Road and New Road, sells antique porcelain, copperware and furniture. Good buys to be found throughout the city include silk items, silver and gold, gems (rubies and sapphires are indigenous to Thailand), pearls, painted umbrellas and fans, ceramics, wickerwork, woodcarvings and leather goods. It is also an ideal place to have clothes made and the quality is of a high standard.

Many stores are open 12 hours a day, seven days a week and the street markets have even longer hours, although some are busier in the mornings and others in the evenings. A *Thailand Duty-Free Shop* is located in the World Trade Centre, on Ratchadamri Road. Tourists can pay for their purchases here and collect them at the airport immediately prior to departure from the country. Value Added Tax (7%) can be refunded on goods bought in shops labelled 'VAT refund for tourists', where there is a minimum transaction of B2000. VAT Refund Application for Tourists forms are completed at the time of purchase and it is necessary to show one's passport. Cash refunds (minimum B5000) can be obtained in the airport departures hall and often the goods purchased must also be shown.

Culture

Bangkok has many traditional dance and theatre groups, which perform around the city, although nowadays they are more popular with tourists than locals, who have generally embraced Western imports. The city does have its own orchestra, the *Bangkok Symphony Orchestra*. Western plays, with famous actors from Britain and America, are often staged for short seasons at some of the international hotels.

Both Thai and international cultural performances, including classical music, dance, ballet and pop concerts, are frequently held in the *Thailand Cultural Centre*, Ratchadaphisek Road (tel: (02) 247 0028; website: www.thaiculturalcenter.com), the *National Theatre*, Rachini Road (tel: (02) 224 1342), and *Queen Sirikit National Convention Centre*, New Ratchadaphisek Road (tel: (02) 229 3000; website: www.qsncc.co.th). Tickets can be obtained in advance from the venues or from *Thai Ticketmaster* (tel: (02) 204 9999; website: www.thaiticketmaster.com).

Music and Dance

Sala Rim Naam (tel: (02) 437 3080 or 6211) is owned by The Oriental hotel and is located on the opposite bank of the Chao Phraya River, next to the Peninsula Hotel. The nightly traditional music and dance show starts at 2030, preceded by dinner at 1900. Although there are numerous traditional shows appearing daily throughout the city, this one – reputed to be the best in Thailand and beautifully located in a traditional teak pavilion-style restaurant – is unmissable. *Baan Thai* (tel: (02) 258 5403), Soi 32

Silver in Chatuchak Market

Photo: Tourism Authority of Thailand

Sukhumvit Road, has a similar nightly music and dance show set in an old Thai house.

The *Bangkok Symphony Orchestra* (website: www. bangkoksymphony.com) usually performs in the *Thailand Cultural Centre* (see above).

Theatre

Classical dramas are very colourful and expressive and these are held on the last Friday and Saturday of each month at the *National Theatre* (see above). The *Bangkok Playhouse*, Phetchaburi Road (tel: (02) 319 7641), puts on modern plays each week on Friday, Saturday and Sunday nights. The *Chalerm Krung Royal Theatre*, Charoen Krung (New Road) (tel: (02) 222 0434), has regular performances of plays and musical dance dramas. For those fascinated by the infamous 'ladyboys' or *katoeys* of Bangkok, there are two performances each night at the *Calypso Cabaret*, in the Asia Hotel, Phayathai Road (tel: (02) 653 3960/216 8937; website: www.calypsocabaret.com), which are always packed out.

Film

Bangkok has a large number of cinemas but not all show English-language films. Some show movies with English soundtracks but many others will have been dubbed into Thai. Cinemas that show films in English or with English subtitles include: *EGV Multiplexes* and *Major Cineplexes* (website: www.majorcineplex .com), both with various venues throughout the city; *Lido Multiplex*, Rama I Road (tel: (02) 252 6498); and *United Artists*, Soi 24 Sukhumvit Road (tel: (02) 664 8711) and Ratchadaphisek Road (tel: (02) 673 6060).

Nineteenth-century Bangkok features in the spectacular film *Anna and the King* (1999). The filming did not take place in the city, as the Thais banned the book on which it was based (see *Literary Notes* below), as well as the earlier film, starring Yul Brynner, claiming they were historically inaccurate. A James Bond movie, *The Man with the Golden Gun* (1974), uses Bangkok, as well as the stunning Phang Nha Bay, as a backdrop. A 2001 epic, *Suriyothai* (directed by Prince Chatrichalerm Yukol), depicts life in the Ayutthaya period of Thai history and the story of the heroic Queen Suriyothai, with some incredible battle scenes.

Cultural Events

The birthdays of the King and Queen of Thailand are widely celebrated throughout Bangkok. Preceding the King's birthday in December is the annual *Trooping of the Colour*, where the Royal Guards renew their allegiance to the monarch, in a colourful ceremony at the Royal Plaza. The *Royal Barge Procession* takes place only occasionally now, because of the age of the barges, although there is a small display on the King's birthday. The last major procession was in November 1999, to mark the 72nd birthday of the King. Prior to that it was in 1996, to celebrate the King's 50th year on the throne. The processions are incredibly spectacular and the 1999 outing saw 52 of the elegantly carved barges rowed by thousands of costumed oarsmen.

Literary Notes

A prolific writer of the darker side of ex-pat life is Christopher G Moore who often uses Bangkok as a backdrop. Particularly well known are *Spirit House* (1992) and *Asia Hand* (1993), the first two books in a series of seven titles featuring the private eye, Vincent Calvino. The latest one, *Minor Wife*, was published in 2002. Jake Needham's novel, *The Big Mango* (1999),

Woman selling hats, Thonburi

depicts the story of an ex-GI returning to Bangkok in search of money stolen from a Vietnamese bank.

The King and I (1956) is probably the most famous film about Bangkok and the royal court. The film is based on the book *Anna and the King of Siam* (1944) by Margaret Landon, which itself is a novel adapted from *The English Governess at the Siamese Court*, the memoirs of Anna Leonowens, recounting her period as a governess in the court of King Mongkut. A more historically accurate account of the time can be found in *The Kingdom and the People of Siam* (1857) by Sir John Bowring, who was responsible for negotiating the treaty with King Mongkut.

Still based around the royal family, *The Bangkok Secret* (1990) by Anthony Grey investigates the mystery surrounding the murder of King Ananda in Bangkok in 1946 – an event that is often glossed over, and the identity of the assailant is still unknown. One of the best-known residents of Bangkok was Jim Thompson, who was responsible for building a major industry – silk – and whose home is a Bangkok landmark (see *Key Attractions*). He mysteriously disappeared in Malaysia in 1967 and William Warren wrote a book about his life and disappearance, called *Jim Thompson: The Legendary American of Thailand* (1976).

SPECIAL EVENTS

New Year's Day, celebrations traditionally begin with merit-making in the mornings, when Buddhists take gifts of flowers, incense or donations to the temples, followed by parties and entertainment for the rest of the day, 1 Jan, Sanam Luang area

Bangkok International Film Festival (website: www.bkkinterfilm.com), Jan, throughout the city

Makha Puja, Buddhist Holy day featuring various day and night candlelit ceremonies, Feb, temples around city

International Kite Festival, kite fighting and demonstrations, Mar/Apr, Sanam Luang

International Bangkok Motor Show (website: www.bangkok-motorshow.com), Mar/Apr, Bangkok International Trade & Exhibition Centre

Bangkok Fringe Festival, innovative theatre productions, Apr, Patravadi Theatre

Songkran (Thai New Year), religious ceremonies and public festivities involving lots of water, Apr, throughout the city

Coronation Day, public holiday, 5 May, throughout the city

Royal Ploughing Ceremony, celebration of the start of the rice-growing season, May, throughout the city

Visakha Puja, Buddhist holiday, May, throughout the city

Asarnha Puja Day/Khao Phansa Day, commemorates Buddha's first sermon and the beginning of Buddhist Lent, Jul, temples throughout the city

Queen's Birthday Celebrations, public holiday with display of lights decorating public buildings, 12 Aug, throughout the city

Chulalongkorn Day, public holiday in memory of Rama V, 23 Oct, throughout the city

Bangkok Marathon, Nov, Sanam Chai

King's Birthday Celebrations, public holiday with display of lights decorating public buildings, 5 Dec, throughout the city

Constitution Day, marks the start of the constitutional monarchy, 10 Dec, throughout the city

BARCELONA

Barcelona is Spain's second city and capital of the autonomous region of Catalonia (*Catalunya*) in the northeast of the country. Despite overlooking the Mediterranean, 200km (124 miles) from the French border, few tourists would have considered visiting the city two decades ago, when it had a rather rundown industrial centre. However, when Barcelona was awarded the Olympic Games for 1992, the city benefited from major redevelopment and renewal. As well as purpose-built sporting developments, with the epicentre on the slopes of Montjuïc, the infrastructure of the city was drastically overhauled and four new beaches were created along the seafront. The process of regeneration continued throughout the 1990s, particularly around the old port. Even the former red-light district of Raval to the southwest of La Rambla has been significantly tidied up in the last few years.

Barcelona was founded by the Carthaginians – one theory is that the city's name is taken from the Carthaginian leader Amilcar Barca – and was later settled by the Romans, the Visigoths, the Moors and the Franks. Under the Empire of Charlemagne, the city became the dominant political and military force in the region. The growth in maritime trade in the Middle Ages was the key to Barcelona's Golden Age, which saw the construction of some of the most impressive buildings in the Gothic quarter. In the 18th century, Barcelona emerged into the modern world at the forefront of the industrial revolution, based on a successful textile industry using cotton imported from the Americas. Prosperity in the 19th century coincided with a resurgence of interest in Catalan culture – Barcelona's civic pride found expression in the World Exhibition of 1888, in the unique urban planning of the Eixample district and in the exuberant architecture of the Modernista movement, a form of Art Nouveau.

The city still enjoys an international reputation as a centre for architecture and design. As well as this unrivalled collection of modernist buildings, in recent years, the world's top architects have flocked here to conjure up an array of modern structures and avant-garde designs. Many have drawn their inspiration from the seminal work of Barcelona's most famous son, the modernist architect, Antoni Gaudí, whose unique style can still be savoured in a number of key buildings around the city, including his masterpiece La Sagrada Família, an unfinished cathedral. The rush of new construction does not dwarf the older buildings at all as Barcelona is the kind of city that happily combines old and new.

As the capital of Catalunya, Barcelona retains a strong sense of regional identity and Catalan is used side by side with Castilian as the official language. The city is also solidifying its position as a major regional economic power, tucked as it is strategically close to the French border and with a wide Mediterranean coastline. Barcelona's key industries include manufacture, textiles, electronics and tourism and its economy has been steadily expanding during the past decade. The locals are very aware of the city's potential and a strong desire still remains among some to create an independent Catalan state with Barcelona at its helm, instead of the current Spanish set-up, where Barcelona plays second fiddle in political terms to Madrid. Although some observers believe that the desire for outright independence has waned since the death of General Franco and the region has seen a greater deal of autonomy, nevertheless, the patriotic feelings still remain strong. Nowhere more so than at Camp Nou, the home of Barça – one of Europe's greatest football teams – arch rivals to Real Madrid.

With a balmy year-round climate – not too steamily hot in summer and with few genuinely cold days in winter – it is not surprising that Barcelona is attracting an increasing number of visitors. Indeed, with cheap air travel becoming ever more popular, Barcelona has entered the millennium as one of Europe's most popular short break destinations. And deservedly so, when it is a thriving modern metropolis with a beautiful Gothic core, a cosmopolitan city that determinedly retains its indigenous traditions and a major business destination with beaches on its doorstep.

Port of Barcelona

TRAVEL

Getting There By Air

El Prat de Llobregat (BCN)

Tel: (93) 298 3838. Fax: (93) 298 3737.
Website: www.aena.es

The airport is located 12km (seven miles) southwest of the city centre and has three terminals (A, B and C). There are daily direct flights between Barcelona and more than 30 international destinations – several further destinations are served by less frequent direct flights. In 1998, the airport was voted Europe's best. The airport served 21 million passengers in 2002, compared with just ten million in 1992, the year of the Barcelona Olympics. A third runway and a new offloading area have been planned for 2006, to cater for the increasing volume of air traffic.

Major airlines: Foreign airlines mostly use terminal A. International flights run by *Iberia* (*IB*), the national airline, usually use terminal B. Information on *Iberia* is available from *Info-Iberia* (tel: (902) 400 500; e-mail: infoib@iberia.com; website: www.iberia.com) or the travel office in Plaza d'Espanya (tel: (93) 325 7358). Other major domestic and international carriers include *Air France*, *American Airlines*, *BMI Baby*, *British Airways*, *Delta*, *EasyJet*, *Iberia*, *KLM*, *Lufthansa*, *SAS*, *Spanair* and *Virgin Airlines*.

Approximate flight times to Barcelona: From London is 2 hours; from New York is 7 hours 30 minutes; from Los Angeles is 13 hours 5 minutes; from Toronto is 14 hours 10 minutes and from Sydney is 25 hours 15 minutes.

Airport facilities: *Banco Exterior de Espana* and *La Caixa* (terminals A and B) are open daily 0700–2300. Bureaux de change (terminals A and B) are open 0700–2300. Car hire services are available from *Atesa*, *Avis*, *Budget*, *Europcar* and *Hertz*. Other facilities include tourist information desks, open daily 0900–2100 (tel: (93) 478 4704), a hotel information desk (terminals A and B), duty-free shopping (terminals A and B), left-luggage (terminal B), post office (terminal C – open mornings only), shops, restaurants and bars. Terminal B has a chemist and 24-hour medical facilities.

Business facilities: There is no business centre at the airport but *Air France*, *British Airways*, *Iberia* and *Spanair* all provide VIP lounges.

Arrival/departure tax: None.

Transport to the city: A *RENFE* (tel: (902) 240 202; website: www.renfe.es) train leaves the airport for the city centre every 30 minutes daily 0600–2200, stopping at Central-Sants (journey time – 15 minutes), Plaça de Catalunya (journey time – 20–25 minutes) and Arc de Triomf and Clot-Aragó for connections to the metro. The fare is €2.30.

An *Aerobús* service (tel: (93) 223 5151; e-mail: info@emt-amb.com; website: www.emt-amb.com) runs to Plaça de Catalunya via Gran Via every 15 minutes Monday to Friday 0600–2400 and every 30 minutes Saturday and Sunday 0630–2400 (journey time – 15–30 minutes). The fare is €3.45, payable by credit card.

Taxis to and from the airport charge a minimum of €10. The ride to a downtown hotel will cost approximately €20, including a €2 airport supplement. Taxi ranks are located outside the terminal buildings.

Getting There By Water

Located close to the city centre, to the west of Montjuïc and below *Barri Gòtic* (Gothic Quarter), the *Port de Barcelona*, run by *Autoritat Portuària de Barcelona* (tel: (93) 298 6000; website: www.apb.es), has re-established its status as one of the major Mediterranean maritime destinations in recent years. In addition to being an important cargo port, it is the second largest Mediterranean cruise centre after Athens. In 2001, the port handled 544 liners and over half a million passengers.

Crueurs del Porte de Barcelona (tel: (93) 412 7914) runs four cruise ship terminals – two at Moll Adossat and two at the World Trade Center – and the *Autoritat Portuària de Barcelona* (tel: (93) 298 6000) runs the Port Vell terminal. All the terminals have tourist information centres, travel agencies, a flight connection service, bureaux de change, first-aid facilities, duty-free and souvenir shops, bars, restaurants and international newspaper stands. Taxis and shuttle buses provide transportation to the city centre. Parking and car hire services are also available.

Ferry services: For ferries to Mallorca, Menorca and Ibiza, the *Estació Marítima Balears* (Balearic Maritime Station) is located at Moll de Sant Bertran 3 (tel: (93) 295 9100). The nearest metro stop is Drassanes (line 3). *Trasmediterránea* (tel: (90) 245 4645 *or* (93) 295 9100; fax: (93) 295 9135; e-mail: correom@trasmediterranea.es; website: www.trasmediterranea.es), runs ferries to Palma, Mahon and Ibiza on the Balearic Islands. They also operate a fast ferry service between Barcelona and Palma. Single fares start from €28 for the standard ferry.

Transport to the city: The *TMB* (tel: (93) 298 7000; website: www.tmb.net) metro links the port to the centre of Barcelona.

Getting There By Rail

RENFE (tel: (902) 240 202 (24-hour information) *or* (93) 490 1122 (overseas); website: www.renfe.es) operates the Spanish rail network, which radiates from Madrid to all the major cities. There are also transversal routes and services running from the French border along the Mediterranean coast. Some of the services are swifter and more reliable than others. The least convenient are *tranvía*, *semidirecto* and *correo* trains, all of which chug along at a leisurely pace. Seat reservations are required on all intercity trains. Supplements are payable on many faster trains,

even for passengers holding Interail and Eurail passes, although the amount is generally worth paying for a more efficient service.

Estació Central-Sants, Plaça del Països Catalans (tel: (93) 495 6215), is the city's main railway station, serving national and international destinations as well as suburban routes. Facilities in the station building include tourist information, hotel information, left-luggage, a bank offering currency exchange (open daily 0800–2200), a restaurant and cafeteria, shops, a first-aid point, showers, lockers and secure parking. Another railway station, *Estació de França*, Avinguda Marqués de l'Argentera, offers mainly southbound regional services. On some train routes, an alternative to both these stations is *Passeig de Gràcia* station, located close to Plaça de Catalunya and La Rambla.

Rail services: There are direct trains to Barcelona from Paris (journey time – 11 hours), Montpellier (journey time – 4 hours 30 minutes), Milan (journey time – 13 hours) and Zurich (journey time – 13 hours). There are eight daily departures to Madrid (journey time – 8 hours), including three sleeper services. A new high-speed rail service linking Barcelona with Madrid and destinations in France is planned for 2004.

Transport to the city: Central-Sants is situated some distance from the city centre but is located at the junction of two *TMB* (tel: (93) 298 7000; website: www.tmb.net) metro lines – the green line (3) and the blue line (5). Estació de França, is situated near the Barceloneta metro stop, while Passeig de Gràcia is located at the junction of three metro lines – the purple line (2), the green line (3) and the yellow line (4).

Getting There By Road

Motorways (*Autopista*) are prefixed by the letter 'A', while highways (*Autovía*) and other major roads (*Carretera Nacional*) are indicated by either two Roman numerals or, more commonly, three digits. Many motorways have tolls. Rates are shown at tollbooths and payment must be made in Euros – cash is preferred, although major credit cards might also be accepted.

Traffic drives on the right. No person under 18 years may hire or ride a vehicle over 75cc. Seatbelts are compulsory for front-seat passengers in cars. Crash helmets must be worn on motorcycles. After sunset, sidelights must be used at all times – spare bulbs and red hazard triangles must be kept in all vehicles. The speed limit for cars and motorcycles is 120kph (74mph) on motorways, 100kph (62mph) on dual carriageways, 90kph (56mph) on roads outside built-up areas and 50kph (31mph) within towns. Fines for traffic offences are strictly enforced. The maximum legal alcohol to blood ratio for driving is 0.05%.

Foreign visitors require a valid driving licence to drive in Spain. National licences from EU countries are accepted, although nationals of other countries, including the USA, Canada and Australia, are advised to obtain an International Driving Permit. Third Party Insurance is required and documents should be carried at all times. A Green Card is strongly recommended for all visitors and is compulsory for those from outside the EU.

Breakdown services and motoring information can be obtained from the *Real Automobile Club de Catalunya* (*RACC*), Avinguda Diagonal 687 (tel: (93) 495 5000 *or* (90) 036 5505 (24-hour information); website: www.racc.es). *Ruta Catalunya* (tel: (93) 230 5000; fax: (93) 230 5001) provides information on driving in Catalonia.

Emergency breakdown services: *RACC* (93) 495 5058 (24-hour line). Alternatively, drivers should contact the *Ayuda en Carretera*, run by the *Guardia Civil*, via the roadside SOS telephones located on both sides of the carriageway at two-kilometre (one-mile) intervals.

Routes to the city: The A7 motorway is the main route to Barcelona from France and runs down the coast past Valencia, as far as Alicante to the south. The A2 heads inland to the west for Zaragoza and

connections to Madrid. The A19 hugs the coast for a short distance to the northeast of the city.

Approximate driving times to Barcelona: From Zaragoza – 3 hours; Valencia – 3 hours; Madrid – 5 hours 30 minutes.

Coach services: *Eurolines* international coach services (tel: (902) 405 040; website: www. eurolines.es) use *Estació Autobuses de Sants*, situated next to the Central-Sants train station, Carrer Viriato (tel: (93) 490 4000), although services to France also stop at *Estació del Nord*, Avinguda Vilanova (tel: (93) 265 6508). Most long-distance coaches from other parts of Spain operate from the Estació del Nord. There are Eurolines services to major European cities, including Amsterdam, Frankfurt, London, Prague and Rome.

CITY STATISTICS

Location: Catalunya (Catalonia), Northeast Spain.
Country dialling code: 34.
Population: 1,505,325 (city); 4,390,413 (metropolitan area).
Ethnic mix: Majority Catalan Spanish, minorities include Roma and African.
Religion: 90% Roman Catholic, 10% Protestant, Muslim and Jewish.
Time zone: GMT + 1 (GMT + 2 from last Sunday in March to Saturday before last Sunday in October).
Electricity: 220 volts AC, 50Hz; round two-pin plugs are standard.
Average January temp: 10°C (50°F).
Average July temp: 25°C (78°F).
Annual rainfall: 590mm (23.2 inches).

Getting Around

Public Transport

With the exception of one metro line, transport in the city is operated by *TMB* (tel: (93) 298 7000; website: www.tmb.net). There are TMB information offices in the foyer of the Universitat metro station, open Monday to Friday 0800–2000. There are also offices at Diagonal, Sants Estació and Sagrada Família metro stations.

Regional rail services and the purple metro line are operated by *Ferrocarrils de la Generalitat de Catalunya – FGC* (tel: (93) 205 1515; website: www.fgc.es). The information office, located in the Catalunya metro station, is open Monday to Friday 0700–2100.

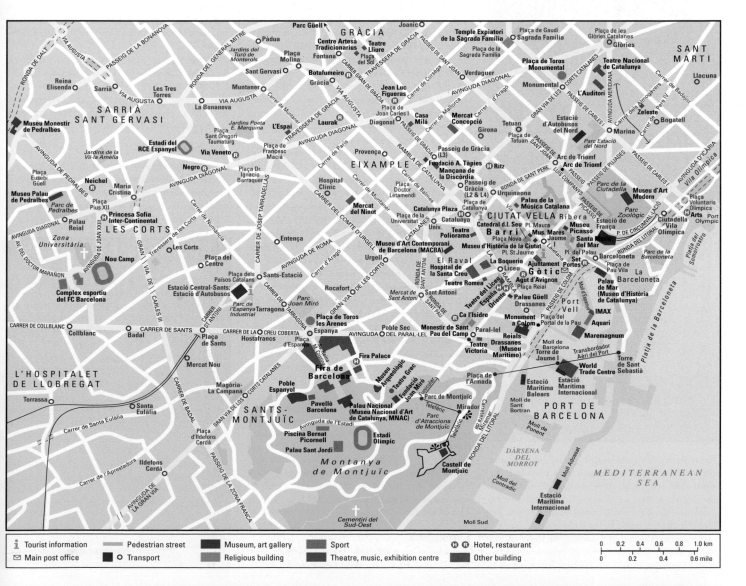

i Tourist information	**==** Pedestrian street	■ Museum, art gallery
✉ Main post office	■ ○ Transport	Religious building

Sport	⊕ Ⓡ Hotel, restaurant	
Theatre, music, exhibition centre	Other building	

0	0.2	0.4	0.6	0.8	1.0 km
0		0.2		0.4	0.6 mile

BUSINESS PROFILE

In business terms, Barcelona is on the up and up. Over the last decade, the city has fully utilised its potential as the gateway between Iberia and the rest of Western Europe – a theme that Barcelona is pushing more than ever in the new millennium. The city has re-established itself as a major Mediterranean port that can compete with the likes of Marseilles and Genoa, thanks in part to the Spanish Ports Law, which has given more independent control to the *Autoritat Portuària de Barcelona.*

Barcelona is one of the largest industrial centres of Spain, with a strong background in manufacturing based on textiles and a large motor industry – *Nissan* and *Seat* have vehicle production plants in the city. Along with the port, these are the main employers in the city. Consumer electronics and chemical and pharmaceutical research are other major industrial sectors and the city is also strong in design, publishing and advertising.

Although Barcelona has a stock market and a bond derivatives markets, it has failed to emerge as a major financial or banking centre to rival Madrid. It is, however, the country's major convention and trade fair centre, with impressive facilities including *Montjuïc 1 and 2,* Avinguda Reina Maria Cristina (tel: (93) 233 2000; fax: (93) 233 2001), which catered for nearly two million visitors in 2002, as well as the state-of-the-art *World Trade Center* (tel: (93) 508 8000; fax: (93) 508 8010) at Port Vell.

The Olympic Games in 1992 was a pivotal event in business terms, as it provided the impetus and investment necessary to improve the infrastructure of the city through US$8 billion of investment. The Games' massive marketing project successfully promoted the city as an efficient, business-like centre and initiated a massive surge of investment in the hotel and tourism sector. In 1998 alone, a quarter of all foreign investment in Spain flowed into Barcelona. The city's economy has been steadily growing over the past decade, reflected in an Arthur Andersen study for *Fortune* magazine in 2000, which ranked Barcelona's economic progress third among cities of the world. Today, around 45% of all foreign visitors come to Barcelona on business. The number of tourists visiting the city has risen too, from 1.7 million in 1990 to over 3.3 million in 2002. Barcelona's unemployment rate, standing at 6% in 2000, is considerably lower than Spain's unemployment rate, which rose from around 9% in 2000 to 12.9% in 2002.

Eixample is the main business district, with Avinguda Diagonal at the very heart of Barcelona's business life. The *Barcelona Chamber of Commerce* (website: www.cambrabcn.es) is located here .

Apart from during the rush hour (0730–0930 and 1800–2030), when it becomes very crowded, the **metro** (*M*) is the most efficient means of transport in the city. Metro lines are all identified by a number and a colour – the direction is shown by the name of the line terminus. A single ticket (*billet senzill*) costs €1 and must be validated in a machine on the platform before boarding and carried at all times to avoid the €30.05 penalty. Tickets are available for purchase at TMB customer service centres, ticket offices and the automatic vending machines at the metro stations. The metro runs from Monday to Thursday 0500–2400, Friday and Saturday until 0200 and Sunday 0600–2400. The FGC line is fully integrated with the rest of the TMB-operated metro system and runs daily until 0130.

Buses in the city run daily from approximately 0630 until approximately 2200. The network is extensive and almost all services run through Plaça de Catalunya, Plaça Urquinaona or Plaça de la Universitat. Single tickets are available for purchase from the driver and cost €1. Travel cards must be validated in machines upon boarding. There are 16 **night bus** routes to limited destinations. These run 2300–0400 every 30 minutes on weekdays and every 20 minutes at weekends and require separate tickets. The *TombBús* is a shopping service that runs during summer between Plaça de Catalunya and Plaça Pius XII, Monday to Friday 0800–2130 and Saturday 0900–2130. A single ticket costs €1.

There are a number of **multi-ride tickets** available – including the *T-10* for ten journeys and *T-50/30* for 50 journeys within 30 days – costing between €5.80 and €93.40, depending on the number of zones, validity period, modes of transport and changes permitted. There is also a variety of **passes** available, including one-day (€4.40) and monthly (€37.65) passes. In addition, for tourists, there are three-day (€11.30), four-day (€14.50) and five-day (€17.30) *Aerobus+Metro+Bus* passes, which cover all transport in the city, including the journey to and from the airport. These are available for purchase at TMB customer service centres, metro ticket offices, automatic vending machines and at FGC railway stations.

For the suburbs and surrounding areas, there are regional **rail** lines run by the *FGC* and *RENFE* (see *Getting There By Rail*). The RENFE local network is known as *Rodalies* or *Cercanías* and the central station in the city is Plaça de Catalunya.

A funicular railway trundles up Montjuïc from the corner of Carrer Nou de la Rambla and Avinguda Parallel to Avinguda Miramar daily 1100–2200 in summer and daily 1045–2000 in winter, costing €1.65 for a single or €2.40 for a return journey. From the amusement park, there is a cable car (*telefèric*) to Montjuïc Castle daily 1200–2000 in summer and Saturday and Sunday 1100–1930 in winter. This costs €3 for a single and €4.21 for a return journey. A further cable car operates every 15 minutes from the San Sebastian Tower in the Barceloneta district to Montjuïc, stopping en route at the Jaume I tower, near the World Trade Center. This operates daily from 1030–1900 (from March to mid-June), 1030–2000 (from mid-June to mid-September), 1030–1900 (from mid-September to mid-October) and 1030–1730 (from mid-October to February). Tickets cost €6.01 for a single or €7.21 for a return journey.

Taxis

There are 11,000 yellow and black registered cabs operating in the city. Not only available on the street, taxis can also be booked in advance. Reliable companies include *Radio Taxi* (tel: (93) 303 3033) and *Servitaxi* (tel: (93) 330 0300). The basic fare is €2, which should be displayed on the meter – each kilometre is charged at €0.80 and a €0.80 supplement is charged for each piece of large luggage. Taxi drivers should be tipped 5–10% of the meter fare.

Limousines

A number of companies offer limousine services with multi-lingual drivers. *Barcelona Limousine Service* (tel: (93) 247 0699; fax: (93) 265 1484; e-mail: bcnlimousine@spain-bcnlimo.com; website: www. spain-bcnlimo.com) charges from €300 for eight hours of limousine hire. *Limousine Rental* (tel: (93) 372 0000; fax (93) 473 6077; e-mail: central@ limorent.com; website: www.limorent.com), hires out limousines from about €230 for a full day.

Driving in the City

The proximity of the main attractions and the excellent public transport system makes driving unnecessary in the city. Driving in Barcelona can be quite daunting, especially at rush hour – early morning, lunchtime and early evening – or on the fast multi-lane avenues in the city centre. A detailed map is a necessity for managing the complicated one-way system and it is advisable for visitors to plan their routes in advance.

Parking is tricky in some areas. Cars require a paid ticket to park in the 'blue' zones 0800–1400 and 1600–2000 daily. Illegal parking results in the offending vehicle being towed away. Parking costs €1–3 per hour or around €20 per day. There are numerous car parks in the city centre, which charge approximately €1.60 per hour and €17.50–20 per day.

Car Hire

Drivers must be 21 years or older to hire a car in Barcelona. A passport and a valid driving licence are required. A valid international insurance policy is also necessary, although this can be purchased at the time of hire.

In addition to companies at the airport, car hire in Barcelona is provided by *Avis*, Carrer Casanova 209 (tel: (93) 209 9533; website: www.avis.com), and *Hertz*, Carrer Tuset 10 (tel: (93) 217 3248; website: www.hertz.com). Hire of a small car costs from €40 per day and from €265 per week.

Bicycle Hire

Barcelona has a limited network of bicycle lanes and bicycle racks. Bicycles can be carried on the public transport system, although there are some peak hour restrictions. Bicycles are available for hire from *Scenic*, Carrer Marina 22 (tel: (93) 221 1666), *Un Coxte*

BUSINESS ETIQUETTE

The business community in Barcelona is accustomed to hosting foreign visitors and many international businesspeople speak English or French. Catalan is used in a business setting among native speakers; otherwise Castilian Spanish is used.

Business hours are generally 0800 or 0900 until 1800 or 1900, with an extended lunch break between 1330 and 1500 or 1600. These hours may vary depending on the size and type of organisation. Punctuality is important. Formal wear is the norm and both men and women should wear a suit for business meetings – men should also wear a tie. Business cards should be exchanged after introduction. All Spaniards have two family names – only the first is used in conversation but any academic or professional titles should be acknowledged.

Invitations to private homes are not common although invitations to pre-dinner drinks and tapas or to dine out might be offered.

Menys, Esparteria 3 (tel: (93) 268 2105), and *Biciclot*, Sant Joan de Malta 1 (tel: (93) 307 7475). Hire charges start at around €5 per hour or €15 per day.

SIGHTSEEING

Sightseeing Overview

Barcelona is neatly framed by the Mediterranean to the east and the hills of Montjuïc and Tibidabo on two of its other flanks. The central section of the city, where most tourists spend their time, is even more conveniently divided by *La Rambla* – the main artery of Barcelona life, which tumbles from *Plaça de Catalunya* southeast towards the Mediterranean and the recently reborn districts of *Port Vell* (Old Port) – and trendy *La Ribera* (The Waterfront). The atmospheric *Barri Gòtic* (Gothic Quarter) is the area to the right of La Rambla if walking towards Plaça de Catalunya. This is the charming heart of the old city, embracing the *Catedral de la Seu* and *Museu Picasso* amid narrow streets and hidden squares. *Plaça de Catalunya* divides the old town from the *Eixample* – a grid of streets laid out in the 19th century – in which much of the city's finest Modernista architecture is to be found, including the celebrated *La Sagrada Família*, a marvel of design by Antoni Gaudí.

An eccentric recluse, Gaudí was the most celebrated practitioner of the Modernista style, the Spanish Art Nouvea movement. In his innovative works, he threw all design rulebooks out of the window in a quest to get architecture to mirror the curves and intricacies of nature. In addition to those sights described in the *Key Attractions* below, further architectural highlights include *Hospital de la Santa Creu I Sant Pau* and the *Palau de la Música Catalana*, both designed by Gaudí's contemporary, Domènech i Montaner. *Passeig de Gràcia*, the most stylish street in the city, is at the heart of the Eixample and intersects with *Avinguda Diagonal* – the city's main thoroughfare – at its northern end.

The *Montjuïc* mountainside has successfully managed the transition from being the site of the 1992 Olympic Games to becoming a permanent tourist attraction, boasting the remaining Olympic installations, such noteworthy museums as *Fundació Joan Miró* and the *Museu Nacional d'Art de Catalunya*, as well as great views of the city.

Key Attractions

Temple Expiatori de la Sagrada Família (Expiatory Temple of the Holy Family)

Gaudí's unfinished masterpiece and the city's most outlandish landmark, the *Expiatory Temple of the Holy Family* towers crazily above the grid-like streets of the Eixample. Despite being very much a building site, the cathedral has a certain beauty that somehow emerges, despite the omnipresent construction. However, it remains the subject of continual controversy over who should pay for its completion. The extraordinary structure has elicited cries of astonishment, awe, amusement and anger from visitors and residents alike, but it remains one of the city's most visited attractions.

Carrer de Mallorca 401
Tel: (93) 207 3031. Fax: (93) 476 1010.
E-mail: informa@sagradafamilia.org
Website: www.sagradafamilia.org

Casa Milá rooftop

Transport: Metro Sagrada Família.
Opening hours: Daily 0900–2000 (Apr–Sep); daily 0900–1800 (Oct–Mar).
Admission: €8.

Museu Picasso (Picasso Museum)

The *Picasso Museum* is the one of the city's main tourist attractions, housed in two 15th-century palaces close to the Parc de la Ciutadella. The impressive permanent collection is devoted to the artist's early work, including a large number of childhood sketches, paintings from the Blue Period (1901–04) and the Pink Period (1907–20), exhibition posters, ceramics and cubist works. There are also two exhibition spaces for temporary exhibitions.

Carrer Montcada 15–23
Tel: (93) 319 6310. Fax: (93) 315 0102.
E-mail: museupicasso@mail.bcn.es
Website: www.museupicasso.bcn.es
Transport: Metro Jaume I.
Opening hours: Tues–Sat 1000–2000, Sun 1000–1500.
Admission: €4.80.

La Rambla

La Rambla is not one street but rather a seamless series of pedestrian avenues stretching from the *Monument a Colom* on the waterfront to *Plaça de Catalunya* in the centre of the city, often known collectivly as Las Ramblas, *La Rambla* has the same place in the psyche of the city as the Champs Elysées in Paris does, although is far less snooty and far more attractive. Lined with trees, cafés, restaurants, flower stalls, shops and newspaper stands, La Rambla is the perfect place in which to stroll and soak up the unique Barcelona atmosphere.

Attractions along the way include Gaudí's first major architectural project, *Palau Güell* (Güell Palace). *Plaça Reial*, just off La Rambla, is one of the most attractive squares in the city – elegant 19th-century houses look down on palm trees, lampposts designed by Gaudí, and an eclectic mix of people enjoying the lively atmosphere at outdoor cafés. Some of La Rambla's most captivating attractions are its famous street entertainers who delight the crowds with their weird and wacky shows. Other points of interest are the *Gran Teatre del Liceu* and

TOURIST INFORMATION

Centre d'Informació Turisme de Barcelona
Plaça de Catalunya 17-S
Tel: (906) 301 282 (within Spain) *or* (93) 368 9730 (international). Fax: (93) 348 9735.
E-mail: teltur@barcelonaturisme.com
Website: www.barcelonaturisme.com
Opening hours: Daily 0900–2100.

Other information desks can be found at the airport, at Central-Sants station and in the City Hall, Rambla de Catalunya 2–4.

Passes
The *Barcelona Card* offers discounts of up to 50% at many of the most interesting tourist attractions, including museums, entertainment and leisure venues, shops and restaurants, as well as free public transport and assistance insurance. Attractions include Museu Picasso, La Sagrada Família and Museu d'Art Contemporani de Barcelona. The card is available for one, two, three, four or five days, for €16.25, €19.25, €22.25, €24 and €26 respectively, from tourist information centres.

The *Articket* gives half-price admission to six of the city's main art galleries and museums – Museu Nacional d'Art de Catalunya, Fundació Joan Miró, Fundació Antoni Tàpies, Centre de Cultura Contemporània de Barcelona, Centre Cultural Caixa de Catalunya and Museu d'Art Contemporani de Barcelona. It is available for €14 from any of the respective box offices and branches of Caixa Catalunya.

La Ruta Modernista pass allows admission to all the best of the city's Modernista architecture (see *Tours of the City*). The pass costs €3.60 and is available from the *Centre del Modernisme*, situated inside *Casa Amatller*, Passeig de Gràcia 41, Monday to Saturday 1000–1900 and Sunday 1000–1400.

Photo: Gary Bowerman

Park Güell

the legendary *Café de l'Opera* opposite, as well as *La Boqueria*, Barcelona's wonderful, bustling food market.

La Rambla
Transport: Metro Liceu or Drassanes; bus 14, 38, 59 or 91.
Palau Güell
Carrer Nou de la Rambla 3–5
Tel: (93) 317 3974.
E-mail: info@gaudiclub.com
Website: www.gaudiclub.com
Opening hours: Mon–Fri 1000–1400 and 1600–1930.
Admission: €2.40.
Gran Teatre del Liceu
La Rambla 51–59
Tel: (93) 485 9900 (information) *or* (902) 332 211 (booking). Fax: (93) 485 9918.
E-mail: informacio@liceubarcelona.com
Website: www.liceubarcelona.com
Opening hours: Performances daily 1700 and/or 2030 (varies).
Admission: From €20 (performances).
La Boqueria
Rambla Sant Josep
Opening hours: Mon–Sat 0800–2000.
Admission: Free.

Parc Güell (Güell Park)

With *Parc Güell*, Gaudí created a fantasy land that seamlessly combines the natural and the man-made, as well as offering good views over the city. The park – originally conceived as a garden city – covers a hill to the north of the city centre. The gardens are enlivened by fantastic pavilions, stairways, columned halls and an organic plaza decorated with stunning broken mosaic work (*trencadís*) by Gaudí's assistant, Josep Maria Jujol. At the base of the hill is a house designed by Francesc Berenguer, which is now home to a collection of Gaudí's furnishings and other memorabilia.
Carrer d'Olot
Tel: (93) 424 3809.
E-mail: info@gaudiclub.com
Website: www.gaudiclub.com
Transport: Metro Vallcarca or Lesseps.

Opening hours: Daily 1000–1800 (Nov–Feb); daily 1000–2100 (May–Aug); daily 1000–1900 (Mar and Oct); daily 1000–2000 (Apr and Sep).
Admission: Free; €1.20 (guided tours).

Casa Milá (Milá House)

Casa Milá, also known as *La Pedrera* (the stone quarry), is an undulating apartment block on the corner of Passeig de Gràcia. The building, inspired by the ocean, is an incredible testament to Gaudí's ability to make stone malleable. Apartments – which are not open to the public – are arranged around elliptical patios with no square corners in sight. The roof terrace is watched over by sentry-like chimneys and offers an excellent view across the city to the spires of La Sagrada Família. The loft space of Casa Milá houses a beautiful museum, *Espai Gaudí*, dedicated to the architect.
Passeig de Gràcia 92/Carrer Provenca 261–265
Tel: (93) 484 5979. Fax: (93) 484 5889.
E-mail: info@gaudiclub.com
Website: www.casamila.com
Transport: Metro Diagonal or Provenca.
Opening hours: Daily 1000–2000; guided tours in English Mon–Fri 1600.
Admission: €7 (concessions available).

Barri Gòtic (Gothic Quarter)

The maze of streets known as the *Barri Gòtic* contains an exemplary collection of Gothic buildings dating from Catalonia's Golden Age, in the 14th and 15th centuries, interspersed with Roman ruins, delightful squares and numerous bars and restaurants. *Plaça Sant Jaume*, at the heart of the district, is the epicentre of the city's political life. The square is overlooked on one side by the Renaissance-style *Palau de la Generalitat* – location of the Catalan government – and on the other by the *Ajuntament* (city hall). Nearby, the *Palau Real* on *Plaça del Rei* houses the *Museu d'Història de la Ciutat*. The remains of the Roman city of Barcino, beneath the palace, were uncovered in 1931; Roman streets are still visible in the vast cellar space that stretches as far as the cathedral. The museum admission fee gives access to the cellar and to a number of beautiful medieval buildings.

Museu d'Història de la Ciutat
Plaça del Rei
Tel: (93) 315 1111. Fax: (93) 315 0957.
E-mail: museuhistoria@mail.bcn.es
Website: www.museuhistoria.bcn.es
Transport: Metro Jaume I.
Opening hours: Tues–Sat 1000–1400 and 1600–2000, Sun 1000–1400 (Oct–Jun); Tues–Sat 1000–2000, Sun 1000–1400 (Jun–Sep).
Admission: €3.60 (concessions available).

Catedral de la Seu

Catedral de la Seu was built between the 13th and 15th centuries, on the site of an earlier basilica, although the spire and façade were not added until the beginning of the 20th century. Highlights include the carved choir stalls, the *Capella de Lepanto* and the tranquil cloisters containing a pond of white geese.
Plaça de la Seu
Tel: (93) 315 1554. Fax: (93) 315 3555.
Transport: Metro Liceu or Jaume I.
Opening hours: Daily 0900–1300 and 1600–1900.
Admission: Free.

Museu Nacional d'Art de Catalunya – MNAC (National Museum of Catalonian Art)

The *Palau Nacional*, on Montjuïc, was the focus of Barcelona's International Fair in 1929. It now houses the *National Museum of Catalonian Art*. The museum boasts a stunning collection of Gothic, Romanesque and medieval treasures and religious artefacts. The most impressive approach to the Palace is along Avinguda Reina Maria Cristina, from Plaça Espanya – the avenue is lined with fountains that are floodlit at night.
Palau Nacional, Parc de Montjuïc
Tel: (93) 622 0360. Fax: (93) 622 0374.
Website: www.mnac.es
Transport: Metro Espanya.
Opening hours: Mon–Wed and Fri–Sat 1000–1900, Thurs 1000–2100, Sun 1000–1430.
Admission: €4.80.

Fundació Joan Miró (Joan Miró Foundation)

Also on Montjuïc, the *Joan Miró Foundation* is one of the most innovative galleries in the city. The foundation was a gift from the artist himself and houses a permanent collection of his paintings, graphics and sculptures.
Parc de Montjuïc
Tel: (93) 443 9470. Fax: (93) 329 8609.
E-mail: fjmiro@bcn.fjmiro.es
Website: www.bcn.fjmiro.es
Transport: Metro Parallel, then funicular to Parc de Montjuïc.
Opening hours: Tues–Sat 1000–1900, Thurs 1000–2130, Sun 1000–1430 (Oct–Jun); Tues–Sat 1000–2000, Thurs 1000–2130, Sun 1000–1430 (Jul–Sep).
Admission: €7.20 (concessions available).

Mançana de la Discòrdia (Block of Discord)

A series of extraordinary houses by Montaner, Gaudí and Puig i Cadafalch comprise the *Mançana de la Discòrdia* (Block of Discord) on the Passeig de Gràcia, between Aragó and Consell de Cent. Gaudí's *Casa Batlló*, at number 43, looks rather like an underwater grotto, with blue-green tiles on the façade, frog-faced balconies and a reptilian roof. The whole block forms part of La Ruta Modernista (see *Tours of the City*). Information and passes for this architectural tour can

be obtained from the first floor of *Casa Lléo Morera*, at number 35. Regrettably, the interiors of all three houses are closed to the public. However, La Ruta Modernista pass-holders are permitted onto the roof of Casa Batlló.
Passeig de Grácia
Transport: Metro Passeig de Grácia.

Santa Maria del Mar

Santa Maria del Mar is counted among the most beautiful churches in the city and is considered a prime example of Mediterranean Gothic architecture. It is located just to the northeast of the Barri Gòtic, at the heart of the fashionable La Ribera district. A 15th-century rose window adds colour to the simple harmony of the columned interior.
Plaça de Santa Maria
Tel: (93) 310 2390.
Transport: Metro Jaume I or Barceloneta.
Opening hours: Daily 0900–1330 and 1630–2000.
Admission: Free.

Museu d'Art Contemporani de Barcelona – MACBA (Museum of Contemporary Arts)

Looking rather incongruous in the down-at-heel surroundings of the Raval district, to the west of La Rambla, the brilliant-white *Museum of Contemporary Arts* is at the forefront of efforts to regenerate this traditionally seedy area of the city. The museum opened amid a blaze of publicity in 1995 and houses a permanent collection of post-1940s international art, as well as various temporary exhibitions.
Plaça dels Angels 1
Tel: (93) 412 0810. Fax: (93) 412 4602.
Website: www.macba.es
Transport: Metro Plaça de Catalunya.
Opening hours: Mon–Fri 1100–1930, Sat 1000–2000, Sun 1000–1500 (Mon–Fri until 2000 25 Jun–24 Sep).
Admission: €4.80 (concessions available).

The Waterfront (La Ribera)

A stroll along the harbourside *passeig* and wooden walkway is an excellent way to see some of the results of Barcelona's epic regeneration programme. The focus of interest and activity in Barcelona is shifting back towards the sea, with the continued development of *Port Vell* (Old Port). The waterfront now boasts a myriad of places to eat and drink, a vast shopping mall and leisure centre (*Maremagnum*) and an excellent aquarium. *Barceloneta*, the old fisherman's quarter, which dates from 1755, still has some of the best fish restaurants in the city and is now also the gateway to Barcelona's cleaned-up beaches. Further to the east, the *Vila Olímpica* at Poble Nou, created for the 1992 Olympic Games, is one of the liveliest and most interesting areas of the city during the warmer months, although it is often deserted during winter.
Passeig de Colom
Transport: Metro Barceloneta or Ciutadella-Vila Olímpica.

Further Distractions

Montjuïc (Mountain of the Jews)

The hill of *Montjuïc* has enough attractions to fill several days and was the main location of the 1992 Olympic Games. In addition to the *Palau Nacional* and the *Fundació Joan Miró*, visitors might also want to explore the *Estadi Olìmpic* and the accompanying museum, the *Museu Arqueològic*, the replica Spanish village (*Poble Espanyol*) or the *Pavelló Barcelona*, created by architect Mies van der Rohe, for the 1929 Exhibition. Other attractions include *Castell de Montjuïc* – an 18th-century fortress – and an amusement park. Half the fun is the funicular ride up the mountainside and the outstanding views from the top.
Montjuïc
Transport: Metro Plaça Espanya, then bus 50; metro Parallel, then funicular; bus 55 from Plaça de Catalunya.

Reials Drassanes and Museu Marítim (Royal Shipyard and Maritime Museum)

The *Maritime Museum* harks back to Barcelona's seafaring past, with a staggering number of nautical exhibits, including a map by Amerigo Vespucci. The museum is housed in the magnificent *Reials Drassanes* (Royal Shipyard), which dates from the 13th century.
Avinguda de les Drassanes
Tel: (93) 342 9920. Fax: (93) 318 7876.
Website: www.diba.es/mmaritim
Transport: Metro Drassanes.
Opening hours: Daily 1000–1900.
Admission: €5.40.

Tours of the City

Official guides can be hired from the *Barcelona Guide Bureau*, Via Laietana 54 (tel: (93) 268 2422 *or* 310 7778; fax: (93) 268 2211; e-mail: bgb@bgb.es; website: www.bgb.es). Guides charge from €160, depending on the language required, for up to four hours Monday to Friday, increasing to €185 at weekends.

Walking Tours

La Ruta Modernista is a book containing a map and details of Modernista sights around the city, linking 50 key Art Nouveau buildings, including La Sagrada Família and sites not usually open to the general public. The self-guided tour departs from *Palau Güell*, Carrer Nou de la Rambla 3–5, and costs just €3.60. The entire walk would take a full day although it is possible to complete just a part. The book also includes half-price entry to various sights en route, including the Palau de la Música, La Pedrera and La Sagrada Família. La Ruta Modernista pass is available from the *Centre del Modernisme*, inside *Casa Amatller*, Passeig de Gràcia 41, Monday to Saturday 1000–1900 and Sundays 1000–1400.

Bus Tours

Two companies run identical tours of the city. *Julià Tours* (tel: (93) 317 6454; website: www.julia-tours.com) departs from Ronda Universitat 5, while *Pullmantur* (tel: (93) 318 0241) sets off from Gran Via de les Corts Catalanes 65. A morning tour concentrates on the Barri Gòtic and Montjuïc, while an afternoon tour includes visits to key examples of Barcelona's architectural heritage and the Picasso Museum. Half-day tours cost around €30.

Casa Batllá

The *Barcelona Bus Turístic*, operated by *TMB* (tel: (93) 298 7000; website: www.tmb.net), allows visitors to hop on and off designated tourist buses. The buses ply two routes at 30-minute intervals or every ten minutes in peak season. The first buses for each route leave Plaça de Catalunya daily at 0900. Tickets cost €15 for one-day validity or €19 for two days.

Boat Tours

There are boat trips around the harbour, offered by *Golondrinas* (tel: (93) 442 3106). These depart regularly from the Port Olímpic daily throughout the year, although times vary. A round trip of the harbour takes approximately 35 minutes and costs €3.15. Energetic visitors can opt for a one-way ticket and then walk the four kilometres (2.5 miles) back to Barceloneta, from the breakwater.

Excursions

For a Half Day

Mount Tibidabo: On a clear day, *Mount Tibidabo* offers unsurpassed views of the city and the Mediterranean in one direction and Montserrat and the Pyrenees in the other. Located on the northwestern edge of Barcelona, the slopes of the mountain are crisscrossed with appealing wooded walks, while the summit is crowned with an old-style amusement park. Transport to the mountain is by FCC metro to Avinguda Tibidabo, then Tramvia Blau tram to Peu de Funicular and funicular railway to the summit.

For a Whole Day

Montserrat: Located some 60km (37 miles) to the northwest of Barcelona, the spectacular peaks of *Montserrat* have been a major pilgrimage destination for centuries. Today, hordes of tourists flock to ride the cable car to this atmospheric monastery that lurks deep in the rugged mountainside. Numerous miracles have supposedly happened here, centred on the icon of *La Moreneta* (Black Virgin), allegedly hidden here by St Peter. In addition to the monastery and accompanying museum (tel: (93) 877 7777), which features paintings by masters such as El Greco, Caravaggio and Picasso, the mountain hides numerous hermitages and caves, which can be reached on foot via a network of mountain paths. The basilica is open daily 0730–2030 (June to September) and 0800–1830 (October to June), while the museum is open daily 1000–1800 (March to December) and 1000–1645 (January to February). FCC trains to Montserrat depart hourly from Espanya station in Barcelona, to the cable car terminus at Aeri de Montserrat.

Teatre-Museu Dalí, Figueres: Located in the town of *Figueres*, 145km (90 miles) northeast of Barcelona and reached by motorway or rail from Passeig de Gràcia, this unusual museum (tel: (97) 267 7500; website: www.dali-estate.org) is a surrealist showcase of the artist's eccentric imagination. Created by Dalí himself, out of the former town theatre where he held his first exhibition, it also holds his surprisingly austere tomb. The museum is open daily 0900–1945 (July to September) and Tuesday to Saturday 1030–1745 (October to June). Entrance costs €9.

Beaches: *Sitges* is a lively Balearic-style resort, situated 40km (25 miles) south of Barcelona, very popular with the Spanish, British and German gay communities and accessible in 40 minutes by train south from Central-Sants. Alternatively, *Tossa de Mar*, located 40km (25 miles) north of Barcelona, boasts several fine beaches and small bays, an attractive old

town and a good museum. Buses from Barcelona are frequent during the summer but private transport might be required at other times. The *Sitges Tourist Office*, Carrer Sínia Morera 1 (tel: (93) 894 4251; fax: (93) 894 4305; website: www.sitges.com), and the *Tossa de Mar Tourist Office*, Avinguda del Pelegrí 25, Edificio La Nau (tel: (97) 234 0108; fax: (97) 234 0712; website: www.infotossa.com), can provide further information.

ACCOMMODATION

Spanish VAT (IVA) is 7% and is added to all hotel bills – usually at the end of the stay, although sometimes it is included within the prices given.

The prices quoted below are the lowest standard rates for a double room, excluding breakfast and IVA, unless otherwise specified.

Business

Catalunya Plaza

A friendly hotel with a personal touch, the three-star *Catalunya Plaza* is located at the very centre of the city, with excellent access to the airport and main traffic routes. It is housed in a pretty 19th-century building, colourfully but tastefully decked out with seasonal themes and featuring stunning stained-glass windows in the reception area. Each of the 46 rooms is fully equipped and includes a fax and generously sized desk. Meeting rooms of various sizes all overlook Plaça de Catalunya and include a multitude of services, including technical back-up and audiovisual equipment. Breakfast is a veritable feast and comes with a choice of newspaper.
Plaça de Catalunya 7
Tel: (93) 317 7171. Fax: (93) 317 7855.
E-mail: catalunya.plaza@h10.es
Website: www.h10.es
Price: €124.

Hotel El Rey Juan Carlos I

Situated on Avinguda Diagonal, Barcelona's vibrant commercial nerve centre, near the Palacio de Congresos, the five-star *Juan Carlos* exudes gravitas, comfort and tranquillity. The 375 rooms, including 37 luxury suites, are spacious, decorated in modern, subtle hues and enjoy panoramic city and sea views. Easy access from the airport coupled with top-notch meeting rooms and facilities make the hotel an obvious choice for visiting politicians and financiers. A tranquil patio restaurant, fringed with palm trees and exotic Mediterranean flora, is just one of a number of excellent eating areas. Leisure facilities include a first-class health and fitness club and indoor and outdoor swimming pools.
Avinguda Diagonal 661–671
Tel: (93) 364 4040. Fax: (93) 364 4264.
E-mail: hotel@hrjuancarlos.com
Website: www.hrjuancarlos.com
Price: From €350.

Hotel Fira Palace

Situated on a quiet, leafy street midway between the Fira de Barcelona exhibition halls and cultural attractions, including the Olympic Stadium and the Miró Museum, the four-star *Fira Palace* has the best of both worlds. The modern and elegantly designed rooms have Italian marble bathrooms and contain a

desk, telephone and fax. An impressive business centre includes separate working areas offering full office services and a number of versatile meeting rooms holding 18 to 2500 delegates. Eating facilities range from restaurant *El Mall*, specialising in regional and international cuisine, to the relaxing *Piano Bar* for snacks. A pool and squash courts are also on site.
Avinguda Rius i Taulet 1–3
Tel: (93) 426 2223. Fax: (93) 424 8679.
E-mail: sales@fira-palace.com
Website: www.fira-palace.com
Price: From €227.

Hotel Princesa Sofia InterContinental

The five-star *InterContinental* is a business hotel *par excellence*. Situated on Avinguda Diagonal, it is the largest hotel conference venue in Barcelona. Decorated in Mediterranean-inspired blues, the light, spacious bedrooms operate as fully functioning offices, featuring large work desks, ergonomically designed chairs and sockets for an array of technology. A superb business centre, comprising 28 meeting and banqueting rooms accommodating ten to 1200 delegates, comes with a full range of secretarial services. A relaxing terrace restaurant, luxurious indoor swimming pool and health club, plus proximity to excellent shopping centres, make it an ideal choice for the seasoned business traveller.
Plaça Pío XII 4
Tel: (93) 508 1000 *or* 1050 (reservations). Fax: (93) 508 1001.
E-mail: barcelona@interconti.com
Website: www.interconti.com
Price: From €250.

Luxury

Hotel Arts

The product of a hugely successful collaboration between New York design and Barcelona money, the *Arts* has been showered with awards, including several for 'Best Hotel'. Forty-four storeys high, it enjoys a relaxing beachside location and all 483 rooms have panoramic views. Decorated with flair and originality throughout, rooms are light and spacious, with full-sized desks and Internet access. Works by leading Spanish artists adorn the public areas. Among the astounding array of services and amenities are top-class restaurants, a fitness club and exceptional business facilities. An in-house conference service team is on hand, as are around-the-clock secretarial services and 'technology butlers'.
Carrer de la Marina 19–21
Tel: (93) 221 1000. Fax: (93) 221 1070.
Website: www.ritzcarlton.com
Price: From €450.

Hotel Ritz

Despite recent changes of name and management, the *Ritz* has maintained all the elegance and grandeur that has made it a by-word for glamour since it opened in 1919. Huge chandeliers, opulent fabrics and a luxurious ambience throughout make it the preferred choice of the rich and famous. The bedrooms are handsomely decorated, with unusual marble bathrooms modelled on ancient Roman spas. The *Scotch Bar Parilla* is ideal for pre-prandial drinks followed by dinner in the pretty *Restaurant Diana* or alfresco in a peaceful interior garden. Business clientele are also well catered for; the conference suites, although traditional in style, benefit from cutting-edge technology.

Gran Via de les Corts Catalanes 668
Tel: (93) 318 5200. Fax: (93) 318 0148.
E-mail: info@ritz-barcelona.com
Website: www.ritz-barcelona.com
Price: From €297.

Moderate

Hostal Jardí

A perennially popular budget option in the busy hub of Barcelona's old quarter, the two-star pension *Jardí* has recently undergone extensive refurbishment, including the addition of a hitherto non-existent breakfast room. The character and original features of this fantastic little hotel have been maintained. Overlooking the shady, café-lined Plaça Sant Josep Oriols and the classic Gothic architecture of the medieval church of Santa Maria del Pi, the Jardí is pretty much unbeatable in terms of price and location, although the improvements have necessitated price rises. All rooms are en suite.
Plaça Sant Josep Oriols 1
Tel: (93) 301 5958. Fax: (93) 318 3664.
Price: From €50 (including IVA).

Hotel Peninsular

Located in a narrow street near the Liceu opera house, the *Peninsular* is a Modernista gem. Built on the site of a former convent, it is one of the oldest hotels in Barcelona, currently managed by the young, humorous offspring of the original owners. Rooms are simple and clean, although not all have their own bathroom facilities. Full of interesting architectural detail, such as the dining room's Moorish-inspired arches, the real *pièce de résistance* is the wonderful interior balcony. Adorned with hanging plants and wicker tables and chairs, it has a serene, almost Oriental atmosphere. Booking well in advance (approximately three months) is almost always necessary.
Carrer Sant Pau 34–36
Tel: (93) 302 3138. Fax: (93) 412 3699.
Price: From €65 (including breakfast and IVA).

Other Recommendations

Hotel España

Designed by one of the leading lights of the Modernista school of architects, Domenèch i Muntaner, and once patronised by the likes of Dalí, the two-star *España* enjoys a privileged location close to La Rambla and the Liceu. Recently renovated, some rooms are superior to others but major compensations include Ramón Casa's striking mural depicting underwater scenes and the elaborate craftsmanship in the high Catalan dining room. The 90 bedrooms are fully equipped; private rooms and a patio garden for meetings and celebrations are also available. It is also one of the few central establishments with parking facilities.
Carrer Sant Pau 9–11
Tel: (93) 318 1758. Fax: (93) 317 1134.
Price: From €80 (including breakfast and IVA).

Hotel Oriente

Situated on the bustling thoroughfare of La Rambla, the three-star *Oriente* is one of Barcelona's original 'grand' hotels. Constructed in 1842 on the site of a Franciscan monastery, the 142-room hotel was once the haunt of the great and the good, counting Maria Callas, Toscanini and Errol Flynn among its illustrious guests. Although recent renovations are perhaps a tad

characterless, the grand dining room and arched ballroom (now a lounge) are still potently redolent of its glorious heyday. Today, the hotel is largely aimed at the business traveller and offers extensive support facilities and 12- and 24-hour 'convention packages'.
La Rambla 45–47
Tel: (93) 302 2558. Fax: (93) 412 3819.
E-mail: horiente@husa.es
Website: www.husa.es
Price: From €131.

RESTAURANTS

The selected restaurants have been divided into five categories: Gastronomic, Business, Trendy, Budget and Personal Recommendations. The restaurants are listed alphabetically within these different categories, which serve as guidelines rather than absolute definitions of the establishments.
Spanish VAT (IVA) is 7% and is included in all menu prices. Where this is not the case, it will be stated that prices are exclusive of IVA.
Tipping is not a widespread practice in Barcelona but, of course, should diners wish to leave a gratuity, it is always appreciated. In the upscale restaurants, it is customary to leave around €3. Occasionally, a cover charge of approximately €1 is added to the bill but the menu should mention this.
The prices quoted below are for an average three-course meal for one person and for a bottle of house wine or cheapest equivalent; they include IVA but not tip.

Gastronomic

Agut d'Avignon

Tucked away in a tiny street in the atmospheric Barri Gòtic, *Agut d'Avignon* is the creation of ex-lawyer and pharmacist Ramón Cabau. Known for his impeccable taste, the restaurant is a haven for writers, artists and politicians; it has attracted diners such as Miró and Yves Montand. Rustic yet elegant, employing top-quality produce and a first-rate wine list, it is evident why this is so. The menu is seasonal, offering regional specialities and such adventurous dishes as partridge pâté and roast wild boar with raspberry sauce.
Carrer de la Trinitat 3/Avinyo 8
Tel: (93) 302 6034. Fax: (93) 302 5318.
Website: www.virtualsd.es/agutdavignon
Price: €40. Wine: €10.

Ca l'Isidre

Run by the Gironés i Salvó family for over 25 years, *Ca l'Isidre* is an intimate restaurant boasting King Juan Carlos among its regular clientele. Isidre Gironés presides over the excellent wine list and exquisite food, personally selecting the best ingredients at the nearby La Boqueria market to conjure up timeless dishes, including duck liver pâté with figs, stuffed artichokes or saddle of lamb. The cosy dining room is a charming 'home from home', thanks to his wife, Montse. Daughter Núria is an excellent *patisera*, whose desserts provide a perfect finale to chef César Pastor's seasonal Catalan dishes. Reservations essential.
Carrer Les Flors 12
Tel: (93) 441 1139. Fax: (93) 442 5271.
Price: €80. Wine: €12.

El Racó de Can Fabes

With three Michelin stars and numerous other awards, *El Racó* is idyllically situated near Montseny, an area of outstanding natural beauty, approximately 50km (32 miles) from Barcelona. Proprietor and chef Santi Santamaria is open, friendly and passionate about Catalan food. His quality-based, customer-orientated philosophy ensures that a visit to his rustic-style restaurant is an exceptional experience. Inspired by products from the sea to the mountains, dishes range from roast kid with sage to prawn ravioli in wild mushroom oil. *Postres* (desserts), such as mango and plum 'lasagne', are deliciously inventive.

Hotel Catalunya Plaza

Photo: Spanish National Tourist Office

Carrer Sant Joan 6, Sant Celoni (A7 from Barcelona, exit 7 for Sant Celoni)
Tel: (93) 867 2851. Fax: (93) 867 3861.
E-mail: canfabes@canfabes.com
Website: www.racocanfabes.com
Price: €90. Wine: €18.

Gaig

Gaig started out as a small family tavern specialising in home cooking in the northern *barrio* of Horta in the 1800s. More than a century later, it is one of the city's top restaurants and the recipient of many awards. Master chef Carles Gaig is at the helm, creating brilliant and innovative versions of old recipes, such as pheasant with plums, *canelones* with truffle sauce and mango ravioli, to name but a few. The wine list is equally impressive. Carles' wife, Fina, presides over the light, modern dining room.
Passeig Maragall 402
Tel: (93) 429 1017.
Price: €60. Wine: €17.

Jean-Luc Figueras

Housed in the former atelier of fashion designer Balanciaga, the elegant, classically Catalan surroundings – all polished wood, lamps and tiled floors – are almost as outstanding as the food. Frenchman Jean-Luc Figueras creates modern, original dishes, such as fried prawn and ginger pasta in mustard and mango sauce, without submitting to the demands of food fads or egoism. The menu tends to lean towards seafood but meat dishes are also included. Master *patisero* Jordi Butrón's sublime puddings are outstanding.
Carrer Santa Teresa 10
Tel: (93) 415 2877.
Price: €55. Wine: €20.

Business

Botafumeiro

Founded in 1973, by Galician José Ramon Neira, in the bohemian *barrio* of Gràcia, *Botafumeiro* has acquired a solid reputation as one of Barcelona's best seafood restaurants, specialising in *mariscos* (lobster, langoustines and oysters), as well as fish and meat stews. The Baroque-inspired dining room is spacious and comfortable, decorated in peachy shades set off by sparkling chandeliers and oil paintings. For the romantic, singers and guitarists are on hand for serenading. An impressive team can help plan business dinners in opulent private dining rooms.
Carrer Gran de Gràcia 81
Tel: (93) 218 4230. Fax: (93) 415 5848.
Price: €40. Wine: €14.

Negro

Conveniently located in the heart of the city's financial district, *Negro* encapsulates the 'less is more' philosophy embraced by the new wave of Barcelona restaurateurs. Fashionably informal and stylishly decorated in minimalist black and white, it is a world away from the somewhat 'folksy', traditional Catalan restaurants. Negro offers an eclectic fusion of Mediterranean and Oriental cuisine, featuring sushi, risotto and unusual salads, served in a cool, cosmopolitan atmosphere. There is live music in the basement on Thursday nights and at the weekend.
Avinguda Diagonal 640 (Caja Madrid Building)
Tel: (93) 405 9444.
Price: €30. Wine: €6.

Neichel

Neichel is one of Barcelona's top restaurants, attracting two Michelin stars and panoply of plaudits for proprietor and chef Jean-Louis Neichel's highly original Alsace–Catalan cuisine. Consommé of black truffles, deer in red wine and honey and lavender ice cream are but a few of the opulent treats to savour. Located in the affluent *barrio* of Pedralbes, the design is modern and the ambience relaxing. The cool cream and white dining room is tasteful and understated and overlooks a colourful Mediterranean garden.
Carrer Beltrán i Rózpide 1–5 (before Avinguda Pedralbes)
Tel: (93) 203 8408. Fax: (93) 205 6369.
E-mail: neichel@relaischateaux.com
Website: www.relaischateaux.fr/neichel
Price: €60. Wine: €12.

Ruccula

Housed in the heart of the spanking new, ultra-smart World Trade Center, *Ruccula* has rapidly become a favourite among the Catalan capital's rich and glamorous. The reasonably priced food, prepared by top-class chefs, is Catalan-based with an ingenious Italian–Asiatic twist. A generous selection of dishes includes fresh pasta salad with langoustines in pesto or chicken yakitori with teriyaki sauce. Designed to resemble a magnificent floating vessel, the WTC is surrounded by sparkling sea views and makes for a luxurious setting.
World Trade Center, Port de Barcelona
Tel: (93) 508 8268. Fax: (93) 508 8269.
Price: €30. Wine: €9.20.

Via Veneto

Since opening in the late 1960s, *Via Veneto* has won a host of awards for its high-class Catalan cuisine and exceptional wines. Dishes include exquisite fish soup, stuffed wild partridge or potatoes with purée of *butifarra* sausage. Located near the business district of Diagonal, the restaurant contains some of the best private dining rooms in Barcelona, accommodating from four to 100 diners. With its pretty Belle Epoque style, wonderful food and welcoming staff, it is little wonder that it became one of Dalí's regular haunts. A mirror, signed by the painter, is on display.
Carrer Ganduxer 10–12
Tel: (93) 200 7244. Fax: (93) 201 6095.
Price: €65. Wine: €20.

Trendy

Arc Café

A recent arrival on the Barcelona scene, *Arc Café* is a 'gastrobar' run by German duo Thomas and Willi. Hearty Mediterranean, Caribbean and Asian-influenced dishes, such as chicken curry salad and sublime spicy veggie burgers, are prepared in the spotless open-plan kitchen, amid warm, softly lit surroundings and a backdrop of mellow sounds. Tending towards the vegetarian, there is nevertheless a good selection of meat dishes too. Its location in a narrow, picturesque street near Plaça Reial makes it an ideal pre-club dinner venue.
Carrer Carabassa 19
Tel: (93) 302 5204.
Price: €15. Wine: €6.

El Racó d'en Baltà

A favourite among hip young Catalans, this design-led restaurant cleverly avoids the 'design over substance'

cliché. This is because it combines a modern approach to traditional dishes – such as meatballs with cuttlefish, fish mousse or *turrón* ice cream – with low prices, a decent wine list and a fascinating array of bizarre creations by British artist, Steve Foster. The upstairs dining room is a relaxing cocoon of gentle greens punctuated with eccentric odds and ends.
Carrer Aribau 125
Tel: (93) 453 1044.
Price: €15. Wine: €7.

Mama Café

Microwaves and processed or tinned foods are strictly prohibited in this stylish, fun vegetarian café-restaurant located in the Raval district, just off La Rambla. Using only the freshest ingredients, a range of innovative dishes, such as melon *gazpacho*, are prepared daily. The use of bold, rainbow colours, recycled materials and laid-back sounds creates a happy and informal atmosphere.
Carrer Doctor Dou 10
Tel: (93) 301 2940.
Price: €15. Wine: €5.

Sikkim

Inspired by their travels to India, the owners have transformed this former grocery into a high temple of exotica, complete with an abundance of candles, Buddhas, wafting incense and rich, mood-enhancing colours. The food is nevertheless Mediterranean, albeit complimented by ingredients from further afield, such as mangoes and yukka. *Sikkim* caters handsomely for vegetarians and carnivores alike, with a decent range of dishes including roast shark, vegetable risottos and homely cheesecakes.
Plaça Comercial 1
Tel: (93) 268 4313.
Price: €25. Wine: €6.

Vildsvin

Urban Barcelona meets old Czechoslovakia in this chic, fusion-inspired *cerveceria* situated near the Generalitat, where modern furnishings and original 19th-century features are stylishly juxtaposed to pleasing effect. The menu is an intriguing mix of Eastern European dishes, such as Hungarian goulash and traditional Spanish *platos* and tapas. A wide range of beers and wines are also available.
Carrer Ferran 38
Tel: (93) 317 9407.
Price: €20. Wine: €7.

Budget

Cantina Machito

Even though the decor verges towards the unsophisticated, with its riotous colours and abundance of Mexican kitsch, the food here is authentic and surprisingly good. Many of the ingredients are imported from Mexico and lovingly prepared by the Mexican-born chef. Standards, such as margaritas, tacos and guacamole, make an appearance, as do unusual puddings, such as lime and tequila mousse.
Carrer Torrijos 47
Tel: (93) 217 3414.
Price: €10. Wine: €5.

Fil Manila

A simple, homely restaurant overlooking a quiet square near Plaça de Catalunya, *Fil Manila* –

Barcelona's only Filipino restaurant – offers excellent value for money. The choice of dishes is vast, with main courses starting at around €4. In addition to meat and fish, there are some appetising coconut milk curries to be had and uncomplicated but mouthwatering puddings, such as fried banana.
Carrer Ramelleres 3
Tel: (93) 318 6487.
Price: €10. Unlicensed.

Habibi

Of the growing number of Lebanese restaurants in Barcelona, *Habibi* is one of the best. A world away from the falafel and kebab brigade, the diverse menu caters for carnivores and vegetarians alike, including excellent houmous and other savoury dips, spicy rice dishes and sweet, succulent Arab puddings to finish. Considering that only organic produce is used, the value for money is almost astonishing.
Carrer Gran de Gràcia 7
Tel: (93) 217 9545.
Price: €10. Wine: €5.

La Fonda

Part of a highly successful, upmarket chain, *La Fonda* offers Catalan classics – such as *butifarra* sausage with haricot beans, or the national dessert, *crema catalana* – in well-designed, attractive surroundings. An abundance of plants, wood and a gallery create a light and spacious atmosphere. The restaurant is very popular, especially at lunchtime, so booking is essential. *Les Quince Nits*, part of the same chain, is just around the corner.
Carrer Escudellers 10
Tel: (93) 301 7515.
Price: €15. Wine: €6.
Les Quince Nits
Plaça Reial 6
Tel: (93) 317 3075.

La Habana Vieja

Retro decor and a plethora of exotic cocktails evoke the exuberant spirit of old Havana in this atmospheric Cuban restaurant, situated in a narrow *passeig* near the Picasso Museum. A feast of dishes – such as shredded beef, coconut and cheese pudding, and fried banana – make for a lively and inexpensive dinner. Cocktails start at just €2.
Carrer Banys Vells 2
Tel: (93) 268 2504.
Price: €15. Wine: €6.

Personal Recommendations

El Convent

El Convent is a sumptuously decorated fin-de-siècle-style restaurant, occupying four storeys of an 18th-century house in a minute street behind La Boqueria market. Individually decorated private rooms are available in addition to the attractive public dining areas. An extensive menu combines *cocina Catalana* and international cuisine, with dishes such as chicken with orange or cod with garlic mousse. Inexpensive group menus start at under €12 per head and include homemade puddings, such as the ubiquitous crème caramel-like 'flan'.
Carrer Jerusalem 3
Tel: (93) 317 1052. Fax: (93) 302 3112.
E-mail: rbmesa@softly.es
Website: www.rbmesa.com/convent.htm
Price: €20. Wine: €5.

Hotel Ritz swimming pool

El Pla de la Garsa

Tucked away amid a tangle of medieval streets near the Picasso Museum, this former dairy and stables has been converted into a cosy, bohemian retreat, retaining many of its original 16th-century features. Antique tiles, an old spiral staircase and low lamps create an agreeable ambience in which to enjoy the wide selection of dishes, high-quality cheeses, pâtés and delicious puddings, such as caramelised figs.
Carrer Assaonadors 13
Tel: (93) 315 2413.
Price: €15. Wine: €6.

Euskal Etxea

Otherwise known as the *Basque Cultural Centre*, some of the best tapas in town are to be had in *Euskal Etxea*. Situated in an idyllic tiny square near the Picasso Museum and the wondrous church of Santa Maria del Mar, the restaurant is an atmospheric bar offering a huge variety of tapas, ranging from the most simple to the most intricate creations. Tapas appear around noon and again around 1900, so the best choice is to be had early.
Placeta Montcada 1–3
Tel: (93) 310 2185.
Price: €10. Wine: €5.

Laurak

Specialising in Basque cuisine, reputedly the best in Spain, *Laurak* is an un-stuffy, top-notch restaurant located near Avinguda Diagonal. The set menus, such as the €17 lunch menu, are amazing value, featuring modern versions of traditional Basque dishes, such as *piquillo* peppers stuffed with salt cod. Extraordinarily creative desserts include cheese mousse with sweet herb syrup. The decor is low-key, as is the friendly and attentive service.
Carrer La Granada del Penedès 14–16
Tel: (93) 218 7165.
Price: €40. Wine: €15.

Set Portes

The building housing *Set Portes* is a national monument and has the distinction of forming the backdrop to the first photograph ever taken in Spain, in 1840. Past diners have included kings, politicians and an array of famous names from Alexander Fleming to Ava Gardner. The large dining room is traditionally Catalan, as are the individually decorated private rooms seating two to 80 diners. Its Old World charm and legendary paella, *zarzuela* (fish stew), *fideuà* (seafood and spaghettini) maintain its status as one of Barcelona's favourite restaurants.
Passeig Isabel II 14
Tel: (93) 319 3033 *or* 2950. Fax (93) 319 3046.
E-mail: admon@setportes.com
Website: www.setportes.com
Price: €25. Wine: €8.

ENTERTAINMENT

Nightlife

Barcelona is increasingly gaining a reputation as one of Europe's great party cities and deservedly so. Things may start slowly with some food and a few drinks after siesta finishes (at approximately 1700) but they soon gather pace and by 2300 the city is buzzing. Friday and Saturday nights are when the city is at its liveliest, although the drinking and dancing keeps going throughout the week. Bars are usually open until 0200 or 0300, while clubs and discos keep going until 0500 or 0600. The legal drinking age in Barcelona is 16 years and the price of tipple ranges from €1 for a small beer or glass of wine to €4 for something stronger, such as a rum and coke, depending also on the type of establishment.
Port Olímpic is particularly buzzing on summer nights, as is *Port Vell*, where the *Maremagnum* shopping complex bizarrely metamorphoses into a nefarious collage of cafés, bars and nightclubs, open late into the night. In the last few years, *bars modernos* with music and designer decor have been popular with a young ultra-hip clientele across the city. The trend is to dress quite smartly when going out in Barcelona.

Photo: Spanish National Tourist Office

Photo: Katharine Bowerman

Olympic Stadium

Available in hostels, the free seasonal guide, *See Barcelona* (website: www.seebarcelona.com), and the *Guía del Ocio* booklet (website: www.guiadelocio.com), available from newsagents and newspaper stands, both provide information on nightlife in Barcelona.

Bars

Xampanyerías (champagne bars) serving sparkling Catalan wine (*cava*) are a speciality of the city. Good places for *cava* include *La Bodegueta del Xampú*, Gran Via de les Corts Catalanes 702, *Xampanyeria Casablanca*, Carrer Bonavista 6, and *El Xampanyet*, Carrer Montcada 22. The latter also serves cider and tapas, in vibrant surroundings. *Bar Pastís*, Carrer Santa Mònica, has the honour of counting Picasso among its former regulars. The artist's other hangout was *El Quatre Gats*, Carrer Montsió 3, a Modernista bar with good beer and live music from 2100. The original menu, designed by Picasso, is on show in the *Museu Picasso* (see *Key Attractions*). *L'Ovella Negra*, Carrer Sitges 5, is as much a favourite with the international backpacker set as it is with local students. *Bar Marsella*, Carrer de Sant Pau 65, is the place to imbibe an *absenta*, a close relative of absinthe. For the style conscious, some of the city's coolest haunts include the spectacular *Torres de Ávila*, Avinguda Marquès de Comillas, Poble Espanyol, on Montjuïc, the perennially stylish *Dry Martini*, Carrer Aribau 162–165, *Ideal Cocktail Bar*, Carrer Aribau 89, and *Mas i Mas*, Carrer Maria Cubi 199. *Mirablau*, Plaça Doctor Andreu, at the foot of the Tibidabo funicular, is especially romantic, with its sweeping views of the city, while popular *Berimbau*, Passeig del Born 17, serves up good cocktails to a background of Brazilian rhythms.

Casinos

Gran Casino de Barcelona, Carrer de la Marina 19–21 (website: www.casino-barcelona.com), is open daily 1300–0500. Visitors must be 18 years or over and carry a passport or driving licence. A smart dress code applies.

Clubs

Barcelona's most beautiful people can be found in *Up And Down*, Carrer Numància 179, the city's most exclusive nightclub, while a younger, more down-to-

earth crowd boogie to the latest sounds at *Bikini*, Carrer Deu i Mata 105. The split-level *Moog Club*, Arc del Teatre 3, in the Chinese Quarter, offers the best of European techno and hosts big international DJs. *Salsitas*, Carrer Nou de la Rambla 22, with a well-designed bar, restaurant and a dancefloor, is one of the city's trendiest hotspots, while stylish *Torres de Ávila*, Avinguda Marquès de Comillas, Poble Espanyol, has long been celebrated for its all-night trance-techno discos on summer weekends. Popular open-air haunts include *La Terrazza*, Avinguda Montanyans – open in the summer months only. *Punto BCN*, Carrer Muntaner 63, is a popular gay club.

For flamenco dancing, try *Tablao Flamenco Cordobes*, La Rambla 35, *Los Tarantos*, Plaça Reial 17, or *Tablao del Carmen*, Arcs 9, Poble Espanyol. *La Paloma*, Carrer Tigre 27, is a beautiful dancehall dating from the turn of the century. The band plays to an enthusiastic crowd, with a menu of pasa doble, tango, salsa, flamenco and more.

Live Music

Large-scale rock and pop concerts by international stars can be heard at the *Palau Sant Jordi*, Passeig Olímpic 5–7, the *Estadi Olímpic*, Montjuïc, and *Camp Nou*, Avinguda de Joan XXII. The best mid-sized venue is *Zeleste*, Carrer Almogàvers 122, in Poble Nou, which hosts Spanish and international pop and rock groups. *Harlem Jazz Club*, Carrer Comtesa de Sobradiel 8, hosts jazz and other live music, daily until 0400. *Jamboree*, Plaça Reial 17, is a long-standing and popular jazz, blues and funk venue, next door to *Los Tarantos* (see *Clubs* above). Traditional folk music from Catalonia, Spain and the rest of Europe is on offer at the *Centre Artesà Tradicionarius*, Travessera de Sant Antoni 6–8, which hosts concerts on Thursday and Friday evenings.

Sport

The 1992 Olympics turned the sporting spotlight of the world onto Barcelona. Most of the action took place on Montjuïc, which gained a new sports stadium, a marina and several swimming pools. Major

annual sporting events in the city include the Barcelona marathon, which takes place in March, the Conde de Godó Trophy tennis tournament in April, and the Formula One Grand Prix, held in Montmeló every May.

Football is ever popular. The local football team, *Fútbol Club Barcelona* (*Barça*), Avinguda Arístides Maillol 12–18 (tel: (93) 496 3600; fax: (93) 411 2219; website: www.fcbarcelona.com), is one of the most successful teams in Europe. The club plays in the massive *Camp Nou* stadium, Avinguda de Joan XXII (tel: (93) 496 3702, for tickets), which also houses a football museum. For visitors who want to break into a sweat themselves, the city authorities have a sports information service (tel: (93) 402 3000) with details of city-run sports centres and facilities. The office is located at Avinguda de l'Estadi 30–40 and is open Monday to Friday 0800–1430 and Monday to Thursday 1600–1815.

Bullfighting

Bullfights are held on Sundays between April and September at the *Monumental* bullring, Gran Via de les Corts Catalanes 749. There is also a museum about the sport at the ring. The official ticket office is at Carrer Muntaner 24 (tel: (93) 453 3821) and fights cost from €15 to €75.

Fitness Centres

There is a fitness centre, which is open to the public, at the *Piscinas Bernat Picornell*, Avinguda de l'Estadi 30–40, on Montjuïc (tel: (93) 423 4041), open Monday to Friday 0700–2400, Saturday 0700–2100 and Sunday 0730–1430.

Golf

There are several golf clubs in the Barcelona area, which are open to non-members. *Real Club de Golf 'El Prat'*, Apartado de Correos 10, El Prat de Llobregat (tel: (93) 379 0278; fax: (93) 370 5102), is a first-rate 36-hole course located near the airport, open to members of a federated club only. The course has hosted the Spanish Open on numerous occasions and is only open to members of a federated club. *Club de Golf Sant Cugat*, in the suburb of Sant Cugat del Valles (tel: (93) 674 3908; fax: (93) 675 5152), some 20km (12 miles) northwest of Barcelona, is a 21-hole course. Visiting players must provide all their own equipment but are entitled to use the club's leisure facilities on payment of the green fee of €65.

Sailing

There are numerous sailing clubs based in Barcelona and several regattas take place during the spring and summer. Further information is available from the *Centre Municipal de Vela*, Moll de Gregal, Port Olímpic (tel: (93) 222 1499).

Swimming

There are seven beaches in the immediate vicinity of Barcelona. Water quality is tested regularly but it is still advisable for bathers to look before they leap into the waves. *Platja de Sant Sebastià* is a nudist beach. At the other beaches, topless bathing is common.

If the beaches do not appeal, the *Club de Natació Atlètic Barceloneta*, Plaça del Mar (tel: (93) 221 0010), has three indoor pools. Alternatively, visitors can relive the Olympic Games in the *Piscines Bernat Picornell*, Avinguda de l'Estadi 30–40, on Montjuïc (tel: (93) 423 4041), open daily 0700–2400. There are also numerous city-run swimming pools; the sports information service (see above) can provide details.

Tennis

Built for the Olympics, the *Centre Municipal de Tennis Vall d'Hebron*, Passeig de la Vall d'Hebron 178 (tel: (93) 427 6500), has several clay courts, which are now open to the public. However, racquets and balls are not provided.

Shopping

Shopping is one of Barcelona's greatest attractions, with a bountiful five-kilometre (three-mile) shopping strip, all the way from the water's edge at Port Vell right up La Rambla to Diagnol. International chains, designer shops and modern department stores can be found in the area around Plaça de Catalunya, Passeig de Gràcia and along Avinguda Diagonal. The most famous shop in the city is the imposing *El Corte Inglés*, on Plaça de Catalunya – part of a national chain, generally considered to be Spain's leading department stores. La Rambla and the Barri Gòtic are the places for tourists to hunt for souvenirs.

A visit to *La Boqueria* market, officially *Mercat de Sant Josep*, off Rambla Sant Josep, is an unmissable experience. The market is open Monday to Saturday 0800–2000, for the sale of fresh fish, meat, vegetables and dairy products. Other food markets for keen shoppers to try are *Concepció*, Carrer Aragó, *Ninot*, Carrer Mallorca, and the *Gastronomic Fair*, which takes place in Plaça del Pi, on the first and third Friday, Saturday and Sunday of the month. For antiques and curios, the *Els Encants* market is held on Plaça de les Glories, every Monday, Wednesday, Friday and Saturday from 0900–1900. Another antiques market is held on Plaça Nova every Thursday (except in August). Representative gifts include Catalan black pottery, handwoven baskets or Barcelona lace.

In recent years, a number of urban-chic orientated fashion stores have opened in the city centre. *Camden Town*, Carrer Hospital 4, has all the latest fashion, as well as some more esoteric PVC and 'erotic' creations. *Jean Pierre Bua*, Avinguda Diagonal 469, is the more conventionally trendy home of designer names such as Gaultier and Miyake.

Shops open at 0900 or 1000 and close again for an extended lunch, between 1330 and 1600 or 1700. In the evening, shops shut at 2000 or 2030. Large department stores do not generally close for lunch. All shops are open on Saturday afternoons but are closed all day on Sunday. IVA (value added tax) of 7% is charged on all goods and services in Spain. Upon departure, visitors from outside the EU, who have been in the EU for less than 180 days, can get an IVA refund from the airport, on goods worth €90 or more. Tax return forms are available from shops on request. IVA on services is not refundable.

Culture

Barcelona's reputation as a world centre for art, architecture and design is growing yearly, with a plethora of cultural activities on offer. As if it needed confirming, in 1999, the entire city was awarded a Royal Gold Medal for Architecture, from the Royal Institute of British Architects. The seminal ghosts of such artistic luminaries as Antoni Gaudí, Pablo Picasso, Joan Miró and Antoni Tàpies permeate

Barcelona's cultural scene. Barcelona is also a showcase for homegrown Catalan traditions – dozens of festivals, religious holidays and special occasions are celebrated in the city each year.

The *Guía del Ocio* booklet, available from newsagents and newspaper stands, provides information on cultural and other events in the city, as well as contact details for ticket agencies. The free seasonal guide, *See Barcelona*, which is available in hostels, is also helpful. Alternatively, there is a cultural information desk at *Palau de la Virrena*, La Rambla 99 (tel: (93) 301 7775). *Caixa Catalunya* run the central ticket agency, *Entrada* (tel: (902) 101 212; website: www.telentrada.com).

Music

Homegrown stars include the cellist Pablo Casals and the international opera singers Josep Carreras and Montserrat Caballé. The latter celebrated her native city in a highly theatrical duet (*Barcelona*) with the late Freddie Mercury of Queen. The main concert hall is the *Palau de la Música Catalana*, Carrer Sant Francesc de Paula 2 (tel: (93) 295 7200; fax: (93) 295 7210; website: www.palaumusica.org). A UNESCO World Heritage building and one of the most extravagant

La Sagrada Família

Photo: Spanish National Tourist Office

music venues in the world, Sunday concerts here are a Barcelona institution. It was designed by Modernista architect Domènech i Montaner as a showcase for the Catalan renaissance and was the main venue for the *Orquesta Sinfónica de Barcelona y Nacional de Catalunya* (website: www.obc.es), until they relocated to *L'Auditori*, Carrera Lepant 150 (tel: (93) 247 9300; fax: (93) 247 9301; e-mail: obc@auditori.org), in 1999. There are free musical events in the city hall's *Saló de Cent*, Rambla de Catalunya 2–4 (tel: (93) 317 2177), on Plaça del Rei, on Thursday at 2000, as well as in various beautiful buildings around the city. Barcelona's opera house, the stunning *Gran Teatre del Liceu*, La Rambla 51–59 (tel: (93) 485 9900; fax: (93) 485 9918; website: www.liceubarcelona.com), was tragically destroyed by fire – for the third time – in 1994. Reconstruction was completed in summer 1999.

Theatre

Barcelona's theatre scene does not enjoy the same international reputation as Madrid's does, however, what it lacks in literary authority, it makes up for in the visual and audio spectacle of its performances. Peformances are lively and well attended and include work by regional and international playwrights. Popular venues include *Teatre Lliure*, Carrer Montseny 47, Gràcia (tel: (93) 218 9251; website: www.teatrelliure.com), *Teatre Tívoli*, Carrer Casp 8 (tel: (93) 412 2063), and *Teatre Poliorama*, La Rambla 115 (tel: (93) 317 7599). A varied programme of drama, music and dance is on offer at *Teatre Nacional de Catalunya*, Plaça de les Arts 1 (tel: (93) 306 5700; fax: (93) 306 5713; e-mail: info@tnc.es; website: www.tnc.es), and *El Mercat de les Flors*, Carrer Lleida 59 (tel: (93) 426 1875).

Music-hall-style shows are also very popular in Barcelona; the *Barcelona City Hall*, Rambla de Catalunya 2–4 (tel: (93) 317 2177), is the main venue.

Dance

The city's main venue for ballet and contemporary dance is the *L'Espai de Dansa i Música de la Generalitat de Catalunya* – referred to simply as *L'Espai* – Travessera de Gràcia 63 (tel: (93) 414 3133; e-mail: espai@qrz.net; website: www.gencat.es). A more relaxed atmosphere is in evidence on Sunday mornings, in the square in front of *Catedral de la Seu*, Plaça de la Seu, when locals flock to watch and participate in the local dance – the *sardana*.

Film

There are a growing number of cinemas that show foreign-language films in the original language, with Spanish subtitles. The 15-screen *Icaria Yelmo Cineplex*, Carrer Salvador Espriu 61, Port Olímpic (tel: (93) 221 7585), and the more convenient one at *Maremagnum*, Port Vell (tel: (902) 333 231), are two of several multi-screen cinemas in the city. There are no notable arthouse cinemas in Barcelona.

Cultural Events

General information on cultural events can be obtained from the *Palau de Congressos*, Avinguda Reina Maria Cristina 1 (tel: (93) 233 2372). The *Grec-Barcelona* festival (tel: (93) 301 7775; website: www.grec.bcn.es), which takes place every summer (June to August), is the focus of the city's cultural life. Theatre, music and dance are performed at venues throughout the city, including the open-air auditoria at *Teatre Grec*, on Montjuïc, and *Convent de Sant Augustí*. October and November see the annual *Festival Internacional de Jazz*, run by *The Project* (tel: (93) 481 7040; fax: (93) 481 4070). Traditional festivities in honour of Sant Jordi (St George) take

Bird's eye view of Eixample district

place on 23 April and again on the night of 23 June, for the *Verbena de Sant Joan* (St John), when bonfires and fireworks illuminate the city. There are two major celebrations in early autumn – *Diada Nacional de Catalunya* (Catalonia National Day), on 11 September, and the spectacular *Fiesta de la Mercé*, in honour of the patron saint of Barcelona, on 24 September. Festivities for the latter include parades, traditional dancing, sporting events and religious celebrations. Human pyramids, known as *castellers*, are constructed in the streets.

Literary Notes

La Ciudad de los Prodigios or *City of Marvels* (1990) by Eduardo Mendoza fictionalises the life of the city, between its two international exhibitions in 1888 and 1929. *Year of the Flood* (1996), by the same author, is set in Barcelona in the 1950s. *La Plaça del Diamant* or *The Time of the Doves* (1962) by Mercè Rodoreda is the best-known Catalan novel and traces the life of Colometa, through the turmoil of the Spanish Civil War. Manuel Vazquez Montalban's detective character, Pepe Carvalho, is a Barcelona native and the city is the setting for the crime novels in which he stars. *Homage to Catalonia* (1937) by George Orwell is the author's first-hand observations of the Spanish revolution in the region. More recently, Colm Toibin's *The South* (1990) is a startling first novel, which depicts the struggles of an Irish woman looking for a new life in Barcelona. Joan Maragall is the region's most celebrated poet.

SPECIAL EVENTS

Epiphany, parades in the streets, 6 Jan, throughout the city
Barcelona Marathon, Mar, throughout the city
Festes de Sant Medir, religious festival with parade and choral singing, 3 Mar, Grácia and various other venues
Trofeo Conde de Godó de Tennis, tennis championship, Apr, Reial Club de Tennis Barcelona
Formula One Grand Prix, May, Circuit de Catalunya, Montmeló
Holy Week festivities, Mar/Apr, various venues
Diade de Sant Jordi (St George's Day), St George book and rose festival, 23 Apr, La Rambla and various venues
Corpus Christi, processions and *L'Ou com Balla* (the dancing egg), May/Jun, various venues
Pasqua Granada, local religious holiday, Jun, throughout the city
Verbena de Sant Joan (St John's Day), bonfires and fireworks, 23 Jun, throughout the city
Fest de Grec-Barcelona, month-long festival celebrating both international and national performing arts (website: www.grec.bcn.es), mid-Jun–mid-July, various venues
Festes de Sant Jaume, religious festival, 25 Jul, throughout the city
Diade Nacional de Catalunya (Catalonia National Day), public holiday, 11 Sep, throughout the city
Fiesta de la Mercé, parades, dancing and sporting events, 24 Sep, various venues
Festival Internacional de Jazz (International Jazz Festival), Oct–Nov, various venues
Fiesta de Santa Llúcia, Christmas fairs, 13 Dec, Plaça de la Seu, Plaça Sant Jaume and various other venues
Christmas, family celebrations, 24–25 Dec, throughout the city

BERLIN

After a fifty-year lull, Berlin is back – back as the capital of a reunified Germany and back as one of Europe's greatest cities. After World War II, Berlin was a crippled pawn, sandwiched between East and West, with a wall deeply dividing the two halves – both physically and spiritually. The northeastern German city even suffered the ignominy of losing its capital status, as the West German government fled to Bonn. Today, the Cold War and the iconic events of November 1989, which saw the Berlin Wall torn to pieces by those whom it had oppressed for so long, are starting to seem like a distant memory and all the talk in Berlin is of the future.

In the biggest construction project in Europe since World War II, a new Berlin has emerged from the forest of cranes dotting the no-man's land that was the divided city's dead heart. Potsdamer Platz is the most voluminous project but the most symbolic recent construction is at the Reichstag. British architect Lord Foster has rejuvenated the German parliament with an impressive glass dome that symbolises the new transparency in German politics – that of a nation with nothing to hide, which is attempting to distance itself from the ghosts of its past.

Coupled with this wave of new construction is a city laden with historical charm – from the old streets of East Berlin, which are slowly being restored after remaining unchanged for 50 years, through to the grand architecture of Museumsinsel and Unter den Linden, and the green lung of the Tiergarten Park. Tourism is on the rise, as visitors come to savour the intoxicating mix of old and new. Big business, too, is booming, as government bodies flock back from Bonn and relocate in the capital, along with investment from many other parts of the country and from all over Europe. Key industries, such as electronics, manufacturing and information technology, reflect the hopes for a brighter future for Berlin.

Contrary to the usual clichés about Germany, Berlin is a city with a laid-back attitude and some of the liveliest nightlife in Europe. In Berlin today, there is everything from authentic beer halls and old Soviet era haunts right through to buzzing style bars and Latino nightclubs. Berlin's climate is equally eclectic, with hot summer days giving way to occasionally freezing temperatures during the long grey winter. Today's quintessential Berlin experience is to laze through a summer day in the Tiergarten with the rabble of construction just out of earshot, sipping on a chilled Pilsner beer, while witnessing a city reinventing itself as one of Europe's finest capitals.

Photo: Corel

Berlin Cathedral

TRAVEL

Getting There By Air

Berlin-Tegel (Otto Lilienthal) (TXL)

Tel: (01805) 000 186 (charged at 12 cents per minute).

Website: www.berlin-airport.de

The airport is located in northwest Berlin, eight kilometres (five miles) from the city centre. Tegel primarily serves Western European destinations, handling flights from 36 scheduled airlines flying to 84 destinations and 26 charter airlines flying to 62 destinations.

Major airlines: *Lufthansa* (tel: (01803) 803 803 (24-hour call centre) *or* 000 074, (arrivals and departures); website: www.lufthansa.com) is Germany's principal airline. Other airlines flying to Tegel include *Air Berlin, Air France, Alitalia, Austrian Airlines, British Airways, CSA Czech Airlines, Deutsche BA, Iberia, KLM, LOT Polish Airlines, Malév, Olympic Airways* and *Turkish Airlines.* Two new low-cost airlines, *Germanwings* and *Hapag-Lloyd Express,* both provide frequent services from Berlin to Cologne/Bonn.

Airport facilities: The airport offers two snack bars, a bistro, a champagne bar and a restaurant. Other facilities include a post office, a bank/bureau de change, ATMs, a florist, newsagents, duty-free shops, left-luggage, baby-care rooms, 24-hour first aid, travel agents, tourist information and clothing shops. Car hire is available from *Avis, Budget, Europcar, Hertz, National* and *Sixt.*

NORTH SEA • DENMARK • BALTIC SEA

Rügen

Helgoland • Kiel • Rostock

Frisian Islands • Lübeck • Greifswald

Hamburg

Bremen

BERLIN

NETHS. • Hanover

Münster • Magdeburg • POLAND • *Oder*

Duisburg • Dortmund • *Harz* • Halle • *SAXONY*

Essen • Kassel • Erfurt • Leipzig

Düsseldorf

Cologne • *Weser*

Aachen • Bonn • **GERMANY** • Chemnitz • Dresden

BELG. • Frankfurt-am-Main

LUX. • Trier • *Rhine* • *CZECH REPUBLIC*

Saarbrücken • *Main* • Nuremberg

Stuttgart • *Black Forest* • *BAVARIA*

FRANCE • *Danube* • **Munich** •

L. Constance (Bodensee) • AUSTRIA

SWITZ.

200km
100mls
✈ international airport

Business facilities: The *LSG* conference centre (tel: (030) 4101 3316), located on the third floor, has four function rooms with a capacity of up to 150 people, as well as a media centre with photocopier, fax, computers with Internet access and printers. Secretarial and translation services can be arranged. The *GSS Airport Service Center* (tel: (030) 4101 3434), opposite gates nine and ten, provide fax services for public use.

There are also four business lounges in the airport, located in the Airport Gallery, above the main hall.

Transport to the city: The *JetExpressBus TXL,* operated by Berlin's public transport provider, *BVG* (see *Getting Around*), leaves the airport every 15 minutes daily 0600–2310, travelling to Potsdamer Platz, Friedrichstrasse and Unter den Linden (journey time – 20–25 minutes). The fare is €2.10. Bus 128 connects to the U6 line at Kurt-Schumacher-Platz, while bus 109 and express bus X9 depart every five to ten minutes daily 0500–2400 and connect to the U7 at Jakob-Kaiser-Platz, before continuing on to Bahnhof Zoo (journey time – 30 minutes on the X9 bus). Taxis are plentiful at the airport and there is a taxi rank immediately outside the arrivals hall. The fare into Berlin is approximately €15–20.

Berlin-Schönefeld (SXF)

Tel: (01805) 000 186 (charged at 12 cents per minute).

Website: www.berlin-airport.de

The airport is located in the southeast of the city, 18km (11 miles) and 22km (13.5 miles) from the Eastern and Western centres respectively. Schönefeld was the primary airport for East Berlin and now handles flights mainly to Eastern Europe and Asia, as well as many charter flights to summer destinations. Some 23 scheduled airlines fly to 53 destinations, while 41 chartered airlines fly to 59 destinations.

Major airlines: *Air Berlin* (tel: (01801) 737 800; website: www.airberlin.de) is the principal German airline operating from Schönefeld. Other airlines include *Aeroflot, Condor, El Al* and *Turkish Airlines.*

Airport facilities: The airport has a restaurant, bars, a florist, a post office, a bank/bureau de change, ATMs, newsagents, duty-free shop and first-aid facilities. Services available 24 hours a day include left-luggage, snack bar, nursery and hotel reservations. Car hire is available from *Avis, Budget, Europcar, Hertz* and *Sixt.*

Business facilities: As well as one business lounge in Terminal A, conference rooms are available at the *Konferenzzentrum Flughafen Berlin-Schönefeld GmbH* (tel: (030) 6091 2222), a ten-minute walk from the terminal. Fax facilities are available at special credit card telephones and at the information desk in Terminal A.

Transport to the city: The easiest way for visitors to get into the city is with the *AirportExpress Schönefeld* train, which is operated by *DB* (see *Getting There By Rail*) and runs every 30 minutes Monday to Friday 0510–0140, Saturday and Sunday 0540–0140. The train stops at four stations in East Berlin before terminating at Bahnhof Zoo (journey time – 30 minutes). The fare is €2.10. The airport station is located half a kilometre (0.3 miles) from the airport and there is a free shuttle bus connecting the two, which runs every ten minutes daily 0430–2330. The station is also served by S-Bahn trains 9 and 45, as well as some mainline and local rail services. Bus 171 connects the airport with the U7 U-Bahn line at Rudow. Taxis are available 24 hours a day and cost approximately €30–35 (journey time – 30 minutes).

Berlin-Tempelhof (THF)

Tel: (01805) 000 186 (charged at 12 cents per minute).

Website: www.berlin-airport.de

The airport is located in the south of the city, three kilometres (two miles) south of Potsdamer Platz. Activities are fairly moderate here, with 15 scheduled airlines serving 25 destinations and five charter airlines serving a total of nine destinations. Most

---

flights are on smaller jets to short-haul domestic and European destinations.

Major airlines: Germany's principal airline, *Lufthansa* (tel: (01803) 803 803 (24-hour call centre) *or* 000 074 (arrivals and departures); website: www.lufthansa.com), operates from Berlin-Tempelhof. Other airlines serving the airport include *City Air, Eurowings* and *Luxair.*

Airport facilities: The airport offers three lounges, snack bars, a florist, a bank/bureau de change, ATMs, newsagents, duty-free shop, left-luggage, first aid, hairdresser, baby-care room, tax refund office and travel agents. Car hire is available from *Avis, Europcar, Hertz, Budget, National, Sixt* and *Westfehling.*

Business facilities: There are a couple of small conference rooms and a 200-seat auditorium offered by *TAG Aviation* (tel: (030) 6951 3880) and *LSG* (tel: (030) 4101 3626). Fax facilities are available at special credit-card telephones.

Transport to the city: The airport is directly connected to Berlin's public transport system (see *Getting Around*), including the U-Bahn network on the U6 line (the station is Platz der Luftbrücke and not, as would be expected, Tempelhof), with quick connections to the city centre (journey time – 10–20 minutes). Bus 119 departs every ten minutes to the Ku'damm area, while buses 104, 184 and 341 (to Potsdamer Platz) also stop near the airport. Nightbuses N4 and N76 leave from Platz der Luftbrücke. Tickets cost €2.10. Taxis are available in front of the main hall for around €12.

Approximate flight times to Berlin: From London is 1 hour 45 minutes; from New York is 8 hours 25 minutes; from Los Angeles is 11 hours 45 minutes; from Toronto is 8 hours 30 minutes and from Sydney is 21 hours 55 minutes.

Arrival/departure tax: Included in the ticket price.

Getting There By Rail

Deutsche Bahn (tel: (0800) 150 7090; website: www.bahn.de), Germany's national rail service provider, operates a comprehensive and efficient rail service, including high-speed *InterCityExpress* (*ICE*) trains. There is a national railway enquiries line (tel: 11861 (within Germany) *or* (01805) 996 633 (from outside Germany, costing 12 cents per minute)). There is a separate hotline for cyclists who wish to take their bikes on the train (tel: (01805) 151 415 (charged at 12 cents per minute)).

The massive new station, *Bahnhof Lehrter*, which will link the main north–south and east–west lines, is due to be completed in 2006. Until then, the busiest station in Berlin will continue to be *Bahnhof Berlin Zoologischer Garten* (or simply 'Bahnhof Zoo'), Hardenbergplatz 11 (tel: (030) 2974 9241; fax: (030) 2974 9159), in the Western centre of the city. Facilities include a travel centre (open daily 0600–2200), tourist information, post office, bank, restaurant, buffet, café, shops, florist, newsagents and left-luggage. Ticket and information offices at *Bahnhof Schönefeld*, near the airport, are open daily 0530–2200 (tel: (030) 2972 9528; fax: (030) 2972 9654). The other major mainline stations are *Bahnhof Lichtenberg*, Weitlingstrasse 22, and *Ostbahnhof*, Am Ostbahnhof 9, in East Berlin. Some mainline services also stop at *Bahnhof Spandau*, to the west, and *Bahnhof Wannsee*, in the southwest.

Rail services: Berlin is part of the *InterCityExpress* (*ICE*) network, with super-fast trains to Hanover (journey time – 1 hour 35 minutes) and Frankfurt (journey time – 3 hours 30 minutes). *ICE* trains also go to Hamburg; at present these trains cost more and their running time is little faster than the other services (journey time – 2 hours 10 minutes). An expanding network of high-speed trains serves destinations across Western Europe. Supplements are incurred for travel on *ICE*, *IC* and *EC* trains.

Transport to the city: The main stations are all located on the S-Bahn spine, which arches from west to east across the city. Connections to the U-Bahn network and north–south S-Bahn lines are available either directly or via a short journey on the main east–west line. Taxi ranks and buses are also available outside the main stations.

Getting There By Road

Germany is covered by an excellent and extensive system of major roads (prefixed 'B') and motorways (prefixed 'A' for *Autobahn*). There are no tolls or speed limits on the *Autobahnen* but a maximum of 130kph (81mph) is recommended. Speed limits are 130kph (81mph) or 100kph (62mph) on major or minor roads outside the cities and 50kph (31mph) in built-up areas. Traffic drives on the right. Seatbelts must be worn at all times and children under 12 years old are forbidden to travel in the front seat without a child restraint.

The minimum age for driving is 18 years. Foreign drivers require proof of insurance and their national driving licence. A Green Card is strongly recommended. A country identification sticker is compulsory. The maximum legal alcohol to blood ratio for driving is 0.05%. Leaded petrol is unavailable; unleaded petrol with a lead additive can be found at some petrol stations.

The *Allgemeine Deutsche Automobil Club – ADAC* (tel: (01805) 101 112; fax: (01805) 302 928 (both charged at 12 cents per minute); website: www.adac.de) provides breakdown services throughout the country. In the Berlin area, *Auto Club Europa – ACE* (tel: (01802) 336 677; website: www.ace-online.de) can also offer assistance.

Emergency breakdown services: *ADAC* (01802) 222 222; *ACE* (01802) 343 536.

Routes to the city: The A10 is an orbital motorway that entirely circles the city. The A111 from the north and A115 from the south connect this to the A100, which wraps part way around the

CITY STATISTICS

Location: Berlin State, northeastern Germany.
Country dialling code: 49.
Population: 3,331,000 (city).
Ethnic mix: 87% German, 6% other European, 4% Turkish nationals, 3% other.
Religion: 54% undeclared, 26.5% Protestant, 10% Roman Catholic, 6% Islamic, 3.5% other.
Time zone: GMT + 1 (GMT + 2 from last Sunday in March to Saturday before last Sunday in October).
Electricity: 220 volts AC, 50Hz; round two-pin plugs are standard.
Average January temp: - 0.5°C (31°F).
Average July temp: 18°C (72°F).
Annual rainfall: 580mm (23 inches).

Western centre. The main roads leading to Berlin from outside the orbital are the A24 (from Hamburg), A9 (from Leipzig and Munich), A13 (from Dresden), A12 (from the Polish border) and A2 (from Hanover, from where the A7 connects to the A5 toward Frankfurt in the south).

Approximate driving times to Berlin: From Dresden – 2 hours 25 minutes; Hamburg – 3 hours 15 minutes; Frankfurt – 5 hours 50 minutes.

Coach services: *Eurolines* international coach services to over 300 destinations are operated by *Bayern Express & P Kühn Berlin GmbH* (tel: (030) 860 960; website: www.deutsche-touring.com or www.bex-berlin.de). Destinations include Paris, Strasbourg, Vienna and London, as well as Frankfurt,

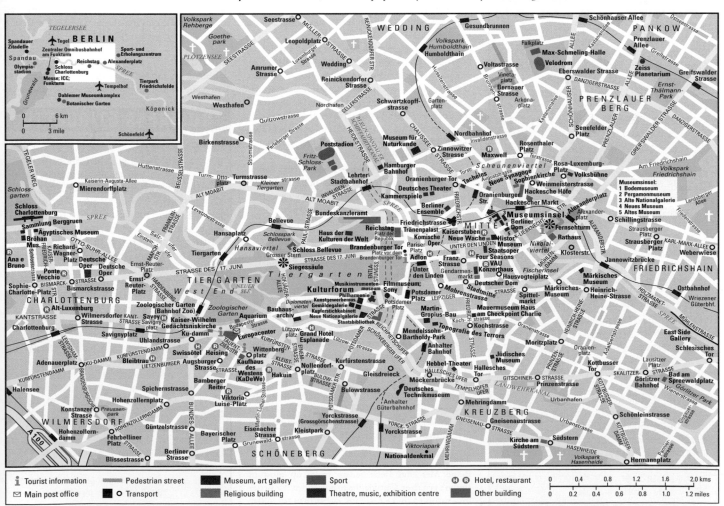

i Tourist information	Pedestrian street	Museum, art gallery	Sport	**H** **R** Hotel, restaurant
✉ Main post office	O Transport	Religious building	Theatre, music, exhibition centre	Other building

BUSINESS PROFILE

With the massive task of marrying a capitalist and a Communist economic system, Germany has had a turbulent time since reunification in 1990. During the Cold War, West Berlin was a heavily subsidised island of capitalism, while East Berlin, under the Communist system, had very little private enterprise. In the intervening years, the city has had to deal with massive unemployment, as inefficient East German industries were shut down. Berlin also had to make a massive investment in modernising and integrating the infrastructure of the city's two halves. Private and public investment is estimated to be €102 billion by 2003.

The city that has emerged from a forest of skyscrapers might look impressive but this façade hides the fact that Berlin is massively in debt – although austerity measures should help to improve the situation. Many new offices lie empty and the rate of unemployment rose from 15% in 1999 to 18.7% in 2003, well above the national average at 11.1%.

Many people in the Berlin business community presumed that the city would emerge as the gateway between East and West, thanks to numerous East Berliners speaking Russian and having a familiarity with the business and social conventions of the former Eastern Bloc. In reality, many international firms have cut out the middleman and saved money by locating directly in Prague and Budapest. However, Berlin's trade with Russia and the Czech Republic increased at a higher rate than average in 2000. And, over the last year or so, there has been a new sense of optimism, as more and more of the colossal building projects become a part of the city's life.

Berlin has regained the status of capital of Germany and the German economy is again growing in strength. Simultaneously the economic decision-making power is shifting from the Western centre in the Ku'damm area to the new centre around Potsdamer Platz, Unter den Linden and Friedrichstrasse.

Among the big names in the new Potsdamer Platz developments are *DaimlerChrysler, Sony, Hertie, Berliner Volksbank and ABB*, while major companies with offices in the city include *Allianz* (insurance), *Bertelsmann* (publishing), *Deutsche Bank, DG Bank* and *KPMG* (finance) and *Sony-Europa* (electronics). Key industries in the city include the electrical, chemical and pharmaceutical industries, food processing and heavy machinery, equipment manufacturing and, increasingly, tourism – Berlin is now Germany's number one tourist destination and the Film Festival alone brings in approximately €30 million a year. A new solar energy centre has also opened in the Eastern area of the city. Overall, 36% of employees work in the service sector, 33% in manufacturing and industry, 13% in trade and transport and 18% in government.

In terms of convention venues, there is the *Internationales Congress Centrum* (*ICC*), Messedamm 22 (tel: (030) 3038 3000; fax: (030) 3038 3030; website: www.messe-berlin.de *or* www.icc-berlin.com). The *Industrie-und Handelskammer Berlin* (Berlin Chamber of Commerce) is located at Fasanenstrasse 85 (tel: (030) 315 100; fax: (030) 3151 0166; website: www.berlin.ihk.de).

Hamburg and Munich. Buses on both international and domestic routes arrive at the *Zentraler Omnibusbahnhof (ZOB) am Funkturm*, Masurenallee, near the western end of the Ku'damm and the Messe Berlin. The station has a restaurant and snack bar; information and tickets are available from the *ZOB-Reisebüro* (tel: (030) 301 0380; fax: (030) 3010 3820) daily 0630–2100. Taxis are available and the U-Bahn Kaiserdamm and S-Bahn Witzleben stations are located nearby. There is a general coach information line (tel: (01805) 250 254 (charged at 12 cents per minute)).

Getting Around

Public Transport

Berlin has a highly integrated transport system comprising **U-Bahn** (underground), **S-Bahn** (commuter rail), **bus**, **tram** and **ferry** services, with easy connections to regional and mainline rail services. The *Verkehrsverbund Berlin-Brandenburg* (*VBB*), Hardenbergplatz 2 (tel: (030) 2541 4141; fax: (030) 2541 4112; e-mail: info@vbbonline.de; website: www.vbbonline.de), co-ordinates activities among the Berlin transport providers and those of the surrounding region.

Berlin's Eastern and Western city centres are linked by the main east–west axis of the **S-Bahn**, which is crossed by the north–south lines at Bahnhof Friedrichstrasse and intersects the S-Bahn ring at Bahnhof Westkreuz and Bahnhof Ostkreuz. Operated by *S-Bahn Berlin GmbH* (tel: (030) 2974 3333; website: www.s-bahn-berlin.de), which has offices at Nordbahnhof (tel: (030) 2971 9843 *or* 2974 3333), the trains run daily 0500–2430; the S1 and S7 run around the clock at the weekend.

The other public transport services are operated daily 0600–2300 by the *Berliner Verkehrsbetriebe – BVG* (tel: (030) 19449 *or* 2562 2562; e-mail: info@bvg.de; website: www.bvg.de). There are nine **U-Bahn** lines, which operate daily 0500–2430; the U9 and U12 run around the clock at weekends. **Bus** services crisscross the city, while the network of 28 **trams** only operates in East Berlin. There are three seasonal and three year-round **ferry** services to the ports of Hamburg, Kiel, Lubeck and Rostock, which are linked by road and rail to Berlin. The *BVG* has an information centre in the pavilion at Hardenbergplatz, in front of Bahnhof Zoo (open daily 0600–2200), as well as a counter at Tegel airport.

Tickets are priced for either two or three zones – almost all visitors will use the *AB* tariff. The standard single fare is €2.10, valid for two hours on all forms of transport. A short journey costs €1.20 (valid for three S-Bahn/U-Bahn stops or six bus/tram stops). Nearly all tickets are available for purchase from automated machines at stations and stops, as well as from service desks and, in the case of buses, from the driver. Bus drivers only sell day tickets, two-hour and short distance tickets.

A number of **passes** are also available. A day ticket, valid until 0300 on the following day of purchase, costs €6.10. Seven-day tickets are valid until 2400 on the seventh day and cost €22. Available from the tourist information office (see *Sightseeing*), the *WelcomeCard* costs €19 and is valid for 72 hours. It also includes reductions on many attractions and performances in Berlin and Potsdam.

Taxis

Beige Mercedes Benz sedans make up most of Berlin's taxi fleet. Outside the main centres, it is better for visitors to find a taxi rank rather than try to flag down a taxi. Taxis are also available by telephone from *Taxi-Funk Berlin* (tel: (030) 69022 *or* 443 322), *Funk Taxi Berlin* (tel: (030) 261 026; website: www.funktaxi-berlin.de), *Würfelfunk* (tel: (030) 210 101; website: www.wuerfelfunk.de) and *Taxi Vorbestellung* (tel: (030) 4228 2828; website: www.taxihaus.de). The initial charge for a taxi is €2.50, rising by €1.50 every kilometre (€1 after the seventh kilometre). A journey from the Ku'damm to Unter den Linden costs approximately €10. It is standard for passengers to tip taxi drivers, usually 5–10% of the fare.

Limousines

Chauffeur and limousine hire is available from *Autovermietung Minex* (tel: (030) 8577 7073; fax: (030) 8577 7070; website: www.minex.de), which charges from €42 per hour for a Mercedes S-Class sedan or €357 for an eight-hour day. Limousine hire is also available from *MC Prestige Limousine Tours* (tel: (030) 262 8259; fax: (030) 262 8269; website: www.mcprestigelimo.de), with prices from €51.13 per hour for a Mercedes E-Class, and €71.58 for a stretch limo, and *United Limousines GmbH* (tel: (030) 343 4600; fax: (030) 3434 6060; website: www.united-limousines.com), charging €203 for three hours in a Mercedes E-Class and €487 for three hours in a stretch limo.

Driving in the City

Weekday rush hours are 0700–0900 and 1600–1900 (until 2300 in some of the popular nightlife districts). The one-way system can be difficult to negotiate but there are plenty of larger, two-way avenues in central Berlin that are easier to use. Parking can be problematic on Saturday, particularly in the shopping areas. Parking lots in the Ku'damm area charge €1.50–2 for the first hour and have day rates of €9–10.

Car Hire

All of the major car hire firms are represented in Berlin and all have multiple locations throughout the

BUSINESS ETIQUETTE

Germans are very businesslike while at work and this shows in their expectations for punctuality, formal manners and attention to detail. It is common to answer the telephone by stating one's last name, rather than saying 'hello'. People should be addressed by their titles (such as Herr Doktor) and last name, until they indicate otherwise. Many businesspeople speak English but might prefer to conduct business in German. Likewise, business cards (which are used extensively) and business letters in English are acceptable, although supporting documentation should be translated. It is best for visitors to err on the conservative side of dress, certainly in the first instance.

Standard business hours are typically Monday to Friday 0800/0900–1600/1700, although, contrary to what many visitors expect, these hours can be less, as Germans have some of the shortest working hours in Western Europe. Meetings are usually between 1100 and 1300 or 1500 and 1700, although late afternoon appointments (other than on Friday) are not unusual. Business lunches are common (the person making the offer is expected to pay) but breakfast meetings are rare. So called 'after-work parties' are becoming increasingly popular ways for workers to meet colleagues and friends for drinks.

city. Some of the most central are *Europcar*, Karl-Liebknecht-Strasse 19–21 (tel: (030) 240 7900 *or* (01805) 800 000 (charged at 12 cents per minute) *or* (030) 417 8520; website: www.europcar.de), *Hertz*, Budapester Strasse 39 (tel: (030) 261 1053 *or* (01805) 333 535 (charged at 12 cents per minute) *or* (030) 4170 4674; website: www.hertz.de), *Sixt*, Nürnbergerstrasse 65 (tel: (030) 212 9880 *or* (01805) 262 525 (charged at 12 cents per minute); website: www.e-sixt.de), and *Avis*, Budapester Strasse 41 (tel: (030) 230 9370 *or* (01805) 557 755 (charged at 12 cents per minute) *or* (030) 4101 3148; website: www.avis.com). Drivers usually must be over 21 years old and require a valid national driving licence. Rates for hire start at around €75 per day (including tax and insurance) and €275 per week. Third party insurance is included.

Bicycle Hire

Bicycles are plentiful in Berlin – the flat terrain and extensive network of bicycle paths make cycling in the city a pleasure. Cycling maps, information and assistance are available at *Das Radlerzentrum*, run by the cycling lobby group *Allgemeine Deutscher Fahrrad-Club (ADFC)*, Brunnenstrasse 28 (tel: (030) 448 4724; website: www.adfc-berlin.de), Monday to Friday 1200–2000 and Saturday 1000–1600. There are a number of bicycle hire outlets, including *City Bike*, Uhlandstrasse 106A (tel: (030) 861 5237; fax: (030) 8639 4363; e-mail: info@citybikeservice.de; website: www.citybikeservice.de), and *Berlin by bike-Fahrradstation* (tel: (01805) 108 000 (charged at 12 cents per minute); website: www.fahrradstation.de), which has offices at Rosenthaler Strasse 40–41 (tel: (030) 2838 4848), Friedrichstrasse 141–142 (tel: (030) 2045 4500), Auguststrasse 29A (tel: (030) 2859 9661), and Bergmannstrasse 9 (tel: (030) 215 1566). Bicycle hire costs around €10 per day or €50 per week (insurance included).

SIGHTSEEING

Sightseeing Overview

Berlin can be a sightseeing nightmare – the vast sprawl that is the city has no definite centre and pockets of attractions are dotted all over. That said, the state museums are grouped in clusters – on the *Museumsinsel*, at the *Kulturforum*, in and around *Schloss Charlottenberg* and in the southwestern suburb of Dahlem. There are also a large number of attractions either at Potsdamer Platz or within walking distance of it, including the Kulturforum to the southwest. To the north lie the *Brandenburger Tor* (Brandenburg Gate) and the *Reichstag*, sporting Lord Foster's new glass dome. The Brandenburg Gate is situated on Berlin's main east–west axis. To the west lies the *Siegessäule* (Victory Column), which provides a view over the surrounding *Tiergarten* and the Western city centre, to the southwest of the column. West Berlin's centre has less to offer and is better for shopping and nightlife than for sightseeing. Nevertheless visitors should take a look at the broken shard of a church, the *Kaiser Wilhelm Gedächtniskirche*, which serves as a brutal reminder of World War II. The nearby *Zoo* and *Aquarium* also provide happy distractions.

The most dense collection of sights lies to the east of the Brandenburg Gate, on either side of Unter den Linden, lined with many 18th- and 19th-century buildings. At its end are the artistic and architectural treasures of the Museumsinsel, where the city's main

cathedral, the *Berliner Dom*, can be found. Further on is the Communist-era *Fernsehturm* (television tower), on Alexanderplatz, which marked the centre of East Berlin. Due to ongoing restoration work, many of the city's museums are prone to closures at present and some of the collections are being temporarily relocated.

Key Attractions

Potsdamer Platz and the New Centre

After lying desolate for decades, except for the platform that allowed Westerners to peer over the Wall into the East, *Potsdamer Platz* is again part of Berlin's thriving centre (in the 1930s, it was the busiest square in Europe). In just a few years, the forest of cranes has given way to a new precinct full of shops, restaurants, bars and entertainment venues. The best place to see it all – as well as terrific views over the rest of Berlin – is from the *Panorama-Point*, at the top of the Kollhof building, reached by what is claimed to be the fastest lift in Europe. One of the more interesting constructions is the *Sony Centre*, with its piazza covered by a futuristic sail-like roof. On the ground floor is the *Filmmuseum Berlin*, which recalls some of the city's great achievements in the early days of cinema and devotes considerable space to Marlene Dietrich, who would have celebrated her 100th birthday on 27 December 2001.
Potsdamer Platz
Transport: U-Bahn/S-Bahn Potsdamer Platz; bus 142, 148, 248 or 348.
Filmmuseum Berlin
Potsdamer Strasse 2
Tel: (030) 300 9030. Fax: (030) 3009 0313.
E-mail: info@filmmuseum-berlin.de
Website: www.filmmuseum-berlin.de
Opening hours: Tues–Sun 1000–1800 (until 2000 Thurs).
Admission: €6.
Panorama-Point
Potsdamer Platz
Tel: (030) 2529 4372 *or* 2554 2104 (guided tours).
Website: www.potsdamerplatz.de
Opening hours: Tues–Sun 1100–1930.
Admission: €3.50.

Reichstag

British architect Lord Foster has transformed the *Reichstag*, which was built at the end of the 19th century and has long since been emblematic of the German State. It was damaged in the fire of 1933, which marked Hitler's consolidation of power, and has now been renovated for the *Bundestag* (People's Assembly) of a reunited Germany. The new dome is meant to symbolise the transparency of the democratic government and visitors can pass between its layers to witness the decision-making chamber of the government. The Plenary is open for free hourly guided tours when parliament is not in session. Parliament is always in session Monday to Friday 0900–1600, Saturday and Sunday 1000–1600. The walk through the dome itself is stunning, culminating in sweeping views of a city in transition. The rooftop restaurant (tel: (030) 2262 9933) provides a way to beat the queues and is open until 2400.
Platz der Republik
Tel: (030) 2273 2152 *or* 2272 2152. Fax: (030) 2273 0027 *or* 2272 0027.
Website: www.bundestag.de
Transport: S-Bahn Unter den Linden; bus 100, 248, 257 or 348.
Opening hours: Daily 0800–2400 (last admission 2200).
Admission: Free.

Kaiser-Wilhelm Gedächtnis

TOURIST INFORMATION

Berlin Tourismus Marketing GmbH
Europa-Center, Budapester Strasse 45 (West Berlin)
Opening hours: Mon–Sat 0830–2030 and Sun 1000–1830, may open later in summer

Brandenburg Gate (South Wing), Pariser Platz (East Berlin)
Opening hours: Daily 0930–1800.

Tel: (0190) 016 316 (Info Hotline, Germany only) or (030) 250 025 (reservations) or (700) 8623 7546 (from outside Germany). Fax: (030) 2500 2424.
E-mail: information@btm.de
Website: www.berlin-tourist-information.de

Other tourist information offices are located at Tegel airport, on the ground floor of *KaDeWe*, Tauentzienstrasse 21–24, and at the Fernsehturm (TV tower) at Alexanderplatz. There is a *Tourist Info Café*, Panoramastrasse 1a, next to the TV tower, open daily 1000–1800. The city of Berlin provides online information (website: www. berlin.de), some of it in English.

Passes
Berlin Tourismus Marketing offers the *WelcomeCard*, which gives discounts of up to 50% on museums and attractions – including Schloss Sanssouci and Zoologischer Garten – as well as guided tours, boat trips and performances in both Berlin and Potsdam. The pass costs €19 and is valid for 72 hours for one adult and up to three children. Also included in the price is unlimited travel on all buses and trains in zones A, B and C. The card is available at tourist offices, transit ticket offices and some hotels.

There is also the SchauLust Museen Berlin three-day tourist ticket, which gives free admission to more than 50 museums, including the *Staatliche Museen zu Berlin*, the *Pergamon Museum* and *Gemäldegalerie*. The pass costs €10 (concessions available) and is available at the main tourist offices.

A two-day pass for all of the region's Prussian palaces and gardens is available at *Schloss Sanssouci* for €15. A one-day pass for all the palaces except Sanssouci costs €12 and is available from any of the participating palaces.

Charlottenburg Palace

Berlin Wall History

Much of the Wall or the 'Anti-Fascist Protection Rampart', as the GDR authorities liked to call it, has succumbed – first to enthusiastic revellers and souvenir hunters and then more significantly to developers; only a few sections remain. The *East Side Gallery*, along Mühlenstrasse (S-Bahn Ostbahnhof), emerged in the post-Wall years as a poignant symbol of new hope, as it was covered with inspiring artwork. Today, its future is in doubt and the faded state of the paintings is symbolic of how far Berlin has come since 1989. The *Gedenkstätte Berliner Mauer* is a graffiti-free stretch of the Wall that has been preserved by the authorities. A visitor centre has information about the Wall years, while a chapel is dedicated to the 80 or so victims that died trying to cross it. Perhaps the best place to get a sense of what the divided city was like is the *Mauermuseum Haus am Checkpoint Charlie*, located next to the site where the famous border-crossing stood. A number of permanent exhibitions document the history of the Wall and place it into context, as well as record the famous paintings on the Western side of the division.

Gedenkstätte
Bernauer Strasse 111
Tel: (030) 2246 41030.
Website: www.the-berlin-wall.de *or* www.berlinermauer.de
Transport: U-Bahn Bernauer Strasse; S-Bahn Nordbahnhof.
Opening hours: Wed–Sun 1000–1700 (visitor centre).
Admission: Free.
Haus am Checkpoint Charlie (Mauermuseum)
Friedrichstrasse 43–45
Tel: (030) 253 7250. Fax: (030) 251 2075.
E-mail: info@mauer-museum.com
Website: www.checkpointcharlie.org
Transport: U-Bahn Kochstrasse or Stadtmitte; bus 129.
Opening hours: Daily 0900–2200.
Admission: €7.50 (concessions available).

Unter den Linden and the Museumsinsel

One of Berlin's most recognisable landmarks, the *Brandenburger Tor* (Brandenburg Gate), stands at the western end of *Pariser Platz*. Stretching eastwards from here is Unter den Linden, along which some of the city's richest cultural treasures lie. These include the *Deutsche Staatsoper* (German State Opera), the *Neue Wache* (New Guardhouse), which is now a memorial to the victims of fascism and tyranny, and the *Zeughaus* (Arsenal), which houses the *Deutsches Historisches Museum* (German Historical Museum). The *Museumsinsel* (Museum Island), at the eastern end of Unter den Linden, offers the *Pergamonmuseum*, containing a host of antiquities, including the enormous Pergamon altar, *Bodemuseum* (closed until 2004) and the massive, neo-Baroque *Berliner Dom* (Berlin Cathedral), built in 1893–1905 and recently renovated. Within the newly restored *Alte Nationalgalerie* (Old National Gallery) is the 'Galerie der Romantik', a large collection of German and Austrian paintings from the first half of the 19th century. These include 24 paintings by Caspar David Friedrich. The *Altes Museum* (Old Museum) is a striking neo-classical building, designed by Karl Friedrich Schinkel, which opened in 1830. The main floor houses a collection of antiquities, while the upstairs galleries house changing exhibitions.

Altes Museum
Am Lustgarten
Tel: (030) 2090 5566 *or* 5555 (recorded info). Fax: (030) 2090 5502.
Website: www.smpk.de/ant
Transport: U-Bahn/S-Bahn Friedrichstrasse or S-Bahn Hackescher Markt; bus 100, 157 or 348.
Opening hours: Tues, Wed and Fri–Sun 1000–1800, Thurs 1000–2200.
Admission: €6; €10 (three-day pass); concessions available; free first Sun of each month.
Deutsches Historisches Museum
Unter den Linden 2
Tel: (030) 203 040. Fax: (030) 2030 4543.
Website: www.dhm.de
Transport: U-Bahn/S-Bahn Friedrichstrasse or S-Bahn Hackescher Markt; bus 100, 157 or 348.
Opening times: Fri–Tues 1000–1800, Thurs 1000–2200.
Admission: Free.

Pergamonmuseum
Am Kupfergraben
Tel: (030) 208 050.
E-mail: vam@smb.spk-berlin.de
Website: www.smpk.de
Transport: U-Bahn/S-Bahn Friedrichstrasse or S-Bahn Hackescher Markt; bus 100, 157, 200 or 348.
Opening hours: Tues, Wed and Fri–Sun 1000–1800, Thurs 1000–2200.
Admission: €6; €10 (for a three-day pass); concessions available.
Alte Nationalgalerie
Bodestrasse
Tel: (030) 2090 5555. Fax: (030) 2090 5502.
Website: www.smpk.de/ang
Transport: U-Bahn/S-Bahn Friedrichstrasse or S-Bahn Hackescher Markt; bus 100, 157 or 348.
Opening hours: Tues–Sun 1000–1800 (until 2200 Thurs).
Admission: €6 (day pass including Pergamonmuseum); €10 (three-day pass); concessions available.

Judische Museum (Jewish Museum)

The striking design of this Daniel Liebeskind-designed memorial to Jewish life in Berlin is based on a shattered Star of David. Even before the installation of the permanent exhibits – recalling the life and history of German Jews through the centuries – visitors came here to experience the evocative spaces within this incredible structure.
Lindenstrasse 9–14
Tel: (030) 2599 3300. Fax: (030) 2599 3409.
E-mail: info@jmberlin.de
Website: www.jmberlin.de
Transport: U-Bahn Hallesches Tor or Kochstrasse; bus 129, 240 or 341.
Opening hours: Daily 1000–2000 (until 2200 Mon); closed on Jewish holidays.
Admission: €5 (concessions available).

Schloss Charlottenburg and museums

The *Charlottenburg Palace* was built in 1790, as a summer residence for Sophie Charlotte, the wife of King Frederick I. Visits to the *Old Palace* are by guided tour only. Prices and hours vary for the *New Wing*, the *Orangerie*, the mausoleum and other parts of the complex. The museums and galleries that are in and around the palace include the *Egyptian Museum*, with its famous bust of Egyptian Queen Nefertiti. The *Berggruen Collection*, opposite the palace, includes 64 artworks by Picasso, as well as a representative collection of his contemporaries.
Schloss Charlottenburg
Luisenplatz
Tel: (0331) 969 4202.
Website: www.spsg.de
Transport: U-Bahn Sophie-Charlotte-Platz or Richard-Wagner-Platz; bus 109, 110, 121, 126 or 145.
Opening hours: Tues–Fri 0900–1700, Sat and Sun 1000–1700, last tour at 1600 (Old Palace); Tues–Fri 1000–1800, Sat and Sun 1100–1800 (New Wing). Grounds open daily 0600–2100 (summer); daily 0600–2000 (winter).
Admission: €8 (Old Palace); €5 (New Wing); concessions available.
Sammlung Berggruen
Westlicher Stülerbau, Schlossstrasse 1
Tel: (030) 2090 5555 (recorded info). Fax: (030) 2090 5502.
Website: www.spmk.de
Transport: U-Bahn Sophie-Charlotte-Platz or Richard-Wagner-Platz; bus 109, 145, 210 or X21.

Photo: Corel

Opening hours: Tues–Fri 1000–1800, Sat and Sun 1100–1800.
Admission €6; €10 (three-day pass); concessions available.

Kulturforum (Cultural Forum)

Located in the west of the city, the *Kulturforum* is a cultural centre, grouping together all the museums that have European art as their chief focus, including a *Musikinstrumentenmuseum* (Musical Instrument Museum) and a new hall for chamber music. The opening of the *Gemäldegalerie* (Painting Gallery) in 1998 brought a stunning collection of 13th- to 18th-century paintings to the site. It joined the *Kunstgewerbemuseum* (Arts and Crafts Museum) and the *Neue Nationalgalerie* (New National Gallery). The latter, built to the designs of Mies van der Rohe, contains German Expressionist and Realist art, as well as other works of the 20th century. There is also a sculpture garden.

Philharmonie und Kammermusiksaal
Herbert-von-Karajan-Strasse 1
Tel: (030) 254 880 *or* 2548 8156 *or* 2548 8999 (ticket hotline). Fax: (030) 261 4887.
Website: www.berlin-philharmonic.com
Transport: U-Bahn/S-Bahn Potsdamer Platz or U-Bahn Mendelssohn-Batholdy-Park; bus 129, 148, 200, 248, 341 or 348.
Opening hours: Performances generally Fri–Sun 1600 and 2000 (depending on programme); guided tours daily at 1300.
Admission: From €7 (performances); €36 (guided tours in English).

Musikinstrumentenmuseum
Tiergartenstrasse 1
Tel: (030) 2548 1178.
E-mail: sim@sim.spk-berlin.de
Website: www.sim.spk-berlin.de
Transport: U-Bahn/S-Bahn Potsdamer Platz or U-Bahn Mendelssohn-Batholdy-Park; bus 129, 142, 148, 200, 248, 341 or 348.
Opening hours: Tues–Fri 0900–1700, Sat and Sun 1000–1700.
Admission: €3; free first Sun of month.

Gemäldegalerie
Kulturforum, Matthäikirchplatz 8
Tel: (030) 266 2010 *or* 2090 5555 (information). Fax: (030) 266 2103.
E-mail: gg@smb.spk-berlin.de
Website: www.smpk.de/gg
Transport: U-Bahn/S-Bahn Potsdamer Platz or U-Bahn Mendelssohn-Batholdy-Park; bus 129, 142, 148, 248, 341 or 348.
Opening hours: Tues–Sun 1000–1800, Thurs 1000–2200.
Admission: €6 (concessions available).

Kunstgewerbemuseum
Kulturforum, Matthäikirchplatz 8
Tel: (030) 266 2002 *or* 2090 5555 (information). Fax: (030) 266 2959.
E-mail: kk@smb.spk-berlin.de
Website: www.smpk.de/kgm
Transport: U-Bahn/S-Bahn Potsdamer Platz or U-Bahn Mendelssohn-Batholdy-Park; bus 129, 142, 200, 248, 341 or 348.
Opening hours: Tues–Fri 1000–1800, Sat and Sun 1100–1800.
Admission: €3 (concessions available).

Neue Nationalgalerie
Kulturforum, Potsdamer Strasse 50
Tel: (030) 2090 5566 *or* 5555 (recorded info). Fax: (030) 2090 5502.

Website: www.smpk.de/nng
Transport: U-Bahn/S-Bahn Potsdamer Platz or U-Bahn Mendelssohn-Batholdy-Park; bus 129, 148, 200, 248, 341 or 348.
Opening hours: Tues, Wed and Fri 1000–1800, Thurs 1000–2200, Sat and Sun 1100–1800.
Admission: €6; special exhibitions cost extra; concessions available.

Centrum Judaicum – Neue Synagogue (Jewish Centre – New Synagogue)

The *Neue Synagogue* was completed in 1866. Its location in the heart of the Scheunenviertel (Berlin's Jewish district) meant that it suffered serious bomb damage in 1943. Thanks to renovation in the mid-1990s, its Moorish dome can now be seen in its original glory. The synagogue houses a *Jewish Centre*, with an exhibition. The *Alter Jüdischer Friedhof* (Old Jewish Cemetery) is a short walk away, at Schönhauser Allee 23–25 (open Monday to Thursday 0800–1600 and Friday 0800–1300).
Oranienburger Strasse 28–30
Tel: (030) 8802 8451 *or* 8316. Fax: (030) 282 1176.
E-mail: office@cjudaicum.de
Website: www.cjudaicum.de
Transport: S-Bahn Hackescher Markt or Oranienburger Strasse; U-Bahn Oranienburger Tor; tram 1 or 13.
Opening hours: Sun–Thurs 1000–1800, Fri 1000–1400 (Sep–Apr); Tues–Thurs 1000–1800, Fri 1000–1700, Mon and Sun 1000–2000 (May–Aug); guided tours Sun 1400 and 1600, Wed 1600; closed on Jewish holidays.
Admission: €3 (concessions available).

Further Distractions

Tiergarten

There are few cities in the world where it is possible to lie naked in the middle of town at noon and not be arrested. Besides having delightful tree-shaded walks, canals and flower gardens, the *Tiergarten* also has a couple of open fields on either side of Hofjägerallee, where the locals sunbathe *au naturel*. While the sunbathers cannot be seen from the *Siegessäule* – the Victory Column in the centre of the park – it does provide a good view of the other major sights around Berlin. The angel at the top of the 69m (226ft) column was the perching place for the angels in Wim Wenders' film *Wings of Desire* (1987).
Strasse des 17 Juni
Transport: Bus 100, 187, 200 or 341; S-Bahn Tiergarten.
Opening hours: Daily 24 hours.
Admission: Free.

Siegessäule
Grosser Stern
Tel: (030) 391 2961.
Opening hours: Mon–Thurs 0830–1830, Fri–Sun 0930–1930 (mid-May–mid-Oct); Mon–Sun 0830–1700 (mid-Oct–mid-May).
Admission: €1.20 (concessions available).

Fernsehturm (TV Tower)

The best views in East Berlin are from the *Fernsehturm* at Alexanderplatz. Looking vaguely like the Death Star on a concrete spit, the television tower is Berlin's tallest structure at 368m (1207ft) and makes for a good reference point, as well as blighting many views of the city skyline. The Communist designers

Victory Column

inadvertently made it so that sunlight reflected on its facets forms a Christian cross. In a sign of changing times, a glare of advertising neon surrounds the base of the tower. Visitors can take an elevator up 203m (666ft) to the viewing platform or the revolving café, for a good look over the city.
Panoramastrasse 1A, Alexanderplatz
Tel: (030) 242 3333. Fax: (030) 242 5922.
E-mail: info@berlinerfernsehturm.de
Website: www.berlinerfernsehturm.de
Transport: U-Bahn/S-Bahn Alexanderplatz; bus 100, 157, 200 or 348; tram 2, 3, 4, 5 or 6.
Opening hours: Daily 0900–0100 (Mar–Oct); daily 1000–2400 (Nov–Feb).
Admission: €6.50 (concessions available).

Spandauer Zitadelle (Spandau Citadel)

This 16th-century fortress is the oldest non-religious building in the city. Its location overlooking the Havel River and the charming old town of Spandau make a trip to this district a lovely excursion within the city. Guided tours of the citadel are available through advance booking.
Am Juliusturm
Tel: (030) 3549 44200 *or* 334 6270 (to book tour). Fax: (030) 3549 44205.
Website: www.zitadelle-spandau.net
Transport: U-Bahn Zitadelle; bus 133.
Opening hours: Tues–Fri 0900–1700, Sat and Sun 1000–1700; guided tours Sat and Sun 1300, 1415 and 1530.
Admission: €2.50 (concessions available).

Tours of the City

Walking Tours

Daily walking tours are offered by *Insider Tour* (tel/fax: (030) 692 3149; website: www.insidertour.com). Walking tours start from the McDonalds opposite Bahnhof Zoo, at 1000 and 1430 (April to October) and at 1000 only (November to March). These take between three and four hours to complete and cost €12 (concessions available). All the major sites, such as the Victory Column, Brandenburg Gate, Potsdamer Platz and the Reichstag, are covered. *Insider Tour* also offers cycling tours with a similar itinerary from May to September for €20.

Bus Tours

A cheap and simple way for visitors to see the sights in Berlin is to first pick up a leaflet at the *BVG* information centre at Hardenbergplatz in front of Bahnhof Zoo and then board bus 100. The leaflet provides information on all the sights along the route, as the bus journeys from the centre of West Berlin to the East, travelling through the Tiergarten and passing the Reichstag and Brandenburg Gate. A similar tour is possible on bus 200, which passes through Potsdamer Platz rather than the Tiergarten.

Guided bus tours are available from a number of companies, which are significantly more expensive at approximately €18–26 for a hop-on, hop-off tour – the summertime (April to October) option of including a one-hour boat tour adds around €7.50 to the price. There are a number of pick-up points along the Ku'damm, between the Europa-Center and Uhlandstrasse. In the Western centre, the best departure point is in front of the large department store, Kaufhas des Westens (KaDeWe), while in the Eastern centre, buses stop at the Brandenburg Gate (in front of the Café Meyerbeer) and at Alexanderplatz (in front of the Hotel Park Inn). Operators include *Berolina* (tel: (030) 8856 8030; fax: (030) 882 4128; e-mail: info@berolina-berlin.com; website: www.berolina-berlin.com), *Severin + Kühn* (tel: (030) 880 4190; fax: (030) 882 5618; e-mail: info@severin-kuehn-berlin.de; website: www.severin-kuehn-berlin.de) and *Tempelhofer Reisen* (tel: (030) 752 4056; fax: (030) 751 7035; e-mail: info@tempelhofer.de; website: www.tempelhofer.de).

Other Tours

Walking tours of Berlin's architecture, neighbourhoods and a variety of cultural institutions off the regular tourist trail are available from *art:berlin*, Oranienburger Strasse 32 (tel: (030) 2809 6390; fax: (030) 2809 6391). A two-hour 'Jewish Life' tour costs €8, departing from Kackescher Markt on Sunday at 1300. *Kultur Büro Berlin* (tel: (030) 444 0936; fax: (030) 444 0939) offers a similar variety of tours, including ones that focus on particular artists such as Max Liebermann or Marlene Dietrich. Tours for both companies are in German but are available in English for group bookings.

Excursions

In addition to the sources mentioned below, information on destinations in Brandenburg, which completely surrounds Berlin, is available from the state tourist office, *Reiseland Brandenburg* (tel: (0331) 200 4747; fax: (0331) 298 7328; website: www. reiseland-brandenburg.de).

For a Half Day

Potsdam: One of the best excursions from Berlin is a visit to Potsdam, with its pleasant main shopping street and Dutch Quarter, as well as the nearby palaces and gardens of *Sanssouci*, *Schloss Cecilienhof* and the *Babelsberg Film Studios*. Potsdam is located approximately 20km (12 miles) from Berlin's centre and is reachable by S-Bahn S7 or the regional train RE1, both leaving from Bahnhof Zoo. The *Potsdam Tourismus GmbH*, Friedrich-Ebert-Strasse 5 (tel: (0331) 275 580; fax: (0331) 275 5899; e-mail: information@ potsdam.de; website: www.potsdam.de), can provide further information.

Haus der Wannsee Konferenz: The *Wannsee Conference House* (tel: (030) 805 0010; e-mail: info@ghwk.de; website: www.ghwk.de) is a place that some Berliners would rather the tourists never see. Nestling in a plush lakeside suburb in the 'Berlin Riviera', this Wannsee villa looks innocuous enough. However, those who walk down the pebble-strewn driveway enter the building where leading Nazis gathered with German industrialists to mechanically plan the deaths of millions of Jews. The free exhibition is open daily 1000–1800 and best reached by S-Bahn to Bahnhof Wannsee, then bus 114.

For a Whole Day

Spreewald: To the southeast of Berlin lies the nature reserve of the *Spreewald* (Spree Forest). Some 48,000 hectares (120,000 acres) of forested land interspersed with a labyrinth of 1000km (621 miles) of waterways marks the headwaters of the Spree River, which flows through Berlin on the way to the sea. This area offers a great opportunity for visitors to get out into nature, either for walks or bicycle rides in the woods or for watersports or boat tours (in punts). The best place to start a tour is from the large harbour in Lübbenau or one of the smaller ones in Lübben or Burg. Spreewald is located 110km (68 miles) on the A13 from Berlin. Regional trains depart hourly from Königs Wusterhausen in southeast Berlin (journey time – 40 minutes) and approximately every two hours from Bahnhof Zoo (journey time – 1 hour 30 minutes) and Ostbahnhof (journey time – 1 hour). *Tourismusverband Spreewald*, Lindenstrasse 1, Raddusch (tel: (035433) 72299; fax: (035433) 72228; e-mail: tourismus@ spreewald.de; website: www.spreewald.de), can provide further information.

ACCOMMODATION

Since becoming Germany's reunited capital, the number of hotel rooms in Berlin has doubled with the growing demand for accommodation. Reservations made well in advance are recommended. Hotel prices usually include VAT at 16% and a buffet breakfast.

The prices quoted below are the lowest standard rates for a double room, including breakfast and VAT, unless otherwise specified.

Business

Hotel Adlon

Voted 'Hotel of the Century' by *Time* magazine in 1999, *Hotel Adlon* is one of the great historical hotels of Berlin. Constructed in 1907, with the help of Kaiser Wilhelm II, over the decades the rich and famous, such as Einstein, Rockefeller, Charlie Chaplin and Marlene Dietrich, have always stayed in this hotel. Located very near to the Brandenburg Gate in central Berlin, the Adlon retains its luxurious and historical feel; the restaurants, bars and banquet rooms – especially the Grand Ballroom – are a wonderful reminder of its glorious past. Yet it also offers the most up-to-date services and facilities, especially for business travellers, with state-of-the-art conference rooms, a business centre and specially designed business suites, which offer a separate working area, with desk and fax machine, as well as a kitchenette. There are even six rooms specifically designed for allergy sufferers.

Unter den Linden 77
Tel: (030) 226 1111 *or* 22610. Fax: (030) 2261 1116 *or* 2261 2222.
E-mail: adlon@kempinski.com
Website: www.hotel-adlon.de
Price: From €330.

Hotel Seehof Berlin

Conveniently situated between the busy Kurfürstendamm and Berlin's fairground and ICC Centre, the *Seehof* overlooks a small, picturesque lake. The hotel is traditionally decorated throughout, with wooden furnishings and high-quality appliances, offering basic business facilities, such as fax and modem connections. Breakfast can be enjoyed on the scenic lake terrace, which, with its open-air bar, also offers great evening entertainment. A large indoor pool provides clean and safe swimming for those who are uncomfortable in the outdoor waters. Most rooms have a relaxing view over the lake, while all rooms are equipped with marble bathrooms, air conditioning, cable TV, video and mini-bar. A concierge service is available around the clock and able to assist with any business, travel or leisure arrangements.

Lietzenseeufer 11
Tel: (030) 320 020. Fax: (030) 3200 2151.
E-mail: info@hotel-seehof-Berlin.de
Website: www.hotel-seehof-Berlin.de
Price: From €165.

Savoy Hotel

The *Savoy Hotel* has been known for its friendliness and comfort for nearly 70 years – famous guest Thomas Mann once declared as much. This small, central hotel is charming and has a classical setting and exceptional service. Shoe cleaning, laundry and ironing services, as well as floral, room and secretarial services, even free newspapers, all complement this traditional establishment. For business travellers, there are fax and modem connections in the rooms and elegant conference facilities. There is also the exclusive *Casa del Habano* bar, with its wide choice of Cuban cigars, where businesspeople and aficionados meet and Cuban delicacies are served.

Fasanenstrasse 9–10
Tel: (030) 311 030. Fax: (030) 3110 3333.
E-mail: info@hotel-savoy.com
Website: www.hotel-savoy.com
Price: From €192.

Swissôtel Berlin

Opened in September 2001, this sleek and comfortable hotel is conveniently situated close to the heart of West Berlin and S-Bahn and U-Bahn stations. There are 316 rooms decorated in an airy, contemporary style, all containing original works of art by the architect/designer, Markus Lupertz. All are spotless and contain hairdryer, iron, mini-bar, safe, modem and Internet connections, satellite TV and coffee machines. Guests are also supplied with fluffy white bathrobes and slippers. There are conference facilities, with 11 rooms seating from two to 350 delegates, and a business centre with fax and Internet access. The reception area has a coffee bar, which is convenient for informal meetings. There is also a small fitness room/sauna and a high-quality restaurant.

Augsburger Strasse 44
Tel: (030) 220 100 *or* 2201 02260 (reservations) Fax: (030) 2201 02222.
E-mail: emailus.berlin@swissotel.com
Website: www.swissotel-berlin.com
Price: From €180.

Luxury

Four Seasons Hotel Berlin

The *Four Seasons* is situated close to Berlin's main attractions and provides an elegant, exclusive environment, where functions for 14 to 150 people unfold flawlessly. With 260 sq metres (2800 sq ft) of banquet and conference space, expert technical support and extensive facilities, any kind of function can easily be arranged. The guest rooms, with their antique furnishings and luxurious rugs, are all equipped with modem points and two-line telephones, big desks and marble bathrooms. Guests are spoilt with oversized cotton bathrobes and slippers, complimentary toiletries and twice-daily housekeeping. There are also spa facilities and a fitness club.
Charlottenstrasse 49
Tel: (030) 20338. Fax: (030) 2033 6166.
Website: www.fourseasons.com
Price: From €300.

The Regent Schlosshotel Berlin

This grandiose hotel was originally built in 1914 as a private mansion and has been restored to its former glory with input from the fashion designer, Karl Lagerfeld. *The Regent Schlosshotel* is located near the main shopping street of Kurfürstendamm and the exhibition centre and yet it is quiet and peaceful, looking out over Grunewald Forest. All 42 rooms and 12 suites have marble baths, two-line telephones, PC connection, cable TVs, videos and stereos, films and CDs. The hotel's recreation facilities are exceptional, including a beauty and physiotherapy studio. All the hotel's services are available 24 hours a day, including secretarial services, babysitting, personal hairdressers, doctors, trainers and butlers.
Brahmsstrasse 10
Tel: (030) 895 840. Fax: (030) 8958 4800.
E-mail: info@lhw.com
Website: www.lhw.com
Price: From €225.

Moderate

Hotel Igel

Located near the Tegeler lake and forest, in the middle of a tranquil, green backdrop, the *Igel* (meaning 'hedgehog') is a newly built hotel block. It is run as a small family business, so guests enjoy the advantages of a very personal service and friendly hospitality. The basic rooms are modern, comfortable and clean; all are en suite. The picturesque surroundings make up for any lack of style or facilities. In this quiet oasis, the turbulent city seems worlds away, although is only around the corner.
Friederikestrasse 33–34
Tel: (030) 436 0010. Fax: (030) 436 2470.
E-mail: igel@hotel-restaurant-igel.de
Website: www.hotel-restaurant-igel.de
Price: From €66.

Pension Modena and Pension Dittberner

These two popular guesthouses, the *Modena* and the *Dittberner*, are both situated in the same building, just off Kurfürstendamm. Although they profit from a very convenient central location, they are situated in a quiet street. Both offer exceptionally good comfort and spotless, spacious accommodation, as well as a friendly, personal service – at a very good price. Bright, generously designed rooms, high ceilings and white walls covered with modern art add a feel of airiness and space to this charming, old house. All rooms are en suite but there are few other facilities. However, business or leisure travellers with a tight budget will find these two places the best value in town.
Wielandstrasse 26
Tel: (030) 885 7010. Fax: (030) 881 5294 (Modena).
Tel: (030) 884 6950. Fax: (030) 885 4046 (Dittberner).
E-mail: hotelpensionmodena@hotmail.com
Price: From €95.

Other Recommendations

Bleibtreu

Classic elegance and a modern ecological philosophy, drawn from local trends, are combined in this centrally located hotel. This is reflected throughout *Bleibtreu*, with furniture made from untreated oak, woollen carpets, door handles made of semi-precious stones and environmentally friendly paints – mainly in vivid blue. Nature is very close by – the ride in the hotel's glass elevator to the fifth floor passes through the branches of a grand chestnut tree. For recreation, the wellness centre features reflex zone massage for hands, feet and ears, acupuncture, lymph drainage and steam baths. Other services include complimentary newspapers, laundry and ironing, secretarial services and a free mini-bar.
Bleibtreustrasse 31
Tel: (030) 884 740. Fax: (030) 8847 4444.
E-mail: info@bleibtreu.com
Website: www.bleibtreu.com
Price: From €192.

Hotel Kronprinz Berlin

This recently renovated hotel boasts an impressive exterior dating from the turn of the century. The antique furniture and traditional style of the foyer is reflected in the rooms and also in its well-known restaurant, where traditional German dishes are served. The concierge will offer service and support wherever needed, giving every guest a warm welcome. Located close to Berlin's fairground, this hotel mainly caters for business travellers, who find comfortable rooms here, as well as a business service that includes fax, modem points, secretarial assistance and three conference rooms. Many guest rooms have balconies or cosy seating areas but all have mini-bar, safe and two telephones. There are 11 French country-style 'romantic rooms', as well as rooms suitable for non-smoking, allergic or disabled guests.
Kronprinzendamm 1
Tel: (030) 896 030. Fax: (030) 893 1215.
E-mail: reception@kronprinz-hotel.de
Website: www.kronprinz-hotel.de
Price: From €145.

RESTAURANTS

The selected restaurants have been divided into five categories: Gastronomic, Business, Trendy, Budget and Personal Recommendations. The restaurants are listed alphabetically within these different categories, which serve as guidelines rather than absolute definitions of the establishments.
Only a small percentage of German restaurants accept credit cards and visitors should check before getting a table. Prices usually include 16% VAT. Normally, a tip of between 5% and 10% is expected for good service. The prices quoted below are for an average three-course meal for one person and for a bottle of house wine or equivalent; they include VAT but not tip.

Gastronomic

Bamberger Reiter

Chef Christoph Fischer has taken over *Bamberger Reiter* – one of the city's leading restaurants – from the famous Franz Raneburger, maintaining the high standards that diners were already accustomed to. He keeps up the tradition of using only the freshest and

The lobby of The Regent Schlosshotel

sometimes rare ingredients, to ensure an international touch to his German cuisine. The menu changes daily but often contains dove or rack of lamb. Decorated with attention to detail in a rustic, farmhouse style, the restaurant is located in Berlin's Schöneberg district. There is a sister bistro next door (no credit cards in bistro). Closed Monday.

Regensburger Strasse 7, Schöneberg
Tel: (030) 218 4282. Fax: (030) 2147 4799.
E-mail: info@bamberger-reiter.de
Price: €77 (restaurant) or €35 (bistro). Wine: €30.

Harlekin

Named after a sculpture by Markus Lüpertz, the *Harlekin* is situated in the Grand Hotel Esplanade, in the Mitte district. The tables are gathered around this sculpture in a strict symmetrical pattern, adding a modern, Japanese feel. Chef Gerd Hammes is expected to win a first Michelin star in the near future, for his personal interpretations of classic international recipes. An extensive wine list and perfect service add to the Harlekin experience. The menu contains highly recommended fish dishes, such as turbot in potato coat on leek and mushroom ragout or venison fillet on lime sauce with broccoli and baby carrots. Closed Sunday and Monday.

Lützowufer 15, Mitte
Tel: (030) 254 780. Fax: (030) 265 1171.
E-mail: info@esplanade.de
Website: www.esplanade.de
Price: €65. Wine: €35.

Heising

Dining at *Heising* is like travelling back in time. Located in Charlottenburg, its Baroque theme with lush curtains, small white statues and traditional china offers an old-fashioned but friendly and high-class dining experience. Traditional dishes with a hint of French influence are served, such as the *croustade* of duck breast with orange butter sauce or the *Loup de Mer* on fennel. No lunch. Closed Sunday.

Rankestrasse 32, Charlottenburg
Tel: (030) 213 3952.
Price: €45. Wine: €26.

VÂU

Created by one of Germany's leading industrial designers, *VÂU*'s interior epitomises relaxed style, with huge pictures by modern artist Oliver Jordan, decorating the walls. This expensive and trendy restaurant is located in the Mitte district and serves excellent German fish and game dishes. Daring combinations include braised oxtail wrapped in truffle dough or turbot with veal sweetbreads on shallots in red wine. Desserts could include wine tart with red wine ice cream. Reservations essential. Closed Sunday.

Jägerstrasse 54–55, Mitte
Tel: (030) 202 9730. Fax: (030) 2029 7311.
E-mail: restaurant@vau-berlin.de
Website: www.vau-berlin.de
Price: €75 (four-course menu). Wine: €26.

Vivaldi

Situated in the impressive Regent Schlosshotel (see *Hotels*), which was recently refurbished under the direction of fashion designer Karl Lagerfeld, *Vivaldi* presents a luxurious setting for gourmet dining in the majestic grandeur of a castle-like building. Award-winning chef Paul Urchs interprets his cooking as quality, luxury, pleasure and zest for life. His scallops on asparagus vinaigrette with violet mustard, the

Brandenburg Gate

lobster on lentil salad with balsamic vinegar or the venison medallions with celeriac purée and juniper sauce are indeed celebrations of vivacity.

Brahmsstrasse 6–10
Tel: (030) 8958 4520. Fax: (030) 8958 4800.
E-mail: info@ritz-carlton.com
Website: www.ritz-carlton.com
Price: €70. Wine: €30.

Business

Alt-Luxemburg

This popular restaurant in Charlottenburg radiates a luxurious yet conservative ambience and is tastefully furnished with antiques. The attentive service enhances its intimate setting. Chef Karl Wannemacher's nouvelle German dishes profit from a hint of intriguing East Asian influence, like his sublime lobster lasagne or monkfish with a saffron sauce.

Windscheidstrasse 31, Charlottenburg
Tel: (030) 323 8730. Fax: (030) 327 4003.
Price: €65. Wine: €26.

Ana e Bruno

Situated in Berlin's Westend, this Berlin classic serves up consistently high-quality Italian food in a rustic setting, elegantly tarted up to suit the rather posh clientele. Although classy and expensive, the atmosphere is still warm and homely, thanks to the hospitality of the owners, Bruno and his wife, Ana. The chef values a healthy, low-calorie interpretation of Mediterranean cuisine, such as grilled salmon in lime sauce, and prefers fresh vegetables and salads to hearty pastas and oily antipasti.

Sophie-Charlotten-Strasse 101
Tel: (030) 325 7110. Fax: (030) 322 6895.
Price: €60. Wine: €25.

Dachgartenrestaurant Kafer

This is probably the most coveted restaurant of the city, as it is located inside the new futuristic parliament building. From within the Reichstag's glass dome, *Dachgartenrestaurant Kafer* offers an amazing view over the heads of the debating ministers to the zoo and the

historic Brandenburg Gate. The menu offers healthy yet traditional cuisine, such as light fish and delicious venison options. Booking is essential, especially in the evening.

Platz der Republik
Tel: (030) 2262 9933.
Price: €45. Wine €30.

Kaiserstuben

Kaiserstuben (Emperor's Parlour) is the perfect place in Mitte for diners to enjoy a meal in a sophisticated yet cosy environment. The young chef, Tim Raue, surprises with his ingeniously prepared dishes that carefully balance regional heritage with influences from all over the world. These include fried goose livers with rhubarb and green pepper kernels.

Am Festungsgraben 1, Mitte
Tel: (030) 2061 0548. Fax: (030) 2061 0550.
E-mail: info@kaiserstuben.de
Website: www.kaiserstuben.de
Price: €49 (four-course menu). Wine: €27.

Ponte Vecchio

This charming Italian restaurant in the Westend, *Ponte Vecchio* ('Old Bridge' in Italian), still boasts one Michelin star. The cluttered, rustic interior might be a matter of preference but the creative dishes, cooked to perfection, definitely do not lack in taste, flavour or style – especially the carpaccio on ossobucco or the duck liver, which are to die for.

Spielhagenstrasse 3
Tel: (030) 342 1999. Fax: (030) 332 4713.
Price: €35. Wine: €21.

Trendy

Bacco

Italian restaurant *Bacco* was established in 1968. Since then, owner-chef Padrone Massimo Mannozzi has been attracting international celebrities with his charm and cooking. The rustic decor reflects his simple Tuscan cuisine, which includes such menu options as fresh Mediterranean fish or homemade tagliata, which comes with white truffle when in season. No lunch Monday. Closed Sunday.

Marburger Strasse 5
Tel: (030) 211 8687. Fax: (030) 211 5230.
E-mail: info@bacco.de
Website: www.bacco.de
Price: €35. Wine: €22.

Borchardt

This is one of the most fashionable meeting places to have appeared in the historic Mitte district. The high ceilings, red plush benches and Art Nouveau mosaic discovered during renovations create the impression of a 1920s café. The cuisine is high-quality French-Mediterranean, including several dishes with veal or fresh fish, such as fillet of stone flounder and lobster with green rice.
Französische Strasse 47, Mitte
Tel: (030) 2038 7110. Fax: (030) 2038 7150.
Price: €50; €19.50 (three-course set menu). Wine: €20.

Florian

The idea of creating a restaurant dedicated to Swabian cuisine might sound unusual but *Florian* has turned out to be a huge success with the trendy crowd in Berlin's Mitte – people from the theatre and film world often can be spotted here. People come to relax in the traditional South German setting, with its wooden furniture and homely ambience, as well as to enjoy the Swabian dishes with a slight French twist, such as the *Hackbraten* (basically a meatloaf) or the potato casserole. No credit cards.
Grolmanstrasse 52, Mitte
Tel: (030) 313 9184.
Price: €38. Wine: €21.

Hamlet

A fascinating ambience is created in *Hamlet*, as European as well as Eastern influences are reflected in its interior design and its menu. The imaginative cuisine covers traditional, French and Arabian tastes, such as vegetable plates or couscous dishes. The diversity of the food is enjoyed by a similarly varied crowd, coming from a range of ethnic backgrounds and social groups.
Uhlandstrasse 47
Tel: (030) 882 1361.
Price: €30. Wine: €22.

Paris Bar

Situated just off the Kurfürstendamm, this trendy restaurant attracts a polyglot clientele of film stars, artists, entrepreneurs and executives who care more for glamour than gourmet food. The atmosphere is created by simple, dark wooden chairs, tables and benches and lots of old French magazine covers and pictures on the walls. The French cuisine, including Jacques oysters and lamb chops with Provençale herbs, is reliable. It is an excellent spot for lunch, as the waiting list for tables is shorter than it is for dinner.
Kantstrasse 152
Tel: (030) 313 8052. Fax: (030) 313 2816.
E-mail: parisbar@sehrgut.de
Website: www.parisbar.de
Price: €30. Wine: €35.

Budget

Carpe Diem

This Spanish restaurant profits from the charm of a typical Berlin setting, located as it is underneath an S-Bahn railway track in Charlottenburg. Many shops and restaurants make use of these railway arches, as they provide an unconventional and cosy setting with their old, impressive brickwork. A variety of inexpensive, tasty tapas is served here. However, the main dishes, such as the paella Valencia or the grilled octopus, are also a delight, especially accompanied by a bottle of Spanish red wine.
Arch 576–577, between Uhlandstrasse and Grolmanstrasse, Charlottenburg
Tel: (030) 313 2728. Fax: (030) 313 2628.
E-mail: info@carpe-diem-restaurant.de
Website: www.carpe-diem-restaurant.de
Price: €28.50 (three-course menu including a glass of sherry). Wine: €17.

Grossbeerenkeller

This cellar restaurant in Kreuzberg, with its massive, dark oak furniture and decorative antlers, is undoubtedly one of the most original dining spots in town. Its old-fashioned and warm Berlin hospitality is hard to equal. Simple, traditional meals, such as diced pork with home fries and herb sauce or boiled salt pork with green cabbage, are served here. The fried potatoes are said to be the best in town.
Grossbeerenstrasse 90, Kreuzberg
Tel: (030) 251 3064.
Price: €20. Wine: €16.75.

Mao Thai

With its gorgeous East Asian interior design and great value for money, *Mao Thai* is always packed, although it is perhaps not the most authentic Thai restaurant in town. The chicken served in a coconut is the signature dish, although other dishes – such as the fried scampi in tomato sauce, with chillies, spring onions, peppers, pineapple and cucumber – are slightly more inventive.
Wörther Strasse 30
Tel: (030) 441 9261. Fax: (030) 4434 2090.
E-mail: maothai@snafu.de
Website: www.thaipage.com
Price: €25. Wine: €15.

Oren

This popular Israeli venue, situated next to the synagogue, is the best place for diners to enjoy traditional Jewish cooking. The restaurant buzzes with loud chatter all evening and the atmosphere and service are friendly. The small backyard is a wonderful spot on a warm summer evening. The *gefilte* fish – a tasty and very salty German-Jewish dish – is recommended.
Oranienburger Strasse 28
Tel: (030) 282 8228. Fax: (030) 2859 9313.
E-mail: info@restaurant-oren.de
Website: www.restaurant-oren.de
Price: €30. Wine: €15 (half-litre).

Pasternak

Normally absolutely packed, this small Russian restaurant attracts an intellectual and alternative crowd, as well as the more chic in-crowd. Decorated in a turn-of-the-century style, it is suitably located in the historic Mitte district, where the atmosphere is buzzing. Food is filling, such as the traditional *borscht*, ample fish plate starters, or the ravioli filled with either meat or potatoes and the hearty beef Stroganoff mains. Reservations essential. No credit cards.
Knaackstrasse 22–24, Mitte
Tel: (030) 441 3399. Fax: (030) 4404 6518.
Website: www.restaurant-pasternak.de
Price: €30. Wine: €28.

Personal Recommendations

Abendmahl

The name means 'Last Supper' and the decor is indeed enlivened with a little Catholic kitsch. The menu changes regularly and all dishes bear wacky names, such as 'News from the Moon' or 'Murder Ahoi'. In most cases, however, they are wonderfully presented, hot fish dishes – such as Thai fish curry – or inventive vegetarian delights. The service is charming and efficient and the ambience laid-back, which makes the trip out to Kreuzberg worthwhile. Reservations recommended. No credit cards.
Muskauer Strasse 9, Kreuzberg
Tel: (030) 612 5170. Fax: (030) 6953 4732.
E-mail: abendmahl@abendmahl-berlin.de
Website: www.abendmahl-berlin.de
Price: €30. Wine: €20.

Fridas Schwester

This relaxed wine bar/bistro in the trendy Mitte district in East Berlin has simple decor with a French feel, characterised by plain wooden floors, wooden tables and chairs and dark walls. There are stools at the bar where guests can sip a glass of wine – there are over 40 varieties to choose from. The clientele is a mixed one, mainly comprised of those working in the creative industries – the bistro at the back is said to attract well-known people seeking privacy. The food is a mix of Austrian, Italian, Mexican and Californian influences and includes dishes such as lemongrass soup, potato gnocchi with olives and parmesan, black fettuccine with shrimps and tomato sauce, and chicken with vegetables and rosemary potatoes in red wine.
Neue Schonhauser Strasse 11
Tel: (030) 2838 4710.
Price: €30. Wine: €18.

Hakuin

Named after a Japanese Zen master, *Hakuin* serves excellent but pricey Buddhist vegetarian food. The restaurant has a quiet Japanese charm, with tables arranged around a fish pool with calming fountain and wild plants. Exotic and delicious vegetable or fruit curries are served on bamboo plates, which complement the overall style. Closed Monday.
Martin-Luther-Strasse 1
Tel: (030) 218 2027. Fax: (030) 213 9862.
E-mail: info@restaurant-hakuin.de
Website: www.restaurant-hakuin.de
Price: €25. Wine: €30.

Maxwell

Situated in the restored former Josty brewery in the Mitte district, this elegant and spacious restaurant spreads over two floors and a big terrace during summer. Chef Uwe Popall insists on using local produce, while the wine list features a wide range of German vineyards. His cuisine is creative, including such delights as red snapper with Merguez sausage and broad beans or duck with black pepper sauce and vegetable spring rolls.
Bergstrasse 22, Mitte
Tel: (030) 280 7121. Fax: (030) 2859 9848.
E-mail: maxwell.berlin@t-online.de
Website: www.maxwellberlin.de
Price: €45. Wine: €20.

Trenta Sei

Situated in the most picturesque square in Berlin, the Gendarmenplatz, *Trenta Sei* is an Italian

Photo: Corel

Part of the Berlin Wall

restaurant with metropolitan character. A row of small tables and chairs are placed along the wall and the windows, the waiters wear long white aprons and the menu is similarly straightforward, with dishes such as *vitello tonnato* (veal in tuna sauce) and cream of crab soup.
Markgrafenstrasse 36
Tel: (030) 2045 2630.
Price: €40. Wine: €25.

ENTERTAINMENT

Nightlife

Berlin is quite simply one of Europe's most effervescent party cities. The old divides are still there when it comes to nightlife and the Western centre, somewhat ironically, lags behind the real action in the resurgent East. Berlin today is a byword for alternative culture and within the city pretty much anything goes. Punk and various forms of anarchy are struggling to survive among the style bars and yuppie haunts in Kreuzberg but the avant-garde cultural scene and accompanying drinking culture has moved on to Mitte, Prenzlauer Berg and increasingly to Friedrichshain. Likewise, the city's gay scene is divided between staid Schöneberg, Kreuzberg and edgier Prenzlauer Berg.

For a first-time visitor, Mitte is probably the better bet, starting around the Hackesche Höfe and working up Oranienburger Strasse to the numerous bars that first greeted the Western hordes after the Wall fell. *Tacheles*, at the end of the street, is worth a visit for the spirit of culture and anarchy it once implied. For the real experience of Berlin, however, it has to be Prenzlauer Berg (Prenzl'berg for short). Some of the more established places are reasonably easy to find but the real fun starts with the wild bars and impromptu clubs that seem to spring up from nowhere one week and disappear forever the next.

Entry to bars is officially restricted to those 18 years and older. There is often a cover charge of around €2.50–10 for discos and nightclubs but most do not have dress codes and there are no fixed closing times. The average price of a drink while out and about in Berlin is €5–6.

Listings can be found in *Zitty* (website: www.zitty.de), *Tip* (website: www.tip-berlin.de) and *Prinz* (website: www.prinz.de) magazines. There are also club listings in the free magazines, *Flyer* (website: www.flyer.de/berlin) and *030* (website: www.berlin030.de).

Bars

For those looking to spend their money in a trendy atmosphere, the *Bar am Lützowplatz*, Lützowplatz 7 (website: www.baramluetzowplatz.com), between the Tiergarten and U-Bahn Nollendorfplatz, offers high-priced cocktails. On the other side of Nollendorfplatz is *Hafen*, Motzstrasse 19, a popular gay bar. Other established bars are *Wirtschaftwunder*, Yorckstrasse 81, with 1950s decor, and the small, crowded *Zoulou Bar*, Hauptstrasse 4, which always has an interesting mix of people.

Bars line the scruffy streets of Oranienstrasse and Wiener Strasse in Kreuzberg, many doubling up as cafés during the day. *Café Bar Morena*, Wiener Strasse 60, is an institution. The nearby *Wiener Blut*, Weiner Strasse 13, is a good local, while *Madonna*, Weiner Strasse 22, is a bit rougher.

In East Berlin, there are too many things happening to list them all here. Good places to start on Oranienburger Strasse (the *geile Meile*) are the funky *Bar Lounge 808*, Oranienburger Strasse 42–43, *Reingold*, Novalisstrasse 11, for cocktails and jazz, or *Mitte Bar*, Oranienburger Strasse 46, which is popular as much with the arty local set as it is with students. There is also the well-established *Obst und Gemuse*, Oranienburger Strasse 48/49. In trendy Prenzlauer Berg, the most buzzing bars are *H20*, Kastanienalle 16, and *Prater*, Kastienalle 7–9, with its beer garden, theatre and bar. You can also try *Icon*, Cantianstrasse 15.

The most unusual bars in the city are the *unsicht-Bar*, Gormannstrasse, and the *Nocti Vagus*, Saarbruecker Strasse 36–38, both of which serve food and drink in complete darkness. During 2003, both venues will stage events such as music evenings and plays.

Cabaret

The legacy of 1930s Berlin and Marlene Dietrich lives on. Over-the-top commercial cabaret is best seen at the *Friedrichstadtpalast*, Friedrichstrasse 107 (website: www.friedrichstadtpalast.de), with musical revues that combine glittering costumes with elements of dance and theatre into the floorshows at one of Europe's largest revue theatres. *Wintergarten –*

Das Varieté, Potsdamer Strasse 96 (website: www.wintergarten-variete.de), offers dinner and variety shows. More off-beat shows can be found at independent venues in the area to the north of the Hackesche Höfe and in Prenzlauer Berg.

Casinos

Spielbank Berlin is part of the new Potsdamer Platz development and is located opposite the Grand Hyatt hotel, Marlene-Dietrich-Platz 1 (website: www.spielbank-berlin.de). There is no specific dress code, although a passport is required, along with the €5.11 entry fee. The casino is open daily 1130–0300 to those aged 18 years and over; guests must bring identification, such as a passport. *Casino Berlin*, situated on the 37th floor of the Forum Hotel, Alexanderplatz, is open daily 1500–0300. The entrance fee is €5 and a jacket and tie are required. Players must be over 18 years and a passport is required for entry.

Clubs

There are a number of tourist-orientated discos in the Ku'damm area but a better bet in West Berlin is *90 Grad*, Dennewitzstrasse 37, with a young crowd dancing to funky beats and house on the gay nights (Thursday and Saturday). *SO36*, Oranienstrasse 190, in Kreuzberg, has different moods and music styles, depending on the night. It also hosts concerts. Then there is the singles-orientated *Balhaus Berlin*, Chausseestrasse 102, where you can invite people to dance via a telephone on your table.

There is an eclectic array of clubs in East Berlin. In Mitte, one of the current hip places to see and be seen is the *Sage-Club*, Köpenicker Strasse 78, with its painfully trendy atmosphere and plenty of up-front house music. In Prenzlauer Berg, *Knaack Club*, Greifswalder Strasse 224, is a multi-level club with a wide variety of sounds and concerts early in the week, while *Havanna*, Haupstrasse 30, offers salsa, merengue and funk. The halcyon days of out-and-out techno (the soundtrack for the fall of the Wall in 1989) live on in *Casino*, Mühlenstrasse, and in *Matrix*, Warschauer Platz 18.

Comedy

Offering quality stand-up, the *Quatsch Comedy Club* can be found on Friedrichstrasse 107 (website: www.quatschcomedyclub.de).

Live Music

In addition to the clubs that double up as live music venues mentioned above, Berlin has a variety of spots in which to witness live bands. The jazz and blues scene is particularly happening and popular spots include *A Trane Jazzclub*, Bleibtreustrasse 1, and *B-Flat*, Rosenthaler Strasse 13, as well as some nights at *Flöz*, Nassauische Strasse 37, and *Quasimodo*, Kantstrasse 12A. Major rock concerts take place at *Columbiahalle*, Columbiadamm 13–21 (website: www.columbiahalle.de), and occasionally at large sporting venues like the *Velodrom*, Paul-Heyse-Strasse 26, Prenzlauer Berg, and *Max-Schmeling-Halle*, Am Falkplatz, Prenzlauer Berg. Open-air concerts are held at the *Waldbühne*, Am Glockenturm, near the Olympic Stadium.

Sport

The *Olympiastadion* (Olympic Stadium), Bismarckstrasse, was built for the 1936 Olympic Games and is now the site for sports events, concerts and conferences. Football is extremely popular and the *Hertha BSC* football team (tel: (01805) 437 842 (charged at €0.12 per minute); website: www.herthabsc.de) plays at the Olympic Stadium, competing valiantly against other top German sides in the *Bundesliga* (First Division). German football was given a massive boost by the announcement that the country will stage the 2006 World Cup, with games scheduled for the capital, although suspicions of alleged bribery surrounded the decision to choose Germany over hot favourite South Africa.

Berlin is home to the *German Women's Open* tennis tournament, which takes place on the clay courts of the *LTTC 'Rot-Weiss'*, Gottfried-von-Cramm-Weg 47–55, Berlin-Grunewald (tel: (030) 895 7550; fax: (030) 8957 5550; e-mail: info@rot-weiss-berlin.de; website: http://rot-weiss.red2pro.net), each May. In men's basketball, *Alba Berlin* (website: www.albaberlin.de) is strong in the German league and competes in Europe. Games can be seen at the *Max-Schmeling-Halle*, Am Falkplatz, Prenzlauer Berg (tel: (030) 443 045; fax: (030) 4430 4709; e-mail: info@velomax.de; website: www.max-schmeling-halle.de).

Fullhouse Service (tel: (030) 3087 85685) sells tickets to basketball matches as well as major annual sporting events. *Showtime* (tel: (0800) 8822 8822; website: www.showtime-berlin.de) also sells tickets to sporting events, with an outlet in the KaDeWe department store.

Fitness Centres

Elixia – Mitte, Behrenstrasse 48, on the corner of Friedrichstrasse (tel: (030) 2063 5300; fax: (030) 2063 5310; website: www.elixia.com), is a centraly located gym with long opening hours (Monday to Friday 0600–2300, Saturday and Sunday 1000–2200). Options include free weights, circuit training, aerobics and other classes, a sauna and a steamroom. A day pass costs €25. The Ostkreuz branch, at Hirschberger Strasse 3, has a 25m (82ft) pool.

Golf

There are 16 golf courses in the Berlin-Brandenburg area and information on these is available in a guide published by the *Association of Golf Timers*, available free from *Golfverband Berlin-Brandenburg*, Forststrasse 34 (tel: (030) 823 6609; fax: (030) 824 4098; website: www.gvbb.de). Public courses charge approximately €18 per round, while the green fees at the various private clubs range from €25 to €50. A public course, *Golf-Zentrum Berlin-Mitte*, Chausseestrasse 94–98 (tel: (030) 2804 7070; website: www.golfzentrum.berlin.de), is a central spot with equipment and training available, where golfers can practice from 0700 until 2200.

Swimming

There is no shortage of places to swim in the city. During summer, locals head to the beaches on *Wannsee* and *Tegeler See*, in West Berlin, or to the larger *Grosser Müggelsee*, in the East. Public swimming pools include the indoor pool at *Bad am Spreewaldplatz*, Wiener Strasse 59, in Kreuzberg (tel: (030) 612 7057; website: www.berlinerbaederbetriebe.de), and an outdoor pool next to U-Bahn Prinzenstrasse station. The *Sport- und Erholungszentrum (SEZ)*, Landsberger Allee 77, in Friedrichshain (tel: (030) 4218 2320), is one of Berlin's largest sport centres and has a swimming pool.

Tennis

There are a number of tennis courts in the city, including *TSF Freizeitcenter Marienfelde*, Richard-Tauber-Damm 36 (tel: (030) 742 1091), and *TSF Freizeitcenter Spandau*, Galenstrasse 33–35 (tel: (030) 333 4083), charging €12–19 in summer and €16–24 in winter. *TSB City Sports*, Brandenburgische Strasse 53 (tel: (030) 873 9097), has rates starting from €8.50 and rising to €17, while *TCW Tenniscenter*, Roelckestrasse 106 (tel: (030) 927 4594), charges €14–26. Rates vary depending on the time of day, with the highest prices falling between 1600 and 2200.

Shopping

For years, the Kurfürstendamm, or Ku'damm for short (website: www.kurfuerstendamm.de or www.berlin-citywest.com), has been the place to shop in Berlin. This elegant boulevard of shops and department stores has designer boutiques and shopping passages tucked down its side streets, particularly around the U-Bahn Uhlandstrasse station. The *Europa-Center* is also unmistakable, as it has a large revolving Mercedes Benz symbol on its roof. However, the most famous address is *Kaufhaus des Westens* or KaDeWe, Tauenzienstrasse 21–24 (website: www.kadewe.de), the largest department store in Europe – its food hall is enormous.

However, the West's pre-eminence for Berlin shoppers is facing challenges from the revitalised areas of East Berlin. Unter den Linden and Friedrichstrasse (website: www.friedrichstrasse.de) have both blossomed since reunification, with boutiques, department stores, such as *Quartier 206*, and the *Galeries Lafayette* shopping centre. Even this is changing with the completion of Potsdamer Platz – already the *Arkaden* shopping mall is luring away shoppers from other, more established areas. Also in the East are the boutiques in the Hackesche Höfe and the many galleries in the Scheunenviertel, just to the north. For innovative clothing, *Heckmannhöfe*, Oranienburger Strasse 32, is the place for shoppers to head, with the likes of *Hut Up*, with its bold woollens, *Nix*, with its urban chic, and *Sterling Gold*, with its array of weird and wonderful second-hand cocktail and evening dresses. Other areas worth exploring are around Rosenhote, Alte Schonhaustrasse and Neue Schonhaustrasse.

For markets, there is the traditional fruit and vegetable market at Winterfeldtplatz, open Wednesday 0800–1300 and Saturday 0800–1530. More interesting objects can be found at the *Trödelmarkt* (Flea Market) and *Arts and Crafts Market*, along Strasse des 17 Juni, open Saturday and Sunday 1000–1700.

Shops are generally open Monday to Friday 0900/1000–2000 and Saturday 0900/1000–1600. Smaller shops might close a little earlier. There is a great online resource (website: www.kauflust.de) in the form of a guide to 250 shops with a clickable map. Visitors from outside the EU can reclaim a portion of the 16% VAT (up to 10%) on goods worth over €30. Shops displaying the 'TAX-FREE' sign issue a receipt that, when stamped by customs, can be redeemed at a tax-free reimbursement office.

Culture

In the decade or so since the fall of the Wall, Berlin has emerged as one of Europe's most culturally vibrant cities, infused with a unique blend of Western and Eastern European cultures. There are world-class theatre and opera performances and a comprehensive array of museums and galleries to choose from.

Beyond this, there are all the expressions of the counter culture for which Berlin is famous. Although remnants remain in Kreuzberg, the most avant-garde artists have moved to Mitte and increasingly to Prenzlauer Berg.

Berlin Tourismus Marketing (see *Tourist Information*) publishes an online event calendar (website: www.berlin-tourist-information.de), as well as the *Berlin Events* leaflet. Tickets to cultural events are available for purchase through *Berlin Tourismus Marketing*, online (website www.berlin.de/tickets) or directly through most venues.

Music

The *Berlin Philharmonic Orchestra* is renowned worldwide. Its performance space, the *Philharmonie*, Herbert-von-Karajan-Strasse 1 (tel: (030) 254 880 or 2548 8132 (information) or 2548 8126 or 2548 8194 (ticket office); fax: (030) 261 4887 (information) or 2548 8323 (bookings); e-mail: kartenbuero@berlin-philharmonic.com; website: www.berlin-philharmonic.com), matches their reputation. Within the venue, the *Kammermusiksaal der Philharmonie* hosts chamber players, soloists and small orchestras.

Berlin's most elegant venue for classical music is the *Konzerthaus Berlin*, Gendarmenmarkt 2 (tel: (030) 2030 92101; fax: (030) 2030 92209; website: www.konzerthaus.de). The *Berliner Sinfonie-Orchester* is based here.

The premier venue for opera, ballet and concerts was built in 1741–43, as the Court Opera House. Today, the *Staatsoper Unter den Linden*, Unter den Linden 7 (tel: (030) 2035 4555 or 4438 (information); fax: (030) 2035 4483; website: www.staatsoper-berlin.de), is under the artistic and musical direction of Daniel Barenboim. The *Deutsche Oper Berlin*, situated in the west of the city, at Bismarckstrasse 35 (tel: (030) 343 8401 or 341 0249; fax: (030) 3438 4232; website: www.deutscheoperberlin.de), stages classical and modern opera, as well as ballet, operettas and concerts.

Performances at the *Komische Oper Berlin*, Behrenstrasse 55–57 (tel: (030) 202 600; fax: (030) 2026 0405; e-mail: info@komische-oper-berlin.de; website: www.komische-oper-berlin.de), which opened in 1947, include music, dance and concerts.

Theatre

The *Deutsches Theater und Kammerspiele*, Schumannstrasse 13A (tel: (030) 2844 1225 or 250 025 (tickets); fax: (030) 282 4117; website: www.deutschestheater.de), mounts contemporary productions as well as 19th- and 20th-century plays. The neo-Baroque *Berliner Ensemble*, Bertolt-Brecht-Platz 1 (tel: (030) 2840 8155; fax: (030) 2840 8115; website: www.berliner-ensemble.de), was built before the turn of the century, as the *Neues Theater*. It was taken over by Bertolt Brecht and Helene Weigel and its resident company continues to show performances from Brecht's works, as well as classical and modern pieces. For non-conformist and unconventional theatre and dance, the *Volksbühne am Rosa-Luxemburg-Platz*, Linienstrasse 227 (tel: (030) 247 6772; fax: (030) 2406 5642; website: www.volksbuehne-berlin.de), is one of the top addresses.

Dance

The *Hebbel-Theater*, Stresemannstrasse 29 (tel: (030) 2590 0427; fax: (030) 2590 0449; website: www.hebbel-theater.de), is one of the centres for contemporary dance and opera in Europe. It also hosts the *Tanz Winter* and *Tanz im August* dance festivals. Classical ballet is staged at the *Deutsche Oper Berlin*, Bismarckstrasse 35 (tel: (030) 343 8401; fax: (030) 343 8455; website: www.deutscheoperberlin.de), which has an excellent resident ballet company, *Ballet der Deutsche Oper Berlin*.

Film

In the early 20th century, Berlin was the cradle of German cinema, with seminal films such as *Metropolis* (1927) and other works of German expressionism. The 1930 film, *Der Blaue Engel* (*The Blue Angel*), starring Marlene Dietrich (website: www. marlene.com), was based on Heinrich Mann's novel, *Professor Unrath* (1905). The movie catapulted Dietrich to stardom, as the sexy cabaret singer Lola Lola. Berlin earned itself a reputation for decadence in the 1920s and 1930s, which were recaptured to good effect in the 1972 film, *Cabaret*. More recent works have included Wim Wenders' 1987 film, *Der Himmel über Berlin* (*Wings of Desire*), in which two angels watch over the divided city from the Siegessäule.

Berlin has over a hundred cinemas and new releases are often screened in the English original (*OV* or *OF*) or the original language with German subtitles (*OmU*). The best place for blockbuster fans to catch the latest big releases, often in the original version, are the 19-screen *CinemaxX Berlin Potsdamer Platz*, Potsdamer Platz (tel: (030) 4431 6316 *or* (0180) 5246 36299; website: www.cinemaxx.de), and the nearby eight-screen *CineStar im Sony Center*, Potsdamer Strasse 4 (tel: (030) 2606 6260; website: www. cinestar.de). Of the mainstream cinemas in the city's western half, *Kant-Kino*, Kantstrasse 54 (tel: (030) 312 5047 *or* 319 9866), sometimes has Hollywood fare in English with German subtitles. Of the numerous repertory, international and arthouse screens, *Arsenal*, Potsdamer Strasse 2 (tel: (030) 2695 5100; website: www.fdk-berlin.de), is a central spot with a lot of English screenings.

The *Berlin Film Festival* (website: www.berlinale.de) is one of the most important on the circuit and the *Berlin Bear* prize is almost as highly valued as the legendary *Palme d'Or*. The film festival takes place in February and celebrated its 50th anniversary in 2000. Weekly film listings are printed on posters that are displayed throughout the city. The magazines *Tip* (website: www.tip-berlin.de) and *Zitty* (website: www.zitty.de) also have listings. During summer there are popular outdoor film screenings in the *Volkspark Hasenheide* and at the *Waldbühne*, near the Olympic Stadium.

Cultural Events

Berlin offers a number of multi-disciplinary venues, which offer a range of cultural events throughout the year. *Haus der Kulturen der Welt*, John-Foster-Dulles Allee 10, in the Tiergarten (tel: (030) 3978 7175; fax: (030) 394 8679; website: www.hkw.de), hosts concerts, theatre, films, readings and events such as the *International Festival of Media Art* in February, with a remit to spotlight non-European cultures. *Tacheles*, Oranienburger Strasse 54–56 (tel: (030) 282 6185; fax: (030) 282 3130; e-mail: office@tacheles.de; website: www.tacheles.de), is an avant-garde, somewhat anarchic, cultural centre in the bombed-out shell of a former department store. One of Berlin's more poignant venues is the *Tränenpalast* (Palace of Tears), Reichstagufer 17 (tel: (030) 206 1000; website: www.traenenpalast.de), which West

The Olympic Stadium

Berliners visiting East Berlin had to pass through. Today, it hosts theatre, films and concerts.

Summer undoubtedly sees most of the cultural action in Berlin, with the largest event of its kind, the massive July *Love Parade* taking over the Strasse des 17 Juni. A multitude of techno ravers gathers to enjoy the vibe, sunshine and the booming sound systems. Other alfresco events that characterise the Berlin summertime are the *Karneval der Kulturen*, a carnival of culture ending in a colourful parade, and the *Christopher Street Day*, when gay and lesbian revellers march through the streets to proclaim their pride. Both take place in June.

Literary Notes

Der Stechlin (1898), Theodor Fontane's late 19th-century novel, has the Stechlinsee in the dark Menzer Forest to the southeast of Berlin as its setting. *Berlin Alexanderplatz* (1929) is Alfred Döblin's epic tale of the city. Also from the inter-war period is Christopher Isherwood's *The Berlin Stories*, comprising the novels *Mr Norris Changes Trains* (1935) and *Goodbye to Berlin* (1939). They depict Berlin in the pre-Hitler years of the decadent Weimar Republic. Bertolt Brecht moved to Berlin in 1924 and stayed there until 1933, when he fled after the burning of the Reichstag. He directed and wrote many of his early plays here, most successfully *Die Dreigroschenoper* (*The Threepenny Opera*), which opened in 1928. Berlin's post-war appearances in English writing have tended to be of the spy novel genre – as the city was the front line of the Cold War. Robert Harris' *Fatherland* (1993) is a disturbing speculative fiction of Berlin based on the premise that the Nazis had not lost the war. Peter Schneider's *The Wall Jumper* (1984) is a mixed genre meditation on the Berlin Wall.

SPECIAL EVENTS

Berlin Cycling Six Days Race, late Jan, Velodrom
Lange Nacht der Museen (Long Night of the Museum), over 100 city museums are open all night long, late Jan/early Feb, various venues
International Festival of Media Art, early Feb, Haus der Kulturen der Welt
Berlinale International Film Festival (website: www.berlinale.de), early Feb, various venues
Annual Berlin Theatre Event, early–mid-May, various venues
Women's Tennis Open, early May, LTTC 'Rot-Weiss'
Berlin-biennale for Contemporary Art, biannual exhibition, with the next event taking place in 2005, mid-May–mid-Jul, Martin-Gropius-Bau
Karneval der Kulturen (Carnival of Cultures), parade and festival, late May/early Jun, Werkstatt der Kulturen, Kreuzberg
German Choir Festival, Jun, various locations
Christopher Street Day, lesbian and gay pride march, late Jun, various venues
Berlin Cycling Six Days Race, late Jan, Velodrom
Classic Open Air, early–mid-Jul, Gendarmenarkt
Berlin Love Parade, mid-Jul, Strasse des 17 Juni (Tiergarten)
Lange Nacht der Museen (Long Night of the Museums), over 100 museums open late with special events, late Aug
Berlin Marathon, late Sep, throughout the city
Tag der Deutschen Einheit (Day of German Unity), 3 Oct, throughout the city
JazzFest Berlin, early Nov, various venues
Jüdische Kulturtage (Jewish Cultural Days), Nov, various venues
Christmas Markets, late Nov–late Dec, next to Europa-Center, at Alexanderplatz, at the Opernpalais (Unter den Linden) and at some local markets
Silvester in Berlin, New Year's Eve celebrations, 31 Dec, huge street party between Brandenburg Gate and the Siegessäule (website: www.silvester-berlin.de), plus numerous balls and parties, throughout the city

BRUSSELS

The European Parliament has found an ideal home in Brussels (*Bruxelles* in French, *Brussel* in Flemish). This inland capital city of Belgium, bordered by The Netherlands, Germany, Luxembourg and France, is a multi-cultural and multi-lingual city at the very heart of Europe. Indeed, it claims, with some justification, to be the 'Capital of Europe'.

Brussels was already a thriving trade centre by the Middle Ages. The *Bruxellois* have inherited the wisdom of ancestors who lived under Roman, Spanish, Austrian, French, Dutch and German domination – their country winning independence only in 1830. Today, Brussels boasts a highly skilled and adaptable workforce. Despite the population of Belgium numbering only 10.2 million, with Brussels itself just some 970,000-strong, the *Bruxellois* have the ability to compensate for their small numbers with skilled diplomacy, compromise and negotiation. These striking traits are followed closely by a highly intellectual and off-beat sense of humour, underpinned by a strong sense of the bizarre. This may help explain why the Surrealist art movement, pioneered by René Magritte, took off in Brussels. A playful and irreverent reaction to life is also revealed in the Belgian love affair with the comic strip, popularised worldwide with Hergé's boy hero, Tintin.

Language is a complex and serious issue in bilingual (French and Flemish) Brussels, as well as being a focus of communal tensions. Some 85% of native *Bruxellois* speak French as their first language. Ironically, Brussels is also the capital of Flemish-speaking Flanders. However, the fierce linguistic debate takes a lighter form, with constant puns and word games forming a complex web. For instance, while a top-notch restaurant is called *Comme Chez Soi* (Just Like Home), a less prestigious establishment calls itself *Comme Chez Moi* (Just Like *My* Home), with more than a twist of irony.

Yet the image of the city suffers abroad, due to its very diversity, as well as the self-effacing nature of its quirky inhabitants, too modest to blow their own trumpet. Brussels has no symbol to rival the skyscraping Eiffel Tower, aside from the tiny but famed Manneken-Pis, a statuette of a urinating boy.

The first visit to Brussels, uncoloured by expectations, is therefore all the more rewarding. Narrow cobbled streets open suddenly into the breathtaking Grand-Place, with its ornate guild houses, impressive Town Hall and buzzing atmosphere. It would be difficult to find a more beautiful square in the whole of Europe. Bars, restaurants and museums are clustered within the compact city centre, enclosed within the *petit ring*, which follows the path of the 14th-century city walls. The medieval city is clearly defined by its narrow, labyrinthine streets, making it easy to distinguish the later additions, such as Léopold II's Parisian-style boulevards – Belliard and La Loi – today lined with embassies, banks and the grand apartments of the bourgeoisie and close to the glitzy new EU quarter. The working class still congregate in the Marolles district, in the shadow of the Palais de Justice, although this area is on the up-and-up. New immigrant communities are settling in the rundown area around the Gare du Nord. Neighbouring *communes*, St-Gilles and Ixelles, draw an arty crowd with their 'in' shops and restaurants. These are worth the trek, if only to glimpse some of Brussels' finest Art Nouveau buildings, the style being developed by *Bruxellois* Victor Horta, the son of a shoemaker.

With a pleasant temperate climate – warm summers and mild winters – and a host of sights and delights to entertain, Brussels offers far more than just beer and chocolate (although excelling in both). The year 2003 marked the city's celebration of its cultural diversity – from its rich architecture to native hero and lyrical singer Jacques Brel – through a series of cultural events, festivals and restoration schemes.

Ommegang procession, Grand-Place

Photo: Belgian Tourist Office – Brussels Wallonia

TRAVEL

Getting There By Air

Brussels Airport (BRU)

Tel: (0900) 70000 (for flight information). Fax: (02) 753 4250.

Website: www.brusselsairport.be

Brussels Airport, operated by *Brussels International Airport Company – BIAC* (tel: (02) 753 4200), is situated 12km (eight miles) northeast of Brussels in Zaventem, offering flights to over 150 destinations worldwide. The number of passengers using the airport in 2001 peaked between July and September when over 20 million passengers passed through Brussels Airport, which is a modern facility quite in keeping with the stature of the city it serves. Comprehensive free information guides are widely available around the airport.

Major airlines: *SN Brussels Airlines* (tel: (02) 723 2323; website: www.flysn.com) has taken on most of the former Sabena routes. Currently, it is one of the two largest Belgian-based airlines, along with *Virgin Express* (tel. (02) 752 0511; website: www.virgin-express.com). SN Brussels Airlines serves 41 European destinations and 13 African destinations, while Virgin Express operates flights to 16 destinations across Europe. Other major airlines include *Air Canada, Alitalia, American Airlines, British Airways, Lufthansa, Singapore Airlines* and *United Airlines*.

Airport facilities: These include post office and medical facilities, bank and bureaux de change, ATMs, bars, restaurants, shops, tourist information and car hire from *Avis, Budget, Europcar, Hertz, National/Alamo* and *Sixt*.

Business facilities: The *Skyport Corporate Meeting Centre* (tel: (02) 714 0200; fax: (02) 714 0201) is located on the fourth-floor 'Promenade' level and offers ten small meeting rooms and secretarial services.

Transport to the city: The *Airport Line* bus service, operated by *MIVB/STIB* (tel: (02) 515 2000; website: www.stib.irisnet.be), runs three to four times per hour daily 0700–2000. The cost of a journey into the city centre (journey time – 40 minutes) is the same as the much faster, more efficient train service, which runs daily 0600–2400. Also operated by STIB, the *Airport City Express* trains to the city (journey time – 15 minutes) depart every 15 minutes to Brussels' three main stations – Gare Centrale, Gare du Nord and Gare du Midi. A first-class one-way ticket costs €3.80, while a second-class ticket costs €2.50.

Taxis to the centre cost about €30. Hotel courtesy coaches go to the Holiday Inn, Novotel and Sofitel.

Brussels South Charleroi Airport (CRL)

Tel: (07) 125 1211. Fax: (07) 125 1202

Website: www.charleroi-airport.com

Brussels' second and smaller airport is located 55km (37 miles) south of Brussels, in Charleroi – a one-hour drive from Lille, in the North of France. The privately owned airport, which belongs to the Walloon region and private investors, is an international airport for passenger and freight traffic, a test and training flight base for aeronautical industry and a centre for general and business aviation. The acknowledged training centre of all Belgian airlines, *Belgian Flight School*, is also based here. Low-cost airline *Ryanair* serves London, Shannon, Dublin, Glasgow Prestwick, Venice, Carcassonne, Pisa, Venice, Rome, Milan and Liverpool.

Major airlines: *Ryanair* (tel: (0900) 10310, French only *or* (0900) 10740, Flemish only; website: www.ryanair.com) operates most passenger flights to and from Charleroi Airport. Other airlines using the airport include *Air Alfa, Air Algérie, bmi British Midland, Futura, Istanbul Airlines, Noubel Air, Turkish Airlines* and *Virgin Express*.

Airport facilities: Facilities include bars, shops, lost property, a bank and duty-free shop. Car hire is available from *Hertz. Avis* (tel: (07) 132 3535) and *All Top Rent a Car* (tel: (07) 132 3334) are based in Charleroi and will deliver cars to the airport.

Business facilities: There is a first-class lounge available in the terminal.

Transport to the city: The *MIVB/STIB* (tel: (02) 515 2000; website: www.stib.irisnet.be) bus 68 runs from Charleroi Airport to the nearby Charleroi train station (journey time – 10 minutes) Monday to Friday 0600–2330 and Saturday and Sunday 0620–2230. From there, a frequent *SNCB* (tel: (02) 528 2828; website: www.sncb.be) train service connects to Brussels' main stations, daily 0500–2400 (journey time – 45 minutes). Tickets cost €10. There are plans to extend the rail link directly to the airport, but this is some years away.

The door-to-door *Airport Transfer Service* (tel: (04) 7342 9490; e-mail: cromexa@yahoo.fr; website: www.cromexa.be) costs between €10 and €25. Taxis also run to central Brussels, costing €85 (journey time – 40 minutes).

Approximate flight times to Brussels: From London is 55 minutes; from New York is 10 hours; from Los Angeles is 16 hours; from Toronto is 7 hours 45 minutes and from Sydney is 27 hours.

Arrival/departure tax: €9.77 departure tax and €6.20 transfer tax is charged as part of the ticket price.

Getting There By Rail

Some €9 billion are being pumped into the *Belgian National Railways – SNCB/NMBS* (tel: (02) 528 2828; website: www.b-rail.be), in a ten-year modernisation plan due for completion in 2005. The service is fast and very efficient. There are three major railway stations in Brussels – *Gare Centrale*, located in the heart of the city, *Gare du Nord*, to the north of the main ring road, and *Gare du Midi*, to the south. They share a rail enquiries line (tel: (02) 555 2555). All three stations have bars, refreshments and disabled access, while Gare du Midi and Gare du Nord both have car parks.

Rail services: Most domestic trains stop at all three stations. *Eurostar* trains (tel: (02) 528 2828; website: www.eurostar.com) from London and *Thalys* express trains (tel: (070) 667 788; website: www.thalys.com) from Aachen, Amsterdam, Cologne and Paris stop at Gare du Midi, the *TGV* (High-Speed Train) terminal. Links to Paris (journey time – 1 hour 30 minutes) and London (journey time – 2 hours 40 minutes) are fast and efficient.

Transport to the city: All three stations are on the métro – Gare du Midi and Gare du Nord have a direct connection to Gare Centrale, as well as to other cities and the main airport.

Getting There By Road

Traffic drives on the right. Major towns are connected by toll-free motorways. Motorways are signposted with a white 'E' on a green background, major roads with an 'N' and minor roads with a 'P'. The speed limit on motorways and dual carriageways is 120kph (75mph), on single carriageways outside built-up areas is 90kph (56mph) and in built-up areas is 50kph (31mph).

The minimum driving age is 18 years. A valid national driving licence is required and national stickers must be displayed. EU nationals taking their own cars to Belgium are advised to obtain a Green Card, as basic insurance is mandatory for driving in Belgium. Children under 12 are forbidden to travel in the front seat without a child restraint. Seatbelts must be worn in the front and back of vehicles. The maximum legal alcohol to blood ratio for driving is 0.05%. Driving licences will be withdrawn for at least six hours if the breathalyser test is positive.

A warning triangle must be displayed at the scene of a breakdown or accident. After paying a membership fee and subscription, at the site of the breakdown, services can be obtained from the *Royal Automobile Club de Belgique*, Rue d'Arlon 53 (tel: (02) 287 0911; website: www.racb.com), or *Touring Club de Belgique*, Rue de la Loi 44 (tel: (02) 233 2212; website: www.touring.be). The latter has a reciprocal agreement with the *AA*, while *VTB VAB Auto Assistance*, Rue Pastoor Coplaan 100, Zwijndrecht (tel: (03) 253 6101), has a reciprocal agreement with the RAC.

Emergency breakdown services: *Royal Automobile Club de Belgique* (02) 287 0900 *or* (078) 152 000; *Touring Club de Belgique* (070) 344 777; *VTB VAB* (070) 344 666.

Routes to the city: The extensive motorway ring road around Brussels offers easy access into the city centre. Routes E19 and A12 lead north to Antwerp – from there, the E19 continues over the border toward Rotterdam and Amsterdam in The Netherlands.

Route E19 also extends south to Paris, becoming E15. Route E40 links Brussels with Ghent – from there, Ostend is reachable via route E17. Route E411 links Brussels to Namur and route E40 to Liège, continuing east over the border towards Cologne, from where the E35 heads toward Frankfurt.

Approximate driving times to Brussels: From Antwerp – 35 minutes; Ghent – 45 minutes; Namur – 45 minutes; Liège – 50 minutes; Ostend – 1 hour 20 minutes; Amsterdam – 2 hours 25 minutes; Paris – 3 hours 20 minutes; Frankfurt – 4 hours 15 minutes.

Coach services: Several companies provide bus services to nearby Belgian cities – all are much slower than the equivalent train routes. *De Lijn* (tel: (02) 526 2828) operates buses between Brussels and Flanders, while *TEC* (tel: (010) 235 353) provides a similar service to the French-speaking Wallonia. Most buses depart from *Gare du Nord*, in the Espace Nord, although some depart from *Place Rouppe*, in the Marolles district. There is a general enquiries line (tel: (02) 515 2000).

Eurolines (tel: (02) 274 1350; website: www. eurolines.com) operates international services to major European destinations – including direct routes to Cologne, Munich and Luxembourg – from *Noord I*, CCN Noordstation, Gare Routière, Vooruitgangstraat 80 (tel: (02) 274 1350), *Noord II*,

CITY STATISTICS

Location: Brussels region, Belgium.
Country dialling code: 32.
Population: 135,000 (city); 970,500 (metropolitan area).
Religion: Majority Catholic, with significant Protestant, Jewish and Muslim communities.
Ethnic mix: Majority Belgian (French and Flemish), with large minorities from other EU states, Morocco and Turkey.
Time zone: GMT + 1 (from 26 September to 30 March), GMT + 2 (from 30 March to 26 September).
Electricity: 220 volts AC, 50Hz; European two-pin round plugs are standard.
Average January temp: 3°C (37.5°F).
Average July temp: 17.5°C (63.5°F).
Annual rainfall: 740mm (29 inches).

Solvayplein 4–Place Solvay 4 (tel: (02) 274 1350) and *Zuid*, Avenue Fonsnylaan 13 (tel: (02) 538 2049).

Getting Around

Public Transport

The integrated **bus**, overground and underground (*prémétro*) **tram** and **métro** network is operated by *Société des Transports Intercommunaux Bruxellois*, known as *STIB* (tel: (02) 515 2000; website: www.stib.irisnet.be). The system operates daily 0600–2400, and the information line is manned Monday to Friday 0800–1900 and Saturday 0800–1600. Although efficient and extremely clean, the network is not without its problems – plans to replace the underground trams with an extended métro system have yet to materialise. However, recent improvements include the addition of lifts for handicapped passengers – at, Maelbeek, De Brouckère and Gare Centrale stations. STIB information points are located at Porte de Namur, Rogier and Midi métro stations, as well as at the Anspach Shopping Centre, Rue de l'Evêque.

Above ground, the **métro** is identified by a sign bearing a white 'M' on a blue background. Many stations display the works of local artists and métro seats are soft and comfortable – the service is pleasant even during rush hour (0730–0930 and 1600–1830). Métro lines 1A and 1B form a giant 'H' shape. Métro line 1A runs northwest to southeast, from Roi Baudouin to Herrmann-Debroux. Line 1B runs southwest to northeast, from Bizet to Stockel. Lines 1A and 1B join in the middle, running along the same lines from Beekhant to Merode, to serve the central part of the city. The incomplete circle of line 2, from Simonis to Clemenceau, follows the inner ring road underground.

Tram and **bus** stops are indicated by red and white signs respectively. The route number and destination are displayed on the front of the vehicle and all stops are request stops. Brussels' bright yellow and blue trams serve the city centre and suburbs. The trams reach their highest speeds underground – the *prémétro* runs south, underneath the heart of the city from Gare du Nord, stopping at Place de Brouckère and Bourse, and Gare du Midi (Eurostar terminal). Some services run on to St-Gilles and Albert.

Tickets for the transport network are available for purchase at métro stations and many newsagents. The tourist reception desk at Rue du Marché-aux-Herbes 63, and at the TIB at the Town Hall in Grand-Place sell day transport tickets (see below) and give out free maps of the network – also available at most métro stations. Tickets must be stamped at the métro ticket barrier, either prior to or upon boarding the bus or tram. Bus and overground tram tickets may also be purchased prior to or upon boarding the vehicle (exact change is required for the latter). Once purchased, the ticket is valid for any form of public transport, including changes. One-hour tickets (*la carte d'une voyage*) cost €1.40, while ten (hour-long) journey tickets (*la carte de dix voyages*) cost €9. A one-day **pass** (*la carte d'un jour*) costs €3.60 and is valid for two persons at weekends and holidays. A one-day group card (maximum five persons) is available for €5.95 and is valid at weekends, holidays and after 0900 on weekdays.

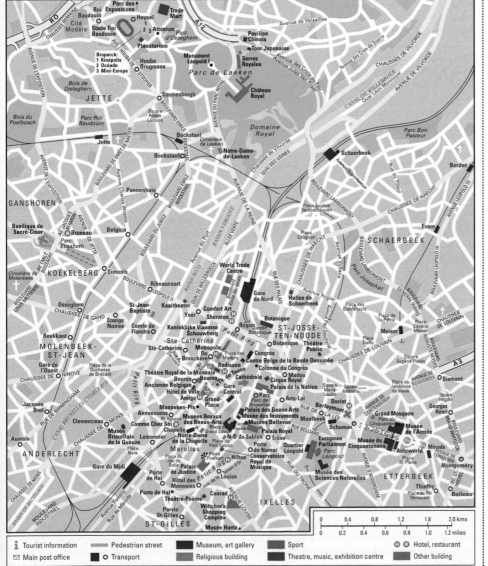

ℹ Tourist information	▦ Pedestrian street
✉ Main post office	▬ Transport

■ Museum, art gallery	
■ Religious building	

■ Sport	
■ Theatre, music, exhibition centre	

Ⓗ Hotel, restaurant	
■ Other building	

BUSINESS PROFILE

Although Brussels accounts for just 0.5% of Belgium's surface area and has a population of under one million, the region generates 15% of the nation's Gross National Product. However, Brussels' unemployment level, at 15%, remains high. The national level is not much better, standing at 12%. This perhaps is explained by the fact that two thirds of Belgium's 40,000-strong asylum seekers are in Brussels and, since 2000 regulations, this population has been entitled to seek work. A further explanation rests on the nature of employment available in Brussels, which relies on a highly skilled, technically proficient and multi-lingual workforce. In this environment, the less skilled find it difficult to slot in. One third of Brussels' labour market comes from the international community, of which 65% are from the European Union.

Most major Belgian companies are based in the capital, including the *Glaverbel*, *Solvay* and *SN Brussels Airlines*. 'Capital' of the European Union, Brussels also plays host to NATO. The presence of these international organisations, combined with Brussels' geographic location at the heart of Europe, excellent transport infrastructure, highly trained multi-lingual workforce and favourable fiscal regimes, draws nearly 2000 foreign companies to Brussels, including 1400 American companies and over 1000 international associations. The presence of some 60 foreign banks has contributed to making Brussels the world's seventh biggest financial market. Along with American companies, France, Germany, Sweden, the United Kingdom, Switzerland and Japan also have strong financial links with Brussels. Foreign companies with a presence in the city include *AT&T*, *Hewlett Packard*, *IBM*, *Price Waterhouse-Coopers*, *Procter & Gamble*, *Sony*, *Toyota* and *Volkswagen* .

The tertiary sector accounts for nearly 80% of all jobs – in various fields such as banking and financial services, tourism and transport. Nonetheless, Brussels remains the nation's second most important industrial centre after Antwerp. Industry is increasingly specialised in high-tech sectors and accounts for 15% of employment.

There are several major business districts. The city centre is where the Belgian financial groups – such as the *FORTIS* and *BBL* – and government ministries are based. The Espace Nord is much favoured by public administrators and private-sector companies, such as *Bankcard Company*, *Belgacom* and *The World Trade Centre*. The Louise area is occupied by national and international companies, while the coveted Léopold area is dominated by the European Parliament. Brussels' international flavour is also evident in the numerous diplomatic missions present and the city welcomes nearly 16,000 business congresses annually. Nearly a third of the capital's population is made up of foreigners, giving Brussels a truly cosmopolitan flair.

In addition to the STIB network, Belgian National Railways (see *Getting There By Rail*) local trains depart from Bruxelles-Chapelle, Bruxelles-Quartier Léopold, Bruxelles–Schuman and Bruxelles–Congrès, linking the inner city to the suburbs.

Taxis

Autolux (tel: (02) 411 1221) are the official taxis in Brussels. These are marked with a blue and yellow plaque and travel from Brussels Airport to the required destination in the city. In central Brussels, taxis are available at centrally located ranks at the major railway stations and at the Bourse, Place de Brouckère and Porte de Namur. Alternatively, radio taxi companies are available to order by telephone. These include *Taxis Verts* (tel: (02) 349 4949), *Taxis Orange* (tel: (02) 349 4343) and *Taxis Bleus* (tel: (02) 268 0000).

The minimum fares are €2.35 in the daytime and €4.21 at night. Trips cost €0.99 per kilometre (double at night) and there is an additional €19.83 per hour for waiting. However, no charge is made for luggage. A €1 or €2 tip is acceptable.

Limousines

Ganax, Brugstraat 24, 1930 Zaventem, (tel: (02) 720 4167; fax: (02) 720 4695), located close to the airport, offers a limousine service. Hire for one day, including a trilingual chauffeur, costs from €430.

Driving in the City

Although commuter traffic is heavy on the outskirts of Brussels during rush hour (0730–0930 and 1600–1830), the centre is relatively easy to negotiate, once the one-way system has been mastered. There is considerable ongoing work to reduce city centre traffic levels, including extensive pedestrianisation and traffic management schemes.

In addition to car parks located in the city centre, there is pay-and-display parking – accepting €0.10, €0.20, €0.50, €1 and €2 coins – in certain streets. The rules for use vary according to the time of day. There is also a large public car park under the Novotel Hotel, Rue de la Montagne. Parking rates are €12 for half a day, €2.50 for two hours and €1 for an hour. Rates apply Monday to Saturday 0900–1300 and 1430–1900, with free street parking available on Sunday and holidays.

Car Hire

Car hire is available to drivers of 23 years and over, on presentation of a passport or identity card and valid national driving licence, held for at least one year. All the major providers are present at Brussels Airport. Other locations throughout the city include *Avis*, Gare du Midi (tel: (02) 527 1705; website: www.avis.be), *Budget Rent-a-Car*, at Avenue Louise 327B (tel: (02) 753 2170; website: www.budget.com), *Europcar*, Gare du Midi and Chaussée de Waterloo 538 (tel: (02) 345 9290 *or* 522 9573; website: www.europcar.com), and *Hertz*, at Gare du Midi, Boulevard Lemonnier 8 and Chaussée de Vleurgat 210 (tel: (02) 513 2886 *or* 524 3100 *or* 649 0015; website: www.hertz.com).

Prices for one day of hire start at around €70 for a small car, rising to €200 for the largest vehicles. Third Party Liability insurance should be covered by the hire rates, however, those hiring a car should always check this.

Bicycle Hire

Pro Vélo, Rue de Londres 15 (tel: (02) 502 7355; fax: (02) 502 8641), offers bicycles for hire at a cost of €20 for a weekend or €12 for a day, as well as guided themed tours, costing €14 for half a day.

BUSINESS ETIQUETTE

A certain degree of business formality is expected in Brussels. It is wise for business visitors to confirm meetings in writing and arrive punctually, armed with business cards and wearing a suit – with a tie for men. Companies are hierarchical and as many managing directors do not delegate, it is advisable to go straight to the top. Standard office hours are Monday to Friday 0830–1730. On introduction, one should address colleagues with their surname, respecting any professional or academic qualifications. English is the standard language of business. Personal relationships are important, so relaxed lunch meetings help develop trust – a stage that must be reached before decisions are made. In Brussels, it is common for business colleagues to be invited for an *apéritif*, followed by dinner at a nice restaurant, although usually not at the first meeting.

SIGHTSEEING

Sightseeing Overview

With the exception of *Grand-Place* and the narrow streets nearby, sightseeing in Brussels is relatively crowd-free. Brussels offers a remarkable choice of 90 museums, some tiny and some international in scale. All museums have bilingual labelling (French and Dutch/Flemish). English is not always used but English-language leaflets are usually available. In recent years, signposting (for drivers and pedestrians) of Brussels' top museums and major monuments has been improved, making sightseeing even easier.

The historic centre around Grand-Place – easily covered on foot – is home to a cluster of alluring museums, including museums dedicated to beer, chocolate and lace-making. Certain sights and sensations are obligatory, such as glimpsing the trickle of water flowing from the *Manneken-Pis* and making a wish while touching the ghoulish bronze statue of *Charles-Everard de T'Serclaes* – said to bring good luck. However, the city has much more to offer. The public transport system works well enough to safely deposit the walk-weary tourist in Brussels' distinct districts: the modern *Quartier des Institutions Européennes*; aristocratic *Sablon*, near the *Place Royal*; vibrant working class *Marolles*, south of Grand-Place; *St-Gilles*, with its splendid examples of Victor Horta's Art Nouveau architecture; and *Heysel*, far out to the northwest, with its memories of the triumph of the 1958 Exhibition and the tragedy of the Heysel stadium disaster.

Key Attractions

Grand-Place

A web of narrow cobbled streets suddenly opens out into the vast *Grand-Place* – the economic and social heart of Brussels since the Middle Ages. The array of filigree Gothic buildings is dominated by the asymmetrical *Hôtel de Ville*, built in the 15th century. Its 96m (315ft) spire is topped with a gilded copper statue of St Michael. Opposite the Town Hall and almost as grand is the *Maison du Roi*, commissioned in 1515 and faithfully rebuilt in the 1890s. Sometime pied à terre of the Hapsburg monarchy, the building now hosts the *Musée de la Ville de Bruxelles* and its small collection includes tapestries and altarpieces, as well as the costumes worn by the Manneken-Pis. A series of lavish *Guildhouses* complete the rectangle of the square – number ten still houses the guild of brewers, *Maison de l'Arbre d'Or*. Events, displays and markets are often held in the Grand-Place.

Grand-Place

Transport: Métro Bourse, De Brouckère or Gare Centrale.

Musée de la Ville de Bruxelles

Tel: (02) 279 4355. Fax: (02): 279 4362.

Opening hours: Tues–Fri 1000–1700, Sat and Sun 1000 –1300.

Admission: €2.48.

Manneken-Pis

The Rue de l'Etuve leads from the grandeur of Grand-Place to this allegory of irreverence and symbol of *Bruxellois* self-mockery – a bronze statuette of a urinating boy. If it were not for the occupation of the young child, the sculpture might resemble an angelic *putto*, such as the ones decorating the façade of the nearby *Bourse* (Stock Exchange), said to have been sculpted by Rodin. Jérôme Duquesnoy cast Manneken-Pis in the 1660s, perhaps as a reference to the peasant lads of legend, who extinguished fires with their urine. Manneken-Pis is regularly kitted out in a choice of some 500 outfits supplied by companies, charities and other organisations wishing to promote their name or brand.

Rue de l'Etuve

Transport: Métro Bourse.

Place du Grand-Sablon

Although the smartest square in town, the *Place du Grand-Sablon* remains laid-back. *Notre-Dame du Sablon* dominates the square. Although it began as a humble chapel for the guild of archers, the arrival of a statue of Mary – with reputed magical healing properties – from Antwerp, in 1348, dramatically increased its popularity. The building was expanded into an impressive Gothic church, which still hosts the annual *Ommegang* procession (see *Cultural Events* and *Special Events*). The area is a major centre for antiques dealers and hosts a busy antique and books market at the weekend.

It is worth a wander around the Sablon district. Intriguing cul-de-sacs lead off from the square to shady spaces – such as the charming *Impasse Saint-Jacques*. The nearby *Place du Petit-Sablon* is a small, green square, surrounded by 48 bronze statuettes representing the 16th-century guilds, with larger statues at its heart, including the martyr-heroes, Egmont and Hornes, and Mercator, the cartographer.

Place du Grand-Sablon

Transport: Bus 20, 34, 48, 95 or 96; tram 92, 93 or 94.

Notre-Dame du Sablon

Opening hours: Mon–Fri 0900–1800, Sat and Sun 1000–1800.

Admission: Free.

Palais Royal (Royal Palace)

Some of Brussels' most opulent buildings and key attractions are clustered around the centrally located *Parc de Bruxelles*, a formal 1870s park with poker-straight tree-lined avenues and a central fountain. The southeast edge is graced by the *Palais des Académies*, a former residence of the Prince of Orange and *Place du Trône*, an impressive statue of Léopold II astride a horse. Opposite the Parc de Bruxelles lies the *Palais Royal*, begun by King William I (1815–30) in the 19th century and later expanded by Léopold II. The royal family now resides in Laeken, in northern Brussels. However, the palace is still

Grand-Place

used as royal office and for state functions. From the end of July until early September, the palace, with its Throne Room, chandeliers, tapestries and gracious dining room, opens to the public.

Rue Bredeorde 16

Tel: (02) 551 2020. Fax: (02) 502 3949.

Website: www.belgium.fgov.be

Transport: Métro Trône or Parc; tram 92, 93 or 94; bus 20, 21, 22, 34, 38, 54, 60, 71, 95 or 96.

Opening hours: Tues–Sun 1030–1730 (late Jul–early Sep).

Admission: Free.

Musées Bellevue (Bellevue Musuems)

The *Musées Bellevue* comprises two sites – the *Musée de la Dynastie* and the *Mémorial Roi Baudouin*. Both are located in the *Hôtel Bellevue*, an 18th-century mansion erected on the ruins of the 11th-century castle of the Dukes of Brabant and standing between the Place des Palais and Place Royale.

The Musée de la Dynastie displays royal memorabilia, from paintings to documents and sculpture, evoking the public and private lives of Belgian royalty and the events that shaped their reign. The Mémorial Roi Baudouin pays homage to the 43-year reign of King Baudouin, much loved by the Belgian people and sadly mourned, following his death in 1993. The memorial traces the life of Leopold III's eldest son, from the untimely death of his mother to his early reign as king – following the abdication of his father – and key events during his reign, from the end of colonisation to the independence of the Congo and federalisation of Belgium.

Hôtel Bellevue, Place des Palais 7

Tel: (02) 512 2821 *or* 545 0801 (guided tours). Fax: (02) 511 4253.

E-mail: bellvue@kbs-frb.be

Website: www.musbellevue.be

Transport: Métro Trône or Parc; tram 92, 93 or 94; bus 20, 21, 22, 34, 38, 54, 60, 71, 95 or 96.

Opening hours: Tues–Sun 1000–1700.

Admission: €6.20 (including audio guide); concessions available.

Muséum des Sciences Naturelles (Museum of Natural Sciences)

Close to the European Parliament and containing what is claimed to be one of the finest dinosaur collections in the world – 'starring' the iguanadons of Bernissart – this fascinating museum additionally features a special presentation on the Arctic and Antarctic regions. It is also possible for visitors to take a 1000m (3281ft) 'dive'

to witness a fight between a sperm whale and a giant squid. All forms of wildlife, extinct and extant, plus mineralogy, are represented here.

Rue Vautier 29

Tel: (02) 627 4238 (guided tours) *or* 4234. Fax: (02) 627 4113.

Website: www.naturalsciences.be

Transport: Métro Maelbeek; bus 12, 20, 21, 22, 34, 38, 54, 59, 60, 80, 95 or 96.

Opening hours: Mon–Fri 0930–1645, Sat and Sun 1000–1800.

Admission: €4 (concessions available).

Musée du Cinquantenaire (Cinquantenaire Museum)

Everything conceived by Léopold II was on a grandiose scale and the *Parc du Cinquantenaire*, built to commemorate the 50th anniversary of Belgian independence, is no exception. The *Musée de l'Armée*, situated in the north wing, has an interesting display of vintage aircraft and free entrance. However, the *Musée du Cinquantenaire*, formerly known as the *Musées Royaux d'Art et d'Histoire* (Royal Art and History Museum), is the major draw card of the area. Boasting collections from five continents, ranging from prehistory to the present, it includes Art Nouveau furniture designed by Victor Horta and fine examples of centuries-old lace.

Photo: Belgian Tourist Office – Brussels Wallonia

Cinquantenaire Museum

Comic strip fans might find some pieces familiar – the large Egyptian collection was the source of inspiration for Belgium's artists, including Hergé.
Parc du Cinquantenaire 10
Tel: (02) 741 7211. Fax: (02) 733 7735.
Transport: Train/métro Mérode or Schuman; tram 81 or 82 (to Mérode); bus 20 or 80 (to Nerviens), 22 (to Cinquantenaire), 61 (to Mérode), 28, 36 or 67 (to Schuman).
Opening hours: Tues–Fri 0930–1700, Sat and Sun 1000–1700.
Admission: €4; free first Wed of month 1300–1700.

Musées Royaux des Beaux-Arts de Belgique (Belgian Royal Museums of Fine Art)
The most important of Belgium's museum complexes is located close to Place Royal. It boasts two rich museums, their collections ranging from the 14th century to the modern day – the *Musée d'Art Ancien*, housed in the former court of Charles de Lorraine, and the underground *Musée d'Art Moderne*, inaugurated in 1984.
The Musée d'Art Ancien (Museum of Ancient Art) – also known as the Museum of Fine Arts – excels in its collection of the Old Masters, with works by Rubens, Bouts and Memling. Collections of Brueghel the Elder and Younger and Hieronymus Bosch are small, as Belgium's foreign masters took most of these treasures away with them. A passageway leads to the Musée d'Art Moderne (Museum of Modern Art), with its splendid collection of the Belgian Surrealists. René Magritte is given pride of place, although the haunting works of Paul Delvaux are also of interest. Picasso, Chagall, Henry Moore and Francis Bacon are also represented.
Rue de la Régence 3
Tel: (02) 508 3211. Fax: (02) 508 3232.
E-mail: info@fine-arts-museum.be
Website: www.fine-arts-museum.be
Transport: Gare Centrale; tram 92, 93 or 94 (to Royale); bus 20, 34, 38, 60, 71, 95 or 96 (to Royale).
Opening hours: Tues–Sun 1000–1200 and 1300–1700.
Admission: €5.

Further Distractions

Centre Belge de la Bande Dessinée (Belgian Centre for Comic Strips)
The history of the Belgian comic strip, including its links with silent movies and animation, is displayed throughout the airy and uplifting *Grand Magasin Waucquez*, designed by Victor Horta. Original drawings by early masters – such as André Franquin, who created accident-prone Gaston Lagaffe, and Georges Remi (Hergé), who breathed life into Tintin – are complemented by modern-day cartoons, temporary exhibitions, an exhaustive academic library, children's library and a brasserie.
Rue des Sables 20
Tel: (02) 219 1980. Fax: (02) 219 2376.
Website: www.cbbd-bcb.org
Transport: Train/métro Gare Centrale, Botanique Rogier; tram 3, 52, 55, 56, 81, 90, 92, 93 or 94; bus 38, 58 or 61.
Opening hours: Daily 1000–1800.
Admission: €6.20 (concessions available); €1.24 (reference library).

Musée Horta (Horta Museum)
Victor Horta (1885–1946) worked to produce some 110 buildings, first in neo-Gothic style, famously in Art Nouveau and latterly in sparse Modernist style. Many – such as the *Hôtel Solvay*, Avenue Louise 224, and *Hôtel Van Eetvelde* at Avenue Palmerston 4 – are still standing. However, the *Musée Horta* – the architect's former home and studio – is beautifully preserved and open to the general public. Attention to detail sweeps through the building, from the vertical letterbox and finely scripted number 25 on the façade to the sculpted staircase and dining room floor, where a marble mosaic encircles the finest American ash. A theatrical arrangement of secret front doors allowed the architect to welcome guests from different social and religious backgrounds without their being aware of each other's presence.
Rue Américaine 25
Tel: (02) 543 0490. Fax: (02) 538 7631.
E-mail: musee.horta@horta.irisnet.be
Website: www.hortamuseum.be
Transport: Tram 81, 82, 91 or 92; bus 54 or 60.
Opening hours: Tues–Sun 1400–1730.
Admission: €4.95.

Atomium and Mini-Europe
In 1909, Léopold II bequeathed the 202-hectare (500-acre) estate of Heysel to the city of Brussels. The large exhibition spaces are located here, to the northwest of the centre. Its most famous landmark, however, is the *Atomium* – a giant model of an oxygen molecule, built for the 1958 World Fair as a temporary structure, although never dismantled. The highest sphere gives a panoramic view of the entire region. The science exhibition is of interest only to young children. Nearby *Mini-Europe* shrinks Europe to a size that can be covered in a short walk, with faithful miniatures of the Eiffel Tower, Westminster and the Berlin Wall in the process of being dismantled. The year 2002 saw the model of the Cathedral of Saint Jacques de Compostella restored to its former glory.
Atomium
Boulevard du Centenaire
Tel: (02) 475 4776. Fax: (02) 475 4779.
Website: www.atomium.be
Transport: Métro Heysel; bus 84 or 99; tram 23 or 81.
Opening hours: Daily 0900–1900 (Apr–Aug); daily 1000–1730 (Sep–Mar).
Admission: €5.45; €15 (combined Atomium and Mini-Europe ticket); concessions available.
Mini-Europe
Bruparck, Boulevard du Centenaire
Tel: (02) 474 1311. Fax: (02) 478 2675.
E-mail: info@minieurope.com
Website: www.minieurope.com
Transport: Métro Heysel; bus 84 or 99; tram 23 or 81.
Opening hours: Daily 0930–1700 (Apr–Jun); Mon–Thurs 0930–1900, Fri–Sun 0930–2300 (Jul–Aug); daily 0930–1700 (Sep–Dec).
Admission: €11; €15 (combined Atomium and Mini-Europe ticket); concessions available.

Musée des Instruments de Musique (Musical Instrument Museum)
Located in the splendid Victor Horta-designed Art Nouveau Old England Building, at the Place Royale, the *Musical Instrument Museum* is home to a collection of instruments as well as information and activities covering ancient, modern and traditional music. A 200-seat concert hall hosts regular concerts (Thursday evenings, from October to May), which are organised to coincide with the various themes of the exhibitions.
Place Royale, Montagne de la Cour 2
Tel: (02) 545 0130. Fax: (02) 545 0178.
Website: www.mim.fgov.be
Transport: Métro line 1A or 1B to Gare Centrale or Park; tram 92, 93 or 94 to Royale; bus 20, 38, 60, 71, 95 or 96 to Royale.
Opening hours: Tues, Wed and Fri 0930–1700, Thurs 0930–2000 (concert at 2000), Sat and Sun 1000–1700.
Admission: €5 (concessions available).

Tours of the City

Walking Tours
The compact city centre of Brussels is tailor-made for walking tours. The *Brussels International Tourism and Congress Office* (tel: (02) 513 8940) offers three-hour guided tours on a variety of themes – architecture, history, culture, cartoons, gastronomy and classical Brussels. Departure points vary depending on the tour chosen. Among the tours offered are a guided tour of 18th-century Brussels, the Charles de Lorraine tour and a walk in the footsteps of Jacques Brel. Tours cost €85. Highly recommended are the underground visits to the Palais Royal to see the original 14th-century streets.

Bus Tours
Open-top, hop-on hop-off bus tours are available from *Visit Brussels Line* (tel: (02) 513 7744; website: www.brussels-city-tours.com), and *City Sightseeing* (tel: (02) 466 1111; e-mail: info@open-tours.com; website: www.open-tours.com). Prices start at €13.50 (concessions available) and tickets are valid for 24 hours. The bus sets off from Gare Centrale and

stops at many famous sights, such as the Atomium, Grand-Place and the Mannekin Pis, on this round trip. Both companies offer a range of other tour options, including excursions to other Belgian cities such as Bruges and Antwerp.

Excursions

For a Half Day

Bruges: The heyday of *Bruges* lasted from the 13th century, when merchants became rich from the cloth trade, until the silting of the Zwin River brought about the city's rapid decline. Nonetheless, Bruges remains one of the most beautifully preserved medieval cities in Europe and is Belgium's top tourist attraction. Visitors can explore charming streets and canals, packed with little restaurants, atmospheric cafés and a cluster of interesting museums and churches. Bruges has recently gained a new concert venue. Michelangelo's delicate marble *Madonna and Child* lies within the *Onze Lieve Vrouwekerk* (Church of Our Lady). Although situated some 80km (50 miles) west of Brussels, Bruges is well connected by public transport and motorways; it is just a one-hour train or bus ride away. The *Tourist Office*, Burg 11 (tel: (050) 448 686; website: www.bruges.be), can provide information and a hotel booking service.

For a Whole Day

Antwerp: Located 40km (25 miles) north of Brussels, *Antwerp* is tucked into the east bank of a bend in the Schelde River. Its largely quadri-lingual inhabitants – known as *Sinjorens* – are proud of the history and culture of their city, which reached its apogee in the 16th century. Masterpieces by Rubens (a former resident) and Van Dyck are on display at the *Museum voor Schone Kunsten* (Royal Museum of Fine Art), Léopold De Waelplaats (tel: (03) 238 7809). Antwerp is also a thriving port, the world's leading diamond centre and now also an international fashion capital. Antwerp is easily reached by train from all three of Brussels' principal stations. The *Tourist Office*, Grote Markt 15 (tel: (03) 232 0103), can provide a wealth of information on the city.

Namur: Located just 45km (28 miles) southeast of Brussels, *Namur* is a picturesque town with a hilltop

Centre Belge de la Bande Dessinée

citadel, which indicates its historic military importance at the confluence of the Meuse and Sambre rivers. Down by the riverbanks, meanwhile, there are pretty pedestrianised streets packed with interesting shops, fine old churches and a handful of decent museums. The pick of these is the *Trésor du Prieuré d'Oignies*, housed in a convent at Rue Julie Billiart 17, and boasting an exquisite collection of gold and silver work. Namur also has some top restaurants and a buzzing nightlife, thanks to its many university students. More information can be obtained from the *Tourist Office*, Place Léopold (tel: (081) 246 449), which is a two-minute walk from the station. Namur is easily accessible from all three stations in Brussels.

ACCOMMODATION

Prices in Belgium generally include a 16% service charge, VAT, which currently stands at 6%, and a 9% city tax.

The prices quoted below are the lowest standard rates for a double room, including breakfast and service charge, VAT and city tax, unless otherwise specified.

Business

Conrad International

Located in the heart of Brussels' centre of chic, on Avenue Louise, the *Conrad International* is a choice for visitors wanting luxury and modern convenience. Although only built in 1993, the Conrad has rapidly become one of Brussels' most established hotels and can already boast a star guest list, including former US president Clinton, Bill Gates and The Rolling Stones. A member of the Leading Hotels of the World group, the Conrad has 269 air-conditioned, individually decorated rooms. Each is equipped with a minimum of three telephone lines, allowing for modem and fax links. There is a business centre, with secretarial, translation and simultaneous translation services available. Of the ten meeting rooms, the largest is a ballroom with the capacity for up to 800 guests. The hotel has two restaurants – the *Maison de Maître* and the less formal *Café Wiltcher's*. For relaxation, there is a cocktail bar, where live piano music is played, and the Brussels *Cigar Club*. Guests are also offered special rates in the recently installed *Champneys* health spa.
Avenue Louise 71
Tel: (02) 542 4242. Fax: (02) 542 4200.
E-mail: brusselsinfo@conradhotels.com
Website: www.conradhotels.com
Price: From €580.

Hilton Brussels

The modern, 27-storey *Hilton Brussels*, located close to the Palais de Justice, towers over the fashionable Boulevard de Waterloo shopping street. The hotel, which was built in 1967, is a short distance from the European Commission and only 16km (ten miles) from the airport. Although business travellers most often fill the 434 air-conditioned rooms, the Hilton is also frequented by wealthy tourists and locals. Facilities include two restaurants – one of which is the gastronomic *Maison du Boeuf* – as well as a bar and a fitness centre. There is also a business centre, which extends over four floors, offering 22 meeting rooms and state-of-the-art business and conference facilities for up to 800 people, with dedicated staff on hand to

help. The four floors of executive rooms are specially equipped with modem points and fax connections.
Boulevard de Waterloo 38
Tel: (02) 504 1111. Fax: (02) 504 2111.
E-mail: bruhitwrm@hilton.com
Website: www.hilton.com
Price: From €320.

Radisson SAS Hotel Brussels

This tailor-made business hotel, which opened in 1989, is an approximate five-minute walk from the Grand-Place and close to Gare Centrale and the main shopping streets. A seven-floor-high atrium endows the hotel with a clinical sheen and a sense of space. The 281 rooms, split into Royal Club, Scandinavian, Oriental and recently renovated Classical floors, offer guests a high level of comfort and come equipped with personal answering machines. There are also rooms for disabled and non-smoking guests. Business facilities are excellent, comprising a business centre for up to 450 delegates, banqueting for up to 296 seated guests (or 600 buffet style), 14 meeting rooms and video-conferencing. There are two bars, the gourmet *Sea Grill* restaurant and the less formal *Atrium* restaurant, which is situated on the ground floor, amid water features and a fragment of the old city wall. Guests are offered preferential rates for the fitness centre (free for those staying in Royal Club rooms), which has a Jacuzzi, as well as solariums and saunas.
Rue du Fossé-aux-Loups 47
Tel: (02) 219 2828. Fax: (02) 219 6262.
E-mail: sales.brussels@radissonsas.com
Website: www.radisson.com
Price: From €275.

Sheraton Brussels Hotel & Towers

This 30-floor tower, located at the heart of Brussels' business district, is the city's largest hotel, offering 533 spacious rooms (including 43 suites) and conference facilities for up to 1000 people. This mini-city comprises bars, shops, a fitness centre and rooftop pool, a 24-hour business centre and *Le Crescendo* restaurant, which serves Mediterranean cuisine. Fans of the *Sheraton* style might prefer to stay in the *Sheraton Brussels Airport Hotel* – located just opposite the main airport terminal, it is a handy stopover for business travellers. The hotel has recently been renovated and offers guests modern yet relaxing rooms, bar and restaurant. Although smaller than the *Sheraton Brussels Hotel & Towers*, the airport hotel boasts excellent conference facilities for up to 600 people.
Sheraton Brussels Hotel & Towers
Place Rogier 3
Tel: (02) 224 3111. Fax: (02) 224 3456.
E-mail: reservations.brussels@sheraton.com
Website: www.sheraton.be
Price: From €335.
Sheraton Brussels Airport Hotel
Brussels Zaventem, 1930 Zaventem
Tel: (02) 710 8000. Fax: (02) 710 8080.
Price: From €400.

Luxury

Amigo

Although within a short walk of the bustling Grand-Place, the *Amigo* is a haven of calm and comfort. Furnished in Spanish Renaissance style with rich tapestries and antiques, the hotel offers a friendly,

Photo: Belgian Tourist Office – Brussels Wallonia

Alfresco café, Grande-Place

personalised welcome, a restaurant and cocktail bar, as well as 176 individually decorated rooms. Each room is air conditioned and has modem points and mini-bar. There are also six meeting rooms for up to 100 people and the *Salle des Ambassadeurs* banqueting suite. These days, the seven luxurious suites are for stars – recent guests include Helmut Kohl and Harrison Ford – but prisoners once stayed here. A prison in the 16th century, the Amigo only opened as a hotel in 1957.
Rue de l'Amigo 1–3
Tel: (02) 547 4747. Fax: (02) 513 5277.
E-mail: hotelamigo@hotelamigo.com
Website: www.hotelamigo.com
Price: From €480.

Hôtel Metropole

The century-old *Hôtel Metropole*, with its gracious Art Nouveau interior, is the first choice for those wishing to combine a lust for nostalgia with a need for modern comfort. Located a stone's throw from the Grand-Place, this palatial hotel offers 303 rooms and ten suites, ten meeting rooms, a fitness centre, steam bath and sauna. Guest rooms are air conditioned and feature modem points and mini-bars. The hotel, designed by French architect Alban Chambon, now also boasts a gastronomic restaurant named in his honour.
Place de Brouckère 31
Tel: (02) 217 2300. Fax: (02) 218 0220.
E-mail: info@metropolehotel.be
Website: www.metropolehotel.be
Price: From €325.

Moderate

Comfort Art Hotel New Siru

This highly individual three-star hotel is located close to the Gare du Nord, a five-minute walk from Parc du Cinquantenaire and a ten-minute walk from the Grand-Place. Each room is decorated with paintings, murals or even sculptures. Guests can choose from

pictures of cavorting angels to Marilyn Monroe. Guest rooms are all en suite and equipped with mini-bar and TV. The *Saint-Germain Brasserie* has a capacity for banquets of up to 100 guests and a meeting room is available for up to 50 delegates. Internet access is available at €5 per hour.
Place Rogier 1
Tel: (02) 203 3580. Fax: (02) 203 3303.
E-mail: art.hotel.siru@skynet.be
Website: www.comforthotelsiru.com
Price: From €90.

Mozart

This pretty 47-room hotel, located just off the Grand-Place, amid a plethora of bars and small eating places, is a wise budget option, offering an attractive lobby decked out in marble and tastefully decorated bedrooms. All rooms are en suite and equipped with TV and mini-bar. A small meeting room with a capacity for around 40 delegates is also available for hire.
Rue du Marché aux Fromages
Tel: (02) 502 6661. Fax: (02) 502 7758.
E-mail: hotel.mozart@skynet.be
Website: www.hotel-mozart.be
Price: From €95.

Other Recommendations

Atlas

This quiet, friendly hotel, approximately a ten-minute walk from the Grand-Place and close to the Bourse, has 92 rooms. The hotel offers reasonable levels of comfort but does not offer meals other than breakfast. It is good value for those who do not mind a slightly longer walk to the main city centre attractions. City bus tours depart from the front door and private parking is available.
Rue du Vieux-Marché aux Grains 30
Tel: (02) 502 6006. Fax: (02) 502 6935.
E-mail: info@atlas.be
Website: www.atlas.be
Price: From €115.

Dorint

This designer hotel with superb conference facilities, located close to the main EU institutions, just to the east of the city centre, opened in 1996. Belgian architect Serge Roose chose a combination of sleek lines and generous curves, gleaming metal and natural materials to create the *Dorint*'s individual style. The unifying theme of photography softens the hotel's minimalist edge – an original print hangs in each of the 212 luxurious rooms and seasonal exhibitions are held in the hallways. All of the rooms are equipped with ISDN connections for fax and modem and non-smoking rooms are available. Business facilities include nine conference rooms with a combined capacity of up to 150 delegates, multimedia presentation equipment and simultaneous translation facilities and booths. Restaurant *Au Plaisir* offers lovely garden views. Alternatively, visitors can keep abreast of world events at the *News Bar* or relax at the *Jacqmotte Coffeeshop*.
Boulevard Charlemagne
Tel: (02) 231 0909. Fax: (02) 230 3371.
E-mail: info@dorintbru.be
Website: www.dorint.be
Price: From €320.

RESTAURANTS

The selected restaurants have been divided into five categories: Gastronomic, Business, Trendy, Budget and Personal Recommendations. The restaurants are listed alphabetically within these different categories, which serve as guidelines rather than absolute definitions of the establishments.
Most restaurants in Brussels include VAT, which currently stands at 6%, and a service charge of 16%, within their prices. Nevertheless, most diners will round up their bill to leave a few extra Euros or leave around an extra 5% of the bill if the service is very good.
The prices quoted below are for an average three-course meal for one person and for a bottle of house wine or cheapest equivalent; they include VAT and service charge, unless otherwise indicated.

Gastronomic

Comme Chez Soi

The fame of this intimate little restaurant, decorated in Belle Epoque style, extends worldwide. Chef Pierre Wynants, with help from his son-in-law Lionel Rigolet, serves food to justify its three Michelin stars. Specialities include fillets of sole with a mousseline of Riesling or prawn and apricot soufflé with crunchy pistachios and red fruits. Reservations strongly recommended. Closed Sunday and Monday.
Place Rouppe 23
Tel: (02) 512 2921. Fax: (02) 511 8052.
E-mail: info:commechezsoi.be
Website: www.commechezsoi.be
Price: €75. Wine: €40.

De Bijgaarden

Situated a 20-minute drive from central Brussels, *De Bijgaarden* is the territory of chef Olivier Schlissinger – his creations in this wooden panelled restaurant have been awarded two Michelin stars. Specialities include duck and goose foie gras and Colchester oysters with champagne. No lunch Saturday. Closed Sunday.

Isidoor van Beverenstrat 20, Groot-Bijgaarden
Tel: (02) 466 4485. Fax: (02) 463 0811.
E-mail: mail@debijgaarden.be
Website: www.debijgaarden.be
Price: €65. Wine: €40.

La Truffe Noire

Italian chef Luigi Ciciriello is passionate about his truffles, used in just about every dish at this gastronomic, Michelin-starred but friendly restaurant. Located close to Avenue Louise in central Brussels, the restaurant is characterised by its rich wood and warm, gentle tones. Specialities include carpaccio truffles with olive oil and parmesan, lobster risotto with truffles, and, for dessert, black chocolate truffle with spun sugar and raspberry sauce. An extensive wine cellar of fine Italian and French bottles offers the perfect accompaniment to any meal. Special business menus are available at lunchtime and private lounges on the first floor may be booked for groups of up to 20 guests. Closed Saturday lunchtime and Monday.

Those with a passion for truffles but without time to linger should head for the sister establishment, the cheaper *L'Atelier de la Truffe Noire*, Avenue Louise 300 (see *Budget* below), which is ideal for a quick but delicious lunch. No lunch Monday. Closed Sunday.
Boulevard de la Cambre
Tel: (02) 640 4422. Fax: (02) 647 9704.
E-mail: luigi.ciciriello@truffenoire.com
Website: www.truffenoire.com
Price: €75; €125 (fixed-price menu including wine).
Wine: €40.

La Villa Lorraine

Located in the Uccle district, on the edge of the Bois de la Cambre, this very smart restaurant, with impeccable, white tablecloths, has large windows overlooking dense greenery. During summer, there is a lovely garden for alfresco dining. The cuisine, created by chef Freddy Vandecasserie, is classical French and specialities include sole Lorraine, broccoli terrine with wild asparagus or lobster with turmeric and coconut milk. There is an extensive wine list, ranging from agreeable, reasonably priced wines to vintage wine from the *Villa's* cellar. To impress a client, there is no better way than to invite them to lunch at La Villa Lorraine. The establishment offers a series of gracious, private rooms, which are ideal for business lunches and banquets – special business menus can be created to order. A suit is required dress here.
Chaussée de la Hulpe 28
Tel: (02) 374 3163. Fax: (02) 372 0195.
E-mail: info@villalorraine.be
Website: www.villalorraine.be
Price: €90, €120 (fixed-price menu including wine).
Wine: €50.

Restaurant Bruneau

Chef Jean-Pierre Bruneau, one of the city's finest and most innovative chefs, has been awarded three Michelin stars for his classic cuisine with a contemporary twist. Located in the Ganshoren district, close to the Koekelberg Basilica, designer dishes are served at *Restaurant Bruneau* against the backdrop of a modern decor and serious atmosphere. This is a temple of fine food – offering a choice of seafood, meat and game dishes. Dishes include *coucou de malines* (chicken stuffed with truffles), ravioli filled with celery and truffles or lobster with truffles and light vinegar sauce. No dinner Tuesday. Closed Wednesday.
Avenue Broustin 73–75
Tel: (02) 427 6978. Fax: (02) 425 9726.

E-mail: bruneau@rest.be
Website: www.bruneau.be
Price: €90; €175 (fixed-price menu including wine).
Wine: €22.

Business

La Maison du Boeuf

The Hilton's gourmet restaurant, *La Maison du Boeuf* ('House of Beef'), specialises in roast beef and steaks, cooked to a Michelin-starred level of perfection. The decor is contemporary and unobtrusive and the service is discreet, making this an ideal venue for high-level business meetings.
Hilton Brussels, Boulevard de Waterloo 38
Tel: (02) 504 1111. Fax: (02) 504 2111.
Website: www.hilton.com
Price: €100. Wine: €40.

La Maison du Cygne

Karl Marx sweated over his Communist manifesto at this address, when it was a bustling tavern. These days, *La Maison du Cygne* ('House of the Swan') is a refined gourmet restaurant, decorated in wooden panelling and beams, with paintings on the wall. It serves classic dishes, such as foie gras and truffles, in the best location possible in Brussels – the Grand-Place. At lunchtime, this is the favoured venue for businesspeople lucky enough to dine on their expense account. No lunch Saturday. Closed Sunday.
Grand-Place 9
Tel: (02) 511 8244. Fax: (02) 514 3148.
E-mail: lecygne@skynet.be
Website: www.lamaisonducygne.be
Price: €65. Wine: €20.

Le Fils de Jules

Close to restaurant *La Quincaillerie* in the Ixelles district (see *Personal Recommendations* below), this popular brasserie, decorated in Art Deco style, specialises in cooking from the Basque country and southwest France, such as hot duck foie gras with prunes or tuna steak with onions. There is also a fine selection of French and Spanish wines. Relaxed, friendly and tourist-free, this is a good place to meet for a business lunch. No lunch Saturday and Sunday.
Rue du Page 35
Tel: (02) 534 0057. Fax: (02) 534 5200.
E-mail: info@filsdejules.be
Website: www.filsdejules.be
Price: €40. Wine: €20.

Sea Grill

Brussels' top fish and seafood restaurant, located in the SAS Radisson Hotel and decorated in muted style, is a cauldron for chef Yves Matagne's creative cooking. Food of this quality – the *Sea Grill* has been awarded two Michelin stars – does not come cheap. However, it is an ideal venue for business lunches for those who are intent on impressing their clients with mouthwatering dishes such as baked sea bass with truffles and thyme. Closed Saturday, Sunday and Monday.
Rue du Fossé-aux-Loups 47
Tel: (02) 227 3120. Fax: (02) 219 6262.
E-mail: sales.brussels@radissonsas.com
Website: www.sasradisson.com
Price: €100. Wine: €25.

Symphony

Symphony, formerly known as *Nico Central*, is located in the Renaissance Hotel (formerly the Swissôtel), close to the European Parliament. This modern restaurant draws a sophisticated, business clientele. Belgian chef Philippe Le Comte, who trained at the Palace Hotel and the Sheraton, serves imaginative and contemporary French cuisine, inspired by London chef Nico Ladenis. The Symphony has a contemporary decor with subtle colours. The varied menu includes gnocci with wild mushrooms, sole *meunière* and foie gras. Closed Saturday and Sunday.
Rue du Parnasse 19
Tel: (02) 505 2929. Fax: (02) 505 2555.
Website: www.renaissancehotel.com
Price: €55. Wine: €20.

Alfesco dining

Photo: Belgian Tourist Office – Brussels Wallonia

Trendy

Bonsoir Clara

Bonsoir Clara distinguishes itself from the host of trendy restaurants in the boutique-lined Rue Antoine Dansaert by its theatrical decor – a whole wall is decorated in colourful, patchwork squares – and imaginative, international cuisine. The menu excels in its fish dishes – a house speciality is salmon marinated in spices – but there are also good meat and vegetarian options. The clientele is chic and arty. No lunch Saturday and Sunday.
Rue Antoine Dansaert 22–26
Tel: (02) 502 0990. Fax: (02) 502 5557.
Price: €50. Wine: €20.

In't Spinnekopke

The name translates as 'In the Spider's Heat' but despite its bizarre appellation, this is an extremely popular venue, offering a wide selection of local beers in this inviting tavern atmosphere. Old beer posters on the walls and wainscot and wooden benches help to concretise this relaxed style. There are also interesting and tempting menu items available at very reasonable prices, including local specialities such as *waterzooi*, poached *kabeljau* and a variety of mussel casseroles – with sauces including white wine, curry or *waterzooi*.
Place du Jardin aux Fleurs 1
Tel: (02) 511 8695. Fax: (02) 513 2497.
Website: www.spinnekopke.be
Price: €35. Wine: €20.

Le Living Room

The open invitation to feel at home in this former hotel turned ultra-trendy restaurant, situated in the St Gilles district, is hard to turn down. On the menu at this light and airy restaurant is East Asian-inspired cuisine, including sushi and sashimi, served in a cosmopolitan atmosphere to a hip clientele. Closed Sunday.
Chaussée de Charleroi 50
Tel: (02) 534 4434. Fax: (02) 539 1590.
Price: €50. Wine: €20.

Les Baguettes Impériales

This Michelin-starred Vietnamese restaurant, decorated in contemporary style, is located in Laeken, close to the Heysel exhibition halls. Specialities include stuffed pigeon and foie gras, and there is an extensive wine list. No lunch Monday and Tuesday. No dinner Sunday.
Avenue Jean Sobieski 70
Tel: (02) 479 6732. Fax: (02) 479 6732.
Price: €75. Wine: €25.

Lola

Located close to the antiques quarter, *Lola* serves classic French cuisine, lifted with a contemporary touch, to an arty, 30-something crowd. The long, narrow interior is sleek and modern but has a 1960s retro feel. Chef Larbi Ouriaghi's specialities include duck with mango, although vegetarians will enjoy the vegetable risotto flavoured with garlic, mushrooms, parmesan and fresh basil, as well as the copious salads.
Place du Grand-Sablon 33
Tel: (02) 514 2460. Fax: (02) 514 2653.
Price: €50. Wine: €20.

Budget

Bleu de Toi

Corinne Ceuleman's intimate two-floor restaurant, with its welcoming blue façade and rich, decadent interior, serves brasserie-style cuisine in a relaxed environment. The house speciality is *bintje* (a special Netherlands-developed potato variety), which come with a wide choice of stuffings, from lobster to smoked salmon, caviar, veal or snails. Desserts include ice cream with *spéculoos* (Belgian ginger biscuit) and oriental nougat. Guests can choose to dine in the chilled-out blue room or more buzzy, red room upstairs. Group bookings (for up to 16 people) are available. No lunch Saturday. Closed Sunday.
Rue des Alexiens 73
Tel: (02) 502 4371. Fax: (02) 502 4371.
Website: www.resto.be/bleudetoi
Price: €20. Wine: €20.

Chez Léon

This popular brasserie chain is best known for its generous portions of *moules frites* (mussels and chips), although it also serves other traditional brasserie fare.

Street cafés

Visitors seeking a relaxing or romantic atmosphere should not opt for *Chez Léon* – the tablecloths are paper and everyone (staff and diners included) seems to be in a bit of a rush. However, this centrally located venue, a stone's throw from the Grand-Place, does offer an authentic experience of basic, Belgian cuisine.
Rue des Bouchers 18
Tel: (02) 511 1415. Fax: (02) 514 0231.
Price: €25. Wine: €15.

Le Grain de Sel

Grégory Yarm's unpretentious family-run restaurant, beside the Ixelles lake and close to Place Flagey, is a top budget option. Specialities include such delights as tomato with goat's cheese, tuna carpaccio, pigeon with lentils or salmon tartare with cucumber and horseradish. Yarm also serves his favourite family recipes, such as his Portuguese grandmother's recipe for sole with Elvira banana. The decor is gentle, with pretty Venetian chandeliers and simple wooden tables. During summer, there is a lovely rose garden for alfresco dining. No lunch Saturday. Closed Sunday.
Chaussée de Vleurgat
Tel: (02) 648 1858. Fax: (02) 646 3579.
E-mail: grandesel@skynet.be
Price: €25. Wine: €15.

Raconte-Moi des Salades

Salad lovers will enjoy the many vegetarian and meaty options offered at this friendly restaurant, decorated with comfortable wicker chairs and candlelit in the evening. Meat dishes include grilled beef with rosemary on a roquette and parmesan salad, while vegetarian options range from five vegetables served with salad and vinaigrette to pasta dishes. The atmosphere is relaxed and prices, bearing in mind the chic location in Ixelles, are very reasonable. During summer, there is the chance to enjoy alfresco dining. Popular with a trendy young crowd, it is wise to book in advance. Closed Sunday.
Place du Châtelain
Tel: (02) 534 2727.
E-mail: salades@resto.be
Website: www.resto.be/salades
Price: €30. Wine: €15.

Touch and Go

A resolutely good-humoured staff serves tasty pitta bread stuffed with a wide variety of salads and sauces at this popular restaurant chain. There are several branches of *Touch and Go* situated across the city – the Rue Saint Boniface branch has colourfully painted walls and large paintings. Closed Sunday.
Rue Saint Boniface 12
Tel: (02) 513 8502.
Price: €25. Wine: €12.
Branches:
Rue Edith Cavell 113
Tel: (02) 347 5494.
Rue de Livourne 131
Tel: (02) 640 5589.

Personal Recommendations

Aux Armes de Bruxelles

The winding streets surrounding the Grand-Place are oozing with restaurants but many are tourist traps. It is always a safe bet for visitors to dine at *Aux Armes de Bruxelles*, which serves Belgian traditional cuisine, such as *waterzooi*, oysters or chips with mayonnaise. The surroundings are crisp and unfussy and the service friendly and efficient. Closed Monday.

Photo: Belgian Tourist Office – Brussels Wallonia

Rue des Bouchers 13
Tel: (02) 511 5550. Fax: (02) 514 3381.
E-mail: arbrux@beon.be
Website: www.armebrux.be
Price: €35. Wine: €25.

Blue Elephant

This popular restaurant, intricately decorated with outsized plants, Buddhist statuary and comfortable bamboo chairs, serves high-class Thai cuisine, using fresh ingredients flown in from Bangkok. Karl Steppe's first venture, Brussels' *Blue Elephant*, opened in the 1980s to great acclaim and the winning formula has now been exported to London, Lyon, Dubai and New Delhi. Specialities include beef paneng and Thai chicken curry, while tofu dishes offer good alternatives for vegetarian diners. The Blue Elephant can cater for banquets and conferences. No lunch Saturday.
Chaussée de Waterloo 1120
Tel: (02) 374 4962. Fax: (02) 375 4468.
E-mail: brussels@blueelephant.com
Website: www.blueelephant.com
Price: €40. Wine: €25.

La Quincaillerie

La Quincaillerie is one of the most renowned of the many restaurants clustered around the Place du Châtelain in the Ixelles district and is always busy. A former ironmonger's shop, the interior retains much of the original decor, including a wrought-iron staircase, designed by students of Victor Horta (Brussels' renowned Art Nouveau architect) in 1903. Chefs Patrick Amourette and Olivier Bellaches serve refined brasserie fare, with an emphasis on fish and seafood dishes, such as red mullet fillets with crab vinaigrette sauce. No lunch Saturday and Sunday.
Rue du Page 43–45
Tel: (02) 533 9833. Fax: (02) 539 4095.
E-mail: info@quincaillerie.be
Website: www.quincaillerie.be
Price: €40. Wine: €25.

La Tour D'y Voir

Located in a 14th-century chapel in the antiques quarter, on the first floor above Les Vieux Sablon art gallery, this is the ideal restaurant for a romantic tête-a-tête in the evening or relaxed business lunch. Brick-face walls, low lighting and high windows create a gothic air of mystery. Owners Pascal and Tania Anciaux create an informal and creative environment with their Surprise and Prestige menu. Guests are invited to choose a fish, meat or vegetarian theme from the menu, leaving it up to the chef to improvise and come up with a mouthwatering and inventive dish. For diners who would rather choose, the menu includes such imaginative delights as grilled ostrich with ratatouille and jacket potatoes or risotto of green Breton crabs and Canadian crabmeat. Closed Monday.
Place du Grand-Sablon 8/9 B6
Tel: (02) 511 4043. Tel: (02) 511 0078.
E-mail: tourdyvoir@skynet.be
Website: www.tourdyvoir.com
Price: €25. Wine: €15.

L'Idiot du Village

This is a tiny but very popular venue serving such specialities as rabbit stew with bacon or sea bass with lentils. It is necessary for guests to book in advance, as there are only eight tables. It is well worth the effort, however. The decor is intimate and refined in blues

Manneken-Pis

and whites, while the menu changes regularly. Diners will, however, most likely be able to choose French favourites such as foie gras, coquilles Saint-Jacques and *tatin de boudin*.
Rue Notre-Seigneur 19
Tel: (02) 502 5582.
Price: €30. Wine: €25.

ENTERTAINMENT

Nightlife

Brussels' location at the heart of Europe encourages top artists and budding stars to tour here. However, the city has a thriving homegrown scene of its own. Jazz has been strong since the 1920s and there is year-round live jazz in a cluster of venues, climaxing in the annual Brussels Jazz Festival. The club scene is relatively new, drawing the crowds after much lingering in the city's many bars and Irish pubs that overflow with expatriates. The legal drinking age in Belgium is 16 years and the price of a beer is around €2.

Aside from the tacky discos for tourists, there is the big-name-DJ-drawing *The Fuse* (see *Clubs* below). The best send out their sounds into the night, around Place de St-Géry, Manneken-Pis and in the Marolles district. Clubs open at 2300, heat up at midnight and survive until about 0600. Being foreign and dressed in tune with the club's image helps the admission process along considerably. Entrance is sometimes free but will more likely cost about €7.

FNAC, in the City 2 complex on Rue Neuve, is the best place for club tickets, although the tourist office on Grand-Place may also be of help. Perhaps the highlight of the clubbing year is the *Klinkende Munt* outdoor music festival, held every July in Brussels at Place de la Monnaie, Petit-Chateau and the Beursschouwburg.

Listings and information on nightlife events in Brussels can be found online (website: www.funinbrussels.com/midnight/discotheque.htm *or* www.noctis.com). *Tèls Quels* magazine (in French) has comprehensive gay nightlife listings.

Bars

Belgium is justly famous for its superb selection of beers, not least those created by Trappist monks at various monasteries around the country. Brussels, furthermore, has its own idiosyncratic varieties, notably *Gueuze* and fruit-flavoured *Kriek* varieties. A wide selection (more than 150) of Belgian beers can be found at the *Loplop Cafe*, Schildknaapstraat 29 (website: www.loplopcafe.com). Other centrally located beer havens include *La Bécasse*, Rue de Tabora 11, *A La Mort Subite*, Rue Montagne aux Herbes Potagères, and *La Rose Blanche*, Grande-Place 11. *Le Soleil*, Rue des Capucins 63, is an intimate little bar, tailor-made for an evening of good beer and good chats. A number of bars transform into clubs as the night wears on, including lively *Le Sud*, Rue de l'Ecuyer 43–5, open Thursday to Saturday. A quieter evening is on offer at the *Théâtre de Toone VII*, Impasse Schuddeveld 6, off Petite Rue de Bouchers, where puppets form a backdrop to the drinking. For the younger audience, the bars around Place St Géry are popular venues.

Casinos

There is a casino in nearby Namur. The *Casino de Naumur*, Avenue Baron Moreau 1, is open daily 1400–0500. Visitors are required to hold a passport or ID document and dress code is smart (strictly no trainers). The minimum age for entry is 21 years.

Clubs

Top international DJs play techno, house and jungle at *The Fuse*, Rue Blaes 208. *Mirano Contintal*, Chemin de Louvain 38, is tacky with a yuppie crowd, while

Photo: Belgian Tourist Office – Brussels Wallonia

Avenue Louise

Le Bal, Boulevard du Triomphe, is just tacky. Tourists might meet other tourists at *Espace de Nuit*, Rue Marché aux Fromages, near Grand-Place, while most of the hipper clubs have a gay (and sometimes lesbian) night. The Brussels trendy set goes to *Les Jeux d'Hiver*, Bois de la Cambre.

Live Music

Jazz dominates the live music scene in Brussels. There is jazz on Saturday and most Sundays at *L'Archiduc*, Rue Antoine Dansaert 6. Frequent concerts at *Fool Moon*, Quai de Mariemont 26, feature anything from jazz-funk to drum'n'bass and Latin music. Although *VK* is a trek away at Rue de l'Ecole 76, this is where alternative sounds – hip hop, rock and indie music – are given a hearing. *Magasin 4*, Rue du Magasin 4, offers a more central venue for indie and hip hop. Folk fans should try *Thunderbird Café*, Quai du Commerce 48, where there are usually twice-weekly gigs on offer, as well as good food. Informal weekend jazz 'jam sessions' are a feature of the *LopLop Café* (see *Bars* above).

The main venues for touring big names are the *Forest National*, Avenue du Globe 36, and *AB* (*Ancienne Belgique*), Boulevard Anspach, for bigger gigs, and *Botanique*, Rue Royale 236, and *Cirque Royal*, Rue de l'Enseignement 81, for smaller acts.

Sport

Football and cycling are the national passions. Brussels' football clubs, *RWDM* (website: www.rwdm.be) and *Union St-Gilloise*, have their fans, but *RSC Anderlecht* (website: www.rsca.be) has a faithful following who support the team at *Stade Constant Vanden Stock*, Avenue Théo Verbeeck 2 (tel: (02) 522 1539). Anderlecht is frequently at the top of the home league and sometimes makes it into the Champions League. Passions were raised to fever pitch in the European Championships 2000, which was hosted jointly by Belgium and The Netherlands in a renamed and reconstructed stadium, *Stade Roi Baudouin*, Heysel (tel: (02) 474 3940). The stadium also hosts the Belgian national team's home games and the cup final. Tickets to football matches are available through *Maison du Football* (tel: (02) 477 1211).

Belgium has an impressive record in cycling and Eddy Merckx did a fine PR job for the country by repeatedly winning the Tour de France in the 1960s and 1970s. His glory still lives on, celebrated annually in the *Eddy Merckx Grand Prix*, on the last Sunday of August. A more amateur affair follows the same 22km (14-mile) trip from the Gare du Nord to Heysel (tel: (02) 502 7355).

The major athletics event is the annual *Ivo van Damme Memorial IAHF Grand Prix* (tel: (02) 878 2025) held in the Stade Roi Baudouin in late August/early September. Amateurs take part in the Brussels 20km (12-mile) circular race held annually in May/June, which starts and finishes at the Esplanade du Cinquantenaire (tel: (02) 511 9000).

Fitness Centres

The vast *Physical Golden Club*, Place du Chatelain 33 (tel: (02) 539 3036), offers weights machines and fitness classes and has the added kudos of being the place where Jean-Claude van Damme started off his action movie career. Martial arts classes are predictably popular. A day pass costs €25. For the ultra well-heeled, *Champneys* (tel: (02) 542 4666/7) has opened up next to the Conran Hotel, Avenue Louise 71B. A 'spa discover day' costs €105.

Golf

The 18-hole *Royal Amicale Anderlecht Golf Club*, Rue Scholle 1 (tel: (02) 521 1687), is located within Brussels itself. The club charges €33 for a day of golfing during the week and €50 at weekends, when prior reservation is recommended. Membership is not required. *Brabantse Golf*, Steenwagenstraat 11, Melsbroek (tel: (02) 751 8205), is situated close to the airport. Membership is required and green fees are €30 weekdays and €45 at the weekend. There are two 18-hole courses at *Royal Zoute Golf Club*, Caddiespad 14, Knokke-le-Zoute (tel: (050) 623 029), located 100km (60 miles) north of Brussels in the seaside town of Knokke-le-Zoute. Visitors are welcome and green fees are €55–95, depending on the handicap of the player. Alternatively, there are 11 courses around Waterloo, just south of Brussels, offering golfing opportunities through a programme called *Golf Pass Walloon Brabant*.

The *Fédération Royal Belge de Golf* (tel: (02) 672 2389) can provide information on Belgium's golf courses. Several golfing packages are available in a programme created by Martins Hotels (website: www.passbw.com).

Tennis and Squash

The *Centre Sportif de Woluwe St-Pierre*, Avenue Salomé 2 (tel: (02) 762 8522), has squash, badminton and tennis courts.

Swimming

There are plenty of pools in Brussels' sports centres. The one at the *Centre Sportif de Woluwe St-Pierre*, Avenue Salomé 2 (tel: (02) 762 8522) is Olympic-sized. *Océade*, Bruparck (tel: (02) 478 4944; website: www.oceade.be), within splashing distance of Mini-Europe (see *Further Distractions*), is a modern 'fun' baths.

Shopping

Brussels' classic souvenir is chocolate. Fresh creamy pralines are for sale at *Wittamer*, Place du Grand-Sablon, who have had almost a century to perfect their recipes. Other names to look out for are the top-quality *Neuhaus*, Grand-Place 27 and Galerie de la Reine 25–27, and *Godiva*, also located in the Grand-Place. Cheaper chocolates are available from the popular *Léonidas* chain, Boulevard Anspach 46. Belgian biscuits are also a gift guaranteed to bring a guilty smile to the receiver. *Dandoy*, Rue au Beurre 31, produce melt-in-your-mouth macaroons and the Brussels speciality *speculoos* – a gingerbread biscuit with a crunch. Beer is best bought at *Bière Artisanale*, Chaussée de Wavre 174 (website: www.users.skynet.be/beermania), which stocks over 400 types of beer and glasses to suit.

Designer clothes are clustered around the smart Avenue Louise and Avenue de la Toison d'Or. Key shopping stops on Avenue Louise include Belgian designers at Shine's new flagship store, located at Avenue Louise 82–84 – fantastic for stunning silk dresses and floaty, Chinese-inspired creations – and more down-to-earth daywear in muted tones at *Caroline Biss*, Avenue Louise 21. Established and up-and-coming Belgian designers – such as Olivier Strelli, Ann Demeulemeester, Dries Van Noten and Carine Lauwers – line the fashionable Rue Antoine Dansaert. Innovative *Stijl* has more avant-garde Belgian clothes, by designers such as Xavier Delcour and Olivier Theyskens, at number 74, underwear at number 47 and children's clothes at *Kat en Muis*, number 32.

Children's and adults' tastes alike are met at Brussels' many comic book shops. Among these is centrally located *La Boutique Tintin*, Rue de la Colline 13. Brussels lace – on show at the *Lace Museum*, Rue de la Violette 6 – is for sale at *F Rubbrecht*, Grand-Place 23, or at the city's largest lace maker, *Manufacture Belge de Dentelle*, Galerie de la Reine 6–8. Most of the souvenir lace shops around Grand-Place are less authentic.

Every day is market day in the different parts of Brussels. Among the best of these is the flower market, open Tuesday to Sunday 0800–1800, at Grand-Place, also the site of the Sunday morning bird market. Antiques are sold at the market on Place du Grand-Sablon, Saturday 0900–1800 and Sunday 0900–1300, and is while the flea market at Place du Jeu de Balle, in the Marolles district, is open daily 0700–1300 and is at its best on weekend mornings. A more high street experience, however, is at hand at *City 2* shopping mall, in the shop-studded Rue Neuve, where shops stay open on Fridays until 2000. Standard shopping hours are 1000–1800/1900 but the Grand-Place area stays open until approximately 2000. Sales tax is 21% and can be refunded to non-EU citizens by any of the shops affiliated to *Global Refund Belgium* (tel: (02) 479 9461; fax: (02) 478 3664; e-mail: taxfree@be.globalrefund.com; website: www.globalrefund.com). Participating shops will issue a global refund cheque, which should be stamped at customs and then cashed upon leaving the country.

Culture

Brussels' cultural life – or lives, rather, as the scene is linguistically split between French and Flemish – is booming, despite a lack of funding partly caused by the language divide. Obviously, some art forms cross all language boundaries. French-Belgian cinema came to prominence in 1994, with Jan Bucquoy's hilarious *La Vie Sexuelle des Belges,* while the more serious Flemish film, *Daens* (1992), directed by Stijn Coninx, was nominated Best Foreign Film at the 1992 Oscars. Contemporary dance came into its own in the 1980s, thanks to Flemish choreographer Anne Teresa De Keersmaeker (Rosas Company) and Wim Vandekeybus (Ultima Vez Company). Theatre is celebrated annually during the *Kunstenfestivaldesarts* (tel: (02) 7022 2199 *or* 219 0707) in May. Opera is performed at the prestigious *Théâtre Royal de la Monnaie*, Place de la Monnaie (tel: (02) 229 1211; website: www.lamonnaie.be), where the rousing performance of an Auber opera provoked the audience into starting the Belgian revolution in 1830. Notable touring companies to perform here include the *RSC* and *Comédie Française*.

The principal cross-cultural venue is the Victor Horta-designed *Palais des Beaux Arts*, Rue Ravenstein 23 (tel: (02) 507 8200), which hosts major temporary art exhibitions, French theatrical productions, classical and contemporary dance, classical music and the finals for the internationally renowned Queen Elizabeth music competition. The *Cirque Royal*, Rue de l'Enseignement 81 (tel: (02) 218 2015; website: www.cirque-royal.org), allows for varied performances in the round, including classical music, dance, musicals and opera. The *Halles de Schaerbeek*, Rue Royale Sainte-Marie 22A (tel: (02) 227 5960), hosts large-scale operatic, theatrical and dance performances and pop acts. Flemish-language theatre and contemporary dance is well represented at the neo-Baroque *Koninklijke Vlaamse Schouwberg* or *Royal Flemish Theatre*, Rue de Laeken 146 (tel: (02) 412 7050 *or* 7070).

The 'What's On' section of English-language *Bulletin*, the Wednesday pull-out section of *Le Soir* and the 'Agenda' section of the *Brussel Deze Week* free newspaper, available every Thursday, all provide cultural listings.

Information and tickets are available at the *Brussels International Tourism and Congress Office*, Hôtel de Ville, Grand-Place (tel: (02) 513 8940; website: www.tib.be), and the *FNAC* store at the City 2

Art market

shopping complex, Rue Neuve (tel: (02) 275 1111). The *FNAC* booking line (tel: (0900) 00600) is for concert, theatre and exhibition theatre tickets. Ticket prices are usually around €13–70 for dance and theatre performances, anything from €15–90 for opera and approximately €6 for cinema.

Music

The national opera house, at the *Théâtre Royal de la Monnaie*, Place du Monnaie (tel: (02) 229 1211; website: www.lamonnaie.be), continues to excel. With only 1200 seats, it is best for visitors to book in advance. For Flemish opera, one should take a trip to *Vlaamse Opera*, Van Ertbornstraat 8, Antwerp (tel: (03) 233 6685; website: www.vlaamseopera.be), or Ghent's *Schouwburg*, Straat 3 (tel: (09) 225 2425). The *Palais des Beaux Arts*, Rue Ravenstein 23 (tel: (02) 507 8200), is home to the *National Orchestra* (website: www.nob-onb.be) and *Philharmonic Society*, which organises most of the major concerts in Brussels. The season, annually consisting of over 350 concerts, runs from September to June.

In addition to these major venues, there is the intimate *Conservatoire Royal de Musique*, Rue de la Régence 30 (tel: (02) 513 4587), which is tailor-made for chamber recitals. The auditorium at *Musée d'Art Ancien*, Rue de la Régence 3 (tel: (02) 508 3211), hosts lunchtime concerts on Wednesday, from Autumn to Easter.

Theatre

There are over 30 theatres in Brussels. The leading French-language *Théâtre National* lost its home at the Centre Rogier (currently being demolished) and has taken up temporary residence in a disused Art Deco cinema palace at Boulevard Anspach 85 (tel: (02) 203 5303). Here aficionados can find polished renditions of classical European theatre. A permanent venue for the National Theatre is under construction at Boulevard Emile Jacqmain – the planned date of completion is 2004. The main Flemish theatre, *Kaaitheater* (tel: (02) 201 5959) has two locations – *Kaaitheater*, Place Sainctelette 20 and *Kaaitheater Studios*, Rue Notre-Dame de Sommeil 81. Innovative productions are

performed in French at the *Théâtre le Public*, Rue Braemt 64–70 (tel: (02) 223 2966), while literary discussions and readings take place at the *Théâtre-Poème*, Rue d'Ecosse 30 (tel: (02) 538 6358). The *American Theatre Company* (e-mail: actbrussels@yahoo.com; website: www.atc-brussels.org) is an English-language theatre group based in Brussels, staging performances at *The Studio Theatre*, Rue Waelhem 73, Schaerbeek (tel: (02) 242 4905).

The one venue not to be missed is the *Théâtre de Toone*, Impasse Schuddeveld 6, Petite Rue de Bouchers 21 (tel: (02) 511 7137), where classics such as *Faust* and *King Lear* are performed by marionettes manipulated by seven puppeteers. Performances are in French (peppered with local dialect), Flemish and occasionally English. It is housed in a 17th-century pub and offers a good range of local beers for refreshment.

Dance

De Keersmaecker's *Rosas Company* is closely linked to the *Théâtre Royal de la Monnaie*, Place de la Monnaie (tel: (02) 229 1211; website: www.lamonnaie.be), while the works of radical choreographers – also contemporary music and avant-garde theatre – are often staged at the *Kaaitheater*, Place Sainctelette 20 (tel: (02) 201 5959), and *Koninklijke Vlaamse Schouwburg* (Royal Flemish Theatre), Rue de Laeken 146 (tel: (02) 412 7050 or 412 7070; website: www.kvs.be). Alternative music, dance and theatre is performed at the trendy *Beursschouwburg*, Rue de la Caserne 37 (tel: (02) 513 8290). The venue is based in Rue Dansaert from September 2003. Although contemporary dance is extremely strong in Brussels, there is no dedicated dance venue. An interest in classical dance is best pursued at the *Royal Ballet of Flanders* (website: www.koninklijkballetvanvlaanderen.be) in Antwerp.

Film

About 50% of films are shown in English ('VO' – *version originale*), with French and Flemish subtitles. Programmes change each Wednesday. Hollywood blockbusters are shown at the 12-screen, ultra-modern *UGC De Brouckère*, Place de Brouckère 38 (tel: (0900) 10440). The cinema also puts on children's films every Sunday morning at 1100, for only €1.60 per person (standard rates are €6.60). State-of-the-art *Kinepolis*, Boulevard du Centenaire 20, Bruparck (tel: (0900) 00555), boasts 28 auditoriums and Europe's largest IMAX screen. The centrally located *Actors Studio*, Petite Rue des Bouchers 16 (tel: (02) 512 1696) specialises in arthouse cinema.

Cultural Events

Each year, Brussels is at the heart of a lively cultural calendar, including the arts festival *Kunstenfestivaldesarts*, in May, and the spectacular *Ommegang* procession in early July. The origins of the traditional Ommegang pageant are rooted in the 13th century, when aristocrats, the nobility and master guildsmen paid homage to the sovereign in a solemn procession. Today, a lively procession recreates the medieval event.

Literary Notes

Brussels sheltered Karl Marx in exile and it was here that he wrote the *Communist Manifesto* in February 1848. Victor Hugo was temporarily protected at Place des Barricades 4, before being exiled once again for protesting against the government's ban on refugees. Perhaps the best literary ambassador of Brussels is the boy reporter, Tintin, created by Hergé (Georges Remy, 1907–1983). Brussels-born Jacques Brel, the celebrated singer-songwriter of *Ne Me Quitte Pas/Don't Leave Me* (1959), has been adopted by the French as their own, as have detective writer Georges Simenon, Marguerite Yourcenar and other Belgian luminaries. But Belgium developed its own national literary identity during the Symbolist movement and writers like Emile Verhaeren, Charles Van Lerberghe and Nobel Prize-winner Maurice Maeterlinck, created a misty, dreamy ambience for Art Nouveau Brussels. This taste for the fantastic and otherworldly, hidden in the hearts of staid Brussels burghers, was continued by Henri Michaux and the surreal visions of Magritte and Delvaux. This vision was shared by comic artists too. Belgians have commandeered the Francophone comic book industry – Hergé is just the tip of the iceberg – proof that Belgians do whimsy and goofy charm far better than the French. For a British take on Brussels, readers should try the modern bestseller, *Travels as a Brussels Scout* (1997), by London-born author Nick Middleton.

SPECIAL EVENTS

International Festival of Films of the Fantastic, Thrillers and Science Fiction, Mar, Passage 44 and Nova
Ars Musica, contemporary music festival, Mar, various venues
Baroque Spring Festival at Sablon, Baroque music festival, Apr, Sablon district
Brussels Film Festival, Apr, Flagey
Zinneke Parade, cultural festival, late May, Grand-Place
Brussels Gay Pride, early May, various venues
Brussels Jazz Marathon, late May, Grand-Place and various venues
Kunstenfestivaldesarts, dance, theatre and opera festival, May, various venues
Couleur Café, world music concerts, late Jun, Thurn et Taxis Building
Visits to the Royal Palace Jul–Sep, Royal Palace
Ommegang, procession, early Jul, Grand Place
Klinkende Munt, dance and outdoor music festival, early Jul, Place de la Monnaie
Mini-Europe by Night, fireworks displays, Friday to Sunday mid-Jul–mid-Aug, Mini-Europe
Meyboom, traditional pageant with maypole dancing, Aug, Place des Sablons to Grand-Place
Flower Carpet, thousands of begonias are laid out in gorgeous designs, Aug, Grand-Place
Brussels Heritage Days, free admission to museums and public buildings not usually open to the general public, mid-Sep, various venues
Audi-Jazz Festival, Oct–Nov, various venues
Sablon Nights, antiques and art galleries festival, Nov, Sablon district
Christmas Market, Dec, Grand-Place
Ice Skating, Dec–Jan, Fish Market

Photo: Belgian Tourist Office – Brussels Wallonia

Ommegang procession

CAPE TOWN

Cape Town is one of the most beautiful cities in the world, with its stunning location, tucked into the arms of a broad bay, surrounded by wild, white-sand beaches and set against the canvas of Table Mountain. Affectionately nicknamed the Mother City, it is the epicentre of South Africa's Western Cape region and the seat of South Africa's parliament. Originally home to the nomadic Khoi people for at least 30,000 years, the Cape Peninsula was first settled, on 6 April 1652, by Dutch sailors led by Jan van Riebeek of the Dutch East India Company. Portuguese explorer Bartholemew Diaz had already discovered the Cape in 1488 and christened it *Cabo Tormentoso* or 'Cape of Storms', but Portugal's King John II later renamed it 'Cape of Good Hope'. In 1795, it became a British colony, when the British Empire extended her borders. The city has been the first port of call for many a European settler, entrepreneur and religious refugee, as well as for Indian, Madagascan and South-East Asian slaves. All these people interspersed with the local Khoi and Xhosa population and the city became a melting pot of cultures, religions, styles and flavours. Nowadays, traders from other African countries – such as Malawi, Zimbabwe, Ethiopia and Nigeria – also favour Cape Town, particularly because there are so many tourists there. The city has a reputation for being the least xenophobic and most welcoming city in South Africa, with a strong diversity and open-minded benevolence.

Capetonians are proud of their easy-going spirit, jokingly known as 'Cape coma', which is so different from their more frenetic counterparts in the north.

On the streets, there is a polyglot of languages spoken, while stalls selling all manner of crafts, food and textiles are squashed among American-style malls, European fashion boutiques, art galleries, luxury hotels, backpacker lodges and the ubiquitous chains. In summer, it is difficult to escape the glitz of the international media, whether film crews, fashion shoots, music videos or commercials, lured by great foreign exchange rates, exotic locations, a world-class infrastructure and seemingly endless supply of drop-dead gorgeous models and extras.

Although Cape Town is undeniably on the up and up, it is still surrounded by the ever-visible legacy of apartheid. The first glimpse of the city coming from the airport is of shanty towns or 'townships', a hangover from the days of the notorious Group Areas Act, which reserved the prime city land for whites only. At the foot of Table Mountain, the area known as District Six (once populated by the local mixed-race community known as 'coloured') is still a ghost town. The inhabitants were moved to the bleak and windswept Cape Flats, which has become notorious as the gangland of disaffected Cape Town youth. Even today, relatively few non-whites live in the more upmarket suburbs, although, some of the former townships are gradually turning into middle-class estates as the economic situation improves.

Nevertheless, beauty spreads out from Cape Town. To the south, the impeccable beaches of the Cape Peninsula are fringed with pretty towns and mansions ending in the beautiful Cape Point. To the east lies the mysterious magnificence of the Overberg, the rolling plains, deserted beaches and lofty mountains of the Southern Cape. To the north and northwest, the misty and severe splendour of the West Coast, the austere wilderness of the Cedarberg and the verdant valley of Ceres await the traveller.

Many visitors think that Cape Town is best during the peak summer months – December to February – but it is attractive all year round. Summer brings long, hot beach days and balmy outdoor evenings, but they could also be described as sweltering and overcrowded and there is the chance of the legendary strong 'southeaster' wind. Spring (August to September) brings blooms of flowers, while autumn (March to April) promises a golden haze of warm days. Winter (May to July), although wet and often very cold, is interspersed with weeks that are both warm and clear. The city is free of tourists and wonderfully green; dolphins and whales stop in the many small bays along the coastline, and waterfalls, the most spectacular sight of this 'secret season', streak silver paths down the mountains.

Photo: South Africa Tourism

Cape Town with Table Mountain as a backdrop

TRAVEL

Getting There By Air

Cape Town International Airport (CPT)

Tel: (021) 937 1200 *or* 934 0407 (flight information).
Fax: (021) 934 2861.
Website: www.airports.co.za
Cape Town International Airport is located 20km (12.4 miles) east of Cape Town's city centre on the N2 highway. The airport has experienced much expansion and renovation over the past decade and its cutting-edge design, clean and efficient interior and extensive facilities have earned it the title of 'Africa's Leading Airport' at the World Travel Awards for four consecutive years (1998–2001) and the African Aviation Award in 2002. The airport is the gateway to the Western Cape and there are direct flights to 23 cities in 19 countries, including London, Munich, Frankfurt, Amsterdam, Istanbul, Kuala Lumpur, Buenos Aires, Singapore, Cairo, Mauritius, Windhoek and Fort Lauderdale. Domestic and regional routes include Johannesburg, Durban, Port Elizabeth, East London and Bloemfontein. The airport handles over four million passengers a year, projected to increase to over six million by 2004.

Major airlines: *South African Airways* (tel: (021) 936 1111 *or* 2389; fax: (021) 936 2487; website: www.flysaa.com) is the national airline. Other major carriers include *British Airways*, *KLM*, *LTU*, *Lufthansa*, *Singapore Airlines* and *Virgin Atlantic*.

Approximate flight times to Cape Town: From London is 11 hours 20 minutes; from New York is 17 hours; from Los Angeles is 25 hours; from Toronto is 19 hours and from Sydney is 16 hours.

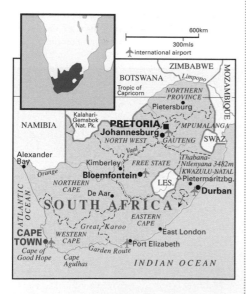

Airport facilities: Facilities include foreign exchange, ATMs, executive car parking services, tourist information, restaurants, bars, snack bars, bookshops, duty-free shops, a pharmacy, mobile phone centre and car hire from *Avis*, *Budget*, *Europcar*, *Hertz*, *Imperial*, *Khaya*, *National/Alamo*, *Siswe* and *Tempest*.
Business facilities: There are four airport business centres, which are open daily, each accommodating between ten and 30 people, with facilities such as e-mail, fax, telephones, projectors, video-conferencing and photocopiers. Mobile phone hire is also available. The new *Airport Training Centre* and

Conference Venue is located near the main control tower. The *Airport VIP Lounge* (tel: (021) 937 1233), located in domestic departures, provides further information on the airport's business facilities.
Arrival/departure tax: An airport tax of R25 is included in the price of all tickets (domestic and international), although this can vary according to the airline and destination.
Transport to the city: There is no rail service or public bus service from the airport. *Legend Tourism Services* (tel: (021) 936 2814; e-mail: info@legendtours.co.za; website: www.legendtours.co.za) operates a shuttle bus service seven days a week 0500–2400, with prices starting at R150 for one passenger to Cape Town (journey time – approximately 20 minutes). *South African Tourism Services* (tel: (021) 510 4552) offers a similar shuttle service between the airport and city, costing R135. Advance booking is recommended. Metered taxis are always available outside the airport from *Touch Down Taxis* (tel: (082) 485 0469), the official airport taxi company, for approximately R160 to the city centre. Most luxury and business hotels will, if notified in advance, provide transport to and from the airport.

Getting There By Water

The superbly located *Cape Town Harbour*, at the heart of the city, off Coen Steytler Avenue and Western Boulevard, is overseen by *South African Port Operations* (tel: (021) 449 2805 *or* 2405; fax: (021) 449 6805; website: www.saponet.co.za), and is the second busiest port in South Africa, handling a huge volume of freight every year. Cruise liners regularly call here and it is also a major fishing port. There are two main sections of the harbour. While the massive working area, the *Duncan Dock*, is off limits to the casual visitor, the *Victoria Basin* and *Alfred Basin*, known collectively as the *V&A Waterfront* (tel: (021) 408 7500; fax: (021) 408 7505; e-mail: info@waterfront.co.za; website: www.waterfront.co.za) is one of South Africa's premier tourist attractions (see *Key Attractions*), as well as a working harbour. There is no dedicated passenger terminal at Cape Town Harbour. Cruise liners longer than 200m (656ft) are accommodated at various terminals at the Duncan Dock, while smaller liners dock at Jetty Two at the V&A Waterfront.
Boat services: *Andrew Weir Shipping* (tel: (021) 425 1165; fax: (021) 421 7485; e-mail: sthelenaline @mweb.co.za; website: www.rms-st-helena.com) offers cruises from Cape Town to St Helena (journey time – 23–31 days) and Tristan Da Cunha (journey time – 20 days) on-board the *RMS St Helena* (an old Royal Mail ship).
Transport to the city: The *Waterfront Shuttle* runs from the V&A Waterfront to Adderley Street, the hub of public transport in the city centre (journey time – approximately 10 minutes), as well as to Sea Point (journey time – approximately 20 minutes).

Getting There By Rail

Shosholoza Meyl (tel: (021) 774 4555 *or* (086) 000 8888 (toll free); website: www.spoornet.co.za) operates all mainline railway services, while *Cape Metrorail* (tel: (021) 449 4210 *or* (083) 123 7245; fax: (021) 449 4610; website: www.capemetrorail.co.za) operates the suburban services (see *Getting Around*). While national travel is easy and comfortable, often

even luxurious, suburban services are unreliable, not very extensive and can be very dangerous, especially after dark. Rail enquiries should be directed to the *Metro Transport Information* central toll-free number (tel: (0800) 656 463; website: www.mti.co.za). *Metrorail* also provides a security emergency number (tel: (0800) 210 081).
Cape Town Station, Adderley Street, services both national and suburban lines. The station is in a vast, vaulted building that houses an array of shops and kiosks – some tacky, others quite compelling. Other facilities include information desks, security lockers for hire (R10 per day), a restaurant and, believe it or not, a doctor, dentist and money-lending services. There is also a daily open-air flea market, located immediately outside the station.
Rail services: Mainline destinations include daily services to Pretoria via Johannesburg, Kimberley and Worcester (journey time – 28 hours), twice-weekly services to East London (journey time – 28 hours) and a weekly service to Durban via Kimberley and Bloemfontein (journey time – 36 hours 30 minutes), as well as international connections to Bulawayo, Gaborone, Harare and Maputo. Trains to Johannesburg and Durban offer a sleeper service and are relaxing alternatives to flying, with dining cars and serviced compartments.
The premier luxury train in South Africa is the *Blue Train* (tel: (021) 449 2672 *or* 334 8459 (reservations); fax: (012) 449 2067 *or* 334 8464; e-mail: bluetrain@transnet.co.za; website: www.bluetrain.co.za), with services between Cape Town and Pretoria (journey time – 25 hours), as well as up the Garden Route from Cape Town to Port Elizabeth (journey time – 43 hours 30 minutes) and to the Victoria Falls (journey time – approximately 50 hours). Most departures are in October, November and February and advance booking is recommended.
Transport to the city: Cape Town Station is situated right in the heart of the city centre. The central public transport bus depot is situated across the road, on Strand Street (in front of the Grand Parade). Metered taxis and minibus taxis are also available outside the station.

Getting There By Road

Cape Town's road network is excellent, with both good highways and scenic routes. This, combined with the fact that there is limited public transport, means that driving is often the preferred mode of transport for many tourists. However, visitors should note that South Africa has a very high accident rate, although most major accidents happen on the national highways outside the cities.

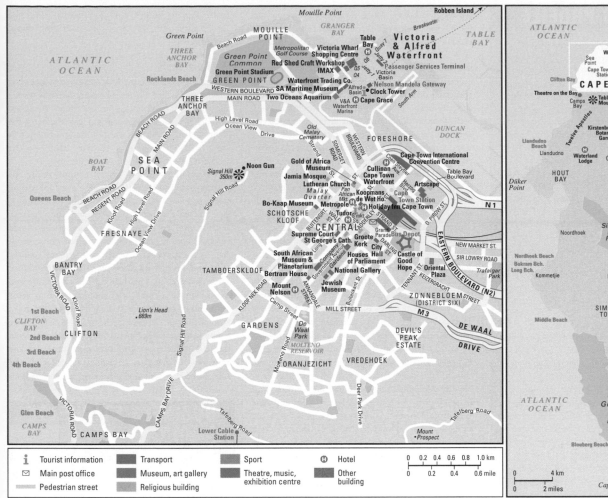

Tourist information	Transport	Sport	Ⓗ Hotel	0 0.2 0.4 0.6 0.8 1.0 km
Main post office	Museum, art gallery	Theatre, music, exhibition centre	Other building	0 0.2 0.4 0.6 mile
Pedestrian street	Religious building			

Roads are designated by an 'M' for motorway, 'N' for national roads and highways (major routes that criss-cross the country) and 'R' for the smaller yet still key routes. Local roads, including gravel or dirt tracks, are commonly designated by a 'C' or 'D', if they are listed at all. The legal driving age is 18 years. Driving is on the left and seatbelts must be worn at all times. The speed limit on highways is 120kph (75mph), 80–100kph (50–62mph) on national roads and 60kph (37mph) in urban areas. Foreign licences are valid if they are printed in English and have a photograph of the holder, otherwise an International Driving Permit is essential. Licences must be carried at all times. Mandatory Personal Accident Insurance is included in the price of the petrol, however, drivers should not rely on this and extra insurance is highly recommended. A recent crackdown on drink-driving has made penalties stringent; so visitors should note that the maximum legal alcohol to blood ratio for driving is lower than many countries at 0.05%.

Foreign drivers need to be aware that car hijacking is rampant in South Africa. Doors should be locked at all times and hitchhikers should be completely avoided. Unfortunately, it is also essential for drivers to carry cash, as petrol stations do not accept credit cards. Nevertheless, almost all petrol stations provide ATM machines.
The *Automobile Association of South Africa* (AA), Shop Five, Parkade Mall, Strand Street (tel: (021) 419 6914; fax: (021) 421 1343; e-mail: aasa@aasa.co.za; website: www.aasa.co.za) provides general information on road travel in South Africa.
Emergency breakdown service: AA (082) 16111 (toll free, 24 hours). Yellow SOS telephones are available along major routes.
Routes to the city: There are three main routes leading into Cape Town. These are the N1 from the Winelands (Paarl and Franschhoek) and northern destinations, such as the Karoo and Johannesburg, the

N2 from the airport, Somerset West and the Overberg via the Garden Route, and the N7 from the West Coast and Namibia.
Approximate driving times to Cape Town: From Somerset West – 30 minutes; Paarl – 45 minutes; Franschhoek – 1 hour; Johannesburg – 17 hours.
Coach services: Cape Town is linked by air-conditioned, deluxe and standard bus services to all major destinations in South Africa, including Johannesburg, Durban and Port Elizabeth, as well as some international destinations, such as Bulawayo and Harare in Zimbabwe, Maputo in Mozambique and Windhoek in Namibia. *Cape Town Station*, Adderley Street, is the departure point for all bus services. Service providers include *Intercape Mainliner* (tel: (021) 386 4400 (information) *or* (0861) 287 287 (central reservations); fax: (021) 386 2488 (reservations); e-mail: info@intercape.co.za; website: www. intercape.co.za), *Greyhound* (tel: (021) 505 6363; website: www.greyhound.co.za), *Translux Express* (tel: (021) 449 3333; fax: (021) 449 2545; website: www.translux.co.za) and *Elwierda* (tel: (021) 418 4673; website: www.elwierdacoachtours.co.za).

Getting Around

Public Transport

Cape Town is a frustrating city to navigate, simply because there is hardly any efficient public transport to speak of. That, and the fact that there is a great big mountain right in the middle of the city, can make getting around quite a daunting task for the tourist. Cape Town is, nevertheless, equipped with some

CITY STATISTICS

Location: Western Cape Province, South Africa.
Country dialling code: 27.
Population: 3.1 million (metropolitan area); 4.5 million (Western Cape Province).
Ethnic mix: 57% 'coloured' or mixed race, 24% white, 18% black, 11% Asian.
Religion: 90% Christian, 6% Muslim, 4% Jewish, Hindu and other.
Time zone: GMT + 2.
Electricity: 220/230 volts AC, 50 Hz; round two- or three-pin plugs are standard.
Average January temp: 23°C (73°F).
Average July temp: 18.5°C (65°F).
Annual rainfall: 509mm (20 inches).

BUSINESS PROFILE

Cape Town is somewhat removed from the business hype of South Africa's major financial and industrial centre, Johannesburg. However, the Western Cape accounts for 14% (R125.7 billion) of the country's Gross Domestic Product (GDP) and the city is home to some of the country's major financial institutions. These include insurance giants Old Mutual and Sanlam, financial houses like the Board of Executives, Investec, Merrill Lynch and Fedsure, and petroleum multinationals BP, Shell and Caltex (Chevron).

The region's economic mainstays are manufacturing, financial and business services, trade, tourism and agriculture. Manufacturing accounts for 20.1% of the GDP, employing 9% of the workforce, while financial and business services account for 17.4% of the GDP, employing 6.3%. Trade brings forth 11.1% of the GDP and employs 8.8%. Ever since the tourism boom in 1995, the city has reaped rich rewards. South Africa experienced an 11.1% increase in total foreign arrivals over 2001 and Cape Town currently enjoys 53% of these tourists.

Since the cessation of apartheid, tourism has provided employment for a large section of the workforce (9.3%), both in the service industry and for street traders and other informal operatives. Cape Town receives 7.6 million foreign and domestic tourists per year and tourism accounts for 9.1% of the GDP. The agriculture industry also employs a large number of people at 9%, producing 5.9% of the GDP – with the emphasis being on wine production and fruit farming. Cape Town is favoured as an ideal location for international film crews, attracted by excellent foreign exchange rates, a good film service industry, stunning locations, excellent weather and well-stocked modelling agencies. Other significant industries centred on Cape Town include advertising, technology and shipping. The Port of Cape Town has an annual turnover of approximately R700 million and expansion of the port is planned.

With an 80% adult literacy (95% in the Western Cape) and five residential universities and technikons, Cape Town boasts a highly skilled workforce, enabling it to attract R1.1 billion in foreign direct investment annually. However, poverty is still rife, with 19% of households suffering from poverty. The city's official unemployment rate stood at 18.9% (17.5% for the Western Cape) in 2001, which is considerably lower than the national rate of 29.3%. Another problem is the increasing HIV infection rate – the Western Cape has an infection rate of 7.1%, which is already one third of the current average South African infection rate.

Cape Town's central business district is situated in the city centre, although business and industrial parks are also found in the southern suburbs and on the outskirts. The new *Cape Town International Convention Centre* (tel: (021) 410 5000; e-mail: info@ctconvention.co.za; website: www.capetown convention.com) on the foreshore, linking the V&A Waterfront and the city centre, opened on 1 July 2003.

The *Cape Chamber of Commerce and Industry*, Cape Chamber House, 19 Louis Gradner Street (tel: (021) 418 4300; fax: (021) 418 4302; e-mail: info@capechamber.co.za; website: www.capechamber. co.za), was founded in 1804 and is a one-stop shop for business information and advice.

trains and buses. *Metro Transport Information* (tel: (0800) 656 463; website: www.mti.co.za) provides centralised information on all trains, buses and taxis. *Cape Metrorail* (tel: (021) 449 4210 *or* (083) 123 7245; fax: (021) 449 4610; website: www.capemetrorail. co.za) runs the suburban network of trains, consisting of four routes, which serve the southern and northern suburbs, Phillipi, Khayelitsha, Paarl, Stellenbosch, Wellington and Strand, completely ignoring the Atlantic seaboard and the airport. The Cape Town–Simon's Town route, which traverses the coastline, just metres from the ocean, is particularly spectacular. Tourists are advised to keep a watchful eye on their possessions, as pickpocketing is rife, and never travel after dark. Trains run daily 0400–2100 (depending on the route travelled), with regular departures, although there is a more limited service at weekends. Since apartheid, there are now only two classes of ticket, although they are known as first class and third class; most people travel in third class, which is basically just the standard service. Tickets vary in price depending on zone and class – a single-zone, third-class ticket costs R5.30 (R14.50 first class). Tickets are available for purchase at *Cape Town Station*, Adderley Street, as are weekly third-class Metrorail passes, costing R19 (R38 for first class). Although extremely chaotic, public buses still run regular and safe services to most destinations – including Camps Bay, Claremont, Hout Bay, Kirstenbosch, Kloof Nek, Sea Point and the Waterfront. However, tourists should probably avoid taking buses to the outlying areas. *Golden Arrow* (tel: (021) 937 8800; fax: (021) 934 4885; e-mail: information@gabs.co.za; website: www.gabs.co.za) has the monopoly on Cape Town's bus services, which run out of the main bus terminal on Strand Street, just opposite Cape Town Station. Buses run daily approximately 0600–2100 (depending on the route), with a more limited service at the weekend. Bus fares are based on the kilometres travelled and prices vary accordingly. For example, a ticket from the city centre toward the southern suburbs (Mowbray) costs R3. Tickets can be purchased upon boarding or from the main terminal (Monday to Friday 0530–1900, Saturday 0700–1815). 'Clipcards' or passes are also available at the Strand Street terminal. Based on travel between the city centre and southern suburbs (Mowbray), these cost R27 for a weekly clipcard.

Water taxis (tel: (021) 418 5806) operate daily from 0800 to sunset, departing from the V&A Waterfront Marina via the Aquarium, Quay Five and Quay Six on specific routes.

Taxis

Metered taxis can be ordered at any time of day or night and can also be hired for day trips. Although the meters are generally accurate, visitors should ask the driver for an estimated price before setting out, as many of the taxi drivers choose to ignore the meter. Taxi rates are approximately R8–10 per kilometre travelled, with a R60 per hour waiting fee. There are taxi ranks at the main railway station and at the top of Adderley Street, just below Company Gardens. Visitors should note that the practice of hailing a taxi on the street is virtually unheard of in Cape Town. Besides finding one at the ranks, visitors can call *Marine Taxis* (tel: (021) 434 0434), *Unicab* (tel: (021) 448 1720) or *City Cabs* (tel: (021) 638 1914). *Rikki's* (tel: (021) 423 4888) also provides a more tourist-orientated taxi service in an open rickshaw-type vehicle; they only run in the city centre and Simon's

Town. Tipping is not common practice in Cape Town, although an extra R10–20 is always appreciated.

Minibus Taxis

A common sight in any South African city, including Cape Town, is the ten- to 12-seater minibus taxis – the preferred transport option of many a car-less local. These can be hailed down anywhere on the streets and are by far the cheapest transport option at about R2.50 a ride from the city centre to the southern suburbs or Atlantic seaboard.

However, the minibus taxis cannot really be recommended to tourists. Although they are getting more organised, especially on the inner city routes, they still have a bad reputation and safety record. Tourists who do choose to use this service should exercise caution and employ common sense at all times. Passengers, particularly women but men as well, should not board an empty bus, nor should they travel alone, at night or beyond the city centre and the immediate suburbs. They should absolutely avoid the minibus taxis that are in dreadful shape – with flat or smooth tyres, alarming dents or just a general state of disrepair. Similarly, tourists should absolutely avoid minibuses where 'co-pilots' lean out of the window or the door to shout the destinations – tourists should only board the minibuses that have the destinations

BUSINESS ETIQUETTE

Business practices in Cape Town and South Africa are very similar to those in the UK and USA. Despite the fact that Cape Town is more informal than Johannesburg, most industries do expect a suit and tie. The more modern or artistic industries, such as information technology and the media, tend to display a more informal attitude to dress – particularly in the summer months. However, it is advisable for foreign business visitors to maintain formality and only resort to the casual uniform of shorts, T-shirts and sandals when the after-hours entertainment begins.

Business hours are 0900–1700, although many companies finish earlier on a Friday. The exchanging of business cards is an important ritual in Cape Town and a firm handshake between both men and women is common. In some instances, the African triple handshake will be used – this is a normal handshake, then a tilt to the hand is executed to clasp the fingers at a 90-degree angle – but without letting go – and then a return to a normal handshake.

Socialising is a big part of the business scene in Cape Town and much business is conducted over lunch. Wine will more than likely be included and visitors should note that South African wines often have a slighter stronger alcohol content than the majority of European wines (usually nearer 13%). Admiration of the local wine will be appreciated, although over-indulgence is certainly not recommended. Capetonians pride themselves on being hospitable to foreign visitors and an invitation to a business contact's home is not unusual. These will, more than likely, take the form of a 'braai' (barbecue), which tends to last throughout the entire afternoon and often into the night. Alcohol flows freely here and a gift of a bottle of wine is always appreciated, unless the host is Muslim, in which instance alcohol is strictly forbidden. In this case, a gift of chocolates, flowers or a speciality gift from the guest's home country is more suitable.

and corresponding route numbers printed on the back of the bus. A ride in a minibus taxi is also a white-knuckle experience, not for the faint-hearted, as the drivers do not pay much attention to the rules of the road.

Limousines

Limousines are something of a novelty in Cape Town and would certainly be stared at in the street. But for an indulgent day of sightseeing – especially wine tasting – a chauffeured limousine is ideal. *Rent-a-Rolls* (tel: (021) 556 7144; e-mail: rentarolls@yahoo.com; website: www.rentarolls.20m.com) hires out limousines for R1500–3000 per day (all-inclusive).

Driving in the City

Due to the lack of efficient and safe public transport, many visitors choose to drive. Driving in the city is usually fairly unstressful, as there are good feeder highways, excellent signage and efficient traffic lights. The scenic routes and meandering country roads are particularly lovely. However, the characteristic Cape Town repose seems to dissolve once the locals are behind the wheel and driving can be hair-raising at times. Drivers are almost always accosted at stop streets and traffic lights, by beggars or entrepreneurs flogging everything from newspapers and roses to bin liners. (However, it can be a treat for hot and bothered motorists to purchase a box of sweet Hanepoot grapes, when in season – late summer.)

Rush hour is generally 0700–0830 and 1630–1800, when some routes, particularly De Waal Drive, heading out of the city, become quite congested. Getting into the city from the southern suburbs can be quite an adventure for the uninitiated. On what is known as 'University Bend', where De Waal Drive rounds the mountain towards feeder roads to the N2 and the Eastern Boulevard, there are many tricky lane changes to tackle, mainly because the exits are to the right of the road despite the fact that driving in South Africa is on the left. A preferred route into the city centre is via Main Road, which feeds into the city centre all the way from Wynberg, through Observatory, Woodstock and Salt River into Cape Town. Although fairly straightforward, here drivers have to keep an eye out for minibus taxis, whose *Mad Max* antics can be quite alarming at times. It is not advisable for drivers to attempt to challenge the minibus taxi drivers, as this can be very dangerous.

Parking is plentiful around the city, with almost every mall equipped with indoor parking. Central car parks are located on Strand Street, the Grand Parade and Plein Street. Indoor parking costs approximately R8 per hour. Other parking lots offer a pay-and-display service. In many free open parking lots, uniformed parking security guards will look after cars for a tip. Tipping is not essential, however, as this is, in most cases, the sole means of support for these security guards, a small tip of around R1 is not much for the average visitor to spare.

Street parking is much less simple. Rather than using coins for the parking meters, they are operated by a prepaid swipe card (tel: (0800) 220 017; website: www.ado.co.za). Cards cost R17 plus R23 of parking credit, which can be topped up; they are available at newsagents, cafés and various other outlets. Street parking generally costs R3 per hour. Once empty, cash can be paid and reloaded on to the card. Parking marshals on the streets of the city centre are on hand to offer assistance with operating the meters and to customers without parking cards. Tipping is not obligatory but is appreciated. The system is in

Table Mountain at night

operation Monday to Saturday during office hours; parking is free of charge after 1800. There are also some pay-and-display parking lots in the suburbs.

Car Hire

Hiring a car is often the visitor's preferred mode of transport in Cape Town, especially for excursions to outlying areas. Hotels can arrange car hire for their guests, while all major car hire companies have booths at the airport. *Cape Town Tourism* (tel: (021) 426 4260; fax: (021) 426 4266) will also arrange car hire for tourists at no extra charge.

Some of the many major car hire companies include *Budget* (tel: (086) 101 6622; e-mail: reservations@budget.co.za; website: www.budget.co.za) and *Hertz* (tel: (0861) 600 136 *or* (021) 400 9600; fax: (021) 400 6886; e-mail: res@hertz.co.za; website: www.hertz.co.za). *Caesars* (tel: (021) 982 8817; fax: (021) 982 8088; e-mail: info@caesars.co.za; website: www.caesarscarhire.com); *Global* (tel: (021) 423 5211; fax: (021) 423 5280; e-mail: info@globalcarrental.co.za; website: www.globalcarrental.co.za); *Tempest* (tel: (086) 103 1666 *or* (021) 424 5000; fax: (021) 424 4190; website: www.tempestcarhire.co.za) and *Cape Car Hire* (tel: (021) 683 2441; fax: (021) 683 2443; e-mail: info@capecarhire.co.za; website: www.capecarhire.co.za) are local providers.

Rates start at around R65–80 per day for a budget vehicle (excluding mileage, which is priced at around R0.85–1.50 per kilometre). Insurance is sometimes included in the rates but is usually offered as an optional extra (some companies make this compulsory, unless proof of individual insurance is provided) and is highly recommended, particularly against theft. Drivers must be at least 23 years old and have a credit card and an International Driving Permit (unless the driver's national licence is printed in English and bears a photograph of the holder).

Bicycle & Scooter Hire

Cycling in the city centre requires nerves of steel and tremendous good luck. It is therefore not recommended. However, country and suburban excursions can be incredibly rewarding, especially through the Winelands and the Cape of Good Hope Nature Reserve. *Rent-n-Ride*, 1 Park Road, Mouille Point (tel: (021) 434 1122; e-mail: bahamba@iafrica.com), hires out bicycles for R85 per day or R350 per week.

To beat the beach parking blues, particularly in the crowded summer months, adventurous tourists often choose to hire out Vespa scooters from *African Buzz*, 202 Long Street (tel: (021) 423 0052; fax: (021) 423 0056; e-mail: skootaz@intekom.co.za), for R145–175 per 24 hours, depending on the season. *Breezes*, 42 Main Road, Sea Point (tel: (021) 434 3461; e-mail: breezes@iafrica.com) also offers scooter hire.

SIGHTSEEING

Sightseeing Overview

There is so much to do and see in Cape Town that the first-time visitor will find it difficult just to fit everything in. Nevertheless, the city centre itself is small and compact, and easy and pleasant to navigate on foot. *Table Mountain* watches over the proceedings, providing not only a beautiful backdrop but also a handy point of orientation, which makes getting lost quite difficult. Having said that, the city centre is deceptively facing north, rather than south, as many visitors believe.

TOURIST INFORMATION

Cape Town Tourism Visitor Information Centre
Corner of Burg Street and Castle Street
Tel: (021) 426 4260. Fax: (021) 426 4266.
E-mail: info@cape-town.org
Website: www.cape-town.org or www.capetourism.org
Opening hours: Mon–Fri 0800–1900, Sat 0830–1400, Sun 0900–1300 (summer); Mon–Fri 0800–1800, Sat 0830–1400, Sun 0900–1300 (winter).

There is also a Visitor Information Centre at the Clock Tower Precinct, at the V&A Waterfront. Many other information centres are situated around the peninsula, including Kirstenbosch Botanical Gardens, The Pavilion in Muizenberg, Sivuyile College in Gugulethu, the Tyger Valley Shopping Centre and Cape Town International Airport.

Passes
There are no tourist passes currently available in Cape Town.

There is an amazing variety of architectural styles, including Cape Dutch, Victorian and Edwardian buildings wedged in between modern skyscrapers. The Foreshore's *V&A Waterfront* is a stunning example of urban regeneration, where old-style harbour warehouses and buildings have been transformed into beautiful shopping centres, luxury hotels and a multitude of restaurants. Spreading west toward *Signal Hill* is the *Bo-Kaap* (Top Cape) area, also known as the *Malay Quarter* (Malay is a misnomer for Cape Muslims of Asian descent). This area was home to the freed slaves – their descendants resisted all attempts at removal by the apartheid authorities and were much more successful than the *District Six* inhabitants, whose homes were bulldozed, following Verwoerd's orders for racial segregation. Offshore, north of Table Bay, lies *Robben Island*, the prison where Nelson Mandela and many of the other current top political leaders of South Africa were jailed by the apartheid regime.

The outlying areas of Cape Town are also of great interest to visitors and an organised 'township tour', which explores the predominantly black and 'coloured' (mixed-race) areas of *Kayalitsha*, *Langa* and *Gugulethu*, is an increasingly popular item on the tourist agenda. A typical tour will include a visit to a significant site of The Struggle, lunch in a shebeen, a visit to a craft market and a stop at a self-help development project. It is inadvisable for visitors to venture into the townships without a guide, as crime levels are high and tourists are often soft targets. A new initiative launched by Cape Town Tourism for the 2002 World Summit on Sustainable Development is the *Trail of Two Cities*, where tourists meet the local communities in some of Cape Town's poorer areas.

To the west of the city centre and extending south toward Cape Point, the Atlantic Seaboard incorporates the *Sea Point*, *Clifton*, *Camps Bay*, *Llandudno*, *Hout Bay*, *Noordhoek* and *Kommetjie* seaside suburbs. Tacky turns to glitzy, dissolving into chic, rustic and downright wild the further from the city centre one travels. Meanwhile, curling around the eastern side of the Table Mountain range is the Southern Suburbs, with the world-renowned *Kirstenbosch Botanical Gardens* and the Constantia and Tokai *Winelands*. These connect to the cosy coastal

towns of False Bay's *Kalk Bay*, *Fish Hoek* and *Simon's Town*. The two sides of the peninsula meet at the windswept and breathtakingly beautiful *Cape of Good Hope Nature Reserve* at *Cape Point*.

Key Attractions

Table Mountain

Cape Town's defining landmark is also one of the city's greatest tourist attractions. A cable car trip to the 1086m (3563ft) summit of *Table Mountain* takes just six minutes and the state-of-the-art gondola – one of just three of its kind in the world – rotates through 360 degrees on the way up (booking is advisable during summer). Once there, more than two kilometres (1.2 miles) of pathways lead walkers over the massif, with breathtaking views of the city and ocean below. A bistro, perched right on the summit, is by far the most incredible sundowner spot in Africa.

A popular option is for day-trippers to take a one-way ticket up and then climb down Platteklip Gorge – although visitors should take care. The local Mountain Rescue teams (tel: (021) 948 9900 or 10177 in an emergency) carry out over 100 rescues a year, many involving foreign tourists. The routes up and down the mountain are treacherous and sheer cliff faces with buffeting winds are a very real danger. Peering over the edge of the mountain, no matter how tempting, is simply not a good idea. The signposts warning of restricted areas must be observed at all costs. Furthermore, the weather can change in a matter of minutes and mist and darkness descend very quickly. Hikers should carry water, food, sunblock, a silver 'space blanket' to prevent hypothermia and a mobile phone.

For the wary wanderer, *The Table Mountain Guiding Company* (tel: (021) 788 8750; e-mail: info@ activeafrica.co.za; website: www.active-africa.com) offers guided hikes up the mountain.

Tafelberg Road (lower cable station)
Tel: (021) 424 8181 or 5148. Fax: (021) 424 3792.
E-mail: marketing@tablemountain.co.za
Website: www.table-mountain.co.za or www. tablemountain.net

Transport: Bus from Adderley Street/Strand Street to Kloof Nek, then a long walk to Tafelberg Road.
Opening hours: Daily 0800–2200 (Jan); daily 0800–2100 (Feb–Apr); daily 0830–1800 (May–mid-Sep); daily 0830–1900 (mid-Sep–Oct); 0830–2000 (Nov); the cable car operates weather permitting.
Admission: R95 (return cable car ticket); R50 (single cable car ticket).

Victoria & Alfred Waterfront

Known universally as the *V&A Waterfront*, the creation of this waterfront was possibly Cape Town's best commercial idea, transforming a rundown harbour area into a booming centre of tourism, culture, leisure and business. The area is now the most visited spot in the city, attracting 85% of international tourists. Renovated Victorian warehouses, offices and buildings created in the Victorian vernacular style, and many dozens of cafés and restaurants complete this waterside area and working harbour. A host of boat and yacht charter operations tout for business and it is worth taking a cruise around the docks, which costs R10–30 (see *Tours of the City*).

The Waterfront is also home to the world-class *Two Oceans Aquarium*. Feeding in the huge predator tanks takes place on Monday, Wednesday, Friday and Saturday at 1530 and should not be missed. Aquarium dives can also be arranged. Then, with over 250 retail outlets, the *Victoria Wharf Shopping Centre* is another premier attraction. The *Waterfront Trading Company* and the *Red Shed Craft Workshop* supply local arts and crafts, while, in summer, various music acts perform on the bandstand.

The newest addition to the V&A Waterfront is the *Clock Tower Precinct*, the departure point for Robben Island cruises. During the initial construction of the area, the ruins of the Dutch East India Military installation, dating back to between 1715 and 1726, were discovered and are now on show to the public. Plans for further expansion of the Waterfront are currently underway. These will include a canal and the creation of a new marina linking the Waterfront to the new convention centre.

Dock Road, off Coen Steytler Avenue or Portswood Road, off Western Boulevard
Tel: (021) 408 7600. Fax: (021) 408 7605.
E-mail: info@waterfront.co.za
Website: www.waterfront.co.za
Transport: Waterfront Shuttle from Adderley Street or Beach Road.
Opening hours: Daily 24 hours.
Admission: Free.
Two Oceans Aquarium
Dock Road
Tel: (021) 418 3823. Fax: (021) 418 3952.
E-mail: aquarium@aquarium.co.za
Website: www.aquarium.co.za
Opening hours: Daily 0930–1800.
Admission: R50 (concessions available).
Waterfront Trading Company
Dock Road
Tel: (021) 408 7840. Fax: (021) 408 7845.
E-mail: craftmarket@waterfront.co.za
Opening hours: Daily 0930–1800.
Admission: Free.
Red Shed Craft Workshop
Victoria Wharf, Quay Five
Tel: (021) 408 7847. Fax: (021) 408 7855.
Opening hours: Mon–Sat 0930–2100, Sun 1000–2100.
Admission: Free.

Photo: South Africa Tourism

Table Mountain cable car

Robben Island

Visiting *Robben Island*, a World Heritage Site, is one of the most profoundly moving experiences to be had in South Africa. The infamous men-only prison and former leper colony was home to a generation of the senior statesmen of Africa, incarcerated because of their political beliefs. The most famous inmate was, of course, Nelson Mandela, who spent 18 years of his 27-year sentence here. The daily Robben Island Tour leaves from the Nelson Mandela Gateway at the V&A Waterfront Clock Tower Precinct. Once on the island, guided tours are all given by former political prisoners here, while the first-class museums, situated both on Robben Island and at the new Clock Tower Precinct, offer a wealth of information on this period of South Africa's history. There is more to Robben Island than politics and history, however. The physical beauty of the island itself is magnificent, with penguin and seal colonies, as well as the fantastic view of Cape Town.

V&A Waterfront and Robben Island

Tel: (021) 413 4200 (information) *or* 411 1006 (museum) *or* 419 1300 (reservations).

Fax: (021) 411 1059 (museum) *or* 419 1057 (reservations).

E-mail: info@robben-island.org.za *or* bookings@ robben-island.org.za

Website: www.robben-island.org.za

Transport: Ferries from the Nelson Mandela Gateway at the Clock Tower Precinct, V&A Waterfront.

Opening hours: Daily 0730–1800 (Nelson Mandela Gateway).

Admission: R100 (ferry ticket and admission).

Kirstenbosch Botanical Gardens

Sprawling over a magnificent 528 hectares (1325 acres) and home to 5000 indigenous plant species, *Kirstenbosch* is rated one of the top seven botanical gardens in the world and was voted top tourism site in the city at the 2001 Premier's MTN Cape Tourism Awards. With stunningly beautiful formal gardens dotted with African stone sculptures, Kirstenbosch is a delightful place for a picnic, a stroll or even an energetic hike through the wild gardens on the lower slopes of Table Mountain. Attractions include trails for the blind, a fragrance garden, a cycad amphitheatre, a greenhouse complete with Boabab tree, an authentic African mud hut, a gift shop, bookshop, restaurants and café. During the summer months (December to March), immensely popular Sunset Concerts are held on Sunday afternoons at 1730, with music that ranges from classical to jazz and African traditional to folk.

Rhodes Drive, Newlands

Tel: (021) 799 8783 (weekdays) *or* 799 8899 (weekends). Fax: (021) 797 6570.

Website: www.nbi.co.za *or* www.kirstenbosch.co.za

Transport: Bus from Adderley Street or Mowbray Station.

Opening hours: Daily 0800–1900 (Sep–Mar); daily 0800–1800 (Apr–Aug).

Admission: R18.

Company Gardens

Jan van Riebeek – the first commander of the Dutch colony at the Cape – ordered the planting of *Company Gardens* in 1652, to serve as a fruit and vegetable supply for the visiting ships, to protect the sailors against scurvy. Nowadays, the gardens are a green lung for the city centre. The park is not just a botanical delight but is also home to *St George's Cathedral*, the *Houses of Parliament*, the

Kirstenbosch Botanical Gardens

South African National Gallery, the *South African Museum* and the *Planetarium*.

The Anglican St George's Cathedral has been in existence for over 100 years but is also a potent symbol of anti-apartheid resistance. It has been the site of many a political rally in the past and, until 1996, Nobel Peace Prize winner Desmond Tutu was archbishop here.

The Houses of Parliament, which flank the eastern edge of the gardens, are a blend of Georgian and Victorian styles of architecture. Designed by the British architect Harry Greaves, they were completed in 1885, when the parliament became the seat of British expansion into Africa. The building is also an important stop on the political tourist's itinerary. This is where the 'architect of apartheid', prime minister Hendrik Verwoerd, was assassinated in 1966. It is also where Nelson Mandela gave his inaugural speech as president of the 'new South Africa' in 1994.

The South African National Gallery contains one of the finest collections of South African and international art in the country and has regular exhibitions of work from around the world. The South African Museum is an excellent place for visitors to spend a couple of hours learning about the natural and political history of South Africa. It also boasts the oldest African artworks, the Lydenburg Heads, which date back to 500BC, as well as a superb whale exhibit and a shop, located on Orange Street. In the Planetarium, the real-time night sky displays are an entrancing introduction to the stellar delights of Southern Africa.

Government Avenue (between Wale Street and Orange Street)

Transport: A short walk from Adderley Street.

Opening hours: Daily 1000–1700.

Admission: Free.

South African National Gallery

Government Avenue

Tel: (021) 465 1628. Fax: (021) 461 0045.

Website: www.museums.org.za/sang

Opening hours: Tues–Sun 1000–1700.

Admission: R5; concessions available; free Sun.

South African Museum

25 Queen Victoria Street

Tel: (021) 424 3330. Fax: (021) 424 6716.

Website: www.museums.org.za/sam

Opening hours: Daily 1000–1700.

Admission: R8; R15 (combined with Planetarium); concessions available; free Sun.

Planetarium

25 Queen Victoria Street

Tel: (021) 481 3900. Fax: (021) 481 3990.

Website: www.museums.org.za/planetarium

Opening hours: Shows Mon–Fri 1400 (excluding first Mon of month), Tues 2000, Sat and Sun 1430.

Admission: R10; R12 (evening shows); R15 (combined with SA Museum); concessions available.

Koopmans De Wet House

Built in 1701, *Koopmans De Wet House* reflects patrician life at the Cape in the 18th century. Designed in the distinctive 'Cape Dutch' architectural style – a style repeated in many of the grand manor houses on rural estates and recognisable by curly gables – the house is also furnished with fine examples of Cape craftsmanship. Many of these hand-carved items of furniture were designed by slave 'fundis' or experts from the East, as was the unique decorative plasterwork on the exterior of this and other buildings. The quiet, cool and darkened interior is also a tranquil retreat from the bustle and heat of the city centre.

35 Strand Street

Tel: (021) 424 2473. Fax: (021) 461 9592.

Website: www.museums.org.za/koopmans

Transport: A short walk from Cape Town Station and Grand Parade.

Opening hours: Tues–Sat 0930–1630.

Admission: R5.

Beaches

Cape Town boasts some of the most spectacular beaches in the world. With a long summer and balmy

Photo: South Africa Tourism

Bakoven from Kasteelpoort, Table Mountain

winter days in between the rain, these are an irresistible attraction all year round. There is a beach to suit just about every taste – from the trendy spots, where tanned bikini bodies are the order of the day, via the more family orientated, easy-swim sites, to wild and rugged sundowner spots. Beaches are overseen by the Cape Peninsula National Park.

Set along the stunning panorama of the Twelve Apostles mountain range, the Atlantic seaboard beaches are several degrees colder than those on the False Bay side, which are warmed by the L'Agulhas current that diffuses into the eastern end of Cape Point.

However, the beaches on the Atlantic seaboard are hugely popular and real estate here is hot property – the stretch of mansions that lines the coast is known as Millionaire's Row. The suburb of *Clifton*, has four beaches, one of which, *Fourth Beach*, is Cape Town's premier beach spot and the preferred place for the beautiful people to pose. All four beaches, however, are often overcrowded in the peak summer months and parking on Victoria Road above the beach is virtually impossible. An alternative, with a California feel and restaurants and bars close at hand, is the nearby *Camps Bay*. Further out is the favourite sundowner spot, *Llandudno*, and the homely *Hout Bay*. The nearby *Mariner's Wharf* fishing harbour (tel: (021) 790 1100; fax: (021) 790 7777; e-mail: mariners@capecoast.co.za; website: www.marinerswharf.com) offers great seafood restaurants, markets, gift shops, boat trips and a fish market selling live lobsters by the kilo, as well as the Cape speciality, smoked snoek. *Noordhoek* and *Kommetjie*, both part of *Long Beach*, are no longer accessible by road from Hout Bay, as Chapman's Peak Drive collapsed into the sea in 2000. Plans to rebuild

it are apparently underway; for now those in search of a stunning view will have to content themselves with driving to the lookout point and no further. These far-flung beaches are still quite deserted and Noordhoek can be dangerous for lone walkers, particularly after dark.

False Bay offers its own set of coastal delights, quite different from the chilly counterparts on the Atlantic side. With warmer waters, the stretch of *Muizenberg* beach and little coves and inlets of *Kalk Bay*, *St James* and *Fish Hoek* offers delightful swimming, with smaller waves and a family feel. Formerly a whaling station and a prisoner of war camp, *Boulders* has a string of delightful coves that are always sheltered from the frequent and blustering 'southeaster' wind. However, visitors to Boulders will have to share their beach with quite a crowd … of African Penguins. The colony of penguins is protected and although these patient birds are happy to pose for photographs, there is a hefty fine for 'wilfully disturbing' them. They also bite – so birdwatchers are encouraged to admire them from a respectful distance. Boulders is just as popular with humans as it is with penguins, so sun-seekers should be sure to arrive early in order to stake their claim to a piece of beach, boardwalk or boulder. When not taking on the might of *Cape Point*'s wind ravaged coastline or enjoying the consistently good waves of Long Beach, surfers mainly head north for Table Bay and the beaches of *Blouberg Strand*, *Dolphin Beach* and *Milnerton*, where the incessant wind promises big waves and the location offers incredible views of Table Mountain.

Clifton, *Camps Bay* and *Llandudno*, access from Victoria Road (M6)
Hout Bay Beach and *Mariner's Wharf*, North Shore

Road or Beach Road, Hout Bay
Noordhoek, Silvermine Road via Ou Kaapse Weg, Noordhoek
Kommetjie, Kommetjie Road (M65), Kommetjie
Muizenberg, Baden-Powell Drive, Muizenberg
Kalk Bay, *St James* and *Fish Hoek*, off Main Road (M4)
Boulders Beach, Miller's Point Road, from Main Road (M4), Simonstown/Miller's Point
Cape Point beaches, several roads off Cape Point Road
Blouberg Strand and *Dolphin Beach*, Otto Du Plessis Road, Blouberg
Milnerton, Marine Drive and Otto Du Plessis, Milnerton
Tel: (021) 731 0260 (Cape Peninsula National Park) *or* 786 2329 (Boulders only). Fax: (021) 713 0604 (Cape Peninsula National Park) *or* 786 5787 (Boulders).
E-mail: capepeninsula@parks-sa.co.za *or* boulders@ parks-sa.co.za
Website: www.cpnp.co.za
Transport: Train to Simon's Town (False Bay beaches); bus to Sea Point, Camps Bay or Hout Bay (Atlantic Seaboard); self-drive for others (see routes above).
Opening hours: Daily 24 hours.
Admission: Free; R10 (Boulders).

Further Distractions

Bo-Kaap Museum
Built in the mid-1760s, the *Bo-Kaap Museum* was originally the home of Turkish scholar, Abu Bakr Effendi, and is the oldest extant residence in the Muslim community, as well as a rare example of urban Cape Dutch architecture. The furnishings are typical of an 18th-century Cape Town Muslim residence, right down to the main bedroom – an authentic bridal suite. Effendi was a revered Arabic teacher and wrote one of the first texts that documented the emergence of South Africa's second language Afrikaans (a mixture of Dutch, Malay, German, Xhosa and English). The Bo-Kaap area is the traditional home of the Cape-Malay community, brought in as slaves from Indonesia. It has some of the city's most interesting history and architecture, as well as fabulous views. The museum is used by the residents for a meeting place and exhibition space.
71 Wale Street
Tel: (021) 424 3846. Fax: (021) 461 9592.
Website: www.museums.org.za/bokaap
Transport: A ten-minute walk from Cape Town Station.
Opening hours: Mon–Sat 0930–1630.
Admission: R5.

Castle of Good Hope
Construction began on this five-pointed, star-shaped castle – originally a Dutch fortress – in 1666, which makes it the oldest colonial building in the country. Perhaps the most visible symbol of the colonial occupation of Cape Town and South Africa, the *Castle of Good Hope* became the apartheid government's military headquarters in 1948. However, since the liberation of South Africa in 1994, South Africa's oldest building has done much to polish up its tarnished image and has become very much a museum of the people. The castle hosts alternative art exhibitions and cultural events. Also within the castle, the *William Fehr Collection* is a superb record of colonial Cape art and culture.
Corner of Darling Street and Castle Street
Tel: (021) 787 1249 *or* 1082/3/4. Fax: (021) 787 1089.

Website: www.castleofgoodhope.co.za
Transport: A short walk from the Grand Parade/Strand Street.
Opening hours: Daily 0900–1600; guided tours daily 1100, 1200 and 1400.
Admission: R15 (including guided tour); R8 on Sun.
William Fehr Collection
Tel: (021) 464 1263/4 *or* 1272 (weekend). Fax: (021) 464 1280.
Website: www.museums.org.za/wfc
Opening hours: Mon–Sat 0930–1600.
Admission: R15; R8 on Sun; concessions available.

Century City

Just ten minutes from the city centre, Africa's largest mall, *Canal Walk*, is located in the massive and architecturally astounding *Century City* development, which is also home to Africa's first full-scale theme park, *Ratanga Junction*, with 30 rides, as well as an entertainment complex, complete with clubs, pubs and restaurants. The *MTN Sciencentre* provides a myriad of scientific distractions, for children of all ages, with over 250 interactive displays and a 200-seat multimedia arena. The 16-hectare (39.5-acre) man-made *Intaka Island*, is a haven for bird life, while boat rides on the four kilometres (2.5 miles) of canals are also available.
Century City, Century Boulevard, Milnerton
Tel: (021) 550 7000. Fax: (021) 550 7021.
E-mail: info@centurycity.co.za
Website: www.centurycity.co.za
Transport: By car, exit 10 off the N1.
Canal Walk Shopping Centre
Tel: (0860) 101 165.
E-mail: touristinfo@canalwalk.co.za
Website: www.canalwalk.co.za
Opening hours: Mon–Fri and Sun 1000–2100, Sat 0900–2100.
Admission: Free; parking charges apply.
Ratanga Junction
Tel: (0861) 200 300.
Website: www.ratanga.co.za
Opening hours: Wed–Fri 1000–1700, Sat 1000–1800, Sun 1000–1700 (20 Nov–4 May).
Admission: R90 (concessions available).
MTN Sciencentre
407 Canal Walk
Tel: (021) 529 8100. Fax: (021) 529 8179.
E-mail: info@mtnsciencentre.org.za
Website: www.mtnsciencentre.org.za
Opening hours: Mon–Thurs 0930–1800, Fri and Sat 0930–2000, Sun 1000–1800.
Admission: R22 (concessions available).

Gold of Africa Museum

Although gold is more often associated with South Africa's 'City of Gold', Johannesburg, Cape Town's new arrival on the museum circuit is entirely based around all that glitters. Located in the historic, 18th-century Martin Melck House, this museum is the first of its kind in the world and is all about the history and artistry of African gold, with a number of dazzling temporary and permanent exhibitions. Highlights include the West African gold artefacts from the Barbier-Mueller Museum in Geneva, the goldsmith workshop and design studio, the wine cellar and a delightful, shady tea garden. Tours are available on request and the museum shop is there to satisfy the jackdaw in all of us.
96 Strand Street
Tel: (021) 405 1540. Fax: (021) 405 1541.
Website: www.goldofafrica.com
Transport: A short walk from Cape Town railway and

bus stations; secure parking on the corner of Buitengracht and Strand streets.
Opening hours: Mon–Sat 1000–1700.
Admission: R20 (concessions available).

Tours of the City

Walking Tours

With its cosmopolitan buzz, street music, markets and busking acts, as well as a multitude of alfresco cafés and restaurants, Cape Town is a great city for exploring on foot. *Cape Town Tourism* (see *Tourist Information*) operates *Wanderlust*'s 'Cape Town on Foot' tours (tel: (021) 426 4260; website: www.wanderlust.co.za), which take two and a half hours to cover the main sights of the city centre. These take place Monday to Friday at 1100 and cost R100 per person.

Bus Tours

Hylton Ross (tel: (021) 511 1784) runs a regular open-topped double-decker bus tour, the 'Cape Town Explorer', which takes in all the major sights of Cape Town, with a running commentary. The two-hour tour can be hailed anywhere along the route and takes in Sea Point, Signal Hill, District Six and Camps Bay. The R80 hop-on hop-off tickets are valid all day and can be purchased on the bus, at the Cape Town Tourism Visitor Information Centres or in advance from *Computicket* (tel: (083) 915 8000; e-mail: info@computicket.com; website: www.computicket.com).
GC Tours (tel: (021) 691 9192; e-mail: gctours@ mweb.co.za; website: www.gctours.active3.com) offers a number of themed tours in air-conditioned microbuses. These include the popular 'Cape Cultural Cross Section' tour of Cape Town's cultural sites and townships. The half-day tour costs R250, while the full-day tour costs R300, which includes a visit to Robben Island. *Grassroute Tours* (tel: (021) 706 1006; fax: (021) 705 0798; e-mail: grasrout@iafrica.com;

website: www.grassroutetours.co.za) and *Roots Africa Tours* (tel: (021) 987 8330; fax: (021) 988 5641; e-mail: rootsafrica@xsinet.co.za; website: www.rootsafrica.co.za) both offer a similar service.

Boat Tours

Waterfront Boat Company (tel: (021) 418 5806; fax: (021) 418 5821; e-mail: info@waterfrontboats.co.za; website: www.waterfrontboats.co.za) offers a range of tours, from harbour tours to excursions and champagne cruises, departing from the V&A Waterfront Quay Five. Tours range from a one-hour cruise (R60) to a full-day fishing trip (R1650). *Fairweather* (tel: (082) 576 4132) offers three-hour luxury catamaran cruises for R100 or sunset cruises for R130, both departing from Quay Five.
The *Waterfront Information Office* (tel: (021) 408 7500 *or* 7600; website: www.waterfront.co.za) provides information on other tours available from the V&A Waterfront.
Boat tours to see the Cape Fur Seals on Duiker Island in False Bay are operated by *Drumbeat Charters* (tel: (021) 438 9208 *or* 790 4859; fax: (021) 438 8554). All cruises, which depart from Hout Bay Harbour, cost R40. There is also a one-way trip from Hout Bay to the Waterfront.

Bicycle Tours

Daytrippers (tel: (021) 511 4766; e-mail: info@ daytrippers.co.za; website: www.daytrippers.co.za) organises a number of bicycle tours, including the 'Cape Point Tour', which follows the Atlantic Coast to the Cape of Good Hope Nature Reserve. The full-day tour costs R325, including picnic lunch and entrance fees. Other cycling tours include a Winelands tour and a whale-watching tour (July to November). *Adventure Village* (tel: (021) 424 1580; e-mail: thrills@adventure-village.co.za; website: www.adventure-village.co.za) operates similar bicycle tours.

Coastal Road, Hout Bay, Cape Peninsula
Photo: South Africa Tourism

Bo-Kaap, Malay Quarter

Other Tours

Civair (tel: (021) 419 5182; fax: (021) 419 5183; e-mail: civair@mweb.co.za; website: www.civair.co.za) and NAC Makana Aviation (tel: (021) 425 3868; fax: (021) 425 3858; e-mail: info@nacmakana.com; website: www.nacmakana.com) both offer 20-minute, 30-minute and one-hour helicopter tours, costing R2000, R3000 and R6000 respectively.

Excursions

For a Half Day

Cape Point: This windswept peninsula, where the cold Benguela current and the warm Mozambique current converge, is the mythical meeting place of the Indian and Atlantic Oceans – the physical meeting place is actually 100km (62 miles) to the east, in Cape L'Agulhas. Cape Point (tel: (021) 780 9010; website: www.capepoint.co.za) is situated in the Cape of Good Hope Nature Reserve at the far tip of the enormous 7750-hectare (19,151-acre) Cape Peninsula National Park (tel: (021) 731 0260; fax: (021) 713 0604; e-mail: capepeninsula@parks-sa.co.za; website: www.cpnp.co.za).

Located 35km (22 miles) from the city centre, along the M4 via Simon's Town, Cape Point is home to a splendid array of wildlife, including zebra, lynx, bontebok, ostrich and baboons, as well as some of the rarest plants on Earth. Visitors should beware of the baboons, however, as they can be dangerous, particularly where food is involved; there is a fine for feeding them. An added bonus is the Two Oceans Restaurant (tel: (021) 780 9200/1; website: www.two-oceans.co.za), which is perched on the cliff above the Atlantic Ocean, as well as curio shops. Admission to the reserve costs R35 per adult and it is open daily 0700–1800 (summer) and 0700–1700 (winter).

Constantia Wine Route: Located approximately 17km (11 miles) or a 25-minute drive south of the city centre, the Constantia Wine Route offers a handy alternative to a longer trip to the Boland. There are over 400 wine producers in South Africa and the Constantia Valley area is home to five of

the Cape's top estates – Groot Constantia, Klein Constantia, Buitenverwachting, Constantia Uitsig and Steenberg Vineyards.

Africa's oldest wine estate, **Groot Constantia**, off the M41 Constantia Road (tel: (021) 794 5128; website: www.grootconstantia.co.za), with its original manor house and wine museum (tel: (021) 794 5067; website: www.museums.org.za/grootcon), gives a fascinating insight into early colonial life in the Cape (admission: R8). There is also the elegant Jonkershuis Restaurant (tel: (021) 794 6255; website: www.jonkershuis.com), while The Tavern (tel: (021) 794 1144) is open daily for wine tasting from 1100. The family-owned **Klein Constantia**, Klein Constantia Road (tel: (021) 794 5188), offers some choice Cape wines for tasting in extremely friendly company. **Buitenverwachting**, Klein Constantia Road (tel: (021) 794 5191), is renowned for its exclusive restaurant (see Restaurants) and pleasant picnic area. **Contantia Uitsig**, Spaanschmat River Road (tel: (021) 794 1810), translates to 'Constantia View' and the farm offers visitors not only excellent wine but the charming Spaanschemat River Café and two superb restaurants; La Colombe is the best (see Restaurants). Finally, **Steenberg Vineyards**, Steenberg Road (tel: (021) 713 2211), makes up for its dubious location opposite Pollsmore Prison with an exclusive hotel, a golf course and a restaurant.

The Kirstenbosch Visitor Information Centre (tel: (021) 762 0687) can provide further information on the Constantia Wine Route. Most of the estates are open for wine tasting at least 0900–1700 (weekdays) and 0900–1300 (Saturdays).

For a Whole Day

The Boland: A tour of the Boland ('uplands' or 'toplands') reveals a world of dramatic mountain ranges, crystal clear rivers teeming with trout, beautiful valleys and the Western Cape's bucolic Winelands, dotted with historic wine estates. There are ten officially designated 'wine routes' incorporating many of the wine estates that are open to the public. Mother City Tours (tel: (021) 448 3817; fax: (021) 448 3844; website: www.mctours.co.za) offers a full-day 'Three Cape Winelands' tour of the

Boland estates. Bacchanalian tourists who choose to go it alone with one of the many route maps obtainable from Cape Town Tourism (see Tourist Information), should always make sure there is a designated driver who abstains from quaffing. The Central Winelands Tourism Office (tel: (021) 872 0686) can also provide further information.

Somerset West is half an hour from the city centre on the R44 off the N2 highway. This bustling town nestles in a basin created by the towering peak of Helderberg ('Clear Mountain') and the Hottentots Holland mountain range. Here, the Vergelegen wine farm, Lourensford Road (tel: (021) 847 1334; website: www.vergelegen.co.za), was built in 1700 and is one of the most gracious and perfectly located of all the old Cape Dutch homesteads, offering wine tasting, cellar tours, a superb restaurant and library containing rare volumes of early Africana. The Helderberg Nature Reserve (tel: (021) 851 4060; website: www.helderbergnaturereserve.co.za) is located just before the turn-off to Vergelegen and comprises several kilometres of hiking trails and paths with magnificent views over the Helderberg Basin.

South Africa's second oldest town, Stellenbosch, produces a third of all the wine in the Cape and boasts the longest wine route in the world. Named after the Dutch governor, Simon van der Stel, this university town is one of the best-preserved South African settlements. The Stellenbosch Village Museum (tel: (021) 887 2948; fax: (021) 887 2902), on the corner of Church and Ryneveld Streets, tells the story and consists of four carefully restored and furnished buildings built between 1709 and 1850. Stellenbosch is located on the R310 off the N2 highway.

South Africa's 'French quarter', Franschhoek, was named after the French Huguenots who fled Catholic persecution and began arriving at the Cape in 1688. Today, the valley is famous for its wine and good food. Located off the N1, the area is key to much of South Africa's distant and recent history. The Huguenot Memorial, Lambrecht Street (tel: (021) 876 2532), traces the history of the Huguenots, while to the west, on the R303, is the Victor Verster Prison, from where Nelson Mandela walked to freedom on 11 February 1990.

Overberg: Over Sir Lowry's pass and beyond South Africa's oldest inn, the Houwhoek Inn, the Western Cape landscape transforms into the harsh beauty of the Overberg, approximately 170km (106 miles) east from Cape Town at its central point. This region is the gateway to Africa's southernmost tip, Cape L'Agulhas – located approximately a three-hour drive southeast of Cape Town, accessible on the N2. Here, the two oceans meet in a spectacular show of natural beauty. The L'Agulhas Lighthouse (tel: (028) 424 2584) and Zuidste Kaap (tel: (028) 435 6034) restaurants both provide a unique location in which to dine out – the fully operational lighthouse, which is over 150 years old, also doubles as a museum and curio shop. However, since a tourist injured herself a few years ago, visitors are no longer permitted up the lighthouse tower. The southernmost point is located one kilometre (0.6 miles) west of the lighthouse. Visitors should take note, however, not to book any tours that involve 4X4 driving on the beaches and dunes as this is not only incredibly harmful to the delicate seafront wildlife – some of which are endangered species – but is also illegal.

Nearby, the 14km (nine miles) of continuous white sand beach – the longest in the Southern Hemisphere – of Struuisbaai offers stunning bathing. Further afield, the virtually untouched charm of *Arniston* delights visitors with a traditional fishing village, *Kassiesbaai*, which has been declared, in its entirety, a national monument. *Hermanus*, another coastal town in the Overberg region, dubbed 'the Riviera of the Overberg' for its wealthy stature, is the principal whale-spotting location, one of the best in the world, with an annual ten-day Whale Watching Festival in September/October (website: www.whalefestival. co.za). The sleepy town of *Grayton* is renowned for its arty locals and this is particularly evident during the winter months, when the Grayton Winter Festival in June (website: www.overberginfo.com/greytonfestivals), which includes a moonlight market among other rustic delights. Many other towns are worth visiting, such as the fruit farming paradise of *Grabouw* and the austere charm of *Napier*. *Southern Tip Tours* (tel: (021) 935 0733/4; website: www.southerntours.co.za) offers tours to the Overberg area (R480), as well as tours for whale watching enthusiasts (R400). For those who wish to spend more than just one day exploring this wonderful region, *Cape Quest* (tel: (021) 674 2555; website: www.capequest.co.za) has a number of bed and breakfast accommodation options in the Overberg. The *Overberg Tourism Office* (tel: (028) 214 1466; fax: (028) 212 1380; e-mail: info@capeoverberg.org; website: www.capeoverberg.org) provides further information on destinations within the Overberg.

ACCOMMODATION

South Africa has a VAT rate of 14% on services, as well as a 1% Tourism Promotion Levy, which is usually included in hotel rates. A complimentary breakfast is also often included. A tip of R5–10 for hotel porters for each piece of luggage is common. The prices quoted below are the lowest standard rates for a double room, including VAT, Tourism Promotion Levy and breakfast, unless otherwise specified.

Business

Cullinan Cape Town Waterfront

This is the first of a cluster of hotels springing up around the brand-new Cape Town Convention Centre, at the entrance to the V&A Waterfront, which makes it excellently located for business and entertainment. The spacious and classically designed guest rooms all have fantastic views of Table Mountain, as well as air conditioning, radio, satellite TV, direct-dial telephone with voice-mail and modem point, safe and workstation. The 416-room hotel also has two restaurants and cocktail bar. Conference facilities are extensive, with five conference rooms, a board room and function room. Video-conferencing is available, as well as fax, photocopying and secretarial services on request. Free parking is available. After a hard day of business, guests can unwind in the hotel gym or at the poolside.
1 Cullinan Street
Tel: (021) 418 6920. Fax: (021) 418 3559.
E-mail: cullinancapetown@southernsun.com
Website: www.southernsun.com
Price: From R1064.

Holiday Inn Cape Town

This massive 32-storey hotel in the heart of the city has been a fixture for many decades. Nowadays, the *Holiday Inn Cape Town* (formerly the *Cape Sun*) primarily caters for the business traveller, as it is home to the largest hotel-based conference facility in Cape Town, with eight configurable rooms and an experienced team on-hand. Other business facilities include secretarial service, fax, printing and a fully equipped business centre. All of the 368 guest rooms (most with glorious views) are air conditioned, have a radio, colour TV, safe, trouser press, a workstation and direct-dial telephone with voice-mail. The 14 executive suites also have a fax

machine and modem point. Cape Malay and Afro-International cuisine is on offer at *Riempies Restaurant*, while the *Noon Gun Bar* is the hotel's cocktail bar. The hotel also offers an indoor plunge pool and a fitness centre with personal trainers and massage facilities.
Strand Street
Tel: (021) 488 5100. Fax: (021) 423 8875.
E-mail: holidayinncapetown@southernsun.com
Website: www.southernsun.com
Price: From R899.

Road Lodge

Conveniently located at Cape Town International Airport, the *Road Lodge* is perfect for business travellers in transit or with an early flight. The city centre is approximately 20 minutes by car along the N2. Part of the City Lodge Hotels Group, this 90-room hotel combines budget business travel with comfort and style. Rooms are functional and stylish with air conditioning and colour TV, a workstation and direct-dial telephone. Hotel facilities include free parking, a 24-hour reception and check-in, fax and photocopying services and a same-day laundry and dry cleaning service.
Cape Town International Airport
Tel: (021) 934 7303. Fax: (021) 934 7473.
E-mail: rlctia@citylodge.co.za
Website: www.citylodge.co.za
Price: From R220 (excluding breakfast).

The Table Bay Hotel

The neo-Victorian *Table Bay Hotel* is perched right on the tip of the historic V&A Waterfront development, looking out across Table Bay to Robben Island or back toward Table Mountain, and linked to the massive Victoria Wharf Shopping Centre. Part of the Sun International group, the hotel has every facility of a luxury hotel, as well as a non-invasive friendly attention to detail that makes guests feel completely at home. There are

Clifton and the Twelve Apostles mountains

Photo: South Africa Tourism

311 guest rooms and 18 suites, stylishly designed in relaxing greens, creams and floral prints, with local artwork on the walls. Facilities include a high-tech, touch-sensitive mini-bar, satellite TV, electronic safe, spacious desks with telephone lines with voice-mail, international direct-dial, fax machine and Internet connection. Conference facilities are extensive and there is a fully equipped business centre; teleconferencing, translation and secretarial services and sophisticated audiovisual equipment are all available. The hotel has an elevated outdoor pool, a health club and spa, an acclaimed restaurant *The Conservatory* (see *Hotels*).
Table Bay Quay 6, V&A Waterfront
Tel: (021) 406 5000 *or* 5889. Fax: (021) 406 5767 *or* 5656.
E-mail: tbhres@sunint.co.za
Website: www.suninternational.com
Price: From R2345 (excluding breakfast and Tourism Promotion Levy).

Luxury

Cape Grace

One of 'The Leading Small Hotels of the World' and certainly Cape Town's loveliest, the 121-room *Cape Grace* exudes contemporary style and elegance. Occupying its own quay in a renovated Victorian harbour building, the hotel is unassuming on the outside and charming inside, with friendly, efficient staff. The spacious guest rooms, suites and apartments (with kitchens, CD players and VCRs) are all impeccably designed with warm, earthy colours, French windows, fresh flowers, contemporary local artwork and books with a local flavour. All rooms include satellite TV, fax and Internet connection, a safe, bathrobes and luxury toiletries. The hotel has a private library that guests can borrow from and also holds a complimentary history presentation and wine-tasting every evening at 1800. Other luxury facilities include in-room massage therapies, beauty treatments and gym equipment, as well as a pool, private luxury transfers and tour guides, even access to a custom-built racing yacht. Business guests are also catered for, with a 12-seat boardroom and fully equipped business centre, while the restaurant *one.waterfront* (see *Restaurants*) is highly acclaimed.
West Quay, V&A Waterfront
Tel: (021) 410 7100. Fax: (021) 419 7622.
E-mail: reservations@capegrace.com *or* info@capegrace.com
Website: www.capegrace.com
Price: From R2795.

Mount Nelson

Voted 'Best Hotel in Africa 2002' by *Condé Nast Traveller*, the city's most prestigious and award-winning hotel proudly upholds the Old World colonial style and traditions that it has excelled in for over 100 years. With palm-lined avenues, classical architecture, pith-helmeted staff and decadent afternoon teas on the shady terrace, the uniquely pink *Mount Nelson* has not changed one bit, save for a few stylish additions. Located right at the heart of the city, the hotel has 145 guest rooms and 56 suites, all individually designed with bespoke furniture, artwork, luxurious fabrics. In-room facilities include workstations with telephone, fax and modem. The business centre is small but well equipped and there are six conference venues. Extras include tennis courts, a fitness centre, a beauty and massage salon, hairdresser and a shuttle service to the V&A Waterfront. An alfresco breakfast feast is served in the hotel's airy *Oasis Restaurant*, next to the main pool, while the *Cape Colony* restaurant (see *Restaurants*) is one of Cape Town's finest dining venues. The dusky hotel bar, the *Lord Nelson*, is the oldest in the city.
76 Orange Street
Tel: (021) 483 1000. Fax: (021) 483 1947.
E-mail: reservations@mountnelson.co.za
Website: www.mountnelsonhotel.orient-express.com
Price: From R4660.

Moderate

Metropole Hotel

One of the oldest addresses on the Cape Town hotel scene, the two-star *Metropole Hotel* has held its own while new venues are popping up all around it. The small hotel, with just 32 rooms, retains an Old World charm, with authentic Art Deco and Victorian furnishings and fixtures, such as the iron-gate lift in the lobby, producing a charming albeit slightly faded ambience. Located on trendy Long Street, the hotel is right at the centre of the city nightlife and close to the V&A Waterfront. All rooms are en suite and equipped with TV, telephones and radio. The adjoining *Coffee Shoppe and Diner* serves breakfast, lunch and dinner, while the hotel bar, *The Office*, keeps the hotel guests' sprits up.
38 Long Street
Tel: (021) 423 6363. Fax: (021) 426 5312.
Price: From R295 (excluding breakfast).

Tudor Hotel

Cape Town's oldest hotel, built in 1870, has recently undergone a refurbishment and is now the epitome of style, all white linen and dark wood. The friendly *Tudor Hotel* is excellently located, right on Greenmarket Square in the city centre. All 28 rooms are en suite, with telephone and TV and now sport simple and stylish bathrooms. The ceiling fans are a lovely old-fashioned touch, making an interesting alternative to noisy air-conditioning. Covered parking is available for R45 per day. Few frills mean good value for such a stylish hotel.
153 Longmarket Street, Greenmarket Square
Tel: (021) 424 1335. Fax: (021) 423 1198.
E-mail: tudorhotel@iafrica.com
Website: www.tudorhotel.co.za
Price: From R495 (excluding breakfast).

Other Recommendations

The Red House

This small, elegant boutique hotel in the upmarket and leafy suburb of Newlands is nothing short of fabulous. A vivid red colour, *The Red House* is a restored Georgian country house, run by a friendly Dutch couple who manage to combine familiarity with professionalism. Accommodation consists of three stunning suites and a secluded cottage, where antique charm meets contemporary style, with white linen, huge beds, antique fireplaces and chandeliers. Facilities include satellite TV, international direct dial telephones and an honesty bar, as well as complimentary tea, coffee, aperitif and airport transfers. With Swedish massages available, a secluded Jacuzzi and sauna, an exquisite rose garden, a sparkling pool, the emphasis is on privacy, luxury and pampering. To top it all off, the breakfasts are outstanding and the service is nothing short of excellent.

4 Hiddingh Avenue, Newlands
Tel: (021) 683 8000. Fax: (021) 683 8006.
E-mail: info@redhouse.co.za
Website: www.redhouse.co.za
Price: From R950.

Waterland Lodge

Although *Waterland Lodge* is situated about 20 minutes from the city centre, it is nestled in the wonderful yet often overlooked Hout Bay valley, a suburb so self-sufficient, with its very own harbour, beach, bars and restaurants, that the locals call it the Republic of Hout Bay. The Waterland Lodge consists of 13 separate units of either self-catering chalets or B&B rooms on a deceptively large estate situated on the banks of the Disa River. The chalets, sporting heavy wood and wild African prints, come with separate *braai* (barbecue) areas, colour TVs and fully equipped kitchens – for guests who want to be completely independent on holiday. While guests who prefer having their breakfast cooked for them in the morning can stay in the homely rooms in the main house, decorated in pastels and wicker. Breakfast is served in the conservatory overlooking the swimming pool, which all guests have access to, as well as the wrap-around views of the surrounding mountains.
Longkloof Road, Hout Bay
Tel: (021) 790 1166 *or* 0361. Fax: (021) 790 7185 *or* 0362.
E-mail: waterland@mweb.co.za
Website: www.waterlandlodge.co.za
Price: From R240 (excluding breakfast).

RESTAURANTS

The selected restaurants have been divided into five categories: Gastronomic, Business, Trendy, Budget and Personal Recommendations. The restaurants are listed alphabetically within these different categories, which serve as guidelines rather than absolute definitions of the establishments.

Cape Point

South Africa has a VAT rate of 14% on services, which is usually included in the prices quoted on menus. Most restaurants do not levy a service charge and waitrons (local term which incorporates waiters and waitresses) expect to be tipped 10–15% tip; however, tables of over six or eight are often charged an automatic 10% service charge.

The prices quoted below are for an average three-course meal for one person and for a bottle of house wine or cheapest equivalent; they include VAT but they do not include tip.

Gastronomic

Blue Danube

One of the very best restaurants in Cape Town, *Blue Danube* is located in a charming Victorian house with polished wooden floors and a living room intimacy. Local art explodes on the walls – some supplied by the master chef, Tomas Sinn, himself. Sinn brought renown to many of the city's better restaurants before venturing out on his own into the world of haute cuisine. Austrian undertones reflect the chef's nationality but his dishes remain faithful to Africa, with tasty morsels such as smoked springbok spätzle in a spicy paprika sauce. The Austrian dessert *Salzburger Nockerln* is not to be missed. No lunch Saturday to Monday.
102 New Church Street, Tamboerskloof
Tel/fax: (021) 423 3624.
E-mail: danube@iafrica.com
Price: R175; R199 (five-course chef's menu). Wine: R59.

Buitenverwachting

Buitenverwachting takes its name from the wine estate upon which this sumptuous, fine dining place is located. The restaurant is stylish, with high-backed chairs and a scheme of dusky blues, burnt reds and understated floral. There is also a conservatory, with views of the vineyards. The cuisine is Italian-French and always excellent; the constantly changing menu might include quail saltimbocca or pan-fried loin of spingbok. The comprehensive wine list has picked up Diners Club Diamond awards in 2001 and 2002. No lunch Saturday. Closed Sunday and Monday and 1 July to mid-August.
Klein Constantia Road, Contantia
Tel: (021) 794 3522. Fax: (021) 794 1351.
Website: www.buitenverwachting.co.za
Price: R250. Wine: R49.

Harbour House

Fresh seafood is the speciality of this small but light restaurant, perched precariously on the edge of Kalk Bay Harbour, with breathtaking views of the mountain, harbour and ocean. Dishes might include West Coast mussels with fresh herb and white wine sauce for starters, followed by a selection of expertly prepared local favourites – kingklip, yellowtail, red steenbras and Cape salmon, depending on what is fresh. There are other options, such as ostrich medallions or French duck breast, but as the name suggests *Harbour House* is really all about fish.
Kalk Bay Harbour, Main Road, Kalk Bay
Tel: (021) 788 4133. Fax: (021) 788 4136.
E-mail: harbourhouse@icon.co.za
Price: R135. Wine: R52.

La Colombe

La Colombe is just one of a handful of excellent dining opportunities at Constantia Uitsig, one of Constantia's

Victoria & Alfred Waterfront

premier wine estates. This homely white and light blue summerhouse-style restaurant also has poolside seating. Chef Franck Dangereux expertly blends Provencal delights with South African influences in an open-plan kitchen, creating such masterpieces as kingklip stuffed with basil pesto with coconut and chilli sauce or springbok medallion with kumquats and a savoy turnip muffin with spicy star annis. With an award-winning wine list, a constantly changing menu and friendly and knowledgeable service, this restaurant is superb. Closed July and August.
Constantia Uitsig, Constantia
Tel: (021) 794 2390. Fax: (021) 794 7914.
E-mail: lc@uitsig.co.za
Website: www.lacolombe.co.za
Price: R220. Wine: R46.

one.waterfront

One.waterfront is the much-celebrated restaurant in the Cape Grace (see *Hotels*). With upholstered high-backed chairs and white linen set against soft beiges, earthy browns and velvety creams, the restaurant displays an understated opulence and local pride, with 95% of the decor and artwork locally produced. In keeping with this attitude, the new executive chef, Bruce Robertson, creates imaginative, beautifully presented and indigenously influenced dishes. For example, for starters a 'spritzer' of West Coast oysters served in chilled verjuice and soda, followed by roasted African quail wrapped in parma ham and stuffed with garlic, anchovies and parmesan.
Cape Grace Hotel, West Quay, V&A Waterfront
Tel: (021) 418 0520.
E-mail: info@capegrace.com
Website: www.onewaterfront.co.za
Price: R175. Wine: R60.

Business

Cape Colony

This award-winning restaurant brings some contemporary chic to the Old World elegance of the Mount Nelson (see *Hotels*). Executive chef Garth Stroebel's cuisine is fresh and modern, blending South African influences with exotic new flavours styles to showcase the new Modern South African cuisine. Classic mains include the Bo-Kaap chicken and prawn curry with fragrant rice or the smoked crocodile with spinach, red onion and samoosa wafer. Nightly jazz helps diners to unwind, while the Saturday night dinner dance is value for money at R165 for a three-course meal including a bottle of wine and mineral water. No lunch.
Mount Nelson Hotel, 76 Orange Street
Tel: (021) 483 1198 *or* 1850. Fax. (021) 424 7472.
E-mail: restaurantreservations@mountnelson.co.za
Website: www.mountnelsonhotel.orient-express.com
Price: R230. Wine: R60.

The Conservatory

Located in the peaceful, cool conservatory of The Table Bay Hotel (see *Hotels*), this restaurant has views of the harbour and Table Mountain. With its attentive waitrons and relaxed decor (palms, wicker, floral prints and gilt-framed mirrors), it is the epitome of easy elegance and graceful charm. From the delicious appetite-wetters of foccacia bread embedded with dried tomato onwards, the menu includes imaginative creations. The tomato and prawn broth starter is beyond compare. Mains might be chargrilled Cape crayfish or double Karoo lamb cutlet with spring roll and barley sprouts, artichoke and bell pepper salad. No lunch, although open for breakfast 0700–1100. Closed Sunday and Monday.
Table Bay Quay 6, V&A Watefront
Tel: (021) 406 5762. Fax: (021) 406 5656.
E-mail: tbfb@sunint.co.za
Website: www.suninternational.com
Price: R160. Wine: R80.

The Foresters Arms

A long time favourite with local businesspeople, looking to clinch a deal over a pint or two, *The Foresters Arms*, or 'Forries' as it is affectionately known, has been serving up good grub in a 'typical British pub' since 1880. The menu is massive and offers interesting salads and lighter meals for lunch, such as baked goat's cheese and cranberry salad, as well as a traditional roast carvery. The British pub theme is also reflected in the menu, with dishes like

Yorkshire pudding and steak and kidney pie and the 'Olde Traditional Favourite Brandy Tipsy Tart', a sponge pudding seeped in brandy.
Newlands Drive, Newlands
Tel: (021) 689 5949/70. Fax: (021) 685 6535.
E-mail: forries@indlovu.co.za
Price: R75. Wine: R32.

Kennedy's Restaurant and Cigar Lounge

Kennedy's attracts the city's business clientele with its shamelessly American affluence and undeniable style. Downstairs is an intimate cigar and cocktail lounge, while the plush restaurant, with live jazz, is upstairs. Sumptuous yet undeniably masculine, the restaurant has a dark wood and leather interior, as well as a terrace outside. Chef Per Menko dabbles in African, Mediterranean, Italian and Californian influences with options such as yellow-fin tuna grilled with mustard and cumin seeds, potato leek gratin and balsamic shallot jus or tomato, celery and pumpkin baklava with olive relish and fennel seed cream. The excellent wine list picked up a Diners Club Platinum award in 2002. No lunch Saturday. Closed Sunday.
251 Long Street
Tel: (021) 424 1212. Fax: (021) 423 0910.
E-mail: kennedys@netactive.co.za
Price: R150. Wine: R56.

Silver Tree

The signature restaurant of Kirstenbosch Botanical Gardens, the *Silver Tree* is crisp and smart with stylish stone and wood and large windows offering views of the mountain and gardens through the restios (fynbos reeds). The food is reliably good with old favourites, such as salmon roulade, brie in filo pastry, Norwegian salmon and a selection of pastas, as well as local creations like ostrich bobotie (a Cape Malay dish with dried fruit and baked savoury custard) and the signature dish of beef fillet with risotto and crayfish sauce. Open for breakfast, lunch and dinner. Free entrance to the gardens for diners after 1700. Closed Sunday.
Kirstenbosch Botanical Gardens, Rhodes Drive, Newlands
Tel: (021) 762 9585.
E-mail: info@kirstenboschrestaurant.co.za
Website: www.kirstenboschrestaurant.co.za
Price: R125. Wine: R30.

Trendy

Anatoli

High ceilings, tiled floors, bare brick walls covered with kilim tapestries, elegant photographs and a trendy locale all conspire to make this Turkish restaurant one of the trendiest in the city. Waitrons bring massive trays filled with a selection of hot and cold mezze, which are usually much tastier than the somewhat ordinary mains. Titbits to look out for (dishes change daily) are the lamb meatballs with walnut purée, dolmades (stuffed vine leaves) and the potato, onion and blackcurrant tahini. Mains are available from the open-plan kitchen's deli-style counter and always include a veggie, meat and chicken option. Closed Monday.
24 Napier Street
Tel: (021) 419 2501.
Website: www.anatoli.co.za
Price: R95. Wine: R40.

La Med

The favourite watering hole for trendy locals, *La Med* is a fantastic sundower spot, with a massive boardwalk terrace for alfresco dining (or just drinking). The venue is somewhat of a chameleon, changing from bar to restaurant to popular live music venue in a matter of hours – and is always busy, especially at the weekend. The grub is quite basic but extremely tasty, with a healthy selection of pizzas, burgers, seafood and salads. The pizzas are particularly good, with creations such as the Clifton First Pizza, with chicken strips, mushroom and avocado. No lunch weekdays May to September.
Glen Country Club, Victoria Road, Clifton
Tel: (021) 438 5600. Fax: (021) 438 2018.
E-mail: lamed@kristensen.co.za
Website: www.lamed.co.za
Price: R70. Wine: R39.

Long Street Café

The sister bar of the Obz Café in Observatory (see *Bars*), this deli-style city café is a magnet for the rich and stylish, with its industrial chic, big-screen TV, floor-to-ceiling windows and fabulous cocktails. Service can be infuriatingly slow – it seems the waitrons are chosen more for good looks than ability – but the atmosphere is excellent, especially on the pavement tables. The food is average but tasty and inexpensive, with dishes including ostrich burgers, coconut chicken strips with Thai curry and creamy chilli or spinach roulade, as well as a range of baguettes and ciabatta toasties. Closed Sunday.
259 Long Street
Tel: (021) 424 2464.
Price: R60. Wine: R34.

Mama Africa

Mama Africa is not just another tourist trap peddling 'authentic' Africana for gullible foreigners; it is created for locals and enjoyed by locals and tourists alike. The big crowd that gathers to enjoy the nightly live music spills over into the dining area so diners should chose a yellow-floorboard table as far from the bar as possible if they prefer eating their food out of the way of gyrating bodies. The decor can only be described as African kitsch – a giant crocodile lamp and a zebra-striped pool table are just some of the oddities. The food is locally flavoured, including specialities like crocodile kebabs, Dovi Zimbabwean chicken and peanut stew, game *potjiekos* (a stew cooked in a cast iron pot over a fire), *mielie pap* (mashed corn) and frozen yoghurt for dessert. Open late. Closed Sunday.
178 Long Street
Tel: (021) 426 1017 *or* 424 8634.
E-mail: mama@gem.co.za
Price: R95. Wine: R38.

Wasabi

In the genteel surroundings of Constantia Village, *Wasabi* has established itself as *the* restaurant for the trendy crowd, who come to enjoy the effortless Japanese food. Sitting beneath the luminous lanterns with a Wasabi seafood platter is a wonderful way to round off a day. The decor dabbles with dark wood, bamboo, wicker and stone floors, while the menu is extensive, including Japanese favourites of ramen, tempura, sushi, wasabi, maki, sashimi-style and flat-top grilled seafood and steak. The dessert spring rolls with choc-almond, choc-strawberry or choc-banana fillings are a glorious must.
Shop 17, Old Village, Constantia Village Shopping Centre, Constantia
Tel: (021) 794 6546. Fax: (021) 794 6549.
E-mail: info@wasabi.co.za
Website: www.wasabi.co.za
Price: R110. Wine: R41.

Budget

The Brass Bell

While all the tourists cram into the trendy bars along the Atlantic Seaboard to watch the sun go down, the locals sit in relative peace on the other side of the mountain in Kalk Bay, enjoying the scruffy charm of this local institution. Although a little rough and ready, the location is stunning, with the Indian Ocean lapping at the wall. *The Brass Bell* is three venues in one: a rugged but friendly pub and *The Water's Edge*, an informal terrace restaurant, downstairs, while upstairs is slightly more formal. The Water's Edge is where the local beach bums and lifesavers gather for a drink and some hearty food, such as the Hunter's Platter (smoked venison and grilled guinea fowl, whole grain mustard and horseradish cream) or fresh local seafood (mussel pots, deep-fried calamari and grilled kingklip).

Mama Africa

Main Road, Kalk Bay
Tel: (021) 788 5456.
Price: R90. Wine: R40.

Don Pedro

This café-restaurant was a meeting place for liberal thinkers during the turbulent 1980s and is still fostering a community spirit and artistic edge in the trendy neighbourhood of Woodstock. Trendy and wallet-friendly, this place is colourful and casual, with some stunning photos and African artwork. The menu is varied with tandoori chicken, sweet and sour lamb, rosemary lamb, spare ribs and vegetable paella all on offer. The Dom Pedro summer salad with tomato, mozzarella, peppadew, avocado, basil and olive oil is a great choice on a hot summer day.
113 Roodebloem Road, Woodstock
Tel: (021) 447 4493. Fax: (021) 447 0482.
E-mail: info@donpedro.co.za
Website: www.donpedro.co.za
Price: R70. Wine: R18.

Hussar Grill

One of Cape Town's best-kept secrets, the unassuming and dimly lit *Hussar Grill* is a welcome alternative to the city's many steakhouse chains. Here, chefs sizzle the steaks right in front of diners in their 1960s-style booths. The house speciality starter is the unusual gin and tomato soup, while mains like grilled ostrich, saddle of lamb, game steaks and other meats come with a variety of sauces (from fresh mushroom, garlic and white wine to creamy mustard and brandy). The ostrich steak has been described as the best in the Cape. More unusual options, such as grilled warthog ribs are also available, as are seafood, pastas and salads. Closed Sunday.
10 Main Road, Rondebosch
Tel: (021) 689 9516.
Price: R90. Wine: R30.

Kuzmas

The posh or pernickety should give *Kuzmas* a wide berth. This dark and arty bar-cum-restaurant has been feeding students and late-night drinkers 24 hours a day for as long as many Capetonians can remember. The decor is Mediterranean-ish, with wrought-iron garden furniture, a dark concrete floor and walls covered in posters for events and parties. Food-wise, Kuzmas has always specialised in schwarma kebabs in pittas, including a number of fillings such as lamb, beef, chicken and calamari, although a number of cheaper toasted pittas are also available. The signature dish of chicken livers Tel Aviv is legendary.
Main Road, Rondebosch
Tel: (021) 689 3762.
Price: R43. Wine: R30.

Ocean Basket

An incredibly popular seafood restaurant chain, this waterfront *Ocean Basket* is by far the best located. The light fishy atmosphere is enhanced by checks, tiles, pastels and pine. Diners might have to wait some time before being seated among the families feasting on fresh fish dishes with Mozambican, Greek and Portuguese influences. Items such as whole lobster, kingklip, calamari steak and line-fish specials are complemented by spectacular platters (all with chips, of course). Starters are primarily Greek, like taramasalata, tzatziki or feta and olives, as are the desserts, which include baklava and kataifi.
Shop 222, Victoria Wharf, V&A Waterfront
Tel/fax: (021) 419 4300.
Website: www.oceanbasket.co.za
Price: R80. Wine: R33.

Other Recommendations

Camel Rock Restaurant

One of the oldest and more remote restaurants in Cape Town, situated near the city's wildest beach, Scarborough, *Camel Rock* makes for an excellent refuelling point while touring the peninsula. Although a bit weatherworn, its rustic charm is undeniable, with tiled floors, green tablecloths, a piano and an African Grey parrot. In summer, diners can sit at the wooden bench tables on the vine-fringed terrace. Although the service might be a bit laid-back for non-locals, the location is worth lingering over. Dishes range from seafood specials, such as grilled fillet of kabeljou served with mussels and deep-fried potatoes, to hearty veggie options, such as lentil curry or mushroom pasta.
Main Road, Scarborough
Tel: (021) 780 1122.
Price: R85. Wine: R30.

Mesopotamia

With tapestries and drapery on the walls, this spacious upstairs restaurant is dark and tent-like but breathtaking. Large kilim rugs and cushions surround circular metal tables although traditional chairs are also available, as is a new balcony space with a brighter ambience. The Kurdish cuisine (the first of its kind in the country), from a team of Kurdish chefs, includes highly spiced mains like *iskender* (oven-roasted diced lamb with bread, garlic yoghurt and tomato sauce) or *beyti* (minced chicken kebab rolled in Nan bread with garlic yoghurt). A cover charge is added on Wednesday, Friday and Saturday when there is a belly dancer. Closed Sunday. All halal.
Corner of Long Street and Church Street
Tel: (021) 424 4664.
E-mail: mesopotamia@diplomats.com
Price: R90. Wine: R30.

Peddlars On The Bend

Teetering on the edge of the Constantia Wine Route, this picturesque restaurant is frequented by tourists and well-heeled locals who come for the award-winning wine list and excellent meat, seafood and veggie dishes on the very comprehensive menu. Dishes range from British pub-grub-style fish and chips, grilled pork chops or chicken and leek pie to international options like the German *eisbein* (gammon on the bone) and *penne salsiccia* (penne with Italian sausage, garlic and tomato sauce). The atmosphere is relaxed, with marble tables under shady oak trees outside and tiled floors, reed ceilings and wooden tables inside, and the service is excellent.
Spaanschemat River Road, Constantia
Tel: (021) 794 7747. Fax: (021) 794 2730.
Price: R130. Wine: R35.

Rhodes Memorial Restaurant

Tucked away behind the monolithic memorial to De Beers big man Cecil John Rhodes is the cosy thatched cottage of *Rhodes Memorial Restaurant*. Sitting underneath the umbrellas on the terrace, there are breathtaking views through the trees and the stone walls and wooden furniture complete the gardener's cottage feel. Dishes on the lunch menu have a mostly English theme, with a selection of pies such as spinach and feta or smoked salmon and line fish. They are best accompanied by the restaurant's own wine from the Hartenberg Estate. This is also a great place for breakfast (such as eggs benedict,

Spanish omelettes or full fry-ups) or tea (possibly the best cheese cake in Cape Town). No dinner.
Groote Schuur Estate, Rondebosch
Tel: (021) 689 9151. Fax: (021) 689 9152.
E-mail: roy@global.co.za
Price: R90. Wine: R39.50.

Zorina's On The Square

Traditional Cape Malay cooking is the mainstay of this small, crisply contemporary restaurant in the Tudor Hotel (see *Hotels*). The menu is a bit on the short side but food is tasty and well prepared, with a number of breyani curries (a dish layered with lentils and meat, poultry or vegetables, flavoured with buttermilk), served with sambals and poppadoms and homemade frikkadel (spicy beef meatball) burgers. Patrons are warned to watch their wallets (and sometimes the food on their plates) if seated next to the large open window, as street children can be a nuisance with their quick fingers. No dinner Sunday. All halal.
Tudor Hotel, Greenmarket Square
Tel: (021) 422 5542.
Price: R70. Wine: Strictly no alcohol allowed.

ENTERTAINMENT

Nightlife

Cape Town is a party town, especially in summer, when tens of thousands of tourists descend upon the city. But even during winter, the action never stops. The city has also become an international Mecca for DJs, running huge rave, trance and ambient parties – often held in stunning locations on beaches or in forests. The city is also firmly entrenched on the international rock music touring circuit.

Much of the nightlife activity is concentrated on a handful of popular city streets and suburbs. Long Street and Kloof Street in the city centre are alive with restaurants, live music clubs, bars, coffee shops and the occasional strip club. On the outskirts of the city centre, the De Waterkant/Green Point area has a string of gay and gay-friendly clubs and restaurants, while the V&A Waterfront is simply awash with nightlife hotspots popular with both tourists and locals. The Camps Bay beachfront brings LA-style outfits, trendy restaurants and some stunning sunsets to Cape Town. Heading towards the southern suburbs, Lower Main Road in the suburb of Observatory and the nearby River Club is another gay-friendly area and the territory of Cape Town's students, offering up a more Bohemian and laid-back style of entertainment. This is the place for local alternative music, slightly seedy pool halls, philosophy, poetry, stand-up comedy and vegetarian food. On the N1 highway, north of the city centre, the Century City development combines a state-of-the-art amusement park with scores of restaurants, several sound stages and the *Dockside* multi-level club and live music venue. The seaside suburbs of Kalk Bay, Fish Hoek and Simon's Town, although traditionally family orientated and 'dry', are becoming increasingly trendy for nightlife beyond the city limits – although this is largely centred upon restaurants.

There are no strict licensing hours in Cape Town and many clubs stay open until the small hours and even sunrise. The dress code is almost always as casual as you wish, although shorts and trainers are not appreciated in some venues and a 'no effort no entry' rule is sometimes enforced. Admission prices to clubs and raves range from R20 to R100 – many are free before 2300. The legal drinking age is 18 years, although some pubs demand a 21-year age limit for entrance. Alcohol is extremely cheap for foreigners, at approximately R8 for a beer.

The bi-monthly *Cape Etc* and monthly *SA Citylife* publications are excellent sources of information and listings for Cape Town's nightlife. The Friday editions of the *Cape Times* and *The Cape Argus* newspapers, as well as the weekly *Mail & Guardian*, all have arts and entertainment sections. Information on Cape Town's club scene is available online (website: www.clubbersguide.co.za).

Bars

South Africa has strange laws concerning the sale of alcohol and bars must, by law, be attached to hotels or alternatively be part of a restaurant/café. For this reason, many bars masquerade as places to eat. In the city centre, the *Long Street Café*, 259 Long Street, is one of the trendiest haunts in town, while its sister, *Café Bardeli*, Longkloof Studios, Kloof Street, is where Cape Town's media and modelling community strut their stuff and sip fantastic summer cocktails. The equally trendy *Café Camissa*, 80 Kloof Street, features live music, stand-up comedy and poetry readings. *Mavericks*, 68 Barrack Street, is a stylish revue bar and restaurant in the heart of the city, attracting business types and cigar smokers.

The V&A Waterfront has dozens of bars and cafés, many with beautiful sea and mountain views. *Den Anker*, Pierhead, V&A Waterfront, is a Belgian bar and restaurant with some very strange bar customs and some fantastic Belgian beers, while *Paulaner Braühaus*, Shop 18/19, Clock Tower Precinct, brings a staggering array of German beers to this trendy brewery-restaurant with beer garden. Situated on the water's edge of the international yacht marina, the *Bascule* whisky bar and cellar, in the Cape Grace hotel, West Quay, is an atmospheric, nautically themed hideaway, with over 375 whiskies on offer and live jazz at the weekend.

Lower Main Road, in the arty district of Observatory, has *Rolling Stones*, a laid-back but crowded pool hall with a balcony, and *Obz Café*, where the terminally hip serve up cocktails to beautiful bohemians. Despite facing east rather than the setting sun, the informal *Brass Bell*, Main Road, St James, has long been a favourite with tippling locals and refugees from the 'dry' Fish Hoek. The Kalk Bay area is exploding into nightlife and earning itself a bohemian and arty reputation with quirky venues such as the ramshackle converted railway shack, *Cape To Cuba*, Main Road.

One of the best venues in which to watch the sun go down is *La Med*, at the Glen Country Club, Victoria Road in Clifton. Bikinis are optional. Another trendy sundowner spot favoured by those who have had a trying day sunbathing on the fabulous beach below is the *Clifton Beach House*, Fourth Beach, Clifton, or *Sunset Beach Bar*, Tuscany Beach, Camps Bay. But for the best view in town, enjoy the sunset from *Table Mountain Bistro* (see *Key Attractions*).

Casinos

There are three casinos in the Cape region and the finest of these is undoubtedly the *Grand West Casino & Entertainment World*, 1 Vanguard Drive, Goodwood (website: www.suninternational.co.za). This massive

complex is a reconstruction of various historic Cape Town buildings and includes two hotels, an Olympic-sized ice rink, several restaurants and, of course, the casino itself, complete with 1750 slot machines and 66 tables, bars, lounges, restaurants, nightclub and revue bar. The gambling areas are open for those over 18 years, dress is smart-casual in the gaming halls and a passport or ID is required.

Clubs

There are literally hundreds of clubs in Cape Town, varying from your average disco playing standard dance fare to deeply alternative clubs where bouncers assess dress, body piercings and language before deciding whether or not patrons make the grade. *The River Club*, Observatory Road, hosts club nights and massive rave parties, such as an annual New Year indoor and outdoor party. *The Purple Turtle*, Long Street, and the *Moomba Club Sociale*, 77 Hout Street, offer a mixed bag of alternative music, theme nights and live music. Meanwhile *The Jet Lounge*, 70 Long Street, and *The Piano Lounge*, corner of Loop Street and Wale Street, play a mix of house, jungle, trance and jazz. More hardcore is *The Shack/Blue Lizard*, 41 De Villiers Street, District Six, with a goth-grunge atmosphere and clientele. Located in Cape Town's 'gay village' of De Waterkant/Green Point, *Bronx Action Bar*, corner of Napier and Somerset Roads, *Rosies*, 125a Waterkant Street, and *Club 55*, 22 Somerset Road, are Cape Town's most popular gay clubs. *Marvel*, Long Street, corners the market of electronica and 'intelligent dance music' every Sunday, while *Chilli 'n Lime*, 23 Somerset Road, combines deep house sounds and live bands with a designer fashion shop and photographic studio. Young clubbers head for *Billy the Bum's*, Main Road, Claremont, for sporty, trendy fun. The *Dockside* complex, Century City (website: www.docksidecapetown.co.za), hosts regular dance parties.

Comedy

Laughter is the best medicine and helped South Africa through the apartheid years, both politically and emotionally. The main venue in Cape Town is the *Comedy Warehouse*, 22 Somerset Road, Green Point, while next door at number 21, *On Broadway* (website: www.onbroadway.co.za), is an extremely popular dinner and cabaret venue. The *Cape Comedy Collective Circuit* provides the laughs at a variety of venues, including the *Baxter Theatre Centre*, Main Road, Rondebosch (website: www.baxter.co.za), which also hosts regular shows of South Africa's finest comic talent.

Live Music

Live music fans would do well to check the local press and listings magazines for details of live music events, as many take place in obscure venues and on an irregular basis. A popular spot for hectic rock, goth noise, local stars and alternative sounds is *Mercury*, 43 De Villiers Street, Zonnebloem. *Marco's African Place*, 15 Rose Lane, Bo-Kaap, is one of the first of a growing number of authentic urban African venues and is a popular spot for Cape Town's rich and famous, who come to enjoy the indigenous cuisine, stylish bar and nightly live music from the best of the local jazz bands. *Mama Africa*, 178 Long Street, also provides great local food (see *Restaurants*), alongside live music in a rowdy atmosphere. The *Drum Café*, 32 Glynn Street, provides African sounds with a drum workshop every Monday. Cape Town excels at jazz and for regular live performances, *The Green Dolphin*,

at the V&A Waterfront, is Cape Town's premier jazz venue. Other swinging venues include *Hanover Street Jazz Club*, Grand West Casino, Goodwood, and *Kennedy's Cigar Bar*, 251 Long Street.

Big-name concerts featuring international artists are usually held at the *Bellville Velodrome*, Durban Road, Bellville (tel: (021) 949 7450), while local stars often shine at the *Baxter Theatre Centre*, Main Road, Rondebosch (website: www.baxter.co.za), and *Dockside* complex (website: www.docksidecapetown.co.za), Century City.

Sport

Sport has proved to be a wonderful way of bringing together the people of South Africa and various steps to break down the traditional racial stereotypes of certain sports seem to be working well. Four big sports dominate life in Cape Town – cricket, rugby, soccer and horseracing.

Despite being knocked out in the early stages, cricket proved to be the most important sport in Cape Town for the year 2003, thanks to the World Cup tournament. With a strong English colonial history, the city is one of the main feeding grounds for the South African international cricket squad, the *Proteas*. The home of Western Province cricket is at the *Newlands Cricket Ground*, 146 Campground Road, Newlands, where the governing body, *Western Province Cricket Association*, 161 Campground Road (tel: (021) 657 2003; e-mail: wpca@cricket.co.za; website: www.wpca.cricket.org), is located. Matches are played most weekends in summer, with international tests between South Africa and its main rivals regularly on the agenda. Night cricket is also one of the most popular pastimes in Cape Town and a good excuse to down beer and cheer at every ball that gets hit.

The city is home to one of rugby's most famous teams, the *Stormers* (website: www.stormersrugby.com), who – despite a run of unsuccessful seasons in the Super 12 series – are still rated as one of the toughest teams in international competition. *Newlands Rugby Stadium*, 11 Boundary Road, Newlands, is home to these local heroes as well as the comprehensive *SA Rugby Museum* (tel: (021) 659 6768). This is a sport that commands a massive following from all sections of the South African public. The home union is the *Western Province Rugby Football Union* (tel: (021) 689 4955; website: www.wprugby.com).

South Africans are also soccer mad, although most of the top teams are based in Johannesburg. The three top local teams – *Ajax Cape Town* (website: www.ajaxct.com), *Hellenic* and *Santos* – all feature strongly in the national Premier League, with Santos the most recent winner, when it took the title of the Premier Soccer League Championship 2002. This was a particularly impressive feat, seeing as the team had been in the Federation League during the apartheid years and sustained itself without a sponsor. Football's governing body, based at *Hartleyvale Stadium*, Willow Road, Observatory (tel: (021) 448 8653 *or* 8652 (bookings)), is the *Western Province Soccer Association* (tel: (021) 448 1648).

Horseracing is as much a social event in Cape Town as it is a sporting one. The hugely popular annual *J&B Met* (website: www.jbmet.co.za) is held at the *Kenilworth Race Track*, Rosmead Avenue.

Tickets to sporting events are available for purchase from *Computicket* (tel: (083) 915 8000; e-mail: info@computicket.com; website: www.computicket.com).

Fourth Beach, Clifton

Photo: South Africa Tourism

Adventure Sports

The spectacular natural setting of the city means that adventurous sports enjoy a huge following. There are several operators who offer a range of adventure sports, from mountain biking to abseiling, rock climbing to sky diving, hiking to bungee jumping, surfing to shark diving and canyonning (known locally as 'kloofing', which entails hiking into romote mountain ranges and then swimming and jumping down the gorges). *Daytrippers* (tel: (021) 511 4766; e-mail: info@daytrippers.co.za; website: www.daytrippers.co.za) offers hiking and kloofing tours, while *Adventure Village* (tel: (021) 424 1580; e-mail: thrills@adventure-village.co.za; website: www.adventure-village.co.za) offers a full range of adventure and extreme sports options, tours and expeditions, including daily abseiling expeditions down the sheer faces of Table Mountain.

Fitness Centres

Virgin Active (tel: (021) 710 8500; fax: (021) 710 8800; website: www.virginactive.co.za) has the monopoly on the fitness centres around the Western Cape, each offering a variety of facilities, including gym, swimming, squash, tennis and other sports. Club locations include *Claremont*, Main Road (tel: (021) 683 2402), *Constantia*, Main Road (tel: (021) 794 5010), *Durbanville Palmgrove Centre*, Main Road (tel: (021) 975 5210) and *N1 City Value Centre*, N1 (tel: (021) 595 3030). A one-day guest fee is about R75.

Golf

There are 55 golf courses in and around Cape Town and many are open to the public. The *Western Province Golf Union* (tel: (021) 686 1668; fax: (021) 686 1669; e-mail: wpga@global.co.za) can provide further information. Eighteen-hole golf courses that are open to the public include the *Rondebosch Golf Club*, 3 Klipfontein Road (tel: (021) 689 4176; e-mail: rgc@mweb.co.za; website: www.rondebosch-golf-club.co.za), the *Royal Cape Golf Club*, 174 Ottery Road, Wynberg (tel: (021) 761 6551; fax: (021) 797 5246), and the *Clovelly Country Club*, Clovelly Road, Clovelly (tel: (021) 782 1118; fax: (021) 782 6853). Green fees vary from R210 for 18 holes at the Rondebosch Golf Club to R280 for 18 holes at the Clovelly Golf Club. Further afield, *Spier Country Club*, located off the R44 toward Stellenbosch (tel: (021) 809 0669), is an 18-hole course situated beneath the Helderberg Mountain range. The club hosts the Golf Summer Festival, as well as a Ladies Day on the last Thursday of every month and a Twilight Round every Friday.

Swimming

The City of Cape Town's *Parks and Bathing Amenities* (tel: (021) 400 4650) oversees Cape Town's public swimming pools. *Newlands Pool*, Sans Souci Road, Newlands (tel: (021) 674 4197), is the centre of competitive swimming, diving and water polo. The *Long Street Baths*, Long Street (tel: (021) 400 3302), is an indoor, heated pool, adjacent to the *Turkish Baths* (tel: (021) 400 2202). Entrance to the pools is R6. Many *Virgin Active* clubs (see *Fitness Centres* above) provide swimming facilities. The *Camps Bay Tidal Pool*, Camps Bay beach (tel: (021) 438 1244), provides alfresco bathing possibilities.

Photo: South Africa Tourism

False Bay coast, Western Peninsula

Tennis

Although there are scores of recreational tennis clubs dotted around the city, it is extremely difficult to access the courts unless accompanied by a member. Several of the golf clubs (see *Golf* above) also provide tennis and lawn bowl facilities. Likewise, many of the *Virgin Active* clubs (see *Fitness Centres* above) also provide tennis courts, as do several major hotels. *Tennis Western Province*, Lovers Walk, Rondebosch (tel: (021) 686 3055; fax: (021) 685 5293), can provide further information.

Watersports

Cape Town is an extremely popular destination for watersports enthusiasts. Zandvlei, in Muizenberg, is still quite popular with windsurfing and small craft yachting, although it is largely considered a learning ground or beginner's beach. Hardcore wave freaks prefer to brave the breakers off Blaauwberg, Long Beach and Cape Point or the Dungeons off Hout Bay. False Bay is considered somewhat dangerous, as this is the favourite spot for other watersports enthusiasts, namely Great White Sharks. *Downhill Aventures* (tel: (021) 422 0388; fax: (021) 423 0127; e-mail: downhill@mweb.co.za) offers day and multi-day surfing courses with instruction and equipment provided, including transport and lunch. *Table Bay Diving* (tel: (021) 419 8822) organises diving charters – including wreck, reef, deep, night and shark cage diving – as well as diving courses. Equipment is available to purchase or hire. Ocean yachting mainly takes place in the Table Bay and False Bay, with regattas held every Wednesday in summer, with the start point at the *Royal Cape Yacht Club*, Duncan Road, Table Bay (tel: (021) 421 1354; fax: (021) 421 6028). The *Wind Report* (tel: (021) 788 8226 or 5965)

provides regular updates on the wind situation, while the *Surf Report* (tel: (021) 788 1350) keeps surfers up to date on wave conditions around the peninsula. Surfing information and tips are also available online (website: www.wavescape.co.za).

Shopping

Primarily thanks to the excellent exchange rate, shopping is a popular pastime for visitors to Cape Town. The city has embraced American mall culture with abandon and most shopping precincts in Cape Town have been decentralised to suburban shopping malls, with hundreds of shops under one roof. The most impressive malls are the *Victoria Wharf* at the V&A Waterfront, *Cavendish Square* in Claremont, *Tyger Valley* in the Northern Suburbs and *Canal Walk* at Century City (see *Further Distractions*). Nevertheless, there are still scores of little shops to be found, all offering plenty of bargains. And the mall culture cannot hold back the markets, mostly informal, that continue to flourish in the city centre and along main roads in the suburban areas. While shopping malls are generally open 0900–2100 Monday to Saturday and even Sunday 1000–1600, central city hours are 0830–1700 Monday to Friday and 0830–1300 on Saturday. Muslim-owned businesses close 1200–1300 on Friday.

Since the end of apartheid, Cape Town has become a Mecca for traders from all over Africa and it is possible to buy African art from all corners of the continent within a few city blocks. A sightseeing destination in its own right, *Greenmarket Square*, Shortmarket Street, in the city centre, has a market that is open Monday to Saturday, stocking an eclectic range of goods, including African art, local jewellery,

handmade clothing, music, books and antiques. Most of the streets that fan out from Greenmarket Square are also packed with street traders selling African goods, while *The Pan African Market*, 76 Long Street, is an experience within itself. Wall-to-wall African art and curios crowd into the double-storey labyrinth of shops, open Monday to Saturday. Tiny tin can sculptures sit alongside wooden behemoths of tribal masks, while leathersmiths, hair braiders, djembe drum tutors and West African tailors practise their crafts and an informal café offers refreshments. For more arts, curios, clothing and crafts, the daily *Waterfront Craft Market*, located in the Blue Shed at the V&A Waterfront, next to the Two Oceans Aquarium, is just the place for visitors to pick up a few trademark Capetonian gifts. The *Green Point Fleamarket*, outside Green Point Stadium, Somerset Road, is held every Sunday and public holidays and is the largest of its kind in the Southern Hemisphere, boasting a vast number of stalls selling everything from African art and antiques to fake international labels. However, pickpockets like this area even more than bargain hunters do.

An excellent lightweight gift that is truly indicative of Cape Town is wire sculpture – from as little as R10 for a wire daisy to R600 for a replica African hut. *Streetwires*, 77 Shortmarket Street, is an initiative to empower unemployed South Africans and supplies various creative wire products, which can be made to order. For a tasty South African speciality, biltong (dried raw meat) is available at *PJ's Biltong Bar* kiosks, located at almost every Pick 'n Pay shopping market throughout the city. Visitors should note, however, that importing biltong might be illegal in some countries. A far safer exportable gift would be wine, which is available en route on a Winelands tour for as little as R20 a bottle. Other South African specialities include Rooibos tea, hand-stitched leather or African rubber sandals and Sangoma herbs.

The *Montebello Design Centre*, Newlands Drive, has wonderful ethnic crafts for sale as well as a charming tearoom, while *African Image*, Hotel Mall Victoria Wharf, V&A Waterfront (website: www.African-image.co.za), specialises in authentic African tribal art and artefacts – a dream for collectors. Antique lovers should stroll up and down Church Street and the section of Long Street just off Church Street. Also in Long Street, the fashion aficionado will be spellbound by the incredible offerings on show at *Yin*, an eclectic boutique that specialises in clothes designed and handmade by women from various African communities and countries. A vast collection of African music can be perused and purchased at *The African Music Store*, 90 Long Street.

VAT stands at 14% on all goods sold in Cape Town, although this is largely ignored in the markets, and visitors can reclaim this upon departure for purchases over R250, provided all receipts have been kept and the appropriate tax invoices have been obtained and filled in. These, along with the goods, must be presented to the VAT Refund Administrator at the airport international departures terminal. A refund is then paid after passing through Passport Control. The *VAT Refund Office*, Victoria Wharf Shopping Centre, V&A Waterfront (tel: (021) 421 1612; website: www.taxrefunds.co.za), provides further information and helps with the necessary paperwork beforehand.

Culture

There are many cultural influences at work in Cape Town, which makes the city a particularly interesting one for the arts. So interesting in fact that the city was recently recognised by *Newsweek* as one of the world's top eight new 'cultural Meccas'. However, much like the rest of South Africa, Cape Town is still attempting to leap a cultural hurdle, as far as organised cultural events go. In the past, homegrown talent has been locally regarded as somehow inferior to international cultural imports – an attitude that still persists in some sections of the public. There is also the issue of an apartheid hangover and the resulting perceptions that cultural institutions are white-orientated and out of touch with the majority of the population. Yet another problem is purely logistical – the segregation laws of the past coupled with an inferior transport system have conspired to make cultural events quite literally inaccessible to large sections of the public. Nevertheless, time, several cultural projects and the natural buoyancy of artistic expression are slowly breaking down these barriers and Cape Town is coming into her own as a culturally rich and diverse city. Cape Town's two biggest contributions to South African culture have probably been in the fine arts and in the unique Cape jazz style, epitomised by musicians like Abdullah Ibrahim, Basil 'Manenberg' Coetzee and Robbie Jansen.

The city's two major cultural centres are the *Baxter Theatre Centre*, Main Road, Rondebosch (tel: (021) 685 7880; website: www.baxter.co.za), and the *Artscape Theatre Centre*, 1–10 DF Malan Street, Foreshore (tel: (021) 410 9800 *or* 421 7839; e-mail: artscape@artscape.co.za; website: www.artscape.co.za). All major cultural events can be booked through *Computicket* (tel: (083) 915 8000; e-mail: info@computicket.com; website: www.computicket.com). Tickets for Artscape events are available through *Artscape Dial-A-Seat* (tel: (021) 421 7695).

Listings information can be found in the Friday editions of the daily press – *The Cape Argus* and *Cape Times*. These are both subsidiaries of *The Independent* and listings can be found online (website: www.iol.co.za). The bi-monthly *Cape Etc* and monthly *SA Citylife* publications are excellent sources of information and listings for Cape Town's nightlife. The *Mail & Guardian* (website: www.mg.co.za) also has cultural listings for Cape Town. There are other websites with listings (www.artthrob.co.za, www.ananzi.co.za and www.capetowntoday.co.za), as well as a good online events guide (www. capetownevents.co.za).

Music

The *Cape Town Philharmonic Orchestra* (tel: (021) 410 9809; fax: (021) 425 1009; e-mail: capephil@ artscape.co.za) performs regularly at the *City Hall*, Grand Parade (tel: (021) 465 2029), as well as various other venues – details are published in the local press. The *Artscape Theatre Centre* (see above) features regular opera from the groundbreaking *Cape Town Opera* (website: www.capetownopera.co.za), famous for successfully 'Africanising' the classics. Both the Artscape and Baxter venues (see above) host classical music, jazz and popular music. Regular performances also take place at the *South African College of Music*, Main Road, Rondebosch (tel: (021) 650 2640). Further afield, the *Spier* complex, Lynedoch Road, Stellenbosch (tel: (021) 809 1100; website: www. spier.co.za), one of the oldest wine cellars in the country, is now well established as one of the Cape's major performing arts and music centres, largely thanks to the annual summer festival taking place from November to March.

Theatre

Besides the *Baxter* and *Artscape* venues (see above), which both host regular and varied theatrical productions and stand-up comedy acts, the *Theatre on the Bay*, Link Street, Camps Bay (tel: (021) 438 3301; e-mail: info@theatreonthebay.co.za; website: www.theatreonthebay.co.za), is the city's other major theatre, staging popular and contemporary theatre. The *High Street Theatre*, off Durban Road, Bellville (tel: (021) 914 7030 *or* 6444; e-mail: highstreet@mweb.co.za; website: www.highstreet.co.za), frequently features well-known South African artists.

Dance

Cape Town's premier contemporary dance company, *Jazzart* (tel: (021) 410 9848 *or* 9828; e-mail: dance@jazzart.co.za; website: www.jazzart.co.za), stages regular performances at *Artscape Theatre Centre* (see above) and other venues. Visiting national and international dance and ballet troupes frequently appear at the Baxter and Artscape venues (see above). The *Cape Town City Ballet* is based at the Artscape Theatre Centre but also performs at the delightful *Maynardville Open-Air Theatre*, Maynardville Park, Wynberg (tel: (021) 410 9800).

Film

Although Cape Town has a huge film and television industry, locally made feature films mainly come out of Johannesburg. The South African film industry, although packed with new talent, is yet to receive the necessary funding and attention it deserves to truly take off. Nevertheless, one of the city's favourite pastimes is cinema. Every major shopping centre has a cinema complex showing mainstream movies, either run by *Ster-Kinekor* or *Nu-Metro*, with advance booking through *Computicket* (tel: (083) 915 8000; e-mail: info@computicket.com; website: www. computicket.com).

Ster-Kinekor outlets are located in various shopping centres, including *Blue Route*, Tokai Road (tel: (021) 713 1280) and *Cavendish Commercial*, Cavendish Square, Dreyer Street, Claremont (tel: (021) 683 6328/9). A 17-screen Nu-Metro Multiplex is located at *Canal Walk*, Century City (tel: (0860) 101 165; website: www.centurycity.co.za). Nu-Metro also provides the big-screen thrills at *Victoria Wharf*, V&A Waterfront (tel: (021) 419 9700/1). Arthouse and independent films are equally well catered for, with Ster-Kinekor's *Cinema Nouveau* outlets located at *Cavendish Nouveau*, Cavendish Square, Dreyer Street, Claremont (tel: (021) 683 4063/4), and *V&A Nouveau*, Kings Warehouse, V&A Waterfront (tel: (021) 425 8222). The *Labia Theatre*, 68 Orange Street (tel: (021) 424 5927; website: www.labia.co.za), is the city's oldest and most Bohemian arthouse movie theatre. Another popular arthouse spot is the *Independent Armchair Theatre*, 135 Lower Main Road, Observatory (tel: (021) 447 1510/4; website: www.armchairtheatre.co.za). Lovers of giant-screen movies are able to visit the *IMAX Theatre*, BMW Pavilion, V&A Waterfront (tel: (021) 419 7365; website: www.imax.co.za).

Cultural Events

There are many cultural, sporting and trade events that take place throughout the city all year round (website: www.capetownevents.co.za). Among the scores of food and wine festivals, flower shows and dog shows, there is the annual summer *Maynardville Shakespeare Season*, which takes place at the *Maynardville Open-Air Theatre*, Maynardville Park, Wynberg (tel: (021) 410 9800), in January and February. One of the most popular annual cultural events of the season is *Kirstenbosch Appeltiser Sunday Summer Concerts* (tel: (021) 799 8783; website: www.kirstenbosch.co.za), held at *Kirstenbosch Botanical Gardens*. Crowds of over 5000 picnickers start gathering from early afternoon, to enjoy an eclectic evening of classical, ethnic, jazz and popular music. The September *Cape Town Festival* celebrates the diversity of the city's people through music, dance, drama, film and other cultural and religious events featuring local artists and personalities. The

Company Gardens

oldest and arguably the most quintessentially Capetonian cultural event is the *Kaapse Klopse* (also, somewhat controversially, known as the '*Coon Carnival*'). This carnival originates from the days of slavery in Cape Town, when the Malay slaves paraded through the streets on the Tweede Nuwe Jaar (Second New Year). The event is largely the mainstay of Cape Town's 'coloured' community, those descended from the Malay slaves, who dress up in elaborate costumes and paint their faces to march in a noisy, jazzy, jubilant and colourful parade through the streets of Cape Town, past the Grand Parade to Green Point Stadium, where prizes are awarded for the best costumes. This is a particularly pertinent event, seeing as it stood the test not only of time but also of apartheid oppression.

Literary Notes

Ever since Sir Francis Drake describe the Cape Peninsula as 'the most stately thing and the fairest cape in all the whole circumference of the earth', Cape Town has featured strongly in international literature. Most often, the city has been used as a metaphor for the system of apartheid and as a symbol of white oppression in black Africa. However, since the release of Nelson Mandela and the end of apartheid, Cape Town has become a symbol of freedom and democracy, with many of the major political works – by figures such as Nelson Mandela, Desmond Tutu and Govan Mbeki – written here.

The writer who has, perhaps more than any other, defined South African literature is J M Coetzee – twice winner of the Booker Prize for literature. His novels, which include *Disgrace* (1999), *Foe* (1986), *The Life and Times of Michael K* (1983), *Waiting for the Barbarians* (1980) and *Dusklands* (1974), go to the very heart of the South African psyche and delve deep into the political and social landscape of the country. Coetzee was born in Cape Town and is Professor of English at the University of Cape Town. Another literary figure at the university is André Brink, three-time winner of South Africa's premier literary prize, the CAN Award and twice shortlisted for the Booker Prize and winner of various other prizes. Brink's eight novels include *Looking on Darkness* (1974), *Rumours of Rain* (1978), *A Dry White Season* (1979) and *An Act of Terror* (1991). Jakes Mda is an internationally acclaimed and award-winning Capetonian poet, playwright and novelist, whose works include *Heart of Redness* (2000), *She Plays With the Darkness* (1995) and *Ways of Dying* (1995).

South Africa's premier playwright, Athol Fugard, based his powerful two-man play, *The Island* (1973), on the political incarcerations on Robben Island. Lesser known internationally but the unofficial king of Cape Town musicals, David Kramer penned a magnificent memoir of Cape Town's darkest moment when he captured not only the grief, hatred and confusion of the relocations but also the spirit and wonder of this tragic area in his musical collaboration with Taliep Petersen, *District Six* (1987). Kramer also achieved acclaim for his musical, *Karoo Kitaar Blues* (2002).

Another lesser known Capetonian writer is Menán du Plessis, whose novel, *Longlive!* (1989), is about a group of students in a politically turbulent Cape Town during the 1980s. On a more factual level, in *A Mouthful of Glass* (1998), Dutch writer Henk van Woerden documents with clarity and remarkable sensitivity the events that took place in Cape Town, when Demitrios Tsafendas stabbed the then Prime Minister, Hendrik Verwoerd, in the chamber of the South African Parliament in 1966.

SPECIAL EVENTS

Kaapse Klopse (Cape Minstrels' Carnival), New Year 'karnaval' with a parade through the city centre, 2 Jan, city centre to Green Point Stadium

Tweede Nuwe Jaar (Second New Year), informal public holiday, 2 Jan, throughout the city

Cape to Rio Yacht Race, international yacht race (website: www.capetorio.org), Jan, Royal Cape Yacht Club

Standard Bank Jazzathon, jazz festival (website: www.joyofjazz.co.za), mid-Jan, V&A Waterfront

Maynardville Shakespeare Season, open-air theatre, Jan–Feb, Maynardville Open-Air Theatre, Wynberg

International Design Indaba, workshops, lectures and the annual Construction New Media Awards (website: www.designindaba.com), Feb, Artscape Theatre Centre

Cape Town Marathon (website: www.topevents.co.za), Feb, Old Mutual Sports Fields, Jan Smuts Drive, Pinelands

Mutt of the Year, the biggest non-pedigree dog show in the Western Cape (website: www.spca-ct.co.za), early Feb, Constantia

J&B Met, Western Cape's premier horserace (website: www.jbmet.co.za), early Feb, Kenilworth Racecourse

Loveparade Cape Town, free street party with DJs and dance music (website: www.loveparade.co.za), mid-Feb, Heerengracht Street

Community Chest Carnival, international food festival, fun fair and fête (website: www.comchest.org.za), late Feb–early Mar, Maynardville Park, Wynberg

Cape Argus/Pick 'n' Pay Cycle Tour, 109km (68-mile) race around the peninsula, attracting 35,000 cyclists (website: www.cycletour.co.za), mid-Mar, around Cape Peninsula

Out in Africa South African Gay & Lesbian Film Festival, most successful film festival in South Africa (website: www.oia.co.za), mid-Mar, Cinema Nouveau, V&A Waterfront

Cape Town Festival, arts, culture and heritage festival to promote unity within the city (website: www.capetownfestival.co.za), mid–late Mar, various venues with focus areas in Company Gardens, the city centre, Tygerberg, Manenberg, Khayelitsha, Langa and Bonteheuwel

Human Rights Day, commemoration of the martyrs of apartheid, 21 Mar, throughout the city

North Sea Jazz Festival, Africa's biggest jazz festival (website: www.espafrika.com/nsj), late Mar, Good Hope Centre, city centre

Red Bull DHX, extreme speed festival with skateboarding, street luging and in-line skating (website: www.redbulldhx.co.za), Apr, Kloof Nek, Camps Bay

Old Mutual Two Oceans Marathon, 56km (35-mile) race (website: www.twooceansmarathon.org.za), mid-Apr, around the peninsula from the Celtic Harriers Athletic Club, Main Road, Newlands

Freedom Day, commemoration of South Africa's first democratic elections, 27 Apr, throughout the city

Cape Gourmet Festival, food and wine festival (website: www.capegourmet.co.za), May, various venues

Red Bull BWA (Big Wave Africa), surfing spectacular (website: www.redbullbwa.com), Jun, Dungeons, The Sentinel, Hout Bay

Youth Day, anniversary of the 1976 student uprising against apartheid, 16 Jun, throughout the city

Documentary Film Festival, Jul, various cinemas

Hout Bay Snoek Derby, festival in celebration of Cape Town's favourite fish, Aug, Hout Bay harbour

National Women's Day, celebration of the role of women in the anti-apartheid struggle, 9 Aug, throughout the city

Cape Times and V&A Waterfront Wine Festival, over 90 of the Cape's top wine estates, producers and wineries gather for exhibitions and tastings (website: www.waterfront.co.za), late Aug, V&A Waterfront

V&A Waterfront-Cape Times Wine Festival, Sep, V&A Waterfront

Cape Town International Kite Festival (website: www.kitefest.co.za), late Sep, Zandvlei, Muizenberg

Smirnoff International Comedy Festival, Oct, Baxter Theatre Centre, Rondebosch

Cape Times/FNB Big Walk, a walk for charity, now in its 100th year (website: www.bigwalk.co.za), mid-Oct, Cape Town and surrounding areas, finishing at the Hartleyvale Stadium

International Dragon Boat Festival, Nov, V&A Waterfront

Sithengi, Southern African international film festival and television market (website: www.sithengi.co.za), mid-Nov, Artscape Theatre Centre

Wiggle Waggle Walkathon, four kilometre (two-and-a-half mile) walk for dogs (website: www.spca-ct.co.za), mid-Nov, Constantia

Spier Summer Festival, jazz, opera, comedy, dance and classical concerts (website: www.spier.co.za), Nov–Mar, Spier Wine Estate, Stellenbosch

Long Street Carnival, music, dance, theatre and arts, Dec, Long Street

Mother City Queer Project Festival, gay and lesbian events and themed costume party (website: www.mcqp.co.za), mid-Dec, various venues with party at the Castle of Good Hope

Reconciliation Day, day of national unity across political divides, 16 Dec, throughout the city

Hout Bay Beach Festival and New Year's Eve Beach Party (website: www.multisportafrica.co.za), late Dec–31 Dec, Hout Bay

New Year's Eve Under the Stars at Kirstenbosch, outdoor ethnic, jazz, light classic, pop and opera music, 31 Dec, Kirstenbosch National Botanical Garden

Obz Festival, street festival, Dec–Feb, Lower Main Road, Observatory

Kirstenbosch Appletiser Sunday Summer Concerts, open-air concerts (website: www.kirstenbosch.co.za), Dec–Mar, Kirstenbosch Botanical Gardens

COPENHAGEN

Canals, lakes and the sea form the backdrop to modern Copenhagen and are a reminder of the city's heritage as a major Baltic port. This role is also reflected in the city's name, *København*, a corruption of *købmanne hafen* (merchants' harbour).

The city's foundation dates back to 1167, when Bishop Absalon built a bastion on the island of Slotsholmen, today the site of Christiansborg Palace and the Danish parliament. In 1417, the city became the royal capital of a huge swathe of Scandinavia that included not only Denmark but also parts of Sweden and Norway. Many of Copenhagen's most impressive buildings were constructed during the celebrated reign of Christian IV (1588–1648). Existing monuments of the monarch's grand building schemes include the *Børsen* (Stock Exchange), the *Rundetårn* (Round Tower) and the Palace of Rosenborg. Christian IV was responsible for Copenhagen's canal network and for the development of Christianshavn – an island across the inner harbour – as a focus for trade and shipping in the city. In the following centuries, an outbreak of plague, two terrible fires, military attacks by the Swedes (in the 17th century) and the British (in the 19th century) caused widespread damage to the city. The central area of Copenhagen is therefore characterised by 17th-, 18th- and 19th-century architecture – buildings constructed on the foundations of the medieval streets.

Modern Copenhagen is the largest city in Scandinavia but nevertheless retains a disarmingly provincial, small-town atmosphere that is instantly appealing. Gabled houses, narrow streets and a skyline that is dominated by delicate spires rather than hulking skyscrapers are all typical of the city. Copenhagen is also, arguably, the greenest capital in Europe – much of the centre is reserved for pedestrians, strict anti-pollution laws are enforced and bicycles often outnumber cars on the streets. Green spaces – including the world-famous Tivoli – abound, while, in the summer, cafés and restaurants occupy the pavements. The citizens of Copenhagen seem justifiably proud of their attractive, well-kept city and enjoy a quality of life that they are keen to share with visitors from other countries.

Copenhagen boasts theatres, museums and a lively, surprisingly cutting-edge nightlife scene. Danish cinema is increasingly making its mark on the international film circuit and Danish furniture, technology and jewellery remain at the forefront of contemporary design. The best the country has to offer can be experienced in the capital city, where design studios rub shoulders with ultra-hip bars and modern architecture boldly occupies the spaces between 17th-century buildings, military installations and the sea. A road bridge to Sweden, completed in 2000, is helping to make Copenhagen a key focal point for Scandinavia, the Baltic and the rest of mainland Europe.

The climate in Copenhagen is a temperate maritime one and generally quite changeable. Winters are cold and cloudy but summers are warm and sunny. Snowfalls are common between January and March and the wettest season is over the autumnal months of August and October.

Copenhagen skyline

Photo: Wonderful Copenhagen

TRAVEL

Getting There By Air

København Lufthavn (CPH)

Tel: 3231 3231. Fax: 3231 3132.
E-mail: cph@cph.dk
Website: www.cph.dk

The airport is among the most modern and efficient in the world and is located eight kilometres (five miles) from the city centre. In 2002, the airport was the only one in Scandinavia to show growth in the number of passengers. It is the main hub serving Scandinavia and the Baltic and is the principal airport for *Scandinavian Airlines* (*SAS*). International flights use terminals two and three. Terminal one handles domestic services to destinations on Jutland and Funen. A free transit bus connects the domestic and international terminals. Flight information is available from *Scandinavian Airlines System* (tel: 3232 0000), *Novia* (tel: 3247 4747) and *ServisAir* (tel: 3231 4055), but, in 2002, the airport introduced a new system enabling registered users to have messages sent directly to their mobile phones, relaying gate and boarding information, any changes or delays and the arrival time of flights and baggage. This service is available through the website.

Major airlines: *Scandinavian Airlines System – SAS* (tel: 7010 2000; website: www.sas.se), located on the ground floor of the Radisson SAS Royal Hotel in the city centre, is the major airline for Denmark, Sweden and Norway. There are 60 other airlines operating to and from 113 cities served worldwide, including *Air France*, *British Airways*, *EasyJet*, *Iberia*, *KLM*, *Lufthansa*, *Thai Airways International* and *Virgin Express*.

Approximate flight times to Copenhagen: From London is 2 hours 50 minutes; from New York is 11 hours 40 minutes; from Los Angeles is 21 hours 10 minutes; from Toronto is 14 hours 40 minutes and from Sydney is 23 hours 20 minutes.

Airport facilities: Branches of *Danske Bank* (terminals one and two) and *Nordea* (terminal three) offer currency exchange services, daily 0630–2200; *Danske Bank* has ATMs in terminals one and three, *Nordea* in terminal three. Other facilities and services include tourist information and hotel reservations in the international arrivals hall, travel agencies, a post office, duty-free shops, restaurants, a family area,

childcare facilities, 24-hour first aid and left-luggage lockers, as well as saunas, showers and solarium. There is a new five-star *Hilton Hotel* (tel: 3250 1501; website: www.hilton.dk) linked to terminal three by a covered walkway, steps and elevators, as well as a transfer hotel (tel: 3231 2455) in terminal two. Car hire is available from *Avis*, *Budget*, *Europcar Pitzner*, *Hertz* and *Sixt*.

Business facilities: There is a brand-new *Airport Business Centre* (tel: 3248 3000; fax: 3248 3001; e-mail: cph.business@ssp.dk; website: www. cphbusinesscentre.dk) in terminal three, including exclusive executive conference rooms, audiovisual equipment, small meeting rooms and a VIP room. *Scandinavian Airlines*, *ServisAir* and *Novia* all provide executive lounges for their passengers.

Arrival/departure tax: None.

Transport to the city: There are three direct *DSB-HT* S-train (*s-tog*) services (tel: 3314 1701; website: www.s-tog.dk) running hourly (at 15, 35 and 55 minutes past the hour) to Central, Hellerup, Østerport, Nørreport, Glostrup and Høje Tåstrup stations (journey time – 15 minutes). Services operate Monday to Friday 0455–0035, Saturday 0535–0015 and Sunday 0635–0015. Tickets cost Dkk22.50 and are available from the ticket office in terminal three. Public buses 9, 58, 250S and 500S (see *Public Transport* in *Getting Around*) run from the airport to the city centre and beyond, operating daily until midnight. Tickets cost Dkk16.50 to the city centre (journey time – 20–25 minutes). Night bus 96N runs 0037–0400 from terminal three to City Hall Square (Rådhuspladsen). A taxi to the city centre costs Dkk200 (journey time – approximately 20 minutes).

Getting There By Water

Københavns Havn (Port of Copenhagen), Nordre Toldbod 24 (tel: 3347 9999; fax: 3347 9933; e-mail: cphport@cphport.dk; website: www.cphport.dk), is Denmark's largest port and the most important cruise destination in Northern Europe. Most cruise ships that dock in Copenhagen are heading for the Norwegian fjords or the Baltic. These big summer cruise ships dock along Langelinie Pier, which is a 15-minute walk further out from Nyhavn, where the year-round ferries listed below currently dock. Ultimately, however, Langelinie Pier will accommodate all ships that dock in Copenhagen. The development of the area is well underway and facilities are extensive, including an information centre, telephones, lounges, various shops and an increasing number of pierside cafés and restaurants.

Ferry services: High-speed catamarans to Malmö in Sweden are run by *Pilen* (tel: 3332 1260; fax: 3332 2794) and depart from Havnegade 28, hourly Monday to Friday 0900–2300 (journey time – 45 minutes), with additional trips on Friday and Saturday at 0900 and 0100. A one-way adult ticket costs Dkk40 Monday to Thursday and Dkk50 Friday to Sunday. Although the ferry is marketed as a commuter service, many Danes and Swedes seem to use it as a booze-cruise.

An alternative service is run by *Scandlines* (tel: 3315 1515; e-mail: scandlines@scandlines.dk; website: www.scandlines.dk). Holders of the *Copenhagen Card* (see *Public Transport* in *Getting Around*) are entitled to a discount on this service. There are also services to Oslo (journey time – 16 hours) run by *DFDS Seaways* (tel: 3342 3342; fax: 3342 3159; website: www.dfdsseaways.com) and Swinoujscie, in Poland (journey time – 10 hours) run by *Polferries* (tel: 4012 1700; fax: 4097 0370).

Bornholmstrafikken (tel: 5695 1866; fax: 5691 0766; website: www.bornholmstrafikken.dk) runs daily ferry trips between Copenhagen and Ronne, on the island of Bornholm, in the Baltic (journey time – 7 hours).

Transport to the city: The port is approximately a ten- to 15-minute walk from the centre of Copenhagen, four kilometres (two and a half miles) from Central Station and 15km (nine miles) from the airport. Bus route 26E passes along Havnegade, past the ferry terminal; taxis are readily available.

Getting There By Rail

Danish State Railways – DSB (tel: 7013 1415 (enquiries) or 1418 (reservations); website: www.dsb.dk) operates punctual, clean and well-equipped trains. Intercity trains are fitted with sockets for radios and computers, while mobile phones are available for hire in first class. Fax facilities are also provided.

All international trains arrive at and depart from *Hovedbanegården* central station (tel: 3314 8800), located on Bernstorffsgade, near Tivoli. Facilities include currency exchange (*Danske Bank* and *Forex*), a post office, shops, fast-food outlets and a supermarket.

Rail services: Direct trains run from Copenhagen to various European destinations, including Stockholm, Oslo and Hamburg; all require seat reservations. *Intercity Lyn Express* trains offer a direct connection between Copenhagen and other major Danish centres, such as Odense (journey time – 1 hour 15 minutes), Fredericia (journey time – 2 hours 30 minutes), Århus (journey time – 3 hours 30 minutes), Esbjerg (journey time – 3 hours 30 minutes) and Aalberg (journey time – 5 hours 10 minutes). There are also frequent regional train departures to cities in the surrounding area, including three trains an hour to Helsingør (Elsinore).

Transport to the city centre: The central station is situated on the southwestern edge of the Old City. From here, there are S-train (*S-tog*) connections to Vesterport, Nørreport, Østerport and other stations in the metropolitan area. Numerous bus routes pass the station and taxis are readily available.

Getting There By Road

Motorways are designated by the letter 'E' followed by two digits, main roads by two digits on a yellow background, and minor roads by three digits on a white background. The speed limit is 110kph (68mph) on motorways, 80kph (50mph) on main roads and 50kph (31mph) in urban areas. Drivers must keep their headlights switched on at all times during the day. Drivers and front-seat passengers must wear seatbelts. The maximum legal alcohol to blood ratio for driving is 0.05%.

An International Driving Permit is not required but may be preferable if the national driving licence is not in English. Although not necessary, Green Card insurance is recommended. The legal driving age in Denmark is 18 years.

The *Danish Road Directorate* operates a *Traffic Information Service* (tel: 3315 6444 *or* 8020 2060, toll free in Denmark).

Emergency breakdown service: *Danks Autohjælp* 7010 8090.

Routes to the city: Highway E20 (with a connection to E45) crosses Denmark from west to east and intersects with E47 and E55 to the southwest of Copenhagen. The E47 runs south to Rodby, with ferry connections to Germany. The toll bridge across the *Store Bælt*, between Sjælland and Fyn, charges Dkk210 for cars. The construction of the Øresund 16km (ten-mile) bridge and tunnel complex, between Sjælland in Denmark and Scania in Sweden, was completed in 2000. Odense is located in Fyn, on the E20, connecting with the E45 highway in Jylland, which travels north to Århus and Aalborg.

Approximate driving times to Copenhagen: From Odense – 1 hour 30 minutes; Århus – 3 hours; Aalborg – 3 hours 40 minutes.

Coach services: The coach station is located in front of the *Sofitel Plaza Hotel*, Bernstorffgade. Only a few companies operate from Copenhagen with permanent international bus services to and from Sweden (Gothenburg, Halmstad, Malmö, Lund and Ystad) and the Czech Republic (Prague). During the year, however, *Gullivers* offer bus tours to Hamburg, Berlin, Amsterdam, Brussels and Paris; information is available from the tourist information office on Bernstorffsgade.

Eurolines Scandinavia, Reventlowsgade 8 (tel: 7010 0030; website: www.eurolines.dk), operates bus services to Berlin, Frankfurt, Vienna, Hamburg, Paris, Munich, London and other destinations in Europe.

Abildskous Rutebilder (tel: 8678 4888) runs services between Århus and Copenhagen, terminating at Valby. *Fjerritslev-København* (tel: 9821 1275) links the capital with various destinations in Jutland. Aalborg buses operated by *Thinggaard Rutebilder* (tel: 9811 6600) terminate at Ryparken. Bus tickets often include the price of ferry crossings, where applicable.

Getting Around

Public Transport

The *Metropolitan Transport Company – HT* (tel: 3613 1415; website: www.ht.dk) runs the urban transport system. Information on trains can also be obtained from the *Danish State Railways* (see *Getting There By Rail*). There is an integrated **bus** and **urban train** network, known as *S-tog* (tel: 3314 1701; website: www.dsb.dk/s-tog), as well as the first section of Copenhagen's new **Metro** (tel: 3311 1700; fax: 3311 2301; website: www.m.dk), with 11 stations currently in use.

Buses and **trains** run daily 0500–2430 and there are additional **night buses** from City Hall Square (Rådhuspladsen) to the suburbs. There is now a **harbour bus** service connecting the Royal Library's Black Diamond building on Christians Brygge with Nordre Toldbod, with stops along the waterfront, including Nyhavn. The shuttle operates six times an hour daily 0600–1800/1900 throughout the year (weather permitting), and tickets cost Dkk30.

The **Metro** opened in 2002 and runs daily 0500–0100 (all night at weekends) from Nørreport via Kongens Nytorv and Christianshavn to Lergravsparken and Vestamager. Other sections

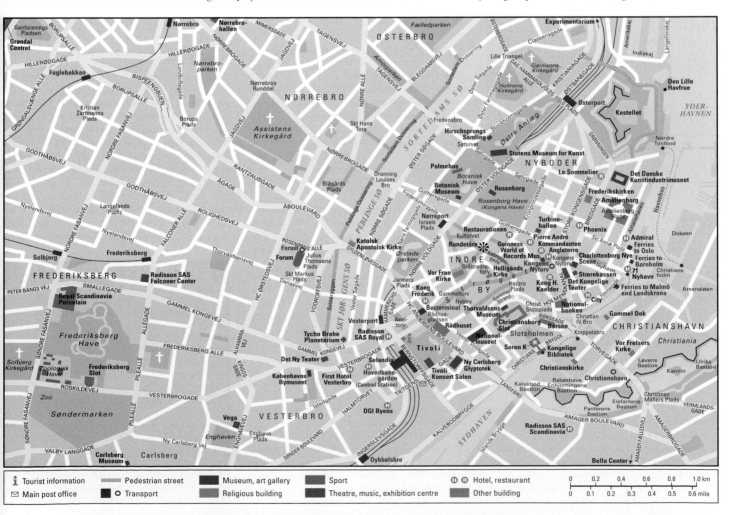

Symbol	Legend		Symbol	Legend
i	Tourist information			Sport
✉	Main post office			Theatre, music, exhibition centre
	Pedestrian street		H R	Hotel, restaurant
O	Transport			Other building
	Museum, art gallery			
	Religious building			

0	0.2	0.4	0.6	0.8	1.0 km
0	0.1	0.2	0.3	0.4	0.5	0.6 mile

BUSINESS PROFILE

Copenhagen's role as a traditional north European transport and trade hub has been strengthened by the economic rise of the Baltic States of Estonia, Lithuania and Latvia, as well as by the democratisation of Eastern Europe. The completion of the fixed road link across the Øresund to Sweden has further cemented Copenhagen's strength in the region.

Greater Copenhagen is home to 41% of companies registered in Denmark and these companies account for 44.5% of total turnover of all Danish companies and 42% of national exports. In 2002, GDP per capita in Copenhagen was 36,400, as compared to a national GDP per capita of 29,400. Unemployment in the city, at a rate of 6.4%, is only slightly higher than the national average of 5.7%.

Denmark's strong economy is characterised by a balanced state budget, low interest rates, low inflation and a stable currency. The generous state welfare system results in high taxes but also provides an excellent climate for education and research. The 980,000-strong workforce in the Greater Copenhagen region tends to be well educated, computer literate and multi-lingual. The IMD/World Economic Forum consistently votes the Danes as the best workforce in Europe. A recent Price Waterhouse Coopers study concluded that the city is the most favourable place in Northern Europe to establish an e-business centre, owing to favourable labour and property costs.

Copenhagen's business strengths lie particularly in energy, design, information technology, biotechnological and medical research, telecommunications, environmental technology and tourism. A recent medico-health sector development is the cross-border initiative with *Skane Regional Federation Council*, to promote foreign investment in pharmaceutical, biotechnology and medical technical industries. The project is centred on the so-called *Medicon Valley*, which brings together a high concentration of academic institutions, industry and investment organisations. International companies based here include *Pharmacia & Upjohn*, *Astra Draco* and *Gambro*. Medicon Valley is a company in the Øresund region, which is the new up-and-coming business district (website: www.orestad.dk).

Denmark leads the world in terms of environmental awareness, with a high proportion of GDP devoted to environmental protection. The first European ministry of the environment was established here in 1975 and the *EU Environment Agency* is still here today. The *Union of International Associations* lists Copenhagen as the eighth most popular congress venue in the world.

opened in 2003, linking the city centre with Frederiksberg and Vanløse. The link to the airport is due for completion by 2007. The trains are fully automatic, however, there is a Metro steward on every train, whose job it is to check the tickets, provide information and help passengers.

Tickets for the Metro, the buses and the trains are all the same. Fares are calculated on a seven-zone structure indicated on colour-coded maps at stations and bus stops. The price of a ticket depends on the number of zones travelled through (minimum two zones). Tickets begin at Dkk15 and are available for purchase from the bus driver, at ticket offices or vending machines at stations and the bus terminus at City Hall Square (Rådhuspladsen). Fares are doubled if you board the Metro or night buses between 0100 and 0500.

Discount cards (*klippekort*) for ten journeys (calculated according to the number of zones you travel but generally saving around 40%) and **24-hour tickets** (Dkk90) are available at stations, the bus terminus or from the tourist information office. It is cheaper per journey to use a discount card than to buy a ticket. The *Copenhagen 'Plus' Card* (see *Tourist Information*) entitles the holder to free, unlimited travel on buses and trains in the metropolitan area, as well as discounts on car hire, canal and harbour tours and express ferries to Sweden. Tickets and discount cards must be held throughout the journey and are subject to inspection.

Taxis

There are five major taxi companies in the city – *Taxa 4 x 35* (tel: 3535 3535), *Codan Taxi* (tel: 7025 2525), *Hovedstadens Taxi* (tel: 3877 7777), *Ryvang Bilen A/S* (tel: 3918 1818) and *Taxamotor* (tel: 3810 1010). All taxis are licensed and can be booked by telephone or hailed in the street. The initial rate is Dkk22, plus Dkk7.70 per km (rising to Dkk9.60 after 1800 and during weekends). Most taxis accept credit cards, although visitors should inform the driver at the beginning of the trip. It is not customary for customers to tip the driver (a service charge is included in the fare) but to round up the final amount instead.

Cheaper cycle taxis, like a back-to-front rickshaw, with space for two passengers at the front, are available from *Quickshaw* (tel: 7020 1375; website: www.quickshaw.biz) and *Cykeltaxa* (tel: 7026 0055; website: www.cykeltaxa.dk). Cycle taxis can be ordered by telephone, hailed in the street or found at dedicated ranks in the centre, such as Tivoli, City Hall Square (Rådhuspladsen) or Kongens Nytorv. They operate within a 14-zone system and the price starts at Dkk25 for a journey in zone one.

Limousines

Limousine services are provided by *VIP Limousine Service* (tel: 3542 4020; fax: 3542 4066; website: www.denmarklimo.com), where a limousine costs Dkk760 per hour (minimum of two hours). *Dankse Limousine Service* (tel: 3315 0630; fax: 3315 0634; e-mail: info@limousine-service.dk; website: www.limousine-service.dk) charges Dkk545 per hour for a sedan. Stretch limos or Rolls Royces are available from *Luxcars* (tel: 7020 1023; e-mail: info@luxcars.dk; website: www.luxcars.dk) for Dkk1200 per hour (minimum of two hours).

Driving in the City

Copenhagen is remarkably and refreshingly free of traffic. Environmental awareness and the compact nature of the city means that many residents prefer to cycle, walk or rollerblade.

Parking meters are in operation in large sectors of the Old City. These are contained within three parking zones, where parking fees are applicable – the Red Zone (Dkk20 per hour Monday to Friday 0800–2000 and Saturday 0800–1400), the Green Zone (Dkk12 per hour Monday to Friday 0800–1800 and Saturday 0800–1400) and the Blue Zone (Dkk7 per hour Monday to Friday 0800–1800). Tickets are available from coin-operated parking meters, which are colour coded to indicate which zone you are in. Beyond the three coloured zones, parking is free, although for two hours only Monday to Friday 0800–1900.

Multi-storey car parks in the city are open 0600/0800–2000/0000. Some are closed Saturday afternoon and Sunday.

Car Hire

Self-drive cars are only hired to people over the age of 21 years, who hold a valid driving licence and an international credit card. Individual car companies may impose their own age restrictions. The prices given below, which reduce significantly for multi-day hire, include unlimited mileage, tax and insurance, although customers should check details of insurance cover.

Avis (tel: 3373 4099; fax: 3373 4090; e-mail: copenhagen@avis.dk; website: www.avis.dk) hires out small cars from Dkk550 per day. *Hertz* (tel: 3317 9020; fax: 3317 9029; e-mail: mail@hertzdk.dk; website: www.hertzdk.dk) charges from Dkk560 per day and drivers must be at least 25 years. *Danecars/National* (tel: 3963 2375; e-mail: info@danecars.dk; website: www.danecars.dk), *EasyBiler* (tel: 3393 0393; e-mail: info@easybiler.dk; website: www.easybiler.dk) and *Europcar/Pitzner* (tel: 3355 9900; fax: 3355 9933; e-mail: cs@europcar.dk; website: www.europcar.dk) charge from Dkk350 to Dkk510 per day for a small or economy car. At the top end of the range, non-Danish residents over 26 years can hire luxury cars from *Luxcars* (tel: 7020 1023; e-mail: info@luxcars.dk; website: www.luxcars.dk), starting from Dkk1375 per day for a BMW.

Bicycle Hire

Cycling is the preferred method of transport for many of Copenhagen's residents and there are cycle routes along all the major streets, through some of the city's most scenic areas. Between April and September, the city provides its visitors with free bicycles on which to get around. There are 125 City Bike Parks (website: www.bycyklen.dk) located around the city, where bikes can be collected for a Dkk20 deposit. Several companies hire bicycles for trips outside the city, including *Københavns Cykelbørs*, Gothersgade 157 (tel: 3314 0717), for Dkk60 per day with a deposit of Dkk200, *Københavns Cykler*, Central Station (tel: 3333 8613), for Dkk75 per day, with a

BUSINESS ETIQUETTE

Business hours are Monday to Friday 0800–1700 and punctuality for appointments is essential. The dress code is relatively formal – a tie for men and suits for both men and women. Business contacts should shake hands on arrival and departure, with business cards exchanged after introduction. Most Danes, particularly those in the international business community, speak excellent English and often speak German and French too.

Business visitors are well looked after, with the provision of lunch, taxis and accommodation, as necessary, and often provided with a day programme too. Nearly all meetings are non-smoking venues, but moderate alcohol consumption over a business lunch or dinner is not inappropriate.

deposit of Dkk500, and *Østerport Cyker*, Oslo Plads 9, Østerport Station (tel: 3333 8513), for Dkk75 per day, with a deposit of Dkk500. ID is required.

SIGHTSEEING

Sightseeing Overview

The heart of Copenhagen is ringed by a series of lakes to the northwest and by the inner harbour to the southeast. It is characterised by narrow and predominantly pedestrian streets lined with gabled houses, enticing shops and cafés. The huge *Rådhuspladsen* (City Hall Square) lies at the western end of the central area. From here, a series of pedestrianised streets (*Strøget*) extend as far as *Kongens Nytorv* (King's New Square). The castles of *Rosenborg* and *Amalienborg* and the seaman's district of *Nyboder* are to be found in the area to the north and east of Kongens Nytorv. *Slotsholmen Island*, the site of Absalon's original bastion, lies to the southwest. The inner harbour separates the main part of the city from *Christianshavn*. This island was first developed in the 17th century, when Christian IV offered tax incentives to encourage merchants, shipbuilders and tradesmen to settle there.

In the 20th century, Denmark has achieved international renown for its contemporary design. Arne Jakobsen's furniture graces cool bars and cafés worldwide (not least in Copenhagen). In the city, the architectural heritage of Christian IV is supplemented by daring 20th-century buildings, including the glittering waterfront extension to the *Royal Library*, known as the 'Black Diamond'.

Key Attractions

Rundetårn (Round Tower)

In the streets to the north of Strøget is the *Rundetårn*, the oldest observatory in Europe. Built by Christian IV in 1642, the building forms part of a scholastic complex that also includes a university library (now an exhibition hall) and student church. A 209m (686ft) spiral ramp leads to the top of the tower, 35m (115ft) above the street, from where there is a good view over the old sections of the city.

Købmagergade 52A
Tel: 3373 0373. Fax: 3373 0377.
E-mail: post@rundetaarn.dk
Website: www.rundetaarn.dk
Transport: Bus 5A, 7, 14, 16, 17, 24, 43, 84; S-train or Metro to Nørreport.
Opening hours: Mon–Sat 1000–2000, Sun 1200–2000 (Jun–Aug); Mon–Sat 1000–1700, Sun 1200–1700 (Sep–May).
Admission: Dkk20 (concessions available).

Tivoli

One of the most famous European amusement parks, *Tivoli* is a charmingly bizarre mixture of the natural and the artificial. Designed by Georg Carstensen as a pleasure ground for the masses, Christian VIII, the then King of Denmark, gave his royal permission for the amusement park in the heart of Copenhagen. 'When the populace are enjoying themselves they forget about politicking,' the widely travelled Georg Carstensen reasoned. When it opened in 1843, visitors had a choice of two amusements – a horse-drawn carrousel and a rollercoaster. Today, there are 25 rides, as well as games and arcades, two theatres, an open-air stage and a

museum. Of the four rollercoasters, the 'Bjergrutschebanen' (the Mountain Roller Coaster) is the oldest (dating from 1914) and still the most popular. Rides cost one, two or three *Tour Tickets* (Dkk10 each). The Tivoli Boys Guard Band parade through the gardens at 1730 and 1930 on weekends and public holidays, with a full orchestra, stagecoach and horses. Crowded, pricey and unbelievably kitsch, Tivoli remains strangely appealing, particularly at night, when the trees are illuminated with lanterns. Numerous concerts and special events are held here every summer (April to September), as well as a Christmas market in December.

Vesterbrogade 3
Tel: 3315 1001 *or* 1012 (ticket centre).
Fax: 3375 0381.
E-mail: info@tivoli.dk
Website: www.tivoli.dk
Transport: Bus 1, 2A, 6, 8, 10, 11, 12, 13, 14, 16, 28, 29, 30 or 39; S-train to Central Station.
Opening hours: Sun–Wed 1100–2300, Thurs and Sat 1100–2400, Fri 1100–0100 (mid-Apr–mid-Jun and mid-Aug–mid-Sep); Sun–Thurs 1100–2400, Fri and Sat 1100–0100 (mid-Jun–mid-Aug).
Admission: Dkk55/Dkk60 (depending on season as above); admission fee also varies according to the day of the week; concessions and discount schemes available.

Waterfront

Nyhavn (New Harbour) is an inlet off the *Inderhavnen*, towards *Kongens Nytorv* (King's New Square). Until recently, brothels and bars serving the visiting sailors dominated this seedy area. Now the multicoloured, 17th-century, gabled buildings accommodate bustling restaurants and pavement cafés serving traditional Danish food beside a pedestrian thoroughfare and the masts of traditional yachts. Hans Christian Andersen lived at three different houses here and, on his birthday (2 April), may still be encountered, in the form of an actor in costume wandering the streets.

It is a very pleasant walk from Nyhavn along Bredgade to Churchill Park or along the waterfront beyond the Admiral Hotel (both routes passing Amalienborg Castle), to the spot in the northeast of the city where *Den Lille Havfrue* (The Little Mermaid) stares wistfully out to sea. Erected in 1913, the statue commemorates the Hans Christian Andersen heroine and has become a global symbol of Copenhagen. Despite being decapitated a few times and being somewhat smaller in stature than might be imagined, the mermaid remains perennially popular with visitors.

Nyhavn
Inderhavnen
Tel: 3312 3233.
Website: www.nyhavn.org
Transport: New harbour bus service; bus 1, 6, 7, 9, 10, 28, 29, 31 or 41.
Den Lille Havfrue
Promenade, Langelinie
Transport: Bus 1 or 6; S-train to Østerport.
Opening hours: Daily 24 hours.
Admission: Free.

Rosenborg Slot (Rosenborg Castle)

Built between 1606 and 1634, *Rosenborg* was the chief residence of Christian IV and the main royal palace until the end of the last century. This redbrick, Dutch Renaissance-style palace displays the crown jewels and other royal treasures, dating from the 16th to the 19th centuries, on the ground floor. In 1999, the Rosenborg Tapestries, woven especially for the banquet room of Rosenborg in the late 1600s, were

Christmas market at Tivoli

returned to their original location after some years at Christiansborg Castle. The gardens (*Kongens Have*) surrounding the palace were laid out in 1606 and are some of the most attractive in the city.

Øster Voldgade 4A
Tel: 3315 3286. Fax: 3315 2046.
E-mail: museum@dkks.dk
Website: www.rosenborg-slot.dk
Transport: Bus 5A, 10, 14, 16, 42, 43, 184, 185, 150S, 173E or 350S; S-train or Metro to Nørreport.
Opening hours: Daily 1000–1600 (May and Sep); daily 1000–1700 (Jun–Aug); Tues–Sun 1100–1400 (Nov–Apr).
Admission: Dkk60 (concessions available).

TOURIST INFORMATION

Wonderful Copenhagen Tourist Information
Bernstorffsgade 1 (at the entrance to Tivoli)
Tel: 7022 2442. Fax: 7022 2452.
E-mail: touristinfo@woco.dk
Website: www.visitcopenhagen.dk
Opening hours: Mon–Sat 0900–1800 (May–Jun); Mon–Sat 0900–2000, Sun 0900–1800 (Jul–Aug); Mon–Sat 0900–1600 (Sep–Apr).

Use It (Youth Information Centre)
Rådhusstræde 13
Tel: 3373 0620. Fax: 3373 0649.
E-mail: useit@ui.dk
Website: www.useit.dk
Opening hours: Mon–Wed 1100–1600, Thurs 1100–1800, Fri 1100–1400 (16 Sep–14 Jun); daily 0900–1900 (15 Jun–15 Sep).

This is a separate tourist information office for young, budget travellers, although a good deal of information useful to all ages and budgets is contained on the website.

Passes
The *Copenhagen Card* allows free admission to various attractions. There are two types of card – 'City' and 'Plus'. The 'City' card is valid for 24 hours and gives free admission to 40 of the most popular museums and attractions; it costs Dkk159. The 'Plus' card is valid for 72 hours (Dkk395) and provides free admission to 70 attractions, as well as free travel on all buses and trains and a comprehensive guide that includes maps and detailed information on more than 100 museums, sights and other services. Both of these cards are available from travel agencies, hotels, railway stations or the main tourist information office.

Photo: Wonderful Copenhagen

Ny Carlsberg Glyptotek garden

Amalienborg Slot (Amalienborg Castle)

Amalienborg Castle has been the winter residence of the Danish royal family since 1794. The four identical Rococo palaces face each other across the octagonal courtyard, where the changing of the guard takes place each day at noon, when the family is in residence. A museum, featuring some of the private chambers and royal treasures dating from 1863–1947, is open to the public.
Amalienborg
Tel: 3312 2186. Fax: 3393 3203.
E-mail: amalienborgmuseet@c.dk
Website: www.rosenborg-slot.dk
Transport: Bus 1, 6 or 10; S-train to Østerport.
Opening hours: Daily 1000–1600 (May–Oct); Tues–Sun 1100–1600 (Nov–Apr).
Admission: Dkk45 (concessions available).

Nationalmuseet (National Museum)

Housed in a 17th-century royal mansion, the *National Museum* is the country's premier historical and cultural institution. Permanent collections include the history of Denmark from the Ice Age to 2000, Egyptian, Greek and Italian antiquities, and a survey of indigenous populations. There is also an interactive children's museum.
Ny Vestergade 10
Tel: 3313 4411. Fax: 3347 3300.
Website: www.natmus.dk
Transport: Bus 1, 2, 5, 6, 8, 10, 28, 29, 30, 32, 33, 550S or 650S.
Opening hours: Tues–Sun 1000–1700.
Admission: Dkk50 (concessions available); free on Wed.

Statens Museum for Kunst (Royal Museum of Fine Art)

The *Royal Museum of Fine Art* houses Denmark's largest art collection, including paintings by Rembrandt, Brueghel and Rubens, works by Titian, Mantegna and Picasso, and an excellent Matisse collection.
Sølvgade 48–50
Tel: 3374 8494. Fax: 3374 8404.
E-mail: smk@smk.dk
Website: www.smk.dk
Transport: Bus 10, 14, 40, 42, 43, 72E, 79E, 173E, 184 or 185; S-train to Østerport or Nørreport; Metro to Nørreport.
Opening hours: Tues and Thurs–Sun 1000–1700; Wed 1000–2000.
Admission: Dkk50 (concessions available); free on Wed; extra charges for temporary exhibitions will apply.

Ny Carlsberg Glyptotek

The *Carlsberg Glyptotek* was built by the Carlsberg brewer, Carl Jacobsen, between 1897 and 1906. Today, it houses a superb collection of Egyptian, Greek and Roman antiquities, as well as Impressionist masterpieces and Danish and French art by Monet, Gauguin, Renoir, Degas and Cézanne.
Dantes Plads 7
Tel: 3341 8141. Fax: 3391 2058.
Website: www.glyptotek.dk
Transport: Bus 1, 2A, 5A, 10, 33, 550S or 650S; S-train to Kobenhavn H.
Opening hours: Tues–Sun 1000–1600.
Admission: Dkk40 (concessions available); free Wed and Sun.

Christiania Free Commune

On the eastern edge of Christianshavn, situated on the derelict site of a former military barracks, *Christiania*, the 'Free City of Copenhagen', is a working experiment in alternative lifestyles and communal living. First occupied in 1970, it is now home to approximately 1000 people and several hundred dogs. Once away from the drug vendors, clothes stalls and eco-cafés, the area is seductively rural, with picturesque farmhouses and wooden cabins overlooking the calm waterways of the *Stadsgraven*. Guided tours can be arranged (see *Tours of the City*).
Prinsessegade/Badsmandsstræde
Tel: 3257 9670. Fax: 3257 6005 (tours).
Website: www.christiania.org
Transport: Bus 8 to Prinsessegade.
Opening hours: Daily 24 hours.
Admission: Free; Dkk30 per person (guided tours).

Further Distractions

Royal Copenhagen Porcelain Factory

The exquisite craftsmanship behind Royal Copenhagen porcelain and an opportunity to see how *Flora Danica* tableware is made is provided during a tour of the *Royal Copenhagen Porcelain Factory* in Frederiksberg. The factory is housed in one of the oldest and most beautiful buildings in Copenhagen, a Renaissance house dating from 1616.
Smallegade 47
Tel: 3814 9297. Fax: 3814 9915.
E-mail: tourism&events@royalskandinavia.dk
Website: www.royalcopenhagen.com
Transport: Bus 1, 14 or 39.

Opening hours: Mon–Fri 1000, 1100, 1300 and 1400 (tours in English).
Admission: Dkk40 (concessions available).

Experimentarium

Experimentarium is Denmark's only science centre, which opened in 1991 in the old bottling hall of the Tuborg Brewery. Visitors of all ages can interact with approximately 300 entertaining and informative sound and water exhibits and experiments. The centre also stages science demonstrations, workshop activities and special exhibitions.
Tuborg Havnevej 7, Hellerup
Tel: 3927 3333. Fax: 3927 3395.
E-mail: info@experimentarium.dk
Website: www.experimentarium.dk
Transport: Bus 6, 21 or 650S; S-train to Hellerup (then bus 21 or 650S) or Svanemøllen (then bus 6 or 650S).
Opening hours: Mon and Wed–Fri 0900–1700, Tues 0900–2100, Sat and Sun 1100–1700.
Admission: Dkk95 (concessions available).

Guinness World Records Museum

Visitors can experience over 500 outstanding world records – from the tallest man to the most poisonous frog – and try what it feels like to drive at 500kph (311mph) or take on the world's best fighter. There is even a chance of bumping into Harry Potter, the latest addition to the museum, because of his phenomenal success.
Østergade 16
Tel: 3332 3131.
E-mail: museum@guinness.dk
Website: www.guinness.dk
Transport: Bus 1, 6, 10, 31, 7E, 15E, 17E or 29; S-train or Metro to Kongens Nytorv.
Opening hours: Sun–Thurs 1000–1800, Fri–Sat 1000–2000 (Sep–May); daily 1000–2200 (Jun–Aug).
Admission: Dkk74 (concessions available).

Carlsberg Visitors Centre and Carlsberg Museum

Carlsberg is, according to its own long-running marketing campaign, 'probably the best lager in the world'. Whether or not visitors agree with that claim, the Visitors Centre is an intoxicating experience. The tour details the history of the brewery, as well as the modern processes of the brewery, with a route through the production plant. At the end, there is a chance to sample the finished product. There is also the *Carlsberg Museum*, situated in a beautiful house dating back to 1882, where extensive exhibits illustrate the cultural and historical relevance of the family and the brewery.
Carlsberg Visitors Centre
Gamle Carlsbergvej 11
Tel: 3327 1314. Fax: 3327 4709.
Carlsberg Museum
Valby Langgade 1
Tel: 3327 1273.
E-mail: visitors@carlsberg.com
Website: www.carlsberg.com
Transport: Bus 6 or 18; S-train to Valby.
Opening hours: Tues–Sun 1000–1600 (Visitors Centre); Mon–Fri 1000–1500 (Museum).
Admission: Free.

Tours of the City

Walking Tours

Two-hour guided walks (in English) to various parts of the Old City are offered by *Wonderful Copenhangen Tourist Information* (tel: 3297 1440; website:

www.visitcopenhagen.dk). These depart from Bernstorffsgade (May to September) and cost Dkk100. During July and August, *Copenhagen Excursions* (tel: 3254 0606; fax: 3257 4905; e-mail: info@cex.dk; website: www.cex.dk), offers two-hour walking tours of the city, starting from the City Hall Square (Rådhuspladsen), for Dkk70. In summer (May/June to September), there are various specialist walking tours; information is available from *Wonderful Copenhagen*. For example, it is possible to step back in time and walk the streets with *Hans Christian Andersen* (tel: 3284 7435; cost: Dkk75 for a 90-minute tour) or with the nightwatchman on one of the *Old Nightwatchman's Rounds* (tel: 3964 4894; cost: Dkk50 for a 90-minute tour).

Throughout the year, on Saturdays and Sundays, *Copenhagen Walking Tours* (e-mail: info@copenhagen-walkingtours.dk; website: www.copenhagen-walkingtours.dk) operates two-hour English-language tours costing Dkk75–100. These start from Bernstorffsgade and cover a range of interests, such as 'Highlights of the Old City', 'Rosenborg Castle', 'Historic Copenhagen' or 'Romantic Copenhagen'. Between June and August, the tours also operate on Thursdays and Fridays.

Guided tours of *Christiania*, the 'Free City of Copenhagen' (tel: 3257 9670; fax: 3257 6005; website: www.christiania.org), depart from the main gate, at 1500 Saturday and Sunday only. The tours are guided by a resident of the commune, take approximately 90 minutes and cost Dkk30 per person.

Bus Tours

Copenhagen Excursions (see *Walking Tours* above) organises a number of bus tours around the city, lasting from 90 minutes to seven hours and starting at Dkk130. All tours depart from the City Hall Square (Rådhuspladsen), next to the Palace Hotel. The company also operates the *Open Top Tours*, one-hour, hop-on hop-off multi-lingual tours of all the main sights in the centre of Copenhagen. From April to October, there are daily departures, also from City Hall Square, every hour 0930–1700. Tickets cost Dkk100–120 depending on the route chosen.

Boat Tours

Boat tours through the harbour and canal networks around Christianshavn and Slotsholmen explain the importance of water in the life and history of the city. *DFDS Canal Tours* (tel: 3342 3320 *or* 3264 0431; fax: 3296 9350; e-mail: canal-tours@canal-tours.dk; website: www.canal-tours.dk) operates multi-lingual guided tours of the harbour and the canal; boats depart every half an hour daily April to October from Nyhavn or Gammel Strand. Tours last about 50 minutes and cost Dkk50. Canal Tours also operates hop-on hop-off *Waterbus* tours without guides. There are two routes, which both depart from Nyhavn; a one-day pass for both routes costs Dkk40. There is also a two-hour two-course 'Dinner Cruise' on-board an elegant restaurant boat, which cruises through historic maritime Copenhagen.

Netto Boats (tel: 3254 4102; website: www.netto-baadene.dk) offers a one-hour guided tour of the harbour and canals for Dkk25. Boats depart frequently April to October from outside Holmens Church, opposite the Old Stock Exchange.

Bicycle Tours

City Safari (tel: 3323 9490; website: www. citysafari.dk) offers a number of themed bicycle tours, including 'Historic Copenhagen' (Dkk150; two and a half hours) and or 'Copenhagen by Night' (Dkk250; three hours). More extensive tours include 'Round Carlsberg', 'In the Footsteps of Hans Christian Andersen' or 'The Big Architecture Ride' (all Dkk350 and four and a half hours). Most tours operate May to September, are conducted in Danish and English and start from the *Danish Centre for Architecture*, in the Gammel Dok Storehouse on Christianshavn (credit cards not accepted). The 'cycle taxi' company, *Quickshaw* (tel: 7020 1375; e-mail: info@quickshaw.biz; website: www.quickshaw.biz), offers four sightseeing tours, lasting one to three hours and costing Dkk100–760 for two people.

Other Tours

Kayak Sightseeing (tel: 4050 4006; fax: 3254 1440; e-mail: kajakole@mail.tele.dk; website: www.kajakole.dk)

offers guided tours of Copenhagen's waterways in kayaks with professional instructors. Tours depart from Gammel Strand and last from 90 minutes to three hours, costing between Dkk165 and Dkk195.

Excursions

For a Half Day

Bakken: Located at Dyrehavevej 62, Klampenborg, in the northern suburbs of Copenhagen, and accessed by S-train C to Klampenborg, the *Bakken* amusement park (tel: 3963 3544; fax: 3963 0138; website: www. bakken.dk) provides an attractive and low-cost alternative to Tivoli. The oldest amusement park in Europe is open daily 1400–2400, from March/April to August, boasting wooded parkland and herds of deer as well as the usual rollercoasters and various rides. Admission to the park is free and all rides are charged at different prices, although it is possible to get a single one-day 'ticket' – in the form of a wristband – for all the rides in Bakken, which costs Dkk198.

The Louisiana Museum of Modern Art: This museum (tel: 4919 0719; fax: 4919 3505; e-mail: curatorial@louisiana.dk; website: www.louisiana.dk) is set in lovely parkland, on the North Zealand coast, 35km (22 miles) north of Copenhagen. It houses a world-class collection of modern art by artists such as Francis Bacon, Max Ernst, Giacometti, Henry Moore, Picasso and Andy Warhol. Humlebæk-Louisiana Station is a 36-minute train ride from Copenhagen. Drivers can take the picturesque coastal road, 'Strandvejen'. The museum is open daily 1000–1700 (until 2200 on Wednesday) and admission costs Dkk72 (concessions available).

Arken Museum of Modern Art: Located at Skovvej 100, in the Køge Bugt Strandpark, this museum (tel: 4354 0222; fax: 4354 0522; e-mail: reception@arken.dk; website: www.arken.dk) was designed by Danish architect Søren Robert Lund to blend into the dune landscape of Ishøj Strand. The museum café affords beautiful views across the bay. Public transport from Copenhagen is by S-train to Ishøj Station or bus 128. Admission costs Dkk55 (concessions available) and opening times are Tuesday to Sunday 1000–1700 (until 2100 on Wednesday).

For a Whole Day

'Castle Tour of North Zealand': *Copenhagen Excursions* (tel: 3254 0606; fax: 3257 4905; e-mail: info@cex.dk; website: www.cex.dk) organises this seven-hour tour for Dkk400. It includes a visit to *Kronborg Slot* in Helsingør (Elsinore) – claimed as the setting for Shakespeare's *Hamlet* – *Fredensborg Slot*, the royal summer residence, and the *Frederiksborg Slot* in Hillrød, a Renaissance palace, built by Christian IV and now a museum.

Roskilde: *Roskilde*, the oldest town in Denmark, is situated approximately ten kilometres (six miles) west of Copenhagen – a 30-minute train journey from the city. It is famed for its Viking heritage, as the *Roskilde Museum*, Sankt Ols Gade 18 (tel: 4631 6500; website: www.roskildemuseum.dk), reveals. The museum is open daily 1100–1600 and admission costs Dkk25. The local tourist information office, Gullandsstræde 15 (tel: 4635 2700; fax: 4635 1474; e-mail: info@destination-roskilde.dk; website: www. destination-roskilde.dk), can provide details of other interesting sites, such as the *Domkirke*, *Ledreborg Castle* and the *Roskilde Fjord*.

The Little Mermaid

Nyhavn at night

ACCOMMODATION

With a number of new openings and some renovations, the hotel scene in Copenhagen has greatly improved over the last few years. As the city is so compact, most hotels are located within walking distance of the centre. Today, the city offers more than 12,000 hotel rooms in total, with another 2200 new rooms opening before the end of 2004.

VAT (*MOMS*) of 25% is automatically included in all hotel prices, as is a city environmental tax. Additionally, it is customary to give porters a small tip.

The prices quoted below are the lowest standard rates for a double room, including VAT but excluding breakfast, unless otherwise specified. Many hotels offer promotional rates, seasonal discounts, special packages and discounts for booking via the Internet.

Business

DGI Byens

One of Copenhagen's newer hotels, the *DGI Byens* is part of a massive sports and business complex located just a short walk from Copenhagen's main railway station. The conference facilities cater for up to 1400 delegates, while the hotel itself has 104 smartly designed rooms. The decor is simple but stylish, with pine floors and mood lighting. Other plus points include a large swimming pool, Internet access through the in-room TVs, and a health spa. For guests staying over the weekend, there are also plenty of family and entertainment facilities, including a water playground and a bowling alley.
Tietgensgade 65
Tel: 3329 8000. Fax: 3329 8080.
E-mail: info@dgi-byen.dk
Website: www.dgi-byen.dk
Price: From Dkk1400 (including breakfast).

First Hotel Vesterbro

Opened at the start of the new millennium, this very central four-star hotel is geared towards the business end of the market. The 403 classically simple rooms all have modem points for high-speed Internet access, as well as ADSL Internet access through the in-room TVs, trouser presses and safes, although some of the rooms are a touch on the small side. A number of rooms have been pitched at the single female traveller and feature such extras as cosmetics and glossy magazines. Disabled travellers are also looked after, with dedicated facilities in some rooms. Other facilities include an IT and business centre.
Vesterbrogade 23–29
Tel: 3378 8000. Fax: 3378 8080.
E-mail: reception.copenhagen@firsthotels.dk
Website: www.firsthotels.com
Price: From Dkk1753.

Hilton Copenhagen Airport

This five-star hotel opened in 2001, mainly to cater for the business market. With Copenhagen Airport now linked to the city centre by a 15-minute shuttle journey and to a number of other Swedish cities by express train, the *Hilton* enjoys a very convenient location right next to the rail terminal at the airport. The hotel has a refreshing modern Scandinavian decor; features include underground parking, an exclusive, well-equipped fitness centre, and a swimming pool. There is also a whole floor of meeting rooms (16 in total) that cater for everything from small groups to larger conferences (up to 450 delegates). Visitors can choose to book a room on one of two exclusive floors, availing themselves of private breakfast facilities, a day-long bar, lounge and direct booking-in service. The hotel's two restaurants serve imaginative dishes of the highest standards with a wine list, service and attention to detail to match.
Ellehammersvej 20
Tel: 3250 1501. Fax: 3252 8528.
Website: www.copenhagen.hilton.com
Price: From Dkk1995 (excluding tax).

Radisson SAS Scandinavia Hotel

This massive hotel boasting 499 rooms and 43 suites is handily located close to Copenhagen's international airport. Features include free parking, a swimming pool, gym, squash courts, the only casino in town, four restaurants and a business centre. There are also non-smoking floors. Room styles vary between what the hotel labels Italian, Oriental and Scandinavian. In terms of conference facilities, the hotel can cater for 1600 delegates, with specialist consultants on hand to tailor each event to the client's needs. One drawback is the 20-minute walk into the city centre.
Amager Boulevard 70
Tel: 3396 5000. Fax: 3396 5500.
Website: www.radissonsas.com
Price: From Dkk1830.

Luxury

Admiral Hotel

Located right on the waterfront, where picturesque old schooners and yachts moor, the four-star *Admiral Hotel* is situated in a listed warehouse building dating from 1787, in close proximity to Amalienborg. Much remains of the original warehouse with its rustic charm, metre-thick brick walls, archways and ancient beams of Pomeranian pine, which provided the framework for a recent and massive refurbishment. All 366 rooms are furnished in solid teak, with fittings and furniture exclusively designed by Danish company Trip Trap. All rooms have modem points, state-of-the-art radio and TV systems with video-on-demand, Internet and e-mail connections. The hotel has a well-equipped business centre, while three modular meeting rooms make this an ideal venue for business meetings and lunches. *SALT* is the name of the bar and restaurant, where head chef Casper Vedel Jensen runs a 'European' kitchen 'with Danish traditions'.
Toldbodgade 24–28
Tel: 3374 1414. Fax: 3374 1416.
E-mail: info@admiralhotel.dk
Website: www.admiralhotel.dk
Price: From Dkk1365.

Hotel d'Angleterre

The *Hotel d'Angleterre* is regarded as the city's finest hotel, offering a world of elegance with traditions

and an atmosphere from a bygone era combined with modern comfort. Royalty, presidents, film and pop stars often stay at this five-star hotel, which is centrally located in a 17th-century building next to the busy Strøget pedestrian thoroughfare. Features include modem points for high-speed Internet access in all rooms, the *Arndal Spa and Fitness Centre* with pool facilities and concierges that are considered to be the most knowledgeable and useful in the city.
Kongens Nytorv 34
Tel: 3312 0095. Fax: 3312 1118.
E-mail: anglehot@remmen.dk
Website: www.remmen.dk
Price: From Dkk2470.

Radisson SAS Royal Hotel

This 260-room five-star hotel opened in 1960 and was originally designed by the world-renowned Danish architect, Arne Jacobsen. However, it has been completely and stylishly refurbished to reflect modern hotel design concepts while retaining the spirit of Jacobsen. There are good business facilities, which include modem points for high-speed Internet access in all rooms and well-equipped computer workstations. The suites are among the best in town, with impressive views over the city skyline, while the *Alberto K* gourmet restaurant offers up to ten courses of outstanding Danish-Italian cuisine.
Hammerichsgade 1
Tel: 3342 6000. Fax: 3342 6100.
Website: www.radissonsas.com
Price: From Dkk2045.

Moderate

Hotel City

Located in the middle of historic Copenhagen, close to Nyhavn, Kongens Nytorv and Amalienborg, this bright and refreshingly designed three-star hotel has been family run since 1955, although, today, it is also part of the Best Western chain. The 81 rooms are all tastefully decorated in modern Danish style and are equipped with basic facilities, such as a writing desk, telephone and cable TV. Although high-speed Internet connections in all the rooms are planned, for now there are two computers on the ground floor providing free Internet access for guests. A small meeting room can comfortably accommodate up to 20 people. Being just off the beaten track, this is a very quiet location, ideal for anyone wanting to get away from the hustle and bustle of the city centre.
Peder Skramsgade 24
Tel: 3313 0666. Fax: 3313 0667.
E-mail: hotelcity@hotelcity.dk
Website: www.hotelcity.dk
Price: From Dkk1250 (including breakfast).

Hotel Selandia

Very handily located in central Copenhagen, near the main railway station and the tourist information office, the *Selandia* is popular with the domestic business community. Booking well ahead for the simple but comfortable, excellent-value rooms is recommended. There are basic business facilities available through reception and trouser presses in all rooms, although some of the rooms are not en suite.
Helgolandsgade 12
Tel: 3331 4610. Fax: 3331 4609.
E-mail: hotel-selandia@city.dk
Website: www.hotel-selandia.dk
Price: From Dkk740 (including breakfast).

Other Recommendations

71 Nyhavn

This trendy hotel is set in the picturesque locale of Nyhavn, a canalside area of the city that teems with bars and cafés. The hotel has 150 rooms and suites and occupies two 19th-century warehouses originally used to store spices and other goods from East Asia. The wood-beamed ceilings and the charming Old World ambience, which make the hotel so special, have been retained. All guest rooms have telephone, radio, cable-TV with in-house video, mini-bar, trouser press and hair dryer. Executive rooms and suites are also equipped with ironing boards, fax machines and bath robes. Early booking is essential to secure one of the rooms facing the waterfront, while the waterfront corner suites are particularly sought after. Business facilities are limited, although there is one meeting room capable of accommodating 16 delegates.
Nyhavn 71
Tel: 3343 6200. Fax: 3343 6201.
E-mail: 71nyhavnhotel@arp-hansen.dk
Website: www.71nyhavnhotelcopenhagen.dk
Price: From Dkk1650 (excluding environmental tax).

Hotel Kong Frederick

This unique four-star hotel is located on the site of a 14th-century pub and until recently it served that very purpose. These days, *Kong Frederick* is something of a local secret – a very comfortable, atmospheric place to stay in the city centre, just a stone's throw from City Hall Square (Rådhuspladsen). Each of the highly individual rooms looks different, although the same English country-house feel remains throughout. Attractive decor touches include the use of plenty of dark woods and paintings of the Danish royal family. All rooms have modem points for high-speed Internet access and standard business services are also available. Complimentary access to the Hotel d'Angleterre's spa and fitness centre is available to guests.
Vester Voldgade 25
Tel: 3312 5902. Fax: 3393 5901.
E-mail: booking.hkf@remmen.dk
Website: www.remmen.dk
Price: From Dkk1440.

Phoenix Hotel

The four-star *Phoenix Hotel* – centrally located in the heart of the financial district and only a short walk from Nyhavn – offers 213 rooms and suites, all lightly and tastefully furnished in a style inspired by the French Louis XVI period. There is a charming, romantic air about the hotel, although it caters equally as well for business visitors as it does for holidaymakers, having modem connections in most rooms and a small business centre offering a full range of facilities.
Bredgade 37
Tel: 3395 9500. Fax: 3333 9833.
E-mail: phoenixcopenhagen@arp-hansen.dk
Website: www.phoenixcopenhagen.dk
Price: From Dkk1990 (reduced rates and inclusive breakfast at weekends).

RESTAURANTS

The days when Copenhagen's restaurants were considered dull and uninteresting are long gone, as various international cuisines have made their mark on the city – most notably French and Oriental. Allied to this growth has been a recent resurgence in Modern Danish, which uses the freshest local ingredients and infuses them with new flavours.
The selected restaurants have been divided into five categories: Gastronomic, Business, Trendy, Budget and Personal Recommendations. The restaurants are listed alphabetically within these different categories, which serve as guidelines rather than absolute definitions of the establishments.
VAT (*MOMS*) of 25% is automatically included in the prices given by Copenhagen restaurants. Service charge is not usually added to the restaurant bill, so a tip of around 5% will be appreciated, perhaps more for cheaper restaurants.
The prices quoted below are for an average three-course meal for one person and for a bottle of house wine or cheapest equivalent; they include VAT but do not include service charge or tip.

Gastronomic

Gastronomique

Gastronomique offers a totally unique restaurant experience, set amid a leafy park, away from the bustle of the city, in a homely yet stylish venue. The cuisine is Modern Danish and the views of the park are part of the relaxing gourmet experience. Specialities include foie gras, grilled turbot and glazed Norway lobster.
Fredericksbergs Runddel 1
Tel: 3834 8436. Fax: 3834 8436.
E-mail: lasse@powerpage.dk
Website: www.gastronomique.dk
Price: Dkk550. Wine: Dkk200.

Kong Hans Kaelder

This one-star Michelin restaurant claims to be housed in the oldest building in Copenhagen. Starters include foie gras and sautéed scallops with wild mushrooms, while mains feature grilled turbot and other fresh seafood, with the signature dessert being chocolate soufflé. The food is served up on metal plates in the charming surrounds of the historical building, where 500-year old Gothic arches and wooden floorboards lend a medieval atmosphere to the restaurant.
Vingaardsstraede 6
Tel: 3311 6868. Fax: 3332 6768.
E-mail: konghans@mail.tele.dk
Website: www.konghans.dk
Price: Dkk700. Wine: Dkk250.

Photo: Wonderful Copenhagen

Danish cuisine

Le Sommelier

Another fine dining temple, complete with white linen tablecloths and immaculately attired waiting staff, that proves how much the Danes love top-class French food. Specialities include foie gras as a starter and a number of seafood and shellfish mains, depending on availability and season. The food is accompanied by a gargantuan wine list that caters for even the most demanding palate; there are rumoured to be almost 1000 different wines, with over 30 sold by the glass. No lunch weekends.
Bredgade 63–65
Tel: 3311 4515. Fax: 3311 5979.
E-mail: mail@lesommelier.dk
Website: www.lesommelier.dk
Price: Dkk350. Wine: Dkk250.

Pierre André

This minimalist restaurant has been offering French cuisine of the highest quality since 1996. It gained its single Michelin star one year later and has held onto it ever since. The roast foie gras is a particular highlight on an innovative and beguiling menu. Other specialities are oysters or lobster as starters and braised sole, pigeon or veal as mains. There are three set menus to choose from, including one mammoth nine-course extravaganza (Dkk695). Another plus is that they bake all their own bread and desserts. No lunch Saturday. Closed Sunday and Monday.
Ny Østergade 21
Tel: 3316 1719. Fax: 3316 1772.
Price: Dkk500. Wine: Dkk250.

Restaurationen

This French restaurant has one Michelin star under its belt and this is well deserved. *Restaurationen* boasts high ceilings and walls adorned with black and white photos of the cooking team. Head chef Bo Jacobsen conjures up an impressive array of dishes with the freshest local produce. The menu follows the changing seasons but, whatever the time of year, booking is essential. The restaurant also bakes its own bread and makes its own sausages and hams, which are made with organic ingredients wherever possible.
Montergade 19
Tel: 3314 9495.
Price: Dkk450. Wine: Dkk250.

Business

Alberto K at The Royal

Alberto K is the centrepiece of the newly refurbished Radisson SAS Royal Hotel. To run a restaurant in the name of Alberto Kappenberger (the first manager of this hotel and an enormous fan of Arne Jacobsen's design) requires something out of the ordinary design-wise, as well as an innovative and expert gastronomy. The *Alberto K* lives up to this high standard. The unusual Scandinavian-Italian symbiosis works well for diners who appreciate the love of ingredients and the care in preparation that is manifest in everything on offer – from the homemade durum bread to that morning's lobster from Thyborøn. Other creations include ham from Parma and its well-smoked counterpart from Løgumkloster, rabbit with truffle oil from Umbria, spring cabbage with polenta, and lump fish with Tuscan rosemary. *Alberto K* also boasts an extensive, mainly Italian, wine list. To top it off, the views from the location on the 20th floor are superb, making this a spectacular setting for a business lunch or a longer dinner.
Hammerichsgade 1
Tel: 3342 6161.
E-mail: salescphzh@cphza.rdsas.com
Website: www.alberto-k.dk
Price: Dkk500. Wine: Dkk250.

Cap Horn

By day, this is the perfect place for a *smørrebrød* sandwich, in the pleasant canalside setting. When the temperature stays up at night, *Cap Horn* is also a good place for a relaxed business dinner by the water's edge, with more substantial Mediterranean options, such as grilled fish and steak, on the menu. The excellent range of desserts at dinner is another plus point, as is the cosy atmosphere of this former jazz club.
Nyhavn 21
Tel: 3312 8504. Fax: 3315 7130.
Price: Dkk300. Wine: Dkk150.

Kommandanten

Denmark's only two-star Michelin restaurant continually delivers and is the perfect venue for impressing clients, as well as severely denting the platinum card. The building, dating from 1698, is a typical burgher's house of the period, with numerous small rooms on several floors. The restaurant enjoys an effortless style, with silver service set against long windows, wooden floors and a quietly contemporary elegance. The main culinary influence is French and the service is first rate. Sample dishes include duck breast with port wine sauce, pork shank with morels, as well as fried Norway lobster à la nage served with aniseed and spring onions, although there is also a 'special' menu offering six small dishes for a fixed price of Dkk690. The wine list contains some 1000 wines, many available in half bottles.
Ny Adelgade 7
Tel: 3312 0990. Fax: 3393 1223.
E-mail: kommandanten@kommananten.dk
Website: www.kommandanten.dk
Price: Dkk600. Wine: Dkk250.

Peder Oxe

Situated right on Grabrodretorv, the city's most beautiful square, *Peder Oxe* specialises in traditional Danish cooking and is a good place to get to grips with the nation's culinary larder. The decor is suitably old fashioned. It may attract too many tourists for some tastes but the quality of the food is still high, with specialities like the eponymous oxe burger and the oxe steak.
Grabrodretorv 11
Tel: 3311 0077.
Website: www.pederoxe.dk
Price: Dkk340. Wine: Dkk147 (70cl carafe).

Søren K

Located in the Black Diamond, the Royal Library, *Søren K* continues to win praise from the Danish press for its super-modern minimalism. This is a splendid venue for impressing clients. The decor is bright and trendy, with modern lines and colours. Fresh seafood – such as grilled halibut with beetroot risotto, balsamic vinegar and oyster vinaigrette – is a speciality but all the produce is of the highest quality.
Søren Kirkegaards Plads 1
Tel: 3347 4949. Fax: 3347 4951.
E-mail: soerenk@kb.dk
Website: www.soerenk.dk
Price: Dkk500. Wine: Dkk300.

Trendy

Barstarten

One of the hottest new nightlife venues in Copenhagen, *Barstarten* also offers very good food. At weekends, locals and savvy visitors flock to this funky venue for the DJ sets and the buzzing atmosphere. The normal menu includes fresh Mediterranean dishes – highlights are the Mediterranean polenta with roast vegetables, and the grilled fish – which are served with fresh salads. The Sunday brunch menu is also good value. Booking is advisable, seeing as only 25 covers can be catered for at once.
Kapelvej 1
Tel: 3524 1100.
E-mail: bar@barstarten.dk
Website: www.barstarten.dk
Price: Dkk250. Wine: Dkk160.

Formel B

Formel B is an unexpected find in a busy part of the city. Head chef Singh Gill performs culinary wonders with the freshest of local produce, in a stylish setting that just manages to avoid being pretentiously hip, with polished wooden floors and a sleek, minimalist look. The cooking is French with a funky accent and

Photo: Wonderful Copenhagen

The entrance to Tivoli

includes codfish with oysters, bouillon of quail with truffles and foie gras, and mushroom pie with walnuts. The restaurant's six-course menu is among the best in the city. Reservations strongly recommended. No lunch. Closed Sunday.
Vesterbrogade 182
Tel: 3325 1066. Fax: 3325 2092.
E-mail: bordbestilling@formel-b.dk
Website: www.formel-b.dk
Price: Dkk550 (six-course set menu, plus Dkk450 wine pairing). Wine: Dkk365.

Konrad

Konrad, one of the leading lights of the modern Scandinavian culinary revolution of the mid-1990s, remains one of the most respected restaurants in the city. In tribute to the English design guru and restaurateur, Terence Conran, Konrad's geometrically clean and stylish interior, DJ bar and cool clientele ensure this venue's continued popularity. A hip restaurant with equally hip clientele, this is the place to see and be seen. The food combines French cuisine with Danish influences in an imaginative way, including such offerings as *boeuf Béarnaise*, beef carpaccio with cauliflower served with lemon and parmesan, and stuffed crab and lemon sole with oyster sauce, saffron and bacon. At weekends, after midnight, the restaurant is transformed into a stylish cocktail bar.
Pilestraede 12–14
Tel: 3393 2929. Fax: 3393 5696.
E-mail: good@living.dk
Website: www.restaurantkonrad.dk
Price: Dkk400. Wine: Dkk225.

La Petite Bourgogne

The three-storey *La Petite Bourgogne*, situated in a corner of the Kultorvet marketplace, specialises in classic Burgundy dishes – something of a novelty so far from its home but definitely worth checking out, especially for lovers of the accompanying Burgundy wine. The decor is a relaxing burgundy red with contemporary paintings on the walls. There are three menus: a taster of five or six courses (from Dkk399), the Burgundy menu and an à la carte menu. Starters include snails in garlic butter, flaky smoked salmon with watercress, or an excellent crayfish and cauliflower soup, while mains, such as Bresse chicken breast served with a morel cream sauce or rabbit in bacon with Dijon sauce, will delight. There is also the classic repertoire of coq au vin and boeuf bourguignon, plus a splendid selection of Burgundy cheeses. Booking recommended. No lunch.
Kultorvet 5
Tel: 3391 0949. Fax: 3369 0581.
E-mail: mail@niscos.dk
Website: www.lapetitebourgogne.dk
Price: Dkk350. Wine: Dkk175.

Restaurant Godt

Run by an Anglo-Danish husband and wife team, this small restaurant more than justifies its Michelin star. The focus is on fresh local meats and seafood given innovative culinary twists. The daily changing set menus (three, four or five courses) might include Norwegian lobster bisque served with monkfish and red caviar, or brill with a beurre blanc of oysters, or veal with a morel sauce. The wine list is extensive but diners can also choose to have a 'wine menu' offering a glass of different wine to accompany each course (Dkk100 per course). The simple two-decked restaurant is very relaxing and tastefully decorated – only pictures of the

Nyhaven

late King Frederick and Queen Ingrid, parents of the present Queen, adorn the dove-grey walls. There is a very limited number of tables and *Godt* is no longer the closely guarded secret that it once was, so booking as far ahead as possible is essential. No lunch. Closed Sunday and Monday.
Gothersgade 38
Tel: 3315 2122.
Price: Dkk445 (set menu). Wine: Dkk250.

Budget

Barock

This bright bar-restaurant, the first restaurant in Nyhavn, is extremely elegant, decorated in the style of Louis XVI with an ornate tiled ceiling and rosehead wall lights. Nevertheless, *Barock* makes it into the 'budget' category as it offers excellent modern Danish cuisine at outstanding value for money. As well as pastas, salads, steak and chicken dishes, the menu includes shrimps with potatoes and avocado, lemon sole poached in white wine, as well as tempting desserts like walnut pie with chocolate and crème fraiche or dark and white chocolate mousse with orange sauce. There is also a fairly comprehensive wine list. From April to October, the waterside terrace is the place to be on a warm summer's evening, enjoying a meal while watching the world go by.
Nyhavn 1
Tel: 3333 0151. Fax: 3333 0311.
Website: www.barock.dk
Price: Dkk280. Wine: Dkk140.

Pasta Basta

This popular budget restaurant offers 15 different types of pasta dishes and the options are imaginative, such as fettuccine in a white wine sauce with grilled salmon strips, garnished with salmon caviar and saffron. The unfussy, unpretentious surroundings are bright and airy and also home to an all-you-can-eat daily buffet. As well as being good value for money, *Pasta Basta* is family friendly and has over 150 seats, able cater for large groups.
Valkendorfsgade 22
Tel: 3311 2131.
Website: www.pastabasta.dk
Price: Dkk200 (à la carte); Dkk79 (fixed-price buffet). Wine: Dkk110.

Restaurant Kultorvet

This bistro is situated on a corner of the Kultorvet market and serves a decent Danish menu, both set (Dkk99.50–140.50) and à la carte. The cubicle layout, decorated with old plates and photographs of Copenhagen in years gone by, makes for intimate conversation. The restaurant is ideal for a light lunch, with its popular open sandwiches (*smørrebrød*) with herring, egg, shrimps or smoked salmon. Alternatively, for a more substantial early evening meal (the bistro closes around 2000), there are good-value standbys, like pork with Béarnaise sauce and salad.
Kultorvet 2
Tel: 3314 7099.
Price: Dkk150. Wine: Dkk155.

Restaurant Puk

This slightly down-at-heel basement bar-restaurant is not the place for those who want a sophisticated or elegant setting. Although its rustic atmosphere, with wooden beams, old photographs and paintings, is enhanced by various objects dotted around – ancient cash registers, dolls, battered musical instruments, books and statuettes – adding to its quirky, off-beat appeal. And for no-nonsense basic Danish cuisine, it is difficult to find anywhere better. House specialities include herrings in various guises – pickled, marinated and curried – Wiener schnitzel, fillet of ox baked on an oak platter (*planksteak*), and 'old cheese' served with a splash of rum.
Vandkunsten 8
Tel: 3311 1417.
Price: Dkk250. Wine: Dkk159.

Shark House Deli

This small, lively deli is perfect for anyone looking for a tasty and quick lunch in the trendy Nørrebro area. The Italian and French deli food on offer – mainly sandwiches, salads, houmous and soup – is among the cheapest in the city and great value for its high quality. Most people grab something 'to go', although there are tables in summer for a more leisurely meal.
Blagardsgade 3
Tel: 3335 3135.
E-mail: sharkhouse@mail.dk
Price: Dkk100. Unlicensed.

Photo: Wonderful Copenhagen

Photo: Wonderful Copenhagen

Copenhagen International Jazz Festival

Personal Recommendations

1.th

This restaurant is something of a local secret and is set to remain that way unless it changes its booking policy. Diners have to book weeks in advance and then receive an 'invitation' to come around for dinner at 1900 in this homely yet impeccably stylish second-floor venue. The set menus take diners on a unique culinary journey, lasting the entire evening, through a variety of cuisines and many different styles of cooking, although primarily Modern Danish with a classical basis. Owner Mette Martinussen's favourite dish is rumoured to be sausages and these do often feature on the menu. There is only space for 16 or so diners and the nine-course dinner has to be paid for in advance (fixed price). Closed Sunday, Monday and Tuesday.
Herluf Trollesgade 9
Tel: 3393 5770. Fax: 3393 6769.
Website: www.1th.dk
Price: Dkk900 (including wine).

Café Victor

A small L-shaped bistro situated on the corner of Ny Østergade and Hovedvagtsgade, *Café Victor* is proving popular with celebrities. Divided into a bar-café and a restaurant, it combines excellent Danish food with fast and friendly service. The menu features herring in various guises, good salads and familiar dishes with pork, steak and fish. Fresh oysters are served daily. This is an excellent, chatty place for a quick lunch, while the restaurant merits a longer stay for a relaxing dinner.
Ny Østergade 8
Tel: 3313 3613. Fax: 3391 1340.
E-mail: cafevictor@sovino.dk
Website: www.cafevictor.dk
Price: Dkk300. Wine: Dkk180.

Cascabel Madhus

Vegetarian heaven is the best way to describe this popular, good-value restaurant. *Cascabel Madhus* is located off the main tourist trail but is still close to the city centre and, as it does not feature in many guidebooks, it is a good place to eat like the locals do, in unfussy surroundings. The eat-in or take-away menu revolves around vegetarian curries and rice dishes but also includes orange pepper and goat's cheese quiche, chick pea, pepper and basil 'meatballs' (*frikadeller*), and mushrooms with pumpkin seeds, as well as three-choice combination dishes. Excellent

value for money. No dinner. Closed weekends.
Store Kongensgade 80–82
Tel: 3393 7797. Fax: 3393 7786.
E-mail: cascabel@restaurant.dk
Website: www.cascabel.dk
Price: Dkk160. Wine: Dkk140.

Il Ristorante

One of the best Italian restaurants in the city, offering a traditional repertoire of classic Italian pasta and dessert dishes, as well as some tasty, more imaginative concoctions. The fillet of lamb in a red wine sauce, the duck in an orange sauce and the tournedos in a light mustard sauce are all rather special. The wine list is modest but well thought out. Subdued lighting and ochre walls adorned with old paintings make this a smart but relaxed restaurant – an easy place to enjoy an inexpensive meal.
Grønnegade 33
Tel: 3315 1565.
Price: Dkk345. Wine: Dkk180.

Restaurant Ida Davidsen

Proving that there is no such thing as 'just a sandwich', Ida takes the Danish *smørrebrød* tradition to new heights. Her 200-plus creations include such delightful toppings as smoked salmon, beef tartar and caviar. This is a real Copenhagen institution, with walls bedecked with old family photos. Diners should remember, however, that *Restaurant Ida Davidsen* is a lunch venue only and it closes at 1700 (the kitchen closes at 1600). Closed weekends.
Store Kongensgade 70
Tel: 3391 3655.
Price: Dkk85–150. Unlicensed.

ENTERTAINMENT

Nightlife

Nightlife in Copenhagen changes fast and starts late, things rarely get going until after midnight on Friday and Saturday night. The city has an ever-changing range of clubs, restaurants and bars catering to all tastes – from pop to cutting-edge dance music or world-class jazz or pop. The city also has a surprise up its sleeve, in the form of several popular

DJ/bar/restaurant 'hybrids' that change mood and function over the course of an evening. There is no one defined nightlife area, although both Nyhavn and Boltens Gaard are popular.
There are late licensing hours in Copenhagen, with cafés typically open until 0100 or 0200, bars close between 0200 and 0500 and clubs close around 0500. The minimum age for drinking is 18 years. A beer costs Dkk25–50, while a gin and tonic averages around Dkk50. In general, the dress code for most places is not strict.
Copenhagen This Week (website: www.ctw.dk) and the *Wonderful Copenhagen* tourist information website (www.visitcopenhagen.dk) both provide further nightlife information.

Bars

A wide range of nightlife venues defy conventional categorisation, such as the pioneering modern Scandinavian restaurant, *Konrad*, Pilestraede 12–14, or *Ultimo*, Hovedvagtsgade 8, *Ketchup*, Pilestræde 19, *BarStarten*, Kapelvej 1, and the trendy *Zoo Bar*, Kronprinsensgade 7. In the daytime, they may function as cafés or restaurants but, in the evening, they become restaurants and/or bars, DJs will appear and suddenly everybody will be on the dancefloor. *Stereo Bar*, Linnésgade 16a, Israels Plads, is a much-loved pre-club joint, with funky 70s decor and an eclectic music policy from easy listening to drum'n'bass. Rather more underground is *Stengade 30*, Stengade 18, in Nørrebro, which blends the best of Danish and overseas rock and dance acts. *The Dubliner*, Amagertorv 5, Strøget, is a genuine Irish restaurant and music pub with nightly live Irish folk/rock music, Irish barmen and a very friendly atmosphere. *Café Victor* (see *Restaurants*) also has a friendly bar area, which is popular with visiting celebrities.

Casinos

Casino Copenhagen, Amager Boulevard 70 (website: www.casinocopenhagen.dk), is open daily 1400–0400 for American and French roulette, blackjack and stud poker. A smart dress code applies and photo ID is required for entrance – entrance is only for those 18 years and older. Admission costs Dkk80 per day.

Clubs

The two top clubs in the city are *Rust*, Guldbergsgade 8, and *Vega*, Enghavevej 40, which are both extremely popular and draw top international DJs and live acts.

The Vega complex is housed in a magnificent 1950s trade union building, while Rust is spread over three floors with a cocktail bar, main bar and large dancefloor. *Park Diskotek*, Østerbrogade 79, close to Parken, the national sports stadium, runs a disco ballroom with DJ music in an authentic 1970s atmosphere. The city's thriving gay scene focuses on *Pan Disco*, Knabrostræde 3, with three floors of lively music, as well as *Sebastian*, Hyskenstræde 10, and *Heaven*, Kompagnistræde 18. For pure dance clubs, head for Boltens Gaard and the *Zero Nightclub and Lounge*, Gothersgade 10B, and *Blue Buddha*, Gothersgade 8F, which was started as a reaction against the high bar prices in the clubs, offering cheap cocktails and beers. If you are still going when the sun is up, head to *Club Blue Note*, Studiestræde 31, which opens at 0500 and serves up techno and house until breakfast.

Live Music

Copenhagen is one of the major European jazz centres, with excellent clubs throughout the city and a festival in July (see *Cultural Events* in *Culture*). The *Copenhagen Jazz House*, Niels Hemmingsensgade 10 (website: www.jazzhouse.dk), is *the* jazz venue, offering top-quality live music followed by a relaxed funk and soul disco. *Vega*, Enghavevej 40, is an established and prestigious cultural institution and Denmark's largest regional venue, annually featuring around 250 concerts. The music profile is rock, modern electric, R'n'B, hip hop, metal and pop. Open-air rock and pop concerts are held at the *Pavillonen*, in Fælledparken, during the summer. The main live music venue in Christiania is *Loppen*, Bådmandsstræde 43, which has regular rock, jazz and other performances. Seedy but hugely atmospheric is *La Fontaine*, Kompagnistræde 11, which is open 2000–0600.

Sport

Denmark hosted the World Badminton Championships in 1999 and is one of the top badminton-playing nations in the world. Local stars include Camilla Martin (1999 World Champion) and Peter Gade. Windsurfing (known as 'boardsailing') is also hugely popular. Football and handball are the favourite team sports. *FC København* (website: www.fck.dk) is the local football team, playing at the national stadium, *Parken*, Øster Allé 50 (tel: 3543 3131; website: www.parken.dk).

Tickets for sporting events are advertised in the Copenhagen papers, however, the easiest way to buy tickets is through the *Call Centre* (tel: 7022 2442).

Badminton

Courts are available for hire at Dkk55 per hour (rackets an extra Dkk25) at *Grøndal Centret*, Hvidkildevej 64 (tel: 3834 1109).

Fitness Centres

Form and Fitness Parken, Øster Allé 42 (tel: 3555 0078; website: www.form-fitness.dk), offers day passes for Dkk200, as do its other outlets – *Form and Fitness Scala*, Vesterbrogade 2–4 (tel: 3332 1002), *Form and Fitness Hotel Scandinavia*, Amager Boulevard 70 (tel: 3254 2888), and *Form and Fitness Radisson SAS Falconer*, Falkoner Allé 9 (tel: 3510 9070). Less costly is the *Hardwork Studio*, Frederiksundsvej 5 (tel: 3581 2283), which charges Dkk250 for four visits.

Golf

The Copenhagen region is a paradise for golfers, with 86 golf courses. The greater Copenhagen area alone has 25, 18-hole courses. Enthusiasts can practise their swings for Dkk126 per hour at the pay-and-play *Copenhagen Indoor Golf Centre*, Refshalevej 177B, Store Stålhal (tel: 3266 1100; e-mail: info@cigc.dk; website: www.cigc.dk). Facilities include an 800m (2624ft) put-and-chip course, 60 driving ranges, a shop and a café. Pay and play at around Dkk150–200 is also available at a number of centres including *Nivå Golf Pay and Play*, Løvbjerggårdsvej 1, Kokkedal (tel: 4914 8888; website: www.nivaa-golfklub.dk), *Smørum Golfcenter*, Skebjergvej (tel: 4497 0111; website: www.smorumgolfcenter.dk), and *Havreholm Slot*, Klosterrisvej 4 (tel: 4975 8600; website: www. havreholm.dk).

Sailing

Boats are available for hire from *Copenhagen Boat Charter*, Rosenborggade 10 (tel: 3393 0333).

Squash

Nørrebrohallen, Bragesgade 5 (tel: 3583 1001; website: www.noerrebrohallen.dk), provides squash courts for Dkk75 per hour. *Copenhagen Squash Club*, Vestersøhus, Vester Søgade (tel: 3311 8638), has courts for hire at Dkk120 per hour.

Swimming

Public pools include *Frederiksberg Swimming Baths*, Helgesvej 29 (tel: 3814 0404), *Vesterbro Swimming Baths*, Angelgade 4 (tel: 3322 0500), and *Øbro-Hallen*, Gunnar Nu Hansens Plads 3 (tel: 3525 7060). Good beaches near the city include *Bellevue* and *Charlottenlund* to the north and *Amager Beach* and the *Beach Park* to the south. There is an open-air pool in *Fælledparken*, Borgmester Jensens Allé 50 (tel: 3539 0804).

Tennis

Booking in advance is necessary at all venues. Indoor and outdoor courts are available for hire for Dkk140–155 per hour at *B93*, Svanemølleanlægget, Ved Sporsløjfen 10 (tel: 3927 1890). *Hotel Mercur*, Vester Farimagsgade 17 (tel: 3312 5711), allows non-residents to use its outdoor courts for Dkk130 per hour. *Københavns Boldklub*, Pile Allé 14 (tel: 3630 2300), and Peter Bangsvej 147 (tel: 3871 4150), charges Dkk115/145 per hour, with an additional Dkk100 per person for non-members.

Windsurfing

Nautic Surf and Ski, Amager beach (tel: 3284 8300), is open all year round.

Shopping

The main international chains and designer boutiques are located around Strøget, interspersed with cafés and restaurants. *Magasin du Nord*, the largest department store in Scandinavia, is situated on Kongens Nytorv. Intriguing second-hand and antique shops are thick on the ground in the Sankt Hans Torv area, while flea markets abound at Israel Plads and Gammel Strand every Saturday.

Shopping hours are normally Monday to Friday 0930/1000 until 1730/1900 and Saturday 0900–1600. Danish shopping hours have now been extended, to allow shops to stay open daily 0600–2000 and smaller outlets at weekends. Most shops are closed on Sunday. Outside normal shopping hours, various kiosks around town are open for the sale of tobacco, newspapers and sweets. Bakeries, florists and confectionery shops remain open most of the time. The Central Station Supermarket is open until late in the evening, as well as all day Sunday. The sale of alcohol is forbidden after 2000.

Typical gifts include Royal Copenhagen porcelain, Scandinavian crystal and amber jewellery. Silver jewellery by designers such as Georg Jensen is also a good option. Contemporary Danish design can be found at *Illums Bolighus*, Amagertorv 10, *Paustian*, Kalkerbrænderilobskaj 2, and *Interstudio Shop*, Dampfærgevej 10. Families might like the plastic classics, *Lego* and *Duplo*, which are also Danish creations.

VAT (*MOMS*) of 25% is charged on most goods. Nationals of countries outside the EU and Scandinavia can claim this back at the airport – only on individual items worth over Dkk300, which have been purchased from shops displaying *Global Refund Denmark* (tel: 3252 5566; website: www.

Strøget

globalrefund.com/denmark) or *Tax Free International* (tel: 4489 2100) emblems. Items must be declared and stamped by customs authorities on departure from the EU.

Culture

Copenhagen is undergoing something of a cultural renaissance with a new Royal Opera House being built at Dokøen, to be opened in 2005, and a new theatre planned for Nyhavn in 2007.

Det Kongelige Teater (The Royal Theatre), Kongens Nytorv (tel: 3369 6933 (information) *or* 6969 (box office); website: www.kgl-teater.dk), has been at the heart of the city's cultural life since the 18th century. The old stage dates from 1874 and is located on the site of a royal theatre since 1748. The Royal Danish Theatre, Royal Danish Opera and Royal Danish Ballet all perform in its opulent circular auditorium, although the opera and ballet will move to the new Royal Opera House at Dokøen.

Tickets for almost all cultural events and performance in the city are sold by *BilletNet* (tel: 3848 1122; website: www.billetnet.dk) at post offices or online. *Copenhagen This Week* (website: www.ctw.dk) and the *Wonderful Copenhagen* tourist information website (www.visitcopenhagen.dk) both provide information on cultural events. The *Copenhagen Post* (website: www.cphpost.dk) is a weekly newspaper, costing Dkk15, which provides Danish news in English, with information on current concerts, films and shows.

Music

Despite the best efforts of numerous Danish composers, it is Danny Kaye's song, 'Wonderful, Wonderful Copenhagen' from the 1952 film, *Hans Christian Andersen*, that buzzes maddeningly in people's heads when they visit the city.

Founded in 1925, the *Danish National Symphony Orchestra* (website: www.dr.dk/rso) is one of the oldest radio symphony orchestras in the world. Closely affiliated to the Symphony Orchestra is the *Danish National Choir*, founded in 1932 (website: www.dr.dk/rk). They both perform at the *DR Concert Hall*, Julius Thomsens Gade, Frederiksberg (tel: 3520 3040).

The *Royal Danish Opera* (website: www.kgl-teater.dk) performs at *Det Kongelige Teater* (see above). The *Royal Danish Orchestra* (website: www.kgl-teater.dk) traces its ancestry to the Royal Trumpet Corps of 1458 and, as such, it is the oldest orchestra in the world. They perform at the *Tivoli Koncertsalen* (Tivoli Concert Hall), Vesterbrogade 3 (tel: 3315 1012; website: website: www.tivoli.dk). This is the city's largest classical music venue, with seating for approximately 1900 people. The hall was decorated by leading Danish artists and stages over 100 concerts, operas and ballets throughout the season (April to September). There are also daily recitals and concerts in the winter garden at the *Ny Carlsberg Glyptotek* (see *Key Attractions*).

Theatre

Det Kongelige Teater (see above) has three stages – the *Gamle Scene* (Old Stage) at Kongens Nytorv, the *Stærekassen* (New Stage) at Tordenskjoldsgade 5, and the *Turbinehallerne* (Turbine Halls), Adelgade 10, in a former power station. Between them, they host classic and contemporary drama, opera and dance performances.

Another major venue is *Det Ny Teater* (The New Theatre), Gammel Kongevej 29 (tel: 3325 5075; fax: 3321 2034; website: www.detnyteater.dk). The *Pantomime Theatre* in Tivoli stages a pantomime daily April to July, usually revolving around the strange relationship between Pierrot and Harlequin.

Dance

The *Royal Ballet* (website: www.kgl-teater.dk) performs at *Det Kongelige Teater* (see above). Founded at the end of the 18th century, under the Italian choreographer, Galeotti, the company achieved its heyday in the 19th century, under August Bournonville. The main venue for contemporary dance is *Dansescenen*, Øster Fælled Torv 34 (tel: 3543 8300; fax: 3543 8110; website: www.dansescenen.dk).

Film

Danish films are now attracting worldwide interest. The director, Lars von Trier, has achieved international acclaim for films such as *Breaking The Waves* (1996) and *The Idiots* (1998). *Festen* (1998), directed by the Danish Thomas Vinterberg, was also a huge success.

The annual *Copenhagen Night Film Festival* (tel: 3312 0005) features films from across the world. Cinema is very popular in the city and most films are shown in the original language with Danish subtitles. Two of the main multiplexes showing the latest blockbusters and action films are *CinemaxX Fisketorvet*, Fisketorvet Shopping Center (tel: 7010 1202), and *Imperial*, Ved Vesterport 4 (tel: 7013 1211). Independent films, shorts and European classics are more the staple repertoire of *Cinemateket*, Gothersgade 55 (tel: 3374 3412), and *Grand Teatret*, Mikkel Bryggers Gade 8 (tel: 3315 1611).

Cultural Events

The *Copenhagen International Jazz Festival* (tel: 3393 2013; fax: 3393 2024; e-mail: info@jazzfestival.dk; website: www.jazzfestival.dk) is held for ten days annually in July. The biggest event of the festival is *Giant Jazz*, in the Circus building, an extravaganza with some of the world's top musicians. Rock is covered in the June *Roskilde Festival* (tel: 4636 6613; fax: 4632 1499; e-mail: info@roskilde-festival.dk; website: www.roskilde-festival.dk), at Roskilde. Despite the tragedy in 2000, when fans of US grunge band Pearl Jam were crushed to death in the crowd, the Roskilde Festival remains one of the most important and popular rock and pop festivals in Europe.

The biannual *Golden Days in Copenhagen Festival* (tel: 3542 1432; fax: 3142 1491; e-mail: info@ goldendays.dk; website: www.goldendays.dk), in September (next 2004), includes exhibitions, concerts, ballet and drama celebrating the Danish Golden Age (1800–50), spearheaded by the likes of Hans Christian Andersen and Søren Kierkegaard. The annual *Kulturnatten* or *Copenhagen Night of Culture* (e-mail: kulturnatten@woco.dk; website: www. kulturnatten.dk) is the night (usually in August, September or October) when locals and visitors wearing a *Culture Badge* can attend special events in the city's museums, galleries, churches, theatres, concert halls, bookshops and cafés.

Literary Notes

Needless to say, Hans Christian Andersen is Copenhagen's most famous literary son. His fairytales, such as the *Little Mermaid* (1837) and the *Ugly Duckling* (1843), are globally recognised. More recently, Peter Høeg has achieved international acclaim for his novel *Miss Smilla's Feeling for Snow* (1992), part of which is set in the city. Karen Blixen (1885–1962), the author of *Out of Africa* (1938), lived a short distance from Copenhagen. Her home at Rungsted Strandvej 111 is now a popular museum – the *Karen Blixen Museet* (tel: 4557 1057; fax: 4557 1058; e-mail: karen-blixen@dinesen.dk; website: www.isak-dinesen.dk).

SPECIAL EVENTS

Ferie: International Travel Exhibition, late Jan, The Bella Centre and Øksnehallen

Copenhagen International Fashion Fair, early Feb, The Bella Centre and Øksnehallen

Night Film Festival, late Mar–early Apr, various venues

Copenhagen Fashion and Design Festival (website: www.nikolaj-ccac.dk), late Mar–earlyApr, Nikolaj Church and various other venues

Queen Margrethe's Birthday Celebrations, 16 Apr, Amalienborg

Scandinavian Furniture Fair, early May, The Bella Centre

Copenhagen Marathon (website: www.sparta.dk), May, Town Hall Square at Vester Voldgade

Midsummer Night's Eve Celebrations, Midsummer Day Jun, throughout the city

Roskilde Festival, rock music festival (website: www.roskilde-festival.dk), late Jun, Roskilde

Copenhagen International Jazz Festival (website: www.jazzfestival.dk), early Jul, various venues

Father Christmas World Congress, Jul, Bakken, north of Copenhagen

Copenhagen International Opera and Ballet season, 14 days in Aug, opera at Søndermarken, Frederiksberg and ballet at Kastellet, near Langelinie

Mermaid Pride Parade, gay parade (website: www.mermaidpride.dk), mid-Aug, route from Nørrebrogade to Town Hall

Festival of Clowns, early Aug, Bakken, north of Copehagen

Kulturnatten (Night of Culture), free performances (website: www.kulturnatten.dk), Aug/Sep/Oct, various venues

Golden Days in Copenhagen Festival, exhibitions, concerts, ballet and drama (website: www.goldendays.dk), biannually Sep, 2004 and 2006, various venues

Copenhagen Blues Festival, third week in Sep, various venues

Copenhagen Gay and Lesbian Film Festival (website: www.cglff.dk), late Oct, various venues

Irish Festival (website: www.irishfestival.dk), early Nov, various venues

Opening of Tivoli's Market, mid-Nov, Tivoli

Christmas in Tivoli, 1–23 Dec, Tivoli

New Year's Eve in Tivoli, 31 Dec, Tivoli

DELHI

Delhi is a daunting city. It sprawls uncontrollably over a vast tract of the Jamuna plain, its population – 13.8 million at the last count – is a seething mass of humanity and its poverty and pollution challenge the sensibilities and respiratory systems of even the most hardened travellers. Those who look beyond the squalor that envelops much of the city, the thundering traffic, the acrid smog and the constant demands of the hustlers will find delights at every turn – historical, architectural, floral and culinary – quite apart from the vivid colour, eastern eccentricity and restless vibrancy that give Delhi its spirit.

Delhi has been the capital of India since Independence in 1947. Even before that, the British moved their capital here from Calcutta in 1911. For much of its history, Delhi was the centre of power for the various Muslim dynasties that ruled swathes of the subcontinent from the 12th century onwards. Modern Delhi is really two cities. Old Delhi, packed into the narrow, filthy streets beneath the Red Fort's imposing walls, is the polar opposite of the grandiose Imperial citadel, broad, leafy boulevards and

well-spaced bungalows of New Delhi, as laid out by Lutyens and Baker in the 1920s. Old Delhi, built by Shah Jahan in the 17th century, is only the latest of seven cities that have existed since the Muslims first arrived. Around New Delhi, particularly in the area known as Transjamuna, across the river from Old Delhi, are the suburbs and slums that have sprung up to accommodate a population that has increased, more by migration than by natural increment, by 46% between 1991 and 2001. This population explosion has brought greater poverty and more wretched degradation in its wake – 45% of Delhi's inhabitants live in slum accommodation and beggars are on every street corner. In India, literacy rates are improving sharply but Delhi's illiteracy rate continues, marginally, to grow.

Delhi is, despite its long history, a city that is in fact very young. At Partition in 1947, Delhi was changed, radically and permanently, more or less overnight. With the creation of a predominantly Hindu India and an exclusively Muslim Pakistan, there was a mass migration of peoples in both directions and sectarian bloodletting on a horrifying scale. Having been largely Muslim before 1947, at Partition, Delhi

became a Hindu and Sikh, Punjabi-speaking city. At the same time, the population virtually doubled, despite the mass exodus of Muslims. This astonishing, artificial demographic change does much to explain Delhi's brashness and insecurity – in many respects, it is a city that is only half a century old.

As well as being a starting-point for visiting Agra – the home of the Taj Mahal – or the cities and forts of Rajasthan, Delhi itself has much to offer. The architectural legacy of the Islamic conquerors is rich and varied, the colonial centre is imposingly impressive, there are some interesting museums and the city's bazaars and shops offer a bewildering array of goods, from spices and silks to car spare parts. The city's restaurants tempt the visitor with a wide variety of delicious food, which – by European standards – is mostly very reasonably priced.

Summer in Delhi is best avoided. From mid-April, the temperature rises inexorably. For much of May, June and July, the thermometer is stuck at around 45°C (113°F), before the monsoon brings some relief. The best time to visit is February or March.

Red Fort

Photo: Government of India Tourist Office

TRAVEL

Getting There By Air

Indira Gandhi International Airport (DEL)

Tel: (011) 2565 2011.

Website: http://delhiairport.com

Indira Gandhi International Airport is located 23km (14 miles) southwest of central Delhi and is the main international gateway to India. Passengers flying to Indian destinations beyond Delhi should be aware that the domestic terminal at Palam (tel: (011) 2567 5140) is located some five kilometres (three miles) away from the international terminal.

Major airlines: *Air India* (tel: (011) 2373 1225; website: www.airindia.com) is the national airline. Other airlines serving the airport include *Air Canada, Air France, Air Lanka, British Airways, Cathay Pacific, Delta Airlines, Gulf Air, Japan Airlines, Jet Airways, Malaysian Airlines, Royal Nepal Airlines, SAS, Singapore Airlines, South African Airways, Swiss, Thai International Airways, United Airlines* and *Virgin.*

Approximate flight times to Delhi: From London is 8 hours 25 minutes; from New York is 16 hours; from Los Angeles is 24 hours; from Toronto is 18 hours and from Sydney is 17 hours.

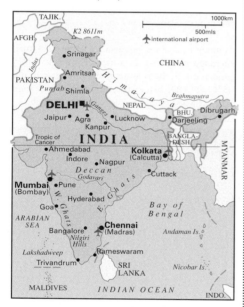

Airport facilities: These include foreign exchange (but no ATM), a tourist information counter, snack bars, a bookshop, duty-free shops, a restaurant and resting rooms. Car hire is available from outside the customs halls at both domestic and international arrivals.

Business facilities: There is a business centre with office facilities including fax, telephones and photocopiers.

Arrival/departure tax: A Foreign Travel departure tax of Rs500 or Rs150 is incorporated into the price of the ticket.

Transport to the city: Although metered taxis are available outside the airport, it is far easier to pre-book at one of the many taxi counters in the arrivals area. Fares should be approximately Rs300–400 for the 30–45-minute drive to central Delhi, although it will cost more at night. The Delhi Traffic Police Pre-Paid Taxi Booth issues a ticket, which is given to the allocated driver in lieu of a cash payment. Hotels and travel agents can, by prior agreement, arrange airport transfer by taxi, which should not cost more than Rs500 in each direction.

Getting There By Rail

Delhi is the hub of the *Indian Railways* (tel: (011) 2334 8787 (reservations) *or* 2375 0114 (general enquiries); website: www.indianrail.gov.in) network. The city has two major railway stations, in New Delhi and Old Delhi. New Delhi station, east of Pahar Ganj (Main Bazaar), is within walking distance of Connaught Place. Main Delhi station (Old Delhi), west of Red Fort, is about seven kilometres (four miles) from Connaught Place. All stations have basic waiting room and restaurant facilities. Railway stations and trains are notorious for theft and luggage should never be left unattended.

Rail services: Delhi offers express trains – known as the *Rajdhani Express* – to all parts of the country. One of the most popular services is the *Shatabdi Express*, the tourist train that travels to Agra, Lucknow and Chandigarh. Tickets are available for purchase at the *International Tourist Bureau* (tel: (011) 2334 6804), located at New Delhi station. This service is for foreigners only and the office takes payment in US Dollars or Pounds Sterling. The main ticket office is at the IRCA building on Chelmsford Road, Pahar Ganj, between New Delhi station and Connaught Place. For a small fee, travel agents take the time-consuming bureaucracy out of the business of booking rail tickets. The *Indrail Pass* is available for half a day up to 90 days; prices include US$70 for a two-day pass, US$135 for a seven-day pass and US$530 for a 90-day pass. It allows unlimited travel for the period of validity but does not dispense with the need to make advance reservations. There are also a number of luxury trains, offering sightseeing tours of Gujarat and Rajasthan, which can be booked as an individual.

Transport to the city: There are plenty of bicycle rickshaws, auto-rickshaws and taxis – pre-paid and otherwise – available at both railway stations. Prices should always be agreed in advance.

Getting There By Road

For those willing to brave Delhi's notorious roads, driving – in principle – is on the left. Foreign drivers must be over 18 years and in possession of an International Driving Permit. Beyond that, there are few rules that are either adhered to or enforced. The consensus is that it is far safer to use taxis or hire a car with a driver for longer journeys. National Highways are designated by a number.

The legal alcohol to blood ratio for driving is 0.03%. Third-party insurance is mandatory as per the Indian Motor Vehicle Act, 1988. Those intending to take their own car to India must obtain a carnet from one of the international motoring associations (such as RAC or AA) before entering the country. This document represents an undertaking that the car will not remain in India for more than six months. Most European motor insurance policies do not extend to India and motorists are advised to seek cover from an Indian insurer, as insurance is compulsory.

The Federation of Indian Automobile Associations (tel: (022) 204 1085) can provide information.

Emergency breakdown service: None.

Routes to the city: Five National Highways pass through Delhi, making the city a hub of the country's road system. The most important of these are the Grand Trunk Road (National Highway 1) from Amritsar in the north, Mathura Road from Agra in the south, National Highway 2 from Calcutta in the

east, and Gurgaon Road (National Highway 8) from Jaipur in the west. The construction of a peripheral expressway to the west of the city, linking it more efficiently to the national road network, has been proposed.

Approximate driving times to the city: From Agra – 2 hours 15 minutes; Jaipur – 2 hours 45 minutes; Amritsar – 4 hours 45 minutes.

Coach services: Delhi is linked by bus services – air conditioned, deluxe and ordinary – to all major destinations in northern India. *The Interstate Bus Terminus* (ISBT), at Kashmir Gate, north of Old Delhi railway station, is the terminus for all intercity bus services. Facilities include left-luggage, a bank, post office, pharmacy and restaurant. There are two other ISBTs in Delhi and together they cater for more than 150,000 passengers and 3300 buses per day. State operators based here include *Delhi Transport Corporation* (tel: (011) 2386 0290; website: http://dtc.nic.in), *Haryana Roadways* (website: (011) 2386 1262), *Himachal Pradesh Roadways* (tel: (011) 2386 3473 *or* 8694), *Punjab Roadways* (tel: (011) 2386 7842), *Rajasthan Roadways* (tel: (011) 2386 1246) and *Uttar Pradesh Roadways* (tel: (011) 2386 8709).

Getting Around

Public Transport

Public transport is not the best in Delhi and tourists will find the easiest way to get around the city is by taxi or auto-rickshaw (see below). Recently, in an attempt to tackle the city's air pollution, the government forced taxis, auto-rickshaws and buses to convert from petrol to Compressed Natural Gas (CNG). This has made some impact – Delhi has moved below Mumbai and Calcutta in the list of India's most polluted cities – and the areas around even the busiest roads do now feel less polluted.

The *Delhi Transport Corporation* (DTC; tel: (011) 2386 0290; website: http://dtc.nic.in) operates a centralised **bus** network of more than 300 routes. These public **buses** have all now been converted to CNG, but finding a seat is an undertaking that challenges all Western notions of courtesy and personal space and, once on, passengers should be prepared for a numbing, bone-crunching ride. However, there are a number of tourist services, including bus 454 between Connaught Place and Nizamuddin, bus 505 to Mehrauli and Qutb Minar, bus 620 to the Diplomatic Enclave (Chanakyapuri) and buses 101 and 139 between Park Hotel and the Red Fort. There is a row of seats on the left of each bus reserved for women, although this rule is observed only on a whim. DTC also operates a night bus service. Bus fares cost between Rs2 and Rs10 (depending on distance), which should be paid upon boarding. Bus **passes** are not available for less than one month.

The Delhi **metro** is still under construction, although the first small section is now in operation – opened by the Indian Prime Minister in December 2002. This short stretch of just over eight kilometres (five miles) is part of the first phase, which will extend to 62km (39 miles), partly overground, partly elevated and partly underground, and which is expected to be in

service by autumn 2005. The system is technologically very advanced: fare collection, for example, is done using 'smart' cards and tokens. The existing section runs from Shahdara in the suburbs of

East Delhi to Tis Hazari, which is just north of Old Delhi; a one-way ticket the full length of the existing line costs Rs7, although shorter journeys are less.

Rickshaws

Auto-rickshaws are open-sided, motorised tricycles, which weave in and out of Delhi's appalling traffic and can be stopped pretty much anywhere in the city. Visitors should be prepared for an uncomfortable ride as they lurch over the bumps and potholes of Delhi's roads, at the same level as the exhaust pipes of most lorries and buses. Four- and six-seater motorcycle rickshaws are also available, running fixed routes at fixed prices, including the route between the Red Fort and Palika Bazaar at Connaught Place. In Old Delhi, bicycle rickshaws are useful for short distances. The authorities have compelled Delhi's taxis and auto-rickshaws to install electronic meters, to counter the widespread overcharging of passengers (according to one recent estimate, Delhi's commuters are overcharged Rs2 billion, approximately £30 million, annually). Unsurprisingly, the meters are extremely unpopular among the taxi and rickshaw wallahs and are rarely used. The official starting meter rate is Rs5 for auto-rickshaws but – even if the meter is used – surcharges can exist over and above the metered price, so fares should be negotiated at the start of the journey. Drivers often expect a tip from foreign tourists and 10% of the fare is satisfactory.

Taxis

Yellow and black Ambassador taxis are readily available, especially at local taxi stands, where taxis can be booked and prices fixed in advance. Taxis can also be booked through hotels. Like auto-rickshaws, there are official rates for taxis (the official starting meter rate is Rs5) but metered prices are generally subject to high surcharges and can be twice as expensive as auto-rickshaws. Prices should be negotiated at the start of the journey. There is a 100% surcharge between 2300 and 0500. Drivers do not usually expect tips unless they have gone to some trouble on their passenger's behalf.

Limousines

For longer journeys or a day of sightseeing, Ambassador cars – of the yellow and black, or plain cream variety – with a driver are a good idea. These can be booked at the Tourist Office (see *Tourist Information*), through hotels or at private travel agents. *Services International* (tel: (011) 2578 2636) provides chauffeur-driven 'luxury' cars, including air-conditioned Mercedes and Fords. In Delhi, hire of a Mercedes plus chauffeur for eight hours would cost Rs6500 and a Ford Icon Rs1560.

Driving in the City

Driving in Delhi takes a certain degree of steeliness. The broad boulevards of New Delhi pose few

CITY STATISTICS

Location: National Capital Territory of Delhi, North India.
Country dialling code: 91.
Population: 13,782,976 (metropolitan area).
Ethnic mix: 72% Indo-Aryan, 25% Dravidian, 3% Mongoloid and other.
Religion: 80% Hindu, 11% Muslim, 1% Sikh, Jain, Christian and Buddhist.
Time zone: GMT + 5.5 (Indian Standard Time).
Electricity: 220 volts AC, 50Hz; round two- or three-pin plugs are used.
Average January temp: 21°C (70°F).
Average July temp: 35°C (95°F).
Annual rainfall: 714mm (27.9 inches). Monsoon season is July and August.

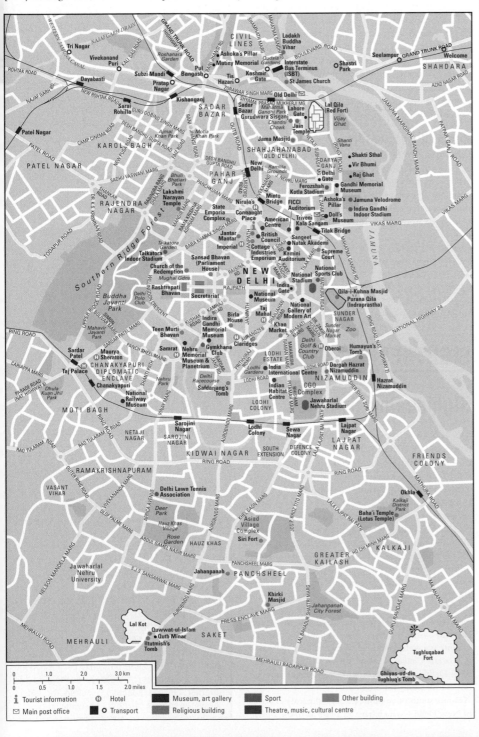

Tourist information
Main post office
Hotel
Transport
Museum, art gallery
Religious building
Sport
Theatre, music, cultural centre
Other building

BUSINESS PROFILE

Mumbai may be the financial capital of India and Bangalore her Silicon Valley but Delhi is the seat of government and enjoys a thriving economy. In 2000/01, Delhi's economy grew at a rate of 4.5% and, since 1993/94, has grown faster than the national economy. Annual per capita income in Delhi, estimated at Rs38,864 (approximately £570), is more than double the national average. Nearly 80% of Delhi's economy is in the so-called tertiary sector, with financial services, insurance, real estate, hotels and restaurants the major contributors.

India's economy has developed significantly, not only since Independence over 50 years ago but also with a decade of reforms under its belt. The economic reforms introduced in the summer of 1991 can, by many measures, be counted a great success. The liberalisation of industry, devaluation of the Rupee and lowering of trade barriers proved a powerful stimulus to the Indian economy. The government is committed to privatisation – the recent sale of part of its stake in Indian Petrochemicals is evidence that the programme is gathering momentum. Inflation has declined from 14% in 1991 to around 5% (estimated 5.5% for 2003/04) and interest rates are at a 30-year low. Direct foreign investment has, since the early 1990s, grown from practically nothing to US$2 billion a year. Exports have reached the US$50 billion mark for the first time in 2002/03, representing growth of 18% over the previous year. The government is confident of achieving US$80 billion of exports by 2007.

However, the continuing crisis in Kashmir threatens political stability, fiscal equilibrium and inward investment. Despite the advances that have been made, immense problems remain. The economic growth of the 1990s has failed to generate the millions of low-skilled jobs that India needs, while agriculture still accounts for a quarter of GDP, which unduly exposes the national economy to the vagaries of the weather. Both central and state governments suffer from enormous deficits, which in turn hinder their capacity to invest in the nation's infrastructure. Unemployment also remains high. Exact figures are difficult to come by, however, the 2001 census records that 'non workers' in Delhi constitute 68.4% of the population, as compared to the national figure of 62.5%. It should be noted that approximately one third of non-workers are students and pensioners.

Multinationals with a presence in Delhi include *Citibank*, *Standard Chartered* and *HSBC* banks, *Price Waterhouse Coopers*, *Microsoft*, *Hewlett Packard*, *Macmillan* and *Penguin*. The central business district of Delhi is situated around Connaught Place, with secondary commercial hubs at Nehru Place and Rajendra Nagar.

potential hazards. However, negotiating the vehicular chaos that is Old Delhi can test the skills of even the most able driver, as bicycles and rickshaws career through the choking traffic of buses, trucks and taxis, not to mention ox carts, lone wandering cows, goats and elephants. Road travel is also subject to the vagaries of VIPs, of which India has an astonishing number, with roads frequently closed for 'VIP movement'. Night driving can be particularly dangerous, with streets and cars lit only sporadically. Car parks are few and far between and, in general, driving oneself around the city is not recommended. There are also several schemes afoot to improve the flow of traffic in the city, the most important of which is the construction of flyovers. Several large-scale road improvement schemes – flyovers, roundabout interchanges and so on – have recently opened, easing the pressure of Delhi's traffic at certain important points. However, Delhi remains addicted to the car – the number of vehicles registered in the city has increased by 90% since 1991 – and congestion, noise and pollution are a constant nuisance.

Car Hire

Although it is more common (and advisable) to hire a car with a driver, the following service providers offer self-drive car hire: *Europcar Inter-Rent* (tel: (011) 2619 1786), *Hertz* (tel: (011) 2678 6681; e-mail: delhi@carzonrent.com), *Mann Tours* (tel: (011) 2336 5544; website: www.carrentalindia.com) and *Wheels Rent A Car* (tel: (011) 2331 8695). Most major hotels can also arrange car hire. An International Driving Permit is essential for driving in India and in most cases the driver must be 25 years or over. Third-party insurance is required by law. Car hire rates start at Rs1500 per day. For chauffeur-driven car hire, see *Limousines* above.

Bicycle & Scooter Hire

Cycling in New Delhi can take some courage but it is a good way of getting around the wide boulevards, which are fairly uncrowded and in relatively good condition. However, bicycle hire is hard to come by. Nevertheless, there is a small unnamed shop, in Pahar Ganj, a few doors down from Hotel Vivek, which has bicycles for hire.

Lovers of vintage motorcycles come to India to indulge a penchant for its locally built Enfields. *Inder Motors*, on Hari Singh Malwa Street (tel: (011) 2572 8579), has new and second-hand Enfields for sale, while *Lucky Auto Accessories*, on Shri Kishan Dass Road, stocks renovated Enfield Bullets.

SIGHTSEEING

Sightseeing Overview

The best-known sights are the two buildings that dominate Old Delhi, the *Red Fort* and *Jama Masjid*. A stroll through the chaotic, raucous, smelly alleyways of Old Delhi – also known as *Shahjahanabad*, after the 17th-century Mughal emperor who built it – is a fascinating experience. The bazaars of *Chandni Chowk* are a riot of colourful exoticism and frenetic activity. Old Delhi is decaying rapidly but it is still possible to glimpse a mosque here or the courtyard of a proud old townhouse there, hidden behind a shop front.

To the south of Old Delhi and in complete contrast to it, is *Rajpath* and the buildings on *Raisina Hill* – *Rashtrapati Bhavan* and the *Secretariat* – which form the centrepiece of British New Delhi. After the clamour of Old Delhi, the calm elegance and Baroque vistas of this most splendidly laid-out scheme is a welcome relief. Between Old Delhi and Rajpath is *Connaught Place*, the arcaded bull's eye of New Delhi, where shops, banks, bars, restaurants and hotels tout loudly for business.

Heading south once more, through the leafy enclaves of New Delhi – which have an allure all of their own,

as they are spacious, shady and lusciously green – the visitor will find the bulk of the ancient monuments of medieval Delhi. *Humayun's Tomb* and the *Lodhi Gardens* are readily accessible from the centre of the city. The *Qutb Minar* complex, the vast and formidable *Tughluqabad* and the remains at *Haus Khaz* are located deeper in the southern suburbs.

The swingeing increases in admission charges to the monuments in the care of the Archaeological Survey of India (ASI), imposed in October 2000, have now been moderated, as a result of protests from the tourist industry. As before, the new rates apply, somewhat controversially, only to foreigners.

The easiest way to get from site to site is by taxi or auto-rickshaw. Sightseeing in Delhi can be exhausting

BUSINESS ETIQUETTE

The Indian Hindu greeting is to put both hands together as if in prayer and tilt the head forward. Indian women may prefer not to shake hands, although men will be quite comfortable with it. Language is a very political issue in India, with 18 official languages and 1600 minor languages and dialects. Government policy encourages the use of Hindi, which is widely spoken in Delhi and the north. However, English is usually sufficient for most business situations.

Corporate entertaining is an important part of Indian business life, making business lunches and dinners a minefield of potential disasters. The first rule is that Indians eat only with the right hand – the left hand may be used to hold a cup or utensil but would not be used to eat or pass food within polite society. Generally, the left hand should be used neither to pass anything nor to point at anyone. Gifts and business cards should be accepted with the right hand or both hands at the same time, as a sign of respect. The other taboo part of the body is the foot. Shoes should be removed when entering a private home and, when sitting, care should be taken to ensure feet are never pointed at anyone.

Indians are very conservative when it comes to dress and women should ensure that they are modestly dressed, with legs and shoulders covered. Trousers are acceptable but short skirts can offend. Regardless of how hot it gets, men are expected to wear suits and should remember the country's British Raj heritage – Indian businessmen still wear blazers for afternoon drinks and dress for dinner.

It has to be said that New Delhi remains very much attached to the days of the Raj, in more ways than one. The legacy of its political and bureaucratic culture means that business is still conducted according to the rather idiosyncratic Indian Standard Time – the same time zone (GMT + 5.5) applies for all areas of this vast country. Business hours are 0930/1000 to 1730/1800. As in the rest of India, however, Delhi is keen to be hooked up to the online world. Hotels and Internet cafés provide sometimes slow and sporadic connection by satellite, frustrated by the fact that India remains a country where it can be difficult to get a telephone line. Laptops can be used to connect to the Internet but the adapters required for Indian telephone sockets can be hard to come by.

– negotiating the urban sprawl and traffic is a long drawn-out and tiring business, particularly in the heat. But it is an experience that the traveller will not regret.

Key Attractions

Lal Qila (Red Fort)

The *Red Fort*'s massive curtain wall and battlements dominate the skyline of Old Delhi. Inside, the bastions – built by Shah Jehan, like the nearby Jama Masjid – are an array of exquisite 17th-century Mughal buildings, which provided the living quarters for the Emperor, his courtiers and family. The flawless balance and proportion of these buildings, as well as the intricate decoration, is wonderful to behold and in complete contrast to the military might of the fort itself. Sadly, the water conduits that would once have cooled the dwellings and gardens are now dry. The *Lahore Gate*, on the west side of the fort, was a potent symbol in the fight for Independence and is still regarded as a shrine for of the Republic. The Indian Tourism Development Corporation runs a daily *son et lumière* show here throughout the year. Times vary.
Entrance from Lahore Gate or Chandni Chowk
Opening hours: Tues–Sun dawn–dusk.
Admission: Rs100 (foreigners); Rs50 (*son et lumière*).

Jama Masjid

Jama Masjid is India's largest mosque and is one of the masterpieces of the Mughal's greatest builder, Shah Jehan. A huge courtyard, bounded by an arcade and pierced with three gates, lies in front of the prayer hall, which achieves a sense of serenity and peace from the perfect harmony of its arches, domes and spaces. The courtyard, which can accommodate 25,000 worshippers, is dominated by two red-and-white-striped sandstone minarets, 70m (230ft) tall. The energetic visitors who climb the 122 narrow steps to the top will be rewarded with a magnificent view of Delhi, smog and all. Shorts and short-sleeved shirts are not permitted – wraps can be borrowed.
Matya Mahal, Bho Jala
Opening hours: Daily dawn–dusk; closed during prayer times.
Admission: Free (mosque); Rs10 to shoe wallah; Rs10 (minaret); Rs100 (for cameras).

Qutb Minar

The *Qutb Minar* is an immense tower, started at the end of the 12th century, to commemorate the Muslim conquest of Delhi. Standing 72.5m (238ft) tall, it is built of fluted red sandstone – which is currently being restored – decorated with calligraphy representing verses from the Koran. The top two levels are faced in white marble. The *Minar* rises above a site that is home to the oldest extant Islamic monuments in India. There is the *Ala-i-Darwaza*, complete with horseshoe-shaped arches, lotus-leaf squinches and elaborate geometric patterns. Next to that, stands the *Quwwat-ul-Islam*, the first mosque to be built in India. So anxious were the new rulers of Delhi to erect a mosque, they shamelessly pilfered 27 Hindu and Jain temples for building materials. Many of the pillars that surround the courtyard are carved with Hindu iconography, which is curiously at odds with the Islamic calligraphy of the Muslim prayer screens. Incongruously, in the centre of the mosque, stands the fourth-century *Iron Pillar*, bearing inscriptions from the Gupta period. Beyond the mosque is the intricately carved *Iltutmish's Tomb*. The site is a must for any visitor to Delhi.

Rashtrapati Bhavan

Qutb Minar complex
Opening hours: Daily dawn–dusk.
Admission: Rs250 (foreigners).

Rashtrapati Bhavan and Rajpath

Rajpath runs between the *Secretariat Buildings* and *India Arch*, the war memorial designed by Lutyens in 1921. Rajpath is a formal conception, lined with trees, fountains and pools, intended by its architects, Lutyens and Baker, as the epicentre of British India. The Secretariat Buildings combine monumental classical and oriental detail and, while not beautiful, are certainly an imposing statement of colonial power. *Rashtrapati Bhavan* is an immense palace, supposedly larger than Versailles, which was built as the residence of the Viceroy and is now the official home of the President of India. Every Saturday morning (0935–1015), guards parade before the iron grille gates. While the apartments are private, the gardens are open to the public every year in February and March.
Rajpath
Opening hours: By appointment; gardens open daily 0900–1600 (Feb–Mar).
Admission: Free.

National Museum

It takes a good few hours to get a decent overview of Indian culture at the *National Museum*, which is filled with exhibits covering over 5000 years of history. Highlights include excavations from Indus Valley civilisation sites, carved pillars and statues from the Maryan empire (250BC), Gupta terracottas dating from AD400, sandstone figures from Pallava temples, stone and bronze Buddhist statues, Tibetan manuscripts, Naga models and masks, silk paintings from Central Asia, a gallery of 300 musical instruments and Mughal clothing, tapestries, ornaments and weapons.
Janpath
Tel: (011) 2301 9538.
Opening hours: Tues–Sun 1000–1700.
Admission: Rs150 (foreigners).

Chandni Chowk

The bazaars that surround *Chandni Chowk*, in Old Delhi, offer a colourful, heaving and pungent slice of Delhi life, with shops and stalls displaying a spectacular array of goods, from fish and poultry to 'second-hand' goods, gemstones and gold, garlands, turbans, tinsel and car parts. They are an unmissable part of any visit to the city. *Naya Bazaar* is the spice market on Khari Baoli, where porters haul sackfuls of spices onto ox carts to be peddled in other parts of the city, while the covered *Gadodial Market*, just off Khari Baoli, is the wholesale spice market with an incredible display of aniseed, turmeric, pomegranate, dried mangoes, ginger, saffron, reetha nuts, lotus seeds, pickles, sugars and chutneys. *Chawris Bazaar* became notorious in the 19th century, for its dancing girls who beckoned to men below from the arched windows and balconies of the huge mansions that once lined the street. Today, the mansions have made way for shops specialising in copper and brass Buddhas, Vishnus and Krishnas.
Chandni Chowk
Opening hours: Daily, approximately 1000–1800; most shops closed Sun.
Admission: Free.

Humayun's Tomb

Often seen merely as a forerunner of the Taj Mahal, *Humayun's Tomb* is, in its own right, a stunning example of the Mughal architectural style, combining dome, mausoleum and plinth in perfect proportion. The Tomb is set in a square garden designed along Persian lines, shaded and geometric, crisscrossed with waterways and paths. In the grounds, there are some other monuments, including the *Tomb of Isa Khan*. The gardens, in particular the watercourses and pools, have recently been magnificently restored, thanks to the generosity of the Aga Khan's Trust, and now the visitor will get a vivid impression of what the tomb and its gardens would have looked like in their pomp.
Lodhi Road and Mathura Road
Opening hours: Daily dawn–dusk.
Admission: Rs250 (foreigners).

Photo: Leonardo

Baha'i Temple

Baha'i Temple

Otherwise known as the Lotus Temple, the modern *Baha'i Temple* has often, somewhat tritely, been compared to the Sydney Opera House. Giant white petals of Rajasthani Macrana marble open out from nine pools and walkways in the shape of an unfolding lotus, symbolising the nine spiritual paths of the Baha'i faith. The crouched yet upright stance and upturned, opening petals hint at the human form in ecstatic prayer. The temple is approached through an attractive formal garden. Inside, the central hall rises to a height of over 30m (98ft), over nine arches, which play a constant and revolving trick of perspective on the eye, creating a sense of perpetual motion. Visitors should take off their shoes before entering.
Kalkaji Hill
Opening hours: Tues–Sun 0930–1730 (Oct–Mar); Tues–Sun 0900–1900 (Apr–Sep).
Admission: Free.

Purana Qila

Humayun's 16th-century Delhi had at its centre the fortress of *Purana Qila*, which reputedly stands on the site of Indraprastha, the city of the Pandavas in the Mahabharata. Of the buildings that survive today, the *Qila-i-Kuhna Masjid* was constructed by Sher Shah in 1541, and represents a successful fusion of the Islamic and Hindu styles. The *Sher Mandal* is an octagonal observatory and library. The north gate, *Talaqi-Darwaza*, has been partially rebuilt and gives an impression of how formidable the fortifications would have been in their heyday. The *chattri* surmounting the west (entrance) gate commands a fine view of New Delhi. Purana Qila is in the throes of an extensive programme of rebuilding and restoration. There is a small archaeological museum just inside the south gate.
Mathura Road
Opening hours: Daily dawn–dusk (fortress); Sat–Thurs 1000–1700 (museum).
Admission: Rs100 inclusive (foreigners).

National Gallery of Modern Art

The *National Gallery of Modern Art* contains a large collection of 20th-century Indian art. There are examples of the work of the painters of the Bengali Renaissance and of the poet and artist, Tagore. The highlight is the room devoted to female Indian artist Amrita Sher-Gil (1913–41), whose portraits – more successful than her genre scenes – are painted with the confident bravura of the youthful Augustus John. The museum is about to embark on an ambitious scheme of building, which, when complete, will provide greatly increased gallery space for the collection. The museum is in Jaipur House – by any yardstick, a grandee's townhouse – formerly the Delhi residence of the Maharaja of Jaipur.
Jaipur House, India Gate
Tel: (011) 2338 2835.
Opening hours: Tues–Sun 1000–1700.
Admission: Rs150 (foreigners).

Tughluqabad

The immense and brutal fortifications of *Tughluqabad* are an impressive monument to the militarism of the Tughluqs, an antidote to any idea that the Delhi Sultans were merely effete builders of mosques and palaces. Nowadays, the only living things that visitors are likely to see at the vast, barren, sun-scorched site are goats, donkeys and the occasional archaeologist, although in the 14th century, the citadel, the third city of Delhi, was the Sultan's capital. Parts of the site are now undergoing restoration. Below the walls is the forbidding tomb of *Ghiyas-ud-din Tughluq*, the builder of Tughluqabad. It is approached from a causeway that crosses a lake, now dry. From the high point of the citadel, there is a sweeping panorama of southern Delhi.
Tughluqabad
Opening hours: Daily dawn–dusk.
Admission: Rs100 (foreigners).

Further Distractions

Raj Ghat

The *ghats* – steps leading down to the water – mark the cremation sites of the leaders and freedom fighters of India. Nowadays, they are situated in a landscaped park, complete with ornamental lake. The most popular, *Raj Ghat*, is a simple square platform of black marble, where Mahatma Gandhi was cremated, after his assassination in 1948. Pilgrims come to touch the petal-strewn platform (*samadhi*) with reverence and emotion and prayers are held in remembrance every Friday evening and on the anniversaries of his birth and death (2 October and 30 January). Nearby, there are memorials to Indira Gandhi and to her son, Rajiv, both of whom were assassinated.
Ring Road
Opening hours: Daily dawn–dusk.
Admission: Free.

Gandhi Memorial Museum

Adjacent to Raj Ghat is the *Gandhi Memorial Musuem*, where the visitor can see a fascinating display of photographs illustrating the Mahatma's life and death. There is a large collection of Gandhi memorabilia, from toothpicks to spinning wheels, via the clothes he was supposedly wearing at his assassination. Among the *bons mots* about Gandhi, which are inscribed on the walls, is George Bernard Shaw's reflection that the Mahatma's murder 'shows how dangerous it is to be too good'.
Ring Road, opposite Raj Ghat
Tel: (011) 2331 0168.
Opening hours: Tues–Sun 0930–1730.

Birla House

Birla House owes its historical resonance to the fact that Mahatma Gandhi was attending an evening prayer meeting here when he was assassinated by a Hindu extremist on 30 January 1948. The house – a large, white bungalow in New Delhi – belonged to the wealthy industrialist G D Birla and Gandhi was a regular guest there while visiting Delhi. The house is now a shrine to the Mahatma's memory and contains a large collection of photographs of his life. The exact spot in the garden where he met his death is marked; as is, rather gruesomely, the exact course of his last few steps, from the house to the prayer meeting.
Akbar Road
Opening hours: Tues–Sun 1000–1700.
Admission: Free.

Lodhi Gardens

An oasis of shaded calm, the *Lodhi Gardens* are a popular and relaxing place in which to escape the heat and clamour of Delhi. The gardens are extensive and boast a fine collection of tropical shrubs and trees. There is even a formal rose garden. There are also a number of monuments of the Lodhi Sultanate (1451–1526), including the *Shish Gumbad*, the *Bara Gumbad* and the *Tomb of Mohammed Shah*, all fine specimens of the Lodhi style.
Lodhi Road, New Delhi
Opening hours: Daily dawn–dusk.
Admission: Free.

Delhi Ridge and the Civil Lines

Delhi Ridge, overlooking Old Delhi, was the centre of the British position for the siege of the city during the Mutiny of 1857. On its southern scarp, is the *Mutiny Memorial*, an ugly neo-Gothic tower commemorating those who took part in the fighting. Higher up the Ridge is one of *Ashoka's Pillars* (third century BC), which was brought to Delhi by Feroz Shah and repaired and re-erected here by the British, in 1867. The *Civil Lines*, nestling below the Ridge, are where the British lived before the construction of New Delhi in the 1920s.
Delhi Ridge
Opening hours: Daily 24 hours.
Admission: Free.

Haus Khaz

Haus Khaz boasts an impressive collection of ruins, the most important of which are the *Tomb of Feroz Shah* (died 1388) and the neighbouring – and contemporary – *madrasa* (college). It was originally the site of the 50-hectare (125-acre) reservoir built by Aladdin (died 1316) to supply his citadel. *Haus*

Khaz Village houses a number of trendy boutiques, galleries and restaurants.
Haus Khaz
Opening hours: Daily dawn–dusk.
Admission: Free.

National Railway Museum

This is a small museum of railway memorabilia, including the skull of an elephant killed when it collided with a mail train in Bengal, in 1894. But the principal glory of the *National Railway Museum* is the open-air display of old steam locomotives and rolling stock. Particularly interesting are the 'special' carriages belonging to British and Indian grandees, such as the Viceregal dining car, the Maharaja of Mysore's personal train, which comprised both sleeping and day compartments, and the Gaekwar of Baroda's Saloon, with its ornate gold and enamel ceiling. Also on display is the last steam engine to see service on the Indian railways – as recently as 1995 – and the first electric-powered engine to do so – as long ago as the 1930s.
Chanakyapuri
Tel: (011) 2688 0939.
Opening hours: Tues–Sun 0930–1700 (Oct–Mar); Tues–Sun 0930–1900 (Apr–Sep).
Admission: Rs10.

Safdarjang's Tomb

The finest extant example of a late Mughal garden tomb, *Safdarjang's Tomb* was built by the Nawab of Avadh to commemorate the life of his father, Safdarjang, who was effectively the prime minister of the Mughal empire. It may lack the perfect proportions and exhilarating simplicity of Humayun's Tomb – which is 200 years older – but is, in its own over-elaborate, almost blowsy way, a splendid building.
Aurobindo Marg and Lodhi Road
Opening hours: Daily dawn–dusk.
Admission: Rs100 (foreigners).

Tours of the City

Walking Tours

Nigel Hankin, an Englishman who has lived in Delhi for many years, runs walking tours of Old Delhi. Places on his tours may be booked at the lodge at the

Taj Mahal

Mughal Gate of the *British High Commission*, Shanti Path, Chanakyapuri. Other than that, self-guided walking tours of a number of areas are possible. Starting at the Jain Temple at the eastern end of Chandni Chowk, by the Red Fort, a walk through this area weaves through the alleyways and takes in the area's best temples and most colourful markets. It takes about an hour and a half to tour the main mosques and mansions of Old Delhi, covering the stretch from Jama Masjid to Ajmeri Gate.

Bus Tours

Delhi Tourism Development Corporation (tel: (011) 2336 3604 *or* 5358; website: http//delhitourism.nic.in) operates sightseeing tours in coaches, covering New and Old Delhi. Between October and April, the tours are in non-air-conditioned coaches, between May and September in air-conditioned ones. The New Delhi tour departs daily at 0900 (finishing at 1315) and includes Jantar Mantar, Birla Mandir, Qutb Minar, the Baha'i Temple and Safdarjang's Tomb. The Old Delhi tour departs daily at 1415 (finishing at 1715), stopping at Red Fort, Jama Masjid, Raj Ghat and Humayun's Tomb. Prices are Rs95 for a half-day tour and Rs180 for a full-day tour. The prices for air-conditioned tours in the hot weather are Rs110 and Rs210 respectively. The four-hour 'Delhi by Evening Tour' includes Birla Mandir, the *son et lumière* show at Purana Qila and a drive past the Parliament House and India Gate. Tickets cost Rs105 and tours depart daily at 1800 (1745 between October and February). Tickets must be purchased in advance at the booking office at N-36 Connaught Place.

Excursions

For a Half Day

Haryana: Bordering the Capital Territory of Delhi to the west and south is the state of *Haryana*. It is one of the most prosperous parts of India, boasting one of the highest per capita incomes in the country. The state government has made great efforts to build up the tourist infrastructure in recent years, with considerable investment in, for example, hotels and golf courses. Its proximity to Delhi and its relatively low tax on alcohol make it a popular destination for weekenders from the capital. Two of the most interesting attractions in the state and the most convenient for Delhi are the *Sultanpur Bird Sanctuary* and *Suraj Kund*. Situated 47km (29.5 miles) from Delhi, approximately 50 minutes by taxi, Sultanpur Bird Sanctuary consists of a small lake and marshland. It is best visited between November and February, when migratory birds, including the greater flamingo, bare-headed and Brahminy ducks from Tibet, flock there. The ruins of *Suraj Kund* are just 16km (ten miles) from the outskirts of Delhi, a journey of about half an hour by taxi. Its tenth-century amphitheatre is the only great Hindu shrine left intact by invading Muslims. The shrine is surrounded by tranquil parklands and a small artificial boating lake and is a popular Sunday lunch picnic destination for middle-class Indian families.
There is an informative website (www.haryana-online.com) that can provide more information about attractions in Haryana.

For a Whole Day

Agra and Taj Mahal: The radiance of early morning is one of the best times to first glimpse the flawless proportions of the *Taj Mahal*, built entirely out of marble, by Shah Jahan, to serve as a mausoleum for his

wife, Mumtaz Mahal. The complex consists of five main elements – the *Darwaza* or main gateway, the *Bageecha* or garden, the *Masjid* or mosque, the *Naqqar Khana* or resthouse and the *Rauza* or the Taj Mahal mausoleum. The actual tomb is situated inside. Most impressive are the four tall minarets (40m/131ft high) at the corners of the structure, the majestic dome in the middle and the black and white chessboard marble floor. The Taj Mahal is open Saturday to Thursday from dawn to dusk and admission costs Rs750 for foreigners (Rs250 for the ASI ticket and Rs500 levied by the municipality of Agra).
The other monument of note in Agra is *Agra Fort*, with high red sandstone ramparts. The foundations of the citadel were laid by the Emperor Akbar in 1565 and successive generations developed it as a stronghold of the Mughal empire. The fort houses the graceful *Diwan-i-Am*, the royal pavilions, the *Hammam-i-Shahi* (royal bath), the *Nagina Masjid* (Gem Mosque) and the *Zenana Meena Bazaar*, where the ladies of the court would linger over silks, jewellery and brocades. The Agra Fort is open daily dawn to dusk and admission costs Rs300 for foreigners.
The *Shatabdi Express*, an air-conditioned tourist train, covers the 199km (124 miles) to Agra in approximately two hours, departing from New Delhi station. Tickets can be purchased at the International Tourist Bureau, on the first floor of New Delhi station, and cost Rs800 for a return, including breakfast. Payment is only accepted in foreign currency or travellers' cheques (US Dollars or Pounds Sterling preferred). Credit cards are not accepted. To circumvent the tiresome queuing necessary to purchase tickets in person, a travel agent will do this for tourists, for a small fee.
The *Government of India Tourist Office* in Agra, 191 The Mall (tel: (0562) 222 6378), can provide further information.

ACCOMMODATION

Delhi boasts a large number of hotels, which offer accommodation ranging from air-conditioned, marbled luxury to cockroach-infested squalor. All hotels listed have air conditioning. The most expensive luxury hotels in Delhi quote their prices in US Dollars – only resident Indians are permitted to pay in Rupees – and the visitor should be aware that the rates that hotels quote do not include substantial local taxes. These are usually 12.5% for the moderate hotels and 20–22.5% for the luxury hotels.
The prices quoted below are the lowest standard rates for a double room, excluding local taxes and breakfast, unless otherwise specified.

Business

Maurya Sheraton Hotel & Towers

A large, well-appointed international hotel, the *Maurya Sheraton* caters for the needs of the business traveller and the tourist alike. The decor is more restrained than that of its next-door neighbour, the *Taj Palace* – the lobby rejects marble in favour of old stone. Guest rooms all have interactive television and Internet access, while business visitors will find a fully equipped business centre and full conference facilities. The lively hotel bar has a golfing theme and drinkers sit among old trophies and other golfing memorabilia. The hotel also boasts a swimming pool,

Photo: Leonardo

Dining at The Imperial

tennis courts and a health club and is a popular venue for lavish Indian weddings.
Sardar Patel Marg, Diplomatic Enclave, New Delhi
Tel: (011) 2611 2233. Fax: (011) 2611 3333.
Website: www.welcomgroup.com
Price: From US$220.

Radisson Hotel

The *Radisson* is an unattractive, modern hotel within easy reach, four kilometres (2.5 miles), of the international airport. It does, however, offer everything that the business traveller could possibly require. There is a fully equipped business centre, extensive meeting and conference facilities, a gym and health club, a swimming pool and ten-pin bowling. It is largely characterless and is designed and run to a formula found the world over but guests can be sure that their cocoon will at least be comfortable and spotlessly clean. Facilities in guest rooms include a mini-bar, hairdryer and fruit basket. Guests are offered free transfers between the hotel and the airport.
National Highway 8, New Delhi
Tel: (011) 2677 9191. Fax: (011) 2677 9090.
E-mail: reservations@radissondel.com
Website: www.radisson.com
Price: From US$225.

Taj Mahal Hotel

The flagship hotel of the Taj Group, the *Taj Mahal Hotel* is a large, modern and well-appointed international hotel, conveniently situated in the heart of New Delhi. The hotel has recently been completely refurbished to the highest specifications and the lobby has emerged as a tasteful contemporary essay in the Mughal style, with domes and enamelled panels offsetting traditional carpets and modern furniture. The hotel has a fully equipped 24-hour business centre and offers the full range of conference facilities. Facilities in the 300 guest rooms include high-speed Internet access, mini-bar, personal safe, in-room fax and international direct dial telephones. The hotel also has a magnificent swimming pool.
1 Mansingh Road, New Delhi
Tel: (011) 2302 6162. Fax: (011) 2302 6070.
E-mail: trn.delhi@tajhotels.com
Website: www.tajhotels.com
Price: From US$255.

Taj Palace Hotel

A large international hotel, the *Taj Palace* is typically glitzy and modern Indian in style. The lobby and public areas positively dazzle the visitor with acres of shiny marble and phalanxes of brassy chandeliers. The corporate traveller will, however, feel at home, as the hotel offers every facility for keeping in touch with clients and the office. It has fully equipped conference halls and meeting rooms, as well as a large swimming pool in which to cool off after the heat of the Delhi day. There are several restaurants offering a wide range of dishes. The 421 guest rooms offer facilities such as international direct dial telephones, voice-mail, mini-bar, personal safe and Internet access.
1 Sardar Patel Marg, Diplomatic Enclave, New Delhi
Tel: (011) 2611 0202. Fax: (011) 2611 0808.
E-mail: palace.delhi@tajhotels.com
or trn.delhi@tajhotels.com
Website: www.tajhotels.com
Price: From US$225.

Luxury

The Imperial

The most famous hotel in Delhi, *The Imperial*, opened in 1933 and was a favourite haunt of Nehru, Mountbatten and other luminaries, who schemed and gossiped in its lush gardens. Historically, it sits on the fault-line between imperial certainty and colonial apology; its clean, modernist lines and unobtrusive Art Deco detail seem to look forward to the Brave New World rather than back to former, faded glories. Its decoration is traditional colonial – 'Lutyens Delhi' – and the ambience calm and sophisticated. The 263 guest rooms are luxurious, with antique furniture and paintings from the hotel's art collection, but they also have modem points for high-speed Internet access and fax hook-up. It has a swimming pool, a number of good restaurants and a stylish bar, the *1911*. This is the first choice among luxury hotels in Delhi.
Janpath, New Delhi
Tel: (011) 2334 1234. Fax: (011) 2334 2255.
E-mail: luxury@theimperialindia.com
Website: www.theimperialindia.com
Price: From US$260.

The Oberoi

A stylish and most luxurious modern hotel, *The Oberoi* occupies a peaceful position overlooking New Delhi's principal golf course. It has every conceivable convenience for the travelling businessperson or well-heeled tourist, including a 24-hour personalised butler service, while guest rooms have two-line telephones, voice-mail and workstations with modem points. In contrast to some of its competitors, the hotel is decorated with an understated, restrained charm, combining luxury and tastefulness. It has a swish bar, a fine swimming pool and four excellent restaurants offering a range of culinary styles. It seems to attract an ostentatiously upmarket clientele.
Dr Zakir Hussain Marg, New Delhi
Tel: (011) 2436 3030. Fax: (011) 2436 0484.
E-mail: reservations@oberoidel.com
Website: www.oberoihotels.com
Price: From US$280.

Moderate

Claridges Hotel

Set in the leafy boulevards of New Delhi, *Claridges Hotel* is of a piece with its surroundings. The building, dating from the 1920s or 1930s, has a mildly Art Deco feel to it and a calm understated elegance, in keeping with the spacious bungalows that line the streets of the city. The lobby, with its fine double-crescent staircase, sets the tone for the rest of the hotel. There is a somewhat primitive business centre, a swimming pool and a health club. The hotel also has a number of restaurants and a congenial bar.
12 Aurangzeb Road, New Delhi
Tel: (011) 2301 0211. Fax: (011) 2301 0625.
E-mail: claridges.hotel@gems.vsnl.net.in
Price: From US$120.

Jukaso Inn

Jukaso Inn is situated in the peaceful enclave of Sunder Nagar ('beautiful place' in Hindi), close to some of the most important sights of New Delhi, including Humayun's Tomb, Purana Qila and the Lodhi Gardens. It is a small, light and airy hotel, having only 50 rooms and suites, but stylish in an old-fashioned way and immaculately clean. All rooms have marble baths. The Jukaso Inn also has business and conference facilities.
49–50 Sunder Nagar, New Delhi
Tel: (011) 2435 0308. Fax: (011) 2435 4402.
E-mail: jukaso@hotmail.com
Website: www.indiamart.com/jukasoinn
Price: From Rs3000.

Other Recommendations

Nirula's Hotel

For those who like to be in the centre of town, *Nirula's Hotel* is the place to stay. Located on Connaught Place, the hub of New Delhi, it overlooks the swirling traffic and many of the best shops, bazaars and restaurants in the city are on its doorstep. Although a small and non-descript hotel, the rooms are comfortable and clean, if on the dark side. Room facilities include colour television, refrigerator and direct-dial telephones. The hotel also offers fax and Internet access for guests' use. Attached to the hotel is the famous Nirula's ice cream parlour and a patisserie.

L-Block, Connaught Place, New Delhi
Tel: (011) 2341 7419. Fax: (011) 2341 8957.
E-mail: delhihotel@nirulas.com
Website: www.nirula.com
Price: From Rs2900.

The Residency

Located in the quiet suburb of Defence Colony – renowned for its market and restaurants, *The Residency* offers rooms and self-contained flats, each with three bedrooms, in light, airy and modern buildings, at reasonable rates. The flats might appeal to families who are visiting Delhi for a week or two, or to visitors who need somewhere to stay while they are searching for permanent accommodation in the city. The atmosphere is friendly and all rooms and flats are provided with a houseboy to do the cleaning and prepare breakfast. Internet access is available.
193 Golf Links, New Delhi
Tel: (011) 2461 1027. Fax: (011) 2464 9008.
E-mail: info@ahujaresidency.com
Price: From Rs1500 per night (rooms); from Rs90,000 per month (flats).

RESTAURANTS

Traditionally, all the best restaurants in Delhi were to be found in the five-star international hotels. When smart Delhiwallahs wished to impress, they would head for one of these places where, in return for five-star prices, they would be guaranteed good food in swish surroundings with obsequious service. To an extent, this is still the case, although beyond the confines of the big hotels, the prosperity of Delhi's enormous middle class has ensured that a huge number of excellent restaurants have sprung up, where one can be assured of delicious food at a fraction of the price that is charged in the big hotel dining rooms.

The question of alcohol is a thorny one in Delhi, where it remains notoriously difficult to secure a drink licence. Therefore many restaurants are unlicensed. Alcohol in Delhi is expensive and wine particularly so – a run-of-the-mill bottle of Pino Grigio could cost up to Rs1800 (approximately £27), before sales taxes – as it is subject to an import tax of more than 200%. Wine lists are almost universally disappointing. Many licensed restaurants do not offer wine, confining themselves to beer, cocktails and spirits. Indian wine does exist and is worth trying, if only for its novelty value. There is an Indian 'champagne' sold under the name 'Marquise de Pompadour', which, at Rs750 a bottle, is a reasonable way to put some sparkle into an evening. Indian beer, however, is excellent and invariably ice cold.

There is also a large number of restaurants in Delhi that are wholly vegetarian. Indeed, the city is a culinary paradise for the non-meat-eater, as even the categorisation of eating houses – 'veg' and 'non-veg' – suggests a presumption in favour of vegetarianism. 'Non-veg' restaurants will all offer a wide variety of 'veg' dishes.

The selected restaurants have been divided into five categories: Gastronomic, Business, Trendy, Budget and Personal Recommendations. The restaurants are listed alphabetically within these different categories, which serve as guidelines rather than absolute definitions of the establishments.

All the restaurants included have air-conditioned dining rooms. Generally, restaurants are subject to a sales tax of 8% on meals and 20% on alcohol – in the five-star hotels, there is an additional impost of 10%. This is called the 'Hotel Expenditure Tax'. There is also a further tax of 12% on soft drinks, although not all restaurants appear to charge it.

The prices quoted below are for an average three-course meal for one person and for a bottle of Indian beer (usually 600ml); they include all taxes but do not include service charges or tip.

Gastronomic

Baan Thai

Baan Thai offers splendid Thai food – some of the best in Delhi – served in stylish surroundings: the restaurant lobby contains a beautiful display of antique Thai artefacts. The ingredients are crisp and fresh and the sauces light yet pungent. Vegetarian and non-vegetarian platters offer diners the traditional favourites; particular recommendations include *yam mamueng* (spicy and sour raw mango and cashew nut salad) and *phanaeng kae* (stir-fried lamb in red curry paste). Patrons at this restaurant in The Oberoi (see *Hotels*) sit on the floor with their feet in a pit beneath the table. There are, however, conventional tables and chairs for the less supple. The service is excellent: prompt, friendly and unobstusive.
The Oberoi, Dr Zakir Hussain Marg, New Delhi
Tel: (011) 2436 3030. Fax: (011) 2436 0484.
E-mail: reservations@oberoidel.com
Website: www.oberoihotels.com
Price: Rs1600. Beer: Rs275.

House of Ming

House of Ming, located in the Taj Mahal Hotel, is one of Delhi's finest restaurants serving genuine Chinese food – as opposed to the (delicious) Indian interpretation of it. The dining room is spacious and the ambience delightful. Seafood dishes are a speciality well worth trying, despite their extra cost.

1 Mansingh Road, New Delhi
Tel: (011) 2302 6162. Fax: (011) 2302 6070.
E-mail: trn.delhi@tajhotels.com
Website: www.tajhotels.com
Price: Rs2200 (with seafood). Beer: Rs250.

La Rochelle

Part of The Oberoi (see *Hotels*), *La Rochelle* is the best French restaurant in Delhi, with prices to match. Not suprisingly, it is rarely crowded. The menu is elaborate and predominantly French; it will excite even the most jaded palate. Dishes include pan-seared foie gras, roast sea bass with white truffle risotto and parmesan, and ravioli of lobster and grilled prawns with crushed pea, tomato and chive velouté. It also boasts the most interesting wine list in Delhi, although diners should beware – a bottle of 1999 Pouilly Fuisse will cost Rs5500 with a 20% alcohol tax to pay on top.
The Oberoi, Dr Zakir Hussain Marg, New Delhi
Tel: (011) 2436 3030. Fax: (011) 2436 0484.
E-mail: reservations@oberoidel.com
Website: www.oberoihotels.com
Price: Rs2500. Beer: Rs275.

Marsala Art

The principal joy of *Marsala Art*, in the Taj Palace Hotel (see *Hotels*), is the 'Instant Sketches' menu, the so-called 'interactive' Indian eating experience. Diners sit at a bar, behind which the chefs cook. There are three set menus to choose from – seafood, vegetarian and non-vegetarian – each comprising ten small dishes. Sample dishes from the non-vegetarian menu include prawns on a sugar-cane stick, chicken cooked on charcoal, spicy lamb kebabs or mutton biriyani. Diner and chef can discuss the courses as these appear. The dining room is modern and unfussy and the food fabulous.
The Taj Palace Hotel, 1 Sardar Patel Marg, Diplomatic Enclave, New Delhi
Tel: (011) 2611 0202. Fax: (011) 2611 0808.
E-mail: palace.delhi@tajhotels.com
Website: www.tajhotels.com
Price: Rs1300. Beer: Rs270.

Lodhi tombs

Photo: Corel

Business

Bukhara Restaurant

Located in the Maurya Sheraton (see *Hotels*), the *Bukhara* is widely touted as the best place for Mughal and Northwest Frontier specialities in Delhi. The food is delicious and everything its reputation suggests – particularly recommended is the kastoori kebab and the paneer tikka, while the delicious dal makes a splendid accompaniment to any meal. Diners sit on benches at elegant low tables. The restaurant is crowded but the service remains attentive. It is one of the few restaurants in Delhi for which one should book a table in advance.
Maurya Sheraton Hotel & Towers, Sardar Patel Marg, Diplomatic Enclave, New Delhi
Tel: (011) 2611 2233. Fax: (011) 2611 3333.
Website: www.welcomgroup.com
Price: Rs1600. Beer: Rs285.

Dhaba

Dhaba is a popular restaurant in Claridges Hotel (see *Hotels*) serving Mughal or Northern Indian specialities. The familiar dishes are all excellent and the restaurant less formal than some others in the large hotels. The atmosphere is intended to be more rustic, suggesting a wayside tavern rather than a nawab's dining room.
Claridges Hotel, 12 Aurangzeb Road, New Delhi
Tel: (011) 2301 0211. Fax: (011) 2301 0625.
E-mail: claridges.hotel@gems.vsnl.net.in
Price: Rs800. Beer: Rs165.

The Host

A staid restaurant in Connaught Place, *The Host* serves Mughal and Chinese specialities to a clientele comprising Delhi businesspeople and well-heeled tourists. The food is good if a little unexciting and, in the case of the Mughal dishes – *bhuna murg*, for example – rich and filling.
F-8 Connaught Place, New Delhi
Tel: (011) 2331 6381 *or* 6576.
Price: Rs550. Beer: Rs125.

The Kashmir Club

The Kashmir Club, in the Ashok Hotel, serves reputedly the best, most authentic Kashmiri food in Delhi. The dining room is slick and modern, the atmosphere calming. The restaurant opened at the beginning of 2003 and currently only offers a buffet, although à la carte dining is planned. Lamb is a staple of Kashmiri cuisine and it appears in several guises in the buffet. The spicy ground lamb 'sausages' are particularly delicious, as is the tomato paneer. The light, fragrant Kasmiri tea is a lovely digestif. It is, sadly, not advised to travel to Kashmir at the moment, but this splendid new restaurant is just as good a place to experience the tastes of 'The Valley'.
Ashok Hotel, 50–B Chanakyapuri, New Delhi
Tel: (011) 2611 0101.
Price: Rs600. Beer: Rs180.

Spice Route

The *Spice Route* is situated in The Imperial (see *Hotels*) and serves top-quality Thai and South Asian food, in a restaurant decorated with antique, gaudily painted, wooden pillars and panels. Even if the food was not excellent – crisp, spicy and fresh – it would be worth eating here for the setting alone. The tangy oriental salads and the piquant vegetable stews are particularly recommended.
The Imperial, Janpath, New Delhi
Tel: (011) 2334 1234. Fax: (011) 2334 2255.
E-mail: luxury@theimperialindia.com
Website: www.theimperialindia.com
Price: Rs1300. Beer: Rs190.

Trendy

Lodi Garden Restaurant

Located in a leafy bower at the southern end of the Lodhi Gardens, the *Lodi Garden Restaurant* invites its patrons to 'indulge in a truly unique Mediterranean experience'. Certainly the menu represents an expansive tour of northern and eastern Mediterranean cuisine, taking in Lebanese, Turkish, Greek, Italian and French dishes. The restaurant provides a welcome change from the staple Mughal cuisine of Delhi and is deservedly popular. The mezze are highly recommended; so too the 'minted Doria', a 'refreshing blend of cucumber and fresh mint'.
Lodhi Road, New Delhi
Tel: (011) 2465 5054 *or* 2808.
Price: Rs650. Beer: Rs180.

Moet's

A well-known and popular restaurant in Defence Colony Market, *Moet's* serves different cuisines in separate but adjacent restaurants – the two original being Indian and Chinese. The Indian establishment serves Mughal and Kashmiri specialities and a range of vegetarian dishes, while the Chinese menu offers a wide range of standard favourites. It has two new annexes: *Grooves@Moets*, which serves European-style brasserie food, and *Sizzlers*, which, as the name suggests, offers kebabs. The food – particularly the *murg haryali* kebab or the *murg achari* in the Indian restaurant – is good and the smart, youngish clientele generates a buzz.
50 Defence Colony Market, New Delhi
Tel: (011) 2462 6814 *or* 2463 5280.
Price: Rs450. Beer: Rs160.

Naivedyam

Situated in the trendy Haus Khaz Village, *Naivedyam* is a South Indian restaurant. The food, which is wholly vegetarian, is fresh, delicious and varied. The restaurant is dark and cool; the black, panelled walls are decorated with gilded Hindu deities, in a style that might be described as 'antique chic'. In common with most South Indian establishments, Naivedyam is unlicensed but has a good selection of interesting 'thirst quenchers' on its drinks menu.
Naivedyam, 1 Haus Khaz Village, New Delhi
Tel: (011) 2696 0426.
Website: http://fhraindia.com/restaurant/delhi/naivedyam
Price: Rs160. Unlicensed.

Photo: Government of India Tourist Office

India Gate

Top of the Village

A rooftop restaurant open to the skies in Haus Khaz Village, *Top of the Village* commands a magnificent view over the remains of Shah Feroz's tomb and madrasa. At night, the ruins are floodlit and make a memorable backdrop to dinner. It is worth going there for the view alone, although the food – Mughal specialities, including particularly good paneer dishes – is more than acceptable. No lunch.
12 Haus Khaz Village, New Delhi
Tel: (011) 2685 2227 *or* 3857. Fax: (011) 2652 2226.
Website: www.fhraindia.com/restaurant/delhi/bistro
Price: Rs600. Beer: Rs175.

Veg Gulati Restaurant

Veg Gulati serves North Indian vegetarian specialities, such as the delicious paneer tikka, tandoori gobhi and tandoori aloo. Although non-descript in terms of decor, it is a popular, family restaurant where patrons will be served quickly and with a smile. Next door is the sister establishment that also serves non-vegetarian food.
8 Pandara Road Market, New Delhi
Tel: (011) 2338 8830 *or* 8863.
Price: Rs450. Unlicensed.

Budget

China Fare

A tiny, prettily decorated and unfussy restaurant in Khan Market, *China Fare* is popular among the expatriate community. It serves delicious Chinese food, cooked in the Indian style (hot and spicy), at reasonable prices. The service is friendly too.
27a Khan Market, New Delhi
Tel: (011) 2461 8602.
Price: Rs400. Unlicensed.

Have More

Located in Pandara Road Market, *Have More* serves the standard Mughal dishes to a large and loyal clientele. The food is fresh and well cooked; the Kashmiri chicken kebab is delicious, spicy and tender. The butter chicken is also highly recommended, as is the vegetarian food. The decor is somewhat tired but diners should not let that put them off.
11–12 Pandara Road Market, New Delhi.
Tel: (011) 2338 7070 *or* 7171.
Price: Rs500. Unlicensed.

Karim's

Established in 1913, *Karim's* is something of a Delhi institution. It serves Mughal food in rudimentary but clean surroundings, off a courtyard that is close behind Jama Masjid in Old Delhi. The tandoori chicken is highly recommended – the bird, surprisingly, arrives whole and spread-eagled but is mouthwateringly good.
Hotel Bombay Orient, 16 Jama Masjid, New Delhi
Tel: (011) 2326 9880 *or* 4981.
E-mail: khpl@del3.vsnl.net.in
Price: Rs300. Unlicensed.

Machan

Part of the Taj Mahal Hotel (see *Hotels*), *Machan* is a 24-hour café that offers a variety of styles of Oriental and European food, including Thai, Vietnamese and Italian, on a constantly changing basis. It is a reasonable place to eat quickly and well – the food is served from a buffet and diners are offered a complimentary glass of wine. It is popular despite the

Jama Masjid

dreadful and instrusive American easy-listening piped music that accompanies every meal.
Taj Mahal Hotel, 1 Mansingh Road, New Delhi
Tel: (011) 2302 6162. Fax: (011) 2302 6070.
E-mail: trn.delhi@tajhotels.com
Price: Rs760. Beer: Rs250.

Sagar

Sagar is located in Defence Colony Market and serves South Indian vegetarian food in a basic environment. The dhosas, idlis and uphapams, light yet filling, make a delicious alternative to the omnipresent Mughal food. The restaurant is very popular, the service swift and polite and the bill pleasingly low. *Sagar* is now a chain, with ten other restaurants across Delhi, although this one is the original.
18 Defence Colony Market, New Delhi
Tel: (011) 2461 7832.
Price: Rs180. Unlicensed.

Turtles Cafe

Turtles is a pleasant café situated above *The Full Circle* bookshop in Khan Market. It is a good place to read a book over a cup of coffee or to take a light snack lunch – such as pasta bake or quiche. The café serves cakes and scones too and is popular with ex-pats of all ages.
The Full Circle Bookshop, 5B Khan Market, New Delhi
Tel: (011) 2465 5641.
Price: Rs150. Unlicensed.

Personal Recommendations

The Curzon Room

Located in the Maidens Hotel, in the Civil Lines, *The Curzon Room* serves an excellent buffet at lunch and dinner; at dinner, there is à la carte dining as well. The buffet offers a mouthwatering variety of well-cooked vegetarian and non-vegetarian North Indian dishes. The dining room is cool and gracious, with a high ceiling and more than a whiff of the Raj about it. Indeed, the hotel was built by the British before New Delhi rose from the dusty Jamuna plain. On the walls, there are some deeply nostalgic photographs of British India, of Maharajahs and Commissioners, elephants, trains and palaces, high ceremonial and tiger shoots.
Maidens Hotel, 7 Sham Nath Marg, New Delhi
Tel: (011) 2397 5464. Fax: (011) 2398 0771.
Website: www.oberoihotels.com
Price: Rs495. Beer: Rs195.

Flavors of Italy

One of the better known Italian restaurants in Delhi, *Flavors of Italy* is a relaxed, café-style restaurant offering reasonably authentic Italian food – pizza and pasta dishes – at reasonable prices. There are often Italian delicacies on sale too, such as good-quality olive oil or parmesan cheese.
52C Moolchand Flyover Complex, opposite Moolchand Hospital, Defence Colony, New Delhi
Tel: (011) 2464 5644.
Price: Rs400. Unlicensed.

The Imperial

The perfect start to the day is breakfast in the garden of The Imperial (see *Hotels*). From a table on the terrace or in the verandah, guests look over the lush lawns and borders of the hotel's celebrated gardens and can admire the tall palm trees along the drive. The buffet provides everything that one could possibly desire at breakfast time, from cornflakes to idlis, via bacon and eggs.
Imperial Hotel, 1, Janpath, New Delhi
Tel: (011) 2334 1234. Fax: (011) 2334 2255.
E-mail: luxury@theimperialindia.com
Website: www.theimperialindia.com
Price: Rs460 (including drinks).

Photo: Government of India Tourist Office

Photo: Government of India Tourist Office

Yoga practice

Lazeez Affaire

In the heart of the Diplomatic Enclave, *Lazeez Affaire* is an elegant, upmarket restaurant, which attracts a smart, well-heeled clientele. The menu is imaginative and the food carefully cooked – the kakori kebab, the *murg hyderabadi* and the stuffed tomato are all particularly recommended. The rogan josh, made with shank of lamb, is a sumptuous rendition of an established favourite. Diners may either sit on the floor, in traditional Indian style, or at tables.

6/48 Shopping Centre, Malcha Marg, Chanakyapuri, New Delhi

Tel: (011) 2687 8155.

Price: Rs850. Beer: Rs170.

Sahara

Sahara is a Japanese restaurant located in the spankingly modern Hotel Metropolitan Nikko, a stone's throw from Connaught Place. It is an airy, spacious and minimal restaurant, serving top-notch Japanese food, supposedly the best in Delhi. The sushi is fabulous and highly recommended: it is swimmingly fresh, tender and succulent. The service is suitably obeisant. A sushi lunch at Sahara is the perfect antidote to a hot morning shopping in Connaught Place.

Hotel Metropolitan Nikko, Bangla Sahib Road, New Delhi

Tel: (011) 2334 2000. Fax: (011) 2334 3000.

Price: Rs1500. Beer: Rs235.

ENTERTAINMENT

Nightlife

Delhi has a long way to go to compete with Mumbai as the capital of Indian nightlife. In Delhi, it is notoriously difficult to obtain an alcohol licence and many of the swishest watering holes and nightclubs are situated in the five-star international hotels – with prices to match. Apart from these hotels, the watering holes of Delhi are concentrated around Connaught Place, with various outposts in the more prosperous southern suburbs. Wine in Delhi is expensive and frequently of indifferent quality – those who wish to drink would be well advised to stick to beer, spirits or cocktails. Although there is no minimum drinking age, the minimum purchasing age in India is 18 years. The price of a beer while out and about in Delhi can vary considerably, depending on the venue, although averages out to approximately Rs200.

Local newspapers (*Hindustan Times* or *Times of India*) carry daily and weekly listings and information on nightlife in Delhi. *City Scan*, *City Guide*, *delhidiary* and *cityinfo* magazines also carry listings. Bars and pubs in Delhi open and close with astonishing regularity, so it is always advisable to consult the listings for the latest developments.

Bars

Anyone who has been to Delhi returns to tell stories about the *Rodeo* bar, A-Block, Connaught Place, because of the mock saddle seats at the bar and its Indian waiters dressed, quite preposterously, as cowboys. *Pegasus*, L-Block, Connaught Place, is the most convincing attempt in Delhi to replicate an English pub. The *Maurya Sheraton*, Sardar Patel Marg, Diplomatic Enclave, has a lively bar behind the hotel lobby, with a golfing theme, while *Henri's*, at the top of the Meridien Hotel, Windsor Place, offers a fine panorama of the city. The celebrated *Cavalry Bar*, in the Maidens Hotel, 7 Sham Nath Marg, Civil Lines, is a relic of the Raj and will appeal to those who like bars to be simple yet smart. *Rick's*, situated in the Taj Mahal Hotel, 1 Mansingh Road, has recently been refurbished in a swish modernist style and offers live music to boot. In Defence Colony Market, there is a new and noisy bar above *Gola* restaurant. Vasant Vihar boasts a *TGI Fridays* – very popular with hip young Delhiites – and the *Golden Dragon*, both situated in C-Block, Market. Expresso bars are increasingly popular and can be found in many areas of the city. The *Barista* chain is the most widely established.

Casinos

There are no casinos in Delhi as gambling in India – except on the racecourse – is illegal.

Clubs

There are about half a dozen discos that have become the regular haunts of elite Delhiites. Most are in the luxury hotels and many of them operate a couples-only policy, as well as a dress code. One of the most popular is *CJ's*, at Le Meridien, Windsor Place. The recently opened *RPM*, above *Lazeez Affaire* restaurant, Shopping Centre, Malcha Marg, Chanakyapuri, has a vibrant atmosphere and is popular among younger, well-heeled Delhiites. *Ssteel*, in the Ashok Hotel, 50-B Chanakyapuri, is a bar that has adopted a blues-based theme. *Annabelles*, at the InterContinental, Barakhamba Avenue, Connaught Place, and *Wheels*, at the Ambassador, Sujan Singh Park, both have an enthusiastic following.

Live Music

The Jazz Bar, at the Maurya Sheraton, Sardar Patel Marg, Diplomatic Enclave, features a live jazz show every evening, performed by Indian musicians. The *Tavern*, at the Hotel Imperial, on Janpath, offers the same in its restaurant-cum-bar.

Sport

In India, cricket reigns supreme and is played everywhere, from smart cricket clubs to the grassy spaces of New Delhi and street corners. The national side is followed with a devotion that borders on the fanatic. India is a consistently strong team, ably doing battle with its mighty Antipodean, South African and UK rivals. In Delhi, Test Matches are played at *Ferozshah Kotla Stadium*, on Bahadur Shah Zhafar Marg, between September and March. Attending a Test Match here is quite an experience and is not for the faint-hearted.

Other popular Indian games include *kabbadi*, a team sport combining the characteristics of wrestling and rugby, and *kho kho*, an evolved game of catch and hockey, in which the Indians regularly produce sides that challenge the best in the world.

Bowling

Indians seem to enjoy bowling and there is a popular bowling alley at the *Qutb Hotel*, off Sri Aurobindo Marg (tel: (011) 2652 1234). Bowlers can also indulge their hobby at *South Delhi Club*, Greater Kailash (tel: (011) 2622 0037).

Fitness Centres

In Delhi, fitness centres mean status and the well groomed keep in shape at *Arya Vaidya Sala*, South Extension (tel: (011) 2462 1790), and *Nelson Health Club*, Hotel Samrat, Chanakyapuri (tel: (011) 2611 0606). *Beyond Looks*, Kalkaji (tel: (011) 2628 2244), provides a comprehensive range of beauty treatments, as well as yoga and meditation sessions. Many of the five-star hotels also provide exercise facilities for their guests.

Golf

Delhi's best-known golf course is the *Delhi Golf and Country Club*, Dr Zakir Hussain Marg (tel: (011) 2436 2768). It boasts a nine-hole and an 18-hole course, both of which are dotted with Mughal mausolea. The timid should note that cobras supposedly lurk in the rough. The 18-hole course is open to the public on weekdays but restricted to members and their guests

at weekends. The nine-hole course is open to all throughout the week. Green fees are Rs1950 (US$40) and a set of clubs can be hired for Rs100. Caddies and ball-spotters are available.

Horseracing

Delhi Racecourse, off Safdarjang Road (tel: (011) 2301 2943), has regular meetings during the racing season, which runs from October until the end of April. Delhi's racecourse is an informal, almost provincial course, in marked contrast to Mumbai's grand stands and spacious lawns. There is a large covered shed, which contains the bookies' pitches. Admission to the Members' Enclosure costs Rs50.

Horseriding and Polo

The *Delhi Riding Club*, Safdarjang Road (tel: (011) 2301 1891), and the *Delhi Polo Club*, Cavalry Cariappa Marg (tel: (011) 2569 9777), both provide equestrian sporting opportunities and facilities. The polo season is from October to March.

Swimming

The safest swimming is in hotel pools, including *Hotel Imperial*, Janpath (tel: (011) 2334 1234), *Hotel Samrat*, Chanakyapuri (tel: (011) 2611 0606), and *Ashok Hotel*, 50-B Chanakyapuri (tel: (011) 2611 0101). All hotels are likely to charge non-guests. Public swimming baths are located at *NDMC Pools*, Nehru Park, Chanakyapuri, *National Stadium Complex*, opposite India Gate, and *Talkatora Pool*, Talkatora Road.

Tennis

Another sport thought to have originated in India, there are tennis facilities at *Delhi Lawn Tennis Association*, Africa Avenue, *Jawaharlal Nehru Stadium*, Bhisham Pitamah Marg, and the *National Sports Club of India*, Mathura Road (tel: (011) 2338 5564).

Watersports

Watersports at Bhaleswa Lake, as well as other adventure activities – local and further afield – are available through *Delhi Tourism's* Adventure Tourism Division (tel: (011) 2341 4011).

Yoga

Sivananda Yoga Vedanta Nataraja Center, Community Centre, Greater Kailash (tel: (011) 2648 0869), offers yoga classes.

Shopping

Silks, gemstones, carpets, antique furniture, spices ... the warehouses and emporia of Delhi are filled with a treasure trove of goods from the far corners of the Indian subcontinent. The intrepid shopper will head for the chowks and alleyways of Old Delhi, while the more cautious will stick to the well-trodden round of Connaught Place and the State Emporia Complex on Baba Kharak Sing Marg, with perhaps an excursion in the direction of Hauz Khas Village and South Extension market.

The most central of the government-run handicraft centres is the *Cottage Industries Emporium*, on Janpath, which is well stocked with leather, textiles, jewellery, silks, cotton and saris. On Baba Kharak Sing Marg, the *Himachal Pradesh Emporium* has soft blankets and shawls in wool, cashmere or pashmina, while the *Poompahar Emporium* stocks the region's glazed Thanjuver pottery and traditional stone carvings of gods and goddesses, and the *Uttar Pradesh Emporium* specialises in leather

Kathakali

goods and copper and brass items. Located in south Delhi, Hauz Khas Village has a centralised collection of furniture shops and bazaars, along with a good selection of frequently changing boutiques offering designer clothes, silks, chiffons and organzas.

There is any number of shops selling carpets in Delhi but the visitor would be well advised to exercise caution and stick to the reputable, fixed-price, non-commission establishments. All the carpets at *Saga*, on Mathura Road, come with a Central Silk Board guarantee.

Delhi's markets come crammed with goods, people and smells. The magnificent bazaars of *Chandni Chowk* are open daily and piled high with gold, nuts, spices, silks, carpets and perfume and are worth visiting for the spectacle alone. *Sunder Nagar Market*, off Mathura Road, is open Monday to Saturday and is a good place to search for antiques and jewellery and boasts a huge variety of other knick-knacks and artefacts spilling out of the shops. One of Delhi's most prestigious markets and a regular haunt of the city's ex-pats, is *Khan Market*, just south of India Gate, open Tuesday to Sunday. There are a number of excellent bookshops here. The wholesale *Spice Market*, on Khari Baoli, in Old Delhi, is where, for centuries, the culinary traditions of North Asia, China, Persia and the Middle East have worked their influence on local cuisine.

Except in the government-run shops, haggling is always the order of the day – it is the only way for shoppers to ensure that they do not pay too far over the odds. Shops tend to open at around 1000 and close between 1800 and 1900. There is no VAT in India at the moment, although the possibility of introducing it has been proposed and discussed in Parliament. However, the idea is so contentious that it is unlikely to be imminent.

Culture

The premier performing arts institute is *Sangeet Natak Akademi*, Firoz Shah Road (tel: (011) 2338 7246),

while the arts complex of *Triveni Kala Sangam*, 205 Tansen Marg (tel: (011) 2371 8833), contains two galleries devoted to fine art and an open-air and indoor theatre, as well as a sculpture park and bookshop. Among the ranks of Delhi's 'chaterati', the *India International Centre*, 40 Lodhi Estate (tel: (011) 2461 9431), is a political icon and post-Independence institution. The capital's premier cultural centre, it organises seminars, lectures, music and dance recitals, as well as screening films on all aspects of Indian culture and environment. Nearby is the huge and recently built *Indian Habitat Centre*, junction of Lodhi Road and Max Mueller Marg, which offers a lively and interesting programme of drama and lectures.

Most of the cultural centres host concerts and exhibitions, as well as screening films in English or their native language. These include, on Kasturba Gandhi Marg, the German cultural centre *Max Mueller Bhavan* (tel: (011) 2332 9506), the *British Council* (tel: (011) 2371 1401), and the *American Centre* (tel: (011) 2331 6841), at D13 NDSE Part II, the *Alliance Francaise* (tel: (011) 2625 8128), on Golf Links, the *Italian Culture Centre* (tel: (011) 2687 1901), and, on Firoz Shah Road, the *Japan Cultural Centre* (tel: (011) 2332 9838) and the *Russian Cultural Centre* (tel: (011) 2332 9102), which houses the Eisenstein Film Club.

Local newspapers (*Hindustan Times* or *Times of India*) carry daily and weekly listings of all events and should be the reference point for anyone interested in sampling the rich cultural life of Delhi. *City Scan*, *City Guide*, *delhidiary* and *cityinfo* magazines also carry listings. While reading the newspapers, it is possible to get insight into another aspect of Indian culture – the marriage columns. 'Brides Sought' and 'Grooms Required' in the weekend newspapers are indispensable reading.

Music

Delhi's concert halls tend to be busy more or less year round, with the *Delhi Symphony Orchestra* performing at the *Kamani Auditorium*, Copernicus Marg (tel: (011) 2338 8084), and the *FICCI Auditorium*, Tansen Marg (tel: (011) 2335 7369). Hindustani music is by far the most popular, closely followed by Karnatic music. Some of Delhi's open-air venues, such as the majestically lit *Qutb Minar* (see *Key Attractions*), provide a dramatic backdrop for select performances. The *Delhi Music Society* (tel: (011) 2611 5331) is based at Nayaya Marg, Chanakyapuri.

Theatre

Delhi is well provided with innovative theatres and the area just to the north of India Gate is home to a number of these, including the *Kamani Theatre*, Copernicus Marg (tel: (011) 2338 8084). The *Abhimanch*, Bahawalpur House (tel: (011) 2338 9402), stages an exciting programme of theatre, dance and films throughout the year.

Dance

Lovers of dance are well catered for in Delhi, seeing as a rich mix of classical – including Kathak, Bharatnatyam and Kathakali – folk and tribal dance, as well as ballet is performed at various auditoria throughout the year. Hauz Khas, Delhi-Mehrauli Road, is a good spot to join well-heeled Delhiites, as they sit back over a meal or a drink while taking in an open-air dance or music performance. The *India International Centre*, 40 Lodhi Estate (tel: (011) 2461 9431), and the *Triveni Theatre*, in Triveni Kala Sangam (see above), are both popular venues for regular, professional dance shows.

Film

Cinema is by far the most popular form of entertainment in India – it has been suggested that 23 million Indians watch a film every day. The glitzy love stories and action movies of Bollywood attract huge audiences and their stars are national figures. There is any number of cinemas in Delhi, some showing only films in Hindi, some only in English and some in both languages. English-language films are shown, among many others, at the *Ritz*, Kasmiri Gate, and the *Chanakya*, Chanakyapuri.

The movie that is closest to Delhi's beating heart is the immensely popular *Monsoon Wedding* (2001), which was set in the city. The busy marketplaces of

Son et lumière show at Red Fort

SPECIAL EVENTS

Dates are calculated according to the Hindu and Nanakshahi Era calendars, which vary from the Gregorian calendar, so they may change. The months listed below are those for 2003.

Birthday of Guru Gobind Singh Ji, Sikh festival, Jan, throughout the city
Republic Day, national holiday, 26 Jan, parade along Rajpath, throughout the city
Martyr's Day, commemoration of Mahatma Gandhi's assassination, 30 Jan, Raj Ghat, throughout the city
Holi, Hindu festival of harvest and fertility, on the day after the full moon, mid-Mar, throughout the city
Baisakhi, Sikh festival, mid-Apr, throughout the city
Janamashtami, anniversary of Krishna's birth, Aug, throughout the city mainly Lakshmi Narayan Mandir
Independence Day, national holiday, 15 Aug, throughout the city
Navratri, Hindu festival, one week in Sep/Oct, throughout the city
Dusshera, Hindu festival, two weeks in Oct, throughout the city
Diwali, Hindu New Year festival, late Oct, throughout the city
Qutub Festival, three-day festival of classical music and dance, Oct, Qutub Minar, Sharad Pournima
Birthday of Guru Nanak Dev Ji, Nov, throughout the city
Martyrdom of Guru Tegh Bahadur Ji, Sikh festival, late Nov, throughout the city

Delhi punctuate director Mira Nair's beautiful celluloid weaving of character, place and drama.

Cultural Events

India's calendar of festivals draws upon the nation's Hindu, Muslim, Jain, Sikh, Parsi, Buddhist and Christian communities, with a sprinkling of non-religious festivals thrown in for good measure. Most will be celebrated, to some extent, somewhere in Delhi. On *Republic Day*, 26 January, a week of celebration kicks off with a military parade along Rajpath. A guard of honour stands to attention at Raj Ghat on *Martyr's Day*, 30 January, to commemorate the anniversary of the assassination of Mahatma Gandhi. Spring exuberance erupts on the day after the full moon in early March, during *Holi*, when people running through the streets bombard each other and stray tourists with brightly coloured powder and water, to celebrate good harvests and fertility of the land. Often an occasion for indulging in a drink or two too many. The *Raslila* is performed across India, recreating the life of Krishna, on the anniversary of his birth, *Janmasthami*, which falls in August/September. The city celebrates most ostentatiously at Lakshmi Narayan Mandir. *Diwali*

(Deepavali), the most pan-Indian of Hindu festivals – coinciding with the onset of the Hindu and Jain new year – symbolises the victory of righteousness and the lifting of spiritual darkness by commemorating Lord Rama's return to his kingdom, Ayodhya, after his 14-year exile. In 2003, Diwali falls on 25 October and is preceded by five days of celebrations.

Literary Notes

At the time of Muhammad Shah Rangila, the poet Mir wrote of Delhi: 'Each glance reveals a picture, each coming of the spring enchains.' The delights of Delhi have been dissected, eulogised and disputed over the generations, by a whole cannon of writers of both Indian and Western origin.

William Dalrymple's *City of Djinns* (1994), the fruit of a year spent in Delhi, is a luminous and penetrative combination of history, observation and anecdote. By weaving the past with the present, he brings the city to life, explaining its mysteries and wonders. The author's Delhi period was just the beginning of years of relentless travelling the length and breadth of the Indian subcontinent, distilled in his collection *The Age of Kali* (1998).

A meaty slice of Indian life viewed from the inside is Vikram Seth's epic *A Suitable Boy* (1993), which follows the lives of four extended families set against the political landscape in a newly independent northern India in the 1950s. The central plot – a love story – runs through a richly populated and eternally varied landscape, with the tension between Hindus and Muslims a constant and dangerous undertow.

Anita Desai, who was educated in Delhi, also focuses on the time of Partition in her first published novel, *Clear Light of Day* (1980), which traces the interweaving, departures and reconciliation of the Das family of Old Delhi. Ahmed Ali's *Twilight in Delhi* (1940) gives a pungent whiff of life in early 20th-century Delhi. Through Ali's wistful eyes, the reader glimpses the rhythms and rituals of Islamic life in the city, before the construction of New Delhi – a world that was destroyed forever by Partition.

One of the most prominent of Indian writers today, Arundhati Roy, who won the Booker Prize with *God of Small Things* (1997), studied and lives in Delhi.

Those interested in the history of India's progress to Independence and beyond should search out a copy of Durga Das's *India: From Curzon to Nehru* (1969). It is a most absorbing book, written by someone – a Delhi man to the core – who was himself on stage as these momentous events unfolded.

t is difficult to believe that a century ago Dubai was little more than a desert-strewn wildscape where Bedouin tribes roamed the sands and a huddle of settlers crowded around the banks of the lifeblood creek. Even as Europe embarked on the mass industrial destruction of World War I, Dubai still had no running water, no real roads and the main mode of transport was the camel.

Dubai first grew as a hub on the ancient trading route between Mesopotamia and the Indus Valley and, by the 19th century, a small fishing village had taken root on the Shindagha peninsula, at the mouth of Dubai Creek. The village was inhabited by the Bani Yas tribe, who were led by the Maktoum family, the dynasty that still presides over Dubai today. The city's remarkable success story really began in the 1960s. During the process of shaking off the shackles of British colonial rule, oil was struck in 1966 and Dubai has never looked back. Since the 1960s, the population has increased tenfold to over a million

people and now over 400 hotels welcome in the temporary ex-pat workers and tourists who help run the economy. Indeed, only 25% of the emirate's population, at last count, were actually ethnically Emirati. Dubai's population mixture has to be one of the world's most cosmopolitan and this diversity discourages any real ethnic tensions despite war or the threat of war elsewhere in the region.

Dubai's evolution has been dramatic, with sweeping skyscrapers and gleaming office blocks rising up on the banks of Dubai Creek. Development has been well managed, with a structure and order to the city that demonstrates that the oil wealth has been well handled and channelled. The rulers of Dubai have a penchant for grand projects – one year a new extension to the port facilities, the next the world's tallest purpose-built hotel and now the Palm Islands, a massive project that will bring 120km (75 miles) of new beachfront, through the creation of the world's two largest man-made islands, as well as hotels, villas,

shopping malls, cinemas and Dubai's first marine park. Dubai seems to know no end to its ambition or have any inhibitions, with new plans constantly on the drawing board.

The US-led war against Saddam Hussein's regime in Iraq in 2003 and regional instability has, however, put a major strain on the city and hit tourism, one of its most successful industries. Until 2003, more and more tourists were flocking to Dubai every year, which is unsurprising, considering the idyllic climate for much of the year, with constant sunshine and only an annual average of five days of rainfall. During summer, however, the heat is extreme, making trips away from air-conditioned vehicles and buildings unbearable.

Despite its sunny disposition, the immediate prospects of the emirate's tourist industry and its economic situation as a whole seem certain to be governed by developments in the rest of the Middle East.

Emirates Towers

Photo: Leonardo

TRAVEL

Getting There By Air

Dubai International Airport (DBX)

Tel: (04) 224 5555. Fax: (04) 224 4074.

Website: www.dubaiairport.com

Dubai International Airport, located five kilometres (three miles) southeast of the city centre, is the busiest airport in the Middle East, handling flights for over 80 airlines, flying to more than 130 destinations worldwide. Over 16 million passengers passed through the airport in 2002. There are two state-of-the-art terminals and first-rate facilities. Despite regional instibility, the national carrier, Emirates Airlines, plans to press ahead with new flights to London and North America. A third terminal is planned for completion by 2006.

Major airlines: *Emirates Airlines* (tel: (04) 214 4444 *or* 800 4444; website: www.emirates.com) is the national airline. *Gulf Air* (tel: (04) 271 3222; website: www.gulfairco.com) is the regional airline. Emirates will have its own terminal by 2005 and the first of its new double-decker Airbus A380 'super-jumbos' is set to arrive in 2006. Other major airlines include *Air France, Air Ukraine, Alitalia, Cathay Pacific, Cyprus Airways, Czech Airlines, Ghana Airways, Gulf Air, Kenya Airways, Kuwait Airways, Lithuanian Airlines, Lufthansa, Malaysia Airlines, Olympic Airways, Oman Air, Qatar Airways, Turkish Airways* and *Yemen Airways*.

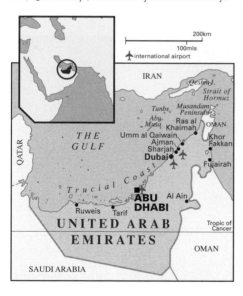

Approximate flight times to Dubai: From London is 7 hours 45 minutes; from New York is 14 hours 50 minutes; from Los Angeles is 19 hours 55 minutes; from Toronto is 14 hours 10 minutes and from Sydney is 16 hours 15 minutes.

Airport facilities: These include ATMs, bureau de change, banking, post office, medical centre, pharmacy, cafés, restaurants, gym, health spa, executive lounges, left-luggage, duty-free shopping, tourist information bureau, smoking areas, children's playrooms and car hire from *Avis, Budget, Fast Rent a Car* and *Hertz*.

Business facilities: There are two airport business centres. The *Global Link Business Centre* is located in the departure lounge, with facilities including six ISD booths, workstations with Internet connection and fax machines, as well as an around-the-clock secretarial service. The second business centre is the *Connect Business Centre*, located in the International

Hotel (tel: (04) 216 4278; fax: (04) 224 5955), which has five meeting rooms and a conference room for up to 60 delegates. Eight workstations include ISDN terminals and fax machines. Secretarial and office services support is offered. There are a number of executive lounges in the airport, some offering excellent business facilities.

Arrival/departure tax: None.

Transport to the city: *Dubai Municipality* (tel: (800) 4848; website: www.dm.gov.ae) airport buses, with air conditioning and extra luggage space, leave for Al Subkha (route 401) and Al Ghubaiba (route 402) bus stations every 30 minutes daily 0600–2200 (journey time – 20 minutes) and cost Dh3. From the bus stations there are regular transfers to all parts of the city. Prepaid airport taxis can be booked in the arrival hall. These charge a fixed Dh30 for destinations in the city centre (journey time – 10 minutes). Otherwise, Dubai Transport taxis are available outside the arrivals terminal, with a hefty Dh20 initial charge.

Getting There By Water

Jebel Ali Port is located 30km (18.5 miles) to the south of the city centre. It is the world's largest man-made port – over 120 shipping lines use the port and it has over 100 berths– but passenger services are limited and are not designed to cater for tourists. A port tax of Dh10 is levied on departures from the UAE. *Dubai Port Authority* (tel: (04) 881 5000; website: www.dpa.co.ae) can provide further information. The government-owned *Dubai Cruise Terminal* (website:www. dubaitourism.co.ae/www/discover/cruiseterminal.asp), which is capable of dealing with two liners at a time, opened at *Port Rashid* in March 2001, with over 50 visiting cruise liners in 2002. Facilities at the cruise terminal include reception, check-in, an information centre, VIP lounge, a relaxation zone and café, rest rooms, a big-screen entertainment centre, duty free, exhibits and an Arabian palm garden.

Ferry services: Ferry services operate to ports in Iran from Sharjah, although these are not recommended for tourists and timetables are erratic. Plans have been mooted for a more developed and comprehensive regional ferry service but these are very much on the back burner at present.

Transport to the city: The fare to Jebel Ali in a metered taxi will cost Dh60–70 (journey time – 20–30 minutes). The fare in a shared taxi to Al-Ghubaiba Bus Station costs Dh7. Dubai Cruise Terminal has its own taxi stand with taxis into Deira or Bur Dubai costing around Dh20–30.

Getting There By Rail

There are no railways in the United Arab Emirates, although there are plans for a public railway system. Construction is supposed to start late in 2003, with a line to the airport first on the drawing board and later extensions as far as Abu Dhabi. However, these developments might take a back seat, due to the current geo-political situation.

Getting There By Road

The United Arab Emirates boasts an impressive network of first-class roads that connect major towns and villages, including a multi-lane highway between

Dubai and Abu Dhabi. Highways and main roads in Dubai and the United Arab Emirates are designated by an Emirate Route Number. Driving in the UAE is on the right. Speed limits are clearly displayed on road signs and are usually 60–80kph (37–50mph) around town and 100–120kph (62–74mph) elsewhere. Seatbelts are compulsory and it is illegal to use handheld mobile phones while driving. Certain minor traffic offences incur on-the-spot fines. Drinking and driving is illegal and the maximum legal alcohol to blood ratio for driving is zero. The police must be called to any road traffic accident – no matter how minor – and those involved in the accident must remain at the scene with their vehicles.

A valid International Driving Permit, a valid national licence and a passport are required to drive in Dubai. Visitors from many European, North American and Pan-Asian countries can obtain a temporary local driving licence if they do not have an international licence – a valid national licence, passport and two passport-sized photographs are required for applicants to obtain this. Drivers must be over 18 years old. Third party insurance is compulsory.

The *Arabian Automobile Association* (tel: (04) 266 9989; fax: (04) 268 2646; website: www.aaa-uae.com) can provide further information.

Emergency breakdown service: *Arabian Automobile Association* (800) 4900 (toll free).

Routes to the city: The main Emirate Route Numbers into Dubai are 77 from Jebel Ali, 88 from Sharjah, 44 from Wajajah, 66 from Al-Ain and 11 from Abu Dhabi.

Approximate driving times to Dubai: From Al-Ain – 1 hour 15 minutes; Abu Dhabi – 1 hour 30 minutes; Muscat – 4 hours.

Coach services: Two buses leave daily for Muscat in Oman, departing from the car park at the *Airline Centre*, Al-Maktoum Road, Deira (tel: (04) 203 3923), at 0730 and 1630. Tickets, costing Dh90 for a return, can be purchased from the driver or the Airline Centre. The *Gold Souk Bus Station*, off Al-Khor Street, and *Al-Ghubaiba Bus Station*, Al-Ghubaiba Road, are the main departure points for local and intercity services, which operate 0600–2300. *Dubai Municipality* (tel: (800) 4848; website: www.dm.gov.ae) can provide further information. There are also buses from Dubai to Jordan, Lebanon and Syria.

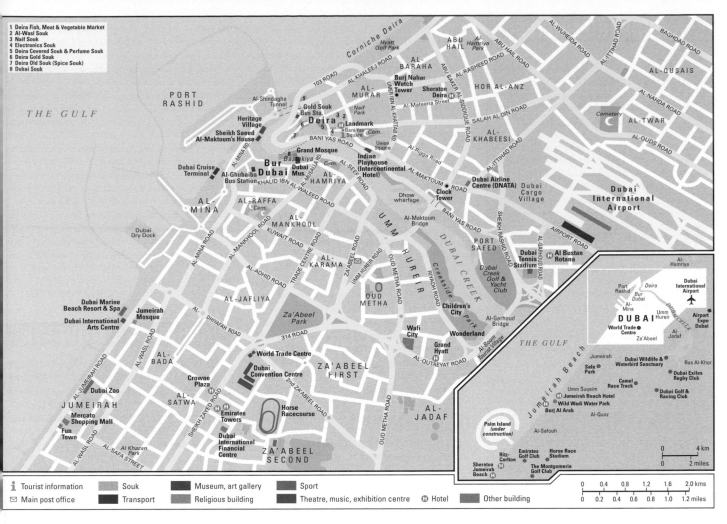

1 Deira Fish, Meat & Vegetable Market
2 Al-Wasl Souk
3 Naif Souk
4 Electronics Souk
5 Deira Covered Souk & Perfume Souk
6 Deira Gold Souk
7 Deira Old Souk (Spice Souk)
8 Dubai Souk

i Tourist information	Souk	Museum, art gallery	Sport
✉ Main post office	Transport	Religious building	Theatre, music, exhibition centre	🏨 Hotel	Other building

0 0.4 0.8 1.2 1.6 2.0 kms
0 0.2 0.4 0.6 0.8 1.0 1.2 miles

Dubai Transport Corporation (tel: (04) 264 1111; website: www.dubaitransport.gov.ae) operates minibus services to the main cities of the UAE, however, it is only possible for travellers to catch these once they are out of Dubai city.

Getting Around

Public Transport

The car is the most popular method of transport in Dubai. In addition, the major tourist hotels provide shuttle bus services for guests. However, *Dubai Municipality* (tel: (04) 285 9401 *or* 221 5555 *or* (800) 4848 (dedicated freephone information line); website: www.dm.gov.ae) operates a reasonable public **bus** service on 36 routes, daily 0600–2300. Adult fares are Dh1–3.50 depending on destination and are paid to the driver upon boarding; it is useful for travellers to have the exact change ready.

Three types of bus **passes** are available. *Smart Cards* give Dh22 worth of transport for Dh20, while monthly passes (called *taufee*) are available at a cost of Dh120 for unlimited travel within the whole city (Blue District) or Dh75 for journeys on one side of Dubai Creek (Red District is Deira and Yellow District is Bur Dubai). Passes, timetables and bus maps are available from the bus stations in Deira and Bur Dubai. Routes and bus numbers are posted in both Arabic and English.

Basic **wooden boats**, locally referred to as *abras*, cross Dubai Creek from Bur Dubai to the Textile Souk area in Deira. These are operated by Dubai Municipality daily 0600–2400 (journey time – 5 minutes) and are excellent value at Dh0.50. New rowing *abras* have recently been brought in as part of a conservation programme, running from Creek Park Station to the Public Library Station, with a one-way fare of Dh1.

Taxis

Air-conditioned taxis can be hailed on the street or prebooked by telephone. Metered taxis, operated by the *Dubai Transport Corporation* (tel: (04) 264 1111), are distinguished by their cream colour and uniformed drivers. Occasionally, drivers do not have detailed knowledge of the city and might ask passengers for directions. For metered taxis, the pick-up fare is Dh3 (Dh3.50 2200–0600) and Dh4 for pre-booked metered taxis. The rate is then charged at Dh1.43 per kilometre. Fixed fares are applied to journeys outside the city boundaries. In non-metered taxis, the fare is generally Dh5 for short journeys and Dh10–15 for longer journeys within the city. It is also possible to hire a taxi for 12 hours, for a fixed fee of Dh500. Tipping is not expected.

Limousines

Limousines are offered by the main car hire companies (see *Car Hire*) and *Dubai Transport Corporation* (tel: (04) 264 1111). The fare from the airport into Deira or Bur Dubai is approximately Dh60, with daily hire from Dh1450.

Driving in the City

Dubai has an excellent and well-signposted road network and the majority of roads have two to four lanes. Unfortunately, driving standards do not match the quality of the roads. Many local drivers travel at speed and change lanes with wild abandon. In addition, drivers are prone to make sudden and dangerous manoeuvres. Accidents occur frequently and visitors are advised to drive defensively. Outside the city centre, signposts are rare, making a good road

---

CITY STATISTICS

Location: Southern shore of the Arabian Gulf, northeastern United Arab Emirates.
Country dialling code: 971.
Population: 1,040,000.
Ethnic mix: 60% Indian, Pakistani and Filipino, 25% Emirati, 12% Arab, 3% Western ex-pats.
Religion: 57% Muslim, 20% Hindu, 20% Roman Catholic, 3% other.
Time zone: GMT + 4.
Electricity: 220 or 240 volts AC, 50Hz; square three-pin plugs are standard.
Average January temp: 24°C (75°F).
Average July temp: 41°C (106°F).
Annual rainfall: 300mm (11.8 inches).

BUSINESS PROFILE

Any economic recovery from the shock waves of the terrorist attacks of 11 September 2001 has been put back in many respects by the US-led war on Saddam Hussein's regime in Iraq in 2003. In recent years, Dubai has been using tourism more and more as a way of decreasing its reliance on oil revenue, which now only accounts for 10% of the economy. Tourist numbers have been rising impressively over the last decade, with especially strong growth in the European market, particulary Britain and Ireland. A recent World Tourism Organisation report stated that Dubai experienced the world's highest growth rate of international visitors in 2002, at 31.1%. Spin-off industries also benefit from tourism, such as retail, with Dubai Duty Free announcing a record annual turnover of Dh1.1 billion in 2002, a 23% increase on the previous year. However, the 2003 war has hit these industries. As the second richest of the emirates, after Abu Dhabi, Dubai has one of the highest per capita incomes in the world. Unemployment is still at an official rate of zero, although the unemployment rate for the UAE is considerably higher at 12%.

The city's main exports are crude oil, natural gas, re-exports, dried fish and dates. Oil itself plays a surprisingly small part in the emirate's economic picture, around 10%. Other sectors that are decreasing in economic importance are traditional small-scale industries, such as fishing, boat-building, handicrafts and pearling, which now only make up a fraction of economic activity. Today, the main emerging industries are international trade, manufacturing, finance and other service-based industries. Dubai has always proved competitive in attracting inward investment, with the 'offshore' Jebel Ali Free Zone (JAFZA) one of the most spectacular success stories. The success of current massive projects, like the *Palm Islands*, depends as much on the regional situation over the coming months as it does on how well they have been planned and constructed. Residential plots have been snapped up on these man-made islands but interest from hoteliers has been more cautious.

The main business district in Dubai is around the World Trade Centre, on Sheikh Zayed Road. The Emirates Towers, the tallest buildings in the Middle East, are one of the business hubs of the city. The focus looks set to shift in part to the new Dubai International Convention Centre (DICC), completed in time for the IMF and World Bank Conference in May 2003. Other major planned infrastructure developments include a revamped Port Rashid container port, the completion of a massive marina in Jumeirah and a new bridge over Dubai Creek.

Multinational companies and international organisations based in Dubai include *Sony, Heinz, AT&T, Shell, IBM* and *General Motors. Etisalat* is the only provider of Internet services within Dubai, exercising heavy control, with all sites accessed and monitored through the company's proxy server. The Dubai Chamber of Commerce (tel: (04) 228 0000; website: www.dcci.org) is often helpful for foreign businesspeople.

map essential, so as to avoid heading aimlessly out into the desert. Increasingly, traffic congestion is also a problem, particularly in Deira and along Jumeirah Beach. Drivers should note that there is a Dh20 tax to pay for driving out of the UAE.

Car parks are operated by *Dubai Municipality* (tel: (800) 4848; website: www.dm.gov.ae) and cost Dh2 per hour. Two centrally located covered car parks are situated near the Spice Souk and Bani Yas Square in Deira.

Car Hire

A valid International Driving Permit, passport and credit card are required to hire a car in Dubai. Visitors from many European, North American and Asian countries can obtain a temporary local driving licence if they do not have an international licence. A valid national licence, passport and two passport-sized photographs are required in order to do this. Fully comprehensive insurance is essential. In the event of an accident, the police must be informed and a written police report obtained, otherwise the hire company's insurance might not cover any damage. Drivers must be at least 21 years old and have held a full licence for one year. The age limit is often raised to 25 years for more expensive models. Payment must be made by credit card.

Major providers include *Avis* (tel: (04) 295 9899; website: www.avis.com), *Budget* (tel: (04) 282 3030; website: www.budgetrentacar.com), *Europcar* (tel: (04) 352 0033; website: www.europcar.com) and *Fast Rent a Car* (tel: (04) 224 5040). Hire of a standard saloon car costs from Dh125 per day and Dh810 per week. Collision damage waiver is sometimes additional at Dh20 per day.

Bicycle Hire

Considering the desert environment, Dubai is not a cyclist's paradise and bicycle hire is not a roaring trade in the city. Nevertheless, some hotels hire out bicycles, although whether or not they will hire them to non–guests varies.

SIGHTSEEING

Sightseeing Overview

Dubai is not a destination that it is easy to explore on foot, with many of the areas of interest, such as Deira and Jumeirah Beach, situated far apart. Sightseeing within the city centre is split mainly between the Deira and Bur Dubai flanks of Dubai Creek. Deira, on the right bank of the waterway, is the business and commercial heart of the city and is also home to the best shopping. Highlights include the myriad *souks*, including the *Spice Souk, Deira Old Souk* and *Dubai Covered Souk*. Deira is also the most atmospheric part of Dubai for a spot of aimless wandering, with a real sense of manic activity and rambling streets that are in sharp contrast to the order and calm of much of the city. Meanwhile, historic Bur Dubai has less of a bustling atmosphere and is home to a number of tourist attractions, including the *Dubai Museum, Grand Mosque* and *Sheikh Saeed Al-Maktoum's House. Dubai Creek* itself is also something of an attraction, whether visitors choose to take the traditional *dhow* cruises along its length or just to stroll along its banks on the promenade on the Bur Dubai side. From here, there are good views back towards the ultra-modern

skyline on the other flank of Dubai Creek. Breaking away, west from the mouth of Dubai Creek, is *Jumeirah Beach*, not really one beach as such but rather a sweeping strip of sand fringed by the warm waters of the Arabian Gulf. Much of the beach these days is officially the private preserve of the ever-increasing string of beach-side luxury hotels, although there is little to stop people wandering where they want to, once on the sand. Many of Dubai's best hotels are located on or nearby Jumeirah Beach, including the unmistakable hulk of the *Burj Al Arab* (or 'Arab Tower'), as well as leisure facilities like *Wild Wadi Water Park* and the more traditional attraction of *Jumeirah Mosque*, which is regarded by both locals and tourists alike as the most charming mosque in Dubai. One new attraction, which visitors can clearly see taking shape just off Jumeirah Beach, are the *Palm Islands*, the twin islands that are set to become the new focus of the city. Away from the city itself, further adventures await in the deserts and mountains, with *wadi bashing* and *dune bashing* jeep safaris both becoming increasingly popular.

BUSINESS ETIQUETTE

It is a major faux pas to break certain conventions when doing business in Dubai. Smart conservative clothing is expected, despite the often soaring heat. Meetings could start late, since this is not frowned upon in Dubai and it should not be commented on. The Arabic handshake involves touching the heart with the palm of the right hand after each shake, although visitors should note that when greeting Arab women they should not offer their hand unless the woman extends hers first. The terms 'Sayed' (Mr) or 'Sayeda' (Mrs), followed by the first name, should be used in greeting, to ensure politeness. It is also very important for visitors never to sit in such a way that their feet are pointing directly at someone else. Causing someone else to lose face, whether a client or colleague, is considered extremely offensive and any criticism or corrections should be kept for private discussions afterwards.

Meetings tend to start with plenty of preliminary chatting before moving onto the serious work, so it is essential for visitors not to rush in. Business meetings in Dubai are often seemingly casual affairs, in cafés or restaurants, although it is easy to be caught off guard, as the pace tends to quicken rapidly and deals are struck in a fraction of the time it can take in Western Europe. Friday is considered a day of prayer and rest, so meetings should not be scheduled for this day. Calls to Arab people should also be avoided on Friday. Similarly, local people will not answer the telephone during siestas, which are usually taken between 1400 and 1700. Business hours are Saturday to Wednesday 0800–1300 and 1600–1900. Businesses run by Western staff might open Sunday to Thursday 0800–1700. Business socialising in Dubai can be quite formal. Lunch meetings are more common than evening meetings and visitors should note that sometimes meals may take place at venues that do not serve alcohol. Asking for it may cause embarrassment and even insult.

With tensions high in the Middle East, visitors are strongly advised not to bring up political matters and, if prompted, to veer on the side of caution, not assuming any common beliefs or opinions.

Key Attractions

Bastakiya

In the days before electricity and air conditioning, Dubai Creek used to be lined by a mass of wind towers that kept the local houses cool. The *Bastakiya* district is a step back in time, laden as it is with traditional courtyard houses, bedecked with these wind towers. The Bastakiya area is currently closed for major renovation, with improved visitor facilities planned for its transformation into a 'tourist village'.
East of Dubai Souk on Al-Fahidi Street
Transport: Bus 19 or *abra* to Bur Dubai.

Sheikh Saeed Al-Maktoum's House

Sheikh Saeed Al-Maktoum's House is one of the oldest houses in the city, as well as one of the best examples of traditional architecture. Built from sandstone in 1896, the house offers sweeping views out towards the sea – although the view has been slightly obscured by recent development. The one-time ruler of Dubai used the house to monitor trade in and out of the country. The house was reopened as a museum in 1986; it also contains an exhibition illuminating Dubai's development from the 1940s to the late 1960s.
Near Al-Shindagha Tunnel, Al-Shindagha Road
Tel: (04) 393 7139.
Transport: Bus 8, 16, 19 or 20.
Opening hours: Sat–Thurs 0830–1930, Fri 1330–1930.
Admission: Dh2.

Jumeirah Mosque

The *Jumeirah Mosque* is the most photographed building in the city and an impressive example of modern Islamic architecture. Built along medieval Fatimid lines, entirely of stone, the mosque and its two minarets are unmistakable. It is particularly attractive at night, when subtle lighting increases its dramatic effect. Non-Muslims are not allowed to enter mosques in Dubai, although they can enter this one if on an organised tour. Visitors should call the tourist office to check if these are available.
Al-Jumeirah Road
Transport: Bus 8 or 20.
Opening hours: Daily 24 hours; access to non-Muslims through organised tours only.
Admission: Free.

Grand Mosque

The *Grand Mosque* was only rebuilt in 1998 and boasts the city's tallest minaret, at 70m (231ft). Located on the Bur Dubai side of Dubai Creek, near the Ruler's Court, the Grand Mosque consists of nine large domes and 45 smaller ones. This huge religious edifice can house up to 1200 worshippers.
Ali ibin Ali Talib Street
Transport: Bus 19.
Opening hours: Daily 24 hours; entrance to non-Muslims is forbidden.
Admission: Free.

Souks (Markets)

The *souks*, or traditional markets, are one of Dubai's greatest attractions (see also *Shopping*). They are located on both sides of Dubai Creek, with the most impressive on the Deira side. The highlight is the colourful *Spice Market*, which abounds with exotic aromas and bustles with locals seeking bargains. Wandering around the atmospheric souks is a good way for visitors to get in touch with how life was in Dubai before oil was discovered.

Deira Covered Souk, Al-Sabkha Road
Deira Old Souk or *Spice Souk*, 67 Street
Deira Gold Souk, Sikkat al-Khali Street
Perfume Souk, Sikkat al-Khali Street
Electronics Souk, Al-Sabkha Road and Al-Maktoum Hospital Road
Dubai Souk, Bur Dubai
Transport: Bus 5, 16, 19 or 20 all stop at souks in both Bur Dubai and Deira.
Opening hours: Sat–Thurs 0700–1200 and 1700–1900, Fri 1700–1900.
Admission: Free.

Children's City

Opened in early 2002, at Dubai Creekside Park, *Children's City* is proving a big hit with both local and international youngsters. The 7700 sq-metre (82,882 sq-ft) development takes young minds on a journey through the human body, science and space, with the help of different 'zones'. There is plenty of hands-on action to keep even the most demanding children occupied. All exhibits are in English as well as Arabic.
Creekside Park
Tel: (04) 334 0808.
Website: www.childrencity.ae
Transport: Bus 19.
Opening hours: Sat–Thurs 0900–2200, Fri 1600–2200.
Admission: Dh15; Dh10 (children under-16); family concessions available.

Dubai Museum

The building that houses the *Dubai Museum*, Al-Fahidi Fort, is an attraction in itself. The historic fort, dating back as far as 1799, was converted into a museum in 1970. The exhibits range from old weapons and pearl-diving outfits to an impressive range of military artefacts. Some of the most fascinating exhibits are those recovered from the 3000 to 4000-year-old graves at Al-Ghusais.
Al-Fahidi Road
Tel: (04) 353 1862.
Transport: Bus 19.
Opening hours: Sat–Thurs 0830–1930.
Admission: Dh3.

Majlis Ghorfat Um-Al-Sheef

At the *Majlis Ghorfat Um-Al-Sheef*, it is possible to delve into the opulent world of the moneyed men of Dubai. The late ruler of Dubai, Ghorfat Um-Al-Sheef, used this building as his 'home from home' but it is now open to the public. The building dates back to 1955 and its most impressive feature are the majlis gardens, which include a reproduction of a traditional Arab irrigation system.
17 Street, off Al-Jumeirah Road
Tel: (04) 394 6343.
Transport: Bus 8.
Opening hours: Daily 0730–1430 and 1630–2100.
Admission: Dh1.

Heritage Village

The *Heritage Village* is an attempt to weave in some local colour among Dubai's rapidly developing 21st-century skyline. The emphasis is on recreating the Bedouin way of life, with locals dressed in traditional garb, displays of traditional handicrafts, song and dance. Local crafts are also available for purchase. There is also a small section for children, with a smattering of things to keep young visitors occupied.
Near Shindagha Tunnel, Al-Shindagha Road
Tel: (04) 393 7151.

Jumeirah District

Transport: Bus 8, 16, 19 or 20.
Opening hours: Sat–Thurs 0800–2200, Fri 1600–2200.
Admission: Free.

Further Distractions

Encounter Zone

Tucked away on the third floor of the Wafi Shopping Centre, the state-of-the-art *Encounter Zone* entertainment centre is a playground for people of all ages. The most popular attractions are the *Crystal Maze*, the horror chamber and the range of 3D films. The emphasis is on fun, fun and more fun, with both kids and big kids enjoying attractions such as the virtual reality rollercoaster and the myriad arcade games.
Wafi Shopping Centre
Tel: (04) 324 7747.
Transport: Bus 14, 16 or 44.
Opening hours: Sat–Tues 1000–2300, Wed–Thurs 1000–2400.
Admission: Free.

Jumeirah Beach

Much of the long expanse of *Jumeirah Beach* is dominated by luxury hotels and their facilities. However, there is a stretch of public beach available, with clean white sand, crystal clear seawater and bath-temperature surf. Some of the hotels allow non-guests to use their pools and stretches of beach if they buy lunch or pay a nominal fee.

TOURIST INFORMATION

Department of Tourism and Commerce Marketing (DTCM) Welcome Bureau
Beni Yas Square, Deira
Tel: (04) 228 5000. Fax: (04) 228 0011.
E-mail: info@dubaitourism.co.ae
Website: www.dubaitourism.co.ae
Opening hours: Daily 0900–2300.

The DTCM has two other Welcome Bureaux located at the airport and 40km (25 miles) out of town, on the Sheik Zayed Road to Abu Dhabi.

Passes
There are no tourist passes currently available in Dubai.

Al-Jumeirah Road, next to Marine Beach Resort
Transport: Bus 8 or 20.
Opening hours: Daily 24 hours.
Admission: Free.

Tours of the City

Walking Tours

Dubai is a sprawling city that can be difficult to walk around and there are no official guided or signposted tours. However, a self-guided stroll around the older central parts of Deira and Bur Dubai is a great way of discovering the delights of the city, exploring its traditional souks or stumbling across hidden mosques or wind towers.

Bus Tours

A number of companies offer half-day city tours, including *Arabian Adventures* (tel: (04) 303 4888; website: www.arabian-adventures.com) and *Net Tours Dubai* (tel: (04) 266 8661; website: www.nettoursdubai.com). Tours vary depending on the operator but most go to the old and new Dubai souks, Jumeirah Mosque, the thriving commercial area and include a Dubai Creek crossing by *abra* (local water taxi). Prices start at Dh110. Another option is to see Dubai by night. Post-tour dinner in one of Dubai's many restaurants is usually a feature of the night-time tours, which also incorporate the mosques, palaces and souks. The tours operate a very organised system, with pick-up at all main hotels.

Boat Tours

Arabian Adventures (see *Bus Tours* above) offers a variety of cruises and sailing, with prices starting at Dh150 for a half-day adventure aboard a 20m (65ft) schooner, which sets off onto the Arabian Gulf from the International Marine Club. Other Arabian Adventure cruises depart from Sheik Zayed Road, next to the Metropolitan Resort and Beach Club. *Alpha Tours* (tel: (04) 294 9888; website: www alphatoursdubai.com) operates evening *dhow* dinner cruises, which take two hours and cost Dh230. Alternatively, tourists should go down to Dubai Creek and charter a traditional *abra* (water taxi), which costs

Dh40–60 for a short river tour lasting 60–90 minutes. The length of the tour and the price should be agreed in advance. Otherwise, visitors can just ride one across Dubai Creek to the other side (journey time – 5 minutes) for Dh0.50.

Excursions

For a Half Day

Dune bashing: An increasingly popular activity is dune bashing, which involves tourists being driven out into the surrounding desert sand dunes in a 4X4 and thrashing up and down the dunes. Visitors should not hire their own vehicles, as desert driving can be dangerous for the inexperienced. *Arabian Adventures* (tel: (04) 303 4888; website: www.arabian-adventures.com) and *Alpha Tours* (tel: (04) 294 9888; website: www.alphatoursdubai.com) both run regular tours and can combine dune bashing with desert dinners in recreated Bedouin camps. Prices start at Dh235, including dinner.
Camel rides: *Arabian Adventures* (tel: (04) 303 4888; website: www.arabian-adventures.com) operates a 'Rides and Slides' tour combining camel rides with sand skiing. Rides on the original 'ships of the desert' offer a totally different perspective on Dubai's desert landscapes. A half-hour journey in a traditional caravan introduces tourists to Dubai's traditional way of life, before throwing them back into the 21st century with the exhilarating new sport of sand skiing. The half-day tour costs Dh195, available Monday, Thursday and Saturday mornings.

For a Whole Day

Hajar Mountains: The *Hajar Mountains*, located 100km (62 miles) south of Dubai city, run along the border with Oman. Four-wheel-drive vehicles are the best way to explore the rugged mountainous terrain. Highlights are the *wadis* (rock pools), which offer the chance to cool off, and the hill town of *Hatta*, which has been recreated along traditional lines, in a mountain oasis. *Arabian Adventures* (tel: (04) 303 4888; website: www.arabian-adventures.com) and *Alpha Tours* (tel: (04) 294 9888; website: www.alphatoursdubai.com) both offer tours to this region, with prices starting at Dh275.

Sharjah: Some dismiss the neighbouring emirate of *Sharjah* as being too industrial and not as glamorous as Dubai. But for those with spare time in Dubai, Sharjah has much to recommend it. Sharjah is located 20km (12 miles) east of Dubai and making a trip there is easy, with regular minibus services, although taxis are perhaps a better idea, as it can be difficult to get a return minibus from Sharjah. This emirate is marginally less developed than Dubai, with a string of more cerebral attractions that are mainly located in its *Heritage District*. These include *Literature Square* with its *House of Poetry*, *Bait al-Gharbi cultural centre*, as well as the *Sharjah Heritage* and *Islamic museums*. Outside this quarter there is also an *Arts Museum* and *Al-Hisn Fort*, a museum that sheds light on the history of Sharjah and shows how, like Dubai, Sharjah has comes a long way in a very short time. Further information on Sharjah is available from the local tourist office (tel: (06) 556 2777; fax: (06) 556 3000; website: www.sharjah-welcome.com).

ACCOMMODATION

Dubai's number and quality of hotels is continuing to grow, with new openings and more hotels planned for the future, with the massive Palm Islands project slated to bring another influx of luxury options to the city. Sales tax of 10% and service charges of 10% are automatically added to the bill at checkout; tipping of porters is also expected.
Due to the current geo-political situation in the region, many hotels have been cutting their rates and offering special deals, with Dubai hotels set to remain good value for the foreseeable future.
The prices quoted below are the lowest standard rates for a double room, including VAT, service charge and breakfast, unless otherwise specified.

Business

Al Bustan Rotana Hotel

This 'Leading Hotels of the World' member, under the leadership of Imad Elias, is one of Dubai's most established five-star luxury business hotels. It is very conveniently located within easy reach of both the airport and the city centre. The 300 guest rooms are split between standard rooms, the 'Club Rotana' executive floor – with its own business centre and secretarial support – and a range of luxurious suites. The first-floor rooms offer direct access to the outdoor pool and the four tennis courts. The largest conference space is the Grand Rashidiya Ballroom, which can seat up to 1500 delegates. Leisure facilities include a private beach club at Jumeirah and the Bodylines Health Club at the hotel.
Al-Garhoud Road, PO Box 30880
Tel: (04) 282 0000. Fax: (04) 282 8100.
E-mail: albustan.hotel@rotana.com
Website: www.rotana.com
Price: From Dh1200.

Emirates Towers

These two ultra-modern skyscrapers are the tallest buildings in the Middle East. Part office, part hotel, the towers are very conveniently located for doing business in Dubai, right at the heart of the Central Business District. Each state-of-the-art room is geared towards business guests – there is access to the Internet via high-speed modem points and the in-room TVs, as well as individual fax/printer/copy

Photo: The Government of Dubai, Department of Tourism and Commerce Marketing

A local water taxi or *abra*

machines, each with their own fax number. The deluxe rooms even have their own chaises longues. The conference centre has 17 meeting rooms and the hotel also has 14 offices for guests to use.

Sheikh Zayed Road, PO Box 72127
Tel: (04) 330 0000. Fax: (04) 330 3030.
E-mail: info@emirates-towers-hotel.com
Website: www.jumeirahinternational.com/towers
Price: From Dh750.

Grand Hyatt Dubai

Bravely opened in March 2003, this new offering from the Hyatt group has quickly established itself as one of Dubai's finest hotels. This 674-room hotel pitches itself at the business crowd, with its great location on Dubai Creek and a conference and convention centre capable of holding up to 2000 delegates. The hotel, with its 15 hectares (37 acres) of grounds, boasts no fewer than 14 venues in which to eat and drink. All of the standard leisure facilities are backed up by the Grand Spa, which has a range of massage treatments and, for those travelling with families, dedicated swimming pools for both children and toddlers. One unusual feature is a 650m (2132ft) jogging track situated in the landscaped grounds.

Al Qutaeyat Road, PO Box 7978
Tel: (04) 317 1234. Fax: (04) 317 1235.
E-mail:dubai.grand@hyattintl.com
Website: www.dubai.grand.hyatt.com
Price: From Dh650.

Sheraton Deira Hotel and Towers

This central 224-room hotel is justifiably popular with both the domestic and international business communities. The rooms have all mod cons, with three telephone lines, voice-mail, trouser presses and large safes. A number of state-of-the-art conference rooms are available to meet the different requirements of its business guests, with the centrepiece – Al Massah Ballroom – catering for up to 1200 people. Other plusses include complimentary airport transfers, a rooftop pool with views over Dubai's skyline and no fewer than nine eating and drinking venues. For days off, there are also free shuttle transfers to the Sheraton at Jumeirah Beach.

Al Mateena Street, PO Box 5772
Tel: (04) 268 8888. Fax: (04) 268 8876.
E-mail: sharaton.deira@sheraton.com
Website: www.sheraton.com
Price: From Dh1100.

Luxury

Burj Al Arab

The 'Arab Tower', which has become one of the most instantly recognisable symbols of Dubai is truly unlike any other hotel on the planet. Rising, like something out of a Bond movie, from its own man-made island in the Arabian Gulf, this multi-storey monster is an oasis of true luxury. All rooms are sumptuously designed suites with wide-screen TVs and all mod cons, although the garish overuse of gold and bright colours will not suit all tastes. Even the cheapest rooms have their own dining tables and individual business centres, complete with laptop and printer. There are also in-room Jacuzzis. As the price of the suites rise, so do the number of facilities, with additional extras like snooker tables, cocktail bars and even private cinemas. The most expensive place to stay in Dubai remains one of the most unique hotels in the world.

Jumeirah Beach, PO Box 74147
Tel: (04) 301 7777. Fax: (04) 301 7000.
E-mail: reservations@burj-al-arab.com
Website: www.jumeirahinternational.com/baa
Price: From Dh4000.

The Ritz-Carlton Dubai

This top-drawer hotel is one of the best on the Jumeirah Beach strip and a model of casual elegance. There are only 138 rooms, making it one of the smaller hotels in this area, which results in more personal standards of service, with over 350 members of staff. The low-rise buildings and soft terracotta hues make this building look more like a European hacienda than a hotel in 21st-century Dubai. Leisure facilities include three swimming pools – one with a swim-up bar – tennis courts, squash courts, a gym and a cigar bar. Business facilities include 209 sq metres (2250 sq ft) of function space and 88 sq metres (950 sq ft) of meeting space, as well as 24-hour secretarial support. Another plus is that all rooms have either a sea-facing patio or a balcony with sea views.

Jumeirah Beach, PO Box 26525
Tel: (04) 399 4000. Fax: (04) 399 4001.
E-mail: rcdubai@emirates.net.ae
Website: www.ritzcarlton.com
Price: From Dh1500.

Moderate

Landmark Hotel

For a budget, four-star hotel that is centrally located, this accommodation is difficult to beat. The 160 en-suite rooms are clean and well kept and the staff is friendly and helpful, although the hotel has few frills. One bonus is the free parking that the hotel provides for its guests. The modern, glass-fronted venue also has a small business centre and a swimming pool.

Nasser Square
Tel: (04) 228 6666. Fax: (04) 228 2466.
Price: From Dh400 (excluding breakfast).

Sheraton Jumeirah Beach Resort and Towers

The *Sheraton Jumeirah Beach* is one of the best-value luxury hotels on Jumeirah Beach and an excellent place to stay for both business and leisure. The 255 rooms are spacious and comfortable, with the 'Towers' floors offering the use of a dedicated lounge, complimentary breakfast and 24-hour butler service. All rooms are en suite. Leisure facilities include an outdoor pool, floodlit tennis courts and a well-equipped gym, while the hotel caters for corporate clients with a business centre and the Al Sufough Ballroom, which can hold up to 350 delegates.

Jumeirah Beach, PO Box 53567
Tel: (04) 399 5533. Fax: (04) 399 5577.
E-mail: sherjum@emirates.new.ae
Website: www.sheraton.com
Price: From Dh700 (excluding breakfast).

Other Recommendations

Al Maha Desert Resort

This luxury retreat draws on the classic image of Dubai in times gone by, as an Arabian desert land, crossed by nomadic tribes. The 'eco-friendly' style is very low key, as the decor and facilities are moulded so as to have as little impact on the surrounding desert as possible. There are 30 suites available in a hotel that also puts an emphasis on personal service, with a staff-to-guest ratio of three to one. *Al Maha* can organise four-wheel desert safari trips or camel treks into the surrounding deserts. The only drawback is that it really does feel a million miles from anywhere and getting to the city centre can take over an hour. In terms of meeting facilities, the hotel can cater for groups of up to 20. The hotel is surrounded by a protected nature reserve.

Al Ain highway (by four-wheel drive vehicle), PO Box 7631
Tel: (04) 343 9595. Fax: (04) 343 9696.
E-mail: almaha@emirates.com
Website: www.al-maha.com
Price: From Dh4400 (including all meals and activities).

Hatta Fort Hotel

This mountain retreat is situated in the Hajar Mountains, a one-hour drive from Dubai city centre. The breathtaking scenery of the mountains is the main attraction in a hotel that is comfortable without being truly luxurious. Sports facilities include a crazy golf course, a shooting range and a gym, while the hotel-organised four-wheel drive 'wadi bashing' safari tours are also very popular. For travellers in a hurry, there is a helipad that can connect with flights to and from Dubai's international airport. The guest rooms are all situated in chalet-style accommodation, spread over the hotel's 32-hectare (80-acre) gardens. The hotel gardens can cater for cocktail and various other theme parties, for up to 2000 guests, while the main conference room can accommodate up to 100 delegates.

Hajar Mountains, PO Box 9277
Tel: (04) 852 3211. Fax: (04) 852 3561.
Website: www.hattafort.com
Price: From Dh600.

RESTAURANTS

The selected restaurants are divided into five categories: Gastronomic, Business, Trendy, Budget and Personal Recommendations. The restaurants are listed alphabetically within these different categories, which serve as guidelines rather than absolute definitions of the establishments.

As Dubai is a Muslim city, many restaurants, especially at the cheaper end of the market, are not licensed to serve alcohol. However, restaurants in the tourist and business hotels almost always serve alcohol. Sales tax at 10% is added to all bills. Service charges at 10–15% are also frequently added – if not, a 10% tip is expected.

The prices quoted below are for an average three-course meal for one person and for a bottle of house wine or cheapest equivalent; they include VAT but they do not include service charge or tip.

Gastronomic

Al Muntaha

Al Muntaha has the best location in Dubai, suspended hundreds of metres above the Arabian Gulf, at the top of the Burj Al Arab hotel. Service is immaculate and the slanted glass windows give the restaurant the feel of a great ocean liner heading out to sea. Al Muntaha also serves up fantastic food, with starters such as lobster Caesar salad or seared scallops and mains the likes of grilled hammour (a local fish) or roasted prime beef rib with mustard crust. An unusual dessert option, created by executive chef John Wood, is the Cranachan, a delicious Scottish oatmeal ice cream.

Burj Al Arab, Jumeirah Beach, PO Box 7147
Tel: (04) 301 7777. Fax: (04) 301 7000.
E-mail: reservations@burj-al-arab.com
Website: www.jumeirahinternational.com
Price: Dh550. Wine: Dh250.

La Baie

Under the expert guidance of head chef Carl Stockenstrom, this fine dining restaurant rather fancies itself to be located in a major European capital, with its mellow piano music, unfaltering service and elegant table settings. The food is similarly impressive and it all adds up to a meal that may stretch the credit card but is guaranteed to be of the highest quality. One of the most exotic starters is the marinated sturgeon carpaccio with caviar and yoghurt sauce, while a highlight among the mains – and rumoured to be the chef's favourite – is the grilled hammour on a bed of green lentils.
The Ritz-Carlton Dubai, PO Box 26525
Tel: (04) 399 4000. Fax: (04) 399 4001.
Price: Dh350. Wine: Dh140.

Signatures

This excellent French restaurant is well worth the trip out to Jebel Ali. The open kitchen allows diners to watch the chefs in action as they conjure up such innovative starters as lobster salad with foie gras and seared scallops wrapped in pastry. The highlight of the main menu is the sea bass served on a bed of red cabbage and cooked to perfection. Candles add to the cosy decor, making this the perfect place to take a loved one for an evening of fine French cooking.
Jebel Ali Hotel, Bur Dubai
Tel: (04) 883 6000. Fax: (04) 883 5543.
Website: www.jebelalihotel.com
Price: Dh300. Wine: Dh120.

Sphinx

Sphinx has been among Dubai's finest restaurants for a number of years now and its reputation is well deserved. The setting is spectacular, in the Wafi Pyramid complex, with Egyptian-style decor and candlelight dining. The service is attentive without being overbearing and food presentation is imaginative. Starters include the excellent lobster bisque and the unusual fried goat's cheese and beetroot sorbet, served with walnut and blue cheese salad. The first-rate 'surf and turf' is the highlight of the main menu.
Pyramids Complex, Wafi City, PO Box 26631
Tel: (04) 324 0000.
Website: www.pyramidsdubai.com
Price: Dh250. Wine: Dh120.

Verre

Gordon Ramsey's Dubai venture, *Verre*, has proved a resounding success and is regarded by many discerning locals as the best place to eat in Dubai. With Britain's only three-star Michelin chef behind things, Verre could not really go wrong. The minimalist decor might not suit all tastes but the simple surrounds and the well-thought-out lighting help focus deserved attention on the food. A nice touch is the chef's specialities – tasty morsels of food that come between the impressive courses. Mains include salmon with a fricassee of peas and horseradish or poached chicken on a bed of tagliatelle. The desserts are divine. The three-course lunch specials offer excellent value.
Hilton Dubai Creek, PO Box 30880
Tel: (04) 227 1111.
Price: Dh300. Wine: Dh150.

Business

Al Boom Floating Restaurant

This is one of Dubai's finest seafood restaurants and is located on-board a traditional-style *dhow*. Diners choose which fish they want from those on display and the chefs cook it to order. There is also a river cruise every night, creating a unique setting for a relaxed business dinner.
Al Boom Tourist Village, PO Box 12650
Tel: (04) 324 3000. Fax: (04) 324 3930.
E-mail: abt@emirates.net.ae
Price: Dh200. Wine: Dh100.

Al Dawaar

Dubai's only revolving restaurant, atop the Hyatt Regency Hotel, on the 25th floor, has some of the best views of any restaurant in the city. Refurbished to a contemporary and sophisticated design in 2002, this restaurant revolves over a two-hour period, offering panoramic views of the entire city and out towards the Arabian Gulf. The most popular dining option is the international buffet, which features dishes from all corners of the globe, including options such as Chinese stir fries, spring rolls and local Dubai dishes. Early diners willing to give up their tables by 2100 are rewarded with a 20% discount.
Hyatt Regency Hotel, PO Box 5588
Tel: (04) 209 1100. Fax: (04) 209 1000.
E-mail: dubai.regency@hyattintl.com
Website: http://dubai.regency.hyatt.com
Price: Dh320. Wine: Dh250.

Casa Mia

Casa Mia is bit of a local secret. Savvy natives know it as the best Italian restaurant in Dubai – far better than the second-rate Italian cuisine that many of the big hotels offer. It is run by an Italian couple who lovingly look after all the cooking and tend to the decent wine list. The decor is authentic too, with an Italian style that just manages to avoid looking kitsch. It is advisable to book well ahead for one of the coveted dinner spots. Starters include beef carpaccio or red mullet and fennel salad, with mains of the likes of potato gnocchi or baked veal cannelloni.
Behind Le Meridien Hotel, PO Box 10001
Tel: (04) 282 4040.
E-mail: casamia@le-meridien-dubai.com
Price: Dh180. Wine: Dh100.

China Times

For diners tired of the Jumeirah Beach Hotel restaurants, *China Times* offers arguably the finest Chinese cuisine in town. Some of the spicier dishes, like the Szechuan chicken or pork, might be toned down a touch for the palates of visiting businesspeople but China Times usually hits the spot. The decor is modern and the service polite without being too stuffy. The open kitchen is fun, as diners can see their meals being prepared.
Jumeirah Plaza, Jumeirah Beach, PO Box 1038
Tel: (04) 344 2930. Fax: (04) 344 3946.
Price: Dh90. Wine: Dh40.

Peacock

This modern and spacious Chinese restaurant is located in the Sheraton Jumeirah Beach (see *Hotels*), at the very end of the beach strip, so it is a good place for business diners to take clients to escape the city. The etched-glass walls allow for fine views of the garden, pool and beach. The cuisine of both Shanghai

and the Hunan provinces, as well as the fiery tastes of the Szechuan region, are explored in this restaurant, which caters for those who normally might not like what is conventionally thought of as 'Chinese' food. Service is friendly and efficient, with highlights on the menu being wonton soup as a starter and aromatic crispy duck or the unusual red snapper fillet served Cantonese style.
Sheraton Jumeirah Beach, PO Box 12650
Tel: (04) 399 5533. Fax: (04) 399 5577.
E-mail: sherjum@emirates.net.ae
Price: Dh110. Wine: Dh70.

Trendy

Café Chic

As French as the name suggests, *Café Chic* is a welcome new addition to the Dubai gastronomic scene. This split-level venue has an open kitchen, so diners can see head chef Pieric Cizeron working his magic. The ground floor is light and airy, while the second floor is a bit more sombre and stylish. Dishes on the menu include healthy starters, such as asparagus salad, or the less healthy fried duck's liver, while the fish dishes are the highlight of the main menu. The sea bream is especially good. Diners should not miss the signature dessert, the chocolate soufflé – a truly divine creation that alone encourages repeat reservations. Decadent Epicureans might want to explore the range of cigars after dinner. Business lunches for Dh66 are especially good value.
Le Meridien Hotel, PO Box 10001.
Tel: (04) 282 4040. Fax: (04) 282 4672.
Price: Dh190. Wine: Dh100.

Indochine

Dubai's first Vietnamese restaurant, *Indochine*, is housed within the new Grand Hyatt Dubai (see *Hotels*) and is predictably chic, with polished wooden floors, discreet palms and stylish lighting. The cooking is light and fresh – lemongrass and lime infuse many dishes with the taste of East Asia. Menu items include prawn dumplings, 'morning glory' (water spinach with garlic) and *tom rang me* (shrimp soup). While Vietnamese dishes are the highlight, responsible for bringing in the crowds, there are also regional excursions into Thai, Malaysian and Chinese cuisine. Attached to Indochine is the *Tea House*, where diners can relax with a calming cup of Asian tea after their meal.
Grand Hyatt Dubai, Al Qutaeyat Road, PO Box 7978
Tel: (04) 317 1234. Fax: (04) 317 1235.
Website: www.dubai.grand.hyatt.com
Price: Dh95. Wine: Dh70.

Legends

This space at the Dubai Creek Golf Club was recently reincarnated as *Legends*, a classic steak house. The views out over Dubai Creek are impressive, particularly from the terrace, which catches the cooling river breezes. Diners should be sure to book a table on this popular terrace, although indoors is equally charming – a luxurious room with the feel of a grand hotel lobby in New York, an ambience enhanced when the pianist is playing. Unsurprisingly, the steaks are the highlight, although the seafood is also good, with a popular main the beef and lobster 'surf and turf' combination. Service is seamless.
Dubai Creek Golf Club, Al-Garhoud
Tel: (04) 295 6000. Fax: (04) 295 6044.
Price: Dh250. Wine: Dh100.

More

More is not a hotel restaurant, which is something unusual among Dubai's better places to eat. This new haunt of the beautiful people is a bright, modern venue with a main space that is awash with colour, comfy seating and black and white photographs. Newspapers and magazines lying around tempt patrons to do the same, although the food is no slouch. The menu is as hard to pin down as the patrons, with Australian steaks mingling with Indonesian *nasi goreng* (fried rice) among the mix of businesspeople and fashion-conscious ex-pats. The patio outside is an alternative space when the weather allows.
Near Welcare hospital, Al-Garhoud
Tel: (04) 283 0224.
Price: Dh220. Wine: Dh100.

Splendido

The local cognoscenti continue their love affair with *Splendido*, which is located at The Ritz-Carlton (see *Hotels*) and is arguably the city's finest Mediterranean restaurant. The setting is luxurious without being overbearing and there is a terrace for days when the sun is not too strong. The menu is fresh and innovative, with starters including marinated salmon with quail egg, pesto and pine nuts, or potato leek soup with lobster. Impressive main courses include rolled homemade pasta filled with ricotta and spinach, or black ink tagliolini with pesto, truffle oil and sautéed prawns. The delicious chocolate crème brûlée is legendary.
The Ritz-Carlton Dubai, Jumeirah Beach, PO Box 26525
Tel: (04) 399 4000. Fax: (04) 399 4001.
Price: Dh250. Wine: Dh110.

Budget

Cactus Jacks

It probably will never win any culinary awards but *Cactus Jacks* seldom disappoints a hungry stomach. A Mexican theme for the decor includes Aztec fabrics and bright designs, as well as multicoloured tiled pillars. Upstairs, there are five tables for diners looking for a touch more privacy. The restaurant has a live DJ at weekends and things can turn quite wild after 2300, when the spicy Tex Mex food and the tequila kick in. Cactus Jacks dishes up all of the usual suspects – fajitas, burritos and tortillas – with plenty of meal deals and drinks specials. Parties of eight diners or more receive a 30% discount on their bill, which gives a good idea of the market that the restaurant is leaning toward.
Airport Hotel, Al-Garhoud
Tel: (04) 282 3464.
Price: Dh100. Wine: Dh75.

Da Vinci's Restaurant

This popular Italian restaurant offers an unpretentious setting and menu in a friendly environment. All of the usual pasta and pizza dishes are on offer and, although there are no real highlights, most dishes are consistently good. One popular offering is the *gamberoni grigliati* (jumbo prawn with capers and potatoes). The dark decor and red, white and green chequered tablecloths might be a touch on the garish side but for an evening meal that does not break the bank or challenge a delicate palate, *Da Vinci's* is a good choice.
Airport Hotel, Al-Garhoud
Tel: (04) 7039 1233.
Price: Dh95. Wine: Dh90.

Deira City Centre Food Court

Of the many food courts that are dotted all around Dubai, this is one of the most popular. On sale is the full *smorgasbord* of international foods, with the only unifying feature being that all the stands are cheap. The most popular stands serve up simple Chinese and Indian specialities accompanied by boiled rice. They also have a play area for kids, which takes some of the pressure off harassed mums and dads.
Deira City Centre Mall, Deira
Tel: (04) 295 1010.
Price: Dh80. Unlicensed.

Thattukada

This excellent South Indian restaurant serves great-value food. Diners sit on long, wooden benches and are surrounded by film posters on the walls. The Kerala-influenced dishes include *kappa erachi* (tapioca and chicken curry) and *karimeem porichathu* (fish fry).
Palm Beach Rotana Inn, PO Box 5822
Tel: (04) 393 1999.
Price: Dh120. Unlicensed.

Woodland Avenue

This ultra-cheap South Indian restaurant has to be one of the best-value places in town. The decor is very plain, with yellow checked tablecloths and little attempt to make things cosy or aesthetically pleasing. Diners do not come here for aesthetic, however, but for the good-value food. The menu is mainly vegetarian and there are few frills but, for value for money, an Indian meal at *Woodland Avenue* seldom disappoints. The vegetable thali is one of the most popular dishes and deservedly so.
Al Karama, PO Box 7529
Tel: (04) 336 6632.
Price: Dh60. Unlicensed.

Personal Recommendations

Al Mansour

This old double-decked *dhow* (a traditional trading ship) has been converted into one of Dubai's most unusual restaurants. It can seat over 150 diners on busy nights, however, booking ahead is still essential for the decent buffet food (stir fries, spring rolls and the like), which is eaten facing the lights of the Dubai skyscrapers glimmering across the waters of Dubai Creek, seen en route during a two-hour gastronomic adventure.
InterContinental Hotel, PO Box 476
Tel: (04) 222 7171. Fax: (04) 228 4777.
Website: www.dubai.intercontinental.com/dining.html
Price: Dh165 (buffet dinner), Dh125 (buffet lunch).
Wine: Dh100.

India Palace

India Palace opened in late 2001 and became popular with the local ex-pat community. The emphasis on Rajasthani cooking is backed up by themed decor and artefacts shipped in from the region. The open kitchen is a nice touch, as are the family booths upstairs, with privacy available at no extra charge. Waiters will only enter the private booths when called upon. The excellent-value menu features starters such as lentil soup and prawn bisque with fresh vegetables, while mains include chicken and vegetarian kebabs and a range of delicately spiced curries. Alcohol is not available but the lassis are excellent, especially an unusual lassi seasoned with salt.
Opposite Dubai Marine Hotel, Bur Dubai
Tel: (04) 286 9600. Fax: (04) 286 5355.
Price: Dh100. Unlicensed.

The Manhattan Grill

The signature restaurant at the newly opened Grand Hyatt Dubai (see *Hotels*) is the *Manhattan Grill*. Housed in the atrium of the hotel, this stylish restaurant is already a favourite with the local smart set, despite only opening in spring 2003. The steaks are to die for, with fresh prime beef flown in from America. Other offerings on the menu include local and international seafood and grilled lamb. Wine is available by the glass or the bottle, with both New and Old World tastes catered for.
Grand Hyatt Dubai, Al Qutaeyat Road, PO Box 7978
Tel: (04) 317 1234. Fax: (04) 317 1235.
Website: www.dubai.grand.hyatt.com
Price: Dh180. Wine: Dh110.

Camel rides

Photo: The Government of Dubai, Department of Tourism and Commerce Marketing

Dubai Racing Club

Noodle House

New for 2002, this funky, laid-back restaurant, in contrast to the stuffy business restaurants that tend to be associated with this part of Dubai, places the emphasis on light, tasty food served up in relaxed surrounds. Patrons can forget table reservations and join the rest of the diners at the long communal tables to enjoy some delightful Asian noodle soups. Also served are spring rolls and more substantial dishes, such as sweet and sour chicken. The desserts are a bit hit and miss but, for a quick and cheerful meal, *Noodle House* is difficult to beat.
Emirates Towers Shopping Boulevard
Tel: (04) 330 0000.
Price: Dh85. Unlicensed.

Venezia

There is no restaurant in Dubai quite like *Venezia*. The recreation of all things Venetian, with mock Venetian buildings, classical musicians and real gondolas drifting around the indoor canal is truly bizarre. The standard Italian cuisine on offer, such as *tortellini arrabiatta* or veal with lemon sauce, is nothing special, although patrons are invited to pick their own wine from their cellar. The sheer surreal ambience of this place makes it worth a visit.
Metropolitan Hotel, Sheik Zayed Road
Tel: (04) 343 0000. Fax: (04) 343 1146.
Price: Dh150. Wine: Dh90.

ENTERTAINMENT

Nightlife

Drinking a pint of beer could land you in prison in some parts of the Middle East, however, in Dubai, alcohol is tolerated, with non-Muslims allowed to imbibe alcohol in the city's bars, restaurants, clubs and hotels. Indeed, it is easy to forget all about the local attitudes to alcohol when on a wild night out in a city whose nightlife is increasingly nefarious. Although non-Muslims are the only people officially allowed to drink, often you can find Dubai Arabs enjoying a pint in one of the many bars.

There are no specific nightlife districts, as many of the best bars are in the big tourist hotels, which are situated throughout the city. Many of these are open until 0100 or 0200. A cheaper and livelier option is the independent bars that are dotted around town. Happy hours are common, with Thursday and Saturday the biggest nights for going out. Tuesdays and Sundays are often 'Ladies Night', with female revellers receiving free drinks. A beer is generally in the region of Dh15–20. The legal drinking age is 21 years. Licensing hours vary greatly, as many of the hotel bars are allowed to open and close whenever they want. Closing time is normally around 0100 or 0200.

The club scene is a curious one, with nightclubs often delineated along ethnic and national lines. Increasingly, big-name DJs are being attracted to Dubai, as a Western-style clubbing scene starts to develop. By law, clubs must close at 0300. Many clubs are over-25 only. Dress codes for bars are generally relaxed, although some bars and all clubs insist on no jeans, trainers or sandals. A more mellow night out can be had at one of Dubai's coffee houses, where you can smoke apple-flavoured tobacco from a *shisha* pipe.

The monthly listings magazine, *Time Out* (website: www.timeout.com), can be found in many hotels, offering a full rundown of what is happening at night in Dubai. Hotel concierges are also often able to provide guests with the latest nightlife information.

Bars

One of the oldest ex-pat bars, *The Irish Village*, Aviation Club, off Al-Garhoud Road, is still going strong, with a good range of beers and an outdoor seating area. It faces stiff competition from more recent arrivals, such as *Carter's*, The Pyramids, Wafi Centre, a stylish haunt of the 20- and 30-something brigade. Monday night happy hour is something of a local institution, with all cocktails priced at Dh10. Even more stylish is the minimalist *Ginseng*, Wafi City, with its mood lighting, Asian-themed decor and

first-rate cocktails. The lowest common denominator is catered for at *Rock Botttom*, Regent Place Hotel, Bur Dubai, a rowdy drinking den with three pool tables, live music and a dance floor. A favourite of Dubai's 'beautiful people' is the swish *Sho Cho*, Dubai Marina Resort, Jumeirah Beach Road, a bar-cum-restaurant with a real buzz, live DJs, great cocktails and an outdoor jetty for special parties. The 'in' crowd can also be found at *Oxygen*, Al Bustan Rotana Hotel, Al-Garhoud Road, which has live music and a dancefloor. The *Fatafeet Café*, Alseef Road, has good views of Dubai Creek and is an atmospheric coffee house in which to try a traditional *shisha*.

Casinos

Dubai adheres to the Muslim ban on gambling and there are no casinos in Dubai.

Clubs

The most popular nightclub in Dubai, housed in the most genuine London-style club venue, is *Planetarium*, Planet Hollywood, Wafi City. Since the closure of the legendary *Lodge*, this has been the main venue for clubbers to head to and is the most likely place in town to attract the big-name international DJs. *Scream*, Ramada Hotel, Al-Mankhool Road, is a warehouse-type venue that blasts out the latest techno to an appreciative crowd. *Pancho Villa's*, Astoria Hotel, Al-Nahda Street, has become a bit of an institution on the Dubai club scene, with a mainstream choice of music, a restaurant and frequent live bands. *Amnesia*, Dubai Park Hotel, Sheik Zayed Road, is becoming more and more popular, especially with its 'Ladies Night' on Thursday.

Live Music

Planet Hollywood, Wafi Pyramids, off Al-Qataiyat Road, is a reliable option, with an eclectic selection of mediocre to good bands and covers outfits. *Bordertown*, Al-Rolla Road, is a Mexican theme bar that stages live bands most nights of the week. The current en vogue music in Dubai is retro throwbacks to the 1970s and 1980s, with stars that are considered washed up in the rest of the world – such as the Human League, Kajagoogoo and Kim Wilde – regularly trooping into Dubai. The *Irish Village*, Aviation Club, off Al-Garhoud Road, also hosts many live acts.

Sport

Sport is very popular in Dubai. As the city is home to few international sporting stars or teams, the trend is to bring in overseas teams to play in glamour friendlies and also to stage major sporting events, with lucrative prize money to attract the big-name stars. In 2003, the regional political tension impacted on sports, with big names like Tiger Woods and Colin Montgomerie pulling out of the *PGA Dubai Desert Golf Classic* (tel: (04) 347 4050; fax: (04) 295 6026; website: www.dubaidesertclassic.com), held in February each year. The *Dubai International Rugby Sevens* (tel: (04) 333 1198; website: www.dubairugby7s.com), is an event usually held at the *Dubai Exiles Rugby Club*, near Dubai Country Club, Al-Awir Road (tel: (04) 333 1198), in December. The *Dubai Open Tennis Championship* is held in February, at the *Dubai Tennis Stadium*, Dubai Aviation Club, Al-Garhoud (tel: (04) 316 6969; website: www. dubaitennischampionships.com).

Horseracing is also very popular among Dubai's moneyed men, who are not content to idly watch and instead opt to actually buy and race horses. *The Dubai World Cup* (tel: (04) 332 2277; website: www. dubaiworldcup.com), organised by the *Dubai Racing Club*, Nad al-Sheba Road (tel: (04) 332 9888), in March, is now the world's richest horseracing event with US$15 million in prize money. A more traditional event is the annual *Emirates Championship Cup*, a 130km (80-mile) endurance horserace through the shifting sands of the desert. Grand sporting projects currently under development include the new *Dubai Cricket Stadium* and the rather unlikely sounding but very characteristic-of-the-city *Dubai Ski Resort*.

There is no umbrella ticketing organisation in Dubai and tourists wishing to buy tickets for sporting events can often get this organised through their hotels.

Fitness Centres

All the luxury hotels offer impressive leisure facilities. Some provide the unusual option of coaching from ex-Soviet Union Olympiads, who have flocked in droves from the economically bankrupt ex-Soviet states to work in Dubai. There are also private leisure clubs geared towards the ex-pat community throughout the city. *Dubai Marine Beach Resort & Spa*, Jumeirah Beach Road (tel: (04) 346 1111; website: www.dxbmarine.com), boasts floodlit tennis courts, two outdoor pools, a children's pool, squash courts, gymnasium and a health spa with public access during the evening. *Le Mirage Health & Leisure Club*, Le Meridien Jumeirah Hotel, Jumeirah Beach (tel: (04) 702 2430), accepts non-members for a fee of Dh55.

Golf

For a nation dominated by so much desert, Dubai somewhat surprisingly has a number of top-quality grass golf courses. *Emirates Golf Club*, Junction 5, Sheik Zayed Road (tel: (04) 347 3222), was the Middle East's first championship grass course, when it opened. Rounds are available for non-members at off-peak times. Green fees are Dh370–425. *Dubai Creek Golf and Yacht Club*, Al-Garhoud Road (tel: (04) 295 6000), is currently host to the Dubai Desert PGA Classic and welcomes guests on a pay-and-play basis. Green fees are from Dh370. *Dubai Golf and Racing Club*, Nad al-Sheba Road (tel: (04) 336 3666), boasts a Scottish-style links floodlit course with green fees for non-members at Dh240–300. *The Montgomerie*, Emirates Hills, off Sheik Zayed Road (tel: (04) 399 9955; website: www.themontgomerie.com), designed by renowned Scottish golfer Colin Montgomerie, opened in 2002 and charges Dh550 per round. Non-members are welcome. It is important for golfing visitors to note that all golf courses in Dubai are spike-free.

Swimming

The four-hectare (12-acre) *Wild Wadi Waterpark* is part of the Jumeirah Beach Hotel complex, Al-Jumeirah Road (tel: (04) 348 4444; website: www.jumeirah-beach.com). This is a paradise for kids and big kids alike, with a thrilling array of 24 interconnected water rides, including the terrifying 'Jumeirah Sceirah', which hurtles the foolhardy at speeds of up to 80kph (50mph). All-day admission is Dh95 for adults and Dh75 for children. Reduced rate 'Sundowner' admission is available after 1600. Most hotel pools are open to the public for Dh25–50.

Tennis

There are a number of tennis clubs that are open to the public. The *Aviation Club*, Al-Garhoud Road (tel: (04) 282 4122), has public courts, as does the *Dubai Tennis Academy*, Jumeirah Beach Hotel, Al-Jumeirah Road (tel: (04) 406 8811). Many of Dubai's hotels also offer tennis facilities.

Watersports

The Arabian Gulf offers a wide range of watersports opportunities. Jet-skiing is available at the *Jumeirah Beach Hotel*, Umm Suqeim Road (tel: (04) 348 0000), for approximately Dh100 per half hour, water-skiing is available at most of the Jumeirah Beach hotels and scuba diving can be organised with *Al-Boom Diving*, Al-Wasl Road (tel: (04) 342 2993), or *Scuba International*, Diving Village, Shindagha (tel: (04) 393 7557).

Shopping

With good reason, Dubai is regarded as the 'Shopping Capital of the Middle East' and increasingly dedicated fans of retail are regarding the emirate as a top-class shopping destination. Shopping is undoubtedly one of the city's greatest draw cards. It is largely divided into two main types – the old souks in Deira and Dubai Souk in Bur Dubai, and the glossy new shopping malls around Beniyas Square, Al-Rigga and Al-Hiyafa Road. New shops and malls seem to pop up every other month, to cater for the seemingly insatiable desire for retail therapy. The airport is also a shopping paradise, with excellent duty-free facilities.

The souks offer an atmospheric shopping experience with sights, sounds and aromas that hint of yesteryear. The *Spice Souk*, Al-Sabkha Road, is more of a tourist attraction, while the buzzing *Gold Souk*, Sikkat al-Khali Street, offers some great deals on gold necklaces, rings, bangles, earrings and brooches, with gold prices among the lowest in the world. The gold souks are strictly regulated, so there is little chance of customers being ripped off in terms of quality, although prices do vary greatly and bargaining is essential. The *Fish Souk* in Deira is more of a tourist attraction, as visitors are unlikely to want to take fresh fish home with them. Early in the morning and late at night, local fishermen unload mountains of fresh fish, which they bargain and haggle over. The *Electronics Souk*, near Beniyas Square, might sound a slightly incongruous idea but this is Dubai, which means that, with shopping, anything goes. Bargaining is the norm in all of the souks, which are generally open daily 0700–1200 and 1700–1900 (closed Friday morning).

The best-value items at the large shopping malls are mainly electrical goods and designer clothing, although interesting local products include carpets, Bedouin jewellery and Arabian souvenirs. The *Dubai Shopping Festival*, held from January to February, and *Dubai Summer Surprises*, held in July and August, are two massive attractions, with all the big stores and almost every shop in Dubai slashing prices in a retail orgy. Other festivals and special promotions run throughout the year, which further enhance Dubai's myriad retail opportunities.

Dubai's shops are open 0800–1300 and 1630–2000/2100. Many shops are closed on Friday. Larger malls are open 1000–2200. Shops, malls and souks are all closed on Friday mornings. There is no sales tax in Dubai and the airport is renowned for having one of the finest duty-free opportunities in the world. This is open to both arriving and departing passengers.

Culture

Dubai's cultural life comes in a distant third to making money and having fun, with cultural activities – where they are available at all – limited in scale. Dubai's cultural life has always suffered from not having a major venue for cultural performances, although the *Dubai Community Theatre* (website: www.dubaitheatre.org) is in the planning stages. With such a small population, there are no major indigenous orchestras or dance companies, although it is possible to find localised groups who occasionally put on public performances. A relative hive of cultural activity is the *Creative Art Centre*, Al-Jumeirah Road (tel: (04) 344 4394; website: www.arabian-arts.com), which runs from Saturday to Wednesday. Mornings are reserved for young children, afternoons for older children and, during winter, evenings are set aside for adult classes. A wide range of cultural and handicraft

Duty-free shopping at Dubai International Airport

Photo: The Government of Dubai, Department of Tourism and Commerce Marketing activities are covered. The *Dubai International Arts Centre*, off Al-Jumeirah Road (tel: (04) 344 4398), offers a similar range, as well as art displays, with works for sale. Visiting international acts occasionally spice up the music scene.

The monthly *Time Out* magazine, which can be found in many hotels, provides information on events and performances in Dubai. *Time Out* also sells tickets for events (tel: (800) 4669; website: www.itp.net/tickets).

Music

Opportunities to hear classical music performed in Dubai are extremely limited. The *Dubai International Congress Centre*, Dubai World Trade Centre, Bur Dubai (tel: (04) 331 4200; website: www.dwtc.com), and *The Crowne Plaza Hotel*, Sheik Zayed Road (tel: (04) 331 1111), are the main venues that host visiting orchestras and musicians from around the world, although performances are far from regular. Many hotels employ a pianist to spice up the lobby, which is often as near to classical music as Dubai gets. Arabic nightclubs (see *Dance*) are the main venues for traditional Arabian music.

Theatre

The *Indian Playhouse*, Intercontinental Hotel (tel: (04) 222 7171), features performances by *Burjor Patel Productions* and hosts the travelling *British Airways Playhouse*, which makes frequent visits to Dubai. *Dubai Drama Group* (tel: (04) 333 1155; website: www. dubaidramagroup.org) is an amateur theatrical company with over 100 members. The *British Touring Shakespeare Company* (website: www.britishtouringshakespeare.co.uk) also frequently visits the emirate. Dubai's first purpose-built *Community Theatre* is still in the fundraising and planning stages.

Dance

There are no real dance companies in Dubai, although there are a number of dance schools, including the renowned *Ballet Centre*, behind Jumeirah Plaza (tel: (04) 344 9776), with ballet, jazz, tap and modern dance on offer. In addition, belly dancing and traditional dance are a mainstay in Arabic nightclubs, such as *Al-Diwan*, Metropolitan Palace Hotel (tel: (04) 227 0000), and *Escoba*, Al-Khaleej Palace Hotel (tel: (04) 223 1000).

Film

Going to the cinema is a very popular pastime in Dubai. There are a number of cinemas for one to choose from, including *Al Massa Bustan*, Al Bustan Centre (tel: (04) 263 3444; website: www.al. bustan.com), and *Frand Cineplex*, adjacent to Wafi City (tel: (04) 324 0000), which provide English-language films. The programmes are currently full of big-budget Hollywood films with little arthouse content.

Cultural Events

Dubai's dominant culture is founded around the Muslim religion, with most of the main cultural events being deeply religious, with little opportunity for tourists to participate. The year's major event is the month-long fasting of *Ramadan*, a Muslim celebration of the truth of the Holy Koran, which takes place in the month of Ramadan. Directly following Ramadan is *Eid Al-Fitr*, a three-day celebration in December. *Eid Al-Adha* is the four-day festival in that follows the main pilgrimage to Mecca (the Haj), celebrated in the Muslim month of Dhulhajj.

On a less spiritual note, *Dubai Summer Surprises* is an attempt to attract more visitors during the slump summer months, from June through to August, with a

wide range of cultural events – including henna tattoo painting and traditional handicraft making – in many of the city's shopping malls and big hotels. *UAE Day*, 2 December, is a public holiday celebrated in all of the seven emirates and increasingly is becoming a cultural event.

Literary Notes

To get right to the heart of Dubai, Graeme Wilson's *Father of Dubai: Sheik Rashid Bin Saeed al Maktoum* (1999) is a detailed tribute to the founder of Dubai. *Arabia Through the Looking Glass* (1979), by Jonathan Raban, covers the region as a whole but also has an illuminating section on Dubai. A local perspective comes from the English translation of Muhammad al-Murr's *Dubai Tales* (1991), with his famed short stories

fleshing a bit of colour into the place. Muhammed al-Murr is one of the most revered local writers and it is worthwhile trying to get a copy of his other famous book, *The Wink of the Mona Lisa* (1994). A good pictorial look at Dubai is Ronald Codrai's mid-20th-century *Dubai – An Arabian Album* (1992). Kevin Higgins' *The Emirates* (1995) is a look at all of the United Arab Emirates and puts Dubai in clear context, while William Facey and Gillian Grant's *The Emirates by the First Photographers* (2002) shows the sheer scale of change in Dubai and the other emirates, over the last century. An insight into the machinations and ambitions of Dubai's ruling family comes through Jason Levin's *From the Desert to the Derby* (2002), a look at their attempt to train a horse to win America's richest horse race.

Beachlife

DUBLIN

Riding on the back of the roaring success of the 'Celtic Tiger' economy, Dublin in the new millennium is a city on the up and up. Business in many sectors is booming and the city overflows with tourists, who flock to the 'party capital of Europe' to sample the infamous Irish *craic* (fun).

But things have not always been so rosy for this thousand-year-old city on the east coast of Ireland. For much of the first half of the 20th century, strife and unrest tore Dublin apart as it was involved in a messy and violent divorce from Britain. Even now, despite ongoing attempts to find a lasting peace settlement, the religious and political troubles further north still dominate Irish politics.

However, it is easy to see why tourists today head to Dublin in such large numbers. This vibrant, fun-loving city on the River Liffey is full of atmospheric pubs where the *craic* is spun with a well-polished finish and the streets echo with the ghosts of artistic luminaries, such as James Joyce and W B Yeats. An excellent time to visit is between April and October, when the weather is at its best, with July and August the busiest months. Increasingly, however, the city is a popular destination throughout the year, with many festivals, cultural and religious events and sporting fixtures.

Sightseeing highlights include the early medieval Christchurch Cathedral (Dublin's oldest building), the cobbled streets of Temple Bar, Phoenix Park (Europe's largest urban park), the National Gallery of Ireland and the treasures of the National Museum of Ireland, containing Europe's finest collection of prehistoric gold artefacts. A plethora of buildings and museums – including Trinity College (Ireland's oldest university) and the Guinness Storehouse – convey a real sense of living history. Indeed, it is this living history, conveyed through the media of music and literature, that has brought Dublin such international acclaim. A string of poets and writers have immortalised the city, none more so than James Joyce, whose seminal *Ulysses* (1922), depicts one day in Dublin and is considered by many literary critics to be the greatest novel of the 20th century.

In the new millennium, Dubliners are no longer content to rest on the laurels of this richly cultural history. Alongside the museums and the folk music in the smoky old pubs, there is a new Dublin of funky bars, rebuilt city streets and confident moneyed 20-somethings – an image that is being carried forward by popular music acts like Westlife, the Corrs and, the biggest of them all, U2.

This new face of the Irish capital stems mainly from the stunning economic success of the country in recent years, which has managed to combine extensive funding from the EU with sound financial acumen to stimulate high levels of growth. Key industries include electronics, teleservices, retail and tourism. Dublin boasts the youngest population in Europe (with 41% under 25 years and 69% under 45 years). Its leafy parks are full of mobile-phone-swinging young professionals enjoying the summer, while during winter, they seek refuge in Dublin's numerous bars. There is no denying Dublin, the 'capital of Euro-cool', is currently booming and its citizens are intent on enjoying it while it lasts.

However, the economic boom has also had negative implications. Prices have increased dramatically and, although long-term unemployment figures have steadily decreased in recent years, the capital is struggling to come to terms with the recent influx of immigrants and asylum seekers, who have imported cultures often at odds with Dublin's own lifestyle.

Despite all these recent changes, essentially the city and its people have remained the same. Alongside trend-setting bars, clubs and designer shops, it is still possible to find quiet, traditional pubs, busking fiddlers in Temple Bar, even horse-drawn carts clip-clopping along cobbled streets. This fascinating blend of tradition and contemporary Irish life means that Irish eyes are well and truly smiling in Dublin today.

O'Connell Street

TRAVEL

Getting There By Air

Dublin Airport (DUB)

Tel: (01) 814 1111.

Website: www.dublin-airport.com

Dublin Airport is located 12km (seven miles) north of the city centre. One of the world's fastest growing airports, with 31 scheduled airlines going to 74 destinations, Dublin Airport served over 15 million passengers in 2002, a 5% increase on the previous year.

Major airlines: Airlines serving the airport include the national airline *Aer Lingus* (tel: (01) 886 8888; website: www.aerlingus.com), Air France, Air Malta, Alitalia, British Airways, bmi, Continental Airlines, Delta, Lufthansa, Manx Airlines, Ryanair and SAS.

Approximate flight times to Dublin: From London is 1 hour; from New York is 6 hours 30 minutes; from Los Angeles is 12 hours; from Toronto is 8 hours 10 minutes and from Sydney is 24 hours.

Airport facilities: These include a tourist office, bureaux de change, duty-free shopping, bank and currency exchange machines, post office, shops and newsagents, pharmacy, telephones, restaurants, bars and car hire from *Avis, Budget, Hertz, Murrays Europcar* and *National*).

Business facilities: The *Anna Livia Executive Lounge* (tel: (01) 814 4501; website: www.dublin-airport.com) contains a business centre with telephones, fax machines, photocopying, Internet access and a meeting room, which is available for hire to anyone in possession of a boarding pass.

Arrival/departure tax: None.

Transport to the city: Buses 16A, 41, 41A/B/C and 46X run to the city centre every ten to 20 minutes daily 0800–2330 (journey time – 40 minutes) and cost €1.60. They are operated by *Dublin Bus* (tel: (01) 873 4222; website: www.dublinbus.ie). The *Airlink Express* (tel: (01) 873 4222) coach service (numbers 747 and 748) links the airport with the Central Bus Station on Store Street and the two main railway stations, Connolly Station and Heuston Station, every ten to 20 minutes daily 0545–2330 (journey time – 30 minutes). Tickets cost €5.00. The

Aircoach (tel: (01) 844 7118; website: www.aircoach.ie) links Dublin Airport with the city centre (O'Connell Street) every 15 minutes daily 0500–2400 and every hour 0000–0500 (journey time – 30 minutes). Tickets cost €6 for a single, €10 return. The *Aerdart Shuttle* (tel: (01) 862 5363; website: www.aerdart.ie) connects Dublin Airport to Howth Junction DART. Station (see *Public Transport*) Monday to Friday 0545–2345, Saturday 0620–2345 and Sunday 0830–2345, thereby avoiding city-centre traffic (journey time – 20 minutes). Tickets cost €5. All bus services depart from bus stops located immediately to the left after exiting the arrivals hall. Taxis are available and a trip into Dublin costs €18–22.

Getting There By Water

Dublin has two main ports, with a series of harbours. *Dublin Ferry Port* (tel: (01) 836 4019) is on Alexandra Road in the east, while *Dún Laoghaire Harbour*, 15 Westmoreland Street (tel: (01) 204 7700; fax: (01) 204 7620), is located 14km (nine miles) south of the city. *Dublin Port Authority*, Alexandra Road (tel: (01) 872 2777; fax: (01) 855 2740; website: www.dublinport.ie), oversees these ports. Facilities at Dublin Ferry Port are limited to a coffee shop and bureau de change. Dún Laoghaire Harbour has several cafés, a tourist office, bureau de change, ATM, newsagent and gift shop.

Ferry services: *Irish Ferries* (tel: (01) 607 5555 *or* (1890) 313 131 (Republic of Ireland only) *or* (01) 661 0715 (24-hour information line); e-mail: info@irishferries.com; website: www.irishferries.com) operates car and foot passenger ferry services five times a day to Dublin Port from Holyhead. *Stena Line* (tel: (01) 204 7777; website: www.stenaline.ie) also operates a car ferry service once a day from Holyhead to Dublin Ferry Port and a high-speed car and foot passenger ferry service from Holyhead to Dún Laoghaire Harbour three times a day. The *Isle of Man Steam Packet Company* (tel: (1800) 805 055 (Republic of Ireland only) *or* (08705) 523 523 (UK number); website: www.steam-packet.com) operates car and foot passenger *Seacat* ferries once a day in winter, twice in summer, from Liverpool to Dublin Port and also from the Isle of Man in summer.

Transport to the city: Bus 53 departs from Dublin Ferry Port daily 0730–1930 (journey time – 10 minutes). Buses 7, 7A and 46A run to the city centre every ten to 15 minutes (less frequently on a Sunday) daily 0630–2300 (journey time – 10–15 minutes). There is a daily DART train 0600–2330 every ten to 15 minutes from Dún Laoghaire Harbour (journey time – 30 minutes). Taxis run from both ports but are difficult to find after busy sailings.

Getting There By Rail

Iarnród Eireann (Irish Rail) provides the national service (tel: (01) 836 6222 (information website: www.irishrail.ie). Services do not cover all parts of the country but are quite reliable. Dublin has two main stations: *Connolly Station*, on Amiens Street (tel: (01) 703 2358), in the centre, and *Heuston Station*, by the Quays (tel: (01) 703 2131). Both have bureaux de change, lockers, luggage minding, shops, a bar and snack bars.

Rail services: Connolly Station serves Belfast (journey time – 2 hours 5 minutes), Rosslare (journey time – 3 hours 10 minutes) and Sligo (journey time – 3 hours). Heuston Station serves Galway (journey

time – 2 hours 40 minutes), Tralee (journey time – 4 hours 30 minutes), Westport (journey time – 3 hours 20 minutes), Kildare (journey time – 30 minutes), Cork (journey time – 2 hours 30 minutes), Kilkenny (journey time – 1 hour 35 minutes), Waterford (journey time – 2 hours 40 minutes), Clonmel (journey time – 4 hours) and Limerick (journey time – 2 hours 30 minutes).

Transport to the city: Connolly is a five-minute walk from the city centre. Heuston is a 20-minute walk to the city centre but there are regular buses (journey time – 10 minutes).

Getting There By Road

Traffic drives on the left and signposts are usually bilingual. Motorways are marked 'M' with a corresponding number (such as M1 and M2), main roads and dual carriageways 'N' and minor roads 'R'. On motorways, a speed limit of 112kph (70mph) applies. The general speed limit is 96kph (60mph), which drops to 64kph (40mph) on approaches to urban areas and 48kph (30mph) in built-up areas. The maximum legal alcohol to blood ratio for driving is 0.08%.

The minimum driving age is 17 years. A valid national driving licence is required and a Green Card and Motor Insurance certificate are recommended. A country identification sticker is compulsory, as is the wearing of seat belts in the front and, where fitted, in the rear of the car.

The *Irish Visiting Motorists Bureau*, Insurance House, 39 Molesworth Street (tel: (01) 676 9944), can provide further information. The *Automobile Association of Ireland* (tel: (01) 617 9999; website: www.aaireland.ie) provides information on reciprocal agreements with other motoring associations.

Emergency breakdown service: *Automobile Association Rescue* (1800) 667 788.

Routes to the city: Dublin can be approached via the N11 dual carriageway from Dún Laoghaire Harbour, the N1 and the M1 motorway from Belfast, the N6 and N4 from Galway and the N8 and N7 from Cork.

Approximate driving times to Dublin: From Belfast – 2 hours 45 minutes; Galway – 3 hours 30 minutes; Cork – 4 hours 15 minutes.

Coach services: *Bus Eireann*, 16 Store Street (tel: (01) 836 6111; website: www.buseireann.ie), operates Ireland's largest coach station, *Busáras* (Central Bus Station), Amiens Street, with routes nationwide. Destinations include Cork, Galway and Limerick, as well as Belfast and Derry in Northern Ireland.

Services are more frequent than those provided by the rail network. Facilities include restaurant, bureaux de change and left-luggage. *Bus Eireann/Eurolines* (tel: (01) 836 6111; website: www.eurolines.ie) has daily services to UK and European destinations, including Amsterdam, Blackpool, Glasgow, Edinburgh, London, Manchester and Paris.

Getting Around

Public Transport

Dublin's public transport system is a **bus** and **rail** network, although a new network of 40 **tram**s is due to be introduced by *Luas Light Rail Lines* (tel: (01) 646 3400; website: www.luas.ie), with passenger services due for commencement in August 2004.
Iarnród Eireann (Irish Rail) runs the clean and speedy electrical *DART* (Dublin Area Rapid Transport) **rail** services (tel: (01) 836 6222; website: www.irishrail.ie), which operate Monday to Saturday 0630–2400 and Sunday 0930–2300. Rail fares vary according to routes. The lowest DART fare is €1 and tickets are available for purchase from any DART station and at 35 Abbey Street Lower.
Bus Atha Cliath (Dublin Bus) runs the city **bus** services (tel: (01) 873 4222; website: www.dublinbus.ie), which operate daily 0600–2330, with a **night bus** service (*Nitelink*) running daily 0030–0430. Bus fares vary according to the number of stops: one to three stops cost €1.60, four to seven stops cost €2.40, eight to 13 stops cost €2.80, 14 stops and over cost €3.20 (concessions available).

CITY STATISTICS

Location: Province of Leinster, Ireland.
Country dialling code: 353.
Population: 495,101 (city); 1,122,600 (metropolitan area).
Religion: 91.6% Catholic, 2.5% Church of Ireland, 5.9% small congregations of Presbyterians, Protestants, Methodists, Jews and other denominations.
Ethnic mix: Majority Irish, with largest minority Chinese, followed by Russian, other minorities include Nigerian and Romanian.
Time zone: GMT (GMT + 1 from last Sunday in March to Saturday before last Sunday in October).
Electricity: 240 volts AC, 50Hz; English-style, square three-pin plugs are standard.
Average January temp: 5°C (41°F).
Average July temp: 17°C (63°F).
Annual rainfall: 73mm (28.5 inches).

Nitelink tickets cost €4–€6, depending on the destination. Drivers prefer exact change. Pre-paid tickets may also be purchased at the CIE Information desk at Dublin Airport, Dublin Bus Head Office or at bus ticket agencies.
Information on fares and timetables are provided at the Dublin Bus Information Office, 59 O'Connell Street Upper, and Dublin Tourism Centre (see *Tourist Information*).
Various **passes** for bus, rail or both combined are available. There are one-, three-, five- and seven-day *Rambler Tickets*, costing €5, €9.50, €14.50 and €17.50 respectively, which offer unlimited travel for consecutive days on all Dublin Bus scheduled services, excluding the night buses. A weekly pass for the DART costs €22 or €26 including the use of buses, while a monthly pass costs €87.50 or €98 including buses. There is also an *Adult Short Hop* pass at €7.70, valid for unlimited travel for one day on all Dublin Bus, DART and suburban rail services, or a *Family Short Hop* pass, costing €11.60.

Taxis

Taxis (standard saloon cars) can be hailed on the street, hired at taxi ranks (O'Connell Street, Dame Street and St Stephen's Green) or booked by telephone. *Radio Link* (tel: (01) 850 0111) is a reputable company. There is often a considerable waiting period for a taxi at peak times, especially Friday and Saturday nights. Taxis cost €2.75 for journeys under three minutes 20 seconds and an extra €0.15 for each additional 30 seconds (or ninth of a mile). There is a €0.50 surcharge for each additional passenger or item of luggage and for journeys during unsociable hours. It is customary for passengers to tip the driver 10–15% of the fare.

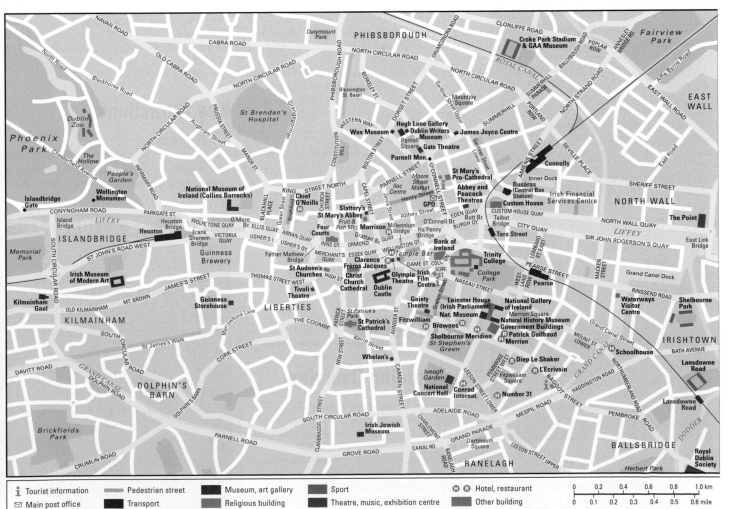

ℹ Tourist information	Pedestrian street	Museum, art gallery	Sport	Ⓗ Ⓡ Hotel, restaurant	
✉ Main post office	Transport	Religious building	Theatre, music, exhibition centre	Other building	

0 0.2 0.4 0.6 0.8 1.0 km
0 0.1 0.2 0.3 0.4 0.5 0.6 mile

BUSINESS PROFILE

The Irish 'Celtic Tiger' economy is currently booming and Dublin is at its heart. As the financial centre of Ireland, Dublin represents 32% of the national labour force and contributes 38% to the GNP. The hub of the national transport system, with a strong educational and research infrastructure, the city looks well set to sustain its current economic boom, which started around 1994, when the 'Celtic Tiger' term was first coined. Unemployment figures for Dublin have steadily decreased in recent years and are among the lowest in Ireland at 4.1%. The national unemployment rate is currently 4.5%.

The number of businesses in Dublin is in the region of 40,000, including over 800 overseas companies. Services account for 77% of all jobs in Dublin (61% on a national level). Dublin's highest growth industry is tourism. Tourism numbers have been growing consistently each year, with figures more than doubled in the past decade. In 2001, 30% of Dublin's overseas visitors travelled for business purposes. This figure is set to expand considerably after the completion of an international convention centre in the city's re-emerging docklands area, once development plans are agreed upon. For the moment, the *Royal Dublin Society* (RDS), Merrion Road, Ballsbridge (tel: (01) 688 0866; fax: (01) 660 4014; e-mail: info@rds.ie; website: www.rds.ie), is one of the main conference venues.

Over the last few decades Dublin has established a reputation as Europe's software capital; over 60% of business application software sold in Europe is manufactured in Ireland. Other significant market sectors include the food industry (including *Cadbury's* and *Guinness*), electronics (with US firms accounting for 82% of total employment), pharmaceuticals and chemicals, teleservices and retail.

Dublin is home to the *Irish Stock Exchange* and the headquarters of the *Bank of Ireland, Central Bank* and *AIB*. The *International Financial Services Centre* (*IFSC*) is an integral part of Dublin's economy, employing around 6000 people and attracting such leading national and international institutions as NatWest, Bank of Ireland, Citibank, *IBM* and *Ulster Bank* to set up branches here. The *IFSC* is located in the old Custom House Docks area, while the traditional business district is in the Dublin 2 area.

The *Dublin Chamber of Commerce* is located at 7 Clare Street (tel: (01) 644 7200; fax: (01) 676 5433; e-mail: info@dubchamber.ie; website: www. dubchamber.ie), while the *Industrial Development Agency* (*IDA*) in Dublin is located at Wilton Park House, Wilton Place (tel: (01) 603 4000; fax: (01) 603 4040; e-mail: idaireland@ida.ie; website: www.idaireland.com).

Limousines

The Limousine Company (tel: (01) 843 9055; website: www.limousine.ie) specialises in corporate hire and offers the latest, conference-seated limousines from €65 per hour (for a minimum four-hour hire period).

Driving in the City

The volume of traffic in Dublin is increasing and parking is expensive and limited, although some hotels and guesthouses provide private parking for guests. Visitors should avoid driving during morning and late afternoon rush hours if possible. Drivers should keep out of bus lanes at all times, whether driving or parking. There are also numerous one-way systems in the centre, including the quays alongside the River Liffey (the south bank flows east to west and the north bank west to east). Street parking is limited in the city centre and official car parks are usually the best bet. The city's main car parks, with various hourly rates, are *Arnotts*, Abbey Street Middle, on the Northside and *Brown Thomas*, 2 Clarendon Street, on the Southside: both are located in the middle of shopping districts. For street parking, kerbside pay-and-display meters are standard; the maximum time for parking is usually three hours. Parking prices on the city centre streets are €2.50 per hour Monday to Saturday 0800–1900. Sunday parking charges are €1.30 per hour between 1200 and 1800. Clamping zones operate within the city centre and the recovery of a clamped vehicle will cost around €80. Recovery of clamped or towed-away vehicles is from *Control Plus* (tel: (01) 602 2500).

Car Hire

A full national driving licence and deposit are necessary for visitors to hire a car in Ireland; most firms require the driver to be over 23 and under 70 years old and to have held a full driving licence for a minimum of two years without endorsements.
Avis, 1 Hanover Street West (tel: (01) 844 4466; website: www.avis.com), *Budget*, 151 Drumcondra Road Lower (tel: (01) 837 9611; website: www.budget.com), and the local *Access Car Rental*, Dublin Airport (tel: (01) 844 4848; website: www.accesscarrentals.com), are among the main providers.
Rates vary on a seasonal basis and start from around €200 per week upwards for the hire of a small car. Pre-booking is strongly recommended in summer, and payment is usually only accepted by credit card.

Bicycle Hire

The best tracks are along Dublin Bay and across the Wicklow Mountains, as central Dublin is sadly lacking in cycle paths.
Cycle Ways, 185–186 Parnell Street (tel: (01) 873 4748; fax: (01) 872 9462; e-mail: cycleway@indigo.ie; website: www.cycleways.com), and *McDonald Cycles Ltd*, 38–39 Wexford Street (tel: (01) 475 2586), both offer a bicycle hire service.
Bicycles are available for hire for around €25 per day or €100 per week. Deposits of at least €100 are usually required.

SIGHTSEEING

Sightseeing Overview

Dublin might not be one of Europe's most visually stunning cities but what it lacks in aesthetics it more than makes up for with its many attractions. Most of the sights are located south of the *River Liffey*, in a district of gracious Georgian mansions and leafy avenues around Grafton Street and elegant St Stephen's Green. The main landmarks here include *Trinity College*, the *National Museum*, *Leinster House* (the home of the *Irish Parliament*) and the *National Gallery of Ireland*.

Nearby, *the Temple Bar* district, once the site of Viking Dublin, has recently reinvented itself. After its promising 1980s resurrection, Temple Bar suffered under the weight of countless British stag and hen nights, scaring off locals and tourists alike. The tourist board and local publicans have since worked hard to deter the worst ravages of the pre-nuptial hordes.
West of Temple Bar, the historic cathedrals, *Christ Church* and *St Patrick's* – both vestiges of Anglo-Norman Dublin – are architecturally impressive. The Norman city walls are on view from neighbouring Cook Street. *Dublin Castle*, the symbol of the Anglo-Irish Ascendancy, stands proud on Dame Street.
The district of the *Liberties* lies to the west of St Patrick's Cathedral and is home to the *Guinness Storehouse* and brewery, *The Irish Museum of Modern Art* and *Kilmainham Gaol* – now a museum recounting Ireland's struggle for independence.
The city is bisected by the River Liffey, which flows west to east and is crossed by a number of bridges. These include the famous *Ha'Penny Bridge* and its newest neighbour, the *Millennium Bridge*, which joins Ormond Quay Lower on the north bank of the Liffey with Wellington Quay on the south bank.
North of the River Liffey the crowds of tourists dissipate in a rougher, grittier area, which Roddy Doyle generously summed up as having more 'soul' than sights. It contains the *General Post Office* (*GPO*), which has a façade pitted with gunfire from the Easter Rising of April 1916, the *Dublin Writers Museum*, the *James Joyce Centre* and the *Hugh Lane Municipal Gallery of Modern Art*. The *Custom House* and *Four Courts* rival the Georgian mansions of the south in grandeur, although the Georgian architecture of *Merrion Square, Fitzwilliam Square* and *St Stephen's Green* is well worth admiring. Other noteworthy sights include *Phoenix Park* to the west, *Collin's Barracks* and the sights located along the Grand Canal (the *Shaw Birthplace, Irish Jewish Museum* and *National Print Museum*), which loops around the south of the centre.

Key Attractions

Trinity College

Visitors can drift through the college among the numerous artistic ghosts in one of the world's most famous centres of learning. Jonathan Swift, Bram

BUSINESS ETIQUETTE

Business meetings are easily fixed but this does not mean that the deal is done. Small talk leading to trust is an important element so plenty of time should be allowed to complete a deal. Due to traffic congestion during rush hour, breakfast meetings are growing in popularity. Lunch meetings are frequent, although meeting in a pub or bar (from around 1730 onwards) for a few beers and/or dinner (at around 2000) is also common. Office hours are generally Monday to Friday 0900–1700/1800.

Business style is informal; first names are used and, although suits are worn, jackets may be taken off. Above all, visitors should avoid treating their Irish hosts as anything other than the modern Europeans that they are. Dublin wit is fast flowing and engaging and is evident in most business situations. Discussion of Irish political issues is best avoided.

Stoker, Oscar Wilde, Samuel Beckett and many other seminal thinkers and writers studied at Ireland's oldest university, which was founded in 1592. With its cobbled squares, gardens and grand buildings, *Trinity College* retains an aura of peace, despite its central location. Its main attraction is the *Book of Kells*, an illuminated manuscript dating from around AD800, which is displayed in the magnificent *Old Library*.

College Street

Tel: (01) 608 2320. Fax: (01) 608 2690.

Website: www.tcd.ie

Transport: All cross-city buses; DART to Tara Street Station.

Opening hours: Old Library/Book of Kells: Mon–Sat 0930–1700, Sun 0930–1630 (Jun–Sep); Mon–Sat 0930–1700, Sun 1200–1630 (Oct–May).

Admission: Old Library/Book of Kells: €7; concessions available.

Trinity College

National Museum of Ireland

Among this rich collection of Irish antiquities, dating from 7000BC to the modern day, are the eighth-century *Ardagh Chalice* and *Tara Brooch* and the 12th-century *Cross of Cong. Ór* (Ireland's Gold) features the finest collection of prehistoric gold artefacts in Europe. There are also major exhibitions on prehistoric Ireland, Viking Ireland, medieval Ireland and Irish history from 1900 to 1921 ('The Road to Independence').

Kildare Street

Tel: (01) 677 7444. Fax: (01) 677 7450.

Website: www.museum.ie

Transport: Bus 7, 7A, 8, 10, 11 or 13; DART to Pearse Station.

Opening hours: Tues–Sat 1000–1700, Sun 1400–1700.

Admission: Free.

National Gallery of Ireland

This impressive collection incorporates some 2500 paintings, as well as watercolours, drawings, prints and sculpture. Although Irish painting holds pride of place, all major European schools of painting are well represented. A major renovation of the museum was completed in 1996 and a new extension opened early in 2002.

Merrion Square West

Tel: (01) 661 5133. Fax: (01) 661 5372.

E-mail: info@ngi.ie

Website: www.nationalgallery.ie

Transport: Bus 5, 7, 7A, 7B, 10, 13A, 44C or 48A; DART to Pearse Station.

Opening hours: Mon–Sat 0930–1730 (until 2030 Thurs), Sun 1200–1730.

Admission: Free; a donation of €3 is requested.

Christ Church Cathedral

Richard de Clare 'Strongbow' (the Earl of Pembroke) founded *Christ Church Cathedral* on the site of a Viking church in 1172. Highlights include the 'leaning wall of Dublin', the north nave wall, which has leaned 46cm (18 inches) since 1562 (when the roof collapsed), a mummified cat and mouse found in an organ pipe, the heart of St Laurence, the patron saint of Dublin and a large crypt full of relics.

Christchurch Place

Tel: (01) 677 8099. Fax: (01) 679 8991.

E-mail: welcome@cccdub.ie

Website: www.cccdub.ie

Transport: Bus 50 or 78.

Opening hours: Mon–Fri 0945–1700, Sat and Sun 1000–1700 (cathedral); Mon–Fri 0945–1700, Sat 1000–1645, Sun 1230–1515 (treasury).

Admission: Free (a donation of €3 is requested); €3 (treasury).

Dublin Writers Museum

First editions, letters, portraits and memorabilia of Swift, Sheridan, Shaw, Wilde, Yeats, Joyce, Beckett and Behan fill this fascinating museum, set in a spectacular Georgian mansion. There is also a room devoted to children's literature.

18–19 Parnell Square North

Tel: (01) 872 2077. Fax: (01) 872 2231.

E-mail: writers@dublintourism.ie

Website: www.writersmuseum.com

Transport: Bus 10, 11, 11A, 11B, 13, 13A, 16, 16A, 19 or 19A; DART to Connolly Station.

Opening hours: Mon–Sat 1000–1700, Sun 1100–1700 (Sep–May); Mon–Sat 1000–1800, Sun 1100–1800 (Jun–Aug).

Admission: €6 (concessions available).

Dublin Castle

Dating from Norman times, the palatial *Dublin Castle* was originally built on the orders of King John, in 1204. The largest visible remaining fragment of the original 13th-century castle is the *Record Tower*. It stands beside the 19th-century Gothic revival *Chapel Royal*. Recently uncovered excavations of Viking fortifications can be viewed at the *Undercroft*. Most of the castle was largely rebuilt in the 18th century, including the gilded *State Apartments* – once the residence of English viceroys. Admission is by guided tour only. Tours run every 20 minutes. Large groups need to book in advance.

Dame Street

Tel: (01) 677 7129. Fax: (01) 679 7831.

E-mail: info@dublincastle.ie

Website: www.dublincastle.ie

Transport: Bus 50, 50A, 54, 56A, 77, 77A or 77B.

Opening hours: Mon–Fri 1000–1700, Sat and Sun 1400–1700.

Admission: €4.25 (concessions available).

Further Distractions

Phoenix Park

Europe's biggest city park boasts more than 707 hectares (1752 acres) of wilderness and landscaped gardens. *Phoenix Park*, Dublin's most famed park, is located on the western edge of the city and originally served as a royal deer park in the 17th century. Today, the Irish president and the US ambassador to Ireland have residences within it. Dubliners enjoy its 12 hectares (30 acres) of landscaped gardens with ornamental lakes, nature trails and grassland. The old duelling ground, *Fifteen Acres*, is now a popular venue for casual sports, while *Nine Acres* is home to the Irish Polo Club. The park also houses *Dublin Zoo* – home to over 700 animals and tropical birds and Ireland's top fee-paying visitor attraction.

Dublin Zoo

Phoenix Park

Tel: (01) 677 1425. Fax: (01) 677 1660.

E-mail: info@dublinzoo.ie

Website: www.dublinzoo.ie

Transport: Bus 10, 25 and 26.

Opening hours: Daily 24 hours (Phoenix Park); Mon–Sat 0930–1800, Sun 1030–1800 (Mar–Sep), Mon–Sat 0930–dusk, Sun 1030–dusk (Oct–Feb) (Zoo).

Admission: €10.10 (concessions available).

Guinness Storehouse

The world's largest single beer-exporting company began in 1759, when Arthur Guinness brewed the first Guinness. The brewery itself is not open to visitors but a visit to this state-of-the-art museum, housed in a converted warehouse and shaped like a mighty pint glass, tells the visitor everything they ever wanted to know about the famous stout. The tour culminates, of course, with a free pint of the legendary black stuff.

Photo: Irish Tourist Board

Photo: Irish Tourist Board

Four Courts

St James's Gate
Tel: (01) 408 4800. Fax: (01) 408 4965.
E-mail: guinness-storehouse@guinness.com
Website: www.guinness-storehouse.com
Transport: Bus 51B, 71A or 123.
Opening hours: Daily 0930–1700.
Admission: €13.50 (concessions available).

Tours of the City

Walking Tours

Dublin Tourism has published a *Ulysses Map of Dublin* (€1.30), for those who wish to conduct a self-guided walk in the footsteps of Joyce's famous character, Leopold Bloom.
Discover Dublin Tours, 20 Stephen Street Lower (tel: (01) 478 0193; website: www.musicalpubcrawl.com), organises a two-and-a-half-hour musical pub crawl in the Temple Bar area for €10. Tickets are available on the night and also from the Dublin Tourism Centre on Suffolk Street. The tour commences upstairs in Oliver St John Gogarty's (corner of Fleet Street and Anglesea Street) and operates nightly at 1930 from the first Friday in May to the last Saturday in October; Fridays and Saturdays only in November, February, March and April.
The Dublin Literary Pub Crawl (tel: (01) 670 5602; fax: (01) 670 5603 *or* 454 5680; e-mail: info@ dublinpubcrawl.com; website: www.dublinpubcrawl. com) is a two-hour tour featuring poetry recitals and singing, as well as visiting Dublin's famed pubs that have literary connections. Tours cost €10 (concessions available), commencing upstairs at the Duke Pub, 9 Duke Street, Monday to Saturday at 1930 from April to October (tickets on sale from 1900); also Sundays at 1200. From November to March, tours operate Thursdays, Fridays and Saturdays at 1930 and Sundays at 1200 and 1930.
Reservations Network, 13 Bachelors Walk (tel: (01) 878 7655), operates self-guided audio tours that take around two hours; a map, personal cassette player and an audio cassette are included in the €8 fee.

Bus Tours

Two bus companies – *Guide Friday* (tel: (01) 872 9010; website: www.irishcitytours.com) and *Dublin Bus* (tel: (01) 873 4222; website: www.dublinbus.ie) offer hop-on, hop-off bus tours covering all the major sights of the city centre, with running commentary from a tour guide. A day ticket costs €14 and tours commence approximately every 15 minutes from O'Connell Street.

Horse and Cart Tours

Guided tours by horse and cart can be picked up at St Stephen's Green during the summer months. The duration and price (usually between €15 and €50) should be negotiated with the driver before setting off.

Excursions

For a Half Day

James Joyce Museum: The Martello tower, located 14km (nine miles) south of Dublin, which was originally built to guard against invasion from Napoleon, is nevertheless an appropriate venue for the *James Joyce Museum* (tel: (01) 280 9265). It was here that Oliver St John Gogarty invited Joyce to stay and the tower overlooking the 'snotgreen sea' became the setting for the opening chapter of *Ulysses* (1922), while Gogarty was transformed into the fictional character, Buck Mulligan. The tower houses a collection that includes the artist's letters, photographs, guitar, walking stick and a copy of *Ulysses* illustrated by Matisse. The opening hours are Monday to Saturday 1000–1300 and 1400–1700 and Sunday 1400–1800, April to October only. Admission costs €6 (concessions available). The tower is easily accessed by DART to Sandycove (a scenic trip) or bus 8 from Burgh Quay.

For a Whole Day

Glendalough: This early Celtic monastery (tel: (0404) 45325), once an important seat of Christian learning, is situated 30km (19 miles) south of Dublin, between Laragh and Hollywood. Its Gaelic name means 'valley of the two lakes' and there are some breathtaking walks around the monastery and on the lakeshore. St Kevin founded the monastery in the sixth century and his body lies in the ninth-century cathedral. The site is adorned with *St Kevin's Cross*, carved in about 1150, and nearby are the remains of *St Kevin's Kitchen*, a thousand-year-old church. The opening hours are daily 0930–1700 (October to March) and 0930–1800 (April to September) and admission costs €2.75 (concessions available). The site is best reached by car. Alternatively, the *St Kevin's Bus Service* departs from St Stephen's Green daily at 1130, with a return service late afternoon. Its route along the Wicklow Way, through the valleys of the Wicklow Mountains, makes for an idyllic journey.

ACCOMMODATION

It is important to remember that prices can double during peak periods; some hotels also offer reduced rates (which may well be lower than the rack rates quoted here), especially during quieter periods and at weekends. Advance booking is generally advised to ensure that rooms are available. Prices usually include service charges and VAT, which currently stands at 21%. The prices quoted below are the lowest standard rates for a double room, including taxes but excluding breakfast, unless otherwise specified.

Business

Chief O'Neills

This modern hotel makes an ideal base for both business and leisure travellers, combining value for money with warm Irish hospitality and comfort. *Chief O'Neills* is situated at the heart of Smithfield, north of the River Liffey. The hotel is named after Irish emigrant Francis O'Neill, a former Chicago Chief of Police and one of the most notable 20th-century private collectors of Irish traditional music. This theme runs through each of the 73 bedrooms, cleverly enhanced by state-of-the-art contemporary Irish home design to create an uncluttered, relaxed atmosphere. All rooms contain a TV, radio and CD player and most also have an ISDN line with their telephone. There are also extensive business facilities on the ground floor for presentations, board meetings and conferences. For extra luxury, the penthouse suites have their own Jacuzzi and rooftop balcony overlooking Smithfield Market.
Smithfield Village, Dublin 7
Tel: (01) 817 3838. Fax: (01) 817 3839.
E-mail: reservations@chiefoneills.com
Website: www.chiefoneills.com
Price: From €180.

Conrad International

This deluxe, modern, international-style chain hotel, geared primarily to business guests, offers no surprises but is known for its reliability, efficiency and friendly, top-notch service. Centrally located, opposite the National Concert Hall and near St Stephen's Green, its first-class facilities include a business centre with 14 conference rooms and an executive boardroom, secretarial services, video-conferencing, complimentary car parking and ISDN lines in each of the 191 generously proportioned bedrooms. Public areas include two popular in-house restaurants, a lively traditional Irish pub with a large outdoor terrace, a hair salon and a state-of-the-art 24-hour fitness centre.
Earlsfort Terrace, Dublin 2
Tel: (01) 602 8900. Fax: (01) 676 5424.
E-mail: dublininfo@conradhotels.com
Website: www.conrad-international.ie
Price: From €167.

The Fitzwilliam Hotel

Luxurious and ultra-modern, *The Fitzwilliam* commands a striking central location, with the calm and tranquillity of St Stephen's Green to one side and Grafton Street, Dublin's most prestigious shopping area, to the other. The dramatic decor, meticulously planned by Terence Conran, is 'Baronial Modern' in design – a stark, minimalist interpretation of typical country-house features, using chrome, frosted glass, large leather sofas and dramatic down-lighting –

creating a chic but restful ambience. Kevin Thornton's two-Michelin-starred restaurant, *Thornton's*, is located on the first floor (see *Restaurants*). Other notable features include a business centre, three conference rooms, Ireland's largest roof garden and complimentary car parking.

St Stephen's Green, Dublin 2
Tel: (01) 478 7000. Fax: (01) 478 7878.
E-mail: enq@fitzwilliamhotel.com
Website: www.fitzwilliamhotel.com
Price: From €240 (including breakfast).

The Merrion Hotel

Dublin's most sumptuous hotel consists of four gracious Grade I-listed Georgian townhouses, sensitively restored to combine period elegance with five-star modern facilities. All 145 bedrooms offer fax machines with e-mail, ISDN lines and modem points, making *The Merrion Hotel* an ideal choice for the business traveller. Within the hotel is celebrated Irish chef Patrick Guilbaud's two-Michelin-starred eponymous restaurant and, for relaxation, a sizeable pool, gym and spa. There are also magnificent formal, landscaped gardens, forming a serene haven far removed from the frenetic city centre on the hotel's doorstep.

Merrion Street Upper, Dublin 2
Tel: (01) 603 0600. Fax: (01) 603 0700.
E-mail: info@merrionhotel.com
Website: www.merrionhotel.com
Price: From €345.

Luxury

Morrison Hotel

Brilliantly located on the north bank of the River Liffey, near the Millennium Bridge, the *Morrison Hotel* is not only an oasis of tranquillity amid the hustle and bustle of the city centre but also a showcase for the talent of Ireland's internationally renowned designer John Rocha. The interior is unashamedly chic, modern and minimalist, juxtaposing wood, stone and steel with exotic fabrics and richly coloured velvets to create a spacious, clutter-free and comfortable environment. All 94 bedrooms are equipped with high-tech efficiency to suit the modern traveller, while the

Grafton Street

hotel's various bars and restaurants, as well as its nightclub, currently rank among the in places to be seen in the city.

Ormond Quay Lower, Dublin 1
Tel: (01) 887 2400. Fax: (01) 878 3185.
E-mail: info@morrisonhotel.ie
Website: www.morrisonhotel.ie
Price: From €270.

Shelbourne Meridien Hotel

A veritable Dublin institution, immortalised in James Joyce's epic *Ulysses* (1922), the five-star *Shelbourne Meridien Hotel* has been home to the rich and famous – and even royalty – since its opening in the 18th century. Irish history has unfolded within its walls; the British garrisoned the hotel during the 1916 Easter Rising and, in 1921, it was the setting for the signing of the Irish Constitution. Today, centrally located beside St Stephen's Green, with its opulent rooms, its celebrated bars and restaurants and a smart new health club, it remains one of Dublin's most distinguished hotels. With extensive boardroom and conference facilities, as well as a state-of-the-art business centre, it is an ideal choice for both business and pleasure.

27 St Stephen's Green, Dublin 2
Tel: (01) 663 4500. Fax: (01) 661 6006.
E-mail: shelbourneinfo@lemeridien.com
Website: www.shelbourne.ie
Price: From €360.

Moderate

Aberdeen Lodge

This small, friendly private guesthouse is situated in an elegant, restored Edwardian house. It combines four-poster beds and other antique furnishings with modern comforts, an elegant drawing room, a large garden and excellent home cooking – including award-winning full cooked breakfasts. All rooms are en suite. Set in a peaceful tree-lined avenue in the stylish southern suburb of Ballsbridge, it is conveniently located near the city's car ferry terminals and is just a five-minute walk from Sydney Parade DART Station, making it an ideal base for accessing both the city centre and the Wicklow Mountains.

53–55 Park Avenue, Dublin 4
Tel: (01) 283 8155. Fax: (01) 283 7877.
E-mail: aberdeen@iol.ie
Website: www.halpinsprivatehotels.com
Price: From €129 (including breakfast).

Number 31

Just a few minutes from St Stephen's Green, overlooking elegant Fitzwilliam Place, at the heart of Georgian Dublin, *Number 31* is the former home of Ireland's leading architect, Sam Stephenson. It has since been converted into a highly sophisticated, award-winning guesthouse, offering bed and breakfast, with the emphasis on detail, luxury and simplicity. This stylish property consists of two impressive buildings – a coach house and a handsome Georgian townhouse – and offers a variety of en-suite accommodation, as well as secure car parking. Guests are encouraged to make themselves at home at any time of day.

31 Leeson Close, Leeson Street Lower, Dublin 2
Tel: (01) 676 5011. Fax: (01) 676 2929.
E-mail: number31@iol.ie
Website: www.number31.ie
Price: From €150 (including breakfast).

Other Recommendations

The Clarence

Undoubtedly the trendiest address in town, this chic, minimalist boutique hotel is owned by U2 band members, Bono and The Edge. Situated on Dublin's 'left bank', overlooking the River Liffey in the Temple Bar district, the hotel was once a 19th-century Customs House. Now thoroughly modernised, with 50 spacious bedrooms and suites, each individually decorated with understated elegance, *The Clarence* offers all the luxuries and amenities expected by the many celebrities who stay here, including a sophisticated cocktail bar and the celebrated *Tea Rooms* restaurant. For the ultimate extravagance, the multi-level penthouse suite has its own outdoor hot tub overlooking the River Liffey.

6–8 Wellington Quay, Dublin 2
Tel: (01) 407 0800. Fax: (01) 407 0820.
E-mail: reservations@theclarence.ie
Website: www.theclarence.ie
Price: From €300.

The Schoolhouse Hotel

The Schoolhouse Hotel is ideal for those seeking somewhere a little bit different. Situated in the leafy, residential suburb of Ballsbridge, just a ten-minute walk from the city centre, this unusual four-star hotel is housed in a former schoolhouse. The hotel has a loyal following and prides itself on its warm, friendly atmosphere, with 31 bedrooms each combining Old World charm with today's modern amenities. Much of the hotel's nostalgic character stems from the many original features preserved from its days as a parochial school – two of its former classrooms now house the intimate *Satchels* restaurant and the popular *Inkwell* bar.

2–8 Northumberland Road, Dublin 4
Tel: (01) 667 5014. Fax: (01) 667 5015.
E-mail: reservations@schoolhousehotel.com
Website: www.schoolhousehotel.com
Price: From €199 (including breakfast).

RESTAURANTS

The selected restaurants have been divided into five categories: Gastronomic, Business, Trendy, Budget and Personal Recommendations. The restaurants are listed alphabetically within these different categories, which serve as guidelines rather than absolute definitions of the establishments.

VAT currently stands at 21% and is generally included in the price of a meal. A service charge of 12.5% is also usually added to restaurant bills and many diners add a discretionary tip of around 5–10% of the bill. If service is not included, a tip of between 12.5% and 15% is usual. Credit cards are accepted in most restaurants.

The prices quoted below are for an average three-course meal for one person and for a bottle of house wine or cheapest equivalent; they include VAT but they do not include service charge or tip.

Gastronomic

L'Ecrivain

Portraits of Irish writers adorn the walls of 'The Writer', a light, airy and sophisticated restaurant specialising in new Irish cuisine. Derry Clarke is

Photo: Irish Tourist Board

Grafton Street

regarded as one of Dublin's most acclaimed chefs and his signature dish – Dublin Bay prawns in Kataifi pastry with chilli jam and tartare sauce – is sensational. During summer visits, diners should ask for a table on the tiny balcony.
109A Baggot Street Lower, Dublin 2
Tel: (01) 661 1919. Fax: (01) 661 0617.
E-mail: enquiries@lecrivain.com
Website: www.lecrivain.com
Price: €70. Wine: €25.

Les Frères Jacques
Located in the city centre, opposite Dublin Castle, Dublin's top French restaurant is celebrated for its classic, seasonal cuisine and its superb seafood, with west coast oysters and grilled lobster favourites. The intimate, traditional decor, combined with crisp white linens, an exemplary wine list and impeccable, formal service, make it an especially popular choice for business lunches.
74 Dame Street, Dublin 2
Tel: (01) 679 4555. Fax: (01) 679 4725.
E-mail: info@lesfreresjacques.com
Website: www.lesfreresjacques.com
Price: €60. Wine: €18.

Restaurant Patrick Guilbaud
The exceptional, contemporary French cuisine of chef Patrick Guilbaud, using the best in-season Irish ingredients, makes this one of Dublin's finest restaurants. It is fully deserving of its two Michelin stars, with prices to match. The elegant ground-floor restaurant, decorated with 20th-century Irish art, opens onto a terrace and landscaped garden, offering alfresco dining in fine weather. The dishes too are works of art – such as Connemara lobster ravioli with toasted almonds or sole and duck confit with a red wine jus – dramatically served from beneath shining silver cloches.
Merrion Hotel, 21 Merrion Street Upper, Dublin 2
Tel: (01) 676 4192. Fax: (01) 661 0052.
Website: www.merrionhotel.com
Price: €100. Wine: €30.

The Tea Rooms
This modish restaurant in U2's celebrated hotel, The Clarence, (see *Hotels*) has handsome light oak furnishings, pristine white linens and designer cutlery and glasses, as well as understated but flattering, blue lighting. *The Tea Rooms* offers a light, sophisticated menu of modern Irish cuisine such as langoustine bisque with Bere Island scallop ceviche, crème fraîche and avocado, followed by lemon and thyme pot roast chicken, served with white asparagus, morel risotto and vanilla jus. Then there is the caramelised peach and rice pudding tart or a platter of scrumptious farmhouse cheeses for dessert. The martinis served at the neighbouring *Octagon Bar* are reputedly the best in town.
The Clarence, 6–8 Wellington Quay, Dublin 2
Tel: (01) 407 0813. Fax: (01) 407 0826.
Website: www.theclarence.ie
Price: €52.50. Wine: €30.

Thornton's
Kevin Thornton is widely considered to be Ireland's top chef. His imaginative two-Michelin-starred cooking – a combination of traditional Irish and southern French cuisine, cooked with refreshing simplicity – can be tasted at surprisingly affordable prices in a plush, formal dining room on the first floor of The Fitzwilliam Hotel (see *Hotels*), overlooking St Stephen's Green. Signature dishes include the sautéed foie gras with scallops and cep sauce and roast suckling pig with poitin sauce. The set lunch menus (€30 for two courses, €40 for three courses) are especially popular with business clients.
The Fitzwilliam Hotel, St Stephen's Green, Dublin 2
Tel: (01) 478 7008. Fax: (01) 478 7009.
Website: www.fitzwilliamhotel.com
Price: €100. Wine: €28.

Business

Brownes Brasserie
This grand Georgian townhouse, overlooking St Stephen's Green, is a popular venue for business entertaining, due to its extensive wine list and sophisticated Mediterranean cuisine. Specialities include shallot tarte tatin and pan-seared scallops served with ratatouille or shellfish salsa.
22 St Stephen's Green, Dublin 2
Tel: (01) 638 3939. Fax: (01) 638 3900.
E-mail: info@brownesdublin.com
Website: www.brownesdublin.com
Price: €60. Wine: €20.

Chapter One
This smart restaurant, decorated with paintings of local literary celebrities, serves modern Irish cuisine within the arched basement of the Dublin Writers Museum. By day, the local business clientele enjoy the three-course set lunch for €28, while the close proximity of the restaurant to the Gate Theatre and Abbey Theatre makes its theatre menu (also €28) equally popular, with two courses served before the show, with dessert and coffee after the performance. Menu items include such delights as herb-crusted loin of lamb with sweetbreads, kidney, minted potatoes and rosemary juice, and seafood options, such as fillet of brill with crab tortellini served in a shellfish sauce with sautéed mushrooms.
18–19 Parnell Square, Dublin 1
Tel: (01) 873 2266. Fax: (01) 873 2330.
E-mail: info@chapteronerestaurant.com
Website: www.chapteronerestaurant.com
Price: €50. Wine: €20.

Diep Le Shaker
Airy and sophisticated, this two-storey restaurant with a stylish cocktail bar is located near Fitzwilliam Square. Cheerful yellow decor, crisp white linen and excellent service attract a chic and glamorous crowd. It is especially popular for business entertaining. The menu offers equally stylish Asian cuisine, with such aromatic dishes as scallops steamed in their shells with garlic, ginger and light soy sauce, or stir-fried beef with chilli and Thai herbs.
55 Pembroke Lane, Dublin 2
Tel: (01) 661 1829. Fax: (01) 661 5905.
E-mail: info@diep.net
Website: www.diep.net
Price: €36. Wine: €20.

Dobbin's Wine Bistro
With its dark, cavernous interior, its jolly red and white gingham tablecloths and sawdust-strewn floor, this sociable bistro is a veritable Dublin institution for 'doing lunch' and is frequented by a loyal following of businesspeople, politicians and locals. Popular dishes include a trio of salmon (smoked, marinated and poached), baked fillet of red mullet with lobster and bacon potatoes or prime fillet of beef served with deep-fried hash browns and lashings of brandy and black pepper sauce.
15 Stephen's Lane, Dublin 2
Tel: (01) 676 4670. Fax: (01) 661 3331.
E-mail: dobbinswinebistro@eircom.net
Price: €50. Wine: €17.50.

La Mere Zou
This bright, cheerful, Provençal-style restaurant serves classical French cuisine with a superb choice of regional French wines within a Georgian basement on the north side of St Stephen's Green. Service is friendly and efficient, while the set lunch menu (at €18.90 for three courses) is especially popular with local business clientele. Dishes include steamed mussels or sautéed young rabbit with rosemary jus and cep mushrooms.

22 St Stephen's Green, Dublin 2
Tel/fax: (01) 661 6669.
E-mail: merezou@indigo.ie
Price: €40. Wine: €17.70.

Trendy

Café Mao

Exotic curries, spicy satays and other innovative Asian dishes are the order of the day in this small, trendy café-restaurant, located near Grafton Street. The interior is stylishly decorated in brilliant blues, reds and yellows. No reservations are accepted and there is frequently a queue but it is well worth the wait.
2–3 Chatham Row, Dublin 2
Tel: (01) 670 4899. Fax: (01) 670 4893.
E-mail: info@cafemao.com
Website: www.cafemao.com
Price: €40. Wine: €16.

Eden

The outdoor terrace of this airy, minimalist restaurant on Meeting House Square makes an ideal venue for an alfresco lunch of modern, market-fresh cuisine. It is also an ideal venue for a relaxed dinner when classic movies are screened in the square on summer evenings. The seafood terrine served with Guinness bread, the chargrilled quail with calvados cream and champ and the rhubarb crème brûlée are especially recommended.
Meeting House Square, Temple Bar, Dublin 2
Tel: (01) 670 5372. Fax: (01) 670 3330.
Price: €50. Wine: €22.

Halo

On the north quay of the River Liffey, the trendiest dining room in town – designed by John Rocha – boasts an imaginative menu of Asian-influenced fusion food in an atrium setting, enhanced by smart minimalist furnishings, dramatic velvet throws and subtle spot lighting. Equally stylish dishes – celery, celeriac and apple soup with gruyère and walnut fritters, followed by fillet of sea bass with yam mash, braised spring onions and aromatic butter sauce – match the setting perfectly. The Valrhona dark chocolate and *griotine* mousse with vanilla sauce is a must for those with a sweet tooth.
Morrison Hotel, Ormond Quay Lower, Dublin 1
Tel: (01) 887 2421. Fax: (01) 878 3185.
E-mail: halo@morrisonhotel.ie
Website: www.morrisonhotel.ie
Price: €50. Wine: €25.

Jacob's Ladder

This is a chic, minimalist restaurant occupying two floors of a Georgian house overlooking the playing fields of Trinity College. Chef Adrian Roche specialises in imaginative, modern Irish cuisine, using seasonal ingredients to create such delicacies as scallops with beetroot and shellfish coddle – a modern version of the traditional Dublin dish – accompanied by an impressive wine list.
4 Nassau Street, Dublin 2
Tel: (01) 670 3865. Fax: (01) 670 3868.
E-mail: dining@jacobsladder.ie
Website: www.jacobsladder.ie
Price: €45. Wine: €20.

Wagamama

There is often a long queue in this basement branch of the stylish Japanese chain of noodle bars, located just off Grafton Street and St Stephen's Green. The cheap, tasty rice and noodle dishes served at long wooden benches are, however, well worth the wait. A gigantic bowl of ramen (noodle soup), the house speciality, is a meal in itself.
King Street South, Dublin 2
Tel/fax: (01) 478 2152.
Website: www.wagamama.com
Price: €25. Wine: €16.95.

Budget

Avoca Café

This stylish café, on the top floor of the well-known Avoca Handweavers craft store, serves hearty soups, home-baked breads, imaginative salads, freshly squeezed juices, tea, coffee and gorgeous cream cakes to weary shoppers.
11–13 Suffolk Street, Dublin 2
Tel: (01) 672 6019. Fax: (01) 672 6021.
E-mail: info@avoca.ie
Website: www.avoca.ie
Price: €20. Wine: €17.

Chief O'Neill's Bar

This modern bar, north of the River Liffey, combines wholesome favourites, such as Irish stew or beef and Guinness pie, with more refined new Irish cuisine, such as roast salmon steak in a garlic and chive sauce with spring onion mash or Bailey's cheesecake. It also features occasional live traditional music.
Smithfield Village, Dublin 7
Tel: (01) 817 3838. Fax: (01) 817 3839.
Website: www.chiefoneills.com
Price: €25. Wine: €18.

Elephant and Castle

This cheerful café-restaurant, with simple decor and large wooden tables, is located at the heart of Temple Bar. It is renowned for its baskets of spicy chicken wings, its homemade burgers and its gigantic bowls of salad, served all day. It is also a popular venue for American-style Sunday brunch.

18 Temple Bar, Dublin 2
Tel: (01) 679 3121. Fax: (01) 679 1399.
Website: www.elephantandcastle.com
Price: €35. Wine: €20.

Ely

This lively wine bar, occupying the ground floor and basement of a splendid Georgian townhouse near St Stephen's Green, serves tasty Irish fare – including Irish stew and genuine Dublin coddle (bacon, bangers and spuds) – and around 80 different wines by the glass.
22 Ely Place, Dublin 2
Tel: (01) 676 8986. Fax: (01) 661 7288.
Price: €25. Wine: €20.

Gallagher's Boxty House

This popular, traditional Irish restaurant, in upbeat Temple Bar, has a simple, homely decor of pine dressers and bookcases. It specialises in boxties – griddled potato cakes containing savoury fillings, such as beef and Beamish stout, smoked fish or bacon and cabbage – and other tasty Irish fare.
20 Temple Bar, Dublin 2
Tel: (01) 677 2762. Fax: (01) 677 9723.
E-mail: info@boxtyhouse.ie
Website: www.boxtyhouse.ie
Price: €25. Wine: €17.95.

Personal Recommendations

Il Baccaro

Hidden in a dark, intimate 17th-century cellar at the heart of Temple Bar, this busy Italian taverna serves tasty regional dishes, including Florentine-style steaks, spaghetti bolognese and all the usual favourites, as well as delicious antipasti, platters of cold cuts and cheeses. House wine is poured straight from the barrel to a young and lively crowd.
Diceman's Corner, Meeting House Square, Dublin 2
Tel: (01) 671 4597.
Price: €25. Wine: €20.

Wicklow-Powerscourt Gardens

Photo: Irish Tourist Board

Kelly & Ping

East meets West with *Kelly & Ping*'s unique blend of Asian cuisine, served in modern Irish surroundings at the centre of Smithfield, north of the River Liffey. The Japanese-style tiger prawns with ginger and lime mayo are particularly tasty, as is the wok-fried chicken with galangal, garlic and mixed Thai herbs. Portions are generous, yet artistically presented, and the menus are helpfully colour-coded for spiciness.
Duck Lane, Smithfield, Dublin 7
Tel: (01) 817 3840. Fax: (01) 817 3841.
E-mail: info@smithfieldvillage.com
Website: www.kellyandping.com
Price: €35. Wine: €16.50.

The Mermaid Café

The Mermaid Café is a small, popular bistro near Dublin Castle, serving homemade American-inspired dishes. Food is served in a relaxed, uncluttered dining room of simple wooden furniture with nautical touches. The speciality of Atlantic seafood casserole is particularly delicious.
69–70 Dame Street, Dublin 2
Tel: (01) 670 8236. Fax: (01) 670 8205.
E-mail: info@mermaid.ie
Website: www.mermaid.ie
Price: €45. Wine: €17.50.

Oliver St John Gogarty

This is a lively pub in Temple Bar offering above-average pub food, including Irish stew, Galway prawns and other Irish favourites, accompanied by live, traditional Irish music daily.
58–59 Fleet Street, Dublin 2
Tel: (01) 671 1822. Fax: (01) 671 7637.
E-mail: info@olivergogartys.com
Website: www.olivergogartys.com
Price: €40. Wine: €15.

Roly's Bistro

This large, lively bistro serving French, Irish and international classics is rated among the top venues in town. The Kerry lamb pie, the Clonakilty black pudding encased in brioche or the Dublin Bay prawns served with mushrooms, leeks and a brandy and tarragon cream butter, are all recommended.

7 Ballsbridge Terrace, Dublin 4
Tel: (01) 668 2611. Fax: (01) 660 8535.
Price: €45. Wine: €19.

ENTERTAINMENT

Nightlife

The nightlife scene in Dublin has changed beyond all recognition in the last few years. Alongside the traditional Irish pubs sit stylish bars and buzzing pre-club haunts. The trendy Temple Bar area is the district most associated with the city's best nightlife hotspots. Pubs are generally open Monday to Saturday 1100–2330 and Sunday 1200/1600–2300, although some serve until 0200. In some parts of the city, the closing times are enforced by patrolling 'Gardai'. Bars close between 2330 and 0100, while clubs stay open until the early hours. The minimum drinking age is 18 years and the price of a pint in a city pub is typically €4–5. On 1 January 2004, new anti-smoking laws, swiftly proposed and passed by the Irish Minster for Health in March 2003, come into effect, banning smoking in any pubs, bars and nightclubs. There is no dress code as such for pubs in Dublin – it depends on the particular establishment in question. Some venues encourage neat dress while casual dress is commonplace in others.
What's on Where (website: www.wow.ie), the free events guide available in cafés and bars throughout the city, and *In Dublin*, the fortnightly magazine, are both useful guides featuring bar, restaurant and club reviews.

Bars

Dublin's watering holes fall into two camps – the traditional drinking haunts and the designer bars for bright young things. Hip bars include *Pravda*, 2–3 Liffey Street Lower, *Zanzibar*, 34–35 Ormond Quay Lower, and *The Chocolate Bar*, Harcourt Street. One of the latest minimalist venues of choice for Dublin's young and moneyed to spend their wealth in is *No 4*, 4 Dame Lane. For a more traditional pub crawl, head to

Temple Bar, where the *Palace Bar*, 21 Fleet Street, *The Temple Bar*, 48 Temple Lane South, and *Oliver St John Gogarty*, 58–59 Fleet Street, are all to be found. On Merrion Row and Baggot Street, there are pubs like *Toner's*, 139 Baggot Street Lower, *O'Donoghue's*, 15 Merrion Row, and *Doheny & Nesbitt*, 5 Baggot Street Lower, where literary ghosts have taken up permanent residence. The *Dawson Lounge*, 25 Dawson Street, is the smallest pub in Dublin, with room for about six people in the basement. *The George*, 89 Great George's Street South, is one of Dublin's most popular gay bars.

Casinos

These are limited to private clubs that are only open to members. Ireland is somewhat anti-gambling and no public casinos exist.

Clubs

Once a clubbing wasteland, Dublin's reputation for top-rack nightclubs is growing year on year. *PoD* (*Place of Dance*), Harcourt Street, is now the style leader and has won awards for its outlandish decor. The exclusive *Lillie's Bordello*, Adam Court, Grafton Street, is where all visiting pop stars, actors and celebrities hang out for after-show parties. *Ri Ra*, Dame Court, combines a chilled bar with a hip club. *D2* (formerly known as *Velvet*), Harcourt Street (open Thursday, Friday and Saturday), was the first club in Dublin to latch on to UK speed garage. In addition to Dublin's clubs, most live music venues (see below) host club nights after gigs.

Comedy

Dubliners are celebrated for their gift of the gab and their wit. Top comedy venues include *The Laughter Lounge*, 4–6 Eden Quay, with local and international stand-up talent Thursday to Saturday at 2100. Other places include pubs like the *Ha'penny Bridge Inn*, 42 Wellington Quay, on Tuesday nights and the *International Bar*, 23 Wicklow Street, on Thursday nights.

Live Music

Eclectic is the key word for Dublin's music scene, with most venues playing something of everything, from jazz, blues and soul to rock and pop, English folk and Irish traditional (known as 'trad'). Trad is played in countless pubs, often in free impromptu 'sessions'. Larger venues or venues hosting high-profile performers could charge on the night or tickets may be bought in advance.
The Temple Bar Music Centre, Curved Street, Temple Bar, is a great venue for spotting new talent. *Spirit* nightclub, 57 Abbey Street Middle (website: www.spiritdublin.com), hosts a variety of international and local acts and has a small, intimate feel to it, similar in style to *Vicar Street*, 58–59 Thomas Street (website: www.vicarstreet.com). The largest concerts (rock and pop) take place at *The Point*, Link Bridge East (website: www.thepoint.ie), where *Oasis*, *U2*, *Westlife*, *All Saints*, *Manic Street Preachers* and *Fatboy Slim* are some of the big names that have performed there over the last few years. The *RDS* (Royal Dublin Society) *Concert Hall*, Merrion Road, Ballsbridge (website: www.rds.ie), also caters for large pop and rock events.
Olympia Theatre, 72 Dame Street, is one of the best venues for early evening and post-midnight gigs in broad-ranging styles in a large and lovely three-floor venue. On a smaller scale, the 18th-century pub, *Whelan's*, 25 Wexford Street, is a hugely popular and innovative live venue, providing a platform for up-and-coming bands. Jazz can be heard regularly at the

Photo: Irish Tourist Board
River Liffey

Viperoom, 5 Aston Quay, while long-established *Slattery's*, 129 Capel Street, offers a wide assortment of music from rock and jazz to traditional Irish. Other popular traditional venues include pubs *O'Shea's Merchant*, 12 Bridge Street Lower, and *O'Donoghue's*, 15 Merrion Row.

Sport

Both hurling (the Irish national game, similar to hockey and one of the fastest field games in the world) and Gaelic football (a cross between soccer, rugby and a street brawl) are played at *Croke Park Stadium*, Croke Park, Dublin 3 (tel: (01) 836 3222). The *Gaelic Athletic Association* (website: www.gaa.ie) can provide information on both sports.

Rugby is played at *Lansdowne Road Stadium*, Lansdowne Road, Ballsbridge, Dublin 4 (tel: (01) 647 3800; website: www.irishrugby.ie), with *Lansdowne FC* (website: www.lansdownefc.com) and *St Mary's College* (website: www.stmaryscollegerfc.com) both consistently doing well in the AIB All Ireland League Division One tables. Soccer takes place at *Tolka Park*, Richmond Road, Dublin 3 (tel: (01) 837 5536) or Lansdowne Road. Dublin has many teams in the National League Premier Division, including *Bohemians FC* (website: www.bohemians.ie), *Shamrock Rovers FC* (website: www.shamrockrovers.ie), *Shelbourne FC* (website: www.shelbournefc.ie), *St Patrick's Athletic FC* (website: www.stpatsfc.com) and *UCD FC Dublin* (website: www.ucd.ie/~soccer).

Race meetings are held at *Fairyhouse*, Ratoath, off the R155 (tel: (01) 825 6167; website: www.fairyhouseracecourse.ie), and *Leopardstown Racecourse*, Leopardstown, Dublin 18 (tel: (01) 289 3607; website: www.leopardstown.com). *Phoenix Park*, Parkgate Street, Conyngham Road, Dublin 8 (tel: (01) 677 0095), contains a racecourse, a motor-racing circuit and is also a popular venue for Gaelic football, cricket, soccer and water polo. Greyhound racing at *Shelbourne Park*, Pearse Street, Dublin 4 (tel: (01) 668 3502; e-mail: racing@shelbournepark.ie; website: www.shelbournepark.com) is a local passion.

The main events in the sporting calendar are the *Dublin Horse Show* (August) and the national hurling and Gaelic football finals (September), during which the whole city goes a little crazy. Tickets are available from *Ticketmaster* (tel: (01) 456 9569 (24-hour credit-card booking line); website: www.ticketmaster.ie).

Fitness Centres

Crunch Fitness, at UCD, Belfield (tel: (01) 260 3155), is open Monday to Friday 0700–2200 and Saturday and Sunday 1000–1730 and charges €12 per visit.

Golf

Within 50km (30 miles) of Dublin, there are over 100 golf courses. Most are private but some are pay-and-play courses. *Sillogue Park Public Golf Course*, Ballymun (tel: (01) 842 9956), is one of the best value, with green fees starting from €7 for nine holes (€15 at the weekend) and €10 for 18 holes (€17 at the weekend). Prices can also vary depending on the time of day. Pre-booking is advisable. The 18-hole course at *Luttrellstown Castle Golf Club*, Clonsilla (tel: (01) 808 9988; fax: (01) 808 9989; e-mail: enquiries@luttrellstown.ie; website: www.luttrellstown.ie), is also open to the public. Green fees for 18 holes are €85 Monday to Thursday and €95 Friday and Saturday.

Traditional live music

Squash

Most squash clubs are open to members only. *Spheres Squash Club*, 14–18 Drimnagh Road (tel: (01) 455 1021), charges €15 per hour (€16 after 1700) for non-members. *Irish Squash* (tel: (01) 450 1564) can provide more information.

Swimming

Most pools are situated in Dublin's suburbs. *St Paul's College Swimming Pool*, Rahen (tel: (01) 831 6283), is located north of the centre and costs €5. A full list of swimming pools is supplied in the *Golden Pages* telephone directory (website: www.goldenpages.ie).

Tennis

Apart from various parks with tennis courts, *Spawell*, Wellington Road, Templeogue (tel: (01) 490 4401), is one of the few venues with courts that are open to the public. Play costs €10 an hour. *Tennis Ireland* (tel: (01) 668 1841) can provide further information.

Shopping

Like the city itself, Dublin's shopping scene is dominated by the fusion of old and new. There is nowhere more traditional than the *Moore Street Market*, on Henry Street (off O'Connell Street), where fresh fruit and vegetables are sold at bargain prices Monday to Saturday 0900–1800. The *Temple Bar Food Market*, in Meeting House Square, on Saturday mornings displays more pricey organic produce.

South of the River Liffey, is the smart Grafton Street shopping precinct with upmarket department store *Brown Thomas* and one of Dublin's finest shopping centres, *The Powerscourt Town House*. The *Design Centre* on the top floor of the Powerscourt Town House shopping centre deals exclusively in Irish designer fashions. Nassau Street, off Grafton Street, is best for traditional Irish gifts, such as hand-blown glass, crafts, knits, Celtic jewellery and Arran sweaters; the *Kilkenny Design Centre*, 6 Nassau Street, and the *Blarney Woollen Mills*, 21–23 Nassau Street, are also good bets.

Good bookshops include *Eason's*, 1 Dawson Street, *Fred Hanna's*, 29 Nassau Street, *Greene's*, 16 Clare Street (second-hand books and rare editions), and *Books Upstairs*, 36 College Green (Irish, gay and lesbian). *Winding Stair*, 40 Ormond Quay Lower, is best for bargain books.

Dublin's fashionable Temple Bar district has good, one-off shops, such as the *DESIGNyard*, a showcase for innovative Irish jewellery, interior design and decorative arts, while the antiques quarter, centred round Francis Street, is particularly lively on a Saturday morning.

Standard shopping hours are Monday to Saturday 0900–1700/1800. Late-night shopping is on Thursday, with the bigger stores and many of the smaller ones remaining open until approximately 2000. Many bookshops keep longer hours and some also open on Sunday afternoon. VAT is levied at different rates on goods and services, with an average rate of 21%. Tax-free shopping is available to non-EU residents, who can redeem the tax at the airport on production of a completed tax-free slip. *Global Refund* (tel: (091) 553 258; fax: (091) 553 403; e-mail: info@globalrefund.ie; website: www.globalrefund.ie) can provide further information.

Culture

Dublin's rich literary culture has led to a flourishing film industry and varied theatre repertoire of Irish classical and contemporary works. The Temple Bar district is the main cultural centre. The annual highlights are the *Dublin Theatre Festival* in late September/early October and the *Dublin Film Festival* in March. In between, there is a richly varied programme to choose from.

Most tickets can be purchased on the night, costing anything from €5 to €70 (for the best seats at the opera). Tickets are also available from *HMV* stores in Henry Street and Grafton Street, from *Dublin Tourism*, Suffolk Street (bookings in person only), or from *Ticketmaster* (tel: (01) 456 9569 (24-hour credit card booking line); website: www.ticketmaster.ie).

There is a very good website for events throughout Ireland (website: www.entertainment.ie). *In Dublin*, the fortnightly magazine, is good for Dublin events listings. *Dublin Tourism* also provides online events listings, which are updated daily (website: www.visitdublin.com).

Temple Bar

Music

Opera Ireland (tel: (01) 478 6041; website: www. operaireland.com) and the innovative *Opera Theatre Company* (tel: (01) 679 4962; website: www.opera.ie) perform regularly at a variety of venues, including the *Gaiety Theatre* (see *Theatre* below) and the *Hugh Lane Gallery*, Charlemont House, Parnell Square North (tel: (01) 874 1903; website: www.hughlane.ie). However, the main classical music venue is the *National Concert Hall*, Earlsfort Terrace (tel: (01) 417 0000; website: www.nch.ie), which is home to the *National Symphony Orchestra*.

The largest concerts (classical and popular) take place at *The Point*, Link Bridge East (tel: (01) 836 3633; website: www.thepoint.ie). This is a thriving venue, where *Riverdance*, classical music and ballet performances are held, as well as major pop performances. The *RDS* (Royal Dublin Society) *Concert Hall*, Merrion Road, Ballsbridge (tel: (01) 688 0866; fax: (01) 660 4014; e-mail: info@rds.ie; website: www.rds.ie), caters for both large pop and rock events and smaller classical concerts.

Theatre

Ireland's national theatre, the *Abbey Theatre*, is located in Abbey Street (tel: (01) 878 7222; website: www.abbeytheatre.ie). Set up by W B Yeats in 1904, it is a historic and reliable venue for high-quality Irish drama. The *Peacock Theatre*, in the same building as the Abbey, has a more experimental repertoire. Orson Welles and James Mason began their acting careers at the *Gate Theatre*, 1 Cavendish Row (tel: (01) 874 4085; website: www.gate-theatre.ie), which is still going strong. The city's first music hall, the *Olympia Theatre*, 72 Dame Street (tel: (01) 679 3323), and the *Gaiety Theatre*, King Street South (tel: (01) 677 1717; website: www.gaietytheatre.com), put on anything from the Irish classics to pantomime. The *Projects Arts Centre*, 39 Essex Street East, in Temple Bar (tel: (01) 679 6622; website: www.project.ie), offers a varied programme of poetry readings, drama and dance.

Dance

Dublin's dance groups include *CoisCéim Dance Theatre*, 14 Sackville Place (tel: (01) 878 0838; website: www.iol.ie/~coisceim), *Rubato Ballet*, 19 Stamer Street (tel: (01) 453 8657; website: www.iol.ie/~rubato), and *Irish Modern Dance Theatre* (tel: (01) 874 9616), who perform a potent mix of poetry, music and drama at Dublin's various theatres. The *Association of Professional Dancers*, 6 Henry Place (tel: (01) 873 4573; website: www.prodanceireland.com), provides information on

performances and festivals, including *Riverdance* (website: www.riverdance.com). Anyone can join in traditional Irish dancing after a pint or two at *O'Shea's Merchant Pub*, 12 Bridge Street Lower (tel: (01) 679 3797).

Film

Dublin's first public screening took place on 20 April 1896 and James Joyce opened the first cinema, *Volta*, in 1909. Irish film culture is considered to be going through a Golden Age, with Dublin at the forefront. John Houston lovingly adapted a short story from James Joyce's *Dubliners* into his final film, *The Dead* (1987). Two years later, Jim Sheridan's film adaptation of Dublin writer-artist Christy Brown in *My Left Foot* (1989) won international acclaim and an Oscar for Daniel Day-Lewis. *Educating Rita* (1983), *Michael Collins* (1996) and *The General* (1999) are among the best-known recent films to have captured Dublin on celluloid, together with Alan Parker's *The Commitments* (1991), telling Roddy Doyle's story of gritty young Dubliners to audiences worldwide. As for Roddy Doyle, he has his own production company: *Deadly Films*.

Art films are shown at the *Irish Film Centre* (*IFC*), 6 Eustace Street (tel: (01) 679 5744; website: www.fii.ie), and the *Screen*, D'Olier Street (tel: (01) 672 5500). Mainstream cinemas include the *Savoy*, 16–17 O'Connell Street Upper (tel: (01) 874 8487), and the vast *Virgin Multiplex*, Parnell Street (tel: (01) 872 8444). The *Irish Times*, *Evening Herald* and *Irish Film Centre* publish cinema listings.

Cultural Events

The main cultural event is *St Patrick's Day*, on 17 March, when the entire city comes to a standstill for the year's greatest celebration of Ireland and all things Irish. During summer, the first two weeks of June bring the *AIB Music Festival*, with top-class chamber music coming to various Georgian houses throughout the city. *Bloomsday*, 16 June, is the major literary event of the year, as the seminal works of James Joyce are celebrated on the anniversary of the day that Joyce's protagonist, Leopold Bloom, took his fictional walk around the city. The first two weeks of October see yet another cultural highlight in the form of the *Dublin Theatre Festival*, which takes place at various venues around the city.

Literary Notes

Dublin's literary history dates back to at least around AD800, with the *Book of Kells*. The real Dublin heavyweights, however, date from the 19th and 20th centuries. In the 19th century, Dublin-born Bram Stoker wrote *Dracula* (1897). Vampire lovers will enjoy a visit to St Michan's Church to see his family crypt. Oscar Wilde, George Bernard Shaw and, most of all, James Joyce, later took up the mantle for European, not just Irish, literature. James Joyce's difficult *Ulysses* (1922) is considered by many literary critics to be the finest novel ever written. The Nobel Prize for literature was won by W B Yeats in 1923, by George Bernard Shaw, author of *Pygmalion* (1916), in 1925, and by Samuel Beckett in 1969. The McDaid's pub on Harry Street inspired famed writer and drinker, Brendan Behan, author of *The Borstal Boy* (1958) and *The Hostage* (1965). Contemporary writers include Christy Brown, author of *My Left Foot* (1989), Maeve Binchy, with numerous bestsellers, including *The Lilac Bus* (1992) and *Circle of Friends* (1991), and Roddy Doyle, whose novel *Paddy Clarke Ha Ha Ha* won the Booker Prize in 1993.

SPECIAL EVENTS

New Year's Day, 1 Jan, throughout the city
National Book Fair, late Jan, Royal Dublin Society
Six Nations Rugby Tournament, Feb–Apr, Lansdowne Road Stadium
Hennessy Cognac Gold Cup Chase, mid-Feb, Leopardstown Racecourse
St Patrick's Day Parade, parades, fireworks, carnival, ceilidh dancing, 17 Mar, throughout the city
Feis Ceoil, classical music festival, last two weeks Mar, 37 Molesworth Street, Temple Bar
Colours Boat Race, rowing race, first weekend Apr, River Liffey between Trinity College and University College Dublin
Dublin Film Festival, third week Apr, various venues including the Savoy, the IFC and the Screen
Heineken Green Energy Music Festival, outdoor concerts at Dublin Castle and smaller indoor gigs at what is rapidly emerging as a landmark event in the city's social calendar, May, Dublin Castle and various other venues
Dublin Garden Festival, late May/early Jun, RDS, Ballsbridge
Bloomsday Festival, a walk around the city in celebration of the life of James Joyce as part of the annual
Dublin Writers' Festival, 16 Jun, walk starts at the James Joyce Centre, 35 Great George's Street North
AIB Music Festival, chamber music festival, first two weeks Jun, Georgian houses throughout the city
Dublin International Organ and Choral Festival, throughout Jun, RDS, Ballsbridge
Music in the Park, series of lunchtime concerts, Jun–Aug, various city parks
Temple Bar Blues Fleadh, live blues festival, third weekend Jul, various venues in Temple Bar
Dublin Horse Show, second week Aug, Royal Dublin Society
The Liffey Swim, first Sat in Sep, River Liffey
All Ireland Hurling Festival, second Sun in Sep, Croke Park
All Ireland Gaelic Football Final, fourth Sun in Sep, Croke Park
Dublin Jazz Festival, mid-Sep, various venues
Irish Antique Dealers Fair, last week Sep, Royal Dublin Society
Dublin Fringe Festival, annual festival celebrating both Irish and world theatre, as well as dance and comedy, Sep, various venues
Dublin Theatre Festival, first two weeks Oct, various venues
Samhain Halloween Festival, 31 Oct, throughout the city
Dublin City Marathon, late Oct, starts Leinster Street South and finishes at Merrion Street West
National Crafts Fair of Ireland, mid-Dec, Royal Dublin Society
Leopardstown Races, annual horseracing event, 26–29 Dec, Leopardstown

This former British imperial enclave – situated at the mouth of the Pearl River Delta, on the southwestern coast of China – has been rapidly changing since the handover from British colonial to Chinese sovereignty in 1997. Hong Kong's role as gateway to China is more in question than ever, with the Bamboo Curtain a distant memory, WTO accession opening the entire mainland to foreign economic penetration and China enjoying surging growth while Hong Kong endures prolonged recession. Hong Kong has also become far more Chinese than ever before, with many ex-pats departed and an overwhelmingly Cantonese government presiding over the Filipinos, Indians, Nepalese and other minorities that comprise the city's ethnic patchwork. Nevertheless, the Hong Kongers resist assimilation, reluctantly yielding to pressures for economic integration while jealously guarding their separate freedoms and identities.

With the political reasons for its creation fast receding into history, Hong Kong's geographical oddity comes into focus. The few square kilometres of territory conceded to the British now top the UN list for urban population density. Hong Kong Island itself is the core of the old imperial possession, with Kowloon just across the harbour forming the other half of the main conurbation. Further north are the New Territories, leased from China in 1898, which form a slightly more rural hinterland. And around this main focus are the large islands of Lamma and Lantau and the smaller Outlying Islands that complete the patchwork.

This assortment of pinnacles and paddies sits slap in the South China Sea's typhoon alley. In winter and early spring, the climate can be mild and fresh but, in May, the ever-present humidity skyrockets and summer is both hot and frequently wet. Typhoons hit during summer and early autumn and, even without

them, ferocious rainstorms fall intermittently. Hong Kong is not the ideal summer holiday destination.

The city's economy has suffered since the Asian economic crisis of 1997, never regaining the same vigour (and insane property prices), although commerce is still its defining characteristic. In the proverbial scale of Cantonese values, money comes first. And Hong Kong still has plenty of that. Hong Kong has a more determined sense of its separate identity than ever before, although it remains a thrustingly commercial city, whose dedication to fast money has never been greater. But the city also has its unsung natural beauties, in the shape of looming mountains, secluded islets, white beaches and island landscapes. The Special Administrative Region government recently branded the entire city 'Asia's World City'. Visitors can judge how true that is but, unquestionably, Hong Kong remains unique.

Photo: Hong Kong Tourism Board

Causeway Bay

TRAVEL

Getting There By Air

Hong Kong International Airport (HKG)

Tel: 2188 7111 *or* 2181 0000 (enquiry hotline).
Fax: 2824 0717.

Website: www.hkairport.com

Twice voted World's Best Airport (2001 and 2002), Hong Kong's airport is located 45km (28 miles) from central Hong Kong, at Chek Lap Kok. It opened on 6 July 1998 – replacing the existing Kai Tak airport – and can handle 49 flights per hour and 45 million passengers per annum; planned ultimately to increase to 87 million. Its cargo capacity – increasingly important as the airport develops as a cargo hub – is planned to rise from its initial three million tonnes to nine million tonnes. This is especially important, since new 'open skies' agreements between incumbent carrier Cathay Pacific and US regulators have opened

terminal building, designed by British architect Sir Norman Foster, is Hong Kong's largest single building and its wing-like roof and glass walls have been hailed as a landmark in modern architecture, although the roof has been known to leak during typhoons.

Major airlines: *Cathay Pacific* (tel: 2747 1888; website: www.cathaypacific.com) is the territory's flag carrier, operating direct flights to most major destinations in the West and Australasia. Other major airlines out of the 62 international carriers that serve the territory include *Air Canada, Air China, Air France, Air India, Air New Zealand, Alitalia, American Airlines, British Airways, China Airlines, Continental Airlines, Delta Airlines, Dragonair, Emirates, Finnair, Garuda Indonesia, Gulf Air, Japan Airlines, Korean Air, Lufthansa, Malaysian Airlines, Northwest Airlines, Olympic Airways, Qantas, Singapore Airlines, Thai International, United Airlines* and *Virgin Atlantic.*

Approximate flight times to Hong Kong: From London is 11 hours 45 minutes; from New York is 20 hours 10 minutes (due to fall by seven hours or more with non-stop New York–Hong Kong services

Internet access lounges are available in the passenger terminal; wireless broadband access is available to passengers with wireless Ethernet cards. Bureaux de change are open daily 0600–2330. The passenger terminal building offers special-needs facilities for passengers with disabilities. Car hire is available at the Ground Transport Centre from *Avis, Hertz* and other major operators.

Business facilities: The *PCCW HKT* business centre (tel: 2883 3863) provides Internet services, fax and telegram facilities, as well as a small conference room accommodating four or five people.

Arrival/departure tax: There is a departure tax of HK$80.

Transport to the city: Rail, bus and taxi links from Hong Kong International Airport to central Hong Kong leave from the Ground Transportation Centre. The easiest connection is via the high-speed *Airport Express* train, operated by *Mass Transit Railway* or *MTR* (tel: 2881 8888; website: www.mtrcorp.com), which runs daily 0550–2448 and leaves every ten minutes, taking passengers from the airport to central Hong Kong in just 23 minutes, via stops at Kowloon and Tsing Yi stations. A single adult ticket costs HK$100 to Hong Kong Station and HK$90 to Kowloon – the likeliest destinations for international travellers. *MTR* also connects districts throughout Kowloon and Hong Kong Island with the airport. A combined Airport Express Tourist Octopus Card, known as the *Three Day Hong Kong Transport Pass*, allows for a single journey into Hong Kong from the airport, plus three days of unlimited rides on the MTR. This costs HK$220 – or HK$300 for two journeys on the Airport Express plus the rest of the package. Passengers can also take advantage of free shuttle buses linking MTR's Hong Kong and Kowloon stations with major hotels; there is also a free check-in service at both stations for up to a day before departure.

By bus, the quickest way to central Hong Kong is on the *Airbus* (tel: 2261 2791) or the *Cityflyer* airport bus (tel: 2873 0818), which depart every 15 minutes (journey time – 1 hour) at a cost of approximately HK$40 for services to Central. About 30 franchised routes serve the airport, including night buses, with 17 pick-up bays. The earliest 'A' route express bus services run 0530–2400, when the 'N' night bus service takes over.

Taxis to Hong Kong are readily available. Red taxis serve Hong Kong Island and Kowloon, green taxis serve the New Territories and blue taxis serve Lantau Island (journey time to Hong Kong – 45 minutes). The fare to Central is typically HK$330, while to Tsim Sha Tsui on Kowloon Side costs HK$270. Limousine hire is available from desks in the arrivals hall, from *International Hire Car* (tel: 2261 2155) and

major international airport

2000km

1000mls

up many direct and onward routes between Hong Kong and US cities. A new commercial project called SkyPlaza – comprising passenger facilities, office and retail space, as well as an international exhibition centre – floated in 2002, is expected to enhance Chek Lap Kok even more.

The airport is one of ten Airport Core Programme (ACP) projects – one of the largest infrastructure projects ever undertaken in the world. It includes the 2.2km (1.4-mile) Tsing Ma Bridge – the world's largest suspension bridge – linking Hong Kong to Lantau. Approximately three quarters of the 12,480 sq kilometres (7800 sq miles) of the airport site was constructed from land reclaimed from the sea, with the rest formed from the excavation of the existing islands of Chek Lap Kok and Lam Chau. The airport

launching); from Los Angeles is 14 hours 35 minutes; from Toronto is 15 hours 15 minutes and from Sydney is 9 hours.

Airport facilities: Hong Kong International Airport has a suite of facilities appropriate to its size and importance. There are 118 immigration desks for arriving passengers and 88 for departing passengers, operated by Hong Kong's Immigration Department. Twelve baggage carousels give an estimated baggage reclaim time of as low as ten minutes. The *Hong Kong SkyMart* shopping centre (open 0600–2430) has over 150 shops, including 26 food and beverage outlets – soon to expand still further. Three information centres (open 0600–2400) provide extensive services, including hotel reservation and touch-screen passenger information kiosks. Free multimedia and

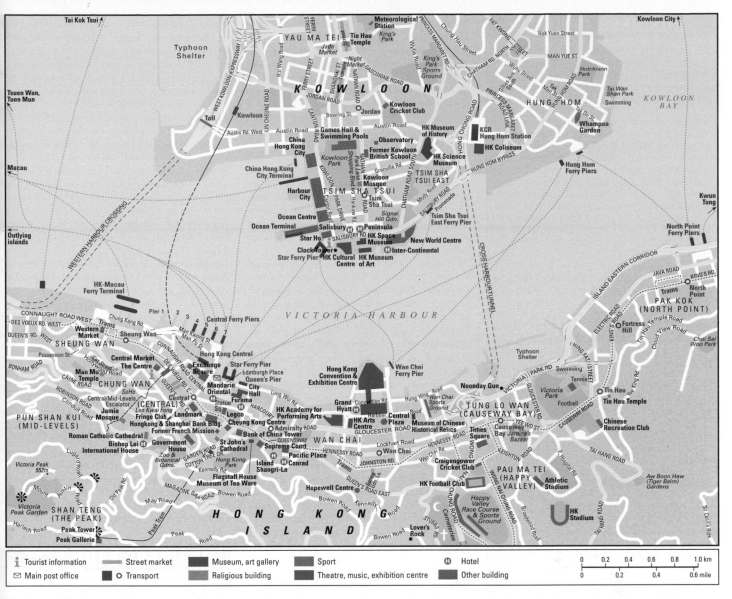

Tourist information | **Street market** | **Museum, art gallery** | **Sport** | **Hotel**
Main post office | **Transport** | **Religious building** | **Theatre, music, exhibition centre** | **Other building**

0 0.2 0.4 0.6 0.8 1.0 km
0 0.2 0.4 0.6 mile

Parklane Limousine (tel: 2261 0303). Ferry links operate between the airport and Tuen Mun in the New Territories daily every 30 minutes and cost HK$15 (journey time – 9 minutes).

Getting There By Water

The *Port of Hong Kong*, situated right at the heart of the territory, between Kowloon and Hong Kong Island, is a major global maritime hub, providing a stream of ocean traffic visible from the city centre. It is administered by the *Marine Department of the Government of Hong Kong* (tel: 2542 3711; fax: 2541 7194; e-mail: mdenquiry@mardep.gov.hk; website: www.info.gov.hk/mardep). The public passenger ferry terminals process approximately 18 million passenger trips a year.

Hong Kong harbour's *Ocean Terminal* (tel: 2118 8951; fax: 2736 2481; website: www.oceanterminal. com.hk), situated on Kowloon Side, is a major cruise destination, able to accommodate the largest liners. Many of the cruise trips, however, are overnight casino trips to international waters, catering for the Chinese passion for gambling. The Ocean Terminal contains 24-hour customs and immigration services at Western Anchorage, left-luggage, banks and bureaux de change. The facilities at the adjacent Harbour City mall are extensive and include banking, duty-free shops, department stores, cafés and a restaurant.

Some hydrofoil and jet catamarans depart from *China Hong Kong City Terminal*, Tsim Sha Tsui, Kowloon. Others depart from the *Shun Tak* hydrofoil terminal in Shueng Wan, Hong Kong Island, which is also the terminal for hydrofoil services to Macau.

Ferry services: Cruise lines serving the Port of Hong Kong include *Club Med Croisieres, Cunard Line, Disney Cruise Line, Holland American, Norwegian Cruiseline, Princess Cruises, Orient Lines, P&O Cruises, Radisson Seven Seas Cruises, Seabourn Cruise Line, Silversea Cruises* and *Star Cruises*. Hovercrafts and jet catamarans link Hong Kong Island and Kowloon with Chinese ports in Guangzhou, Shenzhen and other neighbouring centres, including Shenzhen Airport. *Far East Hydrofoil Co Ltd* (tel: 2921 6688) is the main provider. There are also a number of ships sailing to major Chinese ports, although these are less frequent. There is a fast hydrofoil link to Macau. Ships berth at the *China Hong Kong City Terminal*, in Tsim Sha Tsui. Cruise ships of the *Star Line* also berth at the Ocean Terminal, giving a superb view of central Hong Kong from arriving boats.

CITY STATISTICS

Location: Special Administrative Region (SAR), Guangzhou, People's Republic of China.
Country dialling code: 852.
Population: 6,724,900 (metropolitan area).
Ethnic mix: 95% Chinese, 2% Filipino, 0.8% Indonesian, 0.4% Thai, 0.3% British, 0.3% Indian, 0.2% Nepalese, 0.2% Japanese, 0.2% Pakistani, 0.6% other.
Religion: 90% Buddhist/Taoist, 8% Christian, 1% Muslim, 1% other.
Time zone: GMT + 8 (GMT + 7 summer).
Electricity: 220 volts AC, 50Hz; square three-pin plugs are common, although round three-pin and two-pin plugs are also in use.
Average January temp: 17°C (63°F).
Average July temp: 29°C (84°F).
Annual rainfall: 2214mm (88.5 inches).

BUSINESS PROFILE

The mainstays of Hong Kong's economy are trading, light manufacturing, shipping, media, financial services and tourism, as well as the property sector, which is of huge interest to locals but little to outsiders.

Although transport routes to the newly opened-up ports across coastal China are challenging Hong Kong's pre-eminence, the city's great trading houses remain important. These major international conglomerates, such as *Swire, Jebsen* and *Jardine Matheson*, have widely diversified interests. Li Ka-shing and his *Hutchinson Whampoa* is the quintessence of how Hong Kong's economic power, founded on trade, has spread octopus-like from the Pearl River Delta into vastly diverse locales and commercial holdings, ranging from ports to telecommunications.

Manufacturing is concentrated in textiles, consumer electronics and other consumer goods – Hong Kong is the world's largest producer of children's toys. Increasingly, manufacturing operations are head-quartered in Hong Kong but use infinitely cheaper labour across the border. The shipping and logistics industries are assisted by Hong Kong's natural deep-water harbour, probably the best in the region.

Hong Kong also has a strong media and telecommunications sector, churning out Cantopop, kung fu movies and other fodder for the Greater China public. Companies like *Golden Harvest* and the *Emperor Entertainment Group* dominate the local industry. Internet and telecommunications companies, such as Richard Li's *Pacific Century CyberWorks*, have risen on the backs of established telcos like *Cable and Wireless HongKong Telecom*.

Hong Kong has developed into a major international financial centre since the incorporation of its stock exchange in 1980 – now the tenth largest in the world, as ranked by capitalisation, although soon to be overshadowed by Shanghai and Shenzhen. Banking, insurance and other financial services are provided to local and mainland firms, as well as the many international conglomerates with offices there. The *Hongkong and Shanghai Banking Corporation* is the strongest bank to originate locally and develop an international presence. The *Bank of East Asia* is another notable body. Investment banking houses, such as *Goldman Sachs* and *BNP Prime Peregrine*, are also highly active locally.

Property provides much of the investment funding to support Hong Kong's broader economy, although the sector has been in crisis since the late 1990s. Tourism might yet be Hong Kong's salvation, with the projected completion of the Hong Kong Disneyland on Lantau Island in 2005 and new casinos planned for nearby Macau.

Gross National Product (GNP) for the city stood at HK$1.3 trillion in 2001. The September 2002 census places import and export trade as the largest single employer, followed by financial, insurance, real estate and business services. The headline unemployment rate in Hong Kong was 7.2% in October 2002, almost its highest ever, posing serious challenges for government and industry. Authoritative unofficial surveys suggest the region's unemployment rate is close, at 7%, although official figures give it as 3.6%.

The main financial district is the International Finance Centre (IFC), where the Hong Kong Stock Exchange is housed. Most corporate headquarters are housed around Central, Admiralty and Nathan Road, on Kowloon Side.

Transport to the city: The Ocean Terminal is a major node for bus and taxi services on Kowloon Side and is adjacent to the *Star Ferry* services linking the terminal to Hong Kong Island. Tsim Sha Tsui MTR station is a short walk away. Transport from the Shun Tak hydrofoil terminal is from the nearby Sheung Wan MTR station.

Getting There By Rail

Kowloon–Canton Railway – KCR (tel: 2602 7799; fax: 2601 6602; website: www.kcrc.com) is the service provider for railways leading north from Kowloon. The *KCR Terminal* is located in Hung Hom, Kowloon. Immigration facilities are handled before boarding – passengers are asked to arrive 45 minutes before departure.

Hong Kong Station, located in the International Finance Centre Mall, Exchange Square, Central, serves the *MTR Airport Express* link – passengers wishing to connect to the KCR rail lines must cross to Kowloon by MTR or ferry. The station has a left-luggage service, advance airport check-in, information offices, exchange offices (at the Hang Seng Bank), duty-free shops, banks, restaurants and supermarkets.

Rail services: Kowloon–Canton Railway (KCR) operates a service jointly with *Chinese Railways* (tel: 2947 7888) from Kowloon to Guangzhou, four times a day (journey time – 1 hour 35 minutes). There are also services from Hong Kong to Foshan (journey time – 3 hours) and Changping (journey time – 1 hour 15 minutes). Restaurant cars are only available if travelling first class. Local KCR trains run regularly, daily 0530–2425 (every 5–10 minutes) to Lo Wu – the last stop before the Chinese border – with many passengers joining the trains where the KCR line connects with the MTR at Kowloon Tong. It is possible for travellers to then cross the border to Shenzhen – the first city in China over the border. To go as far as Lo Wu, it is necessary for passengers to hold a visa for China, otherwise it is only possible to get to Sheung Shui. Immigration is handled at the Lo Wu border crossing and there is a last-minute border visa shop, although visitors are recommended to obtain visas earlier. It is also advisable for travellers to leave plenty of time, especially at weekends and public holidays, as it can be crowded at the crossing point. The KCR *WestRail* information line (tel: 2684 8623) can provide further information.

Besides the express service from Kowloon to Guangzhou, there are now direct express links to Beijing (journey time – 16 hours) and Shanghai (journey time – 15 hours 35 minutes), as well as sleeper trains and stopping services to many other Chinese cities.

Transport to the city: The Hung Hom station has plentiful bus and taxi services to destinations in Kowloon and Hong Kong Island. Kowloon Tong station has direct links with the MTR.

Getting There By Road

Hong Kong traffic drives on the left. Routes are designated by a number (such as Route 1, the main expressway route to China, or Route 3 from Hong Kong Island). Speed limits are 50kph (30mph) in built-up areas or 100kph (60mph) elsewhere. An International Driving Permit is recommended, although not legally required. A valid national driving licence is accepted for up to 12 months and the minimum age for driving is 18 years. Third-party insurance is compulsory. Holders of a valid foreign licence who are over 18 years old can drive for their first year of residence, after which they must apply for a local licence. The maximum legal alcohol to blood ratio for driving is 0.05%.

The *Hong Kong Automobile Association* (tel: 2739 5273; fax: 2369 0863; website: www.fia.com/tourisme/infoclub/hkong.htm) can provide more information.
Emergency breakdown service: *HKAA* 2304 4911.
Routes to the city: The most accessible places to drive to are Lantau Island (for the airport) and Guangzhou. Although there is no theoretical reason not to drive to and from the mainland, few visitors do.
Approximate driving times to Hong Kong: From Lantau Island – 1 hour; from Guangzhou – 3 hours.
Coach services: There are bus and coach links to destinations on the Chinese mainland. *Citybus* (tel: 2736 3888) and *CTS* (tel: 2853 3888) offer coach services to Guangzhou and Shenzhen, departing from the *China Hong Kong City Terminal*, Tsim Sha Tsui, Kowloon, and other pick-up points, including the Island Shangri-La Hotel in Admiralty.

Getting Around

Public Transport

Hong Kong has one of the most efficient and diverse public transport systems in the world, incorporating an underground railway, light urban railways, buses, minibuses, boats, ferries and trams. However, the diversity of operators prevents full integration and it is not possible, for example, to transfer from train to minibus on the same ticket, although the Octopus Card is very widely accepted.

BUSINESS ETIQUETTE

Suits are advisable for business – Hong Kong can be surprisingly formal in its outward business standards, in contrast to the casual bucaneering entrepreneurialism of its business practice. Hong Kongers are also not casual about business punctuality – appointments should be fixed in advance and kept. The culture of business cards is prevalent and, if possible, cards should be printed up with Chinese translations on the reverse. Almost all top hotels provide business centres for visiting businesspeople, with typing, photocopying, translation and other services. Normal office hours are 0900–1300 and 1400–1800 Monday to Friday and 0900–1300 Saturday, with some offices staying open later on Saturday and almost every Hong Kong office full of late-night workers long after sunset.

Although business lunches (especially dim sum) and after-hours drinking are a part of the Hong Kong business scene, there is not the same emphasis on drinking parties and bonding evenings as there is in Japan. Hong Kongers are too busy focusing on the bottom line to worry about company camaraderie and many have far lower tolerance for alcohol than their hardened mainland compatriots. Ex-pat workers drink together hugely but this is not a formal part of local business culture – just an unavoidable one.

Photo: Hong Kong Tourism Board

A cruise ship arriving in Hong Kong

The *Mass Transit Railway – MTR* (tel: 2881 8888; fax: 2795 9991; website: www.mtrcorp.com) operates five underground **metro** lines including two cross-harbour lines, as well as the Airport Express link. It is more expensive than the ferry but quicker, particularly for those travelling further into Kowloon than Tsim Sha Tsui. The MTR runs daily 0555–2435. The only other railway line is the *Kowloon–Canton Railway – KCR* (see *Getting There By Rail*), which has 13 stations within Hong Kong. Fares are metered by the number of stations, with only limited zoning. The cheapest fare (for one to two stations) is KH$4 (concessions available).

Bus routes run throughout the territory, with cross-harbour routes via the tunnel. These, however, are often very crowded. Exact change is required for those passengers not in possession of an Octopus Card. Air-conditioned **coaches** operate along certain Hong Kong and Kowloon routes. *Citybus* (tel: 2873 0818; fax: 2857 6179; website: www.citybus.com.hk) and *New World First Bus* (tel: 2136 8888; fax: 2136 2136; website: www.nwfb.com.hk) are the two licensed operators for bus services on Hong Kong Island. *Kowloon Motor Bus* (tel: 2745 5566; website: kmb.com.hk) operates on Kowloon Side. Buses operate daily around 0600–2430. A **night bus** service runs all night. Bus fare is generally around HK$5.

Minibuses operate on fixed routes. These pick up passengers who flag them down like taxis and stop on request – the procedure is for passengers to stand up and yell – except at regular bus stops and other restricted areas. Payment is almost invariably by cash and the kamikaze dash through busy traffic favoured by most drivers is a totally Hong Kong experience. Drivers are not compelled to move without a full load, however, so they often loiter at traffic lights, waiting to pick up more passengers. Fares vary by distance and are usually incomprehensible to

non-locals; most are around HK$5–7 – some minibuses now accept Octopus Card payment. Minibuses run daily around 0600–2430 and a night service operates on specific routes – between Central in Hong Kong and Mongkok or between eastern Hong Kong Island and Kennedy Town in the west.

Trams are only available on Hong Kong Island. They are frequent and cheap, with a standard fare of HK$2 for the entire journey; temporary visitors are unlikely to encounter the far more advanced supertrams in suburban Kowloon. The *Peak Tram*, on the Island, is a funicular tramway to the upper terminus on Victoria Peak (see *Key Attractions*).

The *Star Ferry* (tel: 2367 7065; fax: 2118 6028; e-mail: sf@starferry.com.hk; website: www.starferry.com.hk) ride across Hong Kong harbour is a tourist staple, as well as the cheapest way to make the crossing at HK$1.70 (or HK$2.20 for the nominally air-conditioned upper deck). *Star Ferry* terminals are in Tsim Sha Tsui and Central. Services operate daily 0630–2330. Other **ferry** services also connect with the outlying islands of the territory and other destinations. An *MTR Tourist Ticket*, valid for a full day of unlimited rides, is available at a cost of HK$50. The price of the **pass** includes a map and souvenir ticket. A *Three-Day Hong Kong Transport Pass* is also available for HK$220 for one Airport Express single journey and three days of unlimited MTR rides, or HK$300 for two Airport Express journeys and three days of MTR rides. Both can be upgraded for an additional HK$20 for use on all buses, trams and other public transport services. The price includes a refundable deposit of HK$50; the value of unused travel can be refunded at the end of usage.

However, for visitors staying for a week or more, it is worth getting the *Octopus Card* – a smart card that automatically deducts the cost of the journey when it is placed on a sensor. The card costs HK$150, which

includes a refundable deposit of HK$50. Any other credit remaining is also refunded when the card is handed in. At present, the card may be used on MTR services, as well as on the Kowloon–Canton Railway, major bus routes, some minibuses and some ferries. Plans are underway to extend its use to other routes and means of transport, as Hong Kong's transport system becomes more and more integrated. It can already be used in convenience stores and branches of Starbucks. The MTR Tourist Ticket and Octopus Cards are available for purchase at the ticket kiosk of any MTR station.

Taxis

Taxis are plentiful in Hong Kong and Kowloon and are extremely cheap – most journeys cost less than HK$20. The minimum fare is HK$15 in central Hong Kong (less in the New Territories). There are no specific taxi companies in Hong Kong, as taxis are individually operated. There are taxi ranks in busy locations but taxis can be flagged down anywhere on the street. Red taxis serve Hong Kong Island and Kowloon, green ones serve the New Territories and blue ones Lantau Island. Taxis with a rectangular red plaque on their dashboard are generally cross-harbour taxis. Some journeys incur an extra toll, such as trips through the cross-harbour tunnel (HK$20). Charges are also sometimes added when carrying luggage. It is common for passengers to round up the fare to the nearest Dollar, although this is not mandatory.

Many drivers speak a little English but visitors would be advised to carry a map or have their destination written in Chinese characters. It is also wise for passengers to ask if the taxi is a Hong Kong or Kowloon taxi when boarding, especially late at night – drivers are always happier sticking to their own side of the water.

The more traditional taxis, rickshaws, have disappeared from regular transport and are now purely a tourist

The Peak

attraction, usually found at the Star Ferry terminal in Central. It is advisable for passengers to agree the fare in advance. A typical rickshaw ride lasts some five minutes and runs around the block, costing in the region of HK$50. Supplementary charges will be added for a photograph taken sitting in the rickshaw – this is typically around HK$20.

Limousines

Intercontinental Hire Cars (tel: 2336 6111) and *Oriental Travel Service Ltd* (tel: 2865 2618; fax: 2865 2984; website: www.orientaltravel.com.hk/tours/limousine.htm) both provide chauffeur-driven limousine services with prices starting from around HK$280 per hour.

Driving in the City

Driving in Hong Kong is best left to professionals. With one of the best public transport systems in the world and ubiquitous taxis, there is no need for visitors to risk going behind the wheel. Rates on cars are strong deterrents, with a 100% vehicle import tax and petrol tax, as well as hefty insurance and vehicle registration fees. This does, however, make second-hand cars surprisingly cheap, even once the price of shipping one back home has been factored in. The Ferraris, Maseratis and other premium vehicles lined up in Central in the evenings, show that cars are expensive toys in Hong Kong.

Major car parks in Central are at the Parking Building, Murray Road, and the Airport Express Terminal, Man Cheung Road. In Causeway Bay, the World Trade Centre, near the Excelsior Hotel is the main parking point, while in Kowloon, parking can be found at the Lippo Sun Plaza, Kowloon Park Drive in Tsim Sha Tsui. Parking prices are approximately HK$22 per hour, with a minimum stay of two hours in many locations.

Car Hire

It is wise not to be in charge of a rented vehicle in Hong Kong's vertiginous streets, as the average HK$5000 refundable deposit on hire cars testifies. Car hire companies usually require drivers to be over 25 years. A valid driving licence from the country of residence or an International Driving Permit is required, as well as minimum third-party insurance. Hire rates for a standard saloon car start from about HK$1000 per day. Major operators include *Avis* (tel: 2890 6988; website: www.avis.com) and *Hertz* (tel: 2525 1313; website: www.hertz.com).

Bicycle Hire

It might be consoling to know that if one chooses to cycle in central Hong Kong, the traffic will kill one long before the appalling air quality does. In any event, the Hong Kong authorities actually prohibit bicycle riding in Central. Nevertheless, there are places for visitors to enjoy cycling – out on the islands or in the New Territories.

Bicycles are available for hire from *Hop Cheong Bicycle Shop* (tel: 2896 0816) and *Siu Kee Bicycle* (tel: 2981 1384) in Cheung Chau. The New Territories offer bicycle hire at Tai Po KCR station, where there are numerous small stalls located directly outside. For a standard bicycle, hire prices average HK$50 per day.

SIGHTSEEING

Sightseeing Overview

One should pity the poor locals who never lift their eyes from the streets – Hong Kong can be one of the most riveting and unexpectedly beautiful urban spectacles on earth. A two-minute walk from the bustle of Central reveals a harbour view that the architectural boom of the 1980s and 1990s has turned into a mixture of Manhattan and San Francisco, with added shipping bustle. At night, it just gets better. The view of Hong Kong's glittering lights from the Peak by night is unforgettable – almost as dazzling are the towers of Central seen from the lovers' walk of Kowloon's Tsim Sha Tsui Promenade or the famous glass-walled ladies' toilet of *Felix* in the *Peninsula Hotel*. By contrast, the south side of Hong Kong Island, at Stanley or Repulse Bay, is an entrancing Islandscape straight out of a classical Chinese ink painting. And any backstreet market provides folksy, ethnic charm by the barrow-load.

Old colonial Hong Kong may have been short on grand monuments but the now famous *Bank of China* and the *Hongkong and Shanghai Bank* give the place a 21st-century buzz suited to one of the Pacific Rim's most important economic hubs. These buildings are sharing the limelight with the rainbow-coloured light show of *The Centre* skyscraper, the waterside steel wings of the *Hong Kong Convention and Exhibition Centre* and a host of lesser marvels, with others still under construction – such as *2 International Finance Centre* and *Union Square Phase 7*, due to rank, however briefly, as the world's tallest buildings. Die-hard colonialists can content themselves with *Government House*, the *Former French Mission Building*, the *Former Gate Lodge* on the Peak, the *Former Kowloon–Canton Railway Clock Tower*, the *Former Kowloon British School* and a host of other 'Olds' and 'Formers'.

There are far older relics of the region's past still surviving the relentless forward drive, especially out in the New Territories. These include the Causeway Bay *Tin Hau Temple*, *Law Uk Hakka House*, *Lei Cheng Uk Han Tomb*, *Sam Tung Uk Village*, *Liu Man Shek Tong Ancestral Hall*, *Kun Lung Wai Gate Tower*, *Yeung Hau Temple* and so on. Hong Kong is pinning much of its hopes as a future tourist centre on the *Hong Kong Disneyland*, projected for Lantau Island. However, this is still years away from completion. In the meantime, visitors can ignore the government's ambitions and focus on the plethora of sights already on offer.

Key Attractions

Statue Square

Previously never a feature of traditional Hong Kong tourist itineraries, *Statue Square* is now a must-see, on account of its dazzling ensemble of modern architecture. Richard Rogers' headquarters building for the *Hongkong and Shanghai Banking Corporation* forms the south side of the square and just to the east of it is I M Pei's *Bank of China Tower*. Less distinguished but equally prominent buildings jostle around them, towering over the colonial remnant of *St John's Cathedral*. In more antiquated contrast, the *Legislative Council Building*, formerly the *Supreme Court*, on the east side of the square, houses Hong Kong's partly elected assembly. However, the square should be avoided at weekends, when flocks of Filipino and Indonesian housemaids take time out to chatter and picnic there. The bizarre profile of Norman Foster's masterpiece may not look monumental on paper – it is on most Hong Kong Dollar banknotes – but in the flesh (or steel) it is tremendous. Opened in 1986, the Hongkong and Shanghai Banking Corporation exemplified the fashion for atriums in world architecture and an escalator ride up into the belly of the building, into its towering air-conditioned interior, is a must. The building has no central core – bridge engineering techniques secure the walls and its infrastructure is on the outside – so all 11 storeys of the central atrium are open and unobstructed. Deliberately planned to dwarf the neighbouring Hongkong and Shanghai Bank Building, the Bank of China Tower is now Hong Kong's 'national' monument. The Chinese-American architect, I M Pei, developed Beijing's triumphalist intentions into a soaring, gracefully irregular pinnacle, the design characteristics of which inspire lively debate among connoisseurs of feng shui. The triangular and hexagonal structural logic requires some minutes of puzzled scrutiny. Visitors can ascend to the 43rd of its 74 storeys for a particularly stunning view of Central.

Central
Transport: MTR Central station, exit K.
Hongkong and Shanghai Bank Building
Des Voeux Road, Statue Square
Tel: 2822 1111. Fax: 2868 1646.
Website: www.hsbc.com.hk
Opening hours: Mon–Fri 0900–1630, Sat 0900–1230.
Admission: Free.
Bank of China Tower
2a Des Voeux Road, 1 Garden Road
Tel: 2826 6888. Fax: 2810 5963.
Website: www.bochk.com/en/index.htm
Opening hours: Mon–Fri 0930–2130, Sat and Sun 0930–2330.
Admission: HK$9 (concessions available).

Victoria Peak

A miniature hill station in colonial times, *Victoria Peak* is stratospheric in its social exclusiveness and its rents. Groundlings can still visit, however, ascending by the vertiginous *Peak Tram* – a funicular in use since 1888, which feels more like the Space Shuttle. Atop the hill is the *Peak Tower* – a slightly bizarre viewing platform with displays and other facilities – as well as the *Peak Galleria* shopping arcade. The amusements and shops on offer vary from the appealing to the unforgivably tacky, although there are at least plenty of restaurants and bars to sustain visitors. Dinner at *Café Deco*, in the Peak Galleria, is a must-do Hong Kong experience – the view down into central Hong Kong and across the water to Kowloon defies description, day or night. Hikers can scale the real peak, some 140m (459ft) above the tram terminus, with vistas over Hong Kong Island, Kowloon and the outlying islands.
Garden Road (Lower Peak Tram Terminus)
Tel: 2840 7654. Fax: 2849 6237 (Peak Tram).
E-mail: peaktram@peninsula.com
Website: www.thepeak.com.hk
Transport: Peak Tram from Garden Road; bus from Exchange Square; shuttle bus from Star Ferry terminal.
Opening hours: Daily 0700–2400 (Peak Tram).
Admission: HK$20 (Peak Tram); concessions available.

Western Market

This former market – a four-storey redbrick Edwardian building dating from 1906 and occupying

Trams in Wan Chai

an entire block at the western end of Central – was reopened in 1991, as a shopping centre featuring small shops, souvenir stands and curio sellers. Ground-floor shops sell unique merchandise rather than chain store goods, while the first floor recreates the old 'Cloth Alley', selling silks and fabrics of all kinds. There is also a dim sum restaurant and a fine antique-shop café.
Connaught Road
Tel: 2543 6878. Fax: 2543 6931.
Transport: MTR Sheung Wan, exit B or C; bus or tram along Des Voeux Road to Sheung Wan.
Opening hours: Daily 1000–1900.
Admission: Free.

Times Square

The retail plaza to end them all, *Times Square* is an enormous temple to Hong Kong's number one deity, Mammon. The vast complex houses nine floors of shops and has a spectacular exterior with a huge display screen and electronic clock – the venue for the big millennium countdown in 2000. At the weekend, the hosts of sacrifices ascending the escalator, to be swallowed up in the belly of this huge idol, demonstrate exactly what the Asian economic miracle was all about. Recession has not visibly blunted the shopping frenzy and there are ever more shops and restaurants under this huge pile.
Times Square, Causeway Bay
Tel: 2118 8900. Fax: 2506 2022.
Transport: MTR Causeway Bay; bus or tram along Hennessey Road to Causeway Bay.
Opening hours: Daily 1000–2200.
Admission: Free.

Flagstaff House Museum of Tea Ware

Situated in the beautiful Hong Kong Park and overlooking the ultramodern mania of Central, *Flagstaff House*, dating from 1846, is the former residence of the colonial Commander-in-Chief and the oldest surviving colonial building in Hong Kong. It now houses a fine museum of tea ware, seals and other ceramics.
Cotton Tree Drive, Hong Kong Park, Central
Tel: 2869 0690. Fax: 2810 0021.
Transport: MTR Admiralty, exit F, then up escalator through Pacific Place; bus or tram along Queensway to Pacific Place.
Opening hours: Thurs–Tues 1000–1700.
Admission: Free.

Hong Kong Museum of History

It is somehow fitting that this go-ahead territory has its history commemorated in a dazzling new building. Opened in late 2000, the new museum building, situated next to the *Hong Kong Science Museum* in Kowloon, houses exhibits covering the region's history from prehistoric times, including some spectacular period sets. There are traditional costumes, a huge collection of period photographs, replicas of old village houses and an entire street, circa 1881, with its own Chinese medicine store. There are also numerous temporary exhibitions.
100 Chatham Road South, Tsim Sha Tsui
Tel: 2724 9042. Fax: 2724 9090.
E-mail: hkmh@lcsd.gov.hk
Website: www.lcsd.gov.hk/CE/Museum/History/english

Photo: Hong Kong Tourism Board

Transport: MTR Tsim Sha Tsiu, then walk via Cameron Road; minibus 1 from Kowloon Star Ferry in Tsim Sha Tsiu to Science Museum Road.

Opening hours: Mon, Wed–Sat 1000–1800, Sun 1000–1700.

Admission: HK$10 (concessions available).

Wong Tai Sin Temple

An ornate traditional temple in the heart of Kowloon, *Wong Tai Sin Temple* combines Buddhist, Confucian and Taoist traditions. Wong Tai Sin himself was a Zhejiang shepherd/alchemist who supposedly concocted a marvellous cure-all. His statue in the main building was brought from the mainland in 1915. The building is spectacularly colourful with its red pillars, golden ceiling and decorated latticework, although not particularly distinguished. Far more fascinating are the fortune-tellers in their arcade of booths and the throngs of worshippers. This is also Hong Kong's number one temple for Chinese New Year celebrations.

Tai Sin Road, Kowloon

Tel: 2327 8141. Fax: 2351 5640.

Transport: MTR Wong Tai Sin, exit B3, then follow signs.

Opening hours: Daily 0700–1730.

Admission: Free; donations welcome.

Yuen Po Street Bird Garden

Rearing caged songbirds is a time-honoured Chinese pursuit and the *Yuen Po Street Bird Garden* is Hong Kong's shrine to this obsession. There are about 70 stalls, each with its own chorus, with ornate cages and cage furniture providing added interest. And while conditions in the average Hong Kong poultry market would give an animal welfare activist apoplexy, the birds here are pampered and cosseted, even fed honey nectar to sweeten their songs. Just north of the Bird Garden, there is also a fine flower market and a goldfish market, closer to the MTR station in Tung Choi Street.

Prince Edward Road West, Kowloon

Transport: MTR Prince Edward, exit B1 or B2, then follow signs.

Opening hours: Daily 0700–2000.

Admission: Free.

Further Distractions

Star Ferry

The green and white, or heavily branded, tub-shaped ferries are a familiar sight around Hong Kong and, as such, a symbol of the city. Far more important, however, is the fact that their decks give one of the best available views, day or night, of the waterfronts of Hong Kong Island and Kowloon – not to mention the plethora of ocean traffic surging through the shipping lanes. The boats themselves are cast-iron veterans to delight schoolboys of all ages.

Central, Tsim Sha Tsui, Wan Chai and Hung Hom Star Ferry terminals

Tel: 2367 7065. Fax: 2118 6028.

E-mail: sf@starferry.com.hk

Website: www.starferry.com.hk

Transport: Star Ferry docks are termini for bus and minibus routes, a short walk from MTR stations.

Operating hours: Daily 0630–2330.

Admission: HK$1.70 (lower deck); HK$2.10 (upper deck); concessions available.

Mid-Levels Escalator

Not just any escalator, the *Mid-Levels Escalator* is the world's longest at 800m (2622ft) and was built as a commuter aid for this wealthy residential hillside. The city fathers reportedly balked at the cost of twin stairways, so there is only one escalator, running downhill in the morning and uphill thereafter, until midnight. It gives a fine (and free) view of the streets of fashionable Soho and is a great venue for people-watching by passengers and café patrons alike.

Central Market (corner of Queens Road and Jubilee Street) to Conduit Road

Transport: Bus or minibus to Queen's Road.

Operating hours: Daily 0700–1030 (downhill), 1030–2400 (uphill).

Admission: Free.

Noonday Gun

Yes, there still is a *noonday gun* – as immortalised by Noel Coward – and it is still ceremoniously fired daily at noon. Actually a Hotchkiss three-pounder, the gun is mounted in its own miniature, park-like enclosure overlooking the Causeway Bay typhoon shelter, off Gloucester Road and opposite the Excelsior Hotel. It is reached by an underpass near the World Trade Centre.

Gloucester Road, Causeway Bay

Transport: MTR Causeway Bay, exit D3, then a short walk past World Trade Centre to Excelsior Hotel.

Operating hours: Noon (of course).

Admission: Free.

Tsim Sha Tsui Promenade

Offering another great view of the spectacular Victoria Harbour and Hong Kong Island waterfront, this esplanade is where Hong Kong couples go in the evenings, for a romantic backdrop while necking. However, day or night, the view is superb. The colonial-era Clock Tower at the western end of the promenade, by the Star Ferry piers, makes an attractive historic terminus, while Harbour City with the huge cruise liners is another attractive prospect just to the west.

Star Ferry Terminal to Hung Hom

Transport: MTR Tsim Sha Tsui; Star Ferry to Kowloon.

Opening hours: Daily 24 hours.

Admission: Free.

Tours of the City

Walking Tours

Walking tours of central Hong Kong are apt to involve elbowing one's way through crowds of shoppers or tripping over Filipino maids. But the *Hong Kong Tourism Board*, 99 Queen's Road, Central (tel: 2807 6543; website: www.hktourismboard.com), does have a couple of itineraries, with 'Heritage and Architectural Walks' on Hong Kong Island and in Kowloon. Guides and a rental audio commentary system are available for HK$50. The walks take from two to four hours. The *HKTB Visitor Hotline* (tel: 2508 1234) or any tourist office can provide details. Other operators also run HKTB-approved tours, such as *Gray Line Tours* (tel: 2368 7111; website: www.grayline.com) or *Splendid Tours and Travel* (tel: 2316 2151; website: www.splendidtours.com). Details of these are available on the HKTB website, categorised by theme.

Walkers wishing to range further afield have plenty of well-trodden routes for penetrating the rural New Territories and backwoods of Hong Kong Island, such

Photo: Hong Kong Tourism Board

Chinese New Year

as the 100km (60-mile) MacLehose Trail, the 50km (30-mile) Hong Kong Trail, or even the 3.5km (2.2-mile) Peak Trail. But water bottles are essential for any traveller attempting these routes during the summer.

Bus Tours

Numerous themed bus tours are listed on the *Hong Kong Tourism Board* website (see above), including a 'Heritage Tour', a 'Come Horseracing Tour', a 'Healthy Living Tour', a 'Morning Tea and Tai Chi Tour' and a 'Land Between' coach tour around the more scenic and folksy areas of the New Territories. Tours typically last about five hours and cost from HK$290 to HK$490. Departure points vary depending on the tour – for details, visitors should contact the *HKTB's Visitor Hotline* (tel: 2508 1234) or the *Tour Reservation Hotline* (tel: 2368 7112). *Gray Line Tours* (tel: 2368 7111; website: www.grayline.com), *Splendid Tours and Travel* (tel: 2316 2151; website: www.splendidtours.com) and *Sky Bird Travel Agency* (tel: 2369 9628; website: www. skybird.com.hk) all offer similar bus tours of the city.

Boat Tours

Boat tours of Hong Kong's waters are provided by several companies. *Watertours* (tel: 2926 3868; website: www.watertourshk.com) provides a variety of harbour and island tours from HK$200 to HK$630, while *Star Ferry* (tel: 2118 6241) provides ferry tours for HK$180. Harbour tours take around two to three hours. Watertours has pick-up points throughout Hong Kong Island and Kowloon, although the tours sail from Queen's Pier on Hong Kong side or the Kowloon Public Pier on Kowloon Side. The Star Ferry tours sail from the Star Ferry terminals on either side of the harbour. *HKFF Travel Ltd* (tel: 2533 5339) runs a five-hour tour of the Outlying Islands, departing from the Outlying Islands Ferry Pier in Central daily at 0915. Tours cost HK$320.

Other Tours

A 'Galaxy of Lights' tour is available on an open-topped luxury tram, provided by *JTT Tours* (tel: 2139 3187), under the auspices of the *Hong Kong Tourism Board* (tel: 2807 6543; website: www.hktourismboard. com). This is a night tour on specially modified and illuminated antique trams, travelling along the chief tram route of Hong Kong Island, from the Western District to Causeway Bay, past the lit-up skyscrapers of central Hong Kong. A tour guide provides narrative accompaniment to this 90-minute tour, which costs HK$60 and departs from the Lower Block, City Hall, Central, nightly at 1845.

Excursions

For a Half Day

Stanley Market: Stanley is a small seaside settlement on the south side of Hong Kong Island, with some fine beaches and waterfront restaurants enjoyed by its well-heeled citizens. Visitors flock to *Stanley Market* (open daily 1000–1900), a covered area full of stalls selling clothes, souvenirs, sporting goods, art and many other products of Hong Kong and mainland sweatshops. Other attractions include *Tin Hau Temple*, *Kuan Yin Temple*, *St Stephen's Beach*, the *Old Stanley Fort*, the *military cemetery* with its graves of wartime internees, the *Old Police Station* and fine walks along *Wong Ma Kok Road*. The market, in particular, is like a zoo at the weekend and therefore weekdays make more sense for a visit. Stanley Market can be reached by bus (numbers 6,

Lan Kwai Fong

6A, 6X or 260X) from Exchange Square Bus Terminal, Central, by bus 973 from Tsim Sha Tsui East terminus, by green minibus (number 40) from Hoi Ping Road, Causeway Bay, or by minibus number 14 from Shau Kei Wan.

Lamma Island: Hong Kong's third largest island, *Lamma*, is a green oasis popular with chilled-out ex-pats. Its scenery is beautiful and its beaches are fabulous. Some great pubs, bars and restaurants complement these. Best of all, the island has no cars (and only one ambulance). The main residential village, *Yung Shue Wan*, is the main ferry terminus, while *Sok Kwu Wan*, the second largest village, specialises in open-air seafood restaurants. *Hung Shing Ye* is the largest beach, while *Lo So Shing* is arguably the nicest; *Sek Pai Wan* and *Sham Wan* are perhaps best reached by rented junk. Hikes between the two main villages are popular, as is the climb to *Mount Stenhouse*. Lamma is situated west of Hong Kong Island and ferries to Yung Shue Wan or Sok Kwu Wan on Lamma Island depart from Central.

Repulse Bay: Another seaside destination on Hong Kong Island's southern side, *Repulse Bay* has a superior beach that is good for strolling, on spring days. At the beach's eastern end is a slightly bizarre lifeboat station – bizarre because it is also a temple to Kuan Yin, the Buddhist goddess of mercy, and is adorned with garish plaster statues of figures from Chinese Buddhist mythology. The sea washes into this religious theme park at high tide. At the other end of the beach is a large shopping centre with a selection of fine restaurants. Romantic visitors can finish off their beach stroll with dinner at the *Verandah* restaurant in the Repulse Bay Hotel. Repulse Bay is accessible by bus 6, 6A or 6I from Exchange Square Bus Terminal, Central. Passengers should alight when they see the Repulse Bay Hotel or the strange, curved apartment block with a hole through the middle – put there for good *feng shui*.

For a Whole Day

Shek O: A small village and beach resort on the southeast coast of Hong Kong Island, *Shek O* is secluded enough to be safe from the worst weekend crowds, although weekdays are still the best time to visit. It is also highly exclusive but has some of Hong Kong's best beach space. The further legs of the two-hour trip out have some scenic merits and there are more bluffs and bays within hiking or cycling distance of the village, with its open-air restaurants. Shek O is at the very end of the bus 9 route, which goes from Shau Kei Wan MTR station.

Lantau Island: The new Chek Lap Kok Airport thankfully has not ruined *Lantau*, situated 45km (28 miles) from Central Hong Kong, twice the size of Hong Kong Island itself and with more than half of its territory designated country parkland. Residents at *Discovery Bay* (also known as Disco Bay) enjoy the tranquillity all year round – others visit for a sample. Walking tours and hikes are popular here, although the principal attractions are the *Po Lin Big Buddha* – claimed to be the world's largest seated outdoor Buddha effigy, at 26m (85ft) tall – and the *Po Lin Buddhist Monastery*, definitely Hong Kong's largest. The monastery itself has some fine buildings and has been used as the set for numerous kung fu films. There is a tea garden nearby and the beaches and waterside restaurants along the southern shore are also idyllic. To get to Lantau Island, visitors should take either the MTR Airport Railway link to Tung Chung, followed by bus 23 to Po Lin, or the ferry to Mui Wo from Central, followed by bus 2. The steps up to the Big Buddha are open to visitors daily 1000–1800. *Lantau Tours Ltd* (tel: 2984 8255) offers tours of the island and the monastery for HK$520.

Macau: The quintessential Hong Kong excursion is almost an entirely separate destination and visitors need to remember to take their passports. The last piece of China in foreign hands, reverting from Portuguese rule in December 1999, *Macau*, situated on the southeastern coast of China, approximately one hour from Hong Kong, is an utterly different community – relaxed, hedonistic and even Mediterranean. Its fine colonial architecture gives it far more of a nostalgic air than its big brother territory, only an hour away by jetfoil, adding southern Baroque-style plasterwork to the Latin ambience typified by its restaurants and bars. The pocket-sized territory boasts some fine churches – *St Augustine's Church* and *St Dominic's*, the 17th-century cathedral church, as well as the most famous of all, the façade of *St Paul's Cathedral* – that all survived a fire in 1835. Its *Kun Lam* and *A-Ma Temples* were also founded in the 17th century. The *Monte Fort*, which still has its cannons, was built by the Jesuits, just after 1600. A historic site of enormous interest to Chinese and Sinophiles, the *Sun-Yat Sen Memorial Home* marks where the creator of China's first Republican government practised medicine in his early days.

But newer developments, such as the *Macau Tower*, typify the territory's new drive to be more than a backwater – an ambition due to mature with the opening of the new leisure and casino developments launched since the ending of Stanley Ho's gambling monopoly in 2002. Macau's most important industry is gambling. The Triad warfare associated with it has thankfully diminished with the return of Chinese sovereignty – cheering crowds welcomed the new PLA garrison as deliverers from years of lawlessness. Now Macau has a more robust economy, a more ambitious tourism policy than Hong Kong and awaits its coming transformation into the Vegas of Asia.

Macau can be reached by jetfoil or jet boat from Macau ferry terminal, near Shun Tak Centre, or from China Hong Kong City terminal at Tsim Sha Tsui. *Macau Government Tourist Office*, 9 Largo do Senado (tel: (853) 315 566; fax: (853) 510 104; e-mail: mgto@macautourism.gov.mo; website: www.macautourism.gov.mo), is open daily 0900–1800 and can provide further information.

ACCOMMODATION

All hotel bills are subject to 10% service charge and 3% government tax.

The prices quoted below are the lowest standard rates for a double room, including breakfast and excluding service charge and tax, unless otherwise specified.

Business

Conrad International Hong Kong

One of the Pacific Place hotels in Admiralty, attached to the luxury shopping mall and Hong Kong Park, the *Conrad* vies for supremacy with the Island Shangri-La next door. Some would argue that the Conrad has slightly less elegance but its facilities are exceptional and meals next to its swimming pool overlooking central Hong Kong are a civilised pleasure. Business facilities are second to none, with nine banquet and meeting rooms, including one of Hong Kong's largest ballrooms and a comprehensively equipped business centre.
Pacific Place, 88 Queensway, Admiralty
Tel: 2521 3838. Fax: 2521 3888.
E-mail: hongkonginfo@conradhotels.com
Website: www.conrad.com.hk
Price: From HK$2150.

Grand Hyatt Hong Kong

A waterside hotel with a difference, the *Grand Hyatt* has the most extravagant Babylonian foyer imaginable, with gigantic columns and shining marble. Rooms are appropriately sumptuous for five stars and recently redesigned with state-of-the-art in-room technology. Conference facilities include a grand ballroom and 20 function rooms. The hotel also adjoins the Hong Kong Convention and Exhibition Centre for easy access to events held there. There are full business facilities, including a grand ballroom and 20 function rooms with complete communications infrastructure. Sports and recreational amenities include a full-size pool.
1 Harbour Road, Wan Chai
Tel: 2588 1234. Fax: 2802 0677.
E-mail: info@grandhyatt.com.hk
Website: http://hongkong.grand.hyatt.com
Price: From HK$1840.

Holiday Inn Golden Mile

Kowloon's representative of the *Holiday Inn* chain is situated right on Nathan Road, the Golden Mile of shops and souvenir stalls. Its 600 rooms are furnished and equipped to the usual Holiday Inn standard and it makes an excellent choice for business travellers on a budget, with a luxurious feel that belies its four-star category. Its Crystal Ballroom, three Crystal Rooms and two Jade Suite function rooms provide full resources for events and business functions.
50 Nathan Road, Tsim Sha Tsui West, Kowloon
Tel: 2369 3111. Fax: 2369 8016.
E-mail: reserv@goldenmile.com

Website: www.goldenmile-hk.holiday-inn.com
Price: From HK$890.

Hotel InterContinental Hong Kong

A five-star agglomeration right on the Kowloon waterfront, the *InterContinental* – originally the *Regent*, before it was bought out in 2001 – is a favourite business destination. It offers a magnificent prospect of the skyscrapers of Central from many of its over 600 rooms, surpassing even The Peninsula in this respect. The view over the rim of its outdoor Jacuzzi is just as fabulous, making for stylish late-night dips. The Regent makes some nods to Old World elegance, with trimmings such as Rolls Royce limousines for favoured guests, although its chief focus is decidedly modern. Its ballroom is claimed to be Hong Kong's largest, able to accommodate almost 2000 cocktail guests. Conference and business facilities are equally lavish.
18 Salisbury Road, Tsim Sha Tsui West, Kowloon
Tel: 2721 1211. Fax: 2739 4546.
E-mail: hongkong@interconti.com
Website: www.hongkong-ic.interconti.com
Price: From HK$2900.

Island Shangri-La Hong Kong

Part of the hotel complex on the hillside above the Pacific Place luxury shopping mall in Admiralty, the *Island Shangri-La* is a five-star glass tower offering all international top-level services and amenities, as well as appropriately fabulous views. It boasts that its 565 rooms include the largest on Hong Kong Island. All rooms are data enabled with high-speed Internet connections. The Island Shangri-La's location allows immediate access to transport to everywhere in Hong Kong, from Central to the Peak Tram, while guests desiring a reflective pause from the frantic shopping at Pacific Place can always take a stroll in Hong Kong Park behind the hotel.
Pacific Place, Supreme Court Road, Admiralty
Tel: 2877 3838. Fax: 2521 8742.
E-mail: isl@shangri-la.com
Website: www.shangri-la.com
Price: From HK$2800.

Regal Airport Hotel

Part of the massive infrastructure project at Chek Lap Kok Airport on Lantau Island, the *Regal Airport Hotel* would never win prizes for convenient proximity to Central or Kowloon but it did win *Business Week* and *Bloomberg's* 2001 award for Best Airport Hotel in Asia. It is also a good hotel for transit travellers and anyone else who requires four-star accommodation in this vicinity. With 1103 rooms, this is one of Hong Kong's

Repulse Bay

largest hotels. The airport itself is just a five-minute walk by covered walkway and Airport Express trains put Central only 23 minutes away. The hotel has a grand ballroom and over 16 function rooms for business guests. Its spacious facilities have made it a favourite venue for raves and other parties.
9 Cheong Tat Road, Chek Lap Kok, Lantau
Tel: 2286 8888. Fax: 2286 8686.
E-mail: rah.info@regalhotel.com
Website: www.regalairport.com
Price: From HK$1850.

Luxury

Mandarin Oriental Hong Kong

Overlooking Victoria Harbour, from its perch right in the middle of Central, Hong Kong's five-star representative of the *Mandarin Oriental* chain is a byword for elegance. Its tea rooms and buffets enjoy a loyal following from rich *tai-tai* wives to romancing couples. Business travellers are equally well catered for, with full facilities including Internet access from guest rooms and 13 function rooms to accommodate conferences and events. The black and gold lobby area has style to spare with a somewhat recherché Art Deco flavour. Top-class dining options include *Vong* (see *Restaurants*) and the ground-floor *Mandarin Grill*, while favourite bars include the *Chinnery* and the *Captain's Table*.
5 Connaught Road, Central
Tel: 2522 0111. Fax: 2810 6190.
E-mail: mohkg-reservations@mohg.com
Website: www.mandarin-oriental.com
Price: From HK$3200.

The Peninsula

The jewel in the crown of Kowloon's waterfront hospitality palaces, *The Peninsula* is a colonial foundation dating from 1928, which has kept its supremacy well into the post-colonial era. Comprehensive, modern facilities embellish period grandeur. The tearooms at street level are appropriately magnificent – Noel Coward could walk in any time and feel right at home. Recently given 20 extra storeys, the hotel offers magnificent urban views from some suites, as well as the celebrated glass-walled urinals in *Felix*, the bar-restaurant on the 28th floor.
Salisbury Road, Tsim Sha Tsui
Tel: 2920 2888. Fax: 2722 4170.
E-mail: pen@peninsula.com
Website: www.peninsula.com
Price: From HK$2600.

Moderate

Bishop Lei International House

An economical three-star hotel and hostel on Robinson Road, owned and operated by the Catholic Diocese of Hong Kong, the *Bishop Lei* is on the escalator that runs between Mid-Levels and Central. The rooms are small but comfortable hotel rooms with en-suite bathrooms and many offer splendid panoramic views of Victoria Harbour and the towers of Central. Decor is simple but clean and well maintained. The Bishop Lei offers reasonable, basic business facilities, including a business centre and function room. Other amenities include a swimming pool. There is also a free shuttle bus service to Wan Chai and the Airport Express station in Central.

The Peninsula

4 Robinson Road, Mid-Levels
Tel: 2868 0828. Fax: 2868 1551.
E-mail: resvtion@bishopleihtl.com.hk
Website: www.bishopleihtl.com.hk
Price: From HK$530.

YMCA – The Salisbury

A popular economy hotel in Tsim Sha Tsui, near the main tourist centres on the Kowloon Side of the harbour, *The Salisbury* offers the same harbour views as The Peninsula next door, without the price. The hotel has a business centre, some conference facilities and function rooms, as well as most other modern facilities, although aspects of the hotel, such as the dated Art Deco lobby furniture, do show its age. Rooms are simple but comfortable and hotel rather than hostel style. All rooms have en-suite bathrooms. In true YMCA style, there are also extensive sports and exercise facilities, including two indoor pools.
41 Salisbury Road, Tsim Sha Tsui West, Kowloon
Tel: 2736 0922. Fax: 2405 0922.
Website: www.ymca-hotels.com/hongkong/ymcasalisbury
Price: From HK$600.

RESTAURANTS

The selected restaurants have been divided into five categories: Gastronomic, Business, Trendy, Budget and Personal Recommendations. The restaurants are listed alphabetically within these different categories, which serve as guidelines rather than absolute definitions of the establishments.
A 10% service charge is almost always added to restaurant bills in Hong Kong. In theory, this is discretionary, although in practice, it is better not to challenge it, except in cases of exceptionally poor service. An extra cash tip could be added to this, if desired, to go directly to the staff. Normally this would be no more than 5%.
The prices quoted below are for an average three-course meal for one person and for a bottle of house wine or cheapest equivalent; they do not include service charge or tip.

Gastronomic

The Boathouse

A waterfront special for the seaside retreat of Stanley, *The Boathouse* is not exclusively seafood-focused but offers some fine fish dishes, such as buckets filled with

mussels, prawns or clams, or Cajun sea bass. With its cool marine ambience, it is a touch – and taste – of class, after Stanley Market shopping.
86–88 Stanley Main Street, Stanley
Tel: 2813 4467. Fax: 2810 4467.
Price: HK$250. Wine: HK$190.

M at the Fringe

With a hugely loyal following, *M at the Fringe* has won a reputation as one of Hong Kong's best restaurants, offering splendid continental cuisine – such as bone marrow Bordelaise or salt-encased lamb – in an effortlessly arty ambience.
First Floor, South Block, 2 Lower Albert Road, Central
Tel: 2877 4000. Fax: 2877 0135.
E-mail: reservations@m-atthefringe.com
Website: www.m-atthefringe.com
Price: HK$400. Wine: HK$225.

Tokio Joe

The American version of fashionable Japanese cuisine, this restaurant serves American portions at Tokyo prices in a Tokyo ambience. The decor is a slicker version of a typical Japanese sushi bar, with a large central sushi counter surrounded by booths and tables for foursomes. The dynamite rolls – sushi rolls of crab meat, avocado and mayonnaise – are, well … dynamite. *Tokio Joe* effortlessly dominates Lan Kwai Fong's Japanese scene.
Ground Floor, 16 Lan Kwai Fong
Tel: 2525 1889. Fax: 2840 1234.
Price: HK$450. Wine: HK$250.

Va Bene

The quintessence of Italian dining in Lan Kwai Fong, *Va Bene* has a stellar reputation, comforting wood interior and pretty astronomical prices. Their wonderful selection of breads, mouthwatering ossobucco and other delights can melt even the tightest wad.
58–62 D'Aguilar Street, Central
Tel: 2845 5577. Fax: 2537 6886.
Price: HK$500. Wine: HK$325.

Business

Café Deco Bar and Grill

Café Deco has one of the most breathtaking restaurant views on Earth – the panorama of the harbour from Hong Kong Island's central Peak – especially dazzling

Photo: Hong Kong Tourism Board

Floating restaurant

at night. The cuisine is a hugely diverse array of East and West, from perfect steaks to succulent sashimi and sizzling tandoori platters. What is remarkable is the consistent quality and excellent value; even the Art Deco decor is wonderful.
Peak Galleria, 118 Peak Road
Tel: 2849 5111. Fax: 2849 5188.
Website: www.cafedeco.com
Price: HK$250. Wine: HK$200.

Dan Ryan's Chicago Grill

Dan Ryan's is the classic resort for American cuisine in American portions, in the mall-style surroundings of Pacific Place. The Sunday brunch is a notorious way to blow out a Sunday. Hamburgers, ribs, American beers, American cholesterol … diners can forget California, this is the real McCoy.
114 Pacific Place, 88 Queensway, Admiralty
Tel: 2845 4600. Fax: 2521 8055.
E-mail: info@windy-city.com.hk
Website: www.windy-city.com.hk/dans
Price: HK$200. Wine: HK$220.

Felix

It is debatable whether patrons come here for the top cuisine or the top-level view of Kowloon from *Felix's* glass-walled urinals. The interior was designed by Philippe Starck and has several different themes in its different areas. Full of unexpected treats, such as the capsule-like wine room, a science-fictionesque cocktail bar, a communal dining table and karaoke disco, even the lift decor must be seen to be believed. Crossover food – such as ginger and marinade striped sea bass with wasabe mashed potatoes or hibachi fillet of beef – comes with an incredible skyline and sky-high prices.
28th Floor, The Peninsula Hotel, Salisbury Road, Tsimshatsui
Tel: 2315 3188. Fax: 2315 3190.
E-mail: dining.pen@peninsula.com
Website: www.peninsula.com/hotels/hk/hk.html
Price: HK$450. Wine: HK$300.

The Orange Tree

A consistent award winner, *The Orange Tree* offers 'Dutch Continental' (actually meat-heavy French) cuisine, such as delicate salted herring and lamb fillets.

With a dark wood ambience, the restaurant is situated right beside the Mid-Levels Escalator and is excellent for quiet Sunday dinners and for people-watching.
17 Shelley Street, Central
Tel: 2838 9352. Fax: 2526 0488.
E-mail: restaurant@orangetree.com.hk
Website: www.orangetree.com.hk
Price: HK$260. Wine: HK$160.

Soho Soho

No prizes for guessing where this stylish and contemporary restaurant is located, although its modern British cuisine is far more refined than anything found along Old Compton Street, in London's Soho. So much so that diners can search in vain for the British roots of the diverse delicacies, such as goat's cheese risotto or Gorgonzola and balsamic shallot tart. It is very popular for office lunches, as the excellent set lunch menu offers exceptional quality at HK$120 for three courses.
9 Old Bailey Street, Soho, Central
Tel: 2147 2618. Fax: 2522 3387.
E-mail: soho@hkdining.com
Website: www.soho.hkdining.com
Price: HK$350. Wine: HK$215.

Trendy

Aqua

A glassed-in street corner restaurant with an all-round view, *Aqua* espouses an Australian-tinged international fusion cuisine, which is light, diverse and decidedly popular. Dishes include items like tea-smoked salmon, lime-roasted Barbary duck and yellow-fin tuna. This is a restaurant that dignifies its excellent location, rather than just trying to live off it.
49 Hollywood Road, Central
Tel: 2545 9889. Fax: 2542 3999.
E-mail: rochelle@aqua.com.hk
Website: www.aqua.com.hk
Price: HK$350. Wine: HK$250.

Boca

A Soho bar that deserves a mention on account of its delicious tapas menu, which keeps the tables

packed with lunch and dinner guests. Dishes include grilled black cod, tortillas and marinated chicken strips. Its chain-mail walls and mix of bar-style seating and plush couches keep the ambience light and fresh but no lighter or fresher than the splendid Spanish-style delicacies.
Ground Floor, 65 Peel Street, Soho, Central
Tel: 2548 1717. Fax: 2548 1727.
E-mail: tapasandwine@boca.com.hk
Website: www.boca.com.hk
Price: HK$200. Wine: HK$120.

Jaspa's

Offspring of a much-loved parent in Sai Kung, this bright quasi-Matisse exercise in Australian fusion cuisine on Staunton Street offers great value and fabulous choice for brunch or dinner. Delicious steaks and pastas complement the grilled bugs, yabbies (crayfish) and 'barbie' fare.
28 Staunton Street, Soho, Central
Tel: 2869 0733.
Price: HK$200. Wine: HK$120.

San Marzano PizzaExpress Hong Kong

This beautiful white and plate-glass viewing gallery next to the Mid-Levels Escalator is a surprisingly upscale branch of the UK's PizzaExpress chain. Its pizzas, such as the parmesan and rocket Soho pizza, are good quality and great value.
21 Lyndhurst Terrace, Central
Tel: 2850 7898.
E-mail: info@pizzaexpress.com.hk
Website: www.pizzaexpress.com.hk
Price: HK$130. Wine: HK$180.

Thai Basil Café Bar

One of the most laid-back restaurants in the Pacific Place shopping complex, *Thai Basil* is also one of the best. Not dogmatically Thai but deliciously so, this is an excellent place in which to people-watch, while picking at exquisitely presented dishes, such as Thai green duck curry. The thoroughly contemporary restaurant opens onto the Garden Court of the Pacific Place mall but is shielded by wooden and metal bars. Dining places are arranged bench-style, in a welcoming, restrained and chic ambience.

Shop 5, Lower Ground Floor, Pacific Place, 88 Queensway, Admiralty
Tel: 2537 4682. Fax: 2918 9418.
Price: HK$200. Wine: HK$200.

Budget

El Pomposo

Tucked under the first leg of the escalator to Mid-Levels and part of a string of quasi-Spanish hostelries, *El Pomposo* dishes up imaginative and mouthwatering tapas, such as chicken with goat's cheese or tuna in tomato sauce. Its painted caverns draw crowds in from the rain but its outdoor terrace is also a must in good weather, as one of Hong Kong's few alfresco eating places.
4 Tun Wo Lane, off Hollywood Road, Central
Tel: 2869 7679. Fax: 2973 6589.
Price: HK$150. Wine: HK$220.

Kublai's

A Mongolian barbecue in Wan Chai is a strange pairing but it works, as droves of tourists attest. With tall bar-style stools and tables and a central area for diners to select their own ingredients for the Mongolian-style grill, the concept allows diners to eat imaginative personalised combinations of anything that a buffet full of ingredients and spices can offer, filling their own bowls and handing them to experienced chefs to be cooked. Choices range from most varieties of sliced meats and fish to Oriental vegetables, such as bean sprouts and Chinese cabbage, with a range of sauces from Japanese teriyaki to Thai spice. The result is surprisingly good for Hong Kong's sleazy twilight zone. Half-price Monday nights are hugely popular.
Third Floor, One Capital Place, 18 Luard Road, Wan Chai
Tel: 2529 9117. Fax: 2529 9211.
Price: HK$140. Wine: HK$198.

Ning Po Residents Association

A social institution rather than a restaurant, this is unknown to most Lan Kwai Fong revellers and bears no markings to indicate that it is a restaurant. But anyone who penetrates to the fourth floor of this nondescript building can enjoy Shanghainese delicacies par excellence, such as noodles with green beans or steamed dumplings. The decor is very typically Chinese restaurant, with circular tables, Chinese art on the walls and a rather canteen atmosphere.
Fourth Floor, Yip Fung Building, 10 D'Aguilar Street, Lan Kwai Fong, Central
Tel: 2523 0648.
Price: HK$150. Wine: HK$200.

Taco Loco Taqueria

On the Mid-Levels Escalator, unbelievably convenient, cheap and popular, *Taco Loco* serves very Californian Mexican food – good taste on a low budget. The restaurant has a narrow, darkly painted interior, with bench-style seating and bar-style stools along the windows overlooking the escalator. Menu items such as machaca beef or barbacoa pork tacos for HK$12 or burritos for HK$28 put pricier restaurants to shame. Even the beers are cheap – and Mexican of course.
Lower Ground Floor, 7–9 Staunton Street, Soho, Central
Tel: 2522 1262. Fax: 2522 0757.
Price: HK$40. Beer: HK$20.

Dining out

Tsui Wah

Opposite Yuen Kee, this is Central's venue for post-party bingeing, *Tsui Wah* is where greasy spoon meets noodle bar, with posters of specials and prices plastered all over the walls. Every Chinese snack dish imaginable is served here, such as Hainan chicken rice or stir-fried noodles. Never mind the quality, feel the breadth of the menu and the opening hours.
Ground to Second Floor, 15–19 Wellington Street, Central
Tel: 2525 6338.
Price: HK$80. Beer: HK$40.

Yuen Kee Sweeten Food Expert

Unmissable – for better or worse – *Yuen Kee* sits slap outside Lan Kwai Fong and treats Central to a display of the patrons' classy autos, never mind the food. A crowded but plush traditional Chinese restaurant with wood-panelled walls, gold friezes of dragons and phoenixes, and a circular pool with a fountain in the main stairwell, the restaurant is surprisingly not that pricey. Everyone goes there for desserts – such as lotus seeds in almond paste – and everything else Cantonese. An institution and an asylum.
32–40 Wellington Street, Central
Tel: 2522 1624. Fax: 2840 0888.
Price: HK$100. Wine: Unlicensed.

Personal Recommendations

Café Gypsy

A great venue in which to eat light, delightful French cuisine, while watching Mid-Levels Escalator traffic pass this terrace-style café like fairground shooting gallery ducks. The crêpes make a wonderful brunch treat and the escargot are a speciality.
29 Shelley Street, Mid-Levels
Tel: 2521 0000. Fax: 2521 3613.
Price: HK$200. Wine: HK$190.

Gaia Ristorante

A supremely refined – and supremely pricey – Italian dining experience, *Gaia* has one of Hong Kong's best open-air dining areas. Potted plants screen the large outdoor area from the courtyard outside, while indoors, the white, crescent-shaped dining area is splendid with floor to ceiling windows. The cooking is superb, with an impeccable antipasti buffet and crispy Roman-style pizzas. Buckwheat pasta with vegetable and basil pesto, or goose liver on sweet potato with caramelised blueberries and red pearl onions are delicious, as are the homemade gelati desserts. The selection of Italian wines is particularly fine.
Ground Floor, Grand Millennium Plaza, 181 Queen's Road, Sheung Wan
Tel: 2167 8200. Fax: 2167 8220.
Price: HK$250. Wine: HK$200.

The Stoep

Anyone who makes it out to the lovely seaside village of Cheung Sha on the south side of Lantau Island will certainly not want to leave after sampling the South African beachfront fare, such as mixed barbecue or kebabs. The big beachside verandah, large enough to seat 120 people, is the perfect antidote to the insane bustle of Central.
32 Lower Cheung Sha Village, Lantau
Tel: 2980 2699. Fax: 2980 2699.
Price: HK$100. Wine: HK$150.

Veda

Anything but a usual curry house, *Veda* is a sophisticated and very stylish restaurant with a fine bar below. House dishes, such as roast duck breast with curry leaf or tandoori Boston lobster, are prepared on view in the glass-walled kitchen and are immaculate albeit pricey.
Ground Floor, 8 Arbuthnot Road, Central
Tel: 2868 8885. Fax: 2868 6717.
Website: www.veda.com.hk
Price: HK$400. Wine: HK$220.

The Verandah

A quintessentially romantic place for lovers to end long walks along Repulse Bay beach, *The Verandah* offers opulent international cuisine, along the lines of

Photo: Hong Kong Tourism Board

Old Neighbourhood and Central Plaza

oysters and steamed lobster salad, in a palm-frond and ceiling-fan ambience. The outside courtyard is equally as attractive and far cheaper.
Repulse Bay Hotel, 109 Repulse Bay Road, Repulse Bay
Tel: 2812 2722. Fax: 2812 2176.
Price: HK$500. Wine: HK$180.

ENTERTAINMENT

Nightlife

The 'City of Life' lives by night – most hot in-town venues don't even get going until midnight. Enterprising Sinophiles can try to get invited along to a local karaoke evening and warble into a mike, over buckets of beer, to Cantonese pop videos, or head for one of the unbelievable local discos in darkest Kowloon. Lan Kwai Fong, the famous square inch of Central with the most relaxed drinking hours and the most intense partying, is now losing ground to other locations and its chief developers are now expanding further afield to Shanghai. Soho ('South of Hollywood Road') is a slightly more chic and relaxed concentration of leisure spots, just off the Mid-Levels Escalator. Chinese locals tend to favour Tsim Sha Tsui, riddled with bars and clubs. And anyone seeking

such things will be pleased to hear that they can get all the action they want in the girlie bars and joints of Wan Chai – destination of many a poor Filipino or Thai peasant maiden. Despite the ludicrously strict noise restrictions on open-air events – proof that well-connected residents have huge clout with city hall – live music is also hugely popular and well catered for. Check the free listings in *BC Magazine* and *HK Magazine* for the latest details.

Opening hours in Hong Kong vary by location, while dress code and entrance policies can sometimes be restrictive, particularly in the smarter clubs. Some Lan Kwai Fong venues stay open all night, whereas in Soho, the authorities placate local residents by compelling bars to close around 0200 at weekends and around 2400 on weekdays. What is almost uniformly constant is the high drinks prices – often at least HK$40 for a glass of wine or beer. Bar owners blame this on high rates – extortionate property prices certainly drive up prices in every department. Bars often compensate with happy hours, with two-for-one or half-price deals before 2000 or 2100 common. The minimum drinking age in Hong Kong's public bars is 18 years.

Bars

Escalator watchers can spectate in terrace-like comfort at *Stauntons*, 12 Staunton Street, the prime Soho-watching venue. *Mes Amis*, 81–85 Lockhart Road, is the most relaxed and civilised of the Wan Chai bars. Drinkers wanting a more raw experience should try *Dusk Till Dawn*, 76 Jaffe Road. *La Vie*, 9A Sharp Street, is one of the more chic venues in Causeway Bay's classy bar strip. The staple venue of Lan Kwai Fong, *Insomnia*, 38–44 D'Aguilar Street, creates an air of quality with its stonework and Florentine-style loggia, then promptly contradicts it with Filipino girl bands and relentless disco. *Agave*, 33 D'Aguilar Street, directly opposite, serves a marvellous selection of tequilas and margaritas – a staple for the hot summer months. *The Fong*, a few doors down at 34–36 D'Aguilar Street, is a chic bar-restaurant. *California*, 30–32 Lan Kwai Fong, long the citadel of investment bankers and the women they attract, has recently had a makeover, while *2121*, at 21 D'Aguilar Street, has the most exclusive and relaxed vantage point over the Lan Kwai Fong. Over in Kowloon, *Rick's Café*, 4 Hart Avenue, has some of the longest queues on Saturday night, which must count for something.

Casinos

Hong Kong does not have any casinos; instead they are all a 50-minute jetfoil ride away, in Macau, which is famous as a gambler's paradise (see *Excursions*). Jetfoils run all night just to service the Chinese love of gambling. Passports are needed for both the trip and the casinos – the age limit is nominally 21 years. Gambling in Macau is not a sport for the young or the faint-hearted. Macau boasts nine casinos in all, with dress codes ranging from smart-casual to formal. The best casinos include the *Hotel Lisboa and Casino*, 2–4 Avenida de Lisboa, Macao City, the *Mandarin Oriental Hotel and Casino*, 956–1110 Avenida da Amizade, Macao City, and the *Hyatt Regency & Taipa Resort*, 2 Estrada Almirante Marques Esparteiro, Taipa Island. However, the recent trend is for major international chains to play down their gambling facilities in favour of a broader spa-and-convention strategy.

More adventurous souls can always consider one of the discreet but popular 'leisure' cruises into international waters, operated by *Star Cruises* (tel: 2317 7711; fax: 2317 5551; e-mail: sales@starcruises.com.hk; website: www.starcruises.com), which are carefully packaged

to leave out references to gambling and a very Chinese experience.

Clubs

Dragon-I, in the upper ground floor of the new development, *The Centrium*, above Lan Kwai Fong, 60 Wyndham Street, is the new hangout of the stars; socially exclusive but surprisingly ordinary. *C Club*, 30–32 Lan Kwai Fong, remains Lan Kwai Fong's most reliable dance venue. *Liquid*, 1–5 Elgin Street, stays open till 0400 in crowded Soho, by soundproofing itself with a huge metal airlock. *Drop*, 39–43 Hollywood Road, just down the hill, under the escalator, is another late-night haven with a restrictive door policy and titanically overpriced drinks. The faint of heart should avoid *Joe Bananas*, 23 Luard Road, a pick-up joint par excellence and venue for cheesy model nights, where leggy Suzie Wongs stalk fat cats in three-piece suits. *JJ's*, in the Grand Hyatt Hotel, 1 Harbour Road, Wan Chai, has a similar rep and crowd. Meanwhile, *One-Fifth*, at Starcrest, 9 Star Street, is on a far higher plane of Wan Chai nightlife. *Club Ing*, 4F Convention Plaza, 1 Harbour Road, Wan Chai, is a very inconsistent glass and chrome hotel disco but its Thursday hip-hop 'Ladies' Night' is a staple for ex-pat teens and the businessmen who love them.

Live Music

What passes for stadium rock in Hong Kong is usually found at the *Hong Kong International Trade and Exhibition Centre* (HITEC), 1 Trademart Drive, Kowloon Bay, or the *Hong Kong Convention and Exhibition Centre*, 1 Expo Drive. Filipino live bands, from brilliant to unbearable, swarm across Hong Kong – *Dusk Till Dawn*, 76 Jaffe Road, has some of the best, while its strongest nearby competitor is *The Wanch*, 54 Jaffe Road. *The Edge*, in the otherwise exclusive *The Centrium*, 60 Wyndham Street, has recently been added to the roster of Filipino band venues. *The Jazz Club*, 34–36 D'Aguilar Street, plays far more than just trad and offers a more civilised ambience.

Sport

Hong Kong's favourite sports are few and fervently followed – none more so than horseracing. For example, the government's millennium celebrations were staged at the *Happy Valley Racecourse*, 2 Sports Road, Happy Valley, Hong Kong Island (tel: 2572 2881; website: www.happyvalleyracecourse.com). The other main track is the *Sha Tin Racecourse*, Sha Tin, New Territories (tel: 2966 6520; website: www.shatinracetrack.com). The privileged status of horseracing reached farcical levels in 2002, when soccer betting was officially banned to protect the Hong Kong Jockey Club's official gambling monopoly and the charitable and tax revenues therefrom – with predictable rewards for illegal betting syndicates. The policy has since been reviewed.

The Rugby Sevens are the other chief sporting fixture, taking place at the *Hong Kong Stadium*, 55 Eastern Hospital Road, So Kon Po (tel: 2895 7926; fax: 2895 7962; e-mail: hks@hkstadium.com.hk; website: www.lcsd.gov.hk/leisure/stadium). Competition for seats at this three-day carnival is fierce and, as with most major events internationally, corporate hospitality usually scoops the pool. Despite the enthusiasm for the Sevens and China's performance in the 2002 World Cup, Hong Kong itself does not have any sports teams of note.

Tickets for big global events, such as the Hong Kong Rugby Sevens can be booked online or at the Hong Kong Stadium or similar venues. Tickets for races are available for purchase at the racecourses or by telephone. The *URBTIX* ticketing service for public venues (tel: 2734 9009; website: www.lcsd.gov.hk/CE/Entertainment/Ticket/index.html) and online booking services *Ticketek* (website: www.ticketek.com.hk) and *Cityline* (website: www.cityline.com.hk) handle many major sporting events and venues.

Fitness Centres

California Fitness Centers (tel: 2960 4988; fax: 2960 4933; website: www.calfitnesscenters.com) is Hong Kong's most popular chain of clubs, spread across the territory, including branches on 1 Wellington Street, Central (tel: 2522 5229), and 5–15 Hankow Road, Tsim Sha Tsui (tel: 2366 8666), both open 365 days a year. Meanwhile, *New York Fitness Club*, 32 Hollywood Road, Central (tel: 2543 2280; website: www.nyfhk.com) runs a close second and allows casual visitors to use the extensive facilities for HK200. There are also numerous public facilities, as well as health centres in the large hotels.

Golf

The Asian businessperson's love of golf is catered for in several clubs, with the *Clearwater Bay Golf and Country Club*, Clearwater Bay, New Territories (tel: 2335 3885; fax: 2335 1380; website: www.cwbgolf.org), and the *Hong Kong Golf Club*, Fan Ling, New Territories (tel: 2670 1211), favouring those with the largest expense accounts. Others play at *The Jockey Club Kau Sai Chau Public Golf Course*, Kau Sai Chau, Sai Kung (tel: 2791 3388). Green fees per person are HK$1400 weekdays at Clearwater Bay Golf and Country Club and Hong Kong Golf Club and from HK$330 at the Jockey Club Kau Sai Chau Public Golf Course. Non-members are welcome at all the clubs mentioned, provided they contact the chosen establishment in advance.

Swimming

Hong Kong has 42 officially listed bathing beaches and 13 public pools, to say nothing of the private pools at sports clubs and hotels. Popular (sometimes too popular) public pools include those at *Victoria Park*, Causeway Bay, and *Kowloon Park*, Tsim Sha Tsui. The open season for sea bathing is April to October, although the weather may be good enough to allow swimming outside these times. Pollution and overcrowding plagues the beaches closer to central Hong Kong; the best beaches are in the New Territories and the outlying islands. Summer weekends are predictably busy on the beaches. The *Amateur Swimming Association* (tel: 2572 8594; website: www.hkasa.org.hk) might be able to provide more detailed information.

Tennis

There are public courts available at *Victoria Park*, Causeway Bay (tel: 2570 6186), the *Tennis Centre*, Wong Nai Chung Gap Road, Happy Valley (tel: 2574 9122), and *King's Park*, Kowloon (tel: 2388 8154). Numerous private clubs and courts are also available for the rich and well connected and through major hotels.

Watersports

Another popular sporting pastime, sailing and other watersports are mostly based out of Aberdeen, on the southern side of Hong Kong Island. The exclusive levels of yachting are in the hands of the *Aberdeen*

Marina Club, 8 Shum Wan Road, Aberdeen (tel: 2555 8321; fax: 2873 5681; website: www.amchk.com.hk), and similar institutions, although windsurfing and wakeboarding are far easier to access.

Shopping

If Hong Kong is the 'City of Life', then life is a mall. Some speculate that Hong Kongers need to shop to escape their cramped dwellings. Others simply ascribe the shopping mania to disposable income and greed. The large numbers of missionary churches around town may owe their business to guilt, stemming from the widespread habit of shopping right through Sunday. The prime shopping areas are bedlam at weekends and merely chaotic during the rest of the week.

Once famous for bargain electronics and imitation brand-names, Hong Kong is no longer as cheap as it once was and prices are now closer to European or American averages. Real bargain hunters would be better off going to Bangkok. Shops selling Chinese art objects and souvenirs cluster around the escalator up to the Mid-Levels and along nearby Cat Street. However, any bargain hunter also planning to visit mainland China should do their research in Hong Kong but save their purchases for north of the border. Within Hong Kong, *Shanghai Tang*, right by Central MTR station, is probably the best venue for quality Chinese goods – silks, fabrics, ornaments and furniture.

Mallrats in Hong Kong have plenty of warrens to choose from. *Pacific Place*, in Admiralty, has three floors of almost entirely luxury brands, while *The Landmark* and *Prince's Arcade* vie for the custom of chic Central. *Festival Walk*, Kowloon Tong MTR station, in northern Kowloon, is worth the long trip from Central, for its variety and quality. Causeway Bay has the big Japanese department stores, *Sogo* and *Mitsukoshi*, as well as the towering *Times Square*. Tourist items and souvenirs, often very tacky, are best purchased either along the hotel strip of Nathan Road on Kowloon Side or at Stanley Market (see *Excursions*).

There are computer superstores at Causeway Bay, Wanchai and Mongkok, full of tiny booths selling the silicon equivalent of Hong Kong tailoring and teenage hustlers pushing pirated software. However, for most electrical goods, there are worse places than the many branches of the *Fortress* chain.

Hong Kong also has many markets. One of the most delightful is the Yuen Po Street Bird Garden, on Prince Edward Road West, in Kowloon. Open daily 0700–2000, this market is primarily concerned with the sale of song birds. Nearby, on Tung Choi Street, is a flower market and a goldfish market.

Standard opening hours are daily 0930–1900 and later in many cases. Hong Kongers bridle at the very idea of a sales tax, so visitors can forget about hoarding their receipts until the government finally decides to plug its deficit this way.

Culture

It may seem a laughable idea but culture does exist in Hong Kong. The city's reputation as a brashly philistine capitalist paradise has not exactly enlarged its footprint on the international cultural scene but it should be remembered that this is Greater China's film and media powerhouse and one area where Chinese arts and culture have flourished without political and ideological interference. For instance, the traditional Chinese opera at the China Club

Pacific Place

never had to struggle with all the Maoist impositions that afflicted it on the mainland.

Cityline (tel: 2317 6666; website: www.cityline.com.hk) provides tickets to cultural events. Those looking for events and performances in the city should check the free listings in *BC Magazine* and *HK Magazine* for the latest details.

Music

The *Hong Kong Philharmonic Orchestra* (tel: 2721 2030; website: www.hkpo.com) is the town ensemble and its frequent showings at corporate galas at least bankroll a full year-round programme. The company is resident at the *Hong Kong Cultural Centre*, 10 Salisbury Road (tel: 2734 2009; website: www.lcsd.gov.hk/CE/CulturalService/HKCC), from September to July. It is backed up by the *Hong Kong Chinese Orchestra* (tel: 3185 1600; website: www.hkco.org). Visiting orchestras of all standards frequently tour through Hong Kong. The *Hong Kong Academy for Performing Arts*, 1 Gloucester Road (tel: 2584 8500; website: www.hkapa.edu), also hosts frequent concerts. Traditional Chinese opera is performed at the *China Club*, 13F Old Bank of China Building, Bank Street (tel: 2521 8888). It is very difficult to get an entrée here but it is worth trying, if only to admire the display of modern Chinese art.

Theatre

The *Hong Kong Academy for Performing Arts* (see *Music* above), the *Hong Kong Cultural Centre* (see *Music* above) and the *Hong Kong Arts Centre*, Upper Basement, 2 Harbour Road, Wan Chai (tel: 2582 0200; website: www.hkac.org.hk), are shrines of high theatrical culture. The *Star Alliance Theatre*, Fringe Club, South Block, Lower Albert Road, Central (tel: 2521 7251; website: www. hkfringe.com.hk), gets many of the more wacky acts.

Dance

Hong Kong's classical ballet troupe is the *Hong Kong Ballet* (tel: 2573 7398; website: www.hkballet.com) and preferred venues include the *Hong Kong Cultural Centre* (see *Music* above) and the *Ko Shan Theatre*, 77 Ko Shan Road, Hunghom, Kowloon (tel: 2330 5661). The *Hong Kong Dance Company* (tel: 3103 1888; website: www.hkdance.com) has a traditional Chinese repertoire, while the *City Contemporary Dance Company* (tel: 2326 8597; website: www.ccdc.com.hk) is the more modern dance ensemble. Both perform at a variety of venues.

Film

Jackie Chan and Bruce Lee are still the much-imitated icons of the local film industry, although production has recently diversified into more reflective fare. Meanwhile, John Woo and Chow Yun-Fat propelled the Cantonese gangster genre into *A Better Tomorrow* (1986). The *UA* and *Golden Harvest* cinema chains are Hong Kong's major commercial screening venues. Their principal multiplexes include *UA Pacific Place*, 1 Pacific Place, 88 Queensway, Admiralty (tel: 2869 0322), *UA Times Square*, Times Square, Causeway Bay (tel: 2506 2822), and *Golden Gateway Multiplex*, The Gateway, 25 Canton Road, Tsim Sha Tsui (tel: 2956 3428). English-language movies are mostly screened in the original language with Cantonese subtitles, although some screenings are dubbed. Likewise, Cantonese-language films almost invariably have English subtitles. Arthouse films are mostly screened at the *Lim Por Yen Film Theatre*, in the Hong Kong Arts Centre (see above).

Cultural Events

The *Hong Kong Arts Festival* (tel: 2824 3555; website: www.hk.artsfestival.org), usually based out of Hong Kong City Hall, is the official annual catch-all jamboree of events, with international acts and events of all varieties, held from February to March. Nipping in to the cultural calendar a little earlier, in January through February, is the *City Festival*, which focuses on local acts. Sponsored by the Fringe Club, it is now rivalling its respectable brother in variety and content and arguably excelling it in entertainment value. The *Festival of Asian Arts*, in October/November, gathers the traditional arts of the region, sometimes dovetailing with the *Hong Kong Folk Festival* in November. The *Hong Kong Youth Arts Festival* (website: www.hkyaf.com) runs from October to December.

Literary Notes

Hong Kong has not left a deep impression on global literature. Perhaps, for too long in its history, it lacked the allure of neighbouring Shanghai and the recent economic dynamism has yet to find a literary expression. There is a rich tradition of Cantonese literature but this also has not made much of an impact in translation. Some of the best works on Hong Kong are histories or travel writing rather than pure fiction. Probably the best of the histories is Frank Welsh's *A Borrowed Place: A History of Hong Kong* (1997). Jan Morris' *Hong Kong – Epilogue to an Empire* (1997) is a

typically lyrical summary of the territory's character in the twilight of colonialism, recently updated to cover the latest developments. Mark Roberti's *The Fall of Hong Kong: China's Triumph and Britain's Betrayal* (1996) is an understandably angry survey of events before, during and after the 1997 handover.

As for novels, Paul Theroux's *Kowloon Tong* (1997) focuses on cultural interaction and colonial legacies in the plight of a Hong Kong English trading family on the eve of the handover. Timothy Mo's *An Insular Possession* (1986) is concerned with Macau more than Hong Kong but nonetheless manages to be a subtle and polished work, describing the European enclave of a bygone era. Most recently, John Lanchester's *Fragrant Harbour* (2002) takes his characters, the English Tom Stewart and Catholic nun Sister Maria, through the turbulent trading years and Japanese invasion of Hong Kong in the 1930s and 1940s. Lanchester was born and raised in Hong Kong and provides his readers with a powerful insight into the city.

Otherwise, Hong Kong is a staple of genre fiction. John Le Carré's *The Honourable Schoolboy* (1977) is one of the better spy novels to deal with the territory. Any reader looking for the blockbuster view of Hong Kong should read James Clavell's *Noble House* (1981) and *Tai-Pan* (1966). *The World of Suzie Wong* (1957), by Richard Mason, conjures up more romance than one can find in any of the Filipino pole-dancing bars in Wan Chai. The success of the film it inspired is probably testament enough to the fact that Hong Kong has been best captured on celluloid – Jackie Chan makes as good a swashbuckling cultural hero for the place as anyone.

Wong Tai Sin Temple

SPECIAL EVENTS

New Year's Day, public holiday, street parties and fireworks in the Harbour, 1 Jan, throughout the city

City Festival, local arts festival, Jan–Feb, throughout the city

Chinese New Year, flower markets, lantern parades, fireworks, fortune telling, Feb (first day of first Chinese lunar month), throughout the city

Lantern Festival, lantern parades, matchmaking games, Feb (15th day of first Chinese lunar month), throughout the city

Hong Kong Arts Festival, live performances and artistic events, including music, dance and drama (website: www.hk.artsfestival.org), Feb–Mar, throughout the city

Hong Kong International Machine Tool/Plastics/Packaging Exhibition, Mar, Hong Kong Convention and Exhibition Centre

Interstoff Asia Spring – International Fabric Show, late Mar, Hong Kong Convention and Exhibition Centre

Hong Kong Wedding, Banquet and Honeymoon Travel Expo, early Apr, Hong Kong Convention and Exhibition Centre

Asia Pacific Leather Fair, early Apr, Hong Kong Convention and Exhibition Centre

Ching Ming Festival, visits to ancestral graveyards, Apr (15th day from the spring equinox), throughout the city

Tin Hau Festival, celebrations and parades, Apr (23rd day of third lunar month), Joss House Bay and Yuen Long

Hong Kong Gifts and Premiums Fair, late Apr–early May, Hong Kong Convention and Exhibition Centre

Labour Day, patriotic parades and public holiday, 1 May, throughout the city

Buddha's Birthday, ceremonies at temples and monasteries, May (eighth day of fourth Chinese lunar month), Buddhist holy places throughout the city

International Computer Expo, mid-May, Hong Kong Convention and Exhibition Centre

Dragon Boat Festival, dragon boat racing, Jun (fifth day of fifth Chinese lunar month), various venues

International Travel Expo Hong Kong, mid-Jun, Hong Kong Convention and Exhibition Centre

HKSAR Establishment Day, parades and official festivities, 1 Jul, throughout the city

Hong Kong Fashion Week, mid-Jul, Hong Kong Convention and Exhibition Centre

Hong Kong Comics Festival, early Aug, Hong Kong Convention and Exhibition Centre

Food Expo, mid-Aug, Hong Kong Convention and Exhibition Centre

Mid-Autumn Festival, lantern displays in parks and public places, Sep (15th day of eighth lunar month), throughout the city

Asian IT Expo, late Sep, Hong Kong Convention and Exhibition Centre

National Day, patriotic Chinese celebrations, 1 Oct, throughout the city

Chung Yeung Festival, mountain picnics and family visits to graves, Oct (ninth day of ninth lunar month), throughout the city

Hong Kong Electronics Fair and ElectronicAsia, mid-Oct, Hong Kong Convention and Exhibition Centre

Festival of Asian Arts, traditional arts of the region, Oct–Nov, various venues

Hong Kong Youth Arts Festival (website: www.hkyaf.com), Oct–Dec, various venues

Hong Kong Folk Festival, Nov, various venues

Cosmoprof Asia, international beauty trade fair (website: www.cosmoprof-asia.com), mid-Nov, Hong Kong Convention and Exhibition Centre

Software Exhibition, mid-Nov, Hong Kong Convention and Exhibition Centre

Christmas, parties and festivities, 25 Dec, throughout the city

Vast, vibrant and truly multicultural, London is one of the world's great cities. Located in the southeast of England, on the River Thames, it is the capital of the United Kingdom and has been the heart of its political, cultural and business life for centuries. The now sprawling metropolis is a far cry from the scrabble of dwellings that first sprouted up to house river traders during their voyages towards the sea. It was the Romans who really kick-started the city, by establishing 'Londinium' as an important fortress town, guarding the Thames and protecting against any Celtic tribes trying to invade the then untamed island. The Romans brought with them forts, roads and the rule of law, prompting Roman historian Tacitus to boast of an AD60 city 'filled with travellers and a celebrated centre of commerce.'

Over the centuries, London has developed and expanded, despite the many dangers that might have defeated a lesser place – the Great Plague, the Great Fire, the bitter English Civil War and even a plot to blow up the Houses of Parliament. But most recently and resiliently, London and its citizens survived the German Luftwaffe attempts to bomb the city to oblivion during the World War II 'Blitz'.

Nowadays, the sheer scale of Greater London can be daunting at first, as it sprawls 1500 sq kilometres (580 sq miles) across a voluminous plain. However, it is a city that is surprisingly easy to get around, with the comprehensive and easily navigated London Underground or 'Tube'. The twin axis on which London rests is the Houses of Parliament to the west and the City of London to the east. The seat of government (not far from the home of the royal family) is connected to the City (the financial engine room of London and the whole of the UK) by the River Thames. In between lie most of the tourist attractions and the busiest, liveliest different entertainment areas, such as Knightsbridge and Soho. But London's vivacity and charm stretches far beyond the Circle Line – the Underground route that rings the inner city. Residential areas outside the city centre each have their own beating heart, such as leafy Richmond (southwest) or Hampstead (north), trendy Hoxton (east) or Notting Hill (west).

And as the population of London pushes inexorably towards the ten million mark, the city continues to grow and thrive. Home to 37 distinct immigrant groups, each consisting of more than 10,000 people, this is a city where some three hundred languages are spoken. This very real multiculturalism is evident on every street (and many restaurant plates) and is a key reason why people love the city. Tourists come for London's history or London's royal pageantry but they return for all the charms of the modern London, not least the extraordinary breadth of London's cultural life, with world-class art galleries and theatres, buzzing nightlife, film, music, culinary and fashion scenes. Overseeing the whole lot is a new mayoral government, headed by Mayor Ken Livingstone, who was elected in 2000. Keen to make an impact on the city, various strategies have been developed and quickly implemented – for example, the controversial plan for congestion charging on the inner city roads, which is already a successful reality. But the city skyline is the place where the London's rapid change and optimism is most visible – the Docklands and the City (with its now famous 'Gherkin' tower) have shot up over the last few years.

During summer, London's bountiful green spaces fill up with office workers and tourists enjoying the surprisingly balmy days as café tables sprout across a multitude of pavements. During winter, the grey skies and rain can be forgotten for a while in numerous cosy pubs. But spring or autumn are probably the best seasons to visit the city, when clear crisp sunny days often illuminate London and its landmarks, old and new.

Photo: Visit Britain

Tower Bridge

TRAVEL

Getting There By Air

London Heathrow Airport (LHR)

Tel: (0870) 000 0123. Fax: (020) 8745 4290.
Website: www.baa.co.uk

Heathrow, 24km (15 miles) west of central London, is one of the world's busiest international airports, coping with over 63 million passengers every year. The airport is massive, with terminals one to three linked to terminal four by the Heathrow Express and London Underground services. After a ten-year deliberation and some fierce opposition, plans to build a fifth terminal were approved in 2001 and there is currently talk of a new runway as well.

Major airlines: *British Airways* (tel: (0870) 850 9850; website: www.britishairways.com) operates both national and international flights from Heathrow. There are approximately 90 airlines that operate in and out of Heathrow, serving about 170 destinations worldwide. These include *Air Canada, Air France, Alitalia, Cathay Pacific, Croatia Airlines, Gulf Air, Iberia, Lufthansa, Malaysia Airlines, Qantas, South African Airways, Turkish Airlines, United Airlines* and *Virgin Atlantic*. All domestic flights operate from terminal one.

Airport facilities: Facilities include bureaux de change, ATMs, airport information, hotel reservation and travel information desks, post offices in terminals two and four, left-luggage, showers, telephones and fax machines, shops, duty-free outlets, restaurants, cafés, bars and a *London Tourist Board* centre in the London Underground station. There is Internet access available in terminal four. There is also car hire available in all four terminals, from *Avis, Europcar, Hertz* and *National*.

Business facilities: *The Business Centre Heathrow* (tel: (020) 8759 2434; website: www.the-bch.co.uk) is located in the Queen's Building, between terminals one and two. Open Monday to Friday 0730–1900, it

offers 20 meeting rooms and a conference suite, as well as a communications centre with computers with Internet access, faxes, photocopiers, audiovisual equipment and even showers.

Transport to the city: The *Heathrow Express* (tel: (0845) 600 1515; website: www.heathrowexpress.co.uk) train service to Paddington station operates every 15 minutes Monday to Saturday 0507–2401 and Sunday 0503 –2401 from terminal four (journey time – 23 minutes) and Monday to Saturday 0503–2401 and Sunday 0508–2408 from terminals one, two and three (journey time – 15 minutes). Single tickets cost £13, while a return ticket costs £25. Tickets can be purchased from Heathrow Express desks or self-service ticket kiosks located at the station; tickets are also available for purchase on the train, for a £2 premium, or online, with a 10% discount.

The airport is also on the *London Underground* Piccadilly line (tel: (0845) 330 9880 *or* (020) 7222 1234; website: www.tfl.gov.uk). Trains operate Monday to Saturday 0500–2345 and Sunday 0545–2315. Tickets to the city centre cost £3.70 (journey time – 45 minutes).

There is also a *Central Bus Station* at Heathrow, where the main bus service to central London is the A2 *Airbus* (tel: (020) 7222 1234), which travels to Kings Cross station daily 0530–2145 approximately every 20–30 minutes (journey time – 1 hour 40 minutes). Tickets cost £8 for a single and £12 for a return. At night, the N9 night bus service goes to central London every 30 minutes (journey time – 50 minutes) and costs £1.

The *Airport Travel Line* (tel: (0870) 574 7777) provides coach transport information. The *Travel Line* (tel: (0870) 608 2608) can provide information on all public transport to and from London. Taxis are readily available and cost around £45 for a journey to the city centre (depending on traffic conditions and time of day).

London Gatwick Airport (LGW)

Tel: (0870) 000 2468.
Website: www.baa.co.uk

Gatwick, 45km (28 miles) south of central London, is the second busiest international airport in the UK, serving over 29 million passengers a year. The free *Inter Terminal Transit* train links the two terminals (north and south).

Major airlines: *British Airways* (tel: (0870) 850 9850; website: www.britishairways.com) operates both national and international flights from Gatwick. Over 90 other airlines also use Gatwick airport, serving over 200 destinations worldwide. These include *Alitalia, American Airlines, Britannia Airways, Delta Airlines, Estonian Air, Maersk Air* and *Virgin Atlantic*.

Airport facilities: Both terminals have bureaux de change, ATMs, airport information desks, showers, shops, duty-free outlets, restaurants and bars. There is also a post office and an Internet café situated in the south terminal. Both terminals have car hire from *Avis, Europcar, Hertz* and *National*.

Business facilities: The airport provides a *Fast Track* priority service for business-class travellers, as well as a full range of business services at the *Hilton London Gatwick Airport Hotel* (tel: (01293) 518 080) and *Le Meridien London Gatwick Hotel* (tel: (01293) 567 070).

Transport to the city: The *Gatwick Express* (tel: (0845) 850 1530; website: www.gatwickexpress.co.uk) train service to Victoria station operates every 15 or 30 minutes (depending on the time of day) daily 0520–0135 (journey time – 30 minutes). Single tickets cost £11, while a return ticket costs £21.50. Alternative train services by *Thameslink* (tel: (0845)

748 4950; website: www.thameslink.co.uk) to Kings Cross Thameslink operate daily approximately every 15 minutes during peak hours, with a reduced service at night (journey time – 45–50 minutes). A single ticket costs £9.80. Coaches depart from the ground floor of the south terminal.

The *Flightlink* coach service to Victoria coach station does not exist any more but *Speedlink* (tel: (020) 8990 6300; website: www.speedlink.co.uk) coaches go to Heathrow airport (journey time – 70 minutes) daily approximately 0500–2230. A single ticket costs £17. The *Travel Line* (tel: (0870) 608 2608) can provide information on all public transport to and from London. Chauffeur-driven cars are provided by *Checker Cars* (tel: (01293) 502 808 (south terminal) *or* 501 377 (north terminal); fax: (01293) 569 790). Taxis are readily available and a trip to the centre of London costs around £75 for a journey time of approximately 90 minutes, depending on traffic conditions.

London Stansted Airport (STN)

Tel: (0870) 000 0303. Fax: (01279) 662 066.
Website: www.baa.co.uk

This impressively modern and user-friendly airport is an excellent hub for the increasingly popular budget airlines, which offer cut-price flights to many cities across Europe. One of Europe's fastest growing airports, Stansted is located 48km (30 miles) northeast of central London and serves 16 million passengers per year.

Major airlines: Scheduled flights to over 100 destinations are offered by over 25 airlines. The budget airline *Ryanair* (tel: (0871) 246 0000; website: www.ryanair.com), which now also owns *Buzz*, dominates the Stansted skies, with over 60 destinations covered. The other key low-cost carrier, serving around 20 destinations, is *easyJet* (tel: (0870) 600 0000; website: www.easyjet.com), which bought rival airline Go.

Airport facilities: Newly renovated and expanded facilities include bureaux de change, ATMs, left-luggage, airport information, hotel reservation desk, shops, duty-free outlets, restaurants, bars and car hire from *Avis, Europcar, Hertz* and *National*.

Business facilities: Meeting rooms are available for hire from *easymeeting* (tel: (01279) 662 570), in Enterprise House, situated next to the main terminal building. Broadband wireless Internet access is available from *BT Openzone* (website: www.bt.com/openzone) situated in the departure lounge. A one-hour pass costs £6.

Transport to the city: The *Stansted Express* (tel: (0845) 850 0150; website: www.stanstedexpress.co.uk) train service to Liverpool Street station operates daily 0530–2430, departing every 15 or 30 minutes, depending on the time of day (journey time – 45 minutes). Single tickets cost £13, while a return ticket costs £23.

The main coach service to central London is the A6 *Airbus* (tel: (0870) 575 7747; website: www. nationalexpress.com), which travels to Victoria coach station every 30 minutes, 24 hours a day (journey time – 1 hour 45 minutes). Tickets cost £10 for a single and £15 for a return.

The *Airport Travel Line* (tel: (0870) 574 7777) provides further coach transport information. The *Travel Line* (tel: (0870) 608 2608) can provide information on all public transport to and from London. Taxis are usually available at the airport or can be telephoned; *Airport Carz* (tel: (01279) 662 444) charge around £80 for the 60-minute (depending on traffic and conditions) journey to central London.

London Luton Airport (LTN)

Tel: (01582) 405 100.
E-mail: info@london-luton.co.uk
Website: www.london-luton.co.uk
The UK's seventh largest airport is 52km (32 miles) north of central London. Luton served 6.5 million passengers in 2001.

Major airlines: Luton serves over 60 destinations and is the base for the world's largest charter airline, *Britannia Airways* (tel: (0870) 607 6757; website: www.britanniaairways.com), and the popular low-cost airline *easyJet* (tel: (0870) 600 0000; website: www.easyjet.com). Other airlines include *Monarch Airlines* and *Ryanair*. The new low-cost airline *Now*

CITY STATISTICS

Location: Southeastern England, United Kingdom.
Country dialling code: 44.
Population: 7.4 million (metropolitan area).
Ethnic mix: 72% white, 28% various ethnic groups incorporating over 37 different communities; biggest group is Asian/Asian-British, followed by black/black-British.
Religious mix: 58.2% Christian, 8.5% Muslim, 4% Hindu, 2% Jewish, 1.5% Sikh, 0.8% Buddhist, 0.5% other religions, 24.5% no religion or not stated.
Time zone: GMT (GMT + 1 from last Sunday in March to Saturday before last Sunday in October).
Electricity: 240 volts AC, 50Hz; square three-pin plugs are standard.
Average January temp: 5°C (41°F).
Average July temp: 18°C (64°F).
Annual rainfall: 585mm (23 inches).

(tel: (0845) 458 9737; website: www.now-airlines.com), launching late 2003, is also based here.

Airport facilities: The airport has bureaux de change, ATMs, 11 information kiosks, shops, duty-free outlets, restaurants, bars and car hire from *Avis*, *Budget*, *Europcar*, *Hertz* and *National*.

Business facilities: The *Aviance Executive Lounge* (tel: (01582) 700 898) is located in the international departure lounge. Facilities include fax, telephone, e-mail and Internet.

Transport to the city: *Thameslink* (tel: (0845) 748 4950; website: www.thameslink.co.uk) provides a fast link (approximately 30–40 minutes) to Kings Cross Thameslink from the Luton Airport Parkway station.

A free shuttle bus connects Luton airport with the Parkway station. Trains operate daily approximately every 15–30 minutes, with a reduced service on weeknights. A single ticket costs £10.

Greenline 757 (tel: (0870) 608 7261; website: www.greenline.co.uk) operates a coach service to Victoria coach station, departing every 30–60 minutes 24 hours a day (journey time – 60–90 minutes). Tickets cost £8 for a single.

The *Travel Line* (tel: (0870) 608 2608) provides further information on travel to London. Taxis are available 24 hours and cost approximately £60 for a journey to central London.

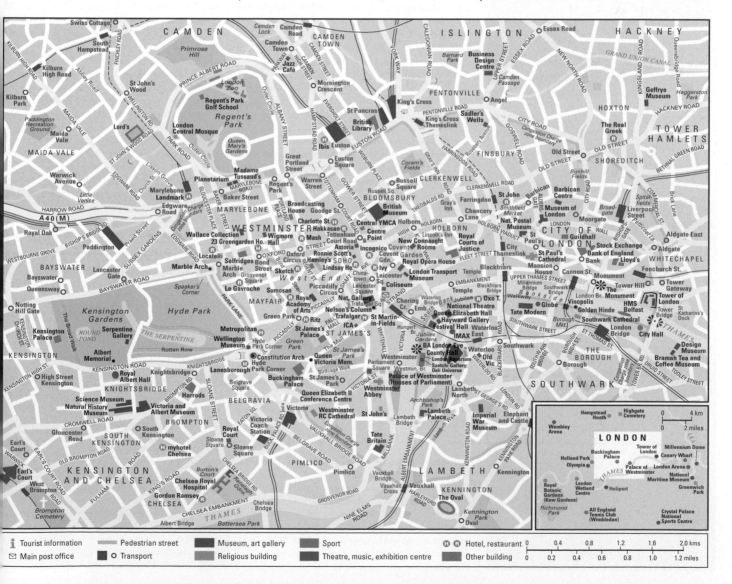

BUSINESS PROFILE

It is impossible to underestimate the importance of London, with an annual GDP of £1043 billion, to the UK's economy. Known as 'the City', the square mile located on the eastern side of central London, the City of London, is the epicentre of British financial life and one of the world's leading international financial centres. It boasts an impressive concentration and variety of banks, insurance companies and other business services. In fact, financial and business services throughout London employ around a third of the Greater London workforce. Over the last few years, the British government has delegated greater responsibility to the Bank of England (website: www. bankofengland.co.uk), while the London Stock Exchange (website: www.londonstockexchange.com) has floated itself.

However, the City and the stock market in particular suffered badly in 2002, continuing into 2003. The 11 September terrorist attacks and the war in Iraq have had an impact on investor confidence and the stock market has reached a six-year low. Major companies seem to be feeling the pinch, which has a knock-on effect on jobs. Beyond the financial heart of London, law, computing, design, media, arts and fashion are all struggling to avoid the global slump, with the advertising sector being worst hit.

One industry that has shown signs of recovery is the tourism industry, which has fought back from the double setback of Foot and Mouth and 11 September, to stage a partial recovery. Although 2001 was one of the worst years on record for tourism in London, 2002 figures (estimated at 29.5 million visitors) are only slightly down on the years preceding the outbreak of Foot and Mouth.

The list of companies based in London is almost endless as most major international companies have offices here, including *IBM*, *Sun Microsystems* and *Warburgs*. London in the 1980s and 1990s saw a decline in production and manufacturing jobs and a growth in the service sector. However, strengths remain in modern product-based manufacturing – specialist firms producing niche products – and high-tech companies. New light industry parks have sprung up out of town, although many businesses (such as computing) still prefer to stay closer to the City. For the more fashionable industries, such as media and design, a West End address is the most sought after, especially one in Soho. To the east of the City, the Docklands has come of age and is now a credible and popular business location with good public transport links and modern office complexes. The centrepiece is Canary Wharf, Britain's tallest building, which has been joined recently by two neighbouring skyscrapers. Nearby, the state-of-the-art ExCeL, is increasingly giving traditional conference venues a run for their money, with the world's largest travel exhibition, World Travel Market, now calling ExCeL home.

Unemployment in Greater London is low by European standards but slightly higher than the UK average at 6.6% (2002 annual rate) compared to a national average of 5.2% (2002 annual rate).

London City Airport (LCY)
Tel: (020) 7646 0088.
E-mail: info@londoncityairport.com
Website: www.londoncityairport.com
The business-orientated London City Airport is the most central of the capital's airports, located just ten kilometres (six miles) east of the City of London. The airport is relatively small, with only ten airlines. However, 1.6 million passengers travel through the airport each year.
Major airlines: *Lufthansa* (tel: (0845) 773 7747; website: www.lufthansa.com) operates the majority of flights from London City Airport, with four connections to Frankfurt per day. Other major airlines are *British European* and *KLM UK*. Scheduled flights are also provided by *Air France*, *Luxair*, *ScotAirways* and *VLM*.
Airport facilities: These include bureaux de change, ATMs, information and hotel reservation desks, postal facilities, duty-free shopping, restaurants, bars, and car hire from *Avis*, *Europcar* and *Hertz*.
Business facilities: The *Meridian Business Centre* (tel: (020) 7646 0900; fax: (020) 7476 3727; e-mail: meridian@londoncityairport.com) offers fully serviced conference suites and office space for hire.
Transport to the city: There are two airport shuttle buses, which operate Monday to Friday approximately 0600–2100, Saturday 0600–1300 and Sunday 1100–2100. The green shuttle bus runs to Canning Town station (journey time – five minutes), costing £2.50. Canning Town is served by *London Underground* (tel: (0845) 330 9880 *or* (020) 7222 1234; website: www.thetube.com), as well as *Silverlink Metro* (tel: (0845) 601 4867; website: www.silverlink-trains.com). The blue bus runs to Canary Wharf (journey time – 10 minutes) and Liverpool Street station (journey time – 30 minutes), with tickets costing £3 and £6 respectively. Canary Wharf and Liverpool Street are both on the London Underground network.
There is a stand with licensed black taxis, located directly outside the terminal building. Fares to central London start from £20. The *Travel Line* (tel: (0870) 608 2608) provides further information on all transport to and from London.

Approximate flight times to London: From New York is 7 hours 40 minutes; from Los Angeles is 10 hours 20 minutes; from Toronto is 7 hours and from Sydney is 23 hours 5 minutes (plus stopover).
Arrival/departure tax: None.

Getting There By Water

London is served by international ferry ports on the south and east coasts of England, including Dover, Newhaven and Harwich. Since the 1980s, the city itself has become a summer cruise destination and cruise ships dock at the *London Cruise Terminal*, in the Port of Tilbury. Facilities here include tourist information, a coffee shop and a bureau de change. There are also smaller *London Central Cruise Moorings*, based either around Tower Bridge or at Greenwich. The *Port of London Authority* (tel: (020) 7743 7900; website: www.portoflondon.co.uk) can provide further information.
Ferry services: The main route across the Channel is Dover–Calais; services are operated by *P&O Ferries* (tel: (0870) 600 0611; website: www.poferries.com), *SeaFrance* (tel: (0870) 571 1711; website: www. seafrance.co.uk) and *Hoverspeed* (tel: (0870) 240 8070; website: www.hoverspeed.com). Services from Harwich go to the Hook of Holland by *Stena Line*

(tel: (0870) 570 7070; website: www.stenaline.com) and to Hamburg and Esjberg by *DFDS Scandinavian Seaways* (tel: (0870) 533 3000 *or* 3111; website: www.scansea.com). Newhaven–Dieppe services are operated by Hoverspeed.
Transport to the city: Rail transport from Dover and Newhaven is provided by *Connex South Eastern* (tel: (0870) 603 0405; website: www.connex.co.uk) to Victoria station. *Great Eastern Railways* (tel: (0845) 950 5000; website: www.ger.co.uk) and *Anglia Railways* (tel: (0870) 040 9090 *or* (0845) 650 4090; website: www.angliarailways.co.uk) run services from Harwich to Liverpool Street station. *National Rail Enquiries* (tel: (0845) 748 4950) can give information on all services.

Getting There By Rail

The British railway network has a bad reputation at the moment – delays, cancellations and poor travelling conditions are common, while fares (particularly on routes via London) are among the highest in Europe. Actual train services are provided by a number of independent operators, while *Network Rail* (tel: (020) 7557 8000; website: www.networkrail.co.uk) is now the company responsible for the infrastructure and the track. The company also owns all the stations but manages only the 17 biggest. In an attempt to avoid the disaster of their predecessor, *Railtrack*, Network Rail is a Company Limited by Guarantee with no shareholders, where all profit is reinvested into the railways.
Railway information is available 24 hours from *National Rail Enquiries* (tel: (0845) 748 4950; website: www.nationalrail.co.uk). London has numerous major stations. These all become very crowded during rush hour (Monday to Friday 0800–0930 and 1700–1830), when services struggle to cope with the sheer volume of passengers. The major national stations in London are *Victoria* (southwest), *Paddington* (west), *Euston* and *Kings Cross* (north), *Liverpool Street* (east), *Waterloo* (south) and *Charing Cross* (central). Station facilities differ but most include ATMs, bureaux de change, shops, cafés and pubs. Tickets should be purchased at the station (from ticket desks and machines) before boarding.

BUSINESS ETIQUETTE

Business hours are officially Monday to Friday 0900 or 0930 until 1700 or 1730, although in practice many companies have much longer hours. Business in London is intense and fast paced. Extended business lunches and post-work drinks were regarded as part of the modern working environment until relatively recently. Nowadays, the emphasis is increasingly on hard work and long hours. Some older establishments can be strictly formal, however, meetings are (as a rule) relatively relaxed and first names are often used after the initial introduction. However, British businesspeople are unlikely to be overtly demonstrative – hand gestures and the use of expressive body language will be minimal and apart from shaking hands, physical contact should be avoided. Standard dress code is a suit and tie for men and a suit (or equivalent) for women but varies greatly depending on the company, with those in the new technologies sectors especially tending towards informality.

Rail services: *Eurostar* (tel: (0870) 518 6186 *or* (01233) 617 575 (from outside the UK); website: www.eurostar.com) services from Calais, Brussels, Lille, Paris Gare du Nord and Disneyland Paris (and Avignon in summer) travel via the English Channel to Waterloo station. Tickets are available at the station, from the *Eurostar Call Centre* or online (see above). Eurostar is extremely convenient and, once time travelling to and from the airport and spent checking in has been taken into account, is usually quicker than flying (approximate journey time to Paris – 3 hours). The construction of the *Channel Tunnel Rail Link*, connecting Kings Cross station with Paris (estimated journey time – 2 hours 20 minutes) is well under way; completion is due in 2007.

The main London termini serve different regions of the country, as follows:. Euston and Kings Cross – Midlands, north of England and Scotland; Liverpool Street – East Anglia; Paddington – Heathrow airport, the West Country, South Wales and the Midlands; Victoria – Gatwick airport and the southeast; and Waterloo – the south coast and the continent. There are also numerous regional stations, including Blackfriars, Charing Cross, London Bridge, Marylebone, St Pancras, Stratford and Clapham Junction (the busiest station in the UK). Overnight sleeper trains, run by *Scotrail* (tel: (0845) 755 0033; website: www. scotrail.co.uk), connect Euston with the Scottish destinations of Edinburgh, Glasgow, Inverness, Fort William, Aberdeen and Dundee. *National Rail Enquiries* (see above) can provide information on all services, including journey prices, times and duration.

Transport to the city: All railway stations are on the London Underground network. Two express bus routes, 205 and 705, cover the major railway stations, with limited key stops in between, often at regional train stations. Both bus routes operate between Paddington to Liverpool Street. Route 205 stops at Marylebone, Euston and Kings Cross St Pancras and operates every 15 minutes daily approximately 0500–2430. Route 705 stops at Victoria (coach and train stations), Waterloo and London Bridge and operates every 30 minutes daily approximately 0800–2000. Tickets cost £1 per trip.

Licensed London taxis are readily available from ranks outside all major railway stations. The *London Travel Information* line (tel: (020) 7222 1234; website: www. tfl. gov.uk) provides information on all the city's transport.

Getting There By Road

Main roads are designated by a letter, followed by up to four numbers: 'M' (motorway), 'A' (major road) and 'B' (minor road). Traffic drives on the left and drivers must be at least 18 years old. The speed limits are 113kph (70mph) on motorways, 97kph (60mph) on single-lane main roads and 48kph (30mph) in built-up areas. Seat belts are compulsory for drivers, front-seat passengers and rear-seat passengers (if fitted). Motorcyclists must wear helmets. The maximum legal alcohol to blood ratio for driving is 0.08%.

Overseas driving licences and International Driving Permits are valid for up to one year. Insurance is mandatory. Overseas visitors bringing their own cars should bring registration documents and check with their insurance company as to whether a Green Card is needed. Breakdown service and general motoring information is available from the *Automobile Association – AA* (tel: (0870) 600 0371; website: www.theaa.co.uk), the *Royal Automobile Club – RAC* (tel: (0870) 572 2722; website: www.rac.co.uk) and

Waterloo Bridge and the River Thames

Photo: Visit Britain

Green Flag (tel: (0800) 328 8772; website: www. greenflag.co.uk).

Emergency breakdown services (toll free): *AA* (0800) *or* (08457) 887 766; *Green Flag* (0800) 400 600; *RAC* (0800) 828 282.

Routes to the city: The M25 encircles Greater London. From this, the M1, M11, M20, M23, M3, M4 and M40 radiate clockwise from the capital to the rest of Britain. The M1 goes north to Leeds, the M3 southwest to Southampton, the M4 west to Heathrow airport and Bristol, the M11 northeast to Cambridge and East Anglia, the M20 southeast to Folkestone (from where the A20 continues to Dover), the M23 goes south to Gatwick airport (and continues as the A23 to Brighton), and the M40 northwest to Oxford and Birmingham.

Motorists and their cars can travel by train through the Channel Tunnel from Calais, France to Folkestone in southeast England, courtesy of *Eurotunnel* (tel: (0870) 535 3535; website: www.eurotunnel.co.uk).

Approximate driving times to London: From Cambridge – 1 hour 30 minutes; Oxford – 1 hour 30 minutes; Folkestone – 1 hour 45 minutes; Birmingham – 2 hours 15 minutes; Bristol – 2 hours 45 minutes; Leeds – 4 hours.

Coach services: National and international services use *Victoria Coach Station*, a short walk from Victoria railway station, at 164 Buckingham Palace Road, SW1 (tel: (020) 7730 3466; website: www. tfl.gov.uk/vcs). Facilities include bureaux de change, ATMs, travel and hotel agencies, information desks, left-luggage office and kiosks. *National Express* (tel: (0870) 580 8080; website: www.nationalexpress.com) operates services throughout the UK. *Eurolines* (tel: (0870) 514 3219; website: www.eurolines.com) has departures to over 500 European destinations.

Getting Around

Public Transport

Transport for London (tel: (020) 7222 1234 (24-hour enquiries); website: www.tfl.gov.uk) provides comprehensive information on all forms of transport within London, as well as operating the **buses**. London's famous red 'Routemaster' double-decker buses are slowly being superseded by more modern single and double deckers. There are now only two fare zones for buses. Any journey that includes the city centre zone one is £1 and any journey outside this zone is 70p. Single tickets are bought from the driver or bus conductor upon boarding and there is a

£5 fine for travelling without a valid ticket. Carnets of six tickets (for any zone) can be purchased from newsagents for £3.90. Services operate 24 hours a day, with **night buses**, prefixed by the letter 'N', replacing the standard services on most routes after midnight. Fares on night buses are the same as regular buses. There are also three **tram** routes at the moment in the Croydon area; it is fairly unlikely that visitors will use these, however, a Cross-River tram from Camden to Brixton via central London is planned for completion in 2011.

The *London Underground* (tel: (0845) 330 9880 *or* (020) 7222 1234; website: www.thetube.com), commonly referred to as the 'Tube', is the oldest and most extensive **underground** system in the world and pervades both the life and layout of London. An on-going programme is replacing old rolling stock, modernising stations and improving efficiency, however, escalator and station closures are still a regular problem. Despite the Mayor of London's opposition, the system will now be partly privatised, with a 30-year investment deal underway as part of the PPP (Public Private Partnership). The network consists of 12 underground lines, each with a different name and colour, supplemented by the *Docklands Light Railway* (website: www.tfl.gov.uk/dlr), connecting the City of London and the Docklands. The entire network is divided into six concentric zones, which determine the price of tickets. Within the city centre (zone one) a single ticket costs £1.60, while to travel from zone one to other zones costs from £2 (to go to zone two) to £3.70 (to go to zone six). *Carnets* of ten zone-one-only tickets cost £11.50. Tickets should be purchased at the station and must be passed through the barrier ticket gates in order for the passenger to enter and leave the system (and avoid a £10 penalty fare). The London Underground operates daily approximately 0530–2430 but should be avoided (where possible) during rush hour (Monday to Friday 0800–0930 and 1700–1830) when it is extremely crowded.

Various regional and commuter **rail** services, such as *Silverlink Metro* (tel: (0845) 601 4867; website: www.silverlink-trains.com) and *Thameslink* (tel: (0845) 748 4950; website: www.thameslink.co.uk), run between numerous stations in the capital and often cover routes not served by the London Underground.

There are a number of **passes** available, including the *One-day Travelcard*, which can be used on buses and London Underground. This costs £4.10 off peak (only valid after 0930) and £5.10 peak (valid from 0001). Both are valid all night until 0430 the next

Photo: Visit Britain

Red 'routemaster' buses and black cabs on Oxford Street

morning. A *Weekend Travelcard*, which is valid all Saturday and Sunday, costs £6.10. Prices quoted are for zones one and two only. The *One-day Bus Pass* is only valid on buses (zones one to four) and costs £2. Weekly, monthly and annual passes must be accompanied by a photocard. All passes, as well as carnets for bus or London Underground, are available for purchase at Tube stations and participating newsagents.

There are a number of transport services operating on the River Thames. *Thames Clippers*, commuter **ferries** running between Savoy Pier (central at Embankment) and Masthouse Terrace (east of Greenwich) are operated by *Collins River Enterprises* (tel: (020) 7977 6892; website: www.thamesclippers.com). A single trip costs £3. The *River Taxi Service*, operated by *Connoisseur Charters* (tel: (020) 7352 5888; website: www.connoisseur.co.uk), is a high-speed commuter service from Chelsea Harbour in the west to Blackfriars; a separate river bus also continues on to Greenland Pier (Greenwich). A single from Chelsea to the Savoy costs £4. This service only operates for commuters on weekdays, in the morning and evening. Full details of all river ferries can be obtained from *Transport for London* (see above). Tickets for the various services available can be purchased on-board.

Interested visitors can trace the history and development of the city's transport system at the *London Transport Museum* in The Piazza, at Covent Garden (tel: (020) 7379 6344 *or* 7565 7299; website: www.ltmuseum.co.uk).

Taxis

London's distinctive black taxi cabs are a pleasant – if pricey – way of getting around the city, as well as meeting the legendary 'cabbies'. Fares always start at £2 and go up in increments of £0.20. The lowest tariff is in effect Monday to Friday 0600–2000 (£0.20 per 180.5m/592.2ft or 38.8 seconds up to £12.40, then £0.20 per 128.9m/422.9ft or 27.7 seconds). Tariffs are higher between 2000 and 2200 weekdays and up to 2200 on Saturdays and Sundays, and then even higher 2200–0600 every day. Increased rates at night were introduced to get more cabs on the street, which has worked, although longer journeys can now

be prohibitively expensive. A tip of 10–15% to 'round up' the bill is customary. Each taxi has a licence number and badged drivers must comply with official regulations. London cabbies have undergone intensive training – known as the 'Knowledge' – which involves riding around London on a moped learning all the street names, followed by a gruelling examination.

Black cabs can be booked through *Dial-a-Cab* (tel: (020) 7251 0581; website: www.dialacab.co.uk) and *Radio Taxis* (tel: (020) 7272 0272; website: www.radiotaxis.co.uk). London taxi drivers' unsurpassed understanding of the city has been tapped by *Black Taxi Tours* (tel: (020) 7935 9363; website: www.blacktaxitours.co.uk), London sightseeing tours in a black cab. Any complaints about black cabs should be directed to the *Public Carriage Office*, 15 Penton Street, London N1 9PU (tel: (020) 7941 7800).

Minicabs (usually standard saloon cars) can be booked over the telephone or direct from local offices throughout London. One particularly efficient and reputable city-wide firm is *Addison Lee* (tel: (020) 7387 8888; website: www.addisonlee.co.uk). Although generally cheaper than black cabs, there are numerous illegal and/or unscrupulous operators, so it is always wise for travellers to check that the company is registered. In particular, offers of lifts by unlicensed drivers off the street, late at night in the West End or anywhere else for that matter, should not be accepted. *Transport for London* (tel: (020) 7222 1234; website: www.tfl.gov.uk) can provide a list of licensed Private Hire companies, as well as information on black taxis.

Limousines

Chauffeur-driven luxury cars can be hired from several companies, including *Carey Worldwide Chauffeur Services* (tel: (020) 7235 0234; website: www.ecarey.com) and *London Chauffeur Drive* (tel: (020) 7633 9410; website: www.lcd.uk.com). On average, stretch limousines cost about £50 (plus VAT) per hour, while a car with chauffeur starts from £30 per hour.

Driving in the City

London Mayor Ken Livingstone's infamous congestion charge (tel: (0845) 900 1234; website:

www.cclondon.com) came into force in February 2003. There is now a daily charge of £5 for all vehicles entering the central London congestion charging zone Monday to Friday between 0700 and 1830. The boundary line of the zone is the Inner Ring Road, which covers Marylebone Road, Euston Road, Pentonville Road, City Road, Commercial Street, Mansell Street, Tower Bridge, New Kent Road, Kennington Lane, Vauxhall Bridge Road and Park Lane (clockwise from northwest point). This is clearly marked on roads and signposts.

The £5 congestion charge can be paid in advance or any time before 2200 on the day. Payment can be made by post in advance or instantly online, by telephone, at BT Internet kiosks and at selected shops, car parks and petrol stations displaying the 'C' sign. Drivers will need their vehicle registration number. If registered, it is possible for drivers to pay up to one year in advance and also by SMS/text message. The charge goes up to £10 if paying between 2200 and 2400 on the day, however, drivers who fail to pay before 2400 will be issued with a penalty charge notice for £80 (reduced to £40 for payment with 14 days).

The attempt to reduce congestion has been fairly successful and there are plans to extend the congestion charging zone. However, the M25 ring motorway and major routes into and out of the city are often at a standstill, particularly on Friday and Sunday evenings.

Off-road parking is available 24 hours at *NCP* garages (tel: (0870) 606 7050; website: www.ncp.co.uk) situated around the city. The tariffs vary, however, from garage to garage. The cheapest NCP garage in London can be found at the Brunswick Centre, Marchmont Street, WC1, with prices here starting from £3.50 for one hour and rising to £12.50 for nine to 24 hours. Street parking in central London can be extremely expensive. Meters, pay-and-display bays or resident's parking bays operate throughout central London. Visitors should read the signs extremely carefully for the operating hours of the different bays and note that, although a pay space might only operate up to 1830, the adjacent resident's parking bays could require permits 24 hours a day. Parking on a single yellow line is prohibited within the hours of operation of the nearest meter or pay-and-display bay. Parking within any area marked with a zigzag or double yellow line is prohibited. On a red line, or a double red line, even stopping is forbidden. The penalty charge for illegal parking is a £100 fine (reduced to £50 for payment within 14 days), however, wheel-clamping and impounding vehicles, both of which incur additional fines, are not uncommon.

Cheap and improved bus services in the capital, combined with the congestion charge and high parking charges, mean that visitors are much better off using public transport than they are driving in central London.

Car Hire

Regulations vary but car hire companies usually require drivers to be around 25 years or older. A foreign national driving licence is valid in Britain for one year, although an International Driving Permit may be preferred if the licence is not in English. A credit card is essential and it is important to check what level of insurance is included in the price of car hire.

All major car firms have locations all over the city, such as *Avis* (tel: (0870) 606 0100; website: www.avis.co.uk), *Budget* (tel: (0800) 181 181; website: www.budget.co.uk) and *Hertz* (tel: (0870) 599 6699; website: www.hertz.co.uk). Rates start from approximately £40 per day. The London congestion charge does apply to all hire cars driven within the zone and drivers will usually be liable for this, in addition to the price quoted for hiring a car. Car hire companies vary but most do not even arrange the payment of the charge and leave it up to drivers to sort this out independently (see *Driving in the City*). There has been a recent growth in budget/Internet car hire companies, spearheaded by *easyCar* (tel: (0906) 333 3333; website: www.easycar.com), the first Internet-only car hire company with prices starting from just £7 per day. The easyCar depot at the Barbican is one of the only places in central London where the congestion charge is included in the price of hiring a car.

Bicycle & Scooter Hire

Both bicycles and motorcycles avoid the congestion charge (as well as traffic and parking charges), so they are sensible modes of transport in London. Mayor Ken Livingstone is trying to make London bicycle friendly and there are many new cycle paths and cycle routes throughout the city. The *London Bicycle Tour Company*, 1A Gabriel's Wharf, 56 Upper Ground SE1 (tel: (020) 7928 6838; website: www.londonbicycle.com), hires out bicycles for £2.50 per hour, £12 per day or £36 per week.

Although *About Town Motorcycle and Scooter Hire* (tel: (020) 8871 1112; fax: (020) 8875 9192; website: www.abouttownbikehire.co.uk) is based in Wandsworth, in the southwest of the city, motorcycles or scooters will be delivered to all London hotels. Prices start from £40/45 per day or £115/135 per week for a scooter/motorcycle, with a deposit of £250 required.

SIGHTSEEING

Sightseeing Overview

Before setting off sightseeing, it is wise for visitors to study a London Underground map, to get a feel for the straightforward colour-coded system. Visitors should also bear in mind, however, that many of the Underground stations are very close to each other and many central areas are easily navigable on foot.

The tourist heart of London lies mainly on the north bank of the River Thames, with the chunk of flat land between South Kensington in the west to Tower Bridge in the east stuffed full of things to do and see. Starting in the west, there are the three major South Kensington museums – the *Victoria & Albert Museum*, the *Natural History Museum* and the *Science Museum*. Moving eastwards, the next key attraction is *Buckingham Palace*, back in vogue after the Jubilee Year in 2002. A short walk away, through *St James's Park*, is Westminster, with the *Houses of Parliament*, *Big Ben* and *Westminster Abbey*. From here, it is another short walk up Whitehall to *Trafalgar Square*, with the *National Gallery* and other attractions. This is where the 'West End' starts, heading slightly north to *Leicester Square* – a busy tourist-infested piazza where many Londoners would not be seen dead – connecting up with *Piccadilly Circus* to the west and *Covent Garden* to the east, with the stately old *British Museum* a little further away to the northeast. In the middle of the West End, *Theatreland* and *Chinatown* merge into *Soho*, with is nightlife and new media offices.

Along the river itself, on the north bank is the *Tate Britain* gallery in the west, followed by Westminster and then the Embankment. Crossing over the River Thames from the Embankment can by done on the new pedestrian *Hungerford Bridge*. The south bank of the river now has its own throngs of tourists, at the *British Airways London Eye* and *London Aquarium*. This side of the river also dominates culturally, with the *South Bank Centre* and, further east, the *Tate Modern* and the *Globe Theatre*. Another pedestrian bridge, Lord Foster's *Millennium Bridge*, connects the Tate Modern with *St Paul's Cathedral*, back on the north bank. From St Paul's, it is possible to walk through the *City of London*, reaching the *Tower of London* further east. *Tower Bridge* connects this ancient seat of power to *City Hall*, on the south bank, the new state-of-the-art home of London Mayor Ken Livingstone and the London Assembly, designed by Lord Foster (website: www.london.gov.uk).

Key Attractions

British Airways London Eye and County Hall

Towering 135m (444ft) into the heavens, right in the heart of London, the *BA London Eye* is literally an unmissable attraction. The world's tallest observation

TOURIST INFORMATION

Britain and London Visitor Centre
1 Regent Street, SW1
Tel: (0906) 133 7799 *or* 866 3344 (24-hour general tourist information).
E-mail: enquiries@londontouristboard.co.uk
Website: www.visitlondon.com
Opening hours: Mon 0930–1830, Tues–Fri 0900–1830, Sat and Sun 1000–1600; Sat until 1700 (Jun–Oct).

There is one other major London Visitor Centre at Waterloo International Terminal, SE1, as well as various London Tourist Information Centres (TIC) situated throughout the city, including one at Pepys House, 2 Cutty Sark Gardens, Greenwich, SE10.

Passes
The *London Pass* (website: www.londonpass.com) allows free access for one adult to over 60 attractions (including the London Dungeon, Tower of London, Hampton Court Palace and Buckingham Palace). The 'with transport' option also includes free transport on all London buses, Tubes and trains. The price varies depending on whether or not the 'with transport' option is taken. A pass for one day costs £23 without transport and £27 with transport, £36 or £47 for two days, £44 or £60 for three days and £62 or £94 for six days. All prices exclude VAT. The London Pass is available for purchase at the airport and tourist information offices around London.

wheel has become one of London's most popular attractions, which usually means a 'flight' requires booking in advance and often queuing as well. However, the experience (one revolution of the wheel, lasting approximately 30 minutes) is absolutely worth it – the unparalleled views of the city reach as far away as 40km (25 miles).

Although the London Eye is the focus of the area, sitting right next door and directly across the River Thames from the Houses of Parliament, *County Hall*, the former home of the Greater London Council (abolished by Margaret Thatcher in 1986), comes a close second. The enormous building is home to the *London Aquarium*, the *Dalí Universe* and, most recently, *The Saatchi Gallery*, majestically situated on the first floor above the rabble. Here, Charles Saatchi's extensive collection of modern British art is displayed, with a permanent exhibition and a changing temporary exhibition. The 3,716 sq metres (40,000 sq ft) of County Hall that make up the gallery have been restored to their original splendour and much of the art is hung in former offices among the oak panelling. The central conference hall contains the most (in)famous pieces, such as Marcus Harvey's portrait of Myra Hindley, Tracey Emin's *Unmade Bed* and Damien Hirst's *The Physical Impossibility of Death in the Mind of Someone Living*, better known as 'the shark in formaldehyde'.

For live sharks in tanks, visitors should go to the London Aquarium, home to over 350 different aquatic species from around the world, including a touch area where visitors can stroke the friendly rays. The Dalí Universe meanwhile contains over 500 works of art by the famous surrealist, including the

British Airways London Eye

The dome of St Paul's Cathedral

painting, *Spellbound*, which was created specially for the set of the 1945 Hitchcock thriller, and the sofa in the shape of Mae West's lips. County Hall is also home to two hotels (Marriott and Travel Inn), numerous bars and restaurants and a *Namco Station*, a vast entertainment centre offering video games, ten-pin bowling, bumper cars, a pool hall, as well as a licensed bar and lounge with big TV screens.

South Bank, SE1

Transport: London Underground Waterloo, Westminster or Embankment.

BA London Eye
Jubilee Gardens, South Bank, SE1
Tel: (0870) 500 0600 (booking line).
Website: www.ba-londoneye.com
Opening hours: Daily 0930–2000 (Oct–Apr); Mon–Thurs 0930–2000, Fri–Sun 0930–2100 (May and Sep); Mon–Thurs 0930–2100, Fri–Sun 0930–2200 (Jun); daily 0930–2200 (Jul and Aug); closed (6–26 Jan).
Admission: £11.

London Aquarium
County Hall, Riverside Building, SE1
Tel: (020) 7967 8000. Fax: (020) 7967 8029.
E-mail: info@londonaquarium.co.uk
Website: www.londonaquarium.co.uk
Opening hours: Daily 1000–1800 (school holidays until 1900).
Admission: £8.75 (concessions available).

Dalí Universe
County Hall, Riverside Building, SE1
Tel: (020) 7620 2720 *or* (0870) 060 2319 (tickets). Fax: (020) 7620 3120.
E-mail: info@daliuniverse.com
Opening hours: Daily 1000–1730.
Admission: £8.50 (concessions available).

The Saatchi Gallery
County Hall, Riverside Building, SE1
Tel: (020) 7823 2363 *or* (0870) 1160 278 (advance tickets).

Website: www.saatchi-gallery.co.uk
Opening hours: Sun–Thurs 1000–1800; Fri and Sat 1000–2200.
Admission: £8.50 (concessions available).

Namco Station
County Hall, Riverside Building, SE1
Tel: (020) 7967 1067. Fax: (020) 7967 1060.
E-mail: countyhall@namco.co.uk
Website: www.namcostation.co.uk
Opening hours: Daily 1000–2400.
Admission: Free.

Tate Modern and Bankside

Opened in 2000, the *Tate Modern* is a £130-million project that is regarded as a model of urban regeneration, with the disused Bankside power station transformed into an avant-garde space dedicated to 20th-century art. The permanent exhibition changes biannually, so that much of the Tate Gallery's collection of modern work can be on show, displayed thematically rather than chronologically. This includes major works by Matisse, Picasso, Rothko and Warhol, as well as contemporary pieces. The Turbine Hall displays changing pieces of artwork, specially commissioned to fit the enormous space; one of the most successful of recent years is Anish Kapoor's *Marsyas*, a vast, fleshy, red plastic sculpture shaped like an ear trumpet.

The Bankside area itself is becoming one of the most exciting corners of the capital, especially now the £14-million *Millennium Bridge* has opened. Designed by Lord Foster, it provides a pedestrian link from the Tate Modern to *St Paul's Cathedral* on the north bank. Bankside's cultural regeneration is enhanced by the beautifully reconstructed *Shakespeare's Globe Theatre & Exhibition*, which is open all year round, although plays are only performed at the outdoor venue during the summer. Other attractions along the river, past Southwark Bridge towards London Bridge, include *Vinopolis*, an interactive celebration of wine, and the

Golden Hinde, a replica of Sir Francis Drake's flagship. *Southwark Cathedral*, with its Visitor Centre and Exhibition, is nestled under London Bridge, on the edge of the nearby *Borough Market* (website: www.boroughmarket.org.uk), a heaven for gourmets.
Bankside, SE1
Transport: London Underground Southwark, Blackfriars or London Bridge.

Tate Modern
Bankside, SE1
Tel: (020) 7887 8000 *or* 8008 (recorded information line).
E-mail: boxoffice@tate.org.uk
Website: www.tate.org.uk
Opening hours: Sun–Thurs 1000–1800, Fri and Sat 1000–2200.
Admission: Free (donations welcome); temporary exhibitions vary.

Shakespeare's Globe Theatre & Exhibition
21 New Globe Walk, Bankside, SE1
Tel: (020) 7902 1400.
Website: www.shakespeares-globe.org
Opening hours: Oct–Apr daily 1000–1700 (exhibition and theatre tour); May–Sep daily 0900–1200 (exhibition and theatre tour) and 1230–1600 (exhibition only).
Admission: £8.

Vinopolis
1 Bank End, Bankside, SE1
Tel: (0870) 444 4777.
Website: www.vinopolis.co.uk
Opening hours: Tues–Thurs and Sun 1200–1800; Mon, Fri and Sat 1200–2100.
Admission: £11.50.

Golden Hinde
St Mary Overie Dock, Cathedral Street, SE1
Tel: (020) 7403 0123 *or* (0870) 011 8700.
Website: www.goldenhinde.co.uk
Opening hours: Daily, hours vary, depending on pre-booked tours and scheduled events.
Admission: £2.75.

Southwark Cathedral
Montague Close, SE1
Tel: (020) 7367 6700.
Website: www.dswark.org/cathedral
Opening hours: Mon–Sat 1000–1800, Sun 1100–1700.
Admission: Free; £3 (exhibition); concessions available.

Palace of Westminster

The *Palace of Westminster* contains the *Houses of Parliament*, part of which is one of the city's most famous landmarks – Big Ben. Big Ben is actually the name of the huge bell, whose tolling tune is instantly recognisable, while the clock tower itself, which rises above the seat of British government, is called *St Stephen's*. The most ancient part of the whole Palace, *Westminster Hall*, is 900 years old. After almost total destruction by fire, the rest of the palace was rebuilt in neo-Gothic style, during the 19th century, to designs by Charles Barry.

All year round, free tours of the Palace of Westminster are available to UK residents, if they contact their MP who can arrange them. It is no longer possible to provide overseas visitors with small group tours. However, during late July/August and mid-September/early October, Parliament is in recess and the *Summer Opening of the Palace of Westminster* takes place. Extensive guided tours are offered for all visitors; these last about 75 minutes and include the *Royal Robing Rooms*, the *House of Lords* and the *House of Commons* and *Westminster Hall*. These are not free

and they must be booked in advance (in person or from *Firstcall*). All visitors who want to watch Parliament at work, rather than tour the Palace, can watch from the *Strangers' Gallery*. When Parliament is in session, there are two long queues (one for the Lords and one for the Commons) outside the Palace.
Parliament Square, SW1
Tel: (020) 7219 4272. Fax: (020) 7219 5839.
Website: www.parliament.uk
Transport: London Underground Westminster.
Summer Opening of the Palace of Westminster
Tel: (0870) 906 3773 (Firstcall).
Website: www.firstcalltickets.com
Opening hours: Mon–Sat 0915–1630 or 1315–1630 (depending on schedules).
Admission: £7 (plus £2 for foreign-language guide).

Westminster Abbey

Across Parliament Square is *Westminster Abbey* – a magnificent Gothic structure where innumerable members of the British royal family have been christened, married, crowned and interred. Consecrated under Edward the Confessor, in the 11th century, it was rebuilt over the next four centuries in Gothic style. Highlights include *Henry VII's Chapel*, *Poet's Corner* and the *Coronation Chair*.
Parliament Square, SW1
Tel: (020) 7654 4900. Fax: (020) 7654 4894.
Website: www.westminster-abbey.org
Transport: London Underground Westminster.
Opening hours: Mon–Fri 0930–1645 and Sat 0930–1445 (sightseeing; last admission one hour before closing); all day Sun (religious services only).
Admission: £6 (concessions available); £5 (pre-booked guided groups); services free.

Trafalgar Square

London Mayor Ken Livingstone is making the once traffic-congested and pigeon-infested *Trafalgar Square* a 'World Square' (website: www.worldsquares.com), pedestrianising more of this famous space and banning seed-sellers, in an attempt to stop what he considers a nuisance. The pedestrianisation will link *Nelson's Column* in the centre with the north side of the square, where the *National Gallery* is to be found. It houses an incredible collection of Western paintings from the 13th to the early 20th century, as well as frequent special exhibitions. Situated around the corner, the *National Portrait Gallery* displays the country's famous, infamous and forgotten, in the media of oil, watercolour, marble and photography. The new *Ondaatje Wing* includes a lecture theatre and restaurant. Opposite the gallery is the beautiful 18th-century neo-classical church, *St Martin-in-the-Fields*, which hosts regular concerts and has a café in the crypt.
Trafalgar Square, WC2
Transport: London Underground Charing Cross or Leicester Square.
National Gallery
Trafalgar Square, WC2
Tel: (020) 7747 2885.
Website: www.nationalgallery.org.uk
Opening hours: Thurs–Tues 1000–1800, Wed 1000–2100.
Admission: Free; temporary exhibitions vary.
National Portrait Gallery
St Martin's Place, WC2
Tel: (020) 7306 0055 *or* 7312 2463 (recorded information).
Website: www.npg.org.uk
Opening hours: Sat–Wed 1000–1800, Thurs and Fri 1000–2100.
Admission: Free.

St Martin-in-the-Fields
Trafalgar Square, WC2
Tel: (020) 7766 1100.
Website: www.stmartin-in-the-fields.org
Opening hours: Daily 0730–1830 (for sightseeing); concerts take place most nights of the week; crypt café opens later.
Admission: Free.

Buckingham Palace

Buckingham Palace, the London home of the Queen, is hugely popular with tourists. They flock to the palace, to witness royal pageantry dating back centuries at the *Changing of the Guard* ceremony, which takes place daily at 1130 April to July and on alternate days at other times of the year. In summer, there is also the chance to see inside a royal residence. The building, by John Nash and Edward Blore, was built around the shell of the older Buckingham House, in the 19th century. The rather drab façade was added in 1913. The 19 *State Rooms* of the palace, including the *Throne Room* and the *Picture Gallery*, are only open to the public during August and September, when the Queen moves to her Scottish residence. The recently refurbished and expanded *Queen's Gallery* is open to the public throughout the year. It displays a changing exhibition of selected works from the Royal Collection, which covers five centuries' worth of art collecting and treasures, now held in trust by the Queen for the nation. The 17-hectare (42-acre) garden, long hidden from view, is now also open to visitors touring the palace.
Buckingham Palace Road, SW1
Tel: (020) 7321 2233. Fax: (020) 7930 9625.
Website: www.royal.gov.uk
Transport: London Underground Green Park, Victoria or Hyde Park Corner.
Opening hours: Daily 0930–1615 (Aug–Sep), visitors should check the website for specific dates (Palace); daily 1030–1730 (Queen's Gallery).
Admission: £12 (Palace); £6.50 (Queen's Gallery); concessions available.

Tower Hill

The infamous royal fortress on *Tower Hill*, the *Tower of London*, was begun by William the Conqueror in 1078 and remained a royal residence until the mid 16th century. Today, it houses the priceless *Crown Jewels* and the *Royal Armouries* collection. The history of the tower is a catalogue of intrigue and bloodshed – key historical figures, including members of the royal family, were imprisoned, tortured and/or executed here. The nearby *Tower Bridge* – a prime example of Victorian architecture and engineering – spans the River Thames. Hydraulic machinery, hidden in twin neo-Gothic towers, lifts the central section to allow ships in and out of the Pool of London. Visitors can learn about the bridge in the *Tower Bridge Experience* or enjoy the excellent views towards Canary Wharf and the City of London. On the northeast side, the harbour at *St Katharine's Dock* marks the beginning of the London Docklands, while the warehouses to the south house the stylish *Design Museum*.
Tower Hill, EC3
Transport: London Underground Tower Hill or London Bridge.
Tower of London
Tel: (0870) 756 6060 (information) *or* 7070 (tickets).
Website: www.tower-of-london.org.uk
Opening hours: Mon–Sat 0900–1800, Sun 1000–1800 (Mar–Oct); Tues–Sat 0900–1700, Sun and Mon 1000–1700 (Nov–Feb); last admission one hour before closing.
Admission: £11.50 (concessions available).
Tower Bridge Experience
Tel: (020) 7403 3761. Fax: (020 7357 7935.
Website: www.towerbridge.org.uk
Opening hours: Daily 0930–1800 (last admission 1700).
Admission: £4.50 (concessions available).
Design Museum
28 Shad Thames, SE1
Tel: (020) 7940 8790.
Website: www.designmuseum.org
Opening hours: Daily 1000–1745.
Admission: £6 (concessions available).

Blackfriars Bridge and Tate Modern

Photo: Visit Britain

Photo: Visit Britain

Richmond Park

St Paul's Cathedral

The dome of *St Paul's Cathedral* is the third largest in the world and one of the most distinctive features of the London skyline. The present building, designed by Sir Christopher Wren, was completed in 1710, on the site of the original cathedral that was destroyed in the Great Fire of London in 1666. On the inside of the dome, the *Whispering Gallery* – named for its incredible acoustics – offers a close-up of the frescoes of the life of St Paul, which decorate the interior of the dome. From there, visitors can climb even higher, up to two further galleries, which are outdoors, offering magnificent views across the whole of London. Guided tours, lasting 90 minutes, are also available at 1100, 1130, 1330 and 1400 Monday to Saturday. Sunday services are held at 0800, 1015, 1130, 1515 and 1800.
Paternoster Square, EC4
Tel: (020) 7246 8348 (information line).
Website: www.stpauls.co.uk
Transport: London Underground St Paul's.
Opening hours: Mon–Sat 0830–1600 (sightseeing); sightseeing is restricted on Sun and religious holidays.
Admission: £6 (cathedral, galleries and crypt); £2.50 (guided tours); concessions available.

British Museum

The *British Museum* – the centrepiece of which is Lord Foster's glass-roofed *Great Court* – is one of the world's finest museums. Visitors must contend with a mind-boggling six million artefacts from all corners of the globe, plucked (or plundered) by collectors. The awesome scale of the museum means it is essential to select just a few of the 94 galleries for close attention. Highlights include the *Rosetta Stone*, a copy of the *Magna Carta* and the controversial *Parthenon Sculptures*, known as the *Elgin Marbles*, taken from the Parthenon in Athens, which Greece want back before the 2004 Olympic Games. A new British Museum souvenir shop next to the museum opened in 2000. A 90-minute 'Highlights' guided tour is available daily at 1030, 1300 and 1500.
Great Russell Street, WC1
Tel: (020) 7323 8299.
Website: www.thebritishmuseum.ac.uk
Transport: London Underground Russell Square.
Opening hours: Sat–Wed 1000–1730, Thurs and Fri 1000–2030.
Admission: Free; £8 (guided tour); concessions available.

South Kensington Museums

The *Victoria & Albert Museum* (*V&A*) is one of three major museums in South Kensington – the others being the *Natural History Museum* and the *Science Museum*. Founded in the 19th century, as a museum of the decorative arts, the V&A's 11km (seven miles) of corridors trace a path through paintings, jewellery, furniture and textiles dating from 3000BC to the present day. Highlights include the *Raphael Cartoons*, the sculpture court, the dress collection from 1700 onwards, as well as the 'British Galleries 1500–1900', a comprehensive history of British design and art.
The *Science Museum* was voted London Visitor Attraction of the Year in 2001 and 2002. It offers interactive exhibits on all kinds of scientific topics, from Space, Time or Weather to Agriculture or Food, from Computing or Mathematics to Nuclear Physics or Veterinary History. One key gallery is 'Making the Modern World', which includes objects such as early cars and computers.
The incredible Victorian building that is the *Natural History Museum* is divided into Earth Galleries and Life Galleries. The Earth Galleries explore our planet, while the Life Galleries explore the creatures that have inhabited it, from the dinosaurs to creepy crawlies. For live specimens, there is the outdoor Wildlife Garden. The new *Darwin Centre* will house the museum's extensive collections of specimens, which date as far back as the 16th century but also include recent new species discoveries. It will also allow visitors to interact with scientists using the collections and carrying out current research. Phase One is now open to the public, with Phase Two completing the project in 2007.
South Kensington, SW7
Transport: London Underground South Kensington.
V&A Museum
Cromwell Road, SW7
Tel: (020) 7942 2000 *or* (0870) 442 0808.
Website: www.vam.ac.uk
Opening hours: Thurs–Tues 1000–1745, Wed and last Fri of the month 1000–2200.
Admission: Free; temporary exhibitions might charge.
Science Museum
Exhibition Road, SW7
Tel: (020) 7942 4000 *or* (0870) 870 4771.
Website: www.sciencemuseum.org.uk
Opening hours: Daily 1000–1800.
Admission: Free.
Natural History Museum
Cromwell Road, SW7
Tel: (020) 7942 5000 *or* 5011.
Website: www.nhm.ac.uk
Opening hours: Mon–Sat 1000–1750, Sun 1100–1750.
Admission: Free.

Tate Britain

The *Tate Gallery of Modern British Art* opened in 1897, around the collection of sugar merchant Henry Tate. It now holds an unrivalled collection of English paintings from 1500 to the present day. Much 20th-century art has moved to the *Tate Modern* (see above), however, some remains on rotation here, from Gaudier Brzeska to Gilbert and George. There is also the 'Art Now' room, which shows a changing contemporary exhibition. The magnificent Turner Bequest is housed in the purpose-built *Clore Gallery*, with hundreds of Turner paintings on display.

Millbank, SW1
Tel: (020) 7887 8000/8.
Website: www.tate.org.uk
Transport: London Underground Pimlico.
Opening hours: Daily 1000–1750.
Admission: Free; temporary exhibitions vary.

Further Distractions

London's Parks

The parkland conurbation of *St James's Park*, *Green Park*, *Hyde Park* and *Kensington Gardens* stretches from Whitehall to Kensington in the west. St James's Park and Green Park are at the heart of royal and governmental London, cantilevered around Buckingham Palace, while Hyde Park's *Speaker's Corner* is the place for soapbox philosophers to harangue passers-by on Sunday mornings. Kensington Gardens contains the delightful *Serpentine Gallery*, as well as the glittering *Albert Memorial*. The more recent memorials to Diana, Princess of Wales currently take the form of a playground and a 11km (seven-mile) *Memorial Walk* through Kensington Gardens, Hyde Park, Green Park and St James's Park, although the official *Memorial Fountain* is due for completion in 2004.
Regent's Park, situated just north of Oxford Circus, is home to *London Zoo*, while immediately next door is *Primrose Hill*, with a fabulous view and chic village atmosphere. Of the many other parks in London, two are huge but located further afield – *Hampstead Heath* in north London and *Richmond Park* in south London. Hampstead Heath boasts acres of natural parkland, the 18th-century *Kenwood House*, numerous bathing ponds and another fantastic view over the capital. Richmond Park is the largest open space in London; first enclosed as a hunting park by King Charles I in 1637, it still boasts deer.
St James's Park
The Mall, Horse Guard's Road and Birdcage Walk, SW1
Tel: (020) 7930 1793.
Website: www.royalparks.gov.uk
Transport: London Underground St James's Park.
Opening hours: Daily dawn to dusk.
Admission: Free.
Green Park
Piccadilly, W1, The Mall and Constitution Hill, SW1
Tel: (020) 7930 1793.
Website: www.royalparks.gov.uk
Transport: London Underground Green Park.
Opening hours: Daily dawn to dusk.
Admission: Free.
Hyde Park
Bayswater Road, W2, Park Lane, W1, and Knightsbridge, SW1
Tel: (020) 7298 2100.
Website: www.royalparks.gov.uk
Transport: London Underground Hyde Park Corner, Marble Arch, Lancaster Gate or Knightsbridge.
Opening hours: Daily 0500–2400.
Admission: Free.
Kensington Gardens
Bayswater Road, W2, and Kensington Road, SW7
Tel: (020) 7298 2100.
Website: www.royalparks.gov.uk
Transport: London Underground Lancaster Gate, Queensway or High Street Kensington.
Opening hours: Daily dawn to dusk.
Admission: Free.

Serpentine Gallery
Kensington Gardens
Tel: (020) 7298 1515.
Website: www.serpentinegallery.org
Transport: London Underground Knightsbridge, Lancaster Gate or South Kensington.
Opening hours: Daily 1000–1800.
Admission: Free.

Regent's Park
Prince Albert Road, NW1/NW8, Albany Street, NW1, Marylebone Road, NW1, and Park Road, NW8
Tel: (020) 7486 7905.
Website: www.royalparks.gov.uk
Transport: London Underground Regent's Park, Great Portland Street, Baker Street, Camden Town or St John's Wood.
Opening hours: Daily dawn to dusk.
Admission: Free.

London Zoo
Outer Circle, Regent's Park
Tel: (020) 7722 3333.
Website: www.londonzoo.com
Transport: London Underground Camden Town.
Opening hours: Daily 1000–1630 (mid-Feb–early Mar); daily 1000–1730 (early Mar–late Oct); daily 1000–1600 (late Oct–mid-Feb).
Admission: £12 (concessions available).

Primrose Hill
Primrose Hill Road, NW3, Regent's Park Road, NW1, and Prince Albert Road, NW1/NW8
Tel: (020) 7486 7905.
Website: www.royalparks.gov.uk
Transport: London Underground Chalk Farm.
Opening hours: Daily 24 hours.
Admission: Free.

Hampstead Heath
East Heath Road, NW3, and Highgate Road, NW5, and others
Tel: (020) 7482 7073.
Website: www.cityoflondon.gov.uk
Transport: London Underground Hampstead, Belsize Park or Highgate; Silverlink Metro Hampstead Heath or Gospel Oak.
Opening hours: Daily 24 hours.
Admission: Free.

Kenwood House
Hampstead Lane, NW3
Website: www.english-heritage.org.uk
Transport: London Underground Hampstead, Belsize Park or Highgate; Silverlink Metro Hampstead Heath or Gospel Oak.
Opening hours: Daily 1000–1730 (Apr–Sep); daily 1000–1700 (Oct); daily 1000–1600 (Nov–Mar); opens at 1030 Wed and Fri.
Admission: Free.

Richmond Park
Roehampton Vale, SW15, Queens Road, Richmond
Tel: (020) 8948 3209.
Website: www.royalparks.gov.uk
Transport: London Underground/Silverlink Metro to Richmond, then bus 371.
Opening hours: Daily dawn to dusk.
Admission: Free.

Highgate Cemetery

Resonating with the ghosts of such luminaries as Karl Marx and George Eliot, *Highgate Cemetery* is one of London's most extraordinary places. With some of the finest Victorian funerary architecture in the country, many of the memorials are architecturally listed sites. The East Cemetery contains Karl Marx's grave and monumental bust.

Nelson above Trafalgar Square

The West Cemetery contains the remarkable Lebanon Circle, formed of 20 family catacombs surrounding an ancient cedar tree, as well as other notable monuments. Visitors can freely explore the East Cemetery but can only visit the West Cemetery by booking the one-hour guided tours in advance (by telephone).
Swains Lane, N6
Tel: (020) 8340 1834.
Website: http://highgate-cemetery.org
Transport: London Underground Archway or Highgate.
Opening hours: East Cemetery: Mon–Fri 1000–1700, Sat and Sun 1100–1700 (Apr–Oct); Mon–Fri 1000–1600, Sat and Sun 1100–1600 (Nov–Mar); last admission half an hour before closing. West Cemetery tours: Mon–Fri 1400 (Mar–Nov only); Sat and Sun 1100, 1200, 1300, 1400 and 1500; Mon–Fri 1400 (Mar–Nov only); Sat and Sun 1100, 1200, 1300, 1400, 1500 and 1600 (Apr–Oct).
Admission: £2 (East Cemetery); £3 (West Cemetery standard tour).

Tours of the City

The *Britain and London Visitor Centre* (see *Tourist Information*) can provide full details on all tour providers in London.

Walking Tours

A variety of guided walks are available from several operators, although the most comprehensive tours are offered by *The Original London Walks* (tel: (020) 7624 3978 *or* 9255 (recorded information); website: www.walks.com). The price is £5 for a two-hour tour. The company also offers themed tours on a huge variety of subjects, including 'Jack the Ripper' and 'The Beatles'. Tours start and finish near a Tube station; there is no need to book and walkers can just turn up at the appropriate station, all of which are listed on the website's 'timetable'. *Mystery Walks* (tel: (020) 8558 9446; website: www.tourguides.org.uk) also offer 'Jack the Ripper' tours, as well as 'Haunted London'. Both cost £5 and take approximately two hours. Booking is required for the 'Haunted London' tour.

Alternatively, for self-guided walks, the *Silver Jubilee Walkway* (website: www.jubileewalkway.com) has been extended from the original three kilometres (two miles) along the South Bank of the River Thames (between Lambeth and Tower bridges) to include much of the City and the West End. Also, starting at the Tower of London, 21 explanatory plaques trace a route along the Roman *London Wall*.

Bus Tours

Various competing companies offer similar bus tours of London's sights. Tickets are usually valid for 24 hours and passengers can hop on and off at various attractions en route. The *Big Bus Company* (tel: (020) 7233 9533; website: www.bigbus.co.uk) offers three different 90-minute sightseeing routes at £16 each, with departure points close to many of London's attractions. *Original London Sightseeing Tours* (tel: (020) 8877 1722; website: www.theoriginaltour.com) also offers various sightseeing bus tours.

Boat Tours

Westminster Pier is the main embarkation point for river trips. From here, there are services east (downstream) or west (upstream). *City Cruises* (tel: (020) 7740 0400; website: www.citycruises.com) operates sightseeing cruises east to Tower Pier, costing £5.20 single or £6.30 return (journey time – 30 minutes each way), and Greenwich Pier, costing £6.50 single or £8 return (journey time – 1 hour each way). City Cruises also offers a 'Red Rover' day pass for its tours, enabling visitors to hop on and off at four different stops for £8.50. Tickets must be purchased at the ticket office before boarding.
Going west, summer services by WPSA (tel: (020) 7930 2062 *or* 4721; website: www.wpsa.co.uk) depart from Westminster Pier upriver to Kew Gardens, Richmond and Hampton Court. Tickets must be purchased before boarding and cost £9 single or £15 return for the 90-minute cruise to Kew, or £12 single or £18 return to Hampton Court, which takes over three hours (each way).
Catamaran Cruises (tel: (020) 7987 1185) provides multi-lingual cruises from Waterloo, Westminster and Embankment piers. These 50-minute non-stop circular cruises cost £7 or £7.50 from June to

Photo: Visit Britain

Hotel dining

August. Catamaran Cruises also operates a hop-on, hop-on service, covering Embankment Pier, Waterloo Pier, Bankside, Tower Pier and Greenwich Pier. Prices start from £3, although a day's worth of unlimited travel on all Catamaran Cruises services is available with the 'River Pass'. Tickets cost £10.50 and must be purchased at the ticket office before boarding.

Other Tours

Frog Tours (tel: (020) 7928 3132; website: www. frogtours.com) runs unconventional tours on an amphibious craft, which depart from County Hall and rumble through London's streets, taking in Whitehall, Trafalgar Square and Buckingham Palace, before plunging into the River Thames for a 30-minute cruise. Single tickets for the 70-minute tour cost £16.50.

Excursions

For a Half Day

Kew Gardens: Situated on the western edge of the city, beside the River Thames, the *Royal Botanic Gardens*, Richmond, Surrey, TW9 (tel: (020) 8940 1171; website: www.rbgkew.org.uk), is a 121-hectare (300-acre) site, first planted in the 17th century and now a horticulturist's heaven – designated a World Heritage Site by UNESCO in 2003. The glasshouses, including the beautiful *Palm House*, shelter rare orchids and palms. Transport to the gardens is by London Underground to Kew Gardens; or by train from Waterloo to Kew Bridge, which is also served by the Silverlink Metro. Admission is £7.50 (concessions available). The gardens are open Monday to Friday 0930–1830, Saturday and Sunday 0930–1930 (April to August), closing earlier as winter sets in.
London Wetland Centre: *London Wetland Centre*, Queen Elizabeth's Walk, Barnes, SW13 (tel: (020) 8409 4400; website: www.wetlandcentre.org.uk), is the first wetland environment ever to be created in a capital city. The former 42-hectare (105-acre) disused reservoir has been transformed into an oasis for a multitude of watery wildlife, with the addition of 30 reformed lakes, ponds and marshland. With 250m (819ft) of boardwalk, three kilometres (two miles) of pathways and seven viewing hides, the centre provides close-up access to water-loving birds, mammals and insects from across Britain and around the world. There is also a visitor centre. The centre is open daily 0930–1800 (summer) and 0930–1700 (winter); admission costs £6.75 (concessions available). Transport is by London Underground to Hammersmith, then bus 283 (the 'Duck Bus' shuttle),

directly to the centre, or by train from Waterloo to Barnes, followed by a short walk.

For a Whole Day

Brighton: Known as 'London on Sea', *Brighton* is located 97km (60 miles) from London, on the south coast. Easily and relatively cheaply accessible from Victoria station or Kings Cross Thameslink, Brighton's young demographic (including residents of the calibre of Fat Boy Slim), vibrant nightlife, top-class restaurants and relaxed vibe certainly make it the trendy coastal retreat of choice. Attractions include the *Royal Pavilion* (George IV's summer retreat), the newly renovated *Museum of Brighton* and the old town around *The Lanes*. The *Brighton Tourist Information Office*, 10 Bartholomew Square (tel: (0906) 711 2255; website: www. tourism. brighton.co.uk), can provide more information.
Oxford: The 'dreaming spires' are located 97km (60 miles) northwest of central London. Harbouring one of the oldest universities in Europe, *Oxford* is not only steeped in history, architecture and traditions (such as punting on the river) but also a bustling commercial city with good shops and excellent pubs. Trains to Oxford depart from Paddington station, while frequent 24-hour coaches leave from Victoria – the *Oxford Express* X90 from Victoria coach station and the *Oxford Tube* from Grosvenor Gardens outside Victoria train station. The *Oxford Tourist Information Office*, The Old School, Gloucester Green (tel: (01865) 726 871; website: www.visitoxford.org), can provide further information.

ACCOMMODATION

All hotel bills are subject to VAT (Value Added Tax) of 17.5%, which is usually added to the bill at the end, although it might be included in the rate given for special deals. Many corporate and weekend rates are available, including the increasingly good-value Internet-only rates for many London hotels.
The prices quoted below are the lowest standard rates for a double room, including VAT and excluding breakfast, unless otherwise specified.

Business

Charlotte Street Hotel

Situated in Charlotte Street, which is a Mecca for restaurants, not far from the media companies of Soho, this hip hotel has a fresh, young feel in comfortable townhouse surroundings. A vast lobby

on the ground floor leads to a drawing room and library – the decor is bright and light throughout, with modern art. The hotel has 52 guest rooms, including four loft suites with high ceilings and large windows, and two spectacular open-plan Penthouse Suites. Each room is equipped with a large writing desk, CD player, video player, two-line telephone with voice-mail, modem point and fax outlet, as well as a personal mobile phone. Private meeting rooms for up to 50 delegates can be hired and there is a state-of-the-art screening room. There is a lively brasserie-style restaurant, which also provides room service.
15–17 Charlotte Street, W1
Tel: (020) 7806 2000. Fax: (020) 7806 2002.
E-mail: charlotte@firmdale.com
Website: www.charlottestreethotel.com
Price: From £220.

Holiday Inn London Heathrow

Opened in August 2000, the *Holiday Inn Heathrow* is a modern, efficient hotel overlooking the airport, with views over the Western runway. Ideal for those who require proximity to Heathrow, all rooms are triple glazed so that the airport activity can be seen but not heard. Designed with function rather than aesthetics in mind, the hotel is comfortable yet impersonal, with 230 almost identical rooms all equipped with power showers, satellite TV, desks and telephone with modem point. For business purposes, there are 16 meeting rooms available for hire, as well as a business centre providing secretarial and translation services. The hotel also has a mini gym.
Bath Road, Heathrow Airport, West Drayton, Middlesex
Tel: (020) 8990 0000. Fax: (020) 8564 7744.
E-mail: enquiries@london-heathrowholidayinn.com
Website: www.london-heathrow.holiday-inn.com
Price: From £155.

The Landmark London

Overlooking Regent's Park, this five-star hotel – awarded the RAC Gold Ribbon award year after year – offers excellent business amenities in luxurious surroundings. The striking Victorian architecture centres on an eight-storey glass-roofed atrium, infusing the hotel with daylight. The 299 guest rooms are spacious and well equipped with desk, high-speed Internet access and three telephone lines. Each guest is given a personal e-mail address and fax number on arrival. There are ten function rooms with the latest audiovisual technology and a secretarial service is available. As an antidote to work, there is a gym, complete with pool and steam rooms. The restaurant, *John Burton-Race at The Landmark*, has two Michelin stars.
222 Marylebone Road, NW1
Tel: (020) 7631 8000. Fax: (020) 7631 8080.
E-mail: info@landmarklondon.co.uk
Website: www.landmarklondon.co.uk
Price: From £175.

The Trafalgar

With its prime location right at the heart of central London, on the corner of Trafalgar Square, *The Trafalgar* is the Hilton's first attempt at a 'style' hotel and a successful attempt at that, making it on to *Condé Nast Traveller's* 'Hot List 2002'. From the ground floor, which houses *Rockwell* (see *Bars* in *Nightlife*), up, this hotel is all about clean, contemporary design. The 129 rooms and suites come in soft, relaxing colours (sky-blue or cream), with simple modern furniture. All rooms include direct-dial telephone, CD player, Sony Playstation and Internet access. The executive rooms and suites all have a view of the City or Trafalgar Square. This hotel is not all style and no substance, however; the facilities for the business traveller are extensive, including meeting rooms, audiovisual and video-conferencing equipment, mobile phone hire and photocopying and secretarial services. As well as the bar, Rockwell, there is the mainly organic, stylish restaurant, *Jago*.

2 Spring Gardens, Trafalgar Square, London SW1
Tel: (020) 7870 2900. Fax: (020) 7870 2911.
Website: www.thetrafalgar.hilton.com
Price: From £169.

Luxury

The Lanesborough

Minutes from Buckingham Palace, this lavish hotel treats its guests like royalty. Formerly Viscount Lanesborough's country home, the hotel is now a St Regis Hotel but remains true to its Regency building, with ornate furnishings and decor. Guests can expect 24-hour butler service, personalised business cards and stationery on arrival. Each of the 95 guest rooms and suites are filled with period furniture and 21st-century technology, including a mobile phone, CD and DVD player, computer with Internet access and the latest software packages and digital television. There are six private dining rooms for entertaining and meetings, as well as a small business centre. Michael Jackson, Madonna and Sylvester Stallone have all stayed here.

Hyde Park Corner, SW1
Tel: (020) 7259 5599. Fax: (020) 7259 5606.
E-mail: info@lanesborough.com
Website: www.lanesborough.com
Price: From £275.

The Ritz

Since 1906, *The Ritz* in London has been providing exemplary service to its well-heeled guests. An elegant building overlooking Green Park, the interior is fastidiously decorated in Louis XVI style with marble columns, rich fabrics and antique furniture. The guest rooms are furnished in soothing pastel colours and two members of staff are on hand to service each room. For business matters, a computer, printer and scanner can be arranged in-room, as can secretarial support. Two large meeting rooms holding up to 100 delegates can be hired. Formal meals can be taken in the chandelier-filled restaurant, while the famous Ritz tea can be enjoyed in the Palm Court at 1530 or 1700, for which it is necessary to book well in advance.

150 Piccadilly, W1
Tel: (020) 7300 2308 *or* 7493 8181. Fax: (020) 7493 2687.
E-mail: enquire@theritzlondon.com
Website: www.theritzlondon.com
Price: From £365.

Moderate

Hampstead Village Guest House

Escape the city's bustle at this charming bed and breakfast situated in one of London's most sought after residential areas, just 20 minutes by Tube from central London and a short walk from beautiful Hampstead Heath. Tucked away from a high street packed with stylish boutiques and bistros, the

Hampstead Village Guest House is a three-storey Victorian house with seven bedrooms and an adjoining self-contained apartment. The family home of proprietor Annemarie van der Meer, paying guests have been welcomed here for the past 20 years. The ambience is distinctly homely with eclectic, bohemian furnishings, a family dog, floor-to-ceiling bookshelves and a rambling garden. Guest rooms have basic facilities, including a small fridge, kettle, tea and coffee, hairdryer, direct-dial telephone and TV.

2 Kemplay Road, NW3
Tel: (020) 7435 8679. Fax: (020) 7794 0254.
E-mail: info@hampsteadguesthouse.com
Website: www.hampsteadguesthouse.com
Price: £72 (shared bathroom) or £84 (en suite).

Ibis Hotel, Euston

This French-owned chain hotel represents excellent value for money in a central location, just seconds from Euston London Underground and railway station. The hotel is basic in design, with 380 bedrooms, an informal restaurant and bar, and a private underground car park. The bedrooms are small, clean and uniformly kitted out with desk, chair and colour TV. The hotel does have a rather sterile, impersonal atmosphere, however, and is lacking any luxury features. However, its bargain rate means that it is almost always full. Conference facilities are available for groups of up to 800 people.

3 Cardington Street, NW1
Tel: (020) 7388 7777. Fax: (020) 7388 0001.
Website: www.ibishotel.com
Price: From £74.95.

Other Recommendations

23 Greengarden House

For those who want to feel like a London resident rather than a visitor, renting a four-star serviced apartment in the heart of the West End could be the perfect option. Set in the pretty, pedestrianised St Christopher's Place, *Greengarden House* contains 15 one-bedroom and eight two-bedroom apartments. Each apartment has its own living room, kitchen and bathroom, and comes fully equipped with every household appliance, including two telephone lines with voice-mail, modem point and ISDN line. Most are decorated with classical furniture in soft, warm colours but there are also five 'contemporary' apartments in cooler colours, with crisper, cleaner lines.

St Christopher's Place, W1
Tel: (020) 7935 9191. Fax: (020) 7935 8858.
E-mail: info@greengardenhouse.com
Website: www.greengardenhouse.com
Price: From £185.

myhotel Chelsea

Situated in a quiet tree-lined street, minutes from Brompton Cross, the designer shopping Mecca, *myhotel Chelsea* is the second London hotel from the myhotel team. Marketed as *Sex and the City* glamour meets *Brideshead Revisited* English country house, the new hotel is already getting noticed (it made *Condé Nast Traveller*'s 'Hot List 2003'). The hotel promises a haven of tranquillity and a stay that is individually tailored to each guest's need. Designed following feng shui principles, the interior has a sexy eclectic style. The 45 guest rooms are decorated in peaceful pastel colours, with contemporary and antique furniture, soft furnishings and fresh flowers. As well as the Eastern-style Thai suite, with its own steam room,

there are the two Red Rooms, situated behind the bar, designed for decadence and indulgence. All rooms have CD/DVD player, flat-screen TVs, telephone and ISDN access, cashmere throws and hot water bottles. The hotel also has two function rooms, a bar-restaurant, a small gym, a spa/treatment room, a resident-only conservatory with complimentary e-mail and refreshments. Guest services include personal shoppers, massage, meditation and botox.

35 Ixworth Place, SW3
Tel: (020) 7225 7500.
E-mail: mychelsea@myhotels.co.uk
Website: www.myhotels.co.uk
Price: From £217.

RESTAURANTS

The selected restaurants have been divided into five categories: Gastronomic, Business, Trendy, Budget and Personal Recommendations. The restaurants are listed alphabetically within these different categories, which serve as guidelines rather than absolute definitions of the establishments.

All restaurant bills are subject to VAT (Value Added Tax) of 17.5%, which is usually included in the prices given. A service charge (usually 12.5%) might be included in the prices stated on the menu but it is more likely to be added to the bill at the end. This is technically an optional charge but it would be very unusual to ask for it to be removed. Where 'Service is not included', a tip of at least 10% is expected, although 12–15% is becoming more common. Diners should check the bill thoroughly, as tipping is not required on top of a service charge.

The prices quoted below are for an average three-course meal for one person and for a bottle of house wine or cheapest equivalent; they include VAT but do not include service charge or tip.

Gastronomic

Le Gavroche

Since its opening in 1967 by brothers Albert and Michel Roux, the smart, formal, dark and classically French *Le Gavroche*, with two Michelin stars, has been setting the culinary benchmark for the British restaurant scene. Currently run by Michel Roux Junior, with the assistance of award-winning maitre d', Silvano Giraldin, diners can expect the highest standards of food, wine and service – at prices to match. Highly praised dishes include the artichoke hearts with foie gras, truffles and chicken mousse, the grilled sea bream with pea and wild mushroom sauce and the baked sea bass with tiger prawns. Reservations essential. No lunch Saturday. Closed Sunday.

43 Upper Brook Street, W1
Tel: (020) 7408 0881. Fax: (020) 7491 4387.
E-mail: bookings@le-gavroche.com
Website: www.le-gavroche.co.uk
Price: £70; £40 (set lunch). Wine: £20.

Lindsay House

Irish-born chef Richard Corrigan has made this Soho townhouse his home and gained a Michelin star in the process, by creating impeccable dishes in a grand but comfortable environment. Arriving at the discreet front door, diners must ring the bell to gain admittance, which heralds the beginning of an evening where the attentive staff treats them like the

A typical London pub

houseguests of a rich, absent host. The 1740s building quietly exudes charm, while guests pad up carpeted stairs to a small, elegant but simple dining room, with white walls, oil paintings, a grand fireplace and comfortable chairs. It is impossible not to feel at home, although there are two private dining rooms for those who really wish to be cocooned, as well as one other public dining room on the ground floor. The menu changes daily (Richard Corrigan tries to source all his ingredients from small suppliers) but, from the tiny wafer-thin cheesy biscuits served with a champagne cocktail, every dish is perfectly balanced, well presented and beautifully cooked.

Recommended starters include the Dutch white asparagus with langoustines and morels or the melt-in-the-mouth foie gras tart with sautéed foie gras and Muscat grape, followed by the best end of lamb with sweetbreads and seared kidneys and the native scallops with pork belly and spiced carrots. For dessert, the Sauternes jelly, poached pear and blue cheese Bavarois is a dreamy dish, where a tiny piece of perfect pear is suspended in a delicate jelly and served with the creamiest Bavarois. With an accessible and distinguished wine list, overseen by Thierry Talibon, *amuse bouche* between every course and petits fours to round the whole thing off, nothing is forgotten in this most memorable establishment. Reservations essential. No lunch Saturday. Closed Sunday.
21 Romilly Street, W1
Tel: (020) 7439 0450. Fax: (020) 437 7349.
E-mail: richardcorrigan@lindsayhouse.co.uk
Website: www.lindsayhouse.co.uk
Price: £48. Wine: £20.

Locanda Locatelli

Giorgio Locatelli, who has been a well-respected chef behind the scenes at various London Italian restaurants for some time, has finally emerged into the limelight with a TV show (*Tony and Giorgio*) and, this, his very own restaurant with one Michelin star. An instant hit, *Locanda Locatelli* serves up delectable Italian dishes in sleek surroundings with a glamorous 1970s feel. Four courses are recommended, so diners are able to enjoy an antipasto – such as the lightest salad of borlotti beans, red onions and tuna – but not miss

out on a pasta dish, such as the rave-worthy veal shank ravioli. Mains include a decent number of fish and meat dishes, served simply with one or two other ingredients, such as John Dory with potatoes and peas (vegetarians might be forced to indulge in a second pasta dish), while desserts should not be missed. Reservations well in advance are essential.
8 Seymour Street, London W1
Tel: (020) 7935 9088 (reservations) *or* 8390 (confirmations/cancellations). Fax: (020) 7935 1149.
Website: www.locandalocatelli.com
Price: £45 (three courses); £55 (four courses). Wine: £12.

Nobu

This devastatingly fashionable restaurant, located on the first floor of the Metropolitan Hotel, provides award-winning Japanese cuisine melded with South American influences in a relaxed yet classy environment. Smiling, uniformed members of staff guide the diner through an extensive menu with head chef Mark Edwards at the helm. The presentation is impeccable and the food itself unique. Signature dishes include black cod marinated in miso, chocolate cake with tea-tree ice cream or sake with gold leaf. The place is also one of the best spots in town for sushi. There is plenty of opportunity for celebrity spotting. Reservations essential. No lunch weekends.
19 Old Park Lane, W1
Tel: (020) 7447 4747. Fax: (020) 7447 4749.
Website: www.noburestaurants.com
Price: £85. Wine: £18.

Restaurant Gordon Ramsay

The only London restaurant with three Michelin stars, this remains the best place to experience Gordon Ramsay at work. In a comfortable but fairly neutral room, the focus is entirely on the food. All dishes are superb and might include the starter of a mosaique of foie gras served three ways – pressed, confit and smoked – with marinated figs and pickled girolles, followed by the fillet of Aberdeen Angus beef with caramelised pig's trotters, quail's eggs, sautéed baby artichokes and truffle sauce. A seven-course set dinner is available for £80 for those who wish to experience the full gastronomic

experience. Reservations essential. Closed Saturday and Sunday.
68 Royal Hospital Road, SW3
Tel: (020) 7352 4441. Fax: (020) 7352 3334.
Website: www.gordonramsay.com
Price: £65; £35 (set lunch). Wine: £25.

Business

Incognico

Nico Ladenis' unfussy West End restaurant provides the best-value set menu in London. For a meagre £12.50, at lunchtime or early evening, diners can enjoy a well-composed three-course meal, with a choice of two dishes per course, from a menu that changes weekly. Dishes might include a brandade of salt cod in crispy pastry, followed by pork belly with fresh sauerkraut and Madeira sauce, and key lime tart. A decent mainly French à la carte menu is also available, including many fish dishes but few entirely vegetarian ones. The interior is cosy and uncluttered but the service can be patchy. A decent wine list has a helpful (or pretentious) adjective describing each wine. Closed Sunday.
117 Shaftesbury Avenue, WC2
Tel: (020) 7836 8866. Fax: (020) 7240 9525.
Price: £40; £12.50 (set lunch/1730–1900). Wine: £15.

The Ivy

The restaurant of choice for many a celebrity, *The Ivy* is notoriously difficult to dine at without a famous name or advance booking of at least six weeks. Telephoning to reserve involves an intimidating call-back system. Once inside, however, the comfortable decor suggests a gentleman's club with dark wooden panelling and diamond-patterned stained-glass windows. The food is simple but of high quality and includes traditional British favourites, such as bangers and mash, potted shrimps or braised beef in stout, along with more European recipes, such as pork tenderloin on lemon polenta. The cosy environment, pleasing food and guaranteed celebrity spotting makes The Ivy an impressive venue for a business meal.
1 West Street, WC2
Tel: (020) 7836 4751. Fax: (020) 240 9333.
Price: £50. Wine: £15.

The Oxo Tower Restaurant, Bar and Brasserie

For panoramic views of London, there is no better place to eat than the restaurant at the top of the Thameside *Oxo Tower*. In good weather, diners can eat on the terrace, otherwise they take a seat in the stylish minimalist interior. At lunchtime, the place is a favourite venue for business meetings, with light, well-prepared food and a set menu available (£28.50 for three courses). In the evening, the place takes on a more festive mood, with its busy bar set against the stunning London nightscape. The cuisine is modern European, with dishes such as monkfish with oxtail, sprouting broccoli and parsnips or spiced tenderloin of lamb, peas, mint and coriander, however, too often the dishes sound promising but fail to shine. The service can also be poor but with those views The Oxo Tower remains perennially popular. Reservations recommended.
Oxo Tower Wharf, Barge House Street, SE1
Tel: (020) 7803 3888. Fax: (020) 7803 3838.
E-mail: oxo.reservations@harveynichols.co.uk
Website: www.harveynichols.com
Price: £45. Wine: £13.95.

Photo: Visit Britain

The Real Greek

This smart restaurant attracts a fair number of 'suits' for lunch, due to its proximity to the City, although a friendly staff and rustic detailing, such as some beautiful plates, make it a relaxed and comfortable place in which to eat. The homemade bread, with its unusual flavours, is a great introduction to the authentic regional Greek cuisine that might be unfamiliar to many diners. As a starter, the delicious plates of three or four different *mezedes* are recommended, such as the one that includes *dolmades, gigandes plaki* (oven-cooked giant beans), *pastourma* (cured beef sirloin) and pan-fried *kefalotiri* (ewe's milk cheese). Mains are simple yet intensely flavoured dishes, usually extraordinarily tender, such as the veal *stifado* (slow-cooked casserole with button onions, spices and red wine) or the lamb fricassee (stew cooked with green dandelions, leeks, cos lettuce and herbs). Prices are expensive but with such a good-value set menu, available at lunchtime and 1730–1900, there is no excuse not to eat here. Knowledgeable staff can help with the all-Greek wine list. Next door, the Mezedopolio serves wine and meze individually. Reservations recommended.
14–15 Hoxton Market, N1
Tel: (020) 7739 8212. Fax: (020) 7739 4910.
Website: www.therealgreek.co.uk
Price: £35; £13.50 (three-course set menu); £10 (two-course set menu). Wine: £11.70.

Sumosan

Stylish Japanese restaurants seem to be the thing at the moment and *Sumosan*, opened in May 2002, is one of the latest pretenders to the crown held by Nobu (see *Gastronomic* above). Executive chef Bubker Behlit has created a menu that pleases lovers of sushi and sashimi, as well as offering tempura, soups, salads and extensive and adventurous appetisers (such as ebi fry, tiger prawns and scallops deep-fried in three different crusts) and mains (such as foie gras teppanyaki). With stunning presentation, luxurious decor and prices to match, this place is good for impressing business clients. Reservations recommended. No lunch Saturday. Closed Sunday.
26 Albemarle Street, W1
Tel: (020) 7495 5999. Fax: (020) 7355 1247.
E-mail: info@sumosan.com
Website: www.sumosan.com
Price: £30. Wine: £13.

Trendy

Cigala

Jake Hodges, one of the original founders of Moro, is the owner-chef of this wonderful Spanish restaurant, with big windows, light wood and simple cream decor. *Cigala* can get busy and noisy, and the tables are a little close together, but it always remains relaxed, friendly and sophisticated, rather like the food. From the starters, the salads are always fresh and delicious combinations, such as the asparagus, broad beans, pea and mint salad. Recommended mains include the fish dishes, such as the skate with garlic, guindilla peppers and balsamic vinegar with braised spinach. There is a charming, small tapas bar in the basement, where it is possible for diners to eat as much of the incredible bread alongside excellent tapas (the meatballs and king prawns are highly recommended). Reservations recommended. Closed Sunday.
54 Lamb's Conduit Street, WC1
Tel: (020) 7405 1717.
E-mail: tasty@cigala.co.uk

Website: www.cigala.co.uk
Price: £25; £18 (three-course set menu); £15 (two-course set menu). Wine: £18.

The Electric Brasserie

Opened in 2002 as part of the refurbishment of Portobello's famous Electric Cinema, England's first purpose-built cinema. A major revamp brought in soft leather seating and chic wooden tables – and a suitably trendy following, coming for breakfast, lunch, dinner or just drinks in the bar area. With a huge range of brasserie-style dishes and great seafood available all day long, this comes as no surprise; it is especially popular for Sunday brunch – comfort food like chunky steak sandwiches or hamburgers with red onion marmalade. The à la carte menu gets slightly grander, with the addition of dishes like grilled dover sole or *chateaubriand* for two. There is also a joint on a trolley, which varies every evening but all Sunday is Aberdeen Angus beef with Yorkshire pudding. Reservations recommended Thursday to Saturday.
191 Portobello Road, W11
Tel: (020) 7908 9696.
Website: www.electricbrasserie.com
Price: £30. Wine: £13.

Hakkasan

This chic restaurant is situated down an alley in central London, which deters passing trade and helps heighten *Hakkasan's* sense of exclusivity. Once down the smart slate steps and past reception, the blue glass doors open on to a stunning, dimly lit room, where a beautiful latticework screen encases the dining area. Unfortunately, the effect is best seen from the lounge-bar area outside, because once within this inner sanctum, with tables too close together and an ill-advised music policy, the magical effect is lost somewhat. Nevertheless, the food makes up for everything – this is one of only five Chinese restaurants with a Michelin star. The lunchtime dim sum is so excellent that it is difficult to single out any one dish. Nevertheless, unmissable mains include the roasted silver cod with champagne and Chinese honey. However, just soaking up the atmosphere with the other trendy people is a viable alternative, given the exquisite, exotic concoctions on the famous cocktail list (all £8). Reservations highly recommended.
8 Hanway Place, W1
Tel: (020) 7927 7000. Fax: (020) 7907 1889.
Price: £45. Wine: £22.

Mash

Brainchild of entrepreneur Oliver Peyton, who also owns the Atlantic Bar and Grill, *Mash* is a novel combination of restaurant, bar, micro-brewery and deli, housed in a bright, open space just off Oxford Street. The bar and micro-brewery downstairs is open until 0200, serving a trendy post-work crowd stylish cocktails, heady own beers and Modern European dishes ranging from the snacky to the more substantial. Enormous beer vats encased in glass line the back wall, while chairs are space-age pods; there is also a sunken cushioned seating area. Upstairs, the quieter restaurant is more exclusive and the food slightly classier, such as roast rack of lamb with ratatouille of courgettes and peppers with green olive tapenade or baked halibut with sautéed potato, artichoke and Swiss chard with anchovy salsa. Trendy places come and go but this remains a reliably stylish West End choice. Closed Sunday.
19–21 Great Portland Street, W1
Tel: (020) 7637 5555. Fax: (020) 7637 7333.
E-mail: info@gruppo.co.uk

Website: www.gruppo.co.uk
Price: £15 (bar); £30 (restaurant). Wine: £13.50. Beer: From £3.20 (pint).

Sketch

French chef Pierre Gagnaire's first venture in London, this enormous 18th-century house has been divided into four different culinary experiences, all extravagantly designed by Mourad Mazouz. *The Parlour* on the ground floor is a frou-frou tea room, with pastries displayed in a jewellery case. *The West Bar*, almost space age with red lighting and pod bar stools, is *the* place to drink at the moment and also serves a 'quick but refined lunch'. *The Gallery* is entirely white and filled with white furniture but has coloured light emanating from the ceiling and a huge frieze of video art; it serves lunch and dinner. However, the piece de resistance is *The Lecture Room*, with its dramatic design featuring luxurious padded walls studded with gold and its dramatic prices (main courses go for £75). The menu is divided into sections, so the starters consist of Red Mullet, Vegetables, Charcuterie, Langoustines and Crab. Mains are famed for unusual pairings, the sections include Poultry and White Truffles, Beef and Caviar, John Dory and Scallops. Reservations essential. Closed Sunday. The Lecture Room closed Monday as well.
9 Conduit Street, W1
Tel: (0870) 777 4488.
Website: www.pierregagnaire.com
Price: £120 (Lecture Room); £60 (Gallery). Wine: £30.

Budget

Café Emm

This brasserie serves the best-value good food in Soho, so its no-booking policy means that a queue is inevitable unless it is very early evening. As well as various starters and snacks, there is a selection of main courses at £5.95,

Photo: Visit Britain

The Oxo Tower

including Cajun-style chicken with potato skins, homemade lentil rissoles and smoked salmon and cream cheese crêpes. For £7.95, diners can choose from classier dishes, such as chargrilled rump steak with new potatoes. The dark-wood interior is packed with candle-lit tables and the service is brisk but not rushed.

17 Frith Street, W1

Tel: (020) 7437 0723. Fax: (020) 580 2947.

Website: www.cafeemm.com

Price: £13. Wine: £9.90.

Golden Dragon

One of Chinatown's best restaurants, the *Golden Dragon* is bedecked in red and gold and has a noisy, bustling atmosphere. In the daytime (1200–1700), the dim sum selection, brought to the table in a never-ending parade of bamboo steamers, is of exemplary quality. Main dishes, available both night and day, are excellent value and come in generously sized portions. As well as all the standard dishes and more, some unusual dishes are on offer, such as eel or jelly fish, roast pigeon or even a whole suckling pig (available on order for £115).

28–29 Gerrard Street, W1

Tel: (020) 7734 2763. Fax: (020) 7734 1073.

Price: £15. Wine: £9.

Mildred's

Mildred's is a tasty and popular Soho establishment that happens to be vegetarian. Although it recently moved a few streets, thankfully, the warm decor, relaxed atmosphere and low prices remain. One improvement is the size, with more space to accommodate the steady stream of regulars and savvy tourists. The healthy menu changes, however, the homemade veggie burger of the day and the pasta of the day are reliable favourites. Vegans are always catered for, as are those with wheat or dairy intolerance. A selection of organic wines and juices is on offer. The staff is young, trendy and helpful. Closed Sunday. Debit cards accepted but no credit cards.

45 Lexington Street, W1

Tel/fax: (020) 7494 1634.

Price: £15. Wine: £10.

Rock and Sole Plaice

It is difficult to beat sitting upstairs at the *Rock and Sole Plaice*, near the fryers, watching the cooking and the takeaway punters and munching on a good plate of fresh fish with crispy batter, chunky chips and mushy peas (optional), while downing a good cuppa. Although, sitting on one of the picnic tables outside on a summer's evening, with a nice bottle of crisp white wine, might pip it. Fish and chips are a British institution and there are few places better to indulge than this, London's oldest surviving chippie. It serves up all the basic fishes (cod, rock, haddock, plaice, skate and scampi) and more specialities (halibut, lemon sole, dover sole, trout, salmon, sardines and mackerel), depending on market availability, as well as other chip-shop standards like pasties and pies.

47 Endell Street, WC2

Tel: (020) 7836 3785.

Price: £10. Wine: £8.

Tokyo Diner

This Japanese canteen on three small floors is a reliable and cheap favourite in Chinatown. With wooden tables and stools, all the floors are fairly similar but the ground floor, with its pale yellow walls and Japanese mask hanging on the wall, is the best, because of the wrap-around windows. With a limited menu that changes seasonally, this is not the place for sushi-lovers, as *Tokyo Diner* only has a few unalterable sushi sets on the menu. However, people come for the 'four-course' bento boxes and the *donburi* (filling rice dishes served in a bowl), a particular favourite being the chicken and onion don. The restaurant also serves Japanese curries and noodle soups. With free Japanese tea, diners who just eat one of the *donburi* pay just £6.60 for their whole meal.

2 Newport Place, WC2

Tel: (020) 7287 8777.

Price: £11.50 (bento box). Wine: £6.90.

Personal Recommendations

Duke of York

A quirky little gastropub in a quiet Bloomsbury street, the *Duke of York* is a relaxed yet vibrant place to spend an evening. Unlike most gastropubs, it is not overly trendy, overly crowded or overly priced. Diners can mingle with pub punters and eat in the brighter red-toned bar area, decorated with contemporary art, or instead sit in private, little booths in the back dining room. The usually tasty dishes range from British classics like Cumberland sausage and mash to more unusual daily specials, such as sea bream tempura with stir-fried noodles, although they can sometimes disappoint. Reservations recommended for dining area.

7 Roger Street, WC1

Tel: (020) 7242 7230.

Price: £15. Wine: £10.50.

La Trompette

La Trompette sneaked into the top ten of *Harden's* 'London Favourites' in 2002 and, despite being situated in a quiet street in Chiswick, it looks set to retain its success. Owner Nigel Platts-Martin and head chef Ollie Couillaud have worked miracles in creating a genuinely world-class menu at out-of-town prices. The menu changes daily but highlights include the starter of tarte fine of wood pigeon, onion and mushrooms or the main of rump of lamb with ratatouille, olives, fondant potato and new season's garlic, while the steak tartar can make a decent claim to be the finest in London. The chic modern interior has a buzz but never becomes too noisy, while most conversations seem to be dominated by discussions about the quality of the food at this fantastic-value restaurant.

5–7 Devonshire Road, W4

Tel: (020) 8747 1836.

Price: £30 or £21.50 (three-course weekday set lunch). Wine: £14.50.

Malabar Junction

The entrance to *Malabar Junction* somewhat belies its smart interior, which opens out into a bright light dining room, almost like a conservatory with its huge central skylight, bamboo chairs, greenery and water fountain. The South Indian restaurant caters for both meat-eaters and vegetarians (although vegetarian dishes get their own kitchen) and *dosas* are the house specialities. The size of a dinner plate, these pancakes are traditionally filled with potato masala and served with *sambar* (lentil curry) and coconut chutney. Recommended mains include the tangy king prawn masala or any of the Keralan dishes, such as *kozhi varutha* (chicken curry).

107 Great Russell Street, WC1

Tel: (020) 7580 5230. Fax: (020) 7436 9942.

Price: £25. Wine: £10.

St John

This restaurant, an old smokehouse, is notorious for being pig heaven, where no bit of the animal is left off the menu. But it also happens to be home to one of the loveliest dining rooms in London. Up some stairs from the courtyard bar, this wonderful, light room is all wooden boards, white paint and chrome hanging lampshades. With tables a decent distance from each other, a friendly staff and an unpretentious mixed bag of diners creating a general hubbub, it is difficult not to recommend this place, even to vegetarians. Although (unless they eat fish), they will be confined to eating the one basic vegetarian dish on offer, such as leeks and red wine. Ultimately, however, this restaurant serves up old-fashioned British classics with absolute panache – boiled ham and parsley sauce, rabbit saddle, roast beef with a stunning horseradish sauce, and eccles cakes with Lancashire cheese for dessert. Although one or two unusual cuts of meat – bone marrow, neck of kid, ox heart, pig's ears, tails, trotters, cheeks – are guaranteed. Whole roast suckling pigs can be pre-ordered for 14 diners, at least seven days in advance, costing £280.

26 St John Street, EC1

Tel: (020) 7251 0848. Fax: (020) 7251 4090.

Website: www.stjohnrestaurant.co.uk

Price: £30. Wine: £12.50.

Truc Vert

This restaurant consists of no more than a few rough and ready wooden tables and chairs at the back of a French deli, surrounded by bottles of wine up to the ceiling. Unfortunately, the prices do not reflect the unpretentious surroundings and the service is terrible, as the staff is split between serving diners and customers of the deli. However, the food is unpretentious and near perfect. The dishes change daily but are not that dissimilar from lunch (1200–1500) to dinner (1800–2100). Starters include pea and fresh mint soup, while mains feature roast duck fillet with roast mushrooms, mash potato and pink peppercorn sauce or seared monkfish with rocket and spring onion risotto. However, at lunch, it is also possible to buy from the deli – cheese, charcuterie, patés and also daily salads, sandwiches and quiches. The smoked salmon quiche is quite possibly the best quiche in London. No dinner weekends.

42 North Audley Street, W1

Tel: (02) 7491 9988.

Price: £30. Wine: £10.90.

ENTERTAINMENT

Nightlife

London's nightlife is currently buzzing with everything, from some of Europe's liveliest nightclubs right through to stylish design bars and traditional old London pubs. Night-time hotspots can be found across the capital, although there is a particular concentration in the West End, where Soho is still the coolest place to drink, although it remains seedy along the edges. Soho is also the best place for gay bars and clubs. Two particularly hip areas in which to drink are the perennially cool Notting Hill/Ladbroke Grove area in the west and the now very up-and-come Old Street/Shoreditch area in the east (where the fashionable art and media crowd has popularised 'Hoxton cool'). Many local areas, such as Camden and

Angel in the north, Brixton and Clapham in the south, have great local pubs and bars and remain the areas where the best of the well-established gastropubs can be found.

The legal drinking age is 18 years and almost all of the clubs exact an admission price (often increasing after 2300 or 2400), which can be pricey, particularly in the West End. Dress codes vary depending on the calibre of the club but it may be wise to leave trainers at home. Although there have been plans for change for a while now, England's licensing laws still mean that pubs and bars traditionally close at 2300 Monday to Saturday and at 2230 on Sunday. However, some places have special licences that allow them to stay open later. Clubs usually open at 2200, fill up by 2400, and stay open until 0200/0300 during the week and usually around 0500 at weekends, although often later. Drink prices are exorbitant in London and can vary from pub to pub and club to club. A pint will cost anything from £2.50 upwards and will be much more like £3 in the West End. Few venues can be defined by their music, featuring different styles on different nights, with regular sets by guest DJs. The best way to keep abreast of goings-on is to check out the listings in the weekly *Time Out* magazine (website: www.timeout.com).

Bars

If a traditional English pub is what you are after, try the 17th-century *George Inn*, 77 Borough High Street, SE1 – the only extant example of a galleried coaching inn in London. Nearby, a popular watering hole for patrons of the Globe Theatre, tourists and locals is *The Anchor*, Bankside, SE1. This 17th-century haunt is quaint and quirky, while its Thames-side terrace is a delight on sunny days. Alternatively, the *Nell Gwyne*, 1–2 Bull Inn Court, just off the Strand, WC2, is one of the smallest and most endearing of the central, old-fashioned pubs, while the hugely popular 17th-century *Lamb and Flag*, 33 Rose Street, WC2, offers two floors connected by a rickety staircase and an outdoor area in summer. For ornate Victorian interiors, *The Salisbury*, 90 St Martins Lane, WC2, with its gin palace atmosphere, is unbeatable. No less popular is the *Lamb*, 94 Lamb's Conduit Street, WC1.

As for bars, many of the best in Soho are members only but *Yo!Below*, in the basement of *Yo!Sushi*, 52 Poland Street, W1, is far more egalitarian, featuring Japanese cartoons, Karaoke-singing staff, self-service beer dispensers and masseuses. For a chilled scruffy kind of Soho cool, try *Two Floors*, Kingly Street, W1; it doesn't have the name above the door but you can tell it by the sofas in the window and the green walls. For stylish, hugely busy, trendy bars that stay open past 2300 and do not require a membership card, *Amber*, 6 Poland Street, W1, is one of the nicest, while *Akbar*, 77 Dean Street, has a touch of exotic decor. The beautiful people go to *The West Bar* at *Sketch*, 9 Conduit Street, W1 (see *Restaurants*). Voted 'Bar of the Year' in 2002, by both the *Evening Standard* and *Time Out*, *Rockwell*, on the ground floor of the Trafalgar Hotel, Trafalgar Square, WC2, is currently one of the city's coolest meeting places, with its sumptuous cocktails and chic decor. *Point 101*, 101 New Oxford Street, WC1, is a late-night West End bar that defies the archaic drinking laws with DJs and an up-for-it clientele.

For gay men in Soho, there is only one street in which to pose. Almost all of the Old Compton Street pubs, bars, cafés and restaurants are gay or very gay-friendly. A new and popular one is *G.A.Y. Bar*, 30 Old Compton Street, W1, run by the unstoppable club night, *G.A.Y.* (see *Clubs* below). Off Old Compton

Soho at night

Street, two male favourites are *The Edge*, 11 Soho Square, W1, and *The Yard*, 57 Rupert Street, W1. For women, the choice is much more limited; the best by far is *The Candy Bar*, 4 Carlisle Street, W1.

Further west, in Notting Hill, one of the newest and best bars in the area is *Under the Westway Bar and Restaurant*, Westbourne Studios, 242 Acklam Road, W10. This bar is set out on the vast open ground floor of a studio/office warehouse – you have to buzz security/reception to be let in, explaining you want to go to the bar. The ceiling of the bar area is actually the concrete flyover known as the Westway. Two pubs about as different from each other as chalk and cheese are the old and unpretentious favourite *Portobello Gold*, 95–97 Portobello Road, W11, and one of the trendiest pubs in the area *The Westbourne*, 101 Westbourne Park Villas, W2.

Heading east, *Vertigo*, Level 42, Tower 42, 25 Old Broad Street, EC2, at 180m (590ft) above the ground, is one of the UK's highest bars and boasts stunning views across the city from the floor-to-ceiling windows, although it is only open on weeknights, as it is in the business-orientated City of London. For pubs in the Old Street area, *The Bricklayers*, 63 Charlotte Road, EC2, is as reliable as ever for a pint and a possible glimpse of a famous artist, while for kitsch cool, the *George and Dragon*, 2 Hackney Road, E1, is your best bet. Table football is the focus of the Brazilian-style *Kick Bar*, 127 Shoreditch High Street, E1. If you are after more of a designer bar, the place to go for DJs is the *Medicine Bar*, 89 Great Eastern Street, EC2, or for food is *Grand Central*, 91–93 Great Eastern Street, EC2, possibly the most beautiful bar-restaurant in London.

Casinos

There are over 20 casinos in London. For contact details and other information, refer to the *British Casino Association*, 38 Grosvenor Gardens, SW1 (tel: (020) 7730 1055; fax: (020) 7730 1050; website: www. britishcasinoassociation.org.uk). By law, only members and their guests over the age of 18 years can enter a British casino; membership usually takes 24 hours.

Clubs

UK garage (becoming ever closer musically to its R&B cousin across the Atlantic) is still the 'in' sound

of London and many clubs across the globe, however, a variety of musical styles pervades clubs throughout the capital. The world-famous super-club *Ministry of Sound*, 103 Gaunt Street, SE1 (website: www. ministryofsound.co.uk), is still going strong a decade on, with its stunning sound system pumping out popular house and garage. Its big rivals today are the more underground *Fabric*, 77A Charterhouse Street, EC1 (website: www.fabriclondon.com), *Pacha*, Terminus Place, Victoria, SW1 (website: www. pachalondon.com), which has brought a touch of Balearic glamour to Victoria, and *The End*, an ultra-stylish club at 18A West Central Street, WC1 (website: www.the-end.co.uk).

However, despite the biggest New Year's Eve party that took place in the vast Millennium Dome, hosted by Ministry of Sound for tens of thousands of revellers, the club scene is probably swinging more towards smaller clubs and DJ-bars. One area that is gaining in popularity for good small-scale clubs is Shoreditch/Old Street, springing up around the now well-established grand-dame of the scene, *333*, at 333 Old Street, EC1. Clubs like the *Bridge and Tunnel*, 4 Calvert Avenue, E2 (with popular electro nights and rocksteady nights), *Cargo*, 83 Rivington Street, EC2 (mostly soulful house), *Herbal*, 12–14 Kingsland Road, E2 (house, breakbeats, hip hop and drum'n'bass), and slightly further away, *93 Feet East*, 150 Brick Lane, E1 (hip hop, deep house and Latin nights). DJ-bars playing various different tunes on most nights of the week include the hugely popular *Market Place*, 11 Market Place, W1, and the relaxed arty vibe of the *Vibe Bar*, 91–95 Brick Lane, E1.

Although the east is running away with things at the moment, the west's *Notting Hill Arts Club*, 21 Notting Hill Gate, W11, is always worth checking out, for its eclectic nights (famous for Latin nights but more recently a rocking punk night). South of the river, Brixton's reputation for nightlife remains unscathed with *The Fridge*, Town Hall Parade, SW2, a long-time favourite, and *Substation South*, 9 Brighton Terrace, SW9, the original and still the best cruisey gay nightclub. The most popular gay night, however, is back in Soho, the inimitable *G.A.Y.* at *The Astoria*, 157 Charing Cross Road, WC2.

Comedy

The *Comedy Store*, Haymarket House, 1A Oxendon Street, SW1 (tel: (020) 7344 0234; website: www.thecomedystore.co.uk), still offers the best comedy in town. *Jongleurs* comedy and cabaret clubs are based in Battersea, Camden and Bow (website: www.jongleurs.com).

Live Music

International acts play at *Earls Court Exhibition Centre*, Warwick Road, Earl's Court, SW5, and *Wembley Arena*, Lakeside Way, Wembley, HA9. Next door, *Wembley Stadium* was once a vast auditorium for massive stars but it is currently being rebuilt. Mainstream pop stars can be heard at the *London Arena*, Limeharbour, E14. For a more unique atmosphere, try *The Astoria (LA1)*, 157 Charing Cross Road, WC2, or the *Brixton Academy*, 211 Stockwell Road, SW9. The *Shepherds Bush Empire*, Shepherds Bush Green, W12, and the *Forum*, 9–17 Highgate Road, NW5, draw medium-sized acts. New and exciting indie acts usually play the *Barfly London*, 49 Chalk Farm Road, NW1, on their way up, while pubs with regular, often unsigned live music include the *Hope and Anchor*, 207 Upper Street, N1, Camden's famous *Dublin Castle*, 94 Parkway, NW1, and the *Swan*, 215 Clapham Road, SW9. For jazz, head to the *Jazz Café*, 5 Parkway, NW1, or to *Ronnie Scott's Jazz Club*, 47 Frith Street, W1, a legendary venue in the heart of Soho.

Sport

The most famous sporting events in the capital are the *London Marathon* (website: www.london-marathon.co.uk) in April and the *Wimbledon Lawn Tennis Championships* at the *All England Lawn Tennis and Croquet Club*, Church Road, Wimbledon, SW19 (tel: (020) 8944 1066; website: www.wimbledon.org) in June and July. Just outside London, *Ascot Racecourse*, Ascot, Berkshire (tel: (01344) 876 876 (tickets); website: www.ascot.co.uk) and *Epsom Downs Racecourse*, Epsom Downs, Surrey (tel: (01372) 470 047; website: www.epsomderby.co.uk) host *Royal Ascot* and *The Derby*. Most Londoners are fanatical about football and the *FA Cup Final* in May was always held at *Wembley Stadium*. However, the famous Towers have been demolished and work has begun on a new national stadium. The FA Cup Final will be held in the Millennium Stadium in Cardiff until Wembly re-opens (at the earliest 2006). Support for one of London's several Premiership football clubs divides the city. *Arsenal* (tel: (020) 7704 4000; website: www.arsenal.com) and *Tottenham Hotspur* (tel: (020) 8365 5000; website: www.spurs.co.uk) are based in north London and are keen rivals, while *Chelsea* (tel: (020) 7385 5545; website: www.chelseafc.co.uk) and *Fulham* (tel: (0870) 442 1234; website: www.fulhamfc.com) are based in the southwest of the city. *West Ham United* (tel: (020) 8548 2748; website: www.westhamunited.co.uk) has a loyal following in the east, while *Charlton Athletic* (tel: (020) 8333 4000; website: www.charlton-athletic.co.uk) represents the Premiership in the southeast of the city. Arsenal were Premiership champions in 2001–2002 and continue to have a high profile nationally and internationally.

National and international Rugby Union (website: www.rfu.com) is based at Twickenham. Successful local clubs include *Harlequins* (website: www.quins.co.uk), *Wasps* (website: www.wasps.co.uk), *Saracens* (website: www.saracens.com) and *London Irish* (website: www.london-irish.com).

The home of cricket's governing body, the *Marylebone Cricket Club – MCC* (tel: (020) 7289 1611), founded in 1787, is *Lord's*, St John's Wood Road, NW8 (tel: (020) 7432 1066 (ticket office); website: www.lords.org), which also hosts league, cup and International Test matches. Major athletic events in London take place at *Crystal Palace National Sports Centre*, Ledrington Road, SE19 (tel: (020) 8778 0131; website: www.crystalpalace.co.uk).

The government is currently making a bid for the Olympic Games to be held in London in 2012.

Tickets to major sporting events can be purchased through *Ticketmaster UK* (tel: (0870) 534 4444; website: www.ticketmaster.co.uk).

Fitness Centres

Public fitness centres where it is not necessary to become a member include *Chelsea Sports Centre*, Chelsea Manor Street, SW3 (tel: (020) 7352 6985; website: www.rbkc.gov.uk/sport/chelseasportscentre), and the massive *Oasis Centre*, 32 Endell Street, WC2 (tel: (020) 7831 1804), situated right in the heart of the West End.

Golf

Regent's Park Golf and Tennis School, Outer Circle, Regent's Park, NW1 (tel: (020) 7724 0643; website: www.rpgts.co.uk), offers professional lessons, costing £30 for half and hour, as well as driving practice at £5 for 50 balls. *The English Golf Union* (tel: (01526) 354 500; website: www.englishgolfunion.org) has information on many of the capital's golf courses.

Swimming Pools

Seasonal open-air swimming pools include *Brockwell Lido*, SW9 (tel: (020) 7274 3088), and *Parliament Hill Lido*, Hampstead Heath, NW3 (tel: (020) 7485 5757). The *Oasis Centre* (see *Fitness Centres* above) has an indoor as well as an outdoor pool and is open year round.

Tennis

Outdoor public courts are available at *Regent's Park*, NW1 (tel: (020) 7486 4216), and at *Islington Tennis Centre*, Market Road, N7 (tel: (020) 7700 1370; website: www.aquaterra.org/tennis), which also has indoor courts.

Watersports

Sailing tuition is offered at *Docklands Sailing and Watersports Centre*, Millwall Dock, 235A Westferry Road, E14 (tel: (020) 7537 2626; website: www.dswc.org).

Shopping

London is one of the world's great shopping cities, with over 30,000 retail outlets dotted across the capital. Typically for London, particular areas of the city have their own shopping characters. In the west, the King's Road in Chelsea, SW1, has a long-standing reputation for fashion, although it is now mainly high-street chains, while the Notting Hill area, once primarily antiques, is now also very popular for fashion boutiques, in particular along Westbourne Grove and Ledbury Road, W11. In the east, the Brick Lane area, E1 and E2, has long been home to up-and-coming fashion designers' studios but now the area is really taking off, with many designers opening boutiques alongside shops selling vintage furniture, second-hand clothes, design objects and other quirky finds (Cheshire Street is especially good for this). More centrally, Oxford Street and Regent Street, W1, attract swarms of shoppers to well-known high-street clothing shops and megastores, including *Hamley's* toy

emporium, 188–196 Regent Street. Department stores are mostly located along Oxford Street – such as the enormous and trendy *Selfridges*, the reliable *Marks & Spencer*, and the back-to-basics *John Lewis* – although the high-fashion *Liberty* is just down Regent Street. Just around the back of Liberty, Carnaby Street, popular in the swinging '60s, is enjoying a revival, although it is mostly filled now with chains. The parallel Newburgh Street has independent trendy boutiques.

Nearby, Tottenham Court Road, WC1, is lined with electrical shops, while directly south, Charing Cross Road, WC2, has long been the centre for bookshops in London, with enticing second-hand shops and bigger chains. London's largest bookshop, *Waterstones*, is situated on Piccadilly, W1. Covent Garden, WC2, is one of the most popular shopping areas. Its Piazza, once the site of the fruit and vegetable market, is now filled with specialist shops, cafés, craft stalls and street performers, while Floral Street is home to trendy clothes shops and Neal Street trendy shoe shops.

Old and New Bond Streets, W1, are home to the flagship stores for big international designers, such as *Prada* and *Gucci*, with nearby Conduit Street providing a home to more off-the-wall designers, such as *Issey Miyake* and *Vivien Westwood*. All these rub shoulders with the home of bespoke tailoring, Savile Row, while high-powered art galleries are scattered throughout the area, particularly Cork Street.

Visitors looking for a gift that is representative of London need look no further than the number of tacky shops and souvenir stalls that line Oxford Street, Piccadilly Circus and other tourist-attracting areas. Passers-by are assaulted with all manner of kitsch, cute and colourful souvenirs, toys and clothes (mostly sporting a Union Jack or member of the royal family). *Harrods*, Knightsbridge, SW1, sells more upmarket souvenirs and attracts huge numbers of tourists (and locals) every year, with its legendary sales and heavenly food hall. Another good place for typical British food stuffs as gifts is *Fortnum and Mason*, on Piccadilly, W1, a classic from the early 20th century.

High-street shopping still dominates in the city centre, however, out-of-town shopping centres are becoming increasingly popular. The massive *Bluewater* (website: www.bluewater.co.uk), 1.6km (one mile) off the M25 ring road, is the biggest of this new breed.

Visiting one or more of London's markets is a way of combining shopping with a cultural experience. The vast market at *Camden Lock*, Chalk Farm Road, NW1, is one of the city's top attractions, open daily but primarily Saturday and Sunday. Visitors also flock to the antiques and flea market on the *Portobello Road*, W10, on Friday and Saturday. In the East End, Sunday markets sell everything from fruit and vegetables to jewellery and junk, such as *Petticoat Lane* and *Brick Lane*, E1, open 0900–1400 and 0600–1300 respectively, as well as the Sunday morning flower market at *Columbia Road*, E2. Despite the imminent redevelopment of half of the original market building, *Spitalfields Market*, E1, continues to thrive. Focused around extensive organic produce stalls, there are also stalls selling arts and crafts, antiques, records and clothes, with a pared-down market on Wednesday. Antiques are available on *Camden Passage*, Islington, N1, on Wednesday and Saturday, and *Greenwich Market*, SE10, on Saturday and Sunday. One of the most wonderful places for shoppers to explore for mainly 20th-century antiques is the massive maze of *Alfie's Antique Market*, 13–25 Church Street, NW8, open Tuesday to Saturday. For foodies, *Borough Market*, SE1, is still the best, open Friday and Saturday, while,

Brixton Market, Electric Avenue, SW9, offers the biggest selection of Caribbean food in Europe, open every day except Friday.

Standard shopping hours are Monday to Saturday 0930–1800, although some shops stay open as late as 2000. Shops rarely close for lunch and many are now also open 1200–1800 on Sunday. Late-night opening (usually until 2000) is on Thursday in the West End and Wednesday in the Knightsbridge area. Most major stores and shops in the West End are part of the *Tax-Free Shopping* scheme run by *Global Refund* (tel: (0800) 829 373; website: www.globalrefund.com), which offers VAT (currently charged at 17.5%) refunds to visitors from outside the EU. To encourage European visitors, the Euro is now increasingly accepted in major shops, with over 45 Oxford Street retailers accepting the currency alongside the Pound Sterling.

Culture

London's cultural scene combines the assurance of long-standing tradition with the verve of regained creativity. The sheer breadth of cultural activities on offer in the capital is breathtaking, with over 150 theatres and 300 art galleries. Contemporary figures like Tracy Emin and Zadie Smith complement the rich heritage of Turner and Shakespeare.

The hulking concrete mass of the *South Bank Centre*, South Bank, SE1 (tel: (020) 7960 4242; website: www.sbc.org.uk), is one of the city's cultural Meccas. It houses the *Hayward Gallery* and three concert halls – the *Royal Festival Hall*, the *Queen Elizabeth Hall* and the *Purcell Room*. Next door is the flagship *Royal National Theatre*, South Bank, SE1 (tel: (020) 7452 3400 (information) *or* 3000 (box office); website: www.nationaltheatre.org.uk). Flying the cultural flag north of the river, the labyrinthine *Barbican Centre*, Silk Street, EC2 (tel: (020) 7638 8891 (box office) *or* 4141 (information); website: www. barbican.org.uk), is an all-inclusive performing and visual arts venue with a varied all-year programme of events.

London Tourist Board's *Visitor Call* service (tel: (0906) 133 7799) and the weekly *Time Out* magazine (website: www.timeout.com) provide details of the week's entertainment. Ticket agencies include *First Call Ticketing* (tel: (0870) 840 1111; website: www.firstcalltickets.com) and *Ticketmaster UK* (tel: (0870) 534 4444; website: www.ticketmaster.co.uk).

Music

The world-famous *Royal Opera House*, Covent Garden, WC2 (tel: (020) 7304 4000; website: www.royalopera.org), is home to the excellent *Royal Opera*. However, despite some attempts to cut the price, ballet and opera tickets are still often fairly expensive. More accessible are performances by the *English National Opera* (website: www.eno.org) at the *London Coliseum*, St Martin's Lane, WC2 (tel: (020) 7632 8300).

Large-scale concerts are staged at the *Royal Festival Hall* (see above), home of the *London Philharmonic Orchestra* (tel: (020) 7840 4200 *or* 4242 (box office); website: www.lpo.co.uk), or the *Barbican* (see above), home of the *London Symphony Orchestra* (tel: (020) 7588 1116; website: www.lso.co.uk). The *Royal Albert Hall*, Kensington Gore, SW7 (tel: (020) 7589 8212 (box office); website: www.royalalberthall.com), can also stage huge concerts, including London's annual musical highlight, the summer series of the *Proms* (see *Cultural Events* below).

Oxford Street

Music connoisseurs should head for the traditional but friendly surroundings of the *Wigmore Hall*, 36 Wigmore Street, W1 (tel: (020) 7935 2141; website: www.wigmore-hall.org.uk), to hear impeccable chamber music and solo recitals. More informal concerts take place in halls and churches all over the capital, including *St Martin-in-the-Fields* (see *Key Attractions*), *St John's*, Smith Square, SW1, and *St James's*, Piccadilly, W1.

Theatre

Within the extraordinary diversity of London's theatre scene, the *Royal National Theatre* (see above) and the *Royal Shakespeare Company* (tel: (01789) 403 404; website: www.rsc.org.uk) compete for audiences with commercial West End theatres, repertory companies, 'off-West End' productions and fringe theatres. The National Theatre's three auditoria – *The Olivier*, *The Cottesloe* and *The Lyttleton* – allow productions of different scale, from classics to new writing. The Royal Shakespeare Company, performing primarily Shakespeare and based out of Stratford-upon-Avon, did use the Barbican as its London home but will now perform in a range of venues including the Barbican.

The *Old Vic*, The Cut, Waterloo, SE1 (tel: (020) 7928 7616; website: www.oldvictheatre.com), offers inspired traditional drama. Meanwhile, down the road, at 66 The Cut, the *Young Vic* (tel: (020) 7928 6363; website: www.youngvic.org) presents modern productions of contemporary and classic plays. The *Royal Court Theatre*, Sloane Square, SW1 (tel: (020) 7565 5000; website: www.royalcourttheatre.com), continues to foster excellent new writing.

Quality innovative productions can also be expected from 'off-West End' theatres, such as the *Donmar Warehouse*, Earlham Street, WC2 (tel: (020) 7369 1732; website: www.donmar-warehouse.com), and the *Almeida*, Almeida Street, N1 (tel: (020) 7359 4404 (box office); website: www.almeida.co.uk). Fringe theatre, ranging from the inspired to the insane, is performed in dozens of local venues, including the *King's Head*, 115 Upper Street, N1 (tel: (020) 7226 1916; website: www.kingsheadtheatre.org), which is the oldest pub-theatre in London.

From May to September, the *Globe Theatre*, New Globe Walk, SE1 (tel: (020) 7401 9919 (box office); website: www.shakespeares-globe.org), stages open-air productions of Shakespeare and his contemporaries. There are also outdoor summer performances in *Regent's Park*, NW1 (tel: (020) 7486 2431; website: www.open-air-theatre.org.uk).

Theatre tickets in the West End cost £15–40. They can be purchased in advance from the theatre box office. Alternatively, for purchases on the day of the performance, there is a booth on the south side of Leicester Square, formerly called the Half-Price Theatre Ticket Booth, now called *tkts* (website: www.tkts.co.uk). This is the official Society of London Theatre's booth; visitors should avoid touts and other outlets in the area. The booth sells mainly half-price tickets, as well as some tickets at 25% discount and some full-price tickets. Because of the booking fee, when only full-price tickets are available for that night's performance, visitors are advised to go to the actual theatre box office.

Dance

Touring dance companies perform mostly contemporary dance at the *Sadler's Wells Theatre*, Rosebery Avenue, EC1 (tel: (020) 7863 8000 (box office); website: www.sadlers-wells.com). Ticket prices are usually more reasonable than at the *Royal Opera House*, Covent Garden, WC2 (tel: (020) 7304 4000), which is home to the *Royal Ballet* (website: www.royalopera.org/ballet).

Film

Local cinemas are less expensive than those in the West End, where tickets cost approximately £10. Two main cinema chains are *Odeon* (tel: (0870) 505 0007; website: www.odeon.co.uk) and *Warner* (tel: (0870) 240 6020; website: www.warnervillage.co.uk), with venues all over London, their biggest in Leicester Square, WC2. *Barbican Screen*, Silk Street, EC2 (tel: (020) 7638 8891; website: www.barbican.org.uk/film), is London's leading independent cinema showing independent, arthouse and blockbuster movies, along with the *National Film Theatre*, on the South Bank, SE1 (tel: (020) 7928 3232; website: www.nft.org.uk). *IMAX* magic can be experienced at the largest cinema screen in the UK, the new *BFI London IMAX Cinema*, South Bank, SE1 (tel: (020) 7902 1234; website: www.bfi.org.uk).

The *Ealing Studios* in west London presented English eccentricity and black humour in a distinctive London setting in the 'Ealing Comedies', such as *Passport to Pimlico* (1949) and *The Ladykillers* (1955). Before the war, Alfred Hitchcock established his reputation at *Elstree Film Studios* (website: www.elstreefilmtv.co.uk), with London-based thrillers such as *The 39 Steps* (1935), featuring Richard Hannay (Robert Donat) hanging precariously from the clock face of Big Ben. Recently, *Sliding Doors* (1997), *Shakespeare in Love* (1998) and *Notting Hill* (1998) have achieved huge success by combining a London setting with the box-office draw of Hollywood stars. The compelling gangster face of East End London has also been portrayed in Guy Ritchie's *Lock, Stock and Two Smoking Barrels* (1998) and *Snatch* (2000). Less blockbuster, more critically acclaimed, London has been portrayed in *Blow Up* (1966), *Mona Lisa* (1986) and *Wonderland* (1999).

Cultural Events

New Year revelry – sometimes of the unruly and even violent sort – has long been a London tradition, with the focus on an overcrowded Trafalgar Square. A few weeks later, Lion Dancers welcome in the *Chinese New Year* in Chinatown, WC2. July brings the fun and festivities of the *Coin Street Festival* (website: www.coinstreetfestival.org) at Gabriel's Wharf, SE1, the arts extravaganza that is the *Greenwich and Docklands Festival* (website: www.festival.org) and a chance for the city's gay and lesbian population to strut their stuff in the *Mardi Gras* parade and festival. The *Notting Hill Carnival* – a two-day celebration of Afro-Caribbean culture during the August Bank Holiday weekend – is Europe's largest street carnival, attended by over two million people. More sedate events include the *Trooping the Colour*, celebrating the Queen's official birthday in June, and the impressive *Lord Mayor's Show* in November, which is a colourful display of the long-standing independence of the City of London. November also sees the two-week *London Film Festival* (website: www.lff.org.uk).

Summer brings the hugely popular music festival known as the *Proms*, with concerts running from July to September. Tickets for these *BBC Promenade Concerts* (website: www.bbc.co.uk/proms) start from £3 (non-seated) and the *Last Night*, led by the *BBC Symphony Orchestra* (website: www.bbc.co.uk/orchestras/so), is one of the few occasions when unabashed patriotism is the order of the day. Summer also brings many other music festivals, including the *City of London Festival* (website: www.colf.org), outdoor performances running from June to July in the gardens of *Kenwood House*, on Hampstead Heath, NW3 (tel: (020) 7973 3427), and outdoor opera at *Holland Park* theatre (tel: (020) 7602 7856; website: www.operahollandpark.com), from June to August.

Literary Notes

London has sheltered and inspired writers for centuries. Bunhill Fields' graveyard has monuments to John Bunyan, Daniel Defoe and William Blake. Bloomsbury gave its name to a literary set that included Virginia Woolf, while the leafy suburb of Hampstead was once home to John Keats, H G Wells and D H Lawrence. Some of the country's most famous writers are commemorated in *Poets' Corner* in Westminster Abbey.

The seething mass of 19th-century London life – and its legendary fog – is vividly recreated in the novels of Charles Dickens. Sinister goings-on in the capital surface in the Sherlock Holmes stories by Arthur Conan Doyle, Robert Louis Stephenson's *The Strange Case of Dr Jekyll and Mr Hyde* (1886) and *The Secret Agent* (1923) by Joseph Conrad. Graham Greene captured the unique atmosphere of wartime London in *The Ministry of Fear* (1943).

More recently, Martin Amis' *London Fields* (1989), a depressing portrait of a London in pre-millennial decline, Chris Petit's *Robinson* (1993), which delves deep into Soho life, Tobias Hill's *Underground* (1999), a poetic murder mystery woven around the Tube, Jake Arnott's *The Long Firm* (1999), set in the London underworld of the 1960s, and Zadie Smith's *White Teeth* (2000) have added their names to the rich London literary canon. A lively and impressively detailed history of London that captures the essence of the city's spirit is Peter Akroyd's *London: A Biography* (2000).

Camden Lock market

LOS ANGELES

Los Angeles, America's second largest city after New York, sprawls along the Pacific coast of southern California. Its coastline actually stretches 122km (76 miles) from Malibu to Long Beach, while inland the city spreads out to fill a vast, flat and once arid basin ringed by the Santa Monica and San Gabriel mountains.

Arriving by aeroplane gives a good first impression of the city. From out of this vast flat grid of streets and buildings, there rises a cluster of imposing skyscrapers to mark Downtown – 26km (16 miles) inland from the coast. To the northeast is Pasadena; to the west and northwest are Hollywood, Beverly Hills and Century City, as well as the wide San Fernando Valley; to the south is Long Beach and along the west coast are Santa Monica and Venice Beach.

Founded in 1781 by Mexican settlers, the city was given the cumbersome name of El Pueblo de Nuestra Señora la Reina de Los Angeles de Porciuncula (the Town of Our Lady Queen of the Angels of Porciuncula). Since then, it has been called everything from La La Land to Tinseltown but is most commonly known simply as LA. However, Los Angeles itself is actually just the largest of 88 different incorporated cities that make up the greater metropolitan area that we think of as Los Angeles.

Over the decades, the city grew from a cowtown to a Gold Rush boomtown to an oil town – and oil pumps can still be seen, bobbing up and down like mechanical donkeys. By the end of the 19th century, settlers were heading west in larger numbers, lured by the same thing that still attracts newcomers today: the mild climate, the sea and the almost continuous sunshine. On average, LA enjoys 329 sunny days each year, cooled by gentle ocean breezes and little rain. And the sunsets can be truly fabulous.

But the turning point in the city's fame came in the 1920s, when the fledgling film industry realised that it was sunshine that was missing from their film-making in New York City – and so it decamped to the West. And Hollywood, then a simple district, became famous. Today, with major studios located here, such as Paramount, Universal, Fox and Warner Brothers, it is labelled the 'Entertainment Capital of the World'.

However, there is more to LA than Hollywood. Disneyland, America's famous fun park, although rather elderly now, is the area's most popular site and well worth a visit. The city is also home to many world-renowned cultural institutions, such as the Museum of Contemporary Art, the LA Philharmonic or the Getty Center. Visitors do come to see the huge Hollywood sign in Griffith Park and the mansions of

the stars in Beverly Hills, but also to experience the nightlife on Sunset Strip, the beach life, the car culture and just to look at the people. LA is exuberant – there are few places in the world where the phrase 'Express Yourself' is taken so literally. From hippy health fanatics to muscled fitness freaks, from Art Deco lovers to devotees of off-beat religions – they all exist alongside the glamorous and the wealthy. From classic cars to silicone, LA represents people's dreams – and thousands come seeking fame and fortune or just a new life. Los Angeles is the country's gateway for immigrants from Asia, the Pacific Rim, Eastern Europe, Mexico and Latin America. People from 160 countries, speaking 96 different languages, make up Los Angeles.

But the population is fairly ghettoised. Afro-Americans live primarily in black suburbs, such as South Central LA and the Crenshaw District, which are poor and rundown and have high crime rates. Visitors are unlikely to go to these areas though and it can feel as though the black population – like the gangster rap that started here – barely touches on the rest of the city. But then much of Los Angeles lives in a bubble anyway. One where it is always sunny and nothing – be it smog, the occasional earthquake or a limited water supply for a growing population – will stop the Angelenos' determination to work hard and live a rich life.

Downtown skyline with San Gabriel mountains

TRAVEL

Getting There By Air

Los Angeles International Airport (LAX)

Tel: (310) 646 5252.

Website: www.lawa.org

Located on Santa Monica Bay, 24km (15 miles) from the city centre, LAX is the world's third busiest airport, handling more than 56 million passengers in 2002. It is particularly important as the US gateway to the Pacific.

Major airlines: Los Angeles is served by almost all major airlines. *United Airlines* (tel: (800) 241 6522; website: www.ual.com) connects Los Angeles to all the major US cities, including daily flights to New York and Chicago. Other major US airlines include *American Airlines, Continental, Delta, Southwest Airlines, TWA* and *US Airways. British Airways* and *Virgin Atlantic* operate daily flights to London, as does *Lufthansa* to Munich. Other international airlines with regular services include *Air Canada, Air France, Air New Zealand, KLM* and *Qantas*.

Airport facilities: Facilities include foreign exchange and banking services, ATMs, locker and baggage storage, medical and first aid, language assistance and a variety of shops and restaurants.

3826; website: www.supershuttle.com), *Xpress Shuttle* (tel: (310) 323 7222 *or* (800) 427 7483; website: www.xpressshuttle.com) and *Prime Time Shuttle* (tel: (800) 733 8267; website: www.primetimeshuttle.com). Charges are US$13–20, depending on the destination. A free shuttle bus runs from the airport to Parking Lot C, where passengers can connect with *MTA* (tel: (800) COMMUTE/266 6883; website: www.mta.net) buses, which run to most places in the city. There is also a free shuttle to Aviation Station on the MTA Metro Green Line. Pick-up is on the lower arrival level under the LAX Shuttle sign. Bus and rail fares into the city are US$1.35.

Ontario International Airport (ONT)

Tel: (909) 937 2700.

Website: www.lawa.org

Located 56km (35 miles) east of Downtown Los Angeles, Ontario International is the city's newest airport (opened 1998) and serves over 6.7 million passengers each year. It handles international and domestic flights and is the closest airport for the heavily settled Orange County.

Major airlines: Among the major airlines serving Ontario Airport are *Alaska Airlines, American Airlines, America West, Continental Airlines, Delta Air Lines, Northwest Airlines, Southwest Airlines, United Airlines* and *United Express*.

Major airlines: *Alaska Airlines, Aloha Airlines, American Airlines, America West, Southwest Airlines* and *United Airlines* all provide regular services to Burbank Airport.

Airport facilities: Facilities include shops and restaurants, ATMs and tourist information. Car hire, located in Terminal B, is provided by *Alamo, Avis, Budget, Hertz* and *National*.

Business facilities: None.

Transport to the city: *Metrolink* (Monday to Friday only) and *Amtrak* (see *Getting There By Rail*) both have nearby stations at Burbank and there are free connecting shuttles to/from the airport. The airport is also connected by many MTA bus lines. Taxis are readily available.

Approximate flight times to Los Angeles: From London is 10 hours 15 minutes; from New York is 5 hours 20 minutes; from Toronto is 5 hours 30 minutes and from Sydney is 14 hours.

Arrival/departure tax: All arrival/departure taxes are paid upon purchase of ticket.

Getting There By Water

Located in San Pedro Bay, approximately 32km (20 miles) south of Downtown, the *Port of Los Angeles*, 425 South Palos Verdes Street, San Pedro (tel: (310) SEA PORT/732 7678; website: www. portoflosangeles.org), is one of the world's biggest and busiest seaports. As well as commercial shipping, the port's *World Cruise Center* handles over one million cruise passengers every year and is a regular stop for visiting cruise ships. The area has also been revamped recently and now includes recreational facilities, such as a Maritime Museum, marina and aquarium.

Ferry services: The majority of the cruise ships are heading south towards Mexico, although Los Angeles is a stop on sailings to Alaska and other international destinations. There is also the *Catalina Express* (tel: (800) 481 3470; website: www.catalinaexpress.com), which operates a service to Santa Catalina Island (see *Excursions*).

Transport to the city: The shuttle bus *Community Connection* 142 operates from Ports O' Call to Long Beach, where various MTA buses are available. Also at Long Beach, the Metro Rail station Transit Mall is on the Blue Line, which goes to Downtown. Taxis are also readily available.

Getting There By Rail

National and regional rail services are provided by *Amtrak* (tel: (800) 872 7245; website: www.amtrak.com). *METROLINK* (tel: (800) 371 5465; website:

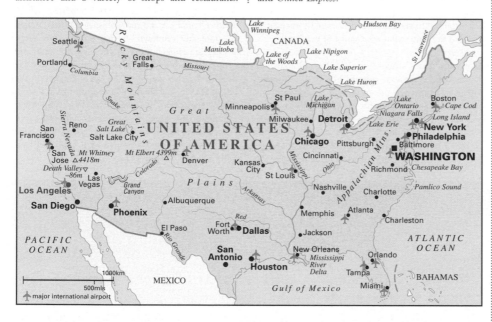

Visitor information booths are located outside the main arrivals building, where staff can advise visitors as to the best route to their destination within the city. Car hire is available from all the major operators, including *Alamo, Avis, Budget, Enterprise, Hertz, National* and *Thrifty*, as well as many local operators.

Business facilities: The *ICE Currency Exchange* booths (tel: (310) 646 0553) offer notary services, fax, photocopying and moneygrams. Internet access is available at many public telephone booths throughout the airport, as well as *Neptune* kiosks (tel: (866) 463 7886). There is also an Internet café in Terminal 4, the *Travel Right Café* (tel: (310) 665 0208).

Transport to the city: Taxis can be found at the lower level. Passengers are presented with a ticket stating typical fares to major destinations. The taxi fare from the airport to Downtown is approximately US$40. Several private shuttle services will drop airport passengers at the door of their hotel or other destinations. These include *Super Shuttle* (tel: (310) 782 6600 *or* (800) 258

Airport facilities: Facilities include information kiosks, ATMs, foreign exchange, lockers and a variety of shops and restaurants. Car hire is available from *Alamo, Avis, Budget, Dollar, Hertz* and *National*.

Business facilities: The business centres have fax service, telephones, Internet ports, mail box/postage vending machines, travel insurance services, money wires and notary public. They are located in the upper level of both terminals.

Transport to the city: Taxis and several shuttle bus services (see above under LAX) provide transportation throughout the region.

Burbank-Glendale-Pasadena Airport (BUR)

Tel: (818) 840 8840.

Website: www.bur.com

Burbank airport handles domestic airlines only, serving some 4.5 million passengers annually. It is the closest airport to Downtown LA (20km/13 miles away), Hollywood and the Valley.

CITY STATISTICS

Location: California, western United States.
Country dialling code: 1 (also required within America, as well as the city code, when dialling from one city code to another).
Population: 3.7 million (city); 9.7 million (Los Angeles County); 16.4 million (Los Angeles Five-County Area).
Ethnic mix: 46.7% white, 32.4% Hispanic, 10.9% Asian, 6.7% African-American, and 3.3% other (including American Aboriginal).
Time zone: GMT - 8 hours (GMT + 7 hours from last Sunday in March to Saturday before last Sunday in October).
Electricity: 110 volts AC; standard two-pin plugs are used.
Average January temp: 14°C (57°F).
Average July temp: 25°C (77°F).
Annual rainfall: 375mm (14.84 inches).

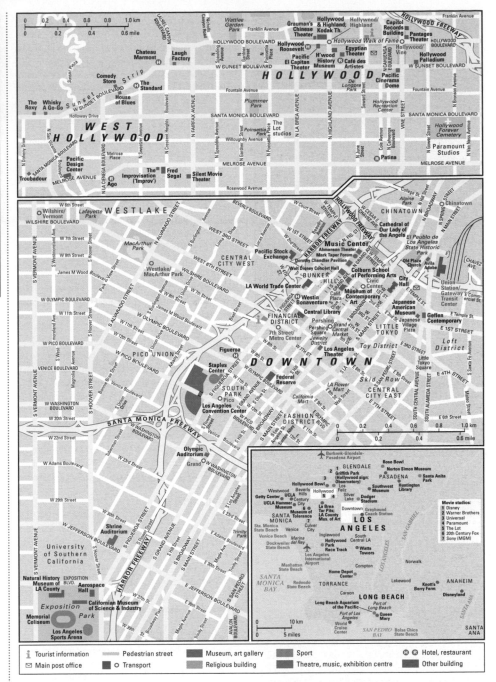

i Tourist information	Pedestrian street	Museum, art gallery
✉ Main post office	○ Transport	Religious building

Sport	**H** ⊕ Hotel, restaurant
Theatre, music, exhibition centre	Other building

www.metrolinktrains.com) is the regional rail system for southern California and connects with most cities in the region. The Los Angeles terminal for both is *Union Station*, located at 800 North Alameda Street on the edge of the Downtown business district. This vast, Art Deco, Spanish-style building, built in 1939, is an attraction itself. Although it still serves over a million passengers a year, rail travel figures have shrunk and many of its huge, arched rooms are fairly empty. Staff are very helpful and can offer advice on special tickets etc. Facilities include checked baggage, passenger information, waiting rooms and snack bar. The trains may not be the swiftest but they are commodious, clean and comfortable.

Rail services: The Los Angeles terminal is situated at the western end of major routes across the southern Rockies and is also the southern terminus of the West Coast line to Seattle (Washington). Frequent services go to stations as far south as San Diego; Amtrak has recently invested US$100 million in new trains to serve this corridor.

Transport to the city: Union Station is a stop on Metro Red Line, which provides the subway service to Downtown LA, Hollywood and beyond. City buses and taxis are also available.

Getting There By Road

Road travel in California is excellent, with good roads connecting Los Angeles to San Diego, Santa Barbara, Monterey and San Francisco.

Driving in the United States is on the right. For UK nationals, a full UK driving licence is sufficient. Other nationalities are required to have an International Driving Permit but it must be accompanied by a full driving licence from their home country. The minimum driving age in the USA is 16 years.

Speed limits are 40kph (25mph) in towns, 88kph (55mph) on highways and 105kph (65mph) on freeways, unless otherwise posted. Drivers may turn right at a red light, after stopping, unless there is a sign that prohibits it. Pedestrians have right of way. The wearing of seatbelts in a private vehicle is mandatory. Children under four years must be protected in car seats. California has strict laws against drink-driving and driving while intoxicated is cause for arrest and a criminal charge. Drink-driving laws are strictly enforced. The maximum legal alcohol to blood ratio for driving is 0.08%. Open containers of alcoholic beverages are not permitted in vehicles.

The *American Automobile Association* (AAA; tel: (800) 222 1333; website: www.aaa-calif.com) can provide information, and may offer reciprocal benefits to members of automobile clubs in other countries.

Emergency breakdown service: *AAA* (800) 400 4AAA/4222 (California) *or* AAA HELP/222 4357 (elsewhere).

Routes to the city: Interstate 5 (I-5) connects Los Angeles with Seattle in the north and San Diego in the south. The Pacific Coast Highway (State Highway 1) is a scenic route north along the California coast to Santa Barbara and San Francisco. Los Angeles is linked to Phoenix (Arizona) by I-10, to Las Vegas (Nevada) and Salt Lake City (Utah) by I-15, and to Oklahoma City (Oklahoma) and Memphis (Tennessee) by I-40.

Approximate driving times to Los Angeles: From San Diego – 2 hours 45 minutes; Las Vegas – 5 hours 30 minutes; San Francisco – 8 hours.

Coach services: The main *Greyhound* (tel: (800) 229 9424; website: www.greyhound.com) coach station is at 1716 East Seventh Street. Greyhound provides coach services to cities nationwide. Facilities at the station include baggage assistance, public toilets and snack bar.

Getting Around

Public Transport

Despite LA being one of the most car-oriented cities in the USA, public transport is good and swift. The *Metropolitan Transportation Authority* (MTA; tel: (800) COMMUTE/266 6883, route information *or* (213) 922 4682, customer relations; website: www.mta.net) actually operates over 1500 **buses** (Metro Bus) – one of the largest fleets in the nation – as well as a **subway** system (Metro Rail). Due to the size of the city, buses can be time consuming and may involve changing but the subway, if it stops where required, is a very good option. For example, visitors could be whisked from Downtown to Hollywood in just 12 minutes.

The Metro Rail system has, at present, nearly 96km (60 miles) of interconnected subway and light rail tracks, covering 50 stations over three lines. The Blue

BUSINESS PROFILE

There's no business like show business – at least not in LA. The city is synonymous with film and television production and most of the nation's leading production facilities for making blockbuster movies and hit TV shows are located here, led by such giants of the industry as Paramount, Universal Warner Brothers, Fox and Disney studios.

Surprisingly, however, although the industry generates US$31 billion annually and is the leading supplier of entertainment to the world, entertainment ranks seventh among the city's major enterprises. In terms of number employed, the leading business sector in the five-county Los Angeles area is actually business services (a category that includes management services, advertising, computer programming, legal services and engineering). It is followed by tourism with over 500,000 employed in the sector, then health services (including medical manufacturing), direct international trade and then wholesale trade. Finally, just above the entertainment industry is technology. The Los Angeles metropolitan area is often called the 'Digital Coast' and multimedia jobs are included in the 277,000 technology jobs that also include digital information technology and advanced transportation technology. The region is also the country's second largest manufacturing centre. Furthermore, with over 172,000 jobs, LA's fashion industry now has a larger workforce than that of New York's garment industry and is the biggest city in America for fashion design and manufacturing.

LA is the leading import/export port in the United States, with US$212 billion worth of trading activity each year in the customs district, which includes the Port of Los Angeles, Port of Long Beach, LAX and smaller ports. LA's main port is located at San Pedro and is the largest man-made port in the world. Major exports include integrated circuits, aircraft, spacecraft, computers, aircraft parts and parts for office machines. Imports include computers, passenger vehicles, integrated circuits, office machine parts and reception apparatus.

Fortune 500 companies based in LA County include *Merrill Lynch* and *Ernst & Young* (accountants), *J P Morgan Chase & Co* (banking) and *Charles Schwab & Co* (medical), as well as the headquarters for *Walt Disney, Occidental Petroleum, Health Net, Mattel* and *Hilton Hotels,* among others.

In general, the LA economy is very healthy, despite the general downturn in the US economy over 2002. The unemployment rate at 6.4% is fairly similar to the national average of 6.5%.

The *Los Angeles County Economic Development Corporation* (website: www.laedc.org) can provide further information.

Line connects Downtown Los Angeles and Long Beach. The Green Line runs along the median of Century Freeway and links Norwalk, El Segundo and Redondo. The Red Line connects Union Station and Downtown LA with either Hollywood, Universal City and North Hollywood or the Wilshire Center. A fourth line, the Gold Line, open in mid-2003, runs from Union Station to Pasadena.

The standard fare for Metro Bus or Metro Rail is US$1.35 one way. Bus tickets can be purchased from the driver (exact change only), while rail tickets should be purchased before boarding from self-service vending machines in stations. A weekly Metro **pass** (US$11) is good for unlimited rides on Metro Bus or Metro Rail, or passengers can buy ten Metro tokens for US$9, which can be used for one-way fares on either bus or rail. Many hotels, local convenience and grocery stores and Metro Customer Centers sell Metro passes and tokens.

Downtown Los Angeles also has a bus system called *DASH*, which operates various routes around the Downtown area. Fares are a low US$0.25. Maps and schedules are available on the bus or from a hotel concierge and signs are posted throughout the Downtown area. DASH is operated by *LADOT* (tel: (818 *or* 310) 808 2273; website: www.ladottransit.com).

Taxis

Although taxis are readily available, the size of Los Angeles makes them expensive and impractical for cross-town journeys. They are more useful for night journeys within one area. There are ten franchise taxi operators in the city. Visitors should look for the official Los Angeles Taxicab Seal before getting in, as those without it are 'bandit' cabs with no legal authorisation to operate. Taxis cannot be hailed on the street but there are ranks at major hotels and they can be telephoned for: *Bell Cab* (tel: (888) BELLCAB/235 5222; website: www. bellcab.com); *LA Yellow Cab* (tel: (800) 200 1085 *or* (877) 733 3305 *or* (888) 793 5569; website: www. layellowcab.com); *Checker Cab* (tel: (323) 938 8130). All official taxis charge the same rates. The basic fare for a taxi ride is US$2 initial charge, then US$2 per mile.

Limousines

Chauffeur-driven cars and limousines are available from *Chauffeurs Unlimited* (tel: (800) 922 8583 *or* (310) 645 8711; website: www.chaufusa.com), *LA Limousine* (tel: (877) 449 7777 *or* (323) 876 3492; website: www.la-limousine.com) and *Orion Limousine Service* (tel: (888) 431 5466; website: www. orionlimo.com). Rates for a limousine start from around US$55 per hour plus 9% sales tax and 15% tip.

Driving in the City

The distances between LA's various points can seem intimidating at first, but it is relatively easy to get around the city in a car. However, it is hard to get a sense of compass points so visitors should try to plan their journey in advance and get to know a map of the major highways. Freeways running east–west have even numbers, while those running north–south have odd numbers. Most have a name as well as a number; and it is wise to ask for both when getting directions. The *Downtown Visitor Information Center* (tel: (213 689 8822) can help here.

The freeways are well marked, although very congested during rush hours (0700–0900 and 1600–1900). Using helicopters, local radio stations broadcast frequent traffic reports 0600–1000 and 1500–1900. Many southern Californian freeways have designated fast lanes for HOVs or High Occupancy Vehicles only – usually cars carrying more than one person. Visitors should not merge into an HOV lane unless their car has the specified number of passengers, as fines are levied. There are call boxes with free telephones every half-mile along the freeways for emergencies.

There are numerous parking lots and garages throughout the city; prices vary widely, starting at around US$4 for a minimum stay. For on-street parking, however, visitors should read all signs carefully, as there is often a complicated system of days or hours when parking is not allowed for street cleaning etc. Illegally parked vehicles are quickly ticketed and may be towed away. A red curb means no parking. A green curb allows parking for a limited time. A white curb is for loading and unloading passengers only. Some streets have metered parking; meters generally take quarters (25-cent coins) and the fees are US$0.25 per 15 minutes in the Downtown area and US$0.25 for 20–30 minutes elsewhere. Meters are generally free after 1800 and on Sundays, but visitors should always check the signs. Many restaurants offer valet parking either free or for a nominal fee; valets should always be tipped US$1–2.

Car Hire

All the major car hire companies have offices around the LA area. These include *Alamo* (tel: (800) 462 5266; website: www.goalamo.com); *Avis* (tel: (800) 230 4898; website: www.avis.com), *Budget* (tel: (800) 404 8033 *or* (800) 527 0700; website: www. budgetrentacar.com), *Dollar* (tel: (800) 800 3665; website: www.dollar.com), *Hertz* (tel: (800) 654 3131; website: www.hertz.com), *National* (tel: (800) 227 7368; website: www. nationalcar.com) and *Thrifty* (tel: (800) 847 4389; website: www.thrifty.com). Drivers must be at least 25

BUSINESS ETIQUETTE

The wide variety of businesses in Los Angeles encourages a variety of styles, depending on the industry involved. In general, Californians cultivate a relaxed, informal atmosphere in keeping with the climate and the LA kind of life: smart-casual dress is a good rule of thumb, especially within industries such as film and TV, computing or multimedia. More conservative suits and business dress are the norm in legal and financial institutions. Increasingly in America, Friday is a dress-down day in many businesses, with employees wearing jeans or other casual attire in anticipation of the weekend. After hours, some top restaurants and hotels require men to wear jacket and tie, but casual-smart is more often de rigueur.

The normal working day runs 0800/0900–1700, although some businesses start early, particularly in the film industry. Breakfast meetings, often as early as 0700, are quite common for busy executives. Lunch is generally between 1200 and 1300, or 1230 and 1330. Where alcohol is concerned, it is best to wait and check the preferences of the host. Many Americans stick to soft drinks, even milk. People are health-conscious: smoking or excessive drinking may be frowned upon in a business environment.

Business associates generally exchange business cards at an appropriate moment, usually towards the end of a meeting. Socialising is normally at lunchtime, sometimes during after-work drinks and/or dinner. LA is a notoriously early-to-bed town, due to the early starts in the film industry, so late nights are not common. Hosts generally do not invite clients or colleagues home unless they know them particularly well. Visitors may be given gifts related to their own business, such as pens or baseball caps complete with company logo on it, so similar gifts from a visitor's company or typical items from his or her country would be appropriate.

years of age, depending on company policy. Weekly car hire rates start at around US$180.

Los Angeles Rent-A-Car (tel: (310) 670 9945 *or* (800) 441 7368; website: www.la-rentacar.com) rents to drivers under 25 years. Los Angeles loves classic cars; to hire these or any slightly more exotic vehicle, visitors could try *Beverly Hills Rent A Car* (tel: (310) 337 1400 *or* (800) 479 5996; website: www. bhrentacar.com).

Bicycle & Motorcycle Hire

LA Bike Tours (tel: (323) 466 5890 *or* (888) 775 BIKE/2453; website: www.labiketours.com) offers bicycles for rental, as well as their more extensive bicycle tours (see *Tours of the City*). Prices are US$20 per day or US$60 per week. *Perry's Beach Café*, 2400 and 2600 Oceanfront Walk, Santa Monica (tel: (310) 372 3138 *or* 452 2399; website: www.perryscafe .com), has bike and skate rentals and easy access to the bike paths either side of Santa Monica Pier. Rates for both bike and skate rentals are US$6 per hour or US$18 per day. *Bikestation*, 105 The Promenade North, Long Beach (tel: (562) 436 BIKE/2453), which links to public transportation and 53km (33 miles) of scenic bike paths, has quality bike rentals. *EagleRider Motorcycle Rental* (tel: (800) 501 8687; website: www.eaglerider.com) has motorcycle rentals, including Harley Davidsons, as well as motorcycle guided tours. Rentals cost US$75–225 per day. Drivers must be at least 21 years of age.

SIGHTSEEING

Sightseeing Overview

The sights of Los Angeles are spread throughout five counties. At off-peak times, the freeways are quick and convenient and it is easy to get around.

Downtown LA comprises the Financial District with skyscrapers that seem the more incredible because the rest of the city is so flat. It is also home to lively local communities with markets (there's a covered market for local produce) and shops. Here are Chinatown, Little Tokyo, the Hispanic centre around Olvera Street, the historic district where the city was founded, with landmarks from the city's early 20th-century heyday, as well as cultural institutions like the *Museum of Contemporary Art* and the *Performing Arts Center*. Joining them in 2003 is the LA Philharmonic's dramatic new home, the *Walt Disney Concert Hall* at Grand Avenue and First Street, designed by Frank Gehry. The completion of the Cathedral of Our Lady of the Angels (website: www.olacathedral.org), LA's new Roman Catholic cathedral designed by architect Jose Raphael Moneo, has also added to the architectural landmarks in the Downtown area.

East of Downtown, the city of **Pasadena**, in the San Gabriel Valley, has a historic centre and two outstanding museums. To the west of Downtown is **Hollywood**, although the actual Hollywood sign is located high above Hollywood Boulevard up in the hills near *Griffith Park*. Although the famous sign is situated on a steep incline, which means that it cannot be visited, the extensive Griffith Park is great for a wander and fantastic panoramas of the whole city. It contains the famous 1935 Art Deco *Griffith Observatory* (website: www.griffithobs.org), although this is closed for renovation until 2005. However, down below in actual Hollywood, the streets and boulevards are less glamorous than their name might suggest and the

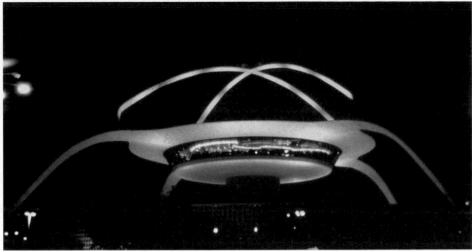

LAX airport

Hollywood Walk of Fame is fascinating but hardly high class. There have been successful attempts to upgrade areas, such as Hollywood and Vine, and there is a string of small museums, mostly connected to films, the famous *Grauman's Chinese Theater*, some notable if occasionally rundown Art Deco buildings and, on its northern edge, the popular *Universal Studios*.

The Westside encompasses trendy, fashionable and primarily gay West Hollywood, rich and handsome Beverly Hills, Miracle Mile, Century City, Westwood Village (where *UCLA* is situated) and Brentwood. Each has its own atmosphere and attractions. West Hollywood has the glitzy stretch of *Sunset Boulevard* known as *Sunset Strip*, with its enormous hand-painted billboards on the sides of buildings, while *Rodeo Drive* is Beverly Hills' most famous street. Stretching along the Pacific coast are the **Beach Cities**, including *Santa Monica* and *Venice Beach*, as well as *Malibu* to the north and *Long Beach*, which lies south of Downtown on San Pedro Bay. Southeast of Downtown is **Orange County**, home of *Disneyland* and *Knott's Berry Farm* theme parks. To the north is the wide **San Fernando Valley**, a largely residential area with several film and TV studios.

Key Attractions

Downtown

El Pueblo de Los Angeles (and Olvera Street)

The birthplace of Los Angeles, just north of the Financial District with its huge skyscrapers, is now a state historic park. In 1781, Father Junipero Serra, founder of many of California's Spanish missions, and Don Felipe de Neve journeyed north from Mexico and established a pueblo here on the site of a former Indian village. Its name – El Pueblo de Nuestra Señora la Reina de Los Angeles de Porciuncula (The Town of Our Lady Queen of the Angels of Porciuncula) – outweighed its size and it was soon shortened to Los Angeles. The 27 historic adobe buildings date from the early 19th century and pay tribute to the city's Spanish heritage. They include the *Avila Adobe*, the city's oldest home; the *Old Plaza Church* and the *Sepulveda House*, which now serves as the El Pueblo Visitor Information Center. The heart of the district is Olvera Street, a lively place with strolling *mariachi* bands, stalls selling Mexican handicrafts and good Mexican restaurants, some still run by the original families.

North Alameda and Spring Streets
Tel: (213) 628 1274 *or* (213) 628 3562.
Website: www.ci.la.ca.us/ELP
Transport: Metro Red Line Union Station/Gateway Transit Center.
Opening hours: Daily 1000–1900; Mon–Sat 1000–1500 (Visitor Center).
Admission: Free.

Photo: Glenn Cormier/Los Angeles Convention & Visitors Bureau

Museum of Contemporary Art

Museum of Contemporary Art (MOCA)

Housed in a striking red sandstone building designed by Japanese architect Arata Isozaki, this celebrated art museum showcases the work of leading modern artists. The permanent collection features the likes of Piet Mondrian and Mark Rothko, while temporary exhibitions highlight contemporary themes and artists of international renown. Pyramid skylights enhance the bright galleries, while the courtyard sports an attractive fountain. *MOCA* has a secondary site, which is located close by and accessible by free shuttle, called *Geffen Contemporary*, which hosts changing contemporary exhibitions in an old warehouse. MOCA's newest third venue is at the *Pacific Design Centre* in West Hollywood, which focuses on contemporary architecture and design.
California Plaza, 250 South Grand Avenue
Geffen Contemporary, 152 North Central Avenue
Pacific Design Centre, 8687 Melrose Avenue, West Hollywood
Tel: (213) 626 6222.
Website: www.moca-la.org
Transport: Metro Red Line Pershing.
Opening hours: Tues–Sun 1100–1700 (until 2000 on Thurs).
Admission: US$8 (concessions available); free all Thurs.

Southwest Museum

Los Angeles' first museum, established in 1907, contains one of the foremost collections of Native American art and artefacts in the nation. Enlightening exhibits on tribal life are well presented and there are fine examples of kachina dolls, native dress and ceremonial costumes, musical instruments, ceramics, weapons, everyday objects and a large display of basketry. The museum lies just north of Downtown, on a hillside beyond Dodger Stadium.
234 Museum Drive
Tel: (323) 221 2164.
Website: www.southwestmuseum.org
Transport: Metro Bus 81 or 83.
Opening hours: Tues–Sun 1000–1700.
Admission: US$6 (concessions available).

Hollywood

Grauman's Chinese Theater and the Hollywood Walk of Fame

Built by showman Sid Grauman in 1927, this is the most famous of the flamboyant picture palaces along this stretch of Hollywood Boulevard. Having undergone an extensive renovation as part of the development of the area (see *Hollywood and Highland* below), the inside has been opulently restored, while the exotic oriental façade is resplendent in its pastel greens, crowned by a red pagoda roof. The ticket booth has been moved from the forecourt – which remains the main attraction here. It is where the hand and footprints of Hollywood celebrities are embedded into the cement. This signature parade started quite by accident, when actress Constance Talmadge stepped in wet cement at the grand opening. Among the more unusual signatures are Jimmy Durante's nose and the hoof prints of Roy Rogers' horse Trigger. The cinema still shows first-run movies, a good way to see its lavish interior. Other Art Deco theatres nearby worth a look are *Pacific El Capitan*, the *Egyptian Theater* and *Pantages Theater*.
The *Hollywood Walk of Fame* passes outside the front of the Chinese Theater. This trail of bronze stars embedded in the paving stones runs 5.5km (3.5 miles) along Hollywood Boulevard between La Brea Avenue and Gower Street, and along Vine Street between Yucca Street and Sunset Boulevard. It honours artists in the film and music industries and the first star embedded in the pavement in 1960 was one for Joanne Woodward. Today, they number well over 2000.
Grauman's Chinese Theater
6925 Hollywood Boulevard
Tel: (323) 464 8111.
Transport: Metro Red Line Hollywood/Highland.
Opening hours: Daily 24 hours (forecourt).
Admission: Free (forecourt); US$10 (film).
Hollywood Walk of Fame
Website: www.hollywoodcoc.org

Hollywood and Highland

Built around the Chinese Theater, as part of a US$615-million plan to revitalise Hollywood Boulevard, this massive new retail and entertainment complex is known as *Hollywood and Highland* because of its location above the Hollywood and Highland subway station. The open-air, five-storey complex includes shops, restaurants, nightclubs, theatres, cinemas, a hotel, a ballroom and the *Hollywood Motion Picture Collection*. It is also home to the *Kodak Theater*, also known as the Academy Awards Theater as it has become the new permanent venue for the Oscars ceremony. There will also be an observation tower, which will offer panoramic views of the Hollywood sign.
6801 Hollywood Boulevard
Tel: (323) 467 6412.
Website: www.hollywoodandhighland.com
Transport: Metro Red Line Hollywood/Highland.
Opening hours: Mon–Sat 1000–2200, Sun 1000–1900.
Admission: Free; attractions cost.

Universal Studios Hollywood

Part film and TV studio, part theme park, *Universal Studios* is one of the most popular attractions in Los Angeles. The visit begins with a behind-the-scenes tram tour of film sets, with a simulated earthquake and collapsing bridge, as well as surprise attacks by the shark from *Jaws* and by King Kong. Stunt shows, musical entertainment and a variety of thrill rides, such as *Back to the Future*, make for a lively day of Hollywood at its best.
100 Universal City Plaza
Tel: (800) UNIVERSAL/864 8377 *or* (818) 508 9600.
Website: www.universalstudios.com
Transport: Metro Red Line Universal City.
Opening hours: Vary from month to month; minimum 1000–1800, maximum 0900–2200.
Admission: US$47 (one-day pass).

Hollywood Roosevelt Hotel

This classic 12-storey 305-room hotel celebrated its 75th diamond anniversary in 2002. The oldest continuously operating hotel in Hollywood, the *Roosevelt Hotel* is listed in the National Registry of Historic Places and is a Hollywood Historic Site. It was founded by a syndicate of Hollywood luminaries in 1927 and was actually the birthplace of the Academy Awards, as the first Oscars ceremony took place here on 19 May 1929. Recently restored to its Spanish Colonial splendour, it is one of the gems on Hollywood Boulevard – great for a drink in the bar.
7000 Hollywood Boulevard
Tel: (323) 466 7000 *or* (800) 950 7667. Fax: (323) 462 8056.
Website: www.hollywoodroosevelt.com

The Westside

Page Museum at the La Brea Tar Pits

Smack in the middle of LA, the *La Brea Tar Pits* are a fascinating survival from prehistoric times. They have yielded more than four million fossils – one of the largest caches in the world – from the Pleistocene Era, dating back 40,000 years. Inside the museum are the skeletons of long-extinct animals, such as the imperial mammoth, giant sloth, sabre-toothed tiger and dire wolf, who became trapped and preserved in the thick black tar, or 'brea', that seeped up through the ground. Visitors can watch palaeontologists cleaning and cataloguing fossils and see excavations from viewing stations beside the tar pits.
5801 Wilshire Boulevard
Tel: (323) 934 PAGE/7243.
Website: www.tarpits.org
Transport: Metro Bus 20, 21, 22 or 217.
Opening hours: Mon–Fri 0930–1700, Sat and Sun 1000–1700.
Admission: US$6 (concessions available).

Los Angeles County Museum of Art

Housed in four main buildings around a courtyard, this outstanding collection of art and artefacts forms one of the leading art museums in the United States. In the

enormous Ahmanson Building, art, sculpture and decorative arts from Asia, Europe and the Americas are on display. Highlights of the collection include the Indian and Southeast Asian art collection, regarded as the finest in the West; the Western Art galleries and pre-Columbian artefacts from Latin America. There is a special Japanese Pavilion, the striking, modern Robert O Anderson Building and the Bing Theater.
5905 Wilshire Boulevard
Tel: (323) 857 6000.
Website: www.lacma.org
Transport: Metro Bus 20, 21, 22 or 320.
Opening hours: Mon, Tues, Thurs 1200–2000, Fri 1200–2100, Sat and Sun 1100–2000.
Admission: US$7 (concessions available).

UCLA Hammer Museum of Art and Cultural Center

The main collection at this museum is an impressive collection of Old Masters, Impressionist and post-Impressionist paintings, which was acquired by the late industrialist Armand Hammer. This collection is shown on a rotating basis and includes works by Constable, Rembrandt, Van Gogh and Monet, as well as a room full of lithographs by Honoré Daumier. Run by UCLA, the museum also displays exhibitions from the *Grunwald Center for the Graphic Arts*, which cover graphic art from the Renaissance to the present day. There is also a distinguished outdoor Sculpture Garden, as well as special exhibitions and programs.
10899 Wilshire Boulevard
Tel: (310) 443 7000.
Website: www.hammer.ucla.edu
Transport: Metro Bus 20, 21 or 22.
Opening hours: Tues–Sat 1100–1900 (until 2100 on Thurs), Sun 1100–1700.
Admission: US$5 (concessions available); free Thurs.

Getty Center

The marble buildings of the *Getty Center*, set in the foothills of the Santa Monica Mountains, were designed by architect Richard Meier. It contains J Paul Getty's painting collection (interesting but hardly top rank), but is also a centre for the study of archaeology, culture, art history and humanities. The galleries also display sculpture, photographs, drawings, furniture and more than 100 illuminated manuscripts. Lectures, concerts and educational programmes are also held. The Getty Center is surrounded by beautiful gardens with rare and native plants and trees, while the terrace affords panoramic views, so visitors should plan to stay for a whole day.
1200 Getty Center Drive
Tel: (310) 440 7300.
Website: www.getty.edu
Transport: Metro Bus 561 or Santa Monica Big Blue Bus 14; or free shuttle bus from car park on Sepulveda Boulevard and Constitution Avenue.
Opening hours: Tues–Sun 1000–1800 (until 2100 Fri and Sat).
Admission: Free. On-site parking: US$5 (reservations essential).

Museum of Tolerance

Visitors should allow at least two hours to experience this thought-provoking museum and last entry is, in fact, two hours before closing time. The main part of the museum is devoted to the Holocaust and is a moving journey from the Jewish ghettos to Hitler's death camps in an hour-long tour. The Tolerancenter contains high-tech, interactive exhibits that explore racism and bigotry in America through events such as the LA riots of 1992. Upstairs are archives and a multimedia learning centre.
9786 West Pico Boulevard
Tel: (310) 553 8403 *or* (800) 900 9036.
Website: www.museumoftolerance.com
Transport: Metro Bus 3, Santa Monica Municipal Bus 5 or 7.
Opening hours: Mon–Thurs 1130–1830, Fri 1130–1700, Sun 1100–1930. Nov–Mar closes at 1500 on Fri. Last admission 2 hours before closing time.
Admission: US$10 (concessions available).

Beach Cities

Santa Monica

Long and wide, Santa Monica Boulevard, if followed to its western end – comes out on Santa Monica itself. With its village feel, its cafés, shops and restaurants, it is one of the more people-friendly areas of Los Angeles – it has the only pedestrianised street in the city. The place is famed for its *Pier*, and jutting out into the Pacific from a wide sandy beach, it is one of the most nostalgic spots in LA. The original fishing pier was built in 1909 and another one for strolling was added in 1921, but by the 1970s both were in a shabby state. In the 1980s, a restoration programme rejuvenated the pier. Besides the original arcades (now *Playland Arcade*) and the carousel dating from 1916, there is now a new aquarium, the *UCLA Ocean Discovery Center*, and *Pacific Park*, an amusement park with rides, ferris wheel and a small rollercoaster. During the summer, there is dancing and live music on Thursday nights. A good time to go is towards the end of the day as the sunsets can be fabulous, especially at the very western end of Sunset Boulevard (obviously enough).
Colorado and Ocean Avenues
Tel: (310) 458 8900.
Website: www.santamonicapier.org
Transport: Metro Bus 4, 20, 22, 33, 320 or 434.
Playland Arcade
Tel: (310) 451 5133. Fax: (310) 394 1587.
Website: www.playlandarcade.com
Opening hours: Sun–Thurs 1000–2400, Fri

1000–0200, Sat 0900–0200. Changes seasonally.
Admission: Free.
UCLA Ocean Discovery Center
Tel: (310) 393 6149. Fax: (310) 393 4839.
Website: www.odc.ucla.edu
Opening hours: Tues–Fri 1500–1800, Sat 1100–1800, Sun 1100–1700 (summer). Sat and Sun 1100–1700 only (winter).
Admission: US$3.
Pacific Park
Tel: (310) 260 8744. Fax: (310) 260 8748.
Website: www.pacpark.com
Opening hours: Sun–Thurs 1100–2300, Fri and Sat 1100–2430. Changes seasonally.
Admission: Free; plus individual rides. Unlimited wristbands: US$10.95/19.95 depending on height.

Venice Beach

Further south along the coast is the slightly more bohemian *Venice Beach*. Its *Boardwalk*, a path alongside the beach, is one of the liveliest places to view LA joie de vivre. Buskers, mime artists, painters, cyclists, palm readers and rollerbladers all mingle here, chilling out, hustling, cruising the sands, wearing colourful attire or, quite often, very little at all. There are shops, stalls and cafés for people-watching. The notorious Muscle Beach, where male and female weight lifters pec-flex in the sun, is a good place for ogling.
Marine Street to the Venice Pier
Tel: (310) 392 4687, ext 6.
Transport: Metro Bus 33.
Website: www.westland.net/venice

Pasadena

Huntington Library, Art Collections and Botanical Gardens

In one visit, it is virtually impossible to fit in everything on this lavish estate. The former home of railroad tycoon Henry E Huntington is filled with French porcelain, tapestries, American paintings and a remarkable collection of British and French art from the 18th and 19th centuries. Famous highlights are Gainsborough's *Blue Boy* and Lawrence's *Pinkie*. Among the four million items in the Library are rare

Universal CityWalk at Universal Studios

Catalina Island

books and manuscripts: a Gutenberg Bible, an early 15th-century manuscript of Chaucer's *Canterbury Tales* and early editions of Shakespeare. Visitors should save some time to stroll in the beautiful *Botanical Gardens*, whose 150 hectares (380 acres) include a Japanese garden, desert garden, rose garden and changing landscapes.
1151 Oxford Road, San Marino
Tel: (626) 405 2100.
Website: www.huntington.org
Transport: Metro Bus 401 from Downtown to Pasadena, Colorado Boulevard/Allen Avenue stop, then 20-minute walk along Allen Avenue.
Opening hours: Tues–Fri 1200–1630, Sat and Sun 1030–1630.
Admission: US$10 (concessions available).

Norton Simon Museum

This renowned collection of European art ranges from the Renaissance to the 20th century. There are works by Rembrandt, Picasso, the Impressionists, a collection of Degas sculptures, as well as leading works by Rodin. The sculptures from Southeast Asia and India, spanning 2000 years, are another highlight, as are the lovely Monet-inspired gardens.
411 West Colorado Boulevard, Pasadena
Tel: (626) 449 6840.
Website: www.nortonsimon.org
Transport: Metro Bus 401 from Downtown to Pasadena, then bus 180.
Opening hours: Wed–Mon 1200–1800 (until 2100 Fri).
Admission: US$6 (concessions available).

Further Distractions

Disneyland

A trip to Los Angeles is arguably not complete without a visit to America's favourite theme park; even adults with a healthy cynicism about the Mouse might find themselves grinning. The park is divided into themed 'lands' – Main Street USA, Tomorrowland, Adventureland, Frontierland, Fantasyland and Toontown – each with a variety of rides and entertainment. Favourite attractions include the Haunted Mansion, Space Mountain, Star Tours and Indiana Jones Adventure. The fabulous Electrical Parade and night-time laser light show are worth staying for.
1313 Harbor Boulevard, Anaheim
Tel: (714) 781 4565 or (714) 781 4400.
Website: www.disney.go.com
Transport: Metro Bus 460.
Opening hours: Daily 0900–2100 (until 2400 on Sat). Extended hours during summer/holidays. Main Street open from 0830. Hours vary; visitors should call.
Admission: US$47.

Knott's Berry Farm

America's oldest theme park began in the 1930s, when Walter Knott built the 'Ghost Town' to entertain customers queuing for his wife's boysenberry pies and chicken dinners. Today, there are several themed areas with shows and attractions, but the park's biggest draw is its hair-raising thrill rides, including Montezooma's Revenge, Supreme Scream and Ghost Rider, one of the tallest and longest wooden rollercoasters in the West.
8039 Beach Boulevard, Buena Park
Tel: (714) 220 5200.
Website: www.knotts.com
Transport: Metro Bus 460.
Opening hours: Mon–Fri 1000–1800, Sat 1000–2200, Sun 1000–1900; extended summer and holiday hours.
Admission: US$42 (concessions available).

Tours of the City

Walking Tours

Walking tours of Downtown Los Angeles are given by *Los Angeles Conservancy Tours* (tel: (213) 623 2489; website: www.laconservancy.org). The tours cover landmark buildings and historic areas, such as Pershing Square, Broadway theatre district and Little Tokyo, and cost US$8 per person. Reservations are required. *Red Line Tours* (tel: (323) 402 1074; website: www.redlinetours.com) offers historic walking tours of Downtown and Hollywood, providing each person with a head set of the live commentary. These tours have rare access to the interiors of buildings and usually cost US$20.
The Los Angeles branch of the Sierra Club (tel: (213) 387 4287; website: www.angeles.sierraclub.org) offers regular hikes, taking in the natural beauty and wildlife of LA and the surrounding areas. *Architours* (tel: (323) 294 5821 *or* (866) 227 2448; website: www. architours.com) gives art and architecture tours of the city.

Bus Tours

LA City Tours (tel: (310) 581 0718 *or* (888) 800 7878; website: www.lacitytours.com) offers a five-and-a-half-hour bus tour of Los Angeles, which includes Downtown, Hollywood, the beaches and movie star homes and costs US$55. They also offer excursions to San Diego, the Grand Canyon and Las Vegas. *Starline Tours* (tel: (800) 959 3131; website: www. starlinetours.com) offers various bus tours of Los Angeles, from the one-hour 'Hollywood Trolley Tour' for US$16 to the seven-and-a-half-hour tour combining 'Grand Tour of Los Angeles' and 'Movie Stars' Homes' for US$63.

Bike Tours

LA Bike Tours (tel: (323) 466 5890 *or* (888) 775 BIKE/2453; website: www.labiketours.com) provides guided group or individual cycling tours of Hollywood Studios, Beverly Hills, the Getty Center, Venice Beach and Santa Monica. Tours include snacks, water, bicycle and helmet and vary in length and in the fitness level required. Prices start from US$49.50. *Perry's Beach Café and Rentals*, 2400 and 2600 Oceanfront Walk, Santa Monica (tel: (310) 372 3138; website: www.perryscafe.com), offers tours along the beach in Santa Monica or Venice and its canals – on bicycle or rollerblade. Prices start from US$30 in winter for a two-hour tour.

Excursions

For a Half Day

Long Beach: The city of *Long Beach*, the second largest in Los Angeles County, is directly south of Downtown LA, an easy drive on the Long Beach freeways (I-710). Alternatively, Metro Blue Line runs from Downtown to the Transit Mall at Long Beach, and from there the Passport Shuttle has a free service to the major Long Beach attractions.
The charming Long Beach was a popular seaside resort in the early 1900s. The discovery of oil in 1921 sparked a boom of industrial and commercial development, including the construction of a harbour. In the 1990s, the city turned to tourism again, restoring historic areas and developing a host of new attractions along its nine kilometres (5.5 miles) of wide and splendid sandy beach. At Long Beach Harbour, visitors can tour the majestic *Queen Mary*, the 1934 luxury liner that once carried celebrities

and royalty on transatlantic voyages (tel: (562) 435 3511; open: daily 1000–1800; admission and self-guided tour: US$24.95). Nearby, the *Long Beach Aquarium of the Pacific* (tel: (562) 590 3100; open: daily 0900–1800; admission: US$18.75) is home to more than 550 species of marine animals in a variety of ocean habitats. Further along the shore are the *Long Beach Museum of Art* (tel: (562) 439 2119; open: Tues–Sun 1100–1700; admission: US$5), the *Shoreline Village* shopping centre and *Gondola Getaway* (tel: (562) 433 9595; trips: 1000–2400; price: US$65 for two people), with gondola cruises through the canals of Naples Island. The *Promenade* walkway from the marina to the business district is lined with restaurants and nightlife venues. Historic walks take in landmark buildings and some of the city's 50 murals. The *Long Beach Area Convention and Visitors Bureau*, Suite 300, One World Trade Center (tel: (562) 436 3645 *or* (800) 452 7829; website: www.visitlongbeach.com).

For a Whole Day

Catalina Island: Just 35km (22 miles) across the ocean from Long Beach is the idyllic *Catalina Island*. This peaceful island where no cars are allowed has long been a favourite retreat for stressed-out Angelenos. The *Catalina Express* (tel: (800) 481 3470; website: www.catalinaexpress.com) runs a ferry service from Long Beach or Los Angeles Port. The journey time from Long Beach is about 1–2 hours depending on the boat and, while the island makes a pleasant day trip, it also rewards a longer stay. Round-trip fares from Long Beach cost US$42.

Avalon, the island capital, sits in the hills above a crescent-shaped harbour, with a beach. At one end is the landmark *Casino*, with its grand ballroom, where people came to dance to the big bands of the 1930s and 40s. A visitor centre on the pier books tours of the Casino, glass-bottom boat rides or visits to the rugged interior where there is a herd of buffalo. Relax on the beach or enjoy a variety of watersports. The *Catalina Island Visitors Bureau & Chamber of Commerce* (tel: (310) 510 1520; website: www.catalina.com) can provide information.

ACCOMMODATION

All hotel bills are subject to a 14% occupancy tax, which is added to the bill at the end; there may be other small individual taxes levied.

The prices quoted below are the lowest standard rates for a double room, excluding tax and excluding breakfast, unless otherwise specified.

Business

Figueroa Hotel and Convention Center

Only one block from Los Angeles Convention Center in the heart of LA's business district, this charming, 12-storey landmark hotel, built in 1926, offers business travellers Moroccan style at reasonable prices. Large, terracotta-coloured rooms feature wrought-iron beds and hand-painted furniture along with private phones, voice-mail, modem points, satellite TV and refrigerators. The hotel's bar and Indian restaurant – or the heated pool and Jacuzzi in a garden of bougainvillea, cacti, fountains and statues – are perfect for relaxing after a hard day's work. The coffee shop and reception are open 24 hours.

939 South Figueroa Street, Downtown
Tel: (213) 627 8971 *or* (800) 421 9092 (reservations).
Fax: (213) 689 0305.
Website: www.figueroahotel.com
Price: From US$114.

Park Hyatt Los Angeles at Century City

This high-tech hotel is within walking distance of Disneyland, 20th Century Fox Studios and ABC Entertainment Center. Each classically furnished room with balcony or patio offers the latest modern technology with two phone lines, voice-mail, fax machine, computer hook-up, remote-control cable TV, in-room movies, video messages, video account reviews and video check-out. Other perks include 24-hour room service, mini-bar, complimentary morning newspaper, coffee and shoeshine. Banquet facilities can accommodate 300 and 12 of the meeting rooms offer spectacular city views. There is a fitness centre, indoor and outdoor pools, restaurant and bar, while golf is 1.6km (one mile) away by courtesy coach.
2151 Avenue of the Stars, Century City
Tel: (310) 277 1234 *or* (800) 233 1234 (reservations).
Fax: (310) 785 9240.
Website: www.hyatt.com
Price: From US$250.

Le Meridien at Beverly Hills

The hotel group *Le Meridien* has renovated the former Hotel Nikko into this 297-room luxury hotel, designed by the French designer Pierre-Yves Rochon. It features antiques, original artworks, imported marble and fine woods, as well as exterior landscaping. The white marble foyer has a fountain and atrium garden, while there is a business lounge, which includes high-speed Internet access and workstations, as well as extensive meeting rooms with state-of-the-art presentation facilities. There is a 24-hour fitness centre and lap pool, as well as a ballroom for up to 450 guests. The *Café Noir* bar and lounge, in the rear of the lobby, has a garden terrace, and features a Petrossian Paris Caviar menu among other things,

while *Le Festival* restaurant offers Mediterranean cuisine with a California twist. Guest rooms and suites are all large and well appointed, with luxurious furnishings and Hermès toiletries. Facilities include double-sided desks, Internet access, 'walk around' telephones, fax/printer/copiers, CD and video players. Underground self-parking for 600 cars is complimentary.
465 North La Cienega Boulevard, Beverly Hills
Tel: (310) 247 0400 *or* (800)645 5624 (reservations).
Fax: (310) 247 0315.
Website: www.lemeridien.com
Price: From US$290.

The Regent Beverly Wilshire

This 73-year-old hotel combines classical grandeur, impeccable service and 21st-century technology. Its ornately carved entrance leads to a magnificent lobby with Grecian columns and tapestries surrounded by an elegant restaurant and wood-panelled piano lounge. Rooms are luxury incarnate with orchids, marble bathrooms, cable TV/video, Internet access (US$10 per day) and electronic privacy and service-page buttons. Some overlook the garden patio and pool (modelled after Sophia Loren's), near the gym and spa. Banquet facilities cater for 820, while ten spacious, fully equipped meeting rooms make this a good choice for the business traveller who wants everything first class.
9500 Wilshire Boulevard, Beverly Hills
Tel: (310) 275 5200. Fax: (310) 274 2851.
Website: www.fourseasons.com
Price: From US$385.

Westin Bonaventure Hotel & Suites

An ideal location for conferences in LA's Financial District, this business-oriented hotel has five towers surrounding a six-storey atrium lobby with a lake and trees. A mini-city, its 20 shops and restaurants cover all tastes, from the rooftop steakhouse to the *Bonavista Bar* and *Lakeview Bistro*. The revolving cocktail lounge on the 34th floor offers 360-degree views of the city. Each room also offers panoramic views, as well as a two-line telephone, modem point, mini-bar, safe, cable TV and in-room movies. Fax/printer/scanners and

The Hollywood sign

Photo: Michele & Tom Grimm/Los Angeles Convention & Visitors Bureau

The Beverly Hills Hotel

computers can be added on request, while the business centre and 26 meeting rooms are fully equipped. A fitness centre and outdoor pool are available.
404 South Figueroa Street, Downtown
Tel: (213) 624 1000. Fax: (213) 612 4800.
Website: www.westin.com
Price: From US$249.

Luxury

The Beverly Hills Hotel

Now owned by the Sultan of Brunei, this is pure Hollywood glamour old-style. Built in 1912, the hotel has seen the honeymoons of six of Elizabeth Taylor's marriages and was featured in the star-studded 1978 movie *California Suite*. The famous *Polo Lounge* – a nostalgic vision in pink and green stripes and palm-printed wallpaper – is still a favourite among film directors and producers who order their salads tossed at the table and discuss deals over the chocolate cake and ganache in pistachio sauce. The rooms have it all, including two cable TVs (one in the bathroom), marble baths and walk-in closets, while bungalows are also available, nestled around the pool area. A whirlpool, fitness centre, tennis courts and business centre complete this paradise on earth.
9641 Sunset Boulevard, Beverly Hills
Tel: (310) 276 2251 *or* (800) 283 8885 (reservations).
Fax: (310) 887 2887.
E-mail: reservations@thebeverlyhillshotel.com
Website: www.thebeverlyhillshotel.com
Price: From US$410.

Shutters on the Beach

The only LA luxury hotel right on the beach, *Shutters* combines sophisticated elegance with a beach holiday atmosphere (although dignity must be maintained and robes as well as bathing suits are recommended at

the breakfast patio). Understated elegance rules. The lobby has comfy couches, a gas-lit fireplace and top-class modern art, including some by David Hockney and Roy Lichtenstein. Each of the 186 rooms has a verandah with table and chairs and an ocean or pool view. All rooms have a four-poster bed, a copy of Hemingway's *Old Man and the Sea*, a private fine wine supply, a TV/video and a whirlpool bath. Business-wise, the hotel is now 'wireless', roaming high-speed Internet access is provided throughout the hotel for US$9.95. Besides the pool, there is a gym, sauna, spa, the *One Pico* restaurant or *Pedals Café*, where brunch includes lemon ricotta pancakes or corned beef hash with perfectly poached eggs.
One Pico Boulevard, Santa Monica
Tel: (310) 458 0030 *or* (800) 334 9000 (reservations).
Fax: (310) 458 4589.
Website: www.shuttersonthebeach.com
Price: From US$395.

Moderate

Beverly Laurel Motor Hotel

This 1960s-style motel near some of the best restaurants in central LA offers retro glamour at very reasonable rates to families and struggling actors. Andy Warhol prints adorn the walls and its *Swingers' Diner*, overlooking the outdoor swimming pool, has become the trendy haunt of young poseurs who like to eat innovative diner food (such as pancakes with jalapeno maple syrup) and those conducting business meetings at unsociable hours (it is open very late). The rooms are all comfortable with basic facilities, including microwaves, fridges, cable TV and modem points, while the staff are friendly.
8018 Beverly Boulevard, Midtown
Tel: (323) 651 2441. Fax: (323) 651 5225.
Price: From US$84.

The Standard

Visitors are shown what to expect from this stylish, modern hotel when they see the sign outside for *The Standard*, spelt backwards – an example of the clever eccentricity that hotel designer André Balazs (who also refurbished Chateau Marmont) is renowned for. Young sophisticates gather in the floor-to-ceiling shag-carpeted lobby with live DJ and performance art shows, the poolside café or the 24-hour restaurant, which serves quality American comfort food. Rooms offer kitsch furniture like beanbag chairs, alongside a voice-mail speaker telephone, mini-bar, CD player, cable TV, modem point and showers (rooms with baths cost more). Balazs' vision of cultural magician meets modern-life convenience at affordable prices is invigorating – but not everyone's cup of tea.
8300 Sunset Boulevard, West Hollywood
Tel: (323) 650 9090. Fax: (323) 650 2820.
Website: www.standardhotel.com
Price: From US$135.

Other Recommendations

Avalon Hotel

This stylish mid-century hotel, in a residential area minutes from Sunset Strip, is where Marilyn Monroe once lived. With furnishings from 1950s to the present day, each room is a designer's dream, with smart, clean lines. Guest rooms are full of practical features, such as two-line telephones with conference/speaker capabilities, Internet access, safe, mini-bar, cassette/CD player and 27-inch cable TV. Every area, from the pool and cabanas to the fitness centre and conference room, is moulded by the same perfectionist eye. Service is of a high standard, with 24-hour room service, dry cleaning/laundry, mobile telephone rental, car hire, taxi/limo service and valet parking available.
9400 West Olympic Boulevard, Beverly Hills
Tel: (310) 277 5221 *or* (800) 535 4715 (reservations).
Fax: (310) 277 4928.
Website: www.avalonbeverlyhills.com
Price: From US$199.

Chateau Marmont

This romantic French chateau-style hotel, perched at the foot of the Hollywood Hills, has been a haven for show-business types since 1929. It has housed Greta Garbo, Warren Beatty and Howard Hughes, and still attracts the movers and shakers of the film and music industries. Through its ornately Gothic lobby and corridors lie rooms uniquely decorated with vintage furniture and appliances from the 1920s to 1950s. However, modern touches – like the attic gym – have been added. The hotel restaurant merges with the garden and pool to create a perfect retreat. Those who might easily forget they are in LA need only look out of a window to see the Sunset Strip below.
8221 Sunset Boulevard, West Hollywood
Tel: (323) 656 1010 *or* (800) 937 8939 (reservations).
Fax: (323) 655 5311.
Website: www.chateaumarmont.com
Price: From US$295.

RESTAURANTS

The selected restaurants have been divided into five categories: Gastronomic, Business, Trendy, Budget and Personal Recommendations. The restaurants are

Photo: Los Angeles Convention & Visitors Bureau

listed alphabetically within these different categories, which serve as guidelines rather than absolute definitions of the establishments.

A sales tax of 9% is always added to restaurant bills in LA. On top of this, a tip of 15% is recommended. An easy and convenient way to calculate the amount suitable for a tip is to double the amount of sales tax that has been added to the bill.

Many restaurants, including some that are licensed and offer wine on the menu, allow customers to bring their own wine. However, a corkage fee will be added to the bill, either as a flat fee or as a fee charged per person partaking of the wine. This can range from about US$3 per person to a US$20 flat fee.

The prices quoted below are for an average three-course meal for one person and for a bottle of house wine or cheapest equivalent; they do not include sales tax or tip.

Gastronomic

Ago

Pronounced 'AHHgo', this Tuscan-style restaurant attracts stars like a magnet. The stylish, modern decor is enriched by candlelight and handsome Italian waiters, who dash around efficiently on split levels that cause havoc with the acoustics. The *bistecca* and the porcini mushroom risotto are good entrées and the extensive dessert menu includes a delicious ricotta cheesecake. No lunch weekends.
8478 Melrose Avenue, West Hollywood
Tel: (323) 655 6333. Fax: (323) 655 6640.
Price: US$41. Wine: US$25.

Campanile

A remarkable building, commissioned in 1926 by Charlie Chaplin, has been designed with new Mediterranean features that reflect the cuisine of former Spago chefs Mark Peel and Nancy Silverton. Graceful arches connect the elegant dining rooms and atrium courtyard to the central sky-lit room, offering views of the building's sheet-metal tower above. The breads, with an extensive selection of olive oils, are good, as is the apple puff pastry with zabaglione. Main courses might include rosemary charred baby lamb, with warm potato salad and sprouted broccoli, spring onion and mustard butter, or seared spot prawns, served with agretti, ginger and lobster butter. No lunch weekends; brunch 0930–1330.
624 South La Brea Avenue, Midtown
Tel: (323) 938 1447. Fax: (323) 938 1447.
E-mail: campanile@campanilerestaurant.com
Website: www.campanilerestaurant.com
Price: US$65. Wine: US$42.

Patina

This is LA's haven for gourmets who never let cost get in the way of fine food. Chef Joachim Spichal whips up Californian-French nouvelle cuisine, while wife/hostess Christine welcomes diners. Elegant espresso-leather decor is complemented by exquisite appetisers, like caramelised scallops grenoblaise with purée of white beans and pressed bread. Entrées are just as good, such as the grilled veal chop served with watercress purée, fondant potatoes, black trumpet mushrooms and a 'gremolata' of crispy sweetbreads. There are four-course fixed-price menus – either 'Ocean' (US$75) or 'Garden' (US$62) for vegetarians – as well as a

five-course tasting menu for US$72. The wine list may be the best in LA. No lunch.
5955 Melrose Avenue, Hollywood
Tel: (323) 467 1108. Fax: (323) 467 0215.
E-mail: patina@patinagroup.com
Website: www.patinagroup.com
Price: US$60. Wine: US$30.

Rockenwagner

Within a Frank Gehry-designed building, chef Hans Rockenwagner and wife Patti serve innovative Euro-Asian/Californian nouvelle cuisine, like the Thai-inspired seafood bouillabaisse or the starter of warm Kumomoto oysters with a champagne-shallot emulsion. The menu changes weekly. The modern decor is enhanced by dim lighting and flowers on the tables; outdoor seating is also available. A tasting menu is available Monday to Thursday from US$58 per person. No lunch. Brunch Sunday 1000–1430.
Edgemar Complex, 2435 Main Street, Santa Monica
Tel: (310) 399 6504. Fax: (310) 399 7984.
E-mail: info@rockenwagner.com
Website: www.rockenwagner.com
Price: US$55 (tasting menu from US$58 per person).
Wine: US$30.

Spago

Chef Wolfgang Puck's flagship restaurant is for the rich and famous. Grandiose entrance doors set the stage for the over-the-top interior decor, with its stained-glass and art by the likes of David Hockney. The centrepiece patio, with olive trees and fountain, is home to the most coveted tables. Puck is particularly renowned for his pizzas, with light, buttery crusts and much mozzarella. The Louisiana spicy shrimp pizza is superb, as are the imaginative desserts, such as the Roasted Pineapple Rugalash Tart, but mains range from Cantonese duck with blood oranges to pan-roasted organic chicken with black truffles. The 22-page wine list satisfies all tastes. No lunch Sunday.
176 North Cañon Drive, Beverly Hills
Tel: (310) 385 0880. Fax: (310) 385 9690.
Website: www.wolfgangpuck.com
Price: US$60. Wine: US$40.

Business

Ca'Brea

Pronounced 'ka-brea', this woody restaurant with high ceilings is known for Italian food that looks as good as it tastes. The appetisers, bread, risottos and pasta dishes, such as rigatoni with braised aubergine, mozzarella and tomatoes, are particularly recommended. Popular with young lawyers and film industry people, reservations are essential for the best spots, as tables are close together and dinner gets very crowded. No lunch weekends.
346 South La Brea Avenue, Midtown
Tel: (323) 938 2863. Fax: (323) 938 8659.
Website: www.cabrearestaurant.com
Price: US$35. Wine: US$22.

Café des Artistes

This country-style cottage in the heart of Hollywood, run by Mimosa owner-chef Jean-Pierre Bosc, is one of the city's hottest spots. The simple French food is cooked to perfection and ranges from starters like Merguez sausages in cumin dip, through salads and sandwiches, bistro

Alfresco dining on Sunset Boulevard

standards like *moules-frites* or *steak-frites*, to full main courses, such as a braised lamb shank Provençale. While the restaurant's hardwood interior is cosy, the charming garden setting of the front and back patios is the most sought-after. No lunch weekends.
1534 North McCadden Place, Hollywood
Tel: (323) 469 7300. Fax: (323) 469 7375.
Website: www.mimosarestaurant.com/cafedesartistes
Price: US$35 (minimum charge of US$25 per person).
Wine: US$20.

Chaya Brasserie

This lively restaurant's Mediterranean-meets-Asian-Pacific-New-Wave cuisine, prepared by a Japanese chef, has been luring Angelenos for years, with its elegant decor, food and staff. Recommended dishes include the lobster ravioli with a pesto cream sauce or the venison with black peppercorns, chestnut purée and champignons. The bar menu, which includes sushi, is cheaper during happy hour (1700–2000) here and in the Venice Beach branch, where the service and decor pale somewhat in comparison. No lunch weekends.
8741 Alden Drive, West Hollywood/Melrose
Tel: (310) 859 8833. Fax: (310) 859 9481.
Website: www.thechaya.com
Price: US$45. Wine: US$22.
Chaya Venice, 110 Navy Street, Venice
Tel: (310) 396 1179.

Maple Drive

This classy restaurant, tucked away in a subdued side street, offers American Dream comfort food to film and record executives in plush, high-backed booths. Tender meatloaf with creamy mashed potatoes or pan-roasted chicken with mushroom kugel, followed by gooey date cake or apple tart, can be savoured by the fireplace or on the open-air terrace, which often has live jazz. No lunch weekends. Closed Sunday.

345 North Maple Drive, Beverly Hills
Tel: (310) 274 9800. Fax: (310) 274 2782.
E-mail: info@mapledriverestaurant.com
Website: www.mapledriverestaurant.com
Price: US$50. Wine: US$22.

Mimosa

This smaller, more authentic version of Café des Artistes, run by owner-chef Jean-Pierre Bosc, offers similar French culinary treasures in an intimate room lined with family pictures and handcrafted pottery. Bread baskets and jam jars of pickles and black olives adorn the tables. The veal daube Provençale with chick pea fritters or the cassoulet are superb. The exceptional wines are described impeccably by amiable waitresses. No lunch. Closed Sunday and Monday.

8009 Beverly Boulevard, Midtown
Tel: (323) 655 8895. Fax: (323) 655 9178.
Website: www.mimosarestaurant.com
Price: US$40. Wine: US$20.

Trendy

The Border Grill

This Mexican restaurant, with its vibrant decor inspired by traditional Central and South American mural art, attracts a young trendy crowd. The party-like atmosphere is further amplified by the consumption of margaritas and top-class tequilas. The green corn tamales topped with sour cream and salsa fresca are excellent, as are the pork chops in citrus adobo marinade served with mashed boniato potatoes, glazed carrots and ancho chilli sauce. For dessert, the chocolate cake with Mexican *crema* or the flans are very good. No lunch Monday.

1455 Fourth Street, Santa Monica
Tel: (310) 451 1655.
E-mail: mail@bordergrill.com
Website: www.bordergrill.com
Price: US$35. Wine: US$17.

Electric Lotus

This Indian restaurant's industrial entrance belies its hot-coloured, Bollywood interior. Techno sitar music accompanies a choice of 80 dishes, including a rich chicken tikka masala, spicy shrimp vindaloo cooled with ginger and lemon, and vegetarian specialities like bertha (stewed aubergine with garlic and ginger). The kablee naan, with raisins, cherries and almond powder, is an adventure. Another branch for vegans, substituting olive oil for ghee and tofu for cheese, opened in central LA.

4656 Franklin Avenue, Los Feliz
Tel: (323) 953 0040.
E-mail: info@electriclotus.com
Website: www.electriclotus.com
Price: US$30. Wine: US$20.
Branch:
8222 West Third Street, Midtown
Tel: (323) 653 2121.

Hugo's

This Italian coffee shop is where celebrities go for breakfast. The huge menu includes substantial, healthy dishes like pumpkin pancakes, tofu scramble, vegetarian Canadian bacon and inspiring freshly squeezed juices and exotic teas. The friendly staff create a comfortable environment but the room's acoustics cause noise levels to soar when only a few tables are full, so intimate conversations are out (although those busy star-spotting probably won't care). On weekends, there are queues. Open 0730–1530 weekdays and 0730–1600 weekends. No dinner. There is another branch in Studio City with longer opening hours.

8401 Santa Monica Boulevard, West Hollywood
Tel: (323) 654 3993. Fax: (323) 654 4089.
Price: US$45. Wine: US$19.
Branch:
12851 Riverside Drive, Studio City
Tel: (818) 761 8985.

The Little Door

Celebrities crowd through this restaurant's little wooden door and into another world of North African cuisine and ambience. The garden patio has romantic vines, flowers and fountains lit-up by candles and fairy lights. Its popularity with the LA set – heightened by being one of the only places in town where diners can smoke – can mean slow service. Sumptuous couscous dishes precede great desserts. No lunch.

8164 West Third Street, Midtown
Tel: (323) 951 1210. Fax: (323) 659 9014.
Price: US$55. Wine: US$22.

Locanda Veneta

Movie stars flock to this lively Italian restaurant, consistently ranked one of the best in town. Tender calamari or carpaccio can be followed by homemade pastas, such as lobster ravioli with creamy saffron sauce. Generous portions leave little room for the rich desserts, such as chocolate *crema* with raspberries. The menu changes weekly. No lunch Saturday. Closed Sunday.

8638 West Third Street, Midtown
Tel: (310) 274 1893. Fax: (310) 274 4217.
Website: www.locandaveneta.com
Price: US$50. Wine: US$20.

Budget

Crocodile Café

Families and large groups love this fun fast-food chain. Large portions of Southwest American food, such as oakwood-grilled salmon in guajillo sauce and spicy buffalo wings, are served by the friendly staff in a casual, bright environment. Kids love the burgers with happy face French fries and huge glasses of lemonade. There are other branches in Santa Monica and Pasadena.

203 North San Fernando Boulevard, Burbank
Tel: (818) 843 7999. Fax: (818) 843 7137.
E-mail: burbank@crocodilecafe.com
Website: www.crocodilecafe.com
Price: US$18. Wine: US$17.
Branches:
101 Santa Monica Boulevard, Santa Monica
Tel: (310) 394 4783. Fax: (310) 395 4743.
Suite 101, 88 West Colorado Boulevard, Pasadena
Tel: (626) 568 9310. Fax: (626) 568 9573.

El Cholo

In 1923, *El Cholo* was the first Mexican restaurant in Los Angeles; today, this chain is excellent value for money for families and large groups. The walls, decorated with colourful Mexican trinkets, add to the lively atmosphere. Specialities include blue corn chicken enchiladas and green corn tamales (available May to October only). The flan is also excellent and the margaritas reliably good. There are also branches in Santa Monica and at Los Angeles airport.

1121 South Western Avenue, Midtown
Tel: (323) 734 2773. Fax: (562) 690 9871.
Website: www.elcholo.com
Price: US$20. Wine: US$18.
Branches:
1025 Wilshire Boulevard, Santa Monica
Tel: (310) 899 1106.
Terminal 5, Los Angeles International Airport (LAX)
Tel: (310) 417 1910.

Mishima

This bright, spacious, modern noodle restaurant offers cheap and delicious Japanese food to a smart Asian clientele and discerning Westerners. Recommendations include fresh swordfish, sweet potato purée, marinated seaweed, seared tuna salad with wasabe dressing or nabeyaki udon soup with spinach, mushrooms, shrimp, chicken, egg and fishcake. There are branches in West LA, Studio City and Torrance.

Suite 108, 8474 West Third Street, West Hollywood/Melrose
Tel: (323) 782 0181.
Website: www.mishima.com/restaurants.html
Price: US$20. Wine: US$18.

Photo: Los Angeles Convention & Visitors Bureau

Santa Monica beach

Branches:

Suite 106A, 11819 Wilshire Boulevard, West LA
Tel: (310) 966 1062.
Suite 112, 12265 Ventura Boulevard, Studio City
Tel: (818) 506 8847.
Suite G, 21605 South Western Avenue, Torrance
Tel: (310) 320 2089.

Newsroom Café

Vegans and the health-conscious will embrace this large bohemian café, complete with designer wall lighting and outdoor patio, which offers veggie burgers, salads and fresh fruit smoothies. Vegetarians who love desserts will be especially at home, as the 'fat-free' desserts include a marble cake, an apple cake and fresh fruit cornbread cobbler with vanilla ice cream – indulge without guilt. There is another branch in Santa Monica.
120 North Robertson Boulevard, West Hollywood/
Melrose
Tel: (310) 652 4444.
Price: US$18. Wine: US$18.
Branch:
530 Wilshire Boulevard, Santa Monica
Tel: (310) 319 9100.

Out Take Café

This small modern yet cosy café – full of aspiring actors and musicians – offers a simple, healthy menu of staples, such as Caesar salad and pasta dishes. The homemade borscht, served hot or cold, is an original Armenian recipe from the owner's mother. The staff are friendly and the prices reasonable. No valet, although parking is available around back.
12159 Ventura Boulevard, Studio City
Tel: (818) 760 1111. Fax: (818) 760 3518.
Price: US$22. Wine: US$18.

Personal Recommendations

James' Beach

An inviting outdoor terrace festooned with lanterns made from colourful boxer shorts leads onto a romantically lit cosmopolitan dining room. This popular restaurant serves up American comfort food with a modern twist, such as fried calamari with jalapeño aioli or pork chops with grilled peaches. The wine list is extensive and the homemade chocolate chip cookies are a must. No lunch Saturday to Tuesday. Brunch Saturday and Sunday 1000–1500.
60 North Venice Boulevard, Venice
Tel: (310) 823 5396.
Price: US$35. Wine: US$20.

Joe's Restaurant

This crisp, stylish restaurant is renowned for reliable yet imaginative food. Breads come with a superb olive tapenade. Dishes like Israeli couscous risotto or chicken, spinach and ricotta ravioli are fantastic and so are simple starters like tomato basil soup. The lunch menu offers a good deal for two courses. The use of mobile phones is forbidden. No lunch weekends.
1023 Abbot Kinney Boulevard, Venice
Tel: (310) 829 7539. Fax: (310) 399 5811.
Price: US$40. Wine: US$25.

Lula Cocina Mexicana

This Mexican cantina is named after chef Lula Bertran – culinary guru to the restaurant's well-known Irish owner Gerri Gilliland, who also owns Santa Monica

Grauman's Chinese Theater

restaurant-bar Jake & Annie's. An oasis on Santa Monica's Main Street, the bright decor and garden patio are the backdrop for top-notch margaritas and regional specialities like lobster taquitos. The chocolate espresso brownie with homemade whipped cream is a dessert must.
2720 Main Street, Santa Monica
Tel: (310) 392 5711. Fax: (310) 392 3391.
Website: www.gerrigilliland.com
Price: US$25. Wine: US$18.

Typhoon

For those who love adventure, this modern Pacific Rim restaurant is a must. Not only is its location – above a runway at Santa Monica airport with neon-lit night views – precarious, but its menu will terrify the timid. Starting out tamely enough with items like coconut soup, pork spare ribs and roasted aubergine, it cuts to the chase with scorpions on shrimp toast, Chambai ants and white sea worms. Yes, the real thing – and they are delicious. There are also less unusual spicy fish and meat dishes. No lunch weekends.
3221 Donald Douglas Loop South (between Centinela Avenue and 23rd Street), Santa Monica
Tel: (310) 390 6565. Fax: (310) 390 8032.
E-mail: typhoon@typhoon-restaurant.com
Website: www.typhoon-restaurant.com
Price: US$40. Wine: US$17.

Woo Lae Oak

This traditional Korean barbecue in Koreatown offers one of LA's best ethnic cuisines in an authentic atmosphere. Marinated meats and exotic vegetables are grilled at each table, while the Korean waitresses, in 1950s-style pink uniforms with white aprons, help with the barbecuing and explain the menu (English menus can be requested). Meals come with a choice of one of 30 kim-chis – Korean spicy pickled cabbage – and soup. The Beverly Hills branch is more upmarket, with suited waiters and a business crowd.

623 South Western Avenue, Koreatown, Midtown
Tel: (213) 384 2244. Fax: (213) 384 8349.
Website: www.woolaeoak.org
Price: US$35. Wine: US$20.
Branch:
170 North La Cienega Boulevard, Beverly Hills
Tel: (310) 652 4187.

ENTERTAINMENT

Nightlife

The 'Entertainment Capital of the World' has a range of nightlife options – bars, nightclubs, cabarets, jazz, rock, blues and country and western can all be found. LA clubs offer a mix of live bands and recorded music on different nights of the week. Comedy clubs are also big in LA.

Sunset Boulevard – with its famous Sunset Strip – still boasts some of the city's most famous clubs but is by no means the only hotspot. Other good nightlife areas are Santa Monica, especially along Third Street Promenade; Hollywood and West Hollywood, the latter a centre for gay nightlife. Pine Avenue in Long Beach and Pasadena's Old Town also have a good number of jazz clubs and other night spots. Admission prices for clubs and live music vary widely according to the entertainment. Entertainment listings can be found in *LA Weekly* (website: www.laweekly.com), a free paper distributed around town. *Where LA* magazine can be found in most major hotels and provides a monthly calendar of events (website: www.wherela.com). The minimum drinking age is 21 years and you should carry photo ID at all times as you may not even be allowed in a venue without it. There is no smoking inside any public place in Los Angeles and this includes bars and nightclubs. However, many offer outdoor areas where smoking is permitted.

Bars

Starting with the Sunset Strip, *Bar Marmont*, next to its famous hotel, Chateau Marmont, 8221 Sunset Boulevard, is a small and intimate bar with a Bohemian feel. The *SkyBar*, at the Philippe Starck-designed Mondrian Hotel, 8440 Sunset Boulevard, is a very glamorous spot for LA's beautiful people. Another hotel bar, *The Standard*, 8300 Sunset Boulevard, is slightly less difficult to get into but equally popular and stylish. Still on Sunset, make sure you stop off at number 8358, the *Argyle Hotel*, a splendid 1920s building, whose authentic Art Deco lounge bar extends to the pool area complete with statues of pink flamingos. The *Cat and Fiddle* is an English-style bar with courtyard and fountain, at 6530 Sunset Boulevard.

For LA gay life, try any bar along Santa Monica Boulevard in West Hollywood, including: the reliable *Gold Coast* at number 8228, the Goth/indie *Parlour Club* at number 7702, the sophisticated *Felt* at number 8279, or the crazy *Fubar* at number 7994, with drag queens and bingo nights. Lesbians in this boys' paradise have *Palms*, at 8572, or the friendly *Normandie Rooms*, at number 8737. For a mixed, hipper crowd, try *Akbar*, 4356 West Sunset Boulevard.

For fans of the film Swingers, it is worth making the trek to Los Feliz, where the *Dresden Room*, 1760 North Vermont Avenue, all white leather upholstery and cork walls, is good for sipping cocktails while listening to the loungey crooning of Marty and Elayne. Over in Hollywood, smokers will love *Tiki Ti*, 4427 Sunset Boulevard, one of the only bars in LA in which the habit is indulged indoors, which also boasts one of the city's largest cocktail menus; while *Star Shoes*, 6364 Hollywood Boulevard, offers patrons the opportunity to try on and purchase shoes while sipping smart cocktails.

The *Observation Bar*, aboard the *RMS Queen Mary* in Long Beach, is an Art Deco joy – a great place for a romantic martini while the sun sets. In the same area, the *Rock Bottom Brewery*, 1 Pine Avenue, is a good place to try handmade beers brewed on the premises. Downtown, the best views of the skyscrapers can be had from the revolving cocktail bar, *BonaVista at Westin Bonaventure Hotel*, 404 South Figueroa Street. With souvenir glasses, floor to ceiling windows and

piped music, it's all very 1980s but hard to beat. Also, *The Roof Bar at The Standard*, 550 South Flower Street, is a stylish place to check out the skyscrapers.

Casinos

Gambling is illegal in Los Angeles.

Clubs

The eclectic *Viper Room*, 8852 Sunset Boulevard, owned by Johnny Depp, is a hip hangout for rock musicians and groupies, although its club nights tend to be more funk and disco.

In Santa Monica, *Gotham Hall*, 1431 Third Street Promenade, is a popular billiards hall frequented by pretty boys and girls. The sophisticated *Club Cohiba*, part of *Mum's Restaurant*, 144 Pine Avenue, Long Beach, features a Cigar and Billiard Room, a Martini Lounge and a Roof Top Terrace with live salsa on Fridays and Saturdays. Swing-dancing is making a comeback in LA and the *Derby*, 4500 Los Feliz Boulevard, is the best place to jive – also featured in the film *Swingers*.

LA is getting a dance club scene, as international DJs start to play there more and more. In the middle of Hollywood, *Blue*, 1642 North Las Palmas Avenue, is popular on its trance-mission night – Fridays – and has an outdoor smoking area. People go on to the *Crush Bar*, 1743 North Cahuenga Boulevard, which turns into an after-hours club from 0230 Friday and Saturday. For cool decor, *Sugar*, 814 Broadway, in Santa Monica, is a good place to go – check out the glass toilets (with blue lights for boys and pink for girls). For serious style, long queues and sexy dancing (including semi-naked dancers on glass-encased podiums), try *Deep*, 1707 Vine Street, on the corner of Hollywood and Vine. Run by the same man (Ivan Kane) as Deep is *Forty Deuce*, 5574 Melrose Avenue, a sultry cabaret-style lounge-bar, complete with burlesque.

For gay clubs, check out Santa Monica Boulevard. The biggest are probably *Rage*, at number 8911, and *Circus Disco*, at 6655. Nearby, *The Abbey*, 692 North Robertson Boulevard, boasts an Indonesian-style outdoor lounge and is mixed and friendly.

Comedy

The Comedy Store, 8433 West Sunset Boulevard, is a good starting point as it has three rooms, which offer

a variety of acts, from mainstream to fledgling. In the past, it has seen the arrival of people like Robin Williams, David Letterman, Whoopi Goldberg and Gary Shandling. The *Laugh Factory*, 8001 West Sunset Boulevard, is a smaller venue where you may see famous names, like Jerry Seinfeld, testing out their routines. *The Improvisation*, 8162 Melrose Avenue, West Hollywood, is another premier venue.

Live Music

The *House of Blues*, 8430 Sunset Boulevard, features top blues and folk names and is also committed to hosting rap and hip hop artists. *Harvelle's*, 1432 Fourth Street, in Santa Monica is another good spot for blues. *The Knitting Factory*, 7021 Hollywood Boulevard, offers live rock, jazz and blues in a high-tech setting. Top jazz entertainers perform at the packed *Catalina Bar & Grill*, 1640 North Cahuenga Boulevard (tel: (323) 466 2210; website: www.catalinajazzclub.com). Booking is essential. Another good spot for jazz is *Lunaria Restaurant & Jazz Bar*, 10351 Santa Monica Boulevard.

Two venerable rock clubs, hosting fairly mainstream acts, are *The Roxy* and *Whisky A Go-Go* at 9009 and 8901 Sunset Boulevard. The *Staples Center*, 1111 South Figueroa Street (tel: (213) 742 7340 or (877) 305 1111; website: www.staplescenter.com), is the venue for mega-concerts and events, such as the Grammy Awards.

Sport

With several top professional teams, Los Angeles offers plenty of opportunities to enjoy spectator sports. Baseball is America's favourite summer pastime, and *Dodger Stadium*, 1000 Elysian Park Avenue (tel: (323) 224 1448), north of Downtown, is the home of the Los Angeles *Dodgers* (website: www.dodgers.com). The season runs from April to October; tickets cost US$6–35. *Staples Center*, 1111 South Figueroa Street (tel: (213) 742 7340; website: www.staplescenter.com), is a new sports/entertainment arena and the home of two basketballs teams, *LA Lakers* (tel: (310) 419 3131; website: www.nba.com/lakers) and *LA Clippers* (tel: (213) 745 0500; website: www.nba.com/clippers), as well as the ice hockey team, *LA Kings* (tel: (888) 556 4752; website: www.lakings.com). Tickets cost from US$10–175. The winter sports season runs from October to April.

LA has not had a resident National Football League team since 1995, so the star collegiate teams ignite Angelenos' passions. *UCLA* games (website: www.uclabruins.com) are at the *Rose Bowl*, 1001 Rose Bowl Drive, Pasadena (tel: (626) 577 3100; website: www.rosebowlstadium.com), the venue for the New Year's Day parade and college football tournament. The *Los Angeles Memorial Coliseum*, 3911 South Figueroa Street (tel: (213) 748 6131; website: www.lacoliseum.com), is the home venue for UCLA's football rival, *USC* (tel: (213) 740 4672; website: www.usctrojans.com).

There is a soccer team, the *LA Galaxy* (website: www.lagalaxy.com), which is in the Major League. It now plays in the new *Home Depot Center* stadium, part of a US$120 million sports complex on the campus of Cal State Dominguez Hills in Carson.

Fitness Centres

Fitness is huge in LA. Fitness centres that allow day membership include: *24-Hour Fitness* (tel: (310) 652

Dodger Stadium

7440; website: www.24hourfitness.com), in Santa Monica, West Hollywood and Beverly Hills; *Gold's Gym* (tel: (310) 392 6004; website: www.goldsgym.com), in Venice Beach and Hollywood; and *Bally Total Fitness* (tel: (800) 258 2006; website: www.ballyfitness.com), with Downtown and Hollywood locations.

Golf

There are numerous public golf courses in the area. A list can be obtained online (website: www.golfcalifornia.com). Green fees start from US$18, although upmarket courses, such as Malibu, will be much higher.

Horseracing

Located 23km (14 miles) northeast of Downtown, *Santa Anita Park*, 285 West Huntington Drive, Arcadia (tel: (818) 574 7223; website: www.santaanita.com), is LA's historic thoroughbred racecourse.

Tennis

The *City of Los Angeles Recreation and Parks Department* (tel: (888) 527 2757; website: www.ci.la.ca.us/rap) maintains over 100 public tennis courts around the metro area. Many are free, on a first-come, first-served basis.

Shopping

The most famous shopping street in Los Angeles is Rodeo Drive, off Wilshire Boulevard in Beverly Hills. Those without hefty bank balances can still go window-shopping at the flagship stores of all the designer names, from Gucci to Tommy Hilfiger. At the end of Rodeo Drive are larger department stores, such as *Barney's* and *Saks*.

Not far away is the *Beverly Center*, a favourite shopping mall of the stars, and *Century City Shopping Center*, an outdoor shopping plaza; both with branches of *Macy's* and *Bloomingdale's*, as well as speciality shops. For eight blocks from Coldwater Canyon to Laurel Canyon, in Studio City, *Ventura Boulevard* also offers smart shopping.

Westwood Village, adjacent to the UCLA campus, is easier on the pocket and has a range of inexpensive shops. Melrose Avenue, between Highland Avenue and Doheny Drive, is lined with 20th-century antique shops and trendy fashion boutiques, from *Mui Mui* to *Red Balls* (featured in the opening credits of the TV show *Melrose Place*). La Brea Avenue, off Melrose Avenue, has more hip boutiques and vintage clothing stores, including the huge *American Rag*. The Silver Lake area, on the border of Los Feliz and Hollywood (Vermont Avenue and Sunset Boulevard), is dubbed the 'Soho of LA'. It has stalls and boutiques selling stylish vintage and retro clothing.

Santa Monica's Third Street Promenade is a pedestrianised mall that runs for several blocks and is lined with shops and outdoor cafés. At one end is Santa Monica Place, an indoor mall with department stores and boutiques. Chic shopping can be found nearby on Montana Avenue, between Seventh and 17th Streets.

Downtown has various shopping complexes and gallerias, including the highly recommended *Grand Central Market* on South Broadway, which is a cornucopia of fresh foods, fruits and vegetables. In the *Jewelry District* (Hill Street between West Fifth and West Seventh Streets), visitors can find good bargains, while the *Fashion District* is a real shopping experience (a 56-block mix of wholesalers, manufacturers and retailers

Rodeo Drive

Photo: Los Angeles Convention & Visitors Bureau

selling merchandise at discounts). The *Downtown Property Owners Association* has maps detailing public transportation routes, the dates of sales and where to find designer merchandise.

The kitsch shops along Hollywood Boulevard are best for the inevitably tacky souvenirs.

Shopping hours are generally 0900–1800 although malls will close at 2100/2200. Sales tax of 9% is not reclaimable.

Culture

Given the fact that LA is the home of the film industry, it might come as a surprise that the city is also home to a wide range of cultural scenes, all thriving. The leading venue in Los Angeles is the *Performing Arts Center* (PAC), a complex of three theatres known as the *Music Center*, which is located at 135 North Grand Avenue (tel: (213) 972 7211; website: www.musiccenter.org), in the heart of Downtown.

The complex stages music, theatre, dance and opera and includes the *Dorothy Chandler Pavilion* (host for many years to the Oscars ceremony), the *Mark Taper Forum* and *Ahmanson Theater*. It also includes the new *Walt Disney Concert Hall* (website: www.disneyhall.org), designed by Frank Gehry, on Grand Avenue and First Street. Starting with the 2003/04 concert season, this is the new home of the *Los Angeles Philharmonic* and the *Los Angeles Master Chorale*.

The best source of up-to-date information on cultural events around the city is the *Los Angeles Convention and Visitors Bureau* (tel: (213) 689 8822).

Tickets can be purchased from *Ticketmaster* (tel: (213) 480 3232; website: www.ticketmaster.com). Other agencies that handle concert, sport and theatre tickets include *Musical Chairs* (tel: (800) 659 1702; website: www.musicalchairstickets.com), *Al Brooks Theatre Ticket Agency* (tel: (800) 341 2766; website: www.albrooks.com) and *V.I.P. Tickets* (tel: (800) 328 4253; website: www.viptickets.com).

Music

The *Los Angeles Philharmonic Orchestra* (website: www.laphil.org) is one of the best in the world and the current Music Director is the acclaimed Essa-Pekka Salonen. The Philharmonic performs at the new Walt Disney Concert Hall, while the *Los Angeles Opera* (website: www.losangelesopera.com) remains at the Dorothy Chandler Pavilion (see above). Chamber music and performances by distinguished alumni can be heard at the *Zipper Concert Hall* at the *Colburn School of Performing Arts*, 200 South Grand Avenue (tel: (213) 621 2200; website: www.colburnschool.org). The classic summer venue to hear music outdoors is the *Hollywood Bowl*, 2301 Highland Avenue (tel: (323) 850 2000; website: www.hollywoodbowl.org), with concerts by the Los Angeles Philharmonic, as well as jazz and pop artists.

Theatre

The *Ahmanson Theater* at the PAC (see above) stages large scale productions. Smaller and more adventurous productions take place in the *Mark Taper Forum*, a theatre-in-the-half-round, also at the PAC. The *Geffen Playhouse*, 10886 Le Conte Avenue (tel: (310) 208 6500; website: www.geffenplayhouse.com), stages classical and contemporary plays in a historic building in Westwood Village. The *Pantages Theater*, 6233 Hollywood Boulevard (tel: (323) 468 1770; website: www.nederlander.com/pantages.html), is an outstanding Art Deco theatre that hosts Broadway musicals and concerts, while the *Pasadena Playhouse*, 39 South El Molino Avenue (tel: (626) 356 7529; website: www.pasadenaplayhouse.org), is an incredible 1925 Spanish Colonial Revival building. *Theatre LA*, 644 South Figueroa Street (tel: (213) 614 0556; website: www.theatrela.org), is an association of some 150 theatres; services include *Web Tix*, a half-price day-of-the-show ticket outlet.

Dance

The *Joffrey Ballet Company* (website: www.joffrey.com) visits the PAC (see above) in June. The *UCLA Center for the Arts*, 4405 North Hillgard, Westwood (tel: (310) 825 2101; website: www.performingarts.ucla.edu), is the venue for touring dance troupes, as well as the *UCLA Dance Company*.

Film

The historic *Grauman's Chinese Theater*, 6925 Hollywood Boulevard (tel: (323) 461 3331), presents first-run movies. *Pacific El Capitan Theater*, 6838 Hollywood Boulevard (tel: (323) 467 7674), also screens first-run films. The *Egyptian Theater*, 6712 Hollywood Boulevard (tel: (323) 466 FILM/3456), shows foreign films and documentaries in Hollywood's oldest restored cinema. The *Pacific Cinerama Dome*, 6360 Sunset Boulevard (tel: (323) 466 3401), has been refurbished in keeping with its late 50s architecture and now has 15 screens. The *Silent Movie Theatre*, 611 North Fairfax Avenue (tel: (323) 655 2520), is the only silent movie theatre in North America and a favourite with the celebrity crowd.

As for films that are shot in the city, it would be easier to compile a list of those that weren't. Films that capture various different moods of LA include Billy Wilder's *Sunset Boulevard* (1950), starring Gloria Swanson, and more recently *LA Confidential* (1997) and *Swingers* (1996).

Cultural Events

The *Grand Performances Festival* is a city-wide arts and music festival held from June through to October, which focuses on LA's diverse ethnic cultures and neighbourhoods, through music, dance, theatre, film and art. The *American Film Institute*, 2021 North Western Avenue (tel: (323) 856 7600; website: www.afi.com), holds an annual film and video festival in October/November time. The *LA Independent Film Festival* takes place in April. The *Shakespeare in the Square Festival* is held annually in July. The *Cinco de Mayo* (5 May) celebrations on Olvera Street highlight LA's Mexican heritage with mariachi music and folk dancing, while *LA Fiesta Broadway*, at the end of April, leads up to the day itself, with local and more famous Latino entertainment making up the world's largest Cinco de Mayo celebrations.

Literary Notes

Los Angeles has inspired many writers and served as the setting for their books and novels. Nathanael West (1903–40) lived in Hollywood from 1933. His novel *The Day of the Locust* (1939) is considered one of the best about Los Angeles. *The Loved One* (1948) by Evelyn Waugh and *After Many a Summer Dies the Swan* (1938) by Aldous Huxley were both set in LA. F Scott Fitzgerald's *The Last Tycoon* (1941), his final unfinished masterpiece, was also set in LA.

SPECIAL EVENTS

For information regarding all festivals and special events in Los Angeles, visitors should consult the Festival Guide (website: www.culturela.com).

Rose Parade, parade prior to the Rose Bowl football game, featuring lavish floats and marching bands (website: www.tournamentofroses.com), 1 Jan, Pasadena
African-American Heritage Celebrations, events include concerts, gallery exhibits and a Children's Village (website: www.africanamericanla.com), Jan–Mar, throughout the city
Chinese New Year Festival (website: www.chinatownla.com), Jan/Feb, Chinatown
Toyota Grand Prix of Long Beach (website: www.longbeachgp.com), Apr, Long Beach
LA Fiesta Broadway, run-up to largest Cinco de Mayo celebrations in the world (website: www.fiestabroadway.net), 27 Apr, Downtown
Cinco de Mayo Celebrations, festivities focusing on Latino culture and music (website: www.cityofla.org/elp/olvera.html), 2–5 May, Downtown
Pershing Square Summer Concerts, mid-May–Sep, Downtown
Grand Performances Festival (website: www.grandperformances.org), Jun–Oct, Downtown
Gay Pride Month and Parade (website: www.laglc.org or www.lapride.org), Jun, throughout the city
Mariachi USA (website: www.mariachiusa.com), Jun, Hollywood
IFP Los Angeles Film Festival, independent film festival (website: www.ifp.org), mid-Jun, Downtown
Shakespeare in the Square (website: www.shakespearefestival.org), throughout Jul, Downtown
Independence Day, loads of neighbourhood celebrations, 4 Jul
Lotus Festival, celebration of Asian culture, mid-Jul, Echo Park
Venice Showcase Festival, features everything that makes Venice unique, including art, music and extreme sport displays, late Aug, Venice
Moon Festival, two-day event featuring the Lion Dance and a lantern parade (website: www.chinatownla.com), Sep, Chinatown
Los Angeles County Fair (website: www.lacountyfair.com), mid–late Sep, Fairplex, Pomona
Halloween Carnival, a Mardi Gras-style street celebration featuring an outlandish costume parade, 31 Oct, West Hollywood
AFI FEST, American Film Institute festival (website: www.afi.com), Oct/Nov, Hollywood
Downtowwn on Ice, outdoor ice-skating, mid-Nov–Jan, Downtown
Doo Dah Parade, tremendously popular parade celebrating the silly side of life (website: www.pasadenadoodahparade.com), late Nov, Pasadena
Hollywood Christmas Parade, features Hollywood stars, fabulous floats and marching bands (website: www.hollywoodchristmas.com), late Nov, Hollywood
Los Angeles Holiday Celebration, seasonally themed concert representing the cultural mosaic of LA (website: www.lacountyarts.org), 24 Dec, Dorothy Chandler Pavilion

LA has attracted many detective writers over the years. The original, Raymond Chandler (1888–1959), lived in LA, and his character, Philip Marlowe, explores its seamier side in the 1930s, in such novels as *The Big Sleep* (1939) and *Farewell My Lovely* (1940). *Raymond Chandler's Los Angeles* by Elizabeth Ward and Alain Silver is an enlightening look at the author's relationship with the city. Another detective writer James Ellroy was born in LA in 1948 and the city inspired his *LA Quartet* of novels – *Clandestine* (1982),

Black Dahlia (1987), *LA Confidential* (1990) and *White Jazz* (1992). William Harrington created another LA detective, Columbo (not from TV). Some novels in the series include *The Helter Skelter Murders* (1994), *The Hoffa Connection* (1995) and *The Game Show Killers* (1996).

Other novels about LA include Joan Didion's *Play It As It Lays* (1970), Alison Lurie's *The Nowhere City* (1965), Walter Mosley's *Black Betty* (1994) and William Penn's *The Absence of Angels* (1995).

Beachlife

According to Arab chroniclers, it was in AD 852 that the Emir of Córdoba, Mohamed I (AD 852–886), ordered a fortress to be built on the left bank of the Manzanares River, the geographical centre of the Iberian Peninsula. He named the settlement 'Mayrit' ('source of water') and in it lay the seeds of the city now known as Madrid. Traces of this flourishing Moorish town survive to this day, in a section of town wall (*muralla Arabe*) near the Royal Palace, as well as in the *mudéjar* architectural style of Madrid's oldest church, San Nicolás de las Servitas.

Mayrit (or Magerit) was situated in a strategically important location and Christians and Arabs fought bitterly over the territory until late in the 11th century, when Alfonso VI finally settled matters by capturing the Alcázar (castle) after a three-year siege. However, it would be another 500 years before Philip II took the historic decision, in 1561, to move his capital from Valladolid to Madrid. Today, Madrid remains Spain's financial and political core, home to the Cortes (Parliament), Senate and Royal Family, as well as the extraordinary cultural riches of the Golden Triangle – the Prado, Reina Sofía and Thyssen-Bornemisza art museums.

With a population of just under three million, Madrid is Europe's fourth largest city – after London, Paris and Milan – and its highest capital, at 650m (2132ft) above sea level. The repression and torpor of the Franco era (1939–75) are now all but forgotten by *Madrileños* who, perhaps more than any other Spaniards, are determined to *vivir a tope* (live life to the full). The craving for conspicuous enjoyment, not to mention the 2800 hours of annual sunshine, turn the streets into bustling centres of public display. Madrid's infectious and colourful fiestas punctuate the year, with each *barrio* (district) trying to outdo the other in its celebrations. The highlights include Reyes Magos (Feast of the Three Kings), Carnival, the religious processions of Holy Week, the San Isidro festival in May (the beginning of the bullfighting season) and Nochevieja (New Year's Eve), when the Puerta del Sol becomes the focal point for several hours of uninhibited partying. Visitors should also look out for the major cultural festivals, notably the Veranos de la Villa in summer and the autumn Festival de Otoño, embracing film, dance, theatre and music of every description. Although Madrid's climate is more extreme than other Spanish locations, the warm dry summers and cool winters still allow for many alfresco activities.

Although anxious to appear 'modern' in clothes, outlook and lifestyle, *Madrileños* remain fiercely traditional, clinging to their customs more noticeably than their cosmopolitan Barcelonese rivals. Most choose to live at home until marriage, divorce remains controversial (particularly in high society) and the family surpasses everything.

While the Comunidad de Madrid (Madrid Province) stretches over 8000 sq kilometres (3090 sq miles), the city's historic heart is easily explored on foot. The narrow, labyrinthine streets of the medieval quarter contrast with the grand boulevards, laid out in the 18th and 19th centuries – the period when Madrid began to take on the trappings of a modern capital. Each *barrio* (district) has its own distinctive atmosphere – Lavapiés, Malasaña and Chueca being the oldest and most interesting. Many visitors first get to know the central area, known as the Madrid of the Austrias (a reference to the Hapsburg era), situated roughly between the Palacio Real and the Puerta del Sol, Madrid's 'mile zero'. It is only a short walk from here to the city's main street, the Gran Vía, lined with shops, banks, offices, bars and cinemas. Fashionable Madrid starts with the Salamanca district and the boutiques of Calle Serrano, while the modern business quarter extends along the north–south axis, known as the Paseo de la Castellana. Distinguished by its skyscrapers and impressive office blocks, this is where the multinationals have their headquarters. At the far (northern) end of the Paseo de la Castellana are the 'leaning towers' of the Puerta de Europa (Gateway of Europe), a daring display of architecture symbolising the city's confidence in its future. Indeed, Madrid has already launched its bid to host the 2012 Olympic Games, which would not only win the city some desirable developments and revenue but also award Madrid the status of one of the world's major players.

Photo: Gary Bowerman

Puerta del Sol

TRAVEL

Getting There By Air

Barajas International Airport (MAD)

Tel: (91) 305 8343/6 (flight information) *or* (902) 353 570. Fax: (91) 393 6203.

Website: www.aena.es

Barajas airport, located 13km (eight miles) from Madrid's city centre, has three terminals serving more than 27 million passengers per year. Terminal one handles all international flights (except Iberia flights to Austria, Belgium, France, Germany, Italy, Luxembourg, the Netherlands and Portugal). Terminal two serves domestic flights and the Iberia international flights listed above. The new terminal three is used primarily for the Madrid–Barcelona shuttle.

Major airlines: In addition to Spain's national airline, Iberia (tel: (91) 722 9600 *or* (902) 400 500 (information); website: www.iberia.es), over 50 airlines serve Barajas, including *Air France, Alitalia, American Airlines, British Airways, Japan Airlines, Lufthansa, Singapore Airlines* and *Thai Airways International.*

Approximate flight times to Madrid: From London is 2 hours 15 minutes; from New York is 7 hours 5 minutes; from Los Angeles is 11 hours 5 minutes; from Toronto is 7 hours 5 minutes and from Sydney is 27 hours 30 minutes.

Airport facilities: These include banks, bureaux de change, ATMs, pharmacies, hotel and rail reservation, tourist information, left luggage, a post office, shops, restaurants, bars, and car hire from *Budget, Europcar* and *Hertz.*

Business facilities: The airport has two business lounges in terminal one, with fax and telephone facilities. Iberia has lounges in both terminals one and two. The *Madrid Chamber of Commerce and Industry* (tel: (91) 305 8807) has a small office in terminal one, with a meeting room for eight people with photocopier, fax and telephone facilities available for €35 (plus VAT) per hour, Monday to Friday 0800–2100.

Arrival/departure tax: None.

Transport to the city: The *EMT* airport bus 89 (tel: (91) 431 6192) departs every 15 minutes, daily 0445–0200, for the underground bus terminal at Plaza de Colón (journey time – 30–45 minutes) and costs €2.50. A taxi journey costs €17–19, including

a €4 airport charge (journey time – 30 minutes). The new extension to metro line 8 (see *Public Transport*) links Barajas (Aeropuerto) with the city centre (Nuevos Ministerios), running daily 0600–0130 (journey time – 12 minutes), costing €1.10. Upon departure, travellers with *Iberia* can now check in at this station rather than at the airport – a service that will eventually become general.

Getting There By Rail

The national Spanish railway network is operated by *RENFE* (tel: (91) 328 9020; website: www.renfe.es). Madrid has two main railway stations – *Estación de Chamartín* (Chamartín Station), Calle Agustín de Foxá, in northern Madrid, and *Estación de Atocha* (Atocha Station), close to Paseo del Prado, at Avenida Ciudad de Barcelona, in southern Madrid. Both stations have exchange facilities, including cafés and car hire on or near the premises. Chamartín also has a post office, tourist information, hotel reservation centre, InterCity Club Room and a large shopping centre.

Mainline services in Spain are reliable and efficient but slow and sometimes crowded – it is essential for travellers to book ahead for long-distance trains. Tickets are available for purchase from stations, the RENFE office on Calle Alcalá 44 (tel: (91) 531 2624), or from travel agents. RENFE also offers a national telephone information and ticket sales service (tel: (902) 240 202).

The *Cercanías* (tel: (902) 444 403) is the suburban network connecting outlying towns beyond the metro (see *Public Transport*). Trains are frequent and reliable and there is less overcrowding than on the metro. Atocha Station is the hub of the Cercanías suburban rail network. *Estación Príncipe Pío* (Príncipe Pío Station), Paseo del Rey 30, also connects with the Cercanías.

Rail services: Madrid's rail network includes services to provincial capitals in Spain and connections to the European railway network. Chamartín Station serves trains from France, Catalonia and northern Spain, including Barcelona (journey time – 6 hours), Bilbao (journey time – 6 hours) and Oviedo (journey time – 6 hours). Atocha is Madrid's largest station, serving trains from the regions of Andalusia, Extremadura and Portugal, including Malaga (journey time – 5 hours) and Valencia (journey time – 3 hours 30 minutes). Many trains stop at both Atocha Station and Chamartín Station. Atocha is the arrival and departure point for *AVE*, the high-speed Madrid–Seville service calling at Córdoba, which leaves twice daily (journey time – approximately 3 hours).

Transport to the city: All three stations are connected to the metro system.

Getting There By Road

Motorways (*Autopista*) are prefixed by the letter 'A', national multi-lane roads connecting towns and cities are prefixed by the letter 'N' and Madrid ring roads by the letter 'M'. Highways (*Autovía*) and other major roads (*Carretera Nacional*) are indicated by two Roman numerals or, more commonly, three digits. Many motorways incur a toll charge.

Traffic drives on the right. No person under 18 years may hire or drive a vehicle over 75cc. Seatbelts are compulsory for front-seat passengers in cars and crash helmets must be worn on motorcycles. After sunset,

sidelights must be used, while spare bulbs and red hazard triangles must be kept in all vehicles. The speed limit for cars and motorcycles is 120kph (75mph) on motorways, 100kph (62mph) on dual carriageways, 90kph (56mph) outside built-up areas and 50kph (31mph) within towns. Fines for traffic offences are strictly enforced. Drivers who are shown to exceed the maximum legal alcohol to blood ratio for driving of 0.05% are fined up to €600.

Foreign visitors require a valid driving licence to drive in Spain. National licences from EU countries are accepted, while nationals of other countries are advised to obtain an International Driving Permit. Third-party insurance is required and documents should be carried at all times. A Green Card is strongly recommended for all visitors and is compulsory for those from outside the EU.

Real Automóvil Club de España – RACE (tel: (91) 594 7400) has reciprocal agreements with the *AA* and *RAC* in Britain and the *AAA* in America.

Emergency breakdown services: RACE (91) 593 3333 (24 hours). Alternatively, drivers in distress can contact the *Ayuda en Carretera* (operated by the *Guardia Civil*) on the roadside SOS telephones, who will contact the breakdown services.

Routes to the city: Motorways radiate outward from Madrid. The NI links Madrid to the French border (via Burgos and Irún), the NII to Barcelona (via Zaragoza) and the French border. The NIII weaves its way to Valencia and Alicante, the NIV to Seville and Cádiz, the NV to Badajoz at the Portuguese border (where the A6/E90 continues to Lisbon) and the N401 to Toledo. There are also two ring motorways, M30 and M40 (a third, M50, is under construction).

Approximate driving times to Madrid: From Barcelona – 7 hours 30 minutes; Seville – 7 hours 45 minutes; Lisbon – 8 hours 45 minutes.

Coach services: *Estación Sur de Autobuses*, Calle Méndez Alvaro 83 (tel: (91) 468 4200 *or* 506 3360), is Madrid's most important bus terminal for long-distance coach travel. Destinations served include Albacete, Alicante, Avila, Barcelona, Benidorm, Santiago and Toledo. *ENATCAR* (tel: (902) 422 242) provides coach services between Spanish cities, operating from this station.

Eurolines (tel: (902) 405 040; e-mail: info@eurolines.es; website: www.eurolines.es) has services to major cities throughout Europe and further afield, including Basel, Berlin, Fez, Frankfurt, Hamburg, Lisbon, Marrakech, Munich, Naples, Prague, Timisoara, Toulouse and Warsaw. Services operate out of the Estación Sur de Autobuses.

Getting Around

Public Transport

Central Madrid is served by a comprehensive network of more than 150 city **bus** routes, a modern and extensive **metro** system and local **trains** to the neighbouring cities and towns. The main hub is Puerta del Sol.

The *Consorcio Regional de Transportes de Madrid* (tel: (902) 444 403; website: www.metromadrid.es *or* www.ctm-madrid.es) **metro** system covers more than 230km (143 miles) and is good value, clean and efficient, although crowded during rush hour. Trains run every three to five minutes, daily 0600–0130. Each of the 11 metro lines is distinguished by a colour and number (at stations and on maps).

EMT (tel: (91) 406 8810) runs Madrid's **bus** service. **Night buses**, known as *buhos* (owls), depart from Plaza de Cibeles for the suburbs, nightly between 0000 and 0600, and cost the same as an ordinary day ticket.

The local train network, operated by *Cercanías* (tel: (902) 444 403), comprises 11 lines in the Madrid area and provides a fast link between Charmartín Station and Atocha Station – as well as to destinations such as Toledo and El Escorial (*see Excursions*).

Single tickets for the metro and city buses – available for purchase on-board and at stations – cost €1.10. *Metrobús* tickets (a carnet of ten tickets) cost €5.20 and are available for purchase at metro stations, *estancos*

CITY STATISTICS

Location: Madrid region, central Spain.
Country dialling code: 34.
Population: 2,938,723 (city); 5,423,384 (Madrid province).
Ethnic mix: Approximately 90% Spanish, 10% other, with the largest minorities from Ecuador, Colombia and Morocco.
Religion: 86% Roman Catholic, 14% other.
Time zone: GMT + 1 (GMT + 2 from last Sunday in March to Saturday before last Sunday in October).
Electricity: 220 volts AC, 50Hz; round two-pin plugs are standard.
Average January temp: 5°C (41.5°F).
Average July temp: 24°C (75.5°F).
Annual rainfall: 439mm (17 inches).

(tobacconists) and EMT information kiosks at Plaza de Callao and Puerta del Sol. The *abono transportes* **pass**, for which a passport photo is required, offers unlimited trips on any combination of public transport – metro, bus and train – within the zone and period of time (month or year) chosen. A one-month ticket costs €32.30 (concessions are available).

Taxis

Oficina Municipal del Taxi (tel: (91) 588 9632) is the governing body for taxis in Madrid. City taxis – white with a diagonal red stripe and a green light on the roof – are available for hire at ranks or on the street. Meters start at €1.35 and rates per kilometre are €0.63 before 2300 and €0.81 thereafter. When entering a taxi, travellers should always check that the meter is not already running, as this is an occasional scam to overcharge passengers. There are surcharges for additional passengers, luggage and telephone or airport pick-up. Taxi touts should be avoided. For tipping, rounding up to the nearest Euro is appreciated.

Major private taxi companies include *TéleTaxi* (tel: (91) 371 2131), *Radio Taxi Independiente* (tel: (91) 405 1213) for long-distance trips and *Radio Taxi* (tel: (91) 447 3232), which also provides a service for the disabled.

Limousines

Limousines are available for hire at Madrid's top hotels and from *Autos Chamartín* (tel: (91) 405 4599) and *Autos Delicias Limousine* (tel: (91) 547 4023). The cost is approximately €344 (plus driver's lunch) for eight hours. To hire a Mercedes with driver costs approximately €231.

Driving in the City

Due to frequent traffic jams, aggressive drivers and problematic parking, driving in central Madrid is not recommended to tourists. Visitors who ignore this advice should make use of centrally located car parks – including Plaza Santa Ana, Plaza Mayor, Plaza de Oriente – costing €0.80 per half hour (€15.20 for a full day). Parking meters now operate in the city centre. These take the full range of coins and have operational instructions in English and other European languages. Illegally parked cars might be towed away. Impounded cars should be recovered as soon as possible as the fines rise every hour (tel: (91) 345 0666).

Car Hire

Cars can be hired by drivers aged 21 years and above, on presentation of a passport and valid driving licence held for at least one year. A valid international insurance policy is also necessary and full insurance is advised. Providers include *Avis*, Charmartín Station (tel: (90) 213 5531; website: www.avis.es), *Europcar*, Atocha Station (tel: (91) 530 0194; website: www.europcar.es), and *Herz*, Barajas airport (tel: (902) 402 405; website: www.hertz.es). Rates start at approximately €65 for one day of car hire.

Bicycle & Scooter Hire

There is no better way to get around Madrid than by bombing along on a moped, thus avoiding the parking problems that car drivers often suffer. *Motoalquiler*, Calle Conde Duque 13 (tel: (91) 542 0657), offers a choice of vehicles, with prices ranging from approximately €30–120 per day. Bicycles are best reserved for trips out of town. *Karacol Sport*, Calle Tortosa 8 (tel: (91) 539 9633), hires out mountain bikes at €12 per bike – a €40 returnable deposit is required – and organises excursions into the surrounding countryside.

| Tourist information | Pedestrian street | Museum, art gallery | Sport | Hotel, restaurant |
| Main post office | Transport | Religious building | Theatre, music, exhibition centre | Other building |

BUSINESS PROFILE

In addition to being Spain's administrative, political and communications hub, Madrid is also the leading financial centre and the country's most important economic region. Over half of Spain's companies have headquarters in Madrid, along with foreign banks, insurance companies and prestigious business consultants and auditing firms. The national stock exchange (*Bolsa*) is also based here. However, rival Barcelona is rapidly overtaking Madrid as the favoured location for international companies.

The financial, insurance and real estate sectors are the most significant contributors to the city's economy, representing 17% of the Spanish total. These activities are supplemented by other successful service industries, including transport and communications, media and publishing, leisure and tourism – Madrid currently receives around five million visitors a year. As well as making a vital economic contribution, these sectors are the main sources of employment in the city, with around 150,000 people working in the transport and communications sector alone.

Foreign companies with a presence in Madrid include *IBM, Peugeot, Proctor & Gamble, Shell* and *Siemens*. Major exhibitions and trade fairs take place at *Institución Ferial de Madrid (IFEMA)* in the grounds of the *Parque Ferial Juan Carlos I*, Campo de las Naciones (tel: (91) 722 5000), and the *Palacio de Congresos de Madrid*, Paseo de la Castellana 99 (tel: (91) 337 8100). The *Comunidad de Madrid* (tel: (902) 100 007; website: www.comadrid.es) has up-to-date information about trade fairs and conventions. The stock exchange is situated near the Plaza de Cibeles, however, most modern businesses and an increasing number of banking headquarters are located in the north of the city, along Paseo de la Castellana – sometimes referred to as *Urbanización Azca*.

Madrid has launched its bid to host the 2012 Olympic Games. To enhance the city's prospects, the developers intend to transform an area to the north of the city – already becoming known as La Nueva Castellana – into an ultra-modern sports and recreation zone. At its heart will be the Palacio Olímpico – a 20,000-seater stadium next to the Real Madrid training ground – and four skyscrapers, each rising to a height of 191m (627ft). The president of Real Madrid, Florentino Pérez, is a major investor in the scheme, estimated to cost more than €275 million.

The unemployment rate in Madrid stands at 8.14% (January 2003) against the national rate of 8.4%. The Madrid economy continues to show strong signs of growth, although some indicators point to a slowing down in demand in the near future. Construction remains the most vital sector. The terrorist attacks on New York and Washington, DC in September 2001 instantly impacted upon the tourist sector, with more than 7800 hotel reservations cancelled in the first nine days following the disaster. The luxury end of the market was worst affected. While the cost of hotel accommodation has continued to rise, visitors may still be able to negotiate bargain rates.

SIGHTSEEING

Sightseeing Overview

Madrid is best known for its 'Golden Triangle' of art museums – *Prado, Reina Sofia* and *Thyssen-Bornomisza*. The celebrated Art Walk, *Paseo del Arte*, links all three. The city's focal point remains the *Puerta del Sol* – the eastern gate (*puerta*) of the city during the 15th century. The monument of the bear and *madroño* (strawberry tree), in the centre of the square, symbolises Madrid. The *Calle Mayor* leads west from Sol, to the *Plaza Mayor*, which evokes the splendour of Spain's 17th-century Golden Age. The *Calle de Alcalá* – a grandiose thoroughfare constructed in the reign of Charles III – leads east of Sol, towards *Plaza de Cibeles*. The fountain, with its statue of a Greco-Roman fertility goddess astride a lion-drawn chariot, is a landmark instantly recognisable to all Spaniards. Visitors might be less impressed with the crazy merry-go-round of traffic encircling her. Overlooking *Plaza de Cibeles* is the imposing *Palacio de Comunicaciones* – the main post office, dating from 1904.

The Madrid cityscape is softened by numerous green spaces – lovely squares, such as the *Plaza de Oriente*, in front of the Royal Palace, and parks, most obviously the landscaped *Parque del Buen Retiro* and *Jardín Botánico* (Botanical Gardens) near the Prado. Further west is the wilder *Casa de Campo*, which also contains the *Parque de Atraciones* funfair and leisure grounds. More unusual is the greenhouse in the Atocha Station (entrance at concourse, gate 14), popular with *Madrileños* and visitors alike.

Key Attractions

Museo del Prado (Prado Museum)

The *Prado Museum* (founded in 1819) is undergoing an extensive programme of renovation to reclaim its position among Europe's greatest galleries. Within its 4000-strong collection of 16th- to early 19th-century paintings, are masterpieces by Fra Angelico, Botticelli, Bosch (El Bosco), Titian, Rembrandt and Velázquez, as well as evidence of the astonishing development of Goya – from his sun-soaked early paintings of dances and festivities to the grim madness of his black period.
Paseo del Prado
Tel: (91) 330 2800. Fax: (91) 330 2856.
E-mail: museo.nacional@prado.mcu.es
Website: http://museoprado.mcu.es
Transport: Metro Atocha or Banco de España; bus 9, 10, 14, 27, 34, 37 or 45.
Opening hours: Tues–Sun 0900–1900.
Admission: €3.01 (concessions available); free Sat 1430–1900 and Sun.

Museo Thyssen-Bornemisza (Thyssen-Bornemisza Museum)

Madrid purchased the private collection of Hans-Heinrich Thyssen-Bornemisza after a nine-and-a-half-year loan, instantly enriching the city's fund of art treasures. The *Museo Thyssen-Bornemisza* collection contains over 800 paintings, sculptures, carvings and tapestries, ranging from primitive Flemish works to contemporary pieces. Highlights include works by Fra Angelico, Van Eyck, Dürer, Caravaggio and Rubens.
Palacio de Villahermosa, Paseo del Prado 8
Tel: (91) 369 0151. Fax: (91) 420 2780.
E-mail: mtb@museothyssen.org

BUSINESS ETIQUETTE

Standard business hours are Monday to Friday 0900–1400 and 1600–1900, although 0800–1500 is quite common during summer. Larger companies and multinationals, however, are increasingly working through the day, in line with the rest of Europe, although smaller and local businesses still take the mid-afternoon break or *siesta*. Punctuality is not the norm. Traffic jams are commonly used and readily accepted as an excuse for arriving 15 minutes late.

Breakfast meetings are popular, perhaps because these are usually accompanied by delicious cakes and strong coffee. Lunch and dinner appointments are also common. Business cards are vital at initial meetings and smart dress, including a suit (and tie for men), is advisable. Small talk is a vital accompaniment to any meeting, as personal relationships must be developed before business can be done. Children, grandchildren, the flight to Madrid and the weather usually occupy the conversation before business rears its ugly head. While *Madrileños* work extremely hard, nothing is of more importance than the family and it is entirely acceptable for an important telephone conversation to be postponed if a family member rings.

Website: www.museothyssen.org
Transport: Metro Banco de España; bus 9, 10, 14, 27, 34, 37 or 45.
Opening hours: Tues–Sun 1000–1900.
Admission: €4.81 (permanent exhibitions); €3.60 (temporary exhibitions); €6.60 (permanent and temporary exhibitions combined); concessions available.

Museo Nacional Centro de Arte Reina Sofía (Reina Sofia National Art Centre Museum)

Housed in a former hospital, built by Francesco Sabatini for Carlos III in the late 18th century but never completed, the museum was designed by the Spanish architect, Antonio Fernánez Alba, in 1977 and completed in 1990. Officially opened by the King and Queen in 1992, it is dedicated to Spanish 20th-century art, pride of place belonging to Picasso's disturbing Civil War canvas, *Guernica*. Dalí, Miró and Juan Gris are among the other artists on show.
Calle Santa Isabel 52
Tel: (91) 467 5062. Fax: (91) 467 3163.
Website: http://museoreinasofia.mcu.es
Transport: Metro Atocha; bus 9, 10 14, 27, 34, 37 or 45.
Opening hours: Mon, Wed–Sat 1000–2100, Sun 1000–1430.
Admission: €3.01; concessions available; free Sat 1430–1900 and Sun.

Palacio Real (Royal Palace)

With the opulence of Versailles in mind, Philip V commissioned Italian architects Giambattista Sacchetti and Francesco Sabatini to build the *Royal Palace*, following a fire that destroyed the medieval *Alcázar* in 1764. The present king, Juan Carlos I, resides in the more subdued Zarzuela Palace outside Madrid, so Philip's 3000-room extravaganza is only used for state functions. The rest of the time, the startling white building in granite and Colmenar stone is open for tours and individual visits. Highlights include the *Hall of Halberdiers* and *Hall of Columns* with their splendid frescoes, the *Throne*

Room with its 17th-century sculptures, and the lavish private apartments of Charles II. Just off the courtyard is the *Royal Armoury* and *Pharmacy* – among Europe's oldest. Visits take approximately two hours. There are spectacular views over Madrid from the gardens.

Plaza de Oriente and Calle Bailén

Tel: (91) 542 0059.

Website: www.patrimonionacional.es

Transport: Metro Opera; bus 3, 25, 39 or 148.

Opening hours: Mon–Sat 0900–1800, Sun 0900–1500 (Apr–Sep); Mon–Sat 0930–1700, Sun 0900–1400 (Oct–Mar); closed during official ceremonies.

Admission: €6 (concessions available).

Plaza Mayor (Main Square)

This beautifully proportioned cobbled square was begun by Philip II and completed by Philip III in 1619 – his statue stands proudly at the centre. Plaza Mayor was both a marketplace and the setting for public spectacles – everything from the ritual condemnation of heretics to bull fights and pageants. Today, tourists outnumber the locals but *Plaza Mayor* is still as lively as it was in the past, with shops and cafés in the covered arcades.

Plaza Mayor

Transport: Metro Sol; any bus route to Sol.

Further Distractions

Parque del Buen Retiro (Retiro Park)

This lush 118-hectare (292-acre) park in the heart of Madrid was originally the private garden of Philip IV. Visitors can enjoy a stroll along the shady avenues and formal gardens, take a rowing boat out on the lake or picnic in the extensive wooded areas. *Madrileños* come here in their thousands on Sunday mornings, where entertainment is provided by fortune tellers, pavement artists and circus acts. There is a children's puppet theatre and numerous refreshment points. Temporary art exhibitions are held in the *Palacio de Cristal*, *Palacio de Velázquez* and the *Casa de Vacas*.

Puerta de Alcalá, Plaza de la Independencia

Transport: Metro Retiro, Atocha or Ibiza; bus 2, 14, 19, 20, 26, 28, 51, 52, 68 or 69.

Opening hours: Daily 0600–2200.

Admission: Free.

Monasterio de las Descalzas Reales (Convent of the Royal Barefoot Sisters)

Founded by Juana de Austria, the daughter of Charles V, in 1559, as a retreat for noblewomen, the *Monasterio de las Descalzas Reales* is still a functioning convent. A superb example of 16th- to 17th-century Baroque architecture, it contains a magpie's hoard of artistic treasures, including Flemish tapestries, Italian and Flemish paintings and sculptures, religious artefacts and more. The convent is open for guided tours only. Tours are in Spanish, although questions are taken in English.

Plaza de las Descalzas Reales 3

Tel: (91) 454 8800.

Website: www.patrimonionacional.es

Transport: Metro Callao or Sol; bus 3, 5, 15, 20, 51, 52 or 150 to Puerta del Sol.

Opening hours: Tues–Thurs and Sat 1030–1245 and 1600–1745, Fri 1030–1245, Sun 1100–1330.

Admission: €4.01 (concessions available).

Faunia Parque Biológico de Madrid (Environmental Park)

The theme of this new, attractively landscaped theme park is bio-diversity. Each of the ten

Palacio Real

pavilions has been specially designed to recreate a different natural environment, with the aim of demonstrating how life – animal life in particular – has learned to adapt to a variety of ecosystems. Thanks to the latest high-tech wizardry, visitors can 'experience' a tropical storm, take a stroll through the rain forest, visit the polar regions with temperatures of - 5°C, or watch rivers of molten lava flowing 1000m (3281ft) beneath the earth's surface.

Avenida de las Comunidades 28

Tel: (91) 301 6210. Fax: (91) 301 6229.

Website: www.faunia.es

Transport: Metro Valdebernardo or Cercanías Vicálvaro; bus 8, 71, 130 or E.

Opening hours: Daily 1000–1800 (Mar and late Sep); daily 1000–2000 (Apr–Jun); daily 1000–2200 (Jul–mid-Sep); Wed–Sun 1000–1800 (Oct–Feb).

Admission: €16.90 (concessions available).

Faro de Moncloa (Light of Moncloa)

The *Faro de Moncloa* observation tower, situated in the university district, is open to the public, offering visitors panoramic views of Madrid from the flying-saucer-shaped viewing deck, 92m (302ft) high. The tower was designed by architect Salvador Arroyo, in 1992, to monitor traffic congestion.

Avenida de los Reyes Católicos/Plaza del Arco de la Victoria

Tel: (91) 544 8104.

Transport: Metro Moncloa; bus 1, 16, 44, 46, 61, 82, 83, 132, 133 or C.

Opening hours: Tues–Sun 1000–1400 and 1700–2100 (Jun–Aug); Tues–Fri 1000–1400 and 1700–1900, Sat and Sun 1000–1800 (Sep–May).

Admission: €1 (concessions available).

Tours of the City

Walking Tours

The *Patronato Municipal de Turismo* (tel: (91) 588 1636) organises a number of 90-minute walking tours (in English), costing €3 each (concessions are available). Two of the more popular tours are 'Hapsburg Madrid', including the Royal Palace, major churches and monasteries and taking place on Saturday 1000, all year round, and 'Legends of Old Madrid', an informative and entertaining introduction to the city (summer only). Both depart from the Oficina Municipal de Turismo, Plaza Mayor.

Bus Tours

Madrid Vision (tel: (91) 779 1888 or 541 6321; fax: (91) 383 0766; website: www.madridvision.es) bus tours depart daily from Puerta del Sol, and run every ten to 25 minutes, depending on the season, 1000–2100 (summer) and 1000–1900 (winter). Cassettes with English

Photo: Spanish National Tourist Office

Photo: Spanish National Tourist Office

Museo del Prado

commentary are provided on the tour, which runs for approximately 75 minutes. There is a choice of three routes – 'Historic Madrid' (including the main sights of the Hapsburg and Bourbon city), 'Modern Madrid' (including the Paseo de la Castellana and Santiago Bernabéu Stadium, Real Madrid's football ground) and 'Monumental Madrid' (exploring the Gran Via). The hop-on-hop-off trip costs €10–12 (concessions are available) and tickets are valid for one or two consecutive days (depending on the option chosen).

Excursions

For a Half Day

Monasterio de San Lorenzo de El Escorial: This monastery lies just 50km (31 miles) northwest of Madrid, in the town of San Lorenzo de El Escorial. The extraordinary rectangular edifice with four spired towers was built by Philip II, as a memorial to his father, Charles V, and is a combination of monastery, church and palace. It contains numerous artistic treasures, an austere 17th-century church and a beautifully decorated library with vaulted, painted ceiling.

Trains depart from Charmartín Station to El Escorial, from where a two-minute bus trip leads to the monastery. Buses also leave from outside Madrid's metro Moncloa, going directly to El Escorial monastery. The road route is along the NVI motorway – turning off on the A6 at 50km (31 miles). The monastery is open Tuesday to Sunday 1000–1700. Admission costs €3.01. Information is available from the *Tourist Office*, Calle Grimaldi 2 (tel: (91) 890 5313), and the *Cultural Centre*, Calle Floridablanca 10 (tel: (91) 542 0059).

For a Whole Day

Toledo: Often described as the 'soul of Spain', *Toledo* lies 70km (43 miles) south of Madrid and is easily reached by bus (from Estación Sur de Autobuses), car (along the N401) or train (regular departures from Atocha Station). The capital of Visigoth Spain (AD 567–711), Toledo is closely associated with the Cretan-born painter, El Greco, who lived and worked here from 1577 until his death in 1614. Regarded as the first great genius of the Spanish School, some of his most famous paintings are on show here, including *El Espolio* (Christ Stripped of His Garments) in the Cathedral and *The Burial of Count Orgaz* in the medieval church of Santo Tomé.

The hilltop city has changed little since medieval times and enjoys a magnificent setting atop the Tagus Gorge. Visitors should look out for the Moorish gate,

Puerta de Bisagrai, the *Sinagoga del Tránsito*, built in the 1360s and now a museum to Sephardic culture and the Jewish Diaspora of the Spanish Jews, the cathedral and the magnificent Renaissance hospital of *Santa Cruz*, now a museum. The *Tourist Office*, Puerta de Bisagra (tel: (92) 522 0843), can provide further information.

ACCOMMODATION

Spanish VAT (IVA) is 7% and is added to all hotel bills. The prices quoted below are the lowest standard rates for a double room, excluding breakfast and excluding IVA, unless otherwise specified.

Business

Hotel Eurobuilding

Located in a modern high-rise building in the north of the city, the *Eurobuilding* is a large hotel with 469 rooms, catering specifically for business travellers. The comprehensive facilities include 20 conference rooms, a business centre and interpreting services, while individual rooms have Internet and fax-modem connection, satellite TV and video. The multi-lingual staff is both friendly and efficient. While the lobby area and lounges are spacious, airy and well suited to informal meetings, they are somewhat lacking in atmosphere (the piped music does not help). The Eurobuilding is just a short walk from the Palacio de Congresos y Exposiciones on Paseo de la Castellana and a short drive to Juan Carlos I Trade Fair Centre and Barajas airport.
Calle Padre Damián 23
Tel: (91) 353 7300. Fax: (91) 345 4576.
E-mail: nheurobuilding@nh-hoteles.com
Website: www.nh-hoteles.com
Price: From €239.

Hotel Opera

A short walk from the Puerta del Sol and the shops of the Gran Via, this modern, medium-sized hotel with 79 rooms is situated just across the street from the Opera House, hence the name. The hotel is comfortable, with traditional, slightly old-fashioned furnishings. The business facilities include fax, interpreting and limousine services and conference rooms for small meetings. All rooms are equipped with video and satellite TV; some have balconies with views of old Madrid. The English-speaking staff is friendly and helpful, while, in the café-

restaurant, evening meals are accompanied by live performances of classical and light opera.
Cuesta de Santo Domingo 2
Tel: (91) 541 2800. Fax: (91) 541 6923.
E-mail: reservas@hotelopera.com
Website: www.hotelopera.com
Price: From €120.

Hotel Santo Mauro

This small luxury hotel with 37 rooms, situated in a leafy corner of the historic Chamberí neighbourhood, is housed in a 19th-century palace that once served as an embassy. It was reconstructed in a tasteful combination of neo-classical and avant-garde styles in 1990. The lounges, ornamented with stucco mouldings, mirrors and fluted pilasters, evoke the refinement of a bygone age and are the perfect setting for entertaining clients. Other facilities include business services, six conference rooms (occupying the former ballrooms), interpreting services, multi-lingual staff and a fitness centre in which to unwind or re-energise after a taxing day of work. All guest rooms are individually designed and are equipped with satellite TV, video and 24-hour room service.
Calle Zurbano 36
Tel: (91) 319 6900. Fax: (91) 308 5477.
E-mail: santomauro@ac-hotels.com
Website: www.ac-hotels.com
Price: From €318.

Suecia

As the plaque outside the hotel explains, the *Suecia's* claim to fame is that writer Ernest Hemingway stayed here during the 1950s, commending it for its proximity to the Prado and the Café del Bellas Artes on Calle Alcalá. The facilities, which include a café-restaurant (with afternoon tea served daily), meeting rooms and a secretarial and translation service, are good value for the price and location. Fitted out in Swedish style – *Suecia* is Spanish for Sweden – the 128 rooms, including nine 'junior suites', are cramped or cosy, depending on one's point of view. To compensate, there is a seventh-floor terrace where guests can stretch their legs.
Calle Marqués de Casa Riera 4
Tel: (91) 531 6900. Fax: (91) 521 7141.
E-mail: bookings@hotelseucia.com
Website: www.hotelsuecia.com
Price: From €172.

Luxury

Hotel Ritz

Designed along the lines of its Parisian counterpart by architect Francis Mewes, the *Hotel Ritz* opened in 1910, in the presence of King Alfonso XIII, who had previously bemoaned the paucity of luxury accommodation in the city. Located only a stone's throw from major cultural attractions like the Prado and the Thyssen-Bornemisza museums, the Ritz also appeals to business travellers, because of its proximity to the Madrid Stock Exchange and the financial district. Rooms are individually designed, with embroidered linen sheets, hand-woven carpets and marble bathrooms. Facilities include fax, telephone, satellite TV and 24-hour room service. Meeting and conference halls cater for up to 500 people, with a simultaneous translation service available. There is also a gym, solarium and sauna. The restaurant, sumptuously decorated in the Belle Epoque style with lashings of marble and gilt, serves a spectacular Sunday brunch, as well as Spanish and International cuisine. The terrace and gardens are the perfect setting for meeting friends and business colleagues.

Plaza de la Lealtad 5
Tel: (91) 701 6767. Fax: (91) 701 6776.
E-mail: reservas@ritz.es
Website: www.ritz.es
Price: From €510.

Palace Hotel

Since first opening its doors in 1913, the *Palace* has been vying with the Ritz in its claims to be Madrid's premier hotel. Built on a grand scale, with 455 rooms, the hotel has been restored to a level of opulence almost in excess of the original. As well as 18 conference and banqueting rooms, a business centre and interpreting service, there are individual guest room-offices equipped with desk, fax/printer and hands-free telephones. The fitness suite is open 24 hours. Although unashamedly glitzy, the Palace is less stuffy than the Ritz and its restaurants and bars are less pricey than one would expect.
Plaza de las Cortes 7
Tel: (91) 360 8000. Fax: (91) 360 8100.
E-mail: reservations.palacemadrid@westin.com
Website: www.palacemadrid.com
Price: From €439.

Moderate

Ingles

This hotel, founded in 1853, enjoys an excellent location in the old part of Madrid, less than 100m (328ft) from Puerta del Sol and equally convenient for cultural attractions, such as the Prado and the bars and restaurants around Calle Huertas. While the modern decor is a little uninspired, all 58 rooms are kept in pristine condition and the 24-hour service is attentive. Rooms overlooking the street may be noisy late at night; those at the back are quieter. All rooms are en suite. Other facilities include a gym, a café and a garage, which is invaluable, considering that parking spaces are at a premium in central Madrid.
Calle Echegaray 8
Tel: (91) 429 6551. Fax: (91) 420 2423.
Price: From €75.

Trafalgar

Less than ten minutes from the centre of town by metro (Iglesia or Bilbao), the *Trafalgar* is a modern hotel that was

completely refurbished a couple of years ago. It lies in a residential neighbourhood, well provided with shops, restaurants and other amenities. The 48 en-suite rooms, while unexceptional, are air conditioned and have direct-dial telephones and TV. There is also a laundry service and currency exchange. The English-speaking staff is friendly and helpful but the real plus – surprising given the price – is the indoor swimming pool.
Calle Trafalgar 35
Tel: (91) 445 6200. Fax: (91) 446 6456.
Price: From €109.

Other Recommendations

Hotel Aristos

The location is the main attraction of this small, modern hotel at the expensive end of the three-star range. Tucked away in a pleasant residential district in the north of the city, the *Aristos* is approximately a 15-minute drive from the centre. It is equally convenient for Barajas airport and the Juan Carlos I Trade Fair Centre, while the Palacio de Congresos y Exposiciones, on Paseo de la Castellana, is even closer. Although a tad soulless, all 23 rooms have air conditioning, satellite TV, a mini-bar, a bath with a hydromassage shower and laundry service. The restaurant (with terrace) serves Mediterranean dishes.
Avenida de Pío XII 34
Tel: (91) 345 0450. Fax: (91) 345 1023.
E-mail: hotelaristos@elchaflan.com
Price: From €163.

Hotel Monaco

Situated in the heart of the lively Chueca *barrio* (district), once home to Madrid's blacksmiths, the *Monaco* was originally a brothel much in vogue with the Spanish nobility, including King Alfonso XIII. Renovated as a hotel in the 1950s, the Art Deco interiors now appear the height of kitsch. Most of the 30 rooms have retained at least some of the original decor – a moulding here, a marble pillar there. The *pièce de resistance*, however, is Room 20, with wall mirrors and a raised central bathtub. The leather booths in the breakfast room are also original – was this where the courtesans entertained their clients, one wonders? Facilities include a ticket agency, fax service, laundry and bar, while rooms have safes, telephones and TVs.

Calle Barbieri 5
Tel: (91) 522 4630. Fax: (91) 521 1601.
Price: From €70.

RESTAURANTS

The selected restaurants have been divided into five categories: Gastronomic, Business, Trendy, Budget and Personal Recommendations. The restaurants are listed alphabetically within these different categories, which serve as guidelines rather than absolute definitions of the establishments.
Spanish VAT (IVA) is 7% and is included in all menu prices. If not, it will be stated that prices are exclusive of IVA. Tipping is not a widespread practice but, of course, should one wish to leave a gratuity, it is always appreciated. In upscale restaurants, it is customary for diners to leave a tip of around 5% of the bill (never more than 10%). Occasionally, a small cover charge is added to the bill – the menu should mention this.
The prices quoted below are for an average three-course meal for one person and for a bottle of house wine or cheapest equivalent; they do not include IVA or tip.

Gastronomic

El Amparo

El Amparo's deserved reputation as one of Madrid's top gourmet restaurants owes a good deal to the creative partnership of culinary consultant Martín Berasategui and head chef Iñigo Pérez and their flair for giving traditional Basque recipes the nouvelle cuisine treatment. Recommended dishes include *millefeuille* of apples with smoked fish and foie gras, hake in a parsley sauce with clams, and for dessert, cinnamon ice cream with dark chocolate and pistachios. Another plus for the restaurant is its setting – a former coach-house in Madrid's smart Salamanca district. The decor is the work of leading Spanish designer Pascua Ortega, who also worked on the refurbishment of the Teatro Real (see *Culture*). The sun streams in through a skylight during the day, while the restaurant space is lit by lanterns at night.
Callejón de Puigcerdá 8
Tel: (91) 431 6456. Fax: (91) 575 5491.
Price: €55. Wine: €19.

El Cenador del Prado

Chef Tomás Herranz has won numerous accolades for his imaginative menus, which showcase the best of Spanish regional cuisine. Salted cod in breadcrumbs with garlic and grape garnishing, medallions of venison with cheese ravioli and quince, beef carpaccio with pig's trotters in a mushroom sauce – all the dishes here are prepared with virgin olive oil and dressed with fresh herbs. The prices are reasonable, the ambience is cool and refined, the service impeccable. The trellised garden room is another plus.
Calle del Prado 4
Tel: (91) 429 1561. Fax: (91) 369 0455.
Price: €30. Wine: €10.

Jockey

Patronised by the rich, famous and discerning, *Jockey* has earned itself the reputation as one of Madrid's top-flight restaurants since opening in 1945. The restaurant is quite small and intimate, with dark

Retiro Park

Photo: Spanish National Tourist Office

wooden panelling and framed prints of jockeys and their mounts. Sea bass, wild fowl and game (when in season) are all to be found on an ambitious and often exciting menu. The wine cellar is also excellent. Typical dishes include lobster ragout with truffles and fresh pasta, marinated partridge in jelée of thyme and lamb à la Provençale.
Amador de los Ríos 6
Tel: (91) 319 1003. Fax: (91) 319 2435.
Price: €60. Wine: €19.

La Broche Sergi Arola

One of the brightest stars in Madrid's culinary firmament, *La Broche*'s master chef, Sergi Arola, has been awarded two Michelin stars for his original interpretations of traditional Catalan and Spanish recipes. The menu changes monthly but signature dishes include *turbot con patas de puerco*, where pan-fried turbot is sprinkled with coriander and served with a jelly of pig's feet wrapped in onion, and *solomillo de buey*, ox steak stuffed with goats' cheese, anchovies, cherries and pine-nut purée. The stark, uniformly white decor helps to create a relaxed and surprisingly informal ambience.
Miguel Angel 29–31 (next to Hotel Occidental Miguel Angel)
Tel: (91) 399 3437.
Price: €85. Wine: €19.

Zalacaín

One of Europe's finest restaurants, *Zalacaín* has gathered just about every gastronomic award, including one Michelin star. Master chef Benjamín Urdaín has spent nearly 30 years fine-tuning a menu that combines classic French recipes with those of his Basque homeland. Only a culinary master with a refreshing unpretentiousness can give humble dishes like pig's trotters and smoked fish equal prominence with lobster, oysters, caviar, truffles and foie gras. Some may find the formality of Zalacaín a touch overdone, with its various dining areas, some of which are well suited to tête à tête, subdued lighting and dark red decor. Jacket and tie are de rigueur.
Alvarez de Baena 4
Tel: (91) 561 5935. Fax: (91) 561 4732.
Price: €110. Wine: €19.

Business

Berceo-Le-Divellec

This gourmet temple in one of Madrid's more exclusive hotels opened in 1998 and has become a by-word for sophisticated eating. Much of its reputation rests on the shoulders of Parisian master chef Jacques Le-Divellec whose culinary *métier* is seafood. However, anyone averse to dishes like sea bass in rum or baked tuna with curry sauce will not be disappointed with the tournedos or the succulent young lamb. The restaurant is formal in style, with a plush, oak-panelled interior; its garden terrace is in great demand during the hot summer months.
Hotel Villa Magna, Paseo de la Castellana 22
Tel: (91) 587 1234. Fax: (91) 431 2286.
E-mail: hotel@villamagna.es
Website: http://villamagna.park.hyatt.com
Price: €45. Wine: €17.

Cabo Mayor

This superb gourmet restaurant, hidden among the office blocks of the Chamartín district, is a showcase for fish dishes from Spain's Cantabrian coast. Hake

with clams in parsley sauce, grilled turbot, sea bream with thyme – there is hardly an item on the menu that does not entice. The atmosphere is pleasantly informal; the main dining area, situated downstairs, is fitted out in nautical style, with brass portholes, wood panels and ship's rigging.
Juan Ramón Jiménez 37
Tel: (91) 350 8776. Fax: (91) 359 1621.
Price: €42. Wine: €12.

Café Gijón

A Madrid institution, this famous literary café first opened its doors in 1888 and is still going strong. Patrons over the years have included the poets Federico García Lorca and Pablo Neruda, the film director Orson Welles and Nobel prize-winning novelist Camilo José Cela. The restaurant boasts a well-lit salon and large, street-facing windows, a terrace and a basement. There are several menus available. The *menu del dia* comprises such dishes as Spanish omelette, stuffed peppers and hake. The tapas menu contains such items as sirloin sandwich, prawns in garlic and anchovies. The à la carte menu boasts Spanish specialities, such as cod in cider. While the Spanish cooking is not outstanding, the set lunch at €9 is good value and the location, a short walk from Cibeles and the Banco de España, can hardly be bettered.
Paseo de Recoletos 21
Tel: (91) 521 5425.
E-mail: info@cafegijon.com
Website: http://cafegijon.com
Price: €25. Wine: €10.

Las Cuatro Estaciones

Rated one of the finest restaurants in Madrid, 'The Four Seasons' celebrated its 20th anniversary in 2001, less than a year after master chef Francisco Ariaz and his team were awarded the top national honours of

Premio Nacional de Gastronomia. Situated to the northwest of the city centre, near the university, *Las Cuatro Estaciones*' floral decor, reflecting the changing seasons, is breathtaking. The cooking is perhaps best described as Mediterranean with a pronounced French accent, including such specialities as *millefeuille de foie gras* or *blanquette* of monkfish.
General Ibáñez Ibero 5
Tel: (91) 553 6305. Fax: (91) 553 0523.
Price: €39. Wine: €14.

Lhardy

This august establishment, less than a one-minute walk from Puerta del Sol, was founded by Frenchman Emile Lhardy in 1839, after being told that there were no decent restaurants in Madrid. The restaurant specialises in traditional Castillian fare, with typical dishes including *solomillo* (entrecôte), roast beef, *cocido* (stew) or tripe cooked Madrid style in a tomato and wine sauce. The tapas bar and delicatessen downstairs preserve the original gilded mirrors, marble counters and brass fittings – the bar is a cheaper option than the plush restaurant on the first floor, with dishes such as soups, paella, tortilla, fish and shellfish dishes, sausages or hams.
Carrera de San Jerónimo 8
Tel: (91) 521 3385. Fax: (91) 523 1171.
E-mail: lhardy@lhardy.com
Website: http://lhardy.com
Price: €54. Wine: €17.

Trendy

Champagnería Gala

Gala is currently one of Madrid's trendier eating places and diners should book ahead to be sure of a table on the canopied garden patio. The Spanish sparkling wines are the ideal accompaniment to the

Plaza Mayor

paellas, risottos and Catalan noodle dishes (*fideuàs*) that are Gala's stock-in-trade. There are more than a dozen of these wines to choose from. The set menu includes a glass of wine, as well as a starter and dessert – a bargain at €11. No credit cards.
Calle Moratín 22
Tel: (91) 429 2562.
Website: www.paellas-gala.com
Price: €11. Wine: €7.

Divina La Cocina

A great location on the fringes of trendy Chueca is one reason why this restaurant, owned by Spanish chef José Luis Castanedo and American Chad Kenyon, is such a hit. Together, they have created their own special brand of Spanish fusion – for example, salted cod in a soya and ginger sauce, seaweed salad with shrimps and eggs of sea urchin or prime beef steak with *pâté de foie gras* in port. Designer Carlos Mayoral's powder blue and terracotta tones add a dash of refinement and sophistication.
Calle Colmenares 13
Tel: (91) 531 3765.
Website: www.divinalacocina.com
Price: €24. Wine: €10.

Las Cuevas de Luís Candelas

While many of the eating places around Plaza Mayor are tourist orientated and overpriced, *Las Cuevas* offers better value and a relaxed convivial atmosphere in the brick-vaulted cellar with tiled bar, wall paintings, wrought iron fittings and an open fire for the suckling pig speciality. Named after a 19th-century highwayman, said to have hidden in one of the cellars (*cuevas*), this bar-restaurant offers a typical range of tapas, as well as substantial main courses. Specialities include *merluza* (hake) and roasts cooked in a wood-fired oven, *jamon serrano* (cured ham), shrimps in garlic or cheese and grilled peppers. An English-language menu is available.
Aarco de Cuchilleros 1
Tel: (91) 366 5428. Fax: (91) 366 4937.
E-mail: info@lascuevasdeluiscandelas.com
Website: www.lascuevasdeluiscandelas.com
Price: €27. Wine: €14.

Lombok

The minimalist decor of this Chueca eating place – with spotlights, bare white walls and steel counter – might seem a trifle passé but *Lombok* is still very much in vogue. Its clientele is young and stylish – perhaps it helps that one of the co-owners is a Spanish TV presenter. The fusion cuisine draws on ingredients and recipes from the far-flung corners of the globe – Thai salad, samosas filled with apple and Roquefort cheese, carpaccio, monkfish kebab and kangaroo steak in port – and it all looks as good as it tastes.
Augusto Figueroa 32
Tel: (91) 531 3566. Fax: (91) 531 3566.
E-mail: info@lombokmadrid.com
Website: www.lombokmadrid.com
Price: €20. Wine: €10.

Robata

Japanese cooking is still not quite as much in vogue in Madrid as in some European capitals but is catching up fast. *Robata* is Japanese for a grill, so grilled meats and fish (Spanish *a la parrilla*) are to the fore on an extensive menu offering combinations of tempura, sashimi, sushi and sukiyaki, as well as soups. The bold black and red colour scheme is eye catching, the ambience relaxed. Diners can sit at a table or around the central sushi bar.

Calle de la Reina 31
Tel: (91) 521 8528. Fax: (91) 531 3063.
Price: €30. Wine: €7 (sake).

Budget

Café del Círculo de Bellas Artes

In its heyday during the 1920s, the *Café del Círculo de Bellas Artes* was the haunt of Madrid's leading intellectuals. Designed by Antonio Palacios, the spacious salon, decorated with classical pillars, chandeliers and an enormous painted ceiling, is known as the goldfish bowl, because of its outlook onto Calle Alcalá. The menu is wide ranging and includes everything from cakes, baguettes and ices to roast beef and smoked salmon. The terrace is a great place to watch the world go by.
Calle Marqués de Casa Riera 2
Tel: (91) 360 5400.
Price: €20. Wine: €7.

La Galette

One of the best things about this well-established vegetarian restaurant is that carnivores are catered for too. From the extensive list of imaginatively prepared vegetable, rice and pasta dishes, one might single out the delicious *tartar de chicle* (cauliflower cheese with a dusting of fresh herbs), followed by apple croquettes. Diners sit elbow-to-elbow in the two small rooms, decked out in an appealing country-kitchen style.
Calle Conde de Aranda 11
Tel: (91) 576 0641.
Price: €18. Wine: €8.

Taberna Carmencita

Once the haunt of artists, soldiers and bullfighters, this rambling inn has been around since 1850. The original hand-painted tiles and the check tablecloths create a homely ambience, appropriate to the *Madrileño* cooking. Croquettes, stuffed peppers, fillet steak, tripe, meatballs, eggs and the hotpot known as *cocido* are the mainstays. While eating à la carte is not especially cheap, the set menu at €9 is good value. It is a pity about the brusque service, however.
Calle Libertad 16
Tel: (91) 531 6612.
Price: €20. Wine: €7.

Vips

This branch of the well-known newsagent and restaurant chain has a great location, close to the Prado and the Thyssen-Bornemisza museums. Open seven days a week until the early hours of the morning, it is nearly always full, on account of the reasonable prices and the diverse menu – everything from ham and eggs to pizzas and bowls of tacos. The atmosphere is busy and bustling and the decor modern and functional. Breakfasts (American, English and continental) are served until midday.
Plaza de las Cortes 7
Tel: (91) 429 4234.
Price: €10. Wine: €7.

Viuda de Vacas

The name 'The Widow Vacas' alludes to the Cánovas Vacas family from Segovia, who founded the restaurant more than a century ago. This homely *taberna*, mainly patronised by young locals, preserves its faded wall tiles, marble-top tables and a spiral staircase leading to the upper floor. The menu, inspired by the Castillian countryside, is only available in Spanish – recommended are *berenjenas* (auberjines stuffed with breadcrumbs in a cream sauce), *jamon al horno* (roast pork), *gallina en pepitoria* (chicken in egg and almond sauce) and *merluza* (hake).
Calle Cava Alta 23
Tel: (91) 366 5847.
Price: €15. Wine: €6.

Plaza de España

Personal Recommendations

Al-Mounia

Ethnic restaurants are not Madrid's strong point but *Al-Mounia* can be counted among the exceptions. Situated just off Paseo de Recoletas, the North African (*Maghreb*) specialities in this restaurant include sublime couscous dishes and tajines. The starters are equally tempting, if pricey – money is better spent on the sticky, finger-licking pastries. The decor, evoking a Moorish palace with ceramic wall tiles and lattice screens, is fun but unconvincing.
Calle Recoletos 5
Tel: (91) 435 0828.
Price: €35. Wine: €13.

Botín

Said to be the oldest restaurant in the world, *Botín* first opened its doors below the Plaza Mayor in 1725. The wonderful old dining rooms retain the original painted tiles, oak beams and wood-burning oven. Traditional Castillian dishes are the speciality here – the roast suckling pig and the tender Aranda lamb are delicious. Reservations strongly recommended.
Calle Cuchilleros 17
Tel: (91) 366 4217. Fax: (91) 366 8494.
Website: www.casabotin.com
Price: €30. Wine: €10.

Café Saigon

Café Saigon opened in February 2001 and consequently made waves among the city's young sophisticates. The cuisine is best described as East Asian, with Vietnamese dishes featuring. There are shades of the 'Paris of the East' too in the lattice woodcarving, hessian drapes, sepia photographs and colonial bric-a-brac in the upstairs dining area. As there is no English-language menu, the safe option is the reasonably priced *menú degustación*.
Paseo de la Castellana 66, corner of Calle de Maria de Molina
Tel: (91) 563 1566.
Price: €30. Wine: €13.

La Dame Noire

'The Black Lady' has a great location in the heart of Chueca, one of Madrid's most colourful neighbourhoods and now the gay quarter. A good deal of its appeal lies in the outlandish decor, a Rococo travesty with *trompe l'oeil* ceiling, red drapes, gilded mirrors, classical statues and leopard skin chair covers. The cooking is French inspired, if a touch eccentric – salted cod in cider may not be to everyone's taste. A safer bet might be trout and almonds in an onion sauce, ox tongue in port or the house speciality of mussels in cream.
Calle Pérez Galdós 3
Tel: (91) 531 0476. Fax: (91) 522 2061.
E-mail: ladamenoire@ladamenoire.com
Website: www.ladamenoire.com
Price: €20. Wine: €10.

Terra Mundi

Galician home cooking is on offer in this delightful restaurant near Plaza Santa Ana. The restaurant has an informal ambience with rustic country-kitchen decor, with pine wood furniture and check tablecloths. The tapas bar is popular with local office workers, while meals are served in the adjoining dining rooms. The menu is inspired by traditional Gallegan recipes; fish and seafood dishes (including octopus) are to the fore, although meat also makes a strong showing – the roast pork in a plum and raisin sauce goes down a treat. Outstanding among the desserts is *filloas* (Galician crêpe).
Lope de Vega 32
Tel: (91) 429 5280.
Price: €20. Wine: €7.

ENTERTAINMENT

Nightlife

Madrileños tend to make not one plan for the evening but three or four. While the busiest nights are Friday and Saturday (with Thursday a close runner-up), the locals go out every night and miraculously manage to work or study during the day. Perhaps the secret lies in the tradition of consuming *tapas* – snacks of olives, anchovies, chorizo sausages, *gambas* (deep-fried shrimp) and local specialities like *orejas* (pig's ears), *callos* (tripe), *mollejas* (sweetbreads), snails in hot sauce and bull's testicles. After a long night on the town, it is customary to breakfast on thick hot chocolate and sweet fried *churros* (dough).

Nightlife centres on three major districts – Chueca (Madrid's gay village, which specialises in trendy restaurants), Calle Huertas (traditional Spanish music, jazz clubs and bars) and Malasaña (mainly bars, and clubs frequented by a mainly young crowd). All bars and clubs are licensed but hours are flexible. It can be hard to tell bars and clubs apart, since bars often have a dancefloor and not all clubs charge for entry. Where they do, €5–10 is the standard admission fee, which usually includes *consumición* (first drink). The legal drinking age in Madrid is 18 years and the price of a tipple ranges from €1.50 for a small beer or glass of wine to €4.50 for spirits and cocktails. It is customary to pay on leaving and certainly worth noting that few bars accept credit cards. Tipping is discretionary (€1 will suffice).

Many venues close during the month of August. There are several listings magazines. The weekly *Guía del Ocio* (website: www.guiadelocio.com/english), published in Spanish only and available from kiosks for €1 has information on concerts, theatre, film and other entertainment options. It also provides restaurant listings. The monthly *What's on* is published in English and Spanish and is less detailed but good on opening times and contact details. *In Madrid* is a monthly English-language newspaper, available from tourist offices, Irish bars or Barajas airport. It is hot on the latest club news, DJs, bars and other aspects of night-time entertainment – and it is free.

Bars

Madrid's bars range from dark, wood-panelled taverns to the fabulous *Viva Madrid*, Calle Manuel Fernández y González 7, with its painted tiles of Madrid scenes from the early 1900s. *The Garamond*, Calle de Claudio Coello 10, has a castle-like interior and suits a smart older crowd. *Chicote*, Grand Vía 12, is Madrid's most famous cocktail bar and has preserved its 1930s interior – it is easy to imagine American novelist Ernest Hemingway relaxing here during the Civil War. A former brothel run by gypsies, with a tiled interior depicting Velázquez's *The Drunkards*, *Los Gabrieles*, Calle Echegaray 17, is now a respectable bar for a young chic clientele. Tapas bars cluster around Plaza de Santa Ana near Sol, Plaza de Santa Bárbara in Calasaña and Cava Baja and Calle de Cuchilleros, behind Plaza Mayor. One of the best is *Taberna los Austrias*, Calle Nuncio 17, situated near metro La Latina. As dawn breaks, revellers head for *Chocolatería San Ginés*, Pasadizo de San Ginés 11, a Mecca for those in search of hot chocolate and *churros*.

Casinos

Casino Gran Madrid, Autovía A6, Km 29 exit from Madrid, Carretera de la Coruna, (website: www. casinogranmadrid.es) is the only officially recognised casino in the area and is located outside the city, near Torrelodones – a free bus service leaves from Plaza Espana 6. The dress code is formal and ties must be worn, the minimum age is 21 years and passports are required for entry.

Clubs

Most tourists head for the clubs around Sol and Gran Vía, although true hedonists might want to try out some of the locals' haunts instead. A typical night might begin around 2300 with the exotic elite at *Serrano 41*, Calle Serrano 41, *Independencia*, Puerta de Alcalá, or the tango-friendly *Sportsman*, Calle Alcalá 65, before moving on to *Fortuny*, Calle Fortuney 23, the laid-back *Café del Foro*, Calle San Andres 38, or super-trendy *Mármara*, Calle Padre Damián, next to Hotel Eurobuilding. There are no admission charges here, although chic dress is recommended. The energetic dance to techno at *Pachá*, Calle Barceló 11. *Gabana 1800*, Calle de Velázquez 6, is another popular venue for stylish 20- and 30-somethings – if the bouncer allows admission.

Live Music

Madrid offers an eclectic choice of flamenco, salsa, jazz, rock, World music and *cantautores* – Spanish singer-songwriters. The *Café de la Palma*, Calle la Palma 62, is the venue of the moment for *cantautores*, as well as flamenco and Cuban music acts. For more Latino sounds, fans should head for *La Negra Tomasa*, Calle Cádiz 9, for live music nightly from 2100. *Moby Dick*, Avenida de Brasil 5, in the Castellana district, plays live pop and rock on weekdays and hosts DJs (reggae and rap) at weekends. The clientele is a charming mixture of foreigners and locals. At *Café Populart*, Calle Huertas 22, punters can experience everything from live jazz to swing, salsa, blues, gospel, African and reggae. There are two shows nightly, at 2300 and 0030. *The Irish Rover* pub, Avenida de Brasil 7, imports Irish, folk and country music. International acts play regularly at the *Café Central*, Plaza del Angel 10, Madrid's top jazz venue. Pop stars and the best salsa bands perform at *La Riviera*, Paseo Bajo de la Virgen del Puerto.

Sport

Nothing has as much power to lift *Madrileños* to the height of joy or drag them into deep depression as sport does – victories and tragedies are passionately recounted in the sports dailies, *Marca* and *As*. Football (*fútbol*) is the major obsession. Madrid has two vast stadiums that fill up on Saturday and Sunday evenings during the September–May season. *Atlético Madrid* (website: www.clubatleticodemadrid.com), now promoted to the first division, plays at *Estadio Vicente Calderón*, Paseo Virgen del Puerto 67 (tel: (91) 366 4707), while the Spanish champions, *Real Madrid* (website: www.realmadrid.es), play at *Estadio Santiago Bernabéu*, Calle Concha Espina Paseo de la Castellana (tel: (91) 398 4300). Another important sporting venue is the top-class *Estadio de la Comunidad de Madrid*, 'La Peineta', Avenida de Arcentales (tel: (91) 720 2400), one of the proposed venues for the 2012 Olympics, should the games be awarded to the city. Basketball (*baloncesto*) is second only to football in the hearts of *Madrileños*. The season runs from September to May, with April marking the climax. Madrid has two top teams – *Estudiantes* (website: www.clubestudiantes.com) and *Real Madrid* (website: www.realmadrid.es). The venue for the former is *Palacio Vistalegre*, Paseo Vista Alegre (tel: (91) 422 0708), and for the latter, *Pabellón Raimundo Saporta*, Paseo de la Castellana 259 (tel: (93) 398 4300).

The enthusiasm for sport does not stop at simply watching and cheering; many *Madrileños* partake in the annual *Maratón Popular de Madrid* (tel: (91) 366 9701), on the last Sunday in April, finishing at Retiro Park/Plaza de Cibeles. Another big event is September's *La Vuelta de España*, the Spanish answer to the Tour de France, a cycle race that whisks its way around Spain before reaching Madrid, where five laps of the Castellana single out the winner.

Tickets to most sporting events are available either from the separate venues or from *Localidades Galicia*, Plaza del Carmen (tel: (91) 531 2732; website: www.eol.es/galicia).

Bullfighting

The bloodthirsty sport of bullfighting takes place at the Madrid bullring, *Plaza de Toros*, Calle de Alcalá 237 (tel: (91) 356 2200). Tickets are available from *Localidades Galicia*, Plaza del Carmen (tel: (91) 531 2732.

Fitness Centres

Most gyms (*gymnasios*) are members only, however, many hotels have their own gyms or agreements with private health clubs. Madrid has some 45 city-run *polideportivos* (sports centres) offering wide-ranging facilities, including gyms, swimming pools and tennis courts. *Polideportivo Municipal Chamartín*, Plaza de Perú (tel: (91) 350 1223), is one of these.

Golf

Golf clubs tend to be expensive. *Golf Olivar de la Hinojosa*, Avenida de Dublin, on the metro Campo de las Naciones (tel: (91) 721 1889), charges approximately €23 for nine holes and €37.50 for 18 holes. Membership is not required and beginners and seasoned golfers are welcome. Facilities include tennis courts.

Swimming

Open-air swimming pools (*piscinas*) are a necessity in Madrid's summer heat, with the season running from the beginning of June to mid-September. The rooftop pool in the *Hotel Emperador*, Calle Gran Vía 53 (tel: (91) 547 2800), offers spectacular views over the city and is open to non-residents for €25 Monday to Friday or €35 at the weekend. One of the best outdoor municipal pools is *Instalación deportiva del Canal de Isabel II*, Avenida Islas Filipinas 54 (tel: (91) 533 1791), near metro Canal – open from 1100–2000, with admission costing €3. Information on Madrid's other public swimming pools is available from *Instituto Municipal de Deportes – IMD* (tel: (91) 540 3939).

Tennis

Madrid has many tennis clubs but most are private. Many *polideportivos* (see *Fitness Centres* above) have tennis courts that are open to non-members. A central polideportivos is *Instalacion deportivo del Canal Isabel II*, Avenida Islas Filipinas 54 (tel: (91) 533 1791 or 554 5153). The standard fee per hour is €4.

Santiago Bernabéu Stadium

Shopping

Madrid's shops are generally open from 0930/1000 to 1330/1400 and 1630/1700 to 2030/2100, with major stores open throughout the lunch hours. The most convenient area for tourists is around Calle de Preciados, between Sol and Gran Vía, home to the *El Corte Inglés* department store, high-street names like *Zara* (Gran Vía 32) and *Casa Jiménez* (Calle de Preciados 42), famed throughout Spain for its lace and embroidered shawls (*mantones* and *mantillas*). The smartest shopping district is Salamanca northeast of the centre, around Calle Serrano. Top designer names like Chanel, Versace, Hermès and Hugo Boss, including the fluid fabrics and elegant cuts of Spanish designer Adolfo Domínguez, are located on Calle Ortega y Gasset. Head for Calle Serrano for Purificación García, Roberto Verino, Ermenegildo Zegna and Yves Saint Laurent. Another trendy area is Chueca, especially Calles Almirante and Conde de Xiquena, while the Mecca for youth fashions is Calle Fuencarral. Bargains can be found during the sales, which take place in January and July.

The main areas for antiques are Salamanca and the arcades on Calle Ribera de Curtidores – *Nuevas Galerías*, at number 12, and *Galerías Piquer*, at number 29. Bargain hunters should make for the *Rastro*, Madrid's famous flea market, also located around Ribera de Curtidores. The market is open on Sunday mornings (closing at 1400). Shoppers should beware of pickpockets in this area.

More unusual shops include: *Mesquida*, Calle Mayor 22, for religious and devotional objects, including crib pieces; the Spanish guitar specialist, *Manuel Gonzales Contreras*, with the store at Calle de la Paz 8, and the workshop at Calle General Margallo 10; *El Flamenco Vive*, Calle Conde de Lemos 7, which sells sheet music, videos and CDs as well as colourful costumes and accessories; and *Seseña*, Calle Cruz 23, makers of traditional Spanish capes.

Serious shoppers might opt for the *Madrid Shopping Tour* (tel: (91) 316 0657; website: www.madridshoppingtour.com). For €25, visitors are taken by minibus on a tour of Salamanca, Las Rozas

shopping centre and downtown Madrid. Advantages include special discounts and guides and lunch is included in the price. Tours depart from Plaza de Neptuno, Tuesday to Thursday at 1000.

Sales tax is 7–16% (luxuries). It is possible for visitors from outside the EU to claim a tax refund from many central shops – shoppers should look for the Global Refund Tax Free Shopping stickers in windows and ask for Tax Free Checks, which should be kept with receipts to be presented at airport customs upon departure. Further information is available from *Global Refund* (tel: (900) 435 482 *or* (91) 729 4380; fax: (91) 729 1299; e-mail: taxfree@es.globalrefund.com; website: www.globalrefund.com).

Culture

Madrid has had its fair share of cultural icons – Surrealist genius Salvador Dalí lived in the city as a student, as did filmmaker Luis Buñuel and poet and dramatist Federico García Lorca. American writer Ernest Hemingway was a war correspondent in Madrid during the Civil War and a regular visitor thereafter. Madrid has its own distinctive dancing style (*chotis*), seen to best effect during the San Isidro festival and light opera (*zarzuela*). The city also boasts an international opera house, as well as numerous cinemas and theatres catering for all tastes.

Ticket prices for cultural events vary from around €5 to €50. While most hotels are happy to book tickets for guests, they will charge for the service. It is cheaper for visitors to book directly at the box offices, not all of which accept credit cards. Keen theatregoers can also make advance bookings at savings banks – for example, *Servicio de Entradas Punto Com* (tel: (902) 488 488). Tickets for sold-out performances are available for purchase (at a price) at *Localidades Galicia*, Plaza del Carmen 10 (tel: (91) 531 2732). Tickets for performances at the state-owned theatres – the Comedia, Teatro de la Zarzuela, Auditoria Nacional and Maria Guerrero – are available from the box offices at each of the four venues.

The English-language monthly publication, *In Madrid*, and the Spanish weekly, *Guía de Ocio* (website:

www.guiadelocio.com/english) print listings on cultural events in and around the city.

Music

Madrid's opera house, the *Teatro Real*, Plaza de Oriente (tel: (91) 516 0660), is one of the most modern opera houses in Europe. The *Teatro de la Zarzuela*, Calle de Jovellanos 4 (tel: (91) 524 5400 website: http://teatrodelazarzuela.mcu.es), is the major venue for *zarzuela* – a genre loosely comparable to Viennese operetta, which encapsulates the idealised *castizo* (authenticity) of working class Madrid. The *zarzuela* season runs from June to September. During summer, outdoor performances take place at *La Corrala*, Calle del Meson de Paredes 65. Classical concerts, including performances by the prestigious *Coro y Orquesta Sinfonica de Madrid* (website: www. orfeoed.com/osm/osm.htm), are held at the *Auditorio Nacional de Música*, Avenida Príncipe de Vergara 146 (tel: (91) 337 0100). At Sunday lunchtime, during the summer, concerts are held at the bandstand in Retiro Park.

Theatre

Madrid's dramatic tradition can be traced back to the classical playwrights of Spain's Golden Age – Lope de Vega (1562–1635), Tirso de Molina (1584–1648) and Calderón de la Barca (1600–81). The season runs from September to June – in summer, there are open-air performances, sponsored by the *Veranos de la Villa* festival (see *Special Events*). The *Compañia Nacional de Teatro Clásico* (website: http://teatroclasico.mcu.es) is based in the *Teatro de la Comedia*, Calle Príncipe 14 (tel: (91) 521 4931), temporarily at Pavón Embajadores 9 (tel: (91) 528 2819). Twentieth-century drama, as well as Spanish classics, are also performed at the impressive *Teatro Español*, Calle Príncipe 25 (tel: (91) 360 1480), which occupies the site of a theatre dating back to 1583. Since opening in 1995, the *Teatro La Abadía*, Calle Fernández de los Ríos 42 (tel: (91) 448 1181), has met with great acclaim for its superb performances of international classics. A good introduction to alternative drama is provided by the *Triángulo*, Calle Zurita 20 (tel: (91) 530 6891), which also hosts English productions by the *ACT* (*American and Classical Theatre*) and the *Madrid Players* (website: www.madridplayers.org). Most theatres are closed on Monday.

Dance

The *Teatro Real*, Plaza de Oriente (tel: (91) 516 0660), and *Teatro de la Zarzuela*, Calle de Jovellanos 4 (tel: (91) 524 5400), juggle Spanish and international dance, along with their commitment to music and opera. Other venues include the *Centro Cultural de la Villa*, Jardines del Descubrimiento, Plaza de Colón (tel: (91) 480 0300), which regularly hosts seasons by visiting companies, and the modern *Teatro de Madrid*, Avenida de la Illustración (tel: (91) 730 1750). *Ballet Nacional de España* (website: www. balletnacional.mcu.es) performs Spanish dance to full houses at the *Teatro Albéniz*, Calle de la Paz 11 (tel: (91) 531 8311), during the *Festival de Otoño* (Autumn Festival). Choreographer Nacho Duato has breathed new life into the *Compañia Nacional de Danza* (website: http://cndanza.mcu.es), which tours widely – brief appearances in Madrid's principal venue, the Teatro Real, are hotly anticipated. Classical ballet is performed at the Teatro de Madrid and Albéniz by Victor Ullate's *Ballet de la Comunidad de Madrid*.

Flamenco dance has developed in the last 20 years, from an outmoded genre to a living passion. Traditional flamenco vies with *nuevo flamenco* (new flamenco) in numerous venues throughout the city. Madrid's talented flamenco dancers and musicians perform at Teatro Albéniz, during the *Festival Flamenco Cajamadrid*, in May.

Film

International stars like Antonio Banderas and Penelope Cruz made their reputations with Spain's leading director, Pedro Almodóvar, who first claimed the world's attention with *Women on the edge of a nervous breakdown* (1988). Although Almodóvar is not a son of the city, he moved to Madrid when he was 16, where he studied cinematic art and made his now highly acclaimed films. His very first film, *Pepi, Luci, Bom and Other Girls on the Heap* (1980) was set and filmed in Madrid. *All About My Mother* (1999) won Almodóvar the Best Director award at the 1999 Cannes Film Festival and Best Foreign Language Film at the 2000 Oscars. His latest movie, *Hable con ella* (*Talk to her*), released in 2002, has won numerous international awards, including a Golden Globe.

Madrileños are great filmgoers, especially on Sunday nights. Prior booking is not the norm, so queues are long. The most popular performances start at around 2200 and earlier screenings are less busy. Reduced tickets are available on Wednesday (*día del espectador*). Cinemas cluster around the Gran Vía, notably the vast *Gran Vía Cinesa*, Calle Gran Via 66 (tel: (902) 333 231), with seating under sparkling chandeliers, for 1000 spectators. English-language screenings are marked 'VO' (*versión original*) in listings and local papers. The most popular venue is *Ideal Yelmo Cineplex*, Calle Doctor Cortezo 6 (tel: (91) 369 2518). Arthouse cinema is on show at *Ciné Doré*, Calle Santa Isabel 3 (tel: (91) 549 0011).

Cultural Events

Each season brings a wave of festivities and parades, where religion, tradition or just sheer energy provides the impetus. Perhaps the most intriguing festival is *Carnaval* (Carnival), accompanying the traditional masked ball, *Entierro de la Sardina* (Burial of the Sardine), the week before Lent (March/April). In May, *San Isidor* is held in commemoration of Madrid's patron saint, with open-air dance performances, theatre productions, *zarzuela*, pop and rock concerts and sports competitions. Summer (July to August) sees in *Veranos de la Villa* (Summer in the City), a season of theatre, dance, ballet, flamenco and concerts (pop

and classical), featuring native and international performers. Autumn (October to November) in Madrid is just as lively, with *Festival de Ontoño* (Autumn Festival), a host of cultural events (film, concerts and theatre), including a number of premieres in English and Spanish.

Literary Notes

Madrid has drawn its share of literary talent. The great novelist, Cervantes, author of the classic 17th-century novel, *Don Quixote de la Mancha* (1605), is buried in Calle de Lope de Vega – named in honour of the great lyric poet of Spain's Golden Age of theatre. (By a strange twist of fate, Lope de Vega's house is located in Calle de Cervantes.) Madrid was also home to poet-dramatist Federico García Lorca. The literati would huddle together in the *barrio literario* in Old Madrid and drink together in the now famous Café Gijón (see *Restaurants*). Hemingway was to join the literary crowd as a reporter in Madrid during the Civil War. His ode to bullfighting, *Death in the Afternoon*, was published in 1932 and *For Whom the Bell Tolls* was published in 1940. The late 20th century has brought its own talent, including the 1989 Nobel Prize winner, Camilo José Cela, who died in 2002, and feminist writers, Ana María Matute and Adelaida Garcia Morales.

Plaza Mayor

Mexico City, an exhilarating and often frustrating megalopolis, was founded in 1525 by the Spaniards, who built upon the remains of the ancient Aztec capital of Tenochtitlán. The Aztecs had arrived at the location in around 1345 and established their stone-built city on an island in the middle of Lake Texcoco. Legend has it that the site was chosen because the Aztecs saw an eagle perched on a cactus and eating a snake there – a sign, they believed, that they should end their wanderings and build a city. The Spaniards arrived in 1519, led by Cortés and his army of only a few hundred men. Superior weaponry, the shock effect of horses (the Indians had never encountered such animals) and the support of the Aztecs' enemies meant that victory was assured. Moctezuma, the Aztec king, believed Cortés to be the feathered serpent-god, Quetzalcóatl, and welcomed the Spaniards, since, centuries previously, Quetzalcóatl was said to have been driven out of Tula and vowed to return to reclaim his throne. The Spanish conquistadores overthrew the Aztec Empire with ease.

Little was left of the original city of Tenochtitlán. Bernal Díaz wrote: 'All that I saw then is overthrown and destroyed; nothing is left standing.' The modern city that has grown out of the original island-city is founded on the beds of several lakes and does not enjoy the most practical location. Many of the earlier buildings began to sink into the soft lakebed and the regular earthquake activity takes its toll.

Situated in the Valle de México, a valley of some 2000 sq kilometres (772 sq miles), Mexico City lies at the very heart of the country of which it is capital, both physically and metaphorically. Mexicans refer to their capital as simply 'México' or more specifically 'el DF' (pronounced *day-effay*). The DF is the 'Distrito Federal' (Federal District), within which the whole of the city centre falls. The city stands alone as the most important economic, cultural, intellectual and political centre in Mexico. The year 2000 saw the end of 71 years of one-party rule under the PRI (Institutional Revolutionary Party), when Vicente Fox was elected President. However, change has been slow in coming and most Mexicans feel the new government has failed to live up to their – albeit high – expectations.

Mexico City is arguably the largest city in the world – around 20 million inhabitants live among the constant hustle and bustle, although no one really knows the true figure. It is the growing population, with two-thirds under the age of 30, that presents the government with the biggest problem. The demand for new jobs is enormous and over half the country's social welfare spending goes to the capital. The inhabitants are engaged in frenetic hustling for a living – the lottery-ticket sellers warble results, street hawkers peddle wares and shoe-shines offer their services, while office workers huddle in doorways eating freshly prepared tacos and impromptu street performances blend with roaming mariachi bands – to provide an ever-present cacophony. The pavements and alleyways burst with Mexico City's daily life – all in the middle of the colonial charm of the *Centro Histórico* (Historic Centre), with its ornate façades and grand buildings. Less than a mile away, in the heart of the city's financial district, modern skyscrapers dominate the skyline, wide boulevards offer open-air eating and the mood is more sedate. Mexico City's Mayor, Andres Manuel Lopez Obrador, with an eye on the 2006 presidential elections, has given the go-ahead to adding a second tier to two major highways in the city, as well as spearheaded various building projects, such as the impressive Torre Mayor, the largest building in Latin America.

Mexico City is ringed by snow-capped mountains and volcanoes, however, the pollution churned out by industry and exacerbated by the traffic is confined by these physical boundaries, so they are rarely visible from the city. The climate is mild but the best months to visit are October to April, as winter slightly dispels the pollution. Nevertheless, this thick yellow cloud hanging in the bowl of the mountains barely causes a shadow over the world's largest city – its energy and life continue unabated.

Photo: Edward Ruiz/Mexico Tourism Promotion Board

Panoramic view of Mexico City

TRAVEL

Getting There By Air

Aéropuerto Internacional Benito Juárez (MEX)

Tel: (55) 5571 3600.

Mexico City's only passenger airport handles some 19 million passengers each year and is situated six kilometres (3.73 miles) east of Mexico City's *Centro Histórico*.

Major airlines: *AeroMéxico* (tel: (55) 5133 4000; website: www.aeromexico.com) and *Mexicana* (tel: (55) 5448 0990; website: www.mexicana.com) are the country's two largest airlines. Several airlines have direct flights from Europe to Mexico City, including *Aeroflot, Air France, British Airways, Iberia, KLM* and *Lufthansa*. Other airlines include *Air New Zealand, American Airlines, America West Airlines, Canadian Airlines, Continental Airlines, Delta Air Lines, Japan Airlines, Northwest Airlines, Qantas* and *United Airlines*.

Approximate flight times to Mexico City: From London is 12 hours; from New York is 5 hours; from Los Angeles is 3 hours 30 minutes; from Toronto is 4 hours 45 minutes and from Sydney (via Los Angeles) is 16 hours 45 minutes.

Airport facilities: These include *casa de cambios* (bureaux de change), ATMs (*Bancomer, Bital* and *Banamex*), travel agents, tourist information, bars, restaurants, 24-hour luggage lockers, a telecommunications office, long-distance telephones and a wide range of duty-free and other shops. Car hire is available from *Avis, Auto Rent, Budget, Europcar, Hertz* and *Thrifty*.

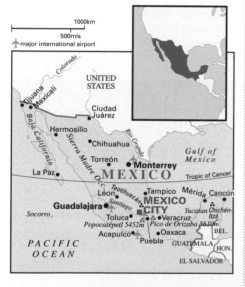

Business facilities: Airlines offer business-class travellers access to their VIP lounges. Although there is a telecommunications office, post office and plenty of long-distance telephones, there is no dedicated business centre.

Arrival/departure tax: Departure tax is US$18 (payable in Dollars or Pesos) on international flights and M$90 on domestic flights.

Transport to the city: Fixed-price *Transportación Terrestre* taxis offer by far the safest and most efficient transport into the city centre. Rates start at M$50 depending on the distance. Tickets are bought in advance from booths at exits A, E and F; visitors should avoid buying tickets from touts, as they tend

to be three times the price. Maps on display show the different zones and prices. There are no direct buses into the city centre. A trolley bus can be taken to Calzada Ignacio Zaragoza and then a bus into the city. This journey takes at least one hour, often much longer, depending on the time of day. The services are available until about 0100. There is a metro station, *Terminal Aérea*, near the exit at the end of hall A but officially no luggage larger than a shoulder bag is allowed on the metro.

Getting There By Rail

Mexico's passenger railway system has been in decline for some years. *Ferrocarriles Nacionales de México* (FNM) or Mexican National Railways (tel: (55) 5541 4213; website: www.ferrocarriles.com) is the service provider. *Estación Buenavista* (Buenavista Station) is a spacious building on Avenida Insurgentes Norte, at the junction of Avenida Jose Antonio Alzate with Avenida Mosqueta. There are left-luggage facilities, long-distance telephone and fax services, an information desk and a cafeteria.

Rail services: Traveling by rail is rare in Mexico. When the government began privatizing the nation's railway system in December 1996, many companies that acquired the rail lines completely phased out passenger travel to use the lines for the transportation of freight. The only passenger services still running from Mexico City go to Querétaro, San Miguel de Allende, San Luis Potosí and Saltillo. These leave three times a week. A monthly timetable is available at the station. These services are extremely slow and subject to change and cancellation at short notice.

Transport to the city: Buses from the station run along Avenida Insurgentes; buses marked 'M(etro) Insurgentes' stop at Metro Insurgentes. The adjacent metro station is Buenavista. There are no authorised taxis – it is advisable to call a radio taxi. *Radio Elite* (tel: (55) 5660 1122) are reliable and quick.

Getting There By Road

Mexico's motorways, although not up to European, Canadian and US standards, are fairly well maintained. They fan out from Mexico City and most large cities can be bypassed. There are more then 6000km (3700 miles) of *cuota* (toll) roads in Mexico. These are often four lanes and in much better condition than the *via libres* (free roads), which have dangerously large potholes, as well as wandering children, livestock and drunks to contend with. *Cuotas* (tolls) vary; on average, it costs around M$10 for every 10–20km (6–12 miles). For example, it costs M$500 to drive to Acapulco. This high cost means toll roads are often empty and are generally much safer. Driving at night in Mexico can be dangerous and is not recommended.

Speed limits are usually 100kph (62mph) on motorways and 30kph (19mph) or 40kph (25mph) in cities. A valid driving licence from the driver's home country is required and an International Driving Permit is recommended. Insurance is not mandatory but is very strongly advised; note that Mexican law *only* recognises Mexican insurance (*seguros*). The minimum age for driving in Mexico is 18 years. There is no legal limit for blood/alcohol levels.

SECTUR, the Mexican Ministry of Tourism, has teams of *Angeles Verdes* (Green Angels) who patrol most of Mexico's main roads and provide free

assistance to motorists in trouble. They have a 24-hour hotline in Mexico City (tel: (55) 5250 8221). Alternatively, there is a 24-hour national tourist assistance number in Mexico City (tel: (55) 5250 0123), as well as a toll-free number for general emergencies throughout Mexico (not in Mexico City) (tel: (800) 903 9200).

Emergency breakdown service: *Angeles Verdes* (55) 5250 8221.

Routes to the city: The 57/57D motorway links Mexico City to the north and Querétaro, San Luis Potosí and Monterrey, with 45D branching west at Querétaro to reach León, Aguascalientes and Zacatecas. Route 150D heads east to Veracruz and Puebla (with branches to Oaxaca and Villahermosa), while 15/15D goes west to Toluca and Guadaljara. To the south, 95D links Mexico City with Cuernavaca and Acapulco, with a branch going to Taxco.

Approximate driving times to Mexico City: From Cuernavaca – 45 minutes; Taxco – 2 hours 30 minutes; Acapulco – 4 hours; Guadalajara – 7 hours.

Coach services: The country's coach services provide an efficient and cost-effective alternative to air travel, with direct buses connecting Mexico City with most other cities in Mexico. The buses vary considerably from non-stop, luxury, air-conditioned services to rickety, second-class affairs.

There are four main long-distance bus terminals in Mexico City, as listed below. All have left-luggage facilities, pay phones and telephone booths (*casetas*) where it is possible to make long-distance telephone calls, post offices, ATMs, cafeterias and a safe taxi rank. Only Terminal Norte and TAPO have *casas de cambio* (bureaux de change).

Terminal Norte (north), Avenida de los Cien Metros 4907 (tel: (55) 5587 5200; Metro Autobuses del Norte), is served by 30 different bus companies linking Mexico City to the north of the country, Guadalajara, Colima and Puerto Vallarta. *Terminal Oriente* (east), Calzada Zaragoza 200 (tel: (55) 5762 5977; Metro San Lázaro), is better known as *TAPO* and serves destinations east and southeast of Mexico City, such as Puebla, Veracruz, Oaxaca and the Yucatán Peninsula. *Terminal Central de Autobuses del Sur* (south), Avenida Tasqueña 1320 (tel: (55) 5689 9745; Metro Tasqueña), offers southward services, including

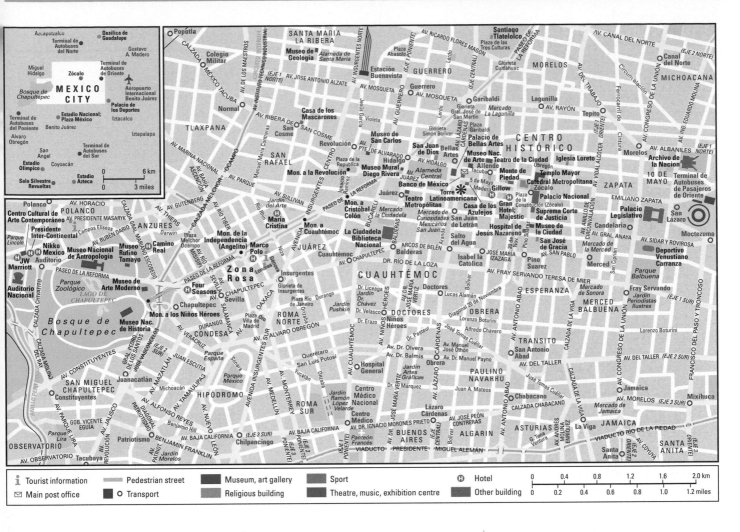

| i Tourist information | Pedestrian street | Museum, art gallery | Sport | H Hotel | 0 | 0.4 | 0.8 | 1.2 | 1.6 | 2.0 km |
| ✉ Main post office | O Transport | Religious building | Theatre, music, exhibition centre | Other building | 0 | 0.2 | 0.4 | 0.6 | 0.8 | 1.0 | 1.2 miles |

Acapulco and Zihuatenejo. *Terminal Poniente* (west), Avenida Sur 122 (tel: (55) 5271 4519; Metro Observatorio), handles westbound services, including frequent shuttles to Toluca.

Getting Around

Public Transport

Considering the sheer size of Mexico City, getting around may seem a daunting prospect, however, the city has a comprehensive and cheap public transport system. The best method of travelling is by **metro**. Mexico City has a modern, efficient and simple-to-use system. There is a flat fare of M$1.50, which includes transfers. It is advisable to buy a number of tickets in advance to avoid queuing. These tickets are simply fed into a turnstile and are valid indefinitely. Trains display their *dirección* (direction); when changing trains, transfers are marked *Correspondencia*. *Lineas* (lines) 1, 2, 3 and A are open Monday to Friday 0500–2430, Saturday 0600–0130, Sunday 0700–

2430; lines 4 through 9 and B open one hour later on weekdays. During rush hour, the carriages get very crowded and are best avoided; between 1800 and 2100 *Solo Mujeres y Niños* (women and children only) carriages operate.

Municipally run Ruta-100 **buses** display their routes on the windscreen and cost M$10. **Minibuses** or *peseros* (also referred to as micro-buses or micros) ply the streets of Mexico City, their routes painted on the windscreen, and are a fun, if slow, way to travel. They can be hailed anywhere and do not have fixed stops, passengers indicate their stop by shouting '*bajan*'. Fares are M$2 for up to five kilometres (three miles), M$2.50 for up to 12km (7.5 miles), M$3 for longer distances and M$4 between 2300 and 0600. This is paid directly to the bus driver on boarding the bus so it is useful to have the correct change.

Visitors should note that pickpockets are rife on all public transport. Metro Hidalgo is a particularly notorious station where pickpockets and bag-snatchers seek out tourists. There have also been a few unpleasant cases of 'express kidnapping', where

people are not only forced to withdraw their daily limit from an ATM at gunpoint but then held overnight or for successive nights and forced to make further withdrawals each day. The only way visitors can guarantee that this does not happen is to not carry any cards and therefore not be worth kidnapping, even if mugged, although the number of police in most of the sightseeing areas has recently greatly increased, so visitors should feel safe in the day. It would be sensible not to carry any cards at night and not to travel on public transport at night.

Taxis

There are several different types of taxi available. The most common are the taxis on unfixed routes. These unofficial taxis are generally green and white Volkswagen Beetles. A *taxímetro* or digital meter should compute the fare – starting at M$4.50 – and there is no need to accept a fixed price. These taxis can be hailed in the street but it is probably more sensible to call for a radio taxi. Unfortunately, in recent years, there has been a rise in taxi crime and violent assaults, robberies and rapes have been reported. Also, unless visitors know exactly where they are going and how to get there (and how to describe that all in Spanish), the drivers may not always know the way. Having said all of that, these taxi-drivers are often extremely charming and friendly, while also fairly streetwise and opinionated and they are widely used by journalists as a barometer of political sentiment on the street.

Radio taxis are much more expensive but far safer and more reliable. These can be telephoned or ordered from hotels and restaurants. Companies include:

CITY STATISTICS

Location: Estado de México, Mexico.
Country dialling code: 52.
Population: 8.5 million (Distrito Federal); 20 million (Mexico City region).
Time zone: GMT - 6 (GMT - 5 from first Sunday in April to last Sunday in October).
Electricity: 110 volts; US-style two-pin plugs are standard.
Average January temperature: 20°C (68°F).
Average July temperature: 25°C (77°F).
Annual rainfall: 660mm (25.7 inches).

BUSINESS PROFILE

From a colonial economy based largely on mining, especially silver, the Mexican economy has diversified to include strong agriculture, petroleum, and industry sectors. Membership in the North American Free Trade Agreement (NAFTA) with the USA and Canada from 1994 has led to hopes of continued economic growth, although resistance to the treaty remains strong among the *campesinos*, or small farmers, who say they cannot compete against heavily subsidised Canadian and US imports. Since the start of 2003, a range of tariffs on foreign farm products were eliminated under the treaty, provoking huge protests nationwide. Mexico is currently the second strongest economy in Latin America after Brazil and its GDP is roughly equivalent to that of Australia, India and Russia. Real incomes are starting to rise again, although Mexicans actually have less purchasing power now than in 1994.

Mexico City is the most important economic centre in the country, home to the entire federal government and the focal point for business. The Mexico City region dominates the national economy, generating nearly half the country's GDP. Major industries in the city include construction; the manufacture of chemicals, plastics, cement, yarns and textiles and, more recently, tourism. Mexico's *Bolsa de Valores* (stock exchange) has its headquarters in Mexico City, as do most major finance, mortgage, insurance and banking companies. The main business areas are found around the *Centro Histórico*, around the Paseo de la Reforma and Avenida Insurgentes and along the Periférico Sur. Most banking headquarters, financial companies and multinationals are found along the Paseo de la Reforma between Avenida Insurgentes and the Bosque de Chapultepec.

Mexico City has the highest cost of living in the country. The gap between rich and poor in the city is enormous – 20% of income earners account for 55% of the income and one-fifth of the city's population are estimated to be living in extreme poverty. The minimum daily wage is about US$3.50 for unskilled labour and US$10 for skilled. It is difficult to gauge levels of unemployment in the city due to the hidden workforce. The 'informal' sector – street hawkers, entertainers and market vendors, who pay no taxes – could account for as many as one third of all workers.

Servitaxis (tel: (55) 5516 6020); *Taxi Radio 24 Horas* (tel: (55) 5566 0077); *Taxi-Mex* (tel: (55) 5538 1440); *Taxi Radio Mex* (tel: (55) 5584 0571); and *Radio Elite* (tel: (55) 5660 1122). From the airport and main bus terminals, fixed-price *Transportación Terrestre* or *autorizado* (authorised) taxis operate. Rates start at M$40, depending on the distance. Tickets are bought in advance from booths, which also display maps indicating the different zones and prices. It is not customary to tip the driver.

Limousines

Several reputable companies offer limousine and other luxury automobile hire with English-speaking chauffeurs and guides. Among them are *Alquimavi* (tel: (55) 5255 5177 *or* 4137), *Creatur Limousine Rental* (tel: (55) 5592 2324) and *Tourismo Leibnitz* (tel: (55) 5488 2435). Many of the hotels catering for business travellers will also be able to organise limousine hire

(or car hire) with bilingual chauffeurs. *Grey Line Tours Rent-a-Car* (see *Car Hire* below) offers English-speaking guides with their cars for US$40 per day, in addition to cost of the car hire.

Driving in the City

Driving in Mexico City is not recommended. Traffic can be dense and infuriating, the one-way systems confusing and signposting less than clear. Visitors should certainly not drive alone at night, as there have been many reports of hijacking, robbery and assaults on lone drivers. Also, the red lights tend to stop operating at night, except on large thoroughfares.

Mexico City has two ring roads, the *Anillo Periférico*, through what used to be the city outskirts, and the *Circuito Interior*, within its circumference. The city has a structure of primary roads called *Ejes Viales* (road axes). The Eje Central runs from south to north passing by *Bellas Artes*. This serves as the focal point for the numbering of all other roads: Ejes to the west are called Eje 1 poniente, Eje 2 poniente, etc; those to the east Eje 1 oriente, Eje 2 oriente and so on; to the north, Eje norte; and to the south, Eje sur.

Mexico City operates a '*Hoy No Circula*' (Don't Drive Today) policy (tel: (55) 5658 1111; website: www.sima.com.mx) in an effort to combat the city's pollution problem. No matter where they are registered, cars without catalytic converters are banned from driving between 0500 and 1000 for one day each week. The last digit of the registration plate denotes when the vehicle must be taken out of circulation: 5 and 6 on Monday; 7 and 8 Tuesday; 3 and 4 Wednesday; 1 and 2 Thursday; 9 and 0 Friday. Some hotels offer off-street parking. Otherwise *estacionamiento público* (supervised public car parks) are recommended and cheap. In the *Centro Histórico*, there are several public car parks south of Avenida Madero, charging around M$10 an hour. Many restaurants have valet parking but it is wise to remove valuables like stereos from the car before leaving it with the valet.

Car Hire

Car hire in Mexico is expensive. A valid driving licence from the driver's home country is required to hire a car, as is a valid passport and a major credit card. The driver must usually be a minimum of 23 years old, although sometimes this is lowered to 21 years. Insurance, tax and fuel are an additional cost to the basic daily or weekly hire rate. Daily rates start from approximately US$40.

Car hire companies include: *Avis*, Hotel Presidente Inter-Continental, Avenida Campos Eliseos 218, Polanco (tel: (55) 5588 8888 (general reservations); website: www.avis.com.mx); *Budget*, Athenas 40, Juárez (tel: (55) 5566 6800 (general reservations); e-mail: reservaciones@budget.com.mx; website: www.budget.com.mx); *Hertz*, Versailles 6, Juárez (tel: (55) 5592 8343; website: www.hertz.com.mx); *Thrifty*, Avenida Campos Eliseos 199B, Polanco *or* Paseo de la Reforma 322, Juárez (tel: (55) 5207 1100; website: www.thrifty.com.mx); and *Grey Line Rent-a-Car*, Londres 166, Juárez (tel: (55) 5208 1163; fax: (55) 5208 2838; e-mail: greyline@supernet.com.mx; website: www.greyline.com.mx).

Bicycle Hire

Bicycles can be hired for about US$5 per hour (Tuesday to Sunday 1000–1700) from Avenida Heroico Colegio Militar, in the *primera sección* of Chapultepec Park.

SIGHTSEEING

Sightseeing Overview

It is not surprising that on arrival most visitors are overwhelmed by the sheer enormity of this megalopolis. It is, however, a great place for a few days' sightseeing – Mexico City offers a fascinating array of Aztec, colonial and modern art and architecture. The city is divided into districts (*colonia*), often indicated with 'Col.' at the beginning. The *Centro Histórico* (Historic Centre), at the heart of the city, was built on the ruins of the original Aztec capital of Tenochtitlán and is packed with fine examples of colonial architecture. At its centre is the *Plaza de la Constitución*, or *Zócalo*, the city's main square and political and religious focus. On two sides of the square are the *Palacio Nacional* (Presidential Palace), with its fine Diego Rivera murals, and the *Catedral Metropolitana* (Metropolitan Cathedral). Close by, the *Templo Mayor* (Main Temple) and the adjacent *Museo del Templo Mayor* are filled with the artefacts unearthed from the original site of Tenochtitlán. The *Alameda Central* is a leafy park in the centre of town favoured by Mexican families at the weekend. At one end is the impressive *Palacio de Bellas Artes*

BUSINESS ETIQUETTE

Machismo is still at the heart of the Mexican ethos and Mexicans believe in the differences between the sexes rather than their equality. The Mexican business world is generally a male domain and, although women are making progress, the top jobs still tend to be held by men. Business attire is very formal – men wear suits and women's clothing should be well tailored and conservative in style. While many people speak some English, it is considered courteous for businesspeople to speak a few words of Spanish, while an interpreter may be required for detailed discussions. It is important to bear in mind that in Mexico 'yes' does not always mean yes, as Mexican social etiquette makes it difficult to say 'no'.

In Mexico City, a lot of business is conducted over a meal, although it is more common for negotiations to take place during a long business breakfast than a lunch. It is polite to accept a drink with your host and customary to shake hands with everyone upon arrival and departure. Business cards are used extensively and it is a good idea to have the cards printed in Spanish and English and to bring plenty of them. Mexicans attach great importance to professional titles – *doctor, profesor, licenciado* (lawyer or graduate) and *ingeniero* (engineer) – and it is courteous to address them by their title. Etiquette includes small talk before getting into business.

The concept of time is fairly flexible, yet while guests might arrive an hour late to social events (to arrive on time is actually considered quite rude), punctuality is observed for most government appointments and functions. In Mexico City, businesses generally open between 0900 or 0930 and work continues until 1900, with a long lunch beginning at 1400 or later. In government offices, work begins at about 1000, with a lunch break beginning at 1400 or 1500, with staff not returning until 1700 or 1800 to work into the evening until 2100.

(Palace of Fine Arts), an arts centre housing some of the greatest works by Mexico's muralists and a must-see for its Art Deco interior. Modern skyscrapers and hotels flank Paseo de la Reforma, the handsome street that runs from the *Centro Histórico* to the *Bosque de Chapultepec* (Chapultepec Park). On the way is *La Zona Rosa* (Pink Zone), a lively neighbourhood popular for shopping, dining and nightlife. Chapultepec Park is the city's largest park and home to many fine museums, including the *Museo Nacional de Antropología* (Museum of Anthropology), one of the most impressive museums of its kind in the world.

Two southern suburbs, *Coyoacán* and *San Angel*, formerly separate villages, have a colonial charm and merit a visit for their markets, museums and memories of their famous residents: Diego Rivera and Frida Kahlo. *El Bazar del Sabado* (Saturday Market) in San Angel offers paintings and quality crafts, while the main square in Coyoacán hosts a colourful market every weekend, accompanied by bands of musicians of varying quality.

Key Attractions

Centro Histórico (Historic Centre)

The focus of the *Centro Histórico*, the *Zócalo*, or *Plaza de la Constitución*, is one of the world's largest plazas and is quite literally the capital's political and religious centre. The area is constantly animated and packed – with official ceremonies and celebrations, demonstrations and marches, impromptu performances and artisans plying their wares. The ceremonial raising and lowering of the huge flag at the square's centre takes place at 0600 and 1800. Mexico's richest man, the telecommunications magnate, Carlos Slim, headed a public-private partnership to revamp the charming but run-down *Centro Histórico* to its former glory, resulting in much construction work throughout 2003.

On the north side of the Zócalo is the *Catedral Metropolitana* (Metropolitan Cathedral). Built in 1573, consecrated in 1667, and completed in 1813, in a Baroque style known as *churrigueresque*, it is the largest and oldest cathedral in Latin America. The cathedral has suffered from subsidence over many years and the restoration work that is under way to build new foundations does detract from its grandeur somewhat. The cathedral is free and open 24 hours but visitors are asked to be respectful during religious services.

Next to the cathedral are the ruins of the *Templo Mayor* (Main Temple), the principal *teocalli* of Aztec Tenochtitlán, which was demolished by the Spaniards in the 1520s and rediscovered in 1978 while telephone cables were being laid in the area. First constructed in 1375, the Aztecs then built a new temple every 52 years – seven have been identified layered one on top of another. The site's museum displays various artefacts found in the main pyramid of Tenochtitlán.

The whole eastern side of the Zócalo is taken up by the *Palacio Nacional* (Presidential Palace), which houses the Federal Treasury and, until recently, the offices of the President of Mexico. Inside are colourful murals by Diego Rivera – his *México a Través de los Siglos* (Mexico Through the Centuries), in the main stairwell leading to the first floor, depicts every major event and personality of Mexican history, from Cortés' conquest of the Aztecs to the Mexican Revolution.

Presidential Palace at night

A few blocks west of Zócalo, the *Museo Nacional de Arte* (National Art Museum), built at the turn of the 20th century in the style of an Italian Renaissance palace, houses an exhaustive collection of Mexican art from every school and style.

Templo Mayor
Plaza de la Constitución
Tel: (55) 5542 0606.
Transport: Metro Zócalo.
Opening hours: Tues–Sun 0900–1700.
Admission: M$35 (free on Sun).

Palacio Nacional
Plaza de la Constitución
Transport: Metro Zócalo.
Opening hours: Mon–Sat 1000–1800.
Admission: Free; identification required for entry.

Museo Nacional de Arte
Tacuba 8
Tel: (55) 5130 3400.
Transport: Metro Bellas Artes.
Opening hours Tues–Sun 1030–1730.
Admission: Free.

Alameda Central

Originally the site of an Aztec marketplace and later a place of execution during the Spanish Inquisition, the *Alameda Central* is Mexico City's largest central park. A welcome green respite where office workers stroll past the many food stalls and hawkers sell a variety of wares; the place throngs with activity on Sunday and there are often open-air concerts. For an artistic impression of the park, the nearby *Museo Mural Diego Rivera* displays the artist's *Sueño de una Tarde Dominical en la Alameda* (Dream of a Sunday Afternoon in Alameda Park), a huge mural painted in 1947. It depicts the many characters from history that Rivera imagined to have walked in the Alameda.

The *Palacio de Bellas Artes* (Palace of Fine Arts), a sumptuous, white-marble concert hall at the eastern end of the Alameda, also houses a museum and theatre within its Art Deco interior. Intended to mark the 1910 centennial celebration of Mexican Independence, work began in 1904, under the Italian architect Adamo Boari, who also designed the spectacular *Correo Mayor* (main post office) nearby. However, it was not completed until 1934, following a number of setbacks, including the Mexican Revolution. The museum on the second and third floors displays old and contemporary paintings, sculptures and handicrafts. Powerful works by the great Mexican muralists – Diego Rivera, Clemente Orozco, David Alfaro Siqueiros and Rufino Tamayo – are on display on the third floor. Operas and orchestral concerts are frequently performed in the theatre, which has a glass curtain designed by Tiffany. Opposite the *Palacio* is the *Torre Latinoamericana* (Latin American Tower), a landmark skyscraper built in the 1950s. Its 43rd-floor viewing platform is 2422m (7950ft) above sea level and affords splendid panoramic views over the city on clear days.

Museo Mural Diego Rivera
Plaza Solidaridad, corner of Balderas and Colón
Tel: (55) 5510 2329.
Transport: Metro Hidalgo.
Opening hours: Tues–Sun 1000–1800.
Admission: M$10 (free for students and on Sun).

Palacio de Bellas Artes
Avenida Juárez, corner of Eje Central Lázaro Cárdenas
Tel: (55) 5512 2593 *or* 5521 9251.
Transport: Metro Bellas Artes.
Opening hours: Tues–Sun 1000–1800 (museum).
Admission: M$25 (free on Sun).

TOURIST INFORMATION

Tourist Information
Oficina de Turismo de la Ciudad de México
Londres 54, corner of Amberes, La Zona Rosa
Tel: (55) 5208 1030.
E-mail: informacionturistica@mexicocity.gob.mx
Website: www.mexicocity.gob.mx
Opening hours: Daily 0900–1900.
Transport: Metro Insurgentes.

SECTUR (National Tourism Ministry)
Avenida Presidente Masaryk 172, corner of Hegel, in Polanco
Tel: (55) 5250 0123 *or* (800) 903 9200 (24-hour help and information Mexico only).
Website: www.mexico-travel.com
Opening hours: Daily 0800–1800.
Transport: Metro Polanco or bus 32.

Passes
There are no passes or discount schemes available for tourists.

Photo: Edward Ruiz/Mexico Tourism Promotion Board

Torre Latinoamericana
Eje Central Lázaro Cárdenas, corner of Avenida Madero
Tel: (55) 5521 0844.
Transport: Metro San Juan Letrán or Bellas Artes.
Opening hours: Daily 0930–2230.
Admission: M$40.

Paseo de la Reforma

The *Paseo de la Reforma*, Mexico City's main boulevard, runs from the Alameda to Chapultepec Park (see below) and is lined with shops, offices, hotels, restaurants and some modern skyscrapers. It is a prestigious address and home to many multinationals, financial institutions and embassies. Based on the Champs Elysées in Paris, this thoroughfare was built to provide a direct path for the Emperor Maximilian between the *Centro Histórico* and his palace in Chapultepec Park and is lined with monuments, fountains and statues of Mexican heroes. In particular, *El Monumento de la Independencia* (Monument to Independence), or *Angelito* as it is affectionately known, is a gilded statue of a winged Victory set atop a 46m-high (150ft) column in a *glorieta* (traffic circle) and the location for demonstrations and sporting and national celebrations. In 1956, the statue toppled to the ground in an earthquake but was completely restored – much to the relief of the Mexican people. Displayed inside the monument is the skull of Hidalgo, the executed leader of a group of rebels who rose against the Spanish in October 1810, which can be seen daily 0900–1700 at no charge. On the night of 2 July 2000, hundreds of thousands of jubilant Mexicans flocked to the monument to celebrate the victory of Vicente Fox in the presidential elections that toppled the 71-year rule of the former Institutional Revolutionary Party.

Lying to the south of the Paseo and bounded by Reforma, Sevilla, Avenida Chapultepec and Avenida Insurgentes Sur, is *La Zona Rosa* (Pink Zone), a busy shopping and entertainment district with many stores, restaurants and nightclubs.
Transport: Metro Insurgentes; *peseros* marked 'Metro Chapultepec', 'Reforma' or 'Auditorio'.

Photo: Corel

Museo Rufino Tamayo

Bosque de Chapultepec (Chapultepec Park)

Bosque de Chapultepec, Mexico City's largest park, is a huge wooded area covering four sq kilometres (2.5 sq miles) and containing lakes, the presidential residences, several of the city's finest museums, an amusement park and a zoo. Legend has it the wood served as a refuge for Toltec and Aztec kings during times of trouble. The park attracts thousands of visitors especially on Sundays when families come to relax and picnic. The park is divided into three sections, with the attractions listed below lying in the *primera sección* (first section), on Paseo de la Reforma. The *segunda sección* (second section) is occupied by *La Feria* (Amusement Park), and the *tercera sección* (third section) by *Atlantis*, a marine park with dolphin and seal shows and an aquarium – both are on Avenida Constituyentes.

The *Castillo de Chapultepec* (Chapultepec Castle), situated on the Chapultepec Hill (the name means 'Hill of Grasshoppers' in the Aztec language Nahuatl), was built in 1785 for the Spanish viceroys and used as a residence for Mexico's presidents until 1940. It now houses the *Museo Nacional de Historia* (National History Museum), filled with hundreds of paintings, murals, ceramics, furniture and carriages depicting the history of Mexico from the Aztecs to the present day. The rooms once used by Emperor Maximilian and Empress Carlotta have been preserved and fine views over the Valley of Mexico can be had from the castle's balconies. A road-train climbs the hill from inside the entrance to the park (M$20).

The *Museo de Arte Moderno* (Museum of Modern Art) has permanent exhibitions of Mexican contemporary art – by Rivera, Siqueiros, O'Gorman, Rufino Tamayo, Frida Kahlo and Dr Atl, to name but a few – and also hosts temporary exhibits of international artists. There is a delightful sculpture garden in the grounds of the museum. *Parque Zoológico de Chapultepec* (Chapultepec Zoological Park) has an impressive collection of animals from around the world and was the birthplace of the first panda born in captivity. The modern *Museo Rufino Tamayo* contains permanent exhibits of work by contemporary Mexican and international painters, donated by Tamayo and his wife, as well as a superb collection of paintings by the artist himself.

Chapultepec Park
Tel: (55) 5515 2697.
Transport: Metro Chapultepec for first section; Metro Constituyentes for second and third sections.
Opening hours: Daily 0500–1700.
Admission: Free.
La Feria
Tel: (55) 5230 2121.
Opening hours: Tues–Fri 1000–1800, Sat and Sun 1000–2230.
Admission: M$60 for an all-ride pass.
Atlantis
Tel: (55) 5271 8618.
Opening hours: Sat and Sun only 1000–1800.
Admission: M$25.
Museo Nacional de Historia
Tel: (55) 5286 0700.
Opening times: Tues–Sun 0900–1700.
Admission: M$35.
Museo de Arte Moderno
Tel: (55) 5211 8331 *or* 8045.
Opening hours: Tues–Sun 1000–1730.
Admission: M$15 (free for students and on Sun).
Parque Zoológico de Chapultepec
Tel: (55) 5553 6229 *or* 6263.
Opening hours: Tues–Sun 0900–1600.
Admission: Free.

Museo Rufino Tamayo
Tel: (55) 5286 6519.
Opening hours: Tues–Sun 1000–1800.
Admission: M$15 (free for students and on Sun).

Museo Nacional de Antropología (National Anthropology Museum)

Perhaps Mexico City's finest museum, the *Museo Nacional de Antropología* is also one of the best of its kind in the world. Situated in an extension of Chapultepec Park, this huge museum houses a vast and spectacular collection centred on a spacious rectangular patio and can take days to explore. Its well-organised collection is dedicated to each major culture that contributed to the evolution of a Mesoamerican civilisation: Pre-Classic, Toltec, Teotihuacán, Aztec, Oaxaca, Gulf Coast, Maya, Northwestern and Western Mexico. Some of the most fascinating exhibits are the famous Aztec 'sun' (or 'calendar') stones, the giant stone Olmec heads from Tabasco and a replica of a Mayan tomb from Palenque. On the upper level, the rooms are dedicated to how modern Mexico's indigenous people live.

Several times a day, *voladores* (fliers) give a daring performance in front of the museum's entrance, re-enacting an ancient ceremony. Men dressed in colourful, traditional costume attach ropes to themselves and scale a tall pole, from where they launch themselves and 'fly' in circles as they unwind until they reach the ground.
Paseo de la Reforma (north of Chapultepec Park)
Tel: (55) 5553 1902 *or* 6381.
Transport: Metro Auditorio.
Opening hours: Tues–Sun 0900–1900.
Admission: M$37 (free on Sun).

Coyoacán

Once a city in its own right, the suburb of *Coyoacán* is the oldest part of Mexico City and was the place from which Cortés launched his attack on Tenochtitlán. Along the peaceful tree-lined avenues are beautiful buildings from the 16th to 19th centuries. Especially at weekends, the craft stalls, musicians and mime artists around the central squares of *Plaza Hidalgo* and *Jardín del Centenario* create a bohemian atmosphere.

The *Museo Frida Kahlo* (Frida Kahlo Museum) occupies the family home of the artist Frida Kahlo. She was born here in 1907 and then lived here with her husband, the revolutionary muralist Diego Rivera, from 1929 until her death in 1954. The couple was part of a glamorous, leftist, intellectual set during the 1930s and the house is full of mementoes of this period. Two rooms are preserved as lived in; the rest display paintings by both artists. The Kahlo work on display is not her best known but expresses something of the pain and torment in her life. The small collection of folk art – a passion of Kahlo's – includes a number of regional costumes worn by the artist.

The *Museo Casa de León Trotsky* (Leon Trotsky House Museum) is the house where the Russian revolutionary spent the last four years of his life. Very little has changed in the house since 1940, when Trotsky was murdered in his study with an ice pick by an assassin sent by the KGB, and it is a very dark and sombre place. There is a tomb in the garden where his ashes were interred.
Museo Casa de Frida Kahlo
Londres 247 (corner of Allende), Coyoacán
Tel: (55) 5554 5999.

Transport: Metro Viveros, Coyoacán or General Anaya; *pesero* marked 'Coyoacán' from Paseo de la Reforma.
Opening hours: Tues–Sun 1000–1740.
Admission: M$30.
Museo Casa de León Trotsky
Avenida Río Churubusco 410, between Gómez Farías and Morelos
Tel: (55) 5658 8732.
Transport: Metro Viveros, Coyoacán or General Anaya; *pesero* marked 'Coyoacán' from Paseo de la Reforma.
Opening hours: Tues–Sun 1000–1700.
Admission: M$30 (half price for students; free on Sun).

San Angel

San Angel is an elegant, colonial neighbourhood about nine kilometres (six miles) south of Paseo de la Reforma. The affluent suburb is best known for its weekly arts and crafts market, the *Bazar Sábado* (Saturday Bazaar), in *Plaza San Jacinto*. The *Museo Estudio Diego Rivera* (Diego Rivera's Studio Museum), where Rivera and his wife, Frida Kahlo, lived in the 1930s, is an avant-garde building designed for them by Juan O'Gorman. There are only a few of the artists' works on display but plenty of memorabilia. The *Museo Carrillo Gil Arte Contemporano* (Carillo Gil Contemporary Art Museum) is a fine art museum containing works by Mexican and international artists.
Museo Estudio Diego Rivera
Diego Rivera 2 (corner of Altavista)
Tel: (55) 5550 1189.
Transport: Metro MA Quevedo, then minibus to San Angel.
Opening hours: Tues–Sun 1000–1800.
Admission: M$10 (free on Sun).
Carrillo Gil Arte Contemporano
Avenida Revolución 1608
Tel: (55) 5550 6289.
Transport: Metro MA Quevedo, then minibus to San Angel.
Opening hours: Tues–Sun 1000–1800.
Admission: M$15 (free on Sun).

Further Distractions

La Basílica de Nuestra Señora de Guadalupe (Basilica of Our Lady of Guadalupe)

In the northern suburbs of Mexico City, *La Basílica de Nuestra Señora de Guadalupe*, often known as *La Villa de Guadalupe*, is the holiest shrine in the country. It is built on the site where, in 1531, the Virgin Mary is said to have appeared three times, in the guise of an Indian princess, to Indian Juan Diego, leaving her image miraculously emblazoned on his cloak. After investigating the story, the church authorities decided to build the shrine and the Pope is set to canonise Juan Diego this year, despite doubts over his existence. The original basilica was built in 1709. When a large crack appeared and it began to sink into the swampy subsoil, a new basilica was constructed in the same plaza and consecrated in 1976. Juan Diego's cloak has been preserved and hangs in the church, behind the main altar. Moving walkways allow visitors to get as close as possible. The original basilica is now a museum displaying many representations of the image on the cloak.
Throughout the year, pilgrims come from all over Mexico to visit. However, for the *Día de Nuestra Señora de Guadalupe* (Patron Saint's Day), on 12 December, millions throng to pray and give thanks to the dark-skinned virgin. Some worshippers hobble on their knees to the church, while others dance their prayers in traditional Indian costumes with feather headdresses and skirts in a festive atmosphere.
Plaza Hidalgo 1, Colonia Villa de Guadalupe
Tel: (55) 5577 6022.
Transport: Metro La Villa; buses marked 'La Villa'.
Opening hours: Daily 0600–2100 (basilica); Tues–Sun 1000–1800 (museum).
Admission: Free (basilica); M$5 (museum).

Tours of the City

Walking Tours

Most places of interest in Mexico City are concentrated in small pockets of the city, so travelling on foot is often the best means of getting around. However, it is worth remembering that, due to the effects of altitude and the pollution, it is not uncommon to feel tired and breathless when walking even short distances for the first few days after arrival. The government's cultural agency *INAH* (*National Institute for History and Archaeology*), Frontera 53, San Angel (tel: (55) 5616 5227/8; website: www.inah. gob.mx), offers walking tours in the city and beyond, which cost around M$250 for a two-hour tour. INAH's tours are cheaper than most and are given by English-speaking specialists but most travel agencies will be able to arrange walking tours.

Bus Tours

Half- or full-day tours of the city typically include pick-up and drop-off at major hotels and visits to the *Centro Histórico* and the Museo Nacional de Antropología accompanied by an English-speaking guide. *Grey Line Tours* (tel: (55) 5208 1163; website: www.greyline.com.mx) offers a variety of city tours. A full-day tour costs US$44, while half-day tours cost US$29. Tours of the pyramids and excursions to Taxco and Puebla can also be arranged. The increasingly popular double-decker *Turibus* (tel: (55) 5212 0260; website: www.turibus.com.mx) cruises around the capital's principal sites every 20 minutes throughout the day. A ride costs M$100 during the week and M$115 on the weekend.

Excursions

For a Half Day

Xochimilco: About 20km (12 miles) south of the Zócalo is a network of canals lined by gardens and agricultural plots known as the 'floating gardens' of *Xochimilco* (the name means 'Place where the Flowers Grow' in the Aztec language of Nahuatl). Within the network of canals, the Pre-Hispanic inhabitants constructed little islands known as *chinampas* on which fruits, vegetables and flowers could be grown. These formed one of the economic bases of the Aztec Empire. Some 180km (112 miles) of canals remain today and the area has become a favourite destination for Mexico City's inhabitants to come for a bit of fun and relaxation. Hundreds of colourful *trajineras* (small, flat-bottomed barges similar to gondolas), each bearing a girl's name, are punted along the canals with parties of revellers on board. As well as the passenger boats, there are waterborne bands of mariachis or marimbas ready to play requests (for a price), vendors selling tacos, soft drinks and flowers, photographers and souvenir sellers adding to the general cacophony. There are nine different

Dome of the Basilica of Our Lady of Guadalupe

embarcaderos (landings), all near the centre of Xochimilco, from where the boats are available for hire (M$130 per hour for a boat holding 18 people, M$110 for up to 12 people) at all hours. Moonlit trips make for an original outing. The *Tourist Office* in Xochimilco is situated at Embarcadero Nativitas (tel: (55) 5653 5209; e-mail: informacionturistica @mexicocity. gob.mx; website: www.mexicocity.gob.mx) and can provide more information. Transport is by buses marked Metro 'Tasqueña', or by taking the metro to Tasqueña and then the *tren ligero* (overground train) to Embarcadero. The *Museo Dolores Olmedo Patino* (Dolores Olmedo Patino Museum) is a renovated 16th-century hacienda, set in three hectares (eight acres) of beautiful grounds, complete with parading peacocks and Xoloitzcuintles, a rare breed of hairless dog indigenous to Mexico. The museum contains some of the best-known works of Diego Rivera and Frida Kahlo, as well as pre-Hispanic artefacts. The collection, which belongs to Señora Olmedo – a rich socialite and prolific patron of Rivera's who still lives in part of the mansion – went on public display in 1994. The museum, open Tuesday to Sunday 1000–1800, is located at Avenida México 5843, on the corner of Antiguo Camino a Xochimilco (tel: (55) 5555 0891 *or* 1221; website: www.arts-history.mx/mdop.html) and costs M$25. Transport is also the *tren ligero* from Metro Tasqueña, although the nearest station is La Noria.

For a Whole Day

Teotihuacán: Situated 50km (30 miles) north of Mexico City is the archaeological zone of *Teotihuacán*. This site is thought to date from around 300–600 BC but the identity of those who built the 'place of the gods' still remains a mystery. Teotihuacán was not just a ceremonial centre – there is evidence it was a functioning city and one of the largest of the pre-industrial world. Tens of thousands of people were employed in crafts and as many as 100,000 in trade and fixed markets. Teotihuacán was also one of the more politically dominant cities, owing to its strategic location in the Valley of Mexico, which provided easy access to trade routes and communication. In the seventh century AD, a fire and

Catedral Metropolitana at night

subsequent looting caused a great exodus of its inhabitants and Teotihuacán was left abandoned. It was left to the Aztecs to name the most important features.

There are three main site areas: the *Ciudadela* (Citadel), *Pirámide del Sol* (Pyramid of the Sun), *Pirámide de la Luna* (Pyramid of the Moon) – all connected by the *Calzada de los Muertos* (Avenue of the Dead). It takes between five and eight hours to see the site properly and it is open daily 0800–1700. The entry fee is M$30 (free on Sunday), plus M$50 for the 45-minute *son et lumière* shows at 1900 (in Spanish) and 2015 (in English). Buses marked 'Los Pirámides' depart from Gate 8 of the *Terminal del Norte* (Metro: Autobuses del Norte) and take about an hour; the cost is US$2 each way. The bus-tour operators listed in the *Tours of the City* section also offer organised excursions to the site, some including a stop at the *Villa de Guadalupe* en route.

ACCOMMODATION

Hotel rates are subject to 15% VAT (Value Added Tax). This, and an additional room tax of around 2%, is usually added to the bill at the end. Payment of hotel bills can usually be made in US Dollars or Mexican Pesos, however, prices are mostly quoted in US Dollars as below. The prices quoted below are the lowest standard rates for a double room, excluding VAT and excluding breakfast, unless otherwise specified.

Business

Hotel Camino Real

This stylish modernistic hotel in convenient Anzures with its bold yellow and pink walls, designed by famous Mexican architect Ricardo Legorreta, offers luxury with originality. A huge mural by Rufino Tamayo hangs in the entrance opposite the hip lobby bar that has live music nightly. Contemporary art works and sculptures adorn the walls and open spaces. Guest rooms are spacious, with views over a delightful garden and large pool with terrace. The hotel has convention facilities, a business centre, a range of shops, a gym and is a pleasant stroll from three important museums.

Calzada Gral. Mariano Escobedo 700, Anzures
Tel: (55) 5263 8888. Fax: (55) 5250 6897 *or* 5263 8889.
E-mail: mex@caminoreal.com
Website: www.caminoreal.com/mexico
Price: From US$275.

Hotel Nikko Mexico

The 744-room, slim, high-rise hotel of the Japanese *Nikko* chain is the third luxury hotel on upmarket Polanco's Avenida Campos Eliseos, adjacent to Chapultepec Park and walking distance from Mexico City's acclaimed Museum of Anthropology. Renovated in 2000, all rooms have views to Chapultepec Park or Polanco. The standard rooms, decorated in muted colours, are functional if unexceptional. The rooms on the executive floor are bigger and brighter. All rooms have two telephone lines and outlets for computer and modem. The hotel has a well-equipped 24-hour business centre and a big athletic club with tennis courts, swimming pool and golf practice range.

Avenida Campos Eliseos 204, Polanco
Tel: (55) 5283 8700. Fax: (55) 5280 9191.
E-mail: nikkosal@nikko.com.mx
Website: www.hotelnikkomexico.com
Price: From US$280.

Hotel Presidente InterContinental

Sandwiched between the Nikko and the Marriott hotels in wealthy Polanco, this 659-room high-rise hotel has a celebrity clientele. Michael Jackson and Bill Clinton, among others, have stayed here. A spacious, modern lobby sets the tone. Decorated in beige and wood, the rooms are comfortable, with pleasant views and king-size beds. The 32nd floor is a ladies-only floor, while the Executive floor has a club lounge with beautiful views, as well as a small library. The well-equipped business centre is open 0700–2300. The hotel has a small exercise room but a bigger sports club with pool is under construction. The many restaurants are popular, especially *Au Pied de Cochon* (see *Restaurants*).

Avenida Campos Eliseos 218, Polanco
Tel: (55) 5327 7700. Fax: (55) 5327 7730.
E-mail: mexicocity@interconti.com
Website: www.interconti.com
Price: From US$220.

JW Marriott Hotel

This 312-room luxury hotel located in the affluent neighbourhood of Polanco, a stone's throw from the impressive Museum of Anthropology, has an understated elegance. The rooms are immaculate, decorated in warm colours and mahogany and many have views over Chapultepec Park. The executive floor has an inviting lounge offering continental breakfast and happy hour. The hotel prides itself on its customer-friendly and personalised service. There are convention facilities, as well as a 24-hour business centre equipped with state-of-the art computers. Guest rooms have two-line telephones, voice-mail, modem points and safes. The spa is small but pleasant with an attractive outdoor pool and enticing sundeck.

Andres Bello 29, Polanco
Tel: (55) 5999 0000. Fax: (55) 5999 0001.
E-mail: jwmbc1@marriott.com.mx
Website: www.marriott.com
Price: From US$315.

Luxury

Four Seasons Hotel

This beautiful hotel, situated on the capital's historic thoroughfare, Reforma, in central Juárez, is well located for visiting tourist sites and getting about easily. The hotel has a simple elegance, decorated with rich, classical prints, furnished with mahogany and with maps and paintings hanging on the walls. Guests can enjoy the tranquillity of the attractive courtyard garden or head for the relaxing pool terrace. The hotel's health spa offers massages, a fully equipped gym and numerous beauty treatments. The hotel has convention facilities and a business centre, while each room has Internet access, TV and two telephone lines.
Paseo de la Reforma 500, Juárez
Tel: (55) 5230 1818. Fax: (55) 5230 1808.
E-mail: mex.res@fourseasons.com
Website: www.fourseasons.com
Price: From US$270.

Marco Polo

A small but very special luxury hotel in the heart of the centrally located La Zona Rosa, the five-star *Marco Polo* offers an attractive alternative to the standard hotel chains. The 60 rooms are bright and tastefully decorated with rustic wooden furniture. They all feature modem points, as well as the usual facilities, such as mini-bar, safe, coffee-maker. The four penthouse suites also have a Jacuzzi and balcony. The hotel has a restaurant-bar, *Il Caffe Milano*, and a gym. For businesspeople, it offers a small business centre, business support services and various meeting rooms and ballrooms.
Amberes 27, Juárez
Tel: (55) 5207 0333. Fax: (55) 5533 3727.
E-mail: reservaciones@marcopolo.com.mx
Website: www.marcopolo.com.mx
Price: From US$161 (including VAT and breakfast).

Moderate

Hotel Gillow

This middle-range hotel is well situated in the heart of the *Centro Histórico*, a stone's throw from the Zócalo and numerous museums and 15 minutes from the airport. *Hotel Gillow* has an attractive Art Deco-style façade and a cheerful, rose-coloured marble lobby hung with plants. Rooms are simple, decorated in pastel colours with TV and bathroom, and they overlook the street or a quiet inner courtyard. The hotel also has a reasonably priced restaurant and bar.
Isabel La Católica 17, Centro Histórico
Tel: (55) 5510 0791 *or* 8585 *or* 2636.
Fax: (55) 5512 2078.
E-mail: hgillow@prodigy.net.mx
Price: From US$50 (including VAT).

Maria Cristina

An easy walk to the centre of La Zona Rosa, this hotel, housed in a beautiful colonial-style building, offers Old World charm. It is one of the best-value deals in this part of town. The 150 comfortable rooms all have TV and fans. The bathrooms are particularly pleasant with Mexican *talavera* tiling. There is a medium-priced restaurant, bar and parking. Other facilities include a travel agency and a beauty salon.
Río Lerma 31, Cuauhtemoc
Tel: (55) 5703 1212. Fax: (55) 5592 3447.
Price: From US$76 (including VAT).

Other Recommendations

El Gran Hotel Ciudad de Mexico

A shrine to Art Nouveau styling, this is one of the most elegant and original hotels in Mexico City. The lobby has a cathedral-like quality, with a stunning coloured-glass window canopy overhead, ornate wrought-iron balconies and lifts at either end. Located conveniently on the Zócalo in the *Centro Histórico* and a 15-minute drive from the airport, the hotel also has convention facilities, making it popular with the business community and upmarket travellers. The 124 rooms all have Art Nouveau touches and TVs. There is a restaurant in the lobby and a terrace café over the square.
Avenida 16 de Septiembre 82, Centro Histórico
Tel: (55) 1083 7700. Fax: (55) 1083 7700, ext 175.
Price: From US$90.

Hotel Majestic

The *Hotel Majestic*, part of the Best Western chain, has one of the prime locations in Mexico City, overlooking the historic Zócalo with its colonial cathedral and national palace and just a 15-minute drive from the airport. The tranquil, mirrored lobby, with its fountain and tiles, offers a welcome retreat from the throngs of vendors, hustlers and tourists outside. The hotel has 85 guest rooms, including five suites. The best overlook the square, while those on Avenida Madero can be noisy. Rooms are simple but comfortable, with TV, mini-bar, coffee-making facilities and rustic wood furniture. The hotel has a popular terrace restaurant overlooking the Zócalo, which serves basic Mexican and international food at reasonable prices.
Avenida Madero 73, Centro Histórico
Tel: (55) 5521 8600 *or* (800) 528 1234 (toll free in USA, Canada and Mexico). Fax: (55) 5512 6262.
E-mail: majestic@supernet.com.mx
Website: www.majestic.com.mx
Price: From US$88.

RESTAURANTS

The selected restaurants have been divided into five categories: Gastronomic, Business, Trendy, Budget and Personal Recommendations. The restaurants are listed alphabetically within these different categories,

Stock Exchange, Centro Bursatil

Photo: Edward Ruiz/Mexico Tourism Promotion Board

Photo: Edward Ruiz/Mexico Tourism Promotion Board

Templo Mayor

which serve as guidelines rather than absolute definitions of the establishments.

Restaurant prices are subject to 15% VAT. This is usually included in the price quoted. In Mexico, it is not common practice to include any service charges in a restaurant bill, so a tip of 10–15%, depending on the quality of the service, is expected. Payment of restaurant bills will usually be expected in Mexican Pesos.

The prices quoted below are for an average two-course meal for one person and for a bottle of house wine or cheapest equivalent; they include VAT but do not include tip.

Gastronomic

Au Pied de Cochon

This fashionable 24-hour bistro in the Hotel Presidente InterContinental (see *Hotels*) has been a hit with Mexico's beautiful people since it opened. Modelled closely on the Parisian original, the restaurant offers sumptuous seafood platters, including oysters and lobster, as well as steaks, pigs' trotters and snails prepared by French chefs. The chocolate profiteroles are delicious. Decor is Art Nouveau and the service is pleasant. An extensive wine list is available.
Hotel Presidente InterContinental, Avenida Campos Eliseos 216, Polanco
Tel: (55) 5327 7756.
Website: www.interconti.com
Price: M$250. Wine: M$180.

El Cardenal

This classical restaurant is always busy thanks to its consistently good Mexican cooking. With formal wood-panelled decor, it offers a haven from the bustle of the *Centro Histórico* outside. *El Cardenal* serves hearty soups and steaks with fried beans, guacamole and enchiladas. Seasonal specialities include grilled Maguey worms and *chile en nogada* (chilli in a sweet creamy sauce with nuts and pomegranate).
Palma 23, Centro Histórico
Tel: (55) 5521 3080 *or* 8815.
Price: M$150. Wine: M$100.

Lando Grill

This elegant bistro-style restaurant in Polanco attracts celebrities, politicians and businesspeople for its outstanding cuisine and discreet charm. With leather chairs, wood panelling and jazz in the background, the *Lando* exudes good taste. An impressive wine list accompanies sophisticated home cooking. Signature dishes are carpaccio of portabello mushroom and artichoke, exquisite lamb chops and an unparalleled chocolate bomb. A wide selection of seafood and steaks is also available.
Emilio Castelar 121, Polanco
Tel: (55) 5282 3052. Fax: (55) 5282 3053.
Price: M$250. Wine: M$150.

Les Moustaches

Situated in Cuauhtemoc, just one block away from the central Monument to Independence, this restaurant has excellent Anglo-French food attentively served in an atmosphere of discreet elegance. The ground floor is an attractive plant-filled patio, while the second floor provides three elegant private rooms for banquets. The food is fresh and sumptuous. They are famous for their mussel soup, duck in orange sauce and spectacular pistachio soufflé.
Río Sena 88, Cuauhtemoc
Tel: (55) 5533 3390 *or* 5525 1265 (reservations).
Fax: (55) 5207 7149.
Website: www.lesmoustaches.com.mx
Price: M$250. Wine: M$180.

Thai Gardens

This beautifully decorated new restaurant has quickly become a favourite among *capitalinos* looking for authentic Thai eats. From vegetarian spring rolls to an impressive array of curries, the extensive menu weds traditional offerings with more fusion-minded dishes and really does have something for everyone. The atmosphere and service are excellent.
Calderon de la Barca 72, Polanco
Tel: (55) 5281 3850.
Price: M$250. Wine: M$150.

Business

Chez Wok

This classy Chinese restaurant, with its yellow and red minimalist decor, is a favourite with Chinese businesspeople. Service is discreet and attentive. The food, prepared by Hong Kong chefs, is superb and its presentation impeccable. Highlights include vegetable dumplings filled with shitake mushrooms, exquisite hot and sour soup, king prawns in black pepper, and duck with prawn sauce and sesame. The menu offers an extensive selection of wines, as well as champagne.
Tennyson 117, Polanco
Tel: (55) 5281 2921.
Price: M$350. Wine: M$150.

La Cava

La Cava is a popular restaurant in the south of the city offering high-quality food in relaxed and comfortable surroundings. The decor is predominantly colonial and the covered patio, with its central fountain, is particularly pleasant. The seafood is recommended, especially the trout and the Portuguese sardines (when in season). All the desserts are excellent.
Avenida Insurgentes Sur 2465
Tel: (55) 5550 1106.
Price: M$150. Wine: M$100.

La Valentina

On the first floor of a plush Polanco mall, this haute cuisine Mexican restaurant is always packed and animated. The colonial hacienda furnishings and the Mariachi musicians adding their voices to the general bustle of the place make this an authentic Mexican dinning experience. It serves one of the best chicken in mole sauces in town.
Avenida Presidente Masaryk 393, Polanco
Tel: (55) 5282 2812 *or* 2514.
Price: M$150. Wine: M$120.

Rincon Argentino

This institution makes no bones about what it is – an unadulterated steak pit in which sides of beef hang next to an open grill and waiters, on request, bring a tray of the choicest cuts to the table. A favourite with visiting Argentines, the price tag packs a wallop but many businesspeople swear by the place as the spot to close a deal. Over 20 different cuts of meat are offered and the three-hour lunch is de rigueur.
Avenida Presidente Masaryk 117, Polanco
Tel: (55) 5254 8775 *or* 8744.
Price: M$300. Wine: M$150.

San Angel Inn

This ex-hacienda with its pretty courtyard is one of the city's most attractive restaurants. Situated in the southern colonial district of San Angel, it serves good Mexican and international food. Signature dishes include the trout, the prawns on a skewer and the *huitlacoche* (corn fungus – a Mexican delicacy) crêpes. The wine list is extensive and the margaritas are delicious.
Diego Rivera 50, San Angel
Tel: (55) 5616 1543 *or* 1402.
Price: M$250. Wine: M$150.

Trendy

Aguila y Sol

This chic Polanco hangout is elegantly designed in a minimalist style with cool mint colours. The food is contemporary Mexican and combines delicious flavours in an original way. Eye-catching starters include foie gras with cacao and guava or squash-flower soup with a touch of curry and almond. Recommended mains include the blue crab enchiladas in a hazelnut and chilli sauce or tuna steak in pepperleaf.

Moliere 42, Polanco
Tel: (55) 5281 8354.
Price: M$250. Wine: M$200.

Blu

Located in the upmarket San Angel district in the south of the city, *Blu* is frequented by the 'beautiful people', who come to enjoy its exceedingly stylish decor and its fresh Mediterranean cuisine. The pasta and seafood are especially recommended. Signature dishes include red snapper in saffron sauce, salmon ravioli and the onion and mushroom focaccia. For dessert, the *Big Mistake* chocolate cake will leave you with no regrets.
Avenida de la Paz 57, San Angel
Tel: (55) 5616 4791.
Price: M$150. Wine: M$100.

Estacion Central

In the hip Condesa neighbourhood, *Estacion Central* offers tasty food in a funky modern setting. The decor is chrome and cream, while the chairs have long triangular backs. Exotic cocktails are served up alongside a tempting choice of international dishes. Starters include veal carpaccio or Roquefort and pear soup, followed by mains such as roast duck in a tamarind and sesame sauce or sea bass with coriander on a black bed of rice in squid ink. Service is helpful.
Avenida Alfonso Reyes 108, Condesa
Tel: (55) 5553 1722.
E-mail: estacioncentral@starmedia.com
Price: M$200. Wine: M$100.

Ixchel

This art gallery turned restaurant is a favourite haunt among Mexican media types and artists. Situated in a beautiful colonial mansion in the heart of bohemian Roma, it houses a terrace bar downstairs, a cool blue velvet lounge and an elegant restaurant upstairs. Presentation is artistic and the food tasty, fusing Oriental and Mexican styles. Recommended dishes are the Thai chicken salad, Oriental salmon fillet on bok choy and the crème brûlée.
Avenida Medellín 65, Roma
Tel: (55) 5525 0730 *or* 5208 4055. Fax: (55) 5525 0730.
Price: M$200. Wine: M$100.

Los Danzantes

Enjoying a prime location on Coyoacán's main square, this pleasant, airy restaurant serves inventive nouvelle Mexican and international cuisine. The service is somewhat languid but it is a good place to talk and people-watch. The coconut-wrapped prawns in sweet and sour sauce make a good starter. An interesting main dish is the medallions of beef in mescal and chilli sauce.
Plaza Jardín del Centenario 12, Coyoacán
Tel: (55) 5658 6451.
Price: M$150. Wine: M$100.

Budget

Agapi Mu

Detailed with arches, vases and wall paintings that recall ancient Greece, *Agapi Mu*'s decor is one of the big attractions of this modest spot for Hellenic cuisine. The moussaka as a main dish is fantastic, while the appetisers are also very good, particularly the dolmades. The staff are always friendly, although weekend evenings can get a bit raucous, with live dancing and plate-smashing.

Tacuba 28, Colonia Condesa
Tel: (55) 5286 1384.
Price: M$100. Wine: M$100.

Café Tacuba

A Mexican institution in the *Centro Histórico*, *Café Tacuba* was founded in 1912 and has since remained popular among Mexicans and tourists alike. The restaurant is a feast for the eye, with painted archways, colourful tiles, stained-glass windows and brass lamps. Prices are low for the traditional Mexican fare, which ranges from tacos and tamales to pork chops, mole and steak.
Tacuba 28, Centro Histórico
Tel: (55) 5512 8482.
Price: M$100. Wine: M$100.

Casa de los Azulejos

The 'House of Tiles', literally covered in Mexican blue and white tiles, is one of the most eye-catching buildings in the *Centro Histórico*. This 16th-century mansion is an ideal stop-off on the way to the Zócalo. The spacious interior is as impressive, with seating around a Moorish fountain in an airy courtyard enlivened by frescoes. Food is basic Mexican, with a good range of soups, salads, fajitas, enchiladas and steaks.
Avenida Madero 4, Centro Histórico
Tel: (55) 5518 0152 *or* 5521 6058. Fax: (55) 5512 7882.
Price: M$100. Wine: M$100.

Oriental

A funky, unpretentious new Chinese restaurant, with orange decor, bare bricks and low lighting, *Oriental* has become a hit with hip Condesa residents. The menu offers tempting starters, such as crab tostadas, pork dumplings and shrimp thai rolls. The crunchy red snapper bites in a sweet sesame sauce make a delicious main course, as do the glazed duck pancakes and the shrimp brochete in black bean

sauce. Service is attentive and the delicious margaritas slip down a treat.
Avenida Nuevo Leon 137, Condesa
Tel: (55) 5286 7526. Fax: (55) 5286 0988.
E-mail: dinastiarest@aol.com
Price: M$150. Wine: M$180.

Saks

This rustic vegetarian restaurant on the busy Avenida Insurgentes heading south of the city has vaulted ceilings and medieval paintings on the walls. Exotic fruit juices and enormous portions of healthy food, combining Mexican and international cuisine, are served up in a relaxed atmosphere. The *Saks* salad of artichokes, palm hearts, asparagus, portobello mushrooms and feta cheese is excellent, as is the chilli filled with squash flower, nopal cactus and mushrooms.
Avenida Insurgentes Sur 1641, Florida
Tel: (55) 5598 6433 *or* 5563 3402. Fax: (55) 5598 7258.
Price: M$100. Wine: M$100.

Personal Recommendations

Bistro Charlotte

This cosy, charming restaurant on a quiet Polanco street is lovingly run by its English owner. The changing menu offers interesting fusion options with an Oriental slant. Recommended dishes include the bay scallops in Hoisin sauce, the Vietnamese duck rolls and the prawn laksa. The dark chocolate bomb with mango and coconut ice cream is a mouthwatering dessert.
Lope de Vega 341, Chapultepec Morales
Tel: (55) 5250 4180.
Price: M$200. Wine: M$100.

El Bodeguita del Medio

Named after Ernest Hemmingway's haunt in Cuba and decorated with clients' signatures on the walls, a

Casa de los Azulejos

good night out is guaranteed at this characterful bar-restaurant in artistic Roma. The atmosphere is lively, with a Cuban band playing most nights, and the *mojitos* (a Cuban cocktail of rum, lime juice, sugar and mint) are the best in town. Specialities of the house include black beans and rice (*moros y cristianos*), shredded beef and tomato stew (*vieja ropa*) and fried chicken with banana.
Cozumel 37, Roma
Tel: (55) 5553 0246.
E-mail: bdelmmex@prodigy.net.mx
Price: M$150. Wine: M$100.

El Mosaico

This newly opened French brasserie-style restaurant is always packed. Located in the fashionable Condesa neighbourhood, *El Mosaico* is a place to while away an afternoon, enjoying superlative food and attentive service. The menu includes typical French fare, such as quiches, steak tartare and black pepper steak, as well as Moroccan dishes like chicken and carrot *tajine* (stew).
Michoacán 10 and Amsterdam, Condesa
Tel: (55) 5584 2932.
Price: M$150. Wine: M$100.

Kohinoor

Indian restaurants are rare in Mexico City but this find, in the new business district of Sante Fe in the north, will satisfy any curry craving with its delicious, rich dishes. The decor is bright and clean, with the focal point being the glass window allowing diners to watch the chefs at work. The chicken tikka masala is very good, the tandoor-baked nan breads are delicious and there is a good variety of vegetarian options.
Guillermo Gonzalez Camarena 999, Sante Fe
Tel: (55) 5292 1291.
Price: M$100. Wine: M$100.

La Opera Bar

Another gem of Mexican history, this saloon-style restaurant-bar, founded in 1870, has bullets lodged in its ceiling, courtesy of revolutionary Pancho Villa, who rode into the bar on horseback – according to legend. Heavy carved wooden ceilings and booths, mirrors and red and gold wallpaper evoke the feeling of being on the set of a Western. The food is an eclectic mix from Spanish tapas, like sardines, to Mediterranean classics, like Caesar salad, and more interesting dishes, like red snapper with olive and tomato sauce.
Avenida Cinco de Mayo, Centro Histórico
Tel: (55) 5512 8959. Fax: (55) 5518 3514.
Price: M$150. Wine: M$150.

ENTERTAINMENT

Nightlife

The nightlife in Mexico City is as lively and varied as everything else the city has to offer. From gentle supper clubs with floorshows to loud, brash nightclubs, from piano bars to *antros* (or *disco-bars*) and bars that offer traditional Mexican music, all tastes are catered for. The most popular districts are Polanco, San Angel, Coyoacán and, more recently, Condesa (a residential neighbourhood just south of La Zona Rosa). La Zona Rosa is still a popular nightspot but has lost ground to Polanco and Condesa in recent years. Nightlife starts late in Mexico and ends late. There are no licensing hours

but many bars and nightclubs are closed on Sundays. Prices of drinks and admission vary enormously depending on the area. When drinking alcohol, it is worth remembering that, because of the high altitude, one drink in Mexico City can have the effect of two at lower altitudes. The minimum age for drinking in Mexico is 18 years. In the popular districts, thieves are rife, so remember to keep your wallet well guarded. *Tiempo Libre* (website: www.tiempolibre.com.mx), published every Thursday, is the weekly listings magazine (in Spanish only) and costs US$1 at newspaper stands.

Bars

In the *Centro Histórico*, *La Opera Bar*, Avenida Cinco de Mayo 10, is a late 19th-century establishment with a lively atmosphere (see *Restaurants*). Look out for a bullet hole in the ceiling, said to have come from Pancho Villa's revolver. For another Mexican speciality, head for *La Casa de las Sirenas*, Guatemala 32, a bar and restaurant offering over 250 varieties of tequila.
In Polanco, the cool bar of the moment is *Lotus*, in the shopping plaza, Plaza Zentro, at Avenida Presidente Masaryk 407. Across the way, *Cosmo* is a funky alternative with a DJ and exotic cocktails. Further down Avenida Presidente Masaryk, at 201, the rooftop bar terrace of the Habitat hotel has a fun atmosphere and is good for people-watching. Less hip but more relaxed is the *Bar Euro*, Avenida Presidente Masaryk 134, with indoor and outdoor seating. *Mezzanote*, also located in Plaza Zentro, Avenida Presidente Masaryk 407, is a lively restaurant and bar, with disco music from Thursday to Saturday. The nostalgic ex-pat *Shelty*, Avenida Campos Eliseos 204 (facing Chapultepec Park), is a wood-panelled English pub in the Hotel Nikko.
In Coyoacán, the popular *Hijo del Cuervo*, Jardín del Centenario 17, attracts a youthful mix of Mexicans and foreigners and occasionally features live music.
In the trendy Condesa neighbourhood, the place to be seen (but with a stuffy door policy) is *Bar Rioma*, Avenida Insurgentes Sur 377. *Barracuda*, Avenida Nuevo Leon 4, is a hip, chilled bar offering food and cocktails and occasionally a DJ spinning tunes. *Rexo*, Saltillo 1, is another bar/restaurant popular with young professionals, as is *Cinna*, Avenida Nuevo Leon, below the cinema. For a more Mexican experience, the *Centenario* cantina, Michoacán 42, is always packed and has live musicians, guaranteeing a good night out.

Casinos

Casinos are illegal in Mexico, although sports books – in which gambling is allowed on sporting events ranging from horseracing to American football – have sprouted up around the city, particularly in the Zona Rosa.

Clubs

The *Colmillo*, Versailles 49, situated in a colonial house in the Juárez district, was founded by two English men and remains one of the hottest clubs in Mexico City, with DJs playing acid jazz upstairs and techno below. The *Pervert Lounge*, Uruguay 70, in the *Centro Histórico*, is another funky alternative. In the bohemian Roma district, *Avant-Garde*, Puebla 310, pumps hardcore techno to a devoted crowd, while the *Living Room*, Orizaba 146, in a delightful high-ceilinged colonial mansion, is one of the most popular gay clubs in town. Also in Roma is the fun *Mama Rumba*, Querétaro 230, an institution with salsa lovers, who groove the night away to live bands.

Mauna Loa, Avenida San Jeronimo 240, is a popular Polynesian nightclub with live music for dancing and a Polynesian floorshow. *Restaurant Chez'ar* in Hotel Aristos, Paseo de la Reforma 276, has a band playing live dance music, from the rumba to the fox trot, while *Antillanos*, Francisco Pimentel 78, is *the* place to go for salsa dancing, with its large dancefloor and enthusiastic crowd. For salsa in a traditional setting, bandleader Pepe Avelavo and his orchestra provide live music at *El Gran Leon*, Querétaro 225, Colonia Roma.

Live Music

Mexico City attracts big-name international rock and pop acts. The main venues are *Auditorio Nacional*, Paseo de la Reforma 50, *Teatro Metropólitan*, Independencia 90, and the *Palacio de los Deportes*, corner of Avenida Río Churubusco and Añil. For more homegrown acts, try *Rockotitlán*, Avenida Insurgentes Sur 953, on Plaza Baja California. *New Orleans Jazz*, Avenida Revolucíon 1655, San Angel, is a classic jazz bar.
Bar Jorongo, in the Sheraton Maria Isabel Hotel, Paseo de la Reforma 325, has been one of the city's popular nightspots for more than 25 years, where big-name mariachis play Mexican music. Alternatively, visit *Plaza Garibaldi*, on Eje Central, between República de Honduras and República de Peru. This square, lined with bars and restaurants, comes alive from about 2000–2400, when the mariachi bands gather, dressed in black, silver-studded suits and large hats. *Café Tenampa* is a long-standing institution on the square, where clients are serenaded by mariachis and can test their virility with a popular electric shock game.

Sport

Mexico City's temperate climate is ideal for outdoor sports and recreation. Football and bullfighting are two national passions. The Mexico City football team, *América*, nicknamed *Las Aguilas* (The Eagles) is the Mexican favourite. Each year, *El Clasico*, a match between *América* and *Guadaljara* (the biggest club outside Mexico City), draws huge crowds of 100,000 and packs the impressive *Estadio Azteca*, Calzada de Tlalpan 3465 (tel: (55) 5617 8080 *or* 3330 *or* 3391) to capacity. The football calendar is divided into two seasons – a *torneo de invierno* (winter season) from August to December and a *torneo de verano* (summer season) from January to May.
The *Monumento Plaza México*, Rodin 241 (tel: (55) 5563 3961), is one of the largest bullrings in the world, holding up to 48,000 spectators. From mid-October to mid-April, *corridas* (bullfights) take place every Sunday at 1600.

Golf

Most golf clubs are private but some hotels offer guest privileges. *Bella Vista Golf Club* (tel: (55) 5366 8050), an 18-hole course off Querétaro Highway 57, is available to guests staying at the Sheraton Maria Isabel Hotel and the Camino Real Hotel. Green fees are US$110 Tuesday to Friday; Saturday, Sunday and holidays US$230.

Fitness Centres

Club San Francisco, Panuco 207 in Cuauhtemoc (tel: (55) 5525 0936), offers aerobics, weights, a sauna (men only) and massage. *Sport's City*, Miguel de Cervantes Saabedra 397, in Irrigacion, near Polanco (tel: (55) 5395 3570), has a pool and offers weights, aerobics, karate and steam baths. One-day membership costs M$410.

Swimming

Many hotels have pools. The public pools are all located far from the city centre.

Shopping

Mexico City offers everything from upmarket department stores to trendy boutiques and from shopping malls to street hawkers. Fixed prices prevail in the upmarket shops and department stores but it is commonplace to bargain in the markets. Favourite shopping areas include Polanco and La Zona Rosa. Shop opening hours are generally 0900/1000– 2000/2100. The larger department stores remain open late into the evening. Smaller stores often close between 1400 and 1600, then reopen until 2000. Mexico City adds VAT at 15%, which cannot be claimed back by visitors.

The largest department stores are *Sanborns*, *Liverpool* and *Palacio de Hierro*. The original stores are in the *Centro Histórico* but all have branches in suburban shopping malls. Particularly interesting is the *Casa de los Azulejos* (House of Tiles), between Avenida Cinco de Mayo and Avenida Madero, a beautiful building, dating from 1596 and covered in handmade blue and white tiles. On the inside, it sports a mural by the painter José Clemente Orozco and a Sanborns department store and restaurant (see *Restaurants*). *Centro Santa Fe*, Vasco de Quiroga 3800, in the western part of the city, is the largest shopping centre in Latin America and boasts 285 shops, with department stores, boutiques, restaurants, play areas for children and ten cinemas, although there is no metro station nearby.

There are a number of markets selling Mexican *artesanías* (handicrafts). The *Bazar Sábado* (Saturday Bazaar), Plaza San Jacinto 11, in San Angel, is located in a colonial mansion and is a showcase for some of Mexico's finest handicrafts, although prices are high. Artisans display their crafts every Saturday 1000–1900. *Mercado de Curiosidades Mexicanos San Juan* (San Juan Market of Mexican Curiosities), at Ayuntamiento and Dolores in the *Centro Histórico*, is a handicraft venue open Monday to Saturday 0900–1900 and Sunday 0900–1600. Nearby, the *Mercado la Ciudadela*, on the corner of Balderas and Dondé (tel: (55) 5512 5064), is a covered market with a wide variety of *artesanía* from all over Mexico. Prices are fair but expect to bargain; open daily 1030–1830.

For more unusual fare, the national pawnshop, the *Monte de Piedad* (Mountain of Compassion), Avenida Cinco de Mayo, opposite the *Catedral Metropolitana*, is also worth a look. It was opened in 1775 as a charitable organisation and still helps finance school construction and retirement homes with its profits. It is open Monday to Friday 0830–1700, Saturday 0830–1300.

Culture

Mexico has a rich cultural heritage – from vibrant Pre-Hispanic folk-art to the works of the great muralists of the 20th century, there is a colourful art tradition as well a thriving music and literature scene. *Tiempo Libre* (website: www.tiempolibre.com.mx), a comprehensive listings guide to all cultural events taking place in the city, comes out every Thursday and costs M$10. The monthly programme, *Guía de Programación*, is available free from the Bellas Artes bookshop and tourist offices. *Ticketmaster* (tel: (55) 5325 9000; website: www.ticketmaster.com.mx) sells tickets for most major events in Mexico City and publishes the monthly entertainment guide, *¿Qué hacemos?* (What shall we do?).

Music

The *Orquesta Filarmónica de la Ciudad de México* (OFCM) (Mexico City Philharmonic Orchestra) has its own concert hall, the *Sala Silvestre Revueltas*, Periferico Sur 5141 (tel: (55) 5606 6089; e-mail: filarmex@prodigy.net.mx). The state-owned *Auditorio Nacional*, Paseo de la Reforma 50 (tel: (55) 5280 9250; e-mail: auditorionacional@com.mx; website: www. auditorio.com.mx), is the biggest music and entertainment venue in Mexico City. Perhaps the most typical Mexican music is the mariachi, where roaming groups of trumpeters, violinists, guitarists and a singer peddle their tunes (see *Live Music* in *Nightlife* for venues).

Theatre

There are plenty of theatres to choose from, although virtually every play staged in Mexico City is in Spanish. Alternatively, there are a number of *Teatro-Bars*, which offer a more informal environment and content for the non-Spanish speaker, as they stage

Photo: Edward Ruiz/Mexico Tourism Promotion Board

Ballet Folclórico de Mexico at Palacio de Bellas Artes

lively variety shows and cabarets with singers, dancers, comedians, ventriloquists and magicians. *La Planta de Luz*, Plaza Loreto, in San Angel (tel: (55) 5616 4761), has such shows from Wednesday to Sunday, complemented by *La Bodega*, Popocatépetl 25, in Condesa (tel: (55) 5511 7390), on Fridays and Saturdays. The avant-garde *El Hábito*, Madrid 13, in Coyoacán (tel: (55) 5554 6414), has Thursday and Friday shows; they also perform at *Teatro La Blanquita*, Avenida Lázaro Cárdenas Sur 16 (tel: (55) 5512 0855). Worth looking out for are the Lebanese-born cabaret artist Astrid Haddad, who packs in the crowds, and the irreverent satirist Jesusa Rodriguez, who makes for an entertaining night out.

Dance

Colourful traditional indigenous dances are an important part of many Mexican regional fiestas. The *Palacio de Bellas Artes*, Avenida Juávez is home to the *Ballet Folclórico de México*, a bright and spectacular performance of Mexican music and dance from all over the country, which takes place every Wednesday and Sunday. The box office opens at 1100, where tickets can be purchased for M$320, M$250 and M$180 for the balcony (these are not recommended as some of the set is obscured).

Film

American and other foreign films (with the exception of animations) are shown in their original language with Spanish subtitles. *Cineteca Nacional*, Avenida México, Coyoacán (tel: (55) 1253 9300; website: http://cineteca.conaculta.gob.mx), *Cinemanía*, Plaza Loreto in San Angel (tel: (55) 5616 4836), and *Centro Cultural Universitario*, Avenida Insurgentes Sur 3000 (tel: (55) 5659 6797), all screen classic and arthouse films. For blockbusters, *Cinemex Casa de Arte*, Avenida Presidente Masaryk 393 (tel: (55) 5280 9156; website: www.cinemex.com), is a modern multi-screen cinema in the Plaza Masaryk; tickets are M$44 and half price on Wednesdays.

Mexican cinema has recently experienced a revival, with Mexicans garnering a record three nominations for the 2003 Academy Awards. Veracruz native Salma Hayek was nominated for best actress for her lead role in *Frida*, while *Y Tu Mama Tambien*, the Mexican hit of 2002, was nominated for best original screenplay and *El Crimen del Padre Amaro* was nominated for best foreign film.

Cultural Events

The *Festival del Centro Histórico* takes place in March and is a three-week festival of classical and popular music, dance, exhibitions and other cultural events. The festival attracts performers from all over Mexico and events are staged in the plazas and theatres throughout the *Centro Histórico*. *Día de los Muertos* (Day of the Dead) is celebrated on 2 November and is a day when the souls of the dead are believed to return to the earth. It is a fabulously colourful and cheerful celebration. Families build altars in their homes and lay decorous garlands on the graves of their loved ones. The Zócalo becomes the focus of the national celebration.

Literary Notes

Pre-Hispanic poems and history have survived in the form of *codices*, colourful inscriptions painted on skin or bark paper, but *History of the Conquest of New Spain* is considered to be the first work of Mexican literature. Written by Bernal Díaz del

SPECIAL EVENTS

Festival del Centro Histórico, three-week festival of classical and popular music, dance, exhibitions and other cultural events, Mar, throughout the *Centro Histórico*

Semana Santa (Holy Week), re-enactment of the crucifixion; hooded penitents hobble to Church on bloodied knees flagellating themselves with thorny whips, 8–15 Apr, Taxco

Día del Trabajo (Labour Day), 1 May, throughout the city

Día de la madre (Mother's Day), Mexicans, for whom the mother is the central figure in the family, hold big fiestas to celebrate Mother's Day, 10 May, throughout the city

Día de la Independencia (Independence Day), commemoration of the start of Mexico's war with Spain for Independence; thousands of people gather the night before to hear the president recite the *Grito de Dolores* (Cry of Dolores) and ring the ceremonial Bell of Dolores, 16 Sep, Zócalo

Día de la Raza, commemoration of Columbus' discovery of the Americas, 12 Oct, throughout the city

Día de Todos Santos (All Saints' Day), when the souls of deceased children are believed to return to earth, 1 Nov, throughout the city

Día de los Muertos (Day of the Dead), when the souls of dead adults are believed to return to the earth; families build extravagant altars in their homes, decorated with candles, flowers and skull-shaped candy and bread; believers cook up a feast for their dead relatives, offering up their favourite food and drink in the hope of enticing them back for the day, 2 Nov, Zócalo and suburb of Mixquic where the graveyard is lit up by waist-high candles and huge bouquets of flowers in traditional style

Día de la Revolución, anniversary of the 1910 Mexican Revolution, 20 Nov, throughout the city

Día de Nuestra Señora de Guadalupe (Patron Saint's Day), 12 Dec, La Basílica de Nuestra Señora de Guadalupe

Castillo, one of Cortés' lieutenants, it is an eyewitness account of the Spanish conquest of the Aztec Empire. Mexico boasts a number of internationally acclaimed writers, including the late Octavio Paz, a Nobel Prize winner and essayist, who wrote the in-depth examination of Mexican myths and the Mexican character *The Labyrinth of the Solitude* (1950). Carlos Fuentes is Mexico's most famous writer – his book, *Where the Air is Clear* (1958), is set in Mexico City and follows the lives of a number of its inhabitants through the decades after the Mexican Revolution. Laura Esquivel is the author of a more contemporary hit, *Como Agua para Chocolate* (*Like Water for Chocolate*, 1990); the film based on the novel also became an instant international success.

Frida Kahlo Museum

MIAMI

Hardly the brash, drug-ridden crime capital of America that was made famous in the 1980s television series, *Miami Vice*, today's booming metropolis has since been dubbed 'America's Casablanca', the 'Magic City' and, more recently, the 'America of the Millennium'. These various appellations touch on one aspect of Miami that distinguishes it from other US cities – its identity as a truly multicultural American city. It is a gateway to South and Central America and the third most popular city in the United States for international visitors (after Los Angeles and New York). In fact, Miami just might be more Latin American than simply American.

For a city famed for its sunny weather, spicy nightlife and fine dining, Miami had surprisingly humble beginnings. Located on the far south coast of Florida, perched between a mangrove swamp and a barrier reef, Miami was founded a hundred years ago, when a tycoon called Henry Flagler extended his railroad to carry citrus fruits from the frost-free South. Development was slow until the Florida land boom in the 1920s. During Prohibition, Al Capone came here when the heat was on in Chicago. After World War II, the Mafia moved in and later, once Fidel Castro seized power in Cuba in 1959, waves of Cuban refugees arrived. Before long, they had established Miami as the Latin capital of the USA – with later mass immigration in the 1980s as well. The cultural climate the Cubans created in Miami inspired residents of other Latin countries – Colombia, Dominica, Puerto Rico, Nicaragua, Haiti and others – to seek an escape from poverty or oppressive governments and emigrate. And now, Spanish is spoken as pervasively in Miami as English.

Embracing its diverse population, Miami has also become one of America's most ultramodern cities – the second largest in Florida (after Jacksonville) but easily its most exciting, exotic and cosmopolitan. Miami, known as Greater Miami and the Beaches or just Greater Miami for short, includes a number of islands and mainland communities, including two cities – Miami and Miami Beach. Much of Miami's appeal is due to its diverse neighbourhoods, which range from the big-city, towering skyscrapers of downtown Miami – the commercial heart of the city – to Little Havana, home to the Cuban community, or to the trendy Miami Beach neighbourhood of South Beach. South Beach is probably most recognisably 'Miami' – with its candy-coloured Art Deco buildings set against a pure South Florida backdrop of cloudless skies, dazzling blue ocean, pale sandy beaches and swaying palm trees.

Greater Miami is also an international crossroads of commerce, finance, culture, sports, entertainment, transportation and tourism, which is, not surprisingly, the city's main source of income. The downtown Port of Miami is the largest cruise ship port in the world, which handles more than three million passengers a year. Besides its importance to cruise travel, Miami Beach is, of course, world-renowned for its 'gold coast' hotel strip, palatial properties and outdoor recreational facilities. Locals give the feeling that nothing could ever be more important than taking a morning run along the beachside path, sunning oneself or shopping during the afternoon, then dining and dancing until dawn. Its subtropical climate ensures warm weather year-round, with plenty of sunshine – and the lifestyle and vibe here emphasise not work but plenty of play.

The city's real genius, however, is that, in recent years, it has successfully absorbed the different cultures of its multi-ethnic population and been influenced by them all – and now Miami is considered a model community for the 21st century and a compelling example of America's changing face. Despite this, not every immigration story is a happy one. Immigrants are not given as hearty a welcome as the Eastern European immigrants to America once were, for example, as the sad story of young Elian Gonzales and his attempted illegal emigration shows, when, in 1999, his mother lost her life in trying to secure US citizenship for her son. This family tragedy began as a hope-filled journey, as Miami is essentially a city founded on the ideals of liberation by immigrants seeking an opportunity to flourish. Now one of the most exhilarating cities in the country, this safe, successful, multicultural metropolis has vibrancy and *savoir faire* and really is a 'City of the Future'.

Photo: Greater Miami Convention and Visitors Bureau

Ocean Drive

TRAVEL

Getting There By Air

Miami International Airport (MIA)

Tel: (305) 876 7000. Fax: (305) 876 7398.
Website: www.miami-airport.com
Located 11km (seven miles) northwest of the city, Miami International Airport is regarded as the 'Hub of the Americas' – the primary connecting point for air travel between the Americas and Latin America and a major gateway to Europe. It has the third highest international passenger traffic in the USA and is number one in the world for international freight trade. Almost 40 airlines serve 34 million passengers per year. The terminal building is in the shape of a horseshoe, with eight concourses (A–H). For easy access to any of the concourses, there is a moving walkway on level 3. International flights arrive at concourses A, B, D, E and F.
Major airlines: National airline *American Airlines* (tel: (800) 433 7300; website: www.aa.com) serves Miami International Airport. Other airlines include *Air Canada, Air France, Air Jamaica, British Airways, Continental, Delta, Lufthansa, Northwest/KLM, TACA, TWA, United, US Airways* and *Virgin Atlantic*.

business-class passengers to access executive lounges. The *Miami International Airport Hotel*, Concourse E, upper level (tel: (305) 871 4100; fax: (305) 871 0800; website: www.miahotel.com), offers conference suites, boardrooms and other meeting facilities, with catering service available.
Arrival/departure tax: US$50–95, depending on airline and destination, included in ticket.
Transport to the city: Some hotels provide a free minibus or limousine service to their visitors. In lieu of this service, perhaps the best mode of transport for the money is the *SuperShuttle* (tel: (305) 871 2000 or (800) 874 8885; website: www.supershuttle.com). Minivans depart from the lower level of the terminal outside baggage claim, with 24-hour service to points as far north as Palm Beach and to some of the Lower Keys. On average, Miami destinations cost US$8–15 one way. Public transport from the airport to Miami is somewhat complicated. A free 24-hour shuttle bus – departing from the ground level of concourse E, directly across from US Customs – connects with the Miami Airport Tri-Rail station. *Tri-Rail* (tel: (954) 942 7248; fax: (954) 788 7878; website: www.tri-rail.com) trains run from Miami Airport station as far as Mangonia Park station in Palm Beach, weekdays 0416–2210 and weekends 0700–2157. To reach downtown Miami by train, passengers must travel two

Taxis charge flat fares (tip is not included) from the airport to most destinations. A trip to the Port of Miami costs US$18, US$24 to Miami Beach and US$31 to Key Biscayne. A trip to downtown Miami or South Beach takes approximately 20 minutes. A porter matches travellers with taxis on the arrivals and departure levels.

Getting There By Water

The *Dante B Fascell Port of Miami* (tel: (305) 371 7678; fax: (305) 347 4843; website: www.co.miami-dade.fl.us/portofmiami), under the authority of *Miami-Dade County Seaport Department* (tel: (305) 371 7678), is the world's busiest cruise port. As the 'Cruise Capital of the World', it serves more than three million passengers a year and handles more 'megaships' (vessels capable of transporting 2000-plus passengers) than any other port in the world. The port, located near Bayside Marketplace, is home to 18 cruise ships and its terminal has smart new facilities, including VIP lounges and an outdoor observation deck, as well as a branch of the *Avis* car hire company.
Boat services: *Carnival Cruise Lines* (tel: (305) 599 2600), *Norwegian Cruise Line* (tel: (305) 436 4000) and *Royal Caribbean International* (tel: (305) 539 6000) are among several cruise lines operating regularly from the port with services to the Caribbean and beyond.
Transport to the city: Bus 3, 16, 95, C or S goes from Bayside (Biscayne Boulevard) to downtown Miami.

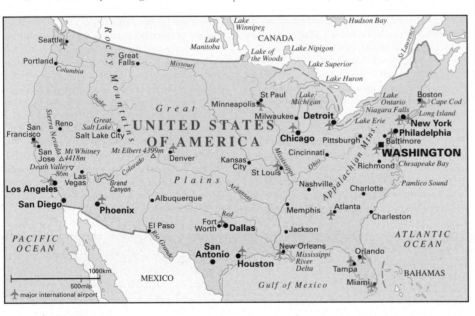

Approximate flight times to Miami: From London is 8 hours 30 minutes; from New York is 3 hours; from Los Angeles is 5 hours; from Toronto is 3 hours 45 minutes and from Sydney is 18 hours.
Airport facilities: Throughout the terminal, there are plenty of restaurants, cafés, snack bars, gift and duty-free shops, newspaper stands and foreign currency exchange booths. A pharmacy (concourse F), a post office (concourse B, level 4) and a unisex hair styling salon cover additional passenger needs. Car hire firms include *Alamo, Avis, Budget, Dollar, Hertz* and *National*. There are five Tourist Information Centers (the main one, at level 2 of Concourse E, is open 0500–2400), a full-service bank (concourse B, level 4) and several ATMs (concourse C and G, level 2).
Business facilities: There are data port connections at various locations throughout the airport terminal. For specific locations, visitors should either pick up a white paging phone or ask at one of the information desks. Many airlines – including American Airlines, Delta and United – belong to the airline VIP club, enabling their

stops on the Tri-Rail to the Tri-Rail/Metrorail Transfer station – the cost is US$2 on weekdays and US$4 at the weekend – and transfer to *Metrorail*, which is operated by *Miami-Dade Transit Agency – MDTA* (tel: (305) 770 3131; fax: (305) 654 6583; e-mail: transit@miamidade.gov; website: www.co.miami-dade.fl.us/mdta). Metrorail trains cost US$1.25 and operate daily 0500–2400.
Alternatively, *Metrobuses*, also operated by the MDTA, leave from the lower level of Concourse E. Services include bus 7, which goes to the Government Center in downtown Miami and the main bus terminal (journey time – 35 minutes), and bus 42, which goes to Coconut Grove; both leave every 40 minutes daily 0600–2200. Bus J goes to Miami Beach every 30 minutes daily 0440–2400 (journey time – approximately 1 hour). The *Metrobus Airport Owl Line* runs hourly 1150–0540 and goes as far as South Beach. The Metrobus costs US$1.25 with an extra US$0.25 for transfers, which should be requested and purchased with the ticket.

Getting There By Rail

Amtrak (tel: (800) 872 7245; website: www.amtrak.com) is the national railway provider. With comfortable trains and a reliable and efficient service, Amtrak is an excellent way to travel. For national rail enquiries, visitors should call the toll-free information line (tel: (800) USA RAIL or 872 7245). Miami's main Amtrak rail terminal is located at 8303 NW 37th Avenue (tel: (305) 835 1223). The station has very basic facilities, including a checked baggage service, an enclosed waiting area, payphones, vending machines and car hire from *Hertz*. The station is also fully accessible to persons using wheelchairs.
Rail services: Amtrak offers a comprehensive rail network to cities throughout the USA and Canada, including Fort Lauderdale (journey time – 4 minutes), Orlando (journey time – 5 hours) and Jacksonville (journey time – 8 hours). *SilverMeteor* and *SilverStar* trains operate up the Atlantic coast from Miami to New York City (journey time – 25 hours) three times a day.
Transport to the city: Bus 42 connects the Amtrak station with downtown Miami.

Getting There By Road

Americans drive on the right-hand side of the road and pass on the left. Right turns at a red light are permitted (unless otherwise indicated) but only after stopping. Speed limits range from 24kph (15mph) to 72kph (45mph) in the city and 88kph (55mph) on most expressways. Speeding fines are hefty. There are also tough penalties for drink driving – the maximum legal alcohol to blood ratio for driving is 0.08%. All passengers must wear seatbelts and children aged under five must be fastened into a child safety seat. All drivers must be over 16 years of age and are required to hold a current driving licence. The State of Florida recognises valid driver's licences from the USA and other countries, as well as International Driving Permits. Visitors who plan on driving should have Personal Accident Insurance (PAI) as part of their standard travel insurance.

The road system is straightforward, consisting of interstate expressways, toll-paying motorways, primary state highways and other state roads, each identified by a number. The general rule for numbering on US freeways and interstates is that the odd numbers go north–south and the even numbers go east–west over their whole length, although at any single, localised point this may seem different.

The *American Automobile Association – AAA* (tel: (800) 222 1333) provides information and road maps and may offer reciprocal benefits to members of automobile clubs in other countries.

Emergency breakdown service: *AAA* (800) AAA HELP *or* 222 4357.

Routes to the city: The I-95 is the major north–south expressway, providing access into Miami from Palm Beach and Fort Lauderdale. It runs through downtown Miami and into US-1 (also called Dixie Highway), which continues south to Key West. Another toll-paying expressway, the Florida Turnpike, heads southwards from Orlando and central Florida to the Golden Glades Interchange in the northern part of Miami. The major east–west expressway to downtown Miami is State Road 836 (Dolphin Expressway), connecting Florida's Turnpike in the west with the I-95 and Miami Beach (via the I-395) in the east.

Approximate driving times to Miami: From Fort Lauderdale – 1 hour; Palm Beach – 2 hours; Key West – 3 hours 30 minutes; Orlando – 5 hours.

Coach services: *Greyhound* (tel: (800) 231 2222; website: www.greyhound.com) operates three main coach stations in Miami – at 4111 NW 27th Street (tel: (305) 871 1810), near the airport, at 100 NW Sixth Street (tel: (305) 374 6160), near Bayside, downtown Miami, and at 16560 NE Sixth Avenue (tel: (305) 945 0801), in North Miami. Facilities at these terminals

range from basic to non-existent. Greyhound operates direct links to Fort Lauderdale, Orlando and Key West, as well as more distant destinations, such as New Orleans, Washington, DC and New York.

Getting Around

Public Transport

Getting around Greater Miami can be difficult, mainly due to the sheer size of the city. Nevertheless, *Miami-Dade Transit Agency – MDTA* (tel: (305) 770

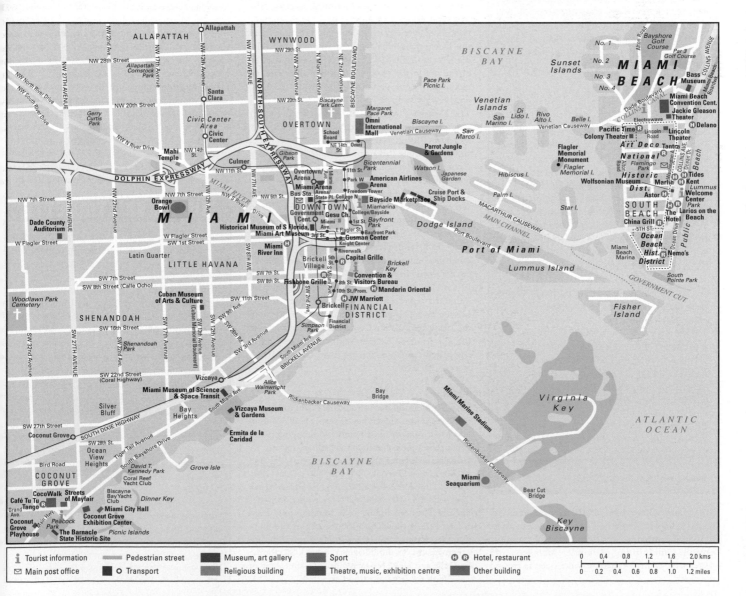

BUSINESS PROFILE

Thanks to its strategic situation at the gateway to the Caribbean, Central and South America, as well as its superior seaport and airport capabilities, Miami is known as the major international trading hub of the Americas. Founded in 1977, the Miami Free Trade Zone – the first and largest privately owned and operated trade zone in the world – is located just west of Miami International Airport and boasts around 200 major international clients. The customs in Miami process 40% of all US exports to Latin America and the Caribbean. Top export trading partners include Brazil, Colombia, Venezuela, Dominican Republic and Argentina.

Recent years have seen the steady economic growth and strengthening of international business opportunities, with trade, construction, manufacturing (clothing, metal fabrication, printing and medical products), real estate and the service sectors showing the strongest potential. The city's main commercial district is at the heart of downtown Miami, where six blocks of government and municipal offices house such prestigious multinationals as *AT&T*, *Apple*, *Johnson & Johnson*, *Kos Pharmaceuticals*, *Sony*, *Texaco* and *Toshiba*. More than 400 multinational companies have operations in Miami and many have their Latin American headquarters here. The city is also emerging as a key international banking centre. Indeed, Brickell Avenue has more international banks (over 100) than any other place in the USA.

The city's chief source of income, however, derives from tourism. The direct economic impact of over 10.5 million visitors to Miami in 2001 was visitor expenditure of US$14 billion. Thanks to its multitude of hotels with conference suites, it is also a major business convention centre. The film and entertainment industry also generates millions annually with film, television, commercial and fashion photography production. Major media organisations located in Greater Miami include *Telemundo* and *Univision* (the top two Spanish-language television networks in the USA), the *Discovery Channel*, *MTV Networks* and the *Travel Channel*.

Employment increased 0.9% in 2002 in Miami-Dade, bringing the city's unemployment rate to 7%. Although this figure tops the national average of 6%, the city's ability to create new jobs in a post-September 11 economic climate is promising. The Miami-Dade County Public Schools, with over 34,000 employees, is the city's largest public sector employer. Miami-Dade County's largest private sector employers include *American Airlines*, *University of Miami*, *Baptist Health Systems of South Florida*, *BellSouth* and *Florida Power & Light Company*. Service industry jobs account for 33% of the labour force, while Miami International Airport apparently generates one out of every six jobs in South Florida.

3131; fax: (305) 654 6583; e-mail: transit@ miamidade.gov; website: www.co.miami-dade. fl.us/mdta) provides a variety of useful transport options, including *Metrorail*, *Metrobus* and *Metromover*. Many of these services operate around the clock.

At 34km (21 miles), the *Metrorail* (tel: (305) 770 3131) is the longest elevated **rapid transit system** in the USA. It runs from Kendall northwards through South Miami, Coral Gables, downtown Miami and then northwest to the Hialeah district. There are 21 stations – each about a mile apart – and the entire journey takes 42 minutes. Trains run 0500–2400 approximately every 15–20 minutes, every six minutes at peak times and every 30 minutes after 2000. Fares are US$1.25 each way – exact change only is placed in the slot at the entrance turnstiles. The trains connect to the Metrobus and Tri-Rail. Transfer to the *Metromover* (see below), at the Government Center station or Brickell station, costs US$0.25 and must be purchased at the original boarding station.

Metrobus (tel: (305) 638 6700) operates a comprehensive **bus** service with 82 routes running Monday to Friday 0400–0213 (with extended hours at the weekend). Blue and green bus-stop signs list the routes and destinations. Fares are US$1.25 each way – exact change only is handed to the driver upon boarding. A transfer from bus to bus or from bus to Metrorail costs US$0.25. Some express routes charge an additional US$1.50.

Downtown Miami is served by the futuristic, driverless *Metromover* (tel: (305) 770 3131), an elevated, three-loop, fully automated **monorail**. This links major business, entertainment and cultural centres, hotels, shopping malls, government buildings and the Brickell Financial District. It also connects with the Metrorail and Metrobus services. The Metromover operates daily 0530–2200, every three minutes or every 90 seconds during rush hour, with the 'Downtown Inner Loop' continuing until 2400. Tickets cost just US$0.25 – exact fare only is placed in the slot at the entrance turnstiles. It is safe, air conditioned and provides unparalleled views of downtown Miami.

The *Electrowave* (tel: (305) 535 9160), South Beach's **electric trolley** service, provides transportation up and down Washington Avenue (between 17th Street and South Pointe Park). Another route covers Collins Avenue and Meridan Avenue (between 16th Street and 23rd Street), with stops at the sights near Dade Boulevard, including the Miami Beach Convention Center. The Electrowave operates every 12–15 minutes (Monday to Wednesday 0800–0200, Thursday to Saturday 0800–0400 and Sunday 1000–0200) and costs just US$0.25 – tickets are purchased on board. It stops at 38 designated stops in the Art Deco Historic District.

A monthly *Metropass*, costing US$60, allows for unlimited travel on the Metrobus, Metrorail and Metromover. This **pass** is available for purchase from the Transit Information Center on the second level of the Government Center Metrorail station and at designated outlets, which are listed on the MDTA website (see above).

Taxis

Taxis are plentiful but it is not the norm for one to hail them in the street. They are easily available from taxi stands outside most hotels and shopping malls, although it is more common to telephone for one. Companies include *Metro Taxi Co* (tel: (305) 888 8888), *Aventura Taxi* (tel: (305) 599 9999), *Coral Gables City Taxi* (tel: (305) 444 4242) and *South Dade Miami Taxi* (tel: (305) 448 8888). All service providers offer flat-rate fares (including tolls but not tips) from Miami International Airport to some of the more popular destinations (see *Getting There By Air*), otherwise visitors should expect to pay US$3 for the first mile and US$2 for each mile thereafter. A tip of 15–20% of the fare is usual and expected.

Water Taxis

The city's waterways are served by a fleet of local ferries, known as water taxis. These operate along two main routes – from Bayside Marketplace to the Fifth Street Marina at the southwestern end of south Beach or to the western end of Lincoln Road – daily 1000–2300. Fares are US$7 one way, US$12 round trip and US$15 for an all-day pass.

Limousines

Dolphin Limousine Service (tel: (305) 651 1641; website: www.dolphin-limo.com), *Extreme Limousines* (tel: (305) 262 7071; website: www.extremelimos.com) and *Royal Limousines* (tel: (305) 442 1414; website: www.royal-limousines.com) all cater for both business and leisure needs.

Visitors should expect to pay around US$150–175 per hour (for a minimum of three hours) or US$170–190 per hour at the weekend.

Driving in the City

Of the 30 municipalities that comprise Greater Miami, familiarisation with the major neighbourhoods is extremely helpful for drivers. Coral Gables (actually a city in itself), Coconut Grove and Little Havana are the popular neighbourhoods in Miami, as well as the downtown area. Miami Beach, a city distinct from Miami, situated to the east, has the lively beachside and shopping centre of South Beach. Visitors should also note that Miami is divided into quadrants. Flagler Street runs east–west, thus dividing the city into north and south sections, while Miami Avenue runs north–south, splitting the city into east and west sections. Most Miami addresses refer to these quadrants.

Highway interchanges can be very confusing, so visitors should be sure to read the signs carefully. Main routes include the major east–west expressway State Road 836 (also called the Dolphin Expressway), which leads from Miami International Airport to the major north–south I-95 expressway and onto Miami Beach via I-195. Four main causeways link Miami and Miami Beach and, once there, the A1A (Collins

BUSINESS ETIQUETTE

Miami's close proximity to Latin America makes it a fascinating place to do business. Throughout the past decade, a large number of companies from the Caribbean, Central and South America have set up offices here and, as a result, Greater Miami's workforce has grown younger, more multi-lingual and more culturally diverse. However, for business purposes, it is still essentially America. Therefore, dress code is smart and business is managed the American way – quickly, efficiently and frankly. Business cards should always be presented. Outside the boardroom, Americans are often informal and will use first names. Business socialising, drinking and dining is popular in Miami.

Office hours are generally Monday to Friday 0900–1700, although these can vary slightly from one organisation to the next. When public holidays occur on a weekday or weekend, they are usually celebrated on the nearest Friday or Monday, thereby creating a three-day weekend. Meetings often take place in social situations and, in keeping with the fast-paced business life of Americans, breakfast meetings are common. Lunch meetings are also popular, sometimes with alcohol. Meetings may also take place over the weekend.

Avenue) is the main thoroughfare running parallel to the coast. The orange 'sun' signs visible on selected highways identify official tourist routes – to Coral Gables, Coconut Grove, downtown Miami, Key Biscayne, Miami Beach and the Port of Miami, as well as to Fort Lauderdale, Orlando and Key West. Construction is all-pervasive in booming Miami. Drivers should look for 'smart' signs, which convey alternate routes and warnings, and also keep an eye out for construction-induced potholes in torn-up areas. Greater Miami traffic can be terrible; cars can come to an absolute standstill along Ocean Drive and Collins Avenue in South Beach during weekday rush hour and weekend nights. Rush hour is Monday to Friday approximately 0630–0845 and again at 1530–1830. Visitors should be aware that short-tempered drivers are as prolific as road construction signs.

There is plenty of metered parking available in Miami but not elsewhere. Visitors should check displayed information for rates and hours of operation. The average rate for parking is approximately US$1 per hour. The fine for an expired meter is US$18 (US$45 if not paid within 30 calendar days). On weekends, parking garages fill up with shoppers during the day and clubbers during the night, especially in Miami Beach and Coconut Grove. Further information on locations of car parks, hours and rates is available from the *Miami Parking System*, 190 NE Third Street, in downtown Miami (tel: (305) 358 7312).

Car Hire

Hiring a car is relatively straightforward. Drivers must be over 25 years old and possess a valid national driving licence and a credit card to hold a deposit of at least US$500. When arranging car hire, visitors should inquire about an all-inclusive rate and ask how this compares to the regular daily rate. An all-inclusive rate should include all taxes, airport fees and car handling fees. CWD (also known as LDW), which makes the hire company, rather than the driver, responsible for damage to the car, and SLI (supplementary liability insurance), also sometimes called top-up liability insurance or EP (extended protection), increases third-party liability coverage. All-inclusive rates may also include a tank of petrol and additional drivers (otherwise around US$5 per driver). There is usually an extra charge for child seats (US$3–5 per day).

It is worth shopping around for the best rates. These vary considerably, from a minimum of around US$170 per week or US$40 per day for a compact car with air conditioning, although this may vary from branch to branch and season to season. Convertible cars for travel in sunny Miami start at a higher rental rate. Free one-way drop-offs are normally possible within Florida, although rarely with the cheapest cars. Major providers include *Alamo*, 3355 NW 22nd Street, Miami International Airport (tel: (305) 633 4132; website: www.goalamo.com), *Avis*, 17760 Collins Avenue, Miami Beach (tel: (305) 932 2350; website: www.avis.com), *Budget*, 3901 NW 28th Street, Miami International Airport (tel: (305) 871 3053; website: www.drivebudget.com), *Hertz*, 3795 NW 21st Street, Miami International Airport (tel: (305) 871 0300; website: www.hertz.com), *Interamerican*, 1789 NW Le Jeune Road, Coral Gables (tel: (305) 871 3030; website: www.interamericancarrental.com), and *Thrifty*, 2875 NW 42nd Avenue, Miami International Airport (tel: (305) 871 5050; website: www.thrifty.com).

Bicycle & Scooter Hire

While Miami has busy thoroughfares, Miami Beach has smaller neighbourhood streets so most rental

Art Deco Historic District

Photo: Greater Miami Convention and Visitors Bureau

outlets are in bike-friendly Miami Beach. The *Miami Beach Bicycle Center*, 601 Fifth Street (tel: (305) 674 0150), charges around US$20 per day. *Bikes to Go*, 6600 SW 80th Street (tel: (305) 666 7702), sells and rents bikes in Miami itself. Visitors interested in hiring an Italian scooter should visit *Ride*, 710 Washington Avenue, Miami Beach (tel: (305) 673 3307).

Bicycle hire rates are around US$20 per day and visitors should ask for a sturdy U-type or Kryptonite lock as bicycle theft is common, and wear a helmet.

SIGHTSEEING

Sightseeing Overview

Miami has long been a premier tourist destination, acclaimed for its physical beauty and its excellent climate. Year round, the fabled white-sand beaches and clear blue waters lapping *Miami Beach* have beckoned visitors to America's 'Riviera'. Others are lured by Miami's world-class shopping and cosmopolitan dining, its international culture and legendary nightlife.

Miami's diverse neighbourhoods offer a range of activities, from cultural to sporting. Residential *Coral Gables* is known for its examples of architectural elegance, including the Biltmore Hotel, Fairchild Tropical Garden and the incomparable Venetian Pool, while the bustling *Bayside* harbour complex in *downtown Miami* offers boat excursions. The distinctly Latin district of *Little Havana*, home to the city's huge Cuban population, has cigar-making shops and is the place to be in March for the lively *Calle Ocho Festival*. Over in Miami Beach, *South Beach* is one of the most-visited neighbourhoods, famed for its pastel Art Deco buildings, where the legendary *Ocean Drive* boulevard is fringed by sidewalk boutiques, bars and restaurants – the favourite haunts of such local celebrities as Gloria Estefan, Ricky Martin and Donatella Versace. Perhaps Miami's biggest crowd-puller is its rich multicultural flavour, which gives the city an undeniably unique atmosphere. Just as the rest of America has embraced the rhythms of heart-throb Ricky Martin, Enrique Iglesias, Shakira and other Hispanic music sensations, Miami has long been swaying to a Latin mix of sensuality, salsa and South Beach style, making it one of the most exciting cities in the USA.

Miami is divided into quadrants and most addresses refer to this. Flagler Street runs east–west, dividing the city into north and south sections, while Miami Avenue runs north–south, splitting the city into east and west sections.

Key Attractions

Downtown Miami

Downtown Miami is the metropolis's nerve centre – the commercial heart of the city – distinguished by its sleek skyscrapers, impressive government buildings and cultural centres and edged by the Port of Miami, the largest cruise ship port in the world. Brickell Avenue is home to major international banks and businesses, as well as Brickell Village, the area around SW Sixth Street, which has power-lunch restaurants cum buzzing nightspots. On the waterfront, the lively *Bayside Marketplace* is a popular shopping and entertainment arcade, clustered around a small harbour and buzzing with bars, shops and market stalls. Bayside is the main stop for the water taxi service (see *Getting Around*) and the starting point for several boat tours (see *Tours of the City*) of Miami Bay. Adjacent to Bayside Marketplace is the *American Airlines Arena*, a 20,000-person entertainment venue and home of the basketball team *Miami Heat* (website:

Dolphins at the Miami Seaquarium

www.nba. com/heat). The nearby historic *Gusman Center for the Performing Arts* hosts the Miami Film Festival and other cultural events under a painted 'starry sky' ceiling. Beyond the port, exclusive *Fisher Island*, accessible only by boat or private plane, is *the* address in Miami and home to many celebrities.
Bayside Marketplace
401 Biscayne Boulevard
Tel: (305) 577 3344.
Website: www.baysidemarketplace.com
Transport: Metrorail Brickell, Government Center or Overtown/Arena.
Opening hours: Mon–Thurs 1000–2200, Fri and Sat 1000–2300, Sun 1100–2100.
Admission: Free.
American Airlines Arena
601 Biscayne Boulevard
Tel: (305) 577 4328 *or* 960 8500.
Website: www.aaarena.com
Transport: Metromover Park West or Freedom Tower.
Gusman Center for the Performing Arts
174 East Flagler Street
Tel: (305) 372 0925.
Website: http://gusmancenter.org
Transport: Metromover Knight Center.

South Beach

Glitzy, glamorous *South Beach* is undoubtedly the trendiest part of town, the place to see and be seen and a magnet for celebrities and fun-lovers who thrive on its cosmopolitan atmosphere, designer shopping, upbeat restaurants and fast-paced nightlife. By day, a young, hip crowd of trendy film-star wannabes, international supermodels, artists, writers, tourists, strollers, strutters and the thriving local gay community all cruise *Ocean Drive* and the pedestrian-friendly *Lincoln Road Mall*, with its art galleries, shops and restaurants – providing the colourful mix that fuels the district's feverish energy levels. By night, salsa or techno music flows from the many and varied dance clubs onto the busy vibrant streets.
South Beach itself, with its white sands, palm trees and dazzling blue sea, stretches from Lincoln Road Mall to South Pointe Park at the southernmost tip (great for surfing, fishing and sunsets). The main access point is *Lummus Park*, bordering Ocean Drive, a favourite park

for in-line skaters and volleyball players. However, the most striking feature of South Beach is its famous *Art Deco Historic District* – over 800 buildings within one and a half sq kilometres (one sq mile), all in the same streamlined architectural style, painted in pastel shades and lit with brilliantly coloured neon lights. Even the Burger King on Alton Road is housed in an Art Deco structure. Tours of the district are offered on Saturday morning or Thursday evening and self-guided tour maps are always available at the *Art Deco Welcome Center*.
Lincoln Road Mall to South Pointe Park
Transport: Bus C, K, M or W; Electrowave trolley.
Art Deco Welcome Center
1001 Ocean Drive
Tel: (305) 531 3484.
Website: www.mdpl.org
Opening hours: Sun–Thurs 1000–2200, Fri and Sat 1000–2400.
Admission: Free; US$10–15 (guided tours).

Miami Beach

Miami Beach is located on a long slender island connected to mainland Miami by four main causeways. It comprises various coastal towns, each with its own personality – including Surfside, the upscale shopping district of *Bal Harbour*, Sunny Isles Beach, South Beach (see above) and Golden Beach. Miami Beach's white sands extend from Lincoln Road Mall northwards to 87th Street, with a scenic boardwalk popular with joggers and strollers, and pastel-coloured Art Deco lifeguard stations dotting the shoreline. Various watersports are available, including windsurfing, sailing, jet-skiing and parasailing.
Lincoln Road Mall to 87th Street
Transport: Bus C, G, H, L, M, S or W.
Bal Harbour Shops
9700 Collins Road
Tel: (305) 866 0311.
Website: www.balharbourshops.com
Opening hours: Daily 1000–1800.
Admission: Free.

Little Havana

After Fidel Castro took power in 1959, refugees fleeing Cuba settled just west of downtown Miami, in a

neighbourhood now known as *Little Havana*. Today, with its 800,000-strong Cuban-American community, this colourful district has a distinctly Latin atmosphere with its Spanish signs, Cuban coffee bars and restaurants, small cigar factories and street-side food stalls, selling such delicacies as *baho* (Cuban stew) and freshly squeezed juices. Monuments to anti-Castro Cubans line the streets, especially around *Calle Ocho* (Eighth Street), the liveliest part of Little Havana and the venue for the Calle Ocho Festival, a famous annual spring carnival – America's largest street party.
Little Havana
Transport: Metrorail Vizcaya; then bus 17 or 24.

Key Biscayne

Key Biscayne combines traditional Florida-style houses with ostentatious mansions belonging to some of Miami's wealthiest residents. The beaches here rank among Florida's best – their fine sand and relatively calm seas make them a popular choice for families. Other top attractions include two beautiful parks – *Bill Baggs Cape Florida State Recreation Area* and *Crandon Park* – both with magnificent beaches, bike trails and nature walks. The small *Crandon Family Amusement Center* in the park has an old-time carousel, playground and outdoor roller rink.
Key Biscayne (linked to the mainland by the Rickenbacker Causeway)
Transport: Bus B.
Bill Baggs Cape Florida State Recreation Area
1200 South Crandon Boulevard
Tel: (305) 361 5811.
Website: www.dep.state.fl.us/parks
Opening hours: Daily 0800–sunset.
Admission: US$2; US$4 per car.
Crandon Park
4000 Crandon Boulevard
Tel: (305) 361 5421 *or* 0099 (Amusement Center).
Website: www.co.miami-dade.fl.us/parks/crandon.htm
Opening hours: Daily 0800–sunset (park); daily 1000–1900 (Amusement Center).
Admission: Free; US$4 (parking); US$1 (three carousel rides).

Miami Seaquarium

Located on beautiful Biscayne Bay, the *Miami Seaquarium* has over 10,000 aquatic creatures on display – including crocodiles, 'gators' and seals, as well as fish of every imaginable shape, size and colour. Star acts include Lolita, a 7000lb killer whale (visitors should sit at least six rows back in the audience to keep dry), Salty the sea lion and TV superstar Flipper the dolphin. The most impressive aspect of Seaquarium, however, is its genuine attempt to preserve and protect marine life. The in-house Marine Mammal Rescue Team is constantly striving to save stranded or injured manatees, dolphins and whales in the waters of South Florida. Other exhibits include *Discovery Bay*, a natural mangrove habitat used to rehabilitate rescued sea turtles; and the special *Manatee Exhibit*, where manatees are nursed back to health, ready for release into the wild.
4400 Rickenbacker Causeway, Key Biscayne
Tel: (305) 361 5705. Fax: (305) 365 0075.
Website: www.miamiseaquarium.com
Transport: Bus B.
Opening hours: Daily 0930–1800.
Admission: US$24.95 (concessions available).

Coconut Grove

Located on the edge of Biscayne Bay, *Coconut Grove* is one of the city's oldest neighbourhoods, with bohemian roots. Settled by a multicultural group of

Photo: Greater Miami Convention and Visitors Bureau

Bahamians and New Englanders, the neighbourhood drew artists and intellectuals, who set up summer homes here. Today, it is a trendy district with a bustling village atmosphere, full of colourful galleries, theatres, nightclubs, fine restaurants, hip sidewalk cafés and shops. The main attraction is *Coco Walk*, a stylish shopping mall packed with restaurants, bars, shops and a cinema. It is also home to the *Vizcaya Museum and Gardens* (see *Further Distractions*).

Biscayne Bay, south of downtown Miami
Transport: Metrorail Coconut Grove.
Coco Walk
3015 Grand Avenue
Tel: (305) 444 0777.
Website: www.cocowalk.com
Opening hours: Sun–Thurs 1100–2200, Fri and Sat 1100–2400 (bars and restaurants until 0200).
Admission: Free.

Coral Gables

This elegant Mediterranean-style residential district was created by local developer George Merrick, during the boom years of the 1920s. Today, it contains some of the city's finest architecture, set amid broad boulevards, canals and parkland. Some buildings are preserved as historic landmarks, including the stunning *Biltmore Hotel*, identified by its 15-storey tower modelled on the Giralda bell-tower in Seville. The remarkable *Venetian Pool*, transformed from a mere rock quarry in 1923, has exotic bridges and waterfalls and was the site of many high-society soirées and beauty pageants in its time, as the vintage on-site photographs reveal. Today, it is the only swimming pool on the National Register of Historic Places. *Coral Gables* is also known for its art galleries, its exclusive *Miracle Mile* shopping street, its neatly manicured golf courses and some of the best hotels and restaurants in town.

Sixteen kilometres (ten miles) southwest of downtown Miami
Transport: Metrorail Douglas Road, then bus 42, 72 or J.
Biltmore Hotel
1200 Anastasia Avenue
Tel: (305) 445 1926. Fax: (305) 913 3152.
Website: www.biltmorehotel.com
Venetian Pool
2701 De Soto Boulevard
Tel: (305) 460 5356.
Website: www.venetianpool.com
Opening hours: Mon–Fri 1100–1930, Sat and Sun 1000–1630 (Jun–Aug); Mon–Thurs 1100–1730, Sat and Sun 1000–1630 (Sep, Oct, Apr and May); Tues–Sun 1000–1630 (Nov–Mar).
Admission: US$9 (Apr–Oct); US$6 (Nov–Mar).

Historical Museum of Southern Florida

This museum offers a fascinating insight into the region's past. It has a small but impressive collection of hands-on displays, archive material, historical objects and multimedia presentations, which covers 10,000 years of Florida history from the first settlers to the present day.

Miami-Dade Cultural Center, 101 West Flagler Street, downtown Miami
Tel: (305) 375 1492. Fax: (305) 375 1609.
E-mail: hasf@historical-museum.org
Website: www.historical-museum.org
Transport: Metrorail Government Center.
Opening hours: Mon, Tues, Wed, Fri and Sat 1000–1700, Thurs 1000–2100, Sun 1200–1700.
Admission: US$5 (concessions available).

Miami Museum of Science and Space Transit Planetarium

The nationally renowned *Miami Museum of Science and Space Transit Planetarium*, associated with the Smithsonian Institute, features interactive scientific exhibits on physics, electricity, light, sound and anatomy, as well as daily astronomy and laser shows in the adjacent planetarium. It also has South Florida's largest natural history collection and a wildlife centre that rehabilitates injured birds of prey and reptiles and displays more than 175 live animals.

3280 South Miami Avenue, Coconut Grove
Tel: (305) 845 4247 (museum) *or* 2222 (planetarium).
Fax: (305) 285 5801.
Website: www.miamisci.org
Transport: Bus 48; Metrorail Vizcaya.
Opening hours: Daily 1000–1800 (last entry 1700).
Admission: US$10 (concessions available).

Wolfsonian Museum

An eccentric world-traveller and Miami native founded the outstanding *Wolfsonian Museum*, affiliated with the Florida International University, from his own collection of modern design and 'propaganda arts'. One-of-a-kind exhibits address 19th- and 20th-century political themes, displaying the arts and crafts that were created to persuade, nationalise or rally citizens. The gift shop sells high-design home decor objects and lovely art books.

1001 Washington Avenue, South Beach
Tel: (305) 531 1001.
Website: www.wolfsonian.fiu.edu
Transport: Bus J; Electrowave trolley.
Opening hours: Mon, Tues, Fri and Sat 1100–1800, Thurs 1100–2100, Sun 1200–1700.
Admission: US$5.

Art Museums

The *Miami Art Museum* (*MAM*) displays international contemporary art since World War II, complemented by art from other periods to provide historical perspective. The museum is located in the new Philip Johnson-designed Cultural Center, which houses several art institutions. The permanent exhibits of the *Bass Museum* focus on European works from the 15th to 18th centuries. A new wing, designed by Japanese architect Arata Isozaki, also has an outdoor sculpture garden.

Miami Art Museum
Miami-Dade Cultural Center, 101 West Flagler Street, downtown Miami
Tel: (305) 375 3000. Fax: (305) 375 1725.
Website: www.miamiartmuseum.org
Transport: Metrorail Government Center.
Opening hours: Tues–Fri 1000–1700, Sat and Sun 1200–1700; third Thurs of the month 1000–2100.
Admission: US$5; concessions available; free on Sun and second Sat of the month.
Bass Museum
2121 Park Avenue, at 21st Street, Miami Beach
Tel: (305) 673 7530.
Website: www.bassmuseum.org
Transport: Bus J.
Opening hours: Tues, Wed, Fri and Sat 1000–1700, Thurs 1000–2100, Sun 1100–1700.
Admission: US$6 (concessions available).

Zoos

Miami MetroZoo, situated just south of Miami, is a state-of-the-art cageless zoo, with over 700 animals of 240 species roaming the 116-hectare (290-acre) grounds, separated from spectators by moats. Wildlife shows, a petting zoo, tram tours, monorail, gift shops, food courts and a playground provide fun for all the family. MetroZoo has also won a number of awards for its successful breeding of rare and endangered animal species.

At *Monkey Jungle*, the humans are kept in caged walkways while the primates roam freely. Here, visitors can see North America's first colony of wild monkeys, crab-eating monkeys diving for treats and hundreds of other exotic primates in lush, tropical jungle surroundings.

Bass Museum

Photo: Greater Miami Convention and Visitors Bureau

Photo: Greater Miami Convention and Visitors Bureau

Gator, Everglades National Park

The relocated *Parrot Jungle and Gardens*, now on its own island between Miami and Miami Beach (opened in June 2003), is a unique bird sanctuary-cum-botanical garden with more than 1100 birds and 100 plant varieties, together with alligators, giant tortoises and apes. Spectacular trained bird shows run throughout the day and children can help hand-feed the birds, hold one of the free-flying macaws or play with the animals at the petting zoo.
Miami MetroZoo
12400 Coral Reef Drive, at SW 152nd Street, Richmond Heights
Tel: (305) 251 0400. Fax: (305) 378 6381.
Website: www.magni.com/metrozoo
Transport: Metrorail Dadeland South; then Metrobus Coral Reef MAX to Miami Metrozoo.
Opening hours: Daily 0930–1730 (last entry at 1600).
Admission: US$8 (concessions available).
Monkey Jungle
14805 SW 216th Street
Tel: (305) 235 1611. Fax: (305) 235 4253.
Website: www.monkeyjungle.com
Transport: Bus 35 to Cutler Ridge Mall.
Opening hours: Daily 0930–1700 (last entry at 1600).
Admission: US$15.50 (concessions available).
Parrot Jungle and Gardens
Watson Island
Tel: (305) 666 7834. Fax: (305) 661 2230.
Website: www.parrotjungle.com
Transport: By car off I-395 MacArthur Causeway; no public transport currently available.
Opening hours: Daily 0930–1800 (last entry at 1700).
Admission: US$15.95 (concessions available).

Further Distractions

Fairchild Tropical Garden

This magnificent 33-hectare (83-acre) botanical garden is located just south of Coconut Grove. It contains extensive collections of rare tropical plants, a 1440 sq-metre (16,000 sq-ft) conservatory, 11 lakes and lily ponds and a rainforest exhibit, set among a waterfall and stream.
10901 Old Cutler Road, Coral Gables
Tel: (305) 667 1651. Fax: (305) 661 8953.
Website: www.fairchildgarden.org
Transport: Bus 65.
Opening hours: Daily 0930–1630.
Admission: US$8 (concessions available).

Vizcaya Museum and Gardens

Vizcaya is a beautiful Italian Renaissance-style palace set in four hectares (ten acres) of picturesque formal gardens, situated south of downtown Miami on Biscayne Bay. Built in 1916, as a winter residence for the Chicago industrialist James Deering, the mansion is modelled on neo-classical designs and its 70 rooms are filled with antique furnishings spanning the 15th to 19th centuries. Tours are available.
3251 South Miami Avenue, Coconut Grove
Tel: (305) 250 9133. Fax: (305) 285 2004.
Website: www.vizcayamuseum.com
Transport: Metrorail Vizcaya.
Opening hours: Daily 0930–1700 (museum); daily 0930–1730 (gardens); last entry at 1630.
Admission: US$10 (concessions available).

Tours of the City

Walking Tours

The *Miami Design Preservation League* (tel: (305) 672 2014; website: www.mdpl.org) conducts 90-minute walking tours of South Beach's Art Deco Historic District twice a week (Saturday at 1030 and Thursday at 1830), departing from its Art Deco Welcome Center, 1001 Ocean Drive, and costing US$15. Self-guided audio tours, lasting 45 minutes, are available daily and cost US$10.

Bus Tours

Dragonfly Expeditions (tel: (305) 774 9019) and *Dade Heritage Trust*, 190 SE 12th Terrace (tel: (305) 358 9572; fax: (305) 358 1162; website: www.dadeheritagetrust.org), operate the 'Miami Magic City Bus Tour', which takes in the city's most famous and historic neighbourhoods in a three- to four-hour tour costing US$40.

Bicycle Tours

The *Miami Beach Bicycle Center*, 601 Fifth Street (tel: (305) 674 0150), organises two-hour bicycle tours of South Beach and the Art Deco Historic District. These depart from the Bicycle Center, on the first and third Sunday of the month, at 1030, and cost US$15, which includes bicycle hire (reservations are essential).

Boat Tours

Island Queen Cruises, Bayside Marketplace, 401 Biscayne Boulevard (tel: (305) 379 5119; website: www.islandqueencruises.com), tour Miami Bay in one and a half hours, travelling past the Port and exclusive Millionaire's Row – home to such celebrities as Gloria Estefan, the Bee Gees, Oprah Winfrey, Boris Becker, Paul Newman and Whitney Houston. The tours depart from Bayside Marketplace daily every hour on the hour 1100–1900 and cost US$15 (concessions available).

Excursions

For a Half Day

Fort Lauderdale: Only 40km (25 miles) north of Miami, this smart east coast resort and international yachting centre is often described as the 'Venice of America' because of its many canals and waterways. It is easily accessible by train from Miami railway station but really has so much to recommend it that a full day could happily be passed here. It boasts magnificent sandy beaches, as well as excellent shopping and nightlife. Attractions include the contemporary collections of the *Museum of Art*, the *Museum of Discovery and Science* and the spectacular *Hugh Taylor Birch State Park and Recreation Area*. The *Greater Fort Lauderdale Convention & Visitors Bureau*, Suite 303, 1850 Eller Drive (tel: (954) 765 4466; fax: (954) 765 4467; website: www.sunny.org), can provide further information.

For a Whole Day

Everglades: South of Miami, the *Everglades National Park* is the second largest national park in America, with its 6070sq kilometres (2344sq miles) of marshes, mangrove forests, freshwater and saltwater areas and open grass prairies. Gator-spotting is one of the main attractions in this vast subtropical wilderness, which is also home to an abundance of rare plants, birds and animals – including wild orchids, Florida panthers, ospreys, manatees, giant loggerhead turtles, the Everglades mink, the Florida black bear and the only saltwater crocodiles in America. There are several entry points, each with Visitor Centers that organise ranger-led walks and talks, boat and tram tours, as well as canoe trails. The main *Visitor Center* (tel: (305) 242 7700; fax: (305) 242 7728; website: www.nps.gov/ever) is just southwest of Homestead, south on the Florida Turnpike (Route 821) until it merges with US-1 at Florida City, where drivers should turn right onto Palm Drive (State Road 9336/SW 344th Street) and follow the signposts. The park is open 24 hours a day, all year round. The Visitor Centers are open daily 0800–1700. Admission costs US$10 per vehicle.
The Keys: This chain of small coral-and-limestone islands ('keys') south of Miami, stretches 180km (113 miles) out across Florida Bay and is linked by just one highway, the US-1. The keys have a unique atmosphere – more slow Caribbean than fast-paced American – and offer some of the best sport fishing, scuba diving, boating, swimming and snorkelling in the world. Further information is available from the *Florida Keys and Key West Visitor's Bureau*, 402 Wall Street, Key West (tel: (305) 294 2587; website: www.fla-keys.com).
The most visited island in the Keys, *Key West*, is at the southernmost point of Continental USA, just 144km (90 miles) north of Cuba. This five-kilometre-long (3.5-mile) sandbar is renowned for its sunset celebrations, its key lime pie, its sizeable gay community and for being the home of Ernest Hemingway (see *Culture*). The *Key West Information Center*, 1601 North Roosevelt Boulevard, Key West (tel: (305) 292 5000; e-mail: info@keywestinfo.com; website: www.keywestinfo.com), can provide further information.

ACCOMMODATION

All hotel bills will have a consumer tax of 6.5% added at the end, as well as a special tax levied on hotels by most municipalities, which varies from 9.5% to 12.5% depending on the district.

On top of this, it is normal to tip porters (around US$1 a bag), valet parkers (US$2) and housekeepers (US$2–5 per night).

The prices quoted below are the lowest standard rates for a double room, excluding all taxes and excluding breakfast, unless otherwise specified.

Business

JW Marriott Hotel Miami

Distinguishing itself from others in the Marriott chain, this 22-storey business hotel brings an upscale feel to Miami's downtown Financial District. The hotel features 300 elegantly furnished guest rooms and luxurious suites, three executive-level floors and a 24-hour business centre. Expansive conference facilities contain state-of-the-art audiovisual, teleconferencing, video-conferencing and Internet capabilities. The top-notch restaurant, the *Trapiche Room*, and the *Spa 1111* go beyond standard. Health club facilities and an inviting tropical outdoor swimming pool provide the perfect opportunity for busy executives to relax and unwind at the start or end of the day.
1109 Brickell Avenue, Brickell Village
Tel: (305) 374 1124. Fax: (305) 374 4211.
Website: www.marriotthotels.com/miajw
Price: From US$240.

Mandarin Oriental Miami

Situated in one of Miami's most prestigious commercial districts, this five-star waterfront hotel is also convenient for the major shopping and nightlife centres of Bayside and Coconut Grove, making it the ideal choice for both business and leisure travellers. Business executives will want for nothing here, with facilities including Internet access from the 329 palatial guest rooms, 12 multiple-sized function and meeting rooms, a 24-hour business centre offering all the latest technology and secretarial services, a first-class restaurant, *Azul*, and a sophisticated cocktail bar. But it is also easy to combine work with pleasure here, thanks to the tennis courts, gorgeous swimming pool and luxury health spa.
500 Brickell Key Drive, Brickell Key
Tel: (305) 913 8288. Fax: (305) 913 8300.
E-mail: momia-reserve@mohg.com
Website: www.mandarinoriental.com
Price: From US$350 (including breakfast).

Marlin

At the heart of Miami Beach's celebrated Art Deco Historic district, this candy-coloured boutique hotel, just one block away from the ocean, is a veritable gem, attracting celebrities, entertainment executives, trendy business clientele and others in the know. Each of the 12 suites contains a state-of-the-art entertainment centre, two-line cordless telephones, web-TV with Internet access and private e-mail addresses for every guest, CD players and CD library. All have kitchenettes. Special massage, aromatherapy and 'energy management' treatments provide the perfect antidote for stressed-out business executives. The *Marlin* is also home to the South Beach Studios, drawing artists such as Aerosmith, U2 and Grace Jones, and enjoys a reputation as the 'rock'n'roll hotel of South Beach'.

1200 Collins Avenue, Miami Beach
Tel: (305) 604 5063. Fax: (305) 673 9609.
E-mail: reservations@islandoutpost.com
Website: www.islandoutpost.com
Price: From US$210 (including breakfast).

Luxury

The Biltmore Hotel

When *The Biltmore Hotel* first opened in 1926, it was advertised as 'the last word in civilisation'. Today, this gigantic hotel in fashionable, prosperous Coral Gables still remains one of Miami's finest, upholding all the high standards of old-fashioned hospitality, craftsmanship and style, with handpainted ceilings, magnificent crystal chandeliers, Italian marble floors and Spanish ceramics. The grand edifice, with its imposing 15-storey tower, modelled on Seville's splendid Giralda bell-tower, is registered as a National Historic Landmark. Inside, there are 280 luxuriously appointed bedrooms and suites, a fitness centre and spa, while outside there are ten tennis courts, an 18-hole golf course and the largest hotel swimming pool in the entire continental United States. The excellent French restaurant, *Palme D'Or*, draws diners from far and wide.
1200 Anastasia Avenue, Coral Gables
Tel: (305) 445 1926. Fax: (305) 913 3159.
Website: www.biltmorehotel.com
Price: From US$259.

Delano Hotel

Considered one of America's coolest hotels and *the* place to stay in Miami, the *Delano* is the choice of celebrities and style-conscious travellers. (James Bond's *Goldfinger* movie was filmed at this impressive Art Deco building on South Beach with its distinctive winged tower.) The interiors, designed by Philippe Starck, are strikingly chic, minimalist and predominantly white. Even the narrow ground-floor hallway, which leads from Collins Avenue to the infinity pool out back, is flanked with tall, gauzy white linens, creating a dreamscape and catwalk in one. The 'beautiful people' come here for modern yet small bedrooms and penthouse beauty spa *Agua*. The poolside *Blue Door* restaurant (see *Restaurants*) and back gardens are adjacent to a lovely stretch of beach, complete with towel service, umbrellas and chairs.
1685 Collins Avenue, Miami Beach
Tel: (305) 672 2000. Fax: (305) 673 0888.
Website: www.ianschragerhotels.com
Price: From US$350.

The Hotel

Marking the merger between architectural preservation and interior prettification, this gorgeous property – built in 1939 – was given an interior makeover by American fashion designer Todd Oldham, in 1998. In the 52 deluxe rooms and suites are blonde-wood beds, bold blue linens, bejewelled drawer pulls, plus perks such as Kiehl's bathroom products. Tiled washbasins with stainless steel sinks and enormous showers with rainforest showerheads justify lingering. The rooftop pool with panoramic ocean views draws envious visitors from other hotels, as does *Wish* (see *Restaurants*), the hotel's restaurant. Both are proof that *The Hotel* is anything but as bland as its name.

Bayside

801 Collins Avenue, Miami Beach
Tel: (305) 531 2222 *or* (877) 843 4683 (for reservations).
Fax: (305) 531 3222.
E-mail: info@thehotelofsouthbeach.com
Website: www.thehotelofsouthbeach.com
Price: From US$275.

Moderate

Kent

One of very few affordable yet trendy Art Deco retreats in the celebrated South Beach district, the *Kent* is also perfectly placed for the ocean, the Miami Beach Convention Center and some of the city's hottest shops, sidewalk cafés and nightspots. The hip lobby, with its brightly coloured cube-shaped furniture, e-mail station and breakfast bar, sets the tone for the uber-modern bedrooms, which are decked out with all mod cons – smart stainless steel accessories, cable TV/VCR, radio and CD players. Most of the 50-odd rooms are funky but the third-floor 'Lucite Suite' is perhaps over the top, as practically every furnishing, from bed to tables, is made from translucent plastic. Business services are available upon request and there is even an attractive garden patio.
1131 Collins Avenue, Miami Beach
Tel: (305) 604 5068. Fax: (305) 531 0720.
E-mail: reservations@islandoutpost.com
Website: www.islandoutpost.com
Price: From US$130 (including breakfast).

Miami River Inn

This famous bed and breakfast inn is listed on the National Register of Historic Places. Built in 1906, it is not only the city's oldest hotel but also one of Miami's best-kept secrets – quiet, atmospheric and set in a charming garden in the heart of downtown Miami. The bedrooms are comfortable and homely, with highly polished hardwood floors and antique furnishings, and the delicious breakfast (including home-baked muffins and freshly squeezed Florida orange juice) is served in the rooms or in the shaded courtyard. Despite Miami's many attractions, guests staying here are often found relaxing by the small pool or on the verandah simply watching cargo ships ply the Miami River.
118 SW South River Drive, Little Havana
Tel: (305) 325 0045. Fax: (305) 325 9227.
E-mail: info@miamiriverinn.com
Website: www.miamiriverinn.com
Price: From US$69 (including breakfast).

Other Recommendations

Claridge Hotel

This spectacularly refurbished boutique hotel dating from 1928 is located just 20 minutes from Miami International Airport, ten minutes from the main business district and a stone's throw from Ocean Drive in Miami Beach, yet far enough away from the crowds to be exclusive. The bright, cheerful guest rooms are situated around an elegant interior courtyard atrium. Global design motifs appear throughout, from Peruvian artwork to European furnishings, together with such state-of-the-art amenities as in-room fax machines, dual-line telephones and modem points with high-speed Internet access. Further facilities include a variety of meeting spaces, an acclaimed restaurant specialising in Mediterranean cuisine and Miami's only in-lobby splash spa.
3500 Collins Avenue, Miami Beach
Tel: (305) 604 8485. Fax: (305) 674 0881.
E-mail: reservations@claridgefl.com
Website: www.claridgefl.com
Price: From US$175.

Tides

Minimalist without being entirely white, this chic hotel offers genuine and sophisticated style, with a sumptuous interior decorated in soft tones of white, taupe and sand. The 45 spacious suites all have incredible views of the beach and the Atlantic and contain complete entertainment centres and three two-line telephones and modem points. Telescopes in every room are a clever bonus (the ultimate tool for people-watching), as are other creative touches, like in-room chalk boards and carefully chosen furnishings. The swimming pool on the Mezzanine Terrace attracts many guests. But not as many as the hip lobby bar and alfresco restaurant, *1220* (see *Restaurants*), overlooking Ocean Drive, the steeped terrace of which is *the* place to see and be seen.
1220 Ocean Drive, South Beach
Tel: (305) 604 5070. Fax: (305) 604 5180.
E-mail: reservations@islandoutpost.com
Website: www.islandoutpost.com
Price: From US$395.

RESTAURANTS

Miami boasts a huge range of restaurants catering to all tastes and pockets. The selected restaurants have been divided into five categories: Gastronomic, Business, Trendy, Budget and Personal Recommendations. The restaurants are listed alphabetically within these different categories, which serve as guidelines rather than absolute definitions of the establishments.
As well as a 6.5% state sales tax, most municipalities levy special taxes on restaurants, which vary from 9.5% to 12.5% according to district. These taxes are not included in menu prices but are added to the bill at the end. A few places also include a service charge in the bill but this is not common. It is normal to leave a tip of 15–20% for service.
The prices quoted below are for an average three-course meal for one person and for a bottle of house wine or cheapest equivalent; they do not include taxes, service charge or tip.

Gastronomic

Blue Door at the Delano

A creative culinary duo, Claude Troisgrois and Elizabeth Barlow, meld tropical and Asian ingredients with French technique and yield remarkable meals. The stylish and sumptuous setting in the Delano Hotel means guests can be seated next to celebs, also here for the well-crafted, seasonal dishes. Examples include the Big Ravioli, filled with crab and scallop mousseline and a fantastic lunchtime Cobb salad, in which the ingredients, each in its own little row, are plated with fanatical detail. Indoor seating is possible but the outdoor dining terrace overlooks the long grassy 'orchard', with private cabanas, beyond which is the pool. Reservations recommended.
Delano Hotel, 1685 Collins Avenue, South Beach
Tel: (305) 674 6400.
Website: www.ianschragerhotels.com
Price: US$75. Wine: US$40.

Chef Allen's

Chef Allen's is an ideal restaurant for a special occasion. Chef-owner Allen Susser is counted among America's most respected chefs, celebrated for his innovative New World and 'Floribbean' cuisine. The stylish Art Deco restaurant, with its contemporary artwork, fresh flowers and pink neon lighting, surrounds a glass-enclosed kitchen. Here, diners can watch Allen create masterpieces from his nightly changing menu, such as Bahamian lobster and crab cakes with strawberry ginger

Photo: Greater Miami Convention and Visitors Bureau

Alfresco dining

chutney or tamarind chilli BBQ dry-aged prime sirloin steak with smoked onion mashed potato and mango ketchup. Reservations recommended. No lunch.
19088 North East 29th Avenue, Aventura
Tel: (305) 935 2900. Fax: (305) 935 2900.
E-mail: reservations@chefallens.com
Website: www.chefallens.com
Price: US$65. Wine: US$28.

Norman's

One of America's most celebrated chefs, Norman Van Aken, is considered by many to be the originator of 'New World cuisine' – a blend of Latin, Caribbean, Asian and American cooking; his restaurant is one of Florida's finest. Among the menu highlights are the starter of yucca-stuffed crispy shrimp with a sour-orange mojo or the main of escabeche spiced Chilean sea bass on a boniato-conch hash cake with grilled scallions, salsa romesco and 'mojo-bayon'. All the exquisite dishes are served from an open kitchen in ultra-modern surroundings to a chic clientele of food aficionados. Reservations recommended.
21 Almeria Avenue, Coral Gables
Tel: (305) 446 6767. Fax: (305) 446 7909.
E-mail: comments@norman.com
Website: www.normans.com
Price: US$65. Wine: US$28.

Pacific Time

From the open kitchen, star-chef Jonathan Eismann prepares innovative and intensely flavoured Asian-American and Pacific Rim dishes, such as seared beef salad, tamarind barbecued salmon and sweet sake-roasted sea bass. Each dish from the predominantly seafood menu is a work of art. The elegant, airy Lincoln Road restaurant with cosy banquettes is packed nightly with a trendy, appreciative crowd. Reservations recommended. No lunch.
915 Lincoln Road, South Beach
Tel: (305) 534 5979. Fax: (305) 534 1607.
Price: US$65. Wine: US$27.

Pascal's on Ponce

While other chefs are busy vying for a place among the trendy, chef-proprietor Pascal Oudin sticks to cooking substantive French fare, such as sautéed sea bass wrapped in a crispy potato crust with braised leeks or tenderloin of beef sautéed with snails and wild mushrooms. The desserts are not to be missed. The restaurant's long-standing accolades are created by the food and enhanced by the small, simply appointed dining room, with its quiet atmosphere and serious table service. Reservations recommended.
2611 Ponce de León Boulevard, Coral Gables
Tel: (305) 444 2024. Fax: (305) 444 9798.
Price: US$40. Wine: US$25.

Business

Caffe Abbracci

Thanks to the upscale cuisine, the efficient but discreet service and the elegant Art Deco-style setting with modern wood and marble, crisp white linens and fresh flowers, the *Abbracci* is a favourite choice for business entertaining. The menu focuses on specialities, such as mouthwatering antipasti, homemade pastas, risottos and carpaccios, as well as a knock-out tiramisu for dessert. Reservations recommended. No lunch weekends.
318 Aragon Avenue, Coral Gables
Tel: (305) 441 0700. Fax: (305) 442 0061.
Price: US$35. Wine: US$22.

Downtown Miami

Photo: Greater Miami Convention and Visitors Bureau

Capital Grille

This upscale, New York-style steakhouse is a popular restaurant for power lunches and dinners and is conveniently located in the heart of the Financial District of downtown Miami. Specialities include dry-aged beef and succulent seafood, while the service is notoriously formal. There is live music in the evenings from Tuesday to Saturday.
444 Brickell Avenue, Brickell Village
Tel: (305) 374 4500. Fax: (305) 374 2777.
Price: US$60. Wine: US$35.

China Grill

The name is misleading. There are no mini pagodas and Chinese dragons on the walls here, as this buzzing, atmospheric restaurant specialises in 'world cuisine', combining ingredients, flavours and techniques from around the globe. Menu highlights include irresistible treats like the crispy duck with caramelised black vinegar sauce or the seared tuna sashimi with a spicy Japanese pepper rim. It is especially popular for business lunches and with the 'beautiful people' of South Beach. Reservations recommended.
404 Washington Avenue, South Beach
Tel: (305) 534 2211. Fax: (305) 534 2565.
Price: US$55. Wine: US$33.

Fishbone Grille

Centrally located in the main business district and ideal for an inexpensive working lunch, this fishmonger-cum-restaurant is acknowledged as one of Miami's best-value seafood joints, serving fresh grouper, snapper, Florida spiny lobster, bay scallops and other local catch prepared almost every possible way. The fantastically popular jalepeño cornbread is known throughout the city. The restaurant atmosphere is warm, funky even, the service has a light touch and the spectacular daily specials are as reliable as the tide. Reservations recommended at weekends.
650 South Miami Avenue, downtown Miami
Tel: (305) 530 1915. Fax: (305) 379 2545.
Price: US$30. Wine: US$15.

The Forge

With its elegant 19th-century façade, plush oak-panelled dining rooms, Tiffany chandeliers and haute cuisine, this veritable institution has catered for the stylish Miami Beach crowd since its opening in 1968. *The Forge* is best known for its succulent steaks but the menu also features a wide variety of Continental seafood and chicken dishes. It also boasts one of Miami's most extensive wine cellars. Reservations recommended. No lunch.
432 Arthur Godfrey Road (41st Street), Miami Beach
Tel: (305) 538 8533. Fax: (305) 538 7733.
Price: US$60. Wine: US$25.

Trendy

1220

Located at the glamorous *Tides* hotel, this beautiful, minimalist restaurant is decorated almost entirely in white, with crisp linens, candles and fresh flowers on all the indoor and outdoor tables. Lighting up the minimalist surroundings is Chef Roger Ruch's 'progressive American' cuisine – nearly every dish is a culinary fireworks display, drawing from a palette of global ingredients. Unfathomably good is the trio of tuna, salmon, and smoked marlin tartares appetizer topped with a quail's egg. Ruch's signature dishes – such as the Colossal Pacific Shrimp with pigeon pea ragout and red pepper-ginger velouté – remind one of the thoughtful possibilities of fusion fare. Save room for the Chocolate Lava Soufflé, although the fruit evident in the Key Lime Cannoli with mango ginger sorbet and the Baked Banana Cobbler has never been elevated to such a scrumptious level.
Tides, 1220 Ocean Drive, South Beach
Tel: (305) 604 5130. Fax: (305) 604 5180.
Website: www.islandoutpost.com
Price: US$70. Wine: US$30.

Café Tu Tu Tango

This hugely popular café-restaurant, at the heart of the action in Coconut Grove, is decorated to resemble an artist's loft in Spain, with dozens of original paintings on the walls. Diners lounge in comfy armchairs or at sturdy wooden tables, entertained by artists poised at easels, strolling musicians and magicians, while chefs at three open kitchens prepare an adventurous menu of hot and cold tapas-style dishes. The choice is bewildering, ranging from pizzas, kebabs, BBQ wings and ribs to specialities such as alligator bites, hurricane shrimp fritters and Cajun chicken egg rolls, all washed down with a jug of sangria, 'Matisse Margarita' or 'Picasso Punch'. Reservations are not accepted.

Ocean Drive

CocoWalk, 3015 Grand Avenue, Coconut Grove
Tel: (305) 529 2222. Fax: (305) 461 5326.
Website: www.cafetututango.com
Price: US$5–8 (per dish). Wine: US$19.

Larios on the Beach

Owned by local heroine, Gloria Estefan, this chic, minimalist café-style restaurant serves *nuevo* (lighter) Cuban cuisine to a trendy crowd of Ocean Drive strollers and strutters, with funky Latin music and lethal *mojitos* (fresh mint, white rum and sugar). Diners enjoy *fabada asturiana* (black bean and sausage soup) or *camarones al ajillo* (shrimp in garlic sauce) on the pavement terrace – one of the best locations in South Beach to see and be seen.
820 Ocean Drive, South Beach
Tel: (305) 532 9577. Fax: (305) 531 5725.
Price: US$30. Wine: US$18.

Tantra

A grassy floor in the entryway and lounge leads into a dining room that appeals to the five senses – touch the velvety throw pillows in the banquettes, smell the incense burning in large lanterns, hear the Middle Eastern music, see someone swinging in the rope hammock and taste Willis Loughhead's delectable cuisine. The forward-thinking dishes are decadent, fusing seafood, chicken or meats with Asian

ingredients, for example, 'ginger kissed' salmon or seared tuna and foie gras over diced Asian pear. At night, the place is packed with members of the stylish set, sipping cocktails and grooving to the DJ. Reservations recommended. No lunch weekends.
1445 Pennsylvania Avenue, South Beach
Tel: (305) 672 4765.
Website: www.tantrarestaurant.com
Price: US$65. Wine: US$25.

Wish

Wish is one of South Beach's culinary hotspots – even considering that it is no longer a newcomer. Located in *The Hotel* – an Art Deco boutique hotel with interiors by fashion designer Todd Oldham – the dining area sprawls mostly into the lush outdoors, with enormous white umbrellas for daytime and globes of lights in the palm trees for night-time dining. Wish's chef, E Michael Reidt, was featured on the cover of *Food & Wine* magazine as one of 'America's Ten Best New Chefs' (July 2001) and is lauded for his innovative Brazilian-French cuisine. Outstanding dishes include Aborio-crusted oysters, cachaça-marinated tuna with seared watermelon (cachaça is a Brazilian spirit made from sugar cane), and pan-seared sea scallops with foie gras emulsion. Diners should not pass on the electric cocktails, such as the green apple martini, powered by a glowing ice cube.
The Hotel, 801 Collins Avenue, South Beach
Tel: (305) 674 9474. Fax: (305) 695 9539.
E-mail: info@thehotelofsouthbeach.com
Website: www.wishrestaurant.com
Price: US$70. Wine: US$30.

Budget

Farolito

Locals love this intimate Peruvian venue, with hearty representative dishes in a low-key storefront space. Typical ingredients include starchy pasta, potatoes and beef, with a few ceviche and seafood choices added into the mix. The potatoes with a white cheese sauce and olives give diners a great impression of what wonders can be done with a spud. More elaborate meals include chicken in garlicky walnut-cream sauce. The prices are also very palatable.
2885 Coral Way, Little Havana
Tel: (305) 446 4122.
Price: US$20. Bottle of beer: From US$3.

Johnny Rockets

The pastel-coloured Art Deco buildings of South Beach provide a suitably light-hearted backdrop for *Johnny Rockets* diner, one of the most popular breakfast venues in the district. Its sensational cooked breakfasts are served on the pavement terrace, in full view of all the film-star wannabes, supermodels, tourists, joggers and rollerbladers cruising on Ocean Drive. For the rest of the day, this classic diner, decked out with old jukeboxes and a Harley Davidson, serves old-time favourites – hamburgers, hot dogs, salads and club sandwiches – along with milkshakes, ice cream sodas and hot fudge sundaes.
728 Ocean Drive, South Beach
Tel: (305) 538 2115. Fax: (305) 538 2567.
Website: www.johnnyrockets.com
Price: US$18. Bottle of beer: From US$3.99.

News Café

A cult address – it is the place where Gianni Versace drank his last cup of coffee, shortly before he was murdered on his own doorstep, just two blocks away

– this trendy, European-style café of minimalist decor is one of South Beach's coolest hangouts. It is an ideal place to while away the hours – all 24 of them, in fact. The adjacent News Store is conveniently stocked with magazines and newspapers. The menu boasts everything from eggs Benedict to bagels and ice cream sundaes; there is also an excellent wine list. The signature 'News Cake' is a must for chocolate lovers.
800 Ocean Drive, South Beach
Tel: (305) 538 6397. Fax: (305) 531 0394.
Website: www.newscafe.com
Price: US$25. Wine: US$22.

Shorty's Bar-B-Q

Located in a log cabin in South Miami and decorated with mounted boar and caribou heads, saddles and cowboy hats, this barbecue house is a veritable institution. The informal, fun menu is served at long wooden picnic tables, with specialities including barbecued ribs and chicken – slow-cooked over hickory logs and smothered in Shorty's own spicy barbecue sauce – accompanied by tangy baked beans, corn on the cob, coleslaw and chilled, thirst-quenching beers.
9200 South Dixie Hwy, South Miami
Tel: (305) 670 7732. Fax: (305) 670 7733.
Website: www.shortys.com
Price: US$12. Pitcher of local beer: US$6.

Versailles

Versailles (pronounced with three syllables in these parts) serves simple, yet amazingly flavourful Cuban fare. This is one of Miami's most ornate budget restaurants, with tuxedoed waiters and an elaborate decor of mirrors, murals and chandeliers. The *sopa de platanos* (plantain soup) and *ropa vieja* (beef stew) are especially tasty, while the *café cubano* (a thimble-sized cup of exceedingly strong, sweet black coffee) is reputedly the strongest shot of caffeine in South Florida.
3555 SW Eighth Street, Little Havana
Tel: (305) 444 0240.
Price: US$20. Wine: US$14.

Personal Recommendations

Aria

The view is what makes a meal at *Aria* particularly memorable – whether from the alfresco tables of the beach or from the dining room into the 'exhibition kitchen'. However, the food would stand on its own without any view. Jeff Vigila's creative repertoire means that although dishes might seem familiar, they take on a whole new life in his kitchen. For example, the asparagus cappuccino with crab frittata and nutmeg foam. And sommelier Marita Leonard gives good advice on the best choice of wines to accompany them. Reservations recommended.
The Ritz-Carlton Hotel, 455 Grand Bay Drive, Key Biscayne
Tel: (305) 365 4500.
Price: US$55. Wine: US$30.

Big Pink

At the heart of the South Beach hustle, this upscale, modern diner and sports bar serves classic all-American fare to a young, hip crowd. Living up to its name, everything is pink – the bar stools, the lamps, the Plexiglas tables … even the menu, which consists predominantly of pizzas, burgers, pasta and salads, all served in hearty, value-for-money portions. The real speciality here, however, is the TV dinner at US$13.95

– a six-compartment metal tray loaded with satisfying comfort food.

157 Collins Avenue, Miami Beach

Tel: (305) 532 4700. Fax: (305) 532 4187.

E-mail: info@bigpinkrestaurant.com

Website: www.bigpinkrestaurant.com

Price: US$20. Wine: US$22.

Joe's Stone Crab

A meal at this venerable institution is undoubtedly one of Florida's most entertaining dining experiences, with its huge baskets of stone crab claws – Florida's tastiest seafood delicacy – boiled, cracked and served with melted butter, piquant mustard sauce, a cracking board, mallet and bib. Opened in 1913 as a simple shack and steeped in tradition, the restaurant has now grown to over a thousand covers – all non-smoking. No reservations are accepted and there are frequently long queues but the delicious fare – also including soups, steaks, salads and other seafood options – is well worth the wait. Closed mid May to mid October. No lunch Monday or Sunday.

11 Washington Avenue, Miami Beach

Tel: (305) 673 0365.

E-mail: QandA@joesstonecrab.com

Website: www.joesstonecrab.com

Price: US$55. Wine: US$22.

Metro Kitchen + Bar

The Hotel Astor restaurant has recently benefitted from a minimalist makeover – and a new menu to boot. The stunning wood-panelled yet airy restaurant has a partial atrium, with views of a small dining terrace. The cascades of a small waterfall here conceal any Washington Avenue noise. By teaming up with Nicola Siervo (of *Mynt* bar fame), restaurateur Karim Masri and Chef Rob Boone, have been filling their reservation book and, by the looks of things, with some pretty hip customers. The menu's cutesy subheadings (Raw and Marinated, Planted Seeds, Land and Sea) might not be in earnest but dishes like spicy octopus carpaccio and sea bass with French Horn mushrooms should be taken very seriously indeed.

Astor Hotel, 956 Washington Avenue, Miami Beach

Tel: (305) 674 6400. Fax: (305) 531 3193.

E-mail: info@hotelastor.com

Website: www.hotelastor.com

Price: US$50. Wine: US$36.

Nemo's

Not only does this ultra-chic restaurant count among America's best but it also represents the epitome of South Beach cool. Chef Michael Schwartz's eclectic menu blends Caribbean, Asian, Middle Eastern and Mediterranean influences with his seafood-oriented cooking, to produce signature dishes such as steamed Mediterranean mussels with tomato-harissa broth, sticky black rice and garlic chips. Other options include wok-charred salmon with four-sprout salad, toasted pumpkin seeds and soy-lime vinaigrette, and key lime and white chocolate cheesecake flan for dessert, served with a drunken tropical salsa. The bright colours of the jewel-studded restaurant create the perfect backdrop for the sophisticated cuisine, while the tree-shaded terrace tables offer a more relaxed seaside atmosphere.

100 Collins Avenue, South Beach

Tel: (305) 532 4550. Fax: (305) 532 4187.

Website: www.nemorestaurant.com

Price: US$55. Wine: US$21.

ENTERTAINMENT

Nightlife

Miami never sleeps. When the sun goes down, the stars come out. Celebrities from the entertainment world spend the balmy tropical evenings sipping martinis at hip lounges and open-air cafés, before hitting the pulsating dance clubs, the cool jazz bars and the countless salsa venues.

The main nightlife district is South Beach. Local celebrities Gloria Estefan and Ricky Martin both have restaurant-bars on Ocean Drive. South Beach's Art Deco buildings – neon-lit with vibrant yellows, blues, pinks and purples – provide a suitably light-hearted backdrop to a hedonistic nightlife. In the evenings, the bars are abuzz with a colourful, cosmopolitan crowd. After midnight, the whole of South Beach throbs to the international rhythms of its club scene, which offers some of the hottest nightlife in America.

Bars close around 0100 and nightclubs around 0600. The average price of a drink while out and about in Miami is US$8–12. The minimum age for admission to all clubs in Miami Beach (including South Beach) is 21 years, which is also the minimum drinking age in Florida; it is advisable to carry ID. Dress codes often require chic attire.

Check out the *New Times* (website: www.miaminewtimes.com) or the Friday section of the *Miami Herald* (website: www.miami.com/mld/miamiherald) for listings.

Bars

The local scene changes frequently; the following are some of the South Beach bars that are currently 'in'. The *Shore Club* hotel's unbelievably decadent indoor–outdoor *Skybar*, 1901 Collins Avenue, is a supremely exclusive spot with the inevitable queues. The setting, a bed-strewn lawn and private pillow-filled nooks surrounding a pool, is worth the wait. With its white egg-shaped chairs and orange lighting, the uber-retro *Pearl Restaurant & Champagne Lounge*, 1 Ocean Drive, amuses a gorgeous crowd with its *Barbarella*-inspired decor. With seemingly endless cache, *The Delano*, 1685 Collins Avenue, serves up fancy cocktails off the airy lobby of the perennially glamorous hotel of the same name. Sensual *Tantra*, 1445 Pennsylvania Avenue, sparked a genre of Miami resto-lounges, proffering a top-notch meal in an exotic setting (grass flooring and Turkish tobacco hookahs) that transforms into a nightclub (the DJ spins Middle Eastern fusion).

A cocktail at 1940s era bar at *The National* hotel, 1677 Collins Avenue, is a refined act and one dating back to 1939, when the wooden bar was installed. Have a martini and a peek at the pool. *Larios on the Beach*, 820 Ocean Drive, is owned by Gloria Estefan and serves lethal *mojitos* (fresh mint, sugar and rum cocktails) alongside nightly funky Cuban music. The *Clevelander Hotel's* legendary outdoor bar and dance club, 1020 Ocean Drive, is a hotspot among the randier 20-somethings. The *News Café*, 800 Ocean Drive, one of the Beach's people-watching hangouts (open 24 hours), was the venue for Gianni Versace's last drink.

Miami Beach Patrol

Photo: Greater Miami Convention and Visitors Bureau

Sunbathers

Casinos

The floating *Casino Princesa* (tel: (305) 379 5825; website: www.casinoprincesa.com) offers Las Vegas-style 'gaming cruises' for up to 600 passengers, with on-board blackjack, craps, roulette and slot machines. Four-and-a-half-hour trips (US$6) leave Bayside Harbour (adjacent to the Hard Rock Café), 315 Biscayne Boulevard. Departure times are daily at 1230 and 1930, and Friday to Sunday at 0100. Dress code is casual, the minimum age is 21 years and ID is required.

Clubs

Super-cool *Mynt*, 1921 Collins Avenue, with its anxiety inspiring door policy, teems with New York socialites, Hollywood actors, and Miami's hippest. Then it admits regular folks. *Nikki Beach Club*, 1 Ocean Drive, is right on the beach and has an indoor/outdoor dance floor and a young, supermodel crowd. Another hot South Beach spot is the *Casa Salsa*, 524 Ocean Drive, a restaurant-cum-dance club, owned by Latin heart-throb Ricky Martin, which moves to the sounds of Puerto Rico. The gay-friendly *Crobar*, 1445 Washington Avenue, has angels on bungee cords above the packed dance floor. Nelly and Queen Latifah have been spotted in *Level*, 1235 Washington Avenue, an old movie house and now a massive clubbing venue reminiscent of New York's Studio 54, while *Privé*, in the *Opium Garden* complex, 136 Collins Avenue, is a streamlined second-storey space with lots of private nooks. Big spenders and celebrities come to enjoy this open-air amphitheatre venue, including Enrique Iglesias and Missy Elliot. In Coconut Grove, try *Chili Pepper*, Streets of Mayfair Mall, 2911 Grand Avenue, one of a handful of dance clubs in the area.

Live Music

For the latest Latin rhythms, try *Café Nostalgia*, 432 41st Street, Miami Beach, which has a small dancefloor and a house band playing authentic salsa music. *La Covacha*, 10730 NW 25th Street, is one of the hottest places in Miami for salsa, merengue and

Latin hip hop, while the hugely popular *Mango's Tropical Café*, 900 Ocean Drive, has flamboyant South Beach salsa with dancing on the tables and in the street. At Miami Beach, the laid-back *Van Dyke Café*, 846 Lincoln Road, and the more upmarket jazz club, *Jazid*, 1342 Washington Avenue, both have live jazz and blues nightly.

Sport

Miami is an excellent city for spectator sports and all the American mainstays are popular in the city. Several major American teams hail from Miami, including basketball heroes, *Miami Heat* (website: www.nba.com/heat), who play at home between November and April, at the *American Airlines Arena*, 601 Biscayne Boulevard (tel: (305) 577 4328 *or* 960 8500; website: www.aaarena.com). Miami's top football team, the *Miami Dolphins* (website: www.dolphinsendzone.com), plays at the *Pro Player Stadium*, 2267 NW 199th Street (tel: (305) 623 6100), from August to December, as do baseball's *Florida Marlins* (website: www.flamarlins.com). Their season runs from April to September.

Tickets to sporting events can be purchased direct from the venues or from *Ticketmaster* (tel: (305) 358 5885; website: www.ticketmaster.com).

Beaches

The public stretch of South Beach from First Street to 15th Street is the wide, pristine sand that everyone refers to when they talk about Miami Beach. The *Third Street Beach* is popular with families, while the *12th Street Beach* area is the gay-friendly section. Toplessness among women on public beaches is common and regarded casually. The only beach where clothing is entirely optional is north of Bal Harbour, at *Haulover Beach Park*, in North Miami Beach. *Bill Baggs* is the most spectacular of Key Biscayne beaches but *Crandon Park* draws equal numbers of sun worshippers to its shores even though it is a bit of a walk from the parking area to the sand.

Diving

The *Biscayne National Underwater Park*, 9700 SW 328th Street, Homestead (tel: (305) 230 7275; website: www.nps.gov/bisc), with over 72,400 hectares (181,000 acres) of marine habitat and live coral reefs, is popular for diving, snorkelling and glass-bottom boat rides. PADI-registered *South Beach Divers*, 850 Washington Avenue (tel: (305) 531 6110; e-mail: info@southbeachdivers.com; website: www.southbeachdivers.com), offers lessons, equipment and daily diving trips.

Fishing

Deep-sea fishing day trips are operated by a variety of companies, including the six-person vessel, *Therapy-IV*, 10800 Collins Avenue, Miami Beach (tel: (305) 945 1578; website: www.therapy4.com), which starts at US$90 per person. *Reward Fishing Fleet*, Miami Beach Marina, off the MacArthur Causeway (tel: (305) 372 9470; website: www.fishingmiami.com), includes all the necessary equipment. Rates start at US$30 per person.

Fitness Centres

Many hotels in body-conscious Miami provide some type of fitness centre. American fitness centre chains have several branches around Greater Miami and sell daily passes, which start at around US$25. *Crunch Fitness*, 1259 Washington Avenue (tel: (305) 674 8222), offers an array of aerobic, yoga and fitness classes. *Gold's Gym*, 1400 Alton Road, South Beach (tel: (305) 538 4653), has a serious weight-training focus. Local gyms, such as *Club Body Tech*, 1253 Washington Avenue (tel: (305) 674 8222), have less expensive rates. Day spas are all the rage in Miami and can be found in many of the big hotels. *Sundari Spa*, owned by model Christie Turlington and situated in the *Shore Club* hotel, 1901 Collins Avenue, Miami Beach, has received a lot of attention for its Asian Ayurvedic scrubs and soaks from its gorgeous rooftop locale. The *Mandarin Oriental Hotel Spa* (see *Hotels*) is popular for its local algae treatments.

Golf

Florida is a golfer's paradise, with favourable weather year round and more courses than any other US state. The *Biltmore Golf Club*, 1210 Anastasia Avenue, Coral Gables (tel: (305) 460 5364), is among Miami's most beautiful courses. Green fees are US$76 before 1400 or US$48 after 1400. *Crandon Golf Course*, 6700 Crandon Boulevard, Key Biscayne (tel: (305) 361 9129), is one of America's top-ranked municipal courses and home to the Royal Caribbean Classic golf tournament. Green fees are US$131 or US$37 after 1500. *Doral Golf Resort and Spa*, 4400 NW 87th Avenue (tel: (305) 592 2000; website: www.doralresort.com), has five championship 18-hole courses, each varying in difficulty, from the Great White course to the notorious Monster Blue. Green fees (depending on course and season) are US$195–275. All golf clubs mentioned are open to the public and do not require membership.

In-line Skating

Visitors can join the South Beach crowd and rent a pair of in-line skates from *Skate 2000*, 1200 Ocean Drive (tel: (305) 538 8282). Free lessons are offered on Sunday. *Fritz's Skate and Bike Shop*, 730 Lincoln Road (tel: (305) 532 1954), hires out skates hourly or daily.

Sailing

Moorings, 2550 South Bayshore Drive, Coconut Grove (tel: (305) 858 8650; website: www. moorings.com), charters yachts from Miami Bay, along with many other outfitters and charter companies that use the marinas and docks along this strip of Bayshore Drive.

Tennis

There are public courts at the *North Shore Tennis Center*, 350 73rd Street, Miami Beach (tel: (305) 993 2022), the *Biltmore Tennis Centre*, 1150 Anastasia Avenue, Coral Gables (tel: (305) 460 5360), and the *Tennis Center at Crandon Park*, 7300 Crandon Boulevard, Key Biscayne (tel: (305) 365 2300), where the NASDAQ-100 Open is held. Crandon Park courts are illuminated for night play, although reservations are required.

Shopping

Shopping opportunities abound in Miami, with a broad assortment of facilities ranging from sophisticated malls to small specialist boutiques. *Miracle Mile* in Coral Gables has quality galleries, boutiques and department stores, while the 6.4-hectare (16-acre) waterfront *Bayside Marketplace*, in downtown Miami, offers an unusual mix of retail shops and local artisan stalls. Other key areas are the funky boutiques of South Beach (most notably the *Lincoln Road* shopping district, nicknamed the 'Fifth Avenue of the South'), *CocoWalk*, the exclusive *Streets of Mayfair* shopping centres in Coconut Grove and the numerous malls scattered about Greater Miami. A stretch of Collins Avenue, between Sixth and Eighth Streets, in South Beach, has a handful of local boutiques and medium-price chain stores like Banana Republic, Urban Outfitters and A/X Armani Exchange.

For chic interiors and objects for the home, nothing surpasses the *Miami Design District* – NE 36th Street to NE 41st Street, between NE Second Avenue and North Miami Avenue – where high-end decor and furniture shops are open to the public.

Cuban cigars, Key Lime cookies, architectural or Art Deco posters of books from the *Wolfsonian Museum Gift Shop* or the *Art Deco District Welcome Centre*, a well designed object for the home from the *Miami Design District* and anything related to the beach all make good souvenirs and gifts from Miami.

Aventura Mall, 19501 Biscayne Boulevard, Aventura (tel: (305) 935 1110; website: www. shopaventuramall.com), is one of the most popular malls, featuring Burdines, Macy's, Bloomingdale's, Sears, JC Penney and over 250 smaller shops. *Bal Harbour*, 9700 Collins Avenue, is renowned for its high-end designer boutiques, such as *Gucci* and *Tiffany*. *Sawgrass Mills*, 12801 West Sunrise Boulevard, in Fort Lauderdale (tel: (954) 846 2300; website: www.sawgrassmillsmall.com), is the place to shop for bargains – it is the world's largest outlet mall with more than 300 discounted brand-name stores.

The *Espanola Way* market, which is held from Thursday to Sunday, is the best exaple of a charming outdoor market in the heart of South Beach. The pedestrian-only street is filled with plants and flowers for sale, along with jewellery, clothing, art, pottery and other handcrafted items. One of the largest flea markets in South Florida, *Opa-Locka/Hialeah Flea Market*, on 12705 NW 42nd Avenue at 127th Street, has more than 1200 vendors all selling new, used and wholesale items, produce, baked goods and about anything else imaginable. The market is open daily 0600–1800.

Most malls are open Monday to Saturday 1000–2100 and Sunday 1200–1800. Most supermarkets open daily 0800–2200, although some are open 24 hours. Sales tax is 6.5% on all goods; there is no system for claiming this back upon leaving the country. Credit cards are widely accepted.

Culture

As home to the *Florida Grand Opera*, the *New World Symphony*, the *Florida Philharmonic Orchestra* and the *Jackie Gleason Theater of the Performing Arts*, Miami's cultural life is very much alive and kicking.

The local newspapers are a good way for visitors to find out what is on – the *New Times* or the Friday edition of the *Miami Herald* are best – or the excellent online events calendar (website: www.miami. nightguide.com) gives daily listings of special events. Tickets can be bought at the various venues or from *Ticketmaster* (tel: (305) 358 5885; website: www. ticketmaster.com).

Music

The *Florida Grand Opera* (website: www.fgo.org) is undergoing a renaissance, breaking box-office records with its repertoire of well-loved classics and lesser known works, at the *Dade County Auditorium*, 2901 West Flagler Street (tel: (305) 547 5414). The *Florida Philharmonic Orchestra* (website: www.florida philharmonic.org), America's premier regional symphony orchestra, also regularly performs there, while the *New World Symphony* (website: www.nws.org), America's unique orchestral academy, plays from late September to early May in the historic *Lincoln Theatre*, 555 Lincoln Road, Miami Beach (tel: (305) 673 3331; website: www.lincolntheatre.com). The only symphony orchestra of its kind in the world, the New World Symphony has been training gifted graduates for careers in music since 1987. Both symphony orchestras sometimes play at the historic *Gusman Center for the Performing Arts*, 174 East Flagler Street (tel: (305) 374 2444; website: http:// gusmancenter.org), a renovated 1920s movie palace, which now stages a huge variety of arts events, including the annual Miami Film Festival.

Theatre

The *Jackie Gleason Theater of the Performing Arts*, 1700 Washington Avenue (tel: (305) 673 7300; website: www.gleasontheater.com), is Miami Beach's top artistic venue, showcasing Broadway shows, concerts and dance from the *Florida Philharmonic*, the *Miami City Ballet*, the *Concert Association of Florida* (website:

New World Symphony, Lincoln Theatre

Photo: Greater Miami Convention and Visitors Bureau

www.concertfla.org), as well as other celebrated productions. Also on South Beach, the intimate Art Deco *Colony Theatre*, 1040 Lincoln Road (tel: (305) 674 1026; website: www.colonytheatre.org), hosts an exciting and varied programme of dance, theatre, music and film. Other major theatres include the *Edge Theater*, 405 Espanola Way, Miami Beach (tel: (305) 531 6083), noted for its comedies and its 20th-century classics, and the *Coconut Grove Playhouse*, 3500 Main Highway, Coconut Grove (tel: (305) 442 4000; website: www.cgplayhouse.com), nationally recognised for its innovative productions.

Dance

Florida's internationally acclaimed dance company, the *Miami City Ballet* (website: www.miamicity ballet.org), performs a wide repertoire of classical and contemporary works, at a variety of venues including the *Jackie Gleason Theater* (see above).

Film

There are cinema complexes at every major shopping mall. Miami's three-dimensional *Imax Cinema at Sunset Place*, 5701 Sunset Drive, South Miami (tel: (305) 663 4629; website: www.imax.com/miami), offers the ultimate 3-D movie-going experience, with a screen the size of a six-storey building and a wraparound sound system as dynamic as a full-sized symphony orchestra. Arthouse aficionados should head to the *Bill Cosford Cinema*, in the University of Miami's Memorial Building, Coral Gables (tel: (305) 284 4861).

Miami's film and entertainment industry has grown dramatically in recent years. Indeed, the city's old reputation for brashness was built on the television series *Miami Vice* in the 1980s. Detective work still continues in the celluloid rendering of the city, with the popular series *CSI: Miami*. This whodunnit – or rather howdunnit, seeing as it focuses on forensics – is a spin-off of the original Las Vegas-set detective show. Miami is the third largest centre for film and TV production in the USA. Recent films set here include *Something about Mary* (1998), *The Birdcage* (1996), *Ace Ventura* (1994), *True Lies* (1994), *Get Shorty* (1995) and the unsuccessful adaptation of Carl Hiaasen's locally set novel, *Striptease* (1996). Not forgetting the classics, such as *Citizen Kane* (1941), *Key Largo* (1948) and three James Bond movies – *Dr No* (1962), *Live and Let Die* (1973) and *Goldfinger* (1964).

Cultural Events

The *Art Deco Weekend* (website: www. artdecoweekend.com) is the world's largest annual festival dedicated to the preservation of this unique design style. It takes place every January, with a huge programme of street theatre, big band concerts and processions in South Beach. The *Miami Film Festival* (website: www.miamifilmfestival.com) is a springtime event (February and March), which showcases films and videos by filmmakers from across the USA, with a forum for smaller, independent works. *The Miami Book Fair International* (website: www.miami bookfair.com) takes place in mid November, leading up to Thanksgiving, with night readings, lectures and workshops with top authors, as well as a book fair.

Literary Notes

Miami itself has little literary history. However, over the years, numerous writers have made Florida their home – in particular Key West. Among them were Ernest Hemingway (1899–1960), author of *A Farewell to Arms* (1929), *For Whom the Bell Tolls* (1940) and *The*

Art Deco Weekend, festival for the preservation and celebration of Art Deco (website: www.artdecoweekend.com), Jan, South Beach

Coconut Grove Arts Festival, multimedia arts event, President's Day weekend, Feb, Coconut Grove

Royal Caribbean Golf Classic, golf tournament (website: www.golfweb.com/tournaments), early Feb, Crandon Park Golf Course, Key Biscayne

Miami International Film Festival, ten-day festival featuring Hollywood and independent films and celebrity parties in the Design District (website: www.miamifilmfestival.com), late Feb–early Mar, Gusman Center for the Performing Arts, downtown Miami, and other venues

Genuity Championship, golf tournament, late Feb–early Mar, Doral Golf Resort and Spa

Florida Derby, horseracing (website: www.gulfstreampark.com), Mar, Gulfstream Park

Carnaval Miami, a nine-day festival, with parades and entertainment, leading up to Calle Ocho Festival, early Mar, Little Havana

Calle Ocho Festival, the largest one-day Cuban-American festival and street party in America, early Mar, Little Havana

NASDAQ-100 Open (formerly the Ericsson Open), tennis competition (website: www.nasdaq-100open.com), late Mar, Crandon Park Tennis Center, Key Biscayne

South Beach Film Festival, one-week independent film festival, mid Apr, Colony Theater and other venues, South Beach

Miami/Bahamas Goombay Festival, three-day Caribbean entertainment and food festival, first weekend in Jun, Coconut Grove

Fourth of July, rides, parade, food stalls and fireworks, 4 Jul, Bayfront Park and Key Biscayne

Marlboro Grand Prix, car racing (website: www.miamirace.com), late Sep, Bayfront Park

Hispanic Heritage Festival, the oldest Hispanic cultural festival in America, with food fair and entertainment for a month, leading up to a street party, Festival of the Americas, Oct, various venues

Festival Miami, six-week international music festival featuring world premieres, concerts, chamber music and jazz, mid–late Oct, various venues

Junior Orange Bowl Festival, the world's largest arts, culture and sports festival for youth, with a special focus on tennis; an accompanying parade takes place between Christmas and New Year's, Oct–Jan, various venues

South Miami Art Festival, a festival and fair of artists and craftspeople, first weekend in Nov, Sunset Drive

Miami Book Fair International, night readings, lectures and workshops with top authors, book fair, mid Nov, leading up to Thanksgiving, downtown Wolfson campus of Miami-Dade Community College and other venues

Annual Winternational Thanksgiving Day Parade, fourth Thurs in Nov, starts at the Orange Bowl

Fed Ex Orange Bowl Parade and Big Orange New Year's Eve Celebration, football season events, 31 Dec, downtown Miami

Old Man and the Sea (1952), Elizabeth Bishop (1911–79), one of the most celebrated American poets of this century, and Tennessee Williams (1911–83), playwright and author of *Cat on a Hot Tin Roof* (1944) and *A Streetcar Named Desire* (1955). Hemingway – the rough, tough, local novelist – built his reputation in the bars of Key West (see *Excursions*).

The beautiful Spanish colonial-style house, 907 Whitehead Street (tel: (305) 294 1136; website: www.hemingwayhome.com), where he wrote some of his finest works, is open to the public. The contemporary American novelist, Alison Lurie, also has a house in Key West and set one of her novels, *The Truth about Lorin Jones* (1989), there.

Downtown Miami

MOSCOW

Formerly the centre of one of the world's two superpowers, Moscow (*Moskva*) is still reeling from the rapid pace of change that the past fifteen years have wrought. Located in the centre of the East-European plain, with its major part occupying the valley of the Moskva River, it is a brash city with pockets of ostentatious new-found (and often ill-gotten) wealth surrounded by the vast majority struggling to live on their meagre salaries or pensions. The spiritual, political and economic capital of the world's largest country, Moscow is quite different from the rest of the Russian Federation and the worst ravages of industrial decline have bypassed the city, as it is more focused on the administrative and service sectors.

Moscow is, at its heart, a medieval city, first mentioned by Prince Dolgorukhy of Vladimir in 1147. From this point, its importance as the capital of a small independent principality grew under the Mongol Golden Horde invaders in the 13th century. However, it was not until Ivan the Great defeated the Mongols in 1480 and was crowned 'Ruler of all Russia' that the city began to assert its pre-eminent status – and it remained the capital of Russia until 1712. Many buildings still date back to this period, however, Muscovites burned the city down in 1812 – rather than let it fall into French hands with the Napoleonic War. After Napoleon's defeat, a huge reconstruction plan was put into action and marks the face of the city today, from the Triumphal Arch on

Tverskaya ulitsa to the Bolshoi Theatre. With another threat of invasion – this time by Germany – Moscow was restored as the capital of Russia by Lenin in 1918.

Communist rule has left a legacy of awe-inspiring architecture around the city, such as Stalin's so-called Seven Sisters – the Gothic-looking Social Realist skyscrapers that humble the individual as they loom large from the outskirts of central Moscow. However, for the greater part of eight centuries, the Kremlin has been at the very heart of Moscow, the seat of power for the grand princes, tsars and presidents who have ruled Russia, as well as an important religious site. And for Westerners, the adjacent Red Square, especially the bulbous, multicoloured domes of St Basil's Cathedral, has been an image synonymous with the Soviet Union and Russian state since the advent of television.

Nowadays, the sight of posturing Soviet military driving their tanks through Red Square for the October Revolution Parades has been replaced by wealthy Muscovites posing with their shiny new Mercedes Benz, while the Stalinist buildings along Tverskaya ulitsa now house glitzy Western franchises. The well-heeled New Muscovites may have greeted capitalism with open arms but after 74 years of Communist-imposed atheism, many in the Russian capital have enthusiastically embraced their once-banned Orthodox faith. This is reflected in the

restoration of old churches, the rapid construction of new ones (most notably the Cathedral of Christ the Saviour, completed on the site of a similar church of the same name, in time for Moscow's 850th birthday in 1997) and the decision to give the remains of Russia's last tsar, Nicholas II, a Christian burial.

As the second democratically elected President of Russia, Vladimir Putin is the youngest and perhaps the most vigorous leader the Kremlin has seen. At home, Putin has drawn praise for his management of the economy and the restoration of a stronger leadership after Yeltsin's last years, but also criticism for turning his back on the *glasnost* of earlier Soviet times by encroaching on press freedom. His apparent indecision in handling incidents such as the Kursk submarine tragedy in 2001 and the Moscow theatre hostages in 2002 have not helped. Internationally, Putin supported the US in Afghanistan, thawing the last of any Cold War ice, but ultimately seems better placed to have a more lasting relationship with Europe, especially since Russia allied itself with France and Germany in opposing the war in Iraq in 2003.

One aspect of the city remains constant and that is the harshness of the Moscow winter, although there is nothing so beautiful as seeing St Basil's Cathedral or the spires of the Kremlin churches in the falling snow. In contrast, summer temperatures over 30°C (86°F) are not unusual.

Photo: Helen Argent

Olympic Stadium and Moscow skyline

TRAVEL

Getting There By Air

Sheremetyevo International Airport (SVO)

Tel: (095) 956 4666.

Website: www.sheremetyevo-airport.ru

Located 30km (19 miles) from Moscow, Sheremetyevo International Airport, known as Sheremetyevo-2, is the largest of Moscow's airports, handling flights from outside the former Soviet Union. There is also a domestic terminal on site, known as Sheremetyevo-1 (tel: (095) 232 6565). Airports Domodedovo (tel: (095) 933 6666), Bykovo (tel: (095) 558 4738) and Vnukovo (tel: (095) 941 9999) are the other purely domestic airports.

Major airlines: *Aeroflot – Russian International Airlines* (tel: (095) 753 5555; website: www. aeroflot.com) is the main national airline and took over the international routes from the old Soviet-era organisation. It flies to 150 destinations in 93 different countries and most of these flights are on Boeing or Airbus aircraft – the fleet of Soviet-made aircraft is primarily used for domestic services. Other airlines flying into Sheremetyevo-2 include *Air France, Alitalia, Austrian Airlines, British Airways, JAL, Lufthansa, KLM* and *SAS*.

to Metro Rechnoi Vokzal and bus 871 goes to Metro Planernaya (journey times – 45 minutes by bus, then 30 minutes by Metro to the city centre). There is also the Autoline fixed-route taxi and Airbus service, which departs every 20 minutes (journey time – 45 minutes). Services operate daily 0545–2430. *Aerovokzal* (tel: (095) 155 0922), the Airport Transportation Terminal and a central point for bus transport to Moscow airports, provides further information.

Getting There By Rail

Moscow has nine railway terminals connected to the Russian Federation's extensive rail network. The state-owned *Russian Railways* (tel: (095) 262 2620 *or* 1531; website: www.css-mps.ru) network is broken into regional divisions. *Moscow Railways* (tel: (095) 266 9006 *or* 9333) operates the majority of the terminals and services in the Moscow area, with passenger services operating on 95% of the network. The three railway stations most likely to be used by visitors to Moscow are: *Belorussky vokzal*, Tverskaya Zastava ploshchad (tel: (095) 973 8191), where trains serve Western Europe; *Kievsky vokzal*, Kievskovo voksala ploshchad (tel: (095) 240 0415), where trains serve Budapest, Prague, Kiev, Sofia, Venice and Belgrade; and *Leningradsky vokzal*, Komsomolskaya

Western European cities via Warsaw, Budapest and Prague. The Trans-Siberian Railway is a great way to see just how massive a country the Russian Federation is, although the journey takes at least a week.

On long-distance services, first-class compartments have two soft berths and obviously provide the most comfort and privacy. However, service in the standard second class is usually very good – the compartments are four berth, the linen is generally clean and each carriage has a *provodnik* (attendant) who will even make Russian tea for travellers who ask nicely.

Transport to the city: The train stations are all connected to the city's Metro system. Belorussky vokzal is on Metro Belorusskaya, Kievsky vokzal on Metro Kievskaya and Leningradsky vokzal on Metro Komsomolskaya and Rizhsky vokzal on Metro Rizhskaya.

Getting There By Road

The network of roads around Moscow is much more comprehensive than in other parts of the country but off the main intercity routes the surfaces are often poor. It is a good idea for driving tourists to plan an itinerary and accommodation beforehand, to avoid difficulty with bureaucratic red tape. There are suggested tourist routes, with some road signs in Latin script. Motorways are prefixed by 'M' and major routes are prefixed by 'A'. Traffic drives on the right. The speed limit is 110kph (68mph), except in built-up areas where it is 60kph (37mph). It is forbidden to use the horn (except in emergencies), carry unauthorised passengers or pick up hitchhikers. Driving under the influence of drugs or any amount of alcohol is forbidden, although this practice is increasingly common and motorists should avoid driving at night, when the risk is greater. Seatbelts, a first aid kit and an emergency triangle or red light are required.

The minimum age for driving in Russia is 18 years and an International Driving Permit or national driving licence with an authorised translation is necessary. Visitors travelling in their own car must also carry, at all times, a passport and visa, as well as an itinerary card. This must contain the following

3000km

1500mls

✈ international airport

Approximate flight times to Moscow: From London is 3 hours 35 minutes; from New York is 8 hours 50 minutes; from Los Angeles is 12 hours 10 minutes; from Toronto is 9 hours 20 minutes and from Sydney is 20 hours 5 minutes.

Airport facilities: These include banks, bureaux de change, a post office, newsagents, a pharmacy, restaurants, bars, cafés, duty-free shops, left-luggage and first-aid facilities. Car hire is available from *Avis* and *Europcar*.

Business facilities: Sheremetyevo-2 has a 24-hour business centre (tel: (095) 578 7252; fax: (095) 956 4652) with fax and e-mail facilities.

Arrival/departure tax: Taxes are included in the price of the airline ticket.

Transport to the city: Most hotels will arrange to pick up their guests in a courtesy van for a fee (Rb1200–1500/US$40–50). Taxis are probably the next simplest and safest way to get to the city, however, they are also the most expensive (Rb1800–2400/US$60–80). The local bus 551 goes

ploshchad (tel: (095) 262 9143), where trains serve Helsinki, St Petersburg, Murmansk and Talin. The Trans-Siberian Express leaves from *Yaroslavsky vokzal*, Komsomolskaya ploshchad (tel: (095) 921 5914), daily at 1400 – destinations include Yaroslavl, Irkutsk, Vladivostock, Ulan Bator and Beijing. Trains to and from Riga, the Latvian capital, leave from *Rizhky vokzal*, Rizhskaya ploshchad (tel: (095) 266 0596). Facilities at the larger stations include toilets, shops and food and drink stalls.

The *Central Railway Inquiry Office*, Maly Kharitonevksy pereulok (tel: (095) 266 9000/9), provides timetable information, rail information and ticket sales (tel: (095) 266 9333). Tickets are also available at the stations.

Rail services: Due to the large distances involved, almost any trip a Western visitor will make in Russia (beyond day trips from Moscow) will be on a night train. Major connecting routes are from Kiev in the south (journey time – 13 hours), St Petersburg (journey time – 8 hours 30 minutes) and Helsinki (journey time – 14 hours) in the north, as well as

information: visitor's name and citizenship; the car registration number; full details of the itinerary (presented upon entry into Russia); a form, provided by customs upon arrival, guaranteeing that the car will be taken out of the Russian Federation on departure; petrol vouchers purchased at the border; and insurance documents.

Road tax is payable upon entry to the country. Motor insurance for travel within the Russian Federation should be arranged prior to departure or upon entry to the country at the offices of *Ingosstrakh*, the Russian Federation foreign insurance agency. The Russian Embassy or a specialist tour operator can provide foreign drivers with further details.

One reputable (although not necessarily English-speaking) automobile association in Moscow is *Avtomobilny Klub Rossii*, Yaroslavskaya ulitsa 4 (tel: (095) 785 1010), which provides information and a 24-hour breakdown service.

Emergency breakdown service: *GAI* (095) 923 5373 *or* 236 4136.

Routes to the city: The Moskovskaya Koltsevaya Avtomobilnaya Doroga (Moscow Ring Road) is an orbital motorway surrounding the city and linking roads arriving from Minsk (M1), Kiev (M2), Nizhny Novgorod (M7), Riga (M9) and St Petersburg (M10).

Approximate driving times to Moscow: From Nizhny Novgorod – 7 hours 15 minutes; St Petersburg – 12 hours 30 minutes; Kiev – 14 hours 15 minutes.

Coach services: The *Central Bus Station* is located at Shchelkovskoe Shosse 75 (tel: (095) 468 0400 *or* 4370), in the eastern suburbs of the city. There are, however, no middle or long-distance coaches available that are of a quality acceptable to most Western travellers.

Getting Around

Public Transport

By far the easiest and most pleasant way to get round the city is on the **Metro** system (tel: (095) 943 5003 *or* 5052; website: www.metro.ru). Moscow's Metro is the largest in the world and features some stunningly

decorated stations that are almost palatial (see *Key Attractions*). Entrances are marked by a large 'M' sign. The system is extremely efficient and good value – a magnetic card valid for one journey costs Rb5, while one valid for ten journeys costs Rb35. The network consists of ten lines – the black Circle Line links the major railway stations, while the other nine lines cover the city centre and radiate out from the Circle Line. Stations often have multiple names – one for each line that intersects there.

There is also an extensive network of **buses**, **trolleybuses** and **trams**, run by *Moscow City Transport*, Raushskaya naberezhnaya 22 (tel: (095) 233 3995). These can be crowded and unpleasant during rush hour, although, at other times, they can be an

CITY STATISTICS

Location: Province of Moscow, west Russian Federation.
Country dialling code: 7.
Population: 8,652,195 (city); 11,552,601 (regional area).
Ethnic mix: Predominantly Russian, with minorities from all over the former Soviet Union.
Religion: Predominantly Russian Orthodox.
Time zone: GMT + 3 (GMT + 4 from last Sunday in March to Saturday before last Sunday in October).
Electricity: 220 volts AC, 50Hz; round two-pin plugs are standard.
Average January temp: - 13°C (- 9°F).
Average July temp: 18°C (64°F).
Annual rainfall: 624mm (24.3 inches).
Annual snowfall: 132mm (5.2 inches).

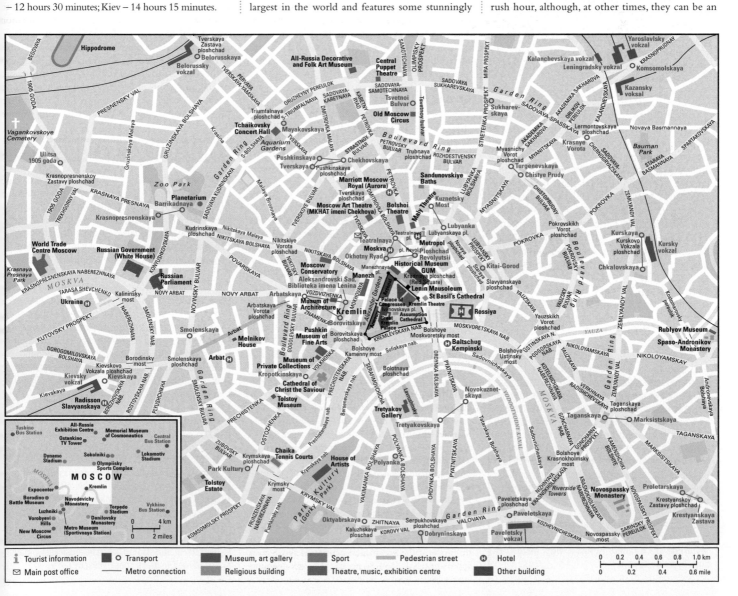

BUSINESS PROFILE

Moscow is the unchallenged economic centre of Russia, although some details of the economic conditions are somewhat hazy due to lax financial reporting and 'unofficial' commerce and employment. However, what is apparent is that, since the last economic crisis of 1998, the Russian economy has shown excellent growth – even through the last years of global economic slowdown since 11 September 2001. During the past five years, the Russian economy has benefited from relatively long-lasting effects of the 1998 Rouble devaluation, three years of high international oil prices and, the cause of the most recent surge of growth, negative interest rates.

At the centre of this growth, Moscow is visibly booming. The total growth of the economy for 2002 was 4.3%. This is down on 2001's growth of 5% and 2000's growth of 9%; however, the economy surged 6.4% in the first quarter of 2003. The government is forecasting annual growth of 4–5% in 2003 and 2004. Key analysts are predicting that the current availability of money for investment is priming big companies for further growth; however, the small and medium-sized businesses that fuel the economies of developed countries are being left out of the windfall. The surge in the economy can clearly be seen by the influx of global corporations returning to the capital. Western manufacturing companies based in the capital include *General Electric*, *Sun Microsystems*, *Rank Xerox*, *Siemens*, *Peugeot*, *IBM* and *Hewlett Packard*.

Heavy industry, including machinery, oil and heavy metals, is the mainstay of the Russian economy, but cuts in military procurement spending over the last ten years have had a devastating impact on the industrial centres circling Moscow. The mix of commerce and industry in Moscow now mirrors Western cities more closely in that most of the employment growth is now in the service sectors, including retail and banking. Russian stock markets also show signs of the strengthening economy, with trading volumes on the MICEX and RTS and in ADRs exceeding half a billion US Dollars. Of Moscow workers employed in large or medium-sized enterprises, 16% work in industrial premises, 12% work in scientific premises, 12% in educational establishments, 9% in physical culture, health and social services, 8% in transport and catering and 7% in construction.

The official newspaper, *Pravda*, lists the unemployment rate for Moscow as 1.6%, compared to the national average of 8%. However, official figures are almost meaningless, as they do not take into account the vast underemployment of Muscovites, including people working off the books for tax reasons (in a city of 10 million, there were only 182,000 filed tax returns in 1999), those working on a barter system because their employer cannot pay wages, and the thousands of people in Moscow without residency permits who officially do not exist.

The main business areas are along Tverskaya ulitsa and at central business centres in the area, such as the World Trade Centre (website: www.wtcmo.ru) and Riverside Towers.

interesting way of sightseeing. Tickets (*bilyeti* or *talony*) can be purchased in advance at Metro stations or kiosks or from the driver and must be validated by punching them into the machines on-board. One journey costs Rb5. Spot fines of about US$5 are levied if travellers do not have a punched ticket.
All forms of transport operate 0530–2430, although some bus and tram routes may stop earlier.
There are no **passes** shorter than monthly passes.

Taxis

Although there are official taxis and private taxis, it is still a common practice for private cars to stop and offer a ride when flagged down. The official taxis are yellow cars with a 'T' and chequered emblems on the door – a green light indicates availability. The private cars, known as 'gypsy cabs', are safe for the most part but best avoided late at night outside nightclubs or tourist bars.
There is a *Central Taxi Reservation Office* (tel: (095) 927 0000), for ordering taxis in advance 24 hours daily. The average taxi fare in Moscow is Rb10 per kilometre. Most drivers will negotiate a flat fare rather than a metered fare; this should be settled before commencing the journey. Tipping is not expected. It is usually possible to hire a taxi by the hour, if desired. Visitors should never share a taxi with a stranger.

Limousines

There are numerous limousine services in Moscow, including *Limousine-Taxi* (tel: (095) 292 2010 *or* 960 2020, ext. 1202), *City Limousine* (tel: (095) 248 5233) and *Limousine-Service* (tel: (095) 257 4000). Hire costs approximately Rb1000/US$30 per hour, with a minimum hire of four hours.

Driving in the City

Moscow's road system is based on a series of concentric rings, connected by arterial roads that radiate from the centre. The innermost, the Garden Ring Road, follows a path similar to the Metro's Circle Line. The outermost arterial is the Moscow Ring Road motorway.
Traffic accidents, many of them caused by drink-driving, are becoming increasingly prevalent and night driving is not recommended. Traffic has increased significantly in the last few years, while improvements to the infrastructure have lagged behind, making driving difficult, especially in the centre. Rush hours are typically 0700–0900 and 1630–1900. With the added hassle of over-zealous police, difficult-to-find parking and Cyrillic-only road signs, many Western visitors find it easier (and often cheaper) to hire a car with a driver. It is advisable to use a guarded parking lot (*platnaya stoyanka*) as theft is common – many hotels offer this facility to non-guests for about US$3 per hour.

Car Hire

Car hire can be expensive in Moscow and large fees may be charged for an airport transfer. Many independent firms hire out cars but only with a driver. International car hire companies based in Moscow include *Avis* (tel: (095) 578 7179; website: www.avis.com), *Budget* (tel: (095) 737 0407; website: www.budget.ru) and *Hertz* (tel: (095) 937 3274; website: www.hertz.com). Drivers must be at least 21 years old and have one year of driving experience and an International Driving Permit or national driving licence with an authorised translation. A small car from one of the companies mentioned above costs approximately US$60–80 per day, although discounts are available if booked in advance.

Bicycle Hire

Cycling can be tricky in Moscow, as there are no cycle paths and bicycles are liable to be stolen if left alone. For these reasons, there are very few, if any, places to hire bicycles from in Moscow. However, some of the major international hotels may be able to help visitors who are keen to cycle.

SIGHTSEEING

Sightseeing Overview

Moscow has grown organically and so, like most old European cities, its treasures – churches, merchant's houses, aristocratic palaces from the 19th and early 20th centuries, Soviet monuments and art – are often stumbled across by chance in side streets. Or in fact, underground, as perhaps the most surprising discovery for first-time visitors are the 'palaces' of the *Moscow Metro*. The capital of Russia until 1712, Moscow retains the atmosphere and architecture of a truly Russian city in a way that St Petersburg, which was modelled on Western architecture, does not. The city centre is still dominated by the Moskva River and the Kremlin as it was in the 15th century; the walls of the Kremlin date from this period. *Kitai Gorod* (literally Chinatown), to the northeast of the Kremlin, is the best area to explore in this part of Moscow. Most of the key tourist sights are within walking distance of the *Kremlin* and the famous *Red Square*, with the gold domes of *St Basil's Cathedral*. This is one of the major orientation points of the city centre, which itself is contained within a series of ring roads. The Moskva River is the other point of orientation, arcing within

BUSINESS ETIQUETTE

The business culture in Moscow has changed dramatically over the past decade. Investment from major Western corporations has brought wealth for a select few, as well as a more Western approach to business. English is far more prevalent than it used to be but it is always worth making sure that there is an interpreter on hand.

Offices are generally open Monday to Friday 0900–1800. Although Russians are not always punctual, it is important for business visitors to arrive on time. Business cards are readily handed out – they should have a Russian translation on the reverse. Business lunches are quite common but evening meetings tend to be more social and occasionally Russians will bring their spouses with them.

If invited to a Russian's home, guests should bring a gift (wine, chocolates or a bouquet of flowers with an uneven number of stems – even numbers are for funerals only) and something small for any children. Visitors should not refuse to drink a toast, although it is not necessary to drain the glass, and, once opened, a bottle will invariably be finished. Business suits should be worn for meetings, otherwise dress is slightly more casual than elsewhere in Europe. A fair amount of sexism still persists in Russian society and businesswomen are advised to dress conservatively.

this ring, along one of the Kremlin's walls and passing Gorky Park (*Park Kultury*) to the southwest.

To the north and east of the Kremlin, along the Moskva River, can be found much of the architecture dating back to the great period of construction after the Napoleonic War. This includes Teatralnaya ploshchad with the *Bolshoi Theatre* and the *Manezh* (imperial stables), as well as the two ring roads, Boulevard Ring and Garden Ring, that enclose this part of the city. This area also contains the main shopping streets (Tverskaya and Petrovka ulitsa) and theatres in Moscow.

For a view of the whole city, head to *Sparrow Hills* where the Moscow University (one of Stalin's so-called 'Seven Sisters') is located, in the southwest of the city. This is the only high point in the city and offers excellent views over the whole of Moscow. It is worth noting that most museums are closed on Monday.

Key Attractions

Kremlin

The heart of Moscow and of the Russian State itself, the *Kremlin* (literally 'fortified town') is a walled fortress dating back to the city's founding in 1147, although the oldest extant walls and churches date from the 15th and 16th centuries. From 1276 to 1712, it was the seat of government for the grand princes and tsars (until the seat of power moved to St Petersburg), while, from 1918, it was home to the Communist government and now the government of the Russian Federation. The redbrick walls and towers enclose a number of spectacular churches and palaces – only the Soviet-era Palace of Congresses provides a reminder of the Communist government's preferred style of architecture.

The *Uspensky Sobor* (Cathedral of the Assumption) is the largest of the churches. It was the burial place for Orthodox patriarchs and was used for the coronations of tsars. The *zakomary* (arched gables) are a visual extension of the vaulting within the cathedral. The pretty *Blagoveshchensky Sobor* (Annunciation Cathedral), with its nine glittering copper-gilt domes, was the private chapel of the tsars. Ivan the Terrible added the *Grosnensky Porch* after he was refused entry to the chapel for contravening church doctrine by marrying for a fourth time. *Archangelsky Sobor* (Cathedral of the Archangel Michael), although built in 1505, houses the remains of the grand princes and tsars who reigned from 1325 to 1696. The *Armoury Museum* and *Diamond Fund* are worth visiting for the state and church treasures they contain, including Fabergé eggs (in the former) and the 180-carat diamond that belonged to Catherine the Great (in the latter). Also within the Kremlin are the Tsar Cannon and Tsar Bell, both the largest of their kind (40 and 200 tonnes respectively) and neither one used for its intended purpose.

English-speaking guides to the Kremlin will often approach tourists outside the main gates. Prices are usually US$10–20 per hour, although there is no set price, so bargaining is necessary.
Krasnaya ploshchad (Red Square)
Tel: (095) 203 0349 *or* 202 4256. Fax: (095) 203 4256.
E-mail: press@kremlin.museum.ru
Website: www.kremlin.museum.ru
Transport: Metro Biblioteka imeni Lenina or Aleksandrovsky Sad.
Opening hours: Fri–Wed 1000–1800.
Admission: Rb290; plus Rb300 (Armoury Museum) and Rb300 (Diamond Fund).

Gorky Park

Krasnaya Ploshchad and Pokrovsky Sobor (Red Square and St Basil's Cathedral)

The site of large May Day parades during the Soviet era and a market before that, *Krasnaya ploshchad* (Red Square – although *krasnaya* also means 'beautiful' in Old Russian) is a dramatic 700m-long (2300ft) space. It also drew crowds to visit Lenin's Mausoleum – a cubic, Russian avant-garde structure built to contain a crystal casket containing the preserved body of the Soviet Union's first leader. The square is dominated by the walls and towers of the Kremlin on one side and the façade of the GUM department store on the other. Yet these provide a frame for one of Russia's most famous images – the multicoloured onion domes of *Pokrovsy Sobor* (Cathedral of the Intercession, better known as St Basil's Cathedral). Each dome has distinctive patterning and colours and the effect of the ensemble is stunning, if a little garish. It was built in the 1550s to commemorate Ivan the Terrible's victory over the Mongols at Kazan.
Krasnaya ploshchad 4
Tel: (095) 298 3304.
Website: www.shm.ru.
Transport: Metro Kitai-Gorod.
Opening hours: Wed–Mon 1000–1700.
Admission: Rb100.

Muzey Izobrazitelnykh Iskusstv imena A S Pushkina (Pushkin Museum of Fine Arts)

Second only in reputation within Russia to the Hermitage in St Petersburg, the *Pushkin Museum* contains a rich collection of artworks from outside Russia, ranging from Egyptian exhibits, treasures of Troy and an awe-inspiring collection of Impressionist and Post-Impressionist masterpieces. Audio tours are available for a fee.
Volkhonka ulitsa 12
Tel: (095) 203 7998 *or* 6974. Fax: (095) 203 4674.
Website: www.museum.ru/gmii
Transport: Metro Kropotkinskaya or Metro Biblioteka imeni Lenina.
Opening hours: Tues–Sun 1000–1700.
Admission: Rb190 (foreign visitors); Rb25 (Russians).

Tretyakov Galereya (Tretyakov Gallery)

The most important collection of traditional Russian painting in the world resides here. The extensive collection of icons is well worth seeing, as it covers the development of this art form from early Byzantine times to the more developed Russian schools of the 17th century. The most famous of these icons is the 12th-century Vladimir Virgin and there

are also works by Theophanes the Greek, Dionysius and Andrey Rublyov – some of Russia's greatest icon painters. The gallery's collection of paintings, sculptures and graphics covers Russian art from the 18th to early 20th centuries.
Lavrushenshy pereulok 10/12
Tel: (095) 230 7788. Fax: (095) 953 1051.
Website: www.tretyakov.ru
Transport: Metro Tretyakovskaya.
Opening hours: Tues–Sun 1000–1930.
Admission: Rb250 (foreign tourists); Rb150 (foreign students); Rb25 (Russians).

Novodevichy Monastyr (Novodevichy Monastery)

Founded by Grand Prince Vassily III in 1524 (although the present towers and walls date from 1685–87), the *Novodevichy Monastery* (Monastery of the New Maidens) contains the *Sobor Smolensk Bogmateri* (Cathedral of the Virgin of Smolensk), with

Photo: Helen Argent

Moskva River

its distinctive bell tower dating from 1690. The cathedral itself was built in 1525 and contains 16th-century frescoes, as well as a magnificent late 17th-century iconostasis. The convent was a place of exile for noblewomen in mourning or disfavour, including Sophia, Peter the Great's sister, who instigated a coup against him from the convent in 1698. The adjacent *Novodevichy Cemetery* contains the graves of distinguished Muscovites, including Nikita Krushchev (the only Soviet leader buried outside the Kremlin), Nikolai Gogol, Sergei Prokofiev and Anton Chekhov.
Novodevichy proezd 1
Tel: (095) 246 8526. Fax: (095) 246 1327.
Transport: Metro Sportivnaya.
Opening hours: Wed–Mon 1000–1700; closed first Mon of month.
Admission: Rb30; Rb65 (combined ticket for cathedral and exhibition).

Moscow Metro

Busier than the New York Subway and the London Underground combined, the *Moscow Metro* transports eight million passengers a day, with a surprising degree of efficiency. Up and running in 1935, just four years after building started, the Metro is one of the Communist regime's few glories. The stations themselves are an attraction, their unique designs are often palatial and provide an introduction to the development of Soviet art and architecture over more than half a century. *Mayakovskaya* station, Tverskaya ulitsa, has a central hall with a ceiling of Social Realist mosaics supported by stainless steel and red marble columns. In *Ploshchad Revolyutsii*, Nikolayskaya ulitsa, bronze scultptures of Red Army soldiers hold up the arches in the passageways. *Komsomolskaya*, Komsomolskaya ploshcad, offers a Russian history lesson in the mosaics near the Circle Line platforms. The *Metro Museum* displays interesting exhibits on the system.
Metro Museum
Sportivnaya Metro station, Sportivnaya ulitsa
Tel: (095) 924 8490.
Transport: Metro Sportivnaya.
Opening hours: Mon–Fri 1000–1700.
Admission: Rb25.

Futher Distractions

Khram Khrista Spasitelya (Cathedral of Christ the Saviour)

The *Cathedral of Christ the Saviour* is a monument to the struggles of 20th-century Moscow. Completed in 1997, the building stands on the site and is a replica of the original cathedral, which was constructed to celebrate Moscow's victory over Napoleon. It was demolished on Stalin's orders in 1930, to make way for a skyscraper (to include a 100m-tall (328ft) statue of Lenin). When the ground turned out to be too soft to support the structure, Muscovites gained the world's largest outdoor swimming pool instead. Moscow mayor Yuri Luzhkov ordered the demolition of this swimming pool and the construction of this new cathedral as part of Moscow's 850th anniversary celebrations. The work was paid for by public donations from groups as diverse as schoolchildren, babushkas, public officials and rich benefactors from new Russia.
Prechistenskaya naberezhnaya 37
Tel: (095) 203 3823.
Transport: Metro Kropotkinskaya.
Opening hours: Daily 0630–2200.
Admission: Free.

Muzey Arkhitecturi imena A V Shusheva (Museum of Architecture)

Moscow's architecture is rich and sharply contrasting, reflecting the seismic changes that the city has undergone over the centuries. The *Museum of Architecture* is a great place to see how cultural transitions have been etched onto the urban landscape. Spanning five centuries, there are over one million exhibits – including street plans, blueprints, draughts, models, engravings, lithographs and photographs.
Vozdvizhenka ulitsa 5/25
Tel: (095) 202 3979 *or* 291 2109.
Transport: Metro Arbatskaya or Biblioteka imeni Lenina.
Opening hours: Tues–Fri 1100–1730, Sat and Sun 1100–1600.
Admission: Rb20.

Muzey-panorama – Borodinskaya bitva (Museum Panorama – Battle of Borodino)

Visitors can experience the epic battle of the Patriotic War of 1812, when the Russian army met Napoleon's Grand Army at Borodino, to the west of Moscow. The main feature is a panoramic painting that shows the decisive battle of 7 September 1812, on a canvas 115m (377ft) wide and 15m (49ft) high. English-language audio guides are available.
Kutuzovsky prospekt 38
Tel: (095) 148 1967. Fax: (095) 148 9489.
Transport: Metro Kotozovskaya.
Opening hours: Sat–Thurs 1000–1800; closed last Thurs of month.
Admission: Rb20 (concessions available); Rb300 for guided tours (groups of 1–14).

Memorialny Muzey Kosmonavtiki (Memorial Museum of Cosmonautics)

The *Memorial Museum of Cosmonautics* is easy to find, thanks to the gigantic titanium rocket sculpture outside it, which was built to commemorate the launch of Sputnik, the world's first artificial satellite. The museum is as much a tour of the lengths the Soviets went to in their bid for world supremacy during the Cold War as it is a tribute to the history of Soviet space technology. Most of the dated spacecraft on display now look like technology turkeys but it is worth a visit, if only to see Yuri Gagarin's original space suit. For a few Roubles, visitors can wriggle into the suit to pose for a photograph.
Mira prospekt 111
Tel: (095) 283 7914 *or* 282 7398 (information).
Fax: (095) 282 8212.
E-mail: mcrus@glasnet.ru
Website: www.museum.ru/kosmonav
Transport: Metro VDNKh.
Opening hours: Tues–Sun 1000–1800; closed last Fri of month.
Admission: Rb50.

Tours of the City

Walking Tours

Private guides can be hired through the major hotels. There are always individuals in the Red Square/Kremlin area who will offer to act as a guide for a fee – visitors should negotiate this before setting off. As a general rule, prices are around US$13 for three hours and US$24 for six hours. *Moscow City Excursion Bureau*, Rozhdesvenka ulitsa 5 (tel: (095) 921 1508 *or* 924 9446), organises various similarly priced three-hour walking tours, taking in the Red Square, China Town, Novodevichy Monastery, Vagankovsky Necropolis and Novy Arbat.

Bus Tours

Astravel, Novoslobodskaya ulitsa, dom 31, Stonyeniye 2 (tel: (095) 926 8700; e-mail: income@astravel.ru), organises group bus tours, which are four-hour city sightseeing tours taking in St Basil's Cathedral, the Vorobyvovy Hills and Moscow State University. The cost of the tour varies, depending on how many people take part, starting at Rb2120/US$70 for an individual tour, down to Rb240/US$8 per person for a tour of 40 people. Bus tours can also be readily arranged through hotels and incoming tour operators. *Intourist* (tel: (095) 923 5089; website: www.intourist.ru) has a representative in most of the major hotels and at Sheremetyevo-2 airport. It is also possible to hire a car and driver who will give a customised tour of the city. *Moscow City Excursion Bureau* (see *Walking Tours*) also offers bus tours of the city.

Boat Tours

One of the more pleasant ways to see the city is to take a boat trip on the Moskva River. Cruises leave half-hourly from a number of landing points in the city centre and last for 90 minutes. Good starting points are Kievskaya, near the Metro station of the same name, the Radisson Slavyanskaya Hotel and the Borodinsky Bridge (the city's oldest, built in 1912). Cruises can generally be booked through hotels or by contacting *Freestyle 21* (tel: (095) 209 0824), which organises a range of tours. The cost of a boat tour is generally Rb150/US$5.

Excursions

For a Half Day

Ostankino: Built by the Sheremetyev family in the 18th century, around an earlier theatre, *Ostankino Palace*, Ostankinskaya 1 5A (tel: (095) 283 4645), in the northeastern part of the city, is open daily 1000–1800 (May–September). The palace contains elegantly furnished rooms and an art collection of 17th and 18th-century works by minor European painters. Admission costs Rb100.

Also in this area is *Ostankino TV Tower*, which, at 540m (1772ft), is one of the tallest free-standing structures in the world. After a fire in August 2000, the tower is no longer open to the public but continues to transmit TV to Muscovites and remains a useful landmark to the area. A visit to nearby *VDNKh* (*Vystavka Dostizheny Narodnovo Khoszyaystvo*), the USSR Economic Achievements Exhibition, now known as the All-Russian Exhibition Centre, can make this a full-day outing. VDNKh is a rather bizarre former showcase of Communism that is now a cross between a bazaar and a world fair of capitalist goods, all with a backdrop of Social Realist art and an excess of gold paint. The nearest Metro is VDNKh, from where tram 11 leads to the palace.

The Tsaritsino Museum: *The Tsaritsina Arts and Nature Historical-Architectural Museum*, Dolgskaya ulitsa 1 (tel: (095) 321 0743 or 6364), is a popular trip for those wanting to escape the grind and grime of the city centre. It houses antique furniture, ceramics and paintings. Perhaps of more interest are the pleasant gardens, which host festivals and concerts. There is also an opera house and restaurant. The nearest Metro stations are Orekhovo and Tsaritsino. The museum is open Wednesday–Friday 1100–1600 and Saturday and Sunday 1000–1700. Admission costs Rb20.

For a Whole Day

Sergiev Posad: One of the most magical sights in Russia is *Troitsko-Sergieva Lavra* (Trinity Monastery of St Sergius), in the town of Sergiev Posad (formerly Zagorsk). Onion domes in gold and bright blue with gold stars come into view from the last rise in the road from Moscow. The monastery is one of Russia's most important pilgrimage sites and one of only four in the Russian Orthodox Church to have the honorific designation 'Lavra'. The town is part of the 'Golden Ring', a group of ancient Russian towns to the northeast of Moscow that have historical significance (including former capitals) and include churches and monasteries that are, in effect, open-air museums.

The monastery complex in Sergiev Posad, begun by St Sergius of Radonezh (the Russian Orthodox Church's greatest saint) in the 1340s, comprises churches, cathedrals and monastic buildings that are once again in use after Soviet neglect. *Troitsky Sobor* (Trinity Cathedral) is the oldest (1422–23) and finest of the churches and its iconostasis included paintings by Rublyov, some of which can now be see in the Tretyakov Gallery (see *Key Attractions*). The monastery (tel: (095) 284 3164 *or* 281 6020) is situated 80km (50 miles) north of the city and can be reached by train from Yaroslavsky vokzal in Moscow. It is open daily 0800–2000 and admission to the church is free (the monastery itself is not open to the public).

ACCOMMODATION

All hotels accept payment in Roubles, while all the hotels listed here also accept major credit cards and US Dollars. Prices in the larger hotels are often quoted in US Dollars and this is reflected below.

Hotels are subject to VAT (20%), which is usually included in the room rate but can sometimes be added to the bill at the end instead. Hotels may also add sales tax of 5% to the bill.

The prices quoted below are the lowest standard rates for a double room, including VAT but excluding optional sales tax and breakfast, unless otherwise specified.

Business

Aerostar Hotel

Form and function merge perfectly at the *Aerostar* – with marble floors and mirrored columns in its lobby, 343 comfortable and modern rooms and a comprehensive conference and business centre. It recently won an award from the local government for the best four-star hotel in Moscow and, while it is not the most interesting or aesthetically pleasing hotel in the city, the management at Aerostar has really made an effort to please. Free champagne is offered to guests on check-in and there is a Star Club 'privilege' scheme to encourage regular guests. There are also two restaurants to choose from and a full fitness centre.
Leningradsky prospekt 37
Tel: (095) 213 9000. Fax: (095) 213 9001.
E-mail: booking@aerostar.ru
Website: www.aerostar.ru
Price: From US$190 (excluding VAT).

Arbat Hotel

The *Arbat Hotel* is a three-star, tasteful and very Russian hotel on a quiet lane, just around the corner from the popular Novy Arbat street, lined with stalls selling everything from the complete works of Gorky to a cosmonaut's helmet. There are 105 crisply decorated and reasonably priced guest rooms, a number of meeting rooms, a swimming pool and a gym. The Arbat also runs a very helpful translation service from

its fully equipped business centre. There is a restaurant (although there are plenty of good places to eat along the Old Arbat), café, bar and winter garden.
Plotnikov pereulok 12
Tel: (095) 244 7635. Fax: (095) 244 0093.
E-mail: hotelarbat@hotmail.com
Website: www.hotelarbat.ru
Price: From US$135 (including breakfast).

Hotel Moskva

The *Hotel Moskva* is a classic piece of Stalinist architecture from the 1950s, whose awkward square angles are explained by the following legend. When the Georgian dictator designed the building, he wrote his name across two different designs; the builders were too scared to ask which one he had decided upon and so constructed the hotel from both plans. Hotel Moskva is ideally located in the city centre, with the Kremlin, Red Square and the Bolshoi Theatre a short walk away. The interior decor is as classic as the outside, with parquet flooring in the superior bedrooms and suites, some of which have been recently decorated. The 1500 rooms all have satellite TV and 24-hour room service, while the hotel also has conference halls seating 20–150 people and smaller meeting rooms. There is one wonderful relic of times past: each floor of the hotel has a *dezhurnaya* – a woman who will perform a whole host of tasks, from sewing on a button to a wake-up call in the morning.
Okhotny ryad 2
Tel: (095) 960 2020. Fax: (095) 960 5938.
Website: www.hotel-moskva.ru
Price: From Rb3150.

Marriott Moscow Royal Hotel

One of three Marriott hotels in Moscow, the *Moscow Royal*, also known as the *Aurora*, opened in 1999 and is as attractive as it is functional. Its peaked towers, reminiscent of the Kremlin just a ten-minute walk away, were completed by the same construction company that helped build Moscow's most recent cathedral, the Cathedral of Christ the Saviour. Its location, its stylish bedrooms, five meeting rooms and exemplary conference facilities make it a popular hotel with businesspeople – on a par with any luxury international hotel. Each room has full room service, direct-dial telephone, air conditioning, mini-bar and a safe. Concierge floor rooms include complimentary

Annunciation Cathedral

Hotel Ukraina at night

continental breakfast, evening hors d'oeuvres, turndown service and international newspapers. It is also the perfect location for evening entertainment at the Bolshoi Theatre.
Petrovka ulitsa 11/20
Tel: (095) 937 1000. Fax: (095) 937 1001.
Website: www.marriott.com
Price: From US$525.

Luxury

Hotel Baltschug Kempinski
This five-star hotel, dating back to 1898, is a very popular, although not cheap, venue for rich tourists and businesspeople on a flexible expense account. From 1989, the hotel underwent a forward-thinking renovation and reopened in 1991, to offer state-of-the-art facilities, including Internet and e-mail on satellite TV in each of the 232 rooms. Its plush ballroom can be used as a conference facility for up to 200 delegates, while there are many other smaller meeting rooms. Many rooms have great views of the Kremlin, St Basil's Cathedral and Red Square. The public areas are stylish, spacious and modern, while the efficient German-led service is typical Kempinski.
Balchug ulitsa 1
Tel: (095) 230 6500. Fax: (095) 230 6502.
E-mail: hbkm.moscow@kempinski.com
Website: www.kempinskimoscow.com
Price: From US$400.

Hotel Metropol Moscow
For a taste of pre-revolutionary Russia as enjoyed by the upper classes, the *Metropol* is the place. Designed by William Walcott in 1898, this establishment has attracted the leading lights of the Russian intelligentsia, including Leo Tolstoy and Rachmaninov, drawn by its modern, Art Nouveau lobby and its restaurants. The tasteful opulence remains today and has been given extra verve when lovingly and thoughtfully restored to its former glory. Despite this sense of past, the marble floors and sweeping staircases, the Metropol has exemplary

business and conference facilities, including a business centre. The 367 guest rooms (including 76 suites) all have satellite TV and a modem point. Other facilities at the hotel include health club, beauty parlour, various restaurants and bars and a casino.
Teatralny proezd 1/4
Tel: (095) 927 6000. Fax: (095) 927 6010.
E-mail: moscow@interconti.com
Website: www.metropol-moscow.ru
Price: From US$480.

Moderate

Alfa Hotel
Not the prettiest hotel in Moscow on the outside, however, for an agenda of sightseeing or breakfast meetings, the *Alfa Hotel* is a clean and efficient option, situated to the northeast of the city centre. Furthermore, the hotel is in perfect striking distance of the legendary Izmailovsky Park – arguably the best tourist market in Moscow, where more can be bought for one US Dollar than in the over-priced tourist shops inside hotels. The service at the Alfa Hotel is functional and friendly; the 1800 rooms may not be the most tastefully decorated but they are well cared for and have satellite TV. There is also a full business centre here, a conference room for up to 80 people and a sauna and massage parlour in which to unwind.
Izmailovskoe shosse 71A
Tel: (095) 166 2698. Fax: (0905) 166 0060.
E-mail: asu@alfa.lvl.ru
Website: www.alfa.lvl.ru
Price: From Rb1400.

Sputnik Hotel
The *Sputnik Hotel* is just a few stops on the Metro to the southwest of the city centre (Metro Leninsky Prospekt). Sputnik means satellite in Russian and the hotel was built ten years after the first satellite was launched by the Soviets – and six years after Yuri Gagarin's first space flight. To honour the first cosmonaut is a huge shining steel statue cast in a modern style. The hotel was refurbished for the

1980 Moscow Olympics and its decor is fairly tasteful with polished parquet floorings and plain furnishings. All rooms are en suite with telephone, satellite TV and fridge. The large conference hall can be hired very cheaply (by Moscow standards) and can seat up to 50 delegates.
Leninsky prospekt 38
Tel: (095) 930 1981 *or* 2287. Fax: (095) 930 6383.
E-mail: hsputnik@dol.ru
Website: www.hotelsputnik.ru
Price: From Rb1677.

Other Recommendations

Hotel Danilovsky
Although situated some way from the centre in South Moscow, *Hotel Danilovsky* has the attraction of being located in the home of the Russian Orthodox Church – Danilovsky Monastery. The setting, with 18th-century churches and well-maintained grounds, makes an ideal place to rest after the pace of central Moscow and the hotel prides itself on offering traditional Russian hospitality. The elegant, modern hotel offers 116 comfortable rooms over five (non-smoking) storeys. All rooms have an en-suite bathroom, TV and views of the monastery. There is also a conference hall and various meeting rooms for business conferences and events, as well as a fine restaurant. The monastery itself has regained a sense of purpose befitting the Church's role in post-Communist Russia and is worth visiting (open daily 0700–1900; admission free).
5 Bolshoi Starodanilovsky Per
Tel: (095) 954 0503. Fax: (095) 954 0750.
E-mail: hotdanil@cityline.ru
Price: US$130 (including breakfast).

Hotel Ukraina
Circling Moscow city centre are Stalin's seven sisters, gigantic peaked buildings that are straight out of a Batman cartoon. One of these is the *Hotel Ukraina*, built in 1957, where a visit feels like a walk through the Soviet history of Russia. Standing at 200m (656ft), it was once the tallest hotel in the world and many of the rooms have great views over the Moskva River and Russian parliament. The hotel is situated very near the Novy Arbat and the Expocentre. With its well-worn red carpets, dark woods and chandeliers,

Ivan the Great Bell Tower

Photo: Helen Argent

The Kremlin

the interior is not quite as impressive as the outside of the building but it is comfortable – if old fashioned. Each of the 1017 rooms is well equipped with en-suite bathroom, mini-bar, fridge, safe, telephone and satellite TV. The business traveller is well catered for, with extensive facilities, including conference rooms that can accommodate up to 180 people.
Kutuzovsky prospekt 2/1
Tel: (095) 933 5656 *or* 243 3030. Fax: (95) 933 6978 *or* 956 2078.
E-mail: reserv@ukraina-hotel.ru
Website: www.ukraina-hotel.ru
Price: From Rb3000 (including breakfast and sales tax).

RESTAURANTS

The selected restaurants have been divided into five categories: Gastronomic, Business, Trendy, Budget and Personal Recommendations. The restaurants are listed alphabetically within these different categories, which serve as guidelines rather than absolute definitions of the establishments.

Restaurant prices are subject to VAT (20%), which is always included within the prices stated. A service charge may be included (around 10%), however, if it is not, it is common (although not obligatory) for diners to leave 5–10% of the total bill for the waiting staff. Even one crisp US Dollar note goes much further than many Roubles.

The prices quoted below are for an average three-course meal for one person and for a bottle of house wine or cheapest equivalent; they include VAT but do not include service charge or tip.

Gastronomic

Bungalo Bar

One of only two Ethiopian restaurants in Moscow, the *Bungalo Bar* serves up traditional east African fare, such as spiced and slow-cooked beef and lamb stews, which are eaten with the fingers between chunks of

large, thick and slightly sour pancakes called *injera*. Once past the thatched canopy and garish sign, the interior becomes more authentic, with parchment paintings and artefacts hung over the snug wooden booths. More adventurous carnivores may like to try the alligator or kangaroo.
Zemlyanoy val 6
Tel: (095) 916 2432.
Price: Rb800. Wine: Rb800.

Noev Kovcheg

Armenian food is similar to Georgian but is more difficult to find, however, *Noev Kovcheg* ('Noah's Ark') is probably the best place to sample it in central Moscow. The restaurant's special is *kyufta* – beef that has been thrashed, salted and sun-dried – and it is delivered fresh from Armenia every week. Enthusiastic carnivores can sample the stuffed suckling pig – they will even deliver it if ordered three hours in advance. Service is efficient and pleasant, while the decor is rustic Asian, with whitewashed walls and plain wooden furniture.
Maly Ivanovsky pereulok 7–9/1
Tel: (095) 917 0717 *or* 4699.
E-mail: kovcheg@noevkovcheg.ru *or* kovcheg@arknoahs.com
Website: www.noevkovcheg.ru
Price: Rb1200. Wine: Rb800.

Pushkin

To dine out in true 19th-century style, the four floors of *Pushkin* are the place. Its food and service are impeccable – with prices to match. The *solyanka* (creamy cabbage soup) and the blini (pancakes) with black caviar are absolute musts. With its old Russia sensibilities, this is where the new Russians like to come and flex the power of their wallets. Ideal for a chic lunch while shopping along the Tverskaya.
Tverskoi bulvar 26A
Tel: (095) 229 5590.
Price: Rb1600. Wine: Rb850.

Settebello

Settebello is an elegant Italian restaurant, with a summer verandah overlooking the fountains nearby.

It has a Rococo conservatory feel to it, with period furniture, white tablecloths and plants. It screens retro films, hosts high-quality live acts and operates a music policy that avoids anything after the 1970s. Most dishes on the menu are very good but the carpaccio, grilled lamb and panna cotta are exceptional.
Sadovaya-Samotechnaya ulitsa 3
Tel: (095) 299 1656 *or* 3039.
Price: Rb1200. Wine: Rb800.

Yar

Yar, a traditional Russian restaurant founded in 1826, was frequented by Pushkin, Tolstoy and Shalyapin. Highlights of the modern menu include black caviar, herring, sturgeon and perch. The beef stroganoff is particularly good, as are the *borscht* (beetroot soup) and *shchi* (cabbage soup). A gypsy band continues a Yar tradition each night by singing love songs to diners in the mirrored hall, which is lined with vaulting serpentine columns stretching up to the ornate domed ceiling.
Leningradsky prospekt 32/21
Tel: (095) 960 2000.
Price: Rb3000. Wine: Rb1200.

Business

Amazonia

Amazonia is a replica rainforest but curiously the menu does not lead off on the trail of South America but serves up Japanese and European dishes. The mixed Spanish cured meat dish (jamon, serrano and chorizo) is particularly tasty and the beef medallions Amazonia are a speciality. Lighter options include algae salad or temaki from the sushi menu, which has become surprisingly popular in Moscow in recent years. On Thursday, the Latin American night offers salsa into the small hours. Prices drop by around a third 1200–1800, although the venue is open until 0600.
Strastnoy bulvar 14
Tel: (095) 209 7487 *or* 9606.
Price: Rb1000. Wine: Rb850.

Photo: Helen Argent

Cathedral of the Assumption

Tibetskie Himalai

Take the most genteel service in Moscow, add the Dalai Lama and Tibetan gods looking down at diners from deep red and yellow walls and the result is an experience that nourishes karma. However, dining at *Tibetskie Himalai* (Tibet Himalaya) will slim the wallet. Dishes to try include the *ongkor* salad (aubergine and rice salad with soya sauce), *chugdzi* salad (cheese, lychee and tomatoes), while sipping *sakura*, a type of cherry wine, or *arag kampu*, wine made from apricots and cinnamon. Carnivores should beware of the full moon, when the restaurant serves a purely vegetarian menu.
Pokrovka ulitsa 19
Tel: (095) 917 3985.
Price: Rb1500. Wine: Rb850.

Uncle Guilly's Steak House

Whether in Moscow for five days or five years, it is almost impossible to avoid one of the myriad of steakhouses across the capital. The best steaks in town can be found at Uncle Guilly's, which has a huge reputation in Moscow with ex-pats hungry for a sizzling taste of home – and a price list to match. In fact, it is so popular that it has a takeaway service too. Set in an old wine cellar, the restaurant prides itself on the freshness of its imported meat. Security is tight here and bookings are usually essential. Tahini spinach salad, *filet mignon* and New Zealand lamb chops are just some of the other highlights of its great menu.
Stoleshnikov pereulok 6
Tel: (095) 229 2050 *or* 4750.
Price: Rb2500. Wine: Rb850.

U Pirosmani

U Pirosmani is a treat indeed. The window seats overlook the golden cupolas of the beautiful Novodevichy Monastery and the pond in front of it. Bill Clinton, Pierre Cardin and Richard Gere have all dined in its warm, folky atmosphere with plain wooden furniture. Fortunately, the traditional Georgian food, such as *kchachapuri* (cheesy bread) or *shashlik* (marinated kebab), have not attracted Hollywood prices.
Novodevichy proezd 4
Tel: (095) 247 1926.
Website: www.upirosmani.ru
Price: Rb1800. Wine: Rb900.

Zen

Zen is an authentic Chinese restaurant, serving familiar Chinese fare – Peking duck, king-size prawns, scallops and sea eel, or vegetarian dishes like fried tofu with Chinese mushrooms. It is the atmosphere that people come for though – the establishment features feng shui touches, like a waterfall over moss-covered limestone rocks and a bridge across a babbling stream to reach the tables. Cheaper deals are on offer 1200–1700, when there is a business lunch for Rb300.
Bolshoi Putnikovsky pereulok 3
Tel: (095) 299 5444.
Price: Rb1500. Wine: Rb900.

Trendy

Kitayskiy Letchik Jao Da

More of a prelude to a big, sweaty, fun night out than a gastronomic gem, *Chinese Pilot Jao Da* is still a

unique dining experience (the counter is made from the wing of an aircraft). Despite the red and green Chinese decor, the food is not traditional Chinese – instead the simple menu includes omelettes, Slavonic *plov* (a rice, cheese and vegetable dish) and a good variety of tasty cheap salads. Live rock bands kick off at 2300 and it usually stays open until around 0800. No credit cards.
Lubyansky proezd 25
Tel: (095) 924 5611.
E-mail: letchik@jao-da.ru
Website: www.jao-da.ru
Price: Rb900. Wine: Rb805.

Orangeya

One of the newer restaurants in Moscow, the *Orangeya* (Orangery), with its orange-painted walls and sleek modern furnishings, reflects the aspirations of young Muscovites. The menu too is a fusion of modern flavours – the Caesar salad could be found in New York and the traditional English trifle could easily be served in London, while the sturgeon steak is a much more local experience. The Orangeya prides itself on its clubby atmosphere and this is reflected in its huge choice of wines and spirits and the cigar room in which to savour them.
Mapaya Gusinskaya 15
Tel: (095) 253 2000 *or* 0253.
Price: Rb1000. Wine: Rb850.

People

With its five dining halls connected by a maze of corridors, there is something redolent of Philippe Starck's designs at *People*, a new restaurant on

Pravdy ulitsa, Moscow's Fleet Street. For really good sushi, diners can book a table in the Japanese room, decorated with bamboo and calligraphy, while in the European restaurant, kangaroo and ostrich (increasingly popular in Moscow) can be ordered. Quite obviously aimed at the hip higher wage earners, the restaurant hosts live music and boasts a sumptuous wood-panelled cigar room, as well as a summer terrace with a mini-golf course.

Pravdy ulitsa 21
Tel: (095) 961 2050.
Price: Rb2000. Wine: Rb900.

Syr

One of the newest restaurants in town, the two-storey turreted *Syr* (Cheese), with model cows at the front door, has attracted a stylish crowd to its two modish dining rooms. The first is light and airy, with milky alabaster walls and twisting columns. The second, with its deep reds and dark greys, is darker and has a much more clubby feel to it. But both floors serve truly fantastic Italian food, such as fresh salmon, carpaccio, and, although the three-course price is rather steep, a pizza will cost around Rb650.

Sadovaya-Samotechnaya ulitsa 16
Tel: (095) 209 7770.
Price: Rb2500. Wine: Rb2000.

Zhyoltoe More

With its round-the-clock service, patrons of *Zhyoltoe More* (Yellow Sea) are said not to live life but glide through it. Its frequenters are described as *pafosno* – knowingly and fashionably pretentious young Muscovites – who can be seen sipping cocktails from the comprehensive drinks menu. From the Japanese breakfast (chicken rolls, vegetable omelette, green tea), served daily 0430–1100, to the karaoke, which only cranks up from midnight, this really is the place to be seen. The restaurant has a great view of two churches, which ring the bells for their daily services. Despite its Japanese decor, the menu also stretches to the cuisine of its gastronomic neighbours – China and Korea.

Bolshaya Polyanka ulitsa 27
Tel: (095) 953 9634.
Price: Rb3000. Wine: Rb1000.

Budget

Genatsvale

Great Georgian food and wine is to be found at *Genatsvale*, not far from Park Kultury (Culture Park). Its authenticity is a particular attraction — it is decorated in traditional *izbushka* (peasant hut) style, while the waiters wear rustic tunics. Georgian food tends to be very meaty and Genatsvale makes no excuses for this with its *kharcho* (beef broth) and *khinkali* (meat-filled dumplings). But the *khachapuri* (cheesy bread) with *lobio* (spicy red beans) make a tasty alternative for vegetarians. What really has people flocking to Genatsvale, however, is the *barabulka*, small fry from the Black Sea.

Ostozhenka ulitsa 12/1
Tel: (095) 202 0445.
Price: Rb800. Wine: Rb800.

Guriya

This cheap traditional Georgian restaurant, just across the Moskva River from Gorky Park, is so popular that diners must arrive early. Russian food is high in fat and sometimes low in taste, which has secured the popularity of the Asiatic flavours from the republic of Georgia. Special dishes include *khachapuri* (cheese-filled bread), *lobio* (a red bean dish), *pelmeni* (dumplings filled with sausage meat) and *goloptsi* (cabbage rolls). The service is friendly and the decor simple (wooden furniture, stone floor). For those wanting to drink, the neighbouring kiosk sells bottles of wine. No credit cards.

Komsomolsky prospekt 7/3
Tel: (095) 246 0378.
Price: Rb600. Wine: Unlicensed; BYO (no corkage fee).

Pizza Sbarro

One of five in the *Sbarro* chain in Moscow, this pizza parlour, just next to the Manezh central exhibition hall, is the best located. Simple metal tables and chairs on a stone-flagged floor with a canteen-style counter add to the efficiency of this cheap and pleasant eating place. The terrace is ideal in summer. As well as a selection of pizzas, Sbarro also serves lasagne, Russian soups and goulash.

Manezhnaya ploshchad 1
Tel: (095) 737 8393. Fax: (095) 737 8390.
Price: Rb300. Wine: Rb800.

Russkoe Bistro

The Americans may have mastered fast food but the Russians invented it – the word bistro comes from Russian and simply means 'fast'. McDonald's has had a strong presence in Moscow since the early 1990s and the *Russkoe Bistro* (Russian Bistro) chain is a riposte to the American burger's dominance. Moscow's mayor, Yuri Luzkov, opened the first in 1995, right across the square from Moscow's first McDonald's, with a billboard showing a hearty Cossack. The Russian interpretation of fast food is pies – *rasstegai* (folded rolls with various fillings) and *kulebyaki* (rolls stuffed with mushrooms or meat) – salads, *kvas* (a semi-alcoholic soft drink), Russian vodkas and *nalivki* (alcoholic fruit drinks served in miniature bottles). A ten-minute walk from Red Square makes this particular franchise in the chain ideal for a filling snack while sightseeing. Closes at 2100.

Tverskaya ulitsa 16
Tel: (095) 290 9834.
Price: Rb150. Vodkas: From Rb60.

Yolki Palki

The *telega* (peasant cart) salad bar at *Yolki Palki* serves Russian salads galore (vegetable salad, marinated mushrooms etc). However, main courses, such as the Mongolian *temircan* plate, where diners choose meats and the spices to go with them, which are then cooked to order, cannot be missed. The *ukha* (fish soup) can be good too, if rather pungent. With rustic, wooden furnishings and waitresses in traditional *sarafan*, there is a definite folk theme running through all these restaurants in the chain.

Klimentovsky per. 14 bulvar 1
Tel: (095) 953 9130.
Price: Rb190 (salad bar); Rb350 (main courses).
Wine: Rb800.
Branch:
Novy Arbat ulitsa 11
Tel: (095) 291 6888.

Personal Recommendations

El Gaucho

El Gaucho's beef steaks are legends in their own right and somehow the restaurant's dark wood

St Basil's Cathedral

Novodevichy Monastery

Photo: Helen Argent

seems an appropriate setting in which to indulge carnivorous instincts. An international franchise, El Gaucho has a strong presence in Israel, which has resulted in kosher specialities. The mixed meat dish comes with chargrilled beef, chorizo, vegetable kebabs, liver and kidneys. El Gaucho has a strong family feel and, on Sunday afternoons, parents pay Rb300 for the children's festival with puppet shows, clowns and a disco to help keep the tots entertained.
Zatsepsky val 6/13
Tel: (095) 953 2876.
Price: Rb1400. Wine: Rb800.

Pancho Villa

Not short of its own revolutionaries, the best Mexican food in Moscow is to be found at *Pancho Villa* – named after the Mexican revolutionary, Pancho (1910–17). Diners can choose from the traditional Tex-Mex menu of quesadilla, fajitas, burritos and enchiladas or the more authentic flavours including *sopa de Carmera* (mutton and haricot bean soup) or *legumbres asados* (aubergines, peppers, tomatoes and mushrooms). In the heart of the tourist zone, Pancho Villa is a busy, popular place and ideal for a quick bite between shopping on the Arbat and a night of high culture at the Bolshoi Theatre. The decor is pure Mexicana – plastic stone walls with robust wooden tables and chairs. The covered street terrace is great in summer.
Novy Arbat 44/1
Tel: (095) 241 9835.
E-mail: panchovilla@mail.ru
Website: http://pvilla.virtualave.net
Price: Rb900. Wine: Rb342 (one-litre carafe).

Taiskii Ban

Despite the garish geometric blue and white decor, *Taiskii Ban* (Baan Thai) should not be missed, as there can be no greater food than Thai to keep out the Moscow cold. This is one of the best places in Moscow for a good winter warmer of *plar kung* (prawn salad with lemongrass and chillies) or *pla sam si* (steamed sturgeon with black mushrooms, ginger and carrot in oyster and soy sauce). Even vegans will not go away hungry, with really tasty dishes, such as the *tao hoo kap het* (stir-fried tofu and mushrooms in peanut sauce), available.
B Dorogomilovskaya ulitsa 11
Tel: (095) 240 0597 *or* 938 8450.
Price: Rb1000. Wine: Rb800.

Taras Bulba

A visit to any of the restaurants in the Ukrainian *Taras Bulba* chain is well worth it. Based on traditional *korchma* (taverns), the rustic furniture and traditional dress worn by the staff takes diners well on the way south to the Black Sea. Special dishes include red meat *borscht*, green spinach *borscht*, as well as chicken, fresh lobster and *vareniki* (a type of meat-filled dumpling).
Petrovka ulitsa 30/7
Tel: (095) 200 6082.
Price: Rb1000. Wine: Rb800.

Tsarskaya Okhota

Reputed to be Boris Yeltsin's favourite restaurant, *Tsarskaya Okhota* (The Royal Hunt) is one of the most expensive places in which to eat in Moscow. However, for those with an elastic expense account or wanting to impress a client, there is no better place to do it. Diners can start with traditional Russian salad (beetroot, potato salad in a mayonnaise and dill dressing) from the *telega* (traditional peasant cart) and then launch into something heavier, such as *rasstegais* (open-top pies), thick soups, *shashlik* (marinated kebab), and great *pelmeni* (dumplings filled with sausage meat). Tsarskaya Okhota nestles in woodland to the northeast of the city, although it is still serviced by the Metro (Molodyozhnaya). Themed as a hunting lodge, it has a roaring open fireplace and its walls are bedecked with antlers of conquests past.
Rublyovo-Uspenskoye shosse 18a, Zhukovka Village
Tel: (095) 418 7982/3.
E-mail: info@tsarshunt.co.ru
Website: www.tsarshunt.com.ru/index_ie.html
Price: Rb2000. Wine: Rb800.

ENTERTAINMENT

Nightlife

Discos are popular in Moscow, although there are also an increasing number of pub-type bars, many of which serve food. These generally offer a happy hour, with two-for-one drink specials. There is no shortage of exotic entertainment and Western men do tend to attract young Russian women. Also, some bars might become violent – it is always best to ask for local advice on the most appropriate places to go.

Moscow has a number of 24-hour bars and 'night restaurants' that are often open until 0500 or 0600 and combine dining, drinking and entertainment under one roof. Otherwise, bars tend to stay open until 2400 or 0100. The minimum drinking age in Russia is 18 years, although the minimum age to purchase alcohol is 21 years. This means that if you are aged 18–20, you are allowed to drink alcohol if seated at a table in a bar but somebody aged 21 or over must actually purchase the drinks at the bar for you. Cover charges at venues vary – some places actually offer free drinks for a limited time, while others charge a cover of Rb600–900/$US20–30 (or more). A beer costs around Rb120–180.

Live music is played all over the city but quality acts are not always easy to come by. Many of the bars and clubs are located in or near the larger hotels and, because of the pace of change in Moscow, bars and clubs tend to close down and open up fairly frequently. Up-to-date information can be found in the Metropolis section of Friday's *The Moscow Times* (website: www.themoscowtimes.com) or the American ex-pat newspaper *eXile* (website: www.exile.ru).

Bars

The *John Bull Pub*, Kutuzovsky proezd 4, has decent music and stays open until 0300 at the weekend. The long-standing Irish pub *Rosie O'Grady's*, Znamenka ulitsa 9/12, is also a popular spot. Homesick Canadians head for the *Moosehead Canadian Bar*, Bolshaya Polyanka ulitsa 54, which serves bar food and is open until 0500. *Chesterfield's*, Zemlyanoy val 26, has the longest bar in Russia (apparently) and draws a mixed ex-pat and Russian crowd. For those who enjoy a cigar and cognac, *The Embassy Club*, Bruysov pereulok 8/10, provides an appropriately swanky environment, while *OGI Project*, Potapovsky pereulok, has become hugely popular with a more hip – vaguely hippy – crowd.

Casinos

There are dozens of casinos in Moscow. Some of the more elegant are attached to the five-star hotels. The 24-hour *Casino Metropol*, located in the hotel of the same name, at Teatralny proezd 1/4, is a classic casino with blackjack, roulette and poker. For lower stakes, the *Olympic Casino Club*, aboard the *Valery Brusov*, Krymskaya naberezhnaya, is open 1900–0600 and offers roulette, blackjack and poker. Another alternative is the *Casino Moskva*, located in the Leningradskaya Hotel, Kalanchevskaya ulitsa 21/40. There is an age restriction of 18 years for gambling, a passport is usually required and the dress code is smart-casual.

Clubs

Propaganda, Bolshoi Zlatoushinsky pereulok 7 (website: www.propagandamoscow.com), is one of the city's best dance clubs and plays non-techno tunes (occasionally acid jazz). Techno-ravers should head for *Khaos*, Timirgazevskaya ulitsa 17. *Brand*, Smolensky ploshchad, has a more upmarket feel, with a disco and bars. The big-name international DJs who appear from time to time at *Club XIII*, Myanitskaya ulitsa, attract foreigners and young Russians with pockets full of cash. *Titanik*, inside the *Young Pioneers Stadium*, Leningradsky prospekt 31, is a well-known techno club with a decent but expensive chill-out area. Clubs catering to a gay crowd are

GUM department store, Red Square

becoming increasingly popular in Moscow. The most frequented of these is *Central Station*, Bolshaya Tatarskaya ulitsa, which could almost compete with any Western gay club. Homophobia is still very much in evidence in Moscow, however, so it is advisable for visitors to avoid going to any of the gay clubs alone.

Live Music

Many of the bars and clubs have live music – usually rock but occasionally country, reggae or folk – for a couple of hours in the evening (generally 2200–2400/0100). For jazz and blues, *BB King*, Sadovaya Samotechnaya ulitsa 4/2, is considered one of the best venues for live acts – concerts and jam sessions continue until 0200. *Bunker*, Tverskaya ulitsa 12, and *Tabula Rasa*, Berezhkovskaya Naberezhnaya 28, both feature live bands – the cover charge depends on the night and who is playing. The *Voodoo Lounge*, Sredny Tishinsky pereulok 5/7 (website: www.voodoolounge.ru), is a hot spot for dancing and includes international music.

Sport

Moscow hosted the Olympic Games in the summer of 1980 and, as a result, has a number of good sporting venues, although the 100,000-seat *Lenin Stadium*, at the Lushiniki stadium complex, which was once the home of Spartak Moscow, is now a giant flea market. *Spartak Moscow* (website: www.spartak.com) now play at the *Lokomotiv Stadium*, Bolshaya Cher-kizovskaya ulitsa 125A (tel: (095) 161 4283), as do *Lokomotiv Moscow* (website: www.lokomotiv.ru). The renowned *Dynamo Moscow* (website: www.fc-dynamo.ru) football club plays at the *Central Dynamo Stadium*, 36 Leningradsky prospekt (tel: (095) 271 8529), while *FC Torpedo Moscow* (website: www.torpedo.ru) plays at the *Torpedo Stadium*, Vostchnaya ulitsa 4 (tel: (095) 275 0745). The fifth premier division football team in the city is that of *Central Sport Club of the Army* (website: www.cska.ru) – abbreviated TSSKA or CSKA – who play at the *CSKA Peschanoe Stadium*, Leningradsky prospekt 39A (tel: (095) 213 7992), as does the popular CSKA ice

hockey team. In fact, many of the teams cross sporting boundaries – Spartak Moscow also have an ice hockey team and CSKA also has a basketball team.

Tennis is currently enjoying a great deal of popularity, not least because it was frowned upon as bourgeois in Soviet times and because of the international success of Russian stars, such as Yevgeny Kafelnikov, Anna Kournikova and Marat Safin. Moscow hosts the country's annual grand slam, the Kremlin Cup, at the *Olympiisky Sports Complex*, Mira prospekt 16 (tel: (095) 288 5453).

The *Moscow Head Office of Theatre, Concert and Sport Ticket Bureaux* (tel: (095) 249 5792) provides information and tickets.

Banya

As sure as a Russian likes tea from a samovar, a Russian likes a *banya* – which usually includes a sauna, massage and a light beating with birch twigs (*veniki*), just to make sure that the circulation is really working. The *Sandunovskiye Baths*, Sandunovskiye pereulok (tel: (095) 925 4631), are the city's grandest and provide a relaxing and very Russian atmosphere in which to experience this. *The Sauna at Chistye Prudy*, Krivokolenny pereulok 14/2 (tel: (095) 923 5854), provides a more 'new Russian' experience.

Diving

Visitors to Moscow can find out about diving clubs from the *Sprut* (Octopus) diving club (tel: (095) 212 5775; website: www.octopus.ru). The oldest diving club in Moscow is the *Moscow State University Diving Club & School*, Serpukovsky val 6 (tel: (095) 105 7799; website: www.dive.ru).

Fitness Centres

The modern sanatorium-style complex *Kimberly Land*, Azovskaya ulitsa 24 (tel: (095) 310 0401; website: www.kimberlyland.ru), offers an aqua park with some swimming pools (whirlpool, kids pool and hills), a fully equipped gym and Turkish baths. *Bitsa Equestrian Sport Club*, 33 Balaklavsky prospect (tel: (095) 318 5366), offers shooting, swimming, tennis, volleyball, aerobics, horseriding and paint-balling, as well as a full fitness centre. *The*

Entertainment Centre na Tulskoi, Kholodilny pereulok 3 (tel: (095) 954 0158), is open 1200–2400 for rollerskating and bowling, as well as 2300–0600 on Friday and Saturday for a roller disco.

Golf

There is a fairly central nine-hole course at the *Moscow City Golf Club*, Dovzhenko ulitsa 1 (tel: (095) 147 1826), where admission costs Rb1661/US$54 for non-members. More challenging 18-hole courses are located further out at *Le Meridien Moscow Country Club*, in Nakhadino (tel: (095) 926 5911). Green fees here cost Rb3000/US$100 at the weekend and membership is required.

Tennis

The *Chaika Tennis Courts*, Korobeynikov pereulok 1 (tel: (095) 202 0474), are conveniently located near Park Kultury Metro station. There is also a swimming pool in the complex. *Petrovsky Park Tennis Club*, Leningradsky prospekt 36 (tel: (095) 212 7392), is another option.

Wintersports

There is a downhill ski jump in the Vorobyevi Hills and cross-country skiing opportunities at Izmailovsky Park and in the countryside outside Moscow. There are numerous places to skate when the water freezes in mid-winter, including Gorky Park.

Shopping

The showpiece of the Soviet economy was the GUM department store, which faces the Kremlin across Red Square and is now full of high-end luxury Western goods. Goods can be found at much cheaper prices elsewhere but it is worth visiting for convenience and for checking what is available. Popular shopping streets in the area include Novy Arbat (a major thoroughfare to the west of the Kremlin) and Arbat ulitsa, which runs parallel to it. Okhotny Ryad, the newest of the arcades in Moscow, is also worth a visit, if only to see Russian aspirational consumerism gone mad. Built by Moscow's mayor, Yuri Luzhkov, for a princely sum of US$350 million, it is as much a tribute to consumerism as his other brainchild, the Cathedral of Christ the Saviour, is a symbol of Russia's religious renaissance. Tverskaya ulitsa, heading north from Red Square, and Petrovka ulitsa, which starts at the Bolshoi Theatre and runs parallel to Tverskaya, are two of Moscow's most fashionable shopping streets and home to some very expensive boutiques. Classic Russian chic can be found at *Valentin Yudashkin*, Kutuzovsky prospekt, which is also home to the exclusive *Moskva* shopping centre.

For the souvenir hunter, Palekh and Kholui lacquered boxes make attractive gifts, as do the traditional Matryoshka dolls (wooden dolls within dolls) and samovars. Other options are Khokhloma wooden cups, saucers and spoons (painted gold, red and black) and Dymkovskaya Igrushka pottery figurines based on popular folklore characters. Engraved amber, Gzhel porcelain, Vologda lace and Fabergé eggs and jewellery are highly sought after. Mementoes from the Red Army abound. The weekend craft market at Izmailovsky Park (Metro Izmailovsky Park) and Novy Arbat are the best places to begin souvenir shopping. Antiques, valuables, works of art and manuscripts, other than those offered for sale in souvenir shops, may not be taken out of the Russian Federation without an export licence.

For a real taste of Russia, *Cheremushinsky Rynok*, on Lomonovsky prospekt, gathers together fresh produce from all corners of the former Soviet Union. The market is open Monday to Saturday 0700–1900 and Sunday 0700–1700. Visitors should not expect pristine hygiene, although bargains are plentiful. The *Konkovo Fair*, located on Profsoyuznaya ulitsa and open daily 0800–2000, is Moscow's largest market and caters to function rather than style, selling clothes, household goods and food.

Shopping hours are generally Monday to Saturday 0900–1800, although larger stores open 1000–2000, while smaller shops still take a lunch break 1300–1500. VAT stands at 20% (10% for certain foodstuffs and items for children), however, it is not reclaimable.

Culture

The city's cultural history spans all the arts and much of the nation's cultural effort has been concentrated here in Mosocw, despite St Petersburg's position as traditional seat of the *intelligentsia*. Notable achievements include the long period of icon painting up to the time of Peter the Great – the most famous icon painter of the Russian Orthodox Church, Andrey Rublyov, had his workshop in Moscow and was buried in the *Spaso-Andronikovsky Monastyr* (Monastery of the Saviour and Andronicus), in the eastern suburbs of the city. The 19th century brought painters such as Ilya Repin, whose Social Realist works portrayed peasants and other ordinary people. The excitement of the Constructivists' avant-garde work in the early 20th century was dampened by Stalin's regime and, until recently, Social Realism has been the only publicly produced art.

The former Soviet Union took great pride in its cultural institutions and these were often of the very highest calibre. A number of these are based in Moscow, notably the Bolshoi Ballet and Opera Company and the Moscow Circus. Advance tickets can be fairly cheap if purchased from the venue or one of the many ticket booths around the city, but those purchased from ticket touts on the evening of the performance are usually comparatively expensive. Concert and theatre tickets can also be purchased

from large hotels or at the *IPS Theatre Box Office*, in the *Metropol Hotel*, Teatralny proezd 1/4 (tel: (095) 927 6000). Tickets for most performances range between Rb600/US$20 and Rb900/US$30.

Moscow Out (website: www.moscowout.ru) is an excellent source of listings and information on cultural events in the city. Film listings can be found in the Metropolis section of Friday's *The Moscow Times* (website: www.themoscowtimes.com).

Music

The *Moscow Conservatory*, Nikitskaya ulitsa 13 (tel: (095) 229 8183), is an important music school, as well as the venue for major concerts – premieres of works by Sergei Prokofiev and Dmitri Shostakovich took place here. Pyotr Tchaikovsky taught at the Conservatory but died before public concerts started in 1898. One of the students whom he commended for his thesis project was none other than Sergei Rachmaninov. Concerts take place in both the Great and Small Halls.

The *Tchaikovsky Concert Hall*, Triumphalnaya ploshchad 4/30 (tel: (095) 299 3957), hosts a full programme of symphony and chamber concerts, as well as special festivals and performances of Russian national dance and organ and choral music. *Arbat-Opera*, Arbat ulitsa 35 (tel: (095) 248 0987), is one of the newest music theatres in Moscow and, although it

is small, it is ideal for chamber operas of Pergolezzi, Rimsky Korsakov, Poulenc and the like.

Theatre

Moscow's pre-eminent theatre company is the *MKHAT imeni Chekhova* (Moscow Art Theatre, named after Chekhov), Kamergersky pereulok 3 (tel: (095) 229 8760; website: http://art.theatre.ru), founded in 1898. It revolutionised drama in Europe, staging plays by Anton Chekhov and providing a venue for the method-acting techniques of Konstantin Stanislavsky. No longer avant-garde, the theatre today continues the tradition of method acting.

The *Maly Teatr* (Small Theatre), Teatralnaya ploshchad 1 (tel: (095) 923 2621), has a history of staging plays of political and social satire, notably during the 19th century. Some of Russia's most famous playwrights, including Nikolai Gogol, staged their first plays here. There are performances daily at 1900. The *Taganka Drama and Comedy Theatre*, Zemlyanov val (tel: (095) 915 1015), has an excellent reputation, earned through its staging of modern classics, such as *Doctor Zhivago* and *The Master and Margarita*.

Dance

One of the world's most renowned ballet and opera companies, the *Bolshoi* (website: www.bolshoi.ru), is based in Moscow from September to June

Tsar Bell

(performance are held daily at 1900, with additional weekend matinees). The company, formed in 1773, began its rise to fame in 1918. Yuri Grigorovich, who directed the company for decades until 1995, raised the Bolshoi's status internationally, aided by some formidable dancers. The *Bolshoi Theatre*, Teatralnaya ploshchad 1 (tel: (095) 292 0050), a grand neo-classical building that was constructed in 1824, is renowned for its size and the quality of the acoustics. If tickets for the Bolshoi are not available, visitors should try the *Stanislavsky and Nemirovich-Danchenko Music Theatre* (known as the Stasic), Bolshoi Dmitrovka ulitsa 17 (tel: (095) 229 0649; website: www.stanislavsky.ru), founded in 1940. Alternatively, the *Kremlin Ballet* and the *Moscow Classical Ballet Theatre* both have a high standard and both perform in the *Kremlin Palace of Congresses* (tel: (095) 928 5232; website: www.kremlin-ballet.ru.tc).

Film

English-language films can be seen at the *American House of Cinema*, located in the *Radisson Slavyanskaya Hotel* (tel: (095) 941 8890), the *Dome Theatre*, located in the *Moscow Renaissance Penta Hotel* (tel: (095) 931 9000), and the *International Cinema Centre*, on Krasnaya Presnaya, Druzhinnikovskaya ulitsa 15 (tel: (095) 255 9057), which screens documentaries, retrospectives and silent movies.

The *Moscow Film Festival* takes place in July (website: www.filmfestivals.com/moscow).

Sergei Eisenstein captured one of Moscow and Russia's harshest rulers in the films *Ivan the Terrible I and II* (1945 and 1958 respectively). The famous director also used the Kolisei cinema (now the *Sovremennik Theatre*, Chistoprudny bulvar 19A) for his Prolecult workers' theatre.

Cultural Events

The *Great Moscow Circus* no longer quite lives up to its reputation but still provides good entertainment. There are performances Tuesday to Friday at 1900, as well as multiple performances at the weekend. The *New Circus* is located at Vernadskovo prospekt 7 (tel: (095) 930 2815), and the *Old Circus* at Tsvetnoi bulvar 13 (tel: (095) 200 0668). The Muscovites make good use of the white nights, which happen during summer, with the annual *White Nights Festival* – a celebration of music, theatre, street events and fireworks. Winter is no less fun, with the *Russian Winter Festival* over Christmas and New Year, when Moscow comes alive with troika rides and traditional folk customs. More sombre annual events include the poetry readings at the Pushkin Monument, celebrating his birthday on 6 June, and annual celebrations of the November Revolution and victory in Russia's significant historical battles.

Literary Notes

Moscow has been home to many important writers and has often been the setting for their works. The houses where playwright Anton Chekhov (Sadovaya-Kudrinskaya ulitsa 6) and novelists Leo Tolstoy (Leo Tolstoy ulitsa) and Maxim Gorky (Malaya Nikitskaya ulitsa) spent part of their lives, are all open to the public.

Philosopher, moral thinker, nobleman, writer of Social Realism and intellectual giant (as well as cobbler), Tolstoy (1828–1910) was born on his family estate, south of Moscow. In many of his works, Tolstoy illustrates life in the capital, particularly in *War and Peace* (1865–69), considered one of the greatest novels ever written, in which he describes the burning of Moscow during the Napoleonic wars.

Chekhov's play, *The Seagull*, premiered at the Moscow Arts Theatre in 1898. Chekhov and the novelist and playwright Nikolai Gogol were both buried in Novodevichy Cemetery, in the southwest of the city (see *Key Attractions*). Fyodor Dostoevsky, although more commonly associated with St Petersburg (the setting for *Crime and Punishment* and many other of his works), was born and spent his early years in Moscow, returning to give a stirring speech (as did Ivan Turgenev) at the unveiling of the monument to Alexander Pushkin in Teatralnaya ploshchad in 1880. This event was the first public recognition of national literature – as Pushkin was seen as the father of Russian literature. His best-known works include *Eugene Onegin* (1825) and *Boris Godunov* (1824).

Mikhail Lermontov (1814–42), the 19th-century poet and novelist, studied at Moscow University and lived just off present-day Novy Arbat. Boris Pasternak (1939–60) lived on the outskirts of Moscow, among the artists and writers in Peredelinko. It was here that he wrote his sweeping romantic novel about the Russian Revolution, *Doctor Zhivago* (1957). Mikhail Bulgakov set parts of his most famous novel, *The Master and Margarita* (written in the 1930s, first published posthumously in 1967), in Moscow – at the Central House of Writers restaurant and the Patriarshiye Prudy (Patriarch's Ponds), where the novel begins.

After glasnost, Anatoly Rybakov published *Children of the Arbat* (1988), in which he traces his Moscow childhood and, more recently, Victor Pelevin, who penned *The Clay Machine Gun* (1996), has been compared to Martin Amis.

There is no shortage of works by Western novelists set during the Cold War – Moscow was a favourite setting for John Le Carré and there is also the eponymous *Gorky Park* (1981), written by Martin Cruz Smith.

Bolshoi Theatre

NEW YORK CITY

New York is a city of superlatives. Besides being a world financial centre, the urban island of Manhattan teems with world-renowned restaurants, architectural masterpieces and venerable art institutions that make it one of the world's greatest cultural cities. Its hectic pace and its alluring promise of 'if you can make it here, you can make it anywhere,' draw visitors and new residents from all over the world, who come in search of a piece of this American pie.

New York has always been a city of the world and its multinational, multicultural inhabitants – who speak over 80 languages – infuse its concrete canyons with a buzz that is every bit as energising and electrifying as that depicted in countless films and TV programmes. With over 20,000 eclectic restaurants, 150 world-class museums and more than 10,000 stores brimming with brand names and bargains from across the globe, New York really does have something for everyone. Away from the mayhem of the 24-hour urban hustle and bustle, New York also boasts the bucolic oasis of Central Park, the breezy park-lined Hudson River and acts as jumping off point for the ritzy beach

towns of Long Island. However, the epicentre of New York life always has been and still very much is the island of Manhattan, which is surrounded by four other distinct city boroughs – the Bronx, Brooklyn, Queens and Staten Island – all of which have their own character and attractions.

New York's location at the confluence of the Hudson River, Long Island and the Atlantic Ocean reflects the city's importance as a port and as the disembarkation point for millions of immigrants to the USA. The first European settlement on Manhattan was by the Dutch, during the 1620s. They named the city New Amsterdam. In 1664, the British took over and renamed it New York. The settlement rapidly flourished, expanding from south to north along the island. Mass immigration in the 19th and early 20th centuries saw the emergence of distinct ethnic quarters, with the island of Manhattan rapidly developing into a unique cultural melting pot housing an entire world within its 58 sq kilometres (23 sq miles). The cultural diversity stemming from the city's rich history contributes to the multiculturalism that New York is famous for.

Today, New York's focus is on its more recent history – the events of 11 September 2001. The ramifications and aftershocks of the terrorist destruction of the city's two tallest buildings – symbols of New York's confidence and success – still permeate many levels of life. Determination to overcome America's worst ever terrorist attack is felt throughout the city, in plans for memorialising the World Trade Center towers and revitalising nearby neighbourhoods. The event has done little to dent the appeal and vitality of the city. In fact, the world seems to have largely rallied around New York and, since the attack, tourists have tended to come not only for the shops, theatres and museums but also for new and thoughtful reasons.

New York is an excellent place to visit at any time of year, although it is particularly pleasant during the spring and autumn, when temperatures hover around 21°C (70°F). New York winters tend to be unpredictable, although cold temperatures bring less snow here than to other nearby cities, while summers are hot and muggy, often lasting until September.

Manhattan

TRAVEL

Getting There By Air

The three airports serving New York City – John F Kennedy, LaGuardia and Newark – are operated by the *Port Authority of New York and New Jersey* (tel: (212) 435 7000; website: www.panynj.gov). Passengers should plan to arrive for international flights at least two and a half hours before take off. Ground transportation information for these airports is available from the port authority (tel: (800) 247 7433) daily 0800–1800.

John F Kennedy International Airport (JFK)

Tel: (718) 244 4444. Fax: (718) 244 3536.
Website: www.kennedyairport.com
Situated in Queens, 24km (15 miles) southeast of central Manhattan, JFK is New York's busiest airport, handling over 30 million passengers a year, travelling to destinations worldwide.
Major airlines: National airlines include *American Airlines* (tel: (800) 433 7300; website: www.aa.com) and *United Airlines* (tel: (800) 241 6522; website: www.ual.com), which both operate international and domestic flights. Primarily domestic national airlines include *Delta* (tel: (800) 221 1212; website: www.delta.com) and *Northwest Airlines* (tel: (800) 225 2525; website: www.nwa.com). Other major carriers include *Aeromexico, British Airways, Canadian Airlines, Cathay Pacific, Continental Airlines, Lufthansa, Qantas, Singapore Airlines* and *Virgin Atlantic.*
Airport facilities: Facilities include banks, bureaux de change, ATMs, bars, refreshments, restaurants, post offices, shops, duty-free shopping and car hire from *Avis, Budget, Dollar, Hertz* and *National.*
Business facilities: The *Radisson Hotel JFK* (tel:

Transport to the city: A free shuttle bus, operating 24 hours at ten-minute intervals daily 0500–2400 and every 30 minutes at other times, travels to the Howard Beach subway station. From there, the connection with the *MTA* 'A' train (tel: (718) 330 1234; website www.mta.nyc.ny.us) costs US$2 and takes approximately 90 minutes to central Manhattan, stopping at a number of stations with further connections on the way. *New York Airport Service* (tel: (718) 875 8200; website: www.nyairportservice.com) express bus operates a direct service to the Port Authority Bus Terminal or Grand Central Terminal, with single tickets costing US$13. Buses depart JFK every 15–30 minutes, daily 0615–2310 (journey time – 45–90 minutes, depending on traffic).
The *Super Shuttle Manhattan* (tel: (212) 258 3826; website: www.supershuttle.com), available on demand 24 hours a day, is a shared door-to-door minibus service that travels anywhere between 23rd and 96th Streets. Prices range from US$13–22. A direct train service to Manhattan is scheduled for completion in late 2003. Taxis to Manhattan are a flat rate US$35, plus tolls and tips.

LaGuardia Airport (LGA)

Tel: (718) 533 3400. Fax: (718) 533 3421.
Website: www.laguardiaairport.com
The airport is located in Queens, 13km (eight miles) east of central Manhattan. LaGuardia handles approximately 20 million passengers a year, although almost all flights are domestic.
Major airlines: Major US carriers with their own terminals at LaGuardia include *Delta* (tel: (800) 221 1212; website: www.delta.com) and *US Airways* (tel: (800) 428 4322; website: www.usairways.com). Other carriers include *America West, Canadian Airlines* and *Continental Airlines.*

Transport to the city: Public transport is available on the *MTA* (tel: (718) 330 1234) bus 60, which intersects with all subway lines as it crosses to the Upper West Side of Manhattan. The bus operates daily 0450–0100 and a single fare is US$2, plus an additional US$2 for the subway (journey time – approximately 1 hour). An express bus service, with departures from LaGuardia every 30 minutes daily 0700–2300, is provided by *New York Airport Service* (tel: (718) 875 8200; website: www.nyairportservice.com), travelling to the Port Authority Bus Terminal or Grand Central Terminal (journey time – 40–50 minutes). A single fare is US$10. Other shuttle services are also available. The *Delta Water Shuttle* (tel: (800) 533 3779 *or* 5935) operates a ferry service from the Marine Air Terminal to 34th Street on the East River or to Pier 11 on Wall Street in downtown Manhattan (journey time – 30–45 minutes). Services operate Monday to Friday 0745–1830. Metered taxis to Manhattan cost around US$20–30, plus tolls and tips.

Newark Liberty International Airport (EWR)

Tel: (973) 961 6000 *or* (888) 397 4636. Fax: (973) 961 6259.
Website: www.newarkairport.com
The airport is located in New Jersey, 27km (16 miles) southwest of central Manhattan. It handles just under 30 million passengers a year, travelling to domestic and international destinations.
Major airlines: *Continental Airlines* (tel: (800) 523 3273; website: www.flycontinental.com) operates both domestic and international flights from Newark airport. Other carriers include *Air Canada, America West, British Airways, Delta, Korean Air, Lufthansa, ProAir* and *Virgin Atlantic.*
Airport facilities: The airport has extensive facilities, including banks, a barber, duty-free and other shops, restaurants, bars and coffee shops, a nursery and car hire from *Avis, Budget, Dollar, Hertz* and *National.*
Business facilities: The *President's Club*, in terminal C (tel: (973) 681 0015), provides workstations, conference rooms, concierge services and even a shower. Access to the lounge for non-members costs US$45. Business-class lounges are provided by the airlines in all terminals. Facilities include showers, a cocktail service and snacks, meeting space, telephones, modem ports and some business facilities.
Transport to the city: The *NJ Transit Airtrain* service (tel: (973) 762 5100 *or* (800) 234 7284; website: www.njtransit.com) connects Newark airport to Penn Station in Manhattan via New Jersey Transit. Trains run daily 0500–0200 (journey time – 20 minutes), with single tickets costing US$11.15.
Olympia Airport Express (tel: (212) 964 6233; website: www.olympiabus.com) offers bus services to Penn

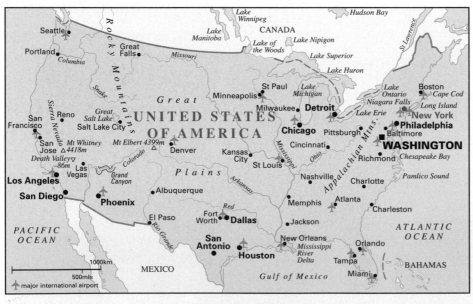

(718) 322 2300; website: www.radissonjfk.com), situated in the airport, has conference space accommodating from ten to 400 delegates, as well as meeting and function rooms. The multi-lingual staff is on hand to help with sales and catering. A concierge service is also available, as is audio-visual hire and services. There is also a 24-hour business centre. Business-class lounges are provided by the airlines in all terminals. The lounges offer private showers, a cocktail service and snacks, meeting space, telephones, modem points and some business facilities.

Airport facilities: Facilities include ATMs, child care, bars, restaurants, shops, duty-free shopping and car hire from *Avis, Budget, Dollar, Hertz* and *National.*
Business facilities: Modem connections, conference space and fully equipped workstations are available at *Laptop Lane* (tel: (718) 424 1301; fax: (718) 397 2357; website: www.wayport.net/laptoplane), in the main terminal, lower level Marketplace. Two *Business Traveler Services* stations, also in the main terminal, have telephone, fax and Internet facilities. Some airlines also provide executive lounges.

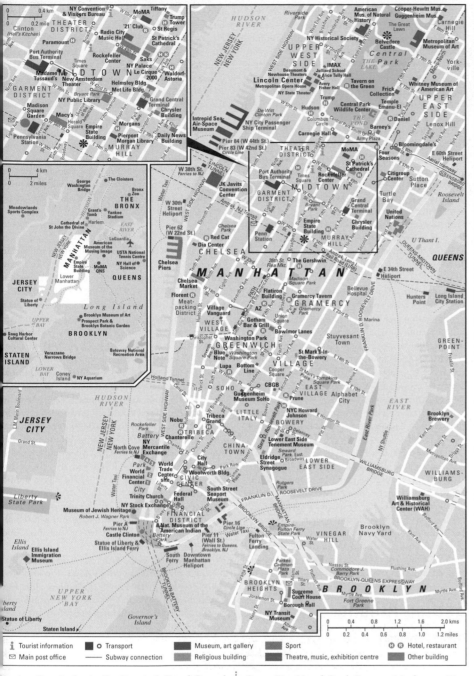

Ferry services: The *Staten Island Ferry* (tel: (718) 727 2508; website: www.siferry.com) operates from Whitehall Terminal in Battery Park, in downtown New York, travelling out past the Statue of Liberty and Ellis Island to its destination of Staten Island every 30 minutes (every 20 minutes during rush hour), daily 24 hours. There are a variety of ferry operators, including *New York Waterway* (tel: (800) 53 FERRY *or* 533 3779; website: www.nywaterway.com), *TNT Hydrolines* (tel: (732) 872 2628 *or* (800) BOAT RIDE *or* 2628 7433; website: www.seastreakusa.com) and *New York Fast Ferry* (tel: (732) 291 2210 *or* (800) 693 6933; website: www.nyff.com), providing services between Manhattan and the other boroughs, as well as to New Jersey.

Transport to the city: Ferry terminals are in or near major transportation centres of the city and are linked to subway and bus lines.

Getting There By Rail

New York City's rail services are primarily operated by Amtrak (tel: (215) 349 2152 *or* (800) 872 7245; website: www.amtrak.com). New high-speed services on the Eastern seaboard are a viable alternative to air travel on shorter routes, such as to Boston and Washington, DC.

The city has two main stations. *Grand Central Terminal*, 42nd Street and Park Avenue, is the terminus for *Metro-North Railroad* (tel: (212) 532 4900; website: www.mta.nyc.ny.us/mnr), with services to upstate New York, New Jersey and Connecticut. *Pennsylvania Station*, referred to locally as *Penn* Station, 34th Street and Sixth Avenue, serves both *Amtrak* and the *Long Island Railroad* (tel: (718) 217 5477; website: www.mta.ncy.ny.us/lirr).

Penn Station and Grand Central both have ATMs, bars, cafés, waiting rooms, shops and taxi ranks and are very well equipped. Grand Central, in aesthetic terms, is a model of station regeneration and undoubtedly the city's most impressive transport hub. Penn Station, on the other hand, is a bit sketchy and institutional, with few comfortable waiting areas. Plans to remodel the station as a glorious and airy iron-and-glass structure in the Farley Building, directly across from the current station on Eighth Avenue, are underway by architectural firm Skidmore, Owings and Merrill. This new building will be the station's third incarnation. The original building, designed by McKim, Mead and White and opened in 1910, was thoughtlessly demolished in the 1960s. This is cited as one of the city's greatest mistakes; the building that currently stands in its place is a poor substitute. A completion date has not been set for the new Penn Station.

Rail travel tends to be expensive, although a number of rail passes are available to visitors from overseas. There is no central rail information number for

Station, Port Authority Bus Terminal, Grand Central Terminal and several Midtown hotels for US$11. Buses run every 15–30 minutes daily 0600–2400 (journey time – 30–60 minutes).

Taxis to Manhattan cost approximately US$40–50 plus tolls and tip.

Approximate flight times to New York: From London is 7 hours and 40 minutes; from Los Angeles is 6 hours; from Toronto is 1 hour and 30 minutes and from Sydney is 21 hours.

Arrival/departure tax: Taxes are included in the price of a ticket.

Getting There By Water

There is no port for international passenger services, although many commuter ferry services operate locally in and around New York. The many terminals include *Lincoln Harbor*, *Hoboken*, *Harborside*, *Liberty Harbor* and *Liberty Landing* on the Hudson River, *St George* on Staten Island, *Hunters Point* in Queens and *West 38th*

Street, *Pier 11* and *South Ferry* on Manhattan. Most ferry terminals have restaurants or snack bars nearby, with passenger facilities limited to ticket sales counters, public telephones and the occasional vending machine. The *Port Authority of New York and New Jersey* (tel: (212) 435 7000; website: www.panynj.gov) provides online information.

CITY STATISTICS

Location: New York State (NY).

Country dialling code: 1.

Population: 7.4 million (city); 18 million (metropolitan area).

Ethnic mix: 29% black, 27 % white, 25% Hispanic, 13% Native American and 6% Asian.

Religion: New York has one of the most religiously diverse populations in the world – figures are constantly changing as the city continues to spiritually evolve.

Time zone: GMT - 5 (GMT - 4 from first Sunday in April to Saturday before last Sunday in October).

Electricity: 110–120 volts, 60Hz; round two-pin plugs are standard.

Average January temp: 0°C (32°F).

Average July temp: 25°C (77°F).

Annual rainfall: 1200mm (47.3 inches).

BUSINESS PROFILE

New York's economy was already contracting before the attacks of September 2001, due to the US recession. Although offices were quickly reopened in new buildings and the stock markets were reopened within a week, the confidence and sense of security in the city's financial district were irreversibly damaged. The benchmark Dow Jones and NASDAQ stock indices both suffered major falls in the weeks after 11 September 2001. Under the presidency of George W. Bush, the nation's economy has been substantially weakened and New York City companies continue to use downsizing as a way to stay afloat, laying off hundreds of thousands of workers. In December 2002, the city's unemployment rate stood at 8.4%, an increase from 6.4% in 2001. The decline in jobs – amounting to a loss of 176,000 jobs in two years – has been more than three times as great, percentage-wise, as in the nation as a whole, which averages an unemployment rate of 6%.

Despite the American economy's recent downturn, New York City remains an international capital of the business world, with nearly 25% of all non-American businesses having headquarters in the city. However, as New York also remains an expensive place in which to do business, this has begun to shift, with businesses moving to the city's borders and New Jersey. Most major global business players still have a strong presence here – including *American Express, Barclays* and *KPMG* – and New York boasts the world's biggest stock exchange, located on Manhattan's Wall Street. Nearly half a million people are employed in banking, real estate and insurance, although the city is also a major international player in the fields of fashion, media and advertising. The real growth industry in New York, over the last three decades – since the brilliant and phenomenally successful 'Big Apple' marketing campaign of the early 1970s – is tourism. In the wake of the September 2001 attacks, however, visitor levels sunk, although Times Square now teems again with the tourists who collectively spend some US$30 million every year.

national rail travel and all enquiries should be directed to the relevant provider.

Rail services: *Amtrak* offers services to Canada – towards Philadelphia (journey time – 1 hour 10 minutes) and Harrisburg, Pennsylvania; to Atlanta, Georgia and New Orleans, Louisiana; and to Baltimore, Maryland, and Florida. There are frequent shuttles to Washington, DC (journey time – 3 hours) and Boston, Massachusetts (journey time – under 4 hours).

Transport to the city: Both stations are centrally located on Manhattan.

Getting There By Road

The general rule for numbering on US freeways and interstates is that the odd numbers go north–south and the even numbers go east–west over their whole length, although at any single, localised point this may seem different. Driving in America is on the right and the speed limit is 48kph (30mph) in the city, 80kph (50mph) outside the city limits and 105kph (65mph) on freeways. Speed limits are clearly indicated along highways and are strictly enforced, with heavy fines imposed. Driving visitors should note that it is illegal

to pass a school bus that has stopped to unload its passengers and all vehicles must stop until the bus has moved back into the traffic stream. Seatbelts must be worn – both front and rear – and drivers must carry their driving licence. The maximum legal alcohol to blood ratio for driving is 0.10% and drink-driving laws are very strict and punishments severe.

The minimum driving age is 16 years. An International Driving Permit is recommended, although it is not legally required and a full national driving licence is accepted. All travellers intending to drive in the USA are strongly advised to acquire supplementary insurance. A yellow 'non-resident, interstate liability insurance card', which acts as evidence of financial responsibility, is available through motor insurance agents.

The *American Automobile Association – AAA* (tel: (212) 586 1166) provides further information and roadside assistance to members.

Emergency breakdown service: *AAA* (800) AAA HELP or 222 4357.

Routes to the city: Travel to Manhattan from New Jersey, Philadelphia and Washington, DC is across the George Washington Bridge or through the Lincoln or Holland Tunnels. The Verrazano–Narrows Bridge connects Brooklyn with Staten Island. Queensborough Bridge links Manhattan and Queens. The Triborough Bridge leads to upstate New York, while the New England Thruway and Bruckner Expressway lead to New England in Boston.

Approximate driving times to New York: From Philadelphia – 2 hours; Boston – 4 hours; Washington, DC – 5 hours.

Coach services: The *Port Authority Bus Terminal*, 40th Street and Eighth Avenue (tel: (212) 564 8484; website: www.panynj.gov/tbt/pabmain.HTM), handles long-distance and regional buses, as well as buses to the airports. *Greyhound* (tel: (800) 231 2222; website: www.greyhound.com) operates bus services that link New York City to points throughout the USA and into Canada and Mexico. Direct services include Washington, DC, Chicago, New Orleans, Orlando and Montreal.

Getting Around

Public Transport

Public transport in New York is run by the *Metropolitan Transit Authority (MTA), New York City Transit* (tel: (718) 330 1234; website www.mta.nyc.ny.us). Services are cheaper and more efficient than the number of private companies also operating in the city.

New York's **subway** is fast, air conditioned, cheap and much safer than it used to be, although it is still best avoided late at night (after 2300). The vast network of 24 routes, identified by letters or by numbers, serves almost 500 stations throughout Manhattan, the Bronx, Brooklyn and Queens. Staten Island is served by the small-scale MTA **Staten Island Railway** (tel: (718) 966 SIRT or 7478), which operates 24 hours a day. Although central Manhattan stations are typically passable, platforms are not always comfortable in terms of temperature or condition. Entrance is gained from a subway *MetroCard* or token (although tokens are not accepted at all entrances), for a flat fare of US$2, available at subway stations and newsagents. Services operate 24 hours a day; on average, subway trains run every two to five minutes during rush hour, every ten to 15 minutes during off-peak times and every 20 minutes daily 0000–0500.

Bus services are extensive and bus stops are located on street corners approximately every two or three blocks. Bus fares cost US$2, paid with a MetroCard, subway token or exact change. Buses operate 24 hours daily.

There are three kinds of *MetroCard* **passes**. *Unlimited Ride MetroCards*, costing US$21 or US$70, are valid for seven or 30 days respectively and expire at midnight on the final day of validity. The one-day unlimited-ride *Fun Pass* costs US$7 and is valid until 0300 the following day. *Pay-Per-Ride MetroCards* offer 12 rides for the price of ten and are available in US$10 or US$20 increments – free transfers to connecting bus or subway routes are included if used within two hours. All passes are available for purchase at subway stations and newsagents.

Taxis

A trip to New York is not complete without a ride in one of the city's famous yellow cabs. Taxis are governed by the *Taxi and Limousine Commission* (tel: (212) NYC TAXI or 692 8294 or 676 1000; website: www.ci.nyc.ny.us/html/tlc) and are hailed on the curb, preferably at intersections. Drivers are required to take passengers to any destination within the five boroughs of New York City or Nassau County, Westchester County and Newark airport. Passengers should provide drivers with the street address and with the nearest cross streets of their destination (for example: 'Fifth Avenue, between 22nd Street and 23rd Street'). Fares begin at US$2, then increase by US$0.30, every fifth of a mile or 90 seconds of waiting time, plus tolls (if any) and a 10–15% tip. There is a US$0.50 surcharge for trips between 2000 and 0600. In the event that there is a problem with the ride, passengers should note the driver's six-digit licence number – located on the roof of the taxi, on the exterior of both passenger doors, on the dashboard and printed on the receipt – and report it to the Taxi and Limousine Commission.

Private car services, unlike taxis, can be called directly and offer point-to-point pre-arranged transport for a fixed rate throughout the five boroughs and beyond. The cost is comparable to that of a metered taxi trip and may be confirmed before pickup. Car services are particularly handy in the outer boroughs, where taxi service is unavailable for trips into Manhattan, or when pre-arranged transport is needed. There are numerous car service companies and hotel concierges can recommend a reliable one.

BUSINESS ETIQUETTE

While on business in New York, normal business courtesies should be observed, although New Yorkers are less formal than Europeans and usually use first names. Both men and women in finance usually wear suits; in other industries, attire might be much less formal. Appointments and punctuality for business meetings are naturally expected. Business hours are officially weekdays, 0900–1730, although an extended working day is very common in certain sectors and it is not unusual for people to be working well into the night or over the weekend. Business meetings frequently take place over breakfast, brunch and lunch. For lunch meetings, alcohol, in moderation, is acceptable.

Limousines

Limousines can be hired from numerous companies throughout the city, including *Affordable New York Limousine* (tel: (888) 888 6569 *or* (516) 897 7605; website: www.affordablenewyorklimousine.com), *Chris Limousines* (tel: (718) 356 3232) and *Executive Town Car* (tel: (516) 538 8551). Trips start from around US$70 and day rates from about US$550.

Driving in the City

Driving in Manhattan is not recommended to visitors. The traffic is horrendous, local drivers impatient, parking fees are exorbitant – approximately US$30 per day – and street parking is elusive. The business and entertainment areas get particularly congested and the fast pace can prove intimidating for tourists. In the unfortunate event of having a car in New York, visitors might want to inquire with their hotel about reasonable local parking and plan to use public transport instead of driving. Drivers should avoid parking on the street, as there are restrictive rules, rampant ticketing and a danger of theft.

Car Hire

A valid national driving licence is required for driving in New York, although an International Driving Permit is required by some car hire firms. Minimum third-party insurance is required and drivers must be at least 25 years old. Branches are located throughout the five boroughs.

Major providers include *Alamo* (tel: (800) 327 9633; website: www.alamo.com), *Avis* (tel: (800) 331 1212; website: www.avis.com), *Budget* (tel: (800) 527 0700; website: www.budget.com), *Dollar* (tel: (800) 800 4000; website: www.dollar.com), *Enterprise* (tel: (800) 736 8227; website: www.enterprise.com), *Hertz* (tel: (800) 654 3131; website: www.hertz.com) and *National* (tel: (800) 227 7368; website: www.nationalcar.com). Prices start from US$70 a day plus tax, for a standard hire car.

Bicycle Hire

Many New Yorkers brave the traffic on bicycles, however, this is not recommended to visitors. Nevertheless, there are 40km (25 miles) of bike paths around the city, where no motorised vehicles are allowed. Cycling around one of New York's parks is also a safe and pleasant option. *Central Park Bicycle Tours/Rentals* (tel: (212) 541 8759; website: www.centralparkbiketour.com) offers individual bicycle hire for US$35 a day, as well as a leisurely two-hour guided bike tour of Central Park, costing US$35 (summer only), including bicycle hire. Much like a walking tour service provider, *Tours By Bike* (tel: (877) 865 0078; website: www.toursbybike.com) offers a range of interesting thematic bike tours for short and longer distances. Tour rates start at around US$50, including bike and helmet hire.

SIGHTSEEING

Sightseeing Overview

Most tourists end up spending the majority of their trip on *Manhattan* and this is where most of the recognisable attractions are located. The remaining four boroughs are primarily residential – the *Bronx* to the north, *Queens* to the east, *Brooklyn* to the southeast and *Staten Island* to the southwest – although there is a sprinkling of

The Statue of Liberty

worthwhile attractions located in them all, which will reward the visitor with time to explore. Almost completely flat and, for the most part, arranged on an easily navigable grid system, Manhattan itself is very easy to walk around, with the excellent subway system handy for the longer hops between attractions. Avenues run north–south and streets run east–west, with just a few neighbourhood exceptions. Fifth Avenue is the city centre and the starting point and zero for all addresses (ie addresses increase the farther they are from Fifth).

The city is packed with things to do and places to see – each street and neighbourhood offers its own varied sights and flavours. The top attractions, like the *Statue of Liberty* and the *Empire State Building*, are renowned throughout the world but there are enough less heralded places to fill weeks of sightseeing.

Manhattan has several distinct areas that are worth wandering around, from the ritzy shopping and residential districts uptown, to the financial district of downtown, taking in the villages in between. *SoHo* is famous for its art galleries and shopping opportunities. *Greenwich Village* traditionally contains a literary and gay community and has the quaint bookstores and cafés to go with it. The young-and-hip *East Village* retains its edgy atmosphere, which is reflected in its quirky shops, record stores, nightclubs and drinking spots. Historical *Lower East Side*, once an immigrant neighbourhood, is now filled with boutiques and vintage shops, nightclubs and restaurants. *Chelsea*, with warehouse conversions mingling with more cutting-edge art galleries, is another gay-friendly neighbourhood. Away from the city, *Long Island* and a number of city beaches provide an escape on hot and humid summer days.

Key Attractions

The Statue of Liberty

The ultimate symbol of the American Dream, Lady Liberty, standing majestically over New York Harbor, is probably the most famous landmark in America. The people of France donated the statue to the United States in 1886, to commemorate the alliance of the two countries during the American Revolution. It was the first sight of the New World to be seen by the 12 million immigrants who passed through *Ellis Island*, the country's principal immigration centre in the early and

mid-20th century. Visitors can usually climb the statue or take the lift, however, the statue is indefinitely closed for security reasons.

Liberty Island, New York Harbor
Tel: (212) 363 3200.
E-mail: stli_info@nps.gov
Website: www.nps.gov/stli
Transport: Circle Line Statue of Liberty Ferry (tel: (212) 269 5755) from South Ferry at Battery Park to Liberty and Ellis islands; free 24-hour Staten Island Ferry (tel: (718) 815 2628) from Battery Park.
Opening hours: Mon–Fri 0930–1700, Sat and Sun 0900–1730.
Admission: Free; US$10 (return ferry trip).

Photo: Corel

Brooklyn Bridge

Ellis Island Immigration Museum

The relatives of over 40% of families living in the United States of America passed through this historical immigration station, which operated from 1892 to 1954. Now a national monument and museum, the *Ellis Island Immigration Museum* has over 30 galleries related to the American immigrant experience. Tours are also on offer, during which visitors will learn how 'undesirables' were weeded out and separated from their families in the Registry Room, after month-long ordeals on often over-crowded boats. For a US$5 fee, visitors can search the Ellis Island archives by computer in the popular *American Family Immigration Center* for information on their ancestors.
Ellis Island, New York Harbor
Tel: (212) 363 3206.
E-mail: moreinfo@ellisisland.com
Website: www.ellisisland.com
Transport: Circle Line Statue of Liberty Ferry (tel: (212) 269 5755) from South Ferry at Battery Park to Liberty and Ellis islands (costing US$10 for a round trip).
Opening hours: Daily 0930–1700.
Admission: Free.

World Trade Center – Ground Zero

In early 2003, the city selected *Memory Foundations* as an architectural design, by Studio Daniel Libeskind, to replace the 110-storey towers and surrounding buildings at the site of the former *World Trade Center*. The new structure will integrate portions of a remaining *slurry wall* (strong enough to hold back the Hudson River). A slightly recessed public space, known as the *bathtub*, will provide the setting for a memorial and a museum. North of this area, a 541-metre (1776ft) spire, the 'Gardens of the World', will grace the skyline. Although the complex's very existence will memorialise the tragedy that occurred here in 2001, each year on 11 September, the sun will shine without a shadow on the *Wedge of Light* piazza. The Lower Manhattan Development Corporation – LMDC (see below) can provide more information on the decision and design.
The viewing platforms that once allowed visitors to pay tribute at the former World Trade Center site, dubbed *Ground Zero,* are no longer in place. A simple viewing area at Liberty Street and Broadway now allows for observation of ongoing work.
Lower Manhattan (on the west side)
Tel: (212) 962 2300. Fax: (212) 962 2431/3 (LMDC).
Website: www.renewnyc.com
Transport: Subway 1 or 9 to Chambers Street or subway E to WTC/Chambers.

Opening hours: Daily 1100–1800.
Admission: Free.

Brooklyn Bridge

Dubbed the eighth wonder of the world, when it was completed after 30-years of construction in 1883, John Augustus Roebling's design remains a masterful feat of engineering. One of the world's first steel wire suspension bridges – and at one time one of the world's longest – links Manhattan to Brooklyn, over the East River. The bridge's mile-long wooden promenade is open to pedestrians and cyclists and offers stunning views of the city.
Park Row
Transport: Subway 4, 5 or 6 to Brooklyn Bridge or City Hall.
Opening hours: Daily 24 hours.
Admission: Free.

Empire State Building

Immortalised by Hollywood cinema – from King Kong and Fay Wray to Tom Hanks and Meg Ryan – this stunning skyscraper is now once again the city's tallest building. Completed in 1931, the 102-storey *Empire State Building* is a wonderful example of Art Deco period architecture and the observatories on the 86th and 102nd floors offer magical and spectacular views of the city; the 86th floor deck is open air. Every night, the top 31 storeys are illuminated with a colour that reflects the season or holiday.
350 Fifth Avenue at East 34th Street
Tel: (212) 736 3100. Fax: (212) 947 1360.
Website: www.esbnyc.com
Transport: Subway B, D, F, N, R, Q or W to 34th Street.
Opening hours: Daily 0930–2400.
Admission: US$10 (concessions available).

Rockefeller Center

Built in 1932–40, the *Rockefeller Center* is a masterpiece of urban design. The best approach is from the *Channel Gardens*, opposite Saks on Fifth Avenue – a popular lunchtime haunt flanked with shops and services – to arrive at the focal point of the complex, the sunken plaza, used as an ice-skating rink in winter and an open-air restaurant in summer. Behind this, the sumptuous GE building dominates the scene with its Art Deco ambience both inside and out. The Rockefeller Center is home to NBC, *Radio City Music Hall* and *Christie's Auction House*. NBC tours, lasting 90 minutes, are available and points of interest include the Today Show studio, the skating rink, the Prometheus and Atlas statues and the Channel Gardens.
Fifth Avenue, 47th Street to 52nd Street
Tel: (212) 332 6868 *or* 632 3975.
Website: www.rockefellercenter.com
Transport: Subway B, D, F, N, Q, R, 1 and 9 to Rockefeller Center.
Opening hours: Daily 0930–1630 (tours run every 30 minutes).
Admission: US$10.

Museum of Modern Art

The *Museum of Modern Art (MoMA)*, 11 West 53rd Street, between Fifth Street and Sixth Street, houses the most important modern art collection in the USA, covering a variety of media from the late 19th and 20th centuries, with impressive touring exhibitions. The museum is currently undergoing a massive regeneration project that will add much needed extra exhibition space by 2005. Its interim outpost, *MoMA QNS*, in Long Island City, Queens – an industrial district just

over the East River – displays permanent collection pieces as well as visiting exhibitions, such as the Matisse Picasso show in a refurbished warehouse space. The subway trip is 10–15 minutes from Midtown.
33rd Street at Queens Boulevard, Long Island City
Tel: (212) 708 9400.
E-mail: info@moma.org
Website: www.moma.org
Transport: Subway 7 to 33rd Street, Queens.
Opening hours: Sat–Mon and Thurs 1000–1700, Fri 1000–1745 (extended during some shows).
Admission: US$12–20 (concessions available).

Soloman R Guggenheim Museum

The *Guggenheim Museum* – a seven-storey conical building designed by US master architect Frank Lloyd Wright – is worth visiting if only for the building alone. Inside, it features an acclaimed collection of late 19th- and 20th-century art works, as well as touring exhibitions.
1071 Fifth Avenue, at 89th Street
Tel: (212) 423 3500.
E-mail: visitorinfo@guggenheim.org
Website: www.guggenheim.org
Transport: Subway 4, 5 or 6 to 86th Street.
Opening hours: Sun–Wed 1000–1745, Fri and Sat 1000–2000.
Admission: US$15; concessions available; patrons may pay what they wish Fri 1600–1800.

Metropolitan Museum of Art

Home to more than two million works of art spanning five millennia, '*the Met*' is a cherished New York institution. It is the largest art museum in the western hemisphere and its collections are outstanding.
1000 Fifth Avenue, at 82nd Street
Tel: (212) 535 7710.
Website: www.metmuseum.org
Transport: Subway 4, 5 or 6 to 86th Street.
Opening hours: Tues–Sun 0930–1730, Fri and Sat 0930–2100.
Admission: US$12 (suggested donation).

Central Park

New York's famous green lung, *Central Park*, is a magnificent city sanctuary situated in the centre of Manhattan. Designed by Frederick Law Olmsted and Calvert Vaux, it opened in 1876 and now offers numerous recreational and cultural outlets. The *Belvedere Castle* – a stone castle built on Vista Rock in the middle of the park at the 79th Street Transverse – offers excellent views from its lookout, while the *Shakespeare Garden*, just west of the castle, contains flowers and herbs mentioned in the Bard's plays. The *Central Park Conservancy* offers various free walking tours of the park. There is also a theatre and sports facilities, including tennis courts, ice rinks and lakes, in addition to the celebrated *Central Park Wildlife Center*. Considered to be one of the world's most appealing small zoos, it has exhibits for each of the world's major environments and houses smaller animals, such as monkeys and penguins. The *Tisch Children's Zoo,* across East 65th Street, is a hands-on animal garden where petting domestic animals, such as goats and pigs, is permitted. The beautifully landscaped *Central Garden* and *Sea Lion Pool* is flanked on three sides by a glass-roofed colonnade, making it accessible even in wet weather. It is considered unwise to visit Central Park after dark, except for events such as ice skating, carriage rides or Summerstage (see *Special Events*).
From 59th Street to 110th Street
Tel: (212) 310 6600 *or* 360 2726 (walking tours hotline).

E-mail: contact@centralparknyc.org *or* tours@
centralparknyc.org

Website: www.centralparknyc.org

Transport: Subway N or R to Fifth Avenue; or bus 4,
5 or 6 to 59th Street.

Opening hours: Daily 24 hours (park); daily
1000–1630 (visitor centre).

Admission: Free.

Belvedere Castle

Mid-Park at 79th Street.

Tel: (212) 772 0210.

Opening hours: Tues–Sun 1000–1700.

Admission: Free.

Central Park Wildlife Centre

830 Fifth Avenue and East 64th Street

Tel: (212) 439 6500 *or* 861 6031.

Website: www.wcs.org/zoos

Opening hours: Mon–Fri 1000–1700, Sat and Sun
1000–1730 (5 Apr–26 Oct); daily 1000–1630 (27
Oct–4 Apr).

Admission: US$6 (concessions available).

Central Park

Further Distractions

American Museum of the Moving Image

A target destination for serious film buffs, the
American Museum of the Moving Image is dedicated to
film, television, video and interactive media.
Attractions and facilities include classic movies
screened daily in the *Tut's Fever Movie Palace*; feature
films shown at weekends in the *Riklis Theater*; and
interactive exhibitions, including a working film set
and film editing demonstrations.

35th Avenue, at 36th Street, Astoria, Queens

Tel: (718) 784 0077 *or* 4520.

Website: www.ammi.org

Transport: Subway N to Broadway, R or G to
Steinway Street.

Opening hours: Tues–Fri 1200–1700, Sat and Sun
1100–1800.

Admission: US$10 (concessions available).

Bryant Park

Bryant Park, behind the *New York Public Library*, is
reminiscent of Paris, with gravel pathways, green
folding chairs and a manicured lawn. It is extremely
popular during summer, especially as it offers free
outdoor concerts and comedy shows. During Fashion
Week, tents concealing the hallowed runways are set
up for the seasonal haute couture fashion shows. Two
lions flank the grand New York Public Library, with
its entrance on Fifth Avenue, where visitors may tour
the impressive reading rooms and literary exhibitions.

Between 40th Street and 42nd Street and Fifth
Avenue and Sixth Avenue

Tel: (212) 768 4242.

E-mail: bprc@urbanmgt.com

Website: www.bryantpark.org

Transport: Subway B, D, F, V and 7 to 42nd Street.

Opening hours: Daily 0700–1900 (Nov–Apr);
Mon–Fri 0700–2300, Sat and Sun 0700–2000 (May,
Sep and Oct); Mon–Fri 0700–2300, Sat and Sun
0700–2100 (Jun–Aug).

Admission: Free.

New York Public Library

Fifth Avenue and 42nd Street

Tel: (212) 930 0800 *or* 0830.

Website: www.nypl.org

Opening hours: Tues–Wed 1100–1930, Thurs–Sat
1000–1800.

Admission: Free.

Grand Central Terminal

Visitors to New York should take the opportunity to
tour *Grand Central Terminal*, familiar to many as Grand
Central Station. Situated in Midtown, just one block
east of Bryant Park, it has historical and architectural
importance, and the celestial ceiling is remarkable.
Free tours take place every Wednesday and Friday at
1230. The Wednesday tour is run by the Municipal
Arts Society and departs from the information booth
of the Grand Concourse, while the Friday tour, run by
the Grand Central Partnership, meets in front of the
Phillip Morris/Whitney Museum on 42nd Street. The
station also boasts a fine dining concourse and a
number of retail opportunities, including the Grand
Central Market.

42nd Street, at Park Avenue

Tel: (212) 935 3960 (Wednesday tour) *or* 697 1245
(Friday tour) *or* 340 2210 (event hotline).

Website: www.grandcentralterminal.com *or*
www.newyorkled.com/grandcentral.htm

Transport: MTA Metro–North Railroad; subway 4, 5,
6, 7 and S; bus 1, 2, 3, 4, 5, 42, 98, 101 and 102.

Opening hours: Daily 0530–0130.

Admission: Free.

Chrysler Building and Daily News Building

Many a tourist has had their breath taken away by the
stunning chrome *Chrysler Building*. Unfortunately,
tours are not available. Further down 42nd Street is
the *Daily News Building*, with its lobby, made famous
in the *Superman* films, which still contains the original
1923 large globe.

Chrysler Building

42nd Street at Lexington Avenue

Tel: (212) 682 3070.

Website: www.chryslerbuilding.org

Transport: Subway B, D, F, V and 7 to 42nd Street.

Opening hours: Visitors usually admitted into the
lobby during weekday working hours; permission is
essential as sneaking in may result in arrest.

Admission: Free.

Daily News Building

220 East 42nd Street

Transport: Subway B, D, F, V and 7 to 42nd Street.

Opening hours: Visitors usually admitted into the
lobby during weekday working hours; permission is
essential as sneaking in may result in arrest.

Admission: Free.

Dia Center

The *Dia Center* is dedicated to large-scale, long-term,
single-artist projects. The most famous is Dan
Graham's site-specific glass installation on the roof,
which reflects and distorts the surrounding views of
Manhattan. Photographs of the bookshop have
appeared in many design magazines.

548 West 22nd Street, between Tenth Avenue and
11th Avenue

Tel: (212) 989 5566. Fax: (212) 989 4055.

Website: www.diacenter.org

Transport: Subway C or E to 23rd Street.

Opening hours: Wed–Sun 1200–1800.

Admission: US$6 (concessions available).

Tours of the City

Walking Tours

New York's streets were made for walking. In fact
walking is the best way for visitors to really explore
the city. There are numerous guided tour operators,
including *Big Onion Walking Tours* (tel: (212) 439
1090; fax: (718) 499 0023; e-mail: bowtnyc@aol.com;
website: www.bigonion.com), who, for over a decade,
have offered entertaining, informative and
contemporary tours of New York's historic districts
and ethnic neighbourhoods. Tours last approximately
two hours and prices start at US$12 (concessions are
available). Departure points vary depending on the
tour – these are clearly listed on the website.

Bus Tours

Gray Line New York Tours (tel: (212) 397 2620 *or* (800)
669 0051; e-mail: greylinenetwork@coachusa.com;
website: www.graylinenewyork.com) offers closed-
and open-top double-decker bus tours, calling at
numerous stops around the city in a two- to three-
hour loop. The 'Essential New York Tour' offers a 40-
stop hop-on hop-off tour of Manhattan for US$69
(concessions are available). Tickets are valid for 48
hours. Gray Line also offers tours of Harlem and
Brooklyn. Buses depart from the Port Authority
Terminal on Eighth Avenue and 42nd Street.

Boat Tours

Circle Line Sightseeing Cruises (tel: (212) 563 3200;
website: www.circleline.com) is the only cruise line
that circles Manhattan Island, with a three-hour

Photo: Corel

SoHo loft buildings

narrated Full Island Cruise, departing from Pier 83 on 42nd Street on the Hudson River and costing US$25. Other options include the two-hour Semi-Circle Cruise, costing US$20, or the evening two-hour Harbor Lights Cruise, costing US$20. At both Pier 83 and Pier 16, South Street Seaport, adventurers can take a spin on the 'Beast' speed boat for a 30-minute thrill ride, costing US$18.

Other Tours

Gray Line New York Tours (see *Bus Tours* above) conducts over two dozen sightseeing trips by different modes of transport. The ten-minute helicopter tour, 'A Bird's Eye View', costs US$138 and allows visitors to see the Empire State Building, the Chrysler Building and Central Park from above. Helicopter flights depart from the West 30th Street heliport.

Scene on TV Tours (tel: (212) 410 9830; website: www.sceneontv.com) operates bus tours of the sites of America's top TV shows, including *Sex and the City* and *The Sopranos*. Basic TV tours covering the sets of *Friends*, *Seinfeld* and *Will & Grace* cost US$20 and are approximately two hours long. The three-hour speciality tours cost US$30–35. Booking is essential for all tours and meeting points vary depending on the tour taken; hotel pick up and drop off is not available.

Excursions

For a Half Day

Coney Island: Located just a 45-minute subway ride from Manhattan (on subway B, D, F or N to Stillwell Avenue), in south Brooklyn, *Coney Island* is a popular haunt for New Yorkers and tourists alike, because of its stretch of beach and historical amusement parks. Major attractions include the *New York Aquarium*, Surf Avenue and West Eighth Street (tel: (718) 265 3400; website: www.nyaquarium.com), located halfway to Brighton Beach. The Aquarium is open daily 1000–1630. Its *Aquatheatre* is home to dolphins and sea lions, the *Sea Cliffs Exhibition* features walrus, penguins and giant Pacific octopus, while *Discovery Cove* is an interactive entertainment complex for children. Entrance is US$11 (concessions available). Coney Island's amusement area comprises several amusement parks, featuring the *Cyclone roller coaster* and the *Wonder Wheel*, the tallest Ferris wheel in the world. Many visitors partake of a *Nathan's Famous* hot dog on the boardwalk – a seaside treat for generations.

For a Whole Day

Long Island: Situated to the east of New York City, *Long Island* stretches for 190km (118 miles) into the Atlantic. Coastal parts of residential Long Island have some of the world's most beautiful white-sand beaches and are popular with New Yorkers and tourists alike for weekend retreats. The north and south shores differ greatly. The south shore is fringed by almost continuous sandy shores, including such public beaches as *Jones Beach* (website: http://mta.info/lirr/beachbrochure/jonesbeach.htm) and gay-oriented *Fire Island National Seashore* (website: www.nps.gov/fiis), a ferry ride away. Meanwhile, the north shore is more immediately beautiful; its cliffs topped with luxurious mansions and estates. The *Hamptons* combines the attractions of the well-to-do, such as shops and excellent restaurants, with wooded nature reserves filled with sand dunes and pristine stretches of accessible beach. A bicycle trip to *The End*, a nickname for the bohemian village of *Montauk* at the island's eastern reach, could well be the pinnacle of a long summer weekend spent in a cottage or inn.

The quickest way to reach Long Island is via the Long Island Railroad from Penn Station, although numerous bus services cover most destinations. Parking permits for Long Island's beaches are issued only to local residents. The *Long Island Convention and Visitors Bureau*, 330 Vanderbilt Motor Parkway (tel: (516) 951 3440 *or* (631) 951 3440 *or* (800) 386 6654; website: www. licvb.com) can provide further information.

ACCOMMODATION

Occupancy rates have dropped slightly in New York, mainly due to new hotels popping up all over the place. This does not always mean lower rates, as the newer venues are usually at the top of the range. To get a good deal, visitors should reserve as far ahead as possible. It is a good idea for travellers to check out the Internet, as hotels often post specials there that they will not mention over the phone.

The prices quoted below are the lowest standard rates for a double room, excluding the 15% city and state taxes, service charges or breakfast, unless otherwise specified.

Business

Hudson

Walking through the front doors of Ian Schrager's trendy *Hudson* can leave visitors feeling a bit disoriented, as they find themselves in a translucent box, with a steep escalator ascending up and out of view. However, at the end of the journey, they reach an airy, exposed brick lobby. Rooms are exceedingly small and appointed with gleaming chrome and crisp, white fabrics and clever space-saving furnishings, such as a rollaway laptop table and wall hooks. A semi-transparent shower wall separates the bath from the bedroom. The popular lobby bar, with a lighted floor and a swirling ceiling mural painted by Francesco Clemente, is jammed with businesspeople, tourists and singles from rush hour onwards. During summer, the rooftop lounge is the place to go – this is New York's only outdoor lounge, strewn with lanterns, plants, chaises, ottomans, pillows and beds for lounging.
356 West 58th Street (between Broadway and Eighth Avenue)
Tel: (212) 554 6000. Fax: (212) 554 6001.
E-mail: hudson@schragerhotels.com
Website: www.ianschragerhotels.com
Price: From US$240.

Morgans

With its laid-back sense of style, *Morgans* does not have to shout to get the visitor's attention. It makes its boldest statement in the lobby, where oversized leather chairs are strewn across the geometrically patterned carpet. Upstairs, things are more sparse, with rooms decorated in shades of taupe and honey, providing a respite from the glaring city just outside the windows. The baths are a study in simplicity, with clear-glass vanities atop polished steel basins. *Morgans Bar*, situated on the ground floor, is a great place to see and be seen. For guests on business, rooms are equipped with modem points, while there is plenty of meeting space downstairs.
237 Madison Avenue (between 37th Street and 38th Street)
Tel: (212) 686 0300. Fax: (212) 779 8352.
E-mail: morgans@ianschragerhotels.com
Website: www.ianschragerhotels.com
Price: From US$290.

New York Palace

Even before *Travel + Leisure* ranked it as one of the world's best places to stay, there was never any doubt that the *New York Palace* is one of the city's most lavish hotels. The hotel is located in the heart of Manhattan and New York's premier cultural, business and shopping districts. Of the two Palace restaurants, the opulent *Le Cirque 2000* should not be missed. The enormous conference centre in the historic *Villard Houses* and state-of-the-art health spa cater to the business class. Luxuriously furnished rooms are also designed with the business traveller in mind – even the in-room safes are big enough to store a laptop computer.
455 Madison Avenue (between 50th Street and 51st Street)
Tel: (212) 212 888 7000. Fax: (212) 212 303 6000.
E-mail: info@nypalace.com
Website: www.newyorkpalace.com
Price: From US$300.

Waldorf–Astoria

Occupying an entire block on Park Avenue, the *Waldorf–Astoria* is the meeting place for the world's movers and shakers. The line of limousines in front of the hotel might signal the arrival of a head of state or a captain of industry. The Art Deco showplace, which opened its doors in 1931, retains the glamour of a long-gone era. The murals that once graced the lobby have been painstakingly restored and the rooms exude elegance, especially those in the soaring *Waldorf Towers*. Yet the Waldorf–Astoria is also the hotel of choice for business travellers, as the rooms have fax machines and modem points. A new executive meeting centre includes high-tech meeting spaces with satellite links and video-conferencing. The hotel is located 45 minutes from JFK airport.
301 Park Avenue (between 49th Street and 50th Street)
Tel: (212) 355 3000. Fax: (212) 872 7272.
Website: www.waldorfastoria.com
Price: From US$300.

Luxury

Four Seasons

Four Seasons is designed by architect I M Pei, so it should not be a surprise that the onyx-trimmed lobby takes the breath away. Even the standard rooms here outshine the suites at other hotels and the most modest accommodations have padded silk walls accented by sycamore furnishings. For guests who need more room to spread out, the executive suites have living rooms with enormous picture windows and terraces with views of Central Park. All have amenities such as walk-in wardrobes and luxurious, quick-filling marble baths. The sophisticated restaurant and bar, *Fifty Seven Fifty Seven*, is a great place to impress that special client. There is everything here that the business traveller needs, from seven high-tech conference rooms to a health spa to relieve all that tension. The hotel is centrally located in Manhattan, with the closest airport being LaGuardia, 19km (12 miles) away; JFK is located 37km (23 miles) from the hotel.

57 East 57th Street (between Park Avenue and Madison Avenue)
Tel: (212) 758 5700. Fax: (212) 758 5711.
Website: www.fourseasons.com
Price: From US$475.

St Regis

This Beaux Arts showplace was built in 1904 and a recent renovation has restored its original grandeur. The marble-floored lobby hints at the luxury found in the guest rooms – silk-covered walls, richly detailed crown molding and crystal chandeliers. The Manhattan hotel is centrally located for New York's main business district and all rooms have everything the business traveller could need, from Internet connections to fax machines. There is no fear about fitting everyone around the conference table, as there are 15 meeting rooms. The *Ballroom*, overlooking the city lights, holds more than 500 people. Guests can dine at *Lespinasse*, one of the city's finest French restaurants, or stop by for something cool at the cosy *King Cole Bar*, where the Red Snapper Cocktail – now known as the Bloody Mary – was first concocted.

2 East 55th Street (at Fifth Avenue)
Tel: (212) 753 4500. Fax: (212) 787 3447.
Website: www.starwood.com/stregis/index.html
Price: From US$425.

Moderate

The Gershwin

Not far from the much-photographed Flatiron Building is *The Gershwin*, one of the city's last remaining bargain hotels. The lollipop left on the pillow when the maid turns down the bed just might match the buttercup yellow walls or cherry-red molding of the simple but comfortable room. The hotel is particularly popular with young people, as the funky Pop Art decor, nightly film screenings, arts events and affordable travel packages aim to please 20-something travellers. All rooms are en suite. Dorm-style rooms, suites and accommodation for families are also available.

7 East 27th Street (between Sixth and Seventh Avenues)
Tel: (212) 545 8000. Fax: (212) 684 5546.
E-mail: reservations@gershwinhotel.com
Website: www.gershwinhotel.com
Price: From US$149 (including breakfast).

New York City Howard Johnson

The first chain hotel to make its way to the crossroads of the East Village and Lower East Side nightlife is a great choice for those who want to be near the city's nightlife but not drain their wallets. The new and simple rooms are motel-style and have a little turning-around room; some have hot tubs or microwaves and mini-refrigerators. All rooms are en suite. The biggest surprise, besides the hotel's move to the neighbourhood, is the ample in-room amenities, such as hairdryers, irons, coffeemakers and free local calls.

The Chrysler Building and the Empire State Building

Photo: NYC & Company

135 East Houston Street (at Forsythe Street)
Tel: (212) 358 8844. Fax: (212) 473 3500.
Website: www.hojo.com
Price: From US$110 (including breakfast).

Other Recommendations

The Paramount

There is nothing traditional about *The Paramount*, a post-modern showplace created by entrepreneur Ian Schrager – who is also responsible for London's St Martin's Lane. For example, in the entrance, red roses are displayed vertically in vases set into the wall. The lobby bar, designed by Philippe Starck, has platinum walls and a glamorous staircase sweeping up to the mezzanine. Guests can gaze down from their tables to the music and theatre industry leaders reclining on the slightly off-kilter furniture below. Half a block to Times Square, the location of this Theater District landmark could not be better. The rooms are rather small but few guests spend much time there anyway.

235 West 46th Street (between Broadway and Eighth Avenue)
Tel: (212) 764 5500. Fax: (212) 575 4892.
E-mail: paramount@ianschragerhotels.com
Website: www.ianschragerhotels.com
Price: From US$275.

Tribeca Grand

Situated in TriBeCa, two blocks south of its sister hotel, the Soho Grand, this historic building has a brick façade with cast-iron detailing. This gorgeous hotel has an eight-storey indoor atrium rising up from the lobby, where the bar, *Church Lounge*, garners a well-heeled clientele. The rooms upstairs are minimalist, modern and yet comfortable; on the stainless steel bathroom counters are Bliss bath products. All have telephones with voice-mail, as well as VCRs and CD players.

2 Avenue of the Americas (at Grand Street)
Tel: (212) 519 6600. Fax: (212) 519 6700.
E-mail: reservations@tribecagrand.com
Website: www.tribecagrand.com
Price: From US$280.

RESTAURANTS

The selected restaurants have been divided into five categories: Gastronomic, Business, Trendy, Budget and Personal Recommendations. The restaurants are listed alphabetically within these different categories, which serve as guidelines rather than absolute definitions of the establishments.

Visitors to New York who wish to dine in that special restaurant should make a reservation well in advance. It is not unreasonable for patrons to call for a table in the trendiest eating places a few months in advance. Sales tax of 8.25% is automatically added to the bill but service charges are only standard for large groups. The prices quoted below are for an average three-course meal for one person and for a bottle of house wine or cheapest equivalent; they include VAT but they do not include tip.

Gastronomic

AZ

Pan-Asian fusion is not the newest culinary invention and yet Patricia Yeo's dishes are inspired enough to make foodies sit up and take notice. Diners could start with lapsang souchon-smoked chicken with black mushroom dumplings and then go for the coriander-crusted tuna with black-bean-braised oxtails or steamed *tatog* and ruby-red shrimp in spicy Thai broth. Much like the food, the restaurant's glass lift and retractable roof are not to be missed. For those on a budget (or a diet), the lounge serves lighter fare.
21 West 17th Street (between Fifth Avenue and Sixth Avenue)
Tel: (212) 691 8888.
Website: www.aznyc.com
Price: US$57 or US$75 (fixed price). Wine: US$30.

Chanterelle

Nothing can distract from the exquisite meals at what must be the most unfussy of the city's top French restaurants. Never mind that the walls have no art and the respectful din of other diners is the only sound to accompany a meal. The lushness of duck consommé with duck and foie gras dumplings, roast squab with black truffles or crisped sweetbreads with Banyuls vinegar and fresh chillies are sensory enough.
2 Harrison Street (at Hudson Street)
Tel: (212) 966 6960. Fax: (212) 966 6143.
E-mail: information@chanterellenyc.com
Website: www.chanterellenyc.com
Price: US$85. Wine: US$40.

Daniel

Named after the renowned chef-owner, Daniel Boloud, this restaurant is consistently ranked as one of the city's best venues for classical French fare, with a decor that exudes classical opulence yet contemporary flare. Seasonal masterpieces have included Maine sea scallops layered with black truffle in golden puff pastry or Morels with duck and foie gras stuffing, each dish accentuating the ingredients to their best. Jacket and tie are required for gentlemen.
60 East 65th Street (between Park Avenue and Madison Avenue)
Tel: (212) 288 0033. Fax: (212) 396 9014.
E-mail: info@danielnyc.com
Website: www.danielnyc.com
Price: US$85. Wine: US$40.

Gramercy Tavern

Danny Meyer's contemporary American restaurant never goes out of fashion. A place New Yorkers take out-of-town guests, the restaurant offers two kinds of dining experiences – the airy first-come-first-served bar serves delicious but uncomplicated meals, while the formal dining room presents extraordinarily skilful fare, such as duck foie gras and roasted cod. Those on an expense account should go all out on the market (fixed-price) menu and get a little taste of nearly everything. Those who cannot get enough of chef Tom Colicchio's wares should try his spectacular second restaurant, Craft.
42 East 20th Street (between Broadway and Park Avenue)
Tel: (212) 477 0777. Fax: (212) 477 1160.
Price: US$75. Wine: US$24.

Le Cirque 2000

With tongue firmly set in cheek, designer Adam Tihany transformed the stately Villard House into a circus as imagined by Salvador Dalí. The presentation of the food is just as overstated, from the enormous gilt-edged plates for entrées to the Venetian-glass fantasies that hold devilishly delicious desserts. The real reason to come here, however, is the food. Diners can taste duck with seared foie gras or veal mignon with potato gnocchi.
455 Madison Avenue (between 50th and 51st Streets)
Tel: (212) 303 7788. Fax: (212) 303 7712.
Website: www.lecirque.com
Price: US$75. Wine: US$25.

Business

'21' Club

Cole Porter sang the praises of this place nearly 70 years ago and it is still worthy of song. With a clientele that has included every president since Teddy Roosevelt, this former speakeasy has a history few New York venues can match. Diners enter below a line of lawn jockeys – 21 of them, naturally – to reach the string of intimate dining rooms. The '21' burger is the classic choice but chef Erik Blauberg has updated the menu of classic American fare to include dishes such as oven-roasted veal chops and hickory-fired filet mignon.
21 West 53rd Street (between Fifth Avenue and Sixth Avenue)
Tel: (212) 582 7200. Fax: (212) 974 7562.
E-mail: info@21club.com
Website: www.21club.com
Price: US$50. Wine: US$28.

Gotham Bar & Grill

At the *Gotham Bar & Grill*, tables are as tightly spaced as in any New York restaurant but the various levels and the soaring ceilings hung with lighting fixtures resembling parachutes give the illusion of space. The staff are harried yet always seems to anticipate the diner's every whim. What is more, chef Alfred Portale, who pioneered the gravity-defying entrées that everyone now emulates, does American food like nobody else. Dishes include the Maine lobster tails or grilled Atlantic salmon.
12 East 12th Street (between Union Square and Fifth Avenue)
Tel: (212) 620 4020. Fax: (212) 627 7810.
E-mail: gothamgm@aol.com
Website: www.gothambarandgrill.com
Price: US$60. Wine: US$25.

Jean George

As they are so often set in basements and backrooms, restaurants in New York rarely get to brag about their view. *Jean George* lets its location in the Trump Hotel speak for itself. Diners can sit on the terrace facing Central Park or enjoy the same view from the Art-Deco influenced dining room. The decor is subdued, allowing chef Jean-Georges Vongerichten's French fare to shine. Few diners will forget dishes like the sliced sea scallops, which sit atop sautéed cauliflower. The wine list is vast and the sommelier is happy to help select a bottle.
1 Central Park West (at 60th Street)
Tel: (212) 299 3900. Fax: (212) 299 3941.
Website: www.jean-georges.com
Price: US$100. Wine: US$27.

Tavern on the Green

This is perhaps the most famous restaurant in New York – with good reason. It is a fantasyland hung with thousands of twinkling lights. Inside is a maze of dining rooms, each more extravagant than the last. Any night of the week, there is a movie premiere party, a reception honouring a local dignitary or a political fundraising event. In terms of food, diners should stick with old favourites, such as the sirloin steak or rack of pork.
Central Park West (at 67th Street)
Tel: (212) 873 3200. Fax: (212) 875 8051.
Website: www.web.tavernonthegreen.com
Price: US$60. Wine: US$20.

Washington Park

Celebrity chef Jonathan Waxman might not be one of the regular faces on US TV's *Food Network*, but that could be about to change. During the 1980s, Waxman helped to popularise the cooking style called 'California cuisine' by offering light and fresh ingredients into a meat-and-potatoes culinary country. *Washington Park* does some of the same and to great success. Seared snapper with lobster broth and sugar snap peas epitomise the sweet-and-light dishes that New York has long missed, prepared here in the open-plan kitchen, in full view of diners. A three-course fixed-price dinner menu changes daily and the wine list covers several grape-growing nooks of the globe. The decor does not attempt to rival the food – where there happens to be wood, it is blonde, while one large abstract artwork stands alone on an otherwise white wall – although the waitrons wear gorgeous Thomas Pink button-down shirts and impeccable blue suits.
24 Fifth Avenue (at Ninth Street)
Tel: (212) 529 4400.
Price: US$45. Wine: US$32.

Trendy

71 Clinton Fresh Food

The Manhattans here are the tastiest (and strongest) in the city, so guests should sample one as they wait for a table at this instantly popular hangout for Lower East Side hipsters. There is no sign on this tiny shop front – diners must look for the stainless-steel façade. The modern yet miniature space means that visitors dine closely among the chic clientele, most likely along the banqueted wall. There are just a handful of options – like the goat-cheese tart topped with applewood-smoked bacon – so that chef Wylie Dufresne can concentrate on creating something truly magical.
71 Clinton Street (between Rivington and Stanton Streets)
Tel: (212) 614 6960. Fax: (212) 614 9426.
Price: US$35. Wine: US$16.

Fressen

It is easy to pass right by the demure façade of this chic eating place in the Meatpacking District without noticing it. Inside, the industrial decor attracts a chic crowd (yes, that is Brad Pitt at the next table), while the menu draws inspiration from across the globe – diners can start with the grilled baby octopus with tzatziki and move on to the pan-roasted Alaskan white salmon. If there are problems getting a table, it is at least worth elbowing through to the sleek bar.
421 West 13th Street (at Washington Street)
Tel: (212) 645 7775. Fax: (212) 255 2713.
Price: US$40. Wine: US$21.

Nobu

Lovely birch trees line the dim dining room at this long-standing favourite in the TriBeCa neighbourhood. The food is most accurately labelled 'Japanese-inspired', which means that chef Nobuyuki Matsuhisa lets his imagination run wild. Newcomers should sample the black cod with miso. Diners who cannot get a seat should try the appropriately named *Next Door Nobu*.
Nobu: 105 Hudson Street (at Franklin Street)
Next Door Nobu: 105 Hudson Street (between Franklin Street and Varick Street)
Tel: (212) 219 0550. Fax: (212) 219 1441.
Website: www.myriadrestaurantgroup.com
Price: US$70. Wine: US$28.

Pastis

This picture-perfect recreation of a slightly faded French bistro is the most democratic place in town – no reservations are accepted, so *everyone* has to wait. Diners belly up to the bar and wait their turn to sample the *steak-frites* or the *croque monsieur*. A better option is to head here early for brunch – the basket of warm breads is well worth the trip.
9 Ninth Avenue (at Little West 12th Street)
Tel: (212) 929 4844. Fax: (212) 929 5676.
E-mail: frontdesk@pastisny.com
Website: www.pastisny.com
Price: US$35. Wine: US$22.

The Red Cat

Moroccan lanterns hanging overhead illuminate this long, narrow restaurant in the newly chic gallery district of Chelsea. There is no pretence here – the warm, welcoming staff guides diners through a menu featuring pan-crisped skate with a marinated cucumber and artichoke salad and chargrilled pork chop with olive purée.
227 Tenth Avenue (between 23rd and 24th Streets)
Tel: (212) 242 1122. Fax: (212) 242 1390.
Website: www.theredcat.com
Price: US$45. Wine: US$24.

Budget

Grange Hall

The Great Depression might seem like an odd theme for a restaurant but *Grange Hall*, tucked away on a side street in Greenwich Village, makes it seem inspired. In a dining room with murals celebrating the heartland, guests can sample cranberry-glazed pork chops with poached apples or grilled lamb steak with rosemary and fried Idaho potatoes. Also recommended is a 'prairie martini' that can be ordered at the lovely carved-wood bar.
50 Commerce Street (at Barrow Street)
Tel: (212) 924 5246. Fax: (212) 255 2117.
Price: US$30. Wine: US$20.

Rockefeller Center ice skating rink

Mama's Food Shop

American comfort food has been on the rise in Manhattan ever since 11 September. But this East Village spot has been serving it long before New Yorkers insatiably craved the stuff. Diners can choose from helpings of fried chicken, roasted salmon and 'mac 'n' cheese', which derive from the 1950s TV dinner era. There is also a large array of oh-so-satisfying vegetable sides – broccoli with garlic, roasted brussel sprouts and mashed potatoes, to name but a few. Diners select a combination of three dishes at the counter and then find a table in the flea-market furnished space. A microwave for re-heating the goods and the tattooed staff are the only reminders of the present era. No credit cards.
200 East Third Street (between Avenue A and Avenue B)
Tel: (212) 777 4425.
E-mail: mamafood@hotmail.com
Website: www.mamasfoodshop.com
Price: US$10. Wine: BYO (no corkage fee).

Max

Everyone knows how much a box of pasta costs in the market. And this link in the chain seems to respect the intelligence of its patrons by not charging a fortune. The house rigatoni and eggplant topped with mozzarella cheese is a mere US$9. Similarly, the owners could get twice the asking price for the melt-in-the mouth gnocchi. Although the restaurant, which also serves scrumptious salads and fish and meat dishes, now has three outposts, the original East Village space is always packed with hipsters getting more than their money's worth. Country-style Italian table and chairs are crammed together in the main dining space, with barely room for diners to move between them and a sideboard teeming with pepper grinders and bowls of parmesan cheese. A walk through the kitchen, which bisects the restaurant, takes one to the narrow bar area and another small dining space. No credit cards.
51 Avenue B (between Third and Fourth Streets)
Tel: (212) 539 0111.
Price: US$20. Wine: US$30.

New York Noodle Town

Although other places will charge more, the noisy and fluorescent-lit *New York Noodle Town* never fails to feed its guests properly. Diners can choose from roasted fowl, salt-baked crab or soups and should be sure to get an order of the city's best Hong-Kong-style noodles. The shared tables are full at almost any hour – the restaurant closes only briefly in the early morning – sometimes with celebrities.
28½ Bowery (at Bayard Street)
Tel: (212) 349 2690.
Price: US$15. Wine: US$12.

Second Avenue Deli

New York's Lower East Side was once overflowing with outstanding Jewish delis but this is one of the last remaining. Diners can eat in the *Molly Picon Room*, filled with memorabilia of the famous Yiddish theatre star. Portions are huge, so guests might want to try half a sandwich (corned beef, naturally) with a bowl of the city's best matzo ball soup.
156 Second Avenue (at Tenth Avenue)
Tel: (212) 677 0606. Fax: (212) 353 1836.
E-mail: 2ndavedeli@2ndavedeli.com
Website: www.2ndavedeli.com
Price: US$20. Wine: US$16.

Personal Recommendations

Do Hwa

The West Village is blocks away from the city's Little Korea and yet the upscale spin on Korean menu favourites does not leave diners feeling like they are missing anything. On the contrary, the comfortable yet semi-industrial space lends a special something to the *bibimbop* (rice, vegetables and sometimes meat served with *kochujang*, the ubiquitous tomato paste condiment, with a fried egg) or meat-heavy tabletop grills, served with a platter of spicy *kimchi* and a dozen other condiments. An East Village sister restaurant, *Dok*

Times Square

Photo: Corel

Suni, is always crowded and more casual, much like the neighbourhood itself.
55 Carmine Street (between Bedford Street and Seventh Avenue)
Tel: (212) 414 1224.
Price: US$28. Wine: US$26.

Florent

No longer alone in the trendy Meatpacking District, this late-night bistro refuses to be outshone by its showier neighbours. A savvy West Village crowd packs the tables and diner-style counter stools for French-influenced fare – the *steak-frites* and the *moules* are great. The sassy message board above the bar and fictitious hand-drawn wall maps are always good for a chuckle.
69 Gansevoort Street (between Greenwich Street and Washington Street)
Tel: (212) 989 5779. Fax: (212) 645 2498.
E-mail: askflorent@restaurantflorent.com
Website: www.restaurantflorent.com
Price: US$30. Wine: US$16.

Gobo

Perhaps the first of its kind, *Gobo* is nearly an upscale vegetarian restaurant. Perhaps this is because the creators of this Zen-like space have given the kind of attention to tofu, *tempeh* and vegetables that other restaurants give to meat dishes. And to many a patron's surprise, the ingredients are not all that different from other Japanese inspired or contemporary meals. Meat-free meals have never looked this good.
401 Sixth Avenue (between Waverly Place and West Eighth Street)
Tel: (212) 255 3242. Fax: (212) 255 0687.
Website: www.goborestaurant.com
Price: US$30. Wine: US$30.

Lupa

Although his upmarket restaurant, *Babbo*, and the new affordable *enoteca*, *Otto*, span the price-range of Italian cuisine, it is Mario Batali's medium-priced restaurant that is just right. To the rustic dinner tables, waiters rush crusty bread and such succulent items as a ricotta-filled eggplant *involtini* appetiser, linguini with walnut *pesto primi*, and a veal *saltimbocca* (with *prosciutto* and sage leaves) *secondi*. Diners who do not deny the importance of ordering the incomparable *tartufo* dessert leave happier than Goldilocks.
170 Thompson Street (between Houston Street and Bleeker Street)
Tel: (212) 982 5089. Fax: (212) 982 5490.
Website: www.luparestaurant.com
Price: US$35. Wine: US$30.

Prune

Despite its old-fashioned name, the creative French fare at this tiny East Village *boite* competes with some of the city's best restaurants. In summer, a wall of French doors opens, to allow for semi-sidewalk dining. Although it is small, many mirrors and sufficiently bright lighting help counter Prune's diminutive size. However, it can be very difficult to get a table here and guests should book reservations early, for a chance to sample the stellar and sometimes eccentric, always decadent fare. Top choices include the grilled sardines appetiser or roast quail stuffed with marrow dressing. Popular entrées, such as the roast suckling pig and a meaty yet juicy capon on a garlic crouton, have guests coming back for more. Simple vegetable sides are also raised to their highest potential under the guidance of Chef Gabrielle Hamilton, whose childhood nickname gives the restaurant its sweet name. *Prune* has added a weekend brunch, too.

54 East First Street (between First Avenue and Second Avenue)
Tel: (212) 677 6221.
Website: www.prunerestaurant.com
Price: US$40. Wine: US$30.

ENTERTAINMENT

Nightlife

The cliché, 'the city that never sleeps', really rings true in New York and especially in Manhattan. This small island buzzes with nocturnal activity, from bustling neighbourhood bars, swank cocktail lounges and ultra hip nightclubs, where some of the world's best DJs entertain the city's 'beautiful people'.

Home to Broadway, the once louche Times Square is enjoying a renaissance, with American theme restaurants, bars and cinemas attracting a huge tourist crowd. The East Village, from 14th Street to Houston (pronounced howston), east of Broadway, is famous for its local bars that stay open late and its small live music clubs, such as the renowned CBGB, a live music venue frequented by a young rock-and-roll set. The Lower East Side, an up-and-coming neighbourhood that borders the East Village at Houston and stretches south to Chinatown at Canal, offers a similar nightlife scene and vibe.

SoHo is the hip capital, with its chic nightclubs attracting artists, models and media types. The gay scene is centred around the bars of the West Village, which also offers a lively mix of jazz clubs. Gramercy, in the 20s on the east side, is the 'new SoHo' with velvet-rope cocktail lounges. Upmarket tastes are also catered for in the sophisticated lounges, clubs and cocktail bars in Midtown and the Upper East and Upper West Sides. Entrance fees to some of the smarter nightclubs can be pricey and can only be paid in cash. The hippest clubs employ strict dress codes, only allowing the cool and the beautiful to break through the velvet ropes. The normal club closing time is 0400, although many are open all night. An ever-changing crop of 'after-hours' places offer entertainment until sunrise, however, alcohol cannot legally be served between 0400 and 0800 or after 2400 on Sunday. The minimum drinking age is 21 and checking of photo ID is mandatory. The average price of a beer is US$5–7, while the average price of a cocktail is US$10. A tip of US$1–2 is expected per drink.

Time Out New York (website: www.timeoutny.com) is a very good source of nightlife event information, published weekly and sold at newsagents and kiosks for US$2.99.

Bars

New York has a massive range of bars, with everything from neighbourhood dives and lively Irish pubs to slick jet-set haunts with DJs and dimly lit, cocktail lounges. Hip bars include the airline-theme bar *Idlewild*, 145 East Houston Street, East Village, *Max Fish*, 178 Ludlow Street, Lower East Side, which fills with a young, T-shirt-and-jeans crowd, *Serena*, 222 West 23rd Street, Chelsea, a subterranean lounge in the cool and legendary Chelsea Hotel, as well as favourite of the 'beautiful people' *Lotus*, 409 West 14th Street, West Village. *Double Happiness*, 173 Mott Street, Chinatown, draws a funky 20-something clientele. At *Hogs & Heifers*, 859 Washington Street, West

Village, on which the mediocre film *Coyote Ugly* (2000) was based, patrons toss their bra on the wall with all the others.

A more sophisticated lounge, the *Campbell Apartment*, Grand Central Terminal, Midtown, is hidden away in this busy rail terminal, serving top-class cocktails and first-rate Martinis. The refined, clubby bar in the *Algonquin Hotel*, 59 West 44th Street, Midtown West, is known for its literary origins. For old-time New York, there is *Chumley's*, 86 Bedford Street, West Village, or the *White Horse Tavern*, 567 Hudson Street, West Village.

Casinos

Gambling is illegal in New York State.

Clubs

The New York clubbing scene is notoriously fickle and difficult to pin down, especially after former mayor Giuliani shoved many of the best promoters underground. Away from the cheesy mainstream venues, two consistently good spots are *Centro-Fly*, 45 West 21st Street, with its big-deal DJs, and *Filter 14*, 432 West 14th Street, at Washington Street, a newcomer that is successfully competing with the tried-and-true spots. *Roxy*, 515 West 18th Street, and *Spa*, 76 East 13th Street, get an appreciative gay and lesbian crowd. *Luxx*, 256 Grand Street, Williamsburg, Brooklyn, is the centre of the city's electroclash scene, which looks back to the electric 80s for contemporary inspiration.

Comedy

New York's leading comedy venues, featuring top-line comedians, include *Carolines on Broadway*, 1626 Broadway, *The Comedy Cellar*, 117 McDougal Street, and *Gotham Comedy Club*, 34 West 22nd Street – dubbed the 'best comedy club in Manhattan'. More off-kilter comedy is on offer at *Surf Reality*, 172 Allen Street, while new faces often appear at *Stand Up NY*, 236 West 78th Street.

Live Music

The famous *Madison Square Garden*, Seventh Avenue between 31st Street and 33rd Street, Manhattan (website: www.thegarden.com), plays host to a number of rock and pop heavies, from Britney Spears to U2. *CBGB*, 315 Bowery, between First Street and Second Street (website: www.cbgb.com), the king of American underground rock venues, was there to provide the stage for new bands such as the Ramones and Blondie during the 1970s. It does the same for similar acts today. *The Bottom Line*, 15 West Fourth Street, which showcases softer folk and blues acts, is another long-standing venue that saw the rise to fame of many of its musicians.

New York is also home to numerous jazz clubs, including *The Blue Note*, 131 West Third Street, and the *Iridium*, 1650 Broadway, which both reel in the best American and international jazz musicians.

Sport

Boasting some of the USA's top sports teams, acres of parkland and beaches and state-of-the-art sports complexes, New York is a sports hotbed, offering the very best in spectator sports and a comprehensive array of activities for lovers of the great outdoors. The city's best indoor participant sports venue is the ultra-modern *Chelsea Piers Sports & Entertainment Complex*, a 12-hectare (30-acre) facility situated on four

beautifully restored early 20th-century piers at 23rd Street at West Side Highway, on the Hudson River. The complex has everything from a rock-climbing wall to an in-line skating rink.

Visitors interested in tickets to the top sporting events in the city should book in advance, as seasonal sell-outs are not uncommon. *Ticketmaster* (tel: (212) 307 7171; website: www.ticketmaster.com) is the best and most recognised way to purchase a ticket to a New York sporting event.

With two Major League teams, the baseball season, which runs from April to October, attracts huge crowds to two major stadiums in the area. *Shea Stadium*, 123–01 Roosevelt Avenue, Flushing, Queens (tel: (718) 507 METS *or* 6387 *or* TIXX *or* 8499 for tickets), is home to the *New York Mets* (website: www.mets.com). The *New York Yankees* (website: www.yankees.com), the most successful baseball team in US history, can be found at *Yankee Stadium*, East 161st Street and River Avenue, in the Bronx (tel: (718) 293 6000).

The local basketball season runs from October to April. *Madison Square Garden*, Seventh Avenue, between 31st Street and 33rd Street, Manhattan (tel: (212) 465 6741; website: www.thegarden.com), is the home of the celebrated *New York Knickerbockers*, or *Knicks* (website: www.nba.com/knicks), as well as

New York Liberty (website: www.wnba.com/liberty), the popular women's team.

American football teams from New York include the *Giants* (tel: (201) 935 8222; website: www.giants.com) and *New York Jets* (tel: (516) 560 8200; website: www.newyorkjets.com). The American football season kicks off in September. These two leading teams now play in New Jersey, at the *Giants Stadium*, in the Meadowlands Sports Complex (tel: (201) 935 3900; website: www.meadowlands.com). Tickets sell out well in advance and there are long waiting lists.

Ice hockey is also hugely popular and the National Hockey League (NHL) teams include the local *New York Rangers* (website: www.newyorkrangers.com). The team plays at Madison Square Garden (see above). Other local teams include *New York Islanders* (tel: (800) 883 ISLES *or* 883 4753; website: www.newyorkislanders.com), whose home ground is the *Nassau Coliseum*, 1255 Hempstead Turnpike, Uniondale (tel: (516) 794 9300; website: www.nassaucoliseum.com), and *New Jersey Devils* (website: www.newjerseydevils.com), who play at the *Meadowlands Sports Complex* (tel: (201) 935 3900; website: www.meadowlands.com).

The Arthur Ashe Stadium, Flushing Meadows, Queens, hosts the US Open Tennis Championships (website:

Broadway at night

www.usta.com), which takes place in late August to early September, featuring some of the world's top seeded players.

Beaches

There are several beaches in New York City, such as *Coney Island, Brighton Beach* and *Manhattan Beach*. The best beaches for sunbathing and swimming, however, are located on Long Island (see *Excursions*).

Bowling

Bowlmor Lanes, 110 University Place, between 12th Street and 13th Street (tel: (212) 255 8188), is Manhattan's premier bowling centre with 42 lanes and an atmosphere of 1950s kitsch. The venue, which serves pricey cocktails, becomes a veritable nightclub on some evenings, when it is open until the wee hours, with a DJ and glow-in-dark bowling on offer.

Fitness Centres

The Sports Center at Chelsea Piers, Pier 60, 23rd Street (tel: (212) 336 6000; website: www.chelseapiers.com), is 14,000 sq metres (150,000 sq ft) of adult sports and fitness facilities. The club has an indoor track and swimming pool, sundecks, basketball courts, an indoor sand volleyball court, boxing ring, rock climbing wall and gym. Day membership passes cost US$50 and allow access to all facilities.

Golf

The Black Course at *Bethpage State Park*, 99 Quaker Meeting House Road, Farmingdale (tel: (516) 249 0700), was the first public golf course to host the US Open. It is located just east of the city, on Long Island. Play costs approximately US$30, depending upon the course chosen. *Clearview Golf Club*, 202–12 Willets Point Boulevard (tel: (718) 225 4653), is open to the public for US$22 (weekdays) and US$24 (weekends). *The Golf Club at Chelsea Piers*, Pier 59, 23rd Street (tel: (212) 336 6400; website: www.chelseapiers.com), is America's most high-tech super range. There is a 200-yard fairway, all-weather driving range, putting green and a full-service Golf Academy. A session on the driving range starts at US$20 and prices rise with the number of balls used in session. *American Golf* (website: www.americangolf.com) allows online booking of tee times.

Horseracing

New Yorkers love the races and the main racetracks include *Aqueduct Racetrack*, Ozone Park, Queens (tel: (718) 641 4700), and *Meadowlands Racetrack*, East Rutherford (tel: (201) 935 8500).

Running

New York Road Runners Club, 9 East 89th Street, between Madison Avenue and Fifth Avenue (tel: (212) 860 4455; website: www.nyrr.org), are the organisers of the NYC Marathon and promote the sport through races, events and publications.

Sailing

Chelsea Marina at Chelsea Piers, West 23rd Street (tel: (212) 336 5600; website: www.chelseapiers.com), is the city's largest marina, featuring a sailing school as well as boats for dinner cruising and deep-sea fishing.

Skating/Ice Skating

The Roller Rinks at Chelsea Piers, Pier 62, 23rd Street (tel: (212) 336 6200; website: www.chelseapiers.com), has two indoor ice skating rinks, two outdoor in-line/roller skating rinks and a skate park. There are two outdoor ice skating rinks with skate hire in *Central Park*, 59th Street to 110th Street, and one in the *Rockefeller Center*, Fifth Avenue, 47th Street to 52nd Street (see *Sightseeing*).

Tennis

The tennis courts at *Central Park*, located at 93rd Street (tel: (212) 280 0201), are open to the public during the summer.

Shopping

A city famous for its sartorial elegance and Bohemian chic, New York is a shopper's paradise, hawking everything from the very latest designer fashions to flea market bargains in addition to foods and goods from every corner of the globe. Clothing is not taxed in New York and the bargains have got even better of late, as the US recession has led to widespread discounting on everything from electrical goods to designer fashion.

The smartest shops are located on *Madison Avenue*, where most top designers have flagship stores. Nearby, Fifth Avenue is a magnet for the label conscious and well heeled. Standing at one of the most famous corners in Manhattan, *Tiffany & Co*, 727 Fifth Avenue, is an icon of the American Dream. Famous department stores include *Saks Fifth Avenue*, 611 Fifth Avenue, *Macy's*, Herald Square, *Bloomingdales*, 1000 Third Avenue, at 59th Street, and *Barney's New York*, 660 Madison Avenue, at 61st Street, which is the trendiest of this retail crop. Both Macy's and Bloomingdales now offer free 'personal shoppers' on request, to help navigate their huge ranges. The famous *Ladies' Mile*, which was the epicentre of uptown fashion 100 years ago, with department stores stretching from 14th Street for a mile along Sixth Avenue, is now a major discount centre. However, the spectacular Victorian buildings have been restored and stores such as *Bed Bath and Beyond*, *Old Navy Clothing Co*; *Barnes & Noble* and *Filene's Basement* have spearheaded a revival of the historic shopping strip.

SoHo is the most European of New York's neighbourhoods and its shops resemble those at Covent Garden, with high-end clothing outlets and shoe stores, make-up and beauty salons, art galleries and antiques shops, and modern furniture showrooms. The East Village and Lower East Side harbour street fashion and cutting-edge young designers, with vintage shops and music stores intermingling with designer boutiques and eclectic outlets. Discount shops selling authentic American goods, such as Levi's, are located throughout the city, particularly along Broadway, between Houston Street and 14th Street.

There are numerous markets to appeal to bargain hunters. The *Annex Flea Market*, known as the 26th Street Flea Market, on Sixth Avenue, made famous by Andy Warhol, is open on Saturday and Sunday from dawn to dusk. The best bargains are vintage clothing and fine linens. Many 'green markets', selling locally grown produce, freshly caught fish, desserts and breads, are located around the city, the most central of which is at Union Square, opening on Monday, Wednesday, Friday and Saturday 0800–1800.

Photo: Karen Henderson

Macy's and the Empire State Building

Shopping hours depend on the neighbourhood. Business areas, such as Wall Street, open as early as 0800, while shops in areas such as SoHo and East Village open late at 1100. Many stay open until at least 1900. Department stores are open 1000–1800 and 1200–1700 Sunday.

In New York, everything but life's most basic necessities is taxable and the sales tax of 8.5% on all consumer goods – apart from clothes under US$110 – is one of the highest in the country. Visitors to New York are unable to claim a tax refund for goods purchased.

Culture

From the bright lights of Broadway to the revered stages at the Lincoln Center and Carnegie Hall, from the high kicks of the Rockettes at Radio City Music Hall to the cutting-edge works performed at BAM, New York City continues to be one of the most diverse and heavily textured urban cultural centres in the world. As author Tom Wolfe wrote: 'Culture just seems to be in the air, like part of the weather.'

The principal entertainment districts are the Theater District in the Broadway/42nd Street/Times Square area and the Lincoln Center for the Performing Arts on the Upper West Side. Most Broadway theatres are located in the blocks just east or west of Broadway, between 41st Street and 53rd Street. Off- and Off-Off-Broadway theatres are sprinkled throughout Manhattan, with a concentration in the East and West Villages, Chelsea and several in the 40s and 50s west of the Broadway theatre district. The *Lincoln Center for the Performing Arts*, 70 Lincoln Center Plaza, Columbus Avenue at 64th Street (tel: (212) 721 6500; website: www.lincolncenter.org), is America's first and largest performing arts complex, containing many venues. It is also the home of the *Metropolitan Opera* (website: www.metopera.org), the *New York City Opera* (website: www.nycopera.com), the *New York City Ballet* (website: www.nycballet.com), the *New York Philharmonic* (website: www.newyorkphilharmonic.org), among others.

New York continues to grow and, as well as these established attractions, offers something new each day. Times Square is one of the prominent areas to receive attention. *Madame Tussaud's* wax museum, 234 West 42nd Street (tel: (800) 246 8872; website: www.nycwax.com), which includes a movie complex, the *New Amsterdam Theater*, 214 West 42nd Street, owned by Disney, as well as a number of similar renovations of historic theatres – such as the *New Victory Theatre*, 209 West 42nd Street (tel: (646) 223 3020; website: www.newvictory.org) and the *Academy/Apollo* (see *Theatre* below) – have ensured that New York remains the cultural capital of the USA.

Tickets are available for purchase through *Telecharge* (tel: (212) 239 6200; website: www.telecharge.com), which handles, Broadway, Off-Broadway and some concerts. *Ticketmaster* (tel: (212) 307 7171; website: www.ticketmaster.com), also offers Broadway and Off-Broadway, as well as tickets to Madison Square Garden and Radio City. Reduced-priced tickets of up to half-price for same-day Broadway and Off-Broadway are available for purchase at the *TKTS* booth, 47th Street and Broadway (website: www.tdf.org/programs/tkts), open daily 1500–2000 for evening performances, 1000–1400 for Wednesday and Saturday matinees and 1200–1830 for all Sunday performances. Credit cards are not accepted.

Information on cultural events in the city is available online (website: www.nycvisit.com and

The Apollo Theatre

Photo: Corel

www.whatsonwhen.com). *Time Out New York* (website: www.timeoutny.com) is also a good source of information – published weekly and sold at newsagents and kiosks for US$2.99.

Music

The Avery Fisher Hall, in the Lincoln Center, 70 Lincoln Center Plaza, Columbus Avenue at 64th Street (tel: (212) 875 5030; website: www.lincolncenter.org), is the permanent home of the *New York Philharmonic* (tel: (212) 875 5709; website: www.newyorkphilharmonic.org) and a temporary one to visiting orchestras and soloists. Tickets for the New York Philharmonic cost approximately US$15–50. Avery Fisher also hosts the very popular annual *Mostly Mozart* festival (tel: (212) 875 5103) in August. *The Alice Tully Hall*, also in the Lincoln Center (tel: (212) 875 5050; website: www.lincolncenter.org), is a smaller venue for chamber orchestras, string quartets and instrumentalists. The greatest names from all schools of music – from Tchaikovsky and Toscanini to Gershwin and Billie Holiday – have performed at *Carnegie Hall*, 154 West 57th Street, at Seventh Avenue (tel: (212) 247 7800; website: www.carnegiehall.org), which boasts an astonishing and eclectic repertoire at moderate prices. Other leading venues that draw the world's top performers include *Kaufman Concert Hall*, in the 92nd Street Y, at 1395 Lexington Avenue (tel: (212) 996 1100), and *Lehman Center for the Performing Arts*, 250 Bedford Park Boulevard West, Bronx (tel: (718) 960 8232; website: www.lehman.cuny.edu/lehmancenter).

Known as the *Met*, the *Metropolitan Opera House*, in the Lincoln Center (tel: (212) 362 6000; website: www.lincolncenter.org), is New York's premier opera venue and home to the *Metropolitan Opera* (website: www.metopera.org), from September to late April. *The New York State Theater*, also in the Lincoln Center (tel: (212) 870 5570; website: www.lincolncenter.org), is where the *New York City Opera* (tel: (212) 870 5630; website: www.nycopera.com) perform. Its wide and adventurous program varies wildly in quality – sometimes startlingly innovative, occasionally mediocre

– but seats go for less than half the Met's prices. Other venues include the *Julliard School*, 155 West 65th Street, at Broadway (tel: (212) 799 5000; website: www.juilliard.edu), where talented students perform with a famous conductor, usually for low prices.

Theatre

Theatre venues in the city are referred to as Broadway, Off-Broadway or Off-Off-Broadway – groupings that represent a descending order of ticket price, production polish, elegance and comfort and an ascending order of innovation, experimentation, and theatre for the sake of art rather than cash. Off-Broadway is still the place for theatre punters to see the works of the world's most innovative playwrights – social and political drama, satire, ethnic plays and repertory ... in short, anything that Broadway would not consider a guaranteed money spinner. Lower operating costs also mean that Off-Broadway often serves as a forum to try out what sometimes ends up as a big Broadway production. Off-Off-Broadway is New York's fringe. Unlike Off-Broadway, Off-Off does not have to use professional actors and shows range from shoestring productions of the classics to outrageous and experimental performance art.

The *National Actors Theatre*, 1560 Broadway, Suite 409 (tel: (212) 719 5331; website: www.nationalactorstheatre.org), presents the classics on Broadway, while *Manhattan Theatre Club*, 311 West 43rd Street, Eighth Floor (tel: (212) 581 1212; website: www.mtc-nyc.org), produces some of the finest new plays in American theatre. Other theatre groups include *Walt Disney Theatrical Productions*, 1450 Broadway, Suite 300 (tel: (212) 827 5412; website: www.disney.go.com/disneyonbroadway), which brings the magic of Disney to life on the Broadway stage. For a more ethnic flavour, Harlem's *Apollo Theatre*, 253 West 125th Street (tel: (212) 531 5300; website: www.showtimeinharlem.com), has celebrated the legacy and culture of African-American music and entertainment since 1934.

Dance

New York has five major ballet companies as well as dozens of contemporary troupes and the official dance season runs from September to January and April to June. *Metropolitan Opera House*, in the Lincoln Center (tel: (212) 362 6000; website: www.lincolncenter.org), is the home of the renowned *American Ballet Theater* (tel: (212) 477 3030; website: www.abt.org), which performs the classics from early May into July. *New York State Theater*, also in the Lincoln Center (tel: (212) 870 5570; website: www.lincolncenter.org), is home to the revered *New York City Ballet* (website: www.nycballet.com), which performs more contemporary ballet for a nine-week season each spring.

Universally known as *BAM*, *Brooklyn Academy of Music*, 30 Lafayette Street, between Flatbush Avenue and Fulton Street, Brooklyn (tel: (718) 636 4100; website: www.bam.org), is America's oldest performing arts academy and one of the busiest and most daring producers in New York. During autumn, *BAM's Next Wave Festival* showcases the hottest international attractions in avant-garde dance and music. Winter brings visiting artists, while, each spring, *BAM* hosts the annual *DanceAfrica Festival*, America's largest showcase for African and African-American dance and culture.

The most eminent and celebrated troupes in modern dance perform at *City Center*, 131 West 55th Street, between Sixth Avenue and Seventh Avenue (tel: (212) 581 1212; website: www.citycenter.org). Big-name companies include *Merce Cunningham Dance Company* (website: www.merce.org), *Paul Taylor Dance Company*, *Alvin Ailey American Dance Theater* (website: www.alvinailey.org), *Joffrey Ballet* (website: www.joffreyballetschool.com) and *Dance Theater of Harlem* (website: www.dancetheatreofharlem.com). *Merce Cunningham Studio*, 55 Bethune St at Washington St (tel: (212) 691 9751; website: www.merce.org/studio.html), the home of the Merce Cunningham Dance Company, stages performances by emerging modern choreographers.

Film

A movie centre second only to Tinseltown itself, New York has hundreds of modern cinema complexes and arthouse cinemas. Cinemas worth visiting include *Sony Lincoln Square*, Broadway at 68th Street (tel: (212) 336 5000 (recorded information) or (212) 336 5020), which is more a theme park than a multiplex, and *The Ziegfeld*, 141 West 54th Street, between Sixth Avenue and Seventh Avenue (tel: (908) 918 2000; website: www.clearviewcinemas.com), which often holds glitzy premieres and is the grandest picture palace in town – once home to the Ziegfeld Follies. Arthouse movies are screened at *Angelika Film Centre*, 18 West Houston Street (tel: (212) 995 2000 or 2570), *Lincoln Plaza Cinemas*, 30 Lincoln Plaza (tel: (212) 757 2280), and *Quad Cinema*, 34 West Street, between Fifth Avenue and Sixth Avenue (tel: (212) 255 8800). General information, show times and advanced tickets are available from *Moviefone* (tel: (212) 777 FILM or 3456).

New York has been portrayed through celluloid in a number of ways, ranging from the ridiculous yet enduring images of *King Kong*, swinging from the Empire State Building, in the 1933 classic starring Fay Wray, to the psychological horrors of Martin Scorsese's *Taxi Driver* (1976). In the latter, Robert De Niro plays the part of a mentally isolated New York cabbie and Vietnam vet, driven to violence by the decadence of the city. It is New York decadence of a slightly different nature that Alan Rudolph explores in *Mrs Parker and the*

SPECIAL EVENTS

Winter Restaurant Week, many of the city's best restaurants set low fixed-price menus corresponding to the year (eg US$20.03 for a three-course lunch in 2003), last week in Jan, various venues
Manhattan Antiques and Collectibles Triple Pier Expo, Feb, Hudson River
Chinese New Year, new lunar year celebrations, early Feb, Chinatown
Westminster Kennel Club Dog Show, more than 2500 champion dogs compete (website: www.westminsterkennelclub.org), one weekend in Feb, Madison Square Garden
New York Flower Show, Mar, 90 and 93 51st Street and 12th Avenue
Art Expo New York, Mar, Javits Convention Centre
St Patrick's Day Parade, Irish-American parade, 17 Mar, Fifth Avenue
Macy's Flower Show, Apr, Macy's department store, Herald Square
Tartan Day, 10,000 pipers and drummers march through city streets in celebration of Scotland, early Apr, Manhattan
Cherry Blossom Festival, the first signs of New York spring (website: www.bbg.org), mid-Apr, Brooklyn Botanic Garden, Washington Avenue
Ninth Avenue International Food Festival, culinary street fair (website: www.9th-ave.com), May, Ninth Avenue
DanceAfrica Festival, African and African-American dance festival, May, Brooklyn Academy of Music (BAM)
Fleet Week, a nautical festival hosted by the Intrepid Sea-Air-Space Museum (website: www.intrepidmuseum.org), Memorial Day weekend, May, Hudson Harbor
Summerstage, free outdoor concerts, May–Aug, Central Park
Summer Restaurant Week, many of the city's best restaurants set low fixed-price menus corresponding to the year (eg US$20.03 for a three-course lunch in 2003), one week in Jun, various venues
Heritage of Pride, annual lesbian and gay pride march, ending in street festival and dance party, late Jun, upper Fifth Avenue to the Village
Mermaid Parade, the city's most informal and most lively parade with a nautical theme (website: www.coneyislandusa.com), late Jun, Coney Island
Fourth of July, annual firework display in celebration of American Independence, 4 Jul, over the East River
Mostly Mozart, music festival, Aug, Avery Fisher Hall
Bryant Park, free outdoor classic films (website: www.bryantpark.org), Aug, Bryant Park, 42nd Street
Feast of San Gennaro, extravaganza of eating, drinking and merry-making, one week in mid-Sep, Little Italy
Greenwich Village Halloween Parade, exuberant fancy dress procession, 31 Oct, along Sixth Avenue
Next Wave Festival, avant-garde dance and music festival, early Oct–Jan, Brooklyn Academy of Music (BAM)
New York City Marathon, early Nov, starts in Staten Island, finishes in Central Park
Macy's Thanksgiving Day Parade, New York institution featuring huge hot-air balloons in the shape of cartoon characters, such as Snoopy, the Pink Panther and Betty Boop, Thanksgiving Day, Nov, 145 Street to 34th Street
New Year's Eve, street party, 31 Dec, Times Square

Vicious Circle (1994), which looks at New York literary life and society during the 1920s. The life and times of one of New York's most famous daughters, the acid and hilarious writer and wit, Dorothy Parker, is brought to life amid a lavish New York setting.

Cultural Events

New York's biggest antiques event, *Manhattan Antiques and Collectibles Triple Pier Expo*, is held at three piers on the Hudson River, in February. The annual harbinger of spring, the *New York Flower Show*, is held on piers 90 and 93, 51st Street and 12th Avenue, in March. Meanwhile, *Art Expo New York*, the world's largest show of popular art, features a wide range of works from paintings and sculpture to posters and decorative arts, at the Javits Convention Centre, also in March. *Ninth Avenue International Food Festival* is a gastronomic feast of a street fair in May, with live bands and hundreds of food stalls selling a wide assortment of ethnic and junk food. *Summerstage*, a festival of free or low-cost concerts in Central Park, features world music, pop, folk and jazz artists throughout the summer.

Literary Notes

The vibrant city of New York has spawned some of America's most celebrated writers and provided the backdrop and inspiration for countless best-selling novels and hit movies. Washington Square, at Fifth

Avenue and Waverley Place, was home to the 19th-century aristocracy and provided the inspiration for the classic study of the American upper classes, *Washington Square* (1881), by New Yorker Henry James. Bohemian Greenwich Village has long been the favoured haunt of America's literati. The Chelsea Hotel, on West 23rd Street, is something of a writers' emporium. Here Arthur Miller penned *After the Fall* (1964) and William Burroughs worked on *Naked Lunch* (1959). New Yorker Arthur Miller is celebrated as America's greatest living playwright, whose numerous works have delighted Broadway and international audiences for decades. His knowledge of the Brooklyn waterfront helped to form his characters in his play *A View From the Bridge* (1955) and powerful reflections upon his home town are revealed in *The Price* (1968).

New York's most famous contemporary novelist is Paul Auster, who won international acclaim for *The New York Trilogy* (1987), a book comprising three novellas – *City of Glass*, *Ghosts* and *The Locked Room* – all set in New York. Edwin G. Burrows and Mike Wallace's *Gotham* (2001) is one of the most illuminating and readable histories of New York. One of the most striking works from the flurry of post-11 September 2001 publications is *September 11: A Testimony* (2001), assembled by press agency Reuters, with some of the most dramatic World Trade Center photographic images.

Paris cannot be approached without expectations and preconceptions. For some, it represents a city of romance, with the image of the celebrated photographer Doisneau's lovers clinched in an eternal embrace. For others, the French capital is a sparkling mix of writers and artists or an unhealthy concentration of proud Parisians. While the first visit to the French capital could surprise, it is unlikely to disappoint. On all sorts of levels – historical, architectural, cultural – this is a fascinating city.

The River Seine splits the city into the *Rive Droite* (Right Bank) north of the river and the *Rive Gauche* (Left Bank) south of the river. Paris is just ten kilometres (six miles) by 11km (seven miles), easily explored on foot or via the efficient transport system. Orientation is facilitated by the 20 *arrondissements* (designated here as 1st to 20th, in French as 1er to 20e), which spiral outwards in the shape of a snail shell from the central Ile-de-la-Cité to Porte de Montreuil on the eastern edge of the city.

The life of the modern city began about 250BC when a Celtic tribe called the *Parisii* established a fishing settlement *Lutétia*, on the Ile-de-la-Cité. The Romans were later drawn to this strategic location, a natural crossroads between Germany and Spain, and took control in 52BC. The first King of France, Hugues Capet, ruled from Paris in AD987. Despite English rule between 1420 and 1436, a series of French kings brought about the centralisation of France, with Paris at its cultural, political and economic heart. The climax of this process was verbalised in Louis XIV's famed claim: *L'Etat c'est moi* (the State is me).

The history of Paris can be uncovered throughout its distinctive districts. Hilly Montmartre, with its village atmosphere, was where the Paris Commune began in 1871; the Marais evokes medieval Paris, its winding streets a sharp contrast to the wide, orderly Haussmann boulevards, envisaged by Napoleon III to keep the mobs at bay. These grand 19th-century avenues still dominate the city, interspersed with modern flourishes. The *grands travaux* (large projects) of President Mitterrand added the Grande Arche de la Défense, the ultra-modern Opéra de la Bastille, the impressive Institut du Monde Arabe, and bravely placed a glass pyramid in the central courtyard of the Louvre.

The varied populations within Paris define the city's atmosphere just as much as its landmarks. The French establishment resides comfortably in the smart 16th *arrondissement*, while African and North African immigrants live less lavishly in areas such as Belleville and the Goutte d'Or. The Jewish quarters include the shabby Sentier and trendy Marais district; the latter is also Paris' gay centre.

Parisians, as a whole, are proud of their city. Yet at the drop of a hat they nip to the provinces (usually Normandy) for a weekend. In August, there is a mass exodus to the south. They go in search of greenery – although central Paris has its own lovely parks, including, most notably, the Jardin de Luxembourg and the Jardin des Tuileries – and to escape from their fast-paced '*boulot, métro, dodo*' (work, métro, sleep) existence. Fortunately, visitors may take the city at a more leisurely pace. The best time to visit is between May and July, when the days are sunny and pleasant. Paris has a moderate climate, with wet winters and little to no snowfall.

Photo: Corel

River Seine and the Eiffel Tower

TRAVEL

Getting There By Air

Aéroports de Paris – ADP (website: www.adp.fr) is responsible for the two major airports in Paris: Roissy Charles de Gaulle and Orly.

Roissy Charles de Gaulle Airport (CDG)

Tel: (01) 4862 2280.
Website: www.adp.fr
The city's main airport is located 23km (14 miles) northeast of the city. There are three terminals: CDG 1 serves international flights; CDG 2 serves national and international flights; and T9 has charter flights only (national and international). CDG 1 and CDG 2 are linked by free shuttle buses. *Air France* coaches and *RER* line B (see below) link Charles de Gaulle airport to Orly airport (journey time – approximately 50 minutes).
Major airlines: France's national carrier is *Air France/Air Inter* (tel: (0820) 820 820 (within France) *or* (01) 4299 2101 (outside France); website: www. airfrance.com). Other airlines include *Air Canada, Alitalia, American Airlines, Cathay Pacific Airways, Delta Airlines, British Airways, Lufthansa, Singapore Airlines* and *US Airways*.

Airport facilities: Facilities include bars, restaurants and boutiques, post offices, newsagents, chemists, banks, ATMs, bureaux de change, insurance facilities and car parks. There is no left-luggage facility. Car hire companies at the airport include *Avis, Budget, Europcar, Hertz, National Citer* and *Sixt*.
Business facilities: Eight fully equipped meeting rooms, three offices and one VIP lounge are located within the *Roissy Charles de Gaulle 1 Business Centre* (tel: (01) 4862 2290; fax: (01) 4862 6129), accessible from the departures level near gate 34 by taking the escalators to the shopping level.
Transport to the city: The *RER* line B (tel: (08) 9268 7714) runs every four to 15 minutes daily 0500–2400, departing from the TGV station of CDG 2 to the Gare du Nord, Châtelet-Les Halles, St-Michel and Denfert-Rochereau, where there are métro stations (journey time – approximately 30–45 minutes). Tickets cost €7.70.
A bus service operated by *Roissybus* (tel: (01) 4925 6187) departs from the three terminals to rue Scribe, métro

Opéra (journey time – approximately 45 minutes). The service operates daily 0600–2300 and costs €8.
RATP buses (tel: (08) 9268 4114 (information in English) *or* (08) 9268 7714; website: www.ratp.fr) depart from CDG 1 (gate 26, departure level); bus 350 stops at Gare du Nord and Gare de l'Est; bus 351 at the Porte de Bagnolet and Nation. RATP tickets cost €1.30.
Air France coaches (tel: (08) 9235 0820) depart every 15 minutes from CDG 1 and CDG 2 – running daily 0545–2300 to place Charles de Gaulle (journey time – approximately 40 minutes); a ticket costs €10. Buses also depart every 30 minutes daily 0700–2130 to Paris-Montparnasse, rue du Commandant Mouchotte, Gare de Lyon and boulevard Diderot (journey time – approximately 50 minutes); a ticket costs €11.50.
The *Airport Shuttle* (tel: (01) 3011 1300; fax: (01) 3011 1309; website: www.airportshuttle.fr) is a door-to-door airport minibus service, often cheaper than a taxi. Places must be reserved at least two days in advance (journey time – approximately 75 minutes) and tickets costs €14.50 per person (cheaper for groups of up to eight). A taxi to the city centre costs approximately €30 (journey time – approximately 60 minutes). The airport's chauffeur-driven limousine service (tel: (01) 4071 8462) costs €100.

Orly Airport (ORY)

Tel: (01) 4975 1515.
Website: www.adp.fr
Orly is located 14km (nine miles) south of the city, on the A6 motorway. There are two terminals linked by shuttle (*navette*). Orly Sud handles mainly international flights, while Orly Ouest handles mainly domestic flights.
Major airlines: The national carrier is *Air France/Air Inter* (tel: (0820) 820 820 (within France) *or* (01) 4299 2101 (outside France); website: www.airfrance.com). These include *Air Algerie, Air France, Air Littoral, Corsair, El Al, Royal Air Maroc, Royal Jordanian* and *Tunis Air*.
Airport facilities: These include bars, restaurants, boutiques, banks, foreign exchange, dry cleaners, supermarket, pharmacy, post office and a hairdresser. There is no left-luggage facility. Car hire companies at the airport include *Avis, Budget, Europcar, Hertz, National Citer* and *Sixt*.
Business facilities: The fully equipped *Orly West Business Centre* (tel: (01) 4975 1233; fax: (01) 4975 0163) has 17 meeting rooms, seven offices and a VIP business lounge in the west terminal. Access is from the departure level by an escalator located at the entrance to hall three.
Transport to the city: A combination service of *RER* line C (tel: (08) 9268 7714) and the *ADP* shuttle bus (*navette*) departs from both terminals and stops at the Gare d'Austerlitz, St-Michel, Invalides and Porte Maillot (journey time – approximately 35 minutes). The service operates daily 0500–2330 and tickets cost €5.25 (includes travel on RER, ADP shuttle and métro services).
Orlyval (tel: (08) 3668 7714) is the frequent Val train shuttle link to the *RER* line B station of Anthony, which has métro connections to Denfert-Rochereau, St-Michel and Châtelet-Les Halles (journey time – approximately 30 minutes). Trains run Monday to Saturday 0600–2230 and Sunday 0700–2300; tickets cost €8.75.
Frequent *RATP* buses (tel: (08) 9268 4114 (information in English) *or* (08) 9268 7714; website: www.ratp.fr) stop at place Denfert-Rochereau. The 'Orlybus' runs to Denfert-Rochereau RER and métro station (journey time – 25 minutes), costing €5.50. The 'Jetbus' runs to métro Villejuif-Louis Aragon (journey time – approximately 15 minutes), costing €4.95.

Air France coaches (tel: (08) 9235 0820) operate daily 0545–2300, stopping at the Porte d'Orléans, Gare Montparnasse, Duroc and Gare des Invalides (journey time – approximately 30 minutes). Tickets cost €7.50. The *Airport Shuttle* (see *Roissy Airport* above) costs approximately €20 for a trip into the city centre (journey time – approximately 1 hour). Taxis from the airport to the centre of Paris also cost approximately €20 (journey time – approximately 35 minutes). The *Airport Limousine* service (tel: (01) 4071 8462) provides chauffeur-driven cars; the price is fixed at €85.
Approximate flight times to Paris: From London is 1 hour 10 minutes; from New York is 7 hours; from Los Angeles is 10 hours 30 minutes; from Toronto is 7 hours and 20 minutes and from Sydney is 23 hours 25 minutes.
Arrival/departure tax: None.

Getting There By Water

The most convenient ports to Paris from Britain all lie on France's northern seaboard and include *St-Malo, Cherbourg, Caen, Le Havre* and *Dieppe*.
Ferry services: The following companies run regular cross-channel ferries. *Brittany Ferries* (tel: (0825) 828 828 *or* (08705) 360 360 (UK number); website: www.brittany-ferries.com) operates services from Plymouth to Roscoff, from Poole to Cherbourg and from Portsmouth to St-Malo and Caen. *Condor Ferries* (tel: (0825) 160 300 *or* (02) 9920 0300 *or* (0845) 345 2000 (UK number); website: www.condorferries.co.uk) operates from Poole, Weymouth, Jersey and Guernsey to St-Malo and from Portsmouth to Cherbourg. *P&O Ferries* (tel: (01) 5569 8228 *or* (0870) 600 0600 (UK number for Dover reservations) *or* (0870) 242 4999 (UK number for Portsmouth reservations); website: www.poferries.com) sail from Dover to Calais and from Portsmouth to Cherbourg and Le Havre. *Hoverspeed* (tel: (0800) 1211 1211 *or* (0870) 240 8070 (UK number); website: www.hoverspeed.com) offers fast hovercraft services from Dover to Calais and from Newhaven to Dieppe.
Transport to the city: The best way for travellers to reach Paris from the ferry ports is by car or by rail.

Getting There By Rail

Société Nationale des Chemins de Fer – SNCF (tel: (01) 5390 2020 (Ile-de-France) *or* (08) 9235 3535 (national); website: www.sncf.com) is the national railway service, which is fast, efficient and generally reliable. Paris has five major stations – *Gare du Nord*, rue Dunkerque, 10th, *Gare St-Lazare*, place du Havre, 8th, *Gare de Lyon*, place Louis-Armand, 12th, *Gare Montparnasse*, boulevard de Vaugirard, 15th, and *Gare d'Austerlitz*, boulevard de l'Hôpital, 13th. Each station has cafés, restaurants, *tabacs*, banks, bureaux de change, ATMs and car hire available on the premises or nearby. The Gare de Lyon also has a tourist office. Information on the French rail network is available directly from *SNCF* or from *Rail Europe* in the UK (tel: (08705) 848 848).

Rail services: Gare du Nord is the French terminus of the international high-speed *Eurostar* (tel: (03) 2855 8212 *or* (08705) 186 186 (in the UK); website: www.eurostar.com) train that runs from London Waterloo (journey time – 3 hours) and Brussels Bruxelles-Midi (journey time – 1 hour 30 minutes). The train station also contains Eurostar's executive lounge. *Eurostar* also runs from London Waterloo to *Disneyland Paris* (tel: (01) 6474 5800; website: www.disneylandparis.com).

The *Eurotunnel* shuttle service is also available for drivers (see *Getting There By Road*).

Transport to the city: All of Paris' major train stations are directly linked to the métro network.

Getting There By Road

Motorways bear the prefix 'A' and national roads 'N'. Minor roads are classed as 'D' (*départementales*) roads. Traffic drives on the right and drivers must give way to the right, unless the route is marked with *Passage Protégé* signs (a broad arrow, a yellow diamond or an 'X' on a triangular background) or the driver is at a roundabout indicating *vous n'avez pas la priorité* ('you do not have the right of way'). Speed limits are 130kph (81mph) on motorways; 110kph (68mph) on dual carriageways separated by a central reservation; 90kph (46mph) outside built-up areas and 50kph (31mph) in built-up areas. Drivers who have held a driving licence for less than two years have different speed restrictions to those who have been driving for longer – a maximum speed limit of 110kph (68mph) is enforced.

The minimum age for driving is 18 years. Seatbelts must be worn by all front- and rear-seat passengers. Under-tens may not travel in the front seat. A national driving licence, the car's registration document and a red warning triangle must be carried at all times or the driver is liable for a fine. EU nationals taking their own cars to France are strongly advised to obtain a Green Card, without which insurance cover is limited to the legal minimum. The Green Card tops this up to the level of cover provided by the car owner's domestic policy. All headlamp beams must be adjusted for right-side driving by use of beam deflectors or by tilting the headlamp bulb-holder. The French police fine motorists on the spot for driving offences such as speeding. Random breath tests for drinking and driving are common; the maximum legal alcohol to blood ratio for driving is 0.05%.

Further details on driving in France are available from French Government Tourist Offices. The *Automobile Club de France* (tel: (01) 4312 4312) can provide

CITY STATISTICS

Location: Ile-de-France region, France.
Country dialling code: 33.
Population: 2,125,000 (city); 10,952,000 (metropolitan area).
Ethnic mix: European majority, with North African, Indochinese and Basque minorities.
Religion: 90% Roman Catholic, 6% non-denominational, 2% Protestant, 1% Jewish, 1% Muslim (North African workers).
Time zone: GMT + 1 (GMT + 2 from last Sunday in March to Saturday before last Sunday in October).
Electricity: 220 volts AC, 50Hz; round two-pin plugs are standard.
Average January temp: 4°C (39°F).
Average July temp: 19.5°C (67°F).
Annual rainfall: 642mm (25.2 inches).

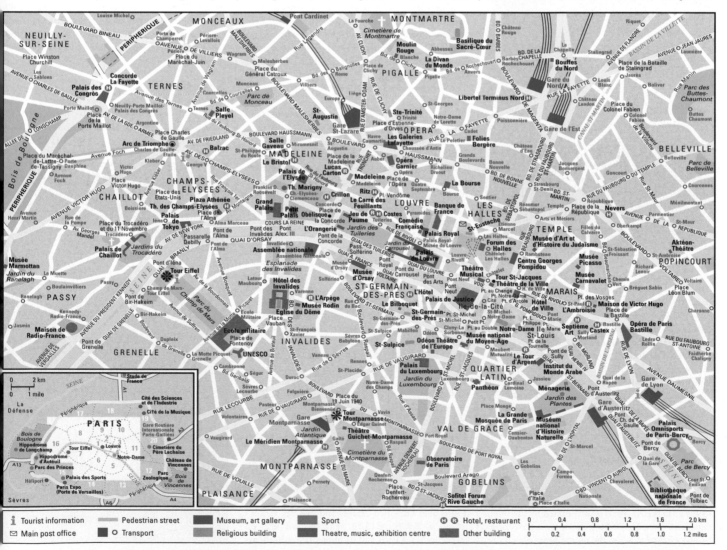

BUSINESS PROFILE

France is the fourth largest economic power in the world in terms of GDP and the second largest exporter of services and agricultural products. Paris and the Ile-de-France region are responsible for 28% of the country's total GDP. The Paris region is predominantly a service economy, followed in importance by commerce, industry, construction and agriculture. Particular strengths are in pharmaceuticals, telecommunications, publishing and research, with Paris ranking first in Europe in terms of research development. Five of the French banks (including *Crédit Agricole*, *BNP* and the *Caisse d'Epargne*) are among the main commercial banks in Europe.

The excellent transport and telecommunications network, highly skilled workforce, quality of life and prestige of Paris have encouraged companies to locate in the city. Many top international companies, including *Sony*, *IBM*, *Hewlett Packard France*, *Siemens* and *Motorola* have a presence in Paris and around 40 companies base their international headquarters here. In total, the French capital has attracted about 2400 foreign companies and numerous foreign banks.

Paris attracts more than 20 million visitors annually and rates among the world's most popular international conference venues. Its thousand-plus annual conventions include over 300 international conferences and 300 trade shows.

That said, the economy is not in a buoyant state at the moment. Unemployment in Paris remains a steady 9.8% (7.7% in the Ile-de-France) and there are said to be nearly 50,000 homeless people on the streets and in the métro stations. The national unemployment rate is similar, standing at 9%.

The main business districts are located in the 8th around avenue des Champs-Elysées, 2nd, where the *Bourse* (Stock Exchange) is located near to rue de la Banque in a grand First Empire building and the smart 16th *arrondissement*. The futuristic business district of La Défense is home to the huge CNIT exhibition hall, as well as *Elf*, *Gan* and *Fiat*.

information and might offer reciprocal benefits to members of automobile clubs in other countries.

Emergency breakdown services: *SOS Dépannage* (tel: (01) 4707 9999); *Adan Dépann Auto* (tel: (01) 4266 6758).

Routes to the city: The Anglo-French *Eurotunnel* shuttle service allows drivers and passengers of cars and coaches to cross the Channel Tunnel (journey time – approximately 35 minutes) from Kent in Southern England to Nord-Pas-de-Calais in Northern France. The tunnel is linked to the UK and French motorway networks. Tickets are available for purchase at check-in on the day of travel or pre-booked with Eurotunnel (tel: (08705) 353 535; website: www.eurotunnel.com). Alternatively, there are numerous daily sea crossings to France (see *Getting There By Water*).

From Boulogne (near Calais), the A16 leads directly into Paris. The E19 motorway leads from Brussels into Paris (via the A2 and A1). Lille is linked directly to Paris via the A1. Paris is surrounded by the often congested *Périphérique* ring road, its intersections (*portes*) are used to access the nearest point of entry to

the desired destination. The N10 leads directly from Bordeaux to Paris, while from Marseille, drivers should take the A7 to Lyon, after which the A6 leads north to Paris.

Approximate driving times to Paris: From Lille – 2 hours 30 minutes; Brussels – 3 hours 30 minutes; London – 5 hours (excluding the Channel crossing); Bordeaux – 6 hours; Marseille – 7 hours 30 minutes.

Coach services: The majority of international coaches arrive and depart from the main coach station, *Gare Routière Internationale Paris-Gallieni*, at Bagnolet, 20th (tel: (08) 9289 9091). Reservations can be made (in English) with *Eurolines* (tel: (08) 9289 9091 or (01) 4972 5780; website: www.eurolines.fr), who offer links to Paris from Amsterdam, Berlin, Brussels, London, Rome and many other European destinations.

Getting Around

Public Transport

The *Régie Autonome des Transports Parisiens* or *RATP* (tel: (08) 9268 4114 (information in English) or 7714; website: www.ratp.fr) is an integrated, five-zone system of **bus**, **métro** and **trains**, which is both cheap and efficient (except during strikes, which are frequent).

The 14 **métro** lines extend into zones one and two in central Paris. Métros operate daily 0530–0115, lines are colour-coded and designated by numbers. They are also clearly signposted with the names of the terminus station. The newest addition – line 14 métro Météor – runs from Madeleine to Bibliothèque François Mitterrand. Free transport maps are available at métro stations, bus terminals and the tourist office.

The **RER** (*Réseau Express Régional*) suburban express **train** network has five lines (A, B, C, D and E) covering five zones and operating daily 0500–0110. The system is linked to the métro network and some SNCF trains.

The **bus** system is easy to use. Bus stops display the buses that stop there, while a map shows all the stops on the route and the bus times. Most buses run Monday to Saturday 0630–2100; some continue until 2430. Services are reduced by approximately half on Sundays and bank holidays. **Night buses** (*Noctambuses*) run on 13 routes, Monday to Saturday 0100–0530 hourly, with a reduced service on Sunday night. The night bus service cuts between place du Châtelet by the Hôtel de Ville and the suburbs.

The same tickets are valid on the bus, métro and RER (within zones one and two only) but not night buses (see below). One ticket is sufficient for a single bus ride, for an RER journey (within zones one and two only) or a métro journey (irrespective of zone). One ticket allows for changes (*correspondances*) of lines on the RER and the métro, however, separate tickets are required for changes between buses or between bus and métro/RER. Tickets should be validated on entry and kept until the end of the journey to avoid on-the-spot fines. One ticket costs €1.30; a carnet of ten tickets costs €9.60. Tickets, carnets and passes are all available for purchase from stations and *tabacs*; only single tickets (€1.30) may be purchased from the bus driver.

Night buses require separate tickets, which cost €2.40 each and allow one change. Weekly or monthly travel passes (see below) may also be used on night buses.

A *mobilis* day **pass** costs €5 for central Paris and €11.70 for five zones including the airports. *Paris Visites* offer one-, two-, three- and five-day visitor's passes at €8.35, €13.70, €18.25 and €26.65 respectively for Paris and its immediate suburbs, or

€16.75, €26.65, €37.35 and €45.70 to include transport to the airports, Versailles and Disneyland Paris. There are reduced prices for children. These are available for purchase at the airports, métro and RER stations and tourist offices.

For longer stays, the *Carte Orange*, with a weekly coupon (*coupon hebdomodaire*), for sale at all métro stations, provides good value. At €13.75, it allows a week's travel in zones one and two. There is also a monthly *Carte Orange* that costs €46.05 for zones one and two. The *Carte Orange* reusable ticket should be validated at the métro turnstile and displayed to the bus driver.

Taxis

Taxis can be hailed at airports, stations and at taxi ranks (*arrêts taxis*) but can be difficult to find, especially when most in demand – Friday and Saturday nights. A yellow light displayed on the roof shows that the taxi is available for hire; an orange light shows the taxi is in use.

A daytime journey in central Paris tends to cost between €6 and €10 (tariff A). Journeys after 1900, on Sundays, bank holidays and in the suburbs are more expensive (tariff B). The most expensive rate (tariff C) applies for the suburbs and airports at night and districts outside Paris during the day. There are additional charges for pick-up (approximately €2) and various other situations, including extra passengers, luggage and waiting. The minimum charge for a taxi ride is €5. Tipping is not compulsory but drivers expect around 10%.

Taxi numbers are displayed at the taxi ranks and listed in the yellow pages. These include *Taxis Bleus* (tel: (01) 4936 2424), *Alpha Taxis* (tel: (01) 4585 8585) and *Artaxi* (tel: (01) 4203 5050).

Limousines

Major providers are *Paris France Limousines*, 34 rue Picpus, 12th (tel: (01) 4344 1272; fax: (01) 7372 2432; website: www.pf-limousines.com), *ExecutiveCar*, 25 rue d'Astorg, 8th (tel: (01) 4265 5420; fax: (01) 4265 2593;

BUSINESS ETIQUETTE

A degree of Parisian aggression and plenty of persistence is necessary when attempting business in the capital. However, firmness, not rudeness, is in order. At the first meeting, non-French speakers should apologise for their lack of linguistic aptitude and respect the local formality, addressing colleagues with the appropriate *Madame*, *Monsieur*, *Professeur* or *Docteur* followed by the surname and a handshake. Business cards (preferably in French and English) should be presented. Small talk is an essential part of doing business, so it is wise to do a quick refresher on French politics and culture prior to the meeting and not to rush straight to talk of business. Smart, conservative, dress is recommended.

Standard business hours are Monday to Friday 0830/0900–1800/1900. Lunches may last for two hours or more – it is best to schedule meetings at 1100 or 1500, unless for lunch itself. Business lunches are popular, working dinners common and breakfast meetings an increasing trend. Whoever fixes the meeting is expected to settle the bill. Conducting business in August – during the Parisian exodus to the south – is to be avoided at all costs.

Arc de Triomphe

website: www.executive-car.com), and *Elite Limousines*, 47 rue de Chaillot, 16th (tel: (01) 4720 2323; fax: (01) 4720 7320; website: www.elitelimousines.com). Rates are approximately €60 per hour.

Driving in the City

Driving in central Paris is not advised. Most hotels do not have garages, parking is difficult (illegally parked cars are towed away) and traffic jams (*embouteillages*) are frequent. While the average speed in the métro is 27kph (17mph), the average road speed is 18kph (11mph) and even slower during the rush hours (Monday to Friday 0730–0900 and 1700–1900).

Parking prices vary throughout the city but are in the region of €1.50 per hour, for a maximum of two hours. Most legal street-side parking spaces are marked '*payant*'; coins of €0.20, €0.50 and €1 may be used for the pay-and-display parking machines (*horodateurs*). Paris also has numerous underground and covered car parks in the city centre, costing around €2.50 per hour or approximately €15 for periods of 12–24 hours. These include the *Arc de Triomphe*, *place de Concorde* and near *Forum des Halles*. Many municipal garages close at around 2300 and some are closed on Sunday. The only good news is that parking is usually free on weekends and on weekdays before 0900 and after 1900.

Car Hire

The minimum age for car hire varies from 21 to 25 years. Drivers must have held a national driving licence for at least one year. It is usually requested that the cost is paid for with the driver's credit card.

Major car hire companies include *Avis* (tel: (01) 5538 6720; website: www.avis.fr), *Budget* (tel: (01) 4884 6029; website: www.budget.com), *National Citer* (tel: (01) 4438 6045; website: www.citer.fr), *Europcar* (tel: (01) 3044 9384; website: www.europcar.fr), *Hertz* (tel: (01) 3938 3000; website: www.hertz.fr) and *Sixt* (tel: (01) 4438 5552; website: www.sixt.fr). In addition, local firms include *ADA*, with numerous branches, the main office being 97 boulevard Magenta (Gare du Nord), 10th (tel: (01) 4770 0606; website: www.ada.fr), *Locabest*, 3 rue Abel, 12th (tel: (01) 4346 0505; website: www.locabest.fr), and *Rent A Car*, 15 rue de Pyramides, 1st (tel: (01) 4296 9595; website: www.rentacar.fr).

Average car hire rates are approximately €40 per day or €90 per week.

Bicycle & Scooter Hire

The Mairie de Paris embarked on a scheme to introduce cycle lanes in 1996, which now total 100km (62 miles). Various maps and cycling guides can be found in bookstores and at some cycle shops. Bicycle hire companies include *Bike'N Roller*, 38 rue Fabert, 7th (tel: (01) 4550 3827), *Bicyclettes Locations-Services* or *BLS*, 23 rue Beaurepaire, 1st (tel: (06) 8066 9558), *Paris à Vélo c'est Sympa*, 37 boulevard Bourdon, 4th (tel: (01) 4887 6001; website: www.parisvelosympa.com), and *Paris Vélo*, 4 rue du Fer-à-Moulin, 5th (tel: (01) 4337 5922). Bicycle hire costs from around €12 per day.

Scooters and motorbikes are available for hire from *Atelier de la Compagnie*, 57 boulevard de Grenelle, 15th (tel: (01) 4579 7724; website: www.atelier-de-la-compagnie.com). Scooter hire costs from around €30 per day.

SIGHTSEEING

Sightseeing Overview

Sightseers can choose their own Paris. The nostalgic should wander around the mansions of the Marais district, past the *Musée Carnavalet*, 23 rue de Sévigné, 3rd; *Hôtel de Sully*, 62 rue St-Antoine, 4th, and *place des Vosges*, home to the *Maison de Victor Hugo*. Monet's *Water Lillies* can be glimpsed at the *Musée de l'Orangerie* when it re-opens in the summer of 2004 and changing exhibitions of modern art at the *Galerie National du Jeu de Paume*, both in the *Jardin des Tuileries*. Those interested in modern art and design should opt for the *Centre Georges Pompidou*, place Beaubourg, 4th; Jean Nouvel's *Institut du Monde Arabe*, 1 rue des Fossés-St-Bernard, 5th; or the *Grande Arche de la Défense* with its high-speed glass lift offering a spectacular view of Paris. The Grande Arche, which lies along the same geographical axis as Napoleon's *Arc de Triomphe* and the Champs-Elysées, was built a century and a half later. This incongruity – the modern city juxtaposed with the old – is all part of the charm of Paris. Serious sightseers might wish to plan their day, others might prefer simply to wander.

Paris is overrun with museums, ranging from the vast collections of the Louvre to the small and quirky – such as the *Musée des Arts Forains*, 53 avenue des-Terroires-de-France, 12th, a shrine to fairground art. Those who have not been to Paris for a few years will be surprised at the number of new additions. The *Musée d'Art et d'Histoire*

du Judaïsme (Museum of Jewish Art and History) is one example, situated in a lovely townhouse in the Marais: Hôtel de St-Aignan, 71 rue du Temple, 3rd. Also now well established are the *Musée de la Musique*, Cité de la Musique, 221 avenue Jean-Jaurès, 19th, and the *Musée de la Mode et du Textile* (Fashion and Textile Museum), Palais du Louvre, 107 rue de Rivoli, 1st. The *Musée de la Publicité* (Museum of Advertising) opened in 1999, also at the Palais du Louvre, 107 rue de Rivoli, 1st.

Key Attractions

Tour Eiffel (Eiffel Tower)

The *Eiffel Tower* literally towers over the Champ de Mars in the smart 7th *arrondissement*. The top (third) floor offers a sweeping panorama of Paris. From directly underneath there is a fascinating view of the delicate ironwork of Gustave Eiffel, who was commissioned to build the tower for the Exposition Universelle in 1889, the centenary of the French Revolution.

Champ de Mars, 7th
Tel: (01) 4411 2323 (recorded information). Fax: (01) 4411 2322.
Website: www.tour-eiffel.fr
Transport: Métro Bir-Hakeim; RER Champ de Mars-Tour Eiffel.
Opening hours: Daily 0930–2300 (Sep–mid-Jun); daily 0900–2400 (mid-Jun–Aug).
Admission: By lift: €3.70 (first floor), €7 (second floor), €10.20 (third floor); by stairs: €3.30 (first and second floors only); concessions available.

Cathédrale de Notre-Dame (Cathedral of Our Lady)

The stocky *Notre-Dame Cathedral*, situated on the Ile-de-la-Cité, could not be more different from the filigree Eiffel Tower. Bishop Maurice de Sully began construction on the cathedral in 1163, to outshine the

Photo: Corel

Notre-Dame Cathedral

new abbey at St-Denis; work was completed in 1345. The result is a Gothic masterpiece, with three stunning rose windows. Visitors should be prepared to climb the 387 spiral steps to the top of the 75m (246ft) north tower. The views over the River Seine and the city centre are well worth the effort. There is also a treasury with various liturgical objects on display.
6 place du Parvis-Notre-Dame, 4th
Tel: (01) 4234 5610 *or* 4432 1672 (information on tower). Fax: (01) 4051 7098.
E-mail: info@cathedraledeparis.com
Website: www.cathedraledeparis.com
Transport: Métro Cité; RER St-Michel-Notre-Dame.
Opening hours: Daily 0745–1845 (cathedral); daily 0930–1845 (towers); Mon–Sat 0930–1130 and 1300–1730 (treasury).
Admission: Free (cathedral); €5.50 (towers); €2.50 (treasury); concessions available.

La Basilique du Sacré-Coeur (The Sacred Heart Basilica)

A long, wide series of steps lead to the snowy-white-domed *Sacré-Coeur,* which dominates the arty district of Montmartre. A mishmash of styles, the Catholic church was built between 1870 and 1919, to fulfil a vow made during the Franco-Prussian war. The interior is splendid with neo-Byzantine mosaics and the domed tower offers a spectacular view over Paris. The crypt contains an interesting collection of religious relics and a slide show on the construction of the basilica.
Parvis du Sacré-Coeur, 18th
Tel: (01) 5341 8900. Fax: (01) 5341 8919.
Transport: Métro Abbesses or Anvers.
Opening hours: Daily 0600–2230 (basilica); daily 1000–1745 (crypt and dome).
Admission: Free (basilica); €5 (dome and crypt); concessions available.

Musée National du Louvre (Louvre National Museum)

The *Louvre* first opened to the public in 1793, following the Revolution, as a showcase for the art treasures of the kings of France. The museum is organised into three wings on four floors – Richelieu (along rue de Rivoli), Sully (around cour Carrée) and Denon (along the River Seine). The vast permanent collection includes Greek, Etruscan, Roman, Egyptian and East Asian antiquities, French, Spanish, Italian and northern European sculpture and 19th-century objets d'art. The painting collection is the strongest, with French, Italian, Dutch, German, Flemish and Spanish

masterpieces from the mid-13th to the mid-19th centuries. The most famed French works include David's *Coronation of Napoléon,* Ingres' *The Turkish Bath,* Géricault's depiction of disaster *The Raft of the Medusa* and Delacroix's ode to revolution *Liberty Leading the People.* The museum's greatest treasure, Leonardo da Vinci's *Mona Lisa,* is in a bulletproof case and will be given its own room by 2004. Until then, it is on display in room 13, on the first floor of the Denon wing.
Excavations have exposed traces of the medieval Louvre, which are on display together with the history of the Louvre under the cour Carrée, in the *entresol* level in the Sully wing.
Cour Napoléon, 1st
Tel: (01) 4020 5050 *or* 5151 (recorded information). Fax: (01) 4020 5442.
E-mail: info@louvre.fr
Website: www.louvre.fr
Transport: Métro Palais Royal-Musée du Louvre.
Opening hours: Thurs–Sun 0900–1800, Mon and Wed 0900–2145 (parts of the museum only); opening hours for temporary exhibitions vary.
Admission: Permanent and temporary exhibitions: €7.50 (until 1500); €5 (after 1500 and Sun). Temporary exhibitions in Napoleon Hall: €7. Temporary exhibitions in Napoleon Hall and permanent exhibitions combined: €11.50 (until 1500), €9.50 (after 1500 and Sun). Free (first Sun of month and 14 July). Concessions available. Advance tickets can be purchased by telephone (tel: (01) 4691 5757), from branches of *FNAC* and on the Internet. All tickets allow same-day re-admission.

Musée Rodin (Rodin Museum)

Auguste Rodin (1840–1917) lived and worked in this 18th-century *hôtel particulier.* Now the *Rodin Museum,* his sculptures populate the interior and gardens. Indoors, *The Kiss* portrays eternal passion frozen in white marble, while *The Hand of God* gives life to creamy white, half-formed figures. Works of Rodin's mistress and pupil, Camille Claudel, and paintings by Van Gogh, Monet, Renoir and Rodin himself are also on display. The gardens are graced by the monumental bronze *The Thinker,* whose godly physique contrasts sharply with the decrepitude of the writhing figures of *The Gates of Hell* and the controversial final portrait of Balzac, once described as 'a block that disgraces its author and French Art'.
77 rue de Varenne, 7th
Tel: (01) 4418 6110. Fax: (01) 4418 6130.
Website: www.musee-rodin.fr

Transport: Métro Varenne.
Opening hours: Tues–Sun 0930–1745, garden until 1845 (Apr–Sep); Tues–Sun 0930–1645, garden until 1700 (Oct–Mar).
Admission: €5; concessions available; free first Sun of month; €1 (garden only).

Musée d'Orsay (Orsay Museum)

The strength of this large museum – housed in a former train station next to the River Seine – lies in its collection of Impressionist and Post-Impressionist art. The collection, covering the decisive 1848–1914 period, is arranged chronologically, beginning on the ground floor, jumping to the third, then descending to the middle level. Among the most famous works are Manet's *Déjeuner sur l'Herbe* (Luncheon on the Grass), rejected from the Salon of 1863, five of Monet's paintings of Rouen Cathedral and the recently acquired realist work, *L'Origine du Monde* (The Origin of the World), by Gustave Courbet, whose graphic depiction of the female sex continues to shock.
Entrances at 1 rue de la Légion d'Honneur and 1 rue de Bellechasse, 7th
Tel: (01) 4049 4814 *or* 4549 1111 (recorded information).
Transport: Métro Solférino; RER Musée d'Orsay.
Opening hours: Tues, Wed, Fri and Sat 1000–1800, Thurs 1000–2115, Sun 0900–1800 (Oct–May); Tues, Wed, Fri–Sun 0900–1800, Thurs 0900–2115 (Jun–Sep).
Admission: €7; concessions available; free first Sun of month.

Musée National Picasso (National Picasso Museum)

Paris-based Pablo Picasso (1881–1973) owned most of this collection, the largest worldwide, housed in a 17th-century mansion in the Marais. All phases of his art are represented, with preparatory sketches and paintings covering the Blue Period, Rose Period, Cubism, Classicism, Surrealism and sculptures ranging from a huge plaster head to a small cat. Memorable works include the Blue Period self-portrait *Paolo as Harlequin,* the surreal *Nude in an Armchair* and poignant paintings of Marie-Thérèse. Photographs are displayed alongside the works they inspired and African masks with Picasso's 'primitive' wood carvings. There is also a glimpse of the artist's personal taste in paintings, with his Matisse and Cézanne paintings displayed alongside his own.
Hôtel Salé, 5 rue de Thorigny, 3rd
Tel: (01) 4271 2521. Fax: (01) 4271 1299.
Transport: Métro Chemin Vert or St-Paul.
Opening hours: Wed, Fri–Mon 0930–1800, Thurs 0930–2000 (summer); Wed, Fri–Mon 0930–1730, Thurs 0930–2000 (winter).
Admission: €5.50; concessions available; free first Sun of month; extra charges for temporary exhibitions.

Centre Georges Pompidou (Georges Pompidou Centre)

Considered outrageous in 1977, the *Pompidou Centre,* designed by Piano and Rogers, has become part of the Parisian landscape, primary coloured tubes and all. Although not yet 25 years old, the building has already been revamped and extended, to cope with the huge numbers of people visiting its expanding collection of contemporary art and multimedia library. The centre reopened on the first day of the new millennium, with the main focus being the 20th-century collection of the *Musée National d'Art Moderne* (*MNAM*).
Place Georges Pompidou, 4th
Tel: (01) 4478 1233.

E-mail: info@cnac-gp.fr
Website: www.centrepompidou.fr
Transport: Métro Hôtel de Ville or Rambuteau; RER Châtelet-Les Halles.
Opening hours: Wed–Mon 1100–2100; late-night openings until 2300 for some exhibitions.
Admission: €10 (museum and all exhibitions); €8.50 (exhibitions); €5.50 (museum); concessions available; free first Sun of month.

Further Distractions

Jardin du Luxembourg (Luxembourg Gardens)

This garden, part formal, part *jardin à l'anglaise*, was created for Marie de Médicis (Henri IV's widow), along with the Palais de Luxembourg, which now houses the French Senate. It is a favoured spot for a Sunday stroll, game of tennis, chess or *boules*, pony ride or yacht trip on the lake.
Boulevard St-Michel, rue de Médicis, rue Guynemer, rue d'Assas, rue Auguste-Comte or rue de Vaugirard, 6th
Tel: (01) 4234 2362.
Transport: Métro Odéon; RER Luxembourg.
Opening hours: Daily 0715–2130 (Apr–Sep); daily 0800–dusk (Oct–Mar).
Admission: Free.

Bois de Vincennes (Vincennes Forest)

Napoléon III transformed the royal forest of Valois into a park complete with lake and cascades in 1860, with the help of Haussmann's landscape artist Alphand. The *Bois de Vincennes* is now Paris' largest park, ideal for cycling and boating; it is also the home of the city's main zoo. The park is situated next to the impressive *Château de Vincennes*, where Henri V died in 1422.
Porte de Vincennes or Porte Dorée, 12th
Transport: Métro Porte Dorée or Château de Vincennes.
Opening hours: Daily dawn–dusk.
Admission: Free.

La Grande Mosquée de Paris (Paris Grand Mosque)

Built between 1922 and 1926, close to the Jardin des Plantes, this Hispano-Moorish mosque oversees

Eiffel Tower

France's Muslim community. There is free access and guided tours to the sunken garden and patios. The prayer room, however, remains closed to the non-Muslim public. There is also an authentic *hammam* (Turkish bath) with masseurs at hand, as well as a wonderful mosaic courtyard complete with fig trees and a fountain – the perfect setting for enjoying a sweet mint tea served in tiny gilded glasses with some honeyed *baklava*. In the adjoining restaurant, couscous and other Arabic dishes are served (see *Restaurants*).
1 place du Puits-de-l'Ermite (access via 39 rue Géoffroy-St-Hillaire), 5th
Tel: (01) 4535 9733. Fax: (01) 4535 1623.
Website: www.mosquee-de-paris.com
Transport: Métro Place Monge or Censier Daubenton.
Opening hours: Mon, Wed, Thurs and Sat 1000–2100, Fri 1400–2100 (women); Tues 1400–2100, Sun 1000–2100 (men). Tours Sat–Thurs 0900–1200 and 1400–1800 (winter); Sat–Thurs 0900–1200 and 1400–2200 (summer). Closed Muslim holidays.
Admission: €3 (guided visit); concessions available. Free (tearoom); €15 (Turkish baths – massages extra).

Tours of the City

Walking Tours

Walks on a variety of themes are offered by *Paris Walks* (tel: (01) 4809 2140; fax: (01) 4243 7551; website: www.paris-walks.com), including 'Hemingway's Paris', 'The Village of Montmartre', 'The Marais Circuit' and many more. 'The Marais Circuit' departs every Tuesday, Thursday, Saturday and Sunday; 'Hemingway's Paris' every Friday and the 'Village of Montmartre' every Wednesday and Sunday. Tours depart from various métro stations (listed on the website), last two hours and cost €10 (concessions available).
Details of most tours are in the weekly *Pariscope* magazine (website: www.pariscope.fr).

Bus Tours

The *Balabus* is an ordinary city bus that is marked Bb on the front. It operates from stops marked 'Balabus' from mid-April to the end of September, passing key sights between the Grand Arche de la Défense and the Gare de Lyon. Details can be obtained from any métro station.
Several companies offer coach tours of Paris, with *Les Cars Rouges* (tel: (01) 5395 3953; website: www.lescarsrouges.com), using distinctive red London double-decker buses. Tickets cost €21, purchased on the bus or at tourist offices (concessions available). There are nine stops at main tourist attractions and a recorded commentary in English. Passengers can get on and off at will, with tickets valid for two days.
L'Open Tour hop-on hop-off buses (tel: (01) 4266 5656; website: www.paris-opentour.com) operate daily throughout the year, offering three different routes with running commentaries in French and English, passing all the major tourist sights in the city. One- and two-day passes cost €24 and €26 respectively and are available from tourist offices, *RATP* offices and also from some hotels and travel agencies. Buses run every ten to 15 minutes 1000–1800 April–October and every 25–30 minutes 0930–1600 November–March. The departure point is 13 rue Auber, although there are stops at various sights along the routes.

Boat Tours

The city's *bâteaux-mouches* and *vedettes* are a popular and instantly recognisable feature of the River Seine. Many companies offer cruises – some with lunch or dinner – including *Vedettes de Paris* (tel: (01) 4418

1950; fax: (01) 4705 7453; website: www.vedettesdeparis.com), *Les Vedettes du Pont-Neuf* (tel: (01) 4633 9838; fax: (01) 4329 8619; website: www.pontneuf.net) and *Bâteaux Parisiens* (tel: (01) 4411 3344; fax: (01) 4556 0788; website: www.bateauxparisiens.com). A basic sightseeing tour costs €8–9 and lasts one hour. Departure points are at various stops along the banks of the River Seine.

Bicycle Tours

Various maps and cycle guides – available at tourist offices, bookshops or bike-hire outlets – detail cycle routes in the city. In addition, there are also routes in the Bois de Boulogne, the Bois de Vincennes and a popular Sunday trip along the River Seine, which is closed to cars 1000–1600.
Paris à Vélo, C'est Sympa!, 37 boulevard Bourdon (tel: (01) 4887 6001; fax: (01) 4887 6101; website: www.parisvelosympa.com), offers a variety of three-hour bicycle tours for €30 (concessions available), including 'Heart of Paris', 'Paris Contrasts', 'Paris at Dawn' and 'Unusual Paris', as well as 'Paris by Night' tours during the summer months. Tours depart from the shop and the price includes bicycle hire and insurance.

Excursions

For a Half Day

Château de Versailles: No sooner had Louis XIV set eyes on his finance minister's château at Vaux-le-Victomte, than he decided to build a bigger and better one. The result is one of the three most visited monuments in France. Construction began in 1664, continuing until Louis XIV's death in 1715. Much of the palace can only be visited with a guide, with the notable exception of the 73m (240ft) *Galerie des Glaces* (Hall of Mirrors), where the Treaty of Versailles was signed, effectively bringing World War I to an end. It is worth queuing for a guided tour, if only to recapture the ritualistic atmosphere of the reign of the Sun King, whose actions were considered as miraculous as the movements of the sun itself. The honoured elite among the 20,000 courtiers and royal ministers were obliged to relocate to the palace and observed these banal rituals with awe.
Entry to the château state apartments (tel: (01) 3083 7800; website: www.chateauversailles.fr) costs €7.50 (concessions available). There is the option of a one-hour guided visit of the King's Chamber (audiotour), which costs €4. The château and gardens are set in a landscaped park, designed by Le Nôtre, which is open daily, except during bad weather, from 0700 in summer and 0800 in winter until sunset. Admission to the park is free, although entry to the formal gardens costs €3 (free in winter months). There are also guided tours of the garden for an extra €5. The château itself is open Tuesday to Sunday 0900–1730 (until 1830 from April to October). The grounds are so large that a little train chugs from the palace to the former royal love nests – the *Grand* and *Petit Trianons* (open daily 1200–1730 – until 1830 from April to October). The Italianate Grand Trianon was built in 1687, for Louis XIV to enjoy the company of Madame de Maintenon. Napoléon also had a penchant for this building, which is on a somewhat more human scale than the château, and stayed there with Marie-Louise. Louis XV had Gabriel build the Petit Trianon in the 1760s, for his mistress, Madame de Pompadour. Admission costs €5 to the Grand Trianon and Petit Trianon combined. The château – and everything on site – is free to everyone on the first Sunday of the month from November to March.

Palais de Luxembourg

Versailles is located 23km (14 miles) west of the city and is easily accessible from central Paris on the RER line C5 to Versailles-Rive Gauche.

For a Whole Day

Giverny: Monet lived in countrified *Giverny* – located 80km (50 miles) northwest of Paris – from 1883 until his death in 1926. The house, in which he painted his last, vast water lily canvas, is open to the public as *Musée Claude Monet*. Although the house retains much of its charm, the artist's studio is now a large and over-commercialised gift shop – Monet is, after all, big business. Although many of the original paintings are now at the *Musée d'Orsay*, the inspiration behind them remains here – the famed water lily pond and Japanese footbridges. The museum, 84 rue Claude Monet (tel: (02) 3251 2821; fax: (02) 3251 5418; website: www.fondation-monet.com), is open from Tuesday to Sunday 1000–1800 (April to October). Admission prices are €5.50 for the house and garden or €4 for the gardens only.

A few minutes away, in 99 rue Claude Monet, the *Musée d'Art Américain* (tel: (02) 3251 9465; fax: (02) 3251 9467; website: www.maag.org), is a shrine to Monet-influenced American artists, such as Winslow Homer and Mary Cassatt. Opening hours are Tuesday to Sunday 1000–1800 (April to October) and admission costs €5.

By car, visitors should take the A13 from Paris to Bonnières, then the D201 to Giverny. Alternatively, the train from Gare St-Lazare station goes to Vernon, from where visitors should take a taxi or bus to Giverny.

ACCOMMODATION

Hotel prices generally include VAT and a room tax (*taxe de séjour*) of between €0.20 and €1 per person per night. This tax is sometimes added to the bill at the end of a visit and guests are advised to check whether it is included when making a reservation. Guests are also advised to tip porters €2 for each bag and chambermaids €2 per day.

The prices quoted below are the lowest standard rates for a double room, including VAT and room tax but excluding breakfast, unless otherwise specified.

Business

Hotel Concorde La Fayette

The towering 1000-room *Hotel Concorde La Fayette* is located close to the Champs-Elysées and La Défense Porte Maillot. All guest rooms are air conditioned and decorated in a modern style, with gentle colours. Conference facilities include 2200 sq metres (25,000 sq ft) of space, shared with the recently revamped Palais des Congrès and its own fully serviced business centre. Secretarial and translation services are available. There are also executive floors with modem points in all rooms, a Vitatop fitness club, two bars – one on the 33rd floor offering a panoramic view – and two restaurants.
3 place du Général Koenig, 17th
Tel: (01) 4068 5068. Fax: (01) 4068 5043.
E-mail: info@concorde-lafayette.com
Website: www.concorde-lafayette.com
Price: From €285.

Le Bristol

A plush business clientele frequent *Le Bristol*. Here, 180 elegant rooms and 41 suites, decorated with original prints and paintings, are complemented by top-notch business facilities, including a business centre, meeting rooms and secretarial and translation services. For relaxation, there is a rooftop indoor swimming pool, a fitness room and an excellent restaurant run by top chef Eric Frechon, as well as fabulous shopping nearby in this smart *arrondissement*.
112 rue du Faubourg-St-Honoré, 8th
Tel: (01) 5343 4300 *or* 4325 (reservations). Fax: (01) 5343 4326.
E-mail: resa@hotel-bristol.com
Website: www.lebristolparis.com
Price: From €630.

Le Meridien Montparnasse

Even those with a poor sense of direction will have no problem finding this impressive skyscraper of a hotel, only a tad shorter than the Montparnasse tower. The TGV glides to within a stone's throw of this 1970s business hotel, equipped with in-room voice-mail, meeting rooms for up to 2000 delegates and secretarial services. Dining options include *Montparnasse 25* restaurant and *Le Justine* buffet.

19 rue du Commandant-Mouchotte, 14th
Tel: (01) 4436 4436. Fax: (01) 4055 6788.
E-mail: resindiv.paris@lemeridien.com
Website: www.lemeridien-paris.com
Price: From €350.

Sofitel Forum Rive Gauche

This top business hotel, which boasts conference space for 2000 delegates, as well as a fully equipped business centre with cyber lounge, simultaneous translation and catering services, is the largest four-star convention hotel in Paris. Located on the left bank of the River Seine, the 18-floor hotel, which was built in the 1970s, is just a few minutes from Gare Montparnasse and the Latin Quarter. Each room is decorated in a contemporary style and equipped with a modem point. The hotel boasts a fitness centre on the 18th floor, which offers panoramic views over Paris. There are three restaurants – calorie-controlled *La Table et La Forme* (where no menu exceeds 1000 calories), *Le Café Français* (an ideal setting for business lunches) and *Le Patio* buffet bar. The jazzy *Nelli's Bar* serves good cocktails.
17 boulevard Saint-Jacques, 14th
Tel: (01) 4078 7980 *or* 7840 (reservations). Fax: (01) 4588 4393.
Website: www.sofitel.com
Price: From €250.

Luxury

Hôtel de Crillon

The hotel of choice for supermodels, movie stars and royalty, this marble palace was built for Louis XV in 1758. As sumptuous as the *Ritz*, the *Crillon* sparkles with chandeliers, gleaming marble, sculptures and gilt. Beautiful people dine in the gastronomic, Michelin-starred *Les Ambassadeurs* restaurant or the lower key *L'Obélisque* brasserie. There is also the *Jardins d' Hiver* tea room and hip *Piano Bar*, designed by Sonia Rykiel. Business guests are catered for with conference rooms, a 24-hour business centre and, a rare asset in centrally located Parisian hotels, a fitness centre. Some of the 95 rooms have recently been refurbished. For those really wishing to splash out, there is a choice of 52 suites.
10 place de la Concorde, 8th
Tel: (01) 4471 1500. Fax: (01) 4471 1502.
E-mail: crillon@crillon.com
Website: www.crillon.com
Price: From €575.

Ritz Paris

Situated on one of the smartest yet most intimate squares in Paris, close to the Louvre, the *Ritz* is the essence of luxury and discretion. The lobby gleams with marble and chandeliers, while the Oriental carpets, soft to the touch, soak up the sound. Pop stars, presidents and people with money to burn have a choice of 135 rooms and 40 suites – all fitted with Internet connection. There is a magnificent swimming pool, fitness room and squash court for guest use. In the labyrinthine underbelly of the hotel, lies the celebrated Ritz-Escoffier cookery school, where master chefs teach their tricks to international acolytes.
15 place Vendôme, 1st
Tel: (01) 4316 3070. Fax: (01) 4316 3668.
E-mail: resa@ritzparis.com
Website: www.ritzparis.com
Price: From €590.

Moderate

Hôtel de Nevers

Just around the corner from the charming Marais district and trendy Oberkampf neighbourhood, the *Hôtel de Nevers* is a friendly, 36-room hotel, with a newly renovated reception. A good location and wise budget option – guests can choose from a range of rooms, the more expensive of which have en-suite bathrooms.
53 rue de Malte, 11th
Tel: (01) 4700 5618. Fax: (01) 4357 7739.
E-mail: reservation@hoteldenevers.com
Website: www.hoteldenevers.com
Price: From €32 (excluding city tax of €0.42 per day).

Hotel du Septième Art

A Hollywood theme runs through this fun and funky 22-room hotel designed with the film buff in mind and adorned with 1950s posters. The hotel is a popular media haunt in the Marais district, set in a 16th-century building. There are no mod cons, such as lifts or air-conditioning, although there are original wooden beams throughout and all rooms have en-suite bathrooms.
20 rue Saint-Paul, 4th
Tel: (01) 4454 8500. Fax: (01) 4277 6910.
E-mail: hotel7art@wanadoo.fr
Price: From €75.

Other Recommendations

Hôtel Costes

Ever since it opened in 1995, the intimate *Hôtel Costes* has been the place to see and be seen – the Parisian hangout of pop stars, media types and fashionistas. Decor is decadent Napoleon III style and many of the 82 rooms and three ultra-luxurious suites overlook an Italianate interior courtyard. A trendy restaurant follows the fad for Asian-inspired food and there is also a health club, swimming pool and hip bar. Meeting rooms are available for guests and each room is equipped with a fax connection.
239 rue Saint-Honore, 1st
Tel: (01) 4244 5000. Fax: (01) 4244 5001.
Price: From €500.

L'Hôtel

Fashionistas, film stars and those hopelessly devoted to kitsch hang out at *L'Hôtel* – located on a quiet street in chic St-Germain. After a year's refurbishment, L'Hôtel has re-opened to showcase the stylish decor of Jacques Garcia, who also decorated the *Hôtel Costes* (see above). There are 20 rooms and four suites to choose from, such as the *Chambre Oscar Wilde* (an ode to decadence) or the mirrored fantasy of the *Chambre Mistinguett* (dedicated to the darling of Parisian music halls). Post-refurbishment, the rooms are larger and the hotel also boasts a steam room, swimming pool and *Le Belier* gourmet restaurant.
13 rue des Beaux-Arts, 6th
Tel: (01) 4441 9900. Fax: (01) 4325 6481.
E-mail: reservation@l-hotel.com
Website: www.l-hotel.com
Price: From €248.

RESTAURANTS

The selected restaurants have been divided into five categories: Gastronomic, Business, Trendy, Budget and Personal Recommendations. The restaurants are listed alphabetically within these different categories, which serve as guidelines rather than absolute definitions of the establishments.

Most restaurants include tax and a 15% service charge in their prices. If service is good, guests will often leave an extra €2 tip or the small change from their bill if they pay in cash. If service is not included, it is customary to leave a 15% tip.

The prices quoted below are for an average three-course meal for one person and for a bottle of house wine or cheapest equivalent; they include tax and service charge.

Gastronomic

L'Ambroisie

The atmosphere in place des Vosges – one of the most beautiful and intimate squares in Paris – exudes into the ultra-chic *L'Ambroisie*, which is situated in a genuine *hôtel particulier*. Classic French cuisine is served to pure perfection in these refined interiors decorated with rich tapestries. The menu changes according to the best fresh produce available and prices are steep. Diners can expect such delights as sea bass with olive oil emulsion, chanterelle and boletus mushrooms, and millefeuille with crystallised rhubarb. Wines are likewise expensive but the range is exceptional. Closed Sunday and Monday.
9 place des Vosges, 4th
Tel: (01) 4278 5145.
Price: €200. Wine: €100.

L'Arpège

Alain Passard has drawn on his family history to produce a restaurant renowned for superb, seasonal cuisine. His grandmother's portrait hangs on the otherwise minimalist walls and it is her cooking and joie de vivre that is the source of Alain Passard's inspiration. The restaurant is named in honour of his musical parents and to set the tone for the harmony of flavours. Passard's menu places emphasis on fresh vegetables, fish and white meat. Dishes include lobster carpaccio with olive oil and caviar, fragrant stuffed tomatoes or strawberries scented with hibiscus petals. Closed Saturday and Sunday.
84 rue de Varenne, 7th
Tel: (01) 4705 0906. Fax: (01) 4418 9839.
E-mail: arpege@alain-passard.com
Website: www.alain-passard.com
Price: €300. Wine: €75.

Lucas Carton

Alain Senderens' three-Michelin-starred restaurant is at the pinnacle of Parisian gastronomy, situated in a grand fin-de-siècle setting in chic place de la Madeleine, amid a wealth of posh shops. The first of the Michelin-starred restaurants to serve wine by the glass, Senderen believes that each dish deserves a wine of its own to perfect the flavours. The wine list is outstanding, with vintage Bordeaux from the 1940s. A wide variety of cigars are also on offer – another way of prolonging the pleasure of the meal. Dishes include pan-fried chicken with cep risotto, roast duck with honey and spices, roast lamb with aubergines, and pan-fried lobster served with polenta. No lunch Saturday and Monday. Closed Sunday.
9 place de la Madeleine, 8th
Tel: (01) 4265 2290. Fax: (01) 4265 0623.
E-mail: lucas.carton@lucascarton.com
Website: www.lucascarton.com
Price: €250. Wine: €200.

Pierre Gagnaire

This sumptuous restaurant has a reputation for being among the most exciting gastronomic addresses in Paris and it is certainly one of the most fashionable. Formerly based in St-Etienne, near the gastronomic capital Lyon, Gagnaire brought flavours of that region to Paris in his imaginative menus, which hold dear both tradition and innovation. A simple but refined decor, with spotless white tablecloths, makes the perfect setting for his challenging but impeccable cuisine. Specialities include *supreme de poularde macérée au lait d'amende* (chicken supreme cooked in almond milk) and *pesto de roquette sauvage* (wild rocket pesto). The five-course *Grand Dessert* is worth getting fat for. Closed Saturday.
Hotel Balzac, 6 rue Balzac, 8th
Tel: (01) 5836 1250. Fax: (01) 5836 1251.
E-mail: info@pierre-gagnaire.com
Website: www.pierregagnaire.com
Price: €150. Wine: €60.

Market shopping

Restaurant Plaza Athénée

Alain Ducasse was awarded three Michelin stars within eight months of first opening his Paris restaurant in 1996, at 59 avenue Raymond Poincare, 16th, where he took over from star chef, Joel Robuchon, after moving to the capital from Monte Carlo. In September 2000, Ducasse moved the restaurant to a chic new venue in the 8th, opening the *Restaurant Plaza Athénée*, a sumptuously stylish venue with soaring ceilings, warm tones and splendid chandeliers. Dishes include creations such as *langoustine avec une crème citronnée* (langoustine in a lemon cream sauce). Advance booking highly recommended. Closed Saturday and Sunday.
Hotel Plaza Athénée, 25 avenue Montaigne, 8th
Tel: (01) 5367 6500. Fax: (01) 5367 6512.
E-mail: adpa@alain-ducasse.com
Website: www.alain-ducasse.com
Price: €250. Wine: €60.

Business

Bistrot de l'Etoile

Parisian brasseries have become a little old fashioned and bistros are now all the rage for filling up late at night. Meals, such as duck foie gras with rocket salad, are served until 2330/2400, well after traditional restaurants have closed. The atmosphere here is best described as *chic decontracté* – smart but relaxed.
19 rue Lauriston, 16th *or* 75 avenue Niel, 17th
Tel: (01) 4067 1116 *or* 4227 8844.
Price: €60. Wine: €20.

Bofinger

This convivial Art Nouveau brasserie exudes the unique atmosphere of Paris, as the business community forgets about the office for an hour or two, while tucking into classics such as *steak tartare, salade mixte* or shellfish.
5–7 rue de la Bastille, 4th
Tel: (01) 4272 8782. Fax: (01) 4272 9768.
Price: €20. Wine: €12.

La Tour d'Argent

This temple of fine food has superb service, expensive but delectable dishes and, best of all, superb views of Notre-Dame and the River Seine. The restaurant has a classic French interior and serves duck specialities, such as *canard au sang* (duck in blood). The midday menu is especially good value for €65 and is always popular for business lunches. Advanced booking and insisting on a table with a view is highly recommended. Closed Monday. No lunch Tuesday.
15 quai de la Tournelle, 5th
Tel: (01) 4354 2331. Fax: (01) 4407 1204.
Website: www.tourdargent.com
Price: €200. Wine: €50.

Le Carré des Feuillants

One of the least understood chefs in Paris – perhaps because he avoids snobbery at any cost – Alain Dutournier brought his love of meat and fine fresh ingredients from the Basque country. The wooden interior of *Le Carré des Feuillants* is cosy but stylish with Murano chandeliers and contemporary artwork. Specialities include roast guinea fowl in a wild mushroom sauce or roast lobster with garlic and pepper nougatine but this is really the place to enjoy a steak to remember.
14 rue de Castiglionne, 1st
Tel: (01) 4286 8282. Fax: (01) 4286 0771.
Price: €125. Wine: €60.

A café-bar

Les Bouchons de François Clerc

François Clerc's *bouchons* (the name of a traditional Lyonnais restaurant-bar) have captivated the French capital. Some have beautiful *terrasses* for dining alfresco. The rue de l'Hotel branch has no terrace but it does have a wooden beamed interior, typical of traditional Lyonnais restaurants. On the menu are specialities from Lyon, such as *cannelles* (a kind of egg pastry that soaks up the flavour of fish or pork sauces), as well as standard bistro fare. An added boost is the wine – sold at cost price. No lunch Saturday. Closed Sunday.
22 rue de la Terrasse, 17th
Tel: (01) 4227 3151. Fax: (01) 4227 4576.
Website: www.lesbouchonsdefrancoisclerc.com
Price: €40. Wine: €20.
Branches:
12 rue de l'Hotel Colbert, 5th
Tel: (01) 4354 1534. Fax: (01) 4634 6807.
7 rue Boccador, 8th
Tel: (01) 4723 5780. Fax: (01) 4723 7454.
32 boulevard Montparnasse, 15th
Tel: (01) 4548 5203. Fax: (01) 4548 5217.

Trendy

La Gare

This light and airy brasserie, located in a former railway station, cooks poultry to perfection. It serves a varied menu of traditional French cuisine, including chicken, lamb, duck and fish dishes, as well as large mixed salads. A fashionable hangout, it is well worth booking in advance, particularly if dining at the weekend.
19 chaussée de la Muette, 16th
Tel: (01) 4215 1531. Fax: (01) 4215 1523.
Price: €30. Wine: €10.

Le Buddha Bar

A giant Buddha, beautiful people and international cuisine are on the menu at the perennially popular *Buddha Bar*, the trendy interior of which was designed by Miguel Cancio (who also took on the task of designing the trendy Man Ray). Located close to place de la Concorde, dishes include spiced chicken, seared tuna and tempura platters.
8 rue Boissy d'Anglas, 8th
Tel: (01) 5305 9000. Fax: (01) 5305 9090.
E-mail: buddha.bar@buddha-bar
Website: www.buddha-bar.com
Price: €100. Wine: €25.

Le Georges

Le Georges, decorated in a style that matches the modern Centre Georges Pompidou, is the latest creation from the trend-setting Costes brothers. The restaurant's location on the sixth floor of the Pompidou Centre draws huge crowds, who come to see the superb views across the city. A chic but trendy clientele dine here, while students often come to take a coffee break before diving back into their studies at the Pompidou library. The menu, which includes both French and international cuisine, changes frequently, although the duck, the lobster risotto and the chocolate tart are firm house favourites. Closed Tuesday.
Centre Georges Pompidou, 19 rue Beaubourg, 4th
Tel: (01) 4478 4799. Fax: (01) 4478 4893.
Price: €50. Wine: €20.

Man Ray

Johnny Depp, Sean Penn, John Malkovich and Mick Hucknall back this East Asian-inspired bar-restaurant, where a chic, sexy clientele are served everything from sushi to Chinese stir-fry and classic European cuisine. Inside the restaurant, which was designed by Miguel Cancio (who also designed the Buddha Bar), Man Ray photographs hang on the deep, copper walls. *Man Ray* also boasts a sunken hall and wooden mezzanine. It is definitely a place to see and be seen.
34 rue Marbeuf, 8th
Tel: (01) 5836 4022. Fax: (01) 4225 3636.
Website: www.manray.fr
Price: €50. Wine: €30.

Spoon Food & Wine

Star chef Alain Ducasse forsakes classic French food for an Asian-inspired international cuisine where

Photo: Corel

Grand Arche de la Défense

anything goes but it is all beautifully blended together. Diners can expect copious portions and a trendy crowd having a quick bite to eat from Japanese-style bento boxes at the bar or indulging in a leisurely meal in the main area. Dishes in this minimalist-style restaurant include tofu and noodles or spiced chicken in coconut milk. The wine list is extensive, with a particularly wide choice of Californian wines. Prior booking is vital. Closed weekends.
14 rue de Marignan, 8th
Tel: (01) 4076 3444. Fax: (01) 4076 3437.
E-mail: info@spoon.tm.fr
Website: www.spoon.tm.fr
Price: €25 (bar); €50 (restaurant). Wine: €30.

Budget

Androuët

Although the *Androuët* restaurant, which was formerly on rue Arsene Houssaye, has closed, there are still two Androuët bars in Paris. Both serve a wide choice of cheeses – approximately 20 varieties – on toasted brown bread, accompanied by salad, to enjoy in a modern decor and convivial atmosphere. The Androuët at rue Saint-Roch is close to the Opéra, while the other venue, at rue des Accacia, is near the Champs-Elysées. Both are closed Sunday.
49 rue Saint-Roch, 1st *or* 23 rue des Accacia, 17th
Tel: (01) 4297 5739 *or* 4068 0012.
Price: €20. Wine: €20.

Crêperie de Josselin

This Breton crêperie serves delicious savoury and sweet pancakes, including ham and cream, spinach and egg with black pepper or banana and chocolate. Always packed and full of atmosphere, the restaurant, decorated in a traditional Breton style, is a good budget option.

67 rue Montparnasse, 14th
Tel: (01) 4320 9350.
Price: €12 (savoury crêpe, sweet crêpe and cider).

La Galerie 88

This smoky little Moroccan restaurant, frequented by an arty young crowd, is just a step away from Notre-Dame, overlooking the quayside. The thick, split-pea soup is delicious – equally good is bread with cumin and the wide range of wholesome salads. Meals are served until 2400 daily.
88 quai de L'Hotel de Ville, 4th
Tel: (01) 4272 1758.
Price: €20. Wine: €12.

La Grande Mosquée de Paris

This beautiful mosque, close to the Jardin des Plantes and Natural History Museum, is an exotic setting for a spicy North African couscous or grillades (spicy meat stew) with *frites* (chips), followed by a tiny glass cup of refreshing mint tea, accompanied by sweet pastries, packed full with honey and pistachios.
39 rue Geoffroy St-Hilaire, 5th
Tel: (01) 4535 9733. Fax: (01) 4535 1623.
Website: www.mosquee-de-paris.com
Price: €20. Wine: No alcohol served.

Web Bar

Tucked away in the Marais, the *Web Bar* is connected to a trendy but casual clientele, keen for a bite to eat – the salads are extremely good – or to see an exhibition, experimental performance or poetry reading. The food is light, including a cheese platter (with St Maure, Brie de Meaux and Roquefort) or cold-meat platter, served with raspberry and sesame jam and a mixed salad with walnuts and apricots, toasted bread and butter. The cafe-restaurant area is downstairs and computers

line the walls on the second level. Internet access is available for €1 per 15 minutes. A trendy address, there always seems to be a film crew catching the vibe or cultural happening.
32 rue de Picardie, 3rd
Tel: (01) 4272 6655.
E-mail: contact@webbar.fr
Website: www.webbar.fr
Price: €25. Wine: €10.

Personal Recommendations

Au Pied de Cochon

This simple, no-frills brasserie originally served the market traders at Les Halles before it was moved to the suburbs. The restaurant continues to offer hearty traditional fare, including oysters, French onion soup with a cheesy crust, steaks and a choice of pork offal dishes, including the hallmark dish – grilled pigs' trotters – all washed down with robust house wine from the owner's own vineyard. And there is an added bonus — it is open 24 hours a day.
6 rue Coquillière, 1st
Tel: (01) 4013 7700. Fax: (01) 4013 7709.
Website: www.pieddecochon.com
Price: €40. Wine: €20.

Jo Goldenberg

In the heart of the Jewish quarter, within the labyrinthine streets of the Marais district, lies this busy restaurant, which serves up popular Ashkenazi dishes, ranging from chicken soup and *kreplach* (triangular noodles filled with chopped meat or cheese) to beef goulash. Reminiscent of a New York deli, the restaurant has a no-frills interior. If visitors are pushed for time, the delicatessen sells fresh pastrami, chopped herring, bagels, plaited cholla bread and cheesecake.
7 rue des Rosiers, 4th
Tel: (01) 4887 2016. Fax: (01) 4887 6408.
Price: €20. Wine: €25.

La Cagouille

Chef Gerard Allemandous' speciality is fresh fish and seafood, simply but beautifully served. The extensive wine list enhances the flavours. Guests can choose from dishes such as scallops in balsamic sauce or mussels cooked on a hot griddle. The restaurant is atmospheric and rustic, with a Cognac-region-style dining room and a lovely terrace for summer dining. Open daily, *La Cagouille*'s last dinner service is at 2130.
10 place Constantin-Brancusi, 14th
Tel: (01) 4322 0901. Fax: (01) 4538 5729.
Website: www.la-cagouille.fr
Price: €44. Wine: €19.

Le Rughetta

Le Rughetta is an unpretentious and surprisingly untouristy Montmartre restaurant serving delicious, garlic-licked pizzas, salads and pasta every day of the week. The restaurant, with a traditional, Italian-style interior, is an excellent choice for dining with friends in an informal and relaxing environment. Service is friendly and prices are very reasonable.
41 rue Lepic, 18th
Tel: (01) 4223 4170.
Price: €25. Wine: €15.

Terminus Nord

Located just opposite the Gare du Nord, this bustling brasserie decorated in an Art Nouveau and Art Deco style, with seafood piled high outside, serves good *bouillabaisse* (fish soup), *choucroute* (a cabbage dish not unlike sauerkraut) and French brasserie fare. Its clientele include locals and international travellers looking for a hearty meal after their Eurostar journey to the capital.

23 rue de Dunkerque, 10th

Tel: (01) 4285 0515. Fax: (01) 4016 1398.

Price: €25. Wine: €20.

ENTERTAINMENT

Nightlife

When planning an evening out in Paris, it is more important to decide where to go than what to do. The Champs-Elysées and Trocadéro areas are full of tourists and overpriced venues but if you are wishing to impress, this could be worth considering. Pigalle is the seedy sex centre of Paris but home to some good music venues and the *Moulin Rouge* cabaret, 82 boulevard Clichy, 18th, where the can-can is still performed. Montmartre is heaving in summer and the views over Paris from Sacré-Coeur are unbeatable (if you can see over the heads of the crowds). Bastille is buzzing with bars and clubs but is a bit too hectic for some. The best area for an evening's café-hopping is the Marais district (also the centre of the gay scene), closely followed by the increasingly fashionable Oberkampf, which suits a younger crowd.

The minimum legal age for drinking alcohol (beer and wine) is 16 years of age, rising to 18 years for stronger drinks and spirits. The average price of a drink while out and about in Paris is €4, although prices can vary drastically depending on the location. Bars are usually licensed until 0100 but it does vary according to the individual venue and area. Bouncers frequently turn potential punters away and many of the smarter clubs are (or claim to be) private. There is no sure way of gaining admission, although being foreign, dressed identically to everyone inside, accompanied by a regular or simply beautiful helps. Admission prices (usually around €15–20) often include one free drink. Clubs open at around 2300 and tend not to close until dawn; it is coolest to arrive around 0300, or at least after midnight. *Pariscope* (website: www.pariscope.com) is one of the best sources of information for nightlife listings.

Bars

Most cafés in Paris are considered bars as well – by virtue of their long opening hours and the fact that in the same place you might have a coffee you could also have a beer. There are, however, a number of specifically evening venues, which are listed below. With the exception of Anglo/Irish bars, beers on tap (*bière à la pression*) are normally served as a *demi* (25cl). The super-trendy *Le Buddha Bar*, 8 bis rue Boissy d'Anglas, 8th, so-called because of the giant kitsch Buddha that defines the decor of this underground beauty parade, continues to be the place to be seen. Another bar of beauties, popular with the wealthy business community, is *Barfly*, 49–51 avenue George V, 8th, which serves a variety of (expensive) cocktails and sushi. The crowd is more laid-back at *L'Armagnac*, 104 rue de Charonne, 11th, an ideal café-restaurant for a cool down after a good night out in the Bastille district. The first bar to make Oberkampf a popular new nightspot was *Café Charbon*, 109 rue Oberkampf, 11th. It is still popular with a young artistic crowd.

Forum des Halles

The DJ plays funk and house Tuesday to Saturday. *Le Mecano Bar*, 99 rue Oberkampf, 11th, so called because of its toolbox decor, is typically Parisian.

Although Pigalle can be seedy, *Le Chào Bà Café*, 22 boulevard Clichy, 18th, with its Chinese decor, is popular and even slightly chic.

The Marais (3rd and 4th) is packed with a happy mélange of gay and straight bars. Vibrant gay bars include the *Coffee Shop*, 3 rue Ste-Croix-de-la-Bretonnerie, and *Amnesia*, 42 rue Vieille-du-Temple, 4th. *Le Central*, 33 rue Vieille-du-Temple, 4th, is one of the city's oldest gay bars, with a more sedate clientele. Paris' sole gay-only hotel is situated above the café. There are also a number of quirky little straight bars in and around rue Vieille-du-Temple, including *La Chaise au Plafond*, 10 rue du Trésor, 4th, with its ceiling decorated with Fresian cows and a lovely terrace, *Au Petit Fer à Cheval*, 30 rue Vieille-du-Temple, 4th, named after its huge horseshoe-shaped bar, and *L'Etoile Manquante*, 30 rue Vieille-du-Temple, 4th. Also in the Marais is the *Web Bar*, 32 rue de Picardie, 3rd, a silversmith's atelier turned into a hip but relaxing cybernet haunt.

There is a cluster of café/bars around the Centre Pompidou. The most famed is the large *Café Beaubourg*, 43 rue St-Merri, 4th, an extremely popular and central meeting place.

Anglophone ex-pats find safety in numbers at the *Café Oz*, 184 rue St-Jacques, 5th, which serves a good range of draught and bottled beers, or *The Frog & Rosbif*, 116 rue St-Denis, 2nd, a traditional British pub.

Casinos

The *Casino d'Enghien les Bains*, 3 avenue de Ceinture, Enghien-Les-Bains (tel: (01) 3934 1300), is a 20-minute drive from Paris on the A15. Visitors must be over 18 years, carry a passport and be formally attired to gain admission, which costs €14.

Clubs

Techno, house, garage and latino are the popular sounds of Paris and, to a lesser extent, hip hop and drum'n'bass. Top DJs play house tunes at *Le Queen*, 102 avenue des Champs-Elysées, 8th, a gay club that is still considered the best club in Paris. Thursday and Saturday is gay only, with drag queens in profusion. *Le Divan du Monde*, located in the Pigalle district, at 75 rue des Martyrs, 18th, once hosted Toulouse Lautrec but now draws a crowd that changes radically according to the evening's programme – Brazilian, tango, indie, rock, house and hip hop nights alternate with top French and international DJs. *Le Saint*, 7 rue St-Séverin, 5th, which plays disco, house and salsa, is inexpensive and relaxed. At the other extreme is *Les Bains Douches*, 7 rue du Bourg-l'Abbé, 3rd, a former Turkish bathhouse transformed into the most pretentious of clubs.

Live Music

Le Divan du Monde (see *Clubs* above) hosts intimate pop concerts, providing a chance to see the stars close up. Live jazz is played by local and international high-calibre musicians at *Le Bilboquet*, 13 rue St-Benoît, 6th, nightly (from around 2200 onwards). There is no admission charge but drinks are priced at approximately €20. A young, unsophisticated crowd is drawn to *La Flèche d'Or*, 102 bis rue de Bagnolet, 20th, a converted station turned live music venue, with a sticky, beer-stained floor. Concerts run from Thursday to Sunday evenings and the music ranges from rock to blues or reggae and satirical French *chansons*. *Chesterfield Café*, 124 rue La Boétie, 8th, situated just off avenue des Champs-Elysées, is popular with ex-pats and hosts US rock and blues bands. To guarantee a seat, it is wise to book a table. Major rock concerts take place at the *Palais des Congrès*, 2 place de la Porte-Maillot, 17th.

Sport

Parisians generally prefer to watch sport rather than participate, although the annual *Paris Marathon* in April is an exception. The major spectator event, however, takes place in late July, when swarms of cyclists hurl down avenue des Champs-Elysées, which is lined with crowds, in the final stages of the *Tour de France*. The purpose-built *Stade de France*, St-Denis-la-Plaine (tel: (08) 9270 0900; website: www.stadefrance.com), has become the venue for international football matches and rugby Six Nations' Cup matches.

Meanwhile, domestic football matches take place at the *Parc des Princes*, 86 rue Regnault, 13th (tel: (08) 2507 5078; website: www.psg.fr), the base for the first-division Paris (St-Germain) football team *Paris-SG* (website: www.psg.fr) and *Le Racing* (website: www.racingclubdefrance.org) rugby team. The sports venue for everything from ballroom dancing to judo is the *Palais Omnisports de Paris-Bercy (POPB)*, 8 boulevard Bercy, 12th (tel: (08) 9269 2300).

The major horseracing events – the *Prix de la République* and the *Grand Prix de l'Arc de Triomphe* – take place in the Bois de Boulogne in October.

L'Officiel des Spectacles details sports events. *Le Guide du Sport à Paris*, available at tourist offices and town halls, lists sports facilities. The *Mairie de Paris* (tel: (08) 2000 7575) offers information on municipal facilities. Tickets for sporting events are available for purchase at *FNAC Forum des Halles*, 1 rue Pierre Lescot, 1st (tel: (01) 4041 4000; website: www.fnac.com), and various other FNAC ticket offices situated around the city. *Virgin Megastore*, 52 avenue des Champs-Elysées, 8th (tel: (01) 4953 5000; website: www.virginmega.fr), and online ticket agencies, *Ticketnet* (website: www.ticketnet.fr) and *Ticketclic* (website: www. ticketclic.fr) also sell tickets to sporting events.

Fitness Centres

A number of companies (such as *Moving* and *Gymnasium*) dominate the gym scene in Paris but these tend to be open to members only. Fitness centres open for one-off visits are listed in the *Squash* section below.

Golf

Golf Disneyland Paris, 77 Marne-la-Vallée (tel: (01) 6045 6890), 32km (20 miles), located east of Paris, has a 27-hole course, which is open all year round from 0830 at weekends and 0900 on weekdays. On weekdays, 18 holes cost €32, rising to €52 at the weekend. Yearly membership is also available.

Squash

Squash Montmartre, 14 rue Achille Martinet, 18th (tel: (01) 4255 3830; website: www.slot-montmartre.com), has four courts, saunas, fitness equipment and a restaurant. It charges €10 per person per half-hour. *Club Quartier Latin*, 19 rue de Pontoise, 5th (tel: (01) 5542 7788; website: www.clubquartierlatin.com), with squash, fitness and swimming facilities, charges €11.50 per hour.

Swimming

The underground *Piscine Suzanne-Berlioux*, Les Halles, 10 place de la Rotonde, 1st (tel: (01) 4236 9844), is extremely central and open daily, costing €3.80 per person. *Aquaboulevard*, 4 rue Louis-Armand, 15th (tel: (01) 4060 1010; website: www.aquaboulevard.com), has a selection of indoor and outdoor swimming pools, which are open daily; admission costs €20 (concessions available).

Tennis

To play on municipal courts, application for a *Carte Paris-Tennis* should be made at the Mairie (see above).

Alternatively, visitors can simply turn up and hope for the best. Courts cost approximately €6 per hour. There are also private clubs, which often charge high membership fees. *Forest Hill Tennis* at *Aquaboulevard* (see *Swimming* above) is open daily and charges €23–31 per visit.

Shopping

The Parisian ideal is elegant rather than funky. Trends come and go but Paris is always at the forefront and there are few cities where you can find so many top-quality designers. These include some British designers – John Galliano at *Dior*, Julian McDonald at *Givenchy* and McDonald's predecessor, Alexander McQueen, who recently signed an 'own label' deal with *Gucci* – as well as that ever-controversial Frenchman, Jean-Paul Gaultier, with his own store near Bastille. The exclusive designer shops are in the 8th, enclosed in the golden triangle formed by avenue des Champs-Elysées, avenue Montaigne and rue François 1er and along rue du Faubourg St-Honoré.

A less rarefied but typically Parisian shopping experience is to be had at the main department stores situated on boulevard Haussmann, 8th. These include *Les Galeries*, with its huge coloured dome, and *Au Printemps*. Métro Temple or Republique take the bargain shopper to the cheapest department store in the city – *Tati*, 172 rue du Temple, 3rd (website: www.tati.fr). Cut-price designer gear can be snapped up at the *Mouton à Cinq Pattes*, 8 rue St-Placide, 6th. The sales sweep through Paris in January and July.

Those who enjoy intimate, friendly boutiques should head for the Marais district, in the 4th *arrondissement*.

La Basilique du Sacré-Coeur

Photo: Corel

Rue des Francs-Bourgeois in the gay quarter sells designer kitsch, while the winding rue des Rosiers, in the Jewish quarter, has plenty of young designers whose works are displayed at *L'Eclaireur*. This area is at its busiest on Sunday, with many shops closed on Saturday due to the Jewish sabbath. It is ideal for a quick falafel snack, while the best ice cream is for sale at *Berthillon*, 31 rue de St-Louis-en-L'Ile, 4th.

The *Carrousel du Louvre*, under the glass pyramid in the Louvre courtyard, is a good place for shoppers to find tasteful gifts but those determined to take home plastic Eiffel Towers should head for rue de Rivoli, home to tourist kitsch.

The American-run *Shakespeare & Co*, 37 rue de la Bûcherie, 5th, has the city's widest selection of second-hand books in English. French books are best purchased at the city's *FNAC* stores, one of which is at the shopping arcade, the Forum des Halles, 1st. *Bouquinistes* sell second-hand books, as well as prints, postcards and gifts, along the River Seine.

Expensive antiques are to be found at *Le Louvre des Antiquaires*, beside the Louvre on place du Palais Royal. For bric-a-brac, there are the renowned flea markets (*marchés aux puces*), including the Porte de Montreuil, 20th, which is open on Saturday, Sunday and Monday 0700–1900, and St-Ouen/Porte de Clignancourt, 18th, open Friday 0600–1400, Saturday 0830–1730, Sunday 1030–1800 and Monday 1030–1700. There are numerous morning food markets in Paris, while the Ile-de-la-Cité has one of the largest flower markets in Paris.

Most shops are open Monday to Saturday 0900/1000–1900/2000 and close between about 1200 and 1430 for lunch. Sales tax is 20.6%, as standard, although it varies widely between what are regarded as essential items and luxury goods. Non-EU visitors can obtain a tax deduction on purchases of over €182.94 in any one establishment, by obtaining a form at the relevant shop and presenting it to customs on departure. *Global Refund* (tel: (01) 4161 5151; fax: (01) 4834 6020; e-mail:taxfree@fr.globalrefund.com; website: www.globalrefund.com) can provide further information.

Culture

The French government takes art and culture very seriously, pumping money into the arts, supporting French cinema against Hollywood imports, and embarking on grandiose *grands travaux*, such as the new *Bibliothèque Nationale de France*, Quai François-Mauriac (tel: (01) 5379 5959; website: www.bnf.fr). The *Opéra Bastille* (see *Music* below) opened in 1989, on the bicentennial of Bastille Day, although the merit of its architecture and the quality of its productions have since been questioned.

Major venues, in addition to those detailed below, include the *Palais des Congrès*, 2 place de la Porte-Maillot, 17th (tel: (01) 4068 2222; website: www.palaisdescongres-paris.com), for opera, ballet and pop performances, and the enormous *Palais des Sports*, Porte de Versailles, 15th (tel: (01) 4828 4010; website: www.palaisdessports.com).

Tickets for concerts of all kinds can be purchased at *FNAC Forum des Halles*, 1 rue Pierre Lescot, 1st (tel: (01) 4041 4000; website: www.fnac.com), or *FNAC Musique*, 2 rue Charenton, 12th (tel: (01) 4342 0404). There is also the *Carrousel du Louvre*, 99 rue de Rivoli, 1st (tel: (01) 4316 4747; website: www.carrouseldulouvre.fr), located directly beneath the Louvre, or *Virgin Megastore*, 52 avenue des Champs-Elysées, 8th (tel: (01) 4953 5000; website: www.virginmega.fr). However long the

La Samaritaine department store

queue, ticket touts at the Opéra and concert venues are to be avoided.

Listings are to be found in *Pariscope* (website: www.pariscope.fr) and *L'Officiel des Spectacles*. Classical concerts are listed in the monthly *Le Monde de la Musique*.

Music

The *Paris Opéra* (website: www.opera-de-paris.fr) performs ballet and opera at the *Opéra Garnier*, place de l'Opéra, 9th (tel: (01) 4001 1789), and *Opéra Bastille*, place de la Bastille, 12th (tel: (01) 4001 1789). Tickets cost €30–110). Large opera productions are also performed at the *Théâtre Musical de Paris*, 1 place du Châtelet, 1st (tel: (01) 4028 2840; website: www.chatelet-theatre.com). The varied programme at the *Cité de la Musique*, at La Villette (website: www.cite-musique.fr), is strongest in contemporary music and home to the internationally renowned *Ensemble Intercontemporain* (website: www.ensembleinter.com). It also features ancient music, jazz, chansons and world music. The *Cité* has two important venues – the *Conservatoire National de Musique*, 209 avenue Jean Jaurès, 19th (tel: (01) 4040 4545), and the *Salle des Concerts*, 221 avenue Jean Jaurès, 19th (tel: (01) 4484 4484). Big names in French contemporary and experimental classical music to listen out for are Pierre Boulez, Pascal Dusapin and Luc Ferrarie.

A series of orchestras, including the *Orchestre Colonne* (website: www.orchestrecolonne.fr), *Orchestre Lamoureux* (website: www.orchestrelamoureux.com) and *Orchestre de Paris* (webiste: www.orchestredeparis.com) are based at *Salle Pleyel*, 252 rue du Faubourg-St-Honoré, 8th (tel: (01) 4561 5300). Other prestigious venues for classical music include the *Salle Gaveau*, 45 rue de la Boétie, 8th (tel: (01) 4953 0507), *Théâtre des Champs-Elysées*, 15 avenue Montaigne, 8th (tel: (01) 4952 5050; website: www.theatrechampselysees.fr), and the *Théâtre Musical de Paris*, 1 place du Châtelet, 1st (tel: (01) 4028 2840; website: www.chatelet-theatre.com).

Theatre

The *Comédie Française*, 1 place de Colette, 1st (tel: (01) 4458 1515; website: www.comedie-francaise.fr), is the national theatre, renowned for its production of the classics. *Théâtre National de la Colline*, 15 rue Malte-Brun, 20th (tel: (01) 4462 5252), plays contemporary French drama. New talent is sought out at fringe theatres, such as *Guichet-Montparnasse*, 15 rue du Maine, 14th (tel: (01) 4327 8861). Peter Brook is based at the *Bouffes du Nord*, 37 bis boulevard de la Chapelle, 10th (tel: (01) 4607 3450). The *Odéon*, 1 place de l'Odéon, 6th (tel: (01) 4441 3636), hosts foreign-language productions but is currently closed for renovations.

Dance

The main ballet venue is the *Opéra Garnier* (see *Music* above). Major productions are also held at the prestigious *Théâtre de la Ville*, 2 place du Châtelet, 4th (tel: (01) 4274 2277), where the works of high-profile choreographers, such as Karine Saporta, Maguy Marin and Pina Bausch, are frequently shown. The *Théâtre Musical de Paris* (see *Music* above) hosts ballet companies from abroad.

Film

The first public film screening ever (*Le train entrant en gare*) was shown by the Lumière brothers in Paris in 1895. Today, Paris remains an important cinema capital – in any given week, over 300 films are shown.

There is no English-language cinema in Paris, however, most movies are shown in the original language, with French subtitles. The city's largest (18-screen) cinema is *UGC Ciné Cité Bercy*, 2 cours St-Emilion, 12th (tel: (08) 9270 0000). There is also a 16-screen *UGC Ciné Cité Les Halles*, place de la Rotonde, Nouveau Forum des Halles, 1st (tel: (08) 9270 0000). Although the multi-screen *UGCs* and *Gaumonts* are on the increase (many based on the

Champs-Elysées and in Montparnasse), Paris is still teeming with small arthouse cinemas, clustered in the 5th and 6th *arrondissements*. Among these are *Le Champo*, 51 rue des Ecoles, 5th (tel: (08) 9268 6921; website: www.cinefil.com), near the Sorbonne, and *Racine Odéon*, 6 rue de l'Ecole-de-Médicine, 6th (tel: (08) 9268 9325; website: www.cinefil.com), known for its all-night showings. Some cinemas are worth seeing just for their decor – one such is kitsch *Le Grand Rex*, 1 boulevard Poisssonnière, 2nd (tel: (01) 4508 9389).

The recently released movies, *Amelie* or *Le Fabuleux Destin d'Amelie Poulain* (2001), directed by Jean-Pierre Jeunet – of *Delicatessen* (1991) fame – and *Moulin Rouge* (2001), directed by Baz Luhrmann, were both set in Montmartre and took box offices worldwide by storm.

Cultural Events

Paris offers plenty of choice and a wide variety of lively festivals. Among these are the free, city-wide *Fête de la Musique* (21 June), the *Festival du Film de Paris* (early April) and the *Festival d'Automne* (September to December) contemporary dance event. Free concerts are held within the city's churches during the *Festival d'Art Sacré*, in the weeks preceding Christmas.

Literary Notes

The written word and words uttered during long café discussions on the Left Bank have done much to create the mythical Paris that visitors still hunt out today.

Victor Hugo's historical novel *The Hunchback of Notre-Dame* (1831) is set in 15th-century Paris and his *Les Misérables* (1862) in the poverty-stricken Parisian underworld. Ernest Hemingway's *A Moveable Feast* (1964) depicts the bohemian Paris of the inter-war years. Henry Miller's *Tropic of Cancer* (1934) and *Tropic of Capricorn* (1939) portray a sexier city. A more reflective image is portrayed in Anais Nin's works. For Nin, Paris allows the development of her sexuality and – perceived as equally sinful – creativity. George Orwell describes the poverty of the 1920s in *Down and Out in Paris and London* (1933).

Traces of literary heroes and heroines and their fictional creations are sought throughout the city – in the lingering smoke of the *Café de Flore* and *Les Deux Magots*, boulevard St-Germain, 6th, where the existential discussions between Jean-Paul Sartre, Camus and Simone de Beauvoir used to rage. Joyce used to drink at chic *Le Fouquet's*, 99 avenue des Champs-Elysées, 8th, while such luminaries as Rousseau, Voltaire and Wilde frequented *Le Procope*, 13 rue de l'Ancienne-Comédie, 6th. Hemingway dined at *La Cloiserie des Lilas*, 171 boulevard du Montparnasse, 6th, still popular with the publishing world, and Samuel Beckett's favourite haunt was *Le Select*, 99 boulevard du Montparnasse, 6th.

The place of literary pilgrimage *par excellence* is the Père Lachaise Cemetery, presumed resting place of medieval lovers Abélard and Héloïse. They lie in good company, along with the great 17th-century playwright Molière and fable-teller La Fontaine, Oscar Wilde, Sarah Bernhardt, Champollion, Delacroix, Ingres, Géricault, Bizet, Balzac, Proust, Colette and Edith Piaf. Contemporary poet, singer and icon Jim Morrison was famously buried here in 1971.

SPECIAL EVENTS

New Year's Day, national holiday, 1 Jan, throughout the city

Salon International de l'Agriculture (International Agriculture Show) animal specimens from rural France displayed alongside regional produce (website: www.salon-agriculture.com), late Feb/early Mar, Paris Expo, place de la Porte de Versailles, 15th

La Nuit des Publivores (The Night of the Adeaters), advertisements (publicités) are fêted by 6000 people in two night-long events, mid-Mar, Grand Rex, 1 boulevard Poisssonnière, 2nd

Festival du Film de Paris (Paris Film Festival), late Mar/early Apr, Cinéma Gaumont Marignan, 27 avenue des Champs-Elysées

Le Marathon de Paris (Paris Marathon), early Apr, starts approximately 0900 on avenue des Champs-Elysées, finishes avenue Foch

Foire de Paris (Paris Fair), fair for tourism, multimedia and gastronomy (website: www.foiredeparis.fr), late Apr/early May, Paris Expo, place de la Porte de Versailles

VE (Victory in Europe) Day, national holiday, May

Fête de la Musique (Musical Fair), free concerts throughout Paris (and the rest of France), 21 Jun, in the streets and various venues, such as Sainte-Chapelle, the Musée d'Orsay and Palais de Justice

Gay Pride March, late Jun, along République and the Bastille plus club events

Bastille Day, national holiday with festivities and fireworks to commemorate the storming of the Bastille in 1789, 14 Jul

Grandes Fêtes de Nuit de Versailles (The Night of Versailles Grand Feast), son et lumière display evoking the era of Louis XIV with costumed dancers and music, Jul, Aug and Sep, gardens of Versailles

Le Cinéma en Plein Air (Open-air Cinema), free outdoor film festival, mid-Jul–end Aug, Parc de la Villette, 19th

Le Tour de France, the grand finale of the world-famous bicycle race, late Jul (finishing on last Sun of Jul), finishes on avenue des Champs-Elysées

Journées du Patrimoine (Heritage Day), nationwide weekend festival; historic buildings, including the president's residence and the Palais de l'Elysée, open their doors to the general public, mid Sep, various historic buildings

Festival de l'Automne (Autumn Festival), international contemporary drama, dance and music festival, mid Sep–Dec, Théâtre de la Ville, Odéon and other venues

Mondial de l'Automobile (Automobile World), biennial international motor show (website: www.mondial-automobile.com), late Sep–mid-Oct (next in 2004), Paris Expo, Porte de Versailles, 15th

Foire Internationale d'Art Moderne et Contemporain (FIAC – Contemporary Art Fair), late Oct, Paris Expo, Porte de Versailles, 15th

Remembrance Day, national holiday with laying of wreaths, military parade and review of troops by the President of the Republic, 11 Nov, place Charles-de-Gaulle, 8th

Mois de la Photo (Photography Month), biennial photography exhibitions, late Nov (next 2004), various museums and galleries throughout Paris

Fête du Beaujolais Nouveau (Nouveau Beaujolais Fair), first availability of the season's Beaujolais Nouveau wine, third Tues of Nov, wine bars and cafés everywhere

Festival d'Art Sacré (Festival of Sacred Art), free concerts, Dec, various churches throughout the city

Réveillon (New Year's Eve), crowds celebrate by the thousand, 31 Dec, along the Champs-Elysées

Street artists

PRAGUE

The City of One Hundred Towers and Spires and Golden Prague are names that evoke the many aspects of this fascinating city, the capital of the Czech Republic. Its rich architectural heritage largely results from centuries of escaping the worst ravages of war and, more recently, nature, with the floods in August 2002. Maintenance, especially of the painted stucco exteriors, is a constant process. Under the Communists, Prague was the showplace of the Warsaw Pact, although in a muted fashion. Since the 1989 Velvet Revolution, the city has thrown off decades of oppression and is now returning to its former glory.

Situated in the valley of the Vltava (*Moldau*) River, Prague is dominated by the castle perched on the Western bluffs. Visitors are drawn to the 'fairytale' aspect of the city but this is only part of its vibrant mixture of styles. Prague is unquestionably a city that is best explored on foot – the entire centre has been designated a UNESCO World Heritage Site. Gothic churches rub shoulders with Cubist, Functionalist and ultra-modern buildings, classical music intermingles with jazz and rock, while monumental statues sit next to abstract works and even a Cubist lamppost. Prague's present form was established by the Přemysl King Otakar II (1253–78), when the town was reorganised into three administrative districts – the Castle precincts (*Hradčany*), the Lesser Town below the Castle (*Malá Strana*) and Old Town (*Staré Město*). Across the river, the Jewish community was moved from Lesser Town to the Josefov ghetto, to provide room for German traders.

The city's golden age commenced when Charles IV of Bohemia was elected Holy Roman Emperor in 1346. The ambitious Gothic building programme – including St Vitus Cathedral, the Charles Bridge, the University, and the New Town (*Nové Město*) – centred on Wenceslas Square and transformed the city into one of the greatest and most powerful in Europe. In reaction to Hapsburg rule, Czech nationalism reasserted itself in the late 16th century. Throughout the 19th century, the development of a nationalistic architectural style brought further changes. Later still, the Jewish ghetto was razed to make way for Art Nouveau buildings. At the end of World War I, Czechoslovakia gained its independence. Freed from the censorship and constraints of the Austro-Hungarian Empire, Prague blossomed as new artistic styles were embraced and developed – Cubism, Art Deco and Functionalism found a niche in its arts and architecture. Strong influences came from America, as Prague was ripe for the importation of popular culture from the Jazz Age. Parallels between that time and the 1990s are inescapable – in both cases, Prague took what it wanted, while retaining its unique identity. Not even decades of Nazi and Communist suppression successfully stifled the Czech spirit – the city reclaimed its reputation for cultural excellence when it dramatically threw off stark social realism in the 1990s.

Prague remains one of the most popular destinations for backpackers, still being relatively cheap, although the gap between Czech prices and European prices gets narrower each year. Changes to the laws regarding foreign workers have made it difficult for non-Czechs to find work but, although the 'great days' as a centre for expatriates may have passed, a substantial number still remain, the majority of whom are generally serious about work and the arts.

The best times to visit Prague are in the early spring and the late autumn – after the majority of tourists have left. If the cold isn't a problem, the winter months are the quietest time. Prague has a generally mild climate, although very high and low temperatures can be encountered. Autumn is the season with the highest rainfall. As one of the European cities of culture for the year 2000, Prague chose the theme of urban transformation – an idea that will continue for a number of years, as it looks forward to its exciting role in the new century.

Prague bridges and the Vltava River

Photo: Czech Tourist Authority

TRAVEL

Getting There By Air

Praha Ruzyně International Airport (PRG)

Tel: (02) 2011 3304. Fax: (02) 2011 5301.
Website: www.csl.cz/en

Ruzyně airport is situated approximately 20km (12.5 miles) northwest of Prague. Modernisation and expansion of the existing facilities was completed in 1997, although work continues on upgrading the airport's capacity – for example, they are building a second terminal at the moment (due for completion in 2005). Praha Ruzyně International provides reasonably good links with Western and Eastern Europe.

All passengers on direct flights to London may be required to go to the British Consulate Office, which is located at the far right of the check-in hall, before checking in. Passports and visas must be given for inspection at this time.

Major airlines: The Czech Republic's national carrier, *CSA* (tel: (02) 2480 6111; website: www.csa.cz), operates international and domestic flights from Ruzyně airport. CSA flies to major cities in Europe and the Middle East, as well as to New York, Chicago, Montreal, Toronto, Bangkok and Singapore. Domestic flights are to Ostrava. International airlines serving Prague include *Air Canada, Air France, Alitalia, Austrian Airlines, British Airways, Delta, easyJet, KLM, Lufthansa* and *SAS*.

Approximate flight times to Prague: From London is 1 hour 50 minutes; from New York is 11 hours; from Los Angeles is 18 hours; from Toronto is 10 hours 20 minutes and from Sydney is 21–28 hours.

Airport facilities: Facilities include a post office, banks, bureaux de change, accommodation agencies, restaurant, shops and even a duty-free casino. Car hire is available from *Alamo, Avis, Budget, Europcar* and *Hertz*.

Business facilities: The airport *VIP Service* (tel: (02) 2011 4499 *or* 3562; fax: (02) 2011 4372) hires out lounges and two meeting rooms (seating up to 25). *Diners Club* operates a business lounge with telephone, fax and Internet access, for members and guests only.

Arrival and departure tax: None.

Transport to the city: Shuttle minibus services to the city centre (Náměstí Republiky) are provided every half-hour 0530–2130, by *Cedaz* (tel: (02) 2011 4296; fax: (02) 2011 4286; website: www.aas. cz/cedaz), at a cost of Kč90, including one piece of luggage (journey time – 30 minutes). Bus 119 (see

Public Transport in *Getting Around*) goes to metro Dejvická (Line A) and operates every ten minutes 0430–2330. Tickets cost Kč12 and are available for purchase from the newspaper stand or the machine in front of the terminal. *FIX s.r.o.* taxis (tel: (02) 2011 3892) are expensive and will charge Kč720–870 depending on city zones (approximately Kč770 to the centre). Other taxis are often unreliable and visitors should avoid these.

Getting There By Rail

České dráhy – CD (tel: (02) 2422 4200 (timetable information) *or* 2461 5249 (for ticket prices); website: www.cdrail.cz), manages Prague's railways and stations. The old-fashioned stock is a delight for travellers and the rail system still displays a great deal of the old Austrian pride in the system – a hangover from the days of the Austro-Hungarian Empire, which was famous for the extent of its railway network and the comfort and punctuality of their trains. Even Communist rule could not eradicate the pride the railroad takes in its service.

Rychlík (also *express* and *spěšný*) trains only stop at major towns and cities. *Osobnývlak* are local trains that stop everywhere and average about 30km (19 miles) an hour. Trains are reliable and usually run on time. In many instances, however, buses will be faster, due to routing. The two main international terminals are *Hlavní nádraží* (main station), Wilsonova, Prague 2, and *Nádraží Holešovice*, Vrbenského, Prague 7. *Masarykovo nádraží*, Hybernská, Prague 1, is the station for trains to Moravia and Slovakia. *Praha-Smíchov* (*Smíchovské nádraží*), Prague 5, is the station for trains to the south of Bohemia, and *Praha-Vysočany*, Prague 5, for eastern Bohemia. All stations have lockers and 24-hour left-luggage facilities, while the international stations also have bureau de change facilities and tourist information services.

Rail services: Direct rail links connect Prague with more than 20 European cities, including Munich (journey time – 5 hours), Vienna (journey time – 4 hours 30 minutes), Berlin (journey time – 5 hours 30 minutes) and Paris (journey time – 10 hours). Seat reservations are strongly recommended on all services.

Transport to the city: The main station (Hlavní nádraží) is only a short walk from the city centre, however, the surrounding park can be very dangerous, especially after dark. It is therefore advisable for visitors to take the metro. Nádraží Holešovice (line B) and Smíchovské nádraží (line C) are on the metro, while tram 3 goes from the main station to Masarykovo nádraží.

Getting There By Road

Motorways (limited in number) are marked 'D' and international routes by 'E'. Minor roads are designated by a number, with two or more digits. An annual toll of Kč1000 (Kč200 for a month and Kč100 for ten days) must be paid to use Czech roads – toll stickers must be displayed and can be bought at border crossings, post offices and petrol stations. The legal driving age is 18 years. Traffic drives on the right. Speed limits are 50kph (31mph) in built-up areas, 90kph (56mph) on main roads and 130kph (81mph) on motorways. Seatbelts are compulsory for drivers and passengers, front and rear (if fitted). On-the-spot fines are high for all motoring offences. There is zero tolerance for drink and drugs (drivers are expected to have a 0% alcohol to blood ratio). EU licence holders must have an International Driving

Permit (IDP) as well as the pink format EU licence. An IDP is required for drivers from all other countries. A car registration document and country sticker are also necessary. Third-party liability insurance is compulsory. For drivers based in the Czech Republic for longer than six months, the car must be registered with the Czech authorities – duty and taxes will cost about half the value of the car and minimum third-party coverage with a *Czech* insurer is also required.

Emergency phone lines are situated every two kilometres (1.24 miles) on motorways and international routes. Both the *Ústřední Automotoklub – ÚAMK, Central Automobile Club* (tel: (02) 6110 4111; website: www.uamk.cz) and the *Autoklub České Republiky – ABA, Czech Automobile Club* (tel: (02) 2422 1820; website: www.autoklub.cz) have reciprocal agreements with many automobile associations and provide a 24-hour breakdown service.

Emergency breakdown services: *Ústřední Automotoklub (ÚAMK)* 1230; *Autoklub České Republiky (ABA)* 1240.

Routes to the city: The main routes to Prague are the D1/D2 from Brno (travellers should avoid the D2/D1 route via Bratislava, as foreigners may experience long delays at the Slovak border). From Belgium, the best route is the E40 to Cologne, then the E31 to Heidelberg and the E50, crossing the German/Czech border at Waidhaus/Rozvadov. From Vienna, the E59 leads to the D1 motorway, the E55 from Dresden and Berlin, the E67 from Wroclaw and Warsaw and the E50 from Paris.

Approximate driving times to Prague: From Bruges – 12 hours 30 minutes; Warsaw – 10 hours 15 minutes; Vienna – 4 hours 15 minutes.

Coach services: International buses depart either from the *Florenc coach station*, Křižíkova 8, Prague 8 (conveniently located on both metro lines B and C at Florenc station), or from the coach park at Želivského station (on metro A), located on the corner of Vinohradská and Jana-Želivského, Prague 3. *Kingscourt Express* (tel: (02) 2423 4583; website: www.kce.cz) is the main bus service provider to Western Europe and the UK. For many destinations within the Czech Republic, coaches are far quicker than trains, which tend to stop at every station. Regional services are provided by the state-run company, *CSAD* (tel: (02) 5731 9016; website: www.csadbus.cz). Buses depart from a number of stations and the most convenient place for travellers to get information and purchase tickets is at *Čedok* (see *Tourist Information*).

Getting Around

Public Transport

Prague's inexpensive and efficient transport system is run by *Dopravní podnik Prahy – DP, Prague Public*

Transit Company (tel: (02) 9619 1817; website: www.dp-praha.cz). The network includes the **metro**, **trams**, **buses** and the **funicular** on Petrín Hill. Public transport is an integrated 24-hour system – daytime services run 0500–2400, when night trams and buses take over.

There are three **metro** lines (A green, B yellow and C red). There are three interchanges – Muzeum (A and C), Mustek (A and B) and Florenc (B and C). Trains run at two-minute intervals 0500–2000 on weekdays and at five- to ten-minute intervals at all other times.

Tickets (*jízdenky*) must be purchased in advance and stamped on entering trams and buses and the transport area of the metro. These are valid for all forms of public transport and can be purchased at station ticket machines, most tobacconists, information centres and any shops displaying the red and yellow DP sticker. Two types of ticket are available. The Kč8 ticket allows one ride of up to four stops on the metro or a 15-minute ride above ground without transfers (not valid on night buses, the funicular or historical tram). The Kč12 ticket is valid on all forms of transport, including transfers, for one hour at peak times or 90 minutes at all other times. The on-the-spot fine for travelling without a valid ticket is Kč400.

A **funicular** railway (*lanovka*) runs every 10–15 minutes 0915–2045, carrying passengers from Újezd in the

Lesser Town to the top of Petrín Hill. Tickets cost Kč12. Travel **passes** cost Kč70 for 24 hours, Kč180 for three days, Kč250 for a week and Kč280 for 15 days. A tourist version of the three-day pass, the *Tourist Pass*, costing Kč690, also allows entrance to 42 tourist attractions (see *Tourist Information*).

Taxis

Many taxi firms are controlled by organised crime, unregistered drivers are widespread and most of the horror stories about exorbitant fares are true and all too frequent. Taxis are best avoided at all times, especially at taxi ranks. However, for those who do wish to take the risk, *Profi Taxi* (tel: (02) 6131 4151), with English-speaking drivers, is usually safe.

Travellers can expect to pay Kč30 for a street pick-up and Kč25 for a call-up. Fares are charged at Kč22 per kilometre and Kč4 per minute of waiting time. Officially licensed taxis are required by law to have a meter – if the driver refuses to switch it on, travellers are strongly advised to find another taxi. Passengers normally round up to the nearest Kč10 at the least. An additional amount of 8–10% of the fare could be tipped for exceptional service.

Limousines

Chauffer-driven Mercedes are available for hire from *Prague Limousines*, Psohlavců 1498, Prague 4 (tel: 07776 37707; e-mail: dispo@praguelimousines.cz; website: www.praguelimousines.cz), *Car Service*, Palác Vltava, Revoluční, Prague 1 (tel: (02) 2482 6262; fax: (02) 2482 6261; e-mail: info@limousineservis.cz; website: www.limousineservis.cz) and *Limousine Car Spiritka*, Sušická 21, Prague 6 (tel: (02) 2431 4857; e-mail: travel@beourguest-limousines.com; website: www.beourguest-limousine.com). Prices start from approximately Kč800 per hour.

Driving in the City

Cobbled streets, tram lines and erratic drivers all contribute to make driving in Prague an unpleasant experience. In addition to this, the historic centre of the city is pedestrianised. Parking is a major problem and it is usually best for tourists to leave the car in the secure hotel car park and use public transport. Illegally parked cars will either be clamped or towed away, with retrieval costing at least Kč1000 (tel: 158). There are three parking zones – orange for stays of up to two hours (Kč40 per hour), green for stays up to six hours (Kč30 per hour) and blue for residents and local businesses only. Cars should be locked and alarmed, valuables or radios should not be on display inside.

To discourage driving in the centre of the city, the city transport authority has set up a series of parking lots with direct links to the metro. Indicated by a P+R (park and ride) sign, these parking lots are guarded and charge a flat rate of Kč10. These include *Praha 4*, Hrncirska (line C, Opatov station), *Praha 5*, Radlická (line B, Radlická station), *Praha 5*, Zličín (line B, Zličín station), *Praha 7*, Nádraží Holešovice railway station (line C, Nádraží Holešovice station), *Praha 9*, Chlumecka (line B, Rajská Zahrada and Černý most stations) and *Praha 10*, V Rybnickach (line A, Skalka station).

CITY STATISTICS

Location: Banks of the Vltava, Bohemia, Czech Republic, Central Europe.
Country dialling code: 420. Telephone numbers in Prague are in the process of being digitised and all numbers will ultimately have eight digits. Many have already changed to eight digits, although many seven-digit telephone numbers still work. However, visitors finding that a seven-digit number doesn't work can try adding a '2' at the beginning of the number. For example, if (02) 123 4567 did not work, (02) 2123 4567 might.
Population: 1.23 million.
Ethnic mix: 94.4% Czech, 3% Slovakian, 0.6% Polish, 0.5% German, 0.3% Roma (gypsy), 0.2% Hungarian, 1% other (of which the largest groups are Russian and Vietnamese).
Religion: 39.8% atheist, 39.2% Roman Catholic, 4.6% Protestant, 3% Orthodox, 13.4% other.
Time zone: GMT + 1.
Electricity: 220–230 volts AC, 50Hz; round two-pin plugs are standard; converters are difficult to find.
Average January temp: - 1°C (30°F).
Average July temp: 19°C (63°F).
Annual rainfall: 67mm (2.64 inches).

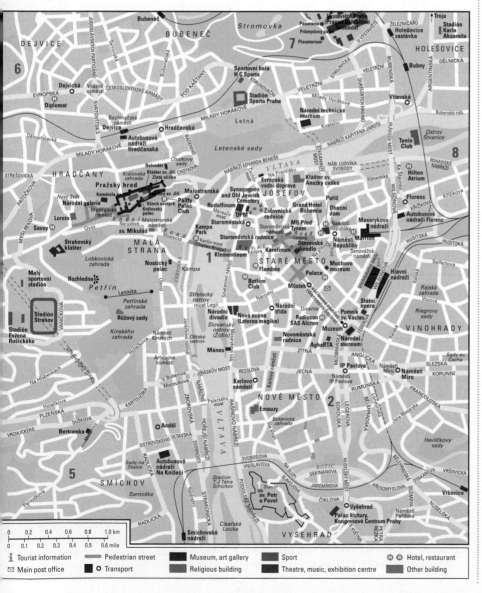

i Tourist information	▬ Pedestrian street
✉ Main post office	■ O Transport
	■ Museum, art gallery
	■ Religious building
	■ Sport
	■ Theatre, music, exhibition centre
	⊕ ⊕ Hotel, restaurant
	■ Other building

BUSINESS PROFILE

The Czech Republic's principal industries are power engineering and fuels, metallurgy, engineering, glass, wood and armaments. The rapidly growing service industry is a major source of income, with the related tourist industry providing enough invisible income to help redress the trade deficit. Global recession in 1996 revealed just how fragile the Czech 'economic miracle' actually was. Increased domestic demand and poor export performance have generated a growing deficit.

Prague is the centre of Czech business – 20% of the country's GDP is created here – although there is no particular central business district and companies are located in all parts of the city and suburbs. As heavy engineering moves outside the city, service industries (financial, retail and telecommunications) and manufacturing industries (electrical, transport and food processing) are becoming increasingly prevalent. Companies to base their Czech or Eastern European headquarters in Prague include *ABB, Philips* and *Siemens*.

Megalithic conglomerates, largely unchanged from their days as nationalised industries, have been a constant drain on bank reserves. Banks were hit by the collapse of the Russian economy in 1999, through exposure to bad debts in the former USSR. Banks are still overly cautious about making loans without sound collateral and sources of venture capital are still very narrow. This has led to a squeeze on the small and medium enterprises (SMEs), which should be at the heart of a dynamic economy. Preparations for admission to the EU have also contributed to the fragility of the economy and the target date of 2004 has been called into question. The EU has identified four main problem areas: the need to reform financial markets, weak disclosure rules and a lack of enforcement have led them to be plagued by insider dealing; the restructuring of the banking system; tightening of national borders to cut down on smuggling; and the need to deal with the rights of the Roma (gypsy) minority.

Current unemployment in the Czech Republic stands at approximately 9.3%. The strong Czech Koruna is also a factor – although good from the standpoint of tourism (and therefore certainly for the Prague economy), exports, especially to the United States, have fallen (by 16% in 2002). Prague's rate of unemployment is only around 3%. Unemployment figures show wide regional variations and some regions of the country, notably those in coal mining and steel production areas, are above 20%. The coal region of Most is above 21.4%.

All is not gloom, however, since much of the Czech workforce is well trained (and willing to retrain), intelligent and hard working. Opportunities for venture capital investment, especially in the SMEs, could reap rich rewards, while low share prices offer attractive bargains. Large conglomerates are being broken up and the companies that emerge should be leaner and better able to compete in a global market.

Car Hire

Car hire is expensive in Prague and – given the pedestrianisation of the city centre – not really necessary other than for trips out of town. Those looking to hire a car should arrange this before arriving, which will guarantee availability and avoid language difficulties. Clients must be over 21 years and have held a full driving licence for at least a year. A valid national driving licence and an International Driving Permit, a passport and a credit card for the deposit are required. Car hire prices generally include collision damage waiver, theft protection and third-party coverage.

Car hire is available at Ruzyně airport, Čedok, American Express offices and many large hotels. Major companies include *Avis*, Klimentská 46, Prague 1 (tel: (02) 2185 1225; website: www.avis.cz), *Budget*, Čistovická 100, Prague 6 (tel: (02) 3532 5713; fax: (02) 3532 5711; website: www.budget.cz), and *Hertz*, Karlovo náměstí 28, Prague 2 (tel: (02) 2223 1010 *or* 2010 2424 (reservation centre); website: www.hertz.cz). Local companies include *Ceník Royal Rent*, Opetalova, Prague 1 (tel: (02) 2224 7515; website: www.royalrent.cz), *Dvořák*, Prague Hotel Hilton, Probezni 8, Prague 8 (tel: (02) 2484 2313; fax: (02) 2484 2407; website: www.dvorak-rentacar.cz), and *Toscar*, Novovysočanská 2A, Prague 9 (tel: (02) 6631 5586; e-mail: info@toscar.cz; website: www. toscar.cz).

Local companies charge from about Kč900 per day, while international companies' rates are much higher, from about Kč2200.

Bicycle Hire

With high pollution levels, unsympathetic drivers and a lack of cycle lanes, cycling in Prague cannot be recommended. Nevertheless, bicycle hire and group tours of Prague are available in the summer from *City Bike*, Královdvorská 5 (tel: 07761 80284; e-mail: citybike@ pragueonline.cz; website: www.pragueonline.cz/ citybike), located not far from the Old Town Square. Rates are Kč700 per day with a passport or ID as a deposit. City Bike does not operate in the winter and it is wise to check with PIS (see *Tourist Information*) to check if this company is open.

SIGHTSEEING

Sightseeing Overview

Wenceslas Square, the Old Town Square and the Charles Bridge serve as the three main navigation points for tourists. The bridge links the Lesser Town and the Castle above with the Old and New Towns. The central tourist area is comprised of five sections – *Hradčany* is the Castle precinct, with *Malá Strana* (Little Town) at its foot, across the *Karlův most* (Charles Bridge) lie *Staré Město* (Old Town), with *Josefov* (the Jewish Quarter) to the north and *Nové M?sto* (New Town) to the south. The 'Royal Road' – the route of major processions in the past – is the main tourist route across the city, beginning at the *Powder Gate* on *Náměstí Republiky* (Republic Square) and continuing along Celetná to the *Old Town Square*. From there, the road passes the *Astronomical Clock* and winds along Karlova to the Charles Bridge. Crossing the bridge, it follows Mostecká through *Malá Strana* to the Baroque square at Malostranské náměstí. Streets off the square lead to the long climb of stairs

to the Castle. To the south, Náměstí Republiky, with its magnificent *Municipal House*, leads via Na přikopě to *Václavské náměstí* (Wenceslas Square), the hub of shopping and nightlife.

Museums and galleries are scattered throughout the city and even the suburbs. Further afield to the south lies *Vyšehrad* (district 4), the site of the original settlement. Less frequented by tourists, the area has much to offer and provides a respite from the bustle of the city centre.

Key Attractions

Karlův most (Charles Bridge)

The construction of Prague's most famous and most photographed location was begun in 1357, as part of Charles IV's monumental building programme that included the Castle, St Vitus Cathedral and the University. All were supervised by the Swabian architect, Peter Parler (although the bridge construction is now known to have been begun by

BUSINESS ETIQUETTE

By and large the Czechs are a warm people who greatly value hospitality. In some instances, when dining with Czech business colleagues, it will emerge that the bill has already been settled quietly. If this happens, business visitors should accept gracefully (considering the disparity in Czech and Western wages, this may also be a matter of personal pride) and try to find some later means of showing appreciation. Czech society is still largely male dominated and, especially with older businessmen, it is unheard of for a woman to pay for a meal, even if she is the senior member of the team. If invited to dine at a colleague's home, a small gift is appropriate – a bottle of wine or flowers are best. When offering or accepting a lift with a business colleague, the favoured location is the backseat.

Initial business meetings are often serious affairs, during which even business partners refer to each other by title and surname. The use of forenames is a mark of friendship, however, using them without permission is seen as insulting or demeaning. Degrees are considered important and should always be used in addressing correspondence (only the doctorate is used in direct address). Meetings can take longer than expected and be more formal than the average Western businessperson is accustomed to. However, as the old Communist bureaucratic ways give ground to capitalism, business lunches and such meetings are gaining popularity, especially with the younger generation. However, one should not expect work-related meals to be the norm.

Office hours are generally Monday to Friday 0830–1700 and punctuality is essential – colleagues should be informed of any unavoidable delays. Dress is conservative for older businesses, while new companies tend to be more relaxed. A jacket and tie for men or smart suit for women is a good bet for first-time business visitors. A firm handshake and maintaining eye contact are seen as signs of honesty and sincerity, while overloud talking and interrupting are construed as attempts to obscure issues. At first meetings, business cards will be exchanged and an offer of coffee or drinks is common.

Jewish Cemetery

Master Otto). The bridge replaced the earlier Judita (Judith) Bridge, the only surviving remnant of which is the plainer of the two towers on the *Malá Strana* gate. The bridge itself is rather drab and it is the later statues (Jesuit additions during the Counter-Reformation), which flank the bridge, that have made it so visually stunning. The first of these – the *Crucifixion* – was erected in 1657, followed soon after by the only bronze statue, that of St John of Nepomuk (who was martyred after being thrown from the bridge). Most of the other statues of the saints – carved from local sandstone, by Josef Brokof and Matthias Braun – were added between 1706 and 1714 (the latest was not added until 1928). Due to pollution, most have been replaced and the originals are housed in the *Lapidarium* in Letná Park. Many tourists wonder about the wooden constructions at the base of the pilings on the upriver side – these protect against ice floes and logjams during the spring melt-off.

The fully pedestrianised bridge serves as a focal point for tourists. There are stalls of various artists and craftspeople lining the bridge, while buskers of all descriptions (from Dixieland jazz bands to puppeteers) provide a constant source of entertainment and often congestion. Work on making the bridge fully weather resistant began in 2003. The first stages are concentrating on research and some work under the bridge arches.

Staré Město (Old Town)
Transport: Metro Staroměstská; tram 17, 18, 51 or 54.

Pražský Hrad (Prague Castle)

From almost any part of Prague, the *Castle*, perched on the ridge in Hradčany, dominates the skyline. Entering under the *Battling Titan* statues, the sheer size of the complex – with three courtyards, fortifications and gardens, almost a small town in its own right – is most striking. Given the wealth of architecture, state apartments, churches, galleries and gardens, it is impossible to see everything in a single day. *Katedrála sv. Víta* (St Vitus Cathedral), the country's largest church, takes up most of the third courtyard. Inspired by the Gothic cathedral at Narbonne, work commenced in 1344, however, reflecting the changing fortunes of the Czechs, was not completed until 1929. The finest of the 22 side chapels is that built to hold the relics of St Wenceslas – the gilded walls are inlaid with hundreds of semi-precious stones that frame the luminous 14th-century paintings. The overly ornate Baroque tomb of St John of Nepomuk, was the work

of Jesuits intent on promoting this martyr as the Czech patron saint in opposition to Wenceslas. The *Coronation Chamber* displays the Bohemian crown jewels but is only infrequently open to the public. The *Crypt* is the resting place of most of the Kings and Queens of Bohemia. *Bazilika sv. Jiří* (St George's Basilica) is a marvel of Romanesque architecture. Founded in AD970, it was rebuilt in the 12th century and acquired its present Baroque façade in the 16th century. The chapel dedicated to Saint Ludmilla, the first Czech martyr, is particularly fine. *Klášter sv. Jiří* (St George's Convent), the oldest monastery in the country, was founded in AD973, for Benedictine nuns. It now houses a remarkable collection of early Czech art from the Gothic to Baroque periods.

In the *Castle Gardens*, the *Belvedere* is Prague's finest Renaissance building. Built in the 1530s, as a summerhouse for Queen Anne, it now houses a changing programme of exhibitions. *Zlatá ulička* (Golden Lane), with its 16th-century houses built into the fortifications, derives its name from being the residences of the court alchemists.

Hradčanské náměstí, Prague 1
Tel: (02) 2437 3368.
E-mail: jaromir.potucek@hrad.cz (tickets and tours) *or* frantisek.kadlec@hrad.cz (information centre)
Website: www.hrad.cz
Transport: Tram 22 to Pražský hrad; metro to Hradčanská.
Opening hours: Daily 0900–1700 (Apr–Oct); daily 0900–1600 (Nov–May).
Admission: Kč220 (castle); free (grounds).

Staroměstské náměstí (Old Town Square)

The 12th-century *Old Town Square* is the focal point for tourists. Stalls selling crafts line the perimeter and horse-drawn carriages await those wishing to take a tour of the historic centre. In summer, tables spill out from the restaurants, while in December, the square hosts the city's largest Christmas Market. The centre is dominated by the monumental memorial to the 14th-century religious reformer, Jan Hus. The *Prague Meridian* is also found here, designating kilometre zero, from which all distances in the city are measured. All of the palaces, churches and houses around the square are of major historical interest. The Gothic *Staroměstská radnice* (Old Town Hall) with its *Astronomical Clock* is a must for visitors. It strikes hourly (0900–2100), when the upper portion – dating from the early 15th century – reveals the Apostles at two windows. Just off the

square, to the east, is the superb Gothic *Chrám Matky boží před Týnem* (Tyn Church), where the tomb of the astronomer, Tycho Brahe, is located.
Staré Město (Old Town)
Transport: Metro Staroměstská; tram 17 or 18.

Josefov (Jewish Quarter)

Until the end of the 19th century, the area north of the Old Town Square constituted the *Jewish Ghetto* – much of the area was cleared to make way for Art Nouveau buildings but some of the flavour still remains. A single ticket, available from the *Jewish Museum*, allows admission to the *Židovnická radnice* (Jewish Town Hall), the *Klausen*, the *Maisel*, the *Pinkas Synagogue* and the *Spanish Synagogue*, the *Old Jewish Cemetery* (in use from the 15th century until 1787) and the *Ceremonial Hall*. A separate ticket is required for the 13th-century *Starovoná synagoga* (Old-New Synagogue), the oldest synagogue in Europe.
Staré Město
Transport: Metro Staroměstská.
Jewish Museum
U Staré školy 1, Prague 1
Tel: (02) 2481 9456 *or* 2231 7191 (ticket reservations).
Fax: (02) 2481 9458 *or* 2231 7181 (ticket reservations).
E-mail: reservacni.centrum@jewishmuseum.cz
Website: www.jewishmuseum.cz
Opening hours: Mon–Fri and Sun 0900–1800 (Apr–Oct); Mon–Fri and Sun 0900–1630 (Nov–Mar).
Admission: Kč490 (Jewish Museum sites); Kč200 (Old-New Synagogue).

TOURIST INFORMATION

Pražská informační služba (PIS – Prague Information Service)
Na příkopě 20, Prague 1
Tel: (02) 12444 (general).
E-mail: tourinfo@pis.cz
Website: www.prague-info.cz
Opening hours: Mon–Fri 0900–1900, Sat and Sun 0900–1700 (Apr–Oct); Mon–Fri 0900–1800, Sat 0900–1500 (Nov-Mar).

PIS branches can also be found in the Old Town Hall, Staroměstské náměstí, Prague 1, Celetná, Prague 1, Hlavní nádraží (main train station), Wilsonova, Prague 1, and, in the summer, at Malostranská mostecká vex (Lesser Town Bridge Tower), Prague 1.

Čedok Travel Agency
Na příkopě 18, Prague 1
Tel: (02) 2419 7241. Fax: (02) 2421 6324.
E-mail: cedok@cedok.cz
Website: www.cedok.cz
Opening hours: Mon–Fri 0830–1800, Sat 0830–1300.

Passes
A three-day *Tourist Pass*, costing Kč690, allows unlimited travel on the metro, trams and buses, as well as admission to 42 major attractions, including Prague Castle, the National Museum and the Museum of Decorative Arts. Passes without the free transport cost Kč400. These passes are available for purchase from tourist information centres and offices of the Prague Public Transit Company (DP).

Obecní dům (Municipal House)

The gem of Art Nouveau in Prague, *Obecní dům*, has been fully restored, after decades of neglect. Designed by A Balsánek and Osvald Polívka, all the major Czech artists made contributions during its construction (1905–10). However, even Karel Spillar's striking mosaic and the sculptural group by Ladislav Šaloun cannot prepare the visitor for the remarkable interiors. Most spectacular of the public areas, the *Lord Mayor's Room* features murals by Alfons Mucha. The restaurant, café and the Amerikanský bar were also the work of Polívka. The centrepiece of the building is the *Smetana Hall*, home of the Prague Symphony Orchestra and one of the major venues for concerts during the Prague Spring Festival. Guided tours are essential for visitors to see the rooms that are not open to the public.
Náměstí Republiky 5, Prague 1
Tel: (02) 2200 2101. Fax: (02) 2200 2100.
E-mail: info@obecni-dum.cz
Website: www.obecni-dum.cz
Transport: Metro Náměstí Republiky; tram 5, 14 or 24.
Opening hours: Daily 1000–1800 (exhibition hall); daily 0730–2300 (café).
Admission: Free; Kč150 (guided tours); approximately Kč60–100 (separate exhibitions).

Václavské náměstí (Wenceslas Square)

Despite its name, *Wenceslas Square* is really a long boulevard. It was here, in 1989, the passive resistance culminating in the Velvet Revolution began. Today, the square is a bustling thoroughfare presenting the best and worst of post-Communist Prague – from the fashionable and expensive stores to the prostitutes and taxis controlled by organised crime rings. Nothing remains of the square's earliest buildings, allthough examples of architectural styles from the last 150 years line its frontage. The lower portion is pedestrianised and contains many of Prague's largest stores – often of more interest for their architecture than for their contents. Newspaper stands at the bottom end are the best place to purchase Czech and foreign-language newspapers. Numerous arcades with winding passages (developed in the 1920s) lead to or surround a cinema (in almost all instances). Many are now being renovated to their original Art Deco splendour, chiefly to house trendy shops. The *Lucerna* (see *Live music* in *Nightlife*) is undoubtedly the finest of these arcades, housing a jazz/rock concert hall, cinema, excellent café and numerous small shops.
Situated on the opposite side of Wenceslas Square, at number 25, the *Grand Hotel Evropa*, (website: www.motylek.com/evropa), is a major landmark of the First Republic. The Evropa's time has not yet returned and service is still reminiscent of the Communist period. Its faded splendour is best enjoyed briefly over coffee or tea. The focal point of the upper end of the square is J.V. Myslbek's monumental bronze equestrian statue of the *Pomník sv. Václav* (St Wenceslas Memorial). The four surrounding statues are of national patron saints – Ludmilla, Procopius, Agnes and Vojtech (Adalbert).
At the top of the square stands the *Národní muzeum* (National Museum). Founded in 1818, this houses the country's oldest and largest collection of antiquities. Although the collections – dedicated to palaeontology, geology, zoology and anthropology – are primarily of interest to specialists, the building itself warrants a visit. Built in the neo-Renaissance style, the façade and interior decorations form a striking celebration of the history of the former Czechoslovakia.

Nové Město (New Town)
Transport: Metro Můstek (bottom) or Muzeum (top).
Národní muzeum (National Museum)
Václavské 68, Prague 1
Tel: (02) 2449 7111. Fax: (02) 2224 6047.
Website: www.nm.cz/english
Transport: Metro Muzeum.
Opening hours: Daily 1000–1800 (May–Sep); daily 0900–1700 (Oct–Apr); closed first Tues of the month.
Admission: Kč80; concessions available; free first Mon of the month.

Further Distractions

Uměleckoprůmyslového Musea (Museum of Decorative Arts)

Only a small fraction of the museum's holding is on display but what is there makes a mockery of fine art's supposed elevation above applied art. The fin-de-siècle building itself is stunning. Divided into two floors, the ground floor hosts temporary exhibitions, while the top floor presents a wide range of crafts. Of particular interest and beauty are the Czech ceramics and glassware.
Ulice 17 listopadu 2, Prague 1
Tel: (02) 2481 1241.
E-mail: komunikace@upm.cz
Website: www.knihovna.upm.cz
Transport: Metro Staroměstská; tram 17 or 18.
Opening hours: Tues–Sun 1000–1800.
Admission: Kč120.

Muchovo Muzeum (Mucha Museum)

Celebrating the life of Czechoslovakia's best-known artist, Alfons Mucha (1860–1934), this collection in the Kaunitz Palace includes many of his Paris posters, including those for performances by Sarah Bernhardt. Paintings, sketchbooks and a recreation of his Paris studio are also on display. There is a pleasant terrace café as well.
Kaunický palác, Panská 7, Prague 1
Tel: (02) 2145 1333.
E-mail: museum@mucha.cz
Website: www.mucha.cz
Transport: Metro Můstek.
Opening hours: Daily 1000–1800.
Admission: Kč120.

Wax Museum Prague

The *Wax Museum Prague* has proved to be a popular attraction and has now moved from its original home to two different locations. The Melantrichová museum features the 'Hall of Celebrities of the 20th Century', the 'Gallery of Totalitarian Rulers' and the multimedia 'Magical Prague' program. The Mostecká musem focuses on Czech history, including a medieval alchemical laboratory and a 19th-century street scene.
Melantrichová 5, Prague 1
Tel: (02) 2493 3349.
Transport: Metro Můstek.
Admission: Kč120 (concessions available).
Mostecká 18, Prague 1
Office tel: (02) 5753 5753.
Transport: Metro Malostranská; tram 12 or 22.
Admission: Kč110 (concessions available).
Tel: (02) 4933 3349.
E-mail: info@waxmuseumprague.cz
Website: www.waxmuseumprague.cz
Opening hours: Daily 0900–2000.
Admission: Kč180 (combined ticket); concessions available.

Small and Temporary Museums

Prague is constantly acquiring new museums, some for the summer season only. These are often strange and extremely interesting. Visitors should look for posters or leaflets in the tourist offices. Among the best to pop up at the moment are the *Muzeum Komunismu* (Museum of Communism), covering the 1948–89 reign of Communism in the city, and the *Sex Machine Museum*, an exposition of mechanical erotic appliances.
Museum of Communism
Na přikopě 10 (first floor)
Tel: (02) 2421 2966.
E-mail: muzeum@muzeumkomunismu.cz
Website: www.muzeumkomunismu.cz
Transport: Metro Můstek.
Opening hours: Daily 0900–2100.
Admission: Kč180 (concessions available).
Sex Machine Museum
Melantrichova 18, Prague 1 (off the Old Town Square)
Tel: (02) 2421 6505. Fax: (02) 2421 6513.
E-mail: info@sexmachinesmuseum.com
Website: www.sexmachinesmuseum.com
Transport: Metro Staroměstská.
Opening hours: Daily 1000–2200.
Admission: Kč250 (concessions available).

Tours of the City

Walking Tours

A Guide to the Capital 'The Silver Line Through Golden Prague' guidebook, part of the *Silver Line* orientation system project (tel: (02) 7400 6565 *or* 6363; e-mail: info@admen.cz; website: www.silver-line.cz), is now available for Kč159 from *PIS* offices (see *Tourist Information*) and bookshops. Linking with the guidebook are numerous silver arrows, placed on pavements throughout the tourist sections of the city, enabling tourists to plan an individual walking tour program, which is also linked to the metro stations.
A number of companies offer excellent walking tours of Prague, some with themes such as ghosts, Kafka and legends. Most charge approximately Kč300 for a two-hour tour. Leaflets are available at all PIS locations (see *Tourist Information*). Most tours start from beneath the Astrological Clock in the Old Town Square. Guides will hold up an umbrella of a particular colour, so that people joining the tour can locate them.
Prague Walks, Nezamyslova 7, Prague 2 (tel: (02) 6121 4603; e-mail: pwalks@comp.cz; website: www. pragueandcountry.cz/pwalks), offers scheduled themed walks, including the 90-minute 'Modern Walk: Life in Communism, Life Today' (Kč300), the one-hour 'Ghost Tour' (Kč300) and the three-hour 'Literary Pub Walk' (Kč300). Departure points vary depending on the tour but is usually underneath the Astronomical Clock in the Old Town Square or a nearby tram or metro station. Guides speak English, French, German, Russian and Spanish. The company also arranges personal guides for individual tours.
Pragotur Guides Centre, Staroměstské náměstí 1, Prague 1 (tel: (02) 2448 2562; fax: (02) 2448 2380; e-mail: guides.pis@volny.cz), also provides qualified guides who speak all European languages. *City Walks* (tel: (02) 2224 4531; website: www.praguer.com) provides a number of walking tours, as well as bicycle and boat tours. *Daily Walks of Prague* (tel: (02) 8191 7642; website: www.walks.cz) and *Prague Travel Ltd* (tel: (02) 2251 6064; website: www.praguetravel.cz) both offer a number of walks. *Wittmann Tours* (tel: (02) 2225 2472; website: www.wittmann-tours.com) specialises in tours of Jewish interest, both in the city and further afield.

Bus Tours

Prague Sightseeing Tours (tel: (02) 2231 4661; e-mail: pstours@pstours.cz; website: www.pstours.cz) depart from Náměstí Republiky and terminate in the city centre – free pick-up from most four-star hotels can also be arranged. The 'Grand City Tour', which takes in all the major sights and includes a walking tour, takes three and a half hours and costs Kč620. The 'Getting Acquainted By Bus Tour' whips tourists around all the major sites – such as the National Museum, Wenceslas Square and the Hradčany Castle district – in two hours, for Kč390. All tours are in English and other major European languages on request.

Bus tours of Prague and other tourist locations are also available through *Best Tour* (tel: (02) 8481 4141; website: www.besttour.cz) and *Bohemia Travel Service* (tel: (02) 2482 6262; website: www.citytours.cz). Numerous tours of the nearby castles, such as Karlštejn and Konopiště, are also available through *Čedok*, Na příkopě 18, Prague 1 (tel: (02) 2419 7241; fax: (02) 2421 6324; website: www.cedok.cz), travel agencies, booths and kiosks throughout the city.

Other Tours

Dopravní podnik Prahy (tel: (02) 2262 3777; website: www.dp-praha.cz) offers tours around the city centre on the Historic Tram 91. The circular route runs from Výstaviste, through Malá Strana, across the Vltava to the National Theatre, through Wenceslas Square and returns to Výstaviste via Náměstí Republiky. The tram runs hourly 1300–2000 on Saturday, Sunday and holidays, from April to October. A ticket costs Kč25 (concessions available) and travellers can board at any stop en route – an entire round trip takes an hour.

Prague Sightseeing Tours (tel: (02) 2231 4661 *or* 4655; e-mail: pstours@pstours.cz; website: www.pstours.cz) offers three special boat tours. A cruise on the Vltava River with lunch and music costs Kč750, taking passengers under the Charles Bridge on this two-and-a-half-hour trip. The two-hour cruise on the Vltava River with coffee and cake is cheaper, at Kč490, travelling past the Prague Castle District and Lesser Town. The 'Prague by Night Tour', costing Kč1290, is three hours of on-board dining and cruising, before a one-hour coach trip to Prague's most beautiful squares. All tours depart by coach from Náměstí Republiky.

Fiacres (horse-drawn taxis of the pre-car era) offer tours of the Old Town centre. Fiacres are found along the west side of the Old Town Square and 20-minute tours cost approximately Kč600.

Old Timer History Trip (tel: (0607) 112 559; website: www.historytrip.cz) and *3 Old Timers* (tel: (0608) 519 333; website: www. 3oldtimers.com) and offer the newest tours in Prague, in beautifully restored cars from the great age of Czech motoring, which took place between the two World Wars. Drivers are suitably attired in 1930s costumes. A 20-minute tour costs Kč900 for one or two passengers or Kč1300 for three or four passengers.

Excursions

For a Half Day

Vyšehrad: No other site is as imbued with as much national history as the fortress at *Vyšehrad*, three kilometres (two miles) south of the centre of Prague. Although recent archaeological evidence does not bear out the traditional theory that this was the first site settled by the Slavic tribes, it clearly indicates that, in the 11th and 12th centuries, Vyšehrad was of far

Karlovy Vary

greater importance than the Castle. Although the neo-Gothic (1880s) church of *sv. Petr a Pavel* (Saints Peter and Paul) is closed to the public, the façade has stunning carvings. Adjacent to the church is the *Vyšehrad Cemetery*, the final resting place for Czech artists, scientists and academics – an indication of the respect in which they have always been held (no politicians or soldiers are buried here). The often highly artistic graves include those of Smetana, Dvorák and Mucha. Within the suburb of Vyšehrad itself, located on Neklanova and Rasínovo nábřeží, are villas, designed by the architect, Josef Chochol, whose designs remain a unique feature of Czech Cubism.

Vyšehrad can be reached on metro and tram 17 (visitors should alight before the road tunnels). *Vyšehrad National Cultural Monument*, V Pevnosti 159 (tel: (02) 4141 0348; e-mail: vyschrad@zris. mepnet.cz; website: www.praha-vysehrad.cz), can provide further information.

Troja (Trojský zámek): Prague's only chateau, *Troja* (tel: (02) 8385 1614), was built by the Sternbeck family in the late 17th century, as a paean to the reigning Hapsburg dynasty. Located in the north of the city, much of the rich Baroque interior decoration celebrates the Hapsburgs, notably Leopold I's victories over the Turks. The exquisite formal gardens lead down to the river, where rowing boats are available for hire (May to October). Visitors can reach Troja by bus 112 from metro Nádraží Holešovice or a pleasant half-hour walk along the banks of the Vltava. Opening hours are Tuesday to Sunday 1000–1800 (April to October) and Saturday and Sunday 1000–1700 (November to March). Admission is Kč100 (free on the first Tuesday of the month).

Parts of the *Prague Zoo*, near Troja (tel: (02) 9611 2230; website: www.zoopraha.cz), are still currently closed in the aftermath of the flood at the end of August 2002. Visitors should check in advance before planning a trip there.

For a Whole Day

Kutná Hora: Now a UNESCO World Heritage Site, located 65km (40 miles) east of Prague, *Kutná Hora* came to prominence in the late 13th century, as a centre for silver mining. With the founding of the Royal Mint in 1308, a boomtown economy developed and, until the veins were exhausted, the town was second only to Prague in importance. The principal point of interest is the extraordinary Gothic *Cathedral of St Barbara*, with its tent-like roof

supported by three needle spires. Like many of the monuments in Prague, the cathedral design came from the workshop of Peter Parler. The building was financed by the miners' guilds, to honour their patron saint. For a taste of what the miners endured, the *Hrádek* in *Barborská Czech Silver Museum* offers tours into the mines (protective clothing is supplied).

Kutná Hora's main station is located in the suburb of *Sedlec* – linked to Prague by trains from Hlavní nádraží or fast trains from Masasykov nádraží, on Wilsonova at the eastern end of Hybernská (journey time – approximately 1 hour). Visitors must change to the local train for the town itself. There is also a bus to Sedlec from Prague, which leaves from outside metro Želivského.

Although most tourists pass swiftly through the dreary suburb of Sedlec, located three kilometres (two miles) northeast of the Kutná Hora town centre, it is worth walking from the train station to view the macabre *ossuary (kostnice)* on Zámecká. Part of the Cistercian Abbey complex – now the largest tobacco factory in Central Europe – the graveyard became internationally famous when Abbot Jindřich returned from Jerusalem with a pot of soil from Golgotha, believed to confer miraculous properties of preservation. Demand for burial came from as far away as Belgium and with the plague of 1318 adding another 30,000 bodies, it became necessary to add a crypt to hold all the bones. The noble Schwarzenberg family acquired the property in 1784. In 1870, they commissioned a local woodcarver to organise the remains. The resulting sculptures, chandeliers and even the Schwarzenberg crest must be seen to be believed. Visitors can reach the monastery with the ossuary by bus 1 or 4 from the town centre. Kutná Hora has a particularly good selection of pictorial signs pointing to all the sights.

The *Tourist Information Office*, Palackého náměstí 377 (tel: (0327) 512 378; website: www.kutnahora.cz), and the *Cultural and Information Centre of Kutná Hora*, Sankturin House, Palackého náměstí 377 (tel: (0327) 515 556; fax: (0327) 512 378; e-mail: infocentrum@kutnohorsko.cz; website: www.kutnohorsko.cz), can provide further information.

Karlovy Vary (Karlsbad): Founded in 1358, the Czech Republic's largest spa town, situated along the river Tepla, has long been a place of decadent extravagance, celebrity visitors and clandestine liaisons. The numerous spas and hotels reflect the past glory of the town. The grandest of all is the *Grand Hotel Pupp*, said to be the most elegant in the country. The town can be exceptionally crowded with tourists, especially during high season. Transport to *Karlovy Vary* is by bus from Florenc station (journey time – 2 hours 30 minutes) or train from Hlavní nádraží (journey time – 4 hours). Further information is available from *Kur-Info*, Vřídelní kolonáda, Karlovy Vary (tel: (017) 322 9312; website: www.karlovyvary.cz).

ACCOMMODATION

Hotel prices in Prague usually include 5% VAT on the room (and breakfast), 22% on any other meals and services (including the mini-bar), as well as city taxes (currently Kč15 per person per night). Many hotels quote their prices in Euros or occasionally US Dollars, however, payment should be made in Czech Koruna. The prices quoted below are the lowest standard rates for a double room, excluding breakfast but including relevant taxes, unless otherwise specified.

Business

Golden Tulip Diplomat Hotel

Very much a business hotel, the modern 400-room *Diplomat* is situated – as the name might suggest – on the edge of the diplomatic quarter, which is at the end of metro line A – convenient for both the city centre and the airport (airport buses stop in front of the hotel). Standard air-conditioned rooms have TV, telephone and voice-mail, while superior rooms include Internet connections. Full business services are available, including video-conferencing and secretarial services, as well as conference planning for up to 350 delegates, with state-of-the-art multimedia equipment. The relax centre on the ninth floor has a wonderful view of Prague Castle and features a fitness area, whirlpool bath, solarium and sauna. For a novel way to unwind, the basement houses Prague's first go-kart track.
Evropská 15, Prague 6
Tel: (02) 9655 9111. Fax: (02) 9655 9215.
E-mail: hotel@diplomatpraha.cz
Website: www.diplomat-hotel.cz
Price: From Kč6600/€210.

Grand Hotel Bohemia

Austrian-owned, this neo-Baroque hotel in the centre of the New Town dates back to 1925 and has now been restored to its original period style. With unobtrusive hospitality, exceptional service and full business facilities and services, the hotel is perfect for the business traveller. The stunning *Boccaccio Ballroom* can cater for up to 140 people. All guest rooms have satellite TV, direct-dial telephone with voice-mail, a modem point, a fax, a working desk and even a trouser press. The gourmet restaurant, *U Prašné Brány*, is complemented by a café and bar.
Králodvorská 4, Prague 1
Tel: (02) 3460 8111. Fax: (02) 2232 9545.
E-mail: office@grandhotelbohemia.cz
Website: www.grandhotelbohemia.cz
Price: From Kč9900/€315 (including breakfast).

Prague Hilton Atrium

This modern hotel, situated on the banks of the Vltava River, close to the International Business Centre, is Prague's largest hotel with 788 rooms and suites. It also has the country's largest atrium. The hotel is almost self-contained – even including a putting green and an indoor swimming pool.

Conference facilities are available for up to 1500 and audiovisual aids can be hired. Full secretarial services and a notary public are available. Standard rooms on floors one to four include telephones with voice-mail, while executive rooms and suites on floors seven and eight include modem connections.
Pobřeží 1, Prague 1
Tel: (02) 2484 1111. Fax: (02) 2484 2378.
E-mail: sales_prague@hilton.com
Website: www.hilton.com
Price: From Kč6500/€205 (excluding VAT).

Prague Marriott Hotel

This 293-room hotel is only a short walk from Náměstí Republiky, the Municipal House and the beginning of the Royal Road. Although the hotel is modern, its atmosphere is reminiscent of a less frantic era. Guests have access to a health club, pool, gym, sauna, as well as local tennis courts and a golf course. There is also an excellent restaurant, *Brasserie Praha* (see *Restaurants*). All rooms have telephones with voice-mail and modem points. There are 11 fully equipped conference rooms, accommodating 30–240 delegates and the business centre provides office hire, secretarial service, translations, Internet services, mobile phone hire and even a shipping service.
V Celnici 8, Prague 1
Tel: (02) 2288 8888. Fax: (02) 2288 8889.
E-mail: prague.marriott@marriott.cz
Website: www.marriott.com
Price: From Kč11,500/€365 (excluding VAT).

Luxury

Hotel Palace Praha

Just minutes south of Wenceslas Square, the *Palace* is one of Prague's finest hotels. Built in 1906, this Art Nouveau hotel has always attracted celebrities, from Caruso and Josephine Baker to Steven Spielberg and the Rolling Stones. The 114 rooms and ten suites are all air conditioned and furnished with period furniture. Telephone with voice-email, Internet access and satellite TV are standard; use of the sauna is also included. There is disabled access and a non-smoking floor, while rooms on the 'business floor' also have fax machines. The *Gourmet Club Restaurant* serves fine Czech and international cuisine, while the café-restaurant offers a bistro menu. There is also a piano bar serving snacks. Conference facilities for 30–250 people include a full range of audiovisual equipment. Secretarial and interpreting services are available.
Panská 12, Prague 2
Tel: (02) 2409 3111. Fax: (02) 2422 1240.
E-mail: palhoprg@palacehotel.cz
Website: www.hotel-palace.cz
Price: From Kč8800/€280.

Hotel Paříž Praha

Adjacent to the Obecní dům, the Hotel Paříž is one of Prague's neo-Gothic landmarks that incorporates Art Nouveau elements. The stunning ambience is complemented by the superb *Restaurant Sarah Bernhardt* (see *Restaurants*) and the *Café de Paris Bistro*. The air-conditioned, soundproof guest rooms are equipped with telephone and voice-mail, Internet connection and satellite TV. Photocopying and fax facilities are available for the business traveller and the Salon Violet caters for conferences of up to 55 people. Full audiovisual and PC equipment can be hired.

The hotel facilities include a fitness room, sauna, a relax room and massage shower.
U Obecního domu 1, Prague 1
Tel: (02) 2219 5195 *or* 2219 5666 (booking). Fax: (02) 2422 5475.
E-mail: pariz@hotel-pariz.cz (info) *or* booking@hotel-pariz.cz (booking)
Website: www.hotel-pariz.cz
Cost: From Kč5400/€170.

Hotel Savoy

The elegant rooms and the library complete with fireplace gives this large five-star hotel (55 rooms and six suites) in the Prague Castle district the ambience of a private club and make it popular with rock divas like Tina Turner and Cher. As well as a small gym and sauna, there is a beauty salon and hairdresser on the premises. Full business facilities are provided and all rooms are air-conditioned and equipped with fax machines with PC connection (ISDN line), telephones, satellite TV and DVD. The *Hradčany* restaurant is highly regarded and Sunday brunches are popular. The *Lobby Bar* is a fashionable meeting place for the Prague elite.
Keplerova 6, Prague 1
Tel: (02) 2430 2430. Fax: (02) 2430 2128.
E-mail: info@hotel-savoy.cz
Website: www.hotel-savoy.cz
Price: From Kč10,000/€320.

Radisson SAS Alcron Hotel

On one of the main streets off Václavské náměstí (Wenceslas Square), Prague's five-star Art Deco gem has been restored to its 1930s glory. The 211 rooms and suites are of a very high standard and all include telephone, fax and modem connections. With eight meeting rooms, including the spectacular glass-roofed *Crystal Ballroom*, the hotel makes a splendid conference venue. The business centre offers secretarial and translation facilities. Restaurants include *La Rotonde*, with terrace dining in the summer, and the Art Deco fish restaurant *Alcron* (see *Restaurants*). The Art Deco *BeBop* bar has nightly jazz. Guests have the use of a modern health club.
Štěpánská 40, Prague 1
Tel: (02) 2282 0000. Fax: (02) 2282 0100.
E-mail: sales.prague@radissonsas.com
Website: www.radisson.com
Price: From Kč7300/€230 (excluding VAT).

Moderate

Betlém Club

Situated on a quiet square opposite the faithful reproduction of Jan Hus' *Bethlehem Chapel*, the hotel's inside walls are filled with armour and old prints. The romance of the location is further enhanced with buffet breakfast served in the 12th-century cellars, although the rest of the hotel is mid-19th century. *Betlém Club* represents excellent value for its location – within walking distance of the Charles Bridge in one direction and Wenceslas Square in the other. All 21 rooms have showers and toilets, satellite TV, telephones and refrigerators.
Betlémské náměstí 9/257, Prague 1
Tel: (02) 2222 1574/5. Fax: (02) 2222 0580.
E-mail: betlem.club@login.cz
Website: www.betlemclub.cz
Price: From Kč3900 (including breakfast).

Hotel Cloister Inn

The *Cloister Inn*, which takes its name from a medieval convent that stood on the site, is located a short walk from the Charles Bridge and the Old Town Square. This quiet and gracious modern hotel in a classic location has 73 guest rooms comprising a bedroom and a sitting area with a comfortable chair and a desk. Some business and interpreting services can be arranged.
Konviktska 14, Prague 1
Tel: (02) 232 7700. Fax: (02) 232 7709.
E-mail: cloister@cloister-inn.cz
Website: www.guideprague.com/cloister/index.php
Price: From Kč3300 (including breakfast).

RESTAURANTS

The selected restaurants have been divided into five categories: Gastronomic, Business, Trendy, Budget and Personal Recommendations. The restaurants are listed alphabetically within these different categories, which serve as guidelines rather than absolute definitions of the establishments.

All restaurant prices in Prague usually include 22% VAT. If a service charge (usually 10–12.5%) has been added to the bill, it is customary to round the bill up to the nearest Kč10. However, where a service charge has not been included, diners should leave a tip of 10–15% of the bill. The prices quoted below are for an average three-course meal for one person and for a bottle of house wine or cheapest equivalent; they include VAT but do not include service charge or tip.

Gastronomic

Alcron

Prague's finest restaurant for fresh seafood, the *Alcron* is a discreet semi-circular room in the Radisson Hotel, with a back wall consisting of a restored floor-to-ceiling Art Deco mural. The seasonal menu includes dishes like roasted turbot, lobster (Canadian or Brittany) with beurre noisette, or mushroom *cordonetti* (thin noodles) with black truffles and grilled scallops. Reservations recommended. No lunch. Closed Sunday.
Radisson SAS Alcron Hotel, Štepánská 40, Prague 1
Tel: (02) 2282 0038.
Website: www.radisson.com
Price: Kč1500. Wine: Kč650.

Francouzská a Plzeňská Restaurace (French Restaurant in the Obecní dům, Municipal House)

The Obecní dům is Prague's greatest Art Nouveau treasure. Situated in Staré Město, the building was constructed between 1905 and 1910, with contributions from all the major Czech artists and architects, and has recently been restored to its original glory. The *French Restaurant*, designed by Osvald Polívka (who also created the façade and the café), mixes the new Baroque and Renaissance styles with Czech Art Nouveau – cylindrical glass and gold chandeliers oversee this wonderful setting. The six-course tasting menu is excellent value at Kč1750, which includes coffee and petits fours, as is the three-course lunch at Kč490 (Kč590 on Saturday). Seasonal dishes might include grilled Breton lobster with herb butter, artichokes filled with roasted vegetables and potato-fennel purée, coq au vin or grilled turbot. Reservations essential.

Obecní dům, Náměstí Republiky 5, Prague 1
Tel: (02) 2200 2770. Fax: (02) 2200 2778.
E-mail: info@obecnidum.cz
Website: www.frenchrest.obecnidum.cz
Price: Kč1700. Wine: Kč580.

Pálffy Palác Club

Situated in Malá Strana, the *Pálffy Palace* was built by the Lamintger family in the 17th century and is one of Prague's best-kept secrets. Acquired by the State in 1895, it housed archives of valuable manuscripts and then, during the Communist period, became a centre for propaganda. After the 1989 Velvet Revolution, the palace was transferred to the Prague Conservatoire and, in 1994, the restaurant on the top floor was opened. The Baroque atmosphere is maintained with period antiques, prints of composers on the walls and fresh flower arrangements. The restaurant holds 60 diners but this is doubled in the summer when the terrace, with its superb views, is open. The excellent dishes include veal tenderloin with chestnut sauce, duck breast grilled with gratinated onions and sun-dried plums, or roasted quails wrapped in bacon with apricot sauce. Sunday brunch and weekday lunch specials are recommended. Reservations recommended.
Valdštejnská 14, Prague 1
Tel/fax: (02) 5753 0522.
E-mail: palffy@seznam.cz
Website: www.palffy.cz
Price: Kč1200. Wine: Kč110 (half-litre carafe).

Restaurant Flambée

Flambée is housed in eighth-century vaults beneath the Betlem Palác in Staré Město and is one of Prague's finest restaurants. The atmosphere is Baroque with light colours, candles on tables and a piano in the evenings. The menu varies but dishes might include roast foie gras with truffle artichokes, stuffed lamb saddle under a pie crust, or young duck Nanteis carved at the table. There is a five-course tasting menu for Kč1760, while the business lunch at Kč490 is exceptional value. The wine vaults date from the eighth century and offer an exceptional and rare selection. Guests have included many heads of state, as well as Hollywood and music stars, like Tom Cruise or Michael Jackson. Reservations recommended.

Betlémský palác, Husova 5, Prague 1
Tel: (02) 2424 8512. Fax: (02) 2424 8513.
E-mail: flambee@flambee.cz
Website: www.flambee.cz
Price: Kč2000. Wine: Kč390.

U Maltézských rytířů (At the Knights of Malta)

Situated in Malá Strana and housed in Gothic and Romanesque cellar dining rooms, this candle-lit restaurant manages to be cosy and cheerful, despite rumours that it is haunted (although apparently the ghost does not appear until after the restaurant closes). Dishes might include venison Chateaubriand, roast fillet of pike-perch filled with smoked salmon and leeks, or roast saddle of boar marinated in wild spices and served with mushroom sauce. The desserts are well known, including homemade apple strudel and nut dough pancakes with homemade pear jam.
Prokopská 10 (off Karmelitská), Prague 1
Tel: (02) 5753 3666.
Price: Kč1000. Wine: Kč140.

Business

Brasserie Praha

Situated in the Marriott Hotel in Staré Město, this comfortable restaurant serves excellent food. The main restaurant has very high ceilings, many windows and tables with plenty of space between them, however, the balcony is for VIP guests. The stuffed boneless quail with truffle sausage and chestnuts over turned vegetables and brandy sauce and the pork medallions with calvados sauce are among the many excellent dishes on offer. The weekday lunch buffet is excellent value at Kč395, as is Sunday brunch at Kč650. There are also good-value themed buffets in the evenings.
Prague Marriott Hotel, V Celnici 8, Prague 1
Tel: (02) 2288 1212.
Website: www.marriott.com
Price: Kč700. Wine: Kč525.

Dobromila

Czech, French and Continental influences mix in this ambitious restaurant in Staré Město. The simple

Crossing the Charles Bridge to the Old Town

Photo: Czech Tourist Authority

exterior is matched inside, with dark pink walls and candles on the tables. The dishes are generally lighter than normal Czech cuisine and are based on recipes by the famous early 19th-century Czech chef, Magdalena Dobromila Rettigová, with a modern French influence. Classic dishes include carp boiled with wind vegetables, pheasant served Jewish style with traditional gnocchi and wild spices, or rabbit saddle with juniper and saffron sauce.
Jungmannova 10, Prague 1
Tel: (02) 9624 6464.
E-mail: dobromila.fr@quick.cz
Price: Kč500. Wine: Kč390.

Hybernia

Providing large portions at modest prices in Staré Město, *Hybernia* has built up a large lunchtime following, which includes heads of state and their bodyguards. The simple ochre decor with arches complements the comfortable high-backed chairs. The main restaurant is divided into smoking and non-smoking sections, while there is a 14th-century basement vault for large parties, as well as a quiet court-yard in summer. Dishes include pork knee Muskateer (with horseradish, mustard and pickled cucumber), and chicken skewer with smoked salmon, bacon and vinegar herb sauce. The steaks are also good here.
Hybernská 7, Prague 1
Tel/fax: (02) 2422 6004.
E-mail: hybernia@volny.cz
Website: www.hyberniapraha.cz
Price: Kč400. Wine: Kč153.

Posezení U Čiriny (Gathering at Cirina's)

This restaurant has dark yellow walls with many old prints and serves predominantly Hungarian/Slovak specialities. The chef, Irena Kosiková, was once the personal chef to President Havel. Dishes include fillet of pork with Hungarian salami and Niva (Czech blue cheese), or pork cutlet filled with chicken liver and bacon, or chicken steak au gratin with ham, peach and cheese.
Navratilova 6, Prague 2
Tel: (02) 2223 1709.
Price: Kč300. Wine: Kč160.

U Prince

Just south of the famous clock tower in Old Town Square in Staré Město, *U Prince* offers outdoor dining under canvas (with very comfortable chairs and excellent heating in the winter) and a large indoor dining room with chandeliers and many old prints on the walls. A wide range of dishes are available, including Prince's Teriyaki (including beef sirloin, pork fillet mignon and chicken breast), roasted zucchini with Niva (Czech blue cheese) on herb butter, or pork medallions on roasted pepper sauce. There is live traditional jazz daily from 2000 inside.
Staroměstské náměstí 29, Prague 1
Tel: (02) 2421 2807. Fax: (2) 2421 3807.
E-mail: reserve@hoteluprince.cz
Website: www.hoteluprince.cz
Price: Kč500. Wine: Kč599.

Trendy

Bazaar Méditerranée

Situated in Malá Strana, this complex with labyrinthine interiors includes a restaurant and wine cellar, while a café and oyster bar are situated in the courtyard. The garden terrace outside also offers dining with excellent views. The vast basement with high ceilings includes a large proper dining room, a bar and a dance area. Every evening, there is live music followed by a DJ. The excellent selection of dishes includes chicken breasts with Niva (Czech blue cheese) and basil sauce, lamb couscous, variace ryb à la Bazaar (fish with crab claw, langouste and vegetables served with three sauces), coq au vin, or Moroccan kefta (lamb meatballs in vegetable ragout).
Nerudova 40, Prague 1
Tel: (02) 5753 5050. Fax: (02) 5753 4438.
E-mail: info@restaurantbazaar.cz
Website: www.restaurantbazaar.cz
Price: Kč700. Wine: Kč295.

Gitanes

Romany, Slavic and Latin influences combine in this colourful restaurant in Malá Strana. The decor is Romany and Balkan with high-back cloth-covered chairs under a blue ceiling painted with flowers. The walls are full of paintings, decorated plates and other memorabilia. Pasta dishes are excellent here but diners should really experiment with dishes like *escalope krardjordje* (pork escalope with thick cream and tartar sauce), hot *pljeskavica* (minced meat with hot peppers and onions), *cevapcici* (spicy mincemeat) and *sarma* (sauerkraut filled with minced meat and rice). The sweet corn bread is excellent and *tafahija* (cooked apple filled with nuts and whipped cream) is an exceptional dessert.
Tržiště 7, Prague 1
Tel: (02) 3334 4800.
Price: Kč500. Wine: Kč250.

Korea House

The understated Korean decor upstairs and the mixed Korean and Japanese decor in the basement complement the excellent food. Korean specialities include *bulgogi* (thinly sliced beef or pork cooked at the table), *shab shab* (beef and seafood with many vegetables) and chicken in hot sauce. For two people, the hot crab stew is especially recommended. The downstairs restaurant can be booked for private parties and karaoke is also possible. Closed Sunday.
Sokolská 52, Prague 2 (near metro I.P. Pavlova)
Tel: (02) 2426 6246. Fax: (02) 2426 6247.
E-mail: info@koreahouse.cz
Website: www.koreahouse.cz
Price: Kč700. Wine: Kč270.

Malý Buddha (Little Buddha)

Up (both horizontally and vertically) the street from Bazaar Méditerranée and another good choice after a day exploring Hradčany (Prague Castle, the museums and the Loreto), *Malý Buddha* is a tearoom serving 51 varieties of tea and a restaurant specialising in Vietnamese temple food. As one would expect, the restaurant is softly Eastern in flavour with cane chairs and candles on tables. Dishes include fried crab with salad, pork with bamboo shoots and soy beans and prawns with Chinese mushrooms and bamboo shoots. There are a number of vegetarian meals and a few unusual items like crocodile or shark with onion and garlic with chilli, and octopus or squid with spicy sauce. Healing wines are also a speciality at Kč45 per glass. No smoking. Closed Monday. No credit cards.
Úvoz 46, Prague 1
Tel: (02) 205 3894.
Price: Kč300. Wine: Kč160.

Scandals

Last year's hot location continues to attract attention and the opening of the basement cocktail bar will only add to its reputation. Its location in Josefov, on a corner site with high ceilings, allows for vast window frontage, which complements the dark walls and narrow modern paintings. As well as excellent steaks and burgers, the menu includes teriyaki-glazed chicken with fried noodles and lemon sauce, or grilled catfish with buttered red wine sauce on a bed of wild mushrooms.
Dlouhá 7/992, Prague 1
Tel: (02) 2481 8320. Fax: (02) 2481 4298.
E-mail: scandals@volny.cz
Price: Kč500. Wine: Kč390.

Budget

Ambiente

A bright and lively American-style basement restaurant, *Ambiente* has yellow walls, blue pillars, palm fans on the ceiling and many old American pictures, adverts and records on the walls. Latino music is played at a volume that permits conversation without shouting. Main dishes include pasta, Creole, Tex-Mex, ribs and steaks, while the salads are particularly good. Special dishes include grilled goose breasts with coriander and rosemary, and beef fillet with turkey breast and bacon. The chocolate fondue with banana, pineapple or seasonal mixed fruits can be ordered with plain, milk or white chocolate.
Trebizského 8, Praha 2 (Vinohrady)
Tel: (02) 2271 4990.
Price: Kč500. Wine: Kč165.

Chilli's

Situated in the New Town, this is possibly the best Tex-Mex restaurant in Prague, with a Southwest American/Mexican decor that matches the food without allowing the restaurant to become a theme restaurant. The menu includes burritos, quesadillos, enchilladas and *huevos rancheros*, as well as a few Czech dishes like roast pork fillet in a potato pancake. The Czech fritters with plum sauce and whipped cream are an extremely good dessert choice. No credit cards.
Vladislavova 18, Prague 1
Tel: (02) 2494 9305.
Price: Kč250. Wine: Kč125.

Příčný Řez (Cross-Cut)

A new restaurant in the New Town that has a steadily growing following, *Příčný Řez* is situated on a corner site, with a balcony area and large windows. The atmosphere is contemporary but cosy; it is hoped that this is the first of a new generation of local restaurants. The basement becomes a dance club most nights. Good dishes include steaks, chicken roll stuffed with ham and cheese served with a light basil sauce, breast of duck in a tarragon lime sauce or salmon on a bed of fettucine with gorgonzola sauce with capers. Service is excellent and the Sunday brunch is well worth a visit. Reservations recommended for the evening. No credit cards.
Příčná 3, at Reznická, Prague 1
Tel: (02) 2223 3283.
Price: Kč225. Wine: Kč159.

Sate

Just up the hill from Malý Buddha (see *Trendy* above) and near to Prague Castle, *Sate* is an excellent Indonesian-inspired restaurant. The basic, slightly Eastern decor is dominated by a large aquarium. Signature dishes include *nasi goreng* (fried rice with meat and prawns) and *opor ayam* (chicken in coconut milk). No credit cards.

Photo: Czech Tourist Authority

Springtime in Prague

Pohořelec 3, Prague 1
Tel: (02) 2051 4552.
Price: Kč250. Wine: Kč110.

Thrakia

A Bulgarian restaurant with decorated wooden plates on the light ochre walls, *Thrakia* is an excellent venue for an inexpensive meal. Kebabs, homemade sausages, *srny* (stuffed cabbage), moussaka, cold cucumber soup and *Mešena skara* (four types of meat roasted on a lava grate) are all good options. No credit cards.
Rubešova 12, Prague 2 (behind the National Museum)
Tel: (02) 2422 3490.
Price: Kč400. Wine: Kč135.

Personal Recommendations

Art Diogenes

Art Diogenes is a proper Greek restaurant featuring classic Greek cuisine in a discreet basement, with a Greek decor that is not overpowering. The restaurant recently moved to a new location in Malá Strana, which has a summer garden. Live music shows are possible for special evenings. Great dishes include pork stuffed with plums, souvlaki, scallops in red wine with cheese and steak Paphos style with asparagus.
Nerudova 23, Prague 1
Tel: (02) 2492 2645.
E-mail: art@diogenes.cz
Website: www.diogenes.cz
Price: Kč700. Wine: Kč290.

Kampa Park

To the right of the Malá Strana end of the Charles Bridge, *Kampa Park* is an excellent choice especially in the summer, when diners can eat beside the Vltava River. Redecorated since the flood in August 2002, the restaurant is primarily painted in dark ochre with lights and chandeliers in holders with glass wings. Signature dishes include the butter poached lobster served with creamy carrot purée, green peas and Jerusalem artichoke foam, the seared venison with parsnip fondant, figs, peach, foie gras and venison reduction, and the pepper steak with crispy potato cake, onions, zucchini and cognac sauce. Guests have included Michael Douglas, Lou Reed, Hillary Clinton and Johnny Depp. Reservations

recommended. Cigars and pipes are not allowed indoors before 2200.
Na Kampe 8B, Prague 1
Tel: (02) 5753 2685. Fax: (02) 5753 3223.
E-mail: kontakt@kampapark.com
Website: www.kampapark.com
Price: Kč1500. Wine: Kč485.

Restaurant Sarah Bernhardt

Around the corner from the Francouzská a Plzeňská Restaurace in the Obecní dům (see *Gastronomic* above) is Prague's other great Art Nouveau restaurant in the Hotel Paříž in Staré Město. The decor is far less ornate than the Obecní dům but still a classic example of this style, with original prints and adverts from the early 20th century. Dishes include duck breast marinated in fresh ginger, honey and lemon grass with Masala sauce, brewery goulash, or barracuda fillets with strong fish volunté. There is a pianist in the evenings and the Sunday brunch is good value.
Hotel Paříž, U Obecního Domu 1, Prague 1
Tel: (02) 2219 5195. Fax: (02) 2422 5475.
Website: www.hotel-pariz.cz
Price: Kč1500. Wine: Kč280.

U Modré kachničky (At the Blue Duckling)

This intimate and esteemed restaurant in Staré Město is one of Prague's best for game. The candlelit dining room – set in a Renaissance-era home with vaulted ceilings and murals painted by the restaurant's artistic owners – is relaxing and appropriate for the quality of the dishes. The seasonal menu can include leg of boar with rosehip sauce, fallow deer medallions with juniper berries flambéed in bororicka (a gin-like spirit), and leg of rabbit in garlic with spinach and potato dumplings. Pancakes with raspberries and strawberries flambéed in armagnac is the exceptional dessert here.
Michalská 16, Prague 1
Tel: (02) 2421 3418.
Price: Kč600. Wine: Kč130.

U Zlatých Andělů (At the Golden Angel)

Most of the restaurants around or near the Old Town Square (Staroměstské náměstí) offer good to excellent meals, although their location often leads to higher prices than one would pay elsewhere. *U Zlatých Andělů* is one of the old-style restaurants with well-spaced

tables under chandeliers. There have been restaurants on this site since the 18th century, with diners including Mozart, the Queen of Denmark and even the Russian anarchist, Bakunin. Old-style Czech dishes include the roast beef with cream sauce, the venison steak with cranberries, and the breast of chicken with peaches. However, the exceptional dish here is the half duck, roasted with sauerkraut, bacon and bread dumplings.
Celetná 29, Prague 1
Tel: (02) 2232 8237. Fax: (02) 2232 8069.
Website: www.pgc.cz/anglicky/r_andele_aj.htm
Price: Kč400. Wine: Kč126.

ENTERTAINMENT

Nightlife

Venues shift in and out of popularity with great rapidity in Prague. With soaring rents in the centre of town, almost all of the clubs around Wenceslas Square have either closed or spread out throughout the city. Establishments tend to be divided to meet the demands of three groups – expensive (for the newly wealthy Czechs and tourists), cheap and trashy (for the young tourists, backpackers and ex-pats) and cheap and innovative (for young Czechs and visitors in the know). Many bars are open late (until 0200 or 0400) and clubs even later (until 0500, 0600 or even later).
In the Czech Republic, however classy, a 'nightclub' usually means a table-dancing club, often with a full strip show and even a sauna and Jacuzzi. Clubs that feature live music are generally known as 'music clubs' or 'jazz clubs', while establishments that offer dancing are known as 'discos' or 'dance clubs'.
Dress codes and admission prices do not feature strongly in Prague's nightlife. The minimum drinking age in the Czech Republic is 18 years and drinks are inexpensive at Kč30 for half a litre of beer or Kč70–100 for imported beers and Kč15–60 for spirits (depending on the drink – vodka is cheaper than whisky, for example).
Weekly listing (in English) of music events can be found in the *Prague Post* (website: www. praguepost.com) and the racier fortnightly *Prague Pill*. *Do města* offers monthly nightlife listings in Czech.

Bars

Currently popular are *Kozička*, Kozí 4, Prague 1, and the grill bar *Belle Epoque*, Křižovnická 8, Prague 1. *Bugsy's*, Pařížská 10, Prague 1 (website: www.bugsysbar.cz), with over 200 cocktails, attracts the business account set. Currently popular with younger Czechs are *Scandals*, Dlouhá 7/992, Prague 1, *Studio A. Rubin*, Malostranské náměstí 9, Prague 1, which has a dancefloor, *Marquis de Sade*, Templová 18, Prague 1, and *Akropolis*, Palác Akropolis, Kubelíkova 27, Prague 3 (website: www.palacakropolis.cz), with three bars (no cover charge), a concert space and the trendy *Kaaba Café*.

Casinos

Gambling plays an important part in the lives of many Czechs and is big business in Prague, with new casinos opening all the time. Most casinos present a sophisticated but relaxed atmosphere, with bets ranging from a minimum Kč20–25 to a maximum of Kč5000 (in a few cases like the Jalta, Kč10,000). The minimum age for gaming is 18 years and a passport or ID is required. Entrance fees are as high as Kč500 in some establishments. Casinos can be found in many of the luxury hotels, where evening dress is essential for admission.

Most of the best casinos are found on Na příkopě and Václavské náměstí. Recommended venues include *Casino Admiral Praha*, Palace of Culture, 5 Kvetna 65, Prague 4, the 24-hour *Casino Jalta Happy Days*, Václavské náměstí 35, Prague 1, the *VIP Club Casino*, Hotel Ambassador, Václavské náměstí 7, Prague 1, and *Casino Palais Savarin*, Na příkopě 10.

Clubs

Prague has more than its fair share of trashy discos but a welcome alternative is the world music that continues to attract great attention in both clubs and live venues in the city. Best for world music is *Akropolis*, Kubelíkova 27, Prague 3 (website: www.palacakropolis.cz), a complex of concert spaces, bars and a café. Latino clubs include *La Habana*, Míšeňská 12, Prague 1, and *Mánes*, Masarykovo nábřeži 250, Prague 1, a 1930s functionalist gallery, which is only open on Friday and Saturday. *Roxy*, Dlouhá 33, Prague 1, caters to the dance crowd and features a hidden tea house. *Radost/FX*, Bělehradská 120, Prague 2 (website: www.radostfx.cz), is one of the few clubs to survive the early post-Revolution period and offers up a glamorous mix of house and techno music. It also includes a vegetarian restaurant and art gallery. *Industry 55*, Vinohradská 40, Prague 2, stays open very late for a youngish crowd, playing techno, house, trance and other dance music. *Klub Lávka*, Novotného Lávka (by the Charles Bridge), is a popular top-40 club with good food and a wonderful riverside terrace. *Karlove Lázné*, also located at Novotného Lávka, claims to be the largest club in central Europe. The four floors all feature different music styles, with synth techno on the fourth floor, retro on the third, radio pop occupying the second and hip hop and funk blasting out on the first floor, complete with MCM café.

Live Music

For Czech folk music, see the *Music* section in *Culture*. Otherwise, *Malostranské beseda*, Malostranské náměstí, Prague 1, features everything from 1920s jazz to contemporary rock. The *Lucerna Music Bar*, Vodičkova 36, Prague 1 (website: www.musicbar.cz), serves up a rich blend of excellent jazz, rock and 80s nights, with plenty of space to dance. Jazz has been popular in Prague since the 1920s and even though the scene has contracted with the growth of rock music, there are still excellent venues for an evening of jazz and blues. *AghaRTA*, Krakovská 5, Prague 1, is undoubtedly the city's best venue (website: www.agharta.net). The *Jazz & Blues Café*, Na příkopě 23, Prague 1, has good programming and sound reproduction that more than make up for the terrible decor. The best local musicians often meet up for late-night jam sessions at *U staré paní*, Michalská 9, Prague 1. *U Malého Glen*, Karmelitská 23, Prague 1, is one of the oldest jazz bars in Malá Strana, with good food and a comfortable, friendly atmosphere. *Reduta*, Národní třída 20, Prague 1, remains infamous as the club where President Clinton attempted to establish a cool image by playing the sax for President Havel but is very touristy.

The image of the cowboy has been inexplicably popular in the Czech Republic since the 1920s. *První Prag Country Saloon Amerika*, Korunní 101, Prague 3, is only open until 2300 but can provide a wild evening of country and western music – dress the part and mosey on down.

Sport

The Czechs' greatest sporting success has come from tennis, with Ivan Lendl, Martina Navrátilová and Jana Novotná being regarded as national sporting heroes. Success was also enjoyed in 1998, when the Czech ice hockey team was the Olympic champion. The Czech national football team can be something of a dark horse, occasionally displaying significant prowess in international events. In the domestic league, the First Division rivalry between *Sparta Praha* (website: www.sparta.cz) and *Slávia Praha* (website: www. slavia.cz) is very strong. Prague's other First Division team, *FK Victoria Žižkov* (website: www. fkviktoriazizkov.cz), is based at the *Viktoria Žižkov Stadium*, Seifertova třída, Prague 3 (tel: (02) 2272 2045). Sparta Praha play at their own *Letna Stadium*, Milady Horákové 98, Prague 7 (tel: (02) 2057 0323), while Slávia Praha play at the new *Eden Stadium*, Vladivostočká 1460/2, Prague 10 (tel: (02) 6731 1102). In the 2002/2003 season, Sparta Praha were second in the league and Victoria Zizkov were third. Although Slavia Praha finished outside the top three, it managed to defeat Sparta Praha in the final of the Czech cup.

Ticketpro, Rytířská 31, Prague 1 (tel: (02) 2161 0162; e-mail: etix@ticketpro.cz; website: www.ticketpro.cz), and other locations around the city, is the best source for tickets to sports events.

Prague has not yet developed a comprehensive network of sports facilities that cater for visitors and facilities for foreign sports fans are limited.

Fitness Centres

As is the case throughout Eastern Europe, fitness centres are appearing everywhere – most are members only and many have questionable levels of supervision. Luxury hotels catering for the business community often are the best option for visitors. *Fitness Club InterContinental*, Náměstí Curieových 43/5 (tel: (02) 2488 1525; website: http://prague. czech-republic.intercontinental.com), and *Fitness Centre Hilton*, Pobřežní 1, Prague 8 (tel: (02) 2484 2913; website: www.hilton.com), both offer a good range of workout machines and are open to non-residents. Other clubs include *Body Island*, Uruguayská 6, Vinohrady, Prague 2 (tel: (02) 2251 7955; website: http://web.quick.cz/bodyisland), and *Sport Centrum*, YMCA, Na Poříčí 12 (tel: (02) 2487 5811). Rates generally start at around Kč70 per day.

Golf

The Czech Republic is poorly lacking in golf courses and Prague's only 18-hole course is members only, although top hotels may be able to arrange access, if given enough advance warning. *Golf Club Prague*, Plzeňská, Prague 5 (tel: (02) 5721 5185), is a nine-hole course and driving range, with green fees of approximately Kč230 per round.

Ice Skating

Skating is an extremely popular sport, however, rinks are only open for one or two-hour periods, usually at weekends. Good rinks include *Sportovní hala* (*HC Sparta*), Za elektrárnou 419, Prague 7 (tel: (02) 7292 8273), and *Vokovice*, Za lány 1, Prague 6 (tel: (02) 362 759). From December, outdoor skating is popular at the reservoirs at Divoká Šárka and Hostivař. The picturesque scenery and the many grog sellers make this an attractive activity, although hire of skates is problematic.

Squash

As this sport is growing in popularity, new squash courts regularly appear in Prague, however, demand still outstrips supply and courts are often booked months in advance. *Squashové centrum*, 15 Václavské náměstí (tel: (02) 2400 9232), offers an unbeatable central location. The three courts are open daily until 2300 and equipment is available for hire.

Swimming

With crowds of children and high chlorine levels at the municipal pools, the smaller pools in luxury hotels are often a better option. The indoor pool at *Aréal*, *Strahov Stadion*, Olympijská, Prague 6 (tel: (02) 3301 4113), is used by competitive swimmers and also offers sauna facilities. The pool is closed during July and August. The *YMCA*, Na Poříčí 12 (tel: (02) 2487 1111), also caters for serious swimmers and is open until 2200. The fee is Kč1.10 per minute. Swimming in the reservoirs outside Prague is extremely popular, although sites can be dirty and crowded.

Tennis

Outdoor courts, generally clay, cost about Kč120–200 per hour, while indoor courts can run to Kč250–550. Most courts are floodlit and open in the evening, some until 2300. Advance booking is essential. *Tenisový klub Slávia Prague*, Letná Park, Prague 7 (tel: (02) 3338 4033), has eight excellent floodlit clay courts, as well as fast-surface indoor courts. Booking is usually essential at the *Český Lawn Tennis Klub*, Ostrov Štranice 38, Hološovice, Prague 7 (tel: (02) 2481 0238; website: www.cltk.cz), with six floodlit courts. *Tenis Club*, Střelecký Island (ostrov), also hires courts to the public.

Shopping

Shopping in Prague can be frustrating or rewarding, depending on the approach taken. Western chains and large stores around Václavské náměstí do not offer bargains and shoppers should seek out the smaller shops to browse and patronise the cafés when it all becomes too much.

Czech crystal and glassware are superb and often extremely good value. There are enough shops for one to spend an entire day on this alone. Cheap Czech crystal jewellery is found throughout the city. Czech garnets are considered the world's best. *Granat*, Dlouhá 28, Prague 1, are the specialists. Amber (*jantar*) can also be found at a bargain price, however, shoppers should stick to the Baltic variety – Russian shops sell a far more brittle and over-priced variety. Even in the markets it is possible to find beautiful and unique wood and ceramic pieces.

The early post-Revolution days, when exquisite pieces of Art Nouveau Daum and Loetz glass or a set of duelling pistols could be purchased at one-sixth of their value, are long gone but antiques still can be good buys. *Jan Hunek Starozitnosti*, Pařížská 1, Prague 1, sells beautiful Czech glass from the 18th century to 1930s Art Deco. *Alma*, Vamentinská 7, Prague 1, specialises in porcelain, lace and folk costumes. Away from the centre, *Bazars* – glorified junk shops – occasionally turn up real finds. Time is needed for one to search them out but the rewards can be worthwhile. Antiquarian books and prints remain good buys but prices are rising. *Antikvariát Galerie Můstek*, 28 Rijna 13/Národní 40, Prague 1, and *Antikvariát Karel Krenek*, Celetná 31, Prague 1, both offer an excellent selection. *Antikvariát Pařížska*, Pařížská 8, Prague 1, specialises in prints and maps from the 16th to 19th centuries. Classical music CDs are often very low in price. The best selections are at *Bonton Megastore*, Palác Koruna, Václavské náměstí 1, Prague 1, and *Bontonland* (*Supraphon*), Jungmannova 20, Prague 1. Supraphon, the privatised state recording company draws on a wealth of stunning Czech music in its archives (website: wwwsupraphon.cz).

Shop opening hours vary widely but are generally Monday to Friday 0800–1000 and 1700–2000 and Saturday 1000–1400. Many tourist shops and larger stores remain open all day including Saturday and Sunday afternoons. Most areas of the city have at least one 24-hour food shop. Almost everything closes on public holidays.

Most markets only sell food and their hours generally correspond to standard shopping hours. The best markets for crafts, hand embroidery, leather goods and charming wooden toys are *Havelská*, Prague 1, and the craft stalls in Staroměstské náměstí. Christmas Markets throughout December are excellent for gifts but visitors should beware of the professional pickpockets and the strength of the hot grog.

VAT stands at 22% for most products and services. Goods must be removed from the Czech Republic within 30 days of purchase, in order for visitors to claim a tax refund. Bills must be confirmed at the border or at the Duty Free Tax desk of the Customs Office in the Departure Hall (Terminal North) of Ryzyně airport upon departure. Actual VAT refunds must be realised by Global Refund at the Thomas Cook cash desk or the Czech Made Products shop in Finger A, or VAT MAX at the transfer desk of Menzies Aviations Group. In Terminal South, actual VAT is refunded in the transit space in Free Shop by Global Refund (website: www.globalrefund.com).

Culture

Music has always been regarded as an important part of education, both through the schools and through town musicians, whose jobs included teaching as well as performing. From its formation in the late 18th century, the *Prague Conservatoire* has been a world-class training ground for musicians and composers. In the 1780s, Dr Charles Burney described Bohemia as 'a nation of musicians' adding: 'It is said by travellers, that the Bohemian nobility keep musicians in their

houses; but in keeping servants it is impossible to do otherwise.' Behind the big four Czech composers – Smetana, Dvořák, Jánaček and Martinů – lie literally hundreds of others, whose talents ranged from good to near great. Virtuoso instrumentalists and conductors have always been manifold. Surprisingly few were actually born in Prague but almost all of them were residents at one time or another.

With the eclipse of Prague by Vienna, under the Hapsburgs, attention shifted from the political sphere to the artistic. Mozart was more highly regarded in Prague than he was in Vienna and every famous composer and virtuoso was welcomed with open arms, with conductors of the Prague opera including Weber, Mahler and Zemlinský. One of the downsides of the fall of Communism was the substantial cutback of state funding and the entire arts scene is experiencing financial difficulties in the shift to a market economy. Artists are still regarded as respected members of the community and every possible effort is made to further their careers. Performance standards have, if anything, risen still higher.

Prague is unquestionably a musical city. Prague Spring Festival is one of the major world-class festivals but concerts abound throughout the year. And this is not the end of the matter – buskers are found everywhere and the streets, squares and bridges echo with everything from talented students from the Conservatoire, to Dixieland jazz, folk and world music and pop.

Tickets can be purchased at *Čedok* (see *Tourist Information*) and *Ticketpro*, Rytířská 31, Prague 1 (tel: (02) 2161 0162; e-mail: etix@ticketpro.cz; website: www.ticketpro.cz). Ticketpro accepts credit cards but does not book for the bigger classical venues. *Bohemia Ticket International* (*BTI*), Na přikopě 16, Prague 1, is the only ticket agency that will accept ticket purchases from abroad (tel: (02) 2422 7832; e-mail: order@ticketsbti.cz; website: www.ticketsbti.cz), although those who choose to do this can expect a substantial booking fee. Ticket agencies tend to mark up ticket prices, especially for foreigners. Purchasing tickets from the relevant box office usually saves quite a bit of money. Unsold tickets costing more than Kč30 can often be purchased 30 minutes before performances. This is especially good value at the National Theatre. Visitors should purchase Spring Festival tickets from the festival office, to avoid a hefty mark-up.

Weekly listings for all musical events can be found in *The Prague Post* (website: www.praguepost.com) and fortnightly in *Prague Pill*. *Do Města* offers monthly cultural listings in Czech.

Music

Prague boasts two world-class orchestras. The *Czech Philharmonic* (website: www.ceskafilharmonie.cz) is based at the neo-classical *Rudolfinum*, Alšovo nábřeží 12, Prague 1 (tel: (02) 2489 3311). The *Prague Symphony Orchestra* (website: www.musica.cz/iso/pso) has now returned to its restored home at the *Smetana Hall* of the Obecní dům, Náměstí Republiky 5, Prague 1 (tel: (02) 2200 2101; fax: (02) 2200 2100; e-mail: info@obecni-dum.cz; website: www.obecni-dum.cz). Various other orchestras also turn in high-quality performances and important venues for chamber music concerts include the *Church of St Nicolas* (*Kostel sv. Mikuláse*), Staroměstské náměstí, Prague 1, the *Nostic Palace*, Maltézské náměstí 1, Prague 1 (tel: (02) 2451 0131), *St Agnes' Convent* (*Kláster sv. Anežky české*), U milosrdných 17, Prague 1 (tel: (02) 2481 0835), and the exquisite Baroque *Chapel of Mirrors* (*Zrcadlová kaple of the Klementinum*), Mariánské náměstí, Prague 1 (tel: (02) 2166 3111, ext 331).

Smetana Hall, Municipal House

The standard opera repertoire is offered at the *State Opera*, Wilsonova 4, Prague 2 (tel: (02) 2422 7266; website: www.sop.cz). The *Estates Theatre*, Ovocný trh, Prague 1 (tel: (02) 2421 5001; website: www.estatestheatre.cz), where *Don Giovanni* was first performed, still presents occasional Mozart operas. Czech repertoire is principally presented at the *National Theatre* (*Národní Divadlo*), Národní 2, Prague 1 (tel: (02) 2490 1111 or 2490 1668; website: www.narodni-divadlo.cz). Performances here tend to be more innovative and ticket prices are lower.

Unusual music shows are presented in the summer at the *Křižíkova Fontana* (*Krizik's Fountain*), in Luna Park, Prague 7, with shows linking music, lights, fountains and water features.

Theatre

Misery Loves Company, Celetná 17, Prague 1 (tel: (02) 2480 9168), presents consistently high-quality productions of international plays and Czech works in English translations. They are active in the summer at the reconstructed *Globe Theatre*, Výstaviště Hološovice, Prague 7 (tel: (02) 2271 1515).

There are currently seven companies presenting shows combining music, dance and 3D effects with black (ultraviolet) light features, known as Black Light Theatre. Performances run from classical to rock and all the companies are excellent. They include *All Colours Theatre*, Rytířská 31, Prague 1 (tel: (02) 2161 0173; website: www.blacktheatre.com), *The Black Light Theatre*, Jiří Grossmann Theatre, Václavské náměstí 43 (tel: (02) 2421 9812; website: www.wow-show.com), *The Black Theatre Prague*, Na přikopě 10 (tel: (02) 2224 4358; website: www.volny.cz/black.theatre), *Image*, Image Theatre, Pařížská 4, Prague 1 (tel: (02) 2231 4448), *Black Light Theatre of Frantisek Kratochvíl*, Národní 25, Prague 1 (tel: (02) 2108 5287), *Ta Fantastika*, Palác Unitaria, Karlova 8, Prague 1 (tel: (02) 2222 1367), and *The Black Light Theatre of Prague of Jiří Srnec*, Divadlo Reduta, Národní třída 20, Prague 1 (tel: (02) 2493 3487).

Photo: Czech Tourist Authority

Old Town by night

Dance

Classical ballet is prevalent at the major theatres but modern dance companies, with their experimental and multimedia techniques, offer a far more exciting evening. *Ponec*, Husitská 24A, Prague 3 (tel: (02) 2481 7886; website: www.divadloponec.cz), a new performance space owned by the dance company, *Tanec Praha* (website: www.tanecpha.cz), presents a constantly varied and challenging programme of Czech and international companies. Folklore shows combining energetic dancing and music with colourful costumes have not lost their exuberance or high standards under the demands of tourists. *Restaurace U Marcanu*, Veleslanínská 14, Prague 6 (tel: (02) 3536 0623), offers a year-round show with a traditional Czech dinner for a reasonable fixed price. Excellent summer shows are presented at the theatres *Divadlo na Klárove*, Nábreží Edvarda Beneše 3, Prague 1 (tel: (02) 2171 1611), and *Divadlo u hasicu*, Římská 45, Prague 2 (tel: (02) 2422 7693).

Film

The majority of foreign films in Prague are screened in the original language – subtitled films are billed as '*titulek*' and films dubbed into Czech are '*dabovat*'. The best cinema for feature films, as well as experimental and late-night programmes, is *64 U Hradeb*, Mostecká 21, Prague 1 (tel: (02) 5753 1158). *Lucerna*, Vodičkova 36, Prague 1 (tel: (02) 2421 6972; website: www.lucerna.cz), for all its faded glory, remains an atmospheric Art Deco movie palace. *Cinema Broadway*, Na příkopě 31, Prague 1 (tel: (02) 2161 3278), is the best venue for epic films. *MAT Studio* at Karlovo náměstí 19, Prague 1 (tel: (02) 2491 5765), shows Czech films with English subtitles at 2200 – with a capacity of 24, advance purchase of tickets is essential. The Czech film archive uses *Ponrepo/Bio Konvikt*, Bartolomějská 13, Prague 1 (website: www.volny.cz/mjos/ponrepo). A one-year membership costs Kč120.

South of Smíchov is the Barrandov Studio. Built by Václav Havel's grandfather, after World War I, it soon became the centre of the Czech film industry. Czech directors, camera operators and technicians were soon in demand across Europe. The earliest important silent films set in Prague, however, were German. Paul Wegener's *The Golem* (1920) vividly brought to life the medieval legend of the Jewish clay automaton – with studio expressionist sets that recreated the claustrophobic ghetto – and Henrik Galeen's *The Student of Prague* (1926), a tale of the *Doppelgänger* (evil double) that recreates the early 19th-century city. Gustave Machatý's *Erotikon* (1929) reveals Art Deco Prague in all its glory, while his *Extase* (1933), winner at the Venice Biennial in 1934, created a sensation with its daring nude scene by Austrian actress Hedy Kiesler (later, in Hollywood, Hedy Lamarr). Czech animation came to prominence in the 1930s and remains influential in the genre.

The implementation of Stalinist doctrine under the Communists largely isolated the industry from the West. However, innovations were still possible and in 1947, Jiří Trnka created the first puppet film, establishing a new genre that helped maintain a Czech presence in cinema in the West. The 1950s also saw the training of a new generation of filmmakers who, with the relaxation of restrictions in the 1960s, gave rise to the superb Czech New Wave. The finest films of this period were undoubtedly *Closely Observed Trains* (1966) and *The Shop on Main Street* (1965). Since the Velvet Revolution, Czech filmmakers seem to have lost their way, remaining in awe of the New Wave and attempting to maintain an identity in the wake of the influx of Hollywood values. Ironically, those values that threaten to swamp Czech films have also served to revive the industry – low costs and quality technicians have made Prague a major location for filming. *Amadeus* (1984), *Mission Impossible* (1996), *Les Miserables* (1998), *From Hell* (2001) and *Frankenstein* (2003) are just a few of the feature films filmed there.

Cultural Events

The Czechs have always been known for their musical ability, as well as their love of music. One of the world's largest festivals, now entering its 59th year, the *Prague Spring International Music Festival* (website: www.festival.cz) continues this fine musical tradition. Every year, the festival starts on 12 May – the day Smetana died in 1884 – and the opening concert always features his great cycle of symphonic poems, *My Country*. *Prague Autumn* (website www.pragueautumn.cz), in September, is a slightly shorter and less intense music festival, which still features many Czech and international performers. Standing outside the main tourist season, it can be a slightly more relaxed event for visitors.

Literary Notes

The German poet, Edward Mörike, wrote a novella called *Mozart's Journey to Prague* (1855), which is a delightful, if fanciful, account of the composer's trip in 1787, to conduct the premiere of *Don Giovanni*. Jan Neruda – the 'Czech Dickens' – provides fascinating 19th-century vignettes in *Lesser Town Tales* (1878), while Gustav Meyrik's *The Golem* (1969) remains the classic version of the story concerning the medieval Jewish automaton. Although also Gothic in character, F Marion Crawford's occult novel, *The Witch of Prague* (1891), provides a wealth of description of the city in the late 1880s. Prague's most famous writer, Franz Kafka, generally took a more jaundiced view of the city, filtered through the bewildering and menacing absurdities of Hapsburg bureaucracy. His masterpieces include *The Trial* (1925), *The Castle* (1926) and *The Transformation and Other Stories* (1915). Just as Kafka has spawned an industry of souvenirs, so too has the anti-hero of Jaroslav Hasek's comic masterpiece of World War I, *The Good Soldier Svejk* (1921). Karel Capek's anti-utopian play, *R.U.R.* (1921), added the word 'robot' to the international vocabulary. Bohumil Hrabal's deservedly famous *Closely Observed Trains* (1965) offers a thoroughly unromantic picture of the final days of World War II. For the Stalinist period, Milan Kundera's *The Joke* (1967) is a far superior work to his better known *The Unbearable Lightness of Being* (1984). Since the Velvet Revolution, literature (often experimental) has flourished in the Czech Republic. Michael Viewegh's *Bringing Up Girls in Bohemia* (1994) offers a wry look at rampant capitalism and sex in modern suburban Prague.

SPECIAL EVENTS

Ball (Ples) Season, Jan–Mar/Apr (the beginning of Lent), various venues

Witches' Night, celebrates the death of winter with bonfires, 30 Apr, throughout the city

Prague Spring (website: www.festival.cz), 12 May–early Jun, various venues

Khamoro, festival of Roma (gypsy) culture, with music, films, theatre, dance, art (website: www.khamoro.cz), late May, various venues

Dance Prague (website: www.tanecpha.cz), Jun, various venues

Prague Autumn (website: www.pragueautumn.cz), mid-Sep, various venues

Burčák Season, sampling the half-fermented new season wines directly from the barrels, late Sep–early Oct, throughout the city

Vokaliza International Jazz Festival, late Oct, Lucerna Music Bar

Musica Iudaica, festival celebrating Jewish composers, Nov, various venues

Prague German-Language Theatre Festival (website: www.theater.cz), Nov, various venues

International Festival of Advent and Christmas Music (website: www.orfea.cz), late Nov–early Dec, various venues, with a final concert of all choirs in the Old Town Square

St Nicholas's Eve, men dress as St Nicholas, an angel and a devil, giving out sweets to good children, 5 Dec, near Charles Bridge, Staroměstské náměstí and Karlovo náměstí

Bohuslav Martinu Festival, music festival featuring the music of this 20th-century Czech composer, including a violin and violoncello competition, as well as concerts of chamber, symphonic and dramatic music (website: www.martinu.cz), early Dec, Lichtenstein Palace and the Ruldophinum

Prague Christmas, festival of carols and customs, mid-Dec, various venues including concerts in the Old Town Square

St Sylvester's Eve, 31 Dec, wild revelry complete with fireworks, especially around Václavské nám?stí and the Old Town Square

RIO DE JANEIRO

Rio de Janeiro is an awe-inspiring city of contrasts: impossibly steep granite mountains jut out of the ocean between glorious stretches of golden sand, impeccable colonial buildings nestle in between modern glass skyscrapers and verdant forests tumble down hillsides into densely populated residential areas. It is a city high on life, a city of beach worship, football, samba and Carnival. And high above all this fun and frivolity stands Rio's ever-present, iconic landmark – the statue of Christ the Redeemer.

The continuing strength of foreign currencies against the Brazilian Real and the national football team's success in the World Cup have both helped to make Brazil – and Rio in particular – an increasingly popular and affordable year-round destination. As well as the city's well-known landmarks of Corcovado and Sugar Loaf mountains, Rio boasts a wealth of attractions and activities, plus great food, music and entertainment – enough to keep a visitor busy for any length of stay.

Situated in southeast Brazil, on the natural port of the Baía de Guanabara (Guanabara Bay), Rio is a city of over ten million people squeezed between the ocean and the mountains. The *cidade marvilhosa* (marvellous city) is a melting pot of cultures and peoples in varying degrees of wealth or poverty. In Rio, the rich and poor live together and the exclusive areas stand in stark contrast and close proximity to the slum areas or *favelas*. But no matter what their background or economic standing, the *Cariocas* – as the citizens of Rio are known – are characterised by a passion and enthusiasm for life, which is on full show during Rio's famous annual Carnival.

Central to the *Carioca* lifestyle is the beach. From dawn until dusk and even after dark, the residents of Rio can be found enjoying the long stretches of sandy coastline with which the city is blessed. The beach is not merely a place to absorb the sun's rays but also an important venue for sports, socialising and even business. It is a people-watcher's paradise – clothing is minimal and bodies are bronzed and beautiful. The famous Copacabana and Ipanema beaches are magnets for Brazilians and tourists alike.

It has taken 500 years for Rio to transform itself into one of the world's greatest cities. On 1 January 1502, Portuguese explorers sailed into Guanabara Bay and named it Rio de Janeiro (River of January), under the mistaken impression that it was an enormous river mouth. The French attempted to gain control of the bay in 1555 but were finally evicted by the Portuguese in 1567.

The Portuguese colony was based on sugar cane and agricultural products throughout the 17th century, until the discovery of gold in the nearby Minas Gerais region led to the city's emergence as a control, export and taxation centre. Black slaves formed the majority of the population in these early days of trading and the African influence is still present in the city's culture. The capital of colonial Brazil was moved from Bahia (now Salvador) in 1763 to Rio de Janeiro and the city began to flourish, especially when coffee became the predominant export in the 19th century. After the Portuguese monarchy was exiled from Portugal, when Napoleon conquered Lisbon, Rio became their home and eventually the capital of an independent Brazilian Empire. Finally, Brazil became a Republic in 1889; Rio de Janeiro remained its capital until 1960, when the Federal government was transferred to Brasilia.

Rio has continued to grow and has become a popular destination not only for tourists but also for migrants from other parts of the country. Despite its development, the city still has more than its fair share of social problems. Strong divisions exist between the 'haves' and the 'have-nots'. Attempts have been made to curtail crime, although both residents and tourists should remain alert to petty thieves.

Rio's best season is undoubtedly the summer months, between December and February, culminating with Carnival. Temperatures can rise to around 40°C (104°F) or more, which is ideal weather if tourists do as the Brazilians do and visit the beaches rather than rush around.

Photo: Brazilian Tourist Office

Bird's eye view of the city

TRAVEL

Getting There By Air

Aeroporto Internacional do Rio de Janeiro/Galeão Antonio Carlos Jobim International Airport (GIG)

Tel: (21) 3398 4106. Fax: (21) 3398 3581.
Website: www.infraero.gov.br
Rio International Airport is an important hub for flights from Europe and North America, as well as for major domestic flights, serving over six million passengers per year. It is located on Ilha do Governador, in Guanabara Bay, some 20km (13 miles) north of Rio. There is easy access from the airport to the city by road.
Major airlines: Brazil's national airline, *Varig* (tel: (21) 2534 0333; fax: (21) 2210 3871; website: www.varig.com.br), connects Rio to international and domestic destinations. Many airlines operate frequent flights to Rio International Airport, including *Aerolineas Argentinas, Air France, American Airlines, British Airways, Continental, Delta Airlines, Iberia, Qantas, TAP, United Airlines* and *Vasp*.
Airport facilities: Facilities include a 24-hour bank, several bureaux de change, ATMs, a selection of restaurants, shops, duty free, a pharmacy, post office, 24-hour hospital, tourist information and car hire from *Avis, Hertz* and *Localiza*.

Business facilities: Guests at the airport's *Luxor Aeroporto* hotel (tel: (21) 2468 8998; fax: (21) 3398 3983; e-mail: aeroporto@luxor-hotels.com.br; website: www.luxor-hotels.com) may use the hotel's business and conference facilities. Diners Club cardholders have access to the *Diners Club VIP Lounge* (tel: (21) 2462 3379), which provides refreshments and business facilities. The lounge is open daily 0630–2300 and is located on the second floor at the international voyages registration desk.
Transport to the city: *Real* (tel: (21) 2560 7041) operates air-conditioned buses from the first floor of the airport to Receiro dos Bandeirantes, via the city centre, the Rodoviária Novo Rio bus terminal, Santos Dumont Airport (see below), Flamengo and along the seafront between Copacabana, Ipanema and Leblon, where many hotels are situated. The bus runs approximately every 15 minutes daily 0500–2300 (journey time – 45 minutes to 1 hour) and costs R$5 (per journey). Fixed-rate taxis can be booked at the kiosk near the airport arrivals gate. The fare is R$56 to Copacabana and R$42 to the city centre.

Aeroporto Santos Dumont (SDU)

Tel: (21) 3814 7070. Fax: (21) 2533 2218.
Website: www.infraero.gov.br
Situated beside the city, on Guanabara Bay, the domestic airport of Santos Dumont serves the Rio to São Paulo shuttle (departing every 30 minutes 0630–1845, with a limited service on weekends) and other small domestic flights, air taxis and private aeroplanes.
Major airlines: *Transbrasil* (tel: (21) 297 4422 *or* (0800) 151 151), *Varig* (tel: (21) 2534 0333; fax: (21) 2210 3871; website: www.varig.com.br) and *Vasp* (tel: (21) 3814 8081; website: www.vasp.com.br/en) all provide domestic services.
Airport facilities: Tourist information, left-luggage, banking and exchange facilities are available, along with car hire from *Avis* and *Hertz*.
Business facilities: Diners Club cardholders have access to the *Diners Club VIP Lounge* (tel: (21) 2532 4167), which provides refreshments as well as business facilities, including a fax machine, photocopying, computers and Internet connection. The lounge is open daily 0600–2000 and is located on the main floor in arrivals.
Transport to the city: The airport is served by the *Real* (tel: (21) 2560 7041) bus service into the city centre (see above), which costs R$5 (journey time – 20 minutes). Taxis are also readily available and cost between R$5 and R$10 to the Centro. A trip to Copacabana costs approximately R$15. It is a 15-minute walk to the Centro from Santos Dumont airport.

Approximate flight times to Rio de Janeiro: From London is 11 hours; from New York is 10 hours; from Los Angeles is 14 hours; from Toronto is 12 hours and from Sydney is 20 hours.
Arrival/departure tax: The international departure tax is US$36. Domestic departure tax is between US$3 and US$5. Both are payable upon departure, in either R$ or US$ although not a combination of the two.

Getting There By Water

The *Cais do Porto do Rio de Janeiro* (tel: (21) 2291 2122) regulates all water traffic in Guanabara Bay. Cruise ships anchor in the port during the summer and during Carnival. Ferry, hydrofoil and catamaran services depart from *Estação das Barcas*, beside the Praça XV de Novembro in the Centro. Tickets are available for purchase here. The ferry terminal is very basic and tourist services are limited. Nevertheless, there are many banks (with ATMs), shops and restaurants in the immediate area.
Ferry and boat services: Boat and yacht hire is available from *Marina da Glória* (tel: (21) 2205 6716). Ferries, hydrofoils and catamarans depart from the *Estação das Barcas* for the commuter route across the Guanabara Bay to Niterói and Paquetá island – both are popular as day trips from Rio. Cheap, regular and scenic, the route is plied by a number of companies. *Barcas S A* (tel: (21) 2533 6661) and *Telebarcas* (tel: (21) 2533 7524) operate daily ferry services, which are cheaper, slower and better for taking in the scenery. *Transtur* (tel: (21) 2533 4343) and *Aerobarcos do Brasil* (tel: (21) 2533 4343) provide daily hydrofoil and catamaran services.
Transport to the city: Regular public buses (see *Public Transport*) run from the *Estação das Barcas* to the Centro, Copacabana and Ipanema. Taxis are also readily available. Barcas Metrô station is situated nearby but the Centro is only a short walk away.

COST OF LIVING

One-litre bottle of mineral water: R$0.70
33cl bottle of beer: R$1.15
***Financial Times* newspaper:** R$13
36-exposure colour film: R$12
City-centre bus ticket: R$1.30 or R$1.50 (air conditioned)
Adult football ticket: From R$10
Three-course meal with wine/beer: From R$20

1 Real (R$1) = £0.22; US$0.33; C$0.48; A$0.53; €0.31

Currency conversion rates as of July 2003

Getting There By Rail

Rail travel in Brazil is extremely limited and is not a viable option for travellers getting to or around the country. There is no single national rail company and any passenger services are few and far between. Trains that do run are often slower than the buses. Information on the trains that do exist is available from *SuperVia* (tel: (21) 2588 9494; website: www.supervia.com.br).
There are two rail terminals located in the city's Centro area – *Estação Dom Pedro II*, Central do Brasil, Praça Cristiano Ottoni (tel: (21) 2296 1244), and *Estação Barão de Mauá*, Leopoldina, Avenida Francisco Bicalho. There are no passenger facilities at either station.
Rail services: Most train services from Rio are for cargo. The overnight train to São Paulo, *Trem de Plata*, has been suspended and there are no replacement services.
Transport to the city: Estação Dom Pedro II is situated right in the Centro area, opposite Central Metrô station. The closest Metrô stations to Estação Barão de Mauá are São Cristóvão and Estácio. Visitors should take the buses marked Centro. Taxis are also available at the stations.

Getting There By Road

Brazil has an expansive system of federal highways, designated by the letters 'BR', which account for 70% of the road network. Minor roads, provided and maintained by the state of Rio de Janeiro, are designated by the letters 'RJ'. Road conditions are poor and lacking in signs. The national speed limit on highways is 110kph (68mph) but drivers seldom adhere to the rule. Accidents and road fatalities are distressingly common.
The minimum driving age is 18 years. Foreigners should carry an International Driving Permit as well as a driving licence from their country of origin and third-party liability insurance is required by law. Driving is on the right-hand side of the road and the rules are generally similar to those in the USA. By law, drivers and passengers must wear their seatbelts. The maximum legal alcohol to blood ratio for driving is 0.06%.
Touring Club Do Brasil (tel: (21) 3824 0070; website: www.touring.com.br) provides information and assistance to foreign motorists in cities and on highways, where the driver is a member of a similar organisation in his/her own country. Car insurance and 24-hour roadside assistance is also offered.
Emergency breakdown service: *Touring Club Brasil* (21) 3824 0070.

Routes to the city: The BR-116 from Porto Alegre passes through Curitiba, where it picks up traffic from Foz do Iguaçu and continues on through São Paulo, all the way to Rio de Janeiro. Coastal highway BR-101 runs from Natal, through Salvador to Rio de Janeiro and beyond. However, there is a faster inland route from Salvador on BR-116, which connects with the BR-040 from Brasilia at Belo Horizonte. The BR-116 and BR-040 lead into Rio along Avenida Brasil. The main highway continues along the coast before emerging from Túnel Novo at Copacabana. From here, the Avenida Atlântica runs alongside the beach to Ipanema and Leblon.

Approximate driving times to Rio: From São Paulo – 6 hours; Brasilia – 20 hours; Foz do Iguaçu – 21 hours; Porto Alegre – 26 hours; Salvador – 28 hours.

Coach services: International and interstate buses operate from the *Terminal Rodoviária Novo Rio*, Avenida Francisco Bicalho, in Santo Cristo (tel: (21) 2291 5151; website: www.novorio.com.br). The station consists of an arrivals and departures side and has a tourist office that is able to help with transportation advice into the city. Facilities include left-luggage and a bureau de change (for cash only). Long-distance coaches also depart from the more conveniently located *Menezes Cortes* terminal, Rua São José, Centro (tel: (21) 2544 6667).

International services go to Asuncion (Paraguay), Buenos Aires (Argentina), Montevideo (Uruguay) and Santiago (Chile). Interstate buses travel to major Brazilian cities and tourist centres. There are many service providers, including *Trans Brasiliana* (tel: (21) 2253 9104; website:

www.transbrasiliana.com.br), with connections to Belem, and *Expresso Brasileiro* (tel: (21) 2253 5121), which operates a service to São Paulo.

Getting Around

Public Transport

There is no unified public transport system in Rio, although *SECTRAN* (tel: (21) 2299 3468; website: www.sectran.rj.gov.br) oversees all forms of organised public transport.

The **underground** service provided by *Metrô Rio* (tel: (21) 3982 3600; website: www.metrorio.com.br) is safe, clean, air-conditioned, fast and efficient, although limited in the area it covers. The two lines operate Monday to Saturday 0600–2300. Line 1 runs from Siqueira Campos (Copacabana) to Sãens Pena (Tijuca), while Line 2 runs from Estácio (Centro) to Pavuna, in the north of the city. Metrô tickets are only available for purchase at the stations – R$1.47 for a single journey or R$14.70 for a carnet of ten tickets. Visitors are advised to keep their wits about them when emerging from stations into unfamiliar surroundings, as pickpockets are common.

Buses are cheap, regular and run to all parts of the city. There is no integrated service – the main providers include *Transbrasiliana* (tel: (21) 2253 4787 or 9104), *Real* (tel: (21) 2263 7689) and *Novo Horizonte* (tel: (21) 2233 7210). Services operate 24 hours and are relatively safe – incidences of crime are rare, although travellers must exercise caution during rush hour and at night, when pickpockets prey. Tickets are available for purchase from the conductor,

who sits next to the turnstile at the back of the bus. These cost R$1.30 per journey or R$1.50 on the air-conditioned *frescão* buses.

An integrated Metrô and bus **pass**, called *Metrô/Ônibus*, is available for R$2.60 at Metrô stations.

Taxis

Yellow taxis operate with a meter and can be hailed on the street. The flag, *bandeira*, indicates the tariff and usually reads '1'. However, after 2300, on Sunday and on holidays the tariff will be '2', which indicates a price hike of about 20%. Taxis are fairly priced, although some late-night drivers might quote excessive fixed prices. Travellers should check that the meter is reset and indicates the correct tariff. The minimum fare is currently R$2.50. Tourists are

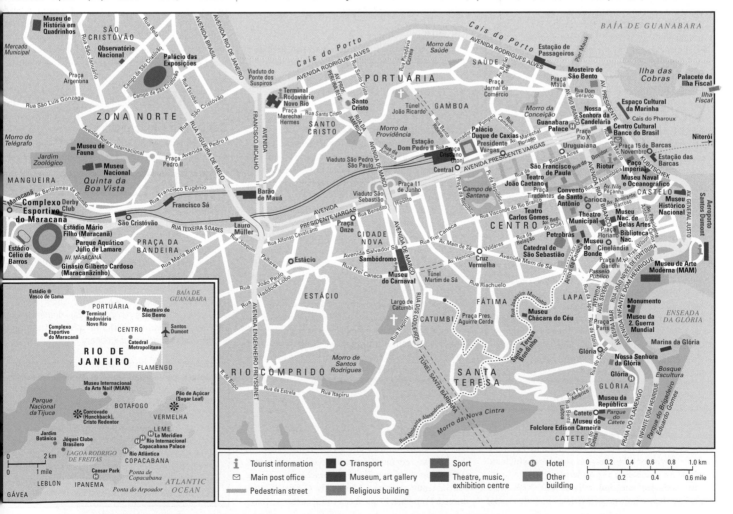

BUSINESS PROFILE

Rio is Brazil's top tourist attraction and consequently the city's main industries revolve around tourism and the service and financial sectors. Banking is important and the city is home to the second most active Stock Exchange in Brazil, the *Bolsa da Valores do Brasil*. As a city, Rio has the second best economy in South America, behind that of São Paulo, also in Brazil. Rio is also a major player in Brazil's industrial production and the city's industries are responsible for producing goods such as processed foods, chemicals, pharmaceuticals, clothing, furniture and textiles.

Brazil has a large economy with well-developed mining, manufacturing, service and agriculture sectors. Despite its wealth and continued growth (GDP growth was 1.51% in 2001), Brazil's inflation (7.5% September 2001–02) and the country's unemployment levels (7.1% in 2000) remain high. The city's unemployment rate of 3.8% in 2000 is considerably lower than the national figure. Nevertheless, the disparity between rich and poor is wide and particularly evident in the city, where crime has become an unofficial industry in its own right.

The economy became stable following the introduction of a new currency, the Real, in 1994. Introduced at a value level with the US Dollar, the development brought renewed confidence and an economic boom to the country. But this success came to an end when world recession and budgetary mismanagement finally led to the devaluation of the Real in 1999. The IMF soon resumed lending to Brazil and the economy bounced back against all expectations. But Argentina's debt default and devaluation of the Peso in January 2002 led to further instability in the region. Brazil's economy and currency looked set to follow suit, until the IMF came forward with a US$10 billion loan package that stabilised the country. The new president, Luiz Inacio Lula da Silva, of the left-wing Partido dos Trabalhadores (PT) took office on 1 January 2003. The business community at first worried that the president's social policies would harm the economy but his government appears to have held confidence and the mood in the country is one of hope.

Foreigners have been allowed to invest in the Brazilian Stock Exchange since 1996. To entice more foreign investment, the government abolished trade restrictions, privatised industries and lowered tariffs. Due to the number of consulates in the city, many companies favour Rio as a South American base. Multinational companies and key Brazilian companies based in Rio include *Shell, Texaco, Esso, Petrobras, Embratel* and *Petroleo Ipiraga.* Most businesses are located in the Centro area of the city or in Barra de Tijuca, where Rio's massive conference centre, *Riocentro*, is situated.

strongly advised only to use taxis that have an official identification sticker in the window.

Special taxis – either blue or red – operate from the airports. Payment is by pre-paid vouchers, which are available for purchase at airport kiosks.

Radio taxis are safe and reliable but 30% more expensive than yellow taxis. Providers include *Central de Táxi* (tel: (21) 2593 2598), *Coopertramo* (tel: (21) 9944; website: www.radio-taxi.com.br) and *Transcopass* (tel: (21) 2560 4888). The minimum fare for radio taxis is currently R$2.50. Brazilians generally do not tip taxi drivers, although rounding the total fare up to the nearest Real is appreciated.

Limousines

Most hotels and travel agencies can provide a private car with an English-speaking guide. A reputable company is *Golden Car* (tel: (21) 2275 4748; e-mail: goldencar@ riomaster.com.br), which provides Rolls Royce cars with English-, Spanish- or Portuguese-speaking drivers, for R$1800 for four hours (minimum). *Grace Festas* (tel: (21) 2516 9297; e-mail: gracefestas@leg.com.br) has a fleet of Mercedes Benz mini-limousines available for approximately R$400 per hour.

Driving in the City

With such a good public transport system, there is little need for tourists to drive in Rio de Janeiro. Those who attempt it need nerves of steel and a solid sense of direction to cope with the hectic traffic and confusing one-way streets. However, driving is a good option for local excursions and visiting some of the further beaches. When driving, seatbelts should be worn and extreme caution employed. Doors should be kept locked. Rio's traffic is a law unto itself and parking is difficult everywhere, although practically impossible in the Centro. Rush hour is Monday to Friday 0800–0900 and 1700–1900, although some areas are bumper to bumper at many hours of the day. For visitors making a day trip to Rio by car, the best option is to park in a secure car park, leaving the car with an attendant. Parking in Rio is very cheap and costs from R$2 per day.

Car Hire

There are many car hire companies in Rio, including international providers. The minimum age to hire a car is 21 years, although this is sometimes higher, depending on company policy. Insurance is essential. A credit card is usually required as security but also for payment, as many companies are reluctant to accept traveller's cheques or US Dollars. Drivers must be in possession of an International Driving Permit along with a driving licence from their country of origin. Rates include the basic third-party cover, although collision waiver and personal accident insurance are extra.

Some major companies with car hire offices in the city include *Avis*, Avenida Princesa Isabel 350, Copacabana (tel: (21) 2543 8481; website: www.avis.com), *Hertz*, Avenida Princesa Isabel 334B, Copacabana (tel: (21) 2275 7440; website: www.hertz.com), and *Localiza*, Avenida Princesa Isabel 214, Copacabana (tel: (21) 2275 3340; website: www.localiza.com.br).

Rates vary according to the model of the car and whether or not it has air conditioning. Prices start at around R$89 per day or R$525 per week for a basic car with unlimited mileage and go up to around R$359 per day or R$2149 per week for an executive vehicle with unlimited mileage. It is sometimes possible for drivers to negotiate discounts and is usually cheaper for visitors to make an advance reservation from abroad.

Bicycle Hire

Rio has 74km (46 miles) of cycle paths that, wherever they exist, are very much preferable to riding in the city's traffic. Most paths run alongside beaches and extend intermittently from the Marina da Glória, Centro, through Flamengo, Copacabana and Ipanema, to Barra da Tijuca. Six kilometres (four miles) of cycle paths exist in the Tijuca National Park.

Energetic visitors can hire bicycles from *Special Bike*, Rua Visconde de Pirajá 135B, Ipanema (tel: (21) 2521 2686; e-mail: sbike@specialbike.com.br; website: www.specialbike.com.br), for R$60 a day. There are other outlets on Rua Figueiredo Magalhães, Copacabana (tel: (21) 2257 1726), and Avenida Borges de Medeiros, in front of Tom Jobin Park, Lagoa.

SIGHTSEEING

Sightseeing Overview

Rio's main attraction is its scenery. There is a stunning view at every turn, as steep, granite mountains – such as *Corcovado* and *Pão de Açúcar* (Sugar Loaf) – rise dramatically above the Centro skyscrapers and curved golden beaches. And it is on these beaches, the most famous of which are *Copacabana* and *Ipanema*, that the energetic and leisurely lifestyle of the *Cariocas* is constantly on show. However, the city is also brimming with a wealth of cultural attractions.

Rio is divided into three zones – the Centro, Zona Norte (north) and Zona Sul (south). *Maracanã Stadium* is located in Zona Norte. Many of Rio's historic buildings and its museums and galleries are located in and around the Centro. However, Rio's biggest attractions, including its beaches, are found in Zona Sul. Because Rio's districts are spread out, it is best for tourists to take public transport to a particular area and then explore it on foot. Although security has been stepped up in many areas, thanks to the increased numbers of tourist police, visitors are still advised to keep their wits about them and carry only the minimum amount of money and possessions required.

Key Attractions

Corcovado (Hunchback)

The *Corcovado* (Hunchback) mountain – so named because of its distinctive shape – is home to probably

BUSINESS ETIQUETTE

Business cards are exchanged by way of introduction and businesspeople expect to deal with someone of an equal business status. Dress code is generally smart and suits are necessary when meeting heads of companies or attending semi-formal social functions in exclusive clubs and restaurants. Normal business hours are Monday to Friday 0900–1800. Quite often, however, business is done over dinner in a restaurant. Visitors would be advised to bring gifts, such as local confectionery.

Brazilians are more casual than their Latin American counterparts but it is important to dress neatly and offer respect. At the beginning of a conversation, at least, strangers should always be addressed with the formal 'o senhor' or 'a senhora' until they use the informal 'tu' or 'você'. Professional people will often be heard being addressed as 'o doutor' ('doctor'), whatever their line of business. Although many executives will speak English, it is advisable for business visitors to conduct business in Portuguese if possible.

the most memorable and identifying image of the city, that of the *Cristo Redentor* (Christ the Redeemer) statue. Inaugurated in 1931, the statue has become an immensely popular visitor attraction and icon for Rio, standing as it does on top of the 710m (2330ft) mountain. French sculptor Paul Landowski created the statue that stands 30m (99ft) high and has an eight-metre (26ft) pedestal containing a chapel capable of holding 150 people.

A road goes almost all the way to the top of Corcovado, although the site is best visited by the train, which travels a steep track through the forest to a station just below the summit. Weather permitting, there are stunning views of the city, beaches and the whole bay area below. After dark, floodlights illuminate the statue, providing a dramatic and spectacular sight visible throughout the city.

Corcovado Railroad Station

Rua Cosme Velho 513, Cosme Velho

Tel: (21) 2558 1329.

E-mail: trem@corcovado.com.br

Website: www.corcovado.com.br

Transport: Bus 180, 181, 182, 183 or 184 from Centro and Flamengo; bus 583 or 584 from Botafago, Copacabana and Ipanema (marked Cosme Velho).

Opening hours: Daily 0830–1900; first train up 0900, last train down 1800 (departures every 30 minutes).

Admission: R$20 (including train and entrance).

Pão de Açúcar (Sugar Loaf)

This conical mountain vies with the *Corcovado* for the visitor's vote of best overall panoramic view. Originally called *Pau-nh-Açquá* (high, pointed peak) by the Tupi Indians, it was renamed *Pão de Açúcar* (Sugar Loaf) by the Portuguese, who thought the shape of the 394m (1293ft) granite rock resembled moulds used to set sugar cane.

Climbers frequently ascend the rock but the less strenuous and most popular route to the top is by cable car – a system that has been in operation since 1912. The present Italian-style cars complete the journey in two stages. The first leg of the ascent takes visitors from Praia Vermelha to a height of 220m (720ft) above sea level, stopping at the summit of Morro da Urca. The second leg completes the journey to the Sugar Loaf over a distance of 750m (2460ft). The final stop offers fine views of the beaches, the city, the mountains of Tijuca National Park and the islands of Guanabara Bay. The area also has several, safe, wooded trails, where it is possible to escape the majority of the tourists who frequently arrive at the summit.

Pão de Açúcar cable car station

Avenida Pasteur 520, Praia Vermelha

Tel: (21) 2546 8400. Fax: (21) 2542 1641.

E-mail: bondinho@bondinho.com.br

Website: www.bondinho.com.br

Transport: Bus 107 from Centro, Flamengo and Botafogo; bus 511 or 512 from Copacabana, Ipanema and Leblon.

Opening hours: Daily 0800–2200.

Admission: R$24.

Copacabana

A large suburb of Rio, *Copacabana* is best known for its amazing, wide, sandy beach that stretches for four kilometres (2.4 miles). The beach is hugely popular with both residents and tourists and usually lies beneath a mass of beautiful and fit bodies. *Carioca* girls, in minimalist bikinis, bask in the scorching sun alongside families with their youngsters. The beach is always a hive of activity. Displaying the Brazilians' passion for sport, joggers and power walkers use the trademark

Rio Carnival

wavy black and white mosaic path that fringes the beach, cyclists whizz by in the cycle lane and the soccer fields and volleyball courts are in constant use. Strong currents can prove dangerous for swimmers, although an excellent lifeguard system exists.

The fishing community of Copacabana only became part of Rio when the Light and Power Company of Canada blasted through rock to establish tunnels for the Rio Tramway. In 1923, the Copacabana Palace Hotel was inaugurated and it quickly became a pivotal point in the area's activities. The establishment of other hotels, nightclubs and casinos attracted the rich and famous during the 1930s and 1940s, although the area fell in popularity when gambling was made illegal in 1946. Housing became important and Copacabana became significant both commercially and residentially. Once the ground surface area had been fully utilised, the only way to build was upwards. Nowadays, hotels and apartment blocks dominate the skyline along the busy avenues and crowded beach. It is advisable for visitors to take the very minimum of possessions and money, seeing as the often easily identifiable tourist is an obvious target for petty thieves.

Túnel Novo to Avenida Atlântica (along the beach)

Transport: Arcoverde Metrô station; bus 119, 121, 123, 127, 128, 173, 177 or 512.

Ipanema

This sophisticated neighbourhood is an enticing blend of beach, bars and boutiques. The area became famous worldwide with the success of the song, 'The Girl from Ipanema'. The song was written by composer Tom Jobim and lyricist and poet Vinicius de Moraes, who were inspired by local beauty Heloisa Pinheiro, who walked past the Velosa Bar each day when returning from school. The very bar where they sat, now known as *Garota de Ipanema* (Girl from Ipanema), is a popular meeting place for locals and a place of pilgrimage for visitors.

The focus of *Ipanema* is undoubtedly the beach, which is nestled between *Aproador* and *Leblon* beaches, beneath the imposing peak of *Pedro Dois Irmãos*. Like Copacabana, many people visit Ipanema to exercise or lie on the sand. But shopping is also a popular pastime and the area boasts a variety of fashionable and expensive outlets. Ipanema is also home to art galleries, a Sunday arts and crafts market

known as the *Hippie Fair* and workshop museums for jewellery shops *Amsterdam Sauer* and *H Stern*.

Avenida Atlântica to Ipanema

Transport: Bus 474, 523, 572, 583 or 584 (marked Ipanema or Leblon).

Centro (Centre)

The Centro provides a worthwhile break to beach life. One of the main attractions is the square, Praça 15 de Novembro, where the 18th-century *Paço Imperial* (Imperial Palace) and other grand buildings are located. Another interesting place is the *Museu Histórico Nacional* (National History Museum), which dates from 1762 and contains a fascinating collection of art, papers, weapons and other assorted artefacts documenting Brazil's history. Many churches are scattered around the area too. One of the most impressive is the *Igreja de Nossa Senhora da Candelária* (Church of Our Lady of the Candles), with its domed roof, marble interior, Portuguese wood carvings and fascinating stained-glass windows. The *Mosteiro de São*

Photo: Brazilian Tourist Office

Sugar Loaf cable car

Bento (Monastery of St Benedict) is a 17th-century monastery and UNESCO World Heritage Site, with an opulent interior of gilded woodcarvings and historic paintings. Art lovers will appreciate the *Museu Nacional de Belas Artes* (National Museum of Fine Arts), where paintings by Brazil's most prominent 19th- and 20th-century artists are exhibited along with examples of African and folk art.

Centro district

Transport: Cinelândia, Carioca or Uruguaiana Metrô stations; any bus marked Centro.

Paço Imperial
Praça 15 de Novembro 48
Tel: (21) 2533 4407. Fax: (21) 2533 4359.
Website: www.pacoimperial.com.br
Opening hours: Tues–Sun 1200–1800.
Admission: Free.

Museu Histórico Nacional
Praça Marechal Âncora
Tel: (21) 2550 9224.
Website: www.museuhistoriconacional.com.br
Opening hours: Tues–Fri 1000–1730, Sat and Sun 1400–1800.
Admission: R$5.

Igreja de Nossa Senhora da Candelária
Praça Pio X
Tel: (21) 2233 2324.
Opening hours: Mon–Fri 0800–1600, Sat and Sun 0900–1300.
Admission: Free.

Mosteiro de São Bento
Rua Dom Gerardo 68
Tel: (21) 2291 7122.
Opening hours: Daily 0800–1100 and 1430–1800.
Admission: Free.

Museu Nacional de Belas Artes
Avenida Rio Branco 199
Tel: (21) 2240 0068.
Website: www.mnba.gov.br
Opening hours: Tues–Fri 1200–1800, Sat and Sun 1400–1800.
Admission: R$4; free Sat and Sun.

Complexo Esportivo do Maracanã (Maracanã Sporting Complex)

Maracanã is the epicentre of Brazilian football and a Mecca for sports fans from around the world. The actual stadium (*Estádio Maracanã*) is also known as *Estádio Mário Filho* after a journalist, although mostly known just as Maracanã. It became the world's biggest stadium, capable of holding around 200,000 people, when it was built to host the 1950 World Cup Final. Tours of the stadium include a visit to the changing rooms, access to the stands for a view of the pitch and the opportunity to stand in the bronzed footprints of Pelé.

Football is a national obsession and even local matches are oversubscribed. Matches take place here up to three times a week, with evening kick-offs (see *Sport*). The atmosphere in the stadium during games is unique to Rio and an experience to remember. The almost Colosseum-like surroundings serve as a fitting venue for a multitude of fireworks, colourful flags, banners and the sounds of samba drums and whistles. The arena has also been used as the location for an address by Pope John Paul II. Frank Sinatra performed here in 1980. When Paul McCartney sang at the stadium in 1991, he gained an entry in the *Guinness Book of Records* for achieving the largest live audience ever for a solo singer.

Rua Prof. Eurico Rabelo, Maracanã
Tel: (21) 2568 9962.
Transport: Maracanã Metrô station; bus 238 or 239 from Centro, 455 from Copacabana or 464 from Ipanema and Leblon.
Opening hours: Daily 0900–1700; match days 0800–1100.
Admission: R$3 (non-match).

Further Distractions

Lagoa Rodrigo de Freitas (Rodrigo de Freitas Lagoon)

This lake is a huge open space in the middle of the city, offering fantastic views over the Ipanema skyline and jagged mountains, including Corcovado and Christ the Redeemer, which stand guard above. At the weekend, visitors can join the city's residents for a stroll or cycle on part of or the entire eight-kilometre (five-mile) path that surrounds it. There are a number of parks, exercise stations and leisure facilities positioned around *Lagoa Rodrigo de Freitas*. Visitors can join families on the lake, by hiring one of the swan-shaped pedalos. Nearby is the *Jardim Botânico*, a landscaped garden containing over 8000 Brazilian and imported species of flora. In the evening, the lakeside remains alive, as people dine at the 25 kiosks, each serving a different cuisine from various parts of Brazil or around the world. Some also provide live music for entertainment.

Bordered by Leblon, Ipanema, Jardim Botânico and Botafogo districts

Transport: Bus marked Leblon, Ipanema or Jardim Botânico (visitors should hop off at the lake or take a map and walk from these districts).

Jardim Botânico
Rua Jardim Botânico
Tel: (21) 2294 9349.
Website: www.jbrj.gov.br
Transport: Bus marked Jardim Botânico.
Opening hours: Daily 0800–1700.
Admission: R$4.

Museu Internacional do Arte Naif (International Naive Art Museum)

The *Museu Internacional do Arte Naif* contains one of the most comprehensive collections of naive art (folk art) in the world. The simplistic, colourful exhibits line the walls of an historic mansion, situated next door to Corcovado Railroad Station. The museum displays a selection of its collection of over 8000 works of folk art, which were created between the 14th century and the present day by artists from Brazil and 130 other countries. Works include a huge painting depicting Rio de Janeiro and Guanabara Bay, as well as a mural, which tells the history of Brazil and is the largest naive art canvas in the world. The

Photo: Brazilian Tourist Office

museum also displays temporary exhibits by renowned naive artists throughout the year.

Rua Cosme Velho 561, Cosme Velho

Tel: (21) 2205 8612. Fax: (21) 2205 8884.

E-mail: mian@museunaif.com.br

Website: www.museunaif.com.br

Transport: Bus 180, 181, 182, 183 or 184 from Centro and Flamengo; bus 583 or 584 from Botafogo, Copacabana and Ipanema (marked Cosme Velho).

Opening hours: Tues–Fri 1000–1800, Sat and Sun 1200–1800.

Admission: R$4.

Tours of the City

Walking Tours

A number of companies provide specialist guided walks in Rio, available on request. *Roteiros Culturais* (tel: (21) 3322 4872; e-mail: culturalrio@uol.com.br) runs cultural sightseeing tours to Rio's historic and colonial landmarks, led by History of Art Professor Carlos Roquette. The average tour takes four hours and costs US$40 per person. The 'Downtown Rio Tour' crosses the best areas of the oldest neighbourhood in town, from the Opera House District to the oldest and richest Baroque church in Rio.

Aventuras Rio (tel: (21) 3813 0312; e-mail: mail@ aventurasrio.com.br; website: www.aventurasrio.com.br) specialises in walks along one or more of the Tijuca forest's 200 trails, passing mountains, ruins and waterfalls. The price is R$75 for a four-hour Tijuca hiking trip, including transportation. *Rio Hiking* (tel: (21) 9271 0594; e-mail: tours@riohiking.com.br; website: www. riohiking.com.br) also provides English-language guided walks in Tijuca forest and up Rio's mountain peaks. The price for a day trip of approximately five to eight hours, including an ascent of Tijuca Peak, is R$165. Pick-up and transportation to Tijuca is included. *Favela Tour* (tel: (21) 9772 1133; e-mail: info@ favela.com.br; website: www.favelatour.com .br) offers guided tours to some of Rio's *favelas* (slum communities), revealing a different and spirited perspective on life in the city. The three-hour tour costs R$45 per person and hotel pick-up can be arranged.

Jeep Tours

Several companies offer jeep tours to out-of-the-way attractions. *Rio by Jeep* (tel: (21) 9693 8800 *or* 2575 8626; e-mail: riobyjeep@riobyjeep.com; website: www.riobyjeep.com) specialises in in-depth tours of Tijuca National Park and out-of-town beaches. Rio by Jeep offers two ecological tours of Tijuca forest. The 'National Park Tour' takes three and a half hours and costs US$30, while the 'Complete Tour' is longer, at five and a half hours, costing US$40. Hotel pick-up can be arranged.

Jeep Tour (tel: (21) 2589 0883 *or* 9977 9610 (24-hour information); e-mail: jeeptour@jeeptour.com.br; website: www.jeeptour.com.br) offers a number of different jeep tours, as well as walking tours, panoramic helicopter tours and combined tours in Rio and further afield. A four-hour tour of Tijuca forest costs US$35, while a three-hour tour of the Favela de Rocinha – the largest slum in South America – costs US$30. Hotel pick-up can be arranged.

Helicopter Tours

For a bird's eye view of the city, *Helisight* (tel: (21) 2511 2141; e-mail: infohsgt@helisight.com.br; website: www.helisight.com.br) offers sightseeing flights of various lengths and itineraries. A 15-minute flight covers the city centre, the Sambódromo, Maracanã stadium, Corcovado and the statue of Christ, Pão de Açúcar and Copacabana and Ipanema beaches and costs R$320. Departures are from one of three helipads, located at Rodrigo de Freitas Lagoon, Dona Marta Belvedere (access routed to the statue of Christ) and Sugar Loaf (cable car's first stop). Helipads are open daily 0900–1800 and night flights are also available from the Sugar Loaf and Rodrigo de Freitas Lagoon helipads.

Boat Tours

Saveiros Tour (tel: (21) 2224 6990; e-mail: saveiros@ saveiros.com.br; website: www.saveiros.com.br) operates a cultural boat tour around Guanabara Bay, providing a unique viewpoint of the city and Niterói island. The two-hour trip departs from the Gloria Marina daily at 0930. Tickets cost R$20 and are available for purchase at the Marina.

Excursions

For a Half Day

Parque Nacional da Tijuca (Tijuca National Park): Occupying an area of 120 sq kilometres (46 sq miles), *Tijuca National Park* (tel: (21) 2492 2252) is the world's largest urban forest and Brazil's only inner-city national park. The thick vegetation tumbles down steep hillsides into the backdoors of many of Rio's neighbourhoods. Much of the forest was cleared for coffee plantations in the 19th century but a successful reforestation project has restored the Atlantic Rainforest habitat, home to hundreds of species of plants and wildlife. Natural attractions include eucalyptus, jacaranda and jakfruit trees, forest flowers, as well as many species of birds, plus ocelots, monkeys, insects and reptiles. There are also waterfalls, grottoes and high viewpoints to be discovered. There are hundreds of walking trails through the forest. Paths are well signposted and maps are available at the park entrance. For travellers who do not want to go alone, many companies offer guided tours (see *Tours of the City*). There are also six kilometres (3.7 miles) of cycle paths to be explored. If all this sounds too strenuous, there are various picnic spots and lookout points for relaxation and enjoyment of the fresh air and natural surroundings.

Buses marked Boa Vista, such as bus 231 from Centro or 454 from Copacabana, go to Tijuca. The entrance to the park is at Praça Afonso Viseu, Alto da Boa Vista. The park is open daily 0600–2100 and admission is free.

For a Whole Day

Paraty: An enchanting colonial town, situated approximately 400km (250 miles) south of Rio, *Paraty* has been declared a UNESCO World Heritage Site. The town's churches, squares and townhouses with flourishing courtyards are still much as they were when Paraty was a chief port for the export of gold and coffee in the 17th and 19th centuries respectively. The winding, cobbled streets are open only to bicycles, horses and pedestrians and are surrounded by a wealth of old buildings containing appealing art galleries, restaurants and handicraft shops. The town sits on the ocean and is backed by lush Atlantic Rainforest. The most imposing church in town is the *Nossa Senhora dos Remédios* (Our Lady of the Remedies). Originally built for the white elite, it now contains works of art by local artists. Approximately a 20-minute walk north of the Old Town is the *Forte*

Christ the Redeemer statue

Defensor Perpétuo (Perpetual Defending Fort), on the Morro de Vilha. Its purpose in 1703 was to defend Paraty from gold-plundering pirates but today it houses the *Museu de Artes e Tradicoes Populares* (Museum of Popular Arts and Tradition).

From Rio, Paraty is best reached by car or bus. Nine buses leave daily from the Terminal Rodoviária Novo Rio in Rio. The journey takes approximately four hours and 30 minutes, although is much quicker by car. No vehicles are allowed in the Old Town itself, however. *Centro de Informações Turisticas*, Avenida Roberto Silveira, Paraty (tel: (24) 3371 2148), can provide further information.

ACCOMMODATION

Room rates incur a sales tax of 5% and a service charge of 10% is usually added to the bill at the end of a stay. Some hotels also charge a room tax of R$3 per night. Tips to individual members of staff are made at the guest's discretion. Tourists planning to visit Rio during Carnival or New Year should book well in advance and bear in mind that many hotels raise prices during these periods.

The prices quoted below are the lowest standard rates for a double room, excluding tax, service charge and breakfast, unless otherwise specified.

Business

Guanabara Palace

Situated in the hub of Rio's commercial district, the *Guanabara Palace* is a reliable option for the business traveller looking for a reasonably priced hotel with a few luxurious touches. The recently renovated façade is ultra modern and the rooms are tastefully decorated, with cream bed linen and wooden floors. All are equipped with telephone, TV, mini-bar and air conditioning. For business purposes, there is a convention centre and a business centre with Internet access, while leisure facilities include a rooftop pool with fine views of Guanabara Bay. The restaurant serves up extravagant buffet meals, as well as à la carte Brazilian and international cuisine. The hotel also offers secure parking, a laundry service, 24-hour room service and the assistance of staff who speak both Portuguese and English.

Avenida Presidente Vargas 392, Centro

Tel: (21) 2216 1313. Fax: (21) 2516 1582.

E-mail: reservas.guanabara@windsorhoteis.com.br

Website: www.windsorhoteis.com.br

Price: From R$240 (including breakfast).

Hotel Rio Internacional

Hotel Rio Internacional is unique in that all of its 117 rooms have wonderful sea views – most with private balconies. The hotel is situated in conveniently close proximity to the business district. The rooms are simply decorated with clean white walls and modern furnishings and are equipped with a safe, air conditioning, mini-bar, cable TV, radio, voice-mail telephone and a second line for Internet connection. Primarily aimed at business travellers, this beachfront hotel offers a bureau de change, three meeting rooms that can be combined into one conference space and a 24-hour business centre comprising two fully equipped offices. For relaxation purposes, a sauna, fitness centre and rooftop swimming pool are available. For wining and dining, there are two bars and the *Sabor e Vista* restaurant, which serves Brazilian and international cuisine. A bilingual staff provides a 24-hour room service.

Avenida Atlântica 1500, Copacabana

Tel: (21) 2546 8000. Fax: (21) 2542 5443.

E-mail: hotel@riointernacional.com.br

Website: www.riointernacional.com.br

Price: From R$462.

Le Meridien

This French-owned hotel is one of Copacabana's top establishments and its close proximity to the business district makes it ideal for corporate guests. The modern structure towers over the seafront with its 496 rooms, including 54 suites, all of which have recently been refurbished in an elegant, tropical style. Business travellers can make use of the hotel's bureau de change, convention centre and business centre – complete with meeting rooms, fax, colour printer and high-speed Internet access. Room service is available 24 hours and the staff is bilingual. Other facilities include laundry, a safe, cable TV, fitness suite, swimming pool and beach service. Live music is played in the *Bar de La Paix* and an executive buffet is served in the *Cafe Fleuri*. The 37th-floor *Le Saint Honoré* restaurant (see *Restaurants*) is considered one of the best in Rio, boasting fantastic views over the city's best-known landmarks of Pão de Açúcar and Corcovado.

Avenida Atlântica 1020, Copacabana

Tel: (21) 3873 8888. Fax: (21) 3873 8777.

E-mail: reservas@lemeridien-riodejaneiro.com

Website: www.meridien-br.com

Price: From R$481.

Pestana Rio Atlântica

Convenient for Rio's main tourist attractions and the city centre, *Pestana Rio Atlântica* is ideally suited to business travellers. The hotel has 218 rooms, 114 of which are luxury suites with ocean views. Rooms are decorated in soft hues and natural woods and feature a mini-bar, cable TV, telephone, Internet connection and air conditioning. Fax machines, mobile phones, computers and secretarial services are available on request and the new business centre features meeting rooms and private office space with Internet access. The hotel also boasts a rooftop pool, fitness centre, sauna, beach service, lobby bar and a recently renovated restaurant serving Portuguese and international dishes.

Avenida Atlântica 2964, Copacabana

Tel: (21) 2548 6332. Fax: (21) 2255 6410.

E-mail: rioatlantica@pestanarioatlantica.com.br

Website: www.pestanahotels.com.br

Price: From R$462.

Luxury

Caesar Park Hotel

Situated along the Ipanema beachfront, this elegant hotel has 193 apartments and 29 suites, all with air conditioning, cable TV, telephone and Internet connection. The rooms are spacious and airy and many have large windows with sea views. The bilingual staff provides an excellent service, which has attracted the custom of distinguished guests over the years, including King Juan Carlos of Spain, Madonna, Pavarotti, Elton John and Pelé. The wide range of facilities includes the renowned *Galani* restaurant (see *Restaurants*), a bar, a rooftop pool, a modern fitness centre, a sauna, shops, 24-hour room service and a bureau de change. Business services include a conference centre and meeting rooms. There is also a secretarial service, as well as fax machines and laptop computers available for in-room use.

Avenida Vieira Souto 460, Ipanema

Tel: (21) 2525 2525. Fax: (21) 2521 6000.

E-mail: reservasrj@caesarpark.com.br

Website: www.caesar-park.com

Price: From R$809.

Copacabana Palace

This elegant establishment has become almost as famous as the beachfront upon which it is located. Since it was built in 1923, many famous figures have granted their seals of approval, including Robert De Niro, Marlene Dietrich, Orson Welles and Princess Diana. The hotel is one of the grandest buildings in Rio and is protected by a preservation order. The plush interior is yet more impressive, with its marble floors, pillars, chandeliers and grand ballroom, which hosts a famous masked ball during Carnival. Facilities include a rooftop tennis court, the largest hotel pool in Rio and a well-equipped fitness centre. No two rooms are the same but all are elegantly decorated and come equipped with a safe, air conditioning, TV, telephone and Internet connection. Business travellers have use of the convention centre and a business centre, which offers laptop connection and communications. There are two restaurants – *Cipriani* specialises in gourmet Italian food (see *Restaurants*) and *Pergula* allows guests to dine on a variety of international dishes while seated by the pool.

Avenida Atlântica 1702, Copacabana

Tel: (21) 2548 7070. Fax: (21) 2235 7330.

E-mail: reservas@copacabanapalace.com.br

Website: www.copacabanapalace.orient-express.com

Price: From R$973.

Moderate

Hotel Glória

Located near Rio's Centro district, *Hotel Glória* is ideal for guests who wish to be close to the city, the airports and beaches. Built in 1922, its French-style architecture and antique interior furnishings give this hotel an aura of the past, yet its facilities are very much up to date. There are two buildings with over 600 suites and rooms, many of which have stunning views over Botafogo Bay to the Pão de Açúcar. All rooms are en suite and decorated in a traditional European style, offering cable TV, telephone and Internet access, as well as 24-hour room service. Two swimming pools (one heated), a sauna, a fitness centre, running track and a garden meditation area are also provided for guests, as well as two restaurants and a comfortable bar. Business travellers are catered for with meeting rooms and a convention centre.

Rua do Russel 632, Glória

Tel: (21) 2555 7572. Fax: (21) 2555 7282.

E-mail: hotel@hotelgloriario.com.br

Website: www.hotelgloriario.com.br

Price: From R$240 (including breakfast).

Rio Copa Hotel

Situated only 200m (656ft) from Copacabana beach, the *Rio Copa* offers easy access to the city centre and both airports. Its 110 rooms are all en suite and smart, comfortable and equipped with a mini-bar, safe, air conditioning, radio, cable TV and telephone. A buffet breakfast is served in *Le Baron Restaurant*, which also offers Brazilian and international snacks throughout the day. The reception staff is bilingual and able to help guests with business facilities, which include a convention room and business centre with fax and Internet access. For relaxation, the hotel has a small roof-terrace swimming pool, a sauna and some exercise bikes.

Avenida Princesa Isabel, Copacabana

Tel: (21) 2275 6644. Fax: (021) 2275 5545.

E-mail: riocopa@riocopa.com

Website: www.riocopa.com

Price: From R$220 (including breakfast).

Other Recommendations

Hotel InterContinental Rio

The *InterContinental Rio* is more of a resort than a hotel. Situated on the beach, in the exclusive São Conrado neighbourhood, it boasts 431 modern, luxurious and spacious rooms, each with an original tapestry woven by a Brazilian artist and many with balconies overlooking the ocean. Facilities include three swimming pools, a fitness centre, three floodlit tennis courts, a nightclub, poolside bar, cocktail lounge and three restaurants, including fine Italian dining in *Alfredo di Roma* (see *Restaurants*). Business travellers can use the fully equipped business centre, the convention centre and the meeting rooms. The hotel is ideal for the golf enthusiast, as the Gavea Golf and Country Club is situated right next door. More adventurous guests can organise a tandem trip on one of the hang-gliders or paragliders that land on the beach.

Avenida Prefeito Mendes de Moraes 222, São Conrado

Tel: (21) 3322 2200. Fax: (21) 3322 5500.

E-mail: rio@interconti.com

Website: www.rio-de-janeiro.interconti.com

Price: From R$335.

Hotel Santa Clara

Located on a quiet street in Copacabana, *Hotel Santa Clara* is one of the cheaper options for comfortable, private accommodation. Rooms are decorated in bright white and blue, featuring wooden furnishings, TV, air conditioning and a communications socket for both telephone and laptop. The hotel's owner seems to have a penchant for art and the halls are decked out with elaborate creations of modern art, while prints of famous paintings by European artists are displayed in the rooms. A continental breakfast is served and the bilingual reception staff are happy to assist guests with tours and visits to attractions.

Rua Décio Vilares 316, Copacabana
Tel: (21) 2256 2650. Fax: (21) 2547 4042.
E-mail: reserva@hotelsantaclara.com.br
Website: www.hotelsantaclara.com.br
Price: From R$105 (including breakfast).

RESTAURANTS

The selected restaurants have been divided into five categories: Gastronomic, Business, Trendy, Budget and Personal Recommendations. The restaurants are listed alphabetically within these different categories, which serve as guidelines rather than absolute definitions of the establishments.

Sales tax of 5% and a service charge of 10–15% are added to most restaurant bills in Rio. Most credit cards are now widely accepted in the city's restaurants, although some of the cheaper or older establishments only accept cash. It is advisable to telephone the restaurant in advance, in order to check whether or not a particular card is accepted.

The prices quoted below are for an average three-course meal for one person and for a bottle of house wine or cheapest equivalent; they include sales tax but they do not include service charge.

Gastronomic

Antiquarius

Antiquarius is generally regarded as one of Rio's best restaurants and has won several prestigious awards for its renderings of classic Portuguese dishes. As well as the elegant splendour of the interior, with its mirror-lined walls and rich furnishings, there is also an antiques shop, which diners can peruse at leisure. As far as gastronomy goes, the leg of lamb is excellent and the menu also features a wide variety of seafood creations, such as shrimp in champagne, lobster thermidor, Cascais-style seafood with rice and over 50 varieties of *bacalhau* (salted cod). The extensive and impressive wine list includes many fine French, Spanish and Portuguese varieties. It is wise for diners to book ahead, as the restaurant is very popular.

Rua Aristides Espinola 19, Leblon
Tel: (21) 2294 1496 *or* 1049. Fax: (21) 2512 5756.
E-mail: informacoes@antiquarius.com.br
Website: www.antiquarius.com.br
Price: R$90. Wine: R$33.

Carême Bistrô

This small and intimate French-style bistro, with its mirrored walls, chequered floor and silver service on crisp white tablecloths, sports an atmosphere that is refined without being too stuffy. The restaurant serves cordon bleu cuisine that changes seasonally and one of its specialities is game, which goes down well with the excellent selection of wines from the cellar. Diners can choose from starters such as salmon in garlic ginger sauce, mains that might include grilled duck breast on puréed potato with caramelised spring onions in a *jus du cassis*, and then a selection of desserts, such as Honfleur apple tart. Reservations are essential and are made to a strict booking schedule. No lunch. Closed Sunday and Monday.

Rua Visconde de Caravelas 113, Botafogo
Tel: (21) 2537 5431.
Price: R$80. Wine: R$24.

Cipriani

The *Cipriani*, one of two dining rooms in the luxurious Copacabana Palace (see *Hotels*), is one of Rio's most exclusive restaurants. In this spacious room with marble floors and French windows, the chef – hailing from the famous Cipriani restaurant in Venice – serves a continually changing selection of North Italian dishes with a Brazilian twist. Tempting appetisers include classic carpaccio with black truffle sauce. Main dishes include veal fillet in lemon and oregano sauce served with eggplant, while the heavenly choice of desserts includes Venetian tiramisu and bitter chocolate soufflé with crème brûlée. Reservations essential at the weekend.

Copacabana Palace, Avenida Atlântica 1702, Copacabana
Tel: (21) 2548 7070. Fax: (21) 2235 7330.
E-mail: reservas@copacabanapalace.com.br
Website: www.copacabanapalace.orient-express.com
Price: R$130. Wine: R$42.

Claude Troisgros

The rather quirky, primrose-coloured Art Deco exterior of *Claude Troisgros* – named after the renowned French chef who founded it over 20 years ago – contains a surprisingly modern and sophisticated restaurant, which is one of the city's finest venues. Although the menu is very much centred on traditional French cuisine, Troisgros has always used fresh Brazilian ingredients, which add a tropical theme to dishes. Mains include sole fillet marinated in banana juice with noisette potatoes covered in herb butter or a side of lamb in a tomato, mozzarella and basil sauce. Closed Sunday.

Rua Custódio Serrão 62, Jardim Botânico
Tel: (21) 2537 8582. Fax: (21) 2527 8775.
E-mail: escritorio@claudetroisgros.com.br
Website: www.claudetroisgros.com.br
Price: R$70. Wine: R$60.

Le Saint Honoré

Located on the 37th floor of Le Meridien (see *Hotels*), this refined and classically stylish restaurant offers spectacular views of Copacabana beach to complement the delightful French cuisine, prepared under the direction of acclaimed chef Paul Bocuse. Brazilian ingredients are used to create exquisite dishes, such as Amazonian *pintado* (mackerel) with mashed sweet potato and Bois de Boudran sauce or

Carioca Arches, Lapa

Copacabana beach

veal fillet encroûte with a mushroom and garlic flan. Desserts might include tart of mango and pistachio or white chocolate and caramelised figs. The smart dress code and extensive list of fine wines and champagnes make this an ideal place for a lavish dinner. Closed Sunday.

Le Meridien, 37th Floor, Avenida Atlântica 1020, Copacabana
Tel: (21) 3873 8880. Fax: (21) 3873 8777.
E-mail: mail@lemeridien-riodejaneiro.com
Website: www.lemeridien-copacabana.com
Price: R$95. Wine: R$30.

Business

Alfredo di Roma

Based in the Hotel InterContinental Rio (see *Hotels*), *Alfredo di Roma* is an Italian restaurant with a relaxed atmosphere. It is a franchise owned by the well-known chef, Alfredo di Lello, who created the fettucine dish that bears his name. The decor is warm and bright – red walls, dark-wood floor, atmospheric lighting and leafy plants reflect the Mediterranean style of the food on offer. Diners might start with a selection of Italian antipasti or mozzarella baked in a pastry crust with basil sauce, before moving on to mains like tortelli stuffed with salmon in a white wine sauce, risotto with clams flavoured with grappa or, of course, the famous fettucine Alfredo. There is an extensive wine list and a separate menu for coffees. No lunch.

Hotel InterContinental Rio, Avenida Prefeito Mendes de Morais 222, São Conrado
Tel: (21) 3323 2200. Fax: (21) 3322 5500.
E-mail: rio@interconti.com
Website: www.rio-de-janeiro.interconti.com
Price: R$65. Wine: R$30.

Barra Grill

Located just ten minutes from Rio's longest beach, in the neighbourhood of Barra da Tijuca, *Barra Grill* is one of the most popular *churrascarias* in the city – and deservedly so. The system is that of a typical Brazilian barbecue – waiters visit each table, carrying a platter of beef, chicken and lamb, from which diners choose as much or as little as they wish to eat, with heaps of salad from the buffet. The dining room has a relaxed atmosphere and the service is informal but attentive. Guests of Barra Grill might notice the whisky bottles lining the dark walls, serving as a testimony to the restaurant's whisky club, where members can entrust their own, labelled bottle to the restaurant and enjoy a tipple whenever they visit. There are live shows in the bar, Tuesday to Saturday.

Avenida Ministro Ivan Lins 314, Barra da Tijuca
Tel: (21) 2493 6060.
Price: R$50. Wine: R$28.

Galani

This exclusive restaurant is located on the 23rd floor of the luxurious Caesar Park Hotel (see *Hotels*) so, as well as dining on sumptuous international cuisine, guests can also enjoy spectacular views of Ipanema beach from the large windows. The decor is plain and simple, with neatly laid tables on a marble floor. Antipasti include Padano cheese in balsamic vinegar or aubergine bruschetta with mussels and salmon caviar. For mains, diners have a choice of pastas, risottos, meats and seafood, such as shrimp in saffron sauce with squid fettucine. A buffet lunch (R$52) is served daily.

Caesar Park Hotel, Avenida Vieira Souto 460, Ipanema
Tel: (21) 2525 2525. Fax: (21) 2521 6000.
E-mail: hotel_rj@caesarpark.com.br
Website: www.caesar-park.com
Price: R$85. Wine: R$45.

Osteria dell 'Angolo

This smart Centro restaurant is popular with the city crowd for business lunches and is warm and inviting yet simple and uncluttered. There is a fine selection of north Italian dishes, including risottos, meats and pastas, such as tagliolini with scampi and saffron, accompanied by a wine selection that is predominantly European. The elegant atmosphere and clientele demand quite formal dress. No dinner (closes 2000). Closed weekends. However, there is another Osteria dell 'Angolo located in Ipanema, which is open every day for dinner only.

Rua Teófilo Otoni 63, Centro
Tel: (21) 2253 8029.
Price: R$70. Wine: R$32.
Branch:
Rua Paul Redfern 40, Ipanema
Tel: (21) 2259 3148.

Siri Mole & Cia

This Brazilian chain specialises in exotic Bahian (northeast Brazilian) seafood dishes. The smart clientele are seated at tables laid with pressed white tablecloths and fine silverware, beside big windows that open out onto the street. The menu boasts six different varieties of *moquecas* (stews cooked with palm oil, coconut milk, peppers, tomatoes, coriander and other spices), including the *sinfonia do mar* (symphony of the sea), a bubbling fish and seafood stew prepared in this traditional Bahian fashion. These dishes are usually big enough for two or three people and are served with rice and *farofa* (ground manioc). The choice of wines includes Brazilian, Chilean, Argentinian and Italian.

Rua Francisco Otaviano 50, Ipanema
Tel: (21) 2267 0894 *or* 2523 4240.
Price: R$90. Wine: R$18.
Branch:
Avenida Rio Branco 1, Centro
Tel: (21) 2233 0107. Fax: (21) 2233 0266.

Trendy

Bar do Arnaudo

Located in a Bohemian corner of the Santa Teresa suburb, *Bar do Arnaudo* is a tiny bar and restaurant that is full of character. The swing doors open onto a

Photo: Brazilian Tourist Office

rustic, wooden interior decorated with handicrafts and antique artwork. Wine is served in tankards, while beer and *caipirinhas* (the name of which translates to 'little peasant girl') are also available to accompany the classic dishes from northeast Brazil. Popular choices include *carne do sol* (sun-dried beef), *feijão de corda* (black beans in herb sauce) and *queijo coalho* (grilled cheese on sticks).
Rua Almirante Alexandrino 316B, Santa Teresa
Tel: (21) 2252 7246.
Price: R$45. Wine: R$19.

Boteco 66

Situated in an old house on a residential street, behind a leaf-covered wall, *Boteco 66* has a surprisingly modern interior. It is part Paris bistro and part Rio corner bar, which reflects the tastes of its owner – the renowned French chef, Claude Troisgros (see *Gastronomic* above), who has adopted Brazil as his home. Troisgros has developed a simple menu of European favourites – such as steaks, pastas, risottos and gourmet burgers – all served with a hint of Brazilian flavour and finesse. The wine list is extensive and includes many French favourites, as well as a selection of champagnes. The atmosphere and attentive service is unmistakably French and the clientele is appropriately sophisticated.
Avenida Alexandre Ferreira 66, Lagoa
Tel: (21) 2266 0838. Fax: (21) 2527 8775.
E-mail: escritorio@claudetroisgros.com.br
Website: www.claudetroisgros.com.br
Price: R$50. Wine: R$30.

Via Sete Grill

This modern Centro restaurant caters for a busy lunchtime crowd of hungry workers. The colourful decor suits the vibrant atmosphere and the staff is fast, efficient and friendly. *Via Sete Grill* offers a selection of grilled meats – beef, lamb or chicken – served burger style with salad, potato with cream cheese and salsa. There is also a choice of filled wraps for the more health-conscious customer. No dinner. Closed weekends.
Rua Sete de Setembro 43, Centro
Tel: (21) 2221 8020.
E-mail: cliente@viasete.com.br
Website: www.viasete.com.br
Price: R$40. Wine: R$18.
Branch:
Rua Garcia D'Avila 125, Ipanema
Tel: (21) 2512 8100.

Zazá

The people of Rio flock to this tropical bistro in Ipanema, voted one of the 'top 100 new restaurants in the world' by *Condé Nast Traveller* magazine in 2001. The three floors of cosy dining rooms have a distinctly eastern flavour, with Moroccan carpets, exotic artefacts and low-level tables. Yet the cuisine is a mixture of Asian and Brazilian dishes. Main meals include tuna steak with passion fruit sauce, fried, crunchy kole and jasmine rice. Or diners can take an 11-course journey through the flavours of *Zazá* for R$105.
Rua Joana Angélica 40, Ipanema
Tel: (21) 2247 9101/2.
E-mail: zazabistro@uol.com.br
Price: R$60. Wine: R$28.

Zuka

Bright, modern *Zuka* is one of the most fashionable new restaurants in Rio. The simple, wooden tables surround a sunken kitchen, where diners can watch their meals being prepared. The food is delicious but it is the presentation that lingers in the memory. Served on big rectangular plates, each dish is a work of art. The selection of grilled steaks and seafood includes shrimps in honey and ginger, with tomato chutney and fresh tagliatelle. Recommended for a light meal is the gourmet burger in *dijonaise* sauce, served with a pile of stacked fries and green salad.
Rua Dias Ferreira 233, Leblon
Tel: (21) 3205 7154.
Price: R$60. Wine: R$18.

Budget

Aipo & Aipim

Perhaps the best budget option for dining is one of the many *quilo* (kilo) or plate-by-weight restaurants that can be found throughout the city. Among these individual and chain restaurants, *Aipo & Aipim* is one of the most popular. The restaurant is decorated with warm, harvest colours and diners eat at basic tables reminiscent of school canteens. The format is the same as any other *quilo* restaurant – diners pick up a plate, load it with a choice of ingredients from the salad bar and hot plates, then place it on the scales and receive a ticket to be paid after eating. It is simple, efficient and very cheap. Aipo & Aipim has the added advantage of also having a *churrascaria*, which serves freshly barbecued fish and meat. Other dishes available include basil farfalle and Brazilian beef jerky with cheese. Diners also can select from tempting desserts, which are carried around on a tray.
Avenida Nossa Senhora Copacabana 391, Copacabana
Tel: (21) 2255 6285.
Price: R$10. Wine: Unlicensed.
Branches:
Avenida Nossa Senhora de Copacabana 605, Copacabana
Tel: (21) 2549 2215.
Avenida Nossa Senhora de Copacabana 920, Copacabana
Tel: (21) 2547 2101.
Avenida Nossa Senhora de Copacabana 1175, Copacabana
Tel: (21) 2513 2403.
Rua Visconde de Pirajá, Ipanema
Tel: (21) 2267 8313.

Casa da Feijoada

The *feijoada* – Brazil's national dish, introduced by African slaves who were brought over by the Portuguese in the 16th century – is a filling concoction of simmered meats, including pig's ear, pig's trotters, dried sausage, salt-cured pork and beef tongue, which are made into a type of stew, along with black beans, spices and orange juice. Although it is traditionally eaten on Saturday, *Casa da Feijoada* serves up the dish on a daily basis and diners can choose the specific ingredients they wish to have incorporated into their portion. For those who prefer something a little lighter, other Brazilian dishes are also on offer, including marinated chicken or prawns with coconut milk, as well as a delicious selection of traditional desserts, such as *doce de abóbora com coco* (sweet pumpkin with coconut) and *doce de leite* (caramel rice pudding). The decor, too, is a celebration of Brazil's national heritage. The walls are painted green and yellow – the two colours of the national flag – and are lined with pictures of the early slaves preparing the *feijoada*.

Rua Prudente de Moraes 10B, Ipanema
Tel: (21) 2247 2776.
Website: www.cozinhatipica.com.br/casa_da_feijoada
Price: R$35. Wine: R$14.

Celeiro

The organic restaurant, *Celeiro*, is always packed with people enjoying its very healthy but nonetheless tasty cuisine. The decor reflects the natural ingredients used, with rustic wooden panelling and skylights built into the ceiling. The pay-by-weight buffet offers an extensive array of scrumptious salads. There are also hot dishes on the menu, including a variety of pasta dishes. Delectable desserts include truffles, chocolate mousse cup and crunchy mango. No dinner. Closed Sunday.
Rua Dias Ferreira 199, Leblon
Tel/fax: (21) 2274 7843.
E-mail: celeiro@celeiroculinaria.com.br
Website: www.celeiroculinaria.com.br
Price: R$28. Wine: Unlicensed.

Mr Ôpi

Mr Ôpi is another of the *quilo* (kilo) restaurants, although this one serves gourmet food at slightly higher prices to a predominantly lunchtime crowd of city workers. The decor is elegant and inviting and the smart waiters in pressed white uniforms spoon selected dishes 'canteen style' onto plates. One side of the buffet bar serves freshly cooked fish, meats, pies, rice and potatoes, while the other serves Brazilian specialities, such as *feijoada* (meat and bean stew). Ingredients and recipes change daily and desserts and drinks are picked up en route to the till, where the plate is weighed. No dinner (closes 2000). Closed weekends.
Rua da Alfândega 91D, Centro
Tel: (21) 2224 5820.
Price: R$20. Wine: Unlicensed.
Branch:
Rua da Quitanda 51, Centro
Tel: (21) 2507 3859.

Pizzaria Guanabara

A good selection of tasty pizzas is served in this simple pizzeria. The restaurant spills out onto the pavement, with a line of large green plants separating the diners from the cars. The interior is comfortable and informal and a mural of the Rio landscape dominates one wall. As well as the usual *margherita* (cheese and tomato) and *quattro formaggi* (four cheese) options, diners can tantalise their palates with sweet pizza toppings, such as banana or peach. Steaks, seafood and paellas also feature on the menu. The busy road outside might be somewhat distracting but the low prices, down-to-earth atmosphere and late – or rather early – opening hours (until 0400) have made this venue one of the most popular in the affluent Leblon district.
Avenida Ataulfo de Paiva 1228, Leblon
Tel: (21) 2294 0797.
Price: R$35. Wine: R$15.

Personal Recommendations

Bira

It is a long trek to this restaurant in Barra da Guaratiba, on the western edges of the city. However, it is definitely worth the effort. Diners with time and transportation will be rewarded with some of the best *Bahian* cooking in the Rio area. Specialities from the menu of dishes from northeast Brazil include *moqueca*

Photo: Brazilian Tourist Office

Rio Carnival

(a seafood stew cooked in coconut milk, peppers, coriander and palm oil), which is cooked in an earthenware pot and served bubbling hot at the table. It is usually eaten with rice, sprinkled with *farofa* (manioc flour) and a hot pepper sauce and is best washed down with a *caipirinha* made with fresh *maracujá* (passion fruit). All this is served on a wooden verandah, surrounded by thick vegetation, overlooking a large lagoon. Tiny monkeys sometimes descend from the trees to see what the diners have overlooked.
Estrada Da Vendinha 68A, Barra da Guaratiba
Tel: (21) 2410 8304.
Price: R$60. Wine: R$30.

Cervantes

This Copacabana bar is a great place for visitors to sit or stand with the locals and enjoy a refreshing glass of *chopp* (beer). It is an old-fashioned venue with frosted windows but has a lively atmosphere. Smartly dressed waiters serve drinks, simple plates and sandwiches to a mixed crowd of customers who drop in at any time of the night for a snack (open until 0500). Meals include filet mignon with broccoli rice, while sandwiches (costing from R$3.50 to R$9.50) feature a variety of meats wrapped in bread with a slice of pineapple. Closed Monday.
Avenida Prado Júnior 335, Copacabana
Tel: (21) 2275 6147.
Price: R$30. Wine: R$18.

Confeitaria Colombo

Walking into the *Confeitaria Colombo* is like stepping back in time. The plush interior of Belgian mirrors, curved glass cabinets and Italian marble counters set the scene of an early 20th-century café where Rio's high society took afternoon tea. Today, a steady stream of city workers, businesspeople and tourists treat themselves to lunch in the opulent interior of one of the city's finest historic landmarks. The surroundings are best viewed from the upstairs gallery, beneath the exquisitely patterned glass roof. The buffet lunch consists of an appetising selection of salad, meat, fish and rice dishes, followed by mouthwatering cakes and pastries, for which the *Confeitaria* is deservedly famous. A traditional *feijoada* (meat and bean stew) buffet is served on Friday. À la carte meals are also available. No dinner. Closed Sunday.

Rua Gonçalves Dias 32, Centro
Tel/fax: (21) 2232 2300.
E-mail: contato@confeitariacolombo.com.br
Website: www.confeitariacolombo.com.br
Price: R$35 (buffet); R$75 (à la carte). Wine: R$22.

Doce Delicia

Although *Doce Delícia* appears classy and upmarket, this restaurant is reasonably priced. It has a welcoming Asiatic theme with its wicker furniture, bamboo walls and calming waterfall features, which cascade like curtains in the middle of the restaurant. The walls are hung with modern paintings and interesting candleholders are scattered throughout the room. Smart, efficient waiters serve simple dishes infused with Brazilian flavour and flair. There are fixed-price plates, daily specials and low-calorie options, including the exquisite *salmão al limone* served with potato noisettes and vegetables. The cakes are as delicious and rich as they look and should not be missed.
Rua Dias Ferreira 48, Leblon
Tel: (21) 2249 2970.
E-mail: sac@docedelicia.com.br
Website: www.docedelicia.com.br
Price: R$35. Wine: R$28.
Branches:
Rua Anibel de Mendança 55, Ipanema
Tel: (21) 2259 0239.
Rua do Ouvidor 60, Centro
Tel: (21) 2262 5200.
São Conrado Fashion Mall, Estrada da Gávea
Tel: (21) 2420 4943.
Shopping Tijuca, Avenida Maracanã 987, Tijuca
Tel: (21) 2284 0455.

Shirley

What started as a front-room eating place serving home-cooked food has grown into one of Rio's most popular seafood restaurants. This unassuming restaurant – hidden away down a side street, just one block from Copacabana beach – serves a superb range of fish, squid and shellfish dishes. Popular choices include lobster thermidor (R$76), shrimps cooked any which way, fish stew and fish *Bahian* style. The cosy wood panelling and weathered sea-inspired artwork give the restaurant an authentic and homely atmosphere. No credit cards.

Rua Gustavo Sampaio 610, Leme
Tel: (21) 2275 1398.
Price: R$35. Wine: R$21.

ENTERTAINMENT

Nightlife

Brazilians know how to party and the *Cariocas* are no exception. Whether it is a post-soccer beer at a beach kiosk, an evening's entertainment at a live music venue or a cocktail at one of the growing number of trendy bars and clubs, a night out in Rio is to be savoured and enjoyed.

Beer seems to be served at all hours of the day and locals can often be seen enjoying a drink with friends at the corner bars that open out onto the streets in all parts of the city. Many bars and pubs have happy hours for people returning from work or the beach and most serve snacks and light meals. But the real action does not really start until around 2300, when the clubs open their doors for music and dancing and stay open until around 0400. Club entry fees cost around R$10 and cards are provided on which drink consumption is recorded. A minimum purchase of R$10 upwards is usually required. It is essential to keep hold of this card or face a forfeit charge, which can be as high as R$300 – much more than the average drinker could possibly consume. Beers are approximately R$5, while spirits or cocktails cost upwards of R$6. The minimum legal drinking age in Brazil is 18 years.

All areas have popular bars and clubs but the beach communities of Copacabana, Ipanema and Leblon are particularly good for a night out. Although clubs do not usually operate formal dress codes, *Cariocas* tend to dress up after dark and it is best to follow suit. Some venues refuse entry to people wearing shorts and T-shirts.

The *O Globo* (website: http://oglobo.globo.com) newspaper publishes *Rio Show*, an excellent entertainment listings magazine on Friday. Good information and discounts for clubbing and nightlife in Rio also can be found online (website: www. caindonanoite.com).

Bars

Outdoor drinking can be enjoyed at the kiosks that line the beach promenades or around the Lagoa. For more of an indoor experience, try *Bar Luiz*, Rua da Carioca 39, Centro, one of the oldest bars in Rio and now popular with the business crowd. *Clipper*, Rua Carlos Góes 263, and *Jobi*, Avenida Ataulfo de Paiva 1166, are both popular bars in Leblon, where drinkers spill out onto the sidewalk. Devotees of 'The Girl From Ipanema' song, will want to visit *Garota de Ipanema*, Rua Vinicius de Moraes 49, Ipanema, where the composition was conceived. The sophisticated atmosphere of *Melt*, Rua Rita Ludolf 47, Leblon, attracts a young and trendy crowd for imported beer and cocktails, with a lounge club upstairs, open from 2300. Those hankering for a pint of ale should visit the *Lord Jim Pub*, Rua Paul Redfern 63, Ipanema.

Casinos

Gambling is illegal in Brazil.

Clubs

The club scene has really taken off in Rio over the last few years, with a number of venues banging out the very best in Brazilian and international dance music.

Most clubs are open Wednesday to Saturday from 2200 onwards. *Bunker 94*, Rua Paul Pompéia 94, Copacabana, *Casa da Matriz*, Rua Henrique de Novais 107, Botafogo, and *Six Electron*, Rua das Marrecas 38, Lapa, are current favourites on the scene. *Studio 54*, Avenida das Américas 5000, Barra da Tijuca, is a techno club based on the famous 1970s New York nightclub. *Help*, Avenida Atlântica 3432, Copacabana, is a huge disco that is popular with the singles crowd.

Live Music

Rio has a wide choice when it comes to live music. Samba, bossa nova, chorinho, rock, MBP (Brazilian pop), classical, blues and jazz can all be enjoyed nightly. An elaborate Carnival-style samba show can be seen at *Platforma 1*, Rua Adalberto Ferreira 32, Leblon, daily from 2200. Favourites for bossa nova include *Bar Ouvidor*, Rua do Ouvidor 43, Centro, on Tuesday and Wednesday evenings, as well as *Vinicius*, Rua Vinicius de Moraes 39, Ipanema, daily from 2300 – in the bar and road named after Vinicius de Moraes of 'The Girl from Ipanema' fame, who penned many of his songs here with Tom Jobim. Another bossa nova hotspot is Thursday to Sunday from 2230 at *Bar do Tom*, Rua Adalberto Ferreira 32, Leblon, named after bossa nova pioneer Tom Jobim. *Esch Café*, Rua do Rosario 107, Centro, and Rua Dias Ferreira 78, Leblon, holds regular jazz evenings. Reputedly the best jazz in Rio can be heard every Thursday 1930–2115 at the open-air venue of *Parque das Ruinas*, Rua Murtinho Nobre 169, Santa Teresa.

Sport

Football is a national obsession in Brazil – even more so nowadays, following the national team's fifth World Cup win in 2002. It takes priority over food, politics and religion. Introduced by Scottish railway engineers in the 1890s, the sport soared in popularity and today, for youngsters living in the *favelas*, football could prove to be their passport to better lives. Pelé (arguably the greatest player of all time), Rivaldo and Ronaldo are just some of the local heroes.

In Rio, the most important teams are *Flamengo* (website: www.flamengo.com.br), *Vasco* (website: www.crvascodagama.com), *Fluminense* (website: www.fluminense.com.br) and *Botafogo* (website: www.botafogo.com). These four teams feature prominently in the national league and cup tournament. The teams and the Brazilian national side play their matches at *Maracanã Stadium*, Rua Prof. Eurico Rabelo, Maracanã (tel: (21) 2568 9962). These are raucous and entertaining affairs. Enthusiastic crowds, drums, flags and endless ticker tape accompany the skill and excitement of the footballers on the pitch.

Tickets cost around R$10 for stand seats, more for Championship and International fixtures. These are available at the gates on match days. *Confederação Brasileira de Futebol* (CBF), Rua da Alfândega 70, Centro (tel: (21) 3221 6100; e-mail: tecnico@cbffutebol.com.br; website: www.cbfnews.bol.com.br), can provide information on Rio's match schedules.

With its vast beaches, Rio is ideal for beach and watersports and the citizens fully exploit the natural resources. Football, beach volley and foot volley are constantly taking place and there is a plethora of tournaments and championships. Hiking, fishing, diving, boating, rowing, body boarding, surfing and windsurfing are also popular and there is ample opportunity to cycle, rollerblade and jog.

Fitness Centres

Fitness is an obsession in Rio. As well as exercise stations on the beaches and around the Lagoa, there are indoor gyms on almost every street, many of which are open to non-members. Of the exclusive clubs, *Estaçaó do Corpo Health Club & Spa*, Avenida Borges de Medeiros 1426, Lagoa (tel: (21) 2219 3131; e-mail: info@estacaodocorpo), is one of the best. Access to its gym, dance studio, spinning centre, running track, soccer pitch, swimming pool and sauna are available at rates of R$40 per day or R$155 per week.

Golf

Players can test their handicap at three local clubs. The first, *Gávea Golf Club*, Estrada da Gávea 800, São Conrado (tel: (21) 3322 4141; e-mail: gaveagol@unisys.com.br), offers a field of 18 holes for R$250 basic green fees. Non-members can play at the invitation of a member. The second, *Itanhangá Golf Club*, Estrada da Barra 2005, Barra da Tijuca (tel: (21) 2494 2507; e-mail: adm@itanhanga.com.br), is a 27-hole course that is only open to members; non-members can play at the invitation of a member. The third, the *Golden Green Golf Club*, Avenida Canal de Marapendi 2901, Barra da Tijuca (tel: (21) 2434 0696; e-mail: ggc@ism.com.br), is a golf clinic with a three-par, six-hole course open to outside players for R$300 basic fees. Further information is available online (website: www.golferio.com.br).

Hang-gliding and Paragliding

A tandem flight from one of Rio's steep mountains is an increasingly popular activity with tourists. There are many pilots and companies offering this, including *Fernando Rocha* (tel: (21) 9429 9497; website: www.bomvoo.com.br), *Fly With Me* (tel: (21) 2522 5586; website: www.guia4ventos.com.br), *Superfly* (tel: (21) 3322 2286) and *Rio by Jeep* (tel: (21) 9693 8800 *or* 2575 8626; e-mail: riobyjeep@riobyjeep.com; website: www.riobyjeep.com).

Tennis

Public tennis courts are situated around the Lagoa. *Rio Sport Center* has two locations with tennis courts, at Avenida Ayrton Senna 2541, Barra da Tijuca (tel: (21) 3325 6644), and Rua Visconde de Pirajá 161, Ipanema (tel: (21) 2267 4192).

Shopping

People do not generally visit Rio specifically for its shopping prowess. Typical Brazilian wares are thin on the ground, with shops orientated towards tourists, selling the usual T-shirts and resort-type souvenirs. Nevertheless, Rio is the place to invest in good-quality beach- and swimwear. Fashion clothes shops are increasingly common and Rio is also recommended for antiques and jewellery. Brazilian soccer shirts make great gifts. Official shirts are available from sports shops and are of a higher quality and more expensive than the cotton replicas found in clothes shops or for sale on the street.

The main shopping streets are Avenida Nossa Senhora de Copacabana and Rua Barata Ribeiro in Copacabana, Rua Visconde de Pirajá in Ipanema and Avenida Ataulfo de Paiva in Leblon. Rio has over 30 shopping centres located throughout the city, most of which contain supermarkets, department stores, fashion boutiques and music outlets, as well as places for one to grab something to eat. The most central is *Rio Sul*, Rua Lauro Muller 116, in Botafogo. Other options include the *São Conrado Fashion Mall*, Estrada da Gávea 899, São Conrado, and *Shopping Center de Copacabana*, Rua Siqueira Campos 143, Copacabana.

Rio also has plenty of good bookstores, many with pleasant cafés located inside. One of the best is *Livraria da Travessa*, with branches at Travessa do Ouvidor 11A, Centro, Avenida Rio Branco 44, Centro, and Rua Visconde de Pirajá 462A, Ipanema.

Good-quality arts and crafts are available at regular outdoor markets, which are colourful and entertaining places for tourists to visit. The *Babilônia Hype Fair*, at Tribune C of the Brazilian Jockey Club Racetrack (tel: (21) 2263 8629; website: www.babiloniahype.com.br), is open over most weekends and gathers together over 150 fashion, art and decoration-themed stalls, also featuring music and dance performances. The *Hippie Fair* takes place every Sunday (0900–1800) around the 18th-century Saracuras Fountain in Ipanema. Stalls feature handicrafts and artwork. The fair is a major attraction for both visitors and locals alike. Antique fairs occur in various parts of the city, every weekend. However, the *Rio Antiques Fair* (tel: (21) 3852 5516), located on the Rua do Lavradio, Centro, is held for two weeks every month. The market provides an excellent opportunity for treasure hunting on this neo-classical street, which was the home and meeting place for the artists, poets, politicians, typographers and writers who have shaped Rio's history.

Jewellery shops *H Stern*, Rua Visconde de Pirajá 490, Ipanema (tel: (21) 2259 7442), and *Amsterdam Sauer*, Rua Garcia D'Avila, Ipanema (tel: (21) 2512 1132), have branches throughout the city, as well as outlets in most of the upmarket hotels, selling intricate and elegant silver, pearl and gemstone designs.

Shops are usually open Monday to Friday 0900–1900 and Saturday 0900–1300, although hours vary according to the location and type of business. Shopping centres are generally open daily 1000–2200, although some have more limited opening hours on Sundays. ICMS (sales tax) in shops is 18%. There is no tax refund scheme in Brazil.

Culture

Rio is and always has been a highly cultured city. The high density and rich ethnic mix of the population has given shape to all forms of artistic expression, which is evident in the music, dance and lifestyle of the *Cariocas* – especially during Carnival. There are many cultural centres, art galleries and performance venues in Rio, hosting an ever-changing series of events. The *Centro Cultural Banco do Brasil*, Rua Primeiro de Março 66, Centro (tel: (21) 3808 2020; website: www.cultura-e.com.br), is one of the city's prime venues for music, plays, exhibitions and films.

The *Rio Show* magazine in the Friday edition of the *O Globo* newspaper has weekly cultural listings. Tickets are available for purchase at the venue box offices and, for some events, through *Ticketmaster* (tel: (11) 6846 6000; website: www.ticketmaster.com.br).

Music

The *Brazilian Symphony Orchestra* (website: www.osb.com.br) is based in Rio, performing at various venues in the city. The *Theatro Municipal*, Praça Floriano, Centro (tel: (21) 2262 3935; website: www.theatromunicipal.rj.gov.br), which has its own resident orchestra, is the main venue for classical concerts and operas.

Rio Carnival

Theatre

Rio has over 60 theatres, cultural centres, museums and cafés designated as spaces for the performing arts. Venues include the 200-seater *Museu Nacional de Belas Artes*, Avenida Rio Branco 199, Centro (tel: (21) 2240 0068; website: www.mnba.gov.br), which stages classic performances, the *Maison de France*, Avenida Carlos 58, Centro (tel: (21) 2262 7527), offering contemporary shows, and the *Theatro Municipal* (see *Music* above), staging both contemporary and classic fare. Theatre is generally staged in Portuguese, with very little in English.

Dance

Rio's ballet company, *Ballet do Theatro Municipal*, is based at the *Theatro Municipal* (see *Music* above). Samba is prevalent in the city. An elaborate Carnival-style samba show is performed daily from 2200 at *Platforma 1*, Rua Adalberto Ferreira 32, Leblon. At *Asa Branca*, Avenida Mem de Sá 17, Lapa (tel: (21) 2224 2342), Adelzon Alves offers *samba de raiz* (root samba). Other famous dance halls (*gafieiras*) in which visitors can sample samba or try some tango include *Elite*, Rua Frei Caneca 4, Centro (tel: (21) 2232 3217), and *Estudantina*, Praça Tiradentes 79 (tel: (21) 2507 8067).

Film

Cariocas are ardent cinemagoers, whether they are watching Brazilian or foreign films. American and European films are released quickly and are screened in the original language with Portuguese subtitles. Mainstream cinemas are situated throughout the city, including *Roxy*, Avenida Nossa Senhora de Copacabana 945, Copacabana (tel: (21) 2236 6245), and *Cinema Largo do Machado*, Largo do Machado 29 (tel: (21) 2205 6842). The arthouse cinema chain, *Estação* (tel: (21) 2537 1112; website: www.estacaovirtual.com), shows an up-to-date selection of international films and has branches all over the city, including the Botafogo, Centro and Leme districts. Cinema tickets cost around R$12.

The most famous film set in Rio is probably the Fred Astaire and Ginger Rogers classic, *Flying Down to Rio*

(1933), which was filmed in the Copacabana Palace Hotel. More recently, *Bossa Nova* (1999), with Antonio Fagundes, was set in Rio. Carlos Diegues' *Orfeu* (1999) and the award-winning 1959 Marcel Camus classic *Black Orpheus* are both celluloid renderings of Vinicius De Moraes' play, which retells the Greek myth of Orpheus, set in the delirium of Rio's Carnival. More recently, a number of movies have explored the gritty reality of Rio's poorer districts, including the internationally acclaimed 2002 film *Ciudade de Deus* (*City of God*).

Cultural Events

The biggest cultural event in Rio is undoubtedly *Carnival*, which takes place annually in late February or early March, over the days running up to and including Shrove Tuesday. People from all over the world are attracted, in hundreds of thousands, to Rio's annual orgy of grandiose fun and frivolity. Balls and street parties are held throughout the city during this frenetic period. Masquerade balls became popular with Rio's elite in the mid-19th century and the

poorer sections of society, not to feel excluded, popularised street celebrations with bands and parades. The main event now takes place in the purpose-built *Sambódromo*, where samba schools compete with music, costume, story, song, rhythm and dance in front of judges and up to 90,000 spectators. Tickets are available from *Riotur* (tel: (21) 2217 7575; website: www.rio.rj.gov.br/riotur), local travel agencies and banks. Advance booking is highly advisable.

Literary Notes

Brazilian literature remains largely untranslated into English. Two notable novelists who have enjoyed worldwide success are Jorge Amado and Paul Coelho. Coelho's *The Alchemist* (1988) is considered a modern classic. Works set in Rio include *Blues For A Lost Childhood* (1989) by Antonio Torres, which depicts the life of a journalist who makes it to the big city but discovers life there to be more akin to a living hell than heaven. Other Brazilian writers include Carlos Drummond, Luis Fernando, Verissimo and Ziraldo.

SPECIAL EVENTS

New Year's Day, national holiday, 1 Jan, throughout the city
Twelfth Night, final Christmas celebrations, 6 Jan, throughout the city
St Sebastian, celebrations in honour of the patron saint of Rio de Janeiro, 20 Jan, throughout the city
Carnival, Feb/early Mar, Sambódromo and throughout the city
Good Friday, religious holiday, Mar/Apr, throughout the city
Rio de Janeiro Pride, gay festival, Jun, throughout the city
Anima Mundi, animation festival (website: www.animamundi.com.br), Jul, throughout the city
Our Lady of Copacabana Week, religious ceremonies, cultural events and candlelit procession, Aug, Copacabana
Independence Day, national holiday, 7 Sep, throughout the city
Brazilian Motorcycle Grand Prix (website: www.riogp.com.br), Sep, Nelson Piquet Circuit
Festival do Rio BR, film festival (website: www.festivaldoriobr.com.br), Sep–Oct, throughout the city
Rio Marathon, Oct, throughout the city
Our Lady Aparecida, religious holiday, 12 Oct, throughout the city
Proclamation of the Republic, national holiday, 15 Nov, throughout the city
Christmas Day, holiday and seasonal festivities, 25 Dec, throughout the city
Iemanjá, religious ceremony and offerings to the sea, 31 Dec, Copacabana, Ipanema and Leblon beaches
Reveillon, outdoor concerts, parties and fireworks, 31 Dec, Copacabana beach and seafront

Photo: Brazilian Tourist Office

Situated on the River Tiber, between the Apennine Mountains and the Tyrrhenian Sea, the 'Eternal City' of Rome (*Roma*) was once the administrative centre of the mighty Roman Empire, governing a vast region that stretched from Britain to Mesopotamia. Today, although Rome is the capital of Italy and the seat of the Italian government, it is superseded by Milan, in the industrial north, for business and finance.

The legendary beginnings of Rome are related in the tale of Romulus and Remus. Princess Rhea Silvia, ravished by Mars (the God of War), gave birth to the twins and abandoned them to fate. The River Tiber carried them to the Palatine Hill, where a she-wolf mothered the babes until their discovery by a shepherd. Romulus later killed Remus, before going on to found Rome in the marshy lowlands of seven hills. The anniversary of Rome's foundation – 21 April 753BC – is now marked by a public holiday. The historians' version is no less astonishing. It traces the rise of the city from an unimportant pastoral settlement – the earliest remains date back to the ninth century BC – to the heart of a vast empire ruled over by a string of emperors. Rome saw a second period of development during the 15th-century Renaissance, when the Papacy took up permanent residence in the city. Although Rome's power has since waned, the city remains the essence of European civilisation.

Ruins dating from Rome's glory days lie within an area known as Roma Antica (Ancient Rome) and include the monumental Colosseum and the Foro Romano (Roman Forum) – a crumbling legacy of pagan temples, broken marble and triumphal arches. Buildings from the Renaissance period are concentrated within the *centro storico* (historic centre), situated between Via del Corso and the Tevere (River Tiber). Here, a labyrinth of narrow, winding, cobbled side streets opens out onto magnificent piazzas presided over by Baroque churches, regal palaces and exquisite fountains. The romantic Piazza Navona with Bernini's Fountain of the Four Rivers, Piazza di Spagna and the sweeping Spanish Steps, and the Trevi Fountain immortalised by Fellini's *La Dolce Vita* (1959), all lie within walking distance of each other. Modern life continues amid this theatre of breathtaking monuments, as thousands of years of history are animated by more recent innovations – sophisticated boutiques, rowdy pizzerias and a merry-go-round of cars, buses and mopeds. Across the river, to the west, lies the Vatican State – home to the Pope and spiritual centre of the Roman Catholic Church. South of the Vatican, one finds the bohemian quarter of Trastevere, packed with trattorias and small wine bars. Further south still is the Testaccio district, renowned for nightclubs and live music.

Tourism is a major source of income and visitors come and go throughout the year. The city is blessed with a warm Mediterranean climate, making Rome particularly pleasant to visit in autumn and spring. In August, it is hot and sticky and most of the locals head for the coast – many shops and bars close for the summer break and the streets are strangely empty, save for visitors. Until recently, Rome was frequently criticised for being noisy, chaotic and poorly maintained. However, celebrations for the year 2000 prompted the completion of a massive urban renewal scheme. Huge amounts of scaffolding were finally dismantled to reveal beautifully restored façades, cleverly revamped museums and a rationalised public transport system. Today, citizens and visitors alike continue to benefit from the improvements carried out for the Jubilee celebrations, when the Eternal City celebrated the fact that the millennium was 2000 years since the birth of Christ.

St Peter's Square

TRAVEL

Getting There By Air

Fiumicino Airport (FCO)

Tel: 066 5951. Fax: 06659 53646.

Website: www.adr.it

Rome's principal airport – also known as *Leonardo da Vinci* – is located 26km (16 miles) southwest of the city centre. Fiumicino handles numerous domestic flights within Italy, as well as international flights to all major European cities and destinations further afield, including New York, Singapore, Buenos Aires, Cairo and Moscow. A free shuttle service links the domestic and international terminals.

Major airlines: Italy's national airline is *Alitalia* (tel: 066 5643; website: www.alitalia.it). Other major airlines are *Air China, Air France, British Airways, Canadian Airlines International, Delta Airlines, Japan Airlines, Lufthansa* and *Singapore Airlines*.

Airport facilities: Facilities include *Banca di Roma* counters, 24-hour bureaux de change, ATMs, left-luggage, a medical office for vaccinations, a pharmacy, a nursery, bars, restaurants, duty-free shops, a post office, *APT* tourist information (tel: 06659 54471; open daily 0800–1900), hotel reservation and car hire (*Avis, Europcar, Hertz, Italy By Car, Maggiore* and *Sixt*).

Business facilities: An 'Executive Center' in Terminal A (open daily 0700–2300) provides meeting rooms, secretarial and translation services and video-conferencing. There are also several airline VIP lounges with telephone and fax facilities.

Transport to the city: *Ferrovie dello Stato* (tel: 892 021; website: www.trenitalia.com) offers a frequent service of non-stop trains to Rome's Termini station. A single fare from the airport costs €8.80 (journey time – 32 minutes). There is also a slower train service (destination Orte or Fara Sabina), which stops at local stations on the way, including the centrally located Trastevere and Tiburtina stations. A single fare costs €4.70 (journey time – 39 and 58 minutes respectively). Tickets can be purchased at vending machines located inside domestic and international arrivals halls. Trains run from the airport to Rome

0637–2337 and from Rome to the airport 0551–2251. During the night, buses run from the airport to Rome 0115–0500 and from Tiburtina station in Rome (stopping at Termini station en route) to the airport 0030–0345. Tickets cost €5 and must be purchased on the bus. Taxis to the centre cost about €42 (more at night).

Ciampino Airport (CIA)

Tel: 0679 4941. Fax: 06794 94400.

Website: www.adr.it

Over 100 airlines use Ciampino, Rome's second airport, located about 15km (nine miles) southeast of the city centre. In addition to charter flights and budget airlines, Ciampino is used as a military airbase.

Major airlines: *Ryanair* (tel: 0505 03770; website: www.ryanair.com) operates flights from London Stansted to Ciampino Airport. Other airlines include *Britannia, Corsair* and *EasyJet*.

Airport facilities: Facilities include a bank, a bureau de change, a bar, a post office, gift shops, information and car hire (*Avis, Europcar, Hertz, Italy By Car, Maggiore* and *Sixt*).

Business facilities: A VIP lounge (open daily 0700–2300) is located inside the General Aviation Terminal.

Transport to the city: *COTRAL* buses (tel: 065 7031 *or* 8004 31784) run from Ciampino airport to Anagnina metro station (line A) and cost €1.50. From Anagnina, it is a direct 30-minute metro journey to Termini station. The bus stops running at 2340, when a taxi journey to the centre – which costs at least €40 – becomes the only option. Many airlines provide their own bus service (for a fee) to the city centre; visitors should ask when purchasing their ticket.

Approximate flight times to Rome: From London is 2 hours 50 minutes; from New York is 8 hours 20 minutes; from Los Angeles is 14 hours 35 minutes; from Toronto is 8 hours 5 minutes and from Sydney is 23 hours 10 minutes.

Arrival/departure tax: None.

Getting There By Water

The port of *Civitavecchia* is approximately one hour by train from Rome. The port is run by the *Autorità Portuale di Civitavecchia*, Molo Vespucci, Civitavecchia (tel: 0766 35993; website: www.port-of-rome.com). Facilities include a waiting room, ATMs, left-luggage and a bar.

Ferry services: Ferries to and from Sardinian ports are run by *Tirrenia Navigazione* (tel: 0648 80854; website: www.gruppotirrenia.it) and *Sardinia Ferries* (tel: 07665 00714; website: www.corsicaferries.com).

Transport to the city centre: Trains from Civitavecchia to Rome run approximately every 30 minutes. A first-class ticket costs about €10, while a second-class one-way ticket costs €7. Taxis to central Rome cost about €80 – if there are no taxis waiting at the port, companies will come out on call (see *Taxis* in *Getting Around*). Some hotels send taxis to pick up their guests, which often works out cheaper.

Getting There By Rail

The Italian State Railway, *Ferrovie dello Stato – FS* (tel: 892 021; website: www.trenitalia.com) runs a fast and efficient service throughout the country. *Stazione Termini*, Piazza Cinquecento, is Rome's main station. Refurbished for the year 2000, its extensive facilities include left-luggage, *carabinieri* (army) and police

stations, a tourist office, an Internet point, money exchange and ATMs (at *Banca di Roma*), many shops, bars and fast-food restaurants. Other important stations include *Tiburtina* at Piazzale della Stazione Tiburtina, *Trastevere* at Piazza F. Biondo, at the end of Viale Trastevere, and *Ostiense* at Piazzale Ostiense. Automatic ticket machines are located in all main stations. Tickets must be validated in the yellow machines located on the station platforms prior to boarding, in order to avoid fines.

Rail services: Most long-distance trains run to Termini station, which is also the main hub for the local transport network (metro and bus). However, the importance of the less centrally located stations – Tiburtina and Ostiense – grows as the night draws on and trains cease to run to Termini station. Ostiense is also the only stop for the *Napoli Express* between Rome and Paris (journey time – 14 hours). All other international trains – including services to Munich (journey time – 10 hours), Vienna (journey time – 14 hours) and London (journey time – 20 hours) – leave from Termini station. *InterCity* trains run from Termini to all major Italian cities – including Florence (journey time – 2 hours), Naples (journey time – 2 hours), Venice (journey time – 5 hours 30 minutes) and Milan (journey time – 5 hours 30 minutes), as well as Nice (journey time – 8 hours). *EuroStar* trains cover the same destinations, however, they are at least 20% more expensive than InterCity ones because they generally provide a faster service, specialising in long-distance trains that only stop at the major cities.

Transport to the city: Termini station is the main hub for the local transport network (metro and bus). Day and night buses run from Tiburtina and Ostiense, while tram 8 runs from Trastevere to Largo Argentina. Taxis are also available.

Getting There By Road

There are over 300,000km (185,000 miles) of roads in Italy – including over 6000km (3700 miles) of motorway – linking all parts of the country. Motorways (*autostrada*) are prefixed by the letter 'A', European roads by the letter 'E' and state roads are prefixed by the letters 'SS'. Many motorways have tolls. Road signs are international and traffic drives on the right. Undimmed headlights are prohibited in towns and cities but are compulsory when passing through tunnels and, since autumn 2002, headlights are required to be turned on whenever driving on motorways or any state roads. The minimum age for driving is 18 years. Passengers are required by law to wear seatbelts. The legal alcohol to blood ratio for driving is 0.05%. Speed limits are 130kph (81mph) on motorways, 90/110kph (56/68mph) on country roads and 50kph (31mph) in urban areas. Fines for speeding and other driving offences are made on the spot and are particularly heavy. All vehicles must carry a red warning triangle, available at border posts.

UK driving licences and EU pink-format licences are valid in Italy, although UK green licences must be accompanied by an International Driving Permit. A Green Card and motor insurance certificate are strongly recommended. A driving licence or a motorcycle driving licence is required for motorcycles over 49cc and it is compulsory to wear a crash helmet. Visitors should note that many petrol stations in town close between 1300 and 1500.

The *AA* or *RAC* in Britain and the *AAA* in America have reciprocal agreements with the *Automobile Club d'Italia – ACI*, Via Marsala 8 (tel: 064 9981; website: www.aci.it), who provide a useful advisory service, as well as dealing with breakdowns.

Emergency breakdown service: *ACI* 803 116.

Routes to the city: Rome is encircled by a network of motorways. The A12 leads into Rome from the west and the A24 from the east. Ciampino airport is connected to the city by Via Appia Nuova (SS7). The A1 runs between Rome, Florence and Milan, while

to reach Venice, drivers should turn off the A1 at Bologna and take the A13.

Approximate driving times to Rome: From Florence – 2 hours 30 minutes; Milan – 6 hours; Venice – 6 hours.

Coach services: *Eurolines Italia* (tel: 0644 04009; website: www.eurolines.it) runs international coaches, with connections to cities throughout Europe, such as London (via Paris). There is no central coach station in Rome, so coaches depart and terminate in front of Tiburtina train station, Via Tiburtina. Domestic coach services covering

northbound routes terminate outside the metro stations of Lepanto, Ponte Mammolo and Tiburtina, while those covering southbound routes terminate outside the metro stations of Anagnina and EUR Fermi.

Getting Around

Public Transport

Termini station is the main hub of Rome's transport system. The city transport authority, *ATAC* (tel:

CITY STATISTICS

Location: Lazio region, western central Italy.
Country dialling code: 39.
Population: 2,655,970 (city).
Ethnic mix: Majority Italian, 6.36% legally registered foreign minority includes Filipino, Polish, North American, Spanish and Romanian.
Religion: Roman Catholic majority, with Russian and Greek Orthodox, Jewish and Muslim minorities.
Time zone: GMT +1 (GMT + 2 from last Sunday in March to Saturday before last Sunday in October).
Electricity: 220 volts AC, 50Hz; round two-pin or three-pin plugs are standard.
Average January temp: 6.5°C (44°F).
Average July temp: 25°C (77°F).
Annual rainfall: 828mm (33 inches).

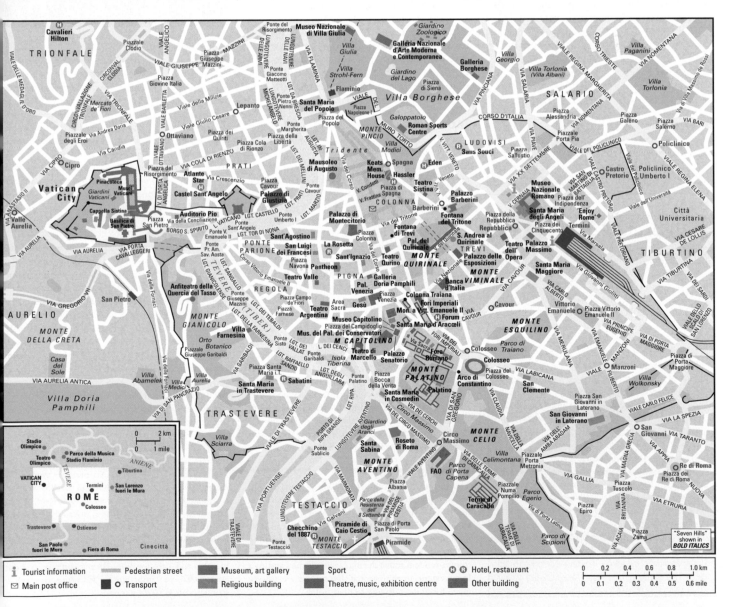

ℹ Tourist information		Pedestrian street		Museum, art gallery	Sport
✉ Main post office	■○ Transport		Religious building		Theatre, music, exhibition centre
					Ⓗ Ⓡ Hotel, restaurant
					Other building

"Seven Hills" shown in **BOLD ITALICS**

BUSINESS PROFILE

Rome's mayor, Walter Veltroni (elected in 2001), has continued work on a major investment programme set up by his predecessor. The scheme aims to maximise the possibilities opened up by tourism and encourage major national and multinational corporations to have a presence in Rome – the political and administrative centre of Italy. These initiatives are set to counter the negative effects of the government's decentralisation programme, which could result in a decreasing role for the capital city as a public sector employer. Mergers and acquisitions, combined with the government-initiated privatisation process, add further elements of risk to the local economy.

The strength of the national economy lies in the service sector, which accounted for 68% of GDP in 2001. Tourism is the country's largest industry, with Rome as the 'number one' destination in Italy. Other significant industries in the capital include finance and banking, insurance, printing, publishing and fashion. Italy's film industry (founded in 1936) is located at nearby Cinecittà. The business district is largely clustered within the *centro storico* (historic centre), partly because no one else can afford to pay the high rents. Trade fairs and large business conventions are normally held in EUR, a modern suburb situated six kilometres (four miles) south of the city centre. The *United Nations Food and Agriculture Organisation (FAO)* is based in Rome, as is the *World Food Programme (WFP)* and the *International Centre for the Study of the Preservation and Restoration of Cultural Property (ICCROM)*.

Unemployment varies dramatically throughout Italy. In 2002, it was 4% in the north, 6.6% in the centre and 18.3% in the south, with a national average of 9%, while Rome's unemployment rate actually dropped to 7.9%, finally falling below the national average.

BUSINESS ETIQUETTE

Although less formal than their Milanese counterparts, business is a serious affair for Romans. Greetings take the form of a handshake (social kissing is reserved for friends and family) and then business cards are exchanged. If possible, it is best to have one side printed in Italian and one in English – all company literature should be provided in Italian. Colleagues should be addressed by their surname and academic/professional titles respected. Although some of the Italian business community will speak some English or French, Italian is the dominant language of business. It is wise to take the precaution of employing an interpreter, to minimise the degree of misunderstandings.

In Rome, appearance counts. It is best to dress in a smart suit (with tie for men and stylish accessories for women). The odd designer label does no harm. Personal relationships are extremely important and it is unlikely that decisions will be made before trust has been established between the two parties. Business lunches provide the ideal opportunity to build relationships and small talk is an essential part of any business meeting. Standard office hours are 0900–1700, with an hour-long lunch break.

06469 52027 *or* 8004 31784; fax: 06469 52032; e-mail: clienti@atac.roma.it; website: www.atac.roma.it), operates the city's large fleet of **buses** and **trams**. The network consists of 282 bus lines and six tram lines, which cover the entire city and run daily 0530–2400. **Night buses** run daily 0000–0530, along 22 routes, and are marked on bus stops (*fermata*) and buses with the letter 'N'.

The regional transport authority, *COTRAL* (tel: 065 7031 *or* 8004 31784; website: www.cotralspa.it), runs **blue buses** throughout the Lazio region. It also runs three **suburban railway lines** departing from Termini, Ostiense and Flaminio stations, as well as Rome's two **metro** lines (A and B), which cross at Termini station. The easily mastered metro service operates daily 0530–2330 (until 2430 Saturday). Plans to forge a new third line have been in the works for years but have not come any closer to fruition. Just extending the two existing metro lines proved to be trouble enough, with the uncovering of archaeological vestiges either postponing or preventing any advances. All tickets must be pre-purchased and are available for sale at ATAC counters, *tabacchi* (newsagents) and at automatic ticket dispensers at metros. Tickets should be validated at the beginning of the journey (to avoid a hefty €51 fine). The cheapest ticket, the *Biglietto Integrato a Tempo (BIT)* costs €0.77 and is valid for up to 75 minutes of travel on *ATAC* buses and trams, or for one trip on the metro or suburban train lines. Day (*BIG*) and week (*CIS*) **passes** – valid on all transport in the municipality – cost €3.10 and €12.40 respectively. Monthly passes are also available. The *BIRG* pass covers a day's worth of transport within the whole Lazio region, and costs between €1.80 and €8 (depending on the number of zones covered).

Taxis

Taxi ranks are located at various points around the city centre. Visitors are recommended to use only the yellow and white official taxis. Surcharges are applied for each item of luggage, for airport transfers and for night service (2200–0700), as well as on Sundays and public holidays. While taxis may be called by telephone, the meter is turned on immediately after the call rather than on pick-up. Tipping of 5–10% is gratefully received, although many Italians do not bother. Companies include *Radio Taxi 3570* (tel: 063 570), *Cooperativa Samarcanda* (tel: 065 551) and *Radio Taxi Tevere* (tel: 064 157). Taxi hire costs, on average, €.78 per kilometre (more out of town).

Limousines

Centrally located providers include *Autonoleggi Bevilacqua*, Via San Nicola da Tolentino 20, Piazza Barberini (tel: 0648 3756), which hires out limousines on an hourly or daily basis, and *Airport Connection Service*, Via A Fava 28/d, Zona Trionfale (tel: 0633 83221; website: www.airportconnection.it), which not only chauffeurs single passengers or groups to the airport but also hires out limousines for day use. Visitors should expect to pay from about €30 per hour.

Driving in the City

The interweaving paths of mopeds, pedestrians and trams, the erratic driving, the one-way systems and the frequent traffic jams make driving in Rome an experience that is best avoided. The authorities have reacted to traffic congestion (and the ensuing pollution) by cutting off large areas of the city centre to non-resident traffic during business hours and, to a lesser extent, in the evening. Exceptions are usually made for visitors driving to their hotels.

Colonnade, St Peter's Square

Parking is as problematic as driving is. Pay-and-display meters charge about €1 per hour (although the fee may be waived in the evenings and at weekends). There are various underground car parks in the city – the one at Villa Borghese is open 24 hours. The wily may snap up a free parking space but anything marked *Sosta Vietata* (no parking) is to be avoided – the municipal police have a nasty habit of towing away illegally parked cars and then charging a huge sum for their return. Unlucky owners should contact the municipal police (tel: 066 7691).

Car Hire

Cars can be hired by drivers aged 21 years (23 for some companies) and above, on presentation of a passport and valid driving licence (held for at least one year). A credit card or cash deposit is requested and a valid international insurance policy is also necessary. Full insurance is advised. A small car costs from around €70 per day to hire. Providers include *Avis* (tel: 0641 9941; website: www.avisautonoleggio.it), *Europcar Italia* (tel: 8000 14410 *or* 0648 82854; website: www.europcar.it), *Hertz* (tel: 1991 12211; website: www.hertz.it), *Sixt* (tel: 0665 9651; website: www.e-sixt.it), and the locally based *Maggiore* (tel: 8488 67067; website: www.maggiore.it), all with various locations throughout the city.

Bicycle & Scooter Hire

Bicycles are available for hire at *Bici & Baci*, Via Viminale 5 (tel: 0648 28443). Scooters are available at *Happy Rent*, Via Farini 3 (tel: 0648 18185; website: www.happyrent.com), and *Roma Scooter Rent*, Via in Lucina 13–14 (tel: 0668 76455), located off Via del Corso, near the Parliament. *RomaRent*, Vicolo de' Bovari 7A, near Campo de' Fiori (tel/fax: 0668 96555; website: www.romarent.net), has scooters, bicycles and cars for hire. Bicycle hire costs from around €4 per hour up to €15 per day, while scooters cost €32–48 per day.

SIGHTSEEING

Sightseeing Overview

There is simply too much to see in Rome – the Vatican City alone can easily swallow up an entire weekend. Most visitors are overwhelmed and remain torn between running from sight to sight in order to 'do' everything or lingering over a couple of monuments and museums. The latter option is strongly recommended – even then, it is best to punctuate cultural trips with ice creams, coffees and serene walks in the city's parks (the *Villa Borghese* is one of the loveliest). As for most holy sites, clothing that covers up midriffs, shoulders and legs is recommended, particularly for the Vatican.

The *centro storico* is the obvious starting point, with the greatest concentration of classical and Christian sites enclosed in a relatively small space. Stumbling upon ancient frescoes, Renaissance fountains and beautiful piazzas is part of the pleasure of wandering around Rome's streets. Rome has over 400 churches and four major basilicas – *St Peter's, St John Lateran, St Mary Major* and *St Paul's*. However, it is *San Clemente* (on Via San Giovanni, in Laterano) that encapsulates the multi-layered labyrinth of Rome. At street level, there is a 12th-century basilica with beautiful mosaics. Down one level is a well-preserved Roman basilica. Deeper still are more ancient Roman remains, until finally, at the deepest level, is the temple to the Oriental cult of Mithras.

The *Ministry of Culture* organises the *Settimana dei Beni Culturali* or Cultural Week (tel: 066 7231; website: www.beniculturali.it), which is usually held in late March or early April and allows free entry to all state-owned museums, public monuments and excavation sites.

Key Attractions

Foro Romano (Roman Forum)

The *Roman Forum* is now a heap of marble fragments, columns and floor layouts. A leap of imagination is required to recreate the former marketplace that was the political, commercial and social heart of ancient Rome and the symbolic centre of an empire stretching to Greece, Sicily and Carthage. Fire, barbarians and pillaging builders in medieval and Renaissance times contributed to the Forum's present state of disrepair, although the Forum was only revealed during the excavation work of the 19th century. A bird's-eye view is gained from behind Piazza del Campidoglio, while a closer look can be had from along Via Sacra that runs through the heart of the Forum. Among the best preserved and most fascinating monuments are the AD203 triumphal *Arch of Septimius Severus* – built to celebrate victory over the Parthinians – and the remains of Caesar's rostra, from where his great speeches were declaimed. Another stunning feature is the former atrium of the *House of the Vestal Virgins* and the adjacent *Temple of Vesta*, a circular building where the vestal virgins were entrusted with keeping the eternal flame alight. Just up from the *Arch of Titus* in the Forum is the *Palatine*, where the palaces of the Roman emperors stood.
Largo Romolo e Romo, Via dei Fori Imperiali
Tel: 06399 67700.
Transport: Metro Colosseo; bus to Via dei Fori Imperiali or Piazza Venezia.
Opening hours: Daily 0900–1830 (Apr–Oct); daily 0900–one hour before sunset (Nov–Mar).
Admission: Free; €8 (Palatine and Colosseum combined ticket).

Colosseum

Colosseo (Colosseum)

Near to Via Sacra and the fourth-century *Arco di Costantino* (Arch of Constantine), lies the gigantic oval of the *Colosseum* – 186m (620ft) long, 153m (510ft) wide and about 47m (157ft) high. Emperor Vespasian began construction in AD72 and work was completed by his son Titus eight years later. It was the scene for entertainment that one can hardly comprehend – gladiatorial conquests between men, lions and wild beasts, with death guaranteed. The 'games' were finally outlawed in the fifth century. The stadium has been pillaged over the centuries and rocked by earthquakes. Today, only its skeletal framework remains, with the winding passages used to force animals up to the battlefield of the arena – formerly underground – now exposed.
Piazza del Colosseo
Tel: 06399 67700.
Transport: Metro Colosseo; bus to Piazza del Colosseo.
Opening hours: Daily 0900–1930 (Apr–Oct); daily 0900–one hour before sunset (Nov–Mar).
Admission: €8 (ticket also allows entry to the Palatine).

Pantheon

The best-preserved and most beautifully proportioned of Rome's ancient monuments, the *Pantheon* has become an emblem of the city. Built by Hadrian between AD119 and AD128, as a temple to the gods, the Pantheon was converted to a Christian church in AD608 – the key to its miraculous survival. The radius of the dome is exactly equivalent to the height and a nine-metre (30ft) hole, known as the *oculus*, in the dome's centre allows light (and rain) into the building. Statues of the deities would once have decorated the interior. Now the focal point of interest is the tomb of Raphael. Most astonishing of all are the large brass doors, which belonged to the original Roman building.
Piazza della Rotonda
Tel: 06683 00230.
Transport: Bus to Largo Argentina or Via del Corso.
Opening hours: Mon–Sat 0830–1930, Sun 0900–1800.
Admission: Free.

Cappella Sistina & Musei Vaticani (Sistine Chapel & Vatican Museums)

An awe-inspiring glimpse of Michaelangelo's depiction of *The Creation* is worth the queues and crowds that go hand-in-hand with a visit to the *Vatican City*. Michaelangelo grudgingly accepted Julius II's commission to paint frescoes on the ceiling of the *Sistine Chapel* – built between 1475 and 1480 as a private chapel of the popes. Work began in May 1508, the frescoes were unveiled in August 1511 and completed in October 1512. It was 21 years later that a reluctant Michaelangelo painted the *Last Judgement* on the wall behind the altar, adding his own aged face below the figure of Christ. Pope Pius IV was scandalised by the display of nudity and the offending genitalia had to be concealed by hastily painted loincloths – most have been removed during restoration work. In fact, the recent restoration of the Old Testament scenes has caused great controversy. The other Renaissance paintings that line the walls, although eclipsed by Michaelangelo's artistry, are fine works, created by the masters – including Michaelangelo's own teacher, Ghirlandaio.

The *Vatican Museums* alone could easily eat up a day or two of a trip to Rome. Highlights include the *Stanze di Raffaello* (Raphael's Rooms), the *Etruscan Museum* – depicting Italy before the Romans – and the *Pio-Clementino Museum* – containing the world's largest collection of classical statues.
Viale Vaticano 100
Tel: 06698 83860. Fax: 06698 85061.
Website: www.vatican.va or www.christusrex.org
Transport: Metro Ottaviano; bus to Piazza del Risorgimento.
Opening hours: Mon–Sat 0845–1545 with last entry at 1420 (Apr–Oct); Mon–Sat 0845–1345 with last entry at 1220 (Nov–Mar); last Sun of month 0845–1345 with last entry at 1220.
Admission: €10; free last Sun of month.

Basilica di San Pietro (St Peter's Basilica)

St Peter's Basilica lies above a former shrine that is said to mark the burial ground of the saint. Despite its venerable age of 1000 years, Pope Julius II pulled down the original structure in 1506 – with his architect Bramante in tow – in order to build a shiny new basilica. Construction lasted 120 years, during which time a team of architects and artists – including Alberti, Bramante, Raphael, Peruzzi, Sangallo the Younger and Michaelangelo – struggled over this enormous edifice. Michaelangelo was responsible for the huge dome and supporting drum but died in 1564, before work was finally completed in 1590. The basilica's interior is an unashamed

TOURIST INFORMATION

Azienda di Promozione Turistica di Roma (APT)
Via Parigi 5
Tel: (06) 488 991 *or* 3600 4399 (call centre).
Fax: (06) 481 9316.
Website: www.romaturismo.com
Opening hours: Mon–Sat 0900–1900.

Other APT branches are at Termini station and Fiumicino airport and there are ten other green tourist information booths dotted around the city at strategic points (open daily 0930–1930).

Another useful source of information is the Anglo-centric *Enjoy Rome*, Via Marghera 8A (tel: (06) 445 1843; website: www.enjoyrome.com), near Termini station. The *Ente Nazionale per il Turismo* (ENIT), Via Marghera 2 (tel: (06) 49711; website: www.enit.it), provides information on Italian areas outside of Rome and the Latium region.

Passes
There are various tourist passes available. *Roma Caput Mundi*, Piazza di Trevi 86 (tel: (06) 678 6136; website: www.romacaputmundi.it), runs the *Itinere Card*, which is a booklet of tickets providing admission to a number of less well-known museums and archaeological sites – including Capitoline Museum, Forum of Trajan and Trajan Markets, Circus of Maxentius, City Museum of Modern and Contemporary Art, Museum of Roman Civilisation and Museum of Folklore. The pass, valid for a week, costs €12.91 and can be purchased from Roma Caput Mundi.

Roma Vision (tel: (06) 4695 4695; website: www.romavision.it) has now introduced a card called *ReadyRoma*. The one-week pass costs €41 and includes the Itinere Card, a tour by boat, a ride on a historic tram and two passes for buses that cover the city's most interesting sites, including the catacombs on the Via Appia. It also offers cheaper one-day options. Cards are available from Roma Vision, who have stands at Termini station, Piazza del Colosseo, Piazza Santa Maria Maggiore and Piazza San Giovanni.

Two other passes are the *Museum Card* and the *Archaeological Card* (tel: (06) 3996 7700, information). The first allows entrance to the National Roman Museum's four sites (Palazzo Massimo alle Terme, Palazzo Altemps, Baths of Diocletian and Crypta Balbi) the second allows entrance to those sites plus the Colosseum, the Palatine, the Baths of Caracalla, the tomb of Cecilia Metella and Villa dei Quintilli. The passes cost €9 and €20 respectively and are valid for seven days from the first day of use. They can be purchased from any of the participating monuments or museums.

display of the power of the Church. Amid the grandeur lies Michaelangelo's *Pietà* (1498/9), in the first chapel on the right. Arnolfo da Cambio's bronze statue of *St Peter* (1296), in the central aisle, has become famed for its foot, worn to a nub by pilgrims' kisses. Bernini's *Throne of St Peter* (1665), made with bronze purloined from the Pantheon on the Pope's orders, is situated above the papal altar and dominates the far end of the nave. Optional extras include a trip (via lift or stairs) into the dome, the *Vatican Gardens* (pre-booked guided tours only), and the *Vatican Grottoes*, containing papal tombs. Access to the *Necropolis* below the Grottoes – the legendary site of St Peter's remains – is only allowed with written permission in advance.
Piazza San Pietro
Tel: 06698 81662 (pilgrim and tourist information centre).
Transport: Metro Ottaviano; bus to Piazza del Risorgimento.
Opening hours: Daily 0700–1900 (Apr–Oct); daily 0700–1800 (Nov–Mar).
Admission: Free.
St Peter's Dome
Opening hours: Daily 0800–1745 (Apr–Oct); daily 0800–1645 (Nov–Mar).
Admission: €4 (without lift); €5 (with lift).
Necropolis
Opening hours: Applications should be made to the *Ufficio Scavi* (tel: 06698 85318; fax: 06698 85518; e-mail: scavi@fsp.va) several days prior to visit.
Admission: €9.
Vatican Gardens/Vatican Guided Tours Office
Tel: 06698 84466. Fax: 06698 85100.
Opening hours: Organised tours can be booked several days in advance.
Admission: €9.

Fontana di Trevi (Trevi Fountain)

A string of legends surround the *Trevi Fountain*, which is situated amid the labyrinthine streets off Via del Tritone. It is said that a virgin came across a three-way (*tre-vie*) spring, causing the original fountain to be built. More recently, the far-from-virginal Anita Ekberg immortalised the fountain in the famous scene of Fellini's *La Dolce Vita* (1959). According to myth, a coin cast in these waters will ensure a return visit to Rome. The Baroque extravaganza was designed by Nicolò Salvi for Pope Clement XII and completed in 1762. The statues – representing Abundance, Agrippa, Salubrity, the Virgin and Neptune guiding a chariot drawn by sea horses – appear as a cast of characters performing a melodrama, with a Renaissance palace for their backdrop and craggy rocks in the foreground.
Piazza di Trevi
Transport: Bus to Piazza San Silvestro.

The Spanish Steps and Keats-Shelley Memorial House

The *Piazza di Spagna* district is little changed from 18th-century prints depicting the area – and is still dominated by the elegant double steps known as the *Spanish Steps*. These were designed by Francesco de Sanctis in 1723–26 to link Via del Babuino with Via Felice – the first great street planned by Sixtus V (1585–90). Reminiscent of the grand ascent to the Sacré Coeur in Paris, the steps lead up to the 16th-century *Trinitá dei Monti*. From here, spectacular views over the city rooftops more than warrant the steep climb. The Spanish Steps acquired their name from the neighbouring Spanish Embassy, although

the area is more intimately associated with England – even acquiring the name of *Ghetto de l'Inglesi* (English Ghetto). The tourists on the Grand Tour of the 18th and 19th centuries – including Keats, Shelley, Byron and the Brownings – helped to establish the district's reputation as a cosmopolitan artistic quarter. At the foot of the steps lies the boat-shaped *Barcaccia* fountain, designed by Bernini in 1627. To the right, stands the modest *Keats-Shelley Memorial House*, where 25-year-old John Keats died of tuberculosis in 1821. Exhibits include pictures and prints, private letters, an urn bearing Shelley's ashes and a lock of Keats' tawny red hair.
Keats-Shelley Memorial House
Piazza di Spagna 26
Tel: 0667 84235. Fax: 0667 84167.
Website: www.keats-shelley-house.org
Transport: Metro Spagna.
Opening hours: Mon–Fri 0900–1300 and 1500–1800, Sat 1100–1400.
Admission: €3.

Piazza Navona

This dramatic piazza – lined with cafés and restaurants – lies at the heart of the *centro storico*. Its oval shape follows the form of the former stadium, built by Emperor Domitian in AD86. During the Renaissance, the site was flooded to stage mock naval battles. The piazza gained its current form in the mid-17th century, when Pope Innocent X commissioned Borromini to design the *Church of Sant'Agnese*. In front of the church, Bernini built the *Fontana dei Quattro Fiumi* (Fountain of the Four Rivers), adorned with powerful figures representing the four great rivers of the world – the Nile, Danube, Ganges and Rio della Plate.
Transport: Bus to Largo Argentina.

Villa & Galleria Borghese

Just to the east of the Spanish Steps lies green relief from sightseeing – these sculpture-scattered gardens, which were landscaped in the 17th century for Cardinal Scipione Borghese (nephew of Pope Paul V).

Roman Forum and Palatine Hill

This area includes the city zoo, Piazza di Siena arena, mock ancient temples, imitation medieval castles and an artificial lake. Unfortunately, the most playful elements of this Baroque extravaganza – trick fountains that sprayed unwitting passers-by – no longer exist. The pull of culture may be strong enough to lure the resting visitor into the *Casino Borghese*, a treasure trove of sculpture and antiquities, the *Etruscan Museum* in nearby *Villa Giulia*, with its remarkable sarcophagus of the reclining 'Bride and Bridegroom' from Cerveteri, or the *Galleria Nazionale d'Arte Moderna e Contemporanea*. However, the *Galleria Borghese* – home to Bernini's most famous work, *Apollo and Daphne* – should be seen first (ticket reservation is obligatory and visitors are only admitted every two hours).

Galleria Borghese
Piazzale Scipione Borghese 5
Tel: 063 2810. Fax: 0685 55952.
Website: www.galleriaborghese.it
Transport: Metro Spagna; bus or tram to Via Veneto.
Opening hours: Tues–Sun 0900–1930.
Admission: €6.50 (reservations required).
Villa Giulia
Piazzale di Villa Giulia 9
Tel: 0632 01951.
Transport: Tram 3 or 19.
Opening hours: Tues–Sun 0900–1930.
Admission: €4.

Further Distractions

Galleria Doria Pamphili

A British voice with a cut-glass accent, issuing from the hand-held cassette, guides visitors through picture-clogged rooms, with lavish furnishings and ageing sculptures – in short, the excessive wealth of the powerful Doria Pamphili family, a pillar of Rome's papal aristocracy. The half-British sibling and heir recalls childhood memories of rollerskating along the parquet floor of the 18th-century ballroom – tiny indentations prove the truth of his tale. The rambling palace is still occupied and a number of the private apartments are open to the public (mornings only) for a small additional fee. Works by Correggio, Caravaggio and Velázquez are on show here, as well as some amusing pieces by lesser known artists.
Piazza del Collegio Romano 2
Tel: 0667 97323. Fax: 0667 80939.
Website: www.doriapamphilj.it
Transport: Bus to Piazza Venezia.
Opening hours: Fri–Wed 1000–1700.
Admission: €7.30.

Campo de' Fiori

From Monday to Saturday, at dawn, stall holders at Rome's best-loved fruit and vegetable market set up their wares at *Campo de' Fiori*. This down-to-earth square – surrounded by tumbledown orange-ochre façades – is a far cry from the more grandiose piazzas of the *centro storico*. Here, one encounters the friendliness and spontaneity for which the *Romani* are so renowned. Come sunset, some of the city's liveliest and most authentic wine bars and trattorias have tables spilling out onto the cobbles, as locals and visitors alike flock here, to eat and drink below the stars.
Campo de' Fiori
Transport: Bus to Largo Argentina.
Opening hours: Mon–Sat dawn–dusk.
Admission: Free.

Tours of the City

Walking Tours

Rome Walks (website: www.romewalks.com) offers a wide variety of group tours. Guides speak English and are experienced in history of art. Departure points vary, depending on the tour. They also arrange personalised tours covering sights that are 'off the beaten track'. Group tours are offered several times a week and include the 'Vatican City Walk', which takes four-and-a-half hours and costs €40 (excluding €10 museum entrance fee) and the highly informative 'Colosseum and Ancient City Walk' (€48 including €8 Colosseum entrance fee). They can also arrange a variety of private tours (for groups of one to four), such as '*La Dolce Vita* in Rome', the catacombs or Nero's Golden Palace.

For those wishing to sample some Roman nightlife, the 'Colosseum Pub Crawls' (website: www.walksofeurope.com) leave every night from both the Colosseum Metro and the Spanish Steps at 2000. The €15 ticket includes free shots, drinks and entrance to a disco-bar at the end. Also *Enjoy Rome* (see *Tourist Information*) offers a number of walking and bike tours around Rome that start at €13.

Bus Tours

The number 110 *ATAC* bus (tel: 06469 52252 (bookings and information)) departs from Piazza dei Cinquecento every half-hour (daily 0900–2000 April to September or 1000–1800 October to March) for a two-hour tour (with commentary in English) around Rome's main sights (there are 11 stops en route). Tickets and a leaflet outlining the itinerary are available in English at any tourist information office. The tour costs €7.75 or €12.91 if you want to get on and off the bus. There are also night tours.

Boat Tours

Tourvisa Italia, Via Marghera 32 (tel: 0644 63481), provides a three-hour round-trip evening boat tour from the bridge Ponte Umberto 1 (Piazza Navona) to Ponte Duca d'Aosta. Boats depart daily at 2000 May to October, weather conditions permitting. The air-conditioned vessel sails past the Vatican, Castel Sant'Angelo and under Rome's bridges. The cruise includes dinner, live music and dancing and costs €65 per person.

View of St Peter's Church across the River Tiber

Excursions

For a Half Day

Ostia Antica: A 40-minute train ride from Piramide station or a pleasant drive along Via del Mare is *Ostia Antica* – Imperial Rome's main port from the second to ninth centuries AD. It was founded by King Ancus Marcius in the seventh century BC and lay abandoned until excavations in the 19th century. The shoreline has now withdrawn three kilometres (two miles) away to the present Lido di Ostia and, at first glance, all that can be seen is a network of thoroughfares with the odd upstanding column. However, a few hours spent in this quiet spot and the imagination will conjure up the former thriving town and the day-to-day lives of its inhabitants. The main artery, the *Decumanus Maximus*, leads to an amphitheatre with fantastic acoustics, which is perfect for a peaceful picnic. Mosaics at the *Forum of the Corporations* depict the produce sold or trade practised, while the bar, *Thermopiliu*, with its wide marble counter and lively fresco, evokes leisure time. Temples to a host of deities summon up the religious

Stone masks from the theatre at Ostia Antica

Photo: Corel

Villa d'Este, Tivoli

life. The homes of Ostia's inhabitants reveal mosaic interiors, while communal latrines are testament to more mundane activities. The museum displays coins, glassware and statues. The site (tel: 06563 58099; website: www.ostia-antica.org) is open daily 0830–1930 April to October or daily 0900–1700 November to March. Admission costs €4.

For a Whole Day

Tivoli: A 30km (20 miles) drive east of Rome (along the A24) lies the hilltop town of Tivoli. Alternatively, travellers can take a *COTRAL* bus from Ponte Mammolo metro station or a train from Termini or Tiburtina stations (direction Avezzano). Both stop at Tivoli.

Conquered by the Romans in 338BC, the town became the prized spot upon which to build luxurious villas and homes for wealthy families. The *Villa d'Este* (tel: 07743 12070) is one such folly, built according to the whim of art patron Cardinal Ippolito d'Este (son of Lucrezia Borgia) in 1550. The state apartment is decorated with the swirling frescoes and paintings of Correggio, Da Volterra and Perrin del Vaga, while outside are the vast Renaissance gardens. Their fountains can only be described as kitsch – the Owl Fountain (designed to echo the owl's hoots) and Fontana dell'Organo Idraulico, which imitated the organ's burblings.

As much, if not more, imagination went into the construction of the *Villa Adriana* or Hadrian's Villa (tel: 07743 82733 *or* 06399 67900 (information and bookings)), which has been included on the UNESCO list of World Heritage Sites. Enough of the Canopus fountain, with its sturdy columns and statues overlooking a central pool, remains to evoke the peace of this domain and country retreat for Rome's great military campaigner. It is thought that his favourite spot was the tiny island, cut off completely from the surrounding man-made pool (*Teatro Marittimo*) by an ingenious retractable bridge.

The standard opening hours for both Villa d'Este and Villa Adriana are daily 0900–1930 (ticket office closes at 1800). Admission to each site costs €6.50.

ACCOMMODATION

As Rome sees a constant stream of visitors throughout the year, there is little difference between low-season and high-season prices. However, if visiting in January, February, October or November, it is worth asking for a reduction.

IVA (value-added tax) at 10% is included in hotel prices but is usually added to the price before it is quoted. The prices quoted below are the lowest standard rates for a double room, including IVA and service charges but excluding breakfast, unless otherwise specified.

Business

Cavalieri Hilton

Undoubtedly Rome's top deluxe hotel, the stylish *Cavalieri Hilton* stands upon Monte Mario hill, affording stunning views over the capital. Set in six hectares (15 acres) of landscaped grounds, it lies 20 minutes from the city centre and 30 minutes from the airport. Its 375 rooms (including 17 suites), each with a balcony, are impeccably furnished in a modern style. With 14 fully equipped congress halls and meeting rooms (seating 15 to 2100), this hotel is ideal for business conventions. The esteemed roof garden restaurant, *La Pergola*, attracts residents and non-residents alike. Other facilities and services include a fitness centre (gym, two pools, Turkish baths, sauna and tennis courts), a shopping arcade and a shuttle bus to the city centre.
Via Cadlolo 101
Tel: 063 5091. Fax: 06350 92241.
E-mail: fom_rome@hilton.com
Website: www.cavalieri-hilton.it
Price: From €465 (including breakfast).

Exedra

Ideally located close to Termini station, the *Exedra* occupies a late 19th-century neo-classical building, renovated and opened to guests in December 2002. Chic and sophisticated, the hotel boasts 236 sumptuous rooms and suites, all with Internet connection and beautifully tiled bathrooms. The underground cellars have been turned into a well–equipped business centre and four meeting halls, hosting from 40 to 250 delegates. New York architect Adam D Tihany designed the hotel's two restaurants. A rooftop spa, with an open-air Jacuzzi, four treatment rooms with sauna and massage, is scheduled to open late 2003.
Piazza della Republica 47
Tel: 0648 9381. Fax: 06489 38777.
E-mail: info@exedra.boscolo.com
Website: www.boscolohotels.com
Price: From €400.

Hotel Atlante Star

Well-managed and friendly, the *Hotel Atlante Star* lies five minutes from the Vatican. Popular with executives, its 70 rooms and 15 suites are the height of luxury, featuring antique furniture and marble bathrooms with Jacuzzi. There is a well-run business centre – a large office space with computers, telephones, fax and photocopier – plus a conference room complete with up-to-date audiovisual equipment and seating for 65 delegates.

Up top, the *Les Etoiles* roof garden restaurant offers a stunning panorama over Rome, with views of St Peter's. A smaller and cheaper sister hotel, the *Hotel Atlante Garden*, lies close by, at Via Crescenzio 78A. Both establishments offer free shuttle pick-up from the airport.
Via Vitelleschi 34
Tel: 0668 73233. Fax: 0668 72300.
E-mail: atlante.star@atlantehotels.com
Website: www.atlantehotels.com
Price: From €290 (including breakfast).

Sheraton Roma

A modern hotel and conference centre aimed at executives, the *Sheraton Roma* is located in EUR, the heart of Rome's commercial life. A hotel shuttle bus makes regular runs to the airport (20 minutes) and the city centre (30 minutes). Besides 650 guest rooms and suites, there are 38 'Smart Rooms' where executives can transact business at all hours. Each unit includes a large desk, a two-line telephone, a printer, fax machine and photocopier. Four congress halls (seating 600 to 2000) and 14 smaller meeting rooms are designed to cater for conferences, exhibitions and seminars. The hotel also offers excellent dining, shopping and sports facilities.
Viale del Pattinagio 100
Tel: 065 4531. Fax: 0659 40689.
E-mail: infosheraton.roma@flashnet.it
Website: www.sheraton.com/roma
Price: From €294 (including breakfast).

Luxury

Hassler–Villa Medici

Located at the top of the Spanish Steps, just a stone's throw from the designer clothes shops of Via Condotti, the elegant *Hassler* commands stunning panoramic views over Rome. Its 100 rooms (including 15 suites) are decorated in classic style, with sweeping floor-to-ceiling curtains, Venetian glass chandeliers and marble bathrooms, while many have either a balcony or terrace. The rooftop restaurant serves dinner by candlelight with piano music and there is an elegant garden bar. Extra facilities include five business meeting rooms, a gym, beauty salon, sun deck and garage space for parking.
Piazza Trinità dei Monti 6
Tel: 0669 9340. Fax: 0667 89991.
E-mail: booking@hotelhassler.it
Website: www.lhw.com/hassler
Price: From €566.

Hotel Eden

Possibly Rome's most glamorous hotel, the *Eden*, located between Via Veneto and the Spanish Steps, dates back to 1889. Frequented by stars and millionaires, former guests range from Ernest Hemingway and Ingrid Bergman, to the more recent names of Cameron Diaz and Daniel Day Lewis. Its 119 rooms (including 14 suites) are richly decorated in turn-of-the-century style, with antique furniture, fine linen sheets and splendid marble bathrooms. Some of the most expensive top-floor rooms have balconies and offer stunning views over the Eternal City, as does the highly acclaimed *La Terrazza dell'Eden* rooftop restaurant. Additional facilities include two elegant business meeting rooms and a well-equipped modern gym.
Via Ludovisi 49
Tel: 0647 8121. Fax: 0648 21584.

E-mail: reservations@hotel-eden.it
Website: www.hotel-eden.it
Price: From €645.

Moderate

Albergo del Sole (al Biscione)
Ideally located in the *centro storico*, this charming but unpretentious hotel lies in a side street between Campo de' Fiori and Piazza Navona, backing onto the ancient Teatro di Pompei. Its 59 bedrooms are simply but comfortably furnished, each with a telephone and satellite TV and some with beamed ceilings. A peaceful roof garden terrace offers some stunning views over the surrounding rooftops and church domes. Breakfast is not served but an early morning cappuccino and a croissant at Campo de' Fiori, watching stallholders set out their wares at the colourful open-air market, more than compensates. Very popular, so it is advisable to reserve in advance.
Via del Biscione 76
Tel: 06688 06873. Fax: 0668 93787.
E-mail: info@solealbiscione.it
Website: www.solealbiscione.it
Price: From €125 (€95 without bathroom).

La Cisterna
Hidden away in a narrow, cobbled side street, a five-minute walk from Piazza Santa Maria in Trastevere, this small, friendly hotel is housed in a recently refurbished 18th-century building. There are 18 homely bedrooms (all have a private bathroom, telephone and satellite TV, while some have wooden beamed ceilings), a bar and a peaceful terrace garden out the back. *La Cisterna* makes an ideal base for cultural travellers on a tight budget. Located in the bohemian district of Trastevere, known for its wine bars and trattorias, the *centro storico* lies just across the river, while the Vatican is a pleasant 15-minute walk along the River Tiber.
Via della Cisterna 8
Tel: 0658 17212. Fax: 0658 10091.
Price: From €130 (including breakfast).

Other Recommendations

Hotel Locarno
This pretty, moderately priced, atmospheric hotel, close to Piazza del Popolo, dates back to 1925, hence the stylish Art Deco details, such as its lift. Each of its 48 rooms is uniquely decorated with antiques and Liberty-style wallpaper and fabrics. They do an extremely generous buffet breakfast, which, during the summer, is served on the roof garden terrace with views over the surrounding rooftops. Within easy walking distance of the chic boutiques and art galleries of Via Margutta, it is popular with people in art and cinema – English film director Peter Greenaway often stays here. A charming extra is the complimentary bicycles available to guests.
Via della Penna 22
Tel: 0636 10841. Fax: 0632 15249.
E-mail: info@hotellocarno.com
Website: www.hotellocarno.com
Price: From €190 (including breakfast).

Raphael Hotel
This romantic hotel lies in a secluded street just behind Piazza Navona, in the heart of the *centro storico*. Its distinctive ivy-clad façade oozes quiet luxurious charm, as does the elegant lobby, decorated with works of art, which include ceramics by Picasso. Each of the 70 rooms is furnished with antiques, while the bathrooms are decorated with marble and hand-painted tiles. Guests have free use of the Finnish sauna and fitness centre and there is an exquisite roof garden, with a restaurant and bar. Although it is popular with politicians and the rich and famous – Robert De Niro likes to stay here – it remains exceptionally friendly and utterly unpretentious.
Largo Febo 2
Tel: 0668 2831. Fax: 0668 78993.
E-mail: info@raphaelhotel.com
Website: www.raphaelhotel.com
Price: From €420.

RESTAURANTS

The selected restaurants have been divided into five categories: Gastronomic, Business, Trendy, Budget and Personal Recommendations. The restaurants are listed alphabetically within these different categories, which serve as guidelines rather than absolute definitions of the establishments.
IVA (value-added tax) at 10% is included in restaurant prices but is usually added to the prices before they are quoted. A 15% service charge is usually added to the bill. Romans are not very generous with tips but an additional 10% on top of the bill, if the meal and service have been good, is very much appreciated.
The prices quoted below are for an average three-course meal for one person and for a bottle of house wine or cheapest equivalent; they include IVA but do not include service charge or tip.

Gastronomic

Checchino dal 1887
The birthplace of Roman cooking, in the heart of Testaccio, *Checchino* has remained in the Mariani family for five generations. Classics, such as *coda alla vaccinara* (braised oxtail) and *abbacchio alla cacciatora* (braised suckling lamb), were invented here. Still on the menu today, they have been adapted to create lighter dishes for the modern palate. Reservations are recommended – it is packed throughout the week, normally with locals. Closed Sunday and Monday and throughout August.
Via Monte Testaccio 30
Tel: 0657 46318. Fax: 0657 43816.
E-mail: checchino_roma@tin.it
Website: www.checchino-dal-1887.com
Price: €50. Wine: €15.

La Pergola
Sublime food and breathtaking views put this roof garden restaurant among Italy's 'Top 20'. The chef, Heinz Beck, shapes the menu according to seasonal produce and personal inspiration. Some of his recent successes include *tortellini di ricotta con pecorino e fave* (ricotta tortellini with pecorino cheese and beans) and *agnello in crosta di olive* (lamb in an olive crust). The cellar stocks some of the best – and most expensive – wines in the world. Closed Sunday and Monday.
Cavalieri Hilton Hotel, Via Cadlolo 101
Tel: 06350 92055. Fax: 06350 92165.
E-mail: fb@cavalieri-hilton.it
Website: www.cavalieri-hilton.it
Price: €100. Wine: €30.

Piazza Santa Maria in Trastevere

La Rosetta
Regarded as Rome's top fish restaurant, *La Rosetta* lies in a quiet side street close to the Pantheon. Upon entering the wood-panelled room, with its wooden furniture and red upholstery, customers receive a complimentary glass of champagne. One might begin with *antipasto misto* (a selection of cold seafood delicacies), followed by *linguine con astice ai tre pomodori* (pasta with lobster and tomato), to be rounded off with *scorfano e verdure grigliate* (grilled sea scorpion and spinach). The wines are truly classy but shockingly expensive. Closed Sunday.
Via della Rosetta 8
Tel: 0668 61002. Fax: 06682 15116.
E-mail: larosetta@tin.it
Website: www.larosetta.com
Price: €80. Wine: €35.

Le Sans Souci
The faded glamour of *La Dolce Vita* lives on at *Le Sans Souci*, just off Via Veneto. It is all rather extravagant – international jet-setters dining below elaborate coffered ceilings, surrounded by impeccably dressed waiters and a *sotto fondo* of romantic guitar music. The chef concocts a blend of Italian and French cuisine – starters include delectable soufflés and truffled terrine of foie gras, with delights such as duck in *millefeuille* pastry or lobster fricassee to follow. No lunch. Closed Monday.
Via Sicilia 20
Tel: 06420 14510. Fax: 0648 21771.
Price: €70. Wine: €25.

Sabatini
Open-air dining is a sheer joy at *Sabatini*, with tables overlooking a delightful piazza backed by the floodlit golden mosaics of the Church of Santa Maria in Trastevere. During winter, the wood-beamed terracotta-floored dining room comes into use. Roman dishes and seafood top the menu – examples include *linguine ai frutti di mare* (pasta with mussels, clams and prawns), followed by delicious grilled scampi.
Piazza Santa Maria in Trastevere 13
Tel: 0658 12026. Fax: 0658 98386.
Website: www.sabatini-fratelli.com
Price: €50. Wine: €9.

Photo: Corel

Roman café

Business

Dal Bolognese

Popular with politicians, artists and businesspeople, this restaurant has a smart summer terrace overlooking Piazza del Popolo and a classic winter dining room decorated with contemporary paintings. The menu features dishes from Bologna, notably homemade pasta in creamy sauces – excellent *tortelloni con ricotta e spinaci* (pasta filled with spinach and ricotta) – and *bollito misto* (mixed boiled meats). For dessert, they do a divine sorbet, served in scooped-out fruit. No lunch Tuesday. Closed Monday.
Piazza del Popolo 1
Tel: 0636 11426. Fax: 0632 22799.
Price: €40. Wine: €16.

Dal Toscano

The Bruni family have run this friendly trattoria for three generations. Close to the Vatican, *Dal Toscano* is known for traditional cooking and speedy service. The interior is simple – vaulted ceilings and plain wooden furniture – and in summer there is a leafy terrace. Both Tuscan and Roman specialities, such as *funghi porcini arrosto* (roast porcini mushrooms) and *abbacchio scottadito* (grilled suckling lamb), are on offer. The Chianti, a robust red, is first-rate. Closed Monday.
Via Germanico 58–60
Tel: 06397 25717. Fax: 06397 30748.
E-mail: info@ristorantedaltoscano.it
Website: www.ristorantedaltoscano.it
Price: €26. Wine: €9.

Enoteca Capranica

Housed within a 15th-century renaissance *palazzo*, close to the Parliament, this elegant restaurant retains old-fashioned charm, with its wood-panelled walls and chintzy covered chairs. Ideal for business lunches, there is also a small room reserved for private meetings. The menu features refined Mediterranean dishes, such as *velluta di patate, cicoria e pepperoncino* (potato and chicory cream soup with hot red pepper), and *anatra alle arance rose con spinaci* (duck with blood orange and spinach). No lunch Saturday. Closed Sunday.
Piazza Capranica 99
Tel: 06699 40992. Fax: 06699 40989.
Website: www.enotecacapranica.it
Price: €40. Wine: €20.

La Tana de Noantri

This is a very popular venue that, despite being situated in the heart of the most touristy part of Trastevere (behind Piazza Santa Maria), has kept up a very high standard of solid Roman cuisine since it opened in 1965. All the dishes use only the very freshest of ingredients, especially the many fish main courses. Another of their specialities are *Tagliolini alla Tana* (thin egg tagliatelle made with tomatoes, mushrooms and fresh oregano). Outdoor seating is available in summer. Closed Tuesday.
Via della Paglia 1–3
Tel: 0658 06404.
Price: €25. Wine: €7.

Taverna degli Amici

Popular with Italian politicians and celebrities from the Roman arts scene, this restaurant nevertheless boasts unpretentious and discreet staff, a tasteful rustic interior and a romantic candlelit terrace overlooking one of the most atmospheric piazzas in Rome's Ghetto (close to Piazza Venezia). The menu changes daily but usually includes many fish dishes. Desserts are homemade and creative (cinnamon mousse and an exquisite crème caramel are just two examples). Closed Monday.
Piazza Margana 37
Tel: 06699 20637. Fax: 06692 90826.
Price: €36. Wine: €15.

Trendy

Cul de Sac

Situated close to Piazza Navona, there is something indefinably French about *Cul de Sac*. The shelves around the walls are stacked high with wine bottles and the staff work from behind a large marble counter. On summer evenings, several candlelit tables are placed outdoors. It is not exactly a restaurant but more an informal retreat where diners can enjoy good wine accompanied by plates of homemade pâté, regional salamis, first-rate cheeses and salads, without running up an exorbitant bill. The few real dishes of food there are, however, are excellent.
Piazza Pasquino 73
Tel: 06688 01094.
Price: €18. Wine: €7.50.

Gusto

This split-level, open-plan restaurant, pizzeria and wine bar is something of a designer showpiece – exposed brickwork, wooden floors, marble-topped tables and industrial-style lighting. The emphasis is on Mediterranean cuisine, primarily meat and fish prepared with aromatic herbs and spices. One classic example is the *Pizza Mediterranea*, topped with ricotta, sliced aubergine and fresh basil leaves. Weekend brunch sees a 'multi-ethnic' menu based on eggs, quiches, muffins and salads, while the 'fitness brunch' combines salad, yoghurt, cereal and freshly squeezed orange juice. Live jazz takes place in the wine bar and there is also an extremely well-stocked shop, selling kitchenware and cookery books.
Piazza Augusto Imperatore 9
Tel: 0632 26273. Fax: 06326 29182.
E-mail: gusto@gusto.it
Website: www.gusto.it
Price: €30. Wine: €15.

Ketumbar

Ketumbar (Malay for 'coriander') is one of several chic restaurants in Testaccio, an area well known for its small, alternative nightclubs. Fusion cuisine fits the bill, with a selection of sushi dishes, curries and *nasi goreng* (rice, egg and greens prepared in a wok). The sleek, minimalist interior – featured in various style magazines – is tastefully decorated with Indonesian furniture, while, in one room, potsherds (pieces of broken Roman amphora that make up Monte Testaccio hill) are subtly lit behind a glass wall. No lunch.
Via Galvani 24
Tel: 06573 05338.
Price: €30. Wine: €18.

Margutta Vegetariano alle Cornacchie

The dining room of this hip vegetarian restaurant hosts temporary art exhibitions, including work by students from the Accademia dei Belli Arti. Out front, in a small square between the Pantheon and Piazza Navona, there is a summer terrace. Dishes include *risotto agli asparagi cremolato al brie* (asparagus and brie risotto), *polpetini al melanzane in umido* (aubergine rissoles with tomato sauce), plus the colourful *Cornacchie* salad, combining endive, rocket, sweetcorn, avocado, radicchio, cherry tomatoes and buffalo mozzarella. They also do pizzas and an all-you-can-eat brunch on Sunday morning.
Piazza Rondanini 53
Tel: 06681 34544. Fax: 06681 31911.
E-mail: maruttavegetariano@maruttavegetariano.com
Website: www.maruttavegetariano.com
Price: €22. Wine: €10.

Testaccio Kitchen Bar

This is another stylish Testaccio venture that is spread over three floors (one disco-bar, one restaurant, one wine bar and terrace). The restaurant's chic interior of exposed steel beams, simple wooden furniture and white linen tablecloths is a breath of fresh air. The kitchen turns out sophisticated Mediterranean dishes, such as *risotto con gamberoni profumati al limone* (king prawn and lemon risotto) and *vitello profumato alla salvia con polenta* (sage-scented veal served with polenta). The pasta and desserts are prepared in-house and there is a selection of farm-produced Italian cheeses. No lunch. Closed Monday.
Via Galvani 20
Tel: 0657 48216.
E-mail: testacciokitchen@tiscali.it
Website: www.testacciokitchenbar.com
Price: €35. Wine: €12.

Budget

Da Agusto

Possibly the last genuine Trastevere *osteria*, a meal at *Agusto's* is an experience in itself. On busy winter evenings, the dining room is packed and steamy, while in summer, rickety wooden tables spill out onto a pretty cobbled piazza. The menu is limited and runs out early. Favourites include *pollo arrosto con patate* (roast chicken and potatoes) and *abbacchio al forno* (lamb cooked in the oven); desserts are homemade. Tables are covered with throwaway paper cloths where waitresses scribble down orders and tot up bills. Closed Saturday and Sunday. No credit cards.
Piazza de' Renzi 15
Tel: 0658 03798.
Price: €18. Wine: €5.

Da Baffetto

One of Rome's best-known pizzerias, *Da Baffetto* is a tiny, rough-and-tumble place, located in a lovely cobbled street close to Piazza Navona. The thin wood-oven pizzas and excellent bruschettas (toast topped with chopped tomatoes, garlic and olive oil) are popular with locals and tourists alike. There is a rapid turnover – the waiters certainly let customers know when it is time to leave. To avoid the crowds, it is best to arrive either very early (before 2000) or very late (after 2400). No lunch. No credit cards.
Via del Governo Vecchio 114
Tel: 0668 61617.
Price: €12. Wine: €5.

Formula 1

As the heart of the student quarter, San Lorenzo is traditionally famous for its cheap and cheerful pizzerias and a growing number of more sophisticated and hip wine bars and eating places. The exceedingly relaxed and slightly chaotic *Formula 1* is one of those basic no-frills pizza places that serve up some of the best in Rome, using real mozzarella (not the factory kind so favoured nowadays). The fried *baccalà* (salted cod) is excellent. No lunch. Closed Sunday. No credit cards.
Via degli Equi 13
Tel: 0644 53866.
Price: €10. Wine: €5.

Insalata Ricca

Surprisingly few Roman restaurants offer creative salads. The founders of *Insalata Ricca* saw a gap in the market and now run a chain of restaurants around town. Popular with diet-conscious Romans and foreigners alike, dishes range from *insalata con gamberetti* (prawns, mushrooms, rocket and radicchio) to *insalata di funghi* (parmesan, fresh mushrooms and rocket). They also do some delicious pasta dishes, including the irresistible *tagliatelle ai funghi porcini* (pasta with porcini mushrooms).
Largo dei Chiavari 85
Tel: 06688 03656.
E-mail: info@linsalataricca.it
Website: www.linsalataricca.it
Price: €15. Wine: €6.

Perilli

A no-frills, down-to-earth trattoria, with menu and waiters to match. Cheerful and slightly chaotic, *Perilli* has served up generous portions of Roman specialities, such as *rigatoni con la pajata* (pasta with veal's intestines), since 1911. Those who feel queasy about offal can

Spanish Steps and Keats-Shelley Memorial House

Photo: Corel

choose the classics – *caprese* (tomato and mozzarella salad) or *saltimbocca alla Romana* (slices of veal rolled in prosciutto). Closed Wednesday and throughout August.
Via Marmorata 39
Tel: 0657 42415.
Price: €22. Wine: €6.

Personal Recommendations

Africa

Ethiopia and Eritrea are former Italian colonies, hence the recent influx of immigrants from these countries. *Africa*, close to Termini station, specialises in Ethiopian and Eritrean cuisine, such as a delicious spicy stew known as *zighini* and highly seasoned cooked vegetables. These are presented on a single large plate, upon a bed of *ingera* (a spongy pancake-like bread). Traditionally, everyone around the table eats from the same plate, using the *ingera* to scoop up the meat and vegetables with their hands. Closed Monday.
Via Gaeta 26
Tel: 0649 41077.
Price: €16. Wine: €7.

Ditirambo

Just off the ever-popular and ever-bustling Campo de' Fiori, this intimate restaurant is a gem of imaginative cuisine and good humour, in a decidedly touristy area. Many dishes are vegetarian but not boring – try the *ravioli di broccoletti in salsa di vongole al tartufo* (ravioli filled with broccoli in a clam and truffle sauce). The interior is warm and inviting, the bread and pasta are homemade, as are the sweets (the fruit and nut sorbets prepared in their skins or shells are divine). No lunch Monday.
Piazza della Cancelleria 74–75
Tel/fax: 0668 71626.
Website: www.ristoranteditirambo.it
Price: €25. Wine: €11.

La Taverna del Ghetto

Rome's Ghetto was created in 1554, when the Pope had a wall built to segregate the Jews from the rest of the Roman population. The community developed their own variation on Roman cooking, which can be sampled at this small, informal, kosher restaurant. Charcoal-grilled meat and fish predominate but there are also delicious pasta dishes, such as *tagliatelle cernia*

e fiori di zucca (pasta with grouper and courgette flowers) and the classic *carciofi alla giudia* (artichoke) side dish. There is an interesting selection of kosher wines. No dinner Friday. No lunch Saturday.
Via Portico d'Ottavia 8
Tel: 06688 09771. Fax: 06682 12309.
Website: www.latavernadelghetto.com
Price: €26. Wine: €12.

Pierluigi

Lying between Campo de' Fiori and the river, this cheerful ivy-clad restaurant extends onto a romantic piazza through summer. It is best known for reasonably priced fish dishes, such as *risotto alla crema di scampi* (shrimp cream risotto) and *calamari e gamberi fritti* (fried squid and prawns), but they also do excellent Roman fare, such as *pasta con fagioli* (pasta with beans) and *fiori di zucca* (fried courgette flowers). Extremely popular, so reservations are recommended. Closed Monday.
Piazza de' Ricci 144
Tel: 0668 61302. Fax: 06688 07879.
E-mail: info@ristorante-pierluigi.it
Website: www.pierluigi.it
Price: €25. Wine: €8.

Taverna de' Mercanti

Hidden away in Trastevere, the atmosphere here is unforgettable – exposed beams, a rough wooden floor, red and white chequered tablecloths, candles and an open fire. It is especially cosy in winter, while, throughout summer, there are tables outside. Start off with a bruschetta served either *al pomodoro* (with tomato) or *al tartuffo* (with truffle cream), to be followed by charcoal-grilled meat – *abbacchio* (suckling lamb), *cinghiale* (wild boar) or *salsicce del montagne* (mountain sausage). For those on a tight budget, pizza makes a cheap option.
Piazza de' Mercanti 3A
Tel: 0658 81693. Fax: 0658 80449.
Price: €25. Wine: €8.

ENTERTAINMENT

Nightlife

Rome may not be the hippest of capitals but, for those who know the right places, it is possible to party all

Trajan's Column

night. Romans go out late and the fun only really commences after dinner. The wine bars and cafés lying between Campo de' Fiori, Piazza Navona and Via della Pace are the places to be seen. Irish pubs have also enjoyed a boom over the last decade. The biggest concentration of nightclubs lies in the Testaccio district, where a plethora of small venues offer dancing and concerts. The gay scene is alive and kicking and accounts for many of the more avant-garde night spots. Both the weekly *Roma C'è* (website: www.romace.it) and the monthly *Time Out Roma* publications have good information on nightlife in Rome.

The legal drinking age in Italy is 16 years and the absence of licensing laws means that drinking is possible at all hours. Most wine bars and *birrerie* stay open until 2400 in winter and 0200 in summer. However, in general, people are more interested in seeing and being seen – alcohol is almost an afterthought. Drink prices vary considerably – a glass of wine at the *Vineria*, Campo de' Fiori, costs €2–5 (depending on the quality), while a cocktail in a nightclub could be €10.50. Half a litre of draught beer usually costs around €4. Drinks and coffees are always cheaper when consumed standing at the bar. Romans tend to dress more casually than their counterparts in Milan and Florence, although most women do their best to look stunning for a night out.

Bars

The *Vineria*, 15 Campo de' Fiori, continues to be one of the best 'in' places and is a perfect rendezvous for an early evening drink. Long-standing customers range from well-known actors to local winos, although lately it has slightly lost its charm, due to its colossal popularity. Just a few doors down, at number 20, is the *Drunken Ship*, good for those in search of English-speaking ex-pats and tourists. Equally popular but rather more refined is *Antico Caffè della Pace*, Via della Pace 5, close to Piazza Navona. The cosy interior is

adorned with antiques, while the ivy-clad façade looks onto a notoriously popular summer terrace. Close by, for late-night drinking, *Bar del Fico*, Piazza del Fico 26–28, serves customers on a large open-air terrace until 0200, with outdoor heaters through winter. For a romantic pre-dinner aperitif, take a table at *Caffè di Marzio*, Piazza Santa Maria in Trastevere 15, and enjoy a glass of wine overlooking this delightful piazza in the heart of Trastevere.

Casinos

Gambling is banned throughout Italy (with the exceptions of Venice, San Remo and Aosta).

Clubs

House music remains a firm favourite here, although a number of smaller and more alternative clubs play rock and other genres. In summer, many clubs close, giving way to the countless unofficial outdoor venues that spring up around town and beside the sea near Ostia. The rich and famous hang out at *Gilda*, Via Mario dei Fiori 97, close to Piazza di Spagna. Disco music dominates the dancefloor, there is a piano bar reserved for private parties and a well-run restaurant. In summer, the establishment moves out to Fregene, on the coast, for *Gilda on the Beach*, Via Lungomare di Ponente 11. Some of Europe's best DJs play at *Goa*, Via Libetta 13, close to Mercati Generali – recent guests include the Chemical Brothers. House and jungle music predominate amid a sophisticated ethnic setting – candles and mirrors, incense and flowers. Sunday is gay night. *Alien*, Via Velletri 13–19, has been refurbished and adorned with candles, rugs and incense, while the 'Sala Rock' is done out exclusively in black and white. House, techno and retro dominate the scene. In Testaccio, *Alibi*, Via Monte Testaccio 39, is for 'gay and friends' and plays predominantly house music with occasional live concerts. Close by, *Zoobar*, Via Monte Testaccio 22, plays rock, funk and retro to a mixed and cheerful crowd.

Live Music

The year 2002 saw the inauguration of the new *Auditorium-Parco della Musica*, Viale Pietro de Coubertin 30 (tel: 0680 2411; website: www. musicaperroma.it). Designed by the renowned Italian architect Renzo Piano, it lies just a ten-minute tram ride from Piazza del Popolo and features three halls with perfect acoustics and a large courtyard for outdoor concerts and events. Jazz lovers should head for *Big Mama*, Vicolo di San Francesco a Ripa 18. It is notoriously cramped but pulls some good up-and-coming musicians, plus a few big names. Likewise, *Fonclea*, Via Crescenzio 82A, in the Prati area (close to the Vatican), stages jazz and rhythm and blues concerts. There is a late-night restaurant and the bar serves excellent cocktails and a wide selection of whiskies. For newer or more rarefied jazz sounds and ethnic music, try the very hip (but with good reason) *La Palma*, Via Giuseppe Mirri 35 (near the Tiburtina metro stop). For an evening of varied music to suit all tastes, visit *Alpheus*, Via del Commercio 36, close to Ostiense station. Lively and fun, there are four large rooms, each with a different theme. Regular live concerts range from rock to rap and Latin to reggae. In Testacccio, *Caffè Caruso*, Via Monte Testaccio 36, hosts performances from local and visiting Caribbean, Cuban and Brazilian musicians, while *Villaggio Globale*, Ex-Mattatoio, Lungotevere Testaccio, offers a nice line in alternative and world music. For something totally different, visit the *Centri Sociali* (see *Culture*). One of these venues that is well known as

a live music hotspot is *Brancaleone*, Via Levanna 11, where an alternative and dressed-down crowd attends concerts, films, art exhibitions and club nights. Likewise, *Circolo degli Artisti*, Via Casilina Vecchia 42, offers an eclectic mix of rap, reggae, cyber punk and grunge.

Sport

Spectator sports claim infinitely more enthusiasm than participatory sports. Romans diligently follow their football clubs' efforts in the *Corriere dello Sport* newspaper. Rome has two main football clubs, both in the *Serie A* (top division) – the traditionally left-wing *AS Roma* (website: www.asromacalcio.it) and right-wing *Lazio* (website: www.sslazio.it). Both perform at the *Stadio Olimpico* (tel: 0632 37333), the 85,000-seat stadium that hosted the 1990 World Cup Final.

The sporting season kicks off in Rome with the Marathon (in March) and then provides a welcome opportunity to show off new hats and outfits at the *Concorso Ippico Internazionale di Piazza di Siena* – International Show Jumping (late April to early May). The Italian Open Tennis championships now attracts some of the biggest names on the circuit and is held in the first week of May.

Tickets to sporting events must be purchased directly from the venue box office or, in some cases, through the club websites.

Fitness Centres

Setting foot in a Roman gym can be overwhelming for those not equipped with the right gym wear (expensive) and body (tanned and toned). Those brave enough could try the *Roman Sport Centre*, Villa Borghese, Via del Galoppatoio 33 (tel: 0632 01667). Rome's largest health centre, it is open to non-members for €26 per day and incorporates two gyms, squash courts, two Olympic-size swimming pools, aerobic courses, massage, sunbeds and saunas.

Golf

Golf is considered quite an upper-crust game in Rome. Most clubs will receive non-members on production of a membership card from their native country, showing their handicap. Fees are usually based on a day's play. *Country Club Castelgandolfo*, Via di Santo Spirito 13 (tel: 0693 12301), is located just outside Rome, within a volcanic crater. Rates rise from €47 on weekdays to €57 at weekends.

Swimming

La Piscina delle Rose, Viale America 20 (tel: 0659 26717), is a large, open-air swimming pool much in favour with the locals. It is open from early May to late September and a passport to a day of relaxation costs €10, while an afternoon stay costs €8. The *Cavalieri Hilton*, Via Alberto Cadlolo 101, Monte Mario (tel: 06350 92950; website: www.cavalieri-hilton.it), also allow non-residents to splash around in their outdoor and indoor pools but rates are higher.

Tennis

Tennis club *Circolo della Stampa*, Piazza Mancini 9 (tel: 0632 32452), is owned by a group of journalists and welcomes non-members. A court costs €9.30 per hour.

Shopping

Romans concur with Parisians that it is better to be chic than shocking. Consequently, Rome's shops are full of (usually expensive and almost identical) fine clothes, leathers, shoes and bags. In winter, real fur is still de rigueur. The smart designer shops, where sales assistants are at their snootiest and price tags absent, are concentrated in the network of streets spanning out from the Spanish Steps. Of these, Via Condotti has most of the big names – *Gucci*, number 8, *Max Mara*, number 17–19A, *Valentino*, number 16, *Louis Vuitton*, number 15, *Salvatore Ferragamo*, numbers 65 and 73, and *Giorgio Armani*, number 77. *Bulgari*, number 10, displays glitteringly expensive watches, while *Damiani*, number 84, stocks alarmingly costly jewellery, worn by Jennifer Aniston in recent publicity campaigns. Nearby, *Dolce e Gabbana*, Piazza di Spagna 82/3, offers slightly more entertaining but equally expensive gear. *Fendi* has a cluster of boutiques along Via Borgognona, numbers 36–39, with a wide range of furs, shoes, bags and its ready-to-wear collection. Other big names here are *Gianni Versace*, number 25, *Moschino*, number 32A, *Gianfranco Ferré*, number 6, and *Laura Biagiotti*, number 44. In the same area, the recently opened *TAD conceptstore*, Via Babuino 155A, specialises in 'ethnic-chic', with departments ranging from furniture to flowers and clothing to music. There is also a hairdresser's and a café. On neighbouring Via Frattina, number 23, the glorious *Pineider* stocks upmarket stationery and desk equipment.

Affordable buys are to be found in the high-street shops lining Via del Corso, Via del Tritone, Via Nazionale and Via Cola di Rienzo. Alternatively, bargains are snapped up in the January and July sales. The antiques quarters lie along Via Margutta, Via del Babuino, Via Giulia, Via dei Banchi Vecchi and Via de' Coronari (the pedestrian street organises fairs in May and October, when its stores are open late). Bric-a-brac and retro clothes are on offer at the increasingly popular flea markets, the best being Via Sannio (Monday to Saturday 0730–1300) and Porta Portese (Sunday 0730–1300).

Although there are supermarkets and shopping malls in Rome – including the 100-shop *Centro Commerciale Cinecittà Due*, Viale Palmiro Togliatti 2, Tuscolana – the Roman shopping style is to visit the local fruit and vegetable markets (Monday to Saturday 0700–1300) and to dip in and out of delicatessens. Luxury goods to take home include assorted vinegar, truffles and olive oil. *Castroni*, Via Cola di Rienzo 196, sells the culinary riches from Italy's regions and comforting imports from around the world (including baked beans). The well-established *Trimani*, Via Goito 20, was founded in 1821 and stocks an excellent selection of Italian wines.

Smaller shops often close for lunch (1300–1630). Larger stores tend to stay open all day (0900–1930). Opening times can be confusing, with many food shops closed on Thursday afternoon (in winter) and other shops not opening until the afternoon on Monday. Summer brings later opening hours (until 2000) but also Saturday afternoon closing and complete closure for at least a fortnight in August.

Value-added tax (IVA) is 20% on clothing and luxury goods. Foreign tourists from non-EU countries can claim a tax refund, provided they spend at least €155 at the same shop on the same day. Those who are eligible should ask the shop assistant for a receipt (with a description of the articles purchased) and a 'tax-free cheque'. Upon departure from the EU (no later than 90 days after the date of purchase), these should be presented to customs. *Global Refund* (website: www.globalrefund.com) can provide more information.

Market shopping

Photo: Corel

Culture

In the past, Rome's cultural life has been hampered by the vagaries of political squabbling and its inhabitants' lack of passion in the arts, however, there has been an increasing desire to step out of the shadows and into the limelight. High-profile international dance and theatre festivals, such as the *RomaEuropa Festival* held in October, and Rome's new state-of-the-art auditorium (see *Music* below) are all helping to make this happen.

Rome's one and only official arts centre, the *Palazzo delle Esposizioni*, Via Nazionale 194, which combines cinema with dance and exhibition spaces is currently closed but should reopen in early 2004. However, major exhibitions have a spectacular venue in the *Scuderie Papali del Quirinale* (tel: 06399 67500; website: www.scuderiequirinale.it), renovated by famous Italian architect Gae Aulenti and located opposite the Quirinal Palace.

Those determined to sample something less conservative should seek out the *Centri Sociali* – non-profit, self-governing social centres originally set up by left-wing students during the 1970s, with support from the Italian Communist Party. Nowadays, they host the most radical concerts, films, theatre and dance events that Rome has to offer. Admission costs are at a minimum here, as are the prices for drinks at the bar. *Centri Sociali* attract an 'alternative' crowd aged 18–30 and vary from well-run places offering educational courses and Internet cafés to suburban squats. See *Live Music* in *Nightlife* for more information.

Tickets for cultural events are in demand and many are for subscribers only, so it is important for culture-keen visitors to rush to the box office with cash (not credit card) in hand some days prior to the performance. Prices start at around €20. Ticket agencies may save hassle. *Orbis*, Piazza Esquilino 37 (tel: 0648 27403), provides tickets for concerts, theatre and sporting events. The weekly *Roma C'è* (website: www.romace.it) and *Time Out Rome* publications provide information on cultural events.

Music

The *Auditorium-Parco della Musica* (see *Live music* in *Nightlife*) is a venue for various touring musicians, however, the classical musical scene bases its reputation on two academies: the *Accademia Nazionale di Santa Cecilia* and the *Accademia Filarmonica*. Rome's principal and most prestigious academy, the *Accademia Nazionale di Santa Cecilia* (tel: 06688 01044; website:

www.santacecilia.it), stages its own concerts or hosts visiting orchestras, at *Auditorio Pio*, Via della Conciliazione 4, all year round, while during the summer, it graces the beautiful Renaissance courtyard of *Villa Giulia*, Piazzale di Villa Giulia 9, with performances. The *Accademia Filarmonica* (tel: 0632 01752 or 26590; website: www.filarmonicaromana.org) performs regular operas and concerts at the *Teatro Olimpico*, Piazza Gentile da Fabriano 17, Flaminio (tel: 0632 65991; website: www.teatroolimpico.it). Rossini and Verdi were once members of this academy (founded in 1821), which offers a varied programme of chamber music, opera and contemporary music.

The *Teatro dell'Opera di Roma*, Via Beniamino Gigli 1 (tel: 0648 1601; website: www.operaroma.it), dominates the opera scene. The season runs from November to May. The box office opens two days before each performance. Free concerts (choral, chamber and organ recitals) are held in churches – including Sant'Ignazio, San Giovanni de' Fiorentini, San Giovanni and Santa Maria Maggiore – during the summer months.

Theatre

The theatre season runs from October to May. The city's official troop, the *Teatro di Roma* (tel: 0668 40001; website: www.teatrodiroma.net), is based at the prestigious *Teatro Argentina*, Largo di Torre Argentina 52 (tel: 06688 04601), which hosts lavish productions directed by renowned directors. The *Teatro Nazionale*, Via del Viminale 51 (tel: 0648 5498), is run by the *Teatro dell'Opera* (website: www.operaroma.it), while the *Ente Teatrale Italiano* (Italian Theatre Board) or *ETI* (tel: 0644 0131; website: www.enteteatrale.it) puts on light and fluffy comedies at various venues, some of which they own, such as *Vascello*, Via Giacinto Carini 72, Monteverde (tel: 0658 81021), and *Teatro Quirino*, Via Marco Minghetti 1 (tel: 0667 94585; website: www.teatroquirino.it).

Musical comedies are performed at the fashionable *Teatro Sistina*, Via Sistina 129 (tel: 0642 00711; website: www.ilsistina.com). Classical works are performed in the *Teatro Valle*, Via del Teatro Valle 23A (tel: 06688 03794; website: www.teatrovalle.it), and in the ETI-owned *Teatro Quirino*, whose varied programme includes the classics, contemporary work and Commedia dell'Arte. Fringe theatre is well represented at ETI's *Vascello* as well.

Best of all are the open-air performances, held in summer in the lovely park, *Giardino degli Aranci*, Via di Santa Sabina, Aventino. Other venues are the *Anfiteatro della Quercia del Tasso*, Passeggiata del Gianicolo (tel: 0657 50827; website: www.anfiteatroquerciadeltasso.com), with stunning views over the city, and the *Teatro Romano di Ostia Antica*, the Roman amphitheatre in Ostia Antica. Information and booking numbers are advertised on posters.

Dance

The *Rome Opera Ballet* performs at the *Teatro dell'Opera di Roma* (see *Music* above), where the regular diet of classical ballet is enriched with guest performances of internationally renowned dancers. The *Teatro Olimpico* (see *Music* above), has a strong dance season, ranging from classical to contemporary. Tickets for dance productions at the *Teatro Argentina* (see *Theatre* above), are snapped up, so early booking is advised.

Film

Italy's grand history in film has been centred in Rome since the *Cinecittà* (Cinema City), Via Tuscolana 1, was opened by Mussolini in 1937. Scenes from Anthony Minghella's *The English Patient* (1996) and Jane Campion's *The Portrait of a Lady* (1996) were filmed in these studios but Italian cinema has failed to match the flowering of the 1940s, 50s and 60s. Among the greats are Rossellini's *Open City* (1946) and Vittorio De Sica's *The Bicycle Thief* (1948), depicting a harsh but touching picture of post-war Rome. Equally popular but highly romanticised was Jean Negulesco's *Three Coins in the Fountain* (1954), focusing on the quest for love and the Trevi Fountain, and Audrey Hepburn's Oscar-winning performance as a besotted princess in *Roman Holiday* (1953). However, it is Fellini's films – *Roma* (1972) and *La Dolce Vita* (1959) – that have indelibly stamped images of Rome on the movie-goer's mind. More recently, Nanni Moretti, Rome's Woody Allen, enjoyed considerable success at home and abroad with a film called *Caro Diario* (1993), which showed a beautiful and virtually empty Rome in August. For shots of the city's piazzas, there is Anthony Minghella's beautiful but tragic *The Talented Mr Ripley* (1999).

Rome is blessed with over 80 cinemas and their numbers are increasing all the time. Tickets cost about €7 (prices are often reduced for matinée performances and on Monday evenings). The *Pasquino Multiscreen*, Piazza San Egidio 10, Trastevere (tel: 0658 15208), shows English-language films daily. *Metropolitan*, Via del Corso 7 (tel: 0632 00933), and *Warner Village Moderno*, Piazza della Repubblica 45–46 (tel: 0647 7791), dedicate one of their screens to English-language films. Films are also shown in their original language on Monday evenings at *Alcazar*, Via Merry del Val 14 (tel: 0658 80099), while *Nuovo Olimpia*, Via in Lucina 16G (tel: 0668 61068), regularly shows original-language films.

There are numerous open-air showings in the summer, including *Cineporto*, Viale Antonio di San Giuliano (tel: 0632 43903; website: www. cineporto.com), close to the Olympic Stadium, and *Notti di Cinema a Piazza Vittorio* (tel: 0644 51208; website: www.agisanec.lazio.it), which shows films in Piazza Vittorio Emanuele II daily in the months of July and August. Weekly showings and details of film festivals are set out in the weekly publication, *Roma C'è* (website: www.romace.it) or in the daily press.

Cultural Events

Each summer, from June to September, *Estate Romana* (website: www.estateromana.it) offers a lively schedule of outdoor cultural events around the city, from rock, ethnic and jazz concerts, through theatre performances and outdoor cinema, to dance lessons and other cultural events hosted in various Roman

Castel Sant'Angelo

piazze and gardens all over town. As home to the Vatican, religious celebrations are important in Rome. The Pope makes an annual appearance at the Colosseum on Good Friday evening and delivers Midnight Mass at St Peter's on Christmas Eve.

Literary Notes

There is nothing like Ovid's *Ars Amatoria* (Art of Love – circa 16–25BC) for bringing Rome to life, with its vivid depiction of a trip to the Colosseum, the site of flirtation and grandiose spectacle. Those interested in political intrigue may turn to *I Claudius* and *Claudius the God* (1934), Robert Graves' portrayals of ancient Rome, or the more measured tones of Gibbon's *History and Decline of the Roman Empire* (1782). The dramatic poetry of Virgil's *Aeneid* (19BC), evokes the glory of the Roman Empire, blessed and cursed by the gods. The Romantics had a soft spot for Rome; indeed Rome is the place where Keats breathed his last and the *Keats-Shelley Memorial House* is situated here (see *Key Attractions*). The tragic tale of Beatrice Cenci, beheaded outside Castel Sant'Angelo in 1599 for plotting to kill the father who had raped her, inspired Shelley's play *The Cenci* (1886). For a taste of life in contemporary Rome, try Elaine Feinstein's glamorous thriller *Dark Inheritance* (2001).

SPECIAL EVENTS

Epifania – La Befana (Epiphany), day of present-giving to Roman children, Jan, throughout the city

Carnevale, children dress up and a few nightclubs put on special parties, week before Lent, various venues

Festa di Primavera (Spring Festival), late Mar–early Apr, Spanish Steps

Settimana Santa & Pasqua (Holy Week and Easter), mass in St Peter's Square on Sat before Palm Sunday, services throughout Rome's churches in Holy Week, and the Pope's evening mass on Good Friday at the Colosseum

Good Friday, Pope makes an appearance, Mar/Apr, Colosseum

Natale di Roma (Rome's Birthday), 21 Apr, fireworks on the Aventine Hill

Festa della Liberazione (Liberation Day), sombre festivities celebrate the Allies' liberation of Italy in World War II, 25 Apr, Mausoleum of the Ardeatine Caves and Tomb of the Unknown Soldier in Piazza Venezia

Festa del Lavoro (Labour Day), free rock concert, 1 May, outside Basilica of San Giovanni

Mostra dell'Antiquariato, antique fairs, mid–end May, Via dei Coronari, near Piazza Navona

Fiera d'Arte di Via Margutta (Margutta Art Fair), four-day art fair, late May, Via Margutta

Estate Romana (Roman Summer), music, dance, literature and film events (website: www.estateromana.it), Jun–Sep, Rome's parks and courtyards

Tevere Expo, arts and crafts fair, late Jun–late Jul, along River Tiber

Festa di San Giovanni, Pope leads the way to the basilica of San Giovanni in Laterano, 23 Jun, Laterano

San Pietro e San Paolo, public holiday in honour of Rome's two patron saints, 29 Jun, church service at Basilica of San Paulo Fouri le Mura

Roma Alta Moda, haute couture collections (website: www.altaroma.it), mid-Jul, Piazza di Spagna and smart hotels

Festa di Noantri, markets and fireworks in honour of Madonna del Carmine, two weeks mid-Jul, Travestere

Mostra dell'Antiquariato, antique fairs, mid–end Oct, Via dei Coronari, near Piazza Navona

Fiera d'Arte di Via Margutta (Margutta Art Fair), four-day art fair, late Oct, Via Margutta

Mercato di Piazza Navona, stalls selling food and craft items, mid-Dec–6 Jan, Piazza Navona

Immacolata Concezione (Immaculate Conception), Mass by the Pope, 8 Dec, Santa Maria Maggiore

Midnight Mass, Pope delivers mass, 24 Dec, St Peter's Basilica

Messa di Natale (Christmas Mass) and 'Urbi et Orbi' Blessing, 25 Dec, St Peter's Basilica

Veglia di Preghiera (Prayer Vigil), for the passage to the new year, 31 Dec, St Peter's Basilica

San Silvestro/Capo d'Anno (New Year's Eve), 31 Dec, festivities throughout the city

Singapore, the diamond-shaped island off the southern tip of Malaysia, is an unlikely success story. Once a simple fishing village, it was founded in 1819 by Sir Stamford Raffles – an official of the British East India Company – who decided it was the perfect location as a trading station. Since then it has thrived and became known as the Lion City.

Singapore City is by far the largest and most significant island alongside the many smaller ones that make up Singapore state. Here, especially at the mouth of the Singapore River, Asian tradition meets modern technology – gleaming skyscrapers tower over traditional architecture, while squat Chinese and Hindu temples stud the city. A curious blend of ancient and modern, the city is home to an ethnic mix of Chinese, Malaysians and Indians, as well as ex-pats from all over the world, in a predominantly English-speaking society. These different races live harmoniously thanks to religious tolerance, increased prosperity, stringent no-nonsense laws and a constant balmy equatorial heat.

Since the island became a Republic in 1965, Lee Kuan Yew, former Prime Minister and now Senior Minister, has pursued a vigorous free-trade policy that has seen an unprecedented rise in the standard of living (most city-dwellers own their own homes) and exponential economic growth. The Asian crisis of 1997 caused mayhem elsewhere, but here it was little more than a slightly worrying blip, although unemployment did rise from a steady 3.2% to 6%. Even after the 11 September terrorist attacks, which caused a downturn in tourism and many other industries, Singapore has made a steady recovery by the end of 2002, although 2003 was also shaky as with much of South-East Asia.

To the visitor stepping into Singapore's world-beating Changi Airport, there is little indication of anything other than impressive efficiency. What can be dangerously beguiling is the safety and cleanliness of this city; dangerous because it has been achieved and maintained at the expense of personal freedom. Canings, corrective work orders and harsh financial penalties can accompany breaking the law. There are the infamous on-the-spot fines for jay-walking or dropping a cigarette, but persistent litterers will find themselves suffering what in Singapore is the huge ignominy of picking up litter themselves, while more serious crimes, such as drug trafficking, are punished by the death penalty.

Yet the financial and business districts are home to a steady stream of well-heeled ex-pats who enjoy a good quality of life. In Singapore, oiling the wheels of success and becoming the best – an economic miracle to show the rest of the world the way – seems paramount. The prestigious *Forbes Magazine* enticed CEOs from around the globe to Singapore for a major business conference in September 2001 (the first one outside America) and now the IMF World Bank Annual Meeting is due to be held here in 2006. For the last 19 years, the city has been voted Asia's top business destination by the Union of International Associations and it boasts a fast-growing market for incentive travel, conventions, conferences and exhibitions.

All of this business thrives amid a constant flow of festivals and events in the ethnic quarters of Chinatown, Little India and Geylang Serai, which mark the many religious and cultural occasions throughout the calendar. Singaporeans still rely on *feng shui* consultants, astrologers and fortune-tellers for advice when moving home, getting married or changing jobs.

There is a budding arts community, which provides something of an outlet for feelings long denied in a series of annual showcases. However, these veer more towards the respectable face of art, often created and marketed by the Singapore Tourism Board, with little wild expression that might rock the establishment. More traditionally, Raffles Hotel and a rank of good museums furnish insights into the past.

But modern consumer culture has a great influence over most aspects of life: the Great Singapore Sale dominates the early summer in the city centre – and increasingly in the suburbs. Most visitors to Singapore at some stage will indulge in the competitive prices and great selection, especially in electronics equipment. And everybody comes to eat: there are food outlets at every step, from traditional hawker centres to modern food courts, Asian specialities to international haute cuisine – reflecting the cuisines of the different ethnic communities that Singapore has long been a home to.

Fountain, Suntec City

Photo: Singapore Tourism Board

TRAVEL

Getting There By Air

Singapore Changi Airport (SIN)

Tel: 6541 2222. Fax: 6542 1231.
Website: www.changiairport.com.sg
Changi is located 20km (12.4 miles) from Singapore centre. It consistently tops international polls as the world's best airport and is currently the 24th busiest. More than 29 million passengers passed through in 2002. A total of 63 airlines operate out of Changi, with 3400 flights weekly to 141 cities in 49 countries worldwide, making it the airport with the most air links in the Asia Pacific region. To cater for growth in demand, an extension to Terminal 1 was completed in 2000 and the building of Terminal 3 is underway, due for completion in 2006.

Major airlines: *Singapore Airlines* (tel: 6223 8888; fax: 6786 6947 (reservations) *or* 6223 6030 (ticketing enquiries); fax: 6786 2937; e-mail: singapore_ticketing@ singaporeair.com.sg; website: www.singaporeair.com.sg) is the national airline, with direct connections to all the major cities in Asia and 116 destinations in 42 countries. Its subsidiary *SilkAir* covers 19 destinations in South-East Asia, plus Trivandrum in India. Other major airlines include *Aeroflot, Air China, Air France, Air India, Air Madagascar, Air Mauritius, Air New Zealand, Alitalia, All Nippon, American Airlines, Biman Bangladesh, British Airways, Cathay Pacific, China Airlines, Continental Airlines, Egypt Air, Emirates, Garuda, Gulf Air, Indian Airlines, Japan Airlines, KLM, Korean Air, Lufthansa, Malaysia Airlines, Pakistan International Airlines, Philippine Airlines, Qantas Airways, Scandinavian Airlines, Sri Lankan Airlines, Swissair, Thai Airways, Turkish Airlines* and *United Airlines.* Passengers may check in up to 48 hours before their flight, at the Singapore Airlines office in the Paragon Shopping Centre, Orchard Road. They may also check in by telephone (tel: 6243 2546) to get a confirmed allocated seat number. In these cases, passengers must still bring their luggage to the airport at least one hour before flying.

Approximate flight times to Singapore: From London is 13 hours; from New York is 20 hours 35 minutes; from Los Angeles is 18 hours; from Toronto is 20 hours and from Sydney is 8 hours.

Airport facilities: While Changi's legendary efficiency means travellers need spend the minimum amount of time in the airport, the facilities on offer mean that days could happily be spent there. These include showers, gym and sauna, fitness centres, putting green, rooftop pool and Jacuzzi, hairdresser's, laundry service, karaoke lounge, Science Discovery Centre, mini supermarket, children's play area, nursery, smoking room, medical centre and prayer room. To get back to nature, even in an airport, there are also cactus, bamboo and orchid gardens and a Koi pond. There are the usual banks, bureaux de change, ATMs, postal and telecommunications offices, shops, restaurants, car hire (*AB Budget Car Rental, Sintat Rent-Acar* and *Hertz*), hotel reservation counters, tourist information and baggage storage facilities. Transit and transfer passengers can also take advantage of free two-hour guided coach tours of Singapore.

Business facilities: The comprehensive range of services includes transit hotels and business-class lounges. There is a business centre located in the Terminal 2 transit hotel, level 3 (tel: 6541 9106/7; fax: 6542 6122). Facilities include workstations with Internet connection, fax and photocopiers. There is a 24-hour Internet centre, with a faster modem server, opposite the Post Office.

Arrival/departure tax: A S$21 Passenger Service Charge is incorporated in the price of the ticket.

Transport to the city: The MRT now has a station at the airport, which is a quick and cheap option for getting anywhere in Singapore. Trains run 0530–2318, approximately every ten minutes. Tickets to the city centre cost S$1.80 (journey time – 30 minutes).

Singapore Bus Service (SBS) (tel: 1800 287 2727; website: www.sbstransit.com.sg) operates regular buses into the city. Public bus stations are located in Terminal 1 at Basement 2 and in Terminal 2 at basement level. Public buses cost S$1.50 (exact fare only) and depart every 6–14 minutes 0600–2400. Bus number 36 goes along Orchard Road (journey time – 50 minutes).

The airport is about 20–30 minutes from Singapore centre by taxi. Taxi fares are about S$15 (plus a standard S$3 airport surcharge, S$5 weekends, as well as any other surcharges – see *Taxis* in *Getting Around*). Limousine taxi service counters are located at the arrival hall on Level 1 of both terminals. They charge a flat rate of S$35 to anywhere in the city and operate 0600–0200 daily.

The six-seater MaxiCab, the airport shuttle service, run by *CityCab* (tel: 6542 8297), costs S$7 and stops at almost every major hotel in the city centre. It leaves from Terminal 1 and 2 every 30 minutes 0600–1800 and every 15 minutes 1900–2100.

Getting There By Water

Singapore is the world's busiest port in terms of shipping tonnage and is also considered the cruise hub of the Asia Pacific. At any one time, there are more than 800 ships in port. Visitors arrive at one of the three terminals (International, Regional or Domestic) of the *Singapore Cruise Centre* (SCC; tel: 6321 2202; fax: 6275 1683; website: www.singaporecruise.com) or at the *Tanah Merah Ferry Terminal* (TMF; tel: 6542 9910; fax: 6540 8007; website: www.singaporecruise.com) near Changi. The Singapore Cruise Centre, situated at the seafront side of the World Trade Centre on Telok Blangah Road, was opened in 1992 to promote Singapore as the cruise gateway to the Asia Pacific. The Tanah Merah Ferry Terminal was opened in 1995 to cater for increasing regional traffic and is for passengers heading for the Indonesian Riau Islands and Malaysian destinations. Facilities for international cruise ships at *SCC* include a Chinese medical hall, post office, electronic lockers, limousine taxis, duty-free goods and medical and dental clinics. At *TMFT*, there is a food hall, travel and resort agencies, duty-free shops and a bureau de change.

COST OF LIVING

One-litre bottle of mineral water: S$1.50
33cl bottle of beer: S$3
***Financial Times* newspaper:** S$4
36-exposure colour film: S$5.20
City-centre bus ticket: S$0.70–1.70
Average round of golf: S$120
Three-course meal with wine/beer: S$45

1 Singapore Dollar (S$1) = £0.36; US$0.57; C$0.80; A$0.89; €0.50

Currency conversion rates as of July 2003

Ferry services: Regular ferries operate between Tanah Merah and the Indonesian islands of Batam and Bintan, as well as Sebana and Tioman on the Malaysian coast. Ferries from the Singapore Cruise Centre go to Kukup in Malaysia, as well as Batam and Bintan. Operators include *Bintan Resort Ferries* (tel: 6542 4369; fax: 6546 1743; website: www.brf.com.sg); *Auto Batam* (tel: 6271 4866; fax: 6275 9861; e-mail: reservation@penguin.com.sg); *Dino Shipping* (tel: 6270 2228; fax: 6270 1113); *Widi Express Ferries PTE Ltd* (tel: 6275 2220; fax: 6275 2219; e-mail: widiexpress@yahoo.com.sg).

Transport to the city: The *Singapore Cruise Centre* is a ten-minute taxi ride from the city centre. Taxis leave from the World Trade Centre or Cable Car Towers in Maritime Square. Tanah Merah is served by regular public buses, operated by *Singapore Bus Service* (SBS) (tel: 6383 7229; fax: 6287 0311), including bus number 35 to Tanah Merah MRT station and bus 14 to Orchard Boulevard. There is a Taxi Order Terminal outside the ferry terminal; however, taxis ordered from here charge an S$8 premium.

Getting There By Rail

Malayan Railway (tel: 6222 5165; e-mail: passenger@ ktmb.com.my; website: www.ktmb.com.my) operates services from *Singapore Railway Station*, on Keppel Road, Tanjong Pagar, just south of the Central Business District. The station has two restaurants, book shops and immigration and customs.

Rail services: Trains depart daily for destinations in Malaysia, including Kuala Lumpur, Johor Bahru and Butterworth. Air-conditioned express trains to Kuala Lumpur leave three times a day with journeys taking between five and six hours. There are also five normal daily services to Kuala Lumpur. The journey to Johor Bahru takes around 30 minutes with four daily departures. Keppel Road is also the departure point for the three-day *Eastern & Orient Express* (tel: 6392 3500; fax: 6392 3600; e-mail: reservation. singapore@orient-express.com; website: www.orient- express.com) to Kuala Lumpur, Kwai, Penang and Bangkok.

Transport to the city: The railway station is not served by the MRT, although Tanjong Pagar MRT is a 20-minute walk away. Buses can be infrequent so the best way into the city is to queue for a taxi or telephone for one (see *Taxis* in *Getting Around*).

Getting There By Road

The road system in Singapore is clear, easy and efficient, but can get very congested at peak times, and especially on weekends and holidays when Singaporeans crowd onto the road causeway to Johor Bahru in Malaysia.

Driving is on the left and the speed limit is 50kph (31mph) in residential areas and 80kph (50mph) on expressways – and visitors should note that there are very high punishments for speeding.

For tourists, a valid driving licence from the country of residence is required for driving in Singapore. An International Driving Permit is recommended, especially if the driving licence is not in English, as it can help expedite proceedings where police are involved. The *Automobile Association of Singapore* (AAS; see below for details) has a helpline (tel: 6831 2195) for information on IDPs, but drivers can expect to pay a S$20 processing fee for an IDP. Foreign residents, however, must convert their national licence (or IDP) into a local licence. The *Traffic Police* (tel: 6547 1818) should be contacted for converting licences, as well as for information on road conditions and reporting all traffic accidents. Anyone driving their vehicle into Singapore must leave it at customs, then go to the AAS with their passport, vehicle registration documents and insurance. They will then be given an International Circulation Permit processed within an hour, which will allow them to collect their vehicle.

Minimum third-party insurance is compulsory and this can be extended to cover Malaysia. The maximum legal alcohol to blood ratio for driving is 0.08%.

Further information can be obtained from the *Automobile Association of Singapore, 336 River Valley*

CITY STATISTICS

Location: Singapore state, South-East Asia.
Country dialling code: 65; but note no city code, just 8 digits to follow, always beginning with '6'.
Population: 3,263,200 (permanent residents); 4,017,700 (total population).
Ethnic mix: 76.8% Chinese, 13.9% Malay, 7.9% Indian, 1.4% other.
Religion: 42.5% Buddhist (Chinese), 8.5% Tao, 14.9% Islam, 14.6% Christian, 4.1% Hindu, 0.6% other, 14.8% no religion.
Time zone: GMT + 8.
Electricity: 220–240 volts AC, 50Hz; square three-pin plugs, or two-pin with adapter.
Average January temp: 26°C (79°F).
Average July temp: 29°C (84°F).
Average humidity: 84.3%.
Annual rainfall: 2792mm (108.5 inches); rainy season Dec–Mar and Jun–Sep.

Road (tel: 6737 2444; fax: 6733 5094; e-mail: aasmail@aas.com.sg; website: www.aas.com.sg).
Emergency breakdown service: *AAS* 6748 9911.
Routes to the city: The main route into Singapore is the kilometre-long causeway, linking the northern district of Woodlands with Malaysia's Johor Bahru. This causeway is usually very busy but, at weekends, the volume of traffic multiplies. The 'Second Link', officially the Malaysia–Singapore Second Crossing, was built to alleviate the traffic and should be faster at busy periods. This second bridge is

located on the western side of Singapore and it links the Tuas checkpoint in Singapore with Tanjung Kupang in Malaysia. The highway then runs up the western part of the Malay peninsular.

The East Coast Parkway (ECP) runs from the airport into the city along the coast; Changi Road and Pan-Island Expressway (PIE) are alternative routes.

Approximate driving times to Singapore: From Johor Bahru – between 20 minutes and 3 hours, depending on traffic; Kuala Lumpur – 3 hours; Malacca – 3 hours 30 minutes.

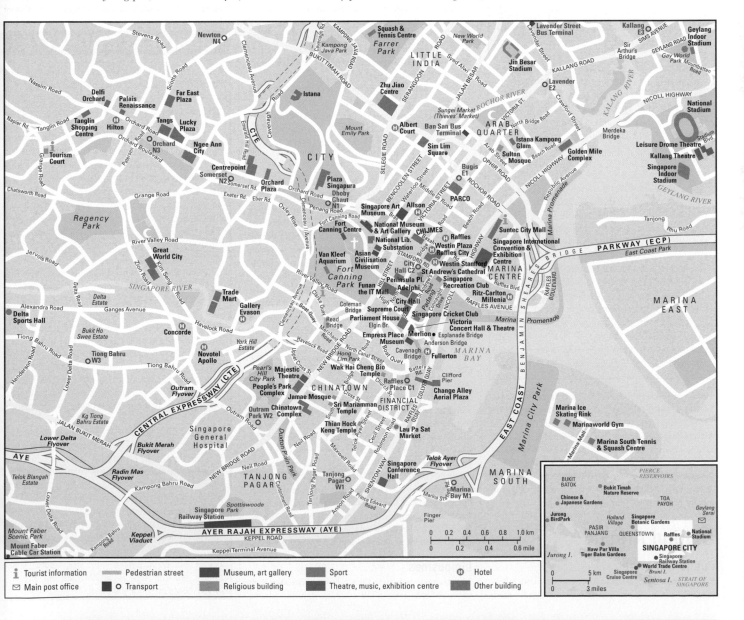

Symbol	Legend				
ℹ Tourist information	▬ Pedestrian street	■ Museum, art gallery	■ Sport	⊕ Hotel
✉ Main post office	■ ○ Transport	■ Religious building	■ Theatre, music, exhibition centre	■ Other building

BUSINESS PROFILE

An obsession with productivity, the high standard of education of its workforce and its location at the heart of ASEAN (Association of Southeast Asian Nations) has made Singapore the most durable economy in the world. In leading surveys during 2002, Singapore had overtaken Hong Kong as the best business centre in Asia. In 2001, it was ranked first in Asia for growth competitiveness by the World Economic Forum, while readers of *Business Traveller Asian Pacific* placed Singapore ahead of Melbourne and Sydney. It gained a further seal of approval from *Forbes Magazine*, which held the Forbes Global CEO Conference in the city in September 2001.

Although productivity growth was lower in the 1990s than in the 1980s, thanks to the Asian financial crisis of 1997, Singapore's slowdown was far less dramatic than its neighbours and its recovery is well underway. GDP growth of 2.2% was shown in 2002. Latest official statistics show that the unemployment rate for 2002 was 4.5%, slightly up on 2001 (3.8%) but significantly better than 2000 (6%).

Of the workforce, 18.2% are employed in manufacturing, 21.3% in commerce, 10.8% in transport and communication, 17.1% in financial and business services and 25.7% in community and personal services.

Most economic sectors, especially tourism, suffered the effects of the 11 September terrorist attacks. The Singapore Tourism Board planned its marketing strategically and focused its efforts on attracting tourists from China and Australia, rather than nervous USA and Japan. Although a slow recovery was in evidence, this was halted after the bomb attack in Bali in October 2002, which meant fewer people going to Bali and therefore not using Singapore as a stopover. Nevertheless, 2002 saw over 7.5 million international visitors (excluding Malaysian arrivals by land) and the Tourism Board has succeeded in developing Singapore into Asia's top convention city and the fifth best in the world.

The business district lies towards the island's east and southernmost tip and includes Orchard Road, Brah Basah Road and Raffles Boulevard, near which are the Singapore International Convention and Exhibition Centre, Pan Pacific and Suntec City. Most major international banks are here as well as international organisations like *IBM, Nokia, National Panasonic, Canon, Toshiba, Hitachi, Sony* and *Nike*.

Coach services: Operators include *Regent Star Travel*, Lavender MRT station (tel: 6292 9009; fax: 6296 1011), *Hasry* (tel: 6294 9306; fax: 6392 7476) and *Malacca-Singapore Express* (tel: 6293 5915; fax: 6292 2436), which are both located at the bus terminal on the corner of Lavender Street and Kallang Bahru. Coach services go to a number of Malaysian destinations, including Kuala Lumpur and Penang, and usually depart every morning and evening.

Getting Around

Public Transport
Public transport in Singapore is efficient, ultra-modern, clean, cheap and mostly air conditioned.

TransitLink Hotline (tel: 1800 767 4222 *or* 6767 4333) is a new one-stop number set up by all the major transport providers to help co-ordinate people's transport needs.

The **train** system is operated by *Singapore Mass Rapid Transit* (tel: 6336 8900; fax: 6334 8051; website: www.smrtcorp.com.sg). The *MRT* system extends north–south and east–west with trains every three to six minutes 0530–2430 daily. Fares range from S$0.80 to S$1.80.

MRT also operates the *Light Rapid Transit System* (LRT; tel: 6893 6455/6; fax: 6762 6732; website: www.slrt.com.sg). There are currently 14 LRT stations – the system runs from Bukit Panjang New Town to Choa Chu Kang in the suburbs. Each trip costs S$0.80–1. Trains run every three to five minutes. The **bus** system is operated by the *Singapore Bus Service* (SBS; tel: 1800 287 2727 *or* 6284 8866; fax: 6282 5204; e-mail: sbscrc@sbs.com.sg; website: www.sbstransit.com.sg) and *Trans Island Bus Service* (TIBS; tel: 6482 3888; fax: 6482 3842; e-mail: webmaster@tibs.com.sg; website: www.tibs.com.sg). SBS buses run 0600–2400 with fares costing S$0.70–1.40 for non-air-conditioned buses and S$0.80–1.70 for air-conditioned buses. TIBS also runs a **Bus-Plus** (tel: 6481 0166; fax: 6484 0129) service, which operates during peak hours to shuttle passengers between residential areas and MRT stations or the Central Business District. Fares are S$3.50–5. **Night buses** operate after these have finished, until around 0400, and cost S$3. Electronic **passes**, known as *ez-link cards* (website: www.ezlink.com.sg), are available from MRT stations (covering MRT, LRT and buses) and cost S$10 plus a deposit of S$5. Once the initial value of S$10 has been used up, the cards can be topped up at ATMs in every station, which makes the fares slightly cheaper. Any remaining value left over may be redeemed at stations.

Taxis
There are more than 18,000 cheap, metered, safe and air-conditioned taxis in Singapore. However, their convenience and reasonable price means that they can be difficult to find during peak hours, especially in the Central Business District (CBD) – and during a downpour. Taxis can be hailed 24 hours a day on the street, as well as at well-marked stands outside most shopping centres and hotels. Fares vary slightly between companies, usually starting at S$2.40 for the first kilometre and rising in increments of S$0.10. They are subject to a number of surcharges – most commonly advance booking fees. Again, different companies vary slightly, but example surcharges are S$1 during peak hours or S$1 for a pick-up in the CBD. There is a 50% surcharge daily 0000–0600, as well as a S$5 surcharge 1700–2400 Friday, Saturday or Sunday. There may also be surcharges for driving along certain highways at certain times.
Despite (or perhaps because of) all the surcharges, it is not customary to tip taxi drivers. Visitors should also note that drivers changing shifts will only take passengers heading in their direction – the red board on the dashboard or windscreen indicates the destination. Although there is no longer a bell that rings if the taxi breaks the speed limit, most drivers adhere strictly to the 80kph (50mph). Taxi firms include *CityCab* (tel: 6552 2222), *Comfort* (tel: 6552 1111) and *TIBS Taxis* (tel: 6555 8888; website: www.tibstaxis.com.sg).

Limousines
More a taxi with style than a limo, *TIBS Taxis* (tel: 6555 8888; fax: 6368 2232; website: www.

etaxis.com.sg) offers Mercedes or London Black Cabs that can be booked for any journey. For example, the journey from the city centre to the airport costs S$39.

Driving in the City
Singapore's highways are all designated by acronyms – AYE, ECP, CTE, AMK, PIE, ORR and CBD. Various tolls are levied in morning and evening peak hours to relieve congestion on expressways and busy roads, using the Electronic Road Pricing Scheme (ERP), which automatically deducts tolls from the In-Vehicle Unit (IU). This is fitted in all Singaporean vehicles and drivers purchase a rechargeable Cashcard and insert it in the IU. Vehicles that are not fitted with the IU must rent one. This can be done from petrol stations and other outlets, at a cost of S$5 daily, minimum of two days (plus a S$120 deposit). To help traffic flow in the Central Business District, all vehicles entering between 0730 and 1900 are also expected to pay a toll, which varies depending on the time. More information is available on the website (www.lta.gov.sg), including where and when the ERP system operates.
The highways are easy to negotiate and traffic generally moves smoothly thanks to the ERP. Wearing seat belts in the front and back is mandatory and it is illegal to use a mobile phone while driving. Offences are treated

BUSINESS ETIQUETTE

English is the official language of business in Singapore and business is conducted very much on a Western model. However, Asian – and especially Chinese – business ethics often prevail. Most offices are designed (interior and exterior) in consultation with a feng shui expert, in order to create the most auspicious environment for generating wealth and harmony, and most feature a fish pond or fountain to ensure that money flows in the right direction. Business cards are exchanged on every social and business occasion; and it is common courtesy to give or receive them with two hands (as with any piece of paper, including money). Corporate entertaining is high on the agenda and long lunches are often taken, with lavish buffets a popular option. Smoking is illegal in many places and is not always socially acceptable, so visitors should check before lighting up.

There are 12 public holidays a year, the most significant being Chinese New Year, usually in February. This is the only occasion when almost everything shuts down – locals spend time visiting their families and ex-pats leave for a long weekend away. During other public holidays, like Christmas Day, banks and offices close but shops stay open.

Business dress is fairly formal, however, men's suits may veer towards lighter shades in Singapore's tropical climate and, except for formal meetings, a jacket is usually dispensed with. Women wear skirt or trouser suits, while their Malay colleagues wear their national dress for formal functions. Some organisations have adopted casual Fridays, although only those departments with no client contact tend to take advantage of this.

Locals and ex-pats alike work long hours. The official working day is 0900–1800 but much longer hours are quite common.

seriously, with tough fines and even jail sentences. Singaporean drivers have a habit of lane drifting but otherwise traffic flows with very few abuses of etiquette. Parking is cheap and easily available all over the city, especially in hotel basement car parks. Rates vary depending on location, management and timing but public car parks cost around S$0.50 per half hour, more inside the Central Business District.

Car Hire

A valid national driving licence is required, although an International Driving Permit (IDP) is preferred and is mandatory where the driver's national licence is not in English. Drivers also require a passport and credit card to hire a car. Minimum third-party insurance is compulsory and can be extended to cover Malaysia. The minimum age limit for hiring a car is 25 years. Major providers include *Avis* (tel: 6737 1668; fax: 6235 4958; e-mail: avissg@singnet.com.sg;website: www.avisworld.com) and *Hertz* (tel: 6734 4646; fax: 6733 0466; e-mail: reservation.hertz@simedarby.com.sg; website: www.hertz.com).

Official rates start at around S$170 per day, with an extra S$40–90 per hour for a driver (minimuim three hours). However, prices vary hugely depending on the time of year, while special offers, corporate accounts, AA membership, even certain credit cards can often bring the official price down considerably.

Bicycle Hire

Cycling in Singapore tends to be restricted to public parks, with *East Coast Park* a popular venue for cyclists and rollerbladers. Bicycle hire is available at several outlets in the park, from about S$1.50 per hour. Bicycles can also be hired at *Sentosa*, *Pasir Ris* and *Bishan* parks. The island of *Pulau Ubin* (see *Excursions*) has mountain bike facilities, with many hire shops near the jetty.

SIGHTSEEING

Sightseeing Overview

Despite a lack of natural resources, or perhaps because of it, Singapore has capitalised on the energy, enterprise and skills of its inhabitants to create something approaching a tourist mecca. Although most tourists only stop over for a couple of days, in transit to somewhere else, many are beginning to stay longer and Singapore has much to merit a longer visit. This is a city where the first impression is that of man's achievements; the efficient and aesthetically pleasing *Changi Airport* is repeatedly voted the world's best. But here, world firsts are becoming commonplace – *Suntec City* boasts the biggest man-made fountain; the *Night Safari* is the first night zoo, and so on.

Heat and humidity not withstanding, the most efficient way to get to know local culture is on foot, especially around *Chinatown*, *Little India* and *Geylang Serai* in the heart of the city. Even in just these areas, it is easy to see how Singapore's successful economy is based upon ancient traditions, rituals and beliefs. It is usually this combination that entices people, but for those wanting pure consumerism and entirely modern architecture, Orchard Road should appeal.

But it is not all urban landscape – great importance is also placed on the natural environment. Areas of natural beauty, albeit with a little help from humans, have been developed heartily. These include *Sungei*

Singapore Botanic Gardens

Buloh Nature Park, *Singapore Zoological Gardens*, the popular *Night Safari* and *Bukit Timah Nature Reserve*. For history lovers and culture vultures, an impressive selection of museums, exhibitions and architectural heritage is available.

Key Attractions

Chinatown

Chinatown's history dates back to 1821 when the first Chinese junk carrying immigrants arrived from Fujian province. Much of it has been rebuilt and the old shop-houses restored and it remains one of the most interesting areas to explore, with a lively street scene rich with traditional architecture and customs. Its four main districts – Kreta Ayer, Telok Ayer, Tanjong Pagar and Bukit Pasoh – each have a distinctive flavour.

Kreta Ayer is the heart of the busy trading area. It contains Smith Street, home to the remains of the once-famed Cantonese Opera House, *Lai Chun Yuen*, and the tradition lives on with daily singing at the *Chinese Theatre Circle*. Newly re-paved, Smith Street is also referred to as Food Street and, along with Trengganu Street, now makes a lively eating and shopping area. Outside the fantastic souvenir and clothes shops, the pavements are crammed with tables and diners eating cheap Chinese food until midnight. At Chinatown Complex, corner of Sago Street and Trengganu Street, fresh food is haggled over at the 'wet market' on the ground floor, while eating stalls on the second floor are also popular until late. This area also has the traditional medicine halls, where a complex array of Chinese herbs are available, with expert advice on hand.

Telok Ayer was the main landing site for the Chinese early immigrants, who formed the backbone of the early Chinese community. The most important Chinese and Muslim temples are here. Tanjong Pagar is on the outskirts of Chinatown. A well-conserved area with old shop-houses, it is now a more upmarket business area, which is quite spacious and good for nightlife. Bukit Pasoh was originally the heart of Chinese culture in Singapore. It has had the reputation for being seedy, with clan associations and prositutes, but is now more upmarket with cafés and boutique hotels.

All of Singapore's major religions are in evidence in Chinatown. Telok Ayer has Singapore's oldest Hindu temple, the *Sri Mariamman Temple* on South Bridge Road, which comes to life during festivals. Also along one stretch of Telok Ayer Street is a magnificent collection of national monuments: *Al-Abrar Mosque*, *Thian Hock Keng Temple*, *Nagore Durgha Shrine* and *Fuk Tak Chi Museum*.

Transport: MRT Outram (W2), then a ten-minute walk to Smith Street.

Little India

North of the colonial district, *Little India* offers a completely different flavour of Singapore with colourful, noisy and crowded streets that reflect an important part of the island's history. When Sir Stamford Raffles arrived in 1819, he had an entourage of 120 Indian assistants and soldiers who resided mainly in Chinatown. Cattle-rearing near the Rochor River brought them into the area now known as Little India and, by the turn of the century, it became a thriving commercial area.

For today's visitor, the attractions are mainly shopping, eating and places of worship, especially along the main hub of Serangoon Road. The smell of spices emerges from the shop-houses, while the

Photo: Singapore Tourism Board

Night Safari

informal restaurants offer some of the best food east of Calcutta in one of the oldest areas of Singapore. The *Little India Arcade* and *Zhujiao Centre* are newly converted shop-houses selling handicrafts, saris and spices, while fortune-tellers use small parrots to pick cards that will tell your future.

A taste of the Indian subcontinent can be devoured, from Ayurvedic (traditional) medicine shops, Bengali tea-houses and flower-garland sellers to the sounds of Bollywood music from the countless CD shops. Traditional and religious life is elaborately displayed at the magnificent temples of *Sri Veerama Kaliamman*, *Sri Srinivasa Perumal* and *Temple of 1000 Lights*. During Hindu festivals, especially Deepavali, the area comes to life even more. Slightly less traditional and more commercial wares are on sale at the *Mustafa Centre*, a three-storey complex selling electronic and household goods at some of the cheapest prices in town – although it is packed at weekends.

Transport: Bus 64, 65, 85, 97 or 111 from Orchard Road.

Raffles Hotel

Built in 1887 and declared a National Monument in 1987, Singapore's most famous landmark is one of the world's greatest Victorian grand hotels. Somerset Maugham, Rudyard Kipling, Noel Coward and Charlie Chaplin made it a favourite retreat and it still oozes tradition, particularly since its S$160 million refurbishment in 1991, which was based on the hotel's heyday of 1915. Afternoon tea in the *Tiffin Room*, a Singapore Sling in the *Long Bar* and a drink under the cool high ceilings of *Bar & Billiard* are all part of the Singapore experience. The new arcade houses 70 regional and speciality shops, as well as restaurants and regular performances at the Victorian-style playhouse, *Jubilee Hall*. The museum on the

upper floor houses fascinating Raffles memorabilia, with photographs of some of its more famous guests over the last 100 years, including Charlie Chaplin and his brother, Elizabeth Taylor and Richard Burton. Noel Coward's diary, which recounts the death of his travelling companion (glossed over elsewhere in the display), is utterly compelling.

Beach Road
Tel: 6337 1886. Fax: 6339 7650.
E-mail: raffles@raffles.com
Website: www.raffles.com
Transport: MRT City Hall Station, then short walk to Beach Road.

Night Safari

Located next to the Singapore Zoological Gardens, the award-winning *Night Safari* is billed as the world's first night zoo. Over 90% of animals are nocturnal, so by opening at night and using clever lighting techniques to recreate an almost authentic natural habitat, this zoo allows visitors an amazing opportunity to see animals when they are at their most active.

Spread over 40 hectares (100 acres), there are more than 1200 animals, covering 110 exotic species in eight zones that recreate geographic regions, including the African savannah, Nepalese river valley, South American pampas and Burmese jungle. There is a 45-minute tram ride, which offers a leisurely alternative to the three Walking Trails. The twice-nightly *Creatures of the Night* show sees employees grappling with some of the less dangerous species (at 2000 and 2100).

180 Mandai Lake Road
Tel: 6269 3411 *or* 3412 (24-hour information). Fax: 6366 3309.

E-mail: info@zoo.com.sg
Website: www.zoo.com.sg
Transport: SBS bus 138 from Ang Mo Kio MRT or TIBS bus 927 from Choa Chu Kang MRT.
Opening hours: Daily 1930–2400.
Admission: S$15.60; S$5 (tram rides); concessions available.

Sentosa Island

Billed as a 'tropical isle of peace and tranquillity' and a contrast to Singapore's frenetic atmosphere, *Sentosa Island* is a purpose-built island theme park. Some of its biggest attractions include: *Underwater World*, one of Asia's largest tropical oceanariums with 2500 marine creatures in an 80m (262ft) submerged tunnel; *Dolphin Lagoon*, a water show with a pink dolphin; *VolcanoLand*, which recreates a journey into the centre of the earth; the 37m (121ft) *Merlion*; and *Magical Sentosa*, a musical fountain show twice every evening. Museums include: *Images of Singapore*, which uses waxwork figures to depict the social and cultural history of Singapore; and *Fort Silosa*, which recreates the bunkers and underground passages used in the island's defence. *Sentosa Island* also offers beaches, golf, hotels and restaurants, regional food and arts – all on an epic scale. There is a free monorail or bus around the island and visitors can jump off at any station.

Sentosa Island
Tel: 6275 0388. Fax: 6275 0161.
E-mail: administrator@sentosa.com.sg
Website: www.sentosa.com.sg
Transport: Orchard bus E from Orchard Road; or Sentosa bus A and C from World Trade Centre and Tiong Bahru MRT; or cable car from Mount Faber.
Opening hours: Attractions vary; usually daily 0900–1900 (or as late as 2200).
Admission: S$2 (excluding transport to the island). Additional charges for individual attractions (S$3–17).

Supreme Court and City Hall

Dating from 1939, the *Supreme Court* is one of the last colonial constructions. Its Corinthian columns surround stately interiors featuring murals by Italian artist Cavaliere Rodolfo Nolli. Next door is *City Hall*, another giant structure, built in 1929 and the site of the Japanese surrender to Lord Mountbatten in 1945. It was on these very same steps that the Prime Minister of the time, Lee Kuan Yew, emotionally declared Singapore's Independence from Malaysia. Organised groups may tour the premises by appointment, with the useful *Guide to the Supreme Court*, and anyone may attend most open court hearings. Those who want to learn more about the local judiciary can visit the *Multimedia Gallery*, where presentations relating to the workings of the court are screened on the hour during office hours.

St Andrew's Road
Tel: 6332 4270. Fax: 6337 9450.
E-mail: supcourt_qsm@supcourt.gov.sg
Website: www.supcourt.gov.sg
Transport: MRT City Hall; then walk across the Padang.
Opening hours: Mon–Fri 0830–1730, Sat 0830–1300.
Admission: Free.

Jurong BirdPark

The largest bird park in all of South-East Asia, *Jurong BirdPark* is a refuge for more than 8000 birds of 600 different species from all over the world. Highlights include *Waterfall Aviary*, at 30m (98ft) the world's highest man-made waterfall; the *South-East Asian Bird Aviary*, where a thunderstorm is simulated every day at

Sv noon; and *Jungle Jewels*, featuring dazzling
Th hummingbirds. At the *Lodge on Flamingo Lake*, visitors
loc can dine surrounded by 1001 flamingos, or breakfast on
ho the Song Bird Terrace. Bird shows and feeding times
kn feature flamingos, macaws, hornbills and cockatoos and
stil one of the biggest attractions is the *Penguin Parade*,
the housing more than 200 penguins of five species. An air-
sitt conditioned monorail covers the entire park.
she 2 Jurong Hill
coi Tel: 6265 0022. Fax: 6261 1869.
bu: E-mail: info@birdpark.com.sg
the Website: www.birdpark.com.sg
fiv Transport: MRT Boon Lay Station, then SBS bus 194
ev or 251 from Interchange.
ead Opening hours: Daily 0800–1800.
fea Admission: S$12; S$3 (monorail); concessions available.
and

Singapore Art Museum

nai This was once the St Joseph's Institution, the island's
mc first all-boys school, which was built by French
Su Catholic monks and is one of the most striking
2 S structures in the city. Now home to the *Singapore Art*
Tel *Museum*, its exhibits are predominantly 20th-
E- century South-East Asian art with paintings,
We sculptures and installations. Although specialising in
Pri regional art, the museum recently broadened its
Ra scope to include the rest of Asia. There are free
2 S guided tours daily in English at 1100 and 1400, as
Tel well as 1530 on Saturdays.
E- 71 Bras Basah Road
We Tel: 6332 3222 *or* 6375 2510 (recorded information).
Pri Fax: 6334 7919.
Website: www.nhb.gov.sg
L Transport: MRT Dhoby Ghaut.
Opening hours: Mon 1200–1800, Tues–Sun
Ra 0900–1800 (until 2100 Fri).
A Admission: S$3; some temporary exhibitions extra;
fou free after 1800 Fri.
on

Singapore Science Centre

At Housing more than 850 exhibits, mostly interactive,
lux the *Science Centre* is Singapore's largest collection
am devoted to the wonder of science – and was recently
to extended. Its exhibition halls include: the *Discovery*
on *Zone*, for young children, the *Human Body*, *Mathemagic*,
val *Space Science*, *Biotechnology*, *Energy*, the *Hall of Aviation*,
anc the *Hall of IT* and the *Web of Life* – all explaining the
in science in ingenious interactive ways. Outside, there is
firs an *Ecogarden* and a *Kinetic Garden*, the first of its kind in
vis Asia, which showcases interactive sculptures and
Ch science displays. There is also an *Omni-Theatre*.
gu 15 Science Centre Road
a d Tel: 6425 2500. Fax: 6565 9533.
a h E-mail: enquiry@science.edu.sg
cei Website: www.science.edu.sg
the Transport: MRT Jurong East, then SBS bus 66 or 335.
1 I Opening hours: Tues–Sun 1000–1800 (last Omni-
Tel Theatre show 2000).
E- Admission: S$6; plus S$10 (Omni-Theatre).
We

Singapore Cable Car

Th This new addition to Singapore's attractions offers
Th views of the city from an impressive height. Spanning
on over 1750m (5740ft), it is the first cable car in South-
roc East Asia and the only one that crosses a harbour. The
ma cable car stops at three stations – and visitors can
coi board at all three. Each has beautiful, very different,
gla views. Mount Faber is the second highest hill in
Gr Singapore and an equatorial rainforest; Cable Car
of i Towers is actually the rooftop of a skyscraper, situated
at t near the World Trade Centre and with a view over
the busy harbour; while the third station is on the

island of Sentosa, so the trip affords fantastic views of
the sea. It is possible to travel in a glass-bottomed car,
making the journey even more spectacular.
Mount Faber, or Cable Car Towers, 3 Maritime
Square, or Sentosa Island
Tel: 6270 8855. Fax: 6273 4639.
E-mail: cablecar@singnet.com.sg
Website: www.cablecar.com.sg
Operating hours: Daily 0830–2100 (last cable car
leaves Sentosa).
Price: S$8.50 (normal cabin); S$15 (glass cabin).

Asian Civilisations Museum

Housed in a restored neo-classical building dating
back to 1910, this museum focuses on the multi-
ethnic heritage of the region, especially Chinese
history, symbolism, art, connoisseurship and the
Chinese scholar tradition. It has a collection of
Buddhist artefacts, Imperial porcelain, 17th-century
Ming-style furniture and displays of Peranakan
culture. It is seen as an important showcase for the
culture's development. There are free daily guided
tours at 1100 and 1400, plus Saturdays at 1530.
39 Armenian Street
Tel: 6332 3015. Fax: 6332 7993.
E-mail: nhb_acm_pa@nhb.gov.sg
Website: www.nhb.gov.sg
Transport: MRT City Hall, then walk along
Stamford Road.
Opening hours: Tues–Sun 0900–1800 (until 2100 Fri).
Admission: S$3 (concessions available).

Changi Prison Chapel & Museum

This chapel and museum is a reminder of Singapore's
more harrowing historical moments. During World
War II, three years of conflict with the Japanese
before capitulation saw 50,000 civilians and soldiers
imprisoned in *Changi Prison*. The chapel, housed
within the open-air courtyard, was first built in 1988
by the wartime prison inmates, and is now a
monument to those prisoners of war. Photographs,
drawings and letters in the museum depict the daily
life of the prisoners, but the highlight of the
exhibition is a series of paintings, called the *Changi
Murals*, recreated from those painted by British PoW
Stanley Warren. Services are conducted by the
Changi Christian Fellowship every Sunday
1730–1900. There are daily guided tours on the hour.
1000 Upper Changi Road North
Tel: 6214 2451. Fax: 6214 1179.

E-mail: changi_museum@pacific.net.sg
Website: www.changimuseum.com
Transport: MRT Tanah Merah, then SBS bus 2.
Opening hours: Daily 0930–1630; guided tours on
the hour from 1000.
Admission: Free; S$6 (guided tours); concessions available.

Singapore Botanic Gardens

The *Singapore Botanic Gardens* are a perfect respite
from the city's urban landscape. They epitomise the
tropical island's luxuriant parks with a combination of
primary jungle and elegantly laid-out flowerbeds and
shrubs. Over 3000 species of plants thrive in the
gardens, which also serve to educate and conserve.
Spread over 52 hectares (128 acres), the gardens hold
more than half a million plants, while the *National
Orchid Garden* has the world's largest orchid display
with over 60,000 plants. The gardens are also a venue
for outdoor concerts.
Cluny Road
Tel: 6471 7808. Fax: 6472 3033.
Website: www.nparks.gov.sg
Transport: SBS bus 7, 105, 106, 123 or 174 from
Orchard Boulevard. Shuttle bus at weekends hourly
0700–1900 from opposite Orchard MRT.
Opening hours: Daily 0500–2400; daily 0830–1900
(National Orchid Garden).
Admission: Free; S$2 (National Orchid Garden).

Further Distractions

Bukit Timah Nature Reserve

This 164-hectare (405-acre) reserve, 12km (7.5 miles)
from the city centre, is one of only two nature
reserves within city boundaries in the world (the
other is in Rio de Janeiro). The reserve contains more
species of trees than the entire North American
continent – and is one of the few attractions in
Singapore that is not man-made. Many species of
larger animals were rendered extinct but today it is
possible to glimpse a flying lemur, long-tailed
macaque monkey or anteater. The reserve has the
island's most challenging walking or cycling trails but
the paths are well marked as they meander through
the jungle, in the company of exotic birds, butterflies,
monkeys and squirrels. *Bukit Timah Hill*, at 164m
(538ft), is Singapore's highest point.
177 Hindhede Drive
Tel: 6468 5736 *or* 1800 468 5736. Fax: 6462 0723.

Chinese Garden

Photo: Singapore Tourism Board

Singapore skyline

RESTAURANTS

The selected restaurants have been divided into five categories: Gastronomic, Business, Trendy, Budget and Personal Recommendations. The restaurants are listed alphabetically within these different categories, which serve as guidelines rather than absolute definitions of the establishments.

Restaurants will add a 10% service charge, 4% GST and 1% government tax to the bill. This 15% is known as 'triple plus' and is mandatory. Tipping is not required on top.

The prices quoted below are for an average three-course meal for one person and for a bottle of house wine or cheapest equivalent; they do not include service charge or tax.

Gastronomic

Alkaff Mansion

This elegant mansion, built in the 1920s, is one of Singapore's finest with high ceilings, wooden beams and antique tiles. Its decadent atmosphere – albeit rather staid – is enhanced by the fantastic view from the top of the hill over acres of park. Start in the Verandah Bar for an apéritif and move upstairs for the fabulous Dutch-Indonesian cuisine. In addition to the à la carte menu, there is an 11-dish Rijsttafel Menu (S$60) with dishes like red snapper with mixed pickles or grilled sliced lamb loin with chilli soy sauce. All ceremoniously served with staff in traditional dress, it is a wonderful way of experiencing this cuisine. For the less adventurous, the Western Menu includes chicken bouillabaisse and tortellini with anchovies and there is a four-course Western set menu at lunchtime for S$27.
10 Telok Blangah Green
Tel: 6415 4888. Fax: 6274 0460.
E-mail: reservations@alkaffmansion.com.sg
Website: www.alkaffmansion.com.sg
Price: S$80. Wine: S$48.

L'Aigle Dor

The Art Nouveau interior of *L'Aigle Dor* creates a cosy yet classy ambience. One of the best authentic French restaurants in town, the cuisine and service are renowned. A meal might start with chilled angel hair pasta with sea urchins or lentil soup with foie gras. Meat dishes dominate the menu, such as roasted pigeon with morels, but there is also seafood, for example, a sole and lobster soufflé. Hazelnut parfait and crêpe suzette or poached cherries in red wine with pistachio ice cream are ideal ways to finish off an evening.
Duxton Hotel, 83 Duxton Road
Tel: 6227 7678. Fax: 6227 1232.
E-mail: berhotel@singnet.com.sg
Price: S$90. Wine: S$55.

Man Fu Yuan

Man Fu Yuan is an elegant restaurant that serves up an exquisite selection of Cantonese dishes with a unique slant. Starters include deep-fried lobster and prawn roll in filo pastry, or a barbecue platter with marinated eel and slivers of chicken liver on toast. The shark fin soup is double-boiled with shark's bone stock. Pork spare ribs are baked and cooked with lemon sauce and, for dessert, the homemade beancurd with sugar syrup or the hasma with red dates are recommended. The serene setting and gracious service merely enhance the finesse of the food.
Hotel InterContinental Singapore, 80 Middle Road
Tel: 6431 1062. Fax: 6431 1139.
Price: S$60. Wine: S$62.

Morton's of Chicago

This slice of America is best known for its superb, succulent steaks, huge portions and unrivalled service. The atmosphere is plush yet intimate, in true gentleman's club style with huge upholstered seats and Sinatra crooning in the background. Entrées like the Maine lobster, tender crab cakes and baked scallops wrapped in bacon come highly recommended. The house speciality is porterhouse, a double delight with one side filet mignon and the other New York strip. Apart from huge succulent hunks of US steak, there is also a good selection of chicken, fish and seafood mains. For the sweet tooth, the Godiva hot chocolate cake is renowned.
The Oriental Singapore Hotel, 5 Raffles Avenue, Marina Square
Tel: 6339 3740. Fax: 6337 3763.
Website: www.mortons.com
Price: S$150. Wine: S$80.

Raffles Grill

The classic French cuisine and top-class service has made the *Grill* the most exclusive restaurant of Raffles Hotel (see *Hotels*). It has previously been named as the island's top restaurant and the current chef has won Michelin stars. The old colonial interior is innately stylish, while the food is exquisite. Pan-seared duck's liver is a house speciality, but other dishes include roasted rack of veal, warm smoked Atlantic salmon and suckling pig with delicious crackling. Diners should finish up with a selection of soufflés or the warm bitter chocolate tart.
Raffles Hotel, 1 Beach Road
Tel: 6337 1886. Fax: 6339 7525.
E-mail: rafflesgrill@raffles.com
Website: www.raffles.com
Price: S$110. Wine: S$80.

Business

Au Jardin Les Amis

This branch of the *Les Amis* group surely wins the prize for the most picturesque setting. Set amid the Botanic Gardens, it overlooks lush greenery and offers fantastic views from its two balconies. Its spacious interior is particularly good for wining and dining clients. The fixed-price menu offers a three-course set lunch for S$55 and a huge six-course dinner for S$150 or four courses for S$135. Favourite dishes include fillet of venison with beetroot purée and black trumpet mushrooms, or seared sea scallops with black pudding. The wine list is highly reputable. Reservations highly recommended.
The group's other branches, *The Lighthouse* and *Les Amis*, also have à la carte menus.

EJH Corner House, Singapore Botanic Gardens, Cluny Road
Tel: 6466 8812. Fax: 6466 8227.
Website: www.lesamis.com.sg
Price: S$150 (six-course set menu). Wine: S$70.
Branches:
Les Amis
16 Shaw Centre, 1 Scotts Road
Tel: 6733 2225. Fax: 6735 0106.
The Lighthouse
The Fullerton Hotel, 1 Fullerton Square
Tel: 6877 8932. Fax: 6877 8931.

Harbour Grill and Oyster Bar

With a cosy, Old World decor, ornate furnishings and an open kitchen area, *Harbour Grill* enjoys a long-standing reputation for classic French and continental food. Good starters are the Scottish smoked salmon, served with blinis and cauliflower salad or the fresh Canadian or Fines de Claire oysters. Main course options include the pan-fried veal loin with potato soufflé or the roasted cod with young vegetables and chicken juice. The exquisite desserts include a mango and passion fruit soup or chestnut soufflé. A four-course set lunch costs S$45, with three courses at S$38. Closed Sunday.
Level 3, Hilton Hotel Singapore, 581 Orchard Road
Tel: 6730 3393. Fax: 6235 4140.
E-mail: harbourgrill@yahoo.com.sg
Price: S$70. Wine: S$75.

Jiang-Nan Chun

Award-winning, personalised, helpful service and an understated chic setting make this restaurant well suited for a business meal. The innovative Chinese cuisine features traditional dishes with a twist, like deep-fried spare ribs with coffee sauce. But classic Chinese favourites include barbecue pigeon, braised shark fin soup with crab rolls, or pork and squid dumplings flavoured with water chestnut.
Four Seasons Hotel, 190 Orchard Boulevard
Tel: 6831 7220. Fax: 6831 7159.
Website: www.fourseasons.com
Price: S$70. Wine: S$65.

Mezza9

Simple Zen and urban chic makes a winning combination in this diverse restaurant of 450 seats. The restaurant serves four cuisines – Chinese, Thai, Japanese and Western – divided into nine dining experiences, including a European Deli, a Chinese steam basket and a sushi and sashimi bar. The à la carte menu has an ever-changing selection of each, including Chinese chilli crab, yakitori (Japanese barbecue) and tom yam gung. Set lunches are available during the week (S$26–39), while the Sunday brunch is fantastic, including the full range of cuisines, plus free-flowing champagne and a chocolate fountain for S$78.
Grand Hyatt Singapore, 10/12 Scotts Road
Tel: 6416 7189. Fax: 6736 3064.
E-mail: mezza9.sg@hyattintl.com
Website: www.restaurants.singapore.hyatt.com
Price: S$65. Wine: S$60.

The Oaks Grill and Bar

Set in a rather inauspicious shopping mall, this restaurant nonetheless has a bright, friendly atmosphere and a popular outdoor terrace. Specialising in Australian steaks and seafood, cooked with an Asian flavour, it originated as a wine store and so not surprisingly boasts a fine wine selection. A

favourite starter is Moreton Bay Bugs skewer with chilli tomato relish, while the grilled kangaroo or ostrich steak mains, or the blue-eyed cod with sautéed spinach and tarragon sauce are recommended. Everything is cooked to perfection and *The Oaks* is a good example of how tasty barbecued food can be.
Tanglin Mall, 163 Tanglin Road
Tel: 6735 8611. Fax: 6735 8600.
Price: S$50. Wine: S$42.

Trendy

Indochine

This group of three restaurants serves authentic food from Indochina. *Indochine Alfresco*, on Waterloo Street, offers casual alfresco dining in a courtyard setting and serves light food like the famous Vietnamese beef noodles. *Indochine Wine Bar and Restaurant* on Club Street is more sophisticated, with dark decor and bold sculptures. It offers more complex dishes, like Loatian pork patties wrapped around lemongrass stalks. The newest addition is the trendy *Waterfront*, on Empress Place, with a huge terrace adjacent to the river and indoor seating behind glass panels. It boasts fusion food like Cambodian chicken with garlic, chilli and basil sauce, and an Indonesian platter including tasters of prawns on sugar cane, dried beef and spring rolls.
Indochine Alfresco
42 Waterloo Street
Tel: 6333 5003. Fax: 6323 2417.
Price: S$50. Wine: S$58.
Indochine Wine Bar and Restaurant
49 Club Street
Tel: 6323 0503. Fax: 6323 2417.
Waterfront
1 Empress Place
Tel: 6339 1720. Fax: 6339 0420.

Marmalade

One of the best and trendiest restaurants on the island, this stylish, upmarket venue has stark, minimalist aesthetics. Based in the heart of the city adjacent to the Metropole Hotel, *Marmalade* has a small but popular American menu serving high-quality food that changes every few months. Starters might include mizune and wildflower salad or tomato and saffron consommé, with mains like the crispy skin fillet of pike or pan-roasted quail served with brioche and foie gras. Desserts include the Jack Daniel's glazed banana or the passion fruit pannacotta. There is also a five-course tasting menu at S$88 or S$118 with wines; the vegetarian equivalent is S$78 and S$108. No lunch. Closed Sunday.
36 Purvis Street
Tel: 6837 2123. Fax: 6837 2124.
Website: www.marmalade.com.sg
Price: S$60. Wine: S$82.

Pierside Kitchen and Bar

The *Pierside Kitchen and Bar*'s trendy waterfront location allows alfresco dining with a harbour view. The modern cuisine has an emphasis on seafood and includes a dash of Japanese. Starters include cumin-spiced crab cakes with marinated cucumber and chilli, and seaweed-wrapped tuna tempura. For main course, the oven-roasted miso cod with new potatoes and sweet peas is highly recommended, as is the Maine lobster linguine. The highlight of the dessert menu is the warm chocolate tart with a molten lava centre. With stylish decor, staff and ambience, *Pierside* has already made its mark as a trendy dining spot.

One Fullerton, 1 Fullerton Road
Tel: 6438 0400. Fax: 6438 3436.
Website: www.piersidekitchen.com
Price: S$60. Wine: S$70.

Saint Pierre

Emmanual Stroobant, a winner of Best Chef of the Year, unites his Belgian roots and Asian experience in an elegant, simple and modern restaurant. The menu includes delicacies like pan-fried foie gras with caramelised apple in port sauce, braised black cod with white miso and the pot-roasted Barbarie duck leg, served with raspberry vinegar reduction and caramelised pear. For dessert, Grandma Stroobant's flourless Belgian chocolate cake lives up to its reputation as unmissable. Reservations recommended. No dinner Sunday. No lunch Saturday.
Central Mall, 3 Magazine Road
Tel: 6438 0887. Fax: 6438 4887.
Website: www.saintpierre.com.sg
Price: S$100. Wine: S$45.

Union Restaurant and Bar

One of the newest and trendiest venues in this hippest of streets, *Union* has an oh-so-cool bar on the ground floor with dim lights and fine cocktails and a restaurant serving modern European cuisine. If pan-fried foie gras is passé, then try the mussels with lemongrass and coconut. The duck is pan-fried with a crispy skin and served with a berry coulis, while the lobster angel hair pasta with caviar is deservedly one of their most popular main courses. Diners can top it all off with chocolate fondue and relax in a simple, clean and spacious setting with seductive lighting and music. A good-value three-course lunch is available for S$25.
81 Club Street
Tel: 6327 4990. Fax: 6327 4989.
E-mail: union@gastronomical.biz
Price: S$60. Wine: S$50.

Budget

Gorkha Grill

This little gem of a dining room, tucked in the busy eating area of Smith Street, is Singapore's first authentic Nepalese restaurant. Small and friendly, with huge murals of mountain scenery, the menu is a great sample of the flavours and spices of Nepal. Filling without being heavy and greasy, *momos* (meat or vegetarian steamed or fried dumplings) are a great way to start. Recommended dishes include the soup made from beans simmered with green vegetables and herbs; *Jheenge papita* (prawns marinated with herbs and vegetables) served in a papaya boat, and *kukhura so makhani* (chicken marinated with herbs and butter gravy). *Gorkha Grill* is tasty and reasonably priced – made more economical by bringing your own wine. A new branch, *Everest Kitchen*, opened in mid-2002 with the emphasis on North Indian cuisine, has a great-value buffet lunch for S$8.
21 Smith Street
Tel: 6227 0806.
Price: S$24. Wine: S$38 or BYO.
Branch:
55 Chander Road, Little India
Tel: 6299 0745.

Komala Vilas

Komala Vilas is one of a plethora of small, casual eating places in the ethnic quarter of Little India. The

Singapore dining

vegetarian menu provides a whole traditional South Indian meal, with favourites such as the *dosai*, a vegetable-filled crêpe, and *thali*, a complete meal comprising rice, lentils and a selection of curries, all served on a banana leaf. A great place for breakfast, open from 0700. No credit cards.
76–78 Serangoon Road
Tel: 6293 6980. Fax: 6392 9385.
E-mail: komala@singnet.com.sg
Price: S$10. Unlicensed.
Branch:
12–14 Buffalo Road
Tel: 6293 3664.

Ling Zhi

With Chinese food being dominated by meat and seafood, it is something of a relief to be able to enjoy pure vegetarian dishes – and at reasonable prices. *Dim sum* is a good place to start – the fried monkey head mushrooms with capsicum and dried chilli must be tried (despite the name), as must the honshimeiji mushrooms, which are stir fried with asparagus, capsicum and macadamia nuts in a crispy yam basket. The chefs in the two outlets have proved that it is possible to turn vegetables and soya into imaginative and tasty dishes. Because of the location and price, lunchtimes are busy but generally cosy, with friendly service.
Liat Towers, 541 Orchard Road
Tel: 6734 3788. Fax: 6734 5788.
E-mail: lingzhi@tunglok.com
Price: S$25. Wine: Unlicensed.
Branch:
Far East Square, 7–10 Amoy St
Tel: 6538 2992. Fax: 6538 7882.

Newton Circus

Eating in a hawker centre is a dining experience special to Singapore, with many around the city, especially in the shopping areas. *Newton Circus* has always been popular with locals and visitors, mainly because it is outdoor and open 24 hours. Diners should ignore the touts who try and entice tourists to their stall and look at what each place offers, then find a table and place an order. As with most food centres, you can order from different stalls and it will all be brought to your table. It does not offer the greatest range of dishes, with few vegetarian options, nor is it the cheapest, but the atmosphere is always lively whether people gather for a late-night meal, for breakfast, or for a beer at 4am.
Newton Circus, next to the Newton MRT
Price: From S$3 per dish. Beer: From S$4.

Orchard Maharajah

This small North Indian restaurant, situated in Orchard Road's shopping district, is ideal for those who like outdoor dining in the midst of activity. Despite its modest location and price, the food is impressive. The tandoori platter comes laden with chicken tikka, fish, shish kebab and prawns. The *Raan e Maharajah* is the house speciality, with lamb marinated overnight and roasted in the tandoor. Vegetarian dishes include the classic *saag aloo* (spinach and potato) and *baigan bartha* (aubergine with spices).
27 Cuppage Terrace
Tel: 6732 6331.
Price: S$26. Wine: S$30.

Personal Recommendations

Broth

Since opening in August 2001, *Broth* has already proved to be a popular place for lunch and dinner in the business district of Chinatown. The Mediterranean atmosphere of the leafy side-street is reflected in the high-ceilinged, cool interior, which only has eight tables, although there are also two on the pavement. The cuisine is Modern European, its dinner menu favouring meaty main courses, such as Middle Eastern chicken or lamb loins in a green coat (herb sauce). There is more variety at lunchtime – starters like snails on brioche with roast garlic, mains like the potato and white truffle gnocchi – while the dessert menu is outstanding. The sticky date pudding should not be missed. A suitable place for a quiet dinner, with relaxing music and friendly service.
21 Duxton Hill
Tel: 6323 3353.
E-mail: broth@singnet.com.sg
Price: S$50. Wine: S$55.

Crossroads Café

The location here is the real gem. Bang in the middle of Orchard Road's shopping and business district on pavement level, its relaxing, terrace-like atmosphere is perfect for people-watching. The extensive menu has snacks, meals and breakfasts with Asian and Western cuisine and the beauty lies in its variety. The Late Breakfast menu includes American pancakes and Eggs Benedict. Dinner might start with a classic Caesar salad with smoked salmon or an Asian combination platter; and move on to the popular Yong chow fried rice with pork, shrimp and chicken satay, or a five-spiced fillet of cod. The café has a long list of sandwiches and side orders, as well as a dessert buffet for S$10, which makes it ideal – whether for an afternoon coffee, a cool beer or a three-course dinner.
Singapore Marriott Hotel, 320 Orchard Road
Tel: 6735 5800. Fax: 6735 9800.
Price: S$40. Wine: S$40.

Doc Cheng's

Specialising in cuisine known as trans-ethnic, *Doc Cheng's* uses unusual combinations of ingredients, which is the restaurant's signature. Fusion cuisine tends to be an over-used description but here is one place that offers the real thing. For starters, Doc's pu-pu plate includes a range of appetisers like samosas, tuna tartare and pork dumplings or Indochine crab cake with butter sauce. Mains include Szechuan rack of lamb marinated with spices, char-boiled miso butter fish, or wok-charred big-eye Hawaiian tuna. A unique dessert would be caramelised bananas baked with sticky rice ice cream. There is a four-course set menu for S$98 (with wine) or S$65 (without wine).
Raffles Hotel Arcade, 328 North Bridge Road
Tel: 6412 1261. Fax: 6339 7013.
E-mail: doccheng@raffles.com
Website: www.raffles.com
Price: S$60. Wine: S$55.

Esmirada

With a heavy Greek accent, *Esmirada* has recently moved to this larger venue and makes for a lively night out, rather than a quiet dinner for two. The salads are full of creamy feta cheese and black olives; main courses include skewered meat and seafood served with bell pepper relish and tzatziki, as well as paella and lamb couscous. The desserts are wonderful, with award-winning tiramisu and lemon crème brûlée. But the pièce de résistance is the Kramat coffee, where, at the table, a waiter prepares a flambéed coffee, loaded with Cointreau, Grand Marnier and Drambuie. Service is informal and friendly yet efficient and there is a huge table seating ten people in a separate dining room, ideal for a more private dinner party.
Orchard Hotel, 442 Orchard Road
Tel: 6735 3476.
Price: S$50. Wine: S$55.

Original Sin

This is one of Singapore's few European vegetarian restaurants, a stylish venue in the ex-pat suburb of Holland Village. There is a tempting choice of bruschettas, salads and starters, the best of which is the mezze plate with six Middle Eastern specialties, like *babaganoush* (roast eggplant dip) and *koresh* (pumpkin, pinenuts and cinammon), served with hunks of pitta bread. The pizzas and calzones are far from predictable, with toppings like roast pumpkin, avocado, smoked cheese and asparagus. The Italian chef excels in risotto, frittata and pasta, and after sampling all that, there is a mouthwatering cheesecake and liqueur coffee to finish. Dishes can also be adapted to cater for vegans – and even non-vegetarians might wish to come back for more.
Chip Bee Gardens, 43 Jalan Merah Saga, Holland Village
Tel: 6475 5605. Fax: 6475 4416.
Website: www.originalsin.com.sg
Price: S$40. Wine: S$49.

ENTERTAINMENT

Nightlife

After-hours drinking and dancing is not as diverse as in many big cities around the world – the range tends to be upmarket, trendy bars and clubs or alternatively karaoke lounges. There is little room for an alternative music scene but the range of clubs and hotel bars is popular, especially at weekends. The bars in the major hotels along Orchard Road are a good bet for a refined drink or even to meet clients. Locals who can't afford the high prices of such places are happy to drink beer in some of the all-night hawker centres or food streets.

Certain areas and venues are popular with wealthier foreign workers and tourists. Boat Quay is filled with tourists; a string of shop-houses converted into noisy bars and restaurants overlook the river and passers-by are enticed in with happy-hour drinks. One of the best-known places is *Harry's Bar*, a former favourite haunt of Baring's Bank fraudster Nick Leeson (and other wealthy ex-pats) with live jazz and jamming sessions most evenings.

The East Coast bars are also renowned as something of an ex-pat enclave, while a more 'creative' clientele hangs out in Tanjong Pagar and Club Street, where many of Singapore's advertising and PR agencies are based. There is also a clubbing centre along Mohammed Sultan Road for trendy locals and Chijmes has plenty of places for eating and drinking. The clubs and bars on and around Orchard Road are popular with locals and tourists, while Emerald Hill, lined with Singapore's most exquisitely converted shop-houses, has a great selection of lively pubs, cosy wine bars and beer taverns. Further to the west, Holland Village is eternally busy, with younger Singaporeans filling its wine bars and retro coffee lounges.

Most clubs are open 2200–0100 Sunday to Thursday and 2200–0300 Friday and Saturday. Dress code is generally smart-casual and the minimum age limit for drinking alcohol is 18 years, although some clubs won't let in anyone under 23. There is normally a cover charge, especially at weekends, usually around S$25 for the more trendy places.

Bars

Singapore has a bar to cater for every taste, from the refined colonial grandeur of Raffles Hotel's *Bar & Billiard* and the *Long Bar*, to the live music at *Muddy Murphy's Irish Pub*, opposite Orchard Towers, Orchard Hotel Shopping Arcade, 442 Orchard Road. The 19th-century Peranakan shop-houses on Emerald Hill contain a good cluster of bars. These include *No. 5*, 5 Emerald Hill, *Ice Cold Beer*, 9 Emerald Hill, and *Que Pasa*, 7 Emerald Hill, the city's oldest wine bar. The *Alley Bar*, 2 Emerald Hill, is a stylish new addition and, as its name suggests, is converted from the narrow space between shop-houses. *Opium*, Empress Place Waterfront, near the Fullerton Hotel and next to *Indochine* (see *Restaurants*), is a fashionable new bar on the waterfront, with tables and huge sofas for alfresco drinking. *Altivo Bar*, 109 Mount Faber Road, sits on top of Mount Faber, good on a hot evening with a club, chill-out area and bar catering to a fairly hip crowd. Duxton Road has lots of small bars, many with karaoke lounges, such as *JJ Mahoney*, 58 Duxton Road, which has three floors featuring a DJ on the first, games on the second and English karaoke on the third floor.

Casinos

Casinos and all other gambling activities are illegal in Singapore. The only legal alternatives are various lotteries and on-course betting on horseraces at *Singapore Turf Club* (see *Sport*).

Clubs

Still going strong is *Zouk*, Jiak Kim Street, one of the best-known clubs in town, and good enough to attract famous foreign DJs (Fat Boy Slim played there

in 2002). It is also home to other clubs within its walls: *Velvet Underground*, which attracts a more mature crowd and offers a mellower brand of cool; *Phuture* and the *Wine Bar*. The place of the moment is *The Gallery Hotel* on Orchard Road, which is home to many bars, including *The Liquid Room*, a dimly lit, retro-style bar, with a large alfresco area and huge dance floor. *Centro 360*, at One Fullerton, is a super-hip huge venue, with gay nights on Sunday. *Bar None*, in the basement of the Singapore Marriott Hotel, has a small dance floor, often has live music and is packed at weekends. *Indigo*, 25 Mohammed Sultan Road, is a new trendy dance club, playing New York house, with plush lounges, private booths and a spacious dance floor, as well as an outdoor terrace. On the same street, *Madamme Wongs* also attracts a young trendy crowd, and *Next Page*, a long-standing favourite with ex-pats, especially journalists.

Karaoke

As in the rest of Asia, karaoke remains an inordinately popular evening's entertainment. *Sparks*, 7th Floor, Tower B, Ngee Ann City, is South-East Asia's largest nightspot with 18 karaoke rooms. At the *Lava Lounge*, Grange Road, you can sing along against the backdrop of its 70s space-age disco lounge and retro music. There are plenty of other karaoke bars off Smith Street in Chinatown and along Duxton Road, like *Fine Night* (number 59) and *Boomerang KTV Lounge* (number 45).

Live Music

The infamous *Harry's Bar*, Boat Quay, features a live jazz band and jam session Tuesday to Sunday nights with pot luck on Mondays, while at *Crazy Elephant*, further along on Clarke Quay, rhythm and blues bands alternate with classic rock'n'roll and alternative underground music daily. Overseas jazz musicians are hosted at *Somerset's Bar* at the Westin Stamford Hotel. The *Hard Rock Café*, Cuscadem Road, features the Malay reggae band Bushmen, every Sunday night.

Sport

Singapore may be renowned for its food-lovers and shopaholics but improving its people's fitness levels is high on the government's agenda – although they have quite a job on their hands. Hardly the most physically dynamic of nations, competitive sports are

not prominent and the nation's favourite sports are listed as swimming and jogging, although there is a rising popularity in hockey and tennis. Every year, the *Singapore Sports Council* (tel: 6345 7111; fax: 6340 9537; website: www.ssc.gov.sg) organises healthy lifestyle activities designed for maximum participation, including national swim and cycle events. SPEX21 is a new initiative to encourage high-performance athletes in soccer, badminton, swimming and table tennis.

There are more than a dozen stadiums and, with fitness such a high priority, there are facilities at every level across the island. Swimming is a favourite pastime, with pools in most residential areas; gyms are equipped with the latest in fitness technology. One of Singapore's major sporting attractions is its acres of golf courses and, as an island, there are plenty of opportunities for watersports.

For spectators, the national soccer team, the *S-league* (website: www.sleague.com), play at home at the *National Stadium*, Kallang. English football is immensely popular with regular televised Premier League and European matches; Liverpool and Manchester United have even toured Singapore over the past few years to play against local sides. Every year sees a boozy fiesta of international rugby, at the *Rugby Sevens* held in April also at the National Stadium. The *Singapore Indoor Stadium*, also at Kallang, hosts the *Heineken Tennis Open* tournament. One of the most popular spectator sports is horseracing, conducted all year round at the *Singapore Turf Club* (tel: 6879 1000; fax: 6879 1010; website: www.turfclub.com.sg) at Kranji, which provides the only legal outlet for gambling. Highlights are the Queen Elizabeth Cup (August) and the lucrative Singapore Airlines International Cup (May). There is a dress code even in the public stands, with no shorts allowed and a smart-casual look for the Hibiscus Room, which allows visitors.

Rugby and cricket matches are held on the *Padang*, an attractive setting at the colonial heart of Singapore. This is the home of the Singapore Cricket Club and is for members only, although it is possible to watch matches away from the clubhouse. There are several other cricket grounds around the city and league matches are held at weekends.

Information on fixtures, events and venues is available through *Singapore Sports Council* (see above), which also offers an online sports facilities reservation system.

Boat Quay

Photo: Singapore Tourism Board

Bowling

Ten-pin bowling is a popular pastime with over 30 bowling alleys in the city. The *Singapore Ten-pin Bowling Congress* (tel: 6440 7388; fax: 6440 7488) can give details of venues. Most are open 0900–0200; some are open 24 hours at weekends.

Fitness Centres

Numerous centres include *Ray Wilson California Fitness Center*, Grange Road (tel: 6834 2100; fax: 6834 2122; website: www.calfitnesscenters.com), and *Takashimaya Fitness Plus*, Ngee Ann City (tel: 6739 9314; fax: 6735 7203; e-mail: fitplus @pacific.net.sg; website: www.fitness-plus.com.sg). Gym facilities are also available at all the major hotels.

Golf

Singapore is said to have more golf courses per capita than any other country in the world (18), several of which are of championship quality. In most clubs, non-members are not allowed at weekends and they are often expected to hold a handicap or proficiency certificate to play at all. Courses include: *Changi Golf Club*, Netheravon Road (tel: 6545 5133; fax: 6545 2531), which has a nine-hole course with green fees from S$40; *Keppel Club*, Bukit Chermin Road (tel: 6273 5522; website: www.keppelclub.com.sg), 18 holes from S$106; *Raffles Country Club*, Jalan Ahmad Ibrahim (tel: 6861 7655; fax: 6861 5563; website: www.rcc.org.sg), two 18-hole courses from S$125; *Sentosa Golf Club*, Bukit Manis Road (tel: 6275 0022; fax: 6275 0654), two 18-hole courses from S$166. More information on golf courses is available from the *Singapore Tourism Board* (website: www.visitsingapore.com).

Karting

Karting Club of Singapore, 2 Fisher Street, Merchant Square (tel: 6354 2319; website: www.kartingclub-sg.com), encourages people to safely try go-karting throughout the week.

Riding & Polo

The *Singapore Polo Club*, Mount Pleasant Road (tel: 6256 4530; fax: 6256 6715), hosts polo matches throughout the year on most Tuesdays, Thursdays and weekends.

Sailing

Seasport Centre, near Lagoon Hawker Centre, East Coast Parkway (tel: 6449 5118; fax: 6449 7181; e-mail: members@bastafrescaseasportscentre.com.sg), can be used by non-members for windsurfing and sailing; while sailing only is available at *Changi Sailing Club*, 32 Netheravon Road (tel: 6545 2876; fax: 6542 4235; e-mail: enquiry@csc.org.sg; website: www.csc.org.sg).

Scuba Diving

Singapore is not a destination offering crystal clear waters or colourful marine life but it is a good location to complete the pool training before heading off to clearer waters in Malaysia or Indonesia for open-water diving. Dive operators include *Big Bubble Centre* (tel: 6222 6862; fax: 6222 5751; e-mail: bbcdiver@starhub.net.sg; website: www. bigbubble.com).

Squash

Courts can be hired at *Kallang Squash and Tennis Centre*, 52 Stadium Road (tel: 6440 6839), and *St Wilfred Squash and Tennis Centre*, 3 St Wilfred Road (tel: 6293 3452).

Swimming

All the top hotels have pools and every residential neighbourhood has a public swimming complex. The *Singapore Sports Council* (tel: 6345 7111; website: www.ssc.gov.sg) can provide information.

Tennis

Courts can be hired at *Singapore Tennis Centre*, East Coast Parkway (tel: 6449 9034; fax: 6449 9036; e-mail: wftennis@singnet.com.sg). See also *Squash* above.

Water-skiing & Wakeboarding

Singapore's waters can be quite sludgy but Singapore is one of Asia's top water-skiing and wakeboarding nations. Several centres rent out equipment and also offer professional instruction: *Cowabunga Ski Centre* at Kallang Riverside Park (tel: 6344 8813; fax: 6346 1780; e-mail: cowabunga@pacific.net.sg); *Ponggol Seasports*, Ponggol Marina (tel: 6386 3891; website: www.uncletomshop.com), and *Williams Water Sports Centre*, 35 Ponggol 24th Avenue (tel: 6257 5859; fax: 6386 3495; e-mail: wiliamteo@yahoo.com.sg; website: www.williamwatersports.som.sg).

Shopping

Whether it is because Singapore offers great shopping or because it is continually being talked up, a reputation as a shopper's paradise is firmly entrenched. The Great Singapore Sale from May to early June, with bargains of up to 70% off, is almost a national obsession and attracts shoppers from throughout the region. Orchard Road is the central retail district and is lined on both sides with one shopping mall after another, ranging from *Lucky Plaza* at the lower end of the market to high-end shopping at the *Palais Renaissance*, the *Hilton Shopping Gallery* and *Paragon*. With its towers looming above the rest, *Ngee Ann City* is the largest mall of all, with more than 100 speciality stores in addition to its flagship Japanese superstore, *Takashimaya*. The top floors of the *Heeren Centre* are a collection of market stalls selling fun and novelty items. The same centre is also home to a huge *HMV*, the largest music store in the city. *Centrepoint*, in the middle of Orchard Road, is home to *Robinsons*, Singapore's oldest and award-winning department store. Orchard Road, however, does not have the monopoly on great shopping. More than 120 malls and arcades co-exist on the island.

Bugis Junction, once Singapore's transvestite locale, has had its shop-houses renovated and integrated into a gleaming, air-conditioned complex known as *PARCO* and there is also a street market selling cheaper items and souvenirs. *Raffles City*, at City Hall, is another popular mall, with the exclusive boutiques at Raffles Hotel just across the road. *Chinatown* (Outram) is a colourful web of streets and alleys with a wealth of artefacts, jewellery, clothes, food and medicines for sale behind traditional Chinese shop-house fronts. The newly paved Smith Street and Trengganu Street are good for cheap clothes and souvenirs. Gold, priced according to weight, is heaped up in the stores crowding the *People's Park Complex*, while hawkers offer durian fruit or grilled pork to passers-by. Nearby is *Yue Hwa Chinese Products*, a five-floor department store selling all things Chinese, while *Chinatown Point* contains the Singapore Handicraft Centre. In January 2003, the Majestic Theatre, a disused venue for Cantonese Opera on Eu Tong Sen Street in Chinatown, was turned into a shopping mall but managed to preserve its famous mosaic façade.

While the major department stores and chains operate fixed prices, bargaining is *de rigeur* in other places and it is always worth comparing prices before buying. The Singapore Gold Circle seal at stores is an assurance of quality and reliability and, unlike much in the ethnic quarters, has the official thumbs up. But it is in those areas where the more interesting buys are likely to be had. Arab Street (Bugis) is lined with shops selling high-quality cottons, silks, velvets and batiks. Otherwise, the only alternative flavours are found at *Far East Plaza* in Scotts Road.

Little India, on and around Serangoon Road, is another treasure trove of sumptuous textiles, as well as spices, jewellery, handicrafts and cheap Indian CDs. At the far end of Serangoon Road is the *Mustafa Centre*, a three-storey emporium mainly selling electrical goods at fixed prices. It offers some of the cheapest deals in town, although visitors should check that there is a full warranty. Its popularity means it is usually packed at weekends.

Singaporeans go to *Sim Lim Square* (Bugis) for discount electronic goods; four levels stacked with cameras, computer equipment, pirate CDs, hi-fi and video equipment. Again, visitors should check for a valid warranty. *Funan The IT Mall* (City Hall) is a shopping centre with dozens of computer shops on each floor offering competitive prices. Across the road, the *Adelphi* is the place to spend thousands of dollars on top-of-the-range audio equipment, while nearby *Peninsula Plaza* is a favourite stop for camera gear.

Some of the most exquisite homes of wealthy Singaporeans are adorned with art and antiques from all over Asia – much of which can be purchased in Singapore. The warehouses on Dempsey Road sell Chinese antiques, original and reproduction furniture, while the cool, dimly lit units at *Tanglin Shopping Centre* (Orchard Road) horde some of Asia's finest statues, carpets, textiles and antique furniture. For a taste of contemporary Asian art, *Art2*, at *The Substation*, Armenian Street, sells works by established as well as up-and-coming local artists.

The flea markets around town offer a totally different shopping experience and bargains and novelty items can be found by browsing through a lot of junk. One of the best is at *Clarke Quay*, 3 River Valley Road, every Sunday 1000–1800. The flea market outside *Tanglin Mall*, 163 Tanglin Road, is mainly for fashion and open the first and third Saturday of every month, 1700–2300. *Thieves Market* on and around Sungei Road is open weekends 1100–1800, with a haphazard collection of second-hand novelty items and handicrafts.

Most stores are open daily about 1000–2100/2200, although boutiques close earlier. All prices include a 4% Goods and Services Tax (GST), which is refundable at Changi Airport's Global Refund Centre (website: www.globalrefund.com) on individual purchases over S$300, or on S$300 made up of several items with a minimum value of S$100. Shoppers need to look out for the Tax-Free Shopping logo, complete the Global Refund Shopping cheque and present it with their goods. Money is refunded either through cash, Changi Airport Shopping Vouchers (where 10% will be added) or through direct transfer to a credit card or bankers cheque.

Culture

Culture and religion remain entwined in Singapore, far more than in the West. Throughout the year, a constant stream of festivals and celebrations in the streets and temples reflects the diverse beliefs and backgrounds of this multicultural society, comprising Buddhists, Taoists, Muslims, Hindus, Christians and Sikhs. Many of the major Buddhist, Muslim and Hindu festivals are marked by public holidays and Christmas is just one more holiday – for which shops stay open. The Chinese calendar dominates and the Chinese New Year is the biggest festival of all, where everything shuts for several days.

The city's art scene, while mainly conventional, reflects the flavours of the region: Malay, Chinese and Indian performances, art and music are on offer. Mainstream performing arts are also well represented, culminating in the *Singapore Arts Festival*, held every year in June, which attracts dance, theatre and music groups from all over the world. Andrew Lloyd Webber productions are a favourite. Year-round performances from overseas tend to be heavily oversubscribed and tickets should be booked well in advance. Domestic performers are of a high standard and easier to experience. Free musical and theatrical performances are held regularly in local parks, for example, the *Singapore's Dance Theatre* performs Ballet Under the Stars twice a year at Fort Canning Park.

Singapore is a good place to view and purchase art from all over Asia, as well as works by local artists. The cultural diversity means that works by local artists cover a broad palette of themes and styles. Notable galleries include the *Singapore Art Museum*, Bras Basah Road (tel: 6332 3222; website: www.nhb.gov.sg); *Artfolio*, Raffles Hotel (tel: 6334 4677; website: www.artfolio.com.sg); *Art2* at The Substation, Armenian Street (tel: 6338 8713); and the galleries on the ground floor of the *Ministry of Information, Communication and the Arts*, MITA Building, 140 Hill Street (tel: 6270 7988; fax: 6837 9480; e-mail: mita_pa@mita.gov.sg; website: www.mita.gov.sg). For arts and antiques, there is a hub of shopping outlets at the *Tanglin Shopping Centre*, 19 Tanglin Road.

Local newspapers (the biggest English-language paper is the *Straits Times*) carry lists of events happening each day, as does the online *National Arts and Entertainment Calendar* (website: www.happening.com.sg). Two free publications to look out for are *I-S Magazine* and *BC*. Both have good listings and reviews for exhibitions, dance, art and music. Additional information can be obtained from the *National Arts Council* (tel: 6746 4622; fax: 6837 3010; website: www.nac.gov.sg) or through the *Singapore Tourism Board*. Tickets can be booked through *Sistic* (tel: 6348 5555; website: www.sistic.com.sg) or *Ticketcharge* (tel: 6296 2929; website: www.ticketcharge.com.sg). Other information is available from *Centre for the Arts* (tel: 6874 2492; website: www.nus.edu.sg/csa), an arts agency that supports various arts groups and organises various festivals as well.

Music

The *Singapore Symphony Orchestra* (tel: 6338 1230; website: www.sso.org.sg) gives performances every Friday and Saturday at the *Victoria Concert Hall*, Empress Place (tel: 6338 6125), as well as open-air concerts. The SSO was founded in 1979 and walks a skilful tightrope between Asian and Western music and has a growing, if still fragile, reputation. The *NUS Symphony Orchestra* performs at the *NUS Forum and Theatrette* (website: www.nus.edu.sg/cfa/symphony_orchestra.html), and the *Singapore Lyric Opera*, Waterloo Street (tel: 6336 1929; website: www.singaporeopera.com.sg), usually performs Western classical pieces, occasionally fusion. The *Chinese Classical Music* plays at various different venues and is worth catching, by checking local press for details. *The Esplanade* (see *Theatre* below) also

Singapore Dragon Boat Festival

hosts local and touring orchestras, as well as other types of music performances.

Theatre

Local groups are extremely energetic in producing contemporary theatre with an Asian flavour, reflecting the ethnic diversity of Singapore. The newest and largest venue for performing arts, *The Esplanade – Theatres on the Bay*, 1 Esplanade Drive (tel: 6828 8222; fax: 6337 3633; e-mail: corporate@esplanade.com; website: www. esplanade.com.sg), is setting out to be one of the biggest and best performing arts centres in Asia. Covering an area of six hectares (15 acres) on the waterfront, it includes a concert hall (capacity of 1800), recital studio (250), two theatres (2000 and 220), and an art gallery. Some of the more prolific theatre companies include: *Singapore Repertory Theatre*, Cecil Street (tel: 6221 5585; website: www.srt.com.sg), which showcases at the *DBS Arts Centre*, 6 Shenton Way; and *TheatreWorks* (tel: 6338 4077; website: www.theatreworks.org.sg), based at the *Black Box* in Fort Canning Centre, Cox Terrace Fort, Canning Park. Other theatres include *Kallang Theatre*, Stadium Walk (tel: 6345 8488; fax: 6344 2340; website: www.sistic.com.sg), and *The Substation*, 45 Armenian Street (tel: 6337 7535 *or* 7800; fax: 6337 2729; website: www.substation.org), which shows modern, experimental drama.

Dance

Ecnad Project Ltd (tel: 6226 6772; website: www. ecnad.org), one of the youngest professional performing arts groups, has built a reputation for also being one of the most dynamic and daring. The company is based around the *Telok Ayer Performing Arts Centre* in Cecil Street. The *Singapore Dance Theatre* (tel: 6338 0611; fax: 6338 9748; website: www.singaporedancetheatre.com) performs classical dance and ballet and is based at the Fort Canning Centre, Cox Terrace Fort, Canning Park. One of the city's most popular events is the *Ballet Under the Stars*, held twice a year at Fort Canning Hill.

Film

Cinemas cater mostly to popular taste. Mainstream films are highly popular and often sold out, although there is a backlash from those who deplore the

censorship allowed through the Film Act of 1981, which bans obscene and pornographic films with a much tighter definition of these than in the West. *NETPAC (Network for the Promotion of Asian Cinema)* was set up in 1994 as an attempt to involve film-makers, critics, festival organisers and the like in a drive for greater artistic freedom in Singapore's film industry. There is also an annual *Singapore International Film Festival* in April, which features documentaries and films from around the globe.

Singapore's main cinemas include *Cathay – Orchard*, 8 Grange Road (tel: 6232 5874), and *Cathay Causeway Point*, 1 Woodlands Square (tel: 6767 1588); and *Lido 8 Ciniplex*, Shaw House, *Bugis*, Parco Bugis Junction, *Balastier*, 360 Balastier Road, and *Prince/Jade*, Shaw Tower, 100 Beach Road (all at tel: 6738 0555; website: www.shaw.com.sg). While there are no art cinemas, the *Alliance Française*, Sarkies Road (tel: 6737 8422), screens mainstream and alternative French films every Tuesday.

Cultural Events

Singapore's calendar of annual events is a real mix of ancient and modern, with old, revered ritual pitted against the new and experimental.

In January, Hindus celebrate *Thaipusam*, a time of devotion, penance and thanksgiving; but the sheer volume of dominant Chinese outshines them with their New Year celebrations. The *Lunar New Year* is the highlight of the Chinese calendar and the streets of Chinatown are lit up in January/February with traditional decorations and fairy lights. After dark, Chinatown becomes a heaving spectacle of the Orient, with hawkers and fortune tellers lining the alleyways as vibrantly coloured dragon and lion dancers parade among the crowds and Chinese opera takes to the streets.

The public holiday for *Vesak Day*, in May, honours the birth, enlightenment and death of Sakyamuni Buddha. Hundreds of caged birds are set free to symbolise the release of captive souls. The annual *Singapore Dragon Boat Festival* in June sends fishermen in search of the Chinese poet and patriot, Qu Yuan. In celebration of the anniversary of Singaporean Independence, a new anthem is composed every year and played incessantly in the month running up to the *National Day Celebration* on 9 August. A National Day Parade is held before thousands of spectators.

The month-long *Festival of the Hungry Ghost* (August to September) is one of the biggest Chinese festivals. According to Taoist belief, the gates of hell are thrown open throughout the seventh month of the lunar year when spirits are allowed to wander the earth. To appease these homeless spirits, sumptuous banquets and 'wayangs' (Chinese street operas) are held, candles and joss-sticks are lit in a row in front of Chinese homes and hell currency notes are burnt as offerings. During the *Lantern Festival* in September, the Chinese Garden becomes a fiesta of light and colour as children and adults pour into the park with their paper lanterns. Also known as the Festival of Lights, *Deepavali* is a Hindu celebration held in October/November to mark the victory of light over darkness and of good over evil. Little India, especially the Hindu temples of Sri Veerama Kaliamman, Sri Vadapathira Kaliamman and Sri Srinivasa Perumal, is decorated with fairy lights, garlands and colourful arches.

Muslims gather for festive shopping for *Hari Raya Puasa*, to mark the end of Ramadan (the month of fasting), usually in November.

The younger generation is engaged in an array of performance and theatre arts that continually push the boundaries of this tightly governed island. *Take Art*, from March to April, is a selection of local and international events with theatre, comedy, art auctions and film. *For Art's Sake!*, from September to mid-November, comprises many performing and creative arts festivals. This includes *WOMAD*, which takes over Fort Canning Park for three days in August; *ARTSingapore*, which showcases contemporary art from South-East Asia, and the *Singapore Music Festival*. *The Singapore Film Festival*, usually in April, continues to try and make cultural headway in a heavily censored society, which would rather give its attention to the *Great Singapore Sale*, the annual shopping bonanza, in May/June.

Literary Notes

'When in Singapore, feed at Raffles.' It was a good piece of marketing for the hotel by Rudyard Kipling, who came to Singapore after leaving India in 1889. In fact, Kipling spoke of 'a place called Raffles Hotel, where the food is as excellent as the rooms are bad'.

Raffles has, for more than one hundred years, been fertile writing ground for a number of authors, including Hermann Hesse, Joseph Conrad, Noel Coward, Somerset Maugham and James Michener – and it is in their honour that the *Writer's Bar* was named. More than any other writer, Somerset Maugham sought inspiration on several visits to the island beginning in 1921. His short stories of Singaporean colonial life include 'The Outstation', 'Yellow Streak' and 'The Casuarina Tree' (1926). Society was outraged by his play, *The Letter* (1927), depicting the real-life murder of her lover by a rubber planter's wife.

More recently, Singapore's success story could be said to be the vision of one man, the island state's Senior Minister Lee Kuan Yew, the grandson of a Hakka coolie from China. His memoirs, *The Singapore Story* (1998), have recently been updated in *From Third World to First – The Singapore Story* (2000) and recount the events leading up to Singapore's Independence, from British colonial rule through Japanese occupation, Communist insurrection, riots, independence and the struggles that followed. *Defending the Lion City* (2000) by Tim Huxley is the first-ever major study of the Singapore Armed Forces and analyses its military strategy, outlook and policies.

Prominent contemporary Singaporean novelists include Hwee Hwee Tan, whose *Foreign Bodies: A Novel* (1999) tells the story of an authoritarian state in which three rootless friends become implicated in the shady dealings of an international soccer gambling syndicate. Catherine Lim's *The Bondmaid* (1997), set in the 1950s, paints a picture of a Singapore far removed from the developed, modern, cosmopolitan society of today and far more entwined with its Chinese roots, traditions and beliefs.

Two popular new books are *Got Singapore* (2002) and *Notes From an Even Smaller Island* (2002). *Got Singapore* is a collection of articles and stories by journalist Richard Lim. He depicts his own perception of the changes that accompanied Singapore's Independence and gives a personal and humorous testimony about life from the 1960s to the 1980s. *Notes From an Even Smaller Island* is written by Neil Humphreys, who gives a slightly different angle, dissecting the culture of Singapore from an ex-pat's viewpoint.

SPECIAL EVENTS

Ponggol, Hindu Harvest Festival, mid-Jan, location

Lunar New Year Light-Up, colourful display in Chinatown to celebrate the Lunar New Year, mid-Jan/early Feb, Chinatown and various locations

Chinese New Year, biggest cultural event of the year, late Jan/early Feb, Chinatown and various locations

Hari Raya Haji, celebrating the return of pilgrims from Mecca, late Feb (15 days earlier each year), various locations

Singapore River Raft Race, a race with rafts made from recycled rubbish, Feb, Singapore River

Singapore International Festival for Children, two-week festival of kids' entertainment, Mar, various locations

Birthday of Lao Zi, one-week Taoist festival to worship founder, Mar, throughout the city

Take Art!, local and international events comprising of many other festivals (website: www.takeart.com.sg), Mar–Apr, various locations

Singapore International Comedy Festival, two-week comedy festival, mid–late Mar, venues throughout the city

Singapore Fashion Festival, two-week fashion festival, late Mar–early Apr, various venues throughout the city, especially shopping malls

Singapore Food Festival, four-week festival (website: www.singaporefoodfestival.com.sg), late Mar–Apr, various locations

International Latin Festival, two-day Latin festival with music and stalls, early Apr, Fort Canning

Qing Ming Festival, Chinese community gives thanks to the ancestors with prayers and gifts, early Apr, various locations

Singapore International Film Festival, two-week film festival (website: www.filmfest.org.sg), mid-Apr

Singapore Rugby Sevens (website: www.ssc.gov.sg), late Apr, National Stadium

Labour Day, public holiday, 1 May

Vesak Day, monks commemorate the Lord Buddha's entry into Nirvana by chanting holy sutras and freeing captive birds, mid-May, all Buddhist temples

Singapore Airlines International Cup, world's richest horse race (website: www.siainternationalcup.com), mid-May, Turf Club

Singapore Arts Festival, three-week eclectic festival of dance, music and drama from around the globe (website: www.singaporeartsfest.com), late May–mid-Jun, various locations

Great Singapore Sale, annual two-week shopping bonanza with prices slashed, late May–Jun, Orchard Road and various locations

Singapore Dragon Boat Festival, fishermen go in search of the Chinese poet and patriot, Qu Yuan, mid-Jun, starts Marina Promenade

Yonex-Sunrise Singapore Open, week-long international badminton tournament (website: www.yonexsunrisesingopen.org.sg), mid-Jun, Singapore Indoor Stadium

International Piano Festival (website: www.ssa.org.sg), mid-Jul, Victoria Concert Hall

Festival of the Hungry Ghost, month-long Taoist festival, with street banquets and operas to entertain and appease homeless spirits, late Jul/early Aug–early Sep, various locations

National Day Celebrations, annual parade celebrating the nation's birthday, 9 Aug, National Stadium and various locations

Manchester United FC exhibition match, Aug, National Stadium

WOMAD Singapore (website: www.womadsingapore.com), late Aug–early Sep, Fort Canning Park

Lantern Festival, late Aug–late Sep, Chinese Garden

For Art's Sake!, international performers (website: www.forartssake.com.sg), Sep–mid-Nov, various venues

International Guitar Festival, international guitar maestros, early Sep, various venues

Mid-Autumn Festival, week-long festival featuring feasting on mooncakes to celebrate the year's fullest moon, Sep, Chinatown and various locations

Birthday of the Monkey God, dramatic and loud procession honouring the hirsute deity, late Sep, Temple of the Monkey God, Seng Poh Road

Nine Emperor Gods Festival, images of the nine gods paraded in sedan chairs, mid-Oct, Nine Emperor Gods Temple

Pilgrimage to Kusu Island, annual Taoist pilgrimage to Pekong Temple on Kusu Island, late Sep–early Nov

Deepavali Light-Up, annual celebration features a three-week festival village in Campbell Lane, early Oct/Nov, Little India

Hari Raya Light-Up, lights go on as Muslim families celebrate the end of Ramadan, late Oct–mid-Dec (15 days earlier every year), Geylang Serai

Hari Raya Puasa, end of Ramadan, Oct

Singapore River Buskers Festival, week-long festival with street performers on the riverbank, mid-Nov, Singapore River

Christmas Light-Up, festive lights for Christmas throughout the city, mid-Nov–Dec

Singapore International Marathon (website: www.singaporemarathon.com), early Dec, starts National Stadium

New Year's Eve, countdown party, 31 Dec, Suntec City

STOCKHOLM

Spread across 24,000 islets and laced with numerous waterways on the southeastern coast of Sweden, Stockholm enjoys one of the most stunning locales of any capital city in the world. Over 30% of the city area is made up of waterways and another 30% is made up of parks and green spaces, giving Stockholm perhaps the freshest air and widest lungs of any European capital. This natural oasis is complemented by the stunning Old Town, which was perfectly preserved by Sweden's neutrality in World War II. This Old Town (or *Gamla Stan*) is the epicentre of the city, with countless hotels, bars, restaurants and shops all prospering – as people in these historical streets have done for centuries.

Away from the charms of the Old Town, the modern city showcases the innovative design standards for which Sweden has become globally renowned. Much of Stockholm's present-day wealth comes from the new light industries, such as information technology and computing, with world-leading companies often occupying prime real estate in the city centre or filling up the new business parks on the city fringes. All this is a far cry from the city's humble beginnings, which stretch back to the 13th century and Birger Jarl – generally accepted as the founder of the city, although various settlements previously existed on the site. The city grew up around the Old Town, as Stockholm emerged as a key trading centre, with influence all over the Baltic Sea region and further afield. Today, Stockholm is a thriving modern European city that dispels all of the anachronistic images about dull Scandinavians.

During the seemingly endless days and bright sunshine of the summer months, the city's chic boutiques and stylish pavement cafés overflow with the 'beautiful people', who enjoy the hedonistic culture and lifestyle that has earned the Swedish capital rave reviews from Europe's style magazines. Stockholm's ethnic make-up is, perhaps surprisingly, very eclectic, with over 15% first generation immigrants and over 100 languages spoken in the city. This increasing diversity has infused the city with a renewed vigour and energy, as the various incoming cultures interact with the indigenous Swedes.

A quintessential summer night is spent bathed in warm sunshine, sitting at a restaurant by the water's edge, savouring fresh seafood plucked straight from the waters around Stockholm, before taking advantage of the midnight light and heading out for a night around the Stureplan, in some of Europe's trendiest bars. When the long winter does come, it is not all Nordic gloom – the locals head for the sanctuary of the cosy pubs that line the city. Stockholm has almost as many restaurants per capita as Paris does, as well as 150 or so museums and galleries, so there is always plenty to do when the winter chill sets in. Then there are the severe winters when many of the waterways around the city freeze up, allowing the unique experience of ice skating around one of the world's most stunning capital cities.

Stockholm city centre

TRAVEL

Getting There By Air

Stockholm-Arlanda (STO)

Tel: (08) 797 6000 *or* 6100. Fax: (08) 797 2096.
Website: www.lfv.se

The city's impressive and modern airport is situated 45km (28 miles) north of Stockholm. Europe's sixth largest airport, Stockholm-Arlanda is a major aviation hub for the Baltic and Scandinavian regions. The airport is used by 57 international airlines and processes approximately 18 million passengers each year.

Major airlines: Sweden's airline is *SAS Scandinavian Airlines System – SK* (tel: (08) 797 0000; website: www.scandinavian.net), an international consortium set up with Denmark and Norway in 1946, which took over Linjeflyg to become the major domestic carrier as well. Other carriers serving the airport include *Air Canada, Air France, American Airlines, Austrian Airlines, British Airways, Finnair, KLM* and *Lufthansa*.

Airport facilities: Services include duty-free shops, banks, bureaux de change, ATMs, restaurants and bars. There is a *Radisson SAS SkyCity* hotel (tel: (08) 5067 4000) at the airport and its health club can be booked for single use for SKr80. *Avis, Europcar* and *Hertz* provide car hire.

Business facilities: Stockholm-Arlanda airport offers business facilities at the *Prime Point* centre (tel: (08) 797 6200; fax: (08) 5936 0920; e-mail: meetings@ primepoint.com; website: www. primepoint.com), located in SkyCity (between terminals four and five). The centre offers a number of conference rooms accommodating from two to 700 delegates, offices and an exhibition hall for up to 1000 delegates. Opening times are Monday to Thursday 0730–2100, Friday 0730–1800 and weekends on request. There are also lounges with business facilities located in terminals two, four and five.

Transport to the city: *Arlanda Express* trains (tel: (08) 5888 9000; website: www.arlandaexpress.com) to Stockholm Central run every 15 minutes daily 0535–2335 (journey time – 23 minutes). The cost is SKr180 or SKr200 for two adults at the weekend. *SL* (tel: (08) 600 1000; website: www.sl.se) or *Flygbussarna* (tel: (08) 600 1000; fax: (08) 686 3797; website: www.flygbussarna.com) bus services run every ten minutes daily 0640–2305 to Stockholm (journey time – 40 minutes) and cost SKr80. Taxis to the city centre should operate at a fixed rate of SKr435, which ought to be posted in the window.

Stockholm Bromma Airport (BMA)

Tel: (08) 797 6874. Fax: (08) 981 010.
Website: www.lfv.se

Located eight kilometres (five miles) west of Stockholm, Bromma Airport is an important hub for domestic flights to 19 airports. The airport processed almost one million passengers in 2000.

Major airlines: *British Airways* (tel: (020) 781 144; website: www.britishairways.com) operates flights from Denmark to Bromma Airport. Domestic carriers include *European Executive Express, Golden Air, International Business Air, Malmö Aviation* and *Skyways*.

Airport facilities: Services at Bromma Airport include a restaurant and shops. There is a *Flyghotellet* located nearby. Car hire is available from *Avis, Europcar* and *Hertz*.

Business facilities: Three conference rooms, accommodating between four and 75 delegates, are available for hire from the *Swedish Civil Aviation Administration* (tel: (08) 797 6874).

Transport to the city: *SL* (tel: (08) 600 1000; website: www.sl.se) or *Flygbussarna* (tel: (08) 600 1000; fax: (08) 686 3797; website: www. flygbussarna.com) airport buses to Stockholm offer connections to the city centre (journey time – 20 minutes). The fare is SKr60 one way or SKr100 return. Buses operate approximately every half hour Monday to Friday 0715–2152, Saturday 0920–1530 and Sunday 1255–1955. A cheaper but more time-consuming option is one of the local SL buses, 110 and 152, which operate approximately 0600–2300 on weekdays and 1000–1730 on Saturday, connecting with the metro for travel into the city centre (journey time – approximately 40 minutes). The journey costs SKr16. *Bromma Taxis/Flygtaxi* (tel: (08) 797 8190) *or* (20) 979 797) operates a taxi service to the city centre, costing approximately SKr170.

Stockholm Skavsta Airport (NYO)

Tel: (015) 528 0400. Fax: (015) 528 0449.
Website: www.skavsta-air.se

Situated 100km (62 miles) south of Stockholm, Skavsta Airport is the terminus for the *Ryanair* international service from London Stansted and has plans for rapid expansion over the next few years. It is also a major cargo airport.

Major airlines: *Ryanair* (tel: (0900) 202 0240; website: www.ryanair.com) is the only passenger airline operating to and from Skavsta, flying from London, Paris, Hamburg, Frankfurt, Oslo, Glasgow and Aarhus.

Airport facilities: These include a FOREX office, hotel booking service, baby changing facilities, duty-free shop, restaurant, bar and coffee shop. Car hire is available from *Avis, Europcar, Hertz* and *National*.

Business facilities: No business facilities or executive lounges are currently available.

Transport to the city: *Flygbussarna* (tel: (08) 600 1000; fax: (08) 686 3797; website: www. flygbussarna.com) buses to Stockholm run four or five times a day, between 1045 and 2150, connecting with all Ryanair flights. These cost SKr130 one way or SKr190 return (journey time – 1 hour 20 minutes). *Skavsta Taxis* (tel: (08) 5503 0000) offers a service to Stockholm (journey time – 1 hour) at a cost of approximately SKr1195, which travellers should book in advance.

Stockholm Vasteras Airport (VST)

Tel: (021) 805 600 *or* 610 (information). Fax: (021) 801 120.
Website: www.vasteras.se/flyg

Situated five kilometres (three miles) from the town of Vasteras, the airport is approximately a one-hour journey from Stockholm. The airport is set to expand; it currently serves routes to Copenhagen, London, Malmö and Oslo.

Major airlines: *Ryanair* (tel: (0900) 200 4040; website: www.ryanair.com) flies from London Stansted to Vasteras. Other airlines operating from Vasteras Airport are *Direkt Flyg, European Executive Express* and *Skyways*.

Airport facilities: Facilities include a café/bar, a shop and car hire from *Avis, Europcar, Hertz* and *Mabi*.

Business facilities: There are currently no business facilities or VIP lounges at the airport.

Transport to the city: *Flygbussarna* (tel: (08) 600 1000; fax: (08) 686 3797; website: www. flygbussarna.com) runs a bus service to Stockholm city centre, meeting all Ryanair flights (journey time – approximately 1 hour 15 minutes). Tickets cost Skr100 for a single and SKr150 return. Taxis are available, costing approximately SKr1490–1600 for a trip into Stockholm (journey time – approximately 1 hour 15 minutes).

Approximate flight times to Stockholm: From London is 2 hours 30 minutes; from New York is 7 hours 45 minutes; from Los Angeles is 14 hours 10 minutes; from Toronto is 12 hours 10 minutes and from Sydney is 24 hours 10 minutes.

Arrival/departure tax: None.

Getting There By Water

Throughout its history, Stockholm has always been a major port. Easy access to the sea, the Stockholm Archipelago and inland waterways, such as the Göta Canal between Stockholm and Gothenburg, make the city an ideal destination for boat travellers. The port authority *Ports of Stockholm Group* (tel: (08) 670 2600; e-mail: info@stoports.com; website: www. portsofstockholm.com), has approximately 150–160 moorings per year and comprises the ports in *Stockholm, Nynäshamn* and *Kapellskär*. Its quays can accommodate ships of up to 245m (800ft) and ferries can tie up within sight of the Old Town. In Stockholm, ferries dock at *Frihamnen*, *Stadsgarden* and *Vartahamnen*, depending on the size of the vessel. The port has immigration facilities for ferry passengers and there are Stockholm Information Service booths offering information, hotel booking and car hire.

Ferry services: There are frequent ferry services to other Baltic ports. *Silja Line* (tel: (08) 222 140; website: www.silja.com) departs from Vartahamnen for Helsinki, Tallinn, Rostock and Turka. *Viking Line* (tel: (08) 452 4000; website: www.vikingline.fi) travels to Helsinki and Turku from Stadsgarden. *Tallink* (tel: (08) 667 0001 *or* 666 6001; website: www.tallink.se) runs a Tallinn–Stockholm service and *Polferries* (tel: (08) 5201 8101; website: www.polferries.com) runs a Gdansk–Nynäshamn service. *DFDS Seaways* (tel: (08705) 333 000 (UK) *or* (0316) 50650 (within Sweden); website: www.dfdsseaways.co.uk) operates a car ferry service from Newcastle to Gothenburg (journey time – 25 hours 30 minutes), sailing from Newcastle on Monday and Friday.

Transport to the city: The city centre is within easy walking distance from the Stockholm port. Taxis are readily available. Nynäshamn, situated 60km (37 miles) south of Stockholm, is linked to the city by the 73 road, as well as by rail, while the E18 road links the city with Kapellskär, 90km (56 miles) north of Stockholm.

CITY STATISTICS

Location: Sodermanland province, southeastern coast of Sweden.
Country dialling code: 46.
Population: 750,348 (city); 1,823,210 (metropolitan area).
Ethnic mix: Predominantly native Swedish, largest minority Finnish, with notable Iraqi, Iranian, Turkish and Somali communities.
Religion: Predominantly Lutheran (Church of Sweden).
Time zone: GMT + 1 (GMT + 2 from last Sunday in March to Saturday before last Sunday in October).
Electricity: 220 volts AC, 50Hz; round two-pin plugs are standard.
Average January temp: From 2°C to –7°C (36°F–19°F).
Average July temp: From 20°C to 25°C (68°F to 77°F).
Annual rainfall: 900mm (35.5 inches).

Getting There By Rail

Swedish State Railways – SJ (tel: (0771) 757 575; e-mail: info@swedenbooking.com; website: www. resor.sj.se) is the efficient and well-organised national rail carrier for the country. *Stockholm Central* station (tel: (08) 762 2000) is located on Vasagatan. As well as left-luggage and other standard facilities, the station also contains Stockholm Central Post Office with all its facilities, a FOREX bureau de change and a Stockholm Information Service booth.

Rail services: Stockholm has international rail links to Copenhagen (journey time – 5 hours) and the rest of Europe, via the X2000 system. Since the opening of the Oresund Link in 2001, the X2000 connects Stockholm with other major European cities without the need for a ferry connection. Trains run to Oslo in Norway twice daily (journey time – approximately 6 hours). The X2000 trains also travel to Gothenburg (journey time – 3 hours).

Transport to the city: Stockholm Central is at the centre of the city's metro network.

Getting There By Road

Sweden uses the standard European road designation system with 'E' indicating European routes. Traffic

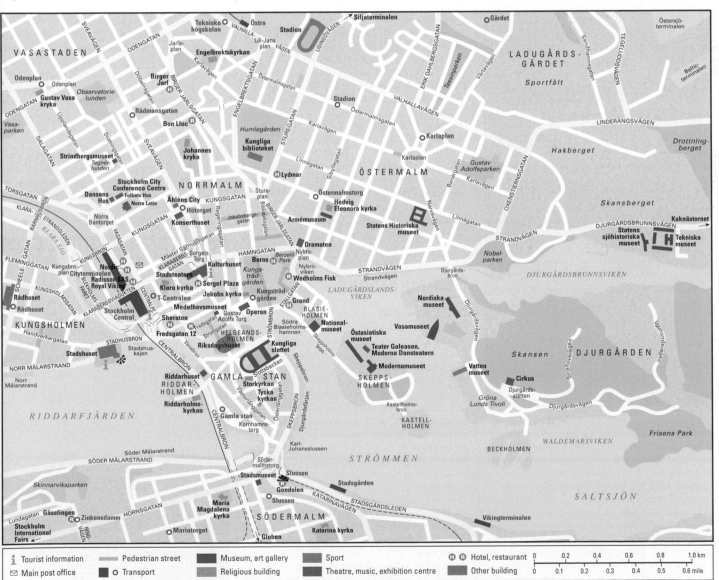

Symbol	Legend	Symbol	Legend	Symbol	Legend
i	Tourist information		Pedestrian street		Museum, art gallery		Sport	H R	Hotel, restaurant
	Main post office		Transport		Religious building		Theatre, music, exhibition centre		Other building

0   0.2   0.4   0.6   0.8   1.0 km
0   0.1   0.2   0.3   0.4   0.5   0.6 mile

BUSINESS PROFILE

Quite simply, Stockholm is the financial, business and economic hub of Sweden, with most major business transactions and major Swedish companies – such as *Electrolux, Ericsson, Ikea, Saab* and *Volvo* – all based in the capital. Further afield, Stockholm is also a major regional player, principally in the merging Baltic markets and within the EU. Although Sweden has opted to stay out of the EMU (European Monetary Union) and thus not adopt the Euro as its currency, the city's major trading partners are all European. The offices around Sergelstog and Hamngatan manage one of the most powerful economies in Europe.

Both Stockholm and the larger Swedish economy have adapted to the decline in its traditional engineering base by diversifying into telecommunications and other ideas- and design-based industries, especially mobile communications and information technology. In 2000, an IDC survey put Sweden ahead of the USA as the world's leading IT nation. However, 2001 was a less positive year for the economy than expected, with GDP growth of only 1.5 % compared to 3.6% in 2000. The country is heavily dependent on exports and the rapid downturn in the IT and telecom sectors affected the economy, particularly in the Stockholm region. Among the countries of the *Organisation for Economic Co-operation and Development* (OECD), Sweden devotes the highest percentage of its GDP to research and development.

Standing at 2.4%, unemployment in the city is considerably lower than the national average of 3.8%. The main employers in the city are Stockholm's municipal authorities and county council, with 67,600 employees, followed by *Ericsson* with 12,375, the post office (*Posten*) with 10,575 and *AstroZeneca* with 8275.

Roughly 75% of the Swedish information and electronics industry is located in the Greater Stockholm area. Global companies with a presence in Stockholm include *KPMG* and *Sheraton*. Stockholm's place in the top ten of international congress and conference venues further reinforces its position in the global trade circuit. Translation services are available from *Activator RW-Consult AB*, Storhagsv 23 (tel (08) 749 0925; website: www.activator.se).

The *Stockholm Chamber of Commerce*, Vastra Tradgardsgatan (tel: (08) 5551 0000; fax (08) 5663 1600; website: www.chamber.se), can provide information on many aspects of doing business in the city.

drives on the right and drivers give way to the right. National speed limits are 110kph (68mph), 90kph (56mph) or 70kph (43mph), depending on the road and traffic density. Speed limits inside built-up areas – virtually all of Stockholm – are 50kph (31mph) or 30kph (19mph) in school areas. The minimum driving age is 18 years for car drivers and 17 years for motorcyclists. The maximum legal alcohol to blood ratio for driving is 0.02% and heavy fines or prison sentences may be imposed on those driving while intoxicated. The use of dipped headlights is compulsory in the daytime for cars and motorcycles,

as are crash helmets for motorcyclists. All car passengers must use seatbelts and children under seven may not travel without specially adapted restraints. Drivers must also carry an emergency warning triangle. Studded tyres are prohibited, except from 1 November to the first Monday after the Easter holiday.

A national driving licence and vehicle registration documents must be carried at all times. The Swedish authorities do not require drivers to carry a Green Card but its use is advisable, as it tops up the level of cover provided to that of the driver's domestic policy. Automatic petrol pumps at service stations accept SKr100, SKr50 and SKr20 notes.

Motormannens Riksforbund, the Swedish automobile association, can provide further information (tel: (08) 690 3800; website: www.motormannen.se), although *Assistancekåren* (tel: (08) 404 1455; website: www.assistancekaren.se) operates the breakdown service for motorists in Sweden.

Emergency breakdown service: *Assistancekåren* (020) 912 912.

Routes to the city: Stockholm is integrated within the European motorway network, however, Oslo is the only other European capital within a convenient distance for direct overland access. The European motorway E18 leads to Oslo, while motorways E20 and E6 lead to Oslo via Gothenburg. European motorway E4 heads south to Malmö for ferry connections to Copenhagen and to Uppsala in the north.

Approximate driving times to Stockholm: From Uppsala – 1 hour; Gothenburg – 5 hours 50 minutes; Malmö – 7 hours 40 minutes.

Coach services: The *Cityterminalen* (City Terminal), Klarabergsviadukten 72 (tel: (08) 762 5997), situated next to Stockholm Central, is the terminus for international coach connections. Facilities include refreshments, left-luggage and a FOREX office. *Eurolines* (tel: (08) 440 8570; website: www. eurolines .se) provides coach links to major European cities, including Amsterdam, Berlin, Copenhagen, Paris and Rome. *Busstop* (tel: (08) 440 8570) provides international bookings and information on domestic services. Coaches from the City Terminal serve most destinations in Sweden, although services to the far north are limited. *Swebus AB* (tel: (08) 762 3500; website: www.swebus.se) runs services out of the capital.

Getting Around

Public Transport

Storstockholms Lokaltrafik – SL (tel: (08) 600 1000; website: www.sl.se) runs Stockholm's well-integrated transport network incorporating **metros**, commuter **trains**, **buses** and **trams**.

The **metro** (*tunnelbana*) is the core of the system; stations are marked with a blue 'T' on a white background and the service runs daily 0500–0100 (later at the weekend). The metro is integrated with the commuter **train** service, although these services are less frequent.

Bus services operate daily approximately 0600–2400 for normal buses, with night buses handling limited routes after that.

There are not many **trams** left in the city, although visitors might find the vintage *Djurgårdslinjen* (tram 7) useful, as it passes many city sights. However, this costs more than other services, at SKr20 per ticket (passes are not valid).

Single tickets, valid on all services, cost SKr16 and are available for purchase on-board buses or at metro

stations. *Rabattkuponger* (discount coupons) are available from newspaper stands; a carnet of 20 coupons costs SKr110.

The *SL Tourist Card* gives free travel on public transport inside the Greater Stockholm area. The **pass** costs SKr80 for 24 hours and SKr150 for 72 hours (concessions available). The *Stockholm Card* (*Stockholmskortet*) gives free public transport along with other benefits. This costs SKr220, SKr380 and SKr540 for 24, 48 and 72 hours respectively (concessions available). See *Passes* in *Tourist Information* for more details of both of these.

Taxis

Taxis can be hailed on the street or ordered by telephone from *Taxi Stockholm* (tel: (08) 150 000 *or* 728 2700; website: www.taxistockholm.se) or *Taxi Kurir* (tel: (08) 300 000 *or* 744 9400; website: www.taxikurir.se). Taxis can also be ordered online with payment by major credit cards.

Taxis normally charge a basic fee of SKr28–36 and a journey of ten kilometres (six miles) will cost approximately SKr100 on weekdays, with higher rates for evenings and weekends. Tips are usually included in the fare.

Limousines

Limousineservice (tel: (08) 222 280) provides chauffeured limousines for SKr780–850 per hour, with a reduced price if the car is hired for more than one day. The higher rate is applicable after 1900 on weekdays, before 0600 weekdays and all weekend. *Prestige Limousine* (tel: (08) 193 300; website: www.prestigelimousine.se) provides limousines and people carriers from SKr700 per hour, while *Bel Air Limousines* (tel: (08) 308 500; website: www.bel-airlimo.se) offers stretch limousines from SKr980 per hour.

Driving in the City

Scattered over 14 islands and governed by strict speed limits, Stockholm is not an ideal city for drivers. The city's planners have imposed numerous restrictions on drivers and petrol prices are among Europe's highest. Visitors might be better advised to use its excellent

BUSINESS ETIQUETTE

Swedes pride themselves on their co-operative, egalitarian spirit in the workplace. In theory at least, issues of status and hierarchy are far less important than in many other countries. Most people use their first names in the workplace and elaborate deference is definitely out of fashion, management style is consensual rather than authoritarian. Since Stockholm is the capital, the city sees itself as setting the tone and pace for the rest of the country. Nevertheless, however relaxed Swedes are about power and authority, they are strict timekeepers and punctuality is expected for both work and play. Standard working hours are Monday to Friday 0900–1800 but flexible hours are common practice. Swedes also tend to stick to the point – personal chat is generally left until the real business is done and dusted. Smart dress is still the norm, although more casual attire is being adopted in the new industries, such as IT and Internet businesses. Most business socialising is done away from the home, at bars and restaurants. Dinners tend to be quite boozy affairs, although lunches will be less so.

Gamla Stan

Photo: Corel

public transport system instead. Principal car parks are the *Galleriangaraget*, at the Gallerian complex, Hamngatan 37, or at *Phus Pub*, Slöjdgatan 3. *Carpark* (website: www.carpark.se) provides a website, complete with maps, which costs focuses on parking in Stockholm. Parking costs on average Kr50 per hour (less at night).

Car Hire

The minimum age for car hire is 18 years, with the proviso that drivers must have held a driving licence for at least one year. Some larger cars are restricted to those over 24 years. A national driving licence, passport and credit card are required for hiring a car in Stockholm. Fire and third party liability is mandatory in Sweden and is included in all car hire deals.

Cars are available from *Avis* (tel: (08) 202 060; website: www.avis.com) and *Hertz* (tel: (08) 240 720; website: www.hertz.com), both of which are located near the Stockholm Central station. Typical rates for car hire are around SKr700 per day for an average saloon.

Bicycle & Scooter Hire

Cykel and Mopeduthyrningen, Strandvägen 24 (tel: (08) 660 7959), and *Cykelstallet*, St Eriksgatan 34 (tel: (08) 650 0804), both provide bicycle and scooter hire. A typical rate for hire of a bicycle is SKr150 per day.

SIGHTSEEING

Sightseeing Overview

Stockholm is an easy city for tourists to navigate, as its centre is largely flat and strolling around is a pleasure. For journeys further afield, there is an excellent public transport system with trams, underground trains, buses and ferries servicing all areas of the city and the surrounding towns and villages.

A good place for one to get acquainted with the city is from the *Gondola Restaurant*, in the Södermalm district, where, over a full gourmet meal or just a drink, visitors can get a good idea of the layout of the city through the venue's panoramic windows. The focus of Stockholm sightseeing is the *Gamla Stan* (or Old Town), which boasts many historical buildings, tourist shops and cafés, as well as the impressive *Royal Palace* – the largest royal palace still in use in the world. North of the Old Town is the main part of the more modern city, whose districts are home to numerous attractions, such as the impressive *City Hall*, the *Museum of National Antiquities* and the *Stringberg Museum*. Across the water, via ferry, is *Djurgarden* – a playground with a funfair park, *Stockholm Zoo* and Sweden's most visited museum, the *Vasa Museum*, which is home to a 17th-century galleon that has been impressively raised from Stockholm's harbour. Many museums are closed on Mondays.

The city has recently gained a reputation for stylish shops, bars and restaurants, making it the Scandinavian capital of cool. Beyond the centre of city, over 10,000 islands and rocky islets in the *Stockholm Archipelago* wait to be explored.

Key Attractions

Vasamuseet (Vasa Museum)

Sweden's most visited museum enshrines the warship, *Vasa*, sunk inside Stockholm harbour while on her

maiden voyage in 1628. The ship was built to the order of the great Vasa king, Gustavus Adolphus, and was the most powerful war galleon of her age. She was raised whole from the harbour bed in 1961, over 330 years after she had last seen the light of day. Carefully preserved, the ship now rests intact in the museum's main hall. Displays recreate life on-board the ship and a film shows how the salvage operation was carried out. The museum's beautiful waterfront site on the island of Djurgården is an added attraction. There are regular guided tours in English.
Galarvarvsvagen 14
Tel: (08) 5195 4800. Fax: (08) 5195 4888.
E-mail: vasamuseet@sshm.se
Website: www.vasamuseet.se
Transport: Bus 47 or 69.
Opening hours: Daily 0930–1900 (10 Jun–20 Aug); Thurs–Tues 1000–1700, Wed 1000–2000 (21 Aug–9 Jun).
Admission: SKr70 (concessions available).

Stadshuset (City Hall)

Voted by the Swedes as the country's finest building, Stockholm's *City Hall* was begun in 1911, to an Art Nouveau design by Ragnar Östberg. Its interior has grand civic apartments, including the *Golden Hall*, with its glass and gold mosaics, while its tower gives a sweeping panorama of Stockholm. The building's *Blue Hall* – which is actually red – is the venue for the annual Nobel Prize banquet. Visitors must join one of the scheduled tours to see the interior, although access to the tower is unrestricted during opening hours.
Hantverkargatan 1
Tel: (08) 5082 9058. Fax: (08) 5082 9059.
Website: www2.stockholm.se/stadshuset
Transport: Five-minute walk from Stockholm Central station; bus 48 or 62.
Opening hours: Tours of the interior: daily 1000, 1100, 1200 and 1400 (Jun–Aug); daily 1000 and 1200 (Sep–May). Tower: daily 1000–1630 (May–Sep).
Admission: SKr50 (interior); SKr15 (tower); concessions available.

Kungliga Slottet (Royal Palace)

Situated in the heart of Stockholm, on the central island of Riddarholmen, the *Royal Palace* is the official residence of the monarchs of Sweden and the chief venue for official state events. With 608 rooms, it is among the largest surviving palaces in Europe. The present glorious Baroque edifice is the work of Nicodemus Tessin the Younger, from a 1692 design, however, parts of the older medieval Castle of Three Crowns still survive. Attractions include the

Banqueting Apartments, the *Apartments of the Orders of Chivalry*, the *Hall of State*, the *Royal Treasury*, Gustav III's *Museum of Antiquities* and the *Royal Chapel*. In addition, the changing of the guard at the palace is as much of a spectacle in Stockholm as it is in London.
Slottsbacken
Tel: (08) 402 6130. Fax: (08) 402 6167.
E-mail info.stockholms-slott@royalcourt.se
Website: www.royalcourt.se
Transport: Metro Gamla Stan; bus 43, 46, 55, 59 or 76.
Opening hours: Tues–Sun 1200–1500 (Feb–mid-May

Photo: Corel

Vasa Museum

and Sep–Dec);Tues–Sun 1000–1600 (mid May–Aug). Admission: SKr110 (combined ticket for all parts of the palace); SKr70 (each separate ticket for selected parts of the palace); concessions available.

Statens Historiska Museet (Museum of National Antiquities)

Sweden's national historical museum, which traces the nation's history from prehistoric times to the present day, is now graced by a spectacular *Gold Room*, housing the gold of the Viking chiefs. These hoards, recovered from tombs or hiding places, show Scandinavian Viking culture at its most prosperous and magnificent. There is also one of the finest European collections of medieval painted wooden religious sculpture on display.
Narvargen 13–17
Tel: (08) 5195 5600. Fax: (08) 5195 5603.
E-mail: info@historiska.se
Website: www.historiska.se
Transport: Metro Karlaplan; bus 44, 47, 56, 69 or 76.
Opening hours: Tues–Sun 1100–1700 (summer); Tues, Wed and Fri–Sun 1100–1700, Thurs 1100–2000 (winter).
Admission: SKr60 (concessions available).

Strindbergsmuseet (Strindberg Museum)

This museum is dedicated to Stockholm's most famous cultural figure. The *Blå Tornet* (Blue Tower) was August Strindberg's last home from 1908 until his death in 1912. His apartment and library have been preserved in their original state. An exhibition showcases his last works, written on the premises. The museum, which also hosts temporary exhibitions and plays, is furnished in a strikingly sparse Nordic Art Nouveau style.
Drottninggatan 85
Tel: (08) 411 5354. Fax: (08) 411 0141.
E-mail: info@strindbergsmuseet.se
Website: www.strindbergsmuseet.se
Transport: Metro Radmansgatan.
Opening hours:Tues–Sun 1200–1600 (summer); Tues 1200–1900,Wed–Sun 1200–1600 (winter).
Admission: SKr40 (concessions available).

Further Distractions

Skansen

This open-air museum and zoological park on Djurgården was founded in 1891 to preserve Sweden's rural culture and is the first such collection to be built. It contains some 160 historic wooden farms and houses from across Sweden. The farms have their own animals – traditional breeds tended by 'farmers' in period costumes – and the zoo and aquarium hold both animals native to the region and more exotic species. The children's circus, zoo and playgrounds make Skansen particularly attractive to families.
Djurgården
Tel: (08) 442 8000. Fax: (08) 442 8280.
E-mail: info@skansen.se
Website: www.skansen.se
Transport: Bus 44 or 47.
Opening hours: Daily 1000–1600 (Oct–Apr); daily 1000–2000 (May); daily 1000–2200 (Jun–Aug); daily 1000–1700 (Sep).
Admission: Mon–Fri SKr30, Sat and Sun SKr50 (Jan–Apr and Sep-Dec.); daily SKr70 (May–Aug), after 1700 SKr30 (May).

Globen (Stockholm Globe)

A vast sporting and events arena, the *Stockholm Globe* is the world's largest spherical building at 85m (279ft) high and 110m (361ft) wide. As well as hosting major sporting contests, it also houses restaurants, bars and a shopping complex. A source of rich controversy when it was first built in the 1980s, the Globe regained its notoriety in the early 1990s, following a spectacular bankruptcy.
Globentorget 2
Tel: (08) 725 1000 *or* (0771) 310 000 (tickets). Fax: (08) 725 1240.
E-mail: info@globearenas.se
Website: www.globen.se
Transport: Metro Globen; bus 4, 150, 164, 803 or 807 to Gullmarsplan.
Opening hours: Daily 0900–1600 (for guided tours).
Admission: SKr50 (tours); concessions available.

Stockholm Metro

Known as the 'world's longest art exhibition', Stockholm's metro is famous for the quality of its subway art. From the mid-1950s, it was official policy to decorate the network with specially commissioned art. *Kungsträdgården* and *Stockholm Central* metro stations are particularly ornate.
Kungsträdgården
Kungsträdgården
Tel: (08) 600 1000.
Website: www.sl.se
Transport: Blue metro line.
Opening hours: Daily 24 hours.
Admission: SKr10 (single metro ticket).
Stockholm Central

Vasagatan
Tel: (08) 600 1000.
Website: www.sl.se
Transport: All metro lines.
Opening hours: Daily 0500–2400.
Admission: SKr10 (single metro ticket).

Tours of the City

Walking Tours

Walking tours are offered by *City Sightseeing* (tel: (08) 5871 4030; website: www.citysightseeing.com). The 'Old Town Walkabout' – a guided stroll through the medieval core of the city – costs SKr90 for 90 minutes, departing from Gustav Adolfs Torg twice a day at 0930 and 1430 (28 June to 31 August).

Bus Tours

City Sightseeing (tel: (08) 5871 4030; website: www.citysightseeing.com) offers a variety of bus tours departing from in front of the Royal Opera House. The 'Stockholm in a Nutshell' tour – combining a 90-minute bus tour around the city centre and a one-hour boat cruise to Djurgarden – is one of the most popular at SKr280.

Boat Tours

A waterborne tour is essential for visitors to Stockholm. The *Stockholm Card* gives free boat tours on certain services during the summer. *Strömma Canal Company* (tel: (08) 5871 4000; website: www. strommakanalbolaget.com) and *Stockholm Sightseeing* (tel: (08) 5871 4020; website: www.stockholmsightseeing.com) both run various boat tours of the city, with departure points from quays near the Royal Dramatic Theatre, the Grand Hôtel and City Hall. Boat tours of the major waterside sights take approximately two hours and cost SKr160. A tour around Djurgården lasts approximately one hour and costs SKr100.

Excursions

For a Half Day

Drottningholms Slott: Just 15km (nine miles) west of central Stockholm, *Drottningholms Slott* (Drottningholm Palace), Flottsforvaltining (tel: (08) 402 6280; website: www.royalcourt.se), is one of the most magnificent legacies of Sweden's imperial age, justly compared to Louis XIV's Versailles in France. Begun by the great Swedish Baroque architects, Nicodemus Tessin the Elder and Younger, in 1662, for the dowager queen Hedvig Eleonora, Drottningholm is a UNESCO World Heritage Site. It is surrounded by equally splendid gardens containing the delightful *Rococo Chinese Pavilion* (tel: (08) 402 6270), almost a palace in itself. It also has the world's best-preserved palace theatre, with its 18th-century stage machinery still in working order – a popular venue for summer concerts and performances. Closed to the public in winter, the palace is the official residence of King Carl Gustaf XVI and the Swedish royal family. Guided tours in English are available on request. Admission to the palace costs SKr50 plus SKr50 to the Chinese Pavilion (concessions available). Drottningholm Palace is open daily 1000–1630 (May to August), daily 1200–1530 (September) and Saturday and Sunday only 1200–1530 (October to April). It can be reached by bus 301 or 323 from Brommaplan metro station or bus 177 or 178 to Drottningholm. There is a regular summer boat service from Stadshuskajen (City Hall Quay) to Drottningholm, operated by *Stockholm Sightseeing*, Skeppsbron 22 (tel: (08) 5871 4020; website: www.stockholmsightseeing.com).

For a Whole Day

Thousand Isles: The classic excursion from Stockholm is a water tour of the entire surrounding archipelago. The 24,000 islands and islets of the Stockholm Archipelago are famed for their beauty and unique atmosphere, especially in summer. The standard package stops at four of the most appealing islands, allowing the option of an overnight stay on one of them. During summer, *Stromma Kanalbolaget* (tel: (08) 5871 4000; fax: (08) 5871 4044; website: www.stromma.se), operates excursions departing from Stockholm Nybroplan and costing SKr875, including lunch, coffee and guided tours.

ACCOMMODATION

Sales tax at 12% is automatically added to the bill. Tipping of porters is common, although tipping for room service is not expected.
The prices quoted below are the lowest standard rates for a double room, including sales tax but excluding breakfast, unless otherwise specified.

Business

Nordic Hotel

Since it opened in 2001, the *Nordic Hotel* has proved a big hit with the Stockholm business community. Within easy walking distance of the evolving IT centre of the city, as well as Stockholm Central station and the new Arlanda Express airport rail link, the location is one of the most convenient in the city. This stylishly designed hotel boasts 542 rooms, as well as a business centre and conference facilities catering for up to 400 delegates. Another plus is Internet access through the in-room TVs. The hotel is split between the Nordic Sea and the Nordic Light buildings, with 367 and 175 rooms respectively, each with their own distinctive decor, including light installations that depict the sun.

Vasaplan
Tel: (08) 5056 3000. Fax: (08) 5056 3060.
E-mail: info@nordichotels.se
Website: www.nordichotels.se
Price: From SKr1300 (including breakfast).

Radisson SAS Royal Viking Hotel

This 351-room hotel is one the best of the numerous Radisson-affiliated hotels in and around Stockholm. The central location, within easy walking distance of the Old Town and the City Hall, is a major advantage. All of the luxuriously appointed rooms have modem points and voice-mail, while 'business class' rooms have extras such as ironing boards, bathrobes and slippers. Non-smoking rooms are available, as are specially equipped rooms to cater for the needs of physically impaired guests. The hotel also boasts 26 conference rooms, as well as a lecture hall that seats 150 people.
Vasagatan 1
Tel: (08) 5065 4000. Fax: (08) 5065 4001.
E-mail: sales.royal.stockholm@radissonsas.com
Website: www.radissonsas.com
Price: From SKr2000.

Scandic Hotel Sergel Plaza

This 405-room five-star hotel in the centre of Stockholm has won the 'Best Hotel in Sweden' award on a number of occasions since opening in 1984. One of the seven floors of the business-orientated *Scandic* is solely occupied by 12 executive suites; the standard rooms are fairly simple. Facilities include 24-hour room service, a swimming pool and a full range of business services. There are conference facilities to cater for 400 delegates.
Brunkebergstorg 9
Tel: (08) 5172 6300. Fax: (08) 5172 6311.
E-mail sergel.plaza@scandic-hotels.com
Website: www.scandic-hotels.com
Price: From SKR2280.

Sheraton Stockholm Hotel and Towers

This 462-room first-class hotel has recently undergone a much-needed revamp, which has restored it to its former high standards. The *Sheraton* offers views over the Old Town, Lake of Malaren and the City Hall; it is just a two-minute walk from Stockholm Central station and airport buses. Room

features include work desk, hairdryer, in-room movies, mini-bar, modem point, cable TV and voice-mail. Business facilities include 12 meeting rooms with a maximum capacity of 400 delegates, as well as a business centre.
Tegelbacken 6
Tel: (08) 412 3400. Fax: (08) 412 3409.
E-mail: sheraton-stockholm@sheraton.com
Website: www.sheratonstockholm.com
Price: From SKr1380.

Luxury

Berns Hotel

Berns is one of the most exclusive places to stay in Stockholm. The 65 rooms (including four suites) marry modern Scandinavian design with the beauty of the building's Belle Epoque architecture. There are fluffy white bathrobes, CD players, satellite TV and hairdryers in all rooms. Eight conference and meeting rooms are available with flexibility in numbers and facilities; the 1200-capacity *China Room* is particularly impressive. There is also a business centre with fax and Internet facilities. The hotel's restaurants and bars have recently undergone a Terence Conran-aided makeover. The *Clock Suite* is legendary and a favourite of younger, trendier celebrity visitors – the older crowd tend to head for the Grând Hotel (see below). Although there are no fitness facilities available on site, guests at Berns can use the extensive facilities at the nearby Grând Hotel, which is owned by the same company.
Berzelii Park, Nackstromsgatan 8
Tel: (08) 5663 2200 *or* 2250 (reservations). Fax: (08) 679 3561.
E-mail: hotel.berns@berns.se *or* info@berns.se
Website: www.berns.se
Price: From SKr2750 (including breakfast).

Grând Hotel

The 310-room *Grând Hotel* has long been the most glamorous place to stay in the city and it seldom disappoints. This deluxe hotel has justifiably been rated as one of the world's great hotels since it opened in 1874 and it is now a member of the *Leading Hotels of the World* group. The Grând Hotel also enjoys an excellent location on the waterfront, with views back across the Old Town, within easy reach of Stockholm's business centre. The 21 luxurious suites are popular with visiting celebrities and royalty – famous past guests include Theodore Roosevelt and Douglas Fairbanks. All rooms have modem points and there are also 19 conference and banqueting rooms, which can cater for anything from two to 2000 delegates. Extensive fitness facilities and beauty treatments were added in 1997.
Sodra Blaisholmshamnen 8
Tel: (08) 679 3500. Fax: (08) 611 8666.
E-mail: hotel.grand@grandhotel.se *or* info@grandhotel.se
Website: www.grandhotel.se
Price: From SKr3400.

Moderate

Central Hotel

This three-star hotel is, as its name suggests, located very conveniently in the heart of modern Stockholm. Although the decor is plain and functional with few luxurious touches, the 93 en-suite guest rooms all have Internet connections through the in-room satellite TVs. There is a conference room available, seating up to 16 delegates.

Grând Hotel

Photo: Corel

Royal Mounted Guard

Vasagatan 38
Tel: (08) 5662 0800. Fax: (08) 247 573.
E-mail: info@profilhotels.se
Website: www.centralhotel.se
Price: From SKr1850.

Scandic Hotel Malmen

This four-star hotel offers good value without sacrificing the level of facilities. The en-suite rooms are modern and comfortable, with extras – such as satellite TV in all rooms, soundproof windows and trouser presses – all geared towards the needs of business visitors. There are, however, no conference rooms.
Gotgatan 49–51
Tel: (08) 5173 4700. Fax: (08) 5173 4711.
E-mail: malmen@scandic-hotels.com
Website: www.scandic-hotels.com
Price: From SKr1240 (including breakfast).

Other Recommendations

Birger Jarl

The revamped *Birger Jarl* hotel has already attracted a steady stream of savvy visitors. This trendy 235-room hotel is the perfect example of the best of modern Scandinavian design without the harshness of too much minimalism. The hotel somewhat uniquely aims to change its mood with the season by changing its decor. Individual designers have also been brought in to create idiosyncratic rooms that can be surveyed on the web before booking. Other plus points include a number of meeting rooms – one with a capacity of up to 150 delegates – and a rooftop gym with views of the city.
Tulegatan 8
Tel: (08) 674 1800. Fax: (08) 673 7366.
E-mail: info@birgerjarl.se
Website: www.birgerjarl.se
Price: From SKr1860 (including breakfast).

Icehotel

Surely one of the most unusual hotels in the world, the *Icehotel* is built every year on the banks of the Torne River, approximately one hour from Stockholm by aeroplane. It might be far from the city centre but the hotel is quite unique. Made, as its name suggests, from ice, the Icehotel has 65 rooms, including 20 suites, all sculpted by different artists. The thick ice provides insulation against the cold – rather like an enormous igloo – and each bedroom has a temperature of around -5⁰C (21⁰F). Guests sleep in thermal sleeping bags on a blanket of reindeer pelts. There are also 30 hotel bungalows with skylights for viewing the northern lights, as well as three conference rooms with a maximum capacity of 120 people.
Jukkasjarvi village
Tel: (980) 66800. Fax: (980) 66890.
E-mail: info@icehotel.com
Website: www.icehotel.com
Price: From SKr2490 (including breakfast).

Lydmar Hotel

The *Lydmar Hotel* is fast becoming the trendiest place to stay in a city whose range of hip hotels is expanding all the time. The hotel's public spaces are often home to temporary art installations and many cultural events are also staged here. Isaac Hayes and Beverly Knight are among the big names to have performed in the hotel's lobby in recent years. All rooms have wide-screen TVs, DVD and voice-mail connections; another six rooms have recently been added. A nice touch is the movies that are provided free of charge. The location is right at the heart of Stockholm's busy nightlife scene and the Lydmar Hotel is a good choice for a business trip that can be extended for a few days of holiday.
Sturegatan 10
Tel: (08) 5661 1300. Fax: (08) 5661 1301.
E-mail: info@lydmar.se
Website: www.lydmar.se
Price: From SKr2300 (including breakfast).

RESTAURANTS

The selected restaurants have been divided into five categories: Gastronomic, Business, Trendy, Budget and Personal Recommendations. The restaurants are listed alphabetically within these different categories, which serve as guidelines rather than absolute definitions of the establishments.

Sales tax of 12% is included in restaurant prices. Some restaurants also add a 10–15% service charge to the bill. If no service charge appears on the bill, a 10% tip is normal and expected. As all wines are imported to Sweden, they are subject to steep price hikes and added tax and therefore tend to be expensive.

The prices quoted below are for an average three-course meal for one person and for a bottle of house wine or cheapest equivalent; they include sales tax but do not include service charge.

Gastronomic

Berns

Recently given a makeover by British style guru Sir Terence Conran, this restaurant in the Berns Hotel (see *Hotels*) has a born-again quality. On a busy night, *Berns* can squeeze in around 250 diners, who come to enjoy the top-rate cooking and the added attraction of the new crustacean bar, which is a must for seafood lovers. There is a wide variety of fresh shellfish served with various sauces and cooked according to the diner's personal preference. Other Berns specialities are the excellent lobster and the dessert option of delicious armagnac ice cream. The restaurant was once a grand theatre hall and the impressive decor, with gilded ceilings and huge chandeliers, creates a remarkable setting for dinner.
Berns Hotels, Berzelii Park, Nackstromsgaten 8
Tel: (08) 5663 2222. Fax: (08) 5663 2323.
E-mail: info@berns.se
Website: www.berns.se
Price: SKr395 (fixed price). Wine: SKr260.

Bon Lloc

Another fine dining temple that proves how much the Swedes love top-quality cooking, *Bon Lloc* has a relaxed atmosphere and food with a Spanish influence. In the dining room, the straight-back, upholstered chairs are teal and wine coloured, with crisp white tablecloths for silver service. With arguably the finest chef in all of Sweden at the helm, Bon Lloc cannot really go wrong. Mathias Dahlgren's 'nouveau Euro-Latino' cooking well deserves its one Michelin star and booking well ahead is essential. One of the best dishes is oven-roasted ham with apple cider glaze, while the willingness to experiment is evident in main courses such as roasted pig's foot. The recent move to a larger, more central location has done nothing to dent the supremacy of Bon Lloc (meaning 'good luck' in Catalan).
Regeringsgatan 111
Tel: (08) 660 6060. Fax: (08) 107 635.
Website: www.bonlloc.nu
Price: SKr650. Wine: SKr250.

Gasslingen

This restaurant serves the finest of French haute cuisine in stylish, although slightly quirky, surroundings – rather like an Alsace cottage, with pictures of geese on the walls. For those who like classical French style and cuisine, this is the place to go. It is a temple to gastronomy, with such delights as foie gras, duck, lobster and truffles.
Brannkyrkagatan 93
Tel: (08) 669 5495. Fax: (08) 848 990.
E-mail: gasslingen@telia.com
Website: www.gasslingen.se
Price: SKr595. Wine: SKr365.

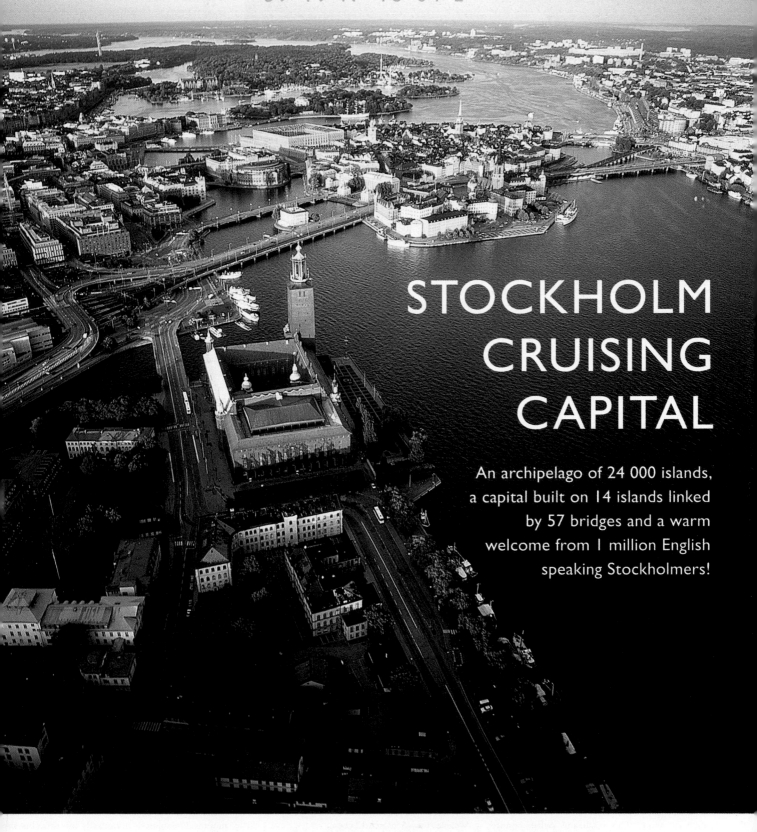

www.stockholmcruise.com
59°19′N 18°04′E

STOCKHOLM CRUISING CAPITAL

An archipelago of 24 000 islands, a capital built on 14 islands linked by 57 bridges and a warm welcome from 1 million English speaking Stockholmers!

Floating restaurant docked near the Old Town

PA & Co

This used to be one of the undoubted stars of the Stockholm restaurant scene but its most fashionable times are now behind it. Once responsible in many ways for helping to kick-start the city's culinary renaissance, *PA & Co* is nevertheless still going strong, despite its detractors. This longevity is largely due to the excellent value of the food on offer. The decor is simple and understated, while the Swedish produce is still as fresh as ever, with well-cooked red meat dishes, including excellent reindeer.
Riddargatan 8
Tel: (08) 611 0845.
Price: SKr300. Wine: SKr230.

Wedholms Fisk

A city that is surrounded by rivers, lakes and the sea, it is no surprise that seafood is very popular in Stockholm. The accolade of best fish restaurant in the city is much fought over, although many locals and discerning visitors agree that the honour goes to *Wedholms Fisk*, whose freshly prepared seafood has earned the restaurant a Michelin star. The creamy sauces that cover the freshly caught sole, turbot and salmon are legendary on the Stockholm culinary scene. The classical cooking style varies between Swedish and classical French, while the decor tends toward the pale and purely stylish. Closed Sunday.
Nybrokajen 17
Tel: (08) 611 7874. Fax: (08) 678 6011.
Price: SKr550. Wine: SKr280.

Business

Bakfickan

Bakfickan is a firm favourite with local businesspeople and is a trusted venue for a business lunch or dinner. This small and stylish counter restaurant is the least formal of the venues located at the State Opera House, serving up a fresh selection of traditional Swedish dishes, including open *smorrebrod* sandwiches. Diners can choose to eat either at the long counter bar or at the small, narrow tables. Closed Sunday.
Operahuset, Karl XII Torg
Tel: (08) 676 5809. Fax: (08) 209 592.
E-mail: info@operakallaren.se
Website: www.operakallaren.se
Price: SKr350. Wine: SKr221.

Franska Matsalen

For unabashed glamour and Old World style, *Franska Matsalen* at the Grând Hotel is hard to beat. A restaurant first opened in these plush surrounds in 1899; today, the setting is still popular among the local business community as a classy place for winning over clients and introducing people to the city for the first time. Fresh fish and red meat feature strongly on the menu and main courses include seared turbot with chanterelles and white wine sauce or peppered glazed reindeer with Jerusalem artichoke and Swiss chard. Savvy diners book a window seat with views across to the Royal Palace.
Grând Hotel, S. Blasieholmskajen 8
Tel: (08) 679 3584. Fax: (08) 611 8686.
Website: www.franskamatsalen.nu
Price: SKr700. Wine: SKr330.

Fredsgatan 12

The classical surroundings of this first-rate restaurant are renowned as a great setting for a business lunch or dinner, with top-quality cuisine to match. The interior is unfussy and cool, reflecting the simple Swedish fusion food on the menu. The cooking has earned *Fredsgatan 12* a Michelin star and the verandah outside is the business place to be seen on a summer day. All courses are starter sized and the restaurant recommends five dishes be chosen. Samples dishes include shellfish tempura, fillet of beef carpaccio, and venison sautéed with pak choi. Diners can also try the delicious yellow cloudberries, when in season.
Fredsgatan 12
Tel: (08) 248 052. Fax: (08) 237 605.
E-mail: info@fredsgatan12.com
Website: www.fredsgatan12.com
Price: SKr650 (five dishes). Wine: SKr280.

Mårten Trotzig

At the most expensive end of the business market, this restaurant hits the mark for those trying to impress clients. During summer, diners can enjoy the sun in the courtyard, but things move inside during winter to the cosy interior rooms, heated by a roaring fire. Specialities include deer and hare, while the homemade ginger beer is legendary. For those on a budget, there is also a cheaper menu that explores a similar mix of Swedish and international dishes. Closed Sunday.
Västerlånggatan 79
Tel: (08) 442 2530. Fax: (08) 204 420.
Website: www.martentrotzig.se
Price: SKr550. Wine: SKr300.

Stadhuskallaren

This is where they cook the dinners for the Nobel Prize ceremonies and it is also a good place for rewarding business contacts and cementing new relationships. Guests can dine in style on white linen tablecloths in the City Hall, under the beauty of the paintings on the ceiling that date back to its opening in 1923. The restaurant is particularly renowned for the quality of its omelettes, which come with a variety of fillings.
City Hall, Hantverkargatan 1
Tel: (08) 650 5454. Fax: (08) 650 5776.
E-mail: stadshuskallaren@profilrestauranger.se
Website: www.profilrestauranger.se
Price: SKr400. Wine: SKr300.

Trendy

Buddah Bar

Buddah Bar is a confirmed favourite on the Stockholm restaurant circuit. The decor tends towards the minimalist but any harshness is taken away by the presence of candles on the tables. This buzzy place might not offer the best value in the city but its menu covers many cuisines and most people come mainly for the atmosphere. Swedish highlights include generous *smorrebrod* and crisp salads, making this a popular venue for a business lunch or a light meal before heading out for a night on the town. During summer, there are tables outside, which make a great place to sit and people-watch.
Biblioteksgatan 9
Tel: (08) 611 8030. Fax: (08) 643 8728.
Price: SKr400. Wine: SKr200.

Folkhemmet

Folkhemmet is an excellent example of the new trend for relaxed restaurants that serve up the best of fresh Swedish produce. A lively crowd occupies the candlelit tables in the main restaurant, which features an open-plan kitchen where the chefs can be seen at work. When the weather allows, there are also tables outside. Menu highlights include starters such as beetroot with goat's cheese and honey or asparagus with hollandaise sauce, and mains such as vegetarian cannelloni. The wine list is good value for Stockholm.
Renstiernas Gata 30
Tel: (08) 640 5595. Fax: (08) 643 8728.
Price: SKr200. Wine: SKr200.

Halv Trappa Plus Gard

This trendy newcomer serves up inspired cooking in highly designed surroundings that recall the glories of the 1970s. Diners can choose between the quirky interior and the tables outside during the warmer months. The menu is not exactly inventive but the fish and meat dishes – such as grilled saddle of lamb or pot au feu – come served with an emphasis and style that reflects the fashionable surroundings.
Lästmakargatan 3
Tel: (08) 611 0277 *or* 665 9422.
Price: SKr350. Wine: SKr250.

Ristorante Paganini

This is a popular Italian restaurant on one of the most bustling streets of the Old Town. Inside, it is cosy and stylish, with large mirrors, plain walls and starched white tablecloths. The menu is a mix of Italian and Swedish dishes with T-bone steaks and pasta courses, such as tortelloni with gorgonzola or with beef.

Västerlånggatan 75
Tel: (08) 406 0607. Fax: (08) 244 121.
Website: www.paganini.lunchinfo.com
Price: SKr300. Wine: SKr198.

Rolfs Kök

One of the trendiest places to eat in Stockholm, *Rolfs Kök* is where the local cognoscenti head. The sparse interior veers towards minimalism and the food tends towards the style (and often small portions) of nouvelle cuisine. The menu is a collage of Swedish and international influences, which are given innovative reinventions in the Rolfs Kök style. Examples of main dishes are confit of tuna with artichokes, bacon and basil, and leg of rabbit with lentils, dried cherries and vanilla.

Tegnergatan 41
Tel: (08) 101 696.
Website: www.rolfskok.se
Price: SKr400. Wine: SKr205.

Budget

Indian Curry House

Laying claim to being the cheapest Indian restaurant in town, this fun place serves up tasty Indian staples – such as samosas and curries – in a typically rich Indian interior. During the summer months, the *Indian Curry House* also has a few tables available outside.

Scheelegatan 6
Tel: (08) 650 2024/5. Fax: (08) 650 2024.
Price: SKr120. Wine: SKr110.

Kungshallen

Located right in the heart of central Stockholm, *Kungshallen* food hall is a great place for the hungry to fill up with cheap goodies, whether diners choose to sit down or take meals away. It offers has a range of international foodstuffs, from Tex-Mex and Indian to Greek and sushi, as well as a range of more esoteric Swedish specialities. There are over a dozen different eateries to choose from here.

Kungsgatan 44
Tel: (08) 218 005.
Website: www.kungshallen.com
Price: SKr160. Unlicensed.

Maharaja

Stockholm has a number of Asian restaurants, however, *Maharaja* is notable, as it offers great value and serves good interpretations of all the usual Indian dishes. The decor incorprates the elaborate embellishment that is synonymous with Indian restaurants. The vegetarian curry and the fresh nan breads are the highlights of the menu. They also prepare a range of very good vegetarian dishes.

Stora Nygatan 20
Tel: (08) 210 404.
Price: SKr175. Wine: SKr160.

Manna Gourmet

This relaxed restaurant offers excellent vegan food in no-nonsense surroundings – the interior is somewhat Spartan, down-to-earth and almost clinical. Dishes are

Södermalm area

healthy and filling and many think it is the best vegetarian restaurant in the city. Menu items include veggie dishes with pasta, potatoes or unpolished rice. Guests can make up their own mix of the main courses on offer or have some hot soup on a cold day. Closes at 2100.

Asogatan 102, Soderhallarna
Tel: (08) 640 5969.
Price: SKr60. Wine: SKr160.

Tranan

This is the type of simple place popular with Swedes who want to dine out without breaking the bank. Not only do few tourists ever make it here but the menu is written in Swedish only, so adventurous visitors will have to trust the friendly staff and other diners to fill them in on translations of the traditional Swedish dishes. One excellent example of the food on offer here is the fillet of beef served with fried potatoes, horseradish and egg yolk. *Tranan* also serves several vegetarian dishes, such as goat's cheese on toast. The decor is that of a typical French bistro, giving it a wonderfully relaxed atmosphere.

Karlbergsvagen 14
Tel: (08) 5272 8100.
E-mail: tranan@tranan.se
Price: SKr360 (fixed price). Wine: SKr230.

Personal Recommendations

Gondolen

Gondolen easily offers the best view of any restaurant in Stockholm. Decor is functional and simple but this purpose-built viewing capsule lends diners panoramic vistas of the Stockholm skyline. The menu mixes French and Swedish cuisine and changes regularly, although dishes usually sound better than they actually taste. Nevertheless, any first-time visit to Stockholm would not be complete

without a pre-dinner cocktail and a meal at Gondolen. Menu highlights include gravadlax (marinated salmon) with asparagus or the roasted reindeer fillet served in cranberry sauce.

Stadsgarden 6
Tel: (08) 641 7090. Fax: (08) 641 1140.
E-mail: info@eriks.se
Website: www.eriks.se
Price: SKr450. Wine: SKr235.

J Restaurang

This restaurant is a boat ride outside the city centre. Its aquatic locale, on a marina in Stockholm's Newport district, complements the cooking, which focuses on seafood. Head chef Mark Phonix is at the helm and works culinary wonders with the day's catch, which often includes turbot and salmon. The menu also includes a range of salads and, in the colder months, hearty soups. The sunny terrace is a heavenly place to be on a hot summer day, although the restaurant is also enjoyable for cosy autumnal dinners.

Augustendalsvagen 52, Newport
Tel: (08) 601 3025. Fax: (08) 601 3029.
E-mail: info@restaurantj.com *or* nackastrand@restaurantj.com
Website: www.restaurantj.com
Price: SKr400. Wine: SKr250.

Nordic Hotel Restaurant

For those either arriving at or leaving from the main international airport, Stockholm - Arlanda, the bright and breezy restaurant at the *Nordic Hotel* is only a two-minute walk from the airport's Arlanda Express train terminal. The restaurant is the perfect alternative to the ramble of fast food joints in Stockholm Central station. Lunches are light and good value, while the evening meals are more interesting, with seafood taking centre stage. One innovative idea for lunch is the 'Swedish platter', a one-dish meal that features Swedish sausages, gravadlax and fish roe.

Skansen open-air museum

Vastaplan 4–11
Tel: (08) 5056 3000. Fax: (08) 5056 3060.
E-mail: info@nordichotels.se
Website: www.nordichotels.se
Price: SKr400. Wine: SKr220.

Sahara

This big outdoor space on the water is the place to be when the sun shines in Stockholm. Once a seafood restaurant, the owners have now introduced a Lebanese menu featuring dishes such as houmous, tabbouleh (salad with tomato, mint, parsley and bulgur wheat), grilled lamb and desserts such as baklava. The modern surroundings and high-quality food are perfect during summer, when the whole evening is bathed in light at this latitude. The bright and friendly staff is another bonus. Closed Sunday.
Norr Malarstrand 75
Tel: (08) 652 4090. Fax: (08) 652 4097.
E-mail: info@restaurangocean.com
Website: www.saharagroup.nu
Price: SKr265 (fixed price). Wine: SKr245.

Salzer Restaurant & Bar

This restaurant is unique in Stockholm for its 1950s interior, which has made it an instant favourite with the city's stylish set. It might remind some diners too much of *Happy Days* but the food is fresh, modern and international. The large portions of the Swedish mainstays keep the locals coming back for more, with dishes such as *Åseda isterband* (a type of smoked sausage) with potatoes in white sauce.
John Ericssons Gate 6
Tel: (08) 650 3028. Fax: (08) 651 3028.
E-mail: info@saltzer.nu
Website: www.salzer.nu
Price: SKr350. Wine: SKr250.

ENTERTAINMENT

Nightlife

The late evening summer sun in Stockholm seems to stretch on forever, while the long winter nights need to be filled with fun. The result is a city committed to its nightlife. Strong jazz traditions and smart bars cater to older or smoother patrons, while the club scene – often Spanish in flavour – parties hard. The area around Stureplan is the most happening place in the city. Admission to clubs can cost anything between SKr5 and SKr100, while a litre of beer will cost SKr70–100 and a shot of vodka around SKr70. The minimum age for buying alcohol is 20 years – 18 years in restaurants or nightclubs. The sale of alcohol is restricted to 1200–2400 (from 1300 on Sunday), although nightclubs or the occasional favoured bar, such as *Kvarnen*, in Södermalm, sell drinks later into the night. Standard hours for bars and clubs are roughly 0900–0200, with restaurant bars opening earlier and some clubs closing later (at around 0500). *What's On* (website: www.whatsonwhen.com) magazine is available locally and provides excellent information on Stockholm's nightlife events.

Bars

Halv Trappa Plus Gård, Lästmakargatan 3, is a ferociously trendy bar-restaurant and a great retreat for local celebrities. Another hot spot is *Spy Bar*, Birger Jarlsgatan 20. *Wih*, Ynglingagatan 26, offers good eating and drinking, while *Gondolen*, Stadsgården 6, serves drinks to match its unbeatable view. The *Sturehof Bar*, Stureplan 2, and its upstairs cousin, *O-bar*, are benchmarks in the style-conscious rebranding of the old Sturehof Restaurant. The Grånd Hotel's *Cadier Bar*, Södra Blasieholmshamnen 8, is the place to enjoy

a classy cocktail, while the *Opera Bar*, Karl X Torg, offers quiet surroundings for a relaxing drink. Conversely, *Kvarnen*, Tjärhovsgatan 4, is a beer hall with a typically rootsy Södermalm charm, open until 0300 and hugely popular. *Tennstopet Bar*, Odengatan 50, is over 100 years old and another solidly traditional drinking hole.

Casinos

The *Radisson SAS Royal Viking Hotel*, Vasagatan 1, and the *Sheraton Stockholm Hotel*, Tegelbacken 6, both operate casinos, as does the *Café Opera*, Kungsträdgården, and *Tre*, Vasagatan 17, near Stockholm Central station. Dress code is smart and only those over 18 years are admitted; passports are required at all venues. All the casinos in Stockholm are similar in games, with blackjack, French roulette and high jack.

Clubs

Some of Stockholm's liveliest clubbing goes on under the palm trees at *Blue Moon*, Kungsgatan 18, which incorporates the *Ice Bar*, as cool as its name suggests, and the *Havana Bar*, dispensing Cuban cigars along with the drinks. Equally Latin in flavour but more upmarket, *Sophie's Bar*, Biblioteksgatan 5, plays host to the rich and funky. *Monkey Bar*, St Eriksgatan 46, is a staple venue with space for chilling out, which has a young crowd. Their parents head for *Penny Lane*, Birger Jarlsgatan 29. *Café Opera*, Kungsträdgården, draws an eclectic crowd of all ages and tastes to its fabulous interior, plying mainstream partygoers with cutting-edge sounds. *Fasching*, Kungsgatan 63, has jazz, soul and Latin American sounds at the weekend. *Tre Remmare*, Vasagatan 17, feeds, waters and entertains night owls long after the other venues close and boasts the *Sinatra bar*, offering cocktails in a mini-shrine to crooner Frank.

Live Music

The hotel bar at the *Lydmar Hotel*, Sturegatan 10, regularly holds unadvertised soul and jazz gigs. Right in the Old Town, *Kristina*, Västerlånggatan 68, offers good food as well as nightly live music. *Stockholms Stadion*, Lidingövägen, is the venue for large-scale stadium rock. Hardcore goths and punks are among those heading for the bashes at *Kafé 44*, Tjärhovsgatan 44.

Sport

The famously healthy Swedes love sport of all kinds. Stockholm's unique location makes it a focus for climbing, sailing, rowing, kayaking and even fishing.
Many of Sweden's main sporting events are held outside the capital. However, events that are held within the city include the annual *Stockholm Marathon*, in June, the world's largest women-only cycling contest, *Tjejtrampet*, in May, and *Tjej-Milen*, an annual running race for women, in August. The *Sandhamn Open*, an annual sailing contest held at the island of Sandhamn in the Stockholm Archipelago, takes place in June. The *Sandhamn Regatta* sets off in July, while *Sailboat Day* is held in September. The *Stockholm Open* tennis tournament takes place in late October.
Like many European countries, the Swedes love football. *AIK Stockholm* (website: www.aik.se) is in the first division and continues to be a good soccer team, emerging over the last few years from the shadow of *IFK Gothenburg* and *FC Malmo* elsewhere in Sweden. The team has its own stadium, *Råsunda Fotbollstadion*, Solnavägen 51, Solna (tel: (08) 735 0935).

Visitors who wish to purchase tickets to sporting events should refer to the AIK Stockholm website (see above), which provides information and tickets for other football and ice hockey games.

Fitness Centres

Urban fitness fanatics can benefit from fitness centres like *Metropolis Gym*, Birger Jarlsgatan 36 (tel: (08) 611 3505; website: www.metropolisgym.nu), or one of the *SATS Sportsclub* (website: www.satssportsclub.com) locations at Sveavägen 20 (tel: (08) 5452 1380), Birger Jarlsgatan 6C (tel: (08) 5450 1460), or Regeringsgatan 47 (tel: (08) 791 2230). Both centres offer a guest pass for SKr200.

Golf

The *Rosenkälla Golfklubb*, Rosenkälla, in Åkersberga (tel: (08) 5102 6260; website: www.golf.se), has a good 18-hole course, with access to guests paying the green fee of SKr180 during the week and SKr220 at weekends. The 18-hole *Drottningholm Golfklubb*, Drottningholm (tel: (08) 759 0085; website: www.drgk.nu), has a lovely setting close to the palace of the same name. Non-members are welcome Monday to Friday 0800–1700 and weekends after 1300, for a green fee of SKr450 for 18 holes. Men must have a handicap of 28 and women 30.

Sailing

The *Royal Swedish Yacht Club* (tel: (08) 717 0856; website: www.ksss.se) can provide information on the waters in and around Stockholm.

Swimming

Visitors not wishing to jump into one of Stockholm's central canals for a bracing dip can go to *Eriksdalsbadet*, Hammarby Slussväg 20 (tel: (08) 5084 0250; website: www.eriksdalsbadet.com), or *Centralbadet*, Drottninggatan 88 (tel: (08) 5452 1300; website: www.centralbadet.com). Bathing in Lake Mälaren or the Baltic is surprisingly popular, given the latitude.

Tennis

Tennisstadion, Fiskartorpsvägen 20 (tel: (08) 215 454; website: www.tennisstadion.se), is a fine old hall in the upmarket Östermalm, where Olof Palme used to play. An hour of play costs SKr180–215. The club, *TSK Malmen*, Siskargortsv 20 (tel: (08) 613 3085; website: www.fly.to/tskmalmen), leases some of its courts and is quiet and cheap at SKr125–160 per hour (concessions available).

Shopping

For decades, the profits of Sweden's post-war prosperity have poured into the boutiques and stores of Stockholm. The result is a shopper's paradise. The area around Biblioteksgatan has most major European fashion designers, while antique shops can be found around Odengatan.

Open all day on Nybrogatan 31, *Östermalmshallen* is arguably northern Europe's loveliest covered food market, although locals will more often be thronging the grocery at *Åhléns City*, Klarabergsgatan 50, Stockholm's last big department store, or malls like *Pk-Huset*, Hamngatan 10. *NK* (Nordiska Kompaniet), Hamngatan 18–20, has over 100 departments, selling everything from crafts to health food. *Gallerian*, Hamngatan 37, claims to be Stockholm's largest shopping complex.

The pick of Swedish glass is on hand at *Nordiska Kristall*, Kungsgatan 9, over 80 years old, or the arts and crafts emporium, *Konsthantverkarna*, at Mäster

NK department store

Samuelsgatan 2. *Agata*, Nytorgsgatan 36, sells stylish modern ceramics, glass and textiles, *Norrgavel*, Birger Jarlsgatan 27, has cool home furnishings, while at *Kallika*, Osterlanggatan 18, traditional wooden furniture and toys are on sale. *Nordiska Galleriet*, Nybrogatan 11, excels in furniture design and *Designtorget*, Götgaten 21, in eclectic curiosities.

Standard Swedish shopping hours are Monday to Friday 0900–1600 and Saturday 0900–1400. In Stockholm, however, many stores are open for longer, as well as late on Sunday. Visitors leaving the country may reclaim the standard VAT rate of 25% within 30 days of purchase – only available at shops displaying the 'tax free shopping' sign. The receipt and unopened goods must be presented at the airport for a refund. *Global Refund* (tel: (04) 104 8450; fax: (04) 104 8469; e-mail: taxfree@se.globalrefund.com; website: www.globalrefund.com) can provide further information.

Culture

Stockholm's cultural history extends back to its Viking beginnings. The city was also the birthplace of Alfred Nobel, whose will instated the famous five prizes for peace, physics, chemistry, medicine and literature – economics was added by the Bank of Sweden in 1968 – and Stockholm's literary set have since brought cultural glory to the city, by winning the Nobel Prize for literature (see *Literary Notes* below).

Stockholm was awarded the title of European Capital of Culture in 1998, an indication of how vibrant and eclectic the city's cultural scene is. The avant-garde architecture of *Modern Museum*, on Skeppsholmen, designed by Rafael Moneo, is a controversial memento to the year, as the style is not to all tastes.

Tickets to cultural events can be booked via the central ticketing agency, *Biljett Direkt* (tel: (0771) 707 070; website: www.ticnet.se). Online information (website: www.musikfestivaler.se) is available for Swedish music festivals. *What's On* magazine (website: www.whatsonwhen.com) is available locally and provides cultural events information.

Music

The blue stuccoed *Konserthuset*, Hötorget (tel: (08) 5066 7788; website: www.konserthuset.se), houses the world-class *Swedish Royal Philharmonic Orchestra*, with guest conductors such as Andrew Davis and Paavo Järvi. The *Royal Palace Music Festival* (tel: (08) 102 247; website: www.royalfestivals.se) and *Stockholm Sinfonietta Riddarhus Festival* annually bring packed concert programmes to splendid venues in the Old Town, while the lovely antique *Drottningholm Court Theatre*, Drottningholms Slott, Flottsforvaltining (tel: (08) 5569 3100; website: www.drottningholmsslottsteater.dtm.se), hosts summer opera and ballet seasons.

Theatre

The *Dramaten*, Nybroplan (tel: (08) 667 0680; website: www.dramaten.se), is Sweden's highly respected national theatre. The *Orionteatern*, Katarina Bangata 77 (tel: (08) 643 8880), is also part of the established scene. The *Stadsteatern*, in the Kulturhuset, Sergels Torg (tel: (08) 5062 0200; website: www.stadsteatern.stockholm.se), has more radical productions and is far cheaper, while *Teater Galeasen*, Slupskjulsvägen, Skeppsholmen (tel: (08) 611 0030; website: www.galeasen.se), is at the cutting edge of contemporary theatre. Stockholm is home to *The English Theatre Company* (tel: (08) 662 4133; fax: (08)

660 1159; e-mail: etc.ltd@telia.com; website: www.englishtheatre.se), based at the *Regina Theatre*, Nybrogatan 35 (tel: (08) 411 6320 *or* (0771) 707 070).

Dance

The *Dansens Hus*, Barnhusgatan 12–14 (tel: (08) 796 4910; website: www.dansenshus.se), was set up in the 1990s, as Sweden's foremost dance venue. Birgit Cullberg, the leading Swedish director and choreographer, frequently stages productions there – her *Cullbergsbaletten* ensemble is the country's foremost. The *Royal Swedish Ballet*, founded in 1773, is one of the oldest companies in the world. It is based at the *Royal Swedish Opera*, Strömgatan (tel: (08) 248 240; website: www.operan.se). *Moderna Dansteatern*, Slupskjulsvägen, Skeppsholmen (tel: (08) 611 3233; website: www.mdt.a.se), hosts more impromptu, innovative performances.

Film

The *Stockholm International Film Festival* (website: www.filmfestivalen.se) is the key event in the city's cinema calendar. All movies in Sweden are shown in their original language with subtitles. Mainstream movies are screened at *Biopalatset*, Medborsplatsen (tel: (08) 678 8548), and *Filmstaden Sergel*, Hotorget (tel: (08) 789 6001), while arthouse movie aficionados should head to *Sture*, Birger Jarlsgaten 28 (tel: (08) 644 3100).

Ingmar Bergman grew up in Stockholm and his schooldays at Palmgren's School in Östermalm were the basis for his 1944 screenplay, *Hets* (*Torment*). His 1952 film, *Sommaren med Monika* (*Summer with Monika*), kicks off with a majestic voyage through Stockholm in a small boat. Many film buffs will also remember Stockholm's crop of Swedish Hollywood sirens – Greta Garbo (born Greta Gustavsson in 1905) and Ingrid Bergman (born in Stockholm in 1915).

Cultural Events

The July *Stockholm Summer Games* (tel: (08) 627 4620; website: www.summergames.se) draws considerable local and international participation and is the kick-off for other events. The customary summer programme (May to August) of opera and ballet at *Drottningholm Court* (tel: (08) 5569 3100; website: www. drottningholmsteatern.dtm.se) is especially popular with music lovers, as is the *Royal Palace Music Festival* (tel: (08) 102 247; website: www. royalfestivals.se) in September. The *Stockholm International Film Festival* (tel: (08) 677 5011; website: www.filmfestivalen.se) takes place in November. The *St Lucia Day* festival, on 13 December, includes singing events and traditional parades of girls crowned with candles.

Literary Notes

The granddaddy of the Swedish literary fraternity is August Stringberg and *The Red Room* (1879) is considered by some to be the first real Swedish novel. Swedish writers have received the Nobel Prize for literature seven times but only Selma Lagerlöf (1909) and Pär Lagerkvist (1951) made any significant impact outside Sweden. Nelly Sachs, winner of the 1966 prize, was a naturalised Swedish citizen of German Jewish extraction who wrote in German. Ingmar Bergman (see *Film* above) spent his career working in the Stockholm film and theatre scenes.

More recent literary works to touch on the city include two hilarious chapters in Bill Bryson's *Neither Here Nor There* (1998) and Colin Forbes' thriller *The Stockholm Syndicate* (1989), which centres on an international conspiracy based in the city.

SPECIAL EVENTS

Viking Run, skating race, mid-Jan, from Appsala to Stockholm

Kiruna Snow Festival, late Jan–early Feb, celebration of winter includes an ice sculpting competition and a reindeer race, Kiruna

International Swedish Furniture Fair, early Feb, Stockholmsmässan

Stockholm International Antiques Fair (website: www.stockholmfurniturefair.com), Feb, Mässvägen 1, Älvsjö

Stockholm International Boat Show, late Feb–early Mar, Stockholmsmässan

Vasaloppet Ski race, historic cross-country ski race, early Mar, Dalarna

Stockholm Art Fair, early Mar, Sollentuna Exhibition Centre

Walpurgle, celebrations for the arrival of spring, late Apr, various venues

Drottingholm Court, ballet and opera events (website: www.drottningholmsteatern.dtm.se), May–Aug, Drottningholm Slottsteater

Swedish National Day, 6 Jun, Skansen

Early Music Festival, features music of pre-1750 (website: www.tidigmusik.com), early Jun, Gamla Stan venues

Stockholm Marathon, mid-Jun, starting and finishing at the Olympic Stadium

Midsummer Night, parties, 21 Jun, throughout the city

Stockholm Summer Games, sports events (website: www.summergames.se), early Jul, various sports venues

Stockholm Pride, the biggest gay and lesbian pride festival in Scandinavia (website: www.stockholmpride.org), late Jul–early Aug, various venues in the city centre

Stockholm Jazz Festival (website: www.stockholmjazz.com), late Jul–early Aug, various venues

Royal Palace Music Festival (website: www.royalfestivals.se), Sep, Kungliga Slottet (Royal Palace)

Stockholm Beer and Whisky Festival, includes tastings, mid–late Sep, Factory Nacka Strand, Augustendalstorget

Stockholm Open, tennis tournament, Kungliga Tennishallen, Lidingövägen 75, mid–late Oct

Scandinavian Sailboat and Scandinavian Motorboat Show, Nov, Mässvägen 1, Älvsjö

Stockholm International Film Festival (website: www.filmfestivalen.se), mid–late Nov, various venues

Christmas Fair in Rosendal Garden (website: www.rosendalstradgard.com), late Nov–end Dec, Rosendal Palace grounds

Nobel Prize Day, award of the Nobel Prizes and banquet (website: www.nobel.se), Dec, Stockholm City Hall

Christmas Fair, seasonal market, Dec, Gamla Stan

Skansen Christmas Market, seasonal market (website: www.skansen.se), Dec, Skansen

St Lucia Day, annual festival of light and procession through central Stockholm (website: www.skansen.se), 13 Dec, Skansen

New Year Concert, 31 Dec, cathedral in Gamla Stan

Folk dancers, Skansen open-air museum

Celebrated as the 'Queen of the Pacific Rim', vast, vibrant Sydney is home to one of the world's most beautiful harbours, with the imposing Opera House as the jewel in its crown.

The state capital of New South Wales, Sydney is a thriving centre for both business and the arts. The city has all the cosmopolitan amenities – top shopping, excellent restaurants and buzzing nightlife – and visitors often find similarities with San Francisco. Carved between the mountains and the sea, the city offers the ultimate in the great outdoors. The Pacific Ocean swells onto golden beaches, while a seasonally shifting palette of colours unfolds further inland, over the Blue Mountains. In addition to the harbour, famously adorned with sailing boats that mirror the distinctive curves of the Opera House, there are numerous inland waterways and national parks.

From its sordid beginnings as a British penal colony in 1788, Sydney rapidly flourished, establishing booming trade links and witnessing large-scale development throughout the 19th and 20th centuries. The Sydney Opera House – a feat of avant-garde architectural vision – epitomises the city's desire to lead the New World in the 21st century. Sydney's architecture is a stunning melange, with little Victorian structures nestling below towering concrete, steel and glass skyscrapers.

All the exuberance and plate-glass sophistication nonetheless fail to compensate for a certain competitive edginess in the city's psyche. After the Australian Federation was created in 1901, the traditional bickering between Sydney and its arch rival, Melbourne, was settled in 1908, by making Canberra the new national capital. However, until 1927, when the city of Canberra was completed, Melbourne remained the seat of national government. Nevertheless, Sydneysiders insist that their city remains the 'true' capital of Australia and indeed, following the triumphant hosting of the 2000 Olympic Games, the world might even agree with this. But the rivalry with Melbourne persists – a rivalry based more on style than on stature for, while Sydney is decidedly Anglo in its ethnic orientation, Melbourne is more continental, with a much more tangibly imported culture.

Australia's white history has eclipsed its indigenous inheritance and, although Sydney has the highest Aboriginal population of any Australian city, a stroll around the city's streets offers little evidence that it has anything other than a white – and latterly, an Asian – heritage. While museums, galleries, theatre and dance troupes pay tribute to the archaeological and cultural legacy of indigenous culture, Aborigines in the city remain very much an invisible minority.

With the Olympics, Sydney came of age as one of the world's great cities. The games' smooth running has been attributed to the thousands of local volunteers, whose helpful, welcoming attitude revealed – much to Sydney's own surprise – that beneath its somewhat vain and self-seeking surface there still exists a bedrock of traditional Australian virtues. But the Games did more than affect the city's mindset; they transformed its physical appearance. Streets and public areas were remodelled, long-neglected eyesores were removed and new street furniture erected, resulting in a city centre that is more pleasant and easier to navigate than ever before. Combine that with semi-tropical summers and mild winters and the result is an excellent city to visit at any time of the year.

Sydney Opera House at night

Photo: Tourism New South Wales

TRAVEL

Getting There By Air

Sydney (Kingsford Smith) Airport (SYD)

Tel: (02) 9667 9111. Fax: (02) 9667 1592.
Website: www.sydneyairport.com.au
Situated on the northern shoreline of Botany Bay, Sydney Airport is Australia's premier gateway, handling 23.2 million passengers per year, arriving on flights from 48 international, domestic and regional airlines.

Major airlines: *Qantas* (tel: (02) 9691 3636 *or* 131 313, Australia only; website: www.qantas.com.au) is the national airline. Other major airlines include: *Air Canada, Air China, Air New Zealand, Alitalia, British Airways, Cathay Pacific, Emirates, Garuda, Japan Airline, Korean Air, Malaysia Airlines, Singapore Airlines, South African Airways, Thai Airways, United Airlines* and *Virgin Blue*.

Approximate flight times to Sydney: From London is 20 hours 10 minutes; from New York is 20 hours 25 minutes; from Los Angeles is 14 hours 40 minutes and from Toronto is 19 hours 30 minutes.

Airport facilities: Sydney Airport is well equipped with restaurants, cafés and a food hall, as well as information desks, lockers, a health care centre, money changing facilities, prayer room, showers and smoking room. There are hotel reservation facilities and car hire from *Avis, Budget, Hertz* and *Thrifty*.

Business facilities: *Sydney Airport Executive Services* (tel: (02) 9667 6534; fax: (02) 8338 4922; e-mail: bookings@syd.com.au; website: www.execservices.com.au) hires out meeting rooms in terminal one and terminal two, as well as VIP rooms and a conference area in terminal two. Equipment and catering is supplied on request. Post, fax and photocopying facilities are available at the *Australia Post Shop* (tel: (02) 9669 1564), while Internet kiosks can be found throughout the international terminal. There are also seven airline lounges.

Arrival/departure tax: Departure, security and baggage screening taxes amounting to A$120.33 are included in the price of the ticket.

Transport to the city: The *CityRail Airport Link* (tel: 131 500, website: www.cityrail.nsw.gov.au) operates every eight minutes to and from Central Station, daily 0510–2300 (journey time – 10 minutes). Fares are A$15.80 return or A$10.40 one way. Taxis to the city centre cost A$22–30.

Getting There By Water

Passenger services dock at *Darling Harbour Passenger Terminal*, located just minutes from the city centre, while cruise ships berth at the *Sydney Cove Passenger Terminal*, Circular Quay. There are no facilities at the terminals, although the nearby Rocks and Darling Harbour both have restaurants, ATM machines and other conveniences. Information is available from the *Department of Shipping* (tel: (02) 9296 4999; website: www.sydneyports.com.au).

Ferry services: There is probably no more dramatic way for one to arrive in Sydney than by water. However, services to Australia are limited. From Europe, the USA and Hong Kong, *P&O* (tel: 132 469, Australia only; fax: (02) 9364 8862; e-mail: information@pocruises.com.au; website: www.pocruises.com.au) and *Cunard* (tel: (02) 9250 6666; website: www.cunard.com.au) include Sydney on their itineraries.

Transport to the city: There are frequent bus, ferry and CityRail connections from both Circular Quay and Darling Harbour.

Getting There By Rail

The New South Wales rail network is run by *Countrylink* (tel: 132 232, Australia only; fax: (02) 9379 1264; e-mail: bookings@countrylink.nsw.gov.au; website: www.countrylink.nsw.gov.au). Countrylink

provides high-speed XPT trains and XPlorer trains for shorter distances. These trains are new, modern and comfortable, featuring air conditioning, wheelchair access, buffet, toilets and satellite telephones. Seats are modelled on the French TGV and there is one sleeping car per journey, with cabins equipped with private bathrooms. Rail travel tends to be expensive, although a number of passes are available to overseas visitors. Sydney's *Central Station*, on Eddy Avenue, just south of the city centre, is a grand old building lined with newsagents, coffee shops and restaurants, as well as transport and tourist information offices.

Rail services: Popular inter-state destinations include Melbourne (journey time – 10 hours), Brisbane (journey time – 12.5 hours), Adelaide (journey time – 26 hours) and Perth (journey time – 64 hours).

Transport to the city: Central Station directly connects to the CityRail line.

Getting There By Road

Driving regulations are not uniform across Australia's states and territories, so visitors should be aware that the laws in Sydney might differ from states outside New South Wales.

Driving in Australia is on the left and the speed limit outside built-up areas is generally 100kph (62mph) or 110kph (68.2mph) on freeways. In built-up areas, the speed limit is 60kph (37.2mph) unless otherwise indicated. Wearing of seatbelts is compulsory in both the front and rear. Roads are usually known by their names – for example, the Hume Highway – although motorways are also identified by a corresponding number.

The legal driving age in New South Wales is 16 years. Overseas driving licences are acceptable, although an International Driving Permit is preferred. Licences must be carried when driving. Visitors are required to take out minimum third-party insurance for driving both their own cars and hire cars. The maximum legal alcohol to blood ratio for driving is 0.05%, which is enforced with random breath tests and curbed by severe penalties.

Visitors who plan to drive in the more remote outback areas should contact one of Australia's motoring organisations beforehand to obtain maps and advice on road and weather conditions, supply points and spare parts to be carried, as these regions are occasionally affected by excessively wet or dry weather. The *Australian Automobile Association* (tel: (02) 6247 7311; website: www.aaa.asn.au) can provide further information. The *National Roads and Motorists' Association – NRMA* (tel: 131 122; website: www.mynrma.com.au) also provides information and motoring services.

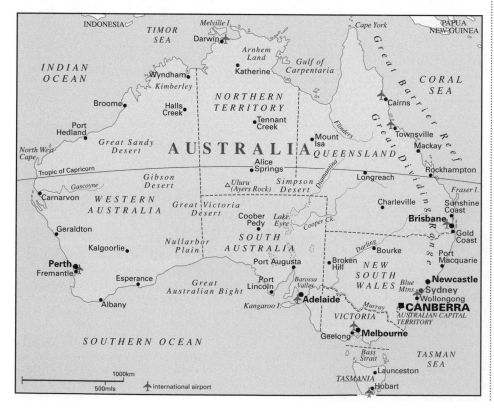

CITY STATISTICS

Location: New South Wales, Australia.
Country dialling code: 61.
Population: 4,140,820 (metropolitan area).
Ethnic mix: 61% white Australian, 4.7% British, 3% Chinese, 2.1% New Zealand, 1.5% Vietnamese, 1.3% Lebanese, 1.2% Italian, 1% indigenous Australian, 0.9% Indian, 0.8% Greek, 22.5% other.
Religion: 30.4% Catholic, 21.9% Anglican, 4.5% Uniting Church, 4.4% Orthodox, 3.3% Presbyterian and Reformed, 2.6% Islamic, 2% Buddhist, 1.6% Baptist, 0.8% Hindu, 0.8% Jewish, 27.7% other or no religion.
Time zone: GMT + 10 (GMT + 11 from last Sunday in October to Saturday before last Sunday in March).
Electricity: 220–240 volts AC, 50Hz; flat three-pin plugs.
Average January temp: 25°C (78°F).
Average July temp: 16°C (61°F).
Annual rainfall: 810mm (31.8 inches).

Emergency breakdown service: *NRMA Emergency Breakdown* 131 111.

Routes to the city: The main routes into Sydney are the Hume Highway (heading northeast from Melbourne), the Pacific Highway (south from Brisbane), the scenic Princes Highway (north from Melbourne via the coast) and the Sturt Highway (linking Adelaide on the west coast to Sydney on the east coast).

Approximate driving times to Sydney: From Melbourne – 11 hours; Brisbane – 13 hours 30 minutes; Adelaide – 18 hours.

Coach services: Operators include *Greyhound Pioneer* (tel: 132 030, Australia only *or* (07) 4690 9888 *or* (02) 9212 3433; e-mail: info@greyhound.com.au; website: www.greyhound.com.au) and *McCafferty's* (tel: 132 030, Australia only *or* (07) 4690 9888 *or* (02) 9212 3433; e-mail: info@mccaffertys.com.au; website: www.mccaffertys.com.au), offering routes to many destinations throughout the country, including Brisbane, Canberra, Adelaide and Melbourne. Buses depart from *Sydney Coach Terminal*, Eddy Avenue, outside Central Station (tel: (02) 9281 9366).

Getting Around

Public Transport

Sydney's mass transit system, incorporating **bus**, **ferry** and various **rail** services, is well developed, efficient and cheap. The *State Transit Infoline* (tel: 131 500, Australia only; website: www.131500.com.au) provides route, timetable and fare information for all buses, ferries and trains.

State Transit (e-mail: info@sydneybuses.nsw.gov.au; website: www.sydneybuses.nsw.gov.au) operates Sydney's **buses** and **ferries**. Buses run daily 0600–2400 and night buses operate on selected routes thereafter. Fares start at A$1.50 for inner-city journeys and tickets are available for purchase from the driver. The commuter **ferry** network that crisscrosses Sydney Harbour is one of the best ways for visitors to see the harbour. Ferries ply between Circular Quay and approximately 30 destinations, daily 0600–2400. Fares start at A$4.30 and tickets are available for purchase at ticket offices and machines located at the ferry stops or, if there is no office or machine, on-board.

CityRail (website: www.cityrail.nsw.gov.au) operates the network of **trains** designed primarily for rapid transit between the suburbs and the city. The stops are not necessarily very convenient for tourists, who tend to remain within the city centre. Trains generally operate daily 0430–2400 with varying times on the different routes and a limited service or no service on some routes on the weekend. Fares start at A$2.20 and tickets are available for purchase from the railway stations.

Sydney Metro (tel: (02) 9285 5600; website: www. metrolightrail.com.au) operates the **monorail** and **light rail** services. The **monorail** shuttles between the city centre, Darling Harbour and the Chinatown areas. Trains operate every three to five minutes Sunday to Thursday 0600–2200 and Friday and Saturday 0600–2400. The fare is A$4. The **light rail** service operates 24 hours between Central Station and Wentworth Park and Sunday to Thursday 0600–2300

and Friday and Saturday 0600–2400 between Central Station and Lilyfield. Fares start at A$2.60 and tickets are available for purchase from the stations.

Numerous money-saving **passes** are available, including the *SydneyPass* – a three-, five- or seven-day pass costing A$90, A$120 and A$140 respectively. This pass allows unlimited travel on public buses, harbour ferries, the Airport Express bus, the Sydney Explorer bus, the Bondi & Bay Explorer bus and the Parramatta Explorer bus, as well as the three sightseeing cruises operated by the State Transit Authority and train travel within the red (city and inner suburban) travel pass zone. Passes are available for purchase from the *New South Wales Travel Centre*, at the international airport, and from the *Sydney Visitor Centre*, 106 George Street, The Rocks. The colour-coded *TravelPass*, valid for one week or more, allows for unlimited travel on public transport within

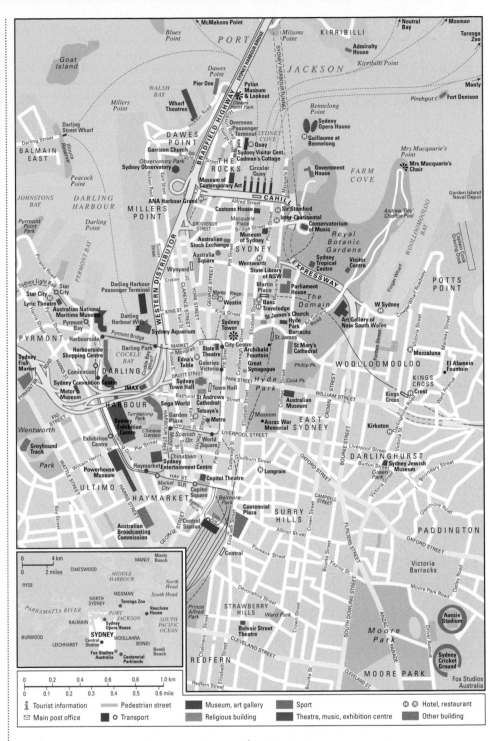

BUSINESS PROFILE

Thanks to the Olympic Games, Sydney's tourism soared in 2000, generating revenue from tourism-related businesses across the board to the tune of an estimated A$7 billion. The publicity that Sydney as a tourist destination has received as a result of the Olympic Games has been valued at more than A$600 million. The event undoubtedly helped boost Sydney's profile in the corporate world and the city is now seen as a genuine contender with Singapore and Hong Kong as a financial hub in the Asia-Pacific region. In 2001, the Australian Stock Exchange was ranked 12th largest internationally. The Olympic Games, together with a falling Australian Dollar, also contributed to a 26% rise in Australian exports. Between 1994 and 2001, Sydney's economic growth rate exceeded 5%. The city's unemployment rate, however, rose to 5.2% for the 2001–02 period, from 4% in 1999. However, this is still low compared to the national rate, which stood at 6.3% in June 2002.

Sydney plays a major part in Australia's economy, accounting for over 25% of Australia's total economic activity. The city is Australia's undisputed financial centre, with 65% of Australia's finance industry located here, including the Reserve Bank, the Australian Stock Exchange and the Sydney Futures Exchange. The strong economic mix encompasses services, manufacturing and mining – with financial, property and retail services together accounting for over 80% of total economic output. Financial and business services account for 47.1% of the city's workforce. Multinationals with Asian-Pacific headquarters here include *3M, American Express, AMP, Boral Ltd, BT, Coca-Cola Amatil, Compuserve, HJ Heinz, IBM, Mastercard, Microsoft, Price Waterhouse Coopers, TNT Ltd* and *Unilever*. Of the nation's top 100 companies, 60% have headquarters in Sydney.

The financial district is centred on Martin Place in the city centre. North Sydney, on the opposite side of the harbour, is a bustling high-rise business district in itself.

a designated area. A weekly blue bus and ferry TravelPass, for example, costs A$27.

A *Daytripper* pass is valid for travel on all buses, ferries and metropolitan area trains and costs A$13.40. A *TravelTen* bus pass is valid for ten bus journeys and starts at A$11.30. A *FerryTen* ticket is valid for ten ferry trips and starts at A$26.50.

There are also travel passes for the Sydney Metro. The *Monorail Supervoucher Day Pass* gives a full day of unlimited use for A$9, while the *Metro Light Rail Day Pass* costs A$8 and the *Weekly Unlimited Trips Pass* is A$19. A *METROConnect* pass is A$28 and allows for unlimited travel on both the light rail and monorail for one week.

All passes are available for purchase from the railway and bus stations, as well as from newspaper stands on bus routes.

Taxis

Taxi ranks can be found outside most bus and railway stations, as well as the larger hotels. The initial charge is A$2.45 and a three-kilometre (two-mile) trip costs approximately A$7. Fares are subject to surcharges for telephone bookings, crossing the Harbour Bridge and using certain parts of the Eastern Distributor, where toll systems operate. Travel between 2200 and 0600 costs an extra 20%. Taxi drivers do not expect a tip, although fares are generally rounded up to the nearest Dollar. Operators include *Taxis Combined Services* (tel: (02) 8332 8888) and *Premier Cabs* (tel: 131 017, Australia only).

Limousines

Chauffeur-driven limousines are available for trips around Sydney, with an optional commentary. Operators include *First National Limousines* (tel: (02) 9948 2728) and *Astra Chauffeured Limousines of Australia* (tel: 132 121, Australia only). Collection from the airport to the city costs from A$66.

Driving in the City

The construction of a new road network for the 2000 Olympic Games left many Sydney routes vastly improved. The Eastern Distributor tunnel, for instance, has made driving to the airport a breeze. The Cross-City Tunnel, due to open in late 2005, will help reduce city congestion by enabling travel from Kings Cross to Darling Harbour, under the CBD.

Nevertheless, Sydney drivers are renowned for speed and intolerance and parking is invariably difficult and/or expensive.

Parking restrictions are clearly signposted and usually specify an hour or two of metered parking during business hours. There are 'clearway' zones that apply at certain times of day and vehicles will be towed away and impounded if they are found parked there during the times indicated. It is probably easiest for visitors to park in one of the car parks situated around the city centre and take public transport from there. A convenient central car park is the Queen Victoria Building (QVB) Car Park in York Street. Metered parking generally costs A$2.20 per hour, while parking stations in the city can charge up to A$50 per day on weekdays.

Car Hire

A national driving licence printed in English is required for driving in Sydney, although some hire firms prefer an International Driving Permit. The minimum age for hiring a car is often 25 years. Minimum third-party insurance is required. Hire rates for a small car start from around A$62 per day. Major operators include *Avis* (tel: (02) 9353 9000 *or* 136 333, Australia only; website: www.avis.com.au), *Budget* (tel: (1300) 362 848 *or* 132 727, Australia only; website: www.budget.com.au), *Hertz* (tel: (03) 9698 2555 *or* 133 039, Australia only; website: www. hertz.com.au) and *Thrifty* (tel: (1300) 367 277; website: www.thrifty.com.au).

Bicycle Hire

Sydney's many steep hills do not make for a leisurely ride and there are limited – and often dangerous – designated cycle lanes. Manly has better paths for cycling but best of all is the popular Centennial Park. Hire companies include *Woolys Wheels*, 82 Oxford Street, Paddington (tel: (02) 9331 8190), and *Inner City Cycles*, 151 Glebe Point Road (tel: (02) 9660 6605). Hire rates start from about A$33 for 24 hours.

BUSINESS ETIQUETTE

In keeping with its distinctly work-hard, play-hard culture, the protocol in Sydney is typically informal. During the week, business is often conducted over a long lunch, with alcohol included, and the weekend can start as early as Friday lunchtime. Both men and women usually wear suits. Business hours are officially weekdays, 0900–1700, although an extended working day is very common in certain sectors and it is not unusual for people to be working well into the night or over the weekend.

Australians are a very friendly people and socialising comes easily. Nevertheless, there are a few things that may offend or annoy. The first is the use of the informal 'G'day' – foreigners should avoid trying to emulate this overused greeting. The second is that, while out drinking, a system of 'rounds' is observed and it is not appreciated when someone skips his or her round by not offering to pay. Gift giving is not a common practice, although a small token – such as chocolate, wine or flowers – is appropriate if invited to a home. If at a loss for conversation topics, sport is always a good choice.

Photo: Tourism New South Wales

Manly ferry heading into Circular Quay, past Fort Denison

SIGHTSEEING

Sightseeing Overview

Who can argue with the claim that Sydney has the most magnificent harbour in the world? Its intricate coastal geography of headlands and secluded bays is the stunning setting for two of the modern world's most ambitious architectural achievements – the *Sydney Opera House* and the *Sydney Harbour Bridge*. It is therefore hardly surprising that much tourist attention is focused on the harbour, with the revived cobbled charm of *The Rocks*, the perpetual motion of people arriving and departing *Circular Quay* and the enduring awe that visitors experience at the steps of the Opera House.

But behind these modern monoliths, there is a wealth of history, culture and tradition. In inner-city Sydney, *Macquarie Place* and *Macquarie Street* are characterised by their imposing Victorian banking chambers and municipal buildings, while further afield, the areas of *Kings Cross, Darlinghurst* and *Paddington* are thriving cosmopolitan communities, each with its own distinct character. Kings Cross, renowned more for its red light district, has a bustling café society, while Darlinghurst comes alive every March for the world-famous *Gay & Lesbian Mardi Gras Parade*. Paddington has a more genteel feel, with its fashionable restaurants, galleries, antique shops and restored Victorian terraces complete with wrought-iron lace verandahs.

Key Attractions

Sydney Opera House

Few architectural feats match that of the *Sydney Opera House*. The roofs are the remaining legacy of Danish architect Jørn Utzon, who left the project halfway through its 14-year genesis, leaving subsequent architects to design the complex of auditoria, theatres, restaurants and bars, which finally opened in 1973. Utzon has never seen the completed building but has been working on designs for a A$70 million interior refurbishment that will bring the building closer to his original vision. The four main auditoria – the *Concert Hall*, the *Playhouse*, the *Opera Theatre* and the *Drama Theatre* – stage a total of 3000 performances per year.
Bennelong Point
Tel: (02) 9250 7111. Fax: (02) 9251 3843.
E-mail: infodesk@sydneyoperahouse.com
Website: www.sydneyoperahouse.com
Transport: CityRail, ferry or bus to Circular Quay; bus 438 to Opera House steps.
Opening hours: Daily 0830–1700 (tours); Mon–Sat 0900–2030 (box office); Sun two hours before show.
Admission: Free; A$17 (front-of-house tour); A$28 (backstage tour).

Sydney Harbour Bridge

Not to be outdone by the imposing grandeur of the Opera House, the *Sydney Harbour Bridge* is, in its own right, a feat of engineering genius. Affectionately known as 'the Coathanger', it took 1400 workers – 16 of whom were killed in the process – eight years to complete the bridge, which opened in 1932. If the views from the *Pylon Lookout* across Sydney Harbour and over the Opera House are not spectacular enough, the *Bridge Climb* gives thrill-seekers the chance to walk to the top of the 50-storey-high bridge

Fireworks, New Year's Eve, Sydney Harbour Bridge

– over the cars and trains rumbling across the deck below – and down the other side. Paul 'Crocodile Dundee' Hogan, a bridge-painter in a former lifetime, was one of the first to climb the bridge.
Sydney Harbour Bridge Pylon Lookout
Access from stairs via Cumberland Street
Tel: (02) 9240 1100. Fax: (02) 9241 2151.
Website: www.pylonlookout.com.au
Transport: CityRail or ferry to Circular Quay.
Opening hours: Daily 1000–1700.
Admission: A$8.50 (concessions available).
Bridge Climb
5 Cumberland Street
Tel: (02) 8274 7777. Fax: (02) 9240 1122.
Website: www.bridgeclimb.com
Transport: CityRail or ferry to Circular Quay.
Opening hours: Daily 0700–2000.
Admission: A$145–175 (concessions available).

The Rocks

Nestled at the foot of the Sydney Harbour Bridge, *The Rocks* – Sydney's historical birthplace – is a neighbourhood of winding streets, sandstone cottages and some of Sydney's oldest pubs. The site of the first landing from Plymouth, England, in 1788, the area is now a busy tourist enclave, with cafés, restaurants, galleries, museums and countless souvenir shops. Among the district's historic buildings are the *Hero of Waterloo* inn (built over a tunnel that was originally used for smuggling), the *Sydney Observatory* (on the site of the colony's first windmill), *Cadman's Cottage* (Sydney's oldest building, built in 1816) and *Susannah Place* (a museum of working-class life). Other attractions include the *Museum of Contemporary Art* and *The Rocks Toy Museum*.
The Rocks, Sydney Harbour
Transport: CityRail or ferry Circular Quay.
Sydney Observatory
Watson Road, Observatory Hill
Tel: (02) 9217 0485. Fax: (02) 9217 0489.
Website: www.phm.gov.au/observe
Opening hours: Daily 1000–1700.
Admission: Free; A$12 (night tour).
Cadman's Cottage
110 George Street
Tel: (02) 9247 8861.
Opening hours: Mon–Fri 0930–1630; Sat and Sun 1000–1630.
Admission: Free.

Museum of Contemporary Art
140 George Street
Tel: (02) 9252 4033.
Website: www.mca.com.au
Opening hours: Daily 1000–1700.
Admission: Free.
The Rocks Toy Museum
2–6 Kendall Lane
Tel: (02) 9251 9793.
Opening hours: Daily 1000–1730.
Admission: Free.
Susannah Place
58–64 Gloucester Street
Tel: (02) 9241 1893.
Opening hours: Sat and Sun 1000–1700.
Admission: A$7 (concessions available).

Photo: Tourism New South Wales

Darling Harbour

A former dockside area, this small harbour has been transformed into a major tourist site, appealing predominantly to children and families. The vast, paved and landscaped recreation ground is packed with restaurants and shops, as well as a number of tourist attractions. These include the *Powerhouse Museum*, *Australian National Maritime Museum*, *Sydney Aquarium*, *LG IMAX Theatre* and the *Chinese Garden of Friendship*, a gift to Sydney from its sister city of Guangdong.
Darling Harbour
Website: www.darlingharbour.com
Transport: CityRail Town Hall; monorail Darling Park or Harbourside; ferry Darling Harbour.
Powerhouse Museum
500 Harris Street
Tel: (02) 9217 0111.
Website: www.phm.gov.au
Opening hours: Daily 1000–1700.
Admission: A$10 (concessions available); some special exhibitions charge an extra entrance fee.
Australian National Maritime Museum
2 Murray Street
Tel: (02) 9298 3777.
Website: www.anmm.gov.au
Opening hours: Daily 0930–1700.
Admission: A$10 (concessions available).
Sydney Aquarium
Aquarium Pier
Tel: (02) 9262 2300.
Opening hours: Daily 0900–2200.
Admission: A$23 (includes return ferry journey to Circular Quay).
LG IMAX Theatre
Tel: (02) 9281 3300.
Website: www.imax.com.au
Opening hours: Daily 1000–2200.
Admission: A$15 (concessions available).
Chinese Garden of Friendship
Tel: (02) 9281 6863.
Opening hours: Daily 0930–1700.
Admission: A$4.50.

Bondi Beach

Bondi is one of the world's most famous beaches, a white crescent of sand strung between two rocky headlands, situated just 15 minutes from the city centre. The waterfront scene, with its street musicians, surf shops and bars is ideal for a summer evening's prowl or a lazy saunter past Campbell Parade's restaurants, cafés and Sunday markets. Topless sunbathing is tolerated and swimmers should stick to the patrolled areas of *North Bondi* or *Bondi Baths*, on the southern rocks. The coastal walk takes in the whole gamut of beach cultures, from the wild surf and gleaming bodies at *Tamarama* to the palm-fringed views of *Bronte* and the soothing sea pools at *Coogee*.
Campbell Parade, off Bondi Road
Website: www.voyeurmagic.com.au
Transport: Bus 380, 382 or L82; CityRail Bondi Junction and then bus 380; ferry from Circular Quay to Rose Bay and then bus 380.
Opening hours: Daily 24 hours.
Admission: Free.

Art Gallery of New South Wales

Featuring the *Yiribana Gallery*, the world's largest permanent exhibition of Aboriginal and Torres Strait Islander art, the *Art Gallery of New South Wales* is one of Australia's foremost art museums. Among its most impressive exhibitions is its Australian art collection, extending from the early colonial period to the mid-20th century, with sculpture and painting exhibited together. Shortlisted portraits in the *Archibald Prize* – Australia's most prestigious art award – are exhibited here annually.
Art Gallery Road, The Domain
Tel: (02) 9225 1700. Fax: (02) 9221 6226.
Website: www.artgallery.nsw.gov.au
Transport: CityRail Martin Place/St James; bus 441.
Opening hours: Thurs–Tues 1000–1700; Wed 1000–2100.
Admission: Free; some special exhibitions charge entrance.

Sydney Tower

Standing 250m (820ft) above Market Street, *Sydney Tower* is the city's tallest building, with views over the city, the Harbour, the Olympic Park and as far as Terrigal Beach, 100km (62 miles) to the north. Entry to the observation deck includes the *Skytour* – a 35-minute virtual tour/ride on the podium level.
100 Market Street
Tel: (02) 9223 0933. Fax: (02) 9223 0233.

Website: www.sydneyskytour.com.au
Transport: CityRail St James/Town Hall; monorail City Centre.
Opening hours: Sun–Fri 0900–2230, Sat 0900–2330.
Admission: A$19.80 (concessions available).

Royal Botanic Gardens

A short walk from the Opera House, the *Royal Botanic Gardens* sits on a slope overlooking the harbour and covers 30 hectares (74 acres) in the heart of the city. Established in 1816, it is Australia's oldest scientific institution and home to over one million specimens. Highlights include the *Sydney Tropical Centre* and the *Rose Garden*; there is a hop-on hop-off trackless train to get around them all.
Macquarie Street (main entrance)
Tel: (02) 9231 8111. Fax: (02) 9231 8054.
Website: www.rbgsyd.gov.au
Transport: CityRail St James, Martin Place or Circular Quay.
Opening hours: Daily 0700–sunset.
Admission: Free.

Sydney Olympic Park

Built on the site of an old rubbish tip, the focal point of the 'best ever Olympics' in 2000 is now an attraction in its own right, comprising 15 architecturally magnificent venues as well as extensive parks and wetlands. Separate guided tours of the venues are given and a *Games Trail* self-guided tour brochure is available from the Visitor Centre.
1 Herb Elliot Avenue, Homebush Bay
Tel: (02) 9714 7888 *or* 131 500, Australia only (bus rides). Fax: (02) 9714 7822.
Website: www.sydneyolympicpark.com.au
Transport: Train to Strathfield, then bus 401 or 403; train to Olympic Park; ferry from Circular Quay to Homebush Bay Wharf.
Opening hours: Daily 0900–1700.
Admission: Free.
Telstra Stadium
Olympic Boulevard, Gate C
Tel: (02) 8765 2300 (tours).
Opening hours: Daily 1030–1530.
Admission: A$26 (60-minute tour), A$15 (30-minute tour); concessions available.
Observation Centre
Level 17, Novotel Hotel, Olympic Boulevard
Tel: (02) 8762 1111.
Opening hours: Daily 1000–1600.
Admission: A$4 (concessions available).
Sydney Aquatic Centre
Olympic Boulevard
Tel: (02) 9752 3666.
Opening hours: Mon–Fri 0500–2045, Sat and Sun 0600–1945.
Admission: A$16 (tour and swim); A$5.80 (swim only); concessions available.
Bicentennial Park
Bennelong Road
Tel: (02) 9714 7545.
Opening hours: Daily 0500–2000.
Admission: Free.

Taronga Zoo

The most desirable residence in Sydney is inhabited not by the upper echelons of society but by a collection of seals, snow leopards, koalas, kangaroos and wallabies. *Taronga Zoo's* location, on Bradley's Head, at Mosman, is one of the most beautiful vantage points on Sydney Harbour, situated on elevated land along the waterfront. The zoo's

Photo: Tourism New South Wales

Manly Beach

attractions include the *Gorilla Forest*, the *Orangutan Rainforest*, *Koala Encounters* and *Cats of Asia*.
Bradleys Head Road (main entrance)
Tel: (02) 9969 2777. Fax: (02) 9969 7515.
Website: www.zoo.nsw.gov.au
Transport: Ferry from Circular Quay; bus 247.
Opening hours: Daily 0900–1700.
Admission: A$23 (concessions available).

Fox Studios Australia

Fox Studios hosted the filming of *The Matrix Trilogy* (1999/2003), *Moulin Rouge* (2001) and *Star Wars Episode II: Attack of the Clones* (2002). The adjoining entertainment precinct includes shops, markets, cinemas, restaurants, mini golf, bungy trampoline and an indoor children's playground.
Lang Road, Moore Park
Tel: (02) 9383 4333. Fax: (02) 9383 4005.
Website: www.foxstudios.com.au
Transport: Bus 335 or 339.
Opening hours: Daily 1000–2400.
Admission: Free.

Further Distractions

Rose Seidler House

The designs for Australia's first modernist home, *Rose Seidler House*, so perplexed local residents they almost succeeded in preventing the building's construction. Created by the great Canadian/Australian architect, Harry Seidler, for his parents, the concrete house has glass walls, a sun-filled deck and panoramic views of *Ku-ring-gai National Park*. The house has been restored to its original scheme, with 1950s furnishings and objects.
71 Clissold Road, Wahroonga
Tel: (02) 9989 8020. Fax: (02) 9487 2761.
Website: www.hht.nsw.gov.au/museums/rose_seidler_house
Transport: Train to Wahroonga.
Opening hours: Sun 1000–1700.
Admission: A$7 (concessions available).

Centennial Parklands

A grand park in the European tradition, the *Centennial Parklands* features landscaped gardens, statues, historic monuments and houses, ponds, formal gardens, wildlife habitat areas and grand avenues. There is a restaurant, café and facilities for every active pursuit under the sun.
Southeast of the city, bordering Paddington, Moore Park and Bondi Junction
Tel: (02) 9339 6699. Fax: (02) 9332 2148.
E-mail: info@cp.nsw.gov.au
Website: www.cp.nsw.gov.au
Transport: Bus 378, 380, 382 or L82 to Paddington/Woollahra Gates, bus 357 or 359 to Musgrave Avenue Gates, bus 355 to Jervois/Robertson Road Gates or bus 339 or 340 to Randwick/Govett Gates.
Opening hours: Daily 24 hours.
Admission: Free.

Tours of the City

Walking Tours

The Rocks Self-guided Tour leaflet is available from the Sydney Visitor Centre (see *Tourist Information*) for A$1 and covers approximately 30 historic buildings and points of interest in The Rocks district. The heritage walk takes one to three hours, beginning at the Visitor Centre – a former sailor's home – and ending

at Cadman's Cottage. *The Rocks Walking Tours* (tel: (02) 9247 6678; website: www. rockswalkingtours. com.au) operates 90-minute guided tours, taking in all the historic sites. Tours cost A$17.50 and depart three times per day (twice per day on the weekend) from Shop K4, Kendall Lane.

Bus Tours

City Sightseeing Sydney (tel: (02) 9567 8400) covers 22 points of interest in the city, Kings Cross, Woolloomooloo and Darling Harbour, with a hop-on, hop-off service. Departures are every 30 minutes daily 0900–1700. Tickets cost A$30 and are valid for 24 hours. Hosted by drag queens, the *Sydney By Diva* (tel: (02) 9360 2227) tour is a comedic expedition of gay Sydney. Setting off from outside the Oxford Hotel in Taylor Square – scene of the demonstrations that launched Mardi Gras in 1978 – every Sunday at 1700, the three-hour tour costs A$75 (first class) and A$55 (economy).

Other Tours

A plethora of harbour cruises is available from a number of operators; many of them based at Circular Quay. *Captain Cook Cruises* (tel: (02) 9206 1111) offers the luxury 'John Cadman Dinner Cruise', departing daily at 1900 from No 6 Circular Quay, ending at 2130 (2230 on Friday and Saturday). The A$99 fee includes an a la carte three-course meal with coffee. The 'Sydney Harbour Explorer' (costing A$25) and 'Sydney Harbour Highlights Cruise' (costing A$20) are fully narrated cruises, leaving from No 6 Circular Quay, with a fixed number of stopping points. The 'Sydney Harbour Explorer' tour takes 105 minutes and departures are every two hours daily 0945–1500. The 'Sydney Harbour Highlights Cruise' takes between 75 and 90 minutes; tours depart approximately once every 90 minutes daily 0930–1930.
For aerial views of Sydney, *Sydney Sights Day & Night* (tel: (02) 9233 1000; website: www. sydneysights.com) offers a half-hour 'Northern Beaches and Harbour Scenic Flight' in a seaplane. Flights depart from Rose Plane Seaplane Base daily at 1000 and cost A$225. The 'Sydney Helicopters Grand Tour of Sydney' tour lasts 35 minutes and departs from Rosehill Airport, 25 Wentworth Street, Granville, every Saturday at 1030. Flights cost A$220.

Excursions

For a Half Day

Manly: New South Wales has *Manly Beach* to thank for its sea and surf culture, for it was here, in 1902, that newspaper editor William Gocher first defied the state law against public bathing. The esplanade is now populated with rollerbladers, joggers and cyclists, while the white sand of the south beaches and the golden sands of the north beaches are crowded with swimmers, sunbathers and surfers. A short ferry ride from Circular Quay, Manly – located 13km (eight miles) northeast of the city centre – can also be reached on foot via the *Manly Scenic Walkway* from Spit Bridge in the city. The walk can take up to four hours but offers some of Sydney's most breathtaking views, as well as skirting some of its most exclusive homes. The *Manly Visitors Information Bureau*, North Steyne, Manly (tel: (02) 9977 1088) can provide further information.

For a Whole Day

Blue Mountains: A 90-minute drive west from the city, along the Great Western Freeway, the

Queen Victoria Building

dramatic, forest scenery of the *Blue Mountains National Park* is a major attraction for nature lovers. The cool eucalyptus forests harbour numerous bush-walks and radiate a blue haze that gives the area its name. More active visitors might like to go abseiling, rock climbing, mountain biking or horseriding. The area's most famous attraction is the *Three Sisters* – a geological feature named after an Aboriginal legend. The easiest way for visitors to see the Blue Mountains is by car, although there are hourly trains to Katoomba from Central Station. *Blue Mountains Tourism* (tel: (1300) 653 408; website: www. bluemts.com.au) can provide further information.
Hunter Valley: One of Australia's premier wine-producing districts, beginning approximately 100km (62 miles) north of Sydney, 'The Hunter' has more than 70 vineyards. Although busiest during the harvest months of March and April, most vineyards remain open to the public on a daily basis and offer a range of tours, restaurants and accommodation. Two of the more popular vineyards are *Lindemans* – one of the largest Australian wine companies – and *Rothbury Estate* – famous for its concerts throughout the March/April *Harvest Festival*, which is an annual celebration of Australian culture, gastronomy and wine. A two-hour drive from Sydney, *Cessnock* is the gateway to Hunter Valley and home to its main visitor centre. Alternatively, trains from Sydney arrive at Newcastle (journey time – approximately 3 hours). *Wine Country Tourism* (tel: (02) 4990 4477; fax: (02) 4991 4518; website: www.winecountry.com.au) can provide full details of tours.

ACCOMMODATION

The central Sydney area has a 10% accommodation levy, commonly known as the 'bed tax'. This is usually included in the prices quoted. Most hostel-type accommodation is exempt from this tax.
The prices quoted below are the lowest standard rates for a double room, including taxes but excluding breakfast, unless otherwise specified.

Business

Hotel InterContinental
This deluxe five-star hotel is housed within the restored Treasury Building – a heritage landmark in the heart of Sydney's business and government area, close to Circular Quay. Many of the 503 rooms have harbour views; some have a panoramic view of the harbour, Royal Botanic Gardens and the Opera House. Lavish executive suites offer a separate study and lounge room, while all rooms are equipped with cable TV, dual telephone line, voicemail and daily newspaper. An outstanding feature of the InterContinental is its private dining rooms, ideal for high-level lunch meetings or special occasions. The business centre boasts two video-conferencing studios along with every other conceivable amenity.
117 Macquarie Street
Tel: (02) 9253 9000. Fax: (02) 9240 1204.
E-mail: sydney@interconti.com
Website: www.intercontinental.com
Price: From A$235.

The Wentworth
A vast 1960s semi-circle of concrete, *The Wentworth* was one of Sydney's first modern prestige hotels and is heritage listed for its space-age design. Located in the heart of the CBD, close to key attractions such as the Opera House and The Rocks, the building's crescent shape encircles the Level 5 Garden Court, a popular dining and bar area. Conventions are a speciality – up to 1100 people can be catered for in the function and meeting rooms and an in-house audiovisual department offers state-of-the-art equipment including satellite teleconferencing. In 2003, the hotel commenced with an upgrading and remodelling programme, to become the Sofitel Wentworth Sydney.
61–101 Phillip Street
Tel: (02) 9230 0700. Fax: (02) 9228 9133.
E-mail: H3665-RE@accor.com.au
Website: www.accorhotels.com.au
Price: From A$215 (including breakfast).

The Westin
The Westin's location in the financial epicentre of Sydney makes it a logical choice for business travellers, as do its superior in-room facilities, such as three telephone lines and Internet connection. The hotel's 'Heritage' rooms have been carved from the 1887 GPO building, offering a charming combination of old and brand new, while the 'Tower' rooms feature glass-walled bathrooms and unobstructed city views. 'Guest Office' rooms are fitted with printer/fax/copiers, speakerphone and an ergonomic chair. The business and conference centre has seven meeting rooms. Incorporating a massive atrium area filled with prestige shops and first-class eating places, this hotel complex blurs the line between business and pleasure.
1 Martin Place
Tel: (02) 8223 1111. Fax: (02) 8223 1222.
E-mail: westin.sydney@westin.com
Website: www.westin.com.au
Price: From A$330.

W Sydney
Arguably the most boldly conceived of the newer hotels in town, *W Sydney* occupies the renovated interior of an old loading wharf, jutting out into the harbour at Woolloomooloo Bay. Retaining the original exterior and many of the interior beams, the refit is an ingenious exercise in industrial chic, which sees a vast central atrium occupied by a bar, restaurant and massive, obsolete conveyor belts – once used for loading bales of wool. Rooms feature sophisticated modern styling alongside photography depicting early 20th-century Sydney, while business travellers are well catered for with oversized work desks, ISDN lines and two telephones. The 24-hour business centre has computers, printers, photocopier and audiovisual equipment for presentations.
6 Cowper Wharf Road, Woolloomooloo
Tel: (02) 9331 9000. Fax: (02) 9331 9031.
E-mail: wsydney@whotels.com
Website: www.whotels.com
Price: From A$425.

Luxury

ANA Harbour Grand
Many Sydney hotels have views. The five-star deluxe *ANA* puts them all to shame. Where else is it possible to view both the Opera House and Harbour Bridge from a guest room's sofa, or to lord it over Darling Harbour from the comfort of the bathtub? Japanese tourists come in their droves to this Japanese-owned hotel with its traditional dining facilities, including sushi bar and teppanyaki restaurant, that are among the best in the country. Rooms are in an Asian-European style and each one boasts a harbour view. The *Horizons Bar* was named Best Sydney Cocktail Bar by the *Daily Telegraph* in 2001.
176 Cumberland Street, The Rocks
Tel: (02) 9250 6000. Fax: (02) 9250 6250.
E-mail: reservations@anahotel.com.au
Website: www.anahotel.com.au
Price: From A$355 (including breakfast).

Sir Stamford at Circular Quay
Formerly the Ritz-Carlton, the *Sir Stamford* has retained a style of traditional European luxury, replete with grand chandeliers, oil paintings, antique furniture and fine bone china. Dining areas and guest rooms are cosy and elegant, bathrooms feature marble double basins and Bulgari toiletries, and personal service is exceptional. The private lounge club is ideal for informal business meetings, with secretarial and IT staff on call for any special requirements. And it is just a short stroll to the Opera House. This hotel was voted number one hotel in Australia by *Condé Nast Traveller* in 2001.
93 Macquarie Street
Tel: (02) 9252 4600. Fax: (02) 9252 4286.
E-mail: sales@sscq.stamford.com.au
Website: www.stamford.com.au
Price: From A$260.

Moderate

The Crest Hotel
Located in the lively nightlife nexus of Kings Cross and Darlinghurst, with Kings Cross train station located just underneath the hotel, *The Crest Hotel* offers a quality Sydney stay that is extremely good value for money. Most rooms have panoramic views of the city or Rushcutters Bay and all have mini-bar, TV and safe; all rooms are en suite. The *Ginseng Bathhouse* on Level 1 is an authentic Korean bathhouse offering specialist saunas, massage and skin treatments and it attracts stressed-out execs from all over town. Guest can enjoy the facilities for half price.
111 Darlinghurst Road, Kings Cross
Tel: (02) 9358 2755. Fax: (02) 9358 2888.
E-mail: reservations@thecresthotel.com.au
Website: www.c-inc.com.au
Price: From A$110.

Travelodge Phillip Street
This no-nonsense hotel in the CBD offers the familiar Travelodge amenities for the budget-minded traveller. Rooms are workmanlike and feature a kitchenette with microwave and cable television. There are also five disabled access rooms. All rooms are en suite. The building houses the *NSW Leagues Club* – guests gain automatic membership – whose four bar areas fill up with after-work revellers. The Quay is a five-minute walk away and Martin Place is just around the corner, although visitors should not expect any views apart from the central atrium's rather unconvincing *trompe l'oeil* mural.
165 Phillip Street
Tel: (02) 8224 9400. Fax: (02) 8224 9500.
E-mail: reservations@travelodge.com.au
Website: www.travelodge.com.au
Price: From A$125.

Other Recommendations

The Kirketon
Named 'Best Boutique Hotel in Australia' at the 2003 Hotel and Management Awards, *The Kirketon* is a byword for stainless steel, mirrors and conspicuous cool. Being a fashion model is not a prerequisite of staying here but it helps. There are 40 guest rooms, as well a small function rooms, the acclaimed *Salt* (see *Restaurants*) and the red, womb-like cigar bar, *Fix*. *The Kirketon* is one of two boutique hotels in Darlinghurst Road, both under the same ownership – the other, *Medusa*, offers a Baroque variation on the minimalist theme.
229 Darlinghurst Road, Darlinghurst
Tel: (02) 9332 2011. Fax: (02) 9332 2499.
E-mail: info@kirketon.com.au
Website: www.kirketon.com.au
Price: From A$275.

Star City
It's big and gaudy – Las Vegas-style. *Star City*, a 24-hour pageant of dedicated gamblers and suave croupiers, is a universe unto itself. This is Australia-as-theme-park – the elaborate and off-putting interior design uses bush and native motifs – but the hotel rooms are big and friendly, with city views and Internet access. The Sydney Convention Centre is a short walk away. Like any good Vegas casino, there is an all-you-can-eat buffet as well as theatres offering big, flashy stage shows. For visitors seeking an action-packed Sydney stay, this is a safe bet.
80 Pyrmont Street, Pyrmont
Tel: (02) 9777 9000. Fax: (02) 9657 8345.
E-mail: reservations@starcity.com.au
Website: www.starcity.com.au
Price: From A$260 (including breakfast and A$10 gaming voucher).

RESTAURANTS

The selected restaurants have been divided into five categories: Gastronomic, Business, Trendy, Budget and Personal Recommendations. The restaurants are listed alphabetically within these different categories, which serve as guidelines rather than absolute definitions of the establishments.

Sydney has a Goods and Services Tax (GST) of 10%. It is highly unlikely that this would be added to the bill as an extra at the end and menus will usually state: 'Prices include GST'. However, on public holidays, many establishments add a 15% service charge to the bill. Tipping is still far from obligatory in Sydney but good service should be rewarded with a gratuity of up to 10%. If the service has been unsatisfactory, it is not necessary for diners to tip.

The prices quoted below are for an average three-course meal for one person and for a bottle of house wine or cheapest equivalent; they include the GST but do not include a service charge or tip. Many restaurants in Sydney are unlicensed but operate a BYO (Bring Your Own) policy. This, including the relevant corkage fee, is listed below.

Gastronomic

Catalina Rose Bay

Catalina Rose Bay is a must for lovers of seafood and ocean views – every year, the Sydney to Hobart Yacht Race begins under the very noses of its patrons. The wrap-around glass windows complement a fresh, nautical decor. Japanese and Spanish influences alternate over a range of fish and shellfish creations that melt in the mouth, such as *crépinette* of crab and snapper, steamed red emperor with fennel, mussels and saffron, and sea scallops with smoked quail. The food's presentation rivals the architectural elegance of this terrific restaurant. Closed Sunday night.
1 Sunderland Avenue, Rose Bay
Tel: (02) 9371 0555. Fax: (02) 9371 0559.
E-mail: catrest@ozemail.com.au
Website: www.catalinarosebay.com.au
Price: A\$95. Wine: A\$40.

Edna's Table

When the craving for emu tartare, crocodile sushi or kangaroo fillet gets too much, *Edna's Table* beckons. Comfortable modern decor, Aboriginal artworks and authentic bush ingredients, including bunya nuts, Kakadu plum and eucalyptus oil, contribute to Edna's truly unique style. A Native Australian *dégustation* menu is also offered with a selection of Australian wines for A\$135.
204 Clarence Street
Tel: (02) 9267 3933. Fax: (02) 9264 9002.
E-mail: ednas@acay.com.au
Website: www.ednastable.com.au
Price: A\$70. Wine: A\$30.

Guillaume at Bennelong

The only Sydney restaurant that is also a world architectural icon, *Guillaume at Bennelong* is the smallest of the three soaring structures making up the Opera House. Jørn Utzon is responsible for designing this vaulted room, with exposed concrete rafters or 'ribs'. Chocolate tones and amber lighting create a warm and sensual space. Under the direction of Guillaume Brahini, a three-Michelin-starred chef, the restaurant's menu embraces local produce cooked with French techniques, such as *ballotine* of ocean trout, rock fish soup with Queensland scallops and mussels, and roasted Glenloth chicken on ravioli of duck *foie gras*. Dining doesn't get much more glamorous than this, although booking well ahead is essential. Closed Sunday. A pre-theatre menu, available from 1730–1900, is good value at A\$65.
Sydney Opera House, Bennelong Point
Tel: (02) 9241 1999. Fax: (02) 9241 3795.
E-mail: enquiries@guillaumeatbennelong.com.au
Website: www.guillaumeatbennelong.com.au or www.sydneyoperahouse.com
Price: A\$80. Wine: A\$35.

Quay

Quay won the *Sydney Morning Herald*'s 'Restaurant of the Year' award for 2003. The restaurant, tastefully decorated in a sombre palette of pastels and greys, is famous for its world-beating views of both the Opera House and the Harbour Bridge – diners should try to reserve a table in the Tower section, which has 320° harbour views. *Quay* now has a menu to match, courtesy of new chef Peter Gilmore. Noted for their geometric presentation, Gilmore's offerings include mud crab stuffed zucchini flower and a *confit* of suckling pig with fungi and sea scallops. Patrons should be sure to leave room for dessert, as the five-textured Valrhona chocolate cake is heavenly.
Overseas Passenger Terminal, West Circular Quay
Tel: (02) 9251 5600. Fax: (02) 9251 5609.
E-mail: gm@quay.com.au
Website: www.quay.com.au
Price: A\$85. Wine: A\$60.

Tetsuya's

Tetsuya Wakuda's name was uttered with quiet awe in the suburb of Rozelle, where he first started serving his ten-course *dégustation* menu of Japanese/French delights. He has since relocated to the centre of town, to a new restaurant, done up in a modern Japanese style with dark wood and chocolate carpet, Arne Jacobsen chairs and glimpses of a Japanese garden. Bookings must be made well in advance but the wait to experience some of Sydney's most decadent gastronomy is well worth it. The set menu consists of small dishes, such as the now famous *confit* of Tasmanian ocean trout with ocean trout roe, as well as lobster ravioli with seaweed vinaigrette and shellfish essence or double-cooked deboned spatchcock with braised daikon (a variety of radish) and bread sauce. Closed Sunday and Monday.
529 Kent Street
Tel: (02) 9267 2900. Fax: (02) 9262 7099.
Price: A\$170. Wine: A\$35.

Business

Banc

One of Australia's most acclaimed restaurants, conveniently located in the heart of the financial district, *Banc*'s luxurious modern interior of marble columns and mirrors is home to the most discerning diners. The menu applies deft twists to traditional haute cuisine, such as baked truffles, fillet of beef Rossini and roast squab, while the cellar boasts over 900 wine labels.
53 Martin Place
Tel: (02) 9233 5300. Fax: (02) 9233 5311.
E-mail: mail@banc.com.au
Website: www.banc.citysearch.com.au
Price: A\$90. Wine: A\$50.

Longrain

A meal at *Longrain* is like a visit to the halls of Valhalla – its converted warehouse space has long wooden dining tables, polished floorboards and a Scandinavian ambience, despite the Thai menu. The food is fit for demigods – betel leaves topped with trout roe and crispy Barossa chicken are two of the highlights. Lunch is served Monday to Friday 1200–0230 but dinner bookings are not taken, so arrival before 1930 is advised. However, the bar is a stylish place in which to wait and the 'stick drinks' (fruit cocktails) go down a treat.
85 Commonwealth Street, Surry Hills
Tel: (02) 9280 2888. Fax: (02) 9280 2887.
E-mail: longrain@iprimus.com.au
Website: www.longrain.com.au
Price: A\$60. Wine: A\$35.

Salt

A fugue of white plastic and metal, *Salt* contrasts severity of design with sumptuousness of menu. Game, such as tempura of quail or roasted rabbit loin, and fish,

The Wentworth

Photo: Leonardo

Photo: Tourism New South Wales

Picnic in the Royal Botanic Gardens

such as baked snapper fillet, are specialities in a venue that has attracted gourmands and serious business folk – as well as the achingly hip – since opening in 1999.
229 Darlinghurst Road, Darlinghurst
Tel: (02) 9332 2566. Fax: (02) 9361 5559.
E-mail: info@saltrestaurant.com.au
Website: www.saltrestaurant.com.au
Price: A$85. Wine: A$40.

The Summit

The world's largest revolving restaurant, *The Summit* has 360-degree views of Sydney, retro-futuristic design based on the space station in the 1968 movie, *2001: A Space Odyssey*, and a good-times atmosphere. The menu is more than adequate, with such dishes as grilled snapper fillet, sirloin steak and Caesar salad. A seafood buffet is available for Sunday lunch, costing A$53.
Level 47, Australia Square, 264 George Street
Tel: (02) 9247 9777. Fax: (02) 9251 2539.
E-mail: summit-rec@accor-hotels.com
Website: www.summitrestaurant.com.au
Price: A$70. Wine: A$30.

Sushi e

Do not be fooled into believing the ubiquitous conveyor belt sushi bars are all that Sydney has to offer in the raw fish department. Part of the Establishment complex (see *Bars*), *Sushi e* is a world-class sushi bar ideal for both a quick business lunch or a protracted gourmet evening. The décor is contemporary chic, with a bright, white interior including such touches as marble-top counters and bubble chairs. The chef's speciality is 'Highly Evolved Sashimi' – kingfish, snapper, squid and other local delights served in white soy or citrus sauces. A rich Balmain bug (crayfish) tempura is another highlight.
Level 4, 252 George Street
Tel: (02) 9240 3041. Fax: (02) 9240 3001.
Website: www.merivale.com
Price: A$75. Wine: A$38.

Trendy

Bill's

There's no better start to a Sydney day than a *Bill's* breakfast – ricotta hotcakes with honeycomb butter, famously creamy scrambled eggs, towering muffins and fresh fruit platters. An enormous communal table is covered with magazines and, thanks to recent renovations, there are enough extra tables for everyone. Lunch is also available, with items ranging from a spicy squid salad to a fillet steak sandwich. No dinner. Closed Sunday.
433 Liverpool Street, Darlinghurst
Tel: (02) 9360 9631. Fax: (02) 9360 7302.
E-mail: bills@billsfood.com.au
Price: A$25. Wine: BYO (free corkage).

Icebergs Dining Room & Bar

Icebergs caused a sensation when it opened in Bondi in late 2002. Built on top of the old Bondi Icebergs swimming club, the venue raised the bar on drinking and dining in the beachside suburb. Offerings include neo-Mediterranean dishes, such as the signature warm salad of King Island crayfish with kipfler potatoes and fresh peas. Icebergs is also a feast for the eye, from the waiters in their deliberately crumpled jackets to the jaw-dropping views straight across the famous beach and out over the Pacific. The restaurant was designed by renowned Australian architect Carl Pickering and features blue banquette seating, polished aluminium screens and a glass wall on the ocean side.
1 Notts Street, Bondi
Tel: (02) 9357 9000. Fax: (02) 9365 9099.
E-mail: idrb@idrb.com
Website: www.idrb.com
Price: A$75. Wine: A$30.

Mezzaluna

When the stars come to town, they head straight for this lively Italian restaurant with its famous view of the Sydney skyline. Sunset is the best time to enjoy a meal or cocktails on the large balcony – covered by tall awnings and heated in winter. Dining here is never less than an occasion, with dishes such as *carpaccio* of venison, *rotolo* of pasta, smoked salmon, mascarpone and salsa verde, as well as double-baked blue swimmer crab with scallop soufflé. All those LA types must have taught them something, as *Mezzaluna* has a separate vegetarian menu.
123 Victoria Street, Potts Point
Tel: (02) 9357 1988. Fax: (02) 9357 2615.
E-mail: mezzaluna@mezzaluna.com.au
Website: www.mezzaluna.com.au
Price: A$70. Wine: A$40.

MG Garage Restaurant

If an MG convertible symbolises the good life, then it makes perfect sense to see several of them parked among the tables and chairs of one of Sydney's most acclaimed restaurants. The plush leather, steel and wood decor is inspired by the automobile, while the menu takes classic French ideas and lightens and

diversifies them, to create dishes such as red mullet with cous cous and a vinaigrette of burnt sugar orange. Despite the high-concept trappings, the place is refreshingly unpretentious. Closed Sunday.
490 Crown Street, Surry Hills
Tel: (02) 9360 7007. Fax: (02) 9360 7005.
E-mail: cnelson@mggaragesydney.com.au
Website: www.mggaragesydney.com.au
Price: A$85. Wine: A$38.

XO

Chef Neil Perry is renowned for simple but perfectly executed Asian cuisine and his latest, moderately priced venture, *XO*, is no exception. The fried salt squid is crunchy and spicy, the duck in tamarind sauce tender and sweet and the combination omelette falls open to reveal crisp sprouts and fresh prawns. The dining room is spread over two floors, with contemporary design and great views. No bookings are taken, except for groups of over six, however, the stylish upstairs bar serves a mean Beetroot Martini (a meal in itself) and smiling staff will look after patrons until a table is free. And if all that was not tempting enough, the city view is sensational.
155 Victoria Street, Potts Point
Tel: (02) 9331 8881. Fax: (02) 9331 8882.
E-mail: xo@rockpool.com
Website: www.rockpool.com
Price: A$50. Wine: A$25.

Budget

Arthur's Pizza

Nothing satiates the hunger after a day's shopping in the chi-chi boutiques of Paddington like a big traditional pizza or pasta at *Arthur's Pizza*. All the classics are served here, along with unusual combinations such as duck sausage with provolone and potato. If the place is full – and it often is – staff are prepared to come and fetch patrons from the pub next door when a table becomes free. Jim Jarmusch film posters fittingly adorn a restaurant that is dark but cheery.
260 Oxford Street, Paddington
Tel: (02) 9360 5257.
Price: A$32. Wine: BYO (corkage A$1.50 per person).

BBQ King

Peking duck hangs in the window and it is Peking duck that attracts the crowds to the authentic if slightly tatty *BBQ King* on the northeastern border of Chinatown. Open until 0200, the menu includes a superb suckling pig and plenty of out-there Chinese delicacies. Frills are not to be expected, although a great meal can.
18–20 Goulburn Street
Tel: (02) 9267 2586. Fax: (02) 9267 2001.
Price: A$30. Bottle of beer: A$6.

Bill & Toni's

The word 'institution' doesn't really cut it for this cheery East Sydney trattoria that has been offering pasta, schnitzel, meatballs and not a whole lot else for a quarter of a century. Big baskets of bread and orange cordial are free, while coffee in the downstairs café is probably the best and most potent in Sydney.
74 Stanley Street, East Sydney
Tel: (02) 9360 4702.
Price: A$22. Wine: BYO (free corkage).

Harry's Cafe de Wheels

Not a restaurant but a waterfront meat pie stand, *Harry's* has been serving the Aussie staple of pies with mash and

gravy to sailors, hoodlums and late-night party casualties since 1945. Consequently, it has become a tourist attraction, decorated with photographs of famous visitors – including, oddly enough, Colonel Sanders. And the pies? Bloody good tucker, mate. *Harry's* is open until 0400 Friday and Saturday.
Cowper Wharf Road, Woolloomooloo
Tel: (02) 9357 3074.
Website: www.harryscafedewheels.com.au
Price: A$4 (per pie). Wine: Unlicensed.

Wok Station

Deliciously peanutty *Pad Thai* noodles are an addictive Sydney treat but not every outlet gets the balance of sweet and tangy just right. *Wok Station's* A$9 *Pad Thai* is always spot on, so it is a good thing that there are also *Wok Station* outlets in Glebe, Pyrmont, Darlinghurst and Leichhardt. For cheap, fresh and delicious Thai food in respectable surrounds, *Wok Station* is the best option.
230 William Street, Kings Cross
Tel: (02) 9326 9343.
Price: A$20. Wine: BYO (corkage A$1 per person).

Personal Recommendations

Bayswater Brasserie

The reliable choice for a civilised lunch, stylish dinner or a few friendly beers, *Bayswater Brasserie* serves modern Mediterranean-style fare – including roast fig and *prosciutto* tartlet, braised lamb shanks, and pan-fried sardine fillets – in an elegant home-style venue. Features include a leafy outdoor dining area, a new oyster bar and cocktail bar.
32 Bayswater Road, Kings Cross
Tel: (02) 9357 2177. Fax: (02) 9358 1213.
E-mail: brasserie@ozemail.com.au
Website: www.bayswaterbrasserie.com.au
Price: A$50. Wine: A$25.

Chinta Ria The Temple Of Love

A gigantic Buddha forms the centrepiece to this large-scale Malaysian eating experience in Cockle Bay Wharf. A shrine to good, inexpensive *laksa* (a spicy sour soup) and noodles, the restaurant serves them up in a carnival atmosphere of chattering diners and steaming woks.
Level 2, 201 Sussex Street, Cockle Bay
Tel: (02) 9264 3211. Fax: (02) 9264 1411.
Website: www.cocklebaywharf.com/chinta.html
Price: A$30. Wine: A$23.50.

Kam Fook

Patrons hoping to sample Sydney's best *yám cha* (lunch) had better arrive before 1000 on weekends or face a 90-minute wait. Luckily, getting a table at dinner time is less of a struggle, although this 800-seater always seems as crowded with people as its enormous tanks are with mud crabs and barramundi. An acclaimed speciality is the deep fried duck, with everything served at a Hong Kong pace.
Level 3, Market City, 9–13 Hay Street
Tel: (02) 9211 8988. Fax: (02) 9211 8882.
Price: A$25. Wine: A$20.

Oh! Calcutta!

Despite the vaudevillian name, *Oh! Calcutta!* has won the *Sydney Morning Herald's* 'Best Indian Restaurant' award, eight years in a row. Why? A captivating menu of unusual dishes from North India, Afghanistan, Pakistan and northwestern China; the best local

produce and exotic meats from camel and goat to kangaroo and crab; stylish mosque-meets-minimalism design; and a charming host.
251 Victoria Street, Darlinghurst
Tel: (02) 9360 3650. Fax: (02) 9331 3701.
Website: www.ohcalcutta.com.au
Price: A$55. Wine: A$33.

Thai Pothong

King Street, Newtown seems to have more Thai restaurants than Bangkok but *Thai Pothong* is the biggest and the best for value. Standards, such as chicken cashew nut and *tom yung* soup, are as good as they come, the service is swift and attentive and the restaurant is filled with the constant buzz of people who know they are eating well at a very reasonable price. The restaurant has a graceful East Asian style, with soft lighting complementing a collection of Thai antiques, pretty parasols and flower arrangements.
294–298 King Street, Newtown
Tel: (02) 9550 6277. Fax: (02) 9519 8050.
Website: www.thaipothong.com.au
Price: A$35. Wine: A$20.

ENTERTAINMENT

Nightlife

Oxford Street, the heart of Sydney's gay area, buzzes with cafés and clubs – gay, straight and mixed – while the established red-light district of Kings Cross continues to cater for the seedier side of life. The Rocks, with its wharves and warehouses, was the original drinking heart of the city and in the early 20th century, the rowdy scene of the ritual 'six o'clock swill', when workers would drink as much as possible before the pubs closed at 1800. Today, the period pubs have been cleaned up for the huge tourist clientele. Drinks at the harbour-side terrace

across the bay, at Bennelong Point, under the curves of the Sydney Opera House, are expensive but worthwhile for the views across the harbour.

Sydney's night owls are predominantly designer-clad. Bouncers at the more fashionable clubs enforce strict dress codes and ID checks. The days of the six o'clock swill are long gone – Sydney's licensing hours are extremely relaxed. At any hour of the day or night, someone somewhere is serving drinks to anyone over the legal age of 18. The price of a drink is approximately A$4–9.

For up-to-date listings, free weekly guides *Drum Media* (website: www.drummedia.com.au), *3D World* (website: www.threedworld.com.au) and *Revolver* (website: www.revolvermag.com.au) are available at most city-centre bookshops and record stores, as is the gay and lesbian *Sydney Star Observer* (website: www.ssonet.com.au). The *Sydney Morning Herald* (website: www.smh.com.au) also carries an entertainment section, 'Metro', in the Friday edition.

Bars

The *Establishment*, 252 George Street, lives up to its name as Sydney's de rigueur after-work drinking place. Chic and enormous, it incorporates the exclusive *Hemmesphere* cocktail lounge. *Middle Bar*, 383 Bourke Street, plays host to many beautiful young things. *East Village*, 234 Palmer Street, offers a sophisticated take on the classic Sydney pub, as does the beautiful Art Deco *Civic*, 388 Pitt Street. *ECQ*, 69 Macquarie Street, has stunning views of the Harbour Bridge – and equally as stunning prices. *The Colombian,* corner of Oxford Street and Crown Street, offers the best of both worlds; straight upstairs and gay downstairs. The *Stonewall*, 175 Oxford Street, is another good place to start a gay night out in Sydney – there are DJs, drag shows and friendly faces galore. The *Darlo Bar*, 306 Liverpool Street, the *Green Park Hotel*, 360 Victoria Street, and the *Bank Hotel*, 324 King Street, are where the younger inner-city crowd converge for pool and beer.

Sydney Harbour Bridge and The Rocks

Casinos

Star City Casino, 80 Pyrmont Street, is a A$60-million casino, theatre, restaurant and hotel complex on the site of a former wharf. Dress code is smart-casual and the gaming section is restricted to persons who are 18 years and over. A passport or other proof of age is required.

Clubs

Sydney takes clubbing very seriously. It is always safer to dress up rather than down and be prepared to queue. *Home*, Cockle Bay Wharf, has four different sections featuring funk, techno, two-step and disco. *Tank*, 3 Bridge Lane, is part of the *Establishment* complex, 252 George Street (see above). *The Chinese Laundry*, 1 Slip Street, combines a blistering sound system with mock East Asian decor. Sydney's well-connected society clubbers go to *Cave*, Pirrama Road, while the old stand-by, *Q Bar*, 44 Oxford Street, is a reliable choice for mid-week clubbing. Other notable venues include *Soho*, 171 Victoria Street, *Sugareef*, 20 Bayswater Road, and *Gas*, 467 Pitt Street. The gay dance scene revolves around *Arq*, 16 Flinders Street.

Comedy

Open from Tuesday to Saturday, Sydney's premier venue showcasing local, national and international stand-up talent is *The Comedy Store*, Fox Studios, Lang Road. Monday night is comedy night at the *Fringe Bar*, Unicorn Hotel, 106 Oxford Street. *The Laugh Garage*, located in the Agincourt Hotel, corner of George Street and Harris Street, is open from Thursday to Saturday.

Live Music

The *Hopetoun Hotel*, 416 Bourke Street, and the *Annandale Hotel*, 17 Parramatta Road, are the best centrally located venues for up-and-coming bands, while leading Australian and international acts perform at the *Sydney Entertainment Centre*, Harbour Street, the *Metro*, 624 George Street, and the *Enmore Theatre*, 130 Enmore Road. Jazz fans can find world-class performers at the *Basement*, 29 Reiby Place, and the *Side-On Cafe*, 83 Parramatta Road, Annandale.

Sport

Sydney's acres of coastline and parkland make it a dream destination for sports enthusiasts and lovers of the great outdoors. During the summer, *Bondi* shows off the bodies beautiful of surfers, rollerbladers and sunbathers. The region boasts some of the world's top surfing conditions and the best beaches for beginners are *Manly*, *Curl Curl*, *Freshwater* or *North Bondi*. Surf aficionados in search of bigger waves should head for the beaches of *North Narrabeen*, *South Maroubra*, *Newport*, *South Bondi* and *Queenscliff*.
Waves aside, the ocean pools offer swimmers a spectacular alternative to chlorinated lanes. Scuba divers are also well served, with a number of local marine parks. For the international yachting set, Sydney Harbour is the starting point for one of the biggest fixtures of the year, the 2000km (1240-mile) Sydney to Hobart race.
Australians adore cricket and Sydney is no exception. The cricket season (October to March) includes Test and World Series Cup matches at the *Sydney Cricket Ground*, Driver Avenue (tel: (02) 9360 6601). During the rugby and football season (March to September) soccer games, rugby league and rugby union matches are held at the *Aussie Stadium*, Moore Park (tel: (02) 9360 6601). Sydney's Aussie Rules football team, the

Sydney Swans (website: www.sydneyswans.com.au), plays at the Sydney Cricket Ground and enjoys considerable support, although the team tends to trail at the bottom end of the AFL ladder.
Tickets to sporting events are available from *Ticketek* (tel: (02) 9266 4800; website: www.ticketek.com).

Bush-walking

The national parks in and around Sydney offer some spectacular bush-walks. Routes and information can be obtained from *Sydney Harbour Parks* (tel: (02) 9247 8861) or the *National Parks and Wildlife Service* (tel: (02) 9585 6444).

Fitness Centres

Body-conscious Sydney has a proliferation of gyms, including *City Gym*, 107 Crown Street (tel: (02) 9360 6247), *Gold's Gym*, 23 Pelican Street (tel: (02) 9264 4496), and *Bayswater Fitness*, 33 Bayswater Road, Kings Cross (tel: (02) 9356 2555). Single entry at these centres costs A$13.50, A$20 and A$15 respectively.

Golf

The Lakes Golf Club, corner of King Street and Vernon Avenue, Mascot (tel: (02) 9669 1311), is among Sydney's most exclusive golf courses. Non-members are welcome on Monday and Thursday. Other clubs include *Marrickville Golf Club*, Wharf Street (tel: (02) 9558 1876), and *St Michael's Golf Course*, Jennifer Street, Little Bay (tel: (02) 9311 0621). Both these clubs are open to the public on selected days and times, including daily afternoon public play. Green fees for 18 holes start at approximately A$20 and can rise to over A$100 at private clubs.

Rollerblading

Rollerbladers are part of the scenery in Sydney, especially at *Bondi Beach* and *Centennial Park*. Blades and protective clothing can be hired at *Bondi Boards & Blades*, 230 Oxford Street, Bondi Junction (tel: (02) 9369 2212; website: www.bondiboardsandblades .com.au), and *Centennial Park Cycles*, 50 Clovelly Road (tel: (02) 9398 5027).

Scuba Diving

Sydney has good visibility and some colourful local marine parks, which are ideal for snorkelling and scuba diving. Operators include *Pro Dive Travel*, 478 George Street (tel: (02) 9281 5066), and *Sydney Dive Academy*, 462 Bunnerong Road, Matraville (tel: (02) 9311 0708).

Squash

The *Surry Hills Squash Centre*, 525 Crown Street (tel: (02) 9699 3233), is centrally located.

Surfing

Outfits such as *Let's Go Surfing*, 128 Ramsgate Avenue, North Bondi (tel: (02) 9365 1800), and *Sydney Safe Surf*, The Pavilion, Marine Parade, Maroubra (tel: (02) 9311 2834), provide courses for beginners.

Swimming

The beaches at Coogee, Avalon, Clovelly and Austinmer have ocean pools. The site of many dramatic Olympic moments, the *Sydney International Aquatic Centre*, Homebush Bay (tel: (02) 9752 3666) is open for public bathing. The underground *Cook & Phillip Park Aquatic Centre*, 4 College Street (tel: (02) 9326 0444), features Olympic pool, wave pool and hydrotherapy bath, right in the city centre.

Tennis

There are plenty of tennis courts all over Sydney. Central ones include *North Sydney Tennis Centre*, 1a Little Alfred Street (tel: (02) 9371 9952), *Rushcutters Bay Tennis Centre*, 7 Waratah Street (tel: (02) 9357 1675), and *Jensen's Tennis Centre*, Prince Alfred Park, Surry Hills (tel: (02) 9698 9451).

Windsurfing

Balmoral Windsurfing, Sailing and Kayaking School is located at 2 The Esplanade (tel: (02) 9960 5344).

Yachting

Every weekend, Sydney Harbour is dotted with the sails of hundreds of yachts. *Sydney Harbour Escapes* (tel: (02) 9328 4748) provides further information for those wishing to join in.

Shopping

The city's flagship department stores are *David Jones*, 86–108 Castlereagh Street, gentlemen's emporium *Gowing Brothers*, corner of Market Street and George Street, which dates back to 1868, and the down-to-earth *Grace Bros*, 436 George Street.
Castlereagh Street is considered Sydney's designer row, although this does not take account of prestige stores in *Chifley Plaza*, 2 Chifley Square, and the *MLC Centre*, 19–29 Martin Place. There are shopping malls galore and two splendid Victorian arcades at the *Strand*, 412–414 George Street, and the palatial *Queen Victoria Building*, 455 George Street, also known as QVB. *Market City*, Thomas Street, Haymarket, has factory outlets and traditional markets.
An impressive homegrown stable of fashion designers has established Sydney as a regional fashion capital, reaching both the Asian and the US markets. Among the most popular designers are Paris Fashion Week regular *Collette Dinnigan*, 33 William Street, Paddington, and *Lisa Ho*, 2a–6a Queen Street.
For gifts with a local flavour, the most exquisite gourmet foods can be found at *Simon Johnson Quality*

Sailing at Balmoral Beach

Foods, 55 Queen Street, Woolahra, Aboriginal artefacts at *Coo-ee Aboriginal Art*, 31 Lamrock Avenue, Bondi Beach, and the trendiest of board gear at *Surfection*, 205 Oxford Street.

It is worth exploring the length of Oxford Street, just to experience the variety of shopping genres, from the camp end at Darlinghurst, past the small fashion stores of Paddington and on into Woollahra and the top-of-the-range antique shops in and around Queen Street. Darling Harbour, Chinatown and The Rocks historic district are teeming with souvenir and craft shops. The Rocks is also the place for shoppers to pick up gems from the major Australian opal fields. *The Rocks Opal Mine*, 13 Clocktower Square, and *Flame Opals*, 119 George Street, both have good selections of stones, as does the downtown *Gemstone Boutique*, 388 George Street. For pearls from the northwest coast of Australia, *Paspaley Pearls*, 142 King Street, has some world-class examples.

There are markets at Balmain, Bondi Beach and The Rocks but perhaps the one with the strongest local flavour is the *Sydney Fish Market*, open daily 0700–1600, in Pyrmont, offering over 100 species of the freshest seafood, sushi bars and fish cafés.

Shop opening hours are generally Monday–Saturday 0900–1800, with late-night shopping until 2100 on Thursday. Increasingly, shops are opening on Sunday. There is a 10% Goods and Services Tax (GST), which is included on the price tags. There are several duty-free shops in the city centre, as well as at the airport. Shoppers must show their passport and onward ticket on collection of goods.

Culture

Sydney's cultural life is uniquely diverse, from high classical at the *Sydney Opera House* to the most cutting-edge contemporary and experimental performance art. The Opera House is the major focus of attention for classical music, opera, theatre and dance.

An important part of Sydney's cultural life is the contribution made by Aboriginal and Torres Strait islanders. The *Survival Festival*, held every year on Australia Day, 26 January, is the Aboriginal alternative to more traditional national celebrations, showcasing Aboriginal and Torres Strait Islander culture with music, dance, art and food. The *Bangarra Dance Theatre* brings that culture right up to date with performances that integrate traditional elements into modern dance.

Cultural productions and events are listed in 'Metro', the Friday edition entertainment section of the *Sydney Morning Herald* (website: www.smh.com.au). Further listings and information are provided in the free booklet, *Sydney Scope* (website: www.sydneyscope.com.au) and online (website: www.sydney.citysearch.com.au).

Tickets are available for purchase from *Ticketek* (tel: (02) 9266 4800; website: www.ticketek.com) and *Ticketmaster7* (tel: 136 100, Australia only; website: www.ticketmaster7.com). The *Halftix* booth, 91 York Street (tel: (02) 9279 0855; website: www.halftix.com.au), offers reduced price tickets on the day of the show.

Music

The *Sydney Opera House*, Bennelong Point (tel: (02) 9250 7111; website: www.soh.nsw.gov.au), is the premier performance venue for classical music,

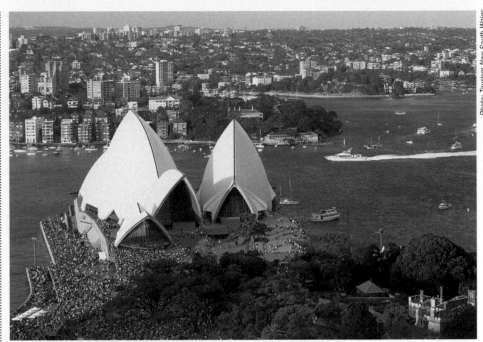
Sydney Festival, Sydney Opera House

although the acoustics in its Concert Hall are notoriously substandard. The *Sydney Symphony* (tel: (02) 9334 4600; website: www.symphony.org.au) has even threatened to boycott it. The *Sydney Philharmonia Choirs* (tel: (02) 9251 2024; website: www.sydneyphilharmonia.com.au), *Opera Australia* (tel: (02) 9319 1088; website: www.opera-australia.org.au) and the *Australian Chamber Orchestra* (tel: (02) 8274 3800; website: www.aco.com.au) still hold most of their performances at the Opera House. The *Eugene Goossens Hall*, ABC Ultimo Centre, Harris Street (tel: (02) 9333 1500), tends to be used for smaller performances, as does *Sydney Town Hall*, 483 George Street (tel: (02) 9265 9189; website: www.cityofsydney.nsw.gov.au), and *City Recital Hall*, Angel Place (tel: (02) 8256 2222; website: www.cityrecitalhall.com). The *Conservatorium of Music*, Macquarie Street (tel: (02) 9351 1222; website: www.usyd.edu.au/su/conmusic), hosts symphony, wind and chamber concerts as well as jazz big bands.

Theatre

The *Sydney Theatre Company* (tel: (02) 9250 1777; website: www.sydneytheatre.com.au) is the city's stylish flagship theatre company. Performances take place at the *Wharf Theatres*, Pier 4, Hickson Road (tel: (02) 9250 1700), and the *Opera House*, Bennelong Point (tel: (02) 9250 7111; website: www.soh.nsw.gov.au). Acting luminaries, such as Geoffrey Rush and Cate Blanchett, have performed at the highly respected *Belvoir Street Theatre*, 25 Belvoir Street (tel: (02) 9699 3444; website: www.belvoir.com.au). *The Performance Space*, 199 Cleveland Street (tel: (02) 9698 7235; website: www.performancespace.com.au), and the *Seymour Theatre Centre*, Cleveland Street and City Road (tel: (02) 9351 7940; website: www.usyd.edu.au/news/seymour), are the main venues for more left-field contemporary performance.

Musicals are staged at the *Capitol Theatre*, 13 Campbell Street (tel: (02) 9320 5000), the *State Theatre*, 49 Market Street (tel: (02) 9373 6852; website: www.statetheatre.com.au), and the *Lyric Theatre*, Star City, Pirrama Road, Pyrmont (tel: (02) 9657 8500; website: www.lyrictheatre.com.au). Newer Australian playwrights stage their work at the

Stables Theatre, 10 Nimrod Street (tel: (02) 9250 7799). Sydney's longest established theatre is the *Ensemble*, 78 McDougall Street, Kirribilli (tel: (02) 9929 0644; website: www.ensemble.com.au).

Dance

The *Australian Ballet* (tel: (02) 9252 5500; website: www.australianballet.com.au) performs mainly traditional pieces during its summer and winter season at the *Sydney Opera House*, Bennelong Point (tel: (02) 9250 7111; website: www.soh.nsw.gov.au). Similarly, the *Sydney Dance Company* (tel: (02) 9221 4811; website: www.sydneydance.com.au), the city's leading contemporary dance group, performs at the Opera House for two seasons per year. The *Bangarra Dance Theatre*, Wharf 4/5 Hickson Road (tel: (02) 9251 5333; website: www.bangarra.com.au), performs a fusion of contemporary and traditional dance at various venues throughout the city. The company also tours extensively, both nationally and internationally.

Film

The city's central cinemas, situated near Town Hall, have all merged into the 17-screen *Village Greater Union Hoyts George Street*, 505 George Street (tel: (02) 9273 7431; website: www.hoyts.com.au). *Fox Studios Australia*, Lang Road, Moore Park (tel: (02) 9383 4333; website: www.foxstudios.com.au), is home to two cinema complexes – *Hoyts* (tel: (02) 9332 1300), which includes the luxury *La Premiere* cinema (tel: (02) 9266 4887), and the arthouse, *Cinema Paris* (tel: (02) 9332 1633). Other arthouse cinemas include the *Academy Twin*, 3a Oxford Street (tel: (02) 9361 4453; website: www.palace.net.au), home to the Gay & Lesbian Mardi Gras Film Festival (tel: (02) 9332 4938), the *Chauvel*, Paddington Town Hall (tel: (02) 9361 5398; website: www.chauvelcinema.com.au), and the Art Deco *Cremorne Hayden Orpheum*, 380 Military Road (tel: (02) 9908 4344; website: www.orpheum.com.au). First-run movies open on Thursday and discount night is on Tuesday.

The *Sydney Film Festival* (tel: (02) 9660 3844; website: www.sydneyfilmfestival.org) takes place every year in June, with most screenings in the magnificent marble auditorium of the State Theatre, 49 Market Street (tel: (02) 9373 6852; website: www.statetheatre.com.au).

Makers of short films enter *Tropfest* (tel: (02) 9368 0434; website: www.tropfest.com.au) every February/March, with finalists shown on open-air screens set up in the Domain – a large open area set on the fringe of the city.

Notable films set or partially set in Sydney include Peter Weir's *The Last Wave* (1977), P J Hogan's *Muriel's Wedding* (1993), Stephan Elliot's *The Adventures of Priscilla, Queen of the Desert* (1993), John Woo's *Mission: Impossible 2* (2000) and Ray Lawrence's *Lantana* (2001).

Cultural Events

Sydney Festival, held in January, features open-air concerts and theatre from around the world, alongside the best of Sydney's performers. *Sydney Biennale*, held from May to July of even-numbered years, is an international art festival held in conjunction with the Museum of Contemporary Art and the Art Gallery of New South Wales. *Gay & Lesbian Mardi Gras* is a month-long festival in February/March, which is famous for its colourful parade along Oxford Street, attracting over half a million spectators every year. *Royal Easter Show* is a traditional 12-day show that brings farm life to the city during April. The *Festival of the Winds* is Australia's largest kite-flying competition, held annually in September at Bondi Beach. *Manly Jazz Festival*, held on the Labour Day long weekend in October, is Australia's largest, longest and best-known jazz festival, featuring traditional, big band, fusion, bop and contemporary jazz. *Sleaze Ball*, a fundraiser for the Mardi Gras Festival, is also held on the Labour Day long weekend in October. Up to 16,000 gay and lesbian revellers dress to a theme and party all night at Fox Studios.

Literary Notes

'One of the finest, most beautiful, vast and safe bays the sun had ever shone upon,' wrote inveterate traveller Joseph Conrad in 1906. Sydney Harbour continues to inspire eulogies from writers, including Miles Franklin who, in 1946, wrote: 'A month would not be long enough to imbibe such beauty.' More recently, Clive James, the writer, satirist, broadcaster and critic, was rather more blunt: 'Sydney is like Venice without the architecture but with more sea.'

SPECIAL EVENTS

Sydney Festival, art, open-air concerts and theatre (website: www.sydneyfestival.com.au), Jan, various venues

Sydney Gay & Lesbian Mardi Gras, the world's largest gay festival, climaxing in costume parade and all-night party (website: www.mardigras.org.au), Feb–early Mar, various venues, parade on Oxford Street

Tropfest, short film festival (website: www.tropfest.com), Feb/Mar, the Domain

Harvest Festival, wine, food and cultural festival (website: www.winecountry.com.au), Mar–Apr, Rothbury Estate, Hunter Valley

Royal Easter Show, traditional farm show (website: www.eastershow.com.au), mid-Apr, Sydney Olympic Park

Mercedes Australian Fashion Week Spring/Summer, runway shows by leading Australian designers featuring international guests (website: www.mafw.com.au), May, Fox Studios

Sydney Writers' Festival, including panel discussions, lectures and readings by local and overseas authors (website: www.swf.org.au), late May, various venues

Sydney Biennale, international art festival, May–Jul of even-numbered years, various venues

Sydney Film Festival (website: www.sydneyfilmfestival.org), Jun, State Theatre

City To Surf, 14km (nine-mile) public marathon (website: www.smh.com.au/marketing/citytosurf), early Aug, from the corner of College Street and Park Street through the city to Bondi Beach

Festival of the Winds, kite flying festival (website: www.aks.org.au/fotw.html), Sep, Bondi Beach

Manly Jazz Festival (website: www.manly.nsw.gov.au/manlyjazz), early Oct, Manly

Sleaze Ball, gay and lesbian theme party (website: www.mardigras.org.au), Labour Day weekend, Oct, Fox Studios

Sculpture By The Sea, temporary art installed along the coastal walk (website: www.sculpturebythesea.com), early Nov, from Bondi to Tamarama

Mercedes Australian Fashion Week Autumn/Winter (website: www.mafw.com.au), Nov, Fox Studios

Sydney to Hobart Yacht Race, world-famous 2000km (1240-mile) yacht race from Sydney Harbour to Hobart, capital of Tasmania (website: www.rolexsydneyhobart.com), 26 Dec, Sydney Harbour

New Year's Eve Party, extravagant fireworks display, 31 Dec, Sydney Harbour

Sydney's literary luminaries include Peter Carey, who lived in the city before moving to New York, and set his Booker Prize-winning *Oscar and Lucinda* (1988) in 19th-century Sydney, where country girl Lucinda dreams of self-reliance and an industrial utopia. David Williamson, Australia's most successful playwright, calls Sydney home. His works include *Up For Grabs* (2000), recently performed on London's West End, starring Madonna, and *Don's Party* (1971). Williamson's *Emerald City* (1987) is a comedic hymn to Sydney's temptations.

An idiosyncratic streak led Sydney-born Thomas Keneally from the priesthood to the life of a full-time novelist. He published his first novel in 1964 and was awarded the Booker Prize for *Schindler's Ark* (1982).

In 1983, he was awarded the Order of Australia for his services to Australian literature.

Modern Sydney receives a sanction of sorts from one of its favourite sons, the art critic Robert Hughes, who wrote: 'The provinciality that seemed to characterise Australian society, and could be plainly seen in Sydney 25 years ago, is all but gone. To a striking degree, the city's habits have softened. Its harsh intolerant machismo ... has toned down. Sydney is no longer quite so keen on the 'ocker' (Pacific redneck) image of the Australian: beer gut, thongs, nasal foghorn voice and a truculent certainty that, short of Paradise itself, Australia is the only ticket and that the rest of the world only displays its inferiority by not necessarily wanting to come here.'

Photo: Tourism New South Wales

Sydney Gay & Lesbian Mardis Gras

TOKYO

Tokyo, symbol of the Japanese success story, is a sprawling megalopolis on the Pacific coast of Honshu, the largest island of the Japanese archipelago. In 1590, the city was founded as Edo, the capital of the *shoguns*, the succession of hereditary absolute rulers of Japan and commander of the Japanese army. Edo boasted its own vibrant culture, the celebrated 'floating world' of pleasure quarters, theatres and cherry blossoms, immortalised in the Japanese woodblock prints of the time. Following the fall of the shoguns in 1867 (and the restoration of the power of the Emperor), the city was renamed Tokyo, the Eastern Capital, heralding its rebirth as a dynamic modern city and the showpiece of a rapidly modernising country. Despite the catastrophic 1923 earthquake and near obliteration during World War II, Tokyo was able to rise from the ashes to host the 1964 Olympics and went on to preside over the Japanese economic miracle.

That this bewildering amalgamation of districts and neighbourhoods is able to function as a coherent whole is largely due to the extraordinarily efficient network of rail and underground lines that crisscross and encircle the city. These are Tokyo's arteries,

transporting legions of businesspeople, office workers and students from the suburbs and depositing them in vast stations. Two million people a day pass through Shinjuku Station alone. The towering business districts swarm with soberly dressed corporate warriors and demure young secretaries known as 'office flowers'. The architectural anarchy and sheer crush of humanity assaults the senses. Amid the frenzy of consumerism, brash electronics outlets are crammed next to refined upscale boutiques and hordes of giggling schoolgirls swoon over pop idols and the latest fashions in glitzy emporiums.

Tokyo enjoys a temperate climate, with warm although sometimes muggy summers and mild, dry winters. The balmy spring days of April to May are the best times to visit the city.

Downtown, old neighbourhoods cluster around antiquated shopping arcades and the clatter of the temple bell echoes across the rooftops. Here, the rhythms of the seasons are still observed. Tokyoites flock to ring in the New Year at the venerable Shinto shrines and springtime brings a flurry of flower-viewing parties and picnics under the cherry

blossoms. Rowdy, traditional festivals punctuate the humid summers and the spirit of the old Edo also survives in the neon-bathed entertainment districts: modern-day 'floating worlds' of karaoke and cinemas, shot bars and bathhouses. Traditional kabuki theatre thrives alongside opera, ballet and symphonic performances, and Tokyoites are passionate about sumo, baseball and now – in the wake of Japan's co-hosting of the 2002 World Cup – football. Another obsession, food, is well catered for in this city of 60,000 restaurants and the world's largest fish market. From bowls of steaming ramen noodles to delicate slices of sashimi, chefs compete to offer the freshest produce, and presentation is elevated to an art form.

The focus of Japan's highly centralised government, business and financial institutions, Tokyo has been hard hit by the country's continuing recession, bank collapses and financial scandals. Many certainties of the past appear to have been swept away, however, opinions differ widely as to the extent of the damage and what might lie ahead. Surprisingly, little of this trepidation will be evident to visitors, as – on the surface, at least – Tokyo and its people remain prosperous and forward-looking.

Nightview with Tokyo Tower

Photo: Japan National Tourist Organisation

TRAVEL

Getting There By Air

Narita Airport (NRT)

Tel: (0476) 322 802. Fax: (0476) 301 571.
Website: www.narita-airport.or.jp/airport_e
Narita Airport (also known as New Tokyo International Airport) is located 66km (41 miles) east of central Tokyo and is the main gateway to Japan, with 47 airlines operating out of its two terminals. The airport is for international flights only; all domestic flights (and *China Airlines* flights to Taiwan) use Haneda Airport (see below).

Major airlines: *JAL* (tel: (03) 5460 0511; website: www.jal.co.jp/en) and *ANA* (tel: (03) 5435 0333; website: http://svc.ana.co.jp/eng/index.html) are Japan's two main international airlines. Other major airlines include: *Air China, Air France, Air India, Alitalia, American Airlines, British Airways, Cathay Pacific, Garuda, Korean Air, KLM, Lufthansa, Malaysia Airlines, Northwest, Qantas, Singapore Airlines, Thai International, United Airlines* and *Virgin Atlantic*.

Airport facilities: These include bureaux de change, ATMs, travel agent, tourist information, numerous restaurants and souvenir shops (including duty-free shopping), left-luggage service, luggage delivery service, showers and day rooms, children's play room, clinic, post office and car hire from *Avis* and *Hertz*.

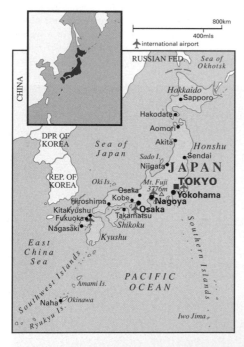

Business facilities: Copy and fax facilities are available at *TEI Lounge*, situated both in terminal one (tel: (0476) 329 450) and in terminal two (tel: (0476) 348 781). Internet access is available in both terminals (website: www.e-airport.jp/en/p_internet/index.html).
Arrival/departure tax: There is no arrival tax. The departure tax of ¥2040 is included in the airfare.
Transport to the city: Japan Railway's *Narita Express* (tel: (03) 3423 0111; website: www.jreast.co.jp/nex/index.htm) and Keisei Railway's *Skyliner* (tel: (0476) 328 505; website: www.keisei.co.jp/keisei/tetudou/accesse) provide fast, very frequent services to the city centre 0600–2200. In addition, both companies run cheaper regular

services. The journey time is 60–90 minutes and tickets cost ¥1000–3000, depending on the type of train and destination within Tokyo. *Airport Limousine* buses (tel: (03) 3665 7220; website: www.limousinebus.co.jp) run several times an hour 0700–2200, serving major hotels in central Tokyo, Haneda Airport and Yokohama. The journey time, depending on traffic and destination, is about 90 minutes and tickets cost approximately ¥3000. Taxis to the city centre are notoriously expensive, costing about ¥25,000. The journey time is about 90 minutes, depending on traffic.

Haneda Airport (HND)

Tel: (03) 5757 8111.
Haneda, Tokyo's domestic airport, is conveniently located 16km (ten miles) south of central Tokyo. Confusingly, Haneda continues to be officially known as Tokyo International Airport, despite the fact that all international flights, other than *China Airlines* flights to and from Taiwan and those carrying high-ranking official visitors from overseas, now use Narita Airport.

Major airlines: All major domestic airlines, including *JAL* (tel: (03) 5460 0522; website: www. jal.co.jp/en) and *ANA* (tel: (03) 3490 8800; website: http://svc.ana.co.jp/eng/index.html), operate from Haneda Airport.

Airport facilities: Facilities include ATMs, travel agent, restaurants and souvenir shops, left-luggage service, luggage delivery service, post office and car hire from *Nissan* and *Toyota*.

Business facilities: None.

Arrival/departure tax: There is no arrival or departure tax.

Transport to the city: The *Tokyo Monorail Co.* (website: www.tokyo-monorail.co.jp/english) connects the airport to Hamamatsu-cho Station on the JR Yamanote loop line, the city's major transport artery (journey time – 22 minutes). The monorail operates 0500–2400 and tickets cost ¥470. The *Keihin* railway (website: www.keikyu.co.jp/english/haneda/index.html) runs to Shinagawa Station (journey time – 19 minutes) and other stations in the centre of the city, operating daily 0530–2400. The fare is ¥400. *Airport Limousine* buses (tel: (03) 3665 7220; website: www. limousinebus.co.jp) run to major Tokyo railway stations. Tickets cost approximately ¥1000. Taxis to central Tokyo cost approximately ¥7000.

Approximate flight times to Tokyo: From London is 11 hours 40 minutes; from New York is 14 hours; from Los Angeles is 11 hours 40 minutes; from Toronto (via Chicago) is 14 hours 30 minutes and from Sydney is 9 hours 30 minutes.

Getting There By Water

Despite being a major port, few passenger services operate out of Tokyo. The *Tokyo Ferry Port* is located at Ariake, on Odaiba Island in Tokyo Bay. Facilities include a snack bar, souvenir shops and luggage lockers. Arrival and departure information is available from the *Ferry Service Centre* (tel: (03) 3501 0889; website: www.tptc.or.jp/eng/ferry.htm).

Ferry services: There are no international ferry services from Tokyo, however, a number of long-distance car and passenger ferries connect Tokyo to Hokkaido, Shikoku, Kyushu and Okinawa. There are services from Okinawa to Taiwan, from Osaka/Kobe to China, and from Fukuoka/Hakata and Shimonoseki to Korea.

Transport to the city: The *Yurikamome Monorail* (tel: (03) 3529 7221) runs from Ariake to Shimbashi Station on the JR Yamanote loop line (journey time – 25 minutes). Tickets cost ¥370.

Getting There By Rail

Japan's extensive *Japan Railways* (JR) rail network provides outstandingly efficient and punctual services and (other than at rush hour and on public holidays) is a pleasure to use. Trains in the Tokyo area and northern Japan are operated by *JR East* (tel: (03) 3423 0111; website: www.jreast.co.jp/e/index.html), while the *Shinkansen* bullet trains on the Tokaido line between Tokyo and Nagoya, Kyoto, Osaka and Fukuoka are operated by *JR Central* (tel: (03) 5818 3510).

Tokyo has several major train stations, with *Tokyo Station*, Marunouchi, Chiyoda-ku, being the city's central hub, while *Ikebukuro Station, Shibuya Station, Shinjuku Station* and *Ueno Station* serve the suburbs. In addition to the JR network, there are a number of private rail companies operating commuter trains to Tokyo's suburbs and an extensive and convenient network of underground lines (website: www.tokyometro.go.jp/e/index.html). All but the smallest stations have coin lockers and newspaper/snack kiosks.

Shinkansen bullet trains and selected express services offer both reserved and non-reserved seats. Some trains also offer first-class 'green car' seats. Reservations for Shinkansen bullet trains and long-distance express services on and around national holidays should be made well in advance – from a major station. Long-distance rail travel is expensive, however, the *Japan Railways Rail Pass* (website: www.japantravel.co.uk/jrp.htm) offers outstanding value for money for those planning to make extensive use of the rail network. It is important to note that the pass must be purchased in advance before entering Japan and is only available to non-resident tourists.

There is no national railways enquiries service and information on rail travel in Japan is provided by the individual stations and travel agents, which are equipped with the latest timetables.

Rail services: All Shinkansen bullet trains depart from and terminate at Tokyo Station, from where commuter and underground trains run to all areas of the city. Shinkansen bullet trains run to northern Japan, Niigata on the Japan Sea, Nagano in the central Alps, Nagoya, Kyoto, Osaka and Hiroshima, and Fukuoka on the southern island of Kyushu. Services run several times an hour. The journey time to Kyoto and Osaka is approximately three hours and to Fukuoka six hours.

Transport to the city: Tokyo Station is very centrally located in the Marunouchi/Ginza area, accessible by numerous train and underground lines including the JR Yamanote loop line. Ikebukuro Station, Shibuya Station, Shinjuku Station and Ueno Station are also all on the JR Yamanote loop line.

Getting There By Road

Heavy traffic congestion tends to make travelling by car in Japan's urban areas a slow and frustrating experience. Fortunately, excellent public transport makes driving in and between cities unnecessary. Hiring a car can, however, be an excellent way for visitors to explore the more remote country areas. Driving in Japan is not as daunting as might be expected – drivers are generally disciplined and courteous and major signs are in both Japanese and English. Expressways, which are all named (for example, The Tokaido Expressway), are toll roads that link the main cities; tolls are expensive at approximately ¥40 per kilometre. Other main roads are numbered (for example, Route 24).

Traffic drives on the left and the wearing of seatbelts is compulsory. The legal driving age in Japan is 18 years for a car and 16 years for a motorbike. Both a national driving licence and an International Driving Permit are required, as is basic travel insurance. Parking can be difficult to find and is a major expense in cities and larger towns. The speed limit outside built-up areas is 50kph (31mph) and 80kph (50mph) on expressways. In built-up areas, the speed limit is usually 40kph (25mph). Driving after having consumed any amount of alcohol is illegal and penalties are severe.

The *Japan Automobile Federation, JAF* (tel: (03) 3436 2811; website: www.jaf.or.jp/e/index_e.htm), provides an English-language 'Rules of the Road' booklet and *JAF Road Service* offers 24-hour breakdown assistance for both members and non-members. In the case of an accident, the police must be informed (tel: 110).

Emergency breakdown service: *JAF* 8139.

Routes to the city: Tokyo is linked by the Tomei–Meishin expressway to Kobe (via Nagoya, Kyoto and Osaka), by the Tohoku expressway to Sendai and northern Japan, and by the Chuo expressway to Nagano and Nagoya.

Approximate driving times to Tokyo: From Nagano – 3 hours 30 minutes; Sendai – 4 hours; Nagoya – 5 hours; Osaka – 7 hours. Note that actual driving times can vary widely depending on traffic conditions.

Coach services: A number of companies together offer a comprehensive network of long-distance bus services. Comfortable overnight coaches with reclining seats serve destinations such as Kyoto, Osaka and the cities of northern Honshu. Coaches leave from terminals outside *Shinjuku Station*, in Shinjuku, and *Tokyo Station*, Marunouchi, Chiyoda-ku. Bookings can be made at *Japan Travel Bureau, JTB* (tel: (03) 5620 9500; fax: (03) 5620 9502; website: www.jtb.co.jp/eng), which has offices all over the city or at large railway stations.

Getting Around

Public Transport

Tokyo has one of the most sophisticated and efficient public transport systems in the world – a combination of an extensive **train** network operated by a number

CITY STATISTICS

Location: Kanto region, eastern Japan.
Country dialling code: 81.
Population: 210,000 (city); 12,170,000 (metropolitan area).
Ethnic mix: 97.5% Japanese, 2.5% other.
Religion: 99% Shinto/Buddhist, 1% Christian.
Time zone: GMT + 9 (GMT + 8 from last Sunday in March to Saturday before last Sunday in October).
Electricity: 100 volts AC, 50/60Hz; flat two-pin American-style plugs are standard.
Average January temp: 4°C (39°F).
Average July temp: 25°C (77°F).
Annual rainfall: 1563mm (62 inches).

of private companies, 12 **underground** lines, **bus** services and several **monorails**. However, the service does not operate 24 hours. Nevertheless, there are many 24-hour pubs and cafés in the city and waiting for the trains to start running in the early morning is a long-established tradition among the revellers wishing to avoid ruinously expensive night-time taxi fares. The *Tokyo Tourist Information Office* (tel: (03) 3201 3331) can provide detailed service and timetable information for all the different service providers.

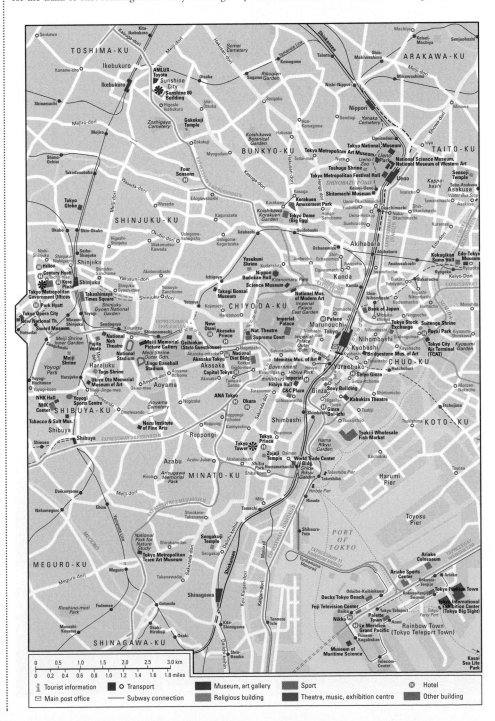

ℹ Tourist information	⬛○ Transport
✉ Main post office	Subway connection
⬛ Museum, art gallery	⬛ Sport
⬛ Religious building	⬛ Theatre, music, exhibition centre
	Ⓗ Hotel
	⬛ Other building

BUSINESS PROFILE

Presiding over the world's second largest economy, Tokyo is the governmental, financial and administrative centre of Japan. Quick to embrace modern developments and fashions, following the 1868 Meiji Restoration, Tokyo has continued to be at the forefront of trends and technology and remains the country's most cosmopolitan city. Japan's current drive towards economic reform and deregulation was initiated in Tokyo and it is here that these measures are having their most immediate effect. Unemployment in the city, at 4.8%, is well below the country's 5.3% average, while per capita income is over 40% higher than in other parts of the country. The service industry is the key employer in the city, followed by construction.

Most major Japanese companies have their head office in Tokyo and for foreign companies a presence in Japan generally means a presence in Tokyo. Companies in the city include *Barclays Bank, Bloomberg, British Aerospace, Citibank, Hewlett Packard, IBM, Kellogg's, Microsoft, Reuters* and *Unilever.* The main business districts are clustered around the National Diet and Ministry buildings to the south and east of the Imperial Palace. The Metropolitan Government is located in West Shinjuku, Tokyo's skyscraper office district.

In addition to the emphasis on the service industries and administration, Tokyo is Japan's publishing and printing centre. Meanwhile, the busy Tokyo Bay port handles a high proportion of the country's imports and exports. Recent deregulation has eased market entry for foreign companies and increasing numbers are now entering the Japanese market. The *Nippon Convention Centre, Makuhari Messe* (website: www.m-messe.co.jp/index_e.html), situated halfway between the city centre and Narita Airport, and the new *Tokyo Big Sight* complex (website: www.bigsight.or.jp/english/index.html), in Tokyo Bay, make Tokyo Japan's major trade fair venue.

After a slow start, the Internet is now increasingly important to Japanese businesses. Hotel rooms are usually equipped with a telephone line supporting Internet use and international public telephones are equipped with modem jacks.

The complexity of the network and the sheer size of some of the stations can be rather daunting. However, public transport is very safe, even after dark, and staff and passers-by are generally quick to help confused foreigners. Despite very frequent services, trains are uncomfortably crowded during rush hours (0730–0900 and 1700–1900); trains run from approximately 0500–2400/0100. Tickets are available for purchase from vending machines located inside stations; most journeys within the centre of the city cost less than ¥200.

The *Tokyo Combination Ticket* (*Tokyo Free Kippu*) is a travel **pass** valid for one day on all *Japan Rail,* underground and bus services within the city and costs ¥1580. The *One-Day Open Ticket* is valid on eight of the 12 underground lines and costs ¥710.

Taxis

Tokyo's taxis are numerous and can easily be hailed on the street or found at taxi ranks. It is also possible to reserve a taxi in advance, from one of the many companies, such as *Nihon Kotsu* (tel: (03) 3586 2151) and *Checker-Musen* (tel: (03) 3573 3751). Approximately ¥500 will be charged for this service. Fares vary slightly between taxi companies but are uniformly expensive at around ¥660 for the first two kilometres (one mile), then ¥80 every 274m (900ft) thereafter. There is a 30% supplement after 2300. Tipping is not customary and could offend.

Taxi drivers are very professional but rarely speak English, so it is advisable for tourists to have their destination written out in Japanese or to be able to point to it on a Japanese map. During rush hour, it is often quicker to take the train. Unoccupied taxis become scarce at around 0100, once the train services have finished. A peculiarity of all Japanese taxis is that the rear doors are operated automatically by the driver – visitors should not try to open or close the doors themselves.

Limousines

Hinomaru Limousine (tel: (03) 3505 1717; e-mail: mailmaster@hinomaru.co.jp; website: www.hinomaru. co.jp/indexe.html) offers a variety of luxury cars and can provide English-speaking drivers. Rates are from ¥6000 per hour, for a minimum of three hours.

Driving in the City

Tokyo's public transport network and taxis are excellent and driving in the city is therefore not advised. Traffic is heavy, navigation is greatly complicated by the fact that streets rarely have names and parking is expensive and difficult to find.

Car Hire

The biggest car hire company, with 150 branches in the Tokyo area, is Nippon Rent-A-Car, 5–5 Kamiyamacho, Shibuya-ku (tel: (03) 3485 7196). Other companies include Avis, 3–13–19 Ginza, Chuo-ku (tel: (03) 5550 1011; website: www.avis.com) and Hertz, 1–8–21 Shiba Koen, Minato-ku (tel: (03) 5401 7651; website: www.hertz.com).

Car hire in Japan costs from ¥5000 per day for the smallest class of car. Basic insurance is usually included in the price. Both a national driving licence and an International Driving Permit are required. Drivers must have held their licence for at least a year and the minimum age for hiring a car varies between 19 and 26, although is usually 21 years.

BUSINESS ETIQUETTE

While Tokyoites are generally the most cosmopolitan of Japanese, many will be reserved in the company of foreigners, particularly when called upon to speak English. Whereas almost everyone under 50 has some basic knowledge of English, very few are able to speak it fluently.

Misunderstandings can easily occur and the use of professional interpreters is advised. Foreigners are not expected to understand the complexities of Japanese etiquette and allowances will be made cheerfully. However, it is worth bearing in mind that shoes must be removed upon entering homes, as well as some offices and restaurants. Also, tips are never expected – the practice is considered vulgar, as is eating while walking. Blowing one's nose in public should also be avoided (it is, however, perfectly acceptable to sniff). Business clothes should be smart but conservative, with suits a must for both men and women. For men, grey and navy are the favoured colours – brown is looked upon with suspicion. It is probably impossible to be over dressed in Japan and business visitors can expect to be judged by their appearance. Business cards are an essential part of introductions – no one can expect to be taken seriously without them.

Corporate entertaining is done mainly in restaurants and *izakaya* beer halls. Invitations to the homes of business associates are unusual. Drinking (beer, whisky and sake) is very much part of the culture, as is smoking. Corporate entertaining remains largely male dominated and business travellers' partners are rarely invited to such events. For the most part, foreign buisnesswomen tend to be treated as 'honorary men' and it is not unknown for them to be taken to strip clubs. There are remarkably few Japanese businesswomen. Gifts are very important – they need not be particularly large or lavish – and are exchanged with great ceremony.

It is usual to refer to colleagues by their surnames and hierarchies should be respected. Business negotiations may require patience as directness is mistrusted and disliked, thus straight 'yes' or 'no' answers are generally avoided. Impatience is frowned upon and confrontation is out of the question, as it is considered a sign of gross weakness. Apologies and thanks are very important and should not be rushed. Normal business hours are Monday to Friday 0900–1700.

Photo: Japan National Tourist Organisation

Meiji Shrine

Bicycle & Scooter Hire

SCS, 2–1–16 Hakusan, Bunkyo-ku (tel: (03) 3827 5432), arranges scooter hire from ¥5000 per day. Bicycles can often be hired at suburban train stations for around ¥1000 per day. However, train stations in the central areas of the city do not offer this service.

SIGHTSEEING

Sightseeing Overview

Tokyo has few specific sights of renown. Instead, the main attraction is the opportunity to experience the life of a city that is on the surface so similar to Western cities, yet at the heart so profoundly unfamiliar. There is no main square, no central landmark or prime focus for tourists, as Tokyo is a collection of distinct areas, a conglomeration of mini-cities.

Ginza's classy boulevards and emporiums cater to the prominent and wealthy; Shinjuku, a hive of office workers by day, reinvents itself as a neon-lit entertainment wonderland at dusk; Shibuya and Harajuku offer trendy shopping, sports grounds and fine parks. Meanwhile, in the old neighbourhoods around Ueno and Asakusa, among the small houses and shops, potted plants and roadside shrines, life continues much as it has for decades. Ginza's glitzy department stores lie less than two kilometres (one mile) from the Pacific Ocean but, curiously, Tokyo gives little feeling of being on the coast. The rapidly developing waterfront rewards the visitor with a different perspective, while an evening stroll through the bustling entertainment areas reveals yet another side to this chameleon city.

Tokyo is many things – a maelstrom of rampant consumerism and oases of serenity, sensory overload and subtle beauty in detail. It is a city rushing into the future but haunted by the past. Most of all, Tokyo is a city that works.

Key Attractions

Sensoji Temple, Asakusa

Tokyo's most revered Buddhist temple and a site of pilgrimage and tourism for many centuries, *Sensoji Temple*, was founded in AD628, to enshrine a gold statuette of the *Kannon Bodhisattva* (the Goddess of Mercy). The temple and its five-storey pagoda are concrete reconstructions but the temple precincts are nevertheless always bustling with worshippers. Smoke from the huge incense burner in front of the temple is said to have healing powers. The impressive *Kaminarimon* (Thunder Gate) is famous for its enormous red paper lantern and fearsome guardian statues, while the temple approach is lined with shops selling traditional sweets and souvenirs. This area was the centre of *Shitamachi* (downtown) during the Edo period and the streets, shops and restaurants surrounding the temple still preserve something of the flavour of old Edo. The great *Sanja festival* takes place annually in Asakusa on the third weekend in May. Over 100 *mikoshi* (portable shrines) are paraded through the streets, accompanied by great celebration and huge crowds.

2–3–1 Asakusa, Taito-ku
Tel: (03) 3842 5566 (Asakusa Cultural and Sightseeing Centre).
Transport: Asakusa Station, eastern terminus of Ginza underground line.
Opening hours: Daily 0600–1700.
Admission: Free.

Ginza at night

Tokyo Tocho (Tokyo Metropolitan Government Offices)

Located in bustling Shinjuku, the *Tokyo Metropolitan Government Offices* are notable both for their extraordinary architecture and the splendid free observation decks on the 45th floor. Designed by Kenzo Tange, one of Japan's top architects, the monumental twin towers are said to be inspired by Notre Dame, although the imposing granite façade rather brings to mind scenes of *Batman*'s Gotham City. The observation decks – one in each tower and both providing a café – are reached by high-speed elevator and give spectacular views over the city. On particularly fine days, visitors can see Mount Fuji.

2–8–1 Nishi-Shinjuku, Shinjuku-ku
Tel: (03) 5320 7890.
Website: www.chijihonbu.metro.tokyo.jp/english/tmg/tmg.htm
Transport: Shinjuku Station, then a ten-minute walk following the underground passage leading west; or Tochomae Station on Toei Oedo underground line.
Opening hours: Tues–Sun 0930–2200.
Admission: Free.

Meiji-jingu (Meiji Shrine)

One of Japan's finest examples of Shinto architecture, the atmospheric *Meiji Shrine* is tucked away in the centre of a dark, cool forest – an unexpected oasis in the centre of the city. Passing through a vast wooden *torii* gate, the visitor follows the wide gravel path through the forest and into the shrine precincts. Completed in 1920, the shrine honours the memory of Emperor Meiji and Empress Shoken, under whose reign Japan rapidly modernised and was opened to the outside world. On weekends, it is often possible for visitors to see a traditional wedding procession and the precincts are one of the best places to witness the finery and festivities of New Year, Coming of Age Day (15 January) and the children's festival of *Shichi-Go-San* (weekends around 15 November). The *Gyoen Inner Garden*, situated in the shrine grounds, is well worth visiting during June, for the spectacular displays of irises.

1–1 Kamizono-cho, Yoyogi, Shibuya-ku
Tel: (03) 3320 5700.
Website: www.meijijingu.or.jp/english
Transport: Harajuku Station on JR Yamanote loop line or Meiji-jingumae Station on Chiyoda underground line.

Opening hours: Daily dawn to dusk (shrine); daily 0900–1630 (Jingu Naien Garden).
Admission: Free (shrine); ¥500 (Gyoen Inner Garden).

Kyoko Higashi Gyoen (Imperial Palace East Garden)

The *Imperial Palace East Garden*, on the site of the old Edo Castle of the shoguns, is the only part of the Imperial Palace that is regularly open to the public. Entered through the *Otemon Gate* – once the main entrance to the castle – it is a pleasant formal garden, surrounded by a section of the original moat and incorporating walls and foundations of the inner castle. Special features include a teahouse, pond and waterfall.

Otemachi, Chiyoda-ku
Tel: (03) 3213 1111.
Transport: Nijubashimae Station on Chiyoda underground line.
Opening hours: Tues–Thurs, Sat and Sun 0900–1600 (Mar–Oct); Tues–Thurs, Sat and Sun 0900–1530 (Nov–Feb).
Admission: Free.

Edo-Tokyo Hakubutsukan (Edo-Tokyo Museum)

Housed in what looks like a colossal white spaceship, the *Edo-Tokyo Museum* is a wonderful place for visitors to get a feel for Tokyo's history and culture, from the Edo of the shoguns up to the post-war reconstruction. There are full-size models of period buildings and the *Nihombashi* 'Bridge of Japan', as well as engaging displays presenting the daily life and customs of the city's past.

Photo: Japan National Tourist Organisation

Photo: Japan National Tourist Organisation

Tsukiji Wholesale Fish Market

1–4–1 Yokoami, Sumida-ku
Tel: (03) 3272 8600.
Website: www.edo-tokyo-museum.or.jp/museum-e/guide.htm
Transport: Ryogoku Station on JR Sobu line.
Opening hours: Tues, Wed, Sat and Sun 0930–1730, Thurs and Fri 0930–2000.
Admission: ¥600.

Ueno Koen (Ueno Park)

Once the site of temples and nobles' mansions, *Ueno Park* is now Tokyo's premier cherry blossom viewing spot and home to several important museums, as well as *Tokyo Zoo*. The park is dotted with historically interesting temples and shrines, including the Tokyo 'branch' of the *Nikko Toshogu Shrine*. The *Tokyo National Museum* houses treasures of Japanese art through the ages, while the *National Museum of Western Art* and the *Tokyo Metropolitan Art Museum* host important visiting exhibitions.
Taito-ku, Tokyo
Tel: (03) 3828 5644.
Transport: Ueno Station on JR Yamanote loop line.
Opening hours: Daily 0500–2300.
Admission: Free (park and shrines).
National Museum of Western Art
Tel: (03) 3828 5131.
Website: www.nmwa.go.jp
Opening hours: Tues–Thurs, Sat and Sun 0930–1700, Fri 0930–2000.
Admission: ¥420.
Tokyo Metropolitan Art Museum
Tel: (03) 3823 6921.
Website: www.tobikan.jp/eng
Opening hours: Tues–Sun 0900–1700.
Admission: Varies according to exhibition, with minor exhibitions from ¥500 to ¥1000 and high-profile exhibitions generally ¥1300.
Tokyo National Museum
Tel: (03) 3822 1111.
Website: www.tnm.jp
Opening hours: Tues–Sun 0930–1700.
Admission: ¥420.
Tokyo Zoo
Tel: (03) 3828 5171.
Website: www.tokyo-zoo.net (Japanese only).
Opening hours: Tues–Sun 0930–1630.
Admission: ¥600.

Tokyo Rainbow Town (Odaiba)

Rainbow Town, also known as *Odaiba*, on the group of artificial islands in Tokyo Bay, is billed as Tokyo's 'Waterfront Town for the 21st Century'. The focus of much futuristic development, the area incorporates prestigious business premises, parks, tourist attractions and spectacular modern architecture. The *Fuji Television Center* (designed by Kenzo Tange), the *Decks Tokyo Beach* shopping and restaurant complex and the *Tokyo International Exhibition Center* (*Tokyo Big Sight*) are fast becoming Tokyo's new landmarks, while the ship-shaped *Museum of Maritime Science* has excellent displays and hands-on exhibits. The driverless monorail ride to and from the island, which gives superb views of the area, is an attraction in itself.
Odaiba, Tokyo Bay
Transport: Yurikamome monorail line from Shimbashi Station.
Museum of Maritime Science
3–1 Higashi-yashio, Shinagawa-ku
Tel: (03) 5500 1111.
Website: www.funenokagakukan.or.jp (Japanese only).
Opening hours: Mon–Fri 1000–1700, Sat and Sun 1000–1800.
Admission: ¥1000.

Further Distractions

Tsukiji Ichiba (Tsukiji Wholesale Fish Market)

The world's biggest fish market, more than 2500 tons of fish pass through the *Tsukiji Wholesale Fish Market* every day, with deals totalling approximately £15 million. The first deliveries take place in the early hours but the main action starts with the tuna auction on the quay at the back of the market at around 0400. The bidding is fast and furious and makes a great show. Spectators are welcome but visitors should bear in mind that this is a business, not a tourist attraction. The auctions are over by 0530, when the focus shifts to the wholesale stalls – at least 1500 of them – offering every imaginable variety of fish and seafood to Tokyo's chefs and food retailers, who come to buy the daily supply. As the city awakes, restaurants situated around the market offer sushi breakfasts, rounded off by a glass of beer. Nowhere in Tokyo can fish be eaten fresher.

5–2–1 Tsukiji, Chuo-ku
Tel: (03) 3542 1111.
Website: www.tsukiji-market.or.jp/tukiji_e.htm
Transport: Tsukiji Station on Hibiya underground line.
Opening hours: Mon–Sat 0500–1000.
Admission: Free.

Tokyo Disneyland

Tokyo Disneyland is a faithful replica of the Californian original, complete with *Adventureland*, *Fantasyland* and *Tomorrowland*, as well as shows, parades and firework displays. The unique and brand-new *DisneySea Park*, set against the backdrop of Tokyo Bay, is proving enormously popular.
1–1 Maihama, Urayasu-shi
Tel: (047) 354 0001 *or* (045) 683 3333 (English-language information).
Website: www.tokyodisneyresort.co.jp/tdr/index_e.html
Transport: Maihama Station on JR Keiyo line from Tokyo Station.
Opening hours: Daily 0800/0900–2200 (varies seasonally).
Admission: ¥5500 (adult all-inclusive one-day 'passport' ticket).

Tours of the City

Walking Tours

The *Tokyo Tourist Information Office* (tel: (03) 3201 3331) provides a leaflet, 'Walking Tour Courses in Tokyo', outlining walking routes in several main areas of the city. *Asakusa's Goodwill Guide Club* gives a free one-hour English-language walking tour of this historical area every Sunday afternoon, setting off from its offices on 2–18–9 Kaminarimon, Taito-ku. Information is available from the *Asakusa Cultural and Sightseeing Centre* (tel: (03) 3842 5566).

Bus Tours

Hato Bus (tel: (03) 3435 6081; fax: (03) 3433 1972; website: www.hatobus.co.jp/english), *JTB Sunrise Tours* (tel: (03) 5796 5454; fax: (03) 5495 0680; website: www.jtb.co.jp/sunrisetour) and *Japan Gray Line* (tel: (03) 3433 5745; fax: (03) 3433 8388; website: www.jgl.co.jp/inbound/index.htm) all offer a wide variety of half-day, full-day and evening bus tours, with English-speaking guides. For example, Hato Bus offers a half-day (0900–1230) 'Tokyo Morning Tour' that departs daily from the Hamamatsucho Bus Terminal. The tour costs ¥5000 and takes in a number of sights, such as the Tokyo Tower and the Imperial Palace Plaza, as well as driving through a number of the cities lively shopping districts. Free hotel pick-up is available. Full day tours usually cost around ¥10,000.

Boat Tours

The *Tokyo Cruise Ship Company* (tel: (03) 3841 9178; website: www.suijobus.co.jp/english) runs a regular waterbus service along the Sumida River, between Asakusa, the Hama Rikyu Gardens, Hinode Pier and Odaiba. The trip takes 40 minutes and costs ¥660 (one way). The company also operates a variety of other waterbus services around Tokyo Bay, lasting between five and 55 minutes and costing ¥200–800. *Vingt-et-Un Cruises* (tel: (03) 3436 2121) and *Symphony Cruises* (tel: (03) 3798 8101; website: www.symphony-cruise.co.jp) offers two-hour daytime and evening boat cruises around Tokyo Bay. The tours cost, on average, ¥5000 and ¥3000 respectively. Symphony cruises depart from the Hinode Pier, while Vingt-et-Un cruises set off from Takeshiba Pier.

Excursions

For a Half Day

Kamakura: A small coastal town surrounded by wooded hills, some ten kilometres (six miles) south of Tokyo, *Kamakura* was the seat of Japan's first military government, the Kamakura Shogunate of 1192–1333. Most famous for the imposing 12m-high (39ft) *Great Buddha*, which dates from the mid-13th century, the town also boasts several fine Zen temples, the impressive *Tsurugaoka Hachiman-gu Shrine* and the nearby *National Treasure Hall*, which displays important Buddhist art of the Kamakura period. Pleasant hiking paths wind through the surrounding hills and the beach is a popular sunbathing and windsurfing spot in summer.

Trains run frequently to Kamakura from Tokyo Station and Shinagawa Station, on the Yokosuka line (journey time – approximately 1 hour). The *Tokyo Tourist Information Center* (tel: (03) 3201 3331) provides a leaflet, *Hakone and Kamakura*, with information on transport and sights.

For a Whole Day

Nikko: One of Japan's most celebrated tourist attractions and a UNESCO World Heritage Site, *Nikko* is celebrated for the dazzlingly ornate mausoleum of the first shogun, Tokugawa Ieyasu (died 1616), who was the model for the fictional warlord of James Clavell's novel *Shogun*. The intricately carved, elaborately painted and gilded gates, halls and storehouses of the mausoleum – known as the *Toshogu Shrine* – today appear almost gaudy but, as a mid-17th-century political representation of shogunal power, they were very much a reflection of the times. Situated amid an ancient cedar forest, the extensive complex also includes *Rinnoji Temple*, *Futarasan Shrine* and the smaller, somewhat less elaborate, mausoleum of the third shogun, Tokugawa Iemitsu. A combination entry ticket for all four attractions is available. Beyond Nikko lies *Lake Chuzenji* and the spectacular *Kegon Waterfall*, reached by a one-hour bus ride up a scenic mountain road of hairpin bends.

Nikko is situated approximately 150km (93 miles) north of Tokyo and trains leave several times an hour from Asakusa Tobu Station on the privately operated Tobu Nikko line (tel: (03) 3621 5202; website: www.tobu.co.jp/english/sight). The journey takes approximately two hours. *JR Rail Pass* holders might prefer to take the slightly longer route of the JR Shinkansen bullet train from Tokyo Station or Ueno Station to Utsunomiya, changing there to a local train for Nikko. The *Toyko Tourist Information Center* (tel: (03) 3201 3331) provides a leaflet, *Nikko*, with information on transport and sights, while the information desk in Tobu Nikko Station (tel: (0288) 534 511) provides leaflets and an English map.

Hakone: The *Fuji-Hakone National Park*, only 80km (50 miles) southwest of Tokyo, offers a spectacular landscape of lakes and mountains, cultural attractions – such as the impressive open-air art museum – and (assuming the weather co-operates) the bonus of magnificent views of Mount Fuji. The popular circular route through the area by toy train, cable car and boat passes through forests and old spa villages before whisking visitors high over sulphurous volcanic valleys and finishing with a leisurely cruise on scenic Lake Ashino. The *Hakone Free Pass* costs

approximately ¥5000 (depending on the starting point) and allows unlimited travel on the area's transport network. Hakone may be reached by Shinkansen Kodama bullet train from Tokyo to Odawara Station, or on the privately operated Odakyu line, which leaves from Tokyo's Shinjuku Station. The *Tokyo Tourist Information Center* (tel: (03) 3201 3331) provides a leaflet, *Hakone and Kamakura*, with information on transport and sights.

ACCOMMODATION

Hotel accommodation is subject to Japan's consumption tax, which currently stands at 5% and is added to the final bill. The Tokyo Metropolitan Government levies a tax on hotel rooms costing over ¥10,000, at a rate of ¥100 per person per night on rooms costing between ¥10,000 and ¥14,999, and ¥200 per person per night on rooms costing ¥15,000 or more. Luxury hotels also add a 10–15% service charge to hotel bills. Tipping is not customary and might offend.

The prices quoted below are the lowest standard rates for a double room, excluding breakfast and excluding consumption tax and service charges, unless otherwise specified.

Business

Hotel New Otani Toyko

A modern mega-hotel towering over the vibrant Akasaka government and entertainment district, the stylish *New Otani's* outstanding feature is its historic four-hectare (ten-acre) Japanese garden complete with waterfall, dining pavilions, tennis courts and an open-air swimming pool. The hotel is an enormously popular venue for everything from society weddings to large-scale conferences and international summits, and regularly welcomes celebrities. The recently refurbished rooms boast high-speed Internet access. During peak periods, the shopping arcades, lounges and spacious lobby are extremely busy, although the traditional teahouse and *New Otani Art Museum* offer tranquil alternatives. Particularly notable among the three dozen

restaurants are *La Tour d'Argent* (see *Restaurants*), *Trader Vic's* and *The Bar*, which offers panoramic views from the 40th floor.
4–1 Kioi-cho, Chiyoda-ku
Tel: (03) 3265 1111. Fax: (03) 3221 2619.
Website: www1.newotani.co.jp/en
Price: From ¥36,000.

Hotel Nikko Tokyo

The spectacular curved edifice of this brand new 'urban resort hotel' is located in Tokyo's up-and-coming waterfront area, close to the *Tokyo Big Sight* international exhibition centre and only 15 minutes from the city's main business districts. Each guest room has a private balcony overlooking the bay and telephone with modem point, while sophisticated rooftop suites boast private gardens and Jacuzzis. An impressive and memorable venue for functions and conferences, the sumptuous banquet halls offer panoramic sea views, as do the impressive *Zen Health Spa*, the continental-style *Terrace Restaurant* and the nautically themed *Captain's Bar*. The hotel's contemporary design features pale colours, natural materials and works of art. The spacious, airy feel and excellent service make it a fine choice for those not requiring a city centre location.
1–9–1 Daiba, Minato-ku
Tel: (03) 5500 5500. Fax: (03) 5500 2525.
Website: www.hnt.co.jp/english
Price: From ¥33,000.

Imperial Hotel

The grande dame of Tokyo's international hotels, the *Imperial's* impeccable service and excellent location between Hibiya and Ginza ensure its continued position among the capital's most prestigious addresses. The *Old Imperial Bar* dates from the 1922 Frank Lloyd Wright building, although today the hotel is a modern 31-storey edifice with over 1000 rooms, each equipped with three telephone, fax and computer-compatible lines, plus a health club, extensive conference facilities and an executive business centre. The vast, lively lobby is a popular meeting place for businesspeople and 'ladies who lunch'. Numerous fine restaurants include the renowned *Les Saisons* (see *Restaurants*). The hotel's shopping arcade is a favourite with visitors, as is the traditional Japanese tea ceremony room.

Rainbow Bridge

Photo: Japan National Tourist Organisation

Park Hyatt Tokyo

1–1–1 Uchisaiwai-cho, Chiyoda-ku
Tel: (03) 3504 1111. Fax: (03) 3581 9146.
Website: www.imperialhotel.co.jp
Price: From ¥39,000.

Keio Plaza InterContinental Tokyo

The two towers of this 47-storey hotel overlook the Nishi-Shinjuku business and shopping area, affording breathtaking views of the surrounding cityscape. The white and gold lobby impresses and 40 function rooms, with a capacity of up to 1800 delegates, put the hotel firmly on the conference and convention map. A rooftop swimming pool, private high-tech karaoke rooms and comprehensive business and computer facilities are further attractions. The comfortable rooms are equipped with video on demand, two telephone lines and modem points. The 45th floor *Pole Star Bar* offers stunning nightscapes, while two dozen restaurants serve Japanese, Chinese, French and Italian cuisine.
2–2–1, Nishi-Shinjuku, Shinjuku-ku
Tel: (03) 3344 0111. Fax: (03) 3345 8269.
E-mail: tokyo@interconti.com
Website: www.tokyo.interconti.com
Price: From ¥24,000.

Luxury

Four Seasons Hotel Chinzan-so

Surrounded by extensive gardens of timeless beauty, this distinguished modern hotel in the suburb of Mejiro is a wonderful retreat from Tokyo's stresses and a firm favourite with dignitaries and international celebrities. High-tech facilities make it a popular conference venue, while the gardens, with their pagoda and summer fireflies, are coveted for upscale functions. The opulent decor and furnishings reflect a sophisticated blend of influences, while recreational facilities include a hot spa and glamorous swimming pool. The guest rooms are among Tokyo's largest and several suites have private garden patios. The hotel's acclaimed restaurants serve a variety of cuisines and the two elegant lounges are perfect for cocktails or afternoon tea.
2–10–8 Sekiguchi, Bunkyo-ku
Tel: (03) 3943 2222. Fax: (03) 3943 2300.
Website: www.fourseasons.com/tokyo/index.html
Price: From ¥41,000.

Park Hyatt Tokyo

The almost decadent luxury of this stunning hotel has quickly established it as Tokyo's most impressive address for both business and pleasure. Located in one of West Shinjuku's most impressive buildings – a towering 52-storey edifice – the host of remarkable facilities include international video-conferencing, a superb health club and extensive private library and art collection. Spacious guest rooms feature oversized bathrooms and personal entertainment centres with large windows providing stunning views of distant Mount Fuji or the Meiji Shrine. The renowned *New York Bar & Grill* and the lively *Girandole* brasserie are both top-class dining options, while the sumptuous breakfast buffet offers a chance to glimpse numerous famous faces.
3–7–1–2 Nishi-Shinjuku, Shinjuku-ku
Tel: (03) 5322 1234. Fax: (03) 5322 1288.
E-mail: mail@parkhyatttokyo.com
Website: www.tokyo.hyatt.com
Price: From ¥52,000.

Moderate

Hotel Tateshina

This well-priced yet superior business hotel is conveniently located near the corporate and transport hub of Shinjuku and the beautiful Shinjuku Gyoen Park. The small Western- and Japanese-style rooms are all en suite and equipped with a desk, telephone, TV and hairdryer. The reception desk offers photocopying, fax and word-processing services, while the hotel's conference and banquet room seats 30 people and is available at reasonable prices. Some English is spoken and foreign guests are most welcome. The hotel's small restaurant, *Noboru*, serves American- and Japanese-style breakfast for ¥800, as well as a Japanese lunch and dinner menu.
5–8–6 Shinjuku, Shinjuku-ku,
Tel: (03) 3350 5271. Fax: (03) 3350 5275.
E-mail: info@tateshina.co.jp
Website: www.tateshina.co.jp/eindex.htm
Price: From ¥11,000.

Shibuya Business Hotel

In a city with notoriously little affordable central accommodation, this conveniently located hotel represents a bargain, despite its lack of facilities and small rooms. A two-minute walk from Shibuya Station, situated in a quiet back street, the efficient receptionists welcome foreign guests, therefore minimising the language barrier problem. The rooms, each with a tiny unit bathroom, are cramped but nevertheless functional, clean and equipped with TV, telephone and hairdryer. There is a small breakfast room, a drinks vending machine and the reception offers a photocopying and fax service. The stylish Chinese restaurant, *Tenchu Saikan,* occupies the hotel's basement and is popular with guests.
1–12–5 Shibuya, Shibuya-ku
Tel: (03) 3409 9300. Fax: (03) 3409 9378.
Website: www.inn-info.co.jp/english/hotels_kanto/kat061e.html
Price: From ¥8600 (excluding breakfast).

Other Recommendations

Radisson Hotel Narita Airport

With Tokyo's Narita Airport a two-hour journey from the city centre, this large, modern airport hotel is an excellent choice for arriving and departing visitors. Located 20 minutes by complimentary shuttle bus from the airport, it offers both Japanese- and Western-style rooms, many of which look onto the hotel's beautiful and extensive gardens, giving the complex something of a resort feel. Impressive executive and recreational facilities include a business centre and meeting rooms, a gym, tennis courts, sauna and two swimming pools. In addition, there is easy access to historic Narita-san Temple and nearby shopping areas.
650–35 Nanae, Tomisato-machi, Inba-gun, Chiba
Tel: (0476) 931 234. Fax: (0476) 934 834.
E-mail: narita@radisson.com
Website: www.radisson.com/tokyojp_narita
Price: From ¥16,500.

Sawanoya Ryokan

Budget-minded visitors wishing to experience something of traditional Japanese culture should consider staying at this old-style Japanese inn (*ryokan*), located in a residential neighbourhood near Ueno Park. Guests sleep on futons in *tatami* rooms and can enjoy a traditional hot bath and Japanese breakfast. The inn is family-run and the hospitable English-speaking owners are eager to make guests feel at home and help them get the most from their stay. Each room has a TV and free Internet access is available in the lobby. *Sawanoya* is a popular member of the *Japanese Inn Group* and reservations should be made well in advance.
2–3–11, Yanaka, Taito-ku
Tel: (03) 3822 2251. Fax: (03) 3822 2252.
E-mail: sawanoya@tctv.ne.jp
Website: www.sawanoya.com
Price: From ¥8800 (excluding breakfast).

RESTAURANTS

The selected restaurants have been divided into five categories: Gastronomic, Business, Trendy, Budget and Personal Recommendations. The restaurants are listed alphabetically within these different categories, which serve as guidelines rather than absolute definitions of the establishments.
A 5% consumer tax is added to restaurant bills and luxury restaurants may also add a 10–15% service charge. Tipping is not customary and might offend.

The prices quoted below are for an average three-course meal for one person and for a bottle of house wine or cheapest equivalent; they include VAT but do not include tip.

Gastronomic

Hai Whan

Located in the upscale Ginza district, *Hai Whan* serves progressive Cantonese haute cuisine in grand surroundings reminiscent of an imperial banquet hall. The emphasis is on seafood and the chefs pride themselves on the freshness of their ingredients, which range seasonally from abalone to lobster, sea bream or crab. Unusual seasonings are incorporated into many dishes and the Chinese-style sashimi is a surprising and delicious addition to the menu.
World Town Building, 5–8–17 Ginza, Chuo-ku
Tel: (03) 3573 0080.
Website: www.haiwhan.co.jp
Price: ¥15,000. Wine: ¥6000.

La Tour d'Argent

Considered by many to offer the very finest French dining in Japan, this branch of the celebrated Parisian restaurant serves classic cuisine in a dramatic setting of period opulence in the *Hotel New Otani* (see *Hotels*). The wine list is renowned for its selection and quality and the seasonally based menu typically features carpaccio with caviar, roast pigeon with fresh truffles or the restaurant's renowned roast duckling.
Hotel New Otani, 4–1 Kioi-cho, Chiyoda-ku
Tel: (03) 3239 3111. Fax: (03) 3221 2619.
Website: www1.newotani.co.jp/en/tokyo/restaurants/westerncuisine
Price: ¥20,000. Wine: ¥9000.

Nobu

Amid the stylish decor of artworks, exposed brickwork and giant pink rose emblems, the 'New Japanese Cuisine' of celebrated chef Nobu Matsuhisa has arrived in Tokyo's upscale Aoyama district. *Nobu's* masterful blending of traditional Japanese ingredients with New World flavours results in exquisite signature dishes such as black cod with miso, squid in light garlic sauce and the renowned 'new-style sashimi'. For a culinary adventure, the *omakase* course (chef's tasting menu) is recommended.
6–10–17 Minami-aoyama, Minato-ku
Tel: (03) 5467 0022. Fax: (03) 5467 0023.
Price: ¥15,000. Wine: ¥6000.

Spago

Wolfgang Puck's *Spago* is one of the originators of New American cuisine and the Tokyo branch will not disappoint. The atmosphere is classic Californian – bright and airy with a cheerful terrace of flowers. In addition to the renowned gourmet pizzas, imaginative entrées, such as prime rib steak with jalapeño garlic gravy sauce, are excellent, as are the Californian wines.
5–7–8 Roppongi, Minato-ku
Tel: (03) 3423 4025. Fax: (03) 3403 1726.
E-mail: spago@wdi.co.jp
Website: www.spagotokyo.co.jp
Price: ¥7000. Wine: ¥4000.

Takamura

Serving *kaiseki* (Japan's haute cuisine and an art form in itself), *Takamura* creates a traditional Japanese dining experience never to be forgotten. Seated in one of eight serene *tatami* rooms overlooking Japanese gardens, guests are presented with a succession of intricately prepared dishes, such as delicate slices of sashimi or quail's eggs, each item seasonal and exquisitely displayed on the finest of Japanese ceramics. Takamura is located on a wooded hill and seems a world away from the bustling city below. Reservations required.
3–4–27 Roppongi, Minato-ku
Tel: (03) 3585 6600.
Price: ¥25,000.

Business

Les Saisons

Long renowned as the top formal French restaurant in Tokyo, the award-winning *Les Saisons* is conveniently located in the Imperial Hotel (see *Hotels*). The elegant opulence of the Provençal-style surroundings is extremely inviting and the seasonal menu features classic dishes such as steak with foie gras, bouillabaisse (fish soup) and cider-roasted lobster. The restaurant is rumoured to be Tokyo's ultimate location for elite political and business 'power breakfasts'.
Imperial Hotel, 1–1–1 Uchisaiwaicho, Chiyoda-ku
Tel: (03) 3539 8087. Fax: (03) 3581 9146.
Website: www.imperialhotel.co.jp
Price: ¥20,000. Wine: ¥6000.

Miyuki

The Japanese restaurant of Tokyo's top-class Four Seasons Hotel (see *Hotels*), *Miyuki* specialises in *kaiseki*, its multiple courses creating the most formal and exquisitely presented of Japanese dining experiences. In addition, the restaurant offers teppanyaki, sushi, tempura and *shabu shabu* menus. The decor is elegantly Japanese and kimono-clad staff present each course on a selection of fine Japanese ceramics. Set lunch menus start from ¥5000.
Four Seasons Hotel, 2–10–8 Sekiguchi, Bunkyo-ku
Tel: (03) 3943 2222. Fax: (03) 3943 2300.
Website: www.fourseasons.com/tokyo/dining/dining_22.html
Price: ¥12,000. Wine: ¥4500.

New York Grill

An oasis of sophistication on the 52nd floor of Shinjuku's Park Hyatt (see *Hotels*), just securing reservations for this award-winning restaurant will impress any Tokyo client. Floor-to-ceiling windows provide magnificent views and the vibrant, contemporary design features bold artworks and an open kitchen. The cuisine is creative American and the honey-glazed rotisserie duck and prime Japanese steaks are particularly notable. Naturally, the Californian wine list is first class and the service impeccable. There is an excellent weekend brunch buffet (¥5800) and the adjacent *New York Bar* features live jazz.
Park Hyatt Toyko, 52F, 3–7–1–2 Nishi-Shinjuku, Shinjuku-ku
Tel: (03) 5323 3458. Fax: (03) 5322 1288.
Website: www.tokyo.hyatt.com
Price: ¥18,000. Wine: ¥6000.

Sabatini di Firenze

This stylish Ginza restaurant is known as one of Tokyo's finest Italian dinner venues. Amid surroundings reminiscent of a grand country villa, freshly made pasta cooked to perfection compliments dishes such as grilled sea bass. The dessert trolley is bursting with temptation and the wine list, featuring an extensive selection of Italian and French wines, rounds off the experience. Set lunch menus start from ¥4500.
Sony Building 7F, 5–3–1 Ginza, Chuo-ku
Tel: (03) 3573 0013.
Price: ¥15,000. Wine: ¥5000.

Teppanyaki Asuka

A favourite for less formal business occasions, the Palace Hotel's teppanyaki restaurant showcases the considerable skills of the chef, as he cooks each meal to order. Guests sit at a crescent-shaped counter and choose from a menu encompassing everything from abalone, prawns and seasonal fish to Kobe beefsteak with Madeira sauce, all accompanied by soup, salad, rice and *kimchee* pickles. Guests may also enjoy cooking for themselves at private tables.

Yakitori

Beer garden

Palace Hotel Tokyo, BF1, 1–1–1 Marunouchi, Chiyoda-ku
Tel: (03) 3211 5211. Fax: (03) 3211 6987.
Website: www.palacehotel.co.jp/english/index.html
Price: ¥6000. Wine: ¥5000.

Trendy

Daidaiya

This upscale Ginza restaurant, serving *nouvelle cuisine Japonaise*, is a treat for the eyes as well as the palate. Theatrical lighting and dramatic avant-garde decor accentuate the succession of unique dining spaces, ranging from rooms to counters and *tatami* areas, plus a cigar bar. The Japanese menu with a twist includes grilled meats and seafood with delicate sauces and excellent sushi and tempura. Set menus start from ¥4500. *Daidaiya* has branches in Shinjuku and Akasaka.
GinzaNine No 1 Building, 2F, 8–5 Saki, Ginza-nishi, Chuo-ku
Tel: (03) 5537 3566. Fax: (03) 5537 3570.
Price: ¥6000. Wine: ¥3500.
Branches:
Shinjuku Nowa Building 3F, 3–37–12 Shinjuku, Shinjuku-ku
Bellvie Akasaka 9F, 3–1–6 Akasaka, Minato-ku

Fujimamas

Asian fusion is the 'in thing' in Tokyo dining and trendy *Fujimamas* is riding the crest of the wave. This Harajuku restaurant, bar and café has a warm, comfortable atmosphere, wooden verandah and rustic-style decor with a stylish twist. Dishes include grilled chilli-marinated pork loin with tomato chutney and sweet potato fries, and crispy tofu steak with Indonesian cucumber sambal. A fine selection of Californian wines rounds off a great meal.
6–3–2 Jingumae, Shibuya-ku
Tel: (03) 5485 2262. Fax: (03) 5485 2261.
E-mail: info@fujimamas.com
Website: www.fujimamas.com
Price: ¥3500. Wine: ¥3000.

Immigrant's Café

Located in trendy Aoyama, this funky café-bar invites guests to 'experience the world' through its Asian fusion menu. Dishes range from clam chowder to Thai fish balls but it is the unusual decor – colourful retro with an industrial edge – that makes the place stand out. A DJ booth, video graphics and lively bilingual staff add the finishing touches to a fun venue. Vegetarian friendly.
Kyodo Building B1, 5–9–15 Minami-Aoyama, Minato-ku
Tel: (03) 5766 8995. Fax: (03) 5766 8996.
Website: www.immigrantscafe.com
Price: ¥2000. Wine: ¥2500.

The Pink Cow

The Pink Cow is a wine bar that is fast becoming a star on Harajuku's trendy café scene. The atmosphere is colourful and relaxed, with funky furnishings and a maze of rooms hung with the work of local artists. The list of Californian wines is excellent and the vegetarian friendly home-style cooking – from burritos and bagels to fudge brownies – is an added bonus. The weekend dinner buffet is ¥2500.
1–10–1 Jingumae, Shibuya-ku
Tel: (03) 5411 6777.
E-mail: cowmail@thepinkcow.com
Website: www.thepinkcow.com
Price: ¥2500. Wine: ¥2500.

TY Harbour Brewery Restaurant and Bar

This large, stylish microbrewery on the Tennozu Isle area of Tokyo Bay offers harbour views and excellent food in addition to a wide variety of fine beers and wines. Californian-style dishes include roasted whitefish with crispy spring roll and light tomato sauce or beer-marinated chicken with thyme and garlic. The flower-filled terrace is the perfect place to enjoy the daily lunch specials and weekend brunch menu.
2–1–3 Higashi-Shinagawa, Shinagawa-ku
Tel: (03) 5479 4555. Fax: (03) 5479 1696.
E-mail: ty-info@tyharborbrewing.co.jp
Website: www.tyharborbrewing.co.jp/eng/index.html
Price: ¥4500. Wine: ¥3000.

Budget

Jangara Ramen

Two minutes from Harajuku Station, an enthusiastic clientele means long peak-time queues. But the bowls of steaming Japanese noodles are well worth the wait. Cheerful staff dish out the standard *Jangara* or richer *Bonchan* with meat, fish and egg added according to choice. Jazz music and quirky artwork add to the colourful atmosphere.
Shanzel Building No. 2 1F/2F, 1–13–21 Jingumae, Shibuya-ku
Tel: (03) 3404 5405.
Website: www.jangara.co.jp (Japanese only)
Price: ¥1000. Beer and sake: From ¥500 (by the glass).

MealMUJI

Just across the railway tracks from the Tokyo International Forum, this bright, spacious café extends the MUJI lifestyle brand to food. Focusing on organic, preservative-free ingredients, the freshly baked breads and 25 deli choices, such as curries, grilled fish and seasonal salads, attract a relaxed, youthful crowd.
3–8–3 Marunouchi, Chiyoda-ku
Tel: (03) 5208 8241.
Price: ¥1200. Wine: ¥400 (by the glass).

Moti

Located in the Roppongi nightlife district, *Moti* has been serving Tokyoites with authentic Indian food for two decades. Vegetable curries such as *palak panir* and *channa masala* offer a haven for vegetarians, while meat eaters will enjoy specialities such as Punjabi chicken *tikka* and mutton *kofta*. Mughal-style arches and murals give an exotic feel to the decor. Lunch specials are just ¥900. Moti also has a branch in Akasaka.

Roppongi Hama Building 3F, 6–2–35 Roppongi, Minato-ku
Tel: (03) 3479 1939.
Website: www.tokyo.to/moti
Price: ¥3000. Wine: ¥2000
Branch:
Kinpa Building 3F, 2–14–31 Akasaka, Minato-ku

Phothai Down Under

This bustling, down-to-earth Thai restaurant is a great place to fill up before hitting the Roppongi nightspots. The extensive menu covers all the favourites, from *tomyam* noodles to beef coconut curry, plus a selection of Australian wines, beers and, somewhat bizarrely, steaks. The tasty lunch buffet (weekdays only) is popular with local office workers and excellent value at ¥1000.
Roppongi Five Plaza Building 2F, 5–18–21 Roppongi, Minato-ku
Tel: (03) 3505 1504. Fax: (03) 3443 7258.
Price: ¥3500. Wine: ¥2500.

Tengu

This cheap and cheerful chain of Japanese-style pubs (*izakaya*) is popular with students and office workers. It offers a wide range of snack foods, such as yakitori grilled chicken and sashimi fish, plus Japanese interpretations of salads and pizza, washed down with reasonably priced beer and sake. Guests can order as little or as much as they want from the convenient picture menu, and the many branches are easily recognised by the red, long-nosed demon mask emblem.
Ginza Roku-chome Branch, 6–13–3 Ginza, Chuo-ku
Tel: (03) 3248 2588.
Website: www.teng.co.jp (Japanese only)
Price: ¥1500. Wine: ¥1000.

Personal Recommendations

Angkor Wat

Just south of Shinjuku, this Cambodian restaurant's extensive menu of tasty dishes, such as beef chilli curry and tangy shredded chicken salad, means that it has been doing a roaring trade for 20 years. The pumpkin cake and coconut ice cream is not to be missed. If the Japanese-only menu is too over-whelming, there are a variety of set meals, starting from ¥1000. Colourful travel posters and lively Cambodian staff liven up the no-frills atmosphere.
Juken Building 1F, 1–38–13 Yoyogi, Shibuya-ku
Tel: (03) 3370 3019. Fax: (03) 3379 0306.
Price: ¥2000. Wine: 2500.

Heiroku Sushi

A landmark in the Omotesando fashion district, this bright and cheery chain sushi restaurant is easy and fun – customers take whatever and as much as they want and pay at the end according to their number of empty plates. A steady stream of customers means that the sushi, ranging from tuna belly and salmon to sea urchin, is always freshly made. Crab mayonnaise, egg and cucumber rolls are also available for more timid pallets. Hot green tea and pickled garlic are free.
5–8–5 Jingumae, Shibuya-kuTel: (03) 3498 3968.
Website: www.heiroku.com (Japanese only)
Price: From ¥120 (per dish). Bottled beer: From ¥600.

Mominoki House

This Harajuku 'food concept house' is often billed as vegan but rather offers healthy, organic dishes, such as grilled tofu burgers or spinach and white radish salad,

amid a menu also featuring fish and meat. Nevertheless, it is a welcome find for vegetarians and Paul McCartney is rumoured to have dropped by. The atmosphere is relaxed and youthful, with a variety of seating arrangements on several levels.
You Building 1F, 2–18–5 Jingumae, Shibuya-ku
Tel: (03) 3405 9144.
Price: ¥3000. Wine: ¥2500.

Nanbantei Yakitori

The concept of yakitori (grilled chicken pieces served on skewers) is extended to a variety of other meats, seafood and seasonal vegetables at this popular traditional-style restaurant in busy Shibuya. Specialities include beef grilled in a tasty miso sauce (*nanban-yaki*), and pork and asparagus rolls (*aspara-maki*). The counter seats allow diners to watch their orders being prepared. *Nanbantei* has branches in Roppongi and throughout the city. Set menus start at ¥3500.
Iwamoto Building 2F, 1–22–7 Jinnan, Shibuya-ku
Tel: (03) 3461 2913. Fax: (03) 3461 2913.
Website: http://gnavi.joy.ne.jp/gn/en/G041701h.htm
Price: ¥3000. Wine: ¥2500.
Branch:
4–5–6 Roppongi, Minato-ku

World Buffet L'Etoile

One of a host of restaurants in Shimbashi's Dai Ichi Hotel, *L'Etoile* offers sumptuous 'all you can eat' lunch and dinner buffets of specialities from around the world, served in a pleasant conservatory-style atmosphere. From sushi and dim sum to smoked salmon roulade, three cheese ravioli and a wide range of cakes, ice cream and sherbets, the enormous selection ensures guests leave satisfied. The all-inclusive price, slightly higher on weekends and during holidays, is discounted for children.
Dai Ichi Hotel Tokyo, 1–2–6 Shimbashi, Minato-ku
Tel: (03) 3501 4411.
E-mail: info@daiichihotel-tokyo.com
Website: www.daiichihotel-tokyo.com/english/topframe.htm
Price: ¥2700 (lunch); ¥5200 (dinner). Wine: ¥4000.

ENTERTAINMENT

Nightlife

It is at night that Tokyo really comes alive. Busy seven nights a week, the vibrant Roppongi district has a profusion of bars, clubs and discos, frequented by the smart ex-pat set as well as servicemen from the US military bases. Shinjuku, on the other hand, offers a more Japanese scene, with an incredible variety of eating and drinking places, from huge beer halls to tiny intimate theme bars, cinemas, clubs, massage parlours and Japan's largest gay scene.

Dress codes are rarely overly strict. Entrance fees to clubs are high but usually include a couple of drinks. Cover charges are common in *izakaya* (Japanese-style pubs) and bars. Drink prices very much depend on the surroundings and range from the reasonable to the stratospheric. If in doubt, do ask before ordering. Should you be tempted by one of the city's many 'hostess clubs', be aware that a beer in the company of an attractive companion can easily cost ¥10,000. Tokyo's gay bars are clustered in the Shinjuku 2–chome area. They are generally wary of foreign customers and are best explored with a Japanese companion. Several major hotels have 'sky bars', offering impressive night views of the city.

There are no specific licensing hours in Tokyo, although the minimum drinking age is 20 years. Admission fees and opening times vary widely and the Tokyo nightlife scene is ever changing – for listings of what's on and information about the latest hotspots, visitors should check the English-language *Metropolis* (website: http://metropolis.japantoday.com/default.asp) or *Tokyo Journal* (website: www.tokyo.to).

Bars

For a typically Japanese 'pub' experience, *izakaya* offer beer, sake and a huge range of Japanese dishes. Among the most accessible to foreigners are the chains, *Murasaki* and *Tengu*. Both have numerous locations across the city and have a lively atmosphere, reasonable prices and convenient picture menus. For a more international scene, head to Roppongi and check out the brash, foreigner-friendly *Gas Panic*, 3–15–24 Roppongi. At nearby *Castillo*, 6–1–8 Roppongi, the non-stop disco classics mean the tiny dancefloor is often busier than the bar. For a pint of Guinness, try *The Dubliners*, 3–28–9 Shinjuku, or experience rock'n'roll Japanese style at the loud and seedy *Rolling Stone*, 3–2–7 Shinjuku. *Las Chicas*, 5–47–6 Jingumae, Harajuku, is a trendy bar/restaurant complex; the leafy courtyard is a fine place to drink on a summer's evening. *Bar Isn't It?*, Roppongi, Minatoku, opposite the Shibuya *Bunkamura* art centre (see *Culture*), is a popular hangout and has the added attraction that all food and drinks are ¥500. For a more refined experience, try Hotel Okura's *Highlander*, 2–10–4 Toranomon, a smart bar offering a selection of over 200 whiskies, or the *New York Bar*, a sophisticated jazz bar on the 52nd

Shinjuku

floor of the swanky Park Hyatt Toyko, 3–7–1–2 Nishi-Shinjuku.

Casinos

Casino gambling is strictly controlled in Japan and although there are currently moves towards liberalisation, venues are still very limited. Central Tokyo's only casino is in the *Tokyo Dome* complex, 1–3 Koraku, Bunkyo Ku. This casino is open to non-members, although Westerners might find the slot machines and blackjack on offer fairly tame. The dress code is smart – a jacket and tie are required for men. The minimum age for entry is 20 years and a passport is required.

Clubs

Club Asia, 1–8 Maruyamacho, Shibuya, hosts major DJ events and 'The Ring', a much-anticipated monthly gay/straight dance party. Take a break from the dancefloor to surf the Internet in an adjacent room. *The Liquid Room*, 1–20–1 Kabukicho, Shinjuku, is a trendy venue for live events and one-off club nights, while *Velfarre*, 7–14–22 Roppongi, is a huge multi-level disco palace with a strict dress code and a high admission charge. The slick *Lexington Queen*, 3–13–14 Roppongi, is much loved by the showbiz/model crowd and a good place to spot celebrities, or you can find the hip student crowd at the progressive venue, *Yellow*, 1–10–11 Nishi-Azabu. For a change of rhythm, try *Salsa Sudada*, 7–13–8 Roppongi, for a heady mix of cocktails and Latin sounds.

Live Music

Tokyo's local pop and rock scene revolves around 'live houses' – dark disco-like venues with a small stage. *Crocodile*, 6–18–8 Jingumae, Harajuku, and *Club Quattro*, 32–13 Udagawacho, Shibuya, are among the best known names. *Milk*, 1–13–3 Nishi-Ebisu, a hip, indie rock music venue, is a club/live house hybrid. Tokyo's premier jazz venue is *Blue Note*, 6–3–16 Minami-Aoyama, which regularly attracts top international acts. The two main venues for major rock acts are *The Budokan*, 2–3 Kitanomaru-Koen, Chiyoda-ku, and *Tokyo Dome*, 1–3 Koraku, Bunkyo-ku. Tickets are pricey and should be reserved well in advance.

Sport

Sumo wrestling is Japan's national sport and the six annual 15-day tournaments excite great interest throughout the country. The January, May and September tournaments are held in Tokyo. Tickets can be purchased at the venue, the *Ryogoku Kokugikan Stadium*, 1–3–28 Yokoami, Sumida-ku (tel: (03) 5237 9310). Further information can be found online (website: www.sumo.or.jp/eng/index.php).

Even greater passion and devotion is aroused by baseball (*yakyu* or *besubaru*). Several of the country's 12 professional teams are based in Tokyo and matches always attract tremendous crowds. One of the best places for one to see a game is *Tokyo Dome*, 1–3 Koraku, Bunkyo-ku (tel: (03) 5800 9999; website: www.tokyo-dome.co.jp/e), home to Japan's most popular team, the *Yomiuri Giants* (website: http://giants.yomiuri.co.jp).

Following Japan's successful co-hosting of the World Cup 2002, football (*sakka*) is more popular than ever. Japan's professional J-League consists of 12 teams and games are regularly played at *Tokyo Dome* (see above) or the *National Stadium*, Kokuritsu Kyogijo (tel: (03) 3403 1151).

Tokyo has two horseracing (*keiba*) tracks, the *Tokyo Keibajo* (tel: (0423) 633 141) and the *Oi Keibajo* (tel: (03) 3763 2151), with races generally taking place on weekends.

Ticket Pia (tel: (03) 5237 9999 for English-language telephone booking) and *Lawson Ticket* (tel: (03) 5537 9999) are the major ticket agencies, with outlets around the city. Events are regularly sold out and bookings should be made well in advance.

Fitness Centres

The *Clark Hatch Fitness Center*, Azabu Towers, 2–1–3 Azabudai Minato-ku (tel: (03) 3584 4092; website: www.clarkhatch.com), offers day membership and the major hotels almost all have fully equipped fitness centres. The Park Hyatt's high rise *Club on the Park*, 3–7–1–2 Nishi-Shinjuku, Shinjuku-ku (tel: (03) 5322 1234), and Hotel Nikko Tokyo's *Bayside Spa 'Zen'*, 1–9–1 Daiba, Minato-ku (tel: (03) 5500 5500), both deserve a special mention.

Golf

Japan is a golf-crazy country and, while Tokyo boasts over 500 driving ranges (often located on rooftops), enthusiasts must be prepared to travel to golf courses. Fees are high and weekends can be amazingly busy. The *Sakawa Royal Golf Club*, Kanagawa Prefecture (tel: (0465) 772 226; fax: (0465) 772 632), two hours by train west of Tokyo, boasts views of Mount Fuji. Non-members may play on weekdays and on weekends outside peak season. The *Kazusa Monarch Country Club*, 856–2 Yanoshiroji Yasurozawa Kimitsu, Chiba (tel: (0439) 293 101; fax: (0439) 293 399; website: www.giganet.net/kmcc/index.html) welcomes non-members at all times. Designed by Jack Nicklaus, the course is 90 minutes by train southeast of Tokyo. Course fees are from ¥13,000. Most golf courses are closed on Monday. The *Tokyo Golf Course Guide* gives additional information (website: www.successstories. com/home.htm).

Jogging

Tokyo's parks are popular with joggers. A favourite is *Yoyogi Park*, reachable via Harajuku Station on the JR Yamanote loop line or Meiji-jingumae Station on the Chiyoda underground line. The outer moat of the Imperial Palace offers an attractive jogging route but runners here might suffer from car fumes.

Tennis

The *Hibiya-koen* tennis courts (tel: (03) 3501 6428) are centrally located in Hibiya Park, near Ginza. They are open 0900–2100 daily and fees are ¥3000–4000 per hour per court. Membership registration is required but can be obtained free of charge. Court reservations should be made well in advance. There is a website that gives information on other places to play (website: www.tokyotennis.com).

Shopping

Despite ongoing economic troubles and a definite move towards being more 'Yen-conscious', the Japanese remain enthusiastic shoppers and indeed the combination of impeccable service, the superb selection of goods and wonderful presentation make shopping in Tokyo very enticing. Although prices are gradually starting to come down and cut price outlets are gaining in popularity, there are still a few bargains to be had, however, the discerning eye will find numerous unique

and affordable items, including ceramics and handicrafts, pearls, electronic goods and toys. The main shopping areas in Tokyo are: stylish Ginza, with its ritzy department stores, designer boutiques and chic galleries; young, trendy Shibuya for clothes, CDs and accessories; the 'youth Mecca' of Harajuku for teenage fashions and kitsch; Akihabara for a vast selection of cut-price electronic goods and computers; and vibrant Shinjuku, known for its camera shops, both new and second hand. *Odaiba Mall* is situated on the Tokyo Rainbow Town development in Tokyo Bay (see *Key Attractions*).

When buying electrical goods, visitors should remember that Japan runs on 100 volts AC, so an adaptor and transformer will be required unless the items have a dual-voltage switch. In addition, many instruction books are only available in Japanese.

The streets around Sensoji Temple in Asakusa are crowded with small shops specialising in Japanese arts and crafts, while the Jimbocho-Kanda area is the place for second-hand books and prints. Worthy of special mention is the *Oriental Bazaar* on Harajuku's Omotesando Avenue, a large arts and souvenir emporium with a wide selection of goods at reasonable prices.

A visit to the basement food hall of a major department store is a must, if only to marvel at the exquisite presentation of the extraordinary selection of foodstuffs. At the other end of the commercial spectrum, lively *Ameyoko Market*, located under the railway tracks just south of Ueno Park, retains echoes of its origins as Tokyo's post-war black market, with raucous vendors, cheap prices and crowds of shoppers. The market is open during standard shopping hours.

Antique/flea markets are held every Sunday – on the first and fourth Sundays of the month at Harajuku's *Togo Shrine*, on the second Sunday of the month at *Nogi Shrine* in Nogizaka and most Sundays at *Hanazono Shrine* in Shinjuku. Starting before dawn, many stalls pack up by early afternoon. These markets are great places for browsing and good buys include old silk kimonos, Japanese dolls, ceramics and lacquer. A smile and a polite request will often yield a discount. Shops are mostly open seven days a week, 1000–1900/2000, with department stores closed one weekday a week. A consumption tax of 5% is added to the price of most goods and services at the till. Major shops and department stores offer tax-free shopping. Visitors can present their passport and receipt at the service desk for an immediate refund. Credit cards are slowly becoming more widely accepted but most transactions are still done in cash. It is sometimes possible for shoppers to bargain at markets and in electronics stores. This generally takes the form of politely asking for the 'best price', although haggling is frowned upon.

Culture

The legacy of the pleasure-loving inhabitants of old Edo, modern Tokyo continues to host an astonishing number of festivals, rituals, observances and celebrations. Starting with the traditional New Year visit to major shrines, to pray for good fortune during the coming year, the Tokyo calendar is full of high days and holidays, from the supremely populist to the positively esoteric. Some events mark a particular anniversary or date in the Buddhist calendar and are restricted to particular neighbourhoods, shrines or temples, while others, such as the spring cherry blossom viewing frenzy, occur citywide.

The traditional arts, too, thrive here, with traditional drama, martial arts, the tea ceremony and flower arranging all widely taught and performed. Tokyo is a stop on the touring schedules of many internationally famous music and dance companies, pop groups and art exhibitions, further adding to the vibrancy of the local arts and entertainment scene. The *Tokyo Tourist Information Center* (tel: (03) 3201 3331) has a database of detailed information on the city's festivals and the English-language magazines *Metropolis* (website: http://metropolis.japantoday.com/default.asp) and *Tokyo Journal* (website: www.tokyo.to) publish listings of events, concerts and exhibitions.

The English-language booking agencies, *Ticket Pia* (tel: (03) 5237 9999) and *Lawson Ticket* (tel: (03) 5537 9999), are the major ticket merchants, with outlets located around the city. Events are regularly sold out and bookings should be made well in advance.

Music

Lovers of classical music are well catered for in Tokyo. There are several resident symphony orchestras, such as the *Tokyo Philharmonic Orchestra* (website: www.tpo.or.jp/english) and the *Tokyo Symphony Orchestra* (website: www.tokyosymphony.com/e-tokyo), as well as regular visits by touring orchestras, choirs and opera companies. There are numerous major venues, among them the *Bunkamura Orchard Hal*, 2–24–1 Dogenzaka, Shibuya-ku (tel: (03) 3477 9999; website: www.bunkamura.co.jp/english/index.html), with transport from Shibuya Station, *Suntory Hall*, 1–13–1 Akasaka, Minato-ku (tel: (03) 3584 9999; website: ww.suntory.co.jp/suntoryhall/english), with transport from Akasaka Station on the Chiyoda underground line, and the stunningly designed new concert hall, *Tokyo Opera City*, 3–20–2 Nishi Shinjuku, Shinjuku-ku (tel: (03) 5353 9999; website: www.operacity.jp) with transport from Shinjuku Station. *Tokyo International Forum*, 3–5–1 Marunochi, Chiyoda-ku (tel: (03) 5221 9000; website: www.tif.or.jp) with transport from Yurakucho Station on the JR Yamanote loop line, stages a variety of musical and cultural performances in its four halls, one being among the largest in the world, with 5000 seats. Traditional Japanese musical performances, such as *taiko* (drum) and *shamisen* (string instrument), are occasionally held at *Bunkamura* (see above) and in smaller local venues.

Theatre

Of Japan's traditional dramatic arts, *kabuki*, with its gorgeous costumes, elaborate staging and complex plots, is probably the most accessible. *Kabuki-za*, 4–12–15 Ginza, Chuo-ku (tel: (03) 3541 3131; website: www.kabuki-za.co.jp), with transport from Higashi-Ginza Station on the Hibiya and Asakusa underground lines, holds regular performances and provides English earphone commentary. Performances are long, sometimes lasting five or six hours, however, it is usually possible to purchase tickets for a single act.

Information on programs of other traditional performing arts, including *noh* (restrained and highly stylised drama, little changed since Japan's medieval era), *bunraku* (puppet theatre) and *kyogen* (short satirical plays, often performed as intervals during *noh* dramas), can be obtained from the *Toyko Tourist Information Center* (tel: (03) 3201 3331).

Contemporary Japanese theatre tends towards the obscure and the language barrier is an additional dissuasion. Far more accessible are the extravagant review-style performances of the glamorous all-

Akihabara

female *Takarazuka* troop, held at the *Tokyo Takarazuka Theatre*, 1–1–3 Yurakucho, Chiyoda-ku (tel: (03) 5251 2001; website: http://kageki.hankyu.co.jp/english/index.html), with transport from Yurakucho Station on the Yamanote loop line.

Dance

Overseas dance companies, ranging from ballet to tango, regularly include Tokyo on their itineraries. Performances are often held at *Bunkamura*, 2–24–1 Dogenzaka, Shibuya-ku (tel: (03) 3477 9999; website: www.bunkamura.co.jp/english/index.html). *Butoh*, an experimental, sometimes grotesque form of expressive dance developed in Japan in the 1960s, has a loyal following among more avant-garde Japanese audiences. Performances take place in various venues, and are listed in the event sections of *Metropolis* (website: http://metropolis.japantoday.com/default.asp) and *Tokyo Journal* (website: www.tokyo.to).

Film

Tokyo's many cinemas are concentrated in Ginza, Shibuya, Shinjuku and Ikebukuro. Foreign films are generally shown in their original language and subtitled in Japanese. However, tickets are expensive and Hollywood releases often lag months behind other countries. The last show generally starts at around 1900, although there is sometimes a later show on weekends. Daily papers and event magazines have listings of what's on. Mainstream cinemas include *Hibiya Chanter Cinema*, 1–2–2 Yurakucho, Chiyoda-ku (tel: (03) 3591 1511), and *Shibuya Tokyu*

Movie Theatre, Tokyu Bunka Kaikan, 2–21–12 Shibuya, Shibuya-ku (tel: (03) 3407 7029). A good arts cinema is *Cinema Rise*, 13–17 Udagawa-cho, Shibuya-ku (tel: (03) 3464 0052).

Rather than literary representations, Tokyo has always inspired powerful images, from the 'ukiyo-e' woodblock prints of the Edo period to the films of the present day. Juzo Itami's *Tampopo* (1986) and Yasujiro Ozu's *Tokyo Story* (1953) explore aspects of life in the city, while Katsuhiro Otomo's acclaimed *Akira* (1988) is a sci-fi animation set in a futuristic vision of Tokyo. However, it is Ridley Scott's *Blade Runner* (1982) with which many Westerners will be most familiar. While actually set in a future Los Angeles and filmed in Hollywood, the scenes of a dark, rainy, neon-studded cityscape have become for many an enduring image of Tokyo.

Cultural Events

Japan's traditional neighbourhood *matsuri* (religious festivals) are still very much a living tradition. Joyous and good-naturedly boisterous, they offer a very different view of the Japanese to that gained in an everyday or business setting. Commencing at the local shrine, *mikoshi* (portable shrines) are paraded through the streets by men, women and children dressed in festival garb, accompanied by traditional music and dancing. Street stalls sell snacks, trinkets and copious amounts of beer. Held in neighbourhoods throughout Tokyo during the summer, the famous 'big three' are the *Kanda Matsuri* held in Kanda and the *Sanja Matsuri* held in Asakusa, both of which take place in mid-May, and the *Sanno Matsuri* held in Akasaka in mid-June.

With thousands of participants and many times that number of spectators, these festivals are great fun but can be incredibly crowded and exhausting.

April is the season for cherry blossom viewing and it seems that the whole population visits the city's parks to picnic and make merry under the blossoms. During August, traditional *Bon-odori* dances are held beneath colourful lanterns to commemorate the spirits of the ancestors. The fun, gaudy and very un-Japanese *Asakusa Samba Carnival* is organised by Brazilian–Japanese returnees and takes place annually in late August on the streets of Asakusa. The annual *Tokyo International Film Festival* is held in late October/early November at *Bunkamura*, 2–24–1 Dogenzaka, Shibuya-ku (tel: (03) 3477 9999; website: www.bunkamura.co.jp/english/index.html), and cinemas in the Shibuya area.

The three main sumo tournaments that take place annually in Tokyo are major events, as is the baseball season, which opens in April and runs through the summer to the championships in October. Meanwhile, Tokyo's two huge trade fair venues host major exhibitions throughout the year, one of the best known being the annual *Tokyo Motor Show*, which is usually held in late autumn.

Literary Notes

Tokyo is home to Japanese authors as diverse as Kenzaburo Oe, 1994 Nobel Laureate in Literature, and Banana Yoshimoto, author of the cult novel *Kitchen* (1993). From the great 'interpreter of Japan', Lafcadio Hearn – an early foreign resident of Tokyo and from the diplomatic wives of the 19th century, who delighted in the cherry blossoms and the dainty manners of the people – to Angela Carter, who pronounced Tokyo 'an exceedingly pleasant place in which to live', Tokyo has merited inclusion in a host of memoirs. These include the writings of William Faulkner, Aldous Huxley, Jean Cocteau and Charlie Chaplin. William Gibson's novel, *Idoru* (1997), explores Tokyo's technological future, while the darker side of the city is vividly portrayed in *Speed Tribes: Children of the Japanese Bubble* (1994) by Karl Taro Greenfeld. A Booker-shortlisted novel set in Tokyo is the *Number 9 Dream* (2001) by David Mitchell.

SPECIAL EVENTS

O-Shogatsu (New Year), families visit temples and shrines to offer prayers for the coming year, 1–3 Jan, temples and Shinto shrines across the city

Special Opening of the Imperial Palace Grounds, crowds flock to the public appearance of the Emperor and Empress, 2 Jan, Imperial Palace Grounds

Dezomeshiki (New Year's Parade of Firemen), Tokyo's firemen perform traditional acrobatic stunts and display the latest equipment, early Jan, Odaiba

Setsubun, ceremony to drive away demons, 3 or 4 Feb, Sensoji Temple, Asakusa, and major temples across the city

Hana Matsuri (The Birth of Buddha), ceremonies are held at Buddhist temples, 8 Apr, throughout the city

Golden Week, a major holiday incorporating several national holidays, during which many offices close and huge numbers of locals take a holiday (a crowded time to travel), 29 Apr–5 May, throughout the city

Cherry Blossom Viewing, picnics and merrymaking beneath the city's thousands of cherry trees, Apr, throughout the city

Kanda Matsuri (Kanda Festival), a major street festival with parades of portable shrines and traditional floats, a weekend in mid-May (odd-numbered years only), Kanda Myojin Shrine

Sanja Matsuri (Sanja Festival), Tokyo's biggest and most famous festival features enormous parades of portable shrines carried by men and women in traditional costume, third weekend in May, Asakusa

Sanno Matsuri (Sanno festival), historic street festival featuring parades of portable shrines and a procession of 500 people in traditional court dress, a weekend in mid-Jun (even-numbered years only), Hie Shrine

Sumida Hanabi (Sumida Fireworks Festival), spectacular fireworks display on Tokyo's Sumida River, late Jul or early Aug, Asakusa

Asakusa Samba Carnival, a riot of colour and sound organised by Brazilian-Japanese returnees, late Aug, Asakusa

Bon-odori dances, dancing takes place beneath colourful lanterns to commemorate the spirits of the ancestors, Aug, various venues

Tokyo International Film Festival, Japan's annual film extravaganza (website: www.tiff-jp.net/e_index.html), 28 Oct–5 Nov, Bunkamura, Shibuya

Tokyo Motor Show, passenger cars and motorcycles featured on odd-numbered years, commercial vehicles featured on even-numbered years (website: www.tokyo-motorshow.com/eng/), late Oct–early Nov, Makuhari Messe, Chiba

Shichi-go-san (Seven, Five, Three Festival), children of these ages are dressed in their best clothes and taken to Shinto shrines to pray for their future. 15 Nov (or closest weekend), Meiji Shrine, Asakusa Shrine, Hie Shrine and others across the city

Tori-no-Ichi (Rake Fair), extraordinarily decorated rakes, believed to bring good fortune, are sold at a great shrine fair, mid-Nov, Otori Shrine, Asakusa

Hagoita-Ichi (Battledore Fair), lavishly decorated battledore paddles of all sizes are sold at a large and popular temple fair in the hope of an auspicious start to the New Year, 17–19 Dec, Sensoji Temple, Asakusa

Omisoka (New Year's Eve), temple bells ring out 108 times and people flock to temples and shrines to see in the New Year, 31 Dec, Meiji Shrine and temples and shrines across the city.

Photo: Japan National Tourist Organisation

Cherry blossom

oronto stands on the northern shore of Lake Ontario and the view of the city across the water is stunning and unmistakable – the CN Tower, thrusting skyward near the water's edge, is the world's tallest building. Framing it is a glimmering collection of skyscrapers, which gives way to a dense city centre with pleasant leafy residential areas and parks, notably along the ravines that cut through the city. The capital of the Province of Ontario, Toronto is Canada's largest city and the fifth largest in North America. A dominant force in the business and economy of the nation, it is also the cultural centre of English-speaking Canada.

Initially claimed by the French in the 18th century, it was not until the American Revolution caused hordes of United Empire Loyalists (loyal to England) to escape to Toronto that the city became an established settlement. Then known as York, the town was exceedingly British in character, functioning as the administrative capital of English-speaking Upper Canada and becoming a thriving manufacturing centre by the 19th century. In 1834, the city was renamed Toronto, a Huron Indian word meaning 'meeting place'.

The Toronto of the 19th and early 20th centuries was a law-abiding city, where rules were made and rarely broken and where the overriding concern was making money. As such, Toronto gained a reputation as a conservative, boring enclave of Protestantism, a reputation that still dogs it to some extent today. Older residents can remember the days when the city would come to a standstill on Sundays and only a handful of the very best restaurants served wine.

Towards the end of the 1950s, a surge in the arrival of immigrants infused Toronto with new foods, new languages and, most importantly, new attitudes. Italians, Portuguese and Eastern Europeans arrived first, followed by immigrants from the Caribbean, Asia and India. They settled into what would become the city's great ethnic neighbourhoods – Greektown, Little Italy and Chinatown. Toronto gradually developed a multiethnic North American character and shrugged off its colonial identity, although vestiges still remain, such as the English-style pubs and the ingrained habit among conservative clubs and societies of toasting the Queen before eating. There is a similar juxtaposition in the architecture of the city itself; at first glance, Toronto does not appear all that different from any other large American city, albeit a clean one, although closer inspection reveals preserved Victorian and Edwardian buildings and a profusion of neighbourhood pubs.

The Toronto of today is a lively, cultured place with hot summers and cold, dry winters. It is the most economically important city in Canada, the centre of finance, media and services and home to more corporate head offices than any other. By night, its people indulge themselves at the city's numerous restaurants, bars and clubs or at the symphony, opera and theatre. More than anything, however, Toronto is defined by its citizens – friendly, efficient and one of the most multicultural in the world.

Photo: Ontario Tourism

Toronto skyline at dusk

TRAVEL

Getting There By Air

Lester B Pearson International Airport (YYZ)

Tel: (416) 247 7678 (T1, T2 and T-New) *or* 776 5100 (T3).
Website: www.gtaa.com
Pearson International Airport is located 27km (17 miles) northwest of downtown Toronto. Canada's busiest and largest airport, it handles over 25 million passengers per year and is served by over 50 scheduled and charter airlines, providing service to 110 destinations in 44 countries. It currently comprises three terminals, although a new terminal (dubbed 'T-New') will replace T1 and T2 and the first phase will open in late 2003.

Major airlines: The national airline is *Air Canada* (tel: (888) 247 2262; website: www.aircanada.ca), which also operates regional flights under the *Air Canada Jazz* banner and low-cost flights as *Tango* (tel: (800) 315 1390; website: www.flytango.com). Other major carriers that serve Pearson International include *Aeroflot, Aeromexico, Air France, Air New Zealand, Air Transat, Alitalia, All Nippon Airways, American Airlines, Austrian Airlines, bmi, British Airways, Cathay Pacific, Continental Airlines, Delta Air Lines, KLM, Korean Airlines, Lufthansa, Northwest Airlines, Qantas, SAS* and *United Airlines.*

the airport to downtown Toronto every 30 minutes 0355–0255 (journey time – 20–35 minutes). The fare is C$14.95 one way or C$25.75 return – a shuttle bus to hotels off the main route costs C$3.25 extra.
Public bus services run by the *TTC* (see *Getting Around*) include bus 192 (the 'Airport Rocket') to Kipling subway station (journey time – 20 minutes), bus 58A to Lawrence West station and night buses 307 to Eglinton station (journey time – 45 minutes) and 300A, which travels along Bloor Street and Danforth Avenue.
GO (tel: (416) 869 3200 *or* (800) 438 6646; website: www. gotransit.com) also runs a bus to Yorkdale and York Mills subway stations (journey time – 35 minutes), costing C$3.50. Buses run Monday to Friday 0550–2402, Saturday 0635–2402 and Sunday 0805–2402. A number of private bus companies operate services to various destinations, including Niagara Falls. Information desks for each company are located in the arrivals area of each terminal. Licensed limousines and taxis are also available at fixed rates based on a zone system, with journeys to downtown Toronto taking approximately half an hour. Taxis cost around C$30 for destinations west of Bathurst or C$40 to Downtown.

Toronto City Centre Airport (YTX)

Tel: (416) 203 6942. Fax: (416) 203 6741.
Website: www.torontoport.com/tcca.htm
Toronto City Centre Airport is situated on an island

Lounge (tel: (888) 247 2262; website: www. aircanada.ca) provides a *Xerox Business Centre* for business-class passengers. Open daily 0445–2115, facilities include Internet connection, photocopying, fax, telephones, workstations and conference rooms.
Transport to the city: *Air Canada* operates a free shuttle bus service to the Royal York Hotel, 100 Front Street West, every 30 minutes daily 0615–1945 (journey time – 10 minutes). A two-minute ferry ride (free of charge to airline passengers) provides transportation every 15 minutes to the mainland, where taxis are available at metered rates. Ferry services operate every 15 minutes daily 0615–2300. Completion of a new bridge is set for spring 2004.

Approximate flight times to Toronto: From London is 8 hours; from New York is 1 hour 30 minutes; from Los Angeles is 4 hours 35 minutes and from Sydney is 18 hours 15 minutes.
Arrival/departure tax: Any departure taxes and airport improvement fees are included in the ticket.

Getting There By Water

The *Port of Toronto* (tel: (416) 863 2000; website: www.torontoport.com), overseen by the *Toronto Port Authority*, is located due south of the city centre and provides transportation, distribution, storage and container services to businesses in Toronto and the surrounding region. It links the city with the rest of the province and the Great Lakes states, as well as Eastern Canada and international destinations on the Atlantic Ocean via the St Lawrence Seaway. The port offers few facilities for passengers, seeing as it is primarily used for commercial storage and transportation; only a half dozen or so cruise ships stop here. There is a food court in the Queen's Quay Terminal shopping centre, situated one block west of the dock for the Toronto Islands ferry.
Ferry services: A publicly operated *Toronto Islands Ferry* (tel: (416) 392 8193; website: www.toronto.ca/ parks/to_islands/ferry.htm), costing C$6 return, links the city with the Toronto Islands. Departures are from the foot of Bay Street. Trips to Niagara Falls and Niagara-on-the-Lake are available aboard *Seaflight Hydrofoils* (tel: (416) 504 8825 *or* (877) 504 8825; website: www.seaflights.com), three to five days per week from mid-May to September (journey time – 1 hour 30 minutes, plus 15 minutes by coach); departures are from 339 Queen's Quay West. There are plans to link Toronto to Rochester, New York, via fast ferry, although these have been repeatedly postponed over the past few years.
Transport to the city: The Port of Toronto is located at the south end of the city centre, near Union Station (rail, subway). Numerous taxi, bus and tram services are available.

Airport facilities: Pearson's three terminals have facilities that include ATMs, bureaux de change, shops, duty-free boutiques, banks, childcare facilities, medical clinics, chapels, porters, left-luggage, traveller's aid, bars and restaurants. Free shuttle buses link the terminal buildings every eight to 15 minutes. Car hire is available from *Avis, Budget, Hertz, National* and *Thrifty*.
Business facilities: *Sheraton Gateway Hotel* (tel: (905) 672 7000) offers a business centre. Some business facilities are available through the various airline executive lounges. There are public Internet stations in T2 and T3.
Transport to the city: *Pacific Western* operates the *Airport Express* bus (tel: (905) 564 6333/3232 *or* (800) 387 6787; website: www.torontoairportexpress.com) from

in Toronto harbour. Handling scheduled commercial, charter, private and corporate flights, the airport primarily services the nearby business community, offering flights from nearby destinations in Canada, such as Montreal, London and Ottawa.
Major airlines: *Air Canada* (tel: (888) 247 2262; website: www.aircanada.ca) is the only airline operating from here, mainly through its domestic subsidiary *Air Canada Jazz*.
Airport facilities: There is a restaurant at the airport. Car hire should be arranged in advance from downtown companies (see *Car Hire* in *Getting Around*), which will arrange for pick-up at the ferry landing.
Business facilities: The *Air Canada Maple Leaf*

Getting There By Rail

VIA Rail (tel: (416) 366 8411 *or* (888) 842 7245; website: www.viarail.ca) is Canada's national rail transport provider. VIA Rail operates from the historic *Union Station*, 65 Front Street West, where tickets and information can be obtained in person. Facilities include restaurants, toilets, bars, lockers, shops, ATMs, bureaux de change, a business centre and car hire from *National*.

Rail services: *VIA Rail* operates services between Toronto and a number of national destinations, including Montreal (journey time – 4–5 hours; night train – 8 hours), Ottawa (journey time – 4 hours) and Niagara Falls (journey time – 1 hour 45 minutes), as well as the USA via Niagara Falls. Both economy and first class (VIA 1) cars are available on services along the Quebec City–Windsor corridor, which accounts for 85% of Canada's passenger rail traffic. The carriages are clean and quiet, with large windows that confer a sense of the country's vastness, as the train passes acres of farmland and mixed conifer and deciduous forests. VIA 1 fares include a surprisingly good meal and complimentary Canadian wines. Longer distance services to Vancouver and the East Coast (changing at Montreal) offer a variety of seated and sleeper accommodation options. Union Station is also the main hub for GO trains (see *Getting Around*), which are overland trains providing frequent commuter service to the city's outlying suburbs.

CITY STATISTICS

Location: Ontario, Canada.
Country dialling code: 1.
Population: 2,481,494 (city); 4,682,897 (metropolitan area).
Ethnic mix (by mother tongue): English 63%, Chinese 6%, Italian 4.5%, Portuguese 2.4%, Polish 1.8%, Spanish 1.6%, Punjabi 1.4%, French 1.3%, Tagalog (Filipino) 1.3%, Tamil 1.1%, Greek 1%, Arabic 0.7%, other 13.9%.
Time zone: GMT - 5 (GMT - 4 from first Sunday in April to last Sunday in October).
Electricity: 110 volts AC, 60Hz; flat two-pin plugs are standard.
Average January temp: - 4.5°C (23°F).
Average July temp: 22°C (72°F).
Annual rainfall: 689mm (27.1 inches).
Annual snowfall: 1350mm (53.1 inches).

Transport to the city: Union Station is located in the city centre and is connected to the city's subway network. Buses, trams and taxis are readily available in the immediate vicinity.

Getting There By Road

An extensive network of secondary highways (designated by two or three digits, such as Highway 35 and Highway 118) and motorways (400-series highways, such as Highway 401) covers the Province of Ontario. The speed limit on secondary highways is 80kph (50mph). On 400-series highways it is 100kph (62mph). Traffic drives on the right. The minimum driving age in Ontario is 16 years. Proof of insurance is compulsory. North American and European visitors may use national driving licences, while visitors from other countries are often required to carry an International Driving Permit as well. The maximum legal alcohol to blood ratio for driving is 0.08%. Seat belts must be worn at all times.

The *Canadian Automobile Association* or *CAA* (tel: (416) 221 4300 *or* (800) 268 3750; website: www.caa.ca) provides a breakdown service throughout Canada and has partnership agreements with various motoring

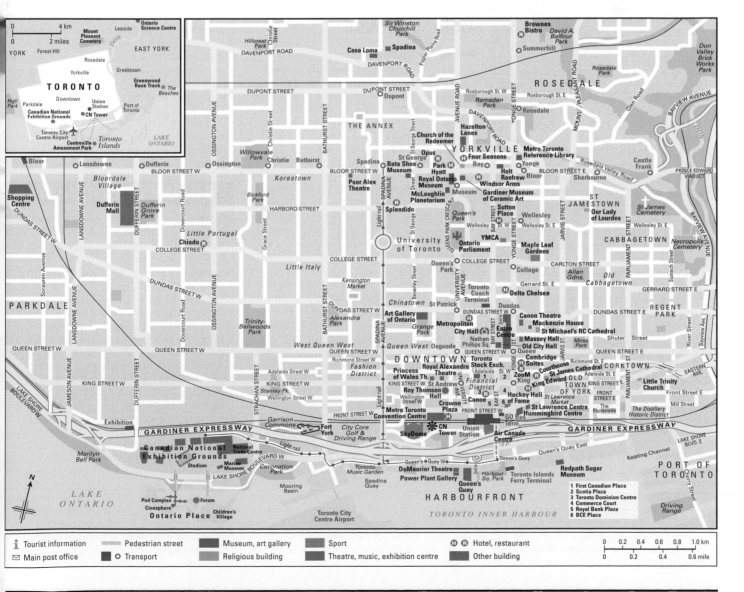

Symbol	Legend
i	Tourist information
✉	Main post office
	Pedestrian street
●	Transport
	Museum, art gallery
	Religious building
	Sport
	Theatre, music, exhibition centre
H R	Hotel, restaurant
	Other building

BUSINESS PROFILE

Toronto is the engine that drives Canada's economy. Virtually all of Canada's major companies situate their head offices within the city's gleaming modern skyscrapers, including half the country's chartered banks, as well as numerous trust companies and insurance firms. Financial service companies in the city include *Sun Life* and *Manulife*, while retailers include *Hudson's Bay Corp* (the world's oldest company) and *Sears Canada*, supermarket chain *Loblaws*, *Onex Corporation* (diverse industries) and, nearby in Brampton, *Nortel Networks Corporation*.

The unemployment rate has been rising slowly over the past couple of years, reaching 7.1% in December 2002, indicative of the sluggish economy, although still below the national average of 7.5%. Although the city historically had a strong manufacturing base, the service economy now dominates, accounting for over 70% of jobs. The city's largest private sector employer is the *Hudson's Bay Company*, a retail giant with historic roots in the country's fur-trading past.

Finance, however, is the city's defining professional industry, employing about 8% of the city's workforce and accounting for a quarter of its GDP. The *Toronto Stock Exchange* is the largest in the country and third largest in North America by value. The Financial District, clustered on and around Bay Street in the heart of the city centre, is marked by tall buildings, men and women in formal business attire and a constant flow of couriers and taxis. The city is Canada's main centre for traditional media, while new media companies are also flourishing in Toronto, with many start-ups locating their offices slightly west of the city centre in and around King Street – all taking advantage of the city's advanced 100% fibre-optic telecommunications system.

Toronto is the largest convention destination in Canada. One of its many convention facilities is the *Metro Toronto Convention Centre* (tel: (416) 585 8000; website: www.mtccc.com), next to the SkyDome, offering over 186,000 sq metres (2,000,000 sq ft) of space – the largest in the country. The region surrounding Pearson International Airport, in the suburb of Mississauga, northwest of the city centre, attracts many businesses taking advantage of the proximity to the airport, particularly those with warehousing requirements.

Although not as all-pervasive as it once was, manufacturing is doing well in Toronto. The largest manufacturing plants produce aeroplanes, computers, electronics and auto parts. Education is also a major employer, as Toronto is home to three universities – University of Toronto, York University and Ryerson University.

organisations, such as the American Automobile Association (AAA).

Emergency breakdown services: *CAA* (416) 222 5222 (Toronto area only) or *CAA/AAA* (800) 222 4357 or ★222 from most mobile phones.

Routes to the city: Toronto is served by a number of 400-series highways. Highway 401 bisects the city north of the city centre, connecting with London and Windsor to the west and Montreal to the east. Detroit

is reached via Windsor. Further north, a new toll motorway, Highway 407, operates as a northern corridor around the city. The QEW (Queen Elizabeth Way) runs along the lake shore from Hamilton and Niagara Falls to downtown Toronto. Buffalo is reached via Niagara Falls. North–south routes include Highway 400, running from Barrie to the city's west end, and Highway 404, running from the distant suburb of Newmarket to the city's east end, becoming the Don Valley Parkway (DVP) as it nears downtown Toronto.

Approximate driving times to Toronto: From Niagara Falls – 1 hour 30 minutes; Buffalo – 2 hours; Detroit – 4 hours; Montreal – 5 hours.

Coach services: A number of private companies operate scheduled services to and from cities throughout Canada and the USA, including Calgary, Montreal, Niagara Falls, Ottawa, Vancouver and Winnipeg. Operators include *Greyhound Canada* (tel: (800) 661 8747; website: www.greyhound.ca), *Coach Canada/Trentway-Wagar* (tel: (800) 461 7661; website: www.coachcanada.com), *Ontario Northland* (tel: (800) 461 8558; website: www.webusit.com), *PMCL* (tel: (800) 461 1767; website: www.pmcl.on.ca) and *Can-ar Coach Service* (tel: (800) 387 7097; website: www.can-arcoach.com). The main terminus is the *Toronto Coach Terminal*, 610 Bay Street (tel: (416) 393 7911), which has bar and restaurant facilities, luggage lockers and traveller's aid services.

Getting Around

Public Transport

Toronto has a well-developed public transport system, operated by two companies. Principal services in the city centre are run by the *Toronto Transit Commission – TTC* (tel: (416) 393 4636; website: www.ttc.ca) and include subway and rapid transit lines, as well as tram and bus routes.

Toronto's three **subway** lines operate Monday to Saturday 0600–0130 and Sunday 0900–0130. The arms of the U-shaped Yonge–University–Spadina subway extend from Union in the south to Finch and Downsview to the north. The Bloor–Danforth subway connects Etobicoke in the west with Scarborough in the east, where the Scarborough Rapid Transit basically provides an eastward extension to the line. The east–west Sheppard subway serves northeast Toronto.

Streetcars (trams) and **buses** operate throughout the city centre approximately 0500–2430/0100 Monday to Saturday and from 0900 on Sunday. These are supplemented by the 'Blue Night Network' **night services** from 0130–0500.

All TTC adult ticket fares cost C$2.25, although prepaid fares, purchased at subway stations or from newsagents, are cheaper at C$9.50 for five tokens or tickets. These are often handier, as exact change is required on buses and trams. Transfers are available for switching between the subway, bus and tram. A day **pass** costs C$7.75 and is valid for two adults or an entire family on Sundays and holidays.

GO Transit (tel: (416) 869 3200 or (800) 438 6646; website: www.gotransit.com) operates **rail** services from Union Station to suburban destinations to the east and west, as well as GO **buses** throughout the Greater Toronto Area. These commuter trains, supplemented by coaches in the outlying area, run Monday to Friday approximately 0600–2405 and weekends 0900–2445. Tickets start at C$3 and are available from GO train stations, bus terminals, transit

ticket agencies and bus drivers. Ticket prices vary depending on distance travelled. Day **passes**, costing C$6 are also available.

Taxis

Within the city centre, taxis can be hailed at almost any time and also can be found at taxi ranks or ordered by telephone. Most taxis operate as part of one of Toronto's major dispatching companies: *Diamond Taxi* (tel: (416) 366 6868), *Crown Taxi* (tel: (416) 750 7878) or *Co-op Cabs* (tel: (416) 504 2667). An initial charge of C$2.50 applies and rises according to the time and distance travelled. A five- to ten-minute trip should not cost more than C$10. Taxi drivers are commonly tipped around 15% of the fare.

Limousines

Chauffeur and limousine services are available from a number of companies, starting at around C$50 per hour for a town car and C$100 per hour or more for a stretch limo. Companies include *Carey Limousine Canada* (tel: (416) 214 1951 or (800) 263 9566; website: www.careycan.com) and *Dynasty Limousine Service* (tel: (416) 493 5579 or (800) 567 0861; website: www.dynastylimoservice.com).

Driving in the City

Traffic is heaviest during rush hour (0730–0930 and 1630–1930), particularly on the major motorways leading in and out of the city, which can make driving to the airport an ordeal. Toronto is laid out on an easy-to-follow grid system, with a few notable exceptions, such as the Don Valley Parkway, snaking along the ravine east of the city centre. Yonge Street, allegedly the longest street in the world, is the city's main thoroughfare, bisecting the city centre into east and west. Its junction with Bloor Street forms the city's most major and central intersection.

Although there is a lot of street parking available, it is notoriously difficult for drivers to find a spot and many opt for the simpler, although slightly more

BUSINESS ETIQUETTE

Toronto has often been ridiculed as a conservative, uptight city – Toronto the Good, as its detractors say. But while this perception is about 20 years out of date, its legacy survives in the city's approach to business.

Torontonians are hardworking, efficient employees. A little chit chat here and there about golf or other sports is welcome but generally people like getting to the point. Men and women wear business suits and rarely drink alcohol at lunch. Entertaining is usually confined to restaurants and bars, rarely in private homes. Business cards are normally exchanged after meals or meetings, not during introductions. The giving of gifts in business situations is unusual and might be treated suspiciously. In the workplace, it is common to answer the telephone by stating one's first and last name. Around the office, however, people – both superiors and co-workers – are usually addressed by first name. Working hours are typically Monday to Friday 0900–1700, although slight variations are not uncommon. The best time to visit Toronto for business purposes is between September and May, as the summer is the most popular time of year for holidays.

expensive, option of parking in a private car park. In the city centre, these typically charge around C$4 per hour, with a daily maximum of between C$5 and C$20 and evening flat rates of C$4–9 (as high as C$15 near nightlife spots on the weekend). *Canpark* (tel: (416) 482 2203) operates a number of 24-hour locations in the city centre.

Car Hire

All major North American car hire companies are represented in Toronto, along with a few local ones, at numerous locations throughout the city. Those with the most central locations and accepting international reservations include *Budget*, 1319 Bay Street (tel: (416) 961 3932; website: www.budgettoronto.com), *Discount*, 730 Yonge Street (tel: (416) 921 1212; website: www.discountcar.com), *Hertz*, 135 Parliament Street (tel: (416) 363 9022; website: www.hertz.com), *National*, Union Station (tel: (416) 364 4191; website: www.nationalcar.com), and *Thrifty*, 191 Parliament Street (tel: (416) 868 0350; website: www.thrifty.com).

Hire charges are approximately C$40–50 per day and C$240–280 per week, not including insurance, which is charged at C$20–26. Drivers must be at least 23 years old and pay by credit card. North American and European visitors may use national licences. Visitors from other countries are often required to have an International Driving Permit as well.

Bicycle Hire

Bicycle hire in Toronto can be arranged through *Cyclepath*, 2106 Yonge Street (tel: (416) 487 1717; website: www.thecyclepath.com), at C$25 per 24-hour day, and *Wheel Excitement*, 5 Rees Street, situated just south of the SkyDome (tel: (416) 260 9000; website: www.wheelexcitement.com), at C$12 for the first hour and C$3 per hour thereafter (maximum C$28 per 24-hour day). *Wheel Excitement* also hires out rollerblades at the same rates. Maps and information on cycling in the city are available from the *Toronto Cycling Committee* (tel: (416) 392 7592; website: www.toronto.ca/cycling), which has a downloadable cycling map, and the *Toronto Bicycling Network* (tel: (416) 760 4191; website: www.tbn.on.ca). Riding a bicycle in the winter is not a good idea, due to possible icy road conditions (not to mention the cold).

SIGHTSEEING

Sightseeing Overview

Like a needle jabbing into the sky, the *CN Tower* dominates Toronto's cityscape and is its most famous attraction. Since its completion in 1976, the tower has attracted company – at its foot stands the *SkyDome* (the world's first retractable dome stadium), while further east is the *Air Canada Centre* (a brand-new, state-of-the-art hockey and basketball arena). Immediately to the north is the dense cluster of office towers that comprise the Financial District, including some architectural wonders by Mies van de Rohe (*Toronto Dominion Centre*) and Santiago Calatrava (the galleria at *BCE Place*). Interspersed between these – and even underneath many of the buildings – are some of the city's main shopping areas, with the theatres and nightclubs of the Entertainment District to the west, and some of Toronto's chief tourist attractions just to the north. The latter include *Toronto*

Toronto City Hall

City Hall, a gem of modern architecture, the nearby *Art Gallery of Ontario*, the vast collections of the *Royal Ontario Museum* and the medieval-inspired 20th-century castle, *Casa Loma*, which stands a bit further to the north. In the city's west end, the enormous, sweeping patch of green known as *High Park* unfurls, while along the waterfront *Ontario Place* and the *Canadian National Exhibition Grounds* provide fun days out for families with children. Beyond the trail-laced ravine of the Don Valley to the east of the centre is *The Beaches*, with chic boutiques and a waterfront promenade.

Toronto is known as a city of neighbourhoods and many of these are a short distance from the Financial District's towers. Unlike many major North American cities, Toronto has a thriving, vital, leafy Downtown that keeps home owners and families from fleeing to the suburbs. The city's most affluent areas are Rosedale and Forest Hill – pleasant for walks and people-watching. Yorkville, a hippy enclave in the 1960s, predictably went chi-chi in the 1970s, today offering elegant cafés and restaurants, a Prada store and even a postmodern park. Spadina Avenue is home to Toronto's Chinatown, arguably North America's best due to Toronto's enormous Chinese community. Danforth Avenue is home to Greektown. Toronto has the highest population of Italians outside Italy and many of them have made their homes in Little Italy, west of the city centre. Near the University of Toronto, the Annex is a trendy, popular neighbourhood known for its lively nightlife and cultural scene. The area around Church Street and Wellesley Street is home to the city's gay and lesbian village.

Key Attractions

CN Tower

At a height of 553m (1815ft), the *CN Tower* is the world's tallest building and the defining symbol of this lakefront city. On a clear day, it offers stunning views of up to 120km (75 miles) across the surrounding cityscape and Lake Ontario. A glass-fronted elevator ride leads to the main section – at the equivalent of 114 storeys high – where a terrifying glass floor enables visitors to stare 342m (1122ft) straight down. A more leisurely view can be had from the revolving *360 Restaurant* on the floor above. Another set of elevators leads to the SkyPod, 33 storeys further up. There is also a

group of entertainment venues at the base of the tower, including two motion-simulator rides.
301 Front Street West
Tel: (416) 868 6937. Fax: (416) 601 4722.
Website: www.cntower.ca
Transport: Subway Union.
Opening hours: Sun–Thurs 1000–2200, Fri and Sat 1000–2300.
Admission: C$16.99; C$23.99 (including SkyPod); concessions available.

Casa Loma

Toronto seems an unlikely location for a castle but, since 1911, the soaring battlements of *Casa Loma* have lent an element of magic to the city. The 98-room castle was completed in 1914 by Sir Henry Pellatt, a charismatic financier, industrialist and philanthropist,

Photo: Ontario Tourism

Casa Loma

to be his home. Financial ruin forced its sale years later and the castle eventually became the popular tourist attraction it is today. The castle is a bizarre hybrid of a medieval-style stonework exterior – replete with turrets and battlements – and an early 20th-century interior. Highlights include the splendidly carved *Oak Room*, secret passageways and pseudo-Gothic *Great Hall*, which has 18m-high (60ft) ceilings. The two-hectare (five-acre) gardens are open between May and October.
1 Austin Terrace
Tel: (416) 923 1171. Fax: (416) 923 5734.
E-mail: info@casaloma.org
Website: www.casaloma.org
Transport: Subway Dupont.
Opening hours: Daily 0930–1700 (last admission 1600).
Admission: C$10 (includes self-guided audio tour); concessions available.

Art Gallery of Ontario (AGO)

Canada's premier art gallery, the *AGO*, contains 50 galleries displaying temporary exhibitions and a large permanent collection of international art. The ground floor houses a European collection covering the Italian Renaissance, Flemish Masters, 17th-century French painting and the Impressionists, right through to 20th-century works by Chagall and Picasso and beyond. The gallery's greatest attraction, however, is the Canadian section on the first floor, featuring a cross-section of work from the Group of Seven, a group of early 20th-century painters whose work embodies the sublime beauty of Canada's boreal wilderness. The gallery is also home to the world's largest collection of Inuit art, as well as works by Henry Moore in the *Henry Moore Sculpture Gallery*. It is worth allowing extra time to visit *The Grange*, a restored 19th-century house, situated adjacent to the gallery.
317 Dundas Street West
Tel: (416) 979 6648. Fax: (416) 204 2711.
E-mail: information@ago.net
Website: www.ago.net
Transport: Subway St Patrick.
Opening hours: Tues, Thurs and Fri 1100–1800, Wed 1100–2030, Sat and Sun 1000–1730.

Admission: C$12 (special exhibitions might cost extra); concessions available; free Wed evenings.

Bata Shoe Museum

The *Bata Shoe Museum* is the only museum of its kind in the world and is housed in an equally unique building, shaped, appropriately enough, like a shoebox. The museum owns some 10,000 items of footwear, dating as far back as 4500 years. Pieces range from Elvis Presley's loafers and Queen Victoria's ballroom slippers to 19th-century beaded Native American shoes and leather broad-toed Tudor shoes.
327 Bloor Street West
Tel: (416) 979 7799. Fax: (416) 979 0078.
Website: www.batashoemuseum.ca
Transport: Subway St George.
Opening hours: Tues, Wed, Fri and Sat 1000–1700, Thurs 1000–2000, Sun 1200–1700.
Admission: C$6 (concessions available); free first Tues of month (winter only).

Royal Ontario Museum (ROM)

The entrance hall alone is reason enough for one to visit the *ROM* – two massive Native Canadian totem poles from British Columbia flank the stairs, underneath a beautiful golden mosaic ceiling. Deeper within, the museum offers a seeming mishmash of different collections. The exhibits representing East Asia include a renowned collection of Chinese art, with wall paintings, snuff bottles and ceramic head cushions, as well as the only complete example of a Ming tomb in the west. Other levels handle the life sciences, the ancient Mediterranean and a Canadian heritage collection. Some galleries might be unavailable during the ongoing C$200-million expansion (designed by Daniel Libeskind).
100 Queen's Park (Bloor Street West at Avenue Road)
Tel: (416) 586 5549 or 8000 (recorded info). Fax: (416) 586 5863.
E-mail: info@rom.on.ca; Website: www.rom.on.ca
Transport: Subway Museum.
Opening hours: Mon–Thurs and Sat 1000–1800, Fri 1000–2130, Sun 1100–1800.
Admission: C$10–16.50 (depending on whether or not there is a special exhibition); concessions available; free Fri 1630–2130.

Ontario Science Centre

The *Ontario Science Centre* was opened in 1969, with a mission to 'open minds to science by creating environments that excite curiosity, inspire insights and motivate learning in science and technology'. This difficult task is successfully accomplished with over 800 fascinating exhibits. Themes explored in depth include the 'Human Body' and the 'Information Highway'. Interactive exhibits include piloting a spacecraft or touching a Van der Graaf generator to make one's hair stand up on end. An *Omnimax Cinema* offers a 24m (79ft) domed screen.
770 Don Mills Road
Tel: (416) 696 1000 or 3127 (recorded info). Fax: (416) 696 3166.
E-mail: webmaster@osc.on.ca
Website: www.ontariosciencecentre.ca
Transport: Subway Eglinton, then bus 34; subway Pape, then bus 25.
Opening hours: Daily 1000–1700.
Admission: C$13 (exhibitions); C$10 (Omnimax Cinema); C$18 (both); concessions available. On-site parking costs C$7.

Toronto Zoo

Situated on a sprawling 287-hectare (710-acre) forested piece of land next to the Rouge Valley, in the suburb of Scarborough, the *Toronto Zoo* is the fourth largest zoo in the world. The collection of over 5000 animals is truly international, since the zoo features pavilions named Africa, the Americas, IndoMalaya, Australasia and the Malayan Woods. Underwater exhibits showcase polar bears, South African fur seals, beavers in their dens and otters swimming at eye level.
Meadowvale Road, two kilometres (one mile) north of Highway 401
Tel: (416) 392 5900. Fax: (416) 392 5863.
E-mail: torontozoo@zoo.metrotor.on.ca
Website: www.torontozoo.com
Transport: Subway Kennedy, then bus 86A; subway Sheppard-Yonge, then bus 85B or 85D; bus routes vary at the weekend.
Opening hours: Daily 0900–1930 (mid-May–early Sep); daily 0930–1630 (early Oct–early Mar); daily 0900–1800 (early Mar-mid-May and early Sep–early Oct); last admission one hour before closing.
Admission: C$18. On-site parking costs C$8. Extra charges apply for some activities; concessions available.

Fort York

Fort York harks back to the days when Toronto, then as British as afternoon tea, was named York. As a colony, the city occasionally had to deal with revolutionaries to the south, so Fort York was founded in 1793 to ensure British control of Lake Ontario. Most of the buildings, however, date from 1814 because, during the War of 1812, the evacuating British blew up the gunpowder magazine – an explosion so unexpectedly large that it killed ten of their own men, 250 advancing Americans and destroyed a good deal of the fort. Highlights of Fort York include blockhouses, barracks, officers' quarters, costumed staff and period demonstrations.
100 Garrison Road, off Fleet Street
Tel: (416) 392 6907. Fax: (416) 392 6917.
E-mail: fortyork@toronto.ca
Website: www.toronto.ca/culture/fort_york.htm
Transport: Subway Bathurst, then tram 511.
Opening hours: Daily 1000–1700 (late May–early Sep); Mon–Fri 1000–1600, Sat and Sun 1000–1700 (early Sep–late May).
Admission: C$5 (concessions available).

Further Distractions

The Distillery Historic District

The collection of 44 stone and red brick buildings that began life as the early 19th-century Gooderham and Worts Distillery – once the largest in the British Empire – has been re-cast as a new arts and cultural district to rival the likes of Boston's Faneuil Hall and Vancouver's Granville Island. What is perhaps the best preserved example of Victorian industrial architecture on the continent is now a brick-paved pedestrian precinct of restaurants, galleries, boutiques, cafés, artists studios and a brewery, enlivened throughout the summer by a host of cultural festivals and events. One-and-a-half-hour tours of the site cover themes like architecture, galleries, cinema – the area was, for many years, used as a location for shooting films – and a brewery tour. These are available by calling in advance (tel: (416) 597 0965 or (866) 821 6422).
55 Mill Street (corner of Parliament Street)
Tel: (416) 364 1177. Fax: (416) 364 4793.
E-mail: jb@thedistillerydistrict.com
Website: www.thedistillerydistrict.com
Transport: Bus 65 or 72; tram 504.
Opening hours: Varies according to individual venue.
Admission: Free; C$8 (tours).

Toronto Islands

Located in Toronto Harbour, facing Downtown and its skyline, the *Toronto Islands* have long been regarded as a place for leisure and relaxation. The islands did not become islands, however, until 1858, when a storm caused a rift between the then peninsula and the mainland. Over the years, the main islands – Ward Island, Centre Island and Hanlan's Point – were popular resort areas and included the baseball park where Babe Ruth hit his first professional home run. In the last 50 years, as a 230-hectare (568-acre) public park, the islands have become popular picnicking places. Facilities include designated picnic areas (with fire pits), wading pools, softball diamonds, beaches, a farm, plenty of restaurants and the *Centreville Amusement Park*. Today, the islands offer an ideal outdoor environment in which to take a waterside walk, relax at a café or enjoy an unparalleled view of the city's skyline. The islands are only accessible by ferry.
Toronto Harbour
Tel: (416) 392 8195 or 8193 (ferry information).
E-mail: parks@toronto.ca
Website: www.toronto.ca/parks/to_islands/island_index.htm
Transport: Subway Union, then any southbound bus or tram to Toronto Island ferry terminal.
Opening hours: Ward Island ferries Mon–Fri 0635–2330, Sat and Sun 0635–2345 (summer); daily 0635–2330 (spring and autumn); daily 0635–2345 (winter). Centre Island ferries daily 0800–2345 (summer); Mon–Fri 0900–2300, Sat and Sun 0800–2345 (spring and autumn). Hanlan's Point ferries Mon–Fri 0900–2230, Sat and Sun 0800–2315 (summer); Mon–Fri 0800–2215, Sat and Sun 0815–2130 (spring and autumn); Mon–Fri 0900–1545 (winter).
Admission: Free; C$6 (return ferry ticket).
Centreville Amusement Park
Centre Island
Tel: (416) 203 0405.
E-mail: info@centreisland.ca
Website: www.centreisland.ca
Opening hours: 17 May–1 Sep daily 1030–1700 (at earliest, closing time varies up to 2000). Early May and Sep Sat and Sun only 1030–1800.
Admission: C$23.

Paramount Canada's Wonderland

Located in the northern suburb of Maple, *Canada's Wonderland* is, as its name suggests, an amusement park. Although not on quite the same scale as a Disney or Universal outfit, it nevertheless features over 200 attractions on its 134 hectares (330 acres) of landscaped grounds and eight-hectare (20-acre) waterpark. Rides include *Cliffhanger*, *Drop Zone*, *Top Gun*, *Scooby-Doo's Haunted Mansion* and *Shockwave*. The latest attractions include the *Psyclone* ride, where visitors are swung around at the end of a giant pendulum, and the *Sledge Hammer*, which pummels riders with accelerated jumps and free-falls. Also new is the *Nickleodeon Central* theme area for kids.
9580 Jane Street (Highway 400, exit 33)
Tel: (905) 832 7000. Fax: (905) 832 7419.
E-mail: info@canadaswonderland.com
Website: www.canadas-wonderland.com
Transport: GO bus from Yorkdale or York Mills stations.
Opening hours: Daily 0900–2200 (Jun–Aug); Sat and Sun 0900–2000 (May, Sep and Oct).
Admission: C$51.91 (unlimited access); C$29.24 (grounds admission only); concessions available.

Tours of the City

Walking Tours

Walking tours of Toronto are available from *Toronto Footsteps* (tel: (416) 483 5483) and *A Taste of the World* (tel: (416) 923 6813; fax: (416) 532 0554; e-mail: info@torontowalksbikes.com; website: www.toronto walksbikes.com), who also offer bicycle tours. True to its name, A Taste of the World offers the 'Kensington Foodies Roots Walk', a three-and-a-half-hour Saturday morning stroll through historic Kensington Market, sampling both the sights and the local delicacies. Tours cost from C$15 (ghost and literary walks) to C$35 (food walk) and are frequently sold out – advance booking is recommended.
Guided tours of the city's natural heritage are available from *Toronto Field Naturalists* (tel: (416) 593 2656; website: www.sources.com/tfn). Architectural walks are available from *Unique Views* (tel: (416) 531 7770). There are also a variety of signposted, self-guided walks that wind through the city's many parks and green spaces. Alternatively, visitors have the option of exploring the vast labyrinth of interconnected shopping areas that lie underneath Downtown's office towers. The ten-kilometre (six-mile) *PATH* network (website: www.toronto.ca/path) links shopping, services and entertainment venues between the two branches of the Yonge–University–Spadina subway, south of Dundas Street.

Bus Tours

Grayline Tours (tel: (416) 594 3310; website: www.grayline.ca/toronto) runs hop-on, hop-off tours of the city centre in open-topped double-decker buses and turn-of-the-century trolley buses. A full circuit lasts two hours and costs C$31 (concessions available). The best places for passengers to hop on are 123 Front Street West (corner of University Avenue) and the corner of Yonge Street and Dundas Street (visitors should call ahead, as tickets are not available at all stops). *Toronto Hippo Tours* (tel: (416) 703 4476 or (877) 635 5510; website: www. torontohippotours.com) offers an 'amphibus' (amphibious bus) from May to October. Departing from 151 Front Street West (corner of Simcoe Street), the hour-long tour of the city takes in the CN Tower, the SkyDome and Toronto City Hall before entering the water at Ontario Place for a half-hour tour around Toronto's harbour. The cost is C$35 (concessions available).

Excursions

For a Half Day

McMichael Canadian Art Collection: Situated 40km (25 miles) northwest of the city centre, in the picturesque village of Kleinburg, the *McMichael* (tel: (905) 893 1121 or (888) 213 1121; website: www.mcmichael.com) possesses one of the largest collections of 20th-century Canadian art. Works on permanent display include many by the country's most prominent painters – Emily Carr, Tom Thomson and the Group of Seven – in a body of work matched in spirit by the gallery's forested setting. The gallery also has a strong collection of contemporary First Nations and Inuit works. Temporary exhibitions are hosted throughout the year. Although it is possible to visit the

Toronto Islands

Photo: Ontario Tourism

Niagara Falls

gallery by public transport, travel by car is recommended (the route is along Highway 400). The gallery is open daily 1000–1600 (November to April) and daily 1000–1700 (May to October). Admission costs C$15 (concessions available) and parking is an additional C$5.

Elora: A pleasant, pastoral town situated approximately 100km (60 miles) from Toronto, *Elora* was founded by settlers harnessing the water of the Grand River to power their mill in the 1830s. The mill still survives, functioning these days as the Elora Mill Country Inn. The town itself offers shopping, restaurants and horse-drawn carriage rides, although its real appeal is as a base from which to explore the surrounding countryside. The *Elora Gorge* is a three-kilometre-long (two-mile) scenic limestone gorge lined with cedars. Admission costs C$3.75 (late April to mid-October); camping permits and inner tube hire cost extra. The surrounding landscape – picturesque, gently rolling fields – is home to various Mennonite communities, a religious sect similar to the Amish, whose members have chosen to live without technology. They can often be seen travelling along the side of the road in horse-drawn wagons and their quaint farms make for soothing roadside scenery. Although coach transport is available, getting there by car is recommended (the route is along Highway 401, then Highway 6 through Guelph, then County Road 7 to Elora). Further details are available from the *Elora Information Centre* (tel: (519) 846 9841; website: www.ferguselora.com) and the *Grand River Conservation Authority* (tel: (519) 846 9742; website: www.grandriver.ca/parks/parks.cfm).

For a Whole Day

Niagara Falls: World-renowned *Niagara Falls* has attracted visitors since the first human inhabitants set eyes upon it and is now one of the most popular tourist destinations in North America. Although Niagara is not the highest waterfall in the world, it carries a staggering 168,000 cubic metres (5.9 million cubic feet) of water per minute over a drop of 51m (167ft). The surrounding town of Niagara Falls (tel: (905) 356 6061 *or* (800) 563 2557; website:

www.discoverniagara.com) is a notorious honeymoon destination, although a tad on the kitsch side. It offers lots of activities for the visitor, including a casino, the *Skylon* observation tower and boat tours of the falls aboard the *Maid of the Mist* (tel: (905) 358 5781; website: www.maidofthemist.com) at a cost of C$13 (April to October). Niagara Falls is located 130km (81 miles) west of Toronto and can be reached by car, coach, train or a hydrofoil and coach trip (see *Getting There By Water*). Further information on the falls is available from the *Niagara Parks Commission* (tel: (905) 371 0254 *or* (877) 642 7275; website: www.niagaraparks.com).

The surrounding region offers winery tours, while the nearby town of *Niagara-on-the-Lake* (tel: (905) 468 1950; website: www.niagaraonthelake.com) is home to a wealth of theatres, tree-lined 19th-century streets and picturesque inns. The main draw for many visitors is the annual *Shaw Festival* (tel: (800) 511 7429; website: www.shawfest.com), which has specialised in the plays of Bernard Shaw and his contemporaries for the last four decades.

Algonquin Provincial Park: For many visitors, *Algonquin Provincial Park* (tel: (705) 633 5572; website: www.algonquinpark.on.ca) captures the archetypal Canadian boreal landscape – shimmering blue lakes, towering pines and granite rock faces carved by the retreating glaciers. The park was established in 1893, in a rugged, beautiful region of southern Ontario – located 300km (186 miles) north of Toronto – and quickly became popular with canoeists and outdoor enthusiasts. For a day trip, it is probably wisest for visitors to take in the natural beauty from Highway 60, which runs right through the park, offering a decent chance for a deer or moose sighting. For a more active experience, visitors could take one of more than a dozen hiking trails, while for educational input there is a Visitors Centre, located on Highway 60, 43km (27 miles) from the west gate and 13km (eight miles) west of the east gate. The centre is open weekends only in winter and daily the rest of the year. Individual transportation is recommended for travelling to and around the park. The park is accessible daily 24 hours; camping is possible all year

round and permits are required – these should be booked in advance, especially during the peak summer dates. There is a C$12 vehicle entry fee and camping permits cost extra.

ACCOMMODATION

Hotel prices are subject to a provincial sales tax, levied at 5% on accommodation, as well as a federal goods and services tax of 7%. The 12% total tax is usually added to the bill at the end. Tipping is expected in Toronto and porters are usually given a C$5 note for their efforts. The prices quoted below are the lowest standard rates for a double room, excluding tax and excluding breakfast, unless otherwise specified.

Business

Cambridge Suites Hotel

Located in the heart of the Financial District, this all-suites hotel is designed with the business traveller in mind. The experienced staff can handle all kinds of business occasions, from state-of-the-art presentations to informal breakfast meetings. The exterior of the hotel is a typically North American 20 floors of green glass, while the 231 guest rooms range from 51 sq-metre (550 sq-ft) apartment-style units to deluxe duplexes, usually decorated in muted browns and creams. All rooms have work areas that are comfortable, well designed and feature two dual-line telephones and a fax machine. The penthouse suites have Jacuzzis, while all guests have complimentary use of the fitness club and racquetball facilities at the nearby Adelaide Club.

15 Richmond Street East, Financial District
Tel: (416) 368 1990 *or* (800) 463 1990. Fax: (416) 601 3751.
E-mail: reservations@tor.cambridgesuites.ns.ca
Website: www.cambridgesuiteshotel.com
Price: From C$250 (including breakfast).

Crowne Plaza Toronto Centre

This modern high-rise hotel is ideal for business travellers. Located next door to the Metro Toronto Convention Centre and a short walk from the heart of the Financial District, the hotel has 15 meeting rooms, as well as a ballroom, boardroom and several smaller hospitality suites. The staff's experience in all varieties of meetings and conferences mean that any business occasion should run smoothly. Following a recent C$20 million refurbishment, the 586 guest rooms are newly appointed with luxurious materials, including comfortable beds and down duvets, made locally, as well as a coffee/tea maker, two telephone lines, high-speed Internet access and complimentary newspaper delivery. In the 90 rooms on the Club Level floors, guests can also expect a complimentary limousine service within downtown Toronto, first-hour complimentary use of the new Club Boardroom, a daily buffet breakfast and evening hors d'oeuvres with an honour bar. The Victoria Spa offers a full range of spa services, while the indoor pool and fitness centre are available to all guests.

225 Front Street West, Financial District
Tel: (416) 597 1400 *or* (800) 422 7969. Fax: (416) 597 8106.
E-mail: reservations@torontocentre.crowneplaza.com
Website: www.torontocentre.crowneplaza.com
Price: From C$249.

Metropolitan Hotel

Located in the north end of the Financial District and a short walk from the Eaton Centre (downtown Toronto's largest shopping mall), this independently owned modern hotel – with majestic lobby ceilings and suites that are contemporary in design – caters to the business traveller. For example, there is complimentary limousine service to guests' first morning appointment and a fully staffed business centre. In addition to telephones with voice-mail, modem and fax points, the guest rooms and meeting rooms have wired broadband Internet access (wireless connectivity is available in the lobby and restaurants). There is complimentary use of the fitness centre and the heated indoor swimming pool, as well as facilities such as express video check-out, in-room dining, same-day dry cleaning and non-smoking floors.
108 Chestnut Street, Financial District
Tel: (416) 977 5000 or (800) 668 6600. Fax: (416) 977 9513.
E-mail: reservations@tor.metropolitan.com
Website: www.metropolitan.com
Price: From C$280.

The Sutton Place Hotel Toronto

Located in Midtown, next to the sprawling green campus of the University of Toronto and Queen's Park, the concrete and glass exterior of *The Sutton Place Hotel* may not take one's breath away but once inside the European styling is luxurious, with antiques and paintings throughout. Although it is the hotel of choice for film celebrities during the Toronto International Film Festival, it also serves the business traveller very well. There are ten individually designed meeting rooms and three breathtaking ballrooms – of which, the newly renovated rooftop ballroom, *Stop 33*, offers a superb view of the city – and a professional staff is on hand to facilitate any type of event. The suites are spacious – some with full kitchens – and all have a large work desk, two-line telephone with voice-mail, fax/modem point, bathrobes and complimentary daily newspaper delivery.
955 Bay Street, Midtown
Tel: (416) 924 9221 or (800) 268 3790. Fax: (416) 924 1778.
E-mail: info_toronto@suttonplace.com
Website: www.suttonplace.com
Price: From C$179.

Luxury

Four Seasons Hotel Toronto

The *Four Seasons* chain was founded and started by Canadian Issy Sharp and, although this hotel is not the original, it is more often than not the one celebrities and well-heeled visitors choose when visiting the city. Located in Yorkville, a chi-chi district littered with boutiques and cafés, the hotel is well known for its service and comfort. Features include corner rooms with balconies, marble bathrooms and family perks, such as child-sized bathrobes and bedtime milk and cookies, as well as time-savers such as complimentary overnight shoeshine and one-hour pressing. In addition to the standard business amenities, including a 24-hour business centre, the hotel provides courtesy limousine service to Downtown on weekdays. Of course, the hotel has not neglected the basics for relaxing either – there is an indoor/outdoor pool, a 24-hour health club (with whirlpool and sauna) and spa services. The chic *Avenue* bar and lounge, and the award-winning restaurant, *Truffles* (see *Restaurants*), are city landmarks.

21 Avenue Road, Yorkville
Tel: (416) 964 0411 or (800) 268 6282. Fax: (416) 964 2301.
E-mail: tfs.reservations@fourseasons.com
Website: www.fourseasons.com/toronto
Price: From C$285.

Le Royal Meridien King Edward

Known affectionately by locals as the 'King Eddy', this elegant century-old hotel was the choice for visiting royalty in the mid-1920s and has continued to draw distinguished guests ever since. Its opulent decor and impressive service have ensured the hotel's reputation, which will be further enhanced by the Art & Tech rooms designed by Yabu Pushelberg (due for completion in early 2004). The hotel's original 1903 façade alone is stunning. Located in Downtown, its locale is ideal for theatregoers, shoppers and businesspeople alike. Although not all rooms are spacious, they are well appointed, tastefully designed and have thoughtful perks, such as complimentary daily newspapers, bathrobes and 24-hour room service. Royal Club level rooms offer complimentary breakfast, cocktails and snacks. A new state-of-the-art business centre joins the list of guest facilities, which includes a 24-hour fitness centre and in-house spa.
37 King Street East, Financial District
Tel: (416) 863 9700 or (800) 543 4300. Fax: (416) 367 5515.
E-mail: reservations@lemeridien-kingedward.com
Website: www.lemeridien-kingedward.com
Price: From C$225.

Moderate

Delta Chelsea

Canada's largest hotel, the glass-clad sky-high *Delta Chelsea* tries to cater for everybody in its 1590 guest rooms. For families, there are Nintendo games, a bottomless cookie jar (in the Family Fun suites only) and kids' discounts at the Delta Chelsea's restaurants. For business travellers, there is a dedicated floor with rooms equipped with cordless speaker telephones, faxes, well-stocked desks and back-friendly chairs. All rooms are en suite. Facilities include two pools –

one with a water slide – and a fitness centre. Many rooms have been designed for travellers with disabilities and there are always staff members on hand to assist with meeting planning or presentation. Weekend packages are often very economically priced.
33 Gerrard Street West, Downtown
Tel: (416) 595 1975 or (800) 268 1133. Fax: (416) 585 4375.
E-mail: reservations@deltachelsea.com
Website: www.deltachelsea.com
Price: From C$129.

The Strathcona

With cheaper rates off-peak (November to April), *The Strathcona* has long been a budget hotel, located as it is directly across from the city's main railway hub, Union Station. Locals might smile when The Strathcona is mentioned, as it is rumoured to be a former flophouse, however, they are probably not aware of the 1999 renovation, where the hotel improved its lobby and added some suites. The Strathcona is now aiming itself at the budget business traveller. It provides corporate rooms – with two telephones, modem points, complimentary morning newspaper and 24-hour fax service – and has added a basic meeting room. The guest rooms are small but efficient and the hotel is just steps away from the Queen's Quay waterfront, with its theatres and great shopping. All rooms are en suite.
60 York Street, Theatre/Financial District
Tel: (416) 363 3321 or (800) 268 8304. Fax: (416) 363 4679.
E-mail: info@thestrathconahotel.com
Website: www.thestrathconahotel.com
Price: From C$109.

Other Recommendations

Park Hyatt Toronto

Formerly known as the Park Plaza, this hotel's rooftop bar-lounge has made appearances in some Canadian novels, such as Margaret Atwood's *Cat's Eye* (1988). Purchased by Hyatt in 1999, over C$60 million was invested in refurbishment of the 65-year-old Art

Delta Chelsea lobby

Deco building – including the addition of the Stillwater Spa. Along with its location in ritzy Yorkville, the hotel boasts typical business amenities of two-line telephones, plush bathrobes, in-room safe, complimentary shoeshine and complimentary Internet access available in each of the guest rooms.
4 Avenue Road, Yorkville
Tel: (416) 925 1234 *or* (800) 977 4197. Fax: (416) 924 4933.
Website: http://parktoronto.hyatt.com
Price: From C$299.

Windsor Arms

Built in 1927, the neo-Gothic *Windsor Arms* was purchased and returned to splendour in 1999. Rated by *Condé Nast Traveller* magazine as one of the world's top boutique hotels, its rooms are second to none – sumptuous linen, butler pantries (an invention by the hotel's owner, designed for those who need room service but do not want to see anybody), plush bathrobes, mood lighting, stereos and ample space. It is a hotel that film stars often frequent and booking one of the 28 rooms during the Toronto International Film Festival (during the first two weeks of September) is next to impossible. Dining downstairs includes the *Courtyard Café* and *Club 22*, which includes a walk-in humidor. There is also a full-service spa and adequate fitness room.
18 St Thomas Street, Yorkville
Tel: (416) 971 9666 *or* (877) 999 2767. Fax: (416) 921 9121.
E-mail: reserve@windsorarmshotel.com
Website: www.windsorarmshotel.com
Price: From C$295.

RESTAURANTS

The selected restaurants have been divided into five categories: Gastronomic, Business, Trendy, Budget and Personal Recommendations. The restaurants are listed alphabetically within these different categories, which serve as guidelines rather than absolute definitions of the establishments.

The city council passed a by-law requiring that all restaurants must be smoke-free. The exceptions to this new and somewhat contentious rule are eating establishments that define themselves as 'bars'.
Restaurant prices are subject to a provincial sales tax (PST) of 8% (10% on alcohol) and a federal goods and services tax (GST) of 7%. All taxes are usually added to the bill at the end of the meal. In addition, it is customary to tip at least 15% for good service.
The prices quoted below are for an average three-course meal for one person and for a bottle of house wine or cheapest equivalent; they do not include taxes or tip.

Gastronomic

Chiado

Located smack in the middle of Little Portugal, Toronto's sizeable Portuguese community could not ask for a better ambassador. The simple, elegant decor is accentuated by the paintings that adorn Chiado's walls. Seafood dominates, with fresh fish flown in daily – anything with tentacles finds a worthy end on the grill. Those partial to land-bound critters will find solace in the braised rabbit, pheasant or veal. No lunch weekends.
864 College Street, Little Portugal
Tel: (416) 538 1910. Fax: (416) 588 8383.
Price: C$70. Wine: C$30.

North 44

Named after Toronto's latitude, *North 44*'s location in Toronto's safe and franchise-ridden Uptown has not stopped this internationally acclaimed restaurant from being the city's most posh eating place for over a decade. Cold and steely from the outside but with a warm and artful interior, the menu changes with the seasons but everything – such as charred tuna sashimi, grilled quail and roasted venison rack – will be prepared to perfection. A recent renovation will likely keep the momentum going for another ten years. No lunch. Closed Sunday.

2537 Yonge Street, Eglinton
Tel: (416) 487 4897. Fax: (416) 487 2179.
E-mail: north.44@rogers.com
Website: www.north44restaurant.com
Price: C$70. Wine: C$26.

Opus

A meal at *Opus*, in an unassuming townhouse on a quaint, leafy street, is much like dinner at a friend's house – only with waiters and an outstanding chef. Servers are attentive, knowledgeable and friendly. The menu changes monthly and reflects the seasons – traditional French fare, such as smoked duck and rack of lamb, made with regional ingredients, often makes an appearance. No lunch.
37 Prince Arthur Avenue, Yorkville/Annex
Tel: (416) 921 3105. Fax: (416) 921 9353.
E-mail: tony@opusrestaurant.com
Website: www.opusrestaurant.com
Price: C$65. Wine: C$30.

Splendido Bar and Grill

Lamborghinis pull up and good-looking people step out and immerse themselves in *Splendido*'s bright yet sophisticated dining room. These discerning patrons come mainly for the adventurous Italian-influenced menu. Dishes include a starter of Tunisian octopus salad and mains like charcoal-grilled New York strip loin with sweet potato, Portobello mushrooms and peppercorn sauce or whole market-fresh fish cooked in a wood-burning oven. Another option is to try one of the tasting menus – five courses for C$65 or seven courses for C$85. There is a large wine list with good New and Old World selections. No lunch. Closed Monday.
88 Harbord Street, Annex
Tel: (416) 929 7788. Fax: (416) 929 3501.
Website: www.splendidoonline.com
Price: C$75. Wine: C$35.

Truffles

The award-winning restaurant of the Four Seasons' flagship hotel (see *Hotels*) and Toronto's only CAA/AAA Five Diamond restaurant (it has won the accolade for nine years running), *Truffles* is, as its name suggests, a celebration of the gourmet. Every detail – from the exotic Uffizi boar sculptures to the exotically sculpted starters, such as rare seared tuna or sautéed foie gras – has been seen to. Fish, fowl and meat are prepared with equal aplomb, with the fresh, light and aromatic cooking style rooted in authentic French flavours. A five-course tasting menu is available for C$85. The long wine list reaches deep into the wallet but includes an impressive selection by the glass. No lunch. Closed Sunday.
Four Seasons Hotel, 21 Avenue Road, Yorkville
Tel: (416) 928 7331. Fax: (416) 964 8699.
Website: www.fourseasons.com/toronto
Price: C$70. Wine: C$40.

Business

Canoe Restaurant and Bar

If there is one truly Canadian restaurant in Toronto, this is it. *Canoe* takes ingredients typical to Canada and creates contemporary gourmet dishes. Maple sugar, Saskatoon berry compote and partridgeberry jus are accessories to such daring and delicious offerings as venison and caribou. *Canoe*'s warm, woody tones add to the whole experience, although the view of Toronto Harbour tends to capture one's attention more. Prices cater to expense accounts and the wine list leans towards

Informal dining

New World selections. Reservations essential. Closed weekends.
54th Floor, Toronto Dominion Bank Tower, 66 Wellington Street West, Financial District
Tel: (416) 364 0054. Fax: (416) 364 4273.
Website: www.canoerestaurant.com
Price: C$75. Wine: C$30.

Courthouse Market Grille

Although the *Courthouse* once held trials and housed a jail, chandeliers now hang from its grand high ceilings and the food is anything but jailhouse rations. Businesspeople and other diners who frequent the Courthouse will be able to delight their palate with fresh market cuisine, while the selection of grilled meats and rotisserie chicken is certain to please. Reservations required. No lunch Saturday. Closed Sunday.
57 Adelaide Street East, Financial District
Tel: (416) 214 9379. Fax: (416) 214 1715.
E-mail: courthouse@libertygroup.com
Website: www.libertygroup.com/restaurants.html
Price: C$45. Wine: C$28.

Indian Rice Factory

The Punjabi-influenced dishes here will appeal to vegetarians and meat-lovers alike. Regular selections include *pakoras* (deep-fried fritters) and dishes such as chicken *khashabad* – a chicken breast stuffed with almonds, cashews and raisins in coconut cream. Antiques and mahogany furnishings contribute to the fine dining experience. Reservations recommended. No lunch weekends.
414 Dupont Street, Annex
Tel: (416) 961 3472. Fax: (416) 962 0199.
Price: C$30. Wine: C$31.

Jump Café and Bar

With its neatly placed palm trees and natural light, this place can be festive, loud and ebullient, although its tucked-away tables allow for a tête-à-tête as well. Since its inception, it has been *the* hangout for Toronto's brokers and traders, so it should come as no surprise that *Jump* serves up food so delicious that it alone might secure any deal. Dishes might include sirloin steak with Yukon-gold potato *frites,* roast chicken or lemon risotto. Fish dishes and other, lighter choices also grace the menu – but if calories are really a concern, the decadent desserts are best seen and not tasted. Reservations required. No lunch Saturday. Closed Sunday.
Commerce Court East, 1 Wellington Street, Financial District
Tel: (416) 363 3400. Fax: (416) 363 3830.
E-mail: jump@oliverbonacini.com
Website: www.jumpcafe.com
Price: C$45. Wine: C$30.

ZooM Caffe and Bar

At one time, this beautifully lit and beautifully peopled restaurant was a bank. Like its award-winning design – featuring small cocktail tables, low lamps, high ceilings and state-of-the-art lighting throughout – the seasonally changing menu is precise. A starter of sesame seed crusted prawns might be followed by red miso marinated pork chops or peanut and coffee crusted beef tenderloin. Four- and five-course tasting menus are available for C$65 and C$85 respectively. Wines tend towards the expensive but there is a large selection available by the glass. *ZooM* is popular for private functions so reservations are recommended. No lunch Saturday. Closed Sunday.

Alfresco dining

18 King Street East, Financial District
Tel: (416) 861 9872. Fax: (416) 861 9251.
E-mail: zoom@zoomrestaurant.com
Website: www.zoomrestaurant.com
Price: C$55. Wine: C$50.

Trendy

Bar One

An island of chic in this up-and-coming part of town, the tall ceilings and narrow walls of this young but firmly established eating place match the converted loft apartments that surround it. The interior is simple and crisp, as is the Italian and international menu, which includes soup (such as spinach and potato), fish and classic pastas like bolognaise, carbonara or marinara. Brunch and dinner only Saturday. Brunch only Sunday. Closed Monday.
924 Queen Street West, Queen West
Tel: (416) 535 1655. Fax: (416) 535 4620.
Price: C$45. Wine: C$24 (per litre).

Lolita's Lust

In an increasingly franchised part of Greektown, *Lolita's Lust* remains a perennial favourite. This intimate, dimly lit hotspot is frequented by stars when they're in town – the signage is subtle and diners should look for a pea-green building with blocked-out windows. The food is mostly Mediterranean fare, including a delicious pan-seared tuna with lentils on the side. Reservations essential. No lunch. Closed Sunday and Monday.
513 Danforth Avenue, Greektown
Tel: (416) 465 1751. Fax: (416) 465 8574.
Price: C$40. Wine: C$23.

The Paddock

The sumptuous, wooden 1940s decor of this bar/restaurant tends to get obscured on Thursday, Friday and Saturday nights by crowds of youngish drinkers. They congregate at the large L-shaped bar in search of draught beer, a well-shaken martini or their inner Humphrey Bogart. On other nights of the week, it is a bit quieter. The menu changes seasonally but highlights might include cassoulet, grilled veal tenderloin with marsala sauce or smoked pork tenderloin with baby turnip, rösti potatoes and a maple-preserved apple jus. No lunch.

178 Bathurst Street, Queen and Bathurst
Tel: (416) 504 9997. Fax: (416) 504 9110.
E-mail: info@thepaddock.ca
Website: www.thepaddock.ca
Price: C$35. Wine: C$35.

Teatro

Decorated in olive green with a red trim, this restaurant in Little Italy is lively but intimate (the small bistro tables are very close together). It is also as popular as they come, because it offers diners a refuge from the storm of pastas and pizzas in the area. The French/Mediterranean bistro menu includes classics like bouillabaisse, *steak-frites*, seafood paella and rack of lamb. Food is served until midnight, although the bar remains open until 0200. No lunch. Closed Sunday and Monday.
505 College Street, Little Italy
Tel: (416) 972 1475.
Price: C$35. Wine: C$38.

Tempo

Low levels of funk music play in the background, while dim halogen lighting and simple metal chairs and tables against muted green walls all give *Tempo* a modern, simple style. Menu items like the tempura, sashimi and sushi may sound distinctly Japanese but the daring, acclaimed food at *Tempo* veers towards fusion. Expect hand rolls (like California Rolls) flavoured with truffle oil or oyster tempura sushi. Daily specials tend toward grilled seafood dressed in strong but not overpowering Thai flavours. And to wash it all down, there are premium domestic or Japanese beers, a thoughtful wine list and a small army of single malts. No lunch.
596 College Street, Little Italy
Tel: (416) 966 5282 (day) *or* 531 2822 (evening). Fax: (416) 966 2525.
Website: www.tempotoronto.com
Price: C$40. Wine: C$24.

Budget

7 West Café

Open 24 hours, this place somehow retains its casual café feel over all three floors. Homemade pizza bagels, delicious sandwiches and salads are good choices during the summer. During the winter, nothing warms as well as the Moroccan chilli con carne (a vegetarian option is available), while the chocolate

Photo: Ontario Tourism

Market shopping

banana cake satisfies late-night sweet cravings. As well as a decent wine and beer list, herbal teas and speciality coffees are also house favourites. Reservations only accepted for large parties.
7 Charles Street West, Yonge and Bloor
Tel: (416) 928 9041.
Price: C$25. Wine: C$30.

Bar Italia

Beyond the bar, choked with well-dressed, good-looking types downing martinis and pints of beer, there is a warm yet minimalist restaurant that serves superb Italian fare. *Insalata di funghi* (warm mushroom salad), *panini Cubano* (pork tenderloin sandwich) and daily pasta specials are but some of the more popular dishes. The wine selection is mostly Italian and French with a decent domestic beer menu. In the summer, a patio seat cannot be beaten for watching the world go by. Brunch is served at the weekend. No lunch weekdays in winter.
582 College Street, Little Italy
Tel: (416) 535 3621. Fax: (416) 535 2348.
Price: C$35. Wine: C$21 (per litre).

Fresh on Bloor

Anybody who wants to eat at this packed health-food restaurant – decorated in relaxing greens and blues – must be prepared to queue. However, despite wooden tables that are set very close together, it is definitely worth the wait. With over 40 different juices from the fruity to the bizarre – including 'Date Almond' for C$6 – there is definitely something to tempt everybody's palate without any guilt. Fresh, organic food is the point here. Portions are plentiful – the Buddha bowl of tofu, rice and organic sprouts being a crowd favourite. Those who can handle a little guilt on the side should go for the sweet potato French fries, served with super-tasty miso gravy. Reservations are not accepted. *Fresh on Crawford*, 894 Queen Street West, offers a similar experience, while *Fresh on Queen*, 336 Queen Street West, is an unlicensed café/juice bar (open daytime only).
521 Bloor Street West, Annex
Tel: (416) 531 2635. Fax: (416) 531 2481.
E-mail: info@juiceforlife.com
Website: www.juiceforlife.com
Price: C$20. Wine: C$13 (per half-litre).

La Tavola Calda

Situated in the heart of Little Italy, *La Tavola Calda* serves better Italian food than most of its neighbours – at half the price. Pasta dishes range from the delicate to the robust, while vegetables are ordered as side dishes – the rapinni (a type of spinach) is excellent. The sausage or the grilled veal must be tasted. The restaurant is long and narrow, with a sparse, bistro-style decor and exposed brick walls; there is a great patio in summer. La Tavola Calda offers one of the cheapest and best meals in town. Closed Monday. Also closed Sunday in winter.
671 College Street, Little Italy
Tel: (416) 536 8328.
Price: C$20. Wine: C$24 (per litre).

Pho Hung

Frequented by students and businesspeople alike, *Pho Hung* offers superb value for money. Authentic Vietnamese selections include tasty beef-broth soups (served with or without noodles) and grilled chicken or pork with vermicelli noodles and spring rolls. The restaurant is bright and airy, with large windows overlooking Bloor Street. Closed Sunday. Visa only.
200 Bloor Street West, Annex
Tel: (416) 963 5080.
Price: C$20. Wine: C$19.
Branch:
350 Spadina Avenue, Chinatown
Tel: (416) 593 4274.

Personal Recommendations

360 The Restaurant at the Tower

Floor-to-ceiling windows, 114 storeys above the lake shore, with a view as good as it gets – blue lake as far as the eye can see to the south and Toronto spreading out in every other direction. And because *360* is the world's largest revolving restaurant, none of the view will be missed. The food is not quite as memorable but it is good enough. Lamb shank, seared salmon and prime rib all make the grade. A reservation at this restaurant also includes a post-dinner walk on the glass-floored lookout – for those who can stomach it. No lunch in winter.

CN Tower, 301 Front Street West, Downtown
Tel: (416) 362 5411. Fax: (416) 601 4895.
E-mail: info@cntower.ca
Website: www.cntower.ca
Price: C$45. Wine: C$35.

Brownes Bistro

Prized by the well-heeled residents of Rosedale, this long-lived neighbourhood bistro is unpretentious, with a lack of culinary adventurousness and hardwood floors and wood panelling reflect the casual bistro ambience. However, its longevity speaks for its quality. Pastas and pizzas change daily, while the meat-and-potatoes dishes, such as braised lamb shank, are regulars. No lunch weekends.
4 Woodlawn Avenue East, Summerhill
Tel: (416) 924 8132. Fax: (416) 924 8145.
Price: C$45. Wine: C$30.

JOV Bistro

Situated in Uptown, this New York-style restaurant – sparsely yet crisply decorated with a wood trim – offers a wonderful dining experience. The standard menu infuses modern French cuisine with Asian touches, applied to really good fish and seafood, as well as the likes of duck confit. The coup de grace, however, is the sauces, applied to game, fish or meat – the chef is a master saucier. A minimum of two people may choose a tasting menu, which contains four courses for C$62 per person . Choices include an exotic array of dishes – emu, rabbit, tiger shrimp, liver – to name but a few. A new glass of wine, specifically chosen to match the dish, arrives with each course; the cost is C$20–33 for four small/large glasses of wine. Reservations recommended. No lunch. Closed Monday and Tuesday.
1701 Bayview Avenue, Uptown
Tel: (416) 322 0530.
Price: C$50. Wine: C$30.

Rol San

Rol San is easy to overlook amid the hundred or so Chinese restaurants that line Spadina Avenue between College Street and the lake shore, especially as it has the same large round tables, plastic tablecloths and bright cardboard signs announcing specials in Chinese. However, Rol San serves delicious dim sum – such as deep fried shrimp and chive cake – by day and crave-worthy portions of fried rice, Szechuan shrimp and crispy chicken until the wee hours (0400).
323 Spadina Avenue, Chinatown
Tel: (416) 977 1128.
Price: C$30. Wine: C$22 (per litre).

ENTERTAINMENT

Nightlife

Toronto's nightlife is yet another aspect of urban life that defies the city's staid reputation. This was recently helped, in no small part, by the provincial government's decision to extend drinking hours until 0200, while nightclubs and after-hours clubs often stay open until dawn. Mixed drinks and pints tend to come in around the C$5 mark and admission is often charged at nightclubs but never at normal bars unless a band is playing. A few self-consciously trendy nightclubs may have no-jeans, no-trainers policies at the door. Since it is illegal in the Province of Ontario to serve alcohol and not serve food, bars can often be considered places to eat as much as to drink. The legal drinking age in Toronto is 19 years.

The free, alternative weeklies, *eye* (website: www.eye.net) and *NOW* (website: www.nowtoronto.com), provide the latest information on club nights and gig listings, while *Xtra* (website: www.xtra.ca) covers the gay scene. The most common nights for locals to spend on the town are Thursday, Friday and Saturday, although enthusiastic crowds can usually be found on most other nights. The most popular area for bars and clubs is in the heart of the city centre, slightly west of the Financial District, around the Theatre District on King Street and Queen Street. For a more ethnic feel, Little Italy offers Italian-flavoured bars and clubs that tend to attract a cooler, more refined crowd in search of pasta, properly mixed drinks and better music. Greektown offers a slew of Greek restaurants and bars that import something of a Mediterranean festive feel even on the darkest of winter nights. Local pubs and bars showing a hockey or baseball game on television can be found almost anywhere and are great spots for a plate of chicken wings and a beer.

Bars

British visitors will feel at home in the many pubs that dot the city, showing up on street corners and in the more commercial neighbourhood high streets. The *Madison Avenue Pub*, 14 Madison Avenue, is something like a super-pub, taking up four floors within two converted Victorian houses. The *Rebel House*, 1068 Yonge Street, a neighbourhood favourite, serves a range of good beer and uncommonly good pub food. For a taste of the excellent lager and ale at the city's best brew pubs, try the *Granite Brewery*, 245 Eglinton Avenue East, or the *Steam Whistle Brewing Company*, 255 Bremner Boulevard, directly south of the CN Tower.

Little Italy's *Bar Italia*, 582 College Street (see *Restaurants*), is a stylish and trendy cocktail bar with reasonably priced and tasty pasta, which attracts the good-looking weekend crowd. The *Rivoli*, 332 Queen Street West, attracts a slightly more alternative crowd. One side of the bar serves fusion cuisine, the other cocktails, while concerts, club nights and spoken-word events take place in the back and there is a large pool hall upstairs. Further west is the *Gypsy Co-op*, 817 Queen Street West, comfortable as a bar/lounge/restaurant earlier in the day or as a nightclub later on. One of the friendliest gay bars in Toronto is the boisterous *Woody's*, 465 Church Street. A sense of the country's ice hockey obsession can be experienced at *Wayne Gretzky's*, 99 Blue Jays Way, owned by one of the game's greatest players ever and a monument to his success on the ice.

Casinos

There are no licensed casinos in Toronto. However, there are three government-run casinos elsewhere in the province. The nearest is *Casino Niagara*, 5705 Falls Avenue, Niagara Falls (website: www.casinoniagara.com). The casino offers slot machines, blackjack, roulette, baccarat, Caribbean stud poker and craps. Patrons must be at least 19 years of age and must possess government-issued identification as proof of age. There is no dress code.

Clubs

Richmond Street is home to many of the city's biggest and best-known clubs. *Joe*, 250 Richmond Street West, has taken over one of the city's longer standing venues (*Whiskey Saigon*) and now offers a lounge and rooftop patio in addition to nights of house and retro hits at its School Disco night. Not far away is *Roxy Blu*, 12 Brant Street, known for modern R&B, garage and house, as well as high-profile DJs occasionally flown into town. A young, tapped-in crowd finds its home at *Sound Emporium*, 360 Adelaide

Street West, for electronic music, trance and breakbeats. Chilled-out spots include *Ciao Edie*, 489 College Street, filled with retro-funk furnishings, and *Fluid Lounge*, 217 Richmond Street West. On the eastern edge of the city centre is *The Government*, 132 Queen's Quay East, a massive warehouse rigged with an industrial-strength sound system that pumps out progressive house and trance Saturday nights until dawn. Gay clubs are scattered throughout the Church and Wellesley area; one of the biggest is the three-floor complex at 418 Church Street, *The Barn* and its adjacent *Stables*.

Comedy

Toronto is home to what is probably North America's most famous comedy club chain, *The Second City* (website: www.secondcity.com). The Toronto branch, situated at 56 Blue Jays Way, however, is of particular pop-cultural significance, seeing as it experienced a golden age in the late 1970s. It witnessed the beginning of the careers of future Hollywood greats, such as Dan Aykroyd, Mike Myers and Martin Short. Toronto's other big venue is *Yuk Yuk's Comedy Cabaret*, 224 Richmond Street West (website: www.yukyuks.com).

Live Music

The *Horseshoe Tavern*, 370 Queen Street West, a gritty down-home venue and the first on the continent to receive The Police, is the best place to hear new rock bands. *Massey Hall*, 178 Victoria Street, hosts everything from jazz, classical, rock and world music to international dance troupes. A more laid-back atmosphere can be found at the *Rex Jazz and Blues Bar*, 194 Queen Street West, and the *Montreal Bistro and Jazz Club*, 65 Sherbourne Street. For more jazz, check out the *Jazz In Toronto* website (website: www.jazzintoronto.com).

Sport

Toronto is first and foremost an ice hockey town, so it comes as no surprise that the *Hockey Hall of Fame*, BCE Place, 30 Yonge Street (tel: (416) 360 7765; website: www.hhof.com), is located here. The city lives and dies according to the success and failure of the *Toronto Maple Leafs* (tel: (416) 703 5323; website: www.mapleleafs.com), one of the NHL's most historic franchises. The Leafs play at the *Air Canada Centre*, 40 Bay Street (tel: (416) 815 5500; website: www.theaircanadacentre.com), as do the *Toronto Raptors* (tel: (416) 366 3865; website: www. raptors.com), the city's professional basketball team. The *Toronto Blue Jays* (tel: (416) 341 1234; website: www.bluejays.com) is the city's professional baseball team, competing in the same American League division as teams like the New York Yankees. The team plays at the *SkyDome*, 1 Blue Jays Way (tel: (416) 341 3663; website: www. skydome.com), the world's first retractable-dome stadium — considered a marvel of beauty and engineering when it was built but slowly gaining the status of a dysfunctional eyesore. During the July to November Canadian Football League season, the *Toronto Argonauts* (tel: (416) 489 2746; website: www.argonauts.ca) also play at the SkyDome.

Tickets for single games for any of the above teams are best purchased from *Ticketmaster Canada*'s sportsline (tel: (416) 872 5000; website: www. ticketmaster.ca).

Canadians are a sports-loving people. In summer months, Torontonians can be found outdoors — jogging, swimming, cycling, walking, playing any number of team sports or having a game of tennis. In winter months, the public tennis courts are iced over and become outdoor community rinks, where anyone (who can skate) is welcome to play in one of the

Nightlife

Photo: Ontario Tourism

impromp-tu games of ice hockey. The City of Toronto *Fun Guide* (website: www.toronto.ca/parks/torontofun .htm), available at any recreation centre, details the activity options available around town.

Fitness Centres

The *YMCA*, 20 Grosvenor Street (tel: (416) 975 9622; website: www.ymcatoronto.org), is a very large, modern venue situated in the heart of the city centre, offering facilities such as a sauna, whirlpool, pool, squash courts and a weight room for C$15 per day.

Golf

Although the season is defined by an icy winter, golf is an immensely popular sport in the city and there are over a hundred courses in the greater Toronto region. Within the city, visitors can play at the *Don Valley Golf Course*, intersection of Yonge Street and William Carsen Crescent (tel: (416) 392 2465; website: www.toronto.ca/parks/recreation_facilities/ golfing/donvalley.htm) for C$50–55 for 18 holes. A short distance northwest of the city centre, in the suburb of Brampton, *Lionhead Golf and Country Club*, 8525 Mississauga Road, Brampton (tel: (905) 455 8400; fax: (905) 455 5815; e-mail: info@ golflionhead.com; website: www.golflionhead.com), is a public course offering two 18-hole courses – its 'Legends' course is considered the most difficult in the country. The price of play is C$125–160, or C$75

after 1700. Most central is *City Core Golf*, 2 Spadina Avenue (tel: (416) 640 9888; website: www. golfcitycore.com), a driving range and green that is only a short putt away from the SkyDome. Play costs C$24 per hour.

Ice Skating

With ice hockey as the national sport, it is not surprising to find many Torontonians enjoying a leisurely skate during the winter. Next to Toronto City Hall, Nathan Phillips Square is iced over when the temperature drops. There is also a rink in the fashionable Hazleton Lanes shopping mall in Yorkville. Information on the city's ice rinks is available by telephone (tel: (416) 338 7465).

Swimming

During the summer, Toronto's beaches attract large crowds to walk, rollerblade and cycle along the meandering boardwalk or frolic in the blue waters of Lake Ontario. Outdoor swimming pools are also popular. *Gus Ryder Sunnyside Pool*, Budapest Park, 1755 Lake Shore Boulevard West (tel: (416) 392 6696), and the *Riverdale Outdoor Pool*, Riverdale Park, 550 Broadview Avenue (tel: (416) 392 0751), are two such options and both offer free entrance. Indoor swimming can be found at the *YMCA* (see above). Information on the city's pools is available by telephone (tel: (416) 338 7665).

Tennis

Tennis courts in Downtown are open to the general public until 1700, after which time various clubs take over. Tennis courts are located in Lytton Park and Otter Creek Park, on Cheritan Avenue.

Shopping

Thankfully, Toronto has not succumbed to mall culture to the same degree as its neighbours in the USA – most malls tend to be firmly located in the suburbs, although there are a number of shopping concourses at the bases of the larger Downtown office towers, linked by underground passageways. The one important mall that has managed to take root in Downtown is the *Eaton Centre*, located at the intersection of Yonge Street and Dundas Street (website: www.torontoeatoncentre.com). The Eaton Centre is a mall for non-mall types – lots of shopping in a more soothing environment, with a huge fountain, a ceiling that is a vast barrel vault of windows and a famous sculpture of flying Canada geese.

As a vital, densely populated hub, the city centre is filled with open-air shopping streets, each with its own character. Queen Street and College Street attract style-conscious 20- and 30-somethings. Fashions are original, often with an emphasis on obscure labels, both domestic and imported. Queen Street West also offers a variety of furniture shops, some offering cutting-edge modern designs and others displaying second-hand pieces from ten to 50 years old. There have been some signs of gentrification, sparking the now hip 'West Queen West' district, beyond Spadina Avenue and Bathurst Street. Yorkville features more upmarket shopping – Prada, Versace, Louis Vuitton – including *Holt Renfrew*, 50 Bloor Street West (website: www.holtrenfrew.com), the Canadian equivalent to New York's Saks or London's Harrods. Yonge Street offers shopping of every variety from its beginnings near the waterfront right to the northern edge of the city.

The bounty of the vast Canadian landscape can be appreciated at St Lawrence Market, at the corner of Jarvis Street and Front Street (website: www.toronto. com/stlawrence). Here, visitors can take in the sight of piles of fresh fish laid out on beds of ice, pick among butcher shops, choose between delicatessens, bakeries and a host of fruit and vegetable shops overflowing with produce. The market is open Tuesday to Thursday 0800–1800, Friday 0800–1900 and Saturday 0500–1700. Across town, Kensington Market, tucked in just behind Chinatown (west of Spadina Avenue, between Dundas Street and College Street) gives a sense of the city's multicultural make-up, with residents from over 30 cultural backgrounds. The market has been around since the 1790s and its narrow streets are filled with fruit stands, butcher shops, cafés, Asian markets and local fashion designers. Normal shopping hours (see below) are observed.

Good gifts or souvenirs include Canadian and Inuit art, local designer threads, Hudson Bay blankets and maple syrup products.

Apart from offering a wealth of good shopping, Toronto is of particular interest to the international traveller, due to the relative weakness of the Canadian Dollar. Shopping is available seven days a week and stores are generally open 1000–1800, although it is common to find some open as late as 2200, especially on Thursday, Friday and Saturday. In addition to the

Photo: Ontario Tourism

Bird's eye view of the city

7% Goods and Services Tax (GST), a provincial sales tax of 8% is added to the listed price of most purchases. The GST portion can be redeemed by non-residents for purchases and short-term accommodation totalling over C$200 (minimum C$50 per individual receipt). The *Canada Customs and Revenue Agency* (tel: (902) 432 5608 *or* (800) 668 4748; website: www.ccra-adrc.gc.ca/visitors) should be contacted for further information and forms. Private companies offer the same service but charge a fee.

Culture

Although Toronto has a reputation as a place of business, it has much to offer the visitor interested in soaking up some local culture – notably its vibrant theatre scene. Toronto has the third most theatres of any city in the world, after London and New York, showing everything from high-budget musicals to experimental fringe theatre.

Toronto's role as the cultural capital of English-speaking Canada is also evident in its major performing arts companies, with ballet, opera and the symphony all well represented during a season that generally runs from September to April. Foremost among the many classical music companies who play at *Roy Thomson Hall*, 60 Simcoe Street (tel: (416) 872 4255; website: www.roythomsonhall.com), is the *Toronto Symphony Orchestra*. Further east, the *Hummingbird Centre for the Performing Arts*, 1 Front Street East (tel: (416) 393 7469; website: www. hummingbirdcentre.com), the largest multi-use facility in the country, is home to the *Canadian Opera Company* and the *National Ballet of Canada*, as well as numerous touring acts.

The *Toronto International Film Festival* is world-famous – now the second largest in the world, after Cannes – but is only one of dozens of annual events and festivals that celebrate the diversity and creativity of Toronto's citizens in a variety of media.

In addition to the daily newspapers, the free weeklies *NOW* (website: www.nowtoronto.com) and *eye* (website: www.eye.net) have listings for major events and obscure fringe offerings. Tickets for most cultural attractions can usually be bought through *Ticketmaster Canada* (tel: (416) 870 8000; website: www. ticketmaster.ca). Tickets for many of the big musicals are available from *TicketKing* (tel: (416) 872 1212 *or* (800) 461 3333; website: www.ticketking.com) or in person (Tuesday to Saturday 1200–1930) from the *T.O. Tix* half-price ticket booth, at the southeast corner of Yonge Street and Dundas Street (tel: (416) 536 6468; website: www.totix.ca).

Music

The *Toronto Symphony Orchestra* (tel: (416) 872 4255; website: www.tso.on.ca) performs over 125 concerts every year at *Roy Thomson Hall* (see above), attracting guest performers of international acclaim. The *Canadian Opera Company* (tel: (416) 363 8231; website: www.coc.ca) has received growing audiences in recent seasons. The city has, for several years, been investigating plans to build its own opera house. For now, however, opera can be appreciated at the *Hummingbird Centre* (see above).

Theatre

The city's Theatre District is focused on King Street West, slightly north of the CN Tower. Built in 1907, the *Royal Alexandra Theatre*, 260 King Street West, is an old, spacious Victorian theatre that shows musicals along

Canadian National Exhibition

with the occasional piece of serious theatre. The nearby *Princess of Wales Theatre*, 300 King Street West, shows similarly popular fare, generally bringing touring versions of major West End and Broadway shows. Both venues are run by Mirvish Productions (tel: (416) 593 0351; fax: (416) 593 9221; e-mail: info@mirvish.com; website: www.mirvish.com) and should be booked through *TicketKing* (see above). The *Canon Theatre*, 263 Yonge Street, restored to its exquisite 1920s design and for many years the Toronto home of *Phantom of the Opera*, is now also a part of the Mirvish stable.

For a more local flavour, the *Poor Alex Theatre*, 296 Brunswick Avenue (tel: (416) 923 1644), is one of the best venues offering innovative new theatre. The *Tarragon Theatre*, 30 Bridgman Avenue (tel: (416) 531 1827; website: www.tarragontheatre.com), specialises in new Canadian writing. The *St Lawrence Centre for the Performing Arts*, 27 Front Street East (tel: (416) 366 7723; website: www.stlc.com), is home to the *Canadian Stage Company* (tel: (416) 368 3110; website: www. canstage.com), producers of modern Canadian plays and productions. Near the waterfront, the *Du Maurier Theatre*, at the Harbourfront Centre, 231 Queen's Quay West (tel: (416) 973 4000; website: www. harbourfront.on.ca), was built as an ice house in the 1920s but was renovated into a modern theatre, showing musicals alongside more serious pieces, in 1992.

Further information on drama in the city is available from the *Toronto Theatre Alliance* (tel: (416) 536 6468; website: www.theatreintoronto.com), which represents over a hundred local companies.

It is worth getting out of the city for two of the country's most important theatre festivals – the *Shaw Festival* (website: www.shawfest.com), held in Niagara-on-the-Lake (see *Excursions*), and the

Stratford Festival (tel: (800) 567 1600; website: www.stratfordfestival.ca), in Stratford, two hours' drive southwest of Toronto. As the name suggests, the focus at the Stratford Festival is on the works of Shakespeare, although the repertoire also includes more recent works by Canadian and international playwrights like Albee and Chekhov.

Dance

The National Ballet of Canada (tel: (416) 345 9686; website: www.national.ballet.ca), the country's best-known dance company, finds its home in Toronto at the *Hummingbird Centre* (see above). The company's most popular show is the annual Christmas production of *The Nutcracker*. One of the best spots for Canadian and international contemporary dance is at the *Harbourfront Centre*, 231 Queen's Quay West (tel: (416) 973 4000; website: www. harbourfront.on.ca).

Film

In recent years, Toronto has gained the nickname 'Hollywood North', due to the large number of American films that are shot on its streets and in its buildings. Around 40 American feature films are shot in Toronto every year. Recent successes include *Angel Eyes* (2001), *American Psycho* (2000) and *X-Men* (2000). A number of television series, including the US version of *Queer as Folk*, are also filmed in the city. Among the films where Toronto actually plays itself are *The City* (1999), *Forever Knight* (1992) and *Exotica* (1994), directed by University of Toronto alumnus Atom Egoyan. Honeymooning couples might want to avoid the noir-ish Marilyn Monroe and Joseph Cotton thriller, *Niagara* (1953), although the

Photo: Corel

spectacular falls do compensate for the acrimony between the newlyweds.

Every September, Toronto is flooded with celebrities and film types; patios are overrun with bruschetta and canapés, as film buffs line up to see major releases and arthouse works from around the world during the *Toronto International Film Festival* (tel: (416) 968 3456; website: www.e.bell.ca/filmfest).

As far as seeing a film in Toronto goes, it is customary for one to purchase tickets at the cinema, which means arriving early if the film is likely to sell out. Seating is always done on a first-come, first-serve basis. *Cineplex Odeon* (website: www.cineplex.com) and *Famous Players* (website: www.famousplayers.ca) operate the vast majority of Toronto's mainstream cinemas, with locations throughout the city. The *Bloor Cinema*, 506 Bloor Street West (tel: (416) 516 2330; website: www.bloorcinema.com), is popular for arthouse and more obscure international films. *Cinémathèque Ontario*, at the Art Gallery of Ontario's Jackman Hall, 317 Dundas Street West (tel: (416) 923 3456; website: www.bell.ca/cinematheque), shows a mixture of English-language and subtitled films.

Cultural Events

Still known to may Torontonians by its former name (Caribana), the *Toronto International Carnival* (website: www.torontointernationalcarnival.info) is the city's annual summer celebration of Caribbean culture and is one of the largest cultural events in North America, attracting hundreds of thousands of people. Taking place in the last two weeks of July, the festival features parades, extravagant costumes, food and music. Late June sees the *Pride Week* gay and lesbian celebration, culminating in the over-the-top *Pride Day Parade* (website: www.torontopride.com), one of the largest in the world. Summertime also sees the annual *Toronto Downtown Jazz Festival* (website: www.tojazz.com), which brings famous jazz acts from all over the world to the city's concert halls and bars, in late June. The *International Festival of Authors* (website: www.readings.org) takes place at the Harbourfront Centre, 235 Queen's Quay West (tel: (416) 973 3000), in late October. The festival attracts local and international authors for readings, lectures, talks and awards.

Literary Notes

Toronto is home to two of the English-speaking world's most talented and well-known writers, Michael Ondaatje and Margaret Atwood. Not surprisingly, their home city features directly in much of their literature. Ondaatje's *In the Skin of a Lion* (1987) follows the early history of Toronto, including the building of the Bloor Street Viaduct and the R C Harris Waterworks. Atwood's *Cat's Eye* (1988) also finds the city as its setting, telling the story of a woman painter returning to Toronto for a retrospective of her own work, which brings on a re-examination of her own and her city's past. Other famous Torontonian writers include recently acclaimed Anne-Marie MacDonald, whose *Fall on Your Knees* (1996), a story of love, abuse and incest on Canada's east coast, won the Commonwealth Prize, and Anne Michaels, whose *Fugitive Pieces* (1997) tells the story of an ageing Holocaust survivor's life and friendships in Toronto.

The famous American author, John Irving, has a particular fondness for Toronto, spending much of his time in the city. His novel, *A Prayer for Owen Meany* (1989), is concerned with a private school for girls in Toronto. And it was also in Toronto that a young American writer, Ernest Hemingway, got his big break – as a journalist on the *Toronto Star*.

Streetlife

SPECIAL EVENTS

Toronto Winterfest, ice skating and fun in the snow (website: www.toronto.ca/winterfest), early Feb, Nathan Phillips Square and Mel Lastman Square

St Patrick's Day Parade, Sunday nearest 17 Mar, Downtown

Canadian Music Week, upcoming bands (website: www.cmw.net), late Mar–early Apr, various venues

World Stage Festival, international theatre festival (website: www.harbourfront.on.ca), Apr, Harbourfront Centre

CONTACT, photography festival (website: www.contactphoto.com), May, throughout the city

Inside-Out, Toronto lesbian and gay film and video festival (website: www.insideout.on.ca), mid–late May, various cinemas

Doors Open Toronto, free access to many of the city's historic properties (website: www.doorsopen.org), late May, throughout the city

Distillery Jazz Festival (website: www.distilleryjazz.com), late May, The Distillery Historic District

Milk International Children's Festival of the Arts, theatre, music, dance, crafts and workshops (website: www.harbourfront.on.ca/milk), late May, Harbourfront Centre

NXNE – North by Northeast Music Festival and Industry Conference, Canadian and international bands (website: www.nxne.com), early Jun, various venues

Toronto International Dragon Boat Race Festival (website: www.torontodragonboat.com), late Jun, Toronto Islands

Queen's Plate Horse Racing (website: www.woodbineentertainment.com), late Jun, Woodbine Racetrack

Toronto Downtown Jazz Festival (website: www.tojazz.com), late Jun, various venues

Pride Week, gay and lesbian pride celebration (website: www.torontopride.com), late Jun, various venues

Toronto Fringe Theatre Festival (website: www.fringetoronto.com), early–mid-Jul, various venues

Molson Indy, CART auto racing (website: www.molsonindy.com), mid-Jul, Exhibition Place

Outdoor Art Exhibition (website: www.torontooutdoorart.org), mid-Jul, Nathan Phillips Square

Beaches International Jazz Festival (website: www.beachesjazz.com), late Jul, The Beaches

Toronto International Carnival (website: www.torontointernationalcarnival.info), late Jul–early Aug, throughout the city

FFIDA – Fringe Festival of Independent Dance Artists (website: www.ffida.org), early–mid-Aug, The Distillery Historic District

Canadian National Exhibition (CNE), agricultural fair, exposition and amusement park (website: www.theex.com), mid-Aug–early Sep, Canadian National Exhibition Grounds

Toronto International Film Festival (website: www.e.bell.ca/filmfest), early–mid Sep, various venues

Niagara Wine Festival, wine tasting, concerts and other events (website: www.grapeandwine.com), late Sep, Montebello Park, St Catherine's

Canadian International Marathon (website: www.runtoronto.com), mid-Oct, throughout the city

International Festival of Authors (website: www.readings.org), late Oct, Harbourfront Centre

Royal Agricultural Winter Fair (website: www.royalfair.org), early–mid-Nov, Exhibition Place

Santa Claus Parade (website: www.thesantaclausparade.org), mid-Nov, Midtown to Downtown

Canadian Aboriginal Festival (website: www.canab.com), late Nov, SkyDome

Toronto Christmas Market (website: www.torontochristmasmarket.com), Dec, opposite St Lawrence Market

Cavalcade of Lights, skating, ice-carving, festive lights and more (website: www.toronto.ca/special_events), late Nov–Jan, Nathan Phillips Square

First Night Toronto, family-oriented New Year's Eve activities (website: www.firstnight.toronto.com), 31 Dec, Toronto City Hall and other venues

VIENNA

Vienna (*Wien*) is a unique blend of the historic and the modern, so full of tradition it can be read on the face of the city, yet with a forward-looking approach that will surprise the visitor. Vienna's role as the seat of the Hapsburg Empire for centuries can be seen in the wealth of architecture and in the city's artistic and musical heritage. Many of the world's most important composers, including Beethoven and Mozart, have lived and performed behind Vienna's Baroque façades. In addition to this Baroque splendour, there are excellent examples of the Art Nouveau (Jugendstil) architecture that also flourished here.

The fall of the Hapsburg Empire, at the end of World War I, allowed Vienna's socialist undercurrents to come to the fore during the 'Red Vienna' period, resulting in numerous social housing and other projects, which still play a role in the city. Vienna's occupation by the Nazis and subsequent partitioning by the four Allied powers tend to be forgotten, as the city instead focuses on its post-war neutrality and the glittering remnants of its imperial glory. This seems to be reinforced by the image of older Viennese walking small dogs or eating cakes in cafés but it ignores the energy of Vienna's alternative and underground scenes, whose members react against the attachment to tradition in a way similar to their Secessionist counterparts a century before.

Vienna is divided into 23 *Bezirke* (districts). The original city that lay within the protective walls comprises the First District of modern Vienna. The demolition of the city walls led to the construction of the Ringstrasse and an impressive parade of buildings along its length. The majority of the tourist attractions lie on and within the Ringstrasse. Districts two to nine are arrayed between the Ringstrasse and the concentric *Gürtel* (Belt). The other districts lie beyond the Gürtel and extend into the foothills of the *Wienerwald* (Vienna Woods), where *Heurigen* (wine taverns) and pretty villages are dotted among the vineyards.

Vienna's climate is generally moderate, although the city can experience heavy snowfalls and low temperatures from December to March, as well as occasionally very high temperatures in July and August. Summer, however, is usually comfortable, with an average daily temperature of 20°C, although heavy thundershowers are likely.

The city is not only the capital of Austria but also a federal province as well, surrounded by Nieder-österreich (Lower Austria). Vienna's location on the east–west trade route along the River Danube played an important part in its history – an empire that once covered a large part of Europe was ruled from here. Even today, Vienna is the financial and administrative capital of Austria and home to a number of international organisations, including the United Nations. And with the fall of Communism, Vienna is once again at the centre of Europe.

View of Vienna and St Stephen's Cathedral

TRAVEL

Getting There By Air

Vienna International Airport (VIE)

Tel: (01) 70070. Fax: (01) 25351.
Website: www.viennaairport.com
Austria's main airport (*Wien Schwechat*) is located 18km (11 miles) southeast of the city. The airport handled 11.84 million passengers in 2001, travelling to destinations worldwide, including London, New York and Bangkok.

Major airlines: The national carrier is *Austrian Airlines* (tel: (05) 1789; website: www.aua.com). Other Austrian airlines serving the airport include *Lauda Air* and *Tyrolean*. There are a number of international carriers including *British Airways, CSA, Iberia, KLM – Royal Dutch Airlines, LOT Polish Airlines* and *Lufthansa*.

Approximate flight times to Vienna: From London is 2 hours 10 minutes; from New York is 8 hours 50 minutes; from Los Angeles is 12 hours 30 minutes; from Toronto is 8 hours 45 minutes and from Sydney is 22 hours 15 minutes.

Airport facilities: The airport offers cafés, snack bars, restaurants and bars, as well as a grocery store, florists, pharmacies, newsagents, duty-free shops and boutiques. In addition, there is a 24-hour Medical Centre (including a vaccination centre) and a Wellness Centre (massage, showers, solarium and Wellness Bar). Car hire is available from *Avis, Budget, Europcar, Hertz, Sixt* and *Thrifty*.

Business facilities: The *VIP & Business Centre* (tel: (01) 7007 23300 *or* 23400 *or* 23406; fax: 7007 23250; e-mail: vip.vie@viennaairport.com) organises events and press conferences. It also provides banqueting, photocopying and telex services. The *Danube Aviator Club* is a lounge for frequent users of Vienna Airport, with work space, telephone, modem, fax and message services, as well as an adjacent conference centre. The airport also offers 12 executive lounges.

Arrival/departure tax: None.

Transport to the city: *Wiener Linien* (tel: (01) 790 9105; website: www.wienerlinien.co.at) operates both an S-bahn commuter train and bus services from Vienna International Airport.

The S7 S-Bahn line runs at least every half an hour 0500–2230 (journey time – 25 minutes) to Wien Mitte and Wien Nord, where visitors can change to the U-Bahn. A single ticket costs €3 (plus €1.50 for onward travel on public transit).

The A4 Airport Motorway and B9 main road connect the airport with the city. Buses depart from the airport to the City Air Terminal every 20–30 minutes 0530–0100 (journey time – 20 minutes). Other buses go to Südbahnhof and Westbahnhof rail stations approximately once an hour 0530–2310 (journey time – 20 and 35 minutes, respectively). A single ticket costs €5.80 or €5 with a *Vienna Card* (see *Public Transport* in *Getting Around*). Buses to Bratislava (Slovak Republic) and Budapest (Hungary) are also available. Taxis to the city (journey time – 30 minutes) are metered but a fixed price of €35–40 to the city centre can be paid at the booking counter. The surcharge for luggage is €1 for 20–50kg and €2 for more than 50kg. For trips from the city to the airport, a charge of €10 may be added to the fare, to cover the driver's return cost. Limousines cost from €23 (journey time – 20 minutes).

Getting There By Water

Vienna is accessible from a number of cities along the River Danube, including Passau (Germany), Bratislava (Slovak Republic) and Budapest (Hungary). The *Reichsbrücke Schiffahrtszentrum* (Navigation Centre), near the Vorgartenstrasse U-Bahn station, is the main dock for passenger boats to and from Vienna. The centre has a café, restaurant with terrace, customs and shipping facilities. The smaller boat terminal, near Schwedenplatz station, is used only for local boat tours. Queries should be directed to *DDSG* (tel: (01) 5888 0442; fax: (01) 5888 0440; e-mail: info@ddsg-blue-danube.at; website: www.ddsg-blue-danube.at).

Boat services: *DDSG Blue Danube Schiffahrt GmbH* (see above) offers hydrofoil crossings from Bratislava Wednesday to Sunday from May to October (journey time – 1 hour 45 minutes), for €21 one way or €32 return. Daily trips from Budapest are available from April to October for €75 one way or €99 return, with additional trips in July and August (journey time – 6 hours 20 minutes). A number of shorter cruise options are also available. Reservations are required.

Transport to the city: The main terminal is *Reichsbrücke*, which is located near the Vorgartenstrasse U-Bahn station. The U1 goes to Stephansplatz in the city centre. Schwedenplatz station, near the smaller boat terminal, is connected by lines U1 and U4.

Getting There By Rail

Österreichischen Bundesbahnen or *ÖBB* (tel: (01) 58000; website: www.oebb.at) operates the 5800km (3600 miles) of rail network in Austria. In addition to the usual onboard services (restaurant and bar cars, snack trolleys and telephones), *ÖBB* offers mini-office compartments (with power points for laptop computers) and women-only compartments for those seeking hassle-free travel. The *ÖBB* also can arrange a pick-up service to greet passengers on the platform and conduct them to their hotels. In Vienna, this service is available at Wien Westbahnhof, in association with the Arcotel Hotel Wimberger.

Vienna's major rail stations and their U-Bahn connections are *Westbahnhof*, Europaplatz, on the U3 and U6 (tel: (01) 5800 31060; fax: (01) 5800 25811), *Südbahnhof*, Südtirolerplatz, on the U1 (tel: (01) 5800 31050; fax: (01) 5800 25830), *Franz-Josefs-Bahnhof*, Franz-Josefs Platz, on the U4 (tel: (01) 5800 31020; fax: (01) 5800 25831), and *Wien Mitte*, Landstrasser Hauptstrasse 1, on the U3 and U4 (tel: (01) 5800

31070; fax: (01) 5800 25815). Facilities at most main stations include bicycle hire, gift shops and a door-to-door luggage service. Timetable information is available 24 hours a day (tel: 1717).

Rail services: Intercity trains within Austria follow the main eastbound route from Bregenz to Vienna (journey time – 8–9 hours) via Innsbruck, Salzburg and Linz, or travel north from Graz (journey time – 2 hours 30 minutes) or Klagenfurt (journey time – 4 hours 30 minutes) via Bruck an der Mur. There are departures to the major cities at least once every two hours. Domestic rail services pass through breathtaking Alpine scenery but this is unfortunately bypassed by the majority of international services. Travellers should watch out for the stunning view of the Melk Abbey on the main line approaching Vienna from the west.

There are international services from most Central and Eastern European capitals. Night trains are available from most Western European countries, including Paris (journey time – 14 hours) and Berlin (journey time – 11 hours) and from as far east as Moscow (although this journey takes one and a half days).

Transport to the city: All of Vienna's railway stations are connected to the U-Bahn network (see above), either directly or by a very short walk.

Getting There By Road

Austria has an excellent network of roads, with *Autobahnen* (motorways indicated by an 'A') between major centres and connecting to the 'E' trans-European routes. *Bundesstrassen* (national roads) have a 'B' prefix. Traffic drives on the right. Speed limits are 130kph (81mph) on motorways, 100kph (62mph) on main roads and 50kph (31mph) in built-up areas. Tolls are payable on a number of mountain roads, tunnels, motorways and main roads. Toll stickers (*Autobahn-vignette*), which must be attached to the windscreen, are available for purchase at €7.60 (valid for ten days), €21.80 (for two months) or €72.60 (for one year) from tobacconists, border-crossing points, filling stations near the border and from automobile clubs *ARBÖ* (website: www.arboe.or.at) and *ÖAMTC* (website: www.oeamtc.at).

The minimum driving age in Austria is 18 years and drivers must carry a European driving licence or an International Driving Permit. Third-party insurance is mandatory. Seatbelts must be worn and children under 12 years may not sit in the front seat. The legal maximum alcohol to blood ratio for driving is 0.08%. Winter tyres are essential during the colder season and travellers who require snow chains can hire them at major border-crossing points.

Information on road conditions is available in English from the *Austrian Automobile Club* (tel: (01) 711 997; fax: (01) 713 1807) daily 0600–2000. Regular road reports in German automatically interrupt the chosen radio station on car radios.

Emergency breakdown services: *ARBÖ* 123; *ÖAMTC* 120.

Routes to the city: The *Westautobahn* (A1) connects Vienna to Linz, Salzburg and Western Europe. The *Südautobahn* (A2) leads to Graz, Klagenfurt and the Italian border. The *Ostautobahn* (A4) passes the airport on its way to Bratislava and Budapest. The A22 connects the city to Prague, in the north.

Approximate driving times to Vienna: From Linz – 2 hours; Budapest – 2 hours 35 minutes; Salzburg – 3 hours.

Coach services: *Eurolines Austria* (tel: (01) 712 0453; fax: (01) 7120 45320; e-mail: info@eurolines.at; website: www.eurolines.at) offers coach services throughout Europe, departing from the *Wien Mitte* bus station, Landrasser Haupstrasse (on the U-Bahn Landstrasse/Wien Mitte). Coach services within Austria are operated in partnership with *Blaguss Internationale Buslinien*, Richard Strauss Strasse 21 (tel: (01) 610 900; fax: (01) 6109 0125; e-mail: office@blaguss.com). National services are also provided by *Postbus* (tel:

(01) 794 440; e-mail: kundenservice@postbus.at; website: www.postbus.at) and a number of private operators. Timetable information (tel: (01) 71101) is available 0700–1900.

Getting Around

Public Transport

The Vienna Transport Authority, *Wiener Linien* (tel: (01) 790 9105; website: www.wienerlinien.co.at), operates the U-Bahn (**underground**), S-Bahn (**commuter rail**), Strassenbahn (**tram**) and **bus** network. Public transport operates between 0500 and 2400. After midnight, half-hourly **night buses** radiate out from Schwedenplatz.

The **U-Bahn** system comprises four lines. The U2 follows the Ringstrasse from Karlsplatz to Schottenring. The U4, with its Art Nouveau stations, completes the ring and leads off into the northern and western suburbs. The east–west U3 and north–south U1 cross in the centre of the Innerestadt (inner town). The U6 is basically a tram on a dedicated track that runs parallel to the Gürtel.

Vienna has one of the largest **tram** networks in the world. The trams are affectionately referred to as 'Bims' because of the noise they make.

A single fare for U-bahn, bus and tram costs €1.50 (€2 if purchased on the tram or bus) and there is no additional charge for transfers. A single night bus fare costs €1. There is a fine of €40 for passengers who are caught without a valid ticket – on-board inspections are carried out at sporadically. Tickets are available at Wiener Linien ticket offices and service centres, vending machines and tobacco/newsagent (*tabak*) outlets.

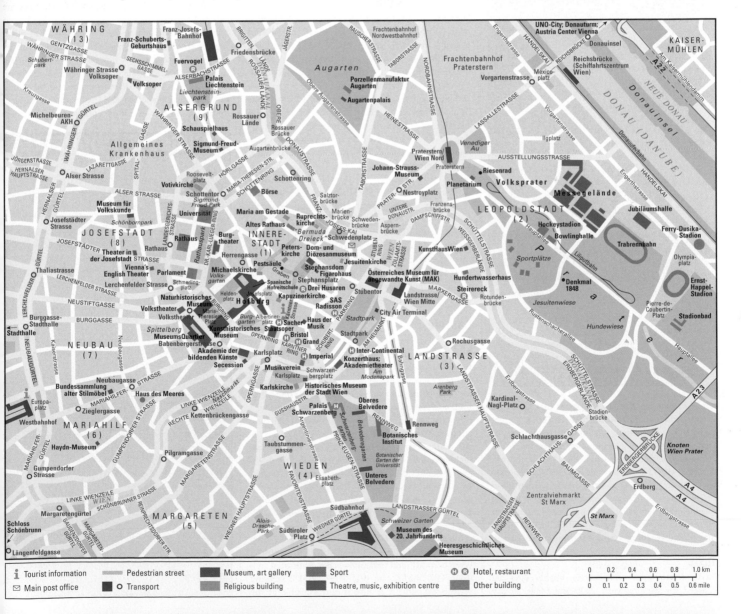

ℹ Tourist information	▬ Pedestrian street	■ Museum, art gallery
✉ Main post office	● ○ Transport	Religious building

Sport · Theatre, music, exhibition centre · H R Hotel, restaurant · Other building

0 0.2 0.4 0.6 0.8 1.0 km
0 0.1 0.2 0.3 0.4 0.5 0.6 mile

BUSINESS PROFILE

In addition to being the capital, Vienna is Austria's economic powerhouse and takes the lead in the administrative, cultural and educational sectors. It is also an important centre for international business and is one of the most sought-after conference venues in the world. Vienna is home to a number of international organisations, including the *United Nations Industrial Development Organisation (UNIDO)*, the *International Atomic Energy Agency (IAEA)*, the *Organisation of Petroleum Exporting Countries (OPEC)*, the *United Nations International Drug Control Programme (UNDCP)* and the *World Federation of Tourist Guides Association (WFTGA)*.

Many of the old small to medium-sized companies have their offices in the main shopping precinct, the First District and Sixth District. Newer businesses have spread out into the suburbs, as far afield as the airport and beyond.

Vienna is the sixth most prosperous region in the EU. One-quarter of Austria's workforce is employed in the city and the Vienna area generates approximately 28% of the country's GDP. Around 40% of all Austrian industrial companies are located here. Most of the industry is small to medium-sized – there are very few Austrian multinationals. The unemployment rate for 2002 was 4%, compared with the national average of 6.3%. Growth has slowed down due to the government's restrictive budgeting policy and to the general slowdown in Europe's economic growth. This remains especially marked in the construction industry and in tourism. The inflation rate remains around the 2% mark.

Since joining the European Union on 1 January 1995, Austria has continued to build on its trade with Western Europe (three-quarters of its trade is with EU nations, with Germany its most important trading partner). At the same time, the country is a major player in the expanding markets of Eastern Europe. Overall, the country has good ties with its neighbours to the east and this translates into strong economic relationships (some 14% of exports are to Eastern European nations). Since it has a small domestic market, Austria is highly dependent on exports. The country has a highly skilled workforce and the fortune of having congenial labour–management relations. Co-operation is mutually beneficial and results in far fewer strike days. Austrians have a high standard of living – within the top 15 countries worldwide – and the competitive marketplace means that consumers demand a high standard of quality and service.

The *Vienna Card* (€16.90) is a **pass** that allows 72 hours of travel on the U-bahn, trams and buses (except night buses) and offers discounts on attractions, at many shops and restaurants (see *Passes* in *Tourist Information*). Other passes include the 24-hour network pass (€5), the 72-hour network pass (€12), the weekly season ticket (€12.50), and the eight-day strip ticket (€24), which can be used for two people travelling together. Passes are available from Wiener Linien ticket offices and service centres. A comprehensive transit map is available for purchase at €1 from ticket offices.

Taxis

Taxis are equipped with meters. Higher fares are charged for trips between 2300 and 0600, all day Sunday and public holidays – a surcharge for luggage is often levied and these rates are clearly posted inside the taxi.

Taxis rates are an initial €2, plus approximately €0.20 for each quarter kilometre or 35.8 seconds of waiting time and a €0.50 final charge. There is also a calling fee of €2 for licensed *Radio Taxis* (tel: (01) 31300 *or* 40100 *or* 60160 *or* 81400) and a €1 surcharge for hailing a taxi from a *Taxistandplatz* (taxi rank). Between 2300 and 0600 and on Sundays, the initial charge rises to €2.10. Within the city, no additional charges for luggage, pets, driving back without passengers and other circumstances are allowed. A tip of 10% or rounding up to the nearest Euro is common.

Limousines

Limousines and minibuses are available from a number of companies, for sightseeing, airport transfers and special occasions. These include *Austria Chauffeur Limousines* (tel: (01) 512 7000; fax: (01) 512 3800; e-mail: acl@aclvienna.at) and *RCV Carey Chauffeur Limousine Service Vienna* (tel: (01) 7007 33340; fax: (01) 7007 33377; e-mail: reservation@rcv.at; website: www.awr.co.at). Hire rates cost around €280 upwards for an eight-hour day, depending on the type of limousine hired.

Driving in the City

While pedestrian tourists may appreciate the jumble of tiny streets in the Innerestadt, motorists will find it a nightmare. The area is best avoided during the day, although even at night it can be almost impossible to find a parking place on the street. Parking lots are often located underneath squares and their entrances are fairly subtle. Parking costs from €5 per hour. Short-term street parking is available in districts one to nine of Vienna's 23 districts. The designated areas are indicated by a blue line on the road, often only marked at the entrance to the short-term parking zone. Tickets – valid for 30, 60 or 90 minutes – are available for purchase at vending machines and newsagents. Hours and restrictions for these areas vary. Parking is strictly policed and fines are high, especially if the car is towed away. Visitors should note that there are restrictions on parking camper vans anywhere near the city centre. Outside the centre, the *Gürtel* (Belt) provides a fairly efficient way of getting around the city but can be slow during rush hour, which is 0730–0900 and 1500–1830.

Car Hire

A national driving licence is sufficient for nationals of EU states – other nationalities should obtain an International Driving Permit. The minimum age for hiring a car is usually 21 years, although many firms have a surcharge for those under 25 years. Third-party insurance is mandatory in Austria and those hiring a car should make sure this is covered in the hire contract. A credit card is required.

All of the major car hire firms are represented, including *Avis*, Opernring 35 (tel: (01) 587 6241; fax: (01) 587 4900; website: www.avis.at), *Budget*, Landstrasser Hauptstrasse 2 (tel: (01) 7146 5650; fax: (01) 714 7238; website: www.budget.com), *Europcar*, Schwechat, Flughafen (tel: (01) 7007 33316; fax: (01) 7007 33716; website: www.europcar.at), *Hertz*, Kärntner Ring 17 (tel: (01) 512 8677; fax: (01) 512 5034; website: www.hertz.at), and *Sixt*, Schwechat, Flughafen (tel: (01) 7007 36517; fax: (01) 7007 36517; website: www.e-sixt.com). Car hire is also available at the airport and at both Westbahnhof and Südbahnhof stations. Car hire rates vary between approximately €80 and €160 per day.

Bicycle Hire

State-owned bicycles are available for hire from *Rent a Bike*, at train stations Westbahnhof (tel: (01) 5800 32985), Bahnhof Wien Nord (tel: (01) 5800 34817), Bahnhof Floridsdorf (tel: (01) 5800 31011), and Südbahnhof (tel: (01) 5800 35886), for €9 per day (€6.50 with a valid rail ticket and photo identification). There are a number of private hire companies in the city, principally near the banks of the River Danube, with easy access to the miles of cycle paths along the Danube Island. *Pedal Power*, Austellungsstrasse 3 (tel: (01) 729 7234; e-mail: office@pedalpower.at; website: www.pedalpower.at), is located just west of the Praterstern U1 underground station. Rates range from €17 for four hours to €27 for one day (24 hours). Bikes can be delivered to hotels, for a surcharge of around €5. Bicycles are available for hire from March to October only.

Rad und Skaterverleih, Copa Cagrana, Donauinsel (tel: (01) 263 5242; fax: (01) 263 5600; e-mail: office@fahrradverleih.at; website: www.fahrradverleih.at), is open from March to October and hires out bicycles for €4.80 per hour, €14.40 for four hours or €24 for a day (six–12 hours). Children's, tandem and family bikes are also available.

Bicycles may be taken on the U-Bahn for a half-price fare, except during rush hour. There is a network of well-marked bicycle paths, however, riders should take care in the Innerestadt and along major routes. *Wien Tourismus* (see *Tourist Information*) provides brochures on cycling in Vienna. The *Rad Weg*, a booklet available from bookshops, shows all the cycle routes.

BUSINESS ETIQUETTE

The Austrians, especially the Viennese, are extremely formal to strangers. It is essential to address business contacts by their title, until familiarity is well established. English is commonly used in international business settings, however, a few words in German – by way of introduction – will not go amiss. Nevertheless, business dress is not too formal in Vienna and it is possible to go to a business meeting without a tie. It is, however, better for business visitors to err on the side of caution in the first instance.

Business hours are generally Monday to Friday 0800–1600/1700, with many offices closing slightly earlier on Friday at 1500/1600. Austrians greatly enjoy eating in restaurants and business meeting are often scheduled over a long lunch. Breakfast and brunch meetings are also becoming increasingly popular. Business visitors should not suggest lunch as a location for a first meeting, however.

Austrians tend to keep work and social life separate. Overtime and weekend work is rare. On those few occasions when one is invited to a business contact or colleague's home for dinner, a gift of flowers for the hostess and a bottle of wine for the host is essential, as is punctuality. Visitors to homes should also at least offer to take off their shoes upon entering. Business meals are more for getting to know people, so family and politics should be avoided in conversation.

SIGHTSEEING

Sightseeing Overview

The heart of Vienna is the *Innerestadt* – the area that lay within the city walls, until they were demolished in the mid-19th century. It is here that some of Vienna's most popular tourist attractions can be found, along with pedestrianised streets lined with countless shops, cafés, bars and restaurants. The centre point is the *Graben* ('moat'), which is a wide square lined with shops and pavement cafés under large umbrellas. Following the demolition of the city walls in 1857, the *Ringstrasse* was laid out and some of Vienna's most beautiful buildings were built along it, between 1858 and 1865. Among the most important are the *Staatsoper* (State Opera House), *Kunsthistorisches Museum* (Museum of Fine Arts), *Naturhistorisches Museum* (Natural History Museum), *Parlament* (Parliament), *Rathaus* (City Hall) and *Burgtheater*.

Although most major attractions are in the First District, the other inner districts have much to offer. *Leopoldstadt* (Second District) lies on the eastern side of the Danube Canal. It is here that the massive *Prater* can be found. *Landstrasse* (Third District) includes the *Schwarzenberg Palace* and the *Konzerthaus*, although the main attraction is the *Belvedere Palace*. *Wieden* (Fourth District) is a small neighbourhood that is just as fashionable as the First District. Most of the city's activity centres are around *Karlsplatz*, with its domed namesake, *Karlskirsch*. *Margareten* (Fifth District) is more residential and the historic homes of Schubert and Gluck still stand here. *Mariahelf* (Sixth District) includes Vienna's busiest shopping street, *Mariahilferstrass*. The *Naschmarkt* (Produce Market) and the *Flohmarkt* (Flea Market), on Saturday morning, add to the excitement, while the surrounding streets are packed with *Beisls* (small restaurants), theatres, cafés and pubs. *Neubau* (Seventh District) includes the *Spittleburg Quarter*, where the old houses have been renovated into boutiques, restaurants, theatres and galleries. *Josefstadt* (Eighth District) was once the area favoured by civil servants – the *Josefstadt Theatre*, the city's oldest (1788), is still in operation. *Alsergrund* (Ninth District) is often called the academic quarter – Freud's home, now a museum, is located here, as is the *Lichtenstein Palace*, which now houses the *Museum of Modern Art*.

Key Attractions

Stephansdom (St Stephen's Cathedral)

The imposing *St Stephen's Cathedral* marks Graben's eastern end and is easily spotted, due to its brightly coloured roof tiles, from more distant viewpoints. Construction began on the cathedral in the 12th century and was completed in 1433. Major restoration and rebuilding work was necessary after the cathedral caught fire at the end of World War II.

Stephansplatz 1
Tel: (01) 5155 23767. Fax: (01) 5155 23191.
Website: www.stephansdom.at
Transport: U-Bahn Stephansplatz.
Opening hours: Daily 0600–2000; services Sat 1900 and Sun 1015 (Sep–Jun), Sun 0930 (Jul–Aug); guided tours Mon–Sat at 1030 and 1500, Sun 1500.
Admission: €2 (south tower); €3 (north tower); €3 (catacombs); €3 (guided tour).

Schönbrunn Palace

Hofburg

The Imperial Palace until 1918, the *Hofburg* is almost a city in itself. Today, it houses the office of the Austrian president, an international conference centre, a number of museums, the chapel where the Vienna Boys' Choir sings and the hall in which the Lipizzaner stallions perform. Visitors can tour the *Kaiserappartements* (Imperial Apartments), including Franz-Josef's private rooms, the great audience hall, dining rooms and staterooms. The *Hofsilber- und Tafelkammer* (Court Silver and Tableware Chamber) is also on show. The *Schatzkammer* (Treasury), Schweizerhof 1, contains stunning exhibits that exemplify the power and wealth of one of Europe's most important empires. The imperial crown of the Holy Roman Empire rests here, as does the crown of the Austrian Empire, the 15th-century Burgundian treasure and the treasure of the Order of the Golden Fleece.

Innerer Burghof 1, Kaisertor
Tel: (01) 533 7570 (Imperial Apartments and Court Silver) *or* 533 7931 (Treasury). Fax: (01) 5337 57033 (Imperial Apartments and Court Silver) *or* 5332 4352 (Treasury).
Transport: Main entrance on Michaelerplatz, at the western end of Kohlmarkt, nearest U-Bahn Herrngasse (U3).
Opening hours: Daily 0900–1700 (Imperial Apartments and Court Silver); Wed and Fri–Mon 1000–1800, Thurs 1000–2100 (Treasury).
Admission: €7.50 (Imperial Apartments and Court Silver), €8 (Treasury).

Spanische Hofreitschule (Spanish Riding School)

For over 400 years, the horses of the *Spanish Riding School* have performed their elegant manoeuvres at the Imperial Stables. The *Lipizzaner Museum Wien* (situated at the stables) traces the history of these renowned performing horses and offers the opportunity to see

Hundertwasserhaus

into the animals' stables. The easiest way for visitors to see the horses in action is at their morning training sessions, Tuesday to Saturday 1000–1200. Tickets to the training sessions, which involve classical dressage exercise to music, are only available at the door on the day. Tickets for the actual performances are in high demand and need to be booked well in advance. The season generally runs from March to June and from September to December. Gala performances vary from month to month, usually Saturday or Sunday mornings and occasionally Friday evenings. Tickets are available on the Internet, by post or by fax and cost €35–105 (seated) or €24–28 (standing room). Final dress rehearsals before the season starts are cheaper (€20) and tickets are available on a first-come-first-served basis.

Michaelerplatz 1 (Riding School ticket office), Reitschulgasse 2 (Lipizzaner Museum)

Tel: (01) 533 9031 (Riding School) *or* 5252 4416 (Lipizzaner Museum). Fax: (01) 535 0186.

E-mail: office@srs.at *or* lipizzaner@khm.at

Website: www.spanische-reitschule.com *or* www. lipizzaner.at

Transport: U-Bahn Stephansplatz; tram D, J, 1 or 2; bus 57A to Burgring.

Opening hours: Daily 0900–1800 (museum); Tues–Sat 1000–1200 (morning training sessions).

Admission: €5 (museum); €11.50 (training sessions); €14.50 (combined ticket); concessions available.

Schloss Schönbrunn (Schönbrunn Palace)

Schönbrunn Palace is Vienna's answer to Versailles and was used as the summer residence of the Hapsburgs from the 18th century until 1918. Of the 1411 rooms in the palace, 40 are open to the public. The golden-yellow palace is set within equally magnificent gardens, landscaped in the Baroque style, with some monumental views. The palace and gardens are included in the UNESCO World Heritage List. The *Gloriette* is a triumphal arch that stands on the hilltop behind the palace and affords a stunning view over the grounds and the city beyond. The *Palmenhaus* (Palm House) and *Schmetterlingshaus* (Butterfly House) are excellent examples of late 19th-century architecture, with cast iron columns delicately holding up the glass walls and roof. The 'Roman ruins' in the garden are a typical folly (built during the Hapsburg's time) and are often used for staging summer productions of *Don Giovanni*. The world's oldest zoo can be found in the park. It was commissioned in 1752, to amuse and educate the court.

Schönbrunner Schloss Strasse 13

Tel: (222) 8111 3239. Fax: (222) 8111 3333.

E-mail: info@schoenbrunn.at

Website: www.schoenbrunn.at

Transport: U-Bahn Schönbrunn or Hietzing (Zoo).

Opening hours: Daily 0830–1700 (Apr–Oct, until 1900 Jul and Aug); daily 0830–1630 (Nov–Mar).

Admission: €8 (audio-guided Imperial Tour of 22 rooms); €10.50 (extended, audio-guided Grand Tour of 40 rooms); €18 (SB Pass Classic, Apr–Oct, including Grand Tour, Privy Garden, the maze and labyrinth, Gloriette, viewing terrace and court bakery).

Belvedere

The *Oberes Belvedere* (Upper Belvedere Palace), which was built in 1721–23, for Prince Eugene of Savoy, offers terrific views across the gardens to the *Unteres Belvedere* (Lower Belvedere) and the city beyond. Artwork from the middle ages and the Baroque era is featured in the *Unteres Belvedere*. The *Oberes Belvedere* houses art from the 19th-century classical, Romantic and Biedermeier periods on the second floor and post-1918 art on the ground floor. The first floor, however, is what draws visitors, with paintings by Gustav Klimt (including *der Küss*), Egon Schiele and other fin-de-siècle artists.

Österreichische Galerie Belvedere, Prinz Eugenstrasse 27

Tel: (01) 79557. Fax: (01) 798 4337.

E-mail: belvedere@belvedere.at

Website: www.belvedere.at

Transport: U-Bahn Südbahnhof; tram D.

Opening hours: Tues–Sun 1000–1800.

Admission: €7.50; special exhibitions cost extra (concessions available).

Kunsthistorisches Museum (Museum of Fine Arts)

This museum was built to house the imperial Hapsburg collections in one place, although these have now grown to such an extent that some are housed in the *Hofburg* and in *Schönbrunn Palace* (see above). The grand staircase in the *Kunsthistorisches Museum* provides passage to the galleries, which include the Antiquities, Egyptian-Oriental and Coin collections. The *Kunstkammer* (art chamber) houses sculpture and decorative arts. The *Gemäldegalerie* (picture gallery) has works by Old Masters – including Dürer, Raphael, Rembrandt, Rubens and Titian – and the most comprehensive collection of Brueghels in the world.

Maria-Theresien-Platz 1

Tel: (01) 525 240. Fax: (01) 5252 4503.

E-mail: info@khm.at

Website: www.khm.at

Transport: U-Bahn Babenbergerstrasse or Volkstheater.

Opening hours: Tues–Sun 1000–1800 (until 2100 Thurs).

Admission: €9 (including special exhibitions); concessions available.

Naturhistorisches Museum (Natural History Museum)

The *Naturhistorisches Museum* is the mirror image of the *Kunsthistorisches Museum*, housing collections of anthropological, geological and palaeontological exhibits, including a variety of dinosaur and ice-age mammal fossils. A highlight among the prehistoric artefacts is the 25,000-year-old 'Venus of Willendorf' sculpture.

Maria-Theresien-Platz 1

Tel: (01) 521 770. Fax: (01) 523 5254.

Website: www.nhm-wien.ac.at

Transport: U-Bahn Babenbergerstrasse or Volkstheater.

Opening hours: Wed–Mon 0900–1800 (until 2100 Wed).

Admission: €6.50 (concessions available).

Further Distractions

Prater

The *Prater* is a giant wooded park, fairground and the location of one of Vienna's most famous sights – the century-old *Riesenrad* (Giant Ferris Wheel). Harry Lime fought here in *The Third Man* (1949) and Ethan Hawke and Julie Delpy fell in love here in *Before Sunrise* (1995).

Prater

Tel: (01) 969 7817.

E-mail: info@wiener-prater.at

Website: www.wiener-prater.at

Transport: S-Bahn or U-Bahn Praterstern; trams O, 5 or 21.

Riesenrad (Giant Ferris Wheel)

Prater 90

Tel: (01) 729 5430. Fax: (01) 7295 43020.

E-mail: info@wienerriesenrad.com

Website: www.wienerriesenrad.com

Opening hours: Daily 0900–2400 (May–Sep); daily 1000–2200 (Mar-Apr and Oct); daily 1000–2000 (Nov–Feb).

Admission: €7.50.

KunstHausWien (Vienna Art House)

KunstHausWien is the unmistakable architectural expression of Friedensreich Hundertwasser's unique vision. Appearing like a Klimt painting as seen through a kaleidoscope, the building contains an exhibition of Hundertwasser's artwork, as well as a bright café with a chic clientele and relaxing garden. The goulash is excellent. The nearby *Hundertwasserhaus* is an apartment project, which can only be viewed from the street.

Untere Weissgerberstrasse 13

Tel: (01) 712 0491. Fax: (01) 712 0496.

E-mail: information@kunsthauswien.com

Website: www.kunsthauswien.com

Transport: Trams N and O to Radetskyplatz.

Opening hours: Daily 1000–1900.

Admission: €8; all exhibitions half price on Mon.

Kaisergruft (Imperial Burial Vault)

The *Imperial Burial Vault* in the *Kapuzinerkirche* (Capuchin Church), which was built between 1622

and 1632, is well worth a visit. The vault became the burial place of the Hapsburgs and the highlight is the double casket of Maria-Theresa and Franz I.
Neuer Markt 1
Tel: (01) 5126 85316.
Website: www.kaisergruft.at
Transport: U-Bahn Stephansplatz or Karlsplatz.
Opening hours: Daily 0930–1530.
Admission: €3.60.

Haus der Musik (House of Music)

The *Haus der Musik* is a major new addition to Vienna's museum scene, offering a link between technology and art. The ground floor has concert spaces and a wine bar, while the first floor houses the museum of the *Vienna Philharmonic Orchestra*, where visitors are given the opportunity to view the last New Year's Day Concert. The second floor is the *Sonosphere*, where many aspects of sound are presented, using hands-on computer technology and giant instruments. The third floor is dedicated to historic displays of great Viennese composers, from Haydn to Berg. One room features the *Virtual Conductor*, where visitors can use virtual technology to conduct the Vienna Philharmonic Orchestra. The fourth floor includes the *Brain Opera*, an interactive musical environment with unique ultramodern musical instruments. The fifth floor includes concert rooms and an excellent café with superb views over St Stephen's Cathedral. All exhibitions are presented in both German and English and anyone can happily spend hours here, whether musically inclined or not.
Seilerstätte 30
Tel: (01) 516 4851. Fax: (01) 516 4848.
E-mail; info@haus-der-musik-wien.at
Website: www.hdm.at
Transport: U-Bahn Stephansplatz, Karlsplatz or Schwarzenbergplatz.
Opening hours: Daily 1000–2200.
Admission: €8.50 (Haus der Musik); €5 (Vienna Philharmonic Museum); €10 (combination ticket).

Tours of the City

Walking Tours

There are 11 tours available in English (and many more in German), as part of the *Vienna Walks* programme (tel: (01) 876 7111; website: www. viennawalks.tix.at *or* www.wienguide.at). These vary from 'Vienna in the Footsteps of *The Third Man*', which scouts out the locations of the famous film, to tours of the homes of Mozart, Beethoven and Schubert. Other popular options include tours focusing on a historical period, Jewish life in Vienna, or the underground city of crypts and wine cellars. Tours take one and a half to two and a half hours and cost €11–16. Any admission fees and transport on the U-bahn, trams or buses are extra. These tours do not need to be pre-booked.
Original Vienna Walks (tel/fax: (01) 889 2896; e-mail: contact@verliebtinwien.at; website: www. verliebtinwien.at) offers a program of walks in both German and English (August to October). The walks vary but include Art Nouveau architecture, medieval quarters and hidden courtyards, or the Imperial Palace. Tours are between 90 minutes and two hours and cost €10.50, with a minimum of three walkers per group.

Bus Tours

Vienna Sightseeing Tours (tel: (01) 7124 68380; fax: (01) 714 1141; e-mail: vst@viennasightseeingtours.com; website: www.viennasightseeingtours.com) offers a

number of half-day city tours, as well as full-day excursions to Prague, Budapest and other locations. The three-and-a-half-hour 'Historical City Tour', which includes a visit to Schönbrunn Palace, costs €32. Hotel pick-up is arranged and participants are given the option of a free transfer to Vienna Sightseeing Tours' hop-on hop-off service, the *Vienna Line*. This sightseeing bus route has 13 stops and departs 1000, 1100, 1300, 1400, 1500 and 1600 from the Staatsoper. A full circuit takes two hours and 45 minutes, while full hop-on hop-off day tickets cost €18. These are available for purchase on the bus, at the Staatsoper stop or from many hotel concierges.
Cityrama (tel: (01) 534 1312; e-mail: office@ cityrama.at; website: www.cityrama.at) offers a similar full city tour, as well as a number of other tours of Vienna and other destinations, in both German and English. The 'Sisi Tour' (Sisi is the name given to Emperor Franz Joseph's wife, Elisabeth) covers the historical sites of the city and includes a visit to St Stephen's Cathedral, Hofburg and a training session at the Spanish Riding School. The three-hour tour costs €33, which does not include entrance to the Spanish Riding School. Free hotel pick-up is arranged.

Boat Tours

The *DDSG Blue Danube Schiffahrt GmbH* (tel: (01) 588 800; fax: (01) 5888 0440; e-mail: info@ddsg-blue-danube.at; website: www.ddsg-blue-danube.at) offers cruises on the River Danube, available daily from mid-April to the end of September. The two sightseeing tours, the 'Grand Danube River Cruise' and the 'Hundertwasser Tour', go between Schwedenplatz and Reichsbrücke (see *Getting There By Water*) and it is possible to take one tour in one direction and return on the other tour. Each tour lasts 70–100 minutes and costs €10.50 (€14 return). DDSG also offers themed cruises and evening dance cruises.

Other Tours

Three- to four-hour bicycle tours are provided by *Pedal Power*, Ausstellungsstrasse 3 (tel: (01) 729 7234; website: www.pedalpower.at), departing from the Prater ferris wheel (daily at 1000 May to September). Tours cost €23, which includes a bike and guide, and cover a number of city sites, such as KunstHausWien, St Stephen's Cathedral and the Danube Canal.
The *Old-Timer Tramway*, is a sightseeing tour on trams that date from 1929. The tour departs from the Art

Nouveau subway pavilion at Karlsplatz on Saturday and Sunday (May to October). Tickets and information are available from the information office of the *Vienna Transport Authority*, Karlsplatz (tel: (01) 587 3186; website: www.wienerlinien.co.at). Points of interest include the Rathskeller, the Burgtheatre, the University of Vienna, the Schönbrunn Palace and the Riesenrad. Tickets for the two-hour tour cost €15 (concessions available).
Alternatively, a romantic, albeit expensive, way for visitors to see the city is by a traditional *Fiaker* (horse-drawn carriage). These are available for hire on Graben and just to the north of St Stephen's Cathedral, at Heldenplatz (near the Hofburg) and at Albertinaplatz (behind the Staatsoper). The cost for up to four people is approximately €40 for 20 minutes (*klein*), €56 for 40 minutes (*gross*) or €95 for one hour (*Stunde*). The exact prices and lengths of the ride must be negotiated in advance.

Excursions

For a Half Day

Krems an der Donau: Along the River Danube, to the west of Vienna, lies *Krems*, a thousand-year-old town surrounded by vineyards. The western end, *Stein*, is the old portion of the town, which contains the street Landstrasse with its old buildings, including the 16th-century town hall. Above Landstrasse, the Renaissance town house, narrow streets and small squares show the structure of the original town. Both the *Piaristenkirche* and the *Wienstadt Museum* celebrate the work of medieval artist Johann Martin Schmidt. The 15th-century *Steiner Tor* gateway marks the end of Stein. Just before the *Kremer Tor*, at the other end of Landstrasse, is the town's new *Kunst Halle Krems*, a major arts venue. The *Gozzoburg*, at the bottom of Hoher Markt, serves reasonably priced local dishes (closed Tuesday), while *Piano*, at An der Donaulände, on the banks of the river, is an attractive place for visitors to enjoy a drink.
Trains leave Vienna Franz Josef Bahnhof every two hours (journey time – 1 hour). The last train back to Vienna is at around 2130. *Austropa Verkehrsbüro*, Undstrasse 6 (tel: (02732) 82676; fax: (02732) 70011; e-mail: austropa.krems@netway.at; website: www.krems.gv.at *or* www.tiscover.com/krems), is located halfway between Stein and Krems and can provide further information.

Museumsquartier entrance

Photo: Austrian National Tourist Office

Photo: Leonardo

Hotel Sacher

For a Whole Day

Wachau Valley: Between Krems an der Donau and Melk, the River Danube winds through one of the most beautiful areas of Austria. A variety of outdoor activities are available on this stretch, including watersports, hiking, cycling, boat cruises and wine-tasting tours. The *Danube Bike Path* follows the river on both banks. *Johann Trautsamwieser*, Siedlung Erlahof 10, Spitz (tel: (0664) 346 9486; e-mail: j.trantsam@aon.at), hires out bicycles throughout the region for €12 per day (€60 per week). He can bring bicycles to any town in the region, for a charge of around €5. Reservations are needed for a group of cyclists.

Trains to Melk, Pöcham and Ybbs depart from the Westbahnhof, while trains to Krems and Spitz depart from Franz Josef Bahnhof. Further information on the region is available from the *Tourismusverband Wachau-Nibelungengau*, Undstrasse 6 (tel: (02732) 85620; fax: (02732) 87471; e-mail: wachau@netway.at; website: www.wachau.at *or* www.tiscover.com/wachau), located halfway between Stein and Krems.

Melk: Founded in 831 and situated on the north bank of the River Danube, approximately half way between Vienna and Linz, *Melk* is an attractive town with a stunning abbey. *Stift Melk*, Abt Berthold Dietmayrstrasse 1 (tel: (02752) 555 225; fax: (02752) 555 226; e-mail: kultur.tourismus@stiftmelk.at; website: www.stiftmelk.at), sits atop an escarpment, commanding a large stretch of the river valley. It is a physical testament to the power and authority of both the Babenbergs, who built it over a thousand years ago, and the Benedictine monks, who have occupied it since 1089. The Abbey, which features in Umberto Eco's novel, *The Name of the Rose* (1983), contains a museum, restaurant, park and garden pavilion. The one-hour guided tour of the abbey is available all year round. The abbey is open to the public daily 0900–1800 (May to September) and 0900–1700 (April and October), however, from November to March, it is only accessible to visitors taking the guided tour. Entrance costs €6.90 or €8.50 with the tour. Entrance to the Abbey Park costs €3. Even those who do not have time to visit the abbey cannot fail to miss it as they approach Vienna by rail or road from the west.

Although a few trains continue on from Krems an der Donau to Melk, there are trains from Vienna's Westbahnhof to Salzburg and travellers for Melk must change at St Pölten Hofbahnhof for the local line to Amstetten. The trip to Melk takes approximately 70 minutes. Returning to Amstetten, one can either go back to Vienna or continue on the InterCity train to Salzburg, Innsbruck or Bregenz.

ACCOMMODATION

Hotel prices quoted will usually include 10% VAT for the room (and for breakfast). VAT of 20% will be included in prices for any other meals or services (including the mini-bar). There is also a city *Ortstaxe* (Tourist Tax) of 2.8% of the total bill.

The prices quoted below are the lowest standard rates for a double room, excluding breakfast but including relevant taxes, unless otherwise specified.

Business

Grand Hotel Wien

Built in the 1860s, from a design by Karl Tietz, the *Grand Hotel Wien* has 250 rooms and suites, a ballroom and five meeting rooms for between 12 and 480 guests – the Quadrille and Galerie rooms can be combined to accommodate 600 delegates. The 24-hour business centre includes PCs, scanner, fax and printers; secretarial and translation services are by arrangement. The well-regarded *Unkai* Japanese restaurant is situated within this centrally located hotel.
Kärntner Ring 9
Tel: (01) 515 800. Fax: (01) 515 1313.
E-mail: reservation@grandhotelwien.com
Website: www.grandhotelwien.com
Price: From €230.

Hotel InterContinental Wien

The 453-room modern five-star hotel faces the Stadtpark, with 16 function rooms and a conference capacity of up to 1100 delegates. Renovated in 2000, all guest rooms include e-mail and cc-mail, while the 24-hour *Reuters Business Centre* and conferencing service is able to fulfil any further business requirements. There also is a health centre. As exclusive caterers to the Hofburg (Imperial Palace),

the *InterContinental* can arrange special events in these exceptional surroundings. Besides the award-winning *Nobile* restaurant, the hotel offers *Mediterraneo*, a lighter restaurant, as well as the *Intermezzo Bar*, with a string trio or pianist in the evenings.
Johannesgasse 28
Tel: (01) 711 220 *or* 2262 (reservations).
Fax: (01) 713 4489.
E-mail: vienna@interconti.com
Website: http://vienna.interconti.com
Price: From €195.

NH Vienna Airport Hotel & Conference Centre

This modern hotel has had many incarnations in the past few years (Astron, Sofitel and Novitel), however, situated at the Vienna Airport and linked by a covered walkway to the World Trade Center, it is always popular. It is ideal for business meetings when it is not possible for delegates to be based in the city centre. There are 328 soundproofed rooms, three restaurants, two bars and 20 function rooms. Facilities include a full business centre, a fitness centre and a sauna. Room facilities include Internet connection, modem point, mini-bar, direct-dial telephone and even a choice of pillows. The city centre is only 20 minutes away by train or bus.
Vienna International Airport
Tel: (01) 701 510. Fax: (01) 706 2828.
E-mail: nhvienna@nh-hotels.com
Website: www.nh-hotels.com
Price: From €170.

Radisson SAS Palais

Dating from 1872, the *Radisson SAS Palais* is, in fact, a combination of two Ringstrasser Palaces – the Leiterberger and Henckel von Donnersmarck. There are 247 rooms and suites, with the best facing the Stadtpark. The decor is an attractive blend of Viennese traditional and Scandinavian modern. With 17 function rooms, suitable for 12–500 delegates, all business services can be arranged, while guest rooms are equipped with modem and voice-mail. Famous guests range from Gorbachev to David Bowie and the AC Milan football team.
Parkring 16
Tel: (01) 515 170. Fax: (01) 512 2216.
E-mail: sales.vienna@radissonsas.com
Website: www.radissonsas.com
Price: From €205.

Luxury

Hotel Bristol, A Westin Hotel

The *Hotel Bristol*, located directly opposite the State Opera House, still retains most of its original fin-de-siècle fixtures and fittings. Since its 1892 opening, the hotel has been an important meeting place for the international aristocracy and masters of industry. There are 140 rooms and seven conference rooms. Following its £10 million refurbishment, the Bristol Executive Club has opened a new *VIP Lounge* and a *Global Business Centre*, equipped with all major telecommunication systems. Besides the *Korso* restaurant (see *Restaurants*), the hotel is also well known for its *Sirk Restaurant and Café*.
Kärntner Ring 1
Tel: (01) 515 160. Fax: (01) 5151 6550.
E-mail: reservations.bristolvienna@westin.com
Website: www.westin.com
Price: From €385.

Hotel Im Palais Schwarzenberg

The *Hotel Im Palais Schwarzenberg* is a superb hotel, located in the 1716 summer palace, next to the Belvedere, and still owned by Fürst (Prince) Schwarzenberg. The 38 air-conditioned double rooms and six suites combine the best of antique and modern furnishings and have CD players besides the usual radio and television. The six Baroque halls, some with frescos by Daniel Gras (1726), and eight seminar rooms for up to 350 people offer possibly the finest venue for business and social events in the city. The *Terrace Restaurant* (see *Restaurants*) is also one of the best in the city and other smaller rooms include a bar and the *Kaminzimmer*, where guests can enjoy pastries in front of an open fire during the winter. There are often events in the 7.2-hectare (18-acre) private park, including ballets and fireworks. The park also includes an outdoor pool, five tennis courts and three kilometres (1.9 miles) of private jogging paths.

Schwarzenbergplatz 9
Tel: (01) 798 4515. Fax: (01) 798 4714.
E-mail: reservierung@palais-schwarzenberg.com
Website: www.palais-schwarzenberg.com
Price: From €330 (including breakfast).

Hotel Imperial

Built in 1869, as one of the Würtemberg Palaces, and located next to the Musikverein Concert Hall, the *Imperial Hotel* was opened by Kaiser Franz Joseph I, in 1873. To this day, it maintains most of its original features, including ceiling frescoes and Old Master paintings. There are 96 rooms and 32 suites, conference facilities for up to 250 delegates and all business facilities can be arranged. Besides the usual apparatus, all rooms include modem and voice-mail. A favourite with state visitors, this hotel offers the ultimate in discretion and service.

Kärntner Ring 16
Tel: (01) 501 100. Fax: (01) 5011 0410.
E-mail: reservations.imperialvienna@luxurycollection.com
Website: www.luxurycollection.com
Price: From €446.

Hotel Sacher

Family run for well over a century, the 105-room *Hotel Sacher* is one of Vienna's great institutions and the art on display in the corridors would rival that in many museums. All rooms include modem, voice-mail and fax connection (fax machines can be hired). Conference facilities are available for up to 250 delegates, with the most modern presentation equipment available. The hotel can also arrange out-of-house services. Besides a café and two bars, Hotel Sacher hosts the famous *Restaurant Anna Sacher*, where Kaiser Franz Josef dined on an almost daily basis, usually choosing *tafelspitz* (boiled beef).

Philharmonikerstrasse 4
Tel: (01) 514 560. Fax: (01) 5145 6810.
E-mail: wien@sacher.com
Website: www.sacher.com
Price: From €260.

Moderate

Nosseck Pension

Totally central and at an excellent price, the 26-room *Nosseck Pension* opens directly on to the pedestrianised Graben, at the heart of central Vienna. This is an extremely attractive pension for its price and prime location, with large and elegantly furnished en-suite rooms. No credit cards.

Graben 17
Tel: (01) 533 7041. Fax: (01) 535 3646.
E-mail: reservation@pension-nossek.at
Website: www.pension-nossek.at
Price: From €105 (including breakfast).

Pension Pertschy

Minutes from the Spanish Riding School, this building, the Palais Cavriana (1734), was once the home of a count. As a four-star pension with a courtyard, flower boxes and period furniture, *Pension Pertschy* is now a national landmark. The 47 rooms are situated between the first and fourth floor and are well equipped with shower or bath, toilet, telephone, TV, mini-bar and hairdryer. There is a free Internet terminal in the hall. Herr Pertschy also owns the Pensions Aviano, Baronesse and Christina.

Habsburgergasse 5
Tel: (01) 534 490. Fax: (01) 534 4949.
E-mail: pertschy@pertschy.com
Website: www.pertschy.com
Price: From €97.

RESTAURANTS

The selected restaurants have been divided into five categories: Gastronomic, Business, Trendy, Budget and Personal Recommendations. The restaurants are listed alphabetically within these different categories, which serve as guidelines rather than absolute definitions of the establishments.

The prices quoted below include 20% VAT. Restaurant bills will also include a service charge of between 10% and 15%, so a tip is not usually necessary. However, it is customary for patrons to round the bill up to the nearest €1.

The prices quoted below are for an average three-course meal for one person and for a bottle of house wine or cheapest equivalent; they include VAT but do not include service charge or tip.

Gastronomic

Altwienerhof

Altwienerhof is a short walk from the Schönbrunn Palace and is one of the city's great restaurants, still with many of its original Biedermeier features and an excellent garden. The restaurant has been in the Kellner family since 1928 and Rudolf Kellner is one of the country's best chefs, well versed in several culinary cultures – his 'grande cuisine' is Austrian with a French bias. The menu changes daily, so recommendations are difficult. Nevertheless, all are excellent. Menu options have included lightly boiled pheasant with goose liver sauce and *loup de mer* (a mild white fish in saffron sauce). The chef prepares a menu dégustation of six or eight courses of each evening's dishes for diners who are having difficulty making up their minds. The 25,000-bottle wine cellar is one of the world's best. Closed Sunday and the last three weeks of January. Jacket and tie are essential.

Herklotzgasse 6
Tel: (01) 892 6000. Fax: (01) 8926 0008.
E-mail: office@altwienerhof.at
Website: www.altwienerhof.at/gb/restaurant.htm
Price: €70. Wine: €22.

Drei Husaren

Founded by members of the aristocracy in 1933, the *Three Hussars* is one of the city's oldest continually running restaurants – not to mention one of the grandest. The atmosphere and decor still suggest the great days of the Hapsburgs, with a stylishly lavish yet intimate interior. The hors d'oeuvres trolley always offers at least 30 superb seasonal dishes, and the house crêpes, *Husarenphannkuchen*, should not be missed. Speciality dishes include the local favourite, *tafelspitz* (boiled beef) with ox marrow, hash brown potatoes, creamed spinach, chive sauce and apple sauce with horseradish, as well as calf's head served in a number of ways, such as with tartar sauce and potato salad or with marjoram-shallot sauce and rice.

Weihburggasse 4
Tel: (01) 5121 0920. Fax: (01) 5121 09218.
E-mail: office@drei-husaren.at
Website: www.drei-husaren.at
Price: €65. Wine: €28.

Kervansaray-Hummerbar

This is the city's finest fish restaurant, where the house specialities comprise a wide variety of lobster dishes. Besides many other fish dishes, such as Norwegian salmon with a horseradish and champagne sauce, excellent meat dishes are also available, even including kebabs and other top Turkish dishes. A special Caviar Menu is available on request. The ground floor *Hummerbar* (Lobster Bar) provides more modest Turkish and international meals. Both floors offer a fashionable but classic decor, with superb service and attention to detail. Closed Sunday.

Mahlerstrasse 9
Tel: (01) 512 8843. Fax: (01) 513 8130.
Price: €50. Wine: €17.

Korso bei der Oper

From the exquisite, classic decor to the exceptional food, produced under the direction of one of Austria's finest chefs, Reinhard Gerer, the *Korso* is considered one of the city's finest restaurants. It specialises in Austrian delicacies, with only the finest ingredients, including *tafelspitz* (boiled beef) and perch in red pepper cream sauce. The wine cellar also is one of the best in Europe. Diners should always save room for the wonderful versions of Viennese desserts. The restaurant has long been a favourite with international opera stars. No lunch Saturday.

Hotel Bristol, Kärntner Ring 1
Tel: (01) 5151 6546.
Website: www.westin.com
Price: €75. Wine: €29.

Restaurant Anna Sacher

Since 1876, dining at the Hotel Sacher has been as much a social experience as a culinary one. Most celebrities visiting Vienna eventually end up at the scarlet dining room, usually to enjoy its most famous – and Austria's national – dish, *tafelspitz* (boiled beef), served with an apple and horseradish and a chive sauce. Diners should always save room for the dessert speciality, Sachertorte, a chocolate tart split in half, spread with apricot jam and iced with chocolate. Each month, there is a new menu reflecting the seasons. Reservations are required and it is best for diners to arrive before 2300, wearing smart clothes.

Hotel Sacher Wien, Philharmonikerstrasse 4
Tel: (01) 514 560. Fax: (01) 5145 6810.
Website: www.sacher.com
Price: €50. Wine: €19.

Terrace Restaurant, Hotel Im Palais Schwarzenberg

Without question, this venue is Vienna's best for outdoor dining in the summer, with a terrace

overlooking the park in the grounds of the 1716 Palais Schwarzenberg (now partly a hotel). Although the restaurant is extremely smart, dining is a tranquil experience here. The seasonal menu presents both Austrian and international cuisine, with dishes including polenta gnocchi with pumpkin and truffles, rabbit ragout and salt-encrusted sea bass with aioli. Desserts, such as chocolate blinis with plums in balsamic vinegar and thyme ice cream, are not to be missed. The wine cellar is exceptional, with many wines available by the glass. It is also possible for diners to enjoy good but smaller meals in the bar.
Hotel Im Palais Schwarzenberg, Schwarzenbergplatz 9
Tel: (01) 798 4515. Fax: (01) 798 4714.
E-mail: hotel@palais-schwarzenberg.com
Website: www.palais-schwarzenberg.com
Price: €60 (€50 in the bar). Wine: €25.

Business

Alef-Alef

Located in the middle of the 'Bermuda Triangle' (see *Nightlife*), next to the synagogue on Siettenstettengasse and just north of the Fleischmarkt, *Alef-Alef* is one of Vienna's best kosher restaurants, with arched ceilings and red velvet upholstery. The classic dishes of German-Jewish cooking, such as *gefilte fisch* (stuffed carp) and *kigel* (potato strudel), are served up here, alongside a wide range of healthier Middle Eastern Jewish dishes of grilled meats and fish, salads and dips.
Seittenstettengasse 2
Tel: (01) 535 2530. Fax: (01) 5352 53033.
Website: www.alef-alef.at
Price: €25. Wine (kosher): €13.80.

Bodega Española

With an antique Spanish decor and a large open fire during the colder seasons, *Bodega Española* looks back to the days when the Hapsburg dynasty had strong connections to the Spanish throne. Located near the Belevedere Galleries, this is one of the finest tapas restaurants in the city. The menu features many small dishes, as well as excellent main courses, like *bacalao á la malagueña* (a fish speciality from Malaga) and lamb steak with lemon-rosemary potatoes. Reservations recommended. Closed Saturday and Monday.
Belvederegasse 10
Tel: (01) 504 5500. Fax: (01) 587 9700.
Price: €25. Wine: €15.

Do&Co Stephansplatz

With the spectacular view from the seventh floor opposite St Stephen's Cathedral, *Do&Co* attracts the jet-set crowd and visitors should book a window table in winter or one on the terrace in summer, to ensure the prime place in this sophisticated and stylish venue. There is a sushi bar (lunchtime) and a better-than-average selection of vegetarian dishes. Meat dishes include the superb king crab and steak combo, Uruguay beef and goose liver on Caesar salad with pumpkinseed oil and lobster St Tropez (sautéed in butter with tomatoes and basil). Sushi, teppanyaki and Thai dishes are also served. Do&Co is also reputed to have the youngest and best looking waitrons in Vienna. The restaurant also runs *Onxy*, a bar and café on the sixth floor, as well as *Aioli*, for antipasti, tapas and Mediterranean dishes, on the third floor.
Stephansplatz 12 (patrons must take Lift Two)
Tel: (01) 535 3969. Fax: (01) 535 3959.

Website: www.doco.com
Price: €45. Wine: €21.

Kupferdachl

Kupferdachl is one of the best choices for moderately priced but excellent quality Styrian dishes, away from the usual tourist haunts. The restaurant is located in the cellar section of the Leupold restaurant and is very much a family affair, with an old-fashioned comfortable atmosphere. Specialities include *raumschnitzel* (creamed veal cutlet), *lungenbraten* (tenderloin of beef stuffed with goose liver, served with cream sauce and dumplings), barbury duck and Wiener schnitzel. There is live music occasionally. Closed Sunday; also Saturday in July and August.
Schottengasse 7 (entrance on Mölker Bastei 1)
Tel: (01) 533 9381.
Price: €26. Wine: €16.70.

Yugetsu

Near the Staatsoper, *Yugetsu* is considered by many to be Vienna's best Japanese restaurant. The ground floor at Yugetsu, comprising a sushi bar and conventional tables, is decorated in a simple and restful Japanese style and offers sushi, sashimi, tempura and a large à la carte menu. Upstairs is lighter, louder and done up for teppanyaki, with comfortable seats arranged around three sides of the double grill, upon which the teppanyaki cooks prepare meals in front of the diners. Closed Sunday.
Führichgasse 10
Tel: (01) 512 2720. Fax: (01) 5122 72021.
Price: €30. Wine: €16.70.

Trendy

MAK

In the Museum of Modern Art, *MAK* is very much a museum restaurant-café, attracting a crowd that is fashionable rather than cultural. The venue is attractive with a combination of painted wooden ceiling and modern bars, as well as a superb courtyard available for summertime dining. The house speciality is *piroghi* – pockets of pastry with many different fillings, such as potato and soft cheese. More substantial meals, such as duck with red cabbage and dumplings, are also available and the desserts are wonderful. Closed Monday. No credit cards.
Steubenring 5
Tel: (01) 714 0121. Fax: (01) 957 7729.
Website: www.mak.at
Price: €13. Wine: €16.

Neu Wien

The venue's casual, cellar-like setting is popular with Vienna's media and avant-garde crowd. The low lighting effectively sets off the many paintings and interesting murals and the restaurant itself was designed by the artist, C L Attersee. *Neu Wien* is one of the finest examples of New Vienna dining, where nouvelle cuisine meets that of the Hapsburgs. The menu changes frequently but could include dishes like *zanderfilet* (crispy pike with cream beet sauce) or veal in truffle sauce. The superb Vranac wines from Montenegro should not be overlooked. Open until 0200 daily, Neu Wien is an excellent choice for late-night dining. No lunch.
Bäckerstasse 5
Tel: (01) 513 0666.
Price: €25. Wine: €17.40.

Novelli

Novelli is one of Vienna's finest modern Italian restaurants, with an open-plan room containing chandeliers and big leather chairs. The antipasti bar is superb and main courses include dishes like steak with sage gnocchi and onions in balsamic vinegar or sea bass poached in tarragon cream. Desserts are well in keeping with Viennese luxury and the Italian wine list is extensive. There is also a discreet bar. Closed Monday.
Bräunerstrasse 11
Tel: (01) 5134 2000. Fax: (01) 5134 2001.
E-mail: novelli@haslauer.at
Website: www.haslauer.at
Price: €35. Wine: €30.

Toko Ri

What began as a small sushi bar has now expanded to three locations, serving probably the best sushi in the city in beautiful interiors. The *ika-natto maki* (squid and fermented soy beans) and the *gyoza* (dumplings) are recommended, as is the fish *maki*, a delicious composition of tuna, salmon, kani and avocado wrapped in nori. Evening reservations are recommended.
Salztorgasse 4
Tel: (01) 532 7777.
Website: www.tokori.at
Price: €30. Wine: €17.
Branches:
Franz-Hochedlinger-Gasse 2
Tel: (01) 214 8940.
Naschmarkt Stand 263–264
Tel: (01) 587 2616.
Naschmarkt Stand 177–178
Tel: (01) 586 1344.

Budget

Lokanta Sarikoç

Lokanta Sarikoç is one of Vienna's best Turkish and Greek restaurants, featuring both buffet and waiter service in a relaxed atmosphere, with a slight accent on Turkish style and decor. There is a wide range of starters, grilled meats, kebabs and fish dishes, as well as many vegetarian options. The Wednesday night special menu is lamb on the spit.
Wahringerstrasse 8
Tel: (01) 319 9987.
Price: €15. Wine: €15.

Reinprecht (Heuriger)

Heurigens are outer suburban wine taverns, usually selling wine from the latest harvest. They are such a separate part of Viennese cuisine that it is only possible to recommend one in the main tourist heurigen area of Grinzing. *Reinprecht* is located in a 300-year-old monastery with a terraced garden and offers grills as well as the usual buffet of cold meats and cheeses, sausages, pickled salads, roast pork and dumplings. *Schrammelmusik* (19th-century Viennese dance music with violins, guitar and clarinet/accordian) is played here nightly and the atmosphere is lively. The best wines are bought by the bottle, with the Pinot Blanc recommended. Reinprecht is closed from mid December to February.
Cobenzlgasse 22, Grinzing (U2 to Schottentor, then tram 38 to end terminus)
Tel: (01) 3201 4710. Fax: (01) 3205 71322.
E-mail: reinprecht@grinzing.net
Price: From €7. Wine: €11.

Wiener Rathauskeller

Throughout the Teutonic world, city halls have traditionally maintained basement restaurants. Even though this Rathaus was only built between 1871 and 1883 and the cellar restaurant not added until 1899, Vienna's city hall is no exception. It features six neo-Gothic rooms, still with all their original stained-glass windows and vaulted ceilings. Besides the usual Viennese dishes, the speciality here is the *Rathauskellerplatte* for two, consisting of various veal, pork and lamb dishes. One portion of the cellar features a Viennese musical evening from 2000, featuring waltzes, operetta and *Schrammelmusik*. Reservations required. Closed Sunday.

Rathausplatz 1
Tel: (01) 4051 2190.
Price: €26. Wine: €18.60.

Wrenkh

Two venues form what is arguably Vienna's top vegetarian restaurant and bar combo, in which Christian Wrenkh serves great seasonal food to a young and elegant crowd. The restaurants have a light and airy designer feel, with the accent on comfort. Firm favourites include miso soup, Greek fried rice with vegetables, feta cheese and olives, and wild rice risotto with mushrooms. The attached bar was designed by Eichinger and Knechtl. Closed Sunday.

Bauernmarkt 10
Tel: (01) 533 1526. Fax: (01) 535 0840.
Price: €15. Wine: €12.
Branch:
Hollergasse 8
Tel: (01) 892 3356.

Zwölf-Apostelkeller (Stadtheurigen)

'City Heurigen' are generally located in the cellars of Vienna's old monasteries and offer a taste of what the outlying wine taverns offer, for those who do not have the time to leave the city. In this one, parts of the '12 Apostles Cellar' predate 1561, with wooden tables under lighting partially provided by streetlights set into the floor. The low prices do not detract from the quality of the traditional food, which includes goulash soup, meat dumplings and *schlachtplatte* (a selection of meats with hot bacon and cabbage salad). As it is from the barrel rather than the bottle, which is common in a Heuriger, wine is sold by the quarter litre. There is music daily from 1830. Closed July.

Sonnenfelsgasse 3
Tel: (01) 512 6777. Fax: (1) 3686 85815.
Price: €18. Wine: €2.25 (quarter-litre carafe).

Personal Recommendations

Abend-Restaurant Fuervogel

A Viennese landmark since World War I, the *Fuervogel* is situated opposite the Lichtenstein Palace and is where one can enjoy the Slavic atmosphere and Gypsy violins. Ideally, a meal should begin with *sakkuska*, a variety platter. In addition to the usual dishes, such as chicken kiev and beef stroganoff, the restaurant offers options like borscht, veal *dulguruki* and other dishes of the Steppes. Dessert should definitely be *plombier* (a rich Russian ice cream). Wonderful fixed-price gourmet dinners of three and five courses ('Kreml Dinners') are also available. Closed Sunday and 15 July to 15 August.

Alserbachstrasse 21
Tel: (01) 317 5391.
Price: €30. Wine: €10.

Fine dining and the dish *tafelspitz*

Café-Restaurant im KunstHausWien

This restaurant is part of the KunstHausWien (see *Key Attractions*). The Hundertwasser style attracts the arty, bohemian and tourist crowds and the restaurant is full of bright primary colours, with undulating floors and vast displays of fresh flowers. Although not the most imaginative of seasonally varied menus – soups, salads, and some Viennese meat dishes like Wiener schnitzel – this still is an extremely attractive and fun place for a meal. The *Midsummer Night's Dream*-like garden is open in the summer.

Weissgerberlände 14
Tel: (01) 712 0497.
E-mail: cafe@kunsthauswien.com
Website: www.kunsthauswien.com
Price: €15. Wine: €15.

Gulashmuseum

Although long a tourist favourite, the *Gulashmuseum*, with at least 15 different traditional versions of goulash, is still an attractive option for a meal. One does not go to this restaurant for its decor, which is very much that of an Austrian country *Gasthaus* (guest house), almost to the point of attractive kitsch. The best starter is the 'national crêpe' of Hungary, *hortobágy palatschinken*, pancakes with minced beef and paprika cream sauce. Goulash is served with beef, pork, veal, chicken liver or vegetables, usually accompanied by boiled potatoes and dark bread. The usual Austrian main courses of meat and fish are also available, as are desserts.

Schulerstrasse 20
Tel: (01) 512 1017.
Price: €19. Wine: €8.40 (litre carafe).

Santo Spirito

The *Holy Spirit* has decor straight from a romantic opera – a dark interior with red velvet curtains and cherubs on the walls – as well as loud classical music and late opening times (until 0200 or 0300). Busts of famous conductors are a feature on the walls. The restaurant has a mixed gay and straight clientele, although everyone is made to feel welcome. Dishes could include Gorgonzola and walnut ravioli in white wine sauce or chicken breast with cranberries, rosemary, marmalade and potato purée. It offers a superb selection of brunches named after famous composers. Reservations necessary. No credit cards.

Kumpfgasse 7
Tel: (01) 512 9998.
Price: €30. Wine: €17.

Steirereck

With one Michelin star, *Steirereck* is one of Vienna's best traditional and nouvelle cuisine restaurants. Located on the Danube Canal, with exposed beams taken from a castle, the restaurant has a cosy atmosphere. The seasonal menu, with a Styrian bias, might include lamb in olive and paprika sauce, or lobster and courgettes on saffron rice. The Austrian wine list is extremely comprehensive, as is their cheese selection – some cheeses are home-made. Brunch (*Weiner Gabelfrühstück*) offers an excellent selection of smaller dishes and the menu changes daily, depending on what is fresh at the markets. Closed weekends. Visa and MasterCard are accepted in the evenings only.

Rasumofskygasse 2 (Tram N to Löwengasse)
Tel: (01) 713 3168. Fax: (01) 7135 1682.
E-mail: wien@steirereck.at
Website: www.steirereck.at
Price: €60; €70 (set menu). Wine: €25.

ENTERTAINMENT

Nightlife

The most popular cluster of bars is around the *Bermuda Dreieck* (Bermuda Triangle), the old Jewish Quarter, in the area around Ruprechtskirche. Other districts with fewer tourists include the Spittelberg area, around Amerlinghaus (in the Seventh and Eighth Districts), and in the Fourth District, adjacent to the Naschmarkt. A lot of the best places in Vienna will not be obvious to tourists, as they are strictly marketed at the locals and are not necessarily in the centre of town. Quite a few clubs are filled with 'schicki-micki' (style-conscious) partygoers and many of these venues operate choosy door policies, where the beautiful or the correctly dressed waltz past the queue. Alternatives to the club and bar scene abound – hip and trendy Viennese still enjoy traditional favourites, such as Heurigen and the city's many balls.
Clubs generally stay open until 0200 during the week and 0400 on the weekend, although there is considerable variation. For late, late nights, there are quite a few bars in the First District that are open until 0300, 0400 or even later. The legal drinking age is 18 years. A beer costs, in general, between €3 and €4, rising to €4.50/5 for a small beer in more upmarket bars and clubs.

For information on what kind of sound and crowd to expect on any given night of the week, pick up the *Der Falter* listings paper (website: www.falter.at) or check out the online information on the club scene (website: www.rave.at).

Balls

The ball season takes place during *Fasching*, Vienna's winter carnival season, from New Year's Eve until the beginning of Lent. Of the 300 or so balls, the most prestigious are the New Year's Eve Imperial Ball and the Opera Ball. The latter is the highlight of the Viennese social calendar and takes place in the elegant surroundings of the *Staatsoper*, Hanuschgasse 3 (website: www.wiener-staatsoper), on the Thursday before Shrove Tuesday. Waltzers in long gowns and dinner jackets twirl under chandeliers, recalling the splendour and romance of a bygone era. New Year's Eve is marked not only by the *Kaiserball* (Imperial Ball) in the *Hofburg*, Innerer Burghof 1, Kaisertor (website: www.hofburg.com/d/va), but also by the conversion of the city centre into the world's largest ballroom.

Bars

The *American Bar*, Kärntnerdurchgang 1, lies just off Kärntnerstrasse. Designed by the famous Austrian architect, Adolf Loos, in 1908, it is a small, quiet space that serves as a good getaway from the crowds. The Spittelberg area (Seventh District) is dotted with bars, including the perennially popular *Amerlingsbeisl*, Stiftgasse 8, with its leafy garden, and *Blue Box*, Richtergasse 8 (website: www.ping.at/bluebox), which hosts a different DJ each night. The Bermuda Triangle, in the Jewish area around Schwedenplatz, also contains many attractive bars. Other popular spots include *Café Europa*, Zollergasse 8, and *Chelsea*, Lerchenfeldergürtel 29–31 (website: www.silverserver.co.at/chelsea), situated under the S-Bahn arches, with regular live concerts and football by satellite from England.

Casinos

The *Casino Wien*, Palais Esterházy, Kärntnerstrasse 41 (website: www.casino-wien.at), is the most central of Vienna's casinos. Casino Wien opens at 1500 and admission is free. The minimum age for admission is 18 years and either an identity card or passport must be shown. Games include roulette, blackjack and poker, as well as 184 slot machines. Dress is smart.

Clubs

One of the hottest clubs in Vienna is *Volksgarten*, Burgring 1 (on the Ringstrasse), which offers raves on Friday and Saturday from 2200 until late in the morning and draws a very dressed-up crowd. *Flex*, Augartenbrücke (website: www.flex.at), draws ravers and all sorts of alternative types, while *U4*, Schönbrunner Strasse 222, is still going strong, with a different theme every night of the week. *P1*, Rotgasse, is a popular spot for a (very) young international crowd. *Club Roxy*, Faulmanngasse 4, *Lindbergh*, Mahlerstrasse 11, and *Atrium*, Schwindgasse 4, are also worth checking out for a change from the techno scene – the music at these venues tends to be the latest dance hits and nothing too heavy.

Coffee Houses (Kaffeehäuser)

The coffee shops are an essential part of Viennese life. For the price of a coffee – anything upwards of €2 – you can sit for hours with the papers, some work, a book, or just watching the world go by. The new 'szene houses' attract a young, trendy crowd. *Stein*, Währingerstrasse 6–8 (website: www.cafe-stein.com),

is the king of the new style, with minimalist decor, Internet facilities, veggie fare and all-day breakfasts. *Café Demel*, Kohlmarkt 14, is the best and most expensive of the old-style cafés – the pastries are not to be missed.

Heurigen

Originally the Viennese word for the wine of the latest harvest, the word *heuriger* now also refers to the place where this wine is sold. Each heuriger can only sell the wine produced on its own estate – and only for a maximum of 300 days per year. Although it is possible to have heurigen in the centre of the city, the best locations are in the small villages in the Tenth to 23rd Districts, such as Grinzing, Nussdorf, Heiligenstadt, Sievering and Stammersdorf. (See also *Restaurants*.)

Live Music

A converted porn cinema, *Porgy & Bess*, Riemengasse 11 (website: www.porgy.or.at), near the Stubentor U-bahn stop, is now Vienna's best jazz club. *Clair Piano Bar*, Naglergasse 23, and *Jazzland*, Franz-Josefs-Kai 23 (website: www.jazzland.at), both offer what their names suggest. Open-air concerts are held on the *Donauinsel* (Danube Island) in summer, while larger rock concerts are performed at the *Ernst-Happel-Stadion*, Meiereistrasse 2. The main indoor venue for large acts is the *Wiener Stadthalle*, Vogelweidplatz 14 (website: www.stadthalle.com).

Sport

Vienna – with its coffee and cakes – does not appear to be a very sporty city and to a certain extent this is true. Most of the sports in which the residents partake are situated outside the city. World-class skiing is available in the Alps, a couple of hours away. There are fantastic opportunities for hiking and mountain biking in the woods to the west of the city – cycling can be dangerous on some of the roads, however, as these are narrow and twisting in the mountains and the Austrians tend to navigate them at speed. There are also good lakes for sailing and other watersports throughout much of the country. Within Vienna itself, however, there are ample bathing spots along the River Danube and the Old Danube (near the UNO-City). The car-free Donauinsel (Danube Island) provides one long cycling and rollerblading track. There is a skating rink, the *Wiener Eislaufverein*, within a 20-minute walk southeast of the cathedral (just outside the Am Stadtpark). The rink hires out skates and is open between late October and early March, although it gets especially crowded at weekends.

In terms of spectator sports, football is most popular, especially since Vienna has two Max Bundesliga (Premier League) teams. Neither team had a particularly good season in 2001/2002, however. *SK Rapid Wien* (website: www.skrapid.at), whose players have been wearing their green strip for a century, finished eighth in the league. Meanwhile *FK Austria Memphis* (website: www.fk-austria.at), formerly *FK Austria Wien*, finished fourth. The teams play at *Gerhard Hanappi Stadion*, Keisslergasse 6 (tel: (01) 914 5510; website: www.stadthalle.com), and *Franz-Horr-Stadion*, Fischhofgasse 14 (tel: (01) 688 0150), respectively.

Tickets to sporting events are usually available at the gate, on the day of the match. However, it is better for visiting spectators to reserve tickets through *Kartenbüro Flamm*, Kärntner Ring 3 (tel: (01) 512

4225), or the *Vienna Ticket Service*, Borsegasse 1 (tel: (01) 534 1363; fax: (01) 534 1328).

Fitness Centres

There are a number of spas in the area surrounding Vienna, including *Thermalbad Oberlaa*, Kurbadstrasse 14 (tel: (01) 6800 99600; website: www.oberlaa.at) which is located in the Tenth District of the city. I offers two indoor and two outdoor swimming pools sauna, solarium, massage and a light-and-sound relaxation bath. Prices start at €9.60 for two hours The adjacent *Wellness Park Oberlaa* offers tennis, squash, badminton and fitness and aerobics facilities To get there, visitors should take the U1 to Reumannplatz, then tram 67 to its terminal. On the other side of the city, the *Sportanlage Marco Polo* Ruthnergasse 170, in the 21st District (tel: (01) 292 3589), offers everything from a six-hole golf course and putting green to tennis, squash, a fitness centre and sauna – most facilities are open 0800–2300. A day membership for fitness costs €6, for golf is €8 and for tennis €15. Transport is by bus 32A or 36A although first-time visitors may find it easier to take a taxi from Florisdorf station on the S-Bahn and U6 U-Bahn lines.

Golf

Golf courses around Vienna are chronically overbooked and it is difficult to get a round at short notice. The nearest 18-hole golf course is the *Wien Golf Club*, Freudenau 65A (tel: (0222) 728 9564), where a round of golf costs €60 and membership is not required. However it is only possible to book a round during the week (weekends only as a guest of a member); golfers must be a member of another club and have a handicap of 28 of less. There are also a number of courses situated outside the city, where it may be possible to book a round on weekdays.

Tennis

Between its three locations, *Tennisplätze Arsenal* (website: www.aufdraht.at/arsenal) offers 57 outdoor courts and eight indoor courts. The most convenient location for visitors is at Arsenalstrasse 3 (tel: (01) 799 0101), in the Third District (near the Südbahnhof rail station). The cost is €10 before 1700 and €13 after. The courts are open 0700–2000.

Shopping

The most interesting shopping locale in Vienna is the inner city, with its narrow streets and elegant façades. The large pedestrian zones on Kärntnerstrasse and Graben meet at the strikingly modern *Haas Haus*, the mirrored façade of which seems to mock St Stephen's Cathedral, standing opposite. In addition to exclusive shops, the Haas Haus has a platform on the top floor, for sightseers who fancy a more face-to-face encounter with the cathedral. There are a number of architectural gems in this district – small shops with façades designed by some of Austria's most famous architects, as well as smaller side streets, often hiding unique and interesting retail opportunities. The *Ringstrassengalerien* offers the convenience of a shopping centre, a short walk from the State Opera House. The traditional shopping street of the Viennese is Mariahilferstrasse, which stretches from the Ringstrasse towards the Westbahnhof rail station (above the U3 U-Bahn line), between the Sixth and Seventh Districts. This street is home to major international stores selling clothing, music and other